DICTIONARY

OF

POLITICAL SCIENCE

DICTIONARY
OF
POLITICAL SCIENCE

Edited by

JOSEPH DUNNER

David Petegorsky Professor of Political Science,
Yeshiva University

PHILOSOPHICAL LIBRARY
NEW YORK

Copyright, 1964, by Philosophical Library, Inc.,
15 East 40th Street, New York 16, N. Y.
Library of Congress Catalog Card No. 63-15600
All rights reserved

Printed in the United States of America

EDITORIAL BOARD

Editor
JOSEPH DUNNER

Associate Editor
JOHN G. STOESSINGER

Assistant Editor
RUTH A. BEVAN

Contributing Editors	Identification
Wolfgang Abendroth University of Marburg Marburg, Germany	W.A.
Henry J. Abraham University of Pennsylvania Philadelphia, Pa.	H.J.A.
William W. Adams, Jr. William Jewell College Liberty, Missouri	W.A.
Charles R. Adrian Michigan State University East Lansing, Michigan	C.R.A.
Benjamin Akzin The Hebrew University of Jerusalem Jerusalem, Israel	B.A.
Spencer D. Albright University of Richmond Richmond, Va.	Sp.D.A.
Marvin H. Alisky Arizona State University Tempe, Arizona	M.A.
Charles W. Anderson University of Wisconsin Madison, Wisconsin	Ch.W.A.
Raymond V. Anderson Wisconsin State University River Falls, Wisc.	R.V.A.
Sheldon Lee Appleton Michigan State University, Oakland Rochester, Michigan	S.L.A.
Satish K. Arora Yale University New Haven, Conn.	S.K.A.
James D. Atkinson Georgetown University Washington, D.C.	J.D.A.
Peter Bachrach Bryn Mawr College Bryn Mawr, Pa.	P.B.
Chester W. Bain University of South Carolina Columbia, S. C.	C.W.B.
Benjamin Baker Rutgers—The State University New Brunswick, N. J.	B.B.

Contributing Editors	Identification
Roger Baldwin U.N. Consultant on Human Rights New York, N. Y.	R.B.
Patricia Barrett Maryville College St. Louis, Mo.	Pa.B.
Russell H. Barrett The University of Mississippi University, Miss.	R.H.B.
Kurt Beermann Gallaudet College Washington, D.C.	K.B.
Daniel M. Berman The American University Washington, D.C.	D.M.B.
Ruth A. Bevan University of Freiburg Freiburg, Germany	R.A.B.
Wilson B. Bishai School of Advanced International Studies (The Johns Hopkins University) Washington, D.C.	W.B.B.
George S. Blair Claremont Graduate School Claremont, California	G.S.B.
Lincoln P. Bloomfield Massachusetts Institute of Technology Cambridge, Mass.	L.P.B.
Imre Boba University of Washington Seattle, Wash.	I.B.
Arnold Brecht New School for Social Research New York, N. Y.	A.B.
James R. Brown University of Hartford Hartford, Conn.	J.R.B.
Ardath W. Burks Rutgers—The State University New Brunswick, N. J.	A.W.B.
Alan K. Campbell Syracuse University Syracuse, N. Y.	A.K.C
Russell B. Capelle Norwich University Northfield, Vt.	R.B.C.

v

Contributing Editors	Identification	Contributing Editors	Identification
Douglas Carlisle University of South Carolina Columbia, S. C.	D.C.	William Fleming Ripon College Ripon, Wisconsin	W.F.
Themistocles Cavalcanti University of Brazil Rio de Janeiro, Brazil	T.C.	Mona Fletcher Kent State University Kent, Ohio	M.F.
John W. Chapman University of Pittsburgh Pittsburgh, Penn.	J.W.Ch.	Peter J. Fliess Louisiana State University Baton Rouge, La.	P.J.F.
Wen Chen Chao Kalamazoo College Kalamazoo, Mich.	W.C.C.	Charles R. Foster DePauw University Greencastle, Ind.	C.R.F.
Ronald E. Chinn Whitworth College Spokane, Wash.	R.E.Ch.	Carl J. Friedrich Harvard University Cambridge, Mass., and University of Heidelberg, Heidelberg, Germany	C.J.F.
Charles B. Clark Upper Iowa University Fayette, Iowa	C.B.C.	Lawrence H. Fuchs U.S. Peace Corps	L.H.F.
Patrick J. Conklin University of Missouri Columbia, Mo.	P.J.C.	Frederick H. Gareau Florida State University Tallahassee, Fla.	F.H.G.
Kenneth E. Davison Heidelberg College Tiffin, Ohio	K.E.D.	Philippe Garigue University of Montreal Montreal, Canada	P.G.
Lowell C. Day The Doherty Foundation Princeton University—Princeton, N. J.	L.C.D.	Kurt Glaser Southern Illinois University Alton, Ill.	K.G.
Irving Dilliard University of Illinois Collinsville, Ill.	I.Di.	Alex Gottfried University of Washington Seattle, Wash.	A.G.
Mary Earhart Dillon Queens College Flushing, N. Y.	M.E.D.	J. A. C. Grant University of California Los Angeles, Cal.	J.A.C.G.
Hanno Drechsler University of Marburg Marburg, Germany	H.D.	Richard B. Gray The Florida State University Tallahassee, Fla.	R.B.G.
Yehezkel Dror The Hebrew University of Jerusalem Jerusalem, Israel	Y.D.	Fritz Grob Olivet College Olivet, Mich.	F.G.
John Paul Duncan University of Oklahoma Norman, Oklahoma	J.P.D.	Franz B. Gross Pennsylvania Military College Chester, Pa.	F.B.G.
Joseph Dunner Yeshiva University New York, N. Y.	J.D.	Leo Gross The Fletcher School of Law and Diplomacy Medford, Mass.	L.G.
Martin B. Dworkis New York University New York, N. Y.	M.B.D	Werner F. Grunbaum University of Houston Houston, Texas	W.F.G.
Je Don A. Emenhiser Utah State University Logan, Utah	J.A.E	Harold Guetzkow Northwestern University Evanston, Illinois	H.G.
Salo Engel The University of Tennessee Knoxville, Tenn.	S.E	Emanuel Gutmann The Hebrew University of Jerusalem Jerusalem, Israel	E.G.
Charles G. Fenwick Department of Legal Affairs Pan American Union Washington, D.C.	C.G.F	Joseph Hajda Kansas State University Manhattan, Kansas	J.H.

Contributing Editors	Identification	Contributing Editors	Identification
J. Oliver Hall Michigan State University East Lansing, Mich.	J.O.H.	Walter Darnell Jacobs University of Maryland College Park, Md.	W.D.J.
Samuel Halperin U.S. Department of Health, Education and Welfare Washington, D.C.	S.H.	Gerald I. Jordan Claremont University College Graduate School Claremont, Calif.	G.I.J.
M. Judd Harmon Utah State University Logan, Utah	M.J.H.	Carey B. Joynt Lehigh University Bethlehem, Pa.	C.B.J.
Guy B. Hathorn University of Maryland College Park, Md.	G.B.H.	Raymond H. Kaaret Ithaca College Ithaca, New York	R.H.K.
Robert D. Hayton Hunter College New York, N. Y.	R.D.H.	Egon K. Kamarasy Southern Illinois University Carbondale, Illinois	E.K.K.
Francis H Heller The University of Kansas Lawrence, Kansas	F.H.H.	Ravi L. Kapil The University of Wisconsin—Milwaukee Milwaukee, Wisc.	R.L.K.
John H. Herz The City College New York, N. Y.	J.H.H.	Morton A. Kaplan The University of Chicago Chicago, Ill.	M.A.K.
Heinz R. Hink Arizona State University Tempe, Arizona	H.R.H.	John J. Karch The American University Washington, D.C.	J.J.K.
Kenneth E. Hoffman Adrian College Adrian, Mich.	K.E.H.	Robert M. W. Kempner (former Chief Legal Advisor of Prussian Police Administration and Nuremberg War Trials Prosecutor) Landsdowne, Pa.	R.M.W.K.
William V. Holloway The University of Tulsa Tulsa, Oklahoma	W.V.H.	Melville T. Kennedy, Jr. Bryn Mawr College Bryn Mawr, Pa.	M.T.K.
Stanley K. Hornbeck (formerly University of Wisconsin and Harvard University) Washington, D.C.	St.K.H.	Hong-Chul Kihm Seoul National University Seoul, Korea	H.C.K.
Ronald F. Howell Emory University Atlanta, Ga.	R.F.H.	George A. King College of the Holy Cross Worcester, Mass.	G.A.K.
S. S. Hsueh University of Hong Kong Hong Kong	S.S.H.	Russell Kirk Post College of Long Island University Brookville, N. Y.	R.K.
Karel Hulicka State University of New York at Buffalo Buffalo, New York	K.Hu.	George Klein Western Michigan University Kalamazoo, Mich.	G.K.
E. J. Immonen University of Helsinki Helsinki, Finland	E.I.	Oscar Kraines New York University New York, N. Y.	O.K.
Vernon R. Iredell The University of Tennessee Knoxville, Tennessee	V.R.I.	Earl Latham Amherst College Amherst, Mass.	E.L.
H. B. Jacobini Southern Illinois University Carbondale, Ill.	H.B.J.	Daniel Lerner Massachusetts Institute of Technology Cambridge, Mass.	D.L.
Dan N. Jacobs Miami University Oxford, Ohio	D.N.J.	Lawrence M. Lew Bradley University Peoria, Illinois	L.M.L.

Contributing Editors	Identification	Contributing Editors	Identification
Edward G. Lewis University of Illinois Urbana, Ill.	E.G.L.	Benjamin Nispel Shippensburg College Shippensburg, Pa.	B.N.
Frank M. Lewis State University of South Dakota Vermillion, S. D.	F.M.L.	Arthur A. North, S.J. Fordham University New York, N. Y.	A.A.N.
J. Ben Lieberman Columbia University New York, N. Y.	J.B.L.	Clark F. Norton DePauw University Greencastle, Indiana	C.F.N.
Henry L. Mason Tulane University New Orleans, La.	H.L.M.	Andrew E. Nuquist The University of Vermont Burlington, Vt.	A.E.N.
John B. Mason California State College at Fullerton Fullerton, Calif.	J.B.M.	Mother Mary O'Callaghan Maryville College of the Sacred Heart St. Louis, Missouri	M.O'C.
Chester C. Maxey President Emeritus, Whitman College Walla Walla, Washington	Ch.C.M.	Eleanor T. Ostrau Stern College for Women Yeshiva University New York, N. Y.	E.T.O.
Charles A. McClelland San Francisco State College San Francisco, Calif.	Ch.A.Mc.	Thomas Payne Montana State University Missoula, Mont.	Th.P.
David W. McCormick Arlington State College Arlington, Texas	D.W.Mc.	Tibor Payzs University of Detroit Detroit, Mich.	T.P.
Charles A. McCoy Temple University Philadelphia, Pa.	C.A.McC.	Victor P. Petrov The George Washington University Washington, D.C.	V.P.P.
Matthew M. McMahon St. Ambrose College Davenport, Iowa	M.M.Mc.	Benigno Mantilla Pineda Universidad De Antioquia Medellin, Colombia, S.A.	B.M.P.
Theodore McNelly University of Maryland College Park, Md.	T.Mc.N.	Dale Pontius Roosevelt University Chicago, Illinois	D.P.
Joseph F. Menez Loyola University Chicago, Ill.	J.F.Me.	Ithiel de Sola Pool Massachusetts Institute of Technology Cambridge, Mass.	I.d.S.P.
Josephine F. Milburn Simmons College Boston, Mass.	J.F.M.	Paul F. Power University of Cincinnati Cincinnati, Ohio	P.F.P.
Emmet V. Mittlebeeler University College of Rhodesia and Nyasaland Salisbury, S. Rhodesia	E.V.M.	Emanuel Rackman Yeshiva University New York, N. Y.	E.R.
Abelardo F. Montenegro Institute of Political Science Fortaleza—Cera, Brazil	A.F.Mo.	Harry Howe Ransom Vanderbilt University Nashville, Tennessee	H.H.R.
Frank Munk Reed College Portland, Oregon	F.M.	John E. Reeves University of Kentucky Lexington, Kentucky	J.E.R.
Fauzi M. Najjar Michigan State University East Lansing, Mich.	F.M.N.	Peter P. Remec Fordham University New York, N. Y	P.P.R.
Wladimir Naleszkiewicz Marquette University Milwaukee, Wisconsin	W.N.	Ross R. Rice Arizona State University Tempe, Arizona	R.R.R.
Robert G. Neumann University of California Los Angeles, Calif.	R.G.N.		

Contributing Editors	Identification	Contributing Editors	Identification
Raimar Richers Escola de Administracao de Empresas de Sao Paulo Sao Paulo, Brazil	R.R.	William D. Spear Eastern Oregon College La Grande, Oregon	W.D.S.
James A. Robinson Ohio State University Columbus, Ohio	J.A.R.	Stanley Spector Washington University St. Louis, Mo.	S.S.
William C. Rogers University of Minnesota Minneapolis, Minn.	W.C.R.	Richard Felix Staar Emory University Atlanta, Ga.	R.F.S.
Alvin Z. Rubinstein University of Pennsylvania Philadelphia, Pa	A.Z.R.	W. J. Stankiewicz The University of British Columbia Vancouver, Canada	W.J.S.
Elie A. Salem American University of Beirut Beirut, Lebanon	E.A.S.	Robert H. Stern State University of New York at Buffalo Buffalo, N. Y.	R.H.S.
Chattar Singh Samra American International College Springfield, Mass.	C.S.S.	John G. Stoessinger Hunter College New York, N. Y.	J.G.St.
Joseph A. Schlesinger Michigan State University East Lansing, Mich.	J.A.S.	John E. Stoner Indiana University Bloomington, Ind.	J.E.S.
Henry J. Schmandt The University of Wisconsin—Milwaukee Milwaukee, Wisc.	H.J.Sch.	Melvin P. Straus Texas Western College of the University of Texas El Paso, Texas	M.P.S.
Royal J. Schmidt Elmhurst College Elmhurst, Ill.	R.J.S.	Robert Strausz-Hupe University of Pennsylvania Philadelphia, Pa.	R.St.-H.
Carl J. Schneider The University of Nebraska Lincoln, Nebraska	C.J.S.	Oscar Svarlien University of Florida Gainesville, Fla.	O.S.
Henry G. Schwarz University of Wisconsin—Racine Racine, Wisc.	H.G.S.	Thor Swanson Washington State University Pullman, Wash.	T.S.
John M. Selig City College of San Francisco San Francisco, Calif.	J.M.S.	Richard W. Taylor Coe College Cedar Rapids, Iowa	R.W.T.
Barbara J. L. Shockley Bloomsburg State College Bloomsburg, Pa.	B.J.L.S.	George B. Telford Drake University Des Moines, Iowa	G.B.T.
T. C. Sinclair University of Houston Houston, Texas	T.C.S.	H. Stanley Thames North Texas State University Denton, Texas	H.S.Th.
Royal Daniel Sloan, Jr. University of Nebraska Lincoln, Nebraska	R.D.S.	Nathaniel P. Tillman, Jr. Howard University Washington, D.C.	N.P.T.
Robert G. Smith Drew University Madison, N. J.	R.G.S.	Jacqueline E. Timm Bowling Green State University, Ohio Bowling Green, Ohio	J.E.T.
Morton J. Sobel Jewish War Veterans of the United States Washington, D.C.	M.J.S.	Roy M. Tollifson Simmons College Boston, Mass.	R.M.T.
Margaret Spahr (formerly Hunter College) Northampton, Mass.	M.Sp.	Peter A. Toma Arizona State University Tempe, Arizona	P.A.T.
		George O. Totten University of Rhode Island Kingston, Rhode Island	G.O.T.

Contributing Editors	Identification	Contributing Editors	Identification
E. G. Trimble *University of Kentucky* *Lexington, Kentucky*	E.G.T.	Chi Kao Wang *Elizabeth City State Teachers College* *Elizabeth City, N. C.*	C.K.W.
Hideo Uchiyama *Keio University of Tokyo* *Tokyo, Japan*	H.U.	William R. Willoughby *University of New Brunswick* *Fredericton, New Brunswick, Canada*	W.W.
Richard W. Van Wagenen *The American University* *Washington, D.C.*	R.W.V.W.	Daniel Wit *Northern Illinois University* *De Kalb, Illinois*	D.W.
Manfred C. Vernon *Western Washington State College* *Bellingham, Wash.*	M.C.V.	Karl A. Wittfogel *University of Washington* *Seattle, Wash.*	K.A.W.
Jorge B. Vivas *Director, Argentine Library of Congress* *Buenos Aires, Argentina*	J.B.V.	George V. Wolfe *The College of Idaho* *Caldwell, Idaho*	G.V.W.
Melvin W. Wachs *Associate Director, Management Institutes* *U.S. Civil Service Commission* *Washington, D.C.*	M.W.W.	Edward Reynolds Wright *Midwestern University* *Wichita Falls, Texas*	E.R.W.
Eric Waldman *Marquette University* *Milwaukee, Wisc.*	E.W.	Theodore Wykoff *Arizona State University* *Tempe, Arizona*	T.W.
Harvey Walker *The Ohio State University* *Columbus, Ohio*	H.W.	Joseph F. Zimmerman *Worcester Polytechnic Institute* *Worcester, Mass.*	J.F.Z.
Richard L. Walker *University of South Carolina* *Columbia, S. C.*	R.L.W.	Victor Zitta *Marquette University* *Milwaukee, Wisc.*	V.Z.

PREFACE

The aim of this dictionary is to provide teachers, students, and laymen interested in the discipline which devotes itself to the study of politics with concise definitions and descriptions of the terms, events, and personalities used most frequently in the writings of political scientists.

In no area of human activities and relationships is there as much semantic confusion (i.e., confusion about the meaning of words) as in politics, and the terminology used by political scientists is not totally immune to this disease. The aim to introduce clarity and generally accepted standards of expression would, of course, be more easily achieved if there were at least a consensus as to what constitutes political science in our time. But, as the introductory essay on "The Meaning and Scope of Political Science" demonstrates, there are serious differences of opinion even among those who form the professional corps of political scientists. Moreover, in the interplay of thought and action, concepts such as "the state," "freedom," "equality," "the rights of people," "peace," have come to mean different things to different people—not only in different times but even at the same time. To give but one illustration, while the vocabulary of the protagonists of totalitarianism may be the same as that of a believer in constitutionalism, liberty, and democracy, the very words "constitutionalism," "liberty," and "democracy," connote one meaning for those who oppose the omnipotent state and an entirely different meaning for those who welcome and defend it.

To represent as wide a variety of viewpoints as possible, I have asked close to two hundred of my professional colleagues in the free world (i.e., in those parts of the world in which there is a chance for freedom of inquiry and expression), many of them chairmen of the political science departments of leading universities and colleges, many of them full professors, all of them teachers with established reputations, to act as contributing editors and to join me in the planning and execution of this project. I owe a profound debt of gratitude to all of them. I am particularly indebted to my friends and former students of Harvard and Grinnell Miss Ruth A. Bevan, B.A., M.A., and Professors Charles Anderson, Daniel Lerner, Wen Chen Chou and John G. Stoessinger who have assumed special work loads to make this dictionary a success.

A word of caution to the reader: the dictionary does not contain every single term, event, and name which he may find in other books dealing with politics. The fact that the verbal expressions of a truly immense field of knowledge had to be compressed within the limits of one volume has made omissions inevitable. If, however, any topics deserve room not accorded them in this edition, it may be possible to include them in a future, somewhat enlarged edition. I welcome suggestions and criticism to that end; and I know that in this respect I may speak in the name of all my colleagues.

It should also be noted that the compilation and production of a work of this kind inevitably leads to omission of last-minute events, after a self-imposed deadline. The entries are to be considered up-to-date as of January 1, 1964.

It is probably superfluous to add that the final responsibility as to the general plan of this dictionary, together with the burden of the shortcomings resulting from inadequate translations and editorial strictures of some contributions, rests with the editor.

The Editor

INTRODUCTION

The Meaning and Scope of Political Science

In the colleges and universities of the United States of America the discipline (i.e., the branch of learning and teaching) which concerns itself with the study of politics is customarily called political science. (In France, the same discipline is usually called *science politique,* and in the Federal Republic of Germany *politische Wissenschaft.*) Like so many other terms, political science is a misnomer. The word "science" is an Anglicized derivative of the Latin word *scientia,* which means knowledge (in the sense of thorough or systematized knowledge). We can endeavor to acquire, and we may eventually succeed in possessing, knowledge of mathematics, chemistry, music, or the various religious traditions of mankind. We can also acquire and possess some knowledge of politics. But a science cannot be political, just as it cannot be mathematical, chemical, musical, or religious. Moreover, in view of the many misconceptions about the role of politics in human existence, political science is a particularly unfortunate word combination, since it might convey the notion that the discipline which devotes itself to the study of politics is itself "politicized," that it pursues narrow partisan objectives and teaches the necessary tricks to achieve these objectives. Appropriate substitutes would be "science of politics," "study of politics," or "politology." In view of the entrenchment of the term "political science," we too shall use it. But let us at least be clear about its meaning. Precise definitions cannot overcome genuine differences of opinion; they help, however, to avert those controversies which are the result of semantic confusion.

To repeat, science means knowledge, and knowledge can presumably be acquired by learning. But what is "political"? What is meant by "politics"?

Both words are derived from the Greek *polis,* a noun which we have come to translate as city-state, or, simply, state.[1] Originally, *polis* was the Greek expression for a fortified place on a commanding height overlooking a city and easier to defend than the city itself. Some 2600 years ago the Athenian Greeks had fortified the hill which rises above the city of Athens, and to this day this hill is known as the Acro-polis, the hill-fortress. Since the Athenians used to repair to the Acropolis whenever they felt the need of deliberating upon their public affairs,[2] the word *polis* gradually came to mean any organized community or

---

[1] The word "state" is an Anglicized derivative of the Latin *status,* used to designate order or rank (e.g., the order of the patricians). What we call "state" today, the ancient Romans used to call *res publica,* a commonwealth.

[2] The word "public" is an Anglicized derivative of the Latin *publicus.* Public affairs are affairs which concern the people as a whole (or at least a substantial part of an organized group) in contrast to private affairs (such as personal feelings and thoughts) which can be directly known only by a single subject.

"power" engaged in relations with similar communities or "powers" or, to be more explicit, any group of people settled in a city and its vicinity, held together by ties of real or fictitious kinship, organized for collective defense, interested in ordered relations among the members of the group and their dependents, having some division of labor in the production of goods and services, and enjoying common facilities for religious worship, sports, and arts.

In the fourth century B.C., Aristotle, who is frequently referred to as "the father of political science," gave a course of lectures which he assembled under the title *Politics*. As the name of this collection indicates, it is concerned with the affairs of the *polis,* or, to be more precise, it describes and analyzes the organization and activities of 158 *poleis* (plural of *polis*) scattered over the Greek peninsula and the Greek island possessions in the Mediterranean during Aristotle's time. Having observed that not only the Greeks but also many settled non-Greeks seemed to feel the need for organizations which resembled the Greek *poleis,* Aristotle deducted that "man is by nature a political animal,"[1] or, as we might say today, that man is by nature a state-builder.

While the exact origin of the state and, therefore, of political life cannot be accurately determined, Aristotle hypothesizes that there were these three major stages of development: (1) the union of male and female for the reproduction of the species, engendering the family (or household); (2) the "sons and the sons of sons" (a phrase stemming from the *Laws* written by Plato, Aristotle's teacher), congregating for the satisfaction of some common needs in villages (or family clans); (3) the *polis,* which in Plato's and Aristotle's view—and this view probably reflects the Hellenistic culture of their time—came into existence as the perfection of human nature, as the whole of which the individuals are organic parts, as man's only chance to attain a civilized and well-ordered life. (Although Aristotle still regards the Athenian *polis* as essentially a kinship organization, he, as well as other writers of his time, were nevertheless aware of the influx of "foreigners" into the membership of the Athenian *polis* and its transformation into a territorial organization, gradually stressing common territory rather than blood relationship.)[2]

While sociology, as the general science of society, endeavors to study the "processes of sociation, association, and dissociation as such,"[3] political science can be said to concern itself primarily with the study of the *"political"* (i.e., the state-building) qualities in man, expressed in *"politics"* (i.e., in all those relationships and activities which characterize man's response to his quest for

---

[1] Aristotle, *Politics*. Great Books of the Western World. Chicago, London, Toronto, 1952. Vol. 9, p. 446.

[2] It should be added, however, that just as the transition of the state as an offspring of kinship organization to the state as a territorial organization did not take place uniformly, it did not produce everywhere the same results. Differences in historical experiences, in climate and material resources, led to different forms of states; and to this day we can observe not only the perpetuation of pre-political social forms but here and there—think of the Eskimos or various tribes of Bedouins—the absence of statal units altogether.

[3] Wiese-Becker, *Systematic Sociology*. John Wiley and Sons, New York, 1932, p. 10.

security and a binding social order). And since these relationships and activities center around the state as their organizational framework, *political science has often been defined as the systematic study of the state and of the processes governing its internal and external relations.* Obviously so comprehensive a field of study will have many subdivisions and many points of common interest with other disciplines.

But before we list the major subdivisions of political science and some of those disciplines with which political science is connected most closely, we must first deal with the frequently made assertion that only a deterministic sequence of data, admitting of prediction, should be called a science and that in view of the relative uniqueness of each political situation man's political relationships and activities do not lend themselves to a science, concluding, therefore, that the term political science is overly pretentious.

Many, if not most, political scientists will admit that, although they search for uniformities and recurrent relationships in politics and try to arrive at some generalizations from their empirical observations, they cannot expect the kind of precision which seems to characterize the generalizations (or "laws") established, for instance, by physicists and chemists. What matters, however, these political scientists say, is the scientific approach to politics, the use of systematic methods of inquiry, and objectivity in the reporting of the subject matter. They will agree that political situations, being intimately connected with the human personality, are indeed unique. But so, they say, are diseases. No case of measles or schizophrenic reaction is exactly like another case. Every disease is a personal and, therefore, a unique event. Yet it is the task of the students of medicine and medical psychology to find the typical in the diversity. A similar task confronts the student of politics. These political scientists will also concede that, in view of the complexity of human behavior and the constantly changing social and political relationships, they cannot predict future political events with the same degree of accuracy which characterizes, for example, the prediction of the chemist that the combination of two parts of hydrogen with one part of oxygen will result in that compound which we call water. However, the prediction that in the United Kingdom of Great Britain and Northern Ireland the passing of a resolution of "want of confidence" by the House of Commons "will almost always lead to general elections"[1] and the formation of a new Cabinet, or the prediction that an internal revolution against a totalitarian dictatorship (such as the Soviet dictatorship of Russia) "is not likely to succeed even if it is begun"[2] has a degree of probability which does not lag very far behind the probability of many predictions of the natural sciences. The first prediction is based on the observations of a custom in the executive-legislative relationships of the British state. The second prediction is

---

[1] Joseph Dunner, "Stabilization of the Cabinet System," *Constitutions and Constitutional Trends Since World War II*, edited by Arnold J. Zurcher, second edition. New York University Press, New York, 1955, p. 87.

[2] Carl J. Friedrich and Z. K. Brzezinski, *Totalitarian Dictatorship and Autocracy*. Harvard University Press, Cambridge, 1956, p. 300.

derived from a painstaking analysis of past and present totalitarian governments[1] and the historical record of the operations and achievements of resistance movements against such governments. Much of political science concerns itself with tradition-grown rules or customs as well as the other set of rules—the enacted laws of the state. Much of political science concerns itself with the study of constitutions, i.e., the basic rules which provide us (though not always conclusively) with an insight into the formal structure of a state and the distribution of political rights (or powers) among the citizens[2] and the various branches and subdivisions of its government. Much of political science deals with the dynamics of political power[3] and contrasts, among others, states favoring a "system of effective restraints upon governmental action"[4] and states which lack such restraints and concentrate political power in the hands of a few specially privileged individuals or groups.

Some political scientists, particularly sensitive to the accusation that political science is not as scientific as, for example, physics, have adopted some of the symbols, tools, and techniques of mathematics and the natural sciences, which they employ in studies of voting behavior and which they hope will introduce a greater scientific objectivity and a chance for more effective communication than achieved by the traditional methods of classification and reflective evaluation of political data. Eager to treat their subject matter with the same detachment which they attribute to the natural scientist, these "behaviorists," or at least some of them, attempt to study political data as given facts; they are skeptical of a normative approach to the discipline and are reluctant to express value judgments.

Those political scientists who reject the "behavioral" approach, readily agree that the study of how men actually behave in a political community is a significant part of political science but suspect, as one of them remarks, that "the behavioral tail may come to wag the philosophical dog."[5] They feel that the behavioral approach tends to conceive of political science as a technique for

---

[1] The word "government" is an Anglicized derivative of the Greek word *kybernan*, meaning steering or guiding. The government of a state is the guiding agency through which the authority of the state is chiefly exercised.

[2] "Citizen" is the Anglicized word of the Latin *civis*, which in antiquity designated a person with full rights of membership in the *civitas*, the Latin equivalent of the Greek *polis*. *Civis* is related to the English "civic" (in Latin *civicus*) used, for example, in "civic rights," the equivalent of "political rights."

[3] Power has been defined as the ability in a given relationship "to command the service or the compliance of others" (Robert M. MacIver, *The Web of Government*. The Macmillan Company, New York, 1947, p. 82.) There is hardly a social relationship which does not involve the use of power, be it in the form of mental persuasion or in the form of coercive force.

[4] Carl J. Friedrich, *Constitutional Government and Democracy*, revised edition. Ginn and Company, Boston, New York, 1950, p. 26.

[5] Russell Kirk, "*Segments of Political Science Not Amenable to Behavioristic Treatment,*" *The Limits of Behaviorism in Political Science*, a symposium sponsored by The American Academy of Political and Social Science, edited by James C. Charlesworth, Philadelphia, 1962, p. 49.

developing means to serve any stipulated end and that this in itself constitutes a value judgment. While they do not depreciate the "clinical" efforts of their colleagues, they maintain that it is not enough to know merely "how" and "why" certain people behave as they do. For they hold that unless a tolerable political order is achieved throughout the world, not much else can be achieved, and that it is the task of political scientists to give due consideration to the "should" or "ought," i.e., to a value judgment on political phenomena. In their opinion any attempt to replace the quest for a good political order by a purely descriptive or analytical political science would be "as absurd as the idea of a medicine which refuses to distinguish between health and sickness."[1]

Another source of disagreement in the discipline of political science concerns the role of power in the affairs of states. There is a school of political scientists (sometimes called "realists") who prefer the "power orientation" in the study of politics as more conducive to the development of a distinctive science of politics than the emphasis given to the architecture of the state and the end of politics seen in a "lawful order" or "human happiness." Equating politics with "the struggle for power," one of the leading spokesmen of the "power-oriented" school of political scientists states that only "the concept of interest defined in terms of power . . . sets politics as an autonomous sphere of action and understanding apart from other spheres, such as economics (understood in terms of interest defined as wealth), ethics, aesthetics, or religion . . . for without it we could not distinguish between political and non-political facts, nor could we bring at least a measure of systematic order to the political sphere."[2] Another leading representative of this school categorically asserts "the study of politics is the study of influence and the influential."[3]

Some political scientists, while sympathetic to the power approach of the "realists," fear, however, that it involves too vast an assignment and envisage nearly insurmountable methodological obstacles in the proper identification of the manifestations of power.[4]

Yet other political scientists reject a single-factor approach to the study of political science and object to the very definition of politics as a "struggle for power" or "struggle for influence." They maintain that it is the conflict of goals which characterizes politics, that the end of politics is the Greek *politeia*, i.e., a plan of action integrating the various conflicting interests among human beings and not an abstract "power" divorced from purposeful motivation. These political scientists will stress that "when power is thought of as the be-all and end-all of the state, a complete reversal of means and ends ensues. Arguments

---

[1] Leo Strauss, *What Is Political Philosophy?* The Free Press of Glencoe, Glencoe, Illinois, 1959, p. 89.

[2] Hans J. Morgenthau, *Politics Among Nations,* third edition. Alfred A. Knopf, New York, 1960, p. 5.

[3] Harold Lasswell, *Politics: Who Gets What, When, How.* Meridian Books, New York, 1958, p. 13.

[4] Cf. Charles S. Hyneman, *The Study of Politics, The Present State of American Political Science,* University of Illinois Press, Urbana, 1959, p. 149.

that once interpreted the state in terms of the functions it undertakes are twisted into arguments in behalf of the power it must employ."[1] And they warn: "When the accumulation of power is viewed as the business of the state, it is a simple next step to argue that what conduces to might is right.... Power may be thought of as unconnected with moral choice and ethical value. The sphere of the state and the processes of politics are deemed amoral or ethically neutral.... In this case it makes no sense to pass judgment on the state, except in terms of whether it succeeds in maintaining that power which is its be-all and end-all. The third possibility is that power may be condemned as evil, on the ground that its control of force involves a coercion which is morally reprehensible. If the state, then, is pre-eminently a power-wielding institution that can employ force, condemnation of force leads to condemnation of the state as something immoral.... Divergent though they be, the various conclusions share a common origin... they spring from a preoccupation with the techniques that the state uses rather than the end which it pursues...."[2]

This emphasis on the normative approach, the (never ending) task of moral reflection, implicitly asking the political scientist to address himself to the problem of choice in political activity, leads us finally to those political scientists who might be classified as the synthesizers of the discipline. They are concerned with the description, analysis, and comparison of political organizations, with public law and public administration; they recognize the significance of control in the political process and the need for understanding of how public policies are achieved; but they are also vitally concerned with the philosophy of the state, and they will not hesitate to point to politically relevant differences among men which, they say, cannot be neutralized by a scientific technology;[3] they will, for example, pass a value judgment on the totalitarian state (as the student of medicine will pass a value judgment on cancer) and they will warn of its implications, risks, and consequences for all who cherish personal and political freedom.[4] Although they do not share Plato's and Aristotle's belief in the identity of state and society, although they realize that the state is but one of many associations and that it is a historical and changing phenomenon, the synthesizers accept—with modifications—the Aristotelian view

---

[1] Leslie Lipson, *The Great Issues of Politics, An Introduction to Political Science,* second edition. Prentice-Hall, Englewood Cliffs, N. J., 1960, p. 87.

[2] Ibid., pp. 87, 88.

[3] "The human child differs fundamentally from the young animal. The latter is largely 'formed' as soon as it is born.... Human beings are in a different position.... Whereas the animal goes straight ahead in the way prescribed by its nature and can rarely be taught to do much else, human beings may develop along a variety of lines. Most of the choices open to them are made for them by their families, and by the other social groups of which they become members, but there does remain a substantial range of free decisions to be made by the individual." (Ferdinand A. Hermens, *The Representative Republic.* University of Notre Dame Press, Notre Dame, Indiana, 1958, p. 6.)

[4] Such research on logical implications and practical consequences constitutes the bridge between the normative and the behavioral school. Cf. Arnold Brecht, *Political Theory, The Foundations of Twentieth-Century Political Thought,* Princeton University Press, 1959, pp. 79, 122, 438, 485, 491 ff.

of political science as the "master" science, in so far as matters involving man's public life are concerned. A clear expression of this concept of political science as an integrator of the findings of all social sciences and the role of the political scientist as an advisor concerning political decisions can be found in the following statement of a political scientist who a little over a decade ago headed the American Political Science Association and who belonged to the founders of the International Political Science Association: "But the almost overwhelming problem of the modern world can be solved only by our most mature minds, and political science is the integrating and synthesizing discipline. The pulling together must be under our auspices . . . I have seen something of the mistakes which are made because too specialized minds are at times on top, and because a broad political judgment was absent. It is the task of the political scientist to synthesize everything which goes into the formulation and implementation of public policy. . . . I would be less than frank with you if I did not assert that foreign and military policy is hardly the task of the nuclear physicist and that power and bureaucracy and other similar concepts are being manhandled by the psychologists. Why? Partly because political scientists have not sufficiently used the other social sciences and partly because we are focusing too much attention on small problems without developing frontal attacks on large, significant ones."[1]

Since there is, quite obviously, no consensus concerning the meaning and scope of political science even among those who constitute the political science profession, there can be and there is no unanimity among political scientists as to the role which they allot to other disciplines in their study of politics. Broadly speaking, the accumulation of human knowledge may be divided into the natural sciences, which study the physical environment in which men live, and the humanities, which deal with man's affairs, organizations, and mental make-up. Political science can, therefore, be classified as a humanistic science, and, particularly, as a social science, since it focuses on man in society and not as an individual.

Depending on their particular bent, political scientists may concern themselves with the problems of birth and death rates, race, and eugenics, to give but a few examples of topics which lie in the border zone of political science, biology, and zoology.

Political scientists will use the findings of the historians to compare contemporary political units with those of the past, and unless they wish to start *de novo* they will remember Sir John R. Seeley's jingle:

> History without political science has no fruit;
> Political science without history has no root.

We have already drawn attention to the sociologist's effort to discover common denominators for all of man's social relationships and activities, be they the relationships and activities of the family, a fraternal order, a religious congregation, or the state; and it stands to reason that many of these studies

---

[1] James K. Pollock, "The Primacy of Politics" (Presidential Address), American Political Science Review, March 1951, p. 15.

could be of value to the student of politics. When the political scientist speaks of "community" or refers to "interests" and "attitudes" he uses sociological terminology. If so inclined, he might also apply sociological methods of stratifying populations, as he might use sociological techniques of questionnaire construction and sampling in endeavors to analyze public opinion and the influence of political parties or special interest groups on political decisions.

Many political scientists draw on the findings of geographers, whose field of study is the surface of the earth with all its physical characteristics and natural resources. While probably most political scientists realize that man's dependence on geographical conditions decreases as he increases his knowledge of utilizing the "laws of nature" for his civilizational purposes, they nevertheless recognize the relationship between geographical factors and many socio-political facts. Some political scientists, preoccupied with problems of military strategy, might stress geopolitics, i.e., political geography as applied to the field of foreign policy.

In a number of universities of the Western world, political science is to this day taught under the heading of "political economy," indicating the close relationship between the study of economics (i.e., the study of the production, distribution, and consumption of material wealth) with the study of the state in so far as it concerns itself with the economic activities of its members. Here, again, we must remember that it is the focus of scientific interest which distinguishes one social science from another, and that there will be many points of overlapping and interpenetration in all social sciences. (This, in turn, may tempt some social scientists to develop deterministic theories of society and stress this or that aspect of social life as the supreme determinant.)[1]

While some political scientists satisfy themselves with the study of objectively (externally) perceivable political relations, others—searching for the motivation which causes human beings to behave as they do—might be inclined to use the methods and findings of psychologists and psychoanalysts who (distinguished largely by differing techniques of inquiry) specialize in the study of the causations of individual behavior.

Those political scientists who assume that man—as distinguished from the animals—seeks a justification for his existence which transcends his physical nature, will stress the intimate relationship of their study to that of philosophy,[2] particularly of ethics or moral philosophy, and explore the immediate and potential problems of politics with a view to their ethical consequences. More

---

[1] Marxists (i.e., the followers of Karl Marx and Friedrich Engels) see the whole sociopolitical order at any given time and in any given place as a superstructure reflecting the mode of economic production and the relationships and institutions which constitute the "economic conditions," making private ownership of the means of production the chief cause of the existence of the state, which, Marxists claim, would "wither away" as the consequence of a "socialist revolution" and the introduction of public ownership of the means of production.

[2] Philosophy, the Anglicized compound of the Greek words *philein* (to love) and *sophia* (wisdom), was originally conceived as the science of sciences, entrusted with the establishment of general principles under which all facts could be understood. Later on, philosophy developed into the science of the first principles of being or of ultimate reality. Among its subdivisions are epistemology, logic, aesthetics, and ethics.

interested in the direction of political events than the efficiency of political techniques and institutions, these political scientists will consider political philosophy an important, if not the most important, aspect of political science.

If one glances through the political science offerings in the catalogues of universities and colleges, one frequently encounters course titles which seem to have but rather tenuous connections with political science and are probably listed in order to accommodate a special fancy of the instructors of such courses. On the other hand, the lack of consensus among political scientists as to the meaning and scope of their field of study leads by necessity to different emphases which are reflected in what the members of a political science department consider to be the major subdivisions of their discipline. Nevertheless (and, one might be inclined to add, miraculously) an international conference of political scientists, held in 1948 under the auspices of UNESCO, was able to indicate what they regarded as the most important subdivisions of political science. They listed these units:

I. *Political Theory*.[1] 1. Political theory. 2. History of political ideas.

II. *Government*. 1. The constitution. 2. National government. 3. Regional and local government. 4. Public administration. 5. Economic and social functions of government. 6. Comparative political institutions.

III. *Parties, Groups, and Public Opinion*. 1. Political parties. 2. Groups and associations. 3. Citizen participation in government and administration. 4. Public opinion.

IV. *International Relations*. 1. International politics. 2. International organization and administration. 3. International law.[2]

In conclusion: The systematic study of politics—circumscribed by the title "political science"—is a most challenging and responsible discipline. By focusing on the political relations and activities in human existence, it clarifies the political scene and helps illuminate the political by-products of social life in general. If carefully and critically studied, political science can be a guide for those who might otherwise be perplexed—if not overwhelmed—by the welter of different political opinions and the multitude and magnitude of political events. But—let us remember—the science of politics is not politics itself. The scientific occupation with politics does not and cannot relieve the student of the burden to make up his mind as to his own position in political life. All it can do—at best—is to tell him that if he takes this or that position, he will

---

[1] A "theory" in the modern technical sense of the term always involves an "explanation" or a "prediction" that is based on an explanation, as distinct from mere descriptions and from unexplained proposals or evaluations. In a broader sense, the term "theory" is frequently used to denote an author's entire thought on a subject matter. Whether a theory is "scientific" or "non-scientific" depends on the author's or critic's use of the term "science." Cf. Arnold Brecht, op. cit.

[2] Cf. William Ebenstein, "Toward International Collaboration in Political Science: A Report on the UNESCO Project, 'Methods in Political Science'," American Political Science Review, December 1948, p. 1186.

have to employ these or those means to bring about a realization of his political intentions. The student must ask himself whether his concept of ethics is consistent with his position and allows him to pursue the means for putting it into political practice. If he desires the end but finds the means detestable, he alone has to decide whether or not "the end justifies the means." As Max Weber wrote in one of his classic essays on the role of science and the scientist, "the teacher can pose the necessity of this choice, but more he cannot do if he wants to remain a teacher and refrain from becoming a demagogue."[1] The teacher of political science has, of course, the right of every citizen to take a political position of his own, and if he is so inclined, he may himself enter the political arena actively. But as a teacher in the classroom he will do well to remember that the privileged relationship between his students and him imposes upon him the obligation not to agitate, not to preach, not to prophesy, but to acquaint his listeners as honestly as is humanly possible with all the ramifications of his subject matter—leaving it to them to be their own historians, political critics, and predictors. This does not preclude the teacher from giving his own preferences and convictions—provided he states that they are his attitudes and are as open to debate as any other statement of preferences and convictions. In fact the mature teacher knows that the best guaranty for an objective comprehension of political data is the full and frank recognition of his own subjective position which, as Sigmund Neumann observed, is frequently the very reason for his preoccupation with his object of inquiry.[2] Most of the masters of political science, i.e., those men whose names withstood the screening process of history, have dedicated themselves to an analysis of political phenomena in times of crisis, when the traditional could no longer be taken for granted and when a reexamination of political structures and relations became imperative. We live in such a time. The contest between Communist totalitarianism and the free world, the massive awakening of hitherto stagnant segments of world humanity —the "revolution of rising expectations"—coupled with the introduction of a technology which tends to revolutionize all of social life (and which also includes the potentiality of obliterating many, if not all, civilizational achievements), makes the scientific clarification of politics a practical necessity.

Joseph Dunner

---

[1] Max Weber, *Soziologie, Weltgeschichtliche Analysen, Politik,* Stuttgart, 1956, p. 333.

[2] Cf. Sigmund Neumann, "Der Demokratische Dekalog," Vierteljahreshefte fur Zeitgeschichte, Stuttgart, January 1963. This article based on Professor Neumann's lecture in the Free University of Berlin was published posthumously. Sigmund Neumann, an outstanding member of the political science profession, for many years chairman of the political science department of Wesleyan University in Middletown, Connecticut, died on October 22, 1962.

A

AAA. See **Agricultural Adjustment Act.**

Abbas, Ferhat. (1899—   )
Algerian political leader, educated in science, he advocated assimilation and moderation until 1943. Later he founded the Union Democratique du Manifeste Algerien and supported a free nation federated with France. Elected to the French and Algerian assemblies, he rejected violence when the national revolution began in 1954. Shifting his position he joined the Front de Liberation Nationale (F.L.N.) and in 1958 became head of the Provisional Government. In its left turn he lost his post to Ben Khedda. Algeria's independence in July 1962 and Ben Bella's rise to Premier obscured Ferhat Abbas who became President of the National Assembly. P.F.P.

Ability Theory.
Taxes as a compulsory contribution to the support of government are levied upon individual taxpayers according to a prescribed formula. Capitation taxes are collected at the same rate from every taxpayer while the general property tax is levied at the same rate for each unit of value. These forms of taxes are said to be unfair to low income taxpayers, and consequently taxes are levied according to "the ability to pay" of each taxpayer, thus following Adam Smith's statement that the compulsory contribution of the taxpayers should be made "according to their respective abilities". Today progressive income tax rates are levied on prescribed segments of net income. This is said to be the best way of levying taxes according to ability, although no real criteria have been fixed to measure its true fairness. A.E.N.

Abjuration.
A repudiation on oath of a principle, right, or privilege; **e.g.**, an alien desiring to become a citizen is required to disclaim allegiance to the country of his birth. J.F.Z.

Ableman v. Booth. 21 Howard 506 (1859).
Wisconsin's highest court attempted to nullify the Fugitive Slave Act of 1850 by releasing through habeas corpus action a violator convicted in Federal district court. The United States Supreme Court held that the federal system precludes State courts from interfering with judicial actions of the United States. J.M.S.

Abolitionism.
The doctrines and policies of American agitators who, in the three decades before the Civil War, worked for the immediate abolition of Negro slavery. Some of the abolitionists, such as William Lloyd Garrison, believed that moral persuasion was the only proper weapon; others, such as James G. Birney, advocated direct political action; while still others, such as John Brown, were quite willing to resort to force. W.W.

Absentee voting.
Provision for the casting of ballots by eligible voters who are unable to cast their vote at their regularly designated polling places during election hours. These provisions, varying greatly from state to state, usually permit eligible voters who are ill or absent from home for business or other reasons to vote by mail. K.E.H.

Absolute.
That which is absolved from limitations or conditions, as in "a. power," "a. sovereignty." More especially: "a. values," i.e. values that are independent of other (ulterior, ultimate) values, of particular conditions, facts, times, personal opinions. See **relativism, value.** A.B.

Abyssinia. See **Ethiopa.**

Academic Freedom.
A body of rights and privileges enjoyed by teachers—and sometimes students—in universities and colleges. In Germany and some other European and Latin-American states, such privileges and immunities often are expressed in statute. In the United States, Britain, and other countries, however, these freedoms are not expressed in positive law, but are rather customary and prescriptive usages, with some claim to origin in the nature of institutions of higher learning.

As a formal concept, academic freedom assumed its present character in the German universities late in the nineteenth century, in order to guarantee professors and students certain well-defined privileges of teaching, studying, and transferring from institution to institution, as related to their particular intellectual disciplines; such statutes were enacted with a view to limiting the otherwise great jurisdiction of state ministers of education.

In the United States, academic freedom is an ill-defined but recognized bundle of rights and claims, always in a debatable zone, rather like the controversy that springs eternal about the character of natural rights. Very generally speaking, advocates of American academic freedom assert that professors and instructors at universities and colleges have a right to secure tenure of their posts without arbitrary interference by the university's administrators, alumni, state legislatures or executives, or groups or persons outside the Academy. This freedom is understood to imply informal guarantees—sometimes backed by tenure—contracts enforceable in courts of law—that a member of a faculty may teach with a considerable latitude of expression and opinion in his discipline, provided he is not deliberately subversive of public order and morality.

Since the middle of the nineteenth century, American controversy concerning the value or abuse of academic freedom has centered, successively, around such questions as bimetallism, Darwinian evolutionary doctrine, involvement in the World Wars, and Communism. Although during the 1940's and much of the 1950's the debate chiefly concerned the question of whether Communists should enjoy rights of tenure in institutions of higher learning, a fresh subject of argument began to appear with the expansion of American universities and colleges: the right of the college instructor to criticize the standards of scholarship and instruction in his institution.

In the United States and most other nations, the claims of academic freedom are applied only in greatly-diminished degree to students and to secondary schools. The general assumption for the existence of academic freedom is this: that a frank exchange of views between competent professors and well-informed college students is necessary for the cultivation of the higher learning. R.K.

Accident Insurance.

Employees who are injured, contract an occupational disease, or are killed in the course of their employment are generally covered by workman's compensation insurance. Statutory rejection of three common law defenses—the fellow servant doctrine, contributory negligence, assumption of the risk, has made employers liable for most injuries received on the job. The States provide that employers may meet this obligation through insurance placed with a government operated fund or with a private carrier, or through self insurance by financially responsible firms. Each of the United States has a workman's compensation insurance law under which awards payable for specific injuries are stipulated. Most States provide for administrative determination of claims. J.M.S.

Accidental War.

An unwanted general war. The dreaded cycle of thermonuclear exchange triggered by something other than the purposeful will of one of the adversaries. Conceivable causes: misinterpretation of intelligence data through human or technical error; unexplained nuclear explosion(s) inadvertently caused by man or machine; deranged personnel; or a malevolent third party. L.P.B.

Accion Democratica.

The Venezuelan reform party founded in 1941, but growing out of earlier organizations of the "generation of 1928," influenced by Romulo Gallegos. "Democratic Action" (AD) can be identified generally with other parties of the anti-Communist "democratic left" in Latin America (e.g., APRA of Peru, National Liberation Party of Costa Rica, Colorado Party of Uruguay and Revolutionary Party of Guatemala). AD's relatively far left orientation has moderated to evolutionary socialism and the welfare state. The program includes: Agrarian reform, universal education, social security, unionization, propagation of democratic ideology (civil liberties, "social rights," free and periodic elections, etc.), abolition of privilege (e.g., of foreign investors and the military), industrial development, increased peasant and worker productivity, and promotion of Latin American economic integration. Romulo Betancourt, AD leader, was elected president of Venezuela in 1958. R.D.H.

Accretion.
The formation of new land through natural causes, such as alluvial deposits or the rise of islands. May lead to the extension of the territorial jurisdiction of the State concerned in which case no formal assertion of jurisdiction is necessary. S.E.

Accumulation (of capital).
Addition of earnings or profits, otherwise distributable as dividends, to the active capital of a corporation. In a nation as a whole the accumulation of capital is made possible by savings of individuals and of business. The inequality of incomes is of considerable help in this economic process, as without it there might be little saving, but the chief source of capital accumulation for business growth is reinvested earnings. W.N.

Acquittal.
A person tried for crime before judge or jury who is found innocent gains acquittal. Under the United States constitutional guarantee against double jeopardy, one may not be tried again for the same offense. A crime which is a violation of both Federal and State laws may be punished by either or both jurisdictions.
Abbate v. United States, 359 U.S. 187 (1959).
Bartkus v. Illinois, 359 U.S. 121 (1959). J.M.S.

Act of Settlement 1701.
Any remnant of doubt about the supremacy of parliament over the crown was removed when the Act of Settlement deliberately changed the line of succession to the throne. But of equal, if not greater, significance, the Act of Settlement assured the independence of the judiciary by stipulating that judges could not be removed except by an "address of both Houses of Parliament." In addition, the act provided for a fixed salary for the judges and thereby raised the status of the judiciary and further assured its independence. C.A.McC.

Act of war. See War.

Action francaise.
Founded in 1899, after the Dreyfus affair, l'Action francaise appeared daily from 1908 to 1944. Charles Maurras, Jacques Bainville, and Leon Daudet preached their doctrine of "integral nationalism" which called for the eradication of republican institutions, removal of "Huguenot" and "Jewish" influences in France. Above all, France needed a monarchy which would authoritatively govern a decentralized France in the Catholic tradition, i.e., Christian sentiment regulated by Graeco-Roman discipline. Disavowed by papacy and pretender, l'Action francaise bitterly opposed Germany until 1933, then changed its line, not because Germany was no longer its enemy, but because it hated the French Republic more. France, although defeated by the Nazis, emerged victoriously in the eyes of Maurras, when Petain proclaimed his **travail, famille, patrie.** K.B.

Adair v. United States. 208 U.S. 161.
Adair v. U.S. declared unconstitutional a provision of Federal law which forbade an interstate railroad from discharging an employee because of membership in a labor union. The Supreme Court stated that the Act deprived the employer of freedom of contract and property rights guaranteed by the due process clause of the Fifth Amendment, and that there was no connection between the commerce power and labor union membership which could justify such regulation. In a related case, Coppage v. Kansas, 236 U.S. 1 (1915), the U. S. Supreme Court invalidated a State law which prohibited an employer from requiring an employee to sign an agreement ("yellow dog contract") not to join or remain a labor union member as a condition of employment. The Court cited Adair v. United States and held the statute un-

constitutional because it interfered with the employer's freedom of contract and property rights contrary to the due process provision of the Fourteenth Amendment. The curbs on union membership imposed by the cases cited were reversed by the Norris—La Guardia Act (1932) which prohibits Federal court enforcement of "yellow dog contracts"; by Phelps Dodge Corp. v. N.L.R.B., 317 U.S. 177 (1941), which held that an employer's refusal to hire because of union membership is an illegal practice under the National Labor Relations Act. J.M.S.

Adams, John. (1735—1826).
Second President of the United States. Adams' Presidency, during the single term of which he provoked sharp criticism from the rising Jeffersonian party and encountered bitter controversy within his own Federalist party as well, was preceded by a long and varied career in public life. He was a leader of the American colonists' protests against British rule from the time of the Stamp Act, a strong supporter of the Declaration of Independence, principal author of the Massachusetts Constitution of 1780, diplomatic agent for the Confederation government and for a period its Minister to Great Britain, and Vice President for both terms under Washington. Adams was, besides, a scholar of political and legal institutions and a writer of substantial works thereon. He is known to American political theory as a conservative who, assuming propensities toward self-aggrandizement to be general among mankind and observing that the "haves" and "have nots" form groups between which there is an inevitable tendency toward conflict, defended the "mixed constitution" as the best means to protect against despotism arising either from within the government or from the unconfined exercise of power by groups in a position to control it. Thus, in his **Defense of the Constitutions of the United States** (1787-88) he argued not only for a functional separation of powers, but for the virtue of a bicameral system which, based upon different levels of property qualification in the electoral constituencies of the two legislative chambers, would insure against **representation becoming** the vehicle for a majority despotism on the one hand or a plutocratic oligarchy on the other. R.H.S.

Adams, John Quincy. (1767—1848.)
Sixth President of the United States and eldest son of President John Adams. Born in Braintree (Quincy), Massachusetts, John Quincy Adams studied in France (1778-79) and Holland (1780), before graduating from Harvard (1787) where he later taught rhetoric and oratory (1806-09). After briefly practicing law in Boston, Adams began a brilliant diplomatic career and helped lay the foundations of American foreign policy as Minister to the Netherlands (1794-96); Prussia (1797-1801); Russia (1809-14); and Great Britain (1815-17). His diplomacy reached one peak in 1814 as head of the American Peace Commission to negotiate the Treaty of Ghent, and another under President James Monroe as Secretary of State (1817-25) when he purchased Florida from Spain (1819), recognized the independence of Spain's Latin American colonies, and promulgated the Monroe Doctrine (1823). A statesman of exceptionally high principle, outspoken, and fiercely independent, Adams suffered bitter disappointments as a politician. He resigned as a Federalist U. S. Senator (1803-18), joined Madison's Republicans, ran second to Jackson in the Electoral College, but became President (1825-29) through election by the House of Representatives with help from Henry Clay. A founder of the Smithsonian Institution, advocate of a national university and internal improvements, disinterested in using patronage power, Adams was ahead of his time, and lost the Presidency to Jackson (1828). As an elder statesman, he served in Congress (1831-48), powerfully opposing slavery and the Mexican War, and successfully contesting the gag rule. K.E.D.

Adams-Clay Republicans.
The wing of the Democratic-Republican party which after 1825 supported John Quincy Adams and Henry Clay and contributed to the eventual creation of the National Republican Party in the U.S.A. W.W.

Aden. See Appendix.

Adenauer, Konrad. (1876—   )
Chancellor of Federal Republic of Germany 1949-1963. Lord Mayor of Cologne, 1917-1933. President, Prussian State Council, 1920-1933. Arrested on several occasions during Hitler period. Chairman, Christian-Democratic Union. President of Parliamentary Council, 1948, entrusted with making Basic Law (Bonn Constitution). Firm exponent of European cooperation and Western defense.   M.C.V.

Ad Hoc Political Committee.
Established (1951) by the UN General Assembly for the duration of its sixth session, re-established at each of the four consecutive sessions, transformed at the eleventh session of the General Assembly (1956) into a Main Committee and renamed "Special Political Committee".   G.V.W.

Adjournment Motion.
A procedure in British-type parliaments which permits debate on a wide variety of subjects and therefore is a normal device for criticism used by the opposition or by backbenchers. Types include adjournment to raise a "matter of urgent public importance," the regular 30 minutes of adjournment debate at the end of each day's business during which several members may make criticisms which are answered by the government, and occasional motions with an obstructive intention which may be ruled "dilatory" by the speaker. Such a motion is also a procedure for interrupting debate on any subject in order to permit preparation for later debate or to permit another subject to be considered.   R.H.B.

Administration.
It is the process by which policy is carried out. Decisions as to what shall be done are made by the people directly, or by representative legislative bodies, or by a monarch or dictator, or even to some extent by judicial and executive organs and officers. These are then put into execution by administrative officials. The application of established general principles to specific cases is often spoken of as administration or management.   H.W.

Administrative County.
One of the two main units of local government in the United Kingdom which includes mainly small towns and rural areas. Sixty-one of these are subdivided into non-county or municipal boroughs, urban districts and rural districts, the last of which are divided into parishes. The County of London is a special case, and it is divided into 28 metropolitan boroughs and the City of London.   R.H.B.

Administrative law.
That law which controls the authority and procedures of governmental administrative agencies in their dealings with private parties. Administrative law involves review by the courts over the rule making (sublegislative) and adjudication (subjudicial power) of these agencies. In addition to decisions of judges, the sources of administrative law include constitutions; statutes; administrative agency rules, decisions, and practices; and customary laws or behavior.   R.D.S.

Administrative Procedure.
Sequence of operations performed by executive and independent regulatory agencies of government to complete an administrative transaction, particularly with relation to rule-making or the issuance of orders. Administrative procedure may involve conference, consultation, investigation, notice and hearing, or research.

In the U.S.A. the increasing need for greater flexibility and informality, specialization and expertness, and continuity than the legislature or judiciary could provide in coping with complex modern industrial and technological developments, led to the emergence of administrative experts in government. Neither the Constitution nor Congress, however, laid down a system of procedures for the administrative experts to make rules and issue orders. Procedures, consequently, were developed by the agencies individually, varying from agency to agency and also from time to time within the same agency.

At the national level, the Federal Administrative Procedure Act of 1946 (60 Stat. 237, 5 U.S.C.A. 1001, June 11, 1946) attempted to formalize and standardize administrative procedure and to set what it described as a "fair administrative procedure." It prescribed three types of procedures with regard to the rule-making and order issuing process: (1) discretionary, (2) administrative, and (3) adjudicatory. Discretionary procedure refers to those areas of rule-making for which a specific procedure is not prescribed by constitution, statute or the courts. Involved here, for example, are military rule-making requiring secrecy and accordingly precluding public hearings, and rule-making relating to public property, grants, loans, benefits, or contracts affecting private rights only indirectly and in which a formal procedure requiring notice and hearing would not serve a useful purpose. Included also in discretionary procedure are interpretative rules, general statements, and rules of agency organization. Administrative procedure, as prescribed by the Federal Administrative Procedures Act, requires publication in the **Federal Register** of: (a) a statement of the time, place, and nature of public rule-making proceedings; (b) reference to the authority under which the rule is proposed; and (c) either the terms or substance of the proposed rule or a description of the subjects and issues involved. Unless these items of public notice are published in the **Federal Register** at least thirty days prior to the designated effective date the rules or orders cannot have legal effect. All persons involved or interested in such matters must be given an opportunity to participate in the rule-making through submission of written data, views or arguments with or without the opportunity of being present. After consideration of all the relevant matter presented, the agency must incorporate in the rules it adopts a statement of their basis and purpose. Adjudicatory procedure is a judicialized kind required where rules must be made, as prescribed by statute, on the record after opportunity for an agency hearing. Accordingly, agency hearings are generally required only when the statutes so demand them. In such cases, the parties concerned are adversaries and the private persons involved seek declarations of rights under existing law.

In the United States, the administrative experts are subject to the ordinary law just as any other person is. If a person believes an administrative rule or order is unjust or discriminatory or violates constitutional rights, he can go to the ordinary courts for judicial review of the administrative action. The Federal Administrative Procedure Act provided generally for such judicial review, but a complainant is required to exhaust administrative remedies before resorting to the courts. The courts may compel an administrative agency to perform legally required action which it has unlawfully withheld or denied or unreasonably delayed. They may invalidate actions that are arbitrary or capricious or which involve abuse of discretionary authority or which violate constitutional rights or which ignore procedures required by law or decisions and rulings which are not supported by substantial evidence or are not warranted by the facts.

While "due process of law" in the Fifth Amendment to the Constitution does not guarantee any particular form of procedure, but rather protects substantial rights, its protection involves the employment of a particular administrative procedure under certain conditions. It is generally accepted, for example, that due process does not require notice and hearing as a condition antecedent to administrative rule-making. That is, if the action taken by an administrative agency is "legislative," preliminary notice and hearing are not required. If, however, the action is "judicial," notice and hearing must be given prior to the determination. At times, though, the difficulty is distinguishing between "legislative" and "judicial" action. Once taken, "legislative" action may be challenged on grounds of being **ultra vires** or depriving a person of life, liberty, or property without due process of law. On the other hand, the statute concerned may specifically require notice and hearing. Nevertheless, even though an agency statute may not expressly demand notice and hearing, the Supreme Court has held that, where notice and hearing may be necessary in order to save the statute from invalidity, this requirement must be read into the law. (**Wong Yang Sung v. McGrath**, 339 U.S. 33 [1950]). This decision has served as a warning to administrative agencies that they are not free from the hearing requirements of the Administrative Procedure Act simply because the statutes they enforce do not specifically provide for notice and hearing.

The Administrative Procedure Act provided also for the hiring within the agencies of trial or hearing examiners as civil servants to make the determinations impartially and independently of the administrative officials and the prosecuting officers. This was the result of many studies made of the administrative rule-making process in which the feeling was generally shared that the prosecuting and judging functions should be separated. This was accomplished by the Administrative Procedure Act's prohibition of the union of these two functions in the same person.

In the past, the area of controversy was centered around the question of whether administrative regulation was necessary or desirable. Today, the critical area is administrative procedure, particularly whether a hearing must be provided and whether judicial review is to be available. Actually, the administrative agencies still enjoy a large measure of independence from judicial review. In addition, they can hire lawyers at public expense to defend their action, whereas the private complainant must assume the high cost of litigation and then finds that the courts tend to favor the administrative experts in technical matters. The problem of administrative procedure is, thus, a complex and continuing one involving our developing concepts of democracy and the integration of an administrative system into the democratic process. O.K.

Administrative Reorganization.

Modern government has grown rapidly as new agencies and services have been added in response to real needs or political pressures. The resulting unwieldy structures proved to be costly and relatively inefficient.

About 1910, in the United States, informed leaders began asking for a streamlining of the executive branches of the several government levels. The subsequent changes are known collectively as "administrative reorganization." Authorizing statutes and executive orders have consolidated related services, tightened lines of communication within and among services, created offices for fiscal administration, and placed greater controls in the hands of the chief executive. To be effective, reorganization must be a continuous process. Many early efforts were considered conclusive, only to be found wanting a generation later, requiring new reform efforts. Among the best known studies which have preceded administrative reorganizations on the national level are the Reports of the first and second "Hoover Commissions." At least 39 states have had their own "little Hoover" commissions, followed by reforms and reorganization on the state level. A.E.N.

Administrative Tribunals.

Bodies regularly constituted to pass judicially on complaints against administrative officers. In a sense supplementary to the regular judicial courts, administrative tribunals represent at their best—as in the French Regional Councils (Tribunaux Administratifs) —the attempt to impose respect for law upon those charged with the day-to-day conduct of administrative operations. Rules of evidence and procedure may be the same as for regular judicial courts, as in the U. S. Court of Claims. P.J.C.

Admiralty Jurisdiction.

Admiralty jurisdiction, according to English law, extended to all acts or torts committed on the high seas, on the streams where the tide ebbed and flowed, and to all maritime contracts concerning trade, navigation or business on these waters. The U.S. Constitution (Art. III sec. 2) confers on the Federal courts jurisdiction over "all cases of admiralty and maritime jurisdiction." Justice Story has suggested that "maritime" was included probably to prevent a narrow interpretation of "admiralty." The Supreme Court has extended the terms to cover commercial activities on public navigable waters of the U.S. including canals and the Great Lakes. (The Genessee Chief [1851] 12 How. 443: Ex-parte Boyer [1884] 109 U.S. 629.) The Federal jurisdiction is exclusive of state control and is exercised through the regular courts beginning in the Federal District Courts. The Constitution and Congressional statutes under it confer and regulate admiralty jurisdiction but the courts themselves determine the scope of admiralty law in the light of a largely unwritten code of international admiralty law. E.G.T.

Admiralty Powers of U.S. Congress.

The Constitutional source of these powers is found in a number of clauses in Article I, Section 8, such as those which empower Congress to define and punish crime and felonies on the high seas; to make rules concerning captures on land and water, the Commerce and the implied powers clauses. American **Admiralty** law is applicable not only to the high seas but also to the Great Lakes and all navigable rivers in the United States. It is derived from the general maritime law of nations modified by Congressional enactments and decisions of the Federal Courts, whose jurisdiction is subject to Congress. A.A.N.

"Admitted" states.

The thirty-seven states admitted to the United States since its formation by the original thirteen states. Two independent nations were admitted as states (Vermont and Texas), one was acquired from Mexico and directly achieved statehood (California), and three were carved out of existing states (Kentucky, Maine, and West Virginia). The remaining thirty-one states were admitted following periods of limited self-government as territories (the latest being Alaska in 1958 and Hawaii in 1959). Art. IV, Sec. 3 of the U.S. Constitution gives to Congress virtually complete authority in admitting new states and determining what conditions are to be met. Traditional requirements have been experience with limited self-government, desire for statehood, and adequacy of population and wealth. New states are admitted on an equal footing with the thirteen original states and the act is irrevocable. R.R.R.

Adoula, Cyrille.

Prime Minister of the Republic of Congo. Born 1923 in Leopoldville, a member of the Mongala tribe. Educated in Catholic mission schools. Early career in trade union activity. In 1959 helped found the leading General Federation of Congolese Workers and was for a time a member of Executive Committee of the International Confederation of Free Trade Unions. Elected Senator from Equator Province in May 1960. Despite early associations with Patrice Lumumba, did not enter his government after independence came to the Congo. Nominated and elected as Premier of the first stable government of the Congo in August 1961. Resigned in July 1964 to head caretaker government. R.L.K.

Advisory ballot.

A poll, or referendum, the results of which are not binding but are designed to determine the attitude of the voters and possibly to instruct their representatives. W.W.

Advisory Commission.

A permanent or **ad hoc** commission appointed by a member of the executive branch and/or the legislative branch of a government to study a governmental problem and submit recommendations. J.F.Z.

Advisory Opinions.

Opinions given by a court before a case arises clarifying the constitutionality of a statute or proposed law. The International Court of Justice gives advisory opinions to the General Assembly and Security Council of the United Nations. In the United States the governor in ten states and the legislature in seven states are authorized by the state constitution to request advisory opinions from the supreme court. Only in Colorado are advisory opinions binding upon the court in future cases. In the other states advisory opinions are considered to be the personal opinions of individual judges. J.F.Z.

Aerial Domain.

Every country claims exclusive and complete sovereignty over air space located above its territory and territorial waters. Route patterns for commercial airlines are determined by diplomatic agreement. There is international discussion concerning national or other jurisdiction over outer space, which is defined as air space beyond the altitude attainable by conventional propelled aircraft.

Who should have authority over such outer space phenomena as interplanetary flight, orbital vehicles, radio frequencies, satellites for communication, observation and weather forecasting? J.M.S.

Aesopian Language.

Manipulation of language constitutes one of the Communists' most potent weapons in their drive for world domination. To the Communists words are tools to achieve effects, not means to communicate in the search for truth. They choose words not to clarify but to produce ambiguities and induce false thinking.

In many instances, the communists make communications serve a dual purpose—to say one thing to Communists while simultaneously conveying quite a different message to non-Communists. This practice has come to be labeled Aesopian language. Every communist communication must convey an orthodox, that is, a revolutionary activating message to the party and its followers. This same communication must convey a different, i.e., soothing, pacifying, and paralyzing message to the opponents of communism. The standard lexicon of the Communists for internal use is replete with terms like "violence" and "class struggle." It is a language of combat designed to win the struggle for the world through force, revolution and war. By contrast, Aesopian terminology—the words employed in external communications—is derived primarily from western political thinking and includes terms which evoke positive response. Communists are eager to create the impression that they are peace-loving and eager to develop an international system of "live and let live." A typical example of the Aesopian vocabulary is "peaceful coexistence." R.St.-H.

Afghanistan.

A land-locked country in Central Asia with an area of approximately 280,000 square miles and a population of roughly 12 million, whose capital is Kabul. The country did not exist as a cohesive entity until the 18th century. In theory Afghanistan is a constitutional monarchy but practically it is ruled by a centralized oligarchy. Afghanistan is a member of the United Nations which it joined in November 1946. J.G.St.

AFL-CIO. See American Federation of Labor—Congress of Industrial Organizations.

Africa, Economic Commission for

A regional commission of the United Nations Economic and Social Council. Established 1958 with headquarters in Addis Ababa. The only regional organization in Africa embracing all states and colonies, irrespective of geographical or ideological position. The ECA functions primarily in the area of economic research, preparation of reports and analyses of trade and investment problems, collection of statistical and economic data and in the training of governmental personnel in economic and developmental fields. The ECA does not provide economic aid or technical assistance, which are handled by other U.N. agencies.

Though an economic body, the ECA's activities have important political implications. So far, the ECA has engaged in studies on the impact of the European Common Market on African trade, the possibilities of a West African Customs Union and the problems of standardizing the collection of statistical and economic data throughout Africa. R.L.K.

Afro-Asian Bloc.

A loose grouping of states which form roughly one-half of the membership of the United Nations. The bloc is unified only on questions of anti-colonialism. On most others, it breaks down into four sub-groupings: (a) the Casablanca Powers — Guinea, Ghana, Mali, Morocco and the United Arab Republic—which are the most left-of-center; (b) the Monrovia group which consists of former British colonies and protectorates; (c) the Brazzaville group constituting the former French colonies and protectorates; these two groups tend to abstain on East-West issues, but in case of strong United States pressure upon them, such as the Congo accreditation question and that of Chinese representation, many of them tend to support the United States; and (d) the Asian group.

J.G.St.

Agency for International Development (AID).

It was set up by the United States Congress in 1961 with the passage of the Foreign Assistance Act. It replaced the International Cooperation Administration (ICA) as the main U.S. economic aid agency. The Administrator of AID has the rank of Undersecretary of State and is responsible to both the President and the Secretary of State. AID has taken over the Development Loan Fund and the Export-Import Bank's program for lending United States-owned foreign currencies.

R.J.S.

Agent Provocateur.

An agent provocateur is one who joins a suspected group in order to encourage its members to commit illegal acts which may then be punished. He pretends to be sympathetic toward the aims of the labor union, political or economic group that he infiltrates. Foreign undercover agents have entered other countries where they have associated with those disaffected for the purpose of promoting sabotage, sedition, treason or warlike acts.

J.M.S.

Aggrandizement.

Enlargement (e.g. the aggrandizement of the territory of one state at the expense of another or the aggrandizement of the executive power at the expense of the judicial); Advancement (e.g. aggrandizement from low estate to social prominence); Exaltation (e.g. the aggrandizement of Peter meant the depreciation of Paul).

G.A.K.

Aggression.

Ever since the establishment of the League of Nations, the problem of defining "aggression" engaged the attention of statesmen and their advisers on international law, but their efforts to establish an authoritative definition of aggression have been depressingly frustrating. At issue has been the legal control of resort to war in international relations. The Covenant of the League of Nations did not expressly prohibit aggression as such, much less define it, although Article 10 required member states to respect and preserve "as against external aggression" the territorial integrity and political independence of member states. And the sanctions of Article 16 were contingent, not upon "aggression" as such, but upon resort to war in breach of the Covenant, especially Article 10. The abortive Geneva Protocol of 1925 made an attempt at definition. Article 10 of the Protocol specified two forms of aggression, namely, first, "resort to war in violation of the undertakings contained in the Covenant and in the present Protocol"; and second, refusal to accept summons before, or to abide by the decisions of a competent court or tribunal, and to abide by the unanimous decision of the League Council.

In 1933, the Committee on Security Questions of the Disarmament Conference considered the meaning of aggression again. Upon lengthy deliberation, the Committee concluded that the definition of aggressor should be reserved for

that state which is the first to commit any of the following actions: (1) declaration of war upon another state; (2) invasion by its armed forces, with or without a declaration of war, into the territory of another state; (3) attack by its land, naval or air forces, with or without a declaration of war, on the territory, vessels, or aircraft of another state; (4) naval blockade of the coasts or ports of another state; (5) provision of support to armed bands formed in its territory which have invaded the territory of another state, or refusal, notwithstanding the request of the invaded state, to take in its own territory all the measures in its power to deprive those bands of all assistance or protection.

The proposals of both the Protocol and the Committee illustrate the difficulty of containing all forms of aggression within a definite formulation. It was, therefore, no accident that the League Special Committee on the definition of aggression reported later that no satisfactory definition could be drawn up, and that the determination of aggressor should be left in each case to the discretion of the League Council.

Insofar as the issue of peace enforcement against aggressor states is involved, the above-mentioned report of the League Special Committee might have offered an escape from a difficult theoretical problem. Indeed, the virtually unlimited power conferred by the Charter of the United Nations upon the Security Council to determine the existence of a "threat to the peace, breach of the peace, or act of aggression," disposes of the difficulty of defining aggression within the confines of any definite verbal formula, although the Great Power veto is likely to operate in the context of the Cold War as a practical barrier against this practical escape.

After World War II, the definition of aggression was made to embrace not only states but also individuals responsible for planning, preparing or waging aggressive war. This crime, enumerated as such in the Charters of the International Military Tribunals at Nuremberg and Tokyo, necessarily involved questions of punishing individuals for the crime of aggressive war. In December 1946, the General Assembly unanimously adopted a resolution in which it affirmed "the principles of international law recognized by the Charter of the Nuremberg Tribunal and the judgment of the Tribunal," although this affirmation does not have the binding force of a treaty.

The Charters of the International Military Tribunals did not attempt a definition, nor did the Tribunals' judgment illuminate the true nature of aggression. When the United Nations General Assembly requested the International Law Commission to establish the meaning of aggression as one of the principles of the Nuremberg Charter, the Commission found itself still faced by the familiar ambiguities. It considered two types of definitions, those using general terms, and those proceeding by enumeration. It soon abandoned enumeration, partly because it could not provide an exhaustive listing of all conceivable forms of aggression, and partly because it might unduly limit the judgment of organs applying the Code in the future. Despite long and earnest effort, the Commission could not agree on any general definition either. By way of compromise, Article 2 of the Commission's Draft Code of Offenses against Peace and Security made an "act of aggression" criminal without defining "aggression." Instead it added the affirmations (1) that an "act of aggression" includes certain specified acts the character of which might otherwise be disputable (such acts, for instance, as threats to resort to an act of aggression, preparation for the employment of armed forces, and fomentation of civil strife in another state) and (2) that an "act of aggression" does not include acts of both collective security and collective self-defense, or acts committed pursuant to a decision or recommendation by a competent organ of the United Nations. Both the inclusions and exclusions, vague and inexhaustive as they are, leave the Draft Code open to a wide variety of interpretation. R.St.-H.

Aggression (Communist definition).

Communist doctrine has taken great pains to distinguish between "just" and "unjust" wars. "Just" wars are by definition those fought by the Soviet Union and its allies to accelerate the global success of communism. By contrast, the communists define any war fought by non-Communists as "unjust." War is thus justified not in terms of the end result but rather in terms of who conducts it. If the "exploiting class" conducts it, it is "unjust"; if the "proletariat," it is "just." Lenin said in 1918:

. . . Legitimacy and justice from what point of view? Only from the point of view of the socialist proletariat and its struggle for emancipation. We do not recognize any other point of view. If war is waged by the exploiting class with the object of strengthening its class rule, such a war is a criminal war, and "defensism" in such a war is a base betrayal of socialism. If war is waged by the proletariat after it has conquered the bourgeoisie in its own country, and is waged with the object of strengthening and extending socialism, such a war is legitimate and "holy." (V. Lenin, " 'Left-Wing' Childishness and Petty-Bourgeois Mentality" [May 3-5, 1918], **Selected Works** [New York: International Publishers, 1943], Vol. VII, p. 357.)

Khrushchev said in Peking in 1959:

... We (the Communists) have always been against wars of conquest. Marxists have recognized, and recognize, only liberating, just wars; they have always condemned, and condemn, wars of conquest, imperialist wars. This is one of the characteristic features of Marxist-Leninist theory. (As reprinted in **The Sino-Soviet Dispute** [Documented and Analyzed by G. F. Hudson, Richard Lowenthal and Roderick MacFarquhar], [New York: 1961], p. 62.)

The Communist definition of aggression is closely related to the Communist concept of "just" and "unjust" wars. Accordingly, the Communists never can be aggressors even if they initiate war. Yet a non-Communist state defending itself against a direct and indirect aggressive attack launched by the Communists is necessarily an aggressor. R.St.-H.

Agrement (consent).

The term used in diplomacy to indicate that a state considers **persona grata** and is willing to receive a particular person as a diplomatic envoy from the sending state. The sending state asks agrément (consent) before accrediting a diplomat. J.E.T.

Agricultural Adjustment Act (AAA).

One of the imaginative measures enacted by the Congress of the United States in response to a national emergency during the famous "one hundred days" after March 4, 1933. Since the Great Depression of late 1920's and early 1930's struck hard against the welfare of the farmers, it was extremely urgent to correct the decline in farm income as one aspect of the massive task of rescuing the nation from the plight into which it had drifted and floundered. The Act provided production controls on specified commodities and authorized payments to cooperating farmers. It also authorized the Secretary of Agriculture to establish State and local farmer committees and bring them into the process of administration. This was done because it was believed that the program would be handled by knowledgeable local farmers more equitably, more responsibly, more acceptably, and more in keeping with democratic ideas. In 1936, the Supreme Court declared the AAA unconstitutional. J.H.

Agricultural Conservation Program.

A cooperative effort of the U. S. Department of Agriculture to share with individual farmers and ranchers the cost of carrying out soil and water conservation measures intended to (1) protect farm and ranch land from wind and water erosion, (2) improve the productivity of the agricultural resources, and (3) protect and improve the source, flow and use of water for agricultural purposes. Through this program, the Federal Government offers to share with farmers the cost of conservation practices authorized for use as a means for achieving the above purposes.

Averaging about 50 percent of the cost of a practice, this cost-sharing is provided in the form of conservation materials, services, and financial assistance. Costs are shared for those approved conservation practices on individual farms, for which cost-sharing is requested, and for which the work is performed according to recognized standards. J.H.

Agricultural Stabilization and Conservation Service.

The largest agency of the U. S. Department of Agriculture. Its principal function is the protection and stabilization of farm income through the administration of the farm programs authorized by law, such as, support of farm prices through loans to farmers on specified commodities and direct purchases of commodities from farmers and processors; management of the commodity inventories acquired by the Government as a result of price-support operations, including storage, transportation, sales, export payments, donations and financing of foreign disposal programs; production adjustment through acreage allotments and marketing quotas for certain basic commodities, retirement of land from crop production, and payments to farmers for diversion of acreage from specific crops, such as feed grains and wheat; payments to sugar and wool producers to protect them against foreign competition; conservation assistance by sharing with farmers the cost of installing needed soil, water, woodland, and wild-life conserving practices; certain marketing agreements and orders, such as milk orders, designed to attain market stabilization; emergency disaster relief by providing feed to farmers whose supplies have been destroyed by flood, drought, or other natural disaster; and planning for national defense in the fields of agricultural production and availability of food reserves and feed stocks. J.H.

Agudat Israel.
(Hebrew "Union of Israel.") World organization of Orthodox Jews, founded in 1912. Until 1947 it opposed Zionism on religious grounds. Its Israeli branch signed the Declaration of Independence and participated in the early governments. The supreme ruling body is the "Great Assembly," and its spiritual guidance is in the hands of the "Council of Sages" composed exclusively of rabbis. In Israel **Poale Agudat Israel** (Labor Agudat Israel) exists as a separate organization. Its close cooperation with Agudat Israel ceased in 1960, when P.A.I. (but not A.I.) joined the government. E.G.

A.I.D. See Agency for International Development.

Air Defense Command.
A part of the joint Continental Air Defense Command and the Canadian-American North American Air Defense Command (NORAD) defending the United States against air attack by missiles or manned aircraft through an extensive network of radio and radar stations, and manned and unmanned counter-weapon systems. T.W.

A.J.C. See Allied Council for Japan.

Alabama Award.
The decision of a celebrated international arbitration between the U.S. and Great Britain in 1871 at Geneva. It denied claims of the U.S. **for indirect** damages resulting from British non-neutral construction of Confederate warships—the **Alabama, Florida** and **Shenandoah**—and the losses they inflicted on American commerce. The award levied a sum of $15,500,000 against Great Britain for **direct** damages to the U. S. M.M.Mc.

Alaska Highway.
A highway from Dawson Creek, British Columbia, to Fairbanks, Alaska, built as a military project by the United States Army Engineers and American and Canadian civilian personnel in 1942-1943. Constructed at an estimated cost of $139,000,000 the road has been widely acclaimed as a notable engineering achievement. Except for the 302 miles lying within the borders of Alaska, since April 3, 1946, the highway has been maintained and operated wholly by Canada. W.W.

Albania.
Albania has an area of 11,097 square miles, largely mountainous. Its population is estimated at 1,700,000, three fourths Moslems. The Ghegs and Tosks comprise the two major groups of Albanians, descendants of ancient Illyrians and Thracians. Some 750,000 Albanians live in Yugoslavia.

A kingdom, established in the third century B.C., was conquered by Rome in 167 B.C. and held until the fall of the Empire. Invasions followed. Despite fierce resistance by national hero Scanderbeg in the 15th century the Turks conquered Albania. In 1878 a League for the Defense of the Albanian Nation was established to seek autonomy. The Albanians rebelled in 1911 and independence was proclaimed on November 28, 1912. The boundaries, established in 1913, are basically those of today.

Occupied during World War I, Albania regained its independence in 1920. In 1924 Ahmet Zogu, former Premier, seized power with Yugoslav support. Albania became a republic in 1925, with Zogu as President and a kingdom in 1928, with him as King Zog. In April 1939 Italy occupied Albania and Zog fled. The National Liberation Movement, created by the Communist Party, assumed power after withdrawal of the occupying armies.

The Constitution of 1946, amended in 1950, declared Albania a People's Republic. Legislative power is vested in the unicameral People's Assembly, elected every four years from a single list of candidates. Executive power resides in the Council of Ministers, headed by the Premier. The judiciary, consisting of lower and higher courts, is elected or appointed for fixed terms. The Workers' (Communist) Party is the only party. Closer Soviet-Yugoslav relations have contributed to Soviet-Albanian differences and in December, 1961 Moscow severed diplomatic relations with Tirana. J.J.K.

Albany Congress of 1754.

An assembly of representatives of American colonies called by Great Britain in 1754 in Albany, to consult in regard to the threatening French and Indian War. The most notable result was a plan of colonial union offered by Benjamin Franklin. It provided for a colonial President and a Grand Council with power to collect taxes, provide for a military establishment, control Indian affairs, purchase lands and control western settlements. It pointed the way to union and federalism, finally adopted by the constitutional convention in 1787. J.E.R.

Alexander the Great (356—323 B.C.).

Son of King Philip II of Macedon. Alexander conquered and hellenized the then known world—today referred to as the Middle East. B.J.L.S.

Alfaro, Eloy (1842—1912).

Born in Montecristo, a little town on the Pacific Coast of Ecuador. He was the son of a Spaniard and an Ecuadorian Indian mother. He did not pursue university studies. He became prosperous in a business devoted to Panamá hats. From his youth he espoused the radical-liberal cause and worked diligently for its triumph in Ecuador. He lived in exile in Panama, Costa Rica and Nicaragua during which time he plotted against oppressive political regimes. From Nicaragua he returned to Ecuador, landing at Guayaquil, and with the triumph of the radical liberal movement, was elected president for the period from 1895 to 1907 and for a second period from 1906 to 1911. Alfaro gave the Ecuatorian people freedom, progress and a revolutionary spirit. Alfaro, following an uprising in Guayaquil, was taken prisoner and transported to Quito, where a mob lynched him (1912). B.M.P.

Algeria. See Appendix.

Algerie Francaise.

The view that Algeria was an integral part of France. This view constituted the official policy of the French government from 1848 to 1958. In the latter year, French Fifth Republic President Charles de Gaulle instigated a policy which led to Algerian independence in 1962. After 1958, the "Algerie Francaise" banner was picked up by European colonists in Algeria, dissident French army officers, and political extremists in France. The most concerted group of opponents to Algerian independence was the Organization Armee Secrete, formed in 1961. The OAS used mainly terroristic methods in attempting to maintain "Algerie Francaise." E.R.W.

Alianza para el Progreso
(Alliance for Progress).

The program for Latin American development approved by the 1961 conference at Punta del Este, Uruguay. In general, this program calls for an investment of $20,000,000,000 in Latin American development over a decade, with the goal of achieving a two and one half per cent annual increase in per capita income for the region during this period. The Latin American nations were called upon to "put their own house in order" as part of this program, through such measures as effective taxation and land reform. Ch.W.A.

Alianza Popular Revolucionaria Americana (American Revolutionary Popular Alliance).

Known throughout Latin America by a contraction of its initials in Spanish, Apra. Officially, Apra is a political party in Peru, whereas Aprismo is the larger movement or philosophy and program for social reform finding adherents in Venezuela within the Accion Democrática political party, in Costa Rica within the Liberacion Nacional political party, and to a lesser extent among political philosophers in Mexico, Uruguay, Chile, Ecuador, and Panama. In addition, Aprismo has had followers clandestinely in the Dominican Republic and in Paraguay. Victor Raul Haya de la Torre, Peruvian social reformer, founded Apra on May 7, 1924, in Mexico City. He stressed that the movement was to serve Indo-America, not Latin America, inasmuch as millions of Latin Americans physically are Indians, and a majority of all Latin Americans are Indian-Spanish hybrids. The alliance was American, not Peruvian, indicating a hemispheric scope. From its Marxist beginnings, Apra grew into a Peruvian socialist political party in no way the pliant tool of the Soviet Union. Finally, Apra became officially anti-Communist and more recently, anti-Castro. Nevertheless, Apra's political platform planks still retain criticisms of United States policies in Latin America. M.A.

Alien.

An alien is a national of one country when present in another country. While each state is free to decide what civil privileges it may choose to confer upon aliens, as distinct from political rights of participation in the government of the state, the general practice is to concede the right to own property, to contract, to engage in the professions and to allow freedom of speech and of religious worship. Domiciled aliens, having permanent residence in the state, may be subject to public duties, such as police and militia service, on the theory that domicile creates a sort of qualified or temporary allegiance.

The controversial international problem arises in connection with the responsibility of the state for the protection of the alien when his fundamental rights of person and of property are violated and there is "denial of justice." Some states maintain that the national standard of justice is final and that the alien is entitled to as much, and no more, protection as the citizen. Other states, including the United States, maintain that there is an international standard of justice, and that if the justice meted out by the national courts is below that standard, then the equality of treatment between the alien and the citizen is not sufficient, and the government of the state of which the alien is a national may intervene or interpose in his behalf. Such interposition is described as diplomatic intervention, and it has met with strong opposition in Latin America when exercised by the United States.

A separate problem is presented when the alien enters into a contract with the foreign government and disputes arise as to fulfillment of the terms of the contract. The so-called "Calvo Clause" is frequently inserted in such contracts, by which the alien agrees that, in the event of dispute as to the terms, he will not have recourse to his government for protection. The Drago Doctrine, proclaimed by Argentina at the beginning of the century, condemned the intervention of foreign powers to enforce the payment of public debts and other contractual claims. C.G.F.

Alien and Sedition Laws.

Acts passed by the U.S. Congress in 1798 authorizing the President of the U.S.A. to effect the deportation of aliens dangerous to domestic peace and punishing the publication of false or malicious statements levied against the President or Congress. J.D.

Alienation.

The concept is very fashionable among Hegelians, Marxists, Existentialists, some sociologists, psychoanalysts, and intellectuals all together. Originally it was used to denote either a voluntary or an involuntary transfer (alienation) of property. It was Rousseau who began to transform modern sensibilities because he expressed in his writings the experience of an emotional impoverishment and estrangement, a disencadrement, which is the phenomenon denoted by the term alienation. Rousseau used the concept explicitly only in his **Social Contract** (1762) however, establishing its dialectic pattern, its Janus-faced character, whereby it contains the opposites of a total impoverishment which, precisely because it is total, topples into its redemptive counterpart. Both the experience, as well as the dialectic pattern of impoverishment-fulfillment, are closely interrelated. Rousseau's alienation expresses a total divestment (or transfer) of rights from which a society is formed where everyone, precisely because participating in so total a divestment, regains his original, primaeval freedom and innocence from suppression. This dialectic recreation of a society of free men through a total alienation of their individual rights corresponds to the dialectic pattern of salvation in religion through a conversion from a completely estranged Self into a regained authentic Self. Rousseau's notion as well as his description of the phenomenon found an echo in German Idealism (Fichte, Hegel) as well as in German Romanticism. Marx, following mainly Hegel and Feuerbach, thought he had discovered the point in history where human labor (the actually creative force rather than merely fictively creative as in Rousseau's Social Contract or partially creative as in Hegel's Mind), alienating (manifesting and articulating) itself through history, attains to its point of total impoverishment and divestment of all humanity and freedom in the 'proletariat' wherefrom it must convert (through revolution) to a restructuring of humanity and freedom through a full realization of its creativity in human labor as well as its redemptive destiny to lead society out of its period of capitalist alienation into true freedom. Marx formulated alienation as 'exploitation' of human labor, denoting with this term ingenuously a remedial legal relationship the feasible removal of which as a target of an organized collectivity can charge history with transformative forces. However, the ultimate goal of his scheme does not seem to be a mere change of remedial legal relationships, but elimination of alienation in the redemption of man from his Fall under Capitalism through the 'proletariat,' the collectivity in which true humanity finds itself crucified. V.Z.

"All-American Cities."

Since 1949 the National Municipal League (more recently with Look magazine) has sponsored the annual selection of eleven "All-American Cities." Any of the 20,000 communities may enter with the size of the community of no bearing on the award. The basis of the coveted award is "energetic, purposeful, intelligent citizen effort in attaining specific civic improvements in the public interest."

The awards have been given for many kinds of unusual community efforts to solve major problems. They include citizen-led campaigns for better government, improved schools, and long-term planning. Cities have also won awards for the energetic way they met some challenge, such as a flood, tornado, or loss of a major industry.

The "All-American Cities" are not necessarily perfect places, but generally are sound-functioning communities displaying a combination of leadership and citizen participation, and serve as sound examples for other communities wanting to better themselves. Continuing, intelligent citizen participation is needed, says the National Municipal League, for any community to make self-government effective and forward-looking. W.D.S.

Allegiance, oath of.

A solemn declaration of loyalty to a state by a person who is, or is to become, its citizen. J.D.

Alliance.

In international law and relations, a contractual relationship between two or more states by which undertakings are exchanged for mutual support in the event of war. A policy of alliance is an alternative to a policy of isolation, which rejects any assumption of responsibility for the security of another state. It is distinguished also from the policy of collective security, which in principle universalizes the policy of alliance in order to deter and if necessary combat wars of aggression. The policy of alliance has been associated historically with balance of power politics, and together with the principle of collective security has been criticized both in principle and on grounds of historical evidence as tending to make war both more likely to occur and more widespread.

H.S.Th.

Alliance for Progress.

See Alianza para el Progreso.

Allied Control Council for Germany.
Formed (June 5, 1945) by the British, French, U. S., and U. S. S. R. Commanders-in-Chief in Germany, it exercised supreme authority in defeated Germany. The chairmanship rotated. Its decisions had to be unanimous. The A. C. C. became ineffective when the Soviet representative walked out (20/3/48). E.K.K.

Allied Council for Japan (A.J.C.).
Established at the same time as the F.E.C., in December, 1945. Its headquarters was in Tokyo, and the countries represented on it were the U.S., Great Britain, China and the U.S.S.R. It was intended to advise the Far Eastern Commission (F.E.C.) in the formulation of policy for SCAP (Supreme Command Allied Powers) during the occupation of Japan. In reality the AJC was almost completely impotent since SCAP refused to discuss policy with the Council or to accept its advice. S.S.

Alsace-Lorraine.
The present French departments of Bas-Rhin, Haut-Rhin, and Moselle, 14,577 sq. km.; pop., 2,230,770 (1961). The last forms parts of French Lorraine which, together with the departments of Meuse, and Meurthe-et-Moselle, was joined to France in 1766. Alsace became part of France by the Treaty of Westphalia (1648). Bismarck's incorporation of Alsace-Lorraine in the German Empire (1871) severely embittered Franco-German relations. The recovery of Alsace-Lorraine was one of the French war aims; it also was point VIII of Wilson's Fourteen Points. Alsace-Lorraine was restored to France in 1918, 14,522 sq. km.; pop., 1,874,014 (1910). Between 1940 and 1944 Germany again held control of Alsace. K.B.

Althusius, Johannes. (1557-1638)
A professor and Syndic of the Town of Emden in Switzerland, he was an ardent Calvinist and wrote extensively on legal questions. His main work, **Politica Methodice Digesta** (1603), may be considered the first systematic treatise of politics since the Ancients. He advocated in it a form of pluralism by developing the idea of the individual's dependence on a great variety of groupings besides the political. He also developed the notion of 'popular sovereignty' that cannot be surrendered by, or alienated from, the people —an idea which Rousseau developed further. Althusius was also among the foremost exponents of the 'Social Contract' idea, and he formulated a principle of federalism suggesting integration of autonomous countries into larger units. V.Z.

Amalgamated Security-Community.
A security-community (q.v.) which has been formed from the formal merger of two or more previously independent units into a single larger unit, with some type of common government after amalgamation. This common government may be unitary or confederal or anything in between, provided that it has one supreme decision-making center on at least certain important matters. Example: United States of America. R.W.V.W.

Ambedkar, Bhimrao Ramji.
(1892—1956)
Son of an Untouchable soldier, Ambedkar was born in Indore. After graduating from the Bombay University, he studied at Columbia University under Gaekwar Baroda's sponsorship and earned his Ph.D. in 1916. Later, he attended Bonn University and the London School of Economics. Qualifying as a barrister, he returned home in 1924 and began law practice. He organized the Scheduled Castes Federation and represented the Untouchables at the Round Table Conference in 1930. During World War II, he served in the Viceroy's Council. Later, he became Chairman of the Drafting Committee of the Constituent Assembly. He served as Law Minister until his resignation in 1951 in protest over unfair treatment of the Untouchables. Becoming a Buddhist in 1950, he advised his followers to do likewise. A strong critic of Nehru's neutralism and policy toward China, Ambedkar died in 1956. C.S.S.

Ambrose, Saint. (340?—397).
Descended from an ancient and distinguished Roman family which at an early period had embraced Christian-

ity. Brilliant student and practitioner of the law, he was appointed by Emperor Valentinian consular prefect in Upper Italy with his court at Milan. Unanimous choice of both Catholics as well as heretical Arians, he was consecrated Bishop of Milan (374) only eight days after he had been baptized. He was especially notable for his strong stand on the autonomy of the Church in spiritual matters. Thus he warned Emperor Valentinian that in matters of faith "bishops are wont to judge of Christian emperors, not emperors of bishops." Later, on a famous occasion he brought the Emperor Theodosius to repentance and public penance for his part in the cruel Thessalonian massacre. He is best remembered not as an excellent statesman, learned bishop, nor eloquent preacher but for his influence on the brilliant Augustine whom he converted and baptized on Easter Eve, 387. G.A.K.

Amendment Process.
The means by which the fundamental political institutions and power relationships of a constitution are formally changed. Informally, all states periodically modify their political systems by customary practices, legislation, executive orders and authoritative interpretations of existing arrangements. In addition, however, more formal means of amendment may also be authorized in systems other than outright personal dictatorships. In federal systems, a special amendment process customarily exists because any serious changes in either the functional or territorial distribution of power inevitably affect existing guarantees to member-states. Therefore, formal amendment normally requires both popular approval (usually through elected legislators) and approval by a special majority (absolute, two-thirds or more) of member-states and/or their representatives in the federal house of a bi-cameral national legislature. The United States, West Germany, and Switzerland are examples. Similarly, the pseudo-federal Soviet Union requires a two-thirds majority of both the federal and popular houses of its Supreme Soviet. Unitary states, however, may employ simpler methods since no constitutional self-government guarantees are provided territorial components. If a parliamentary form of government exists, action by the popularly elected house of the constitutionally supreme parliament may suffice (e.g., Great Britain or the Fourth French Republic). However, unitary states with particularly delicate or otherwise insecure constitutional arrangements may also introduce more complicated procedures to help preserve the system; the Fifth French Republic, for example, requiring ratification either by a special popular referendum after initial parliamentary approval or else by a special two-thirds majority of both houses of parliament. D.W.

American Civil Liberties Union.
A national organization, first of its kind in the U.S.A., founded in 1920 to protect and extend the liberties embodied in the federal and state constitutions, particularly those guaranteeing freedom of speech, press, association, religion, and due process of law. It is supported solely by private contribution, with a national membership, hundreds of cooperating volunteer lawyers and many local affiliates throughout the country. Its activities are centered mainly in challenging violations of civil liberties by federal, state, and local officials through court action, in advocating or opposing legislation, and urging or contesting executive action. (No distinction is made among those whose liberties are defended. Its services are given freely to all those with appropriate grievances. A national board of directors under a New York corporation determines its policies and activities subject to consultation with its affiliates and a national advisory committee.) R.B.

American Farm Bureau Federation.
An organization of U.S. farm families with local bureaus in most of the states. Local organizations were first created about 1915 in order to bring pressure on county boards to employ county agents under the extension program of the U.S. Department of Agriculture and were united as the AFBF in Chicago, Illinois, in November 1919. Today the AFBF is the most

powerful of the general farm organizations and promotes a program of adequate prices for its more than 1½ million members with great zeal and ability. Its strength is mainly in the corn belt of the Middle West and in parts of the South. C.W.B.

American Federation of Labor—Congress of Industrial Organizations.

A federation of essentially independent national labor unions in the U.S.A. formed in 1955 by the merger of the American Federation of Labor and the Congress of Industrial Organizations. The AFL was a federation of trade unions founded in 1886 as opposition to the more radical Knights of Labor. A growing schism over organization on craft versus industrial lines led eight AFL unions to organize a Committee for Industrial Organization in 1935. When the AFL suspended ten unions in 1936, they organized a rival body which held its first convention as the Congress of Industrial Organizations in 1938. The merged AFL-CIO encompasses about two-thirds of the total American union membership. C.W.B.

American Institute of Public Opinion (Gallup).

An organization created in 1935 by George H. Gallup to measure public opinion. Presently located in Princeton, New Jersey, it conducts polls to ascertain public attitudes on political candidates and public affairs. M.B.D.

American Legion.

An ex-servicemen's organization established after World War I to defend the interests of U.S. war veterans and to promote loyalty to the principles of American democracy. J.D.

American Municipal Association.

Founded 1924. The central organization of the 43 voluntary state associations of cities, towns and villages ("state leagues of municipalities"). Performs coordinating, communication, secretariat, and research services for member leagues, as well as maintaining representation of Association views in Washington, D.C. P.J.C.

American Samoa.

(76 sq. mi.; 20,051 inhabitants.) All the islands of the Samoan group east of 171° W. Long., including Tutuila and Aunu's (1900) and the island of the Manu's group (1904), and also Swain's Island (1925) are an unincorporated territory of the United States known as American Samoa. Since the adoption of a Constitution in 1960, the Territory's previously advisory bicameral legislature, the lower house elected by ballot and the upper house elected in mass meetings, now has limited legislative authority. The Governor, Secretary, and Supreme Court Justice are under the U. S. Department of the Interior. Fagatogo is the capital city, and Pago Pago with a good harbor is the major commercial center. Principal export products are canned tuna and copra. J.A.E.

Amicus Curiae.

Literally, a friend of the court; one who, while not a party to the controversy itself, may inform the court in matters of law. While an amicus curiae may be one requested by the court to conduct an investigation or other proceeding, in U.S. law the term is mostly used to refer to persons or groups of persons who enter into a judicial proceeding to offer information or urge adoption of some specific solution to the case at bar. F.H.H.

Amnesty.

Since Anglo-Saxon times there has been a practice which permits the executive authority to issue group pardons. These are usually for political offenders. In the U. S. A. Congress has this power; but the use of a presidential proclamation is the customary procedure. M.F.

Amparo.

A federal writ in Mexico, a constitutional suit of a summary nature, the object of which is to protect, at the request of the allegedly injured party, an individual whose rights have been violated through arbitrary acts or misapplication of the laws by authorities, federal or state or local. This writ can be issued only by federal judges. A writ of amparo has overtones of the writs of habeas corpus, injunction, and error in the United States. In Latin American countries other than Mexico, amparo means "legal protection" in unspecific terms. M.A.

Analytic.
Logical reasoning is analytic if it adds nothing to the meaning of a given term or proposition but merely makes explicit what is implied in that meaning. The meaning of the sentence "all men are mortal" implies that, if Socrates is a man, he too is mortal. To bring this out is an example of purely analytic reasoning. Whether the sentence is true is a different question that cannot be answered by analytic reasoning. A.B.

Anarchism.
Rejection of state and of governmental compulsion, and the fight necessary to obtain society without state control to be accomplished through use of violence, or technique of passive resistance or education.
M.C.V.

Anarchy.
Society based solely on voluntary cooperation without coercion and without any interference with individual liberties. M.C.V.

Ancestor worship (in Japan).
Ancestor worship in Japan has been closely associated with the Shinto religion, some of the deities of which are considered ancestors of the Emperor and the people, and with the patriarchal social and political structure. Confucian and Buddhist influences from China further strengthened the ancestor cult, but in Japan genealogical records were normally kept only by the nobility. The traditional family system in Japan, which embodied the principles of primogeniture and the subordination of women, has undergone great changes in recent years, because of industrialization and urbanization as well as reforms in the Constitution and the Civil Code accomplished during the Allied occupation following World War II. T.Mc.N.

Andorra. See Appendix.

Angola.
Portugal's largest overseas province with an area of almost 500,000 square miles. Portuguese navigators discovered Angola in 1482 and have administered it ever since. Since 1960, in the wake of the Congo's independence, there has been increasing unrest. In December 1962 the Seventeenth General Assembly of the United Nations recommended sanctions against Portugal unless that country granted speedy independence to Angola. It is today one of the last remaining overseas dependencies of a Western power.
J.G.St.

Annapolis Convention.
The Virginia Legislature summoned all of the states to meet at Annapolis in 1786 to consider trade regulations. No trade agreement materialized but the convention issued an urgent call to all states to send delegates to Philadelphia in May 1787; this meeting drafted the Constitution of the United States. J.E.S.

Annexation. See Appendix.

Annexation (of a city in U.S.).
The legal process for adding territory to a city. Normally, the territory is not unincorporated, of smaller size than the annexing city. In American practice it is most common for the process to require the consent of those dwelling in the area to be incorporated.
P.J.C.

Anschluss.
Hitler's annexation of Austria, 13 March 1938. Faced with the presence of German troops, Austrian voters approved the absorption of Austria in a Greater Germany by the plebiscite of 20 April 1938. K.B.

Antarctic Claims.
Seven Nations lay formal claim to territories in the south polar region: United Kingdom (Falkland Islands Dependencies, a sector from 20° to 80° West Long.), New Zealand (Ross Dependency, sector 160° East to 150° West Long.), France (Adelie Land, sector 136° to 142° East Long.), Australia (Australian Antarctic Territory, sector 45° to 160° East Long., less the French sector), Norway (Queen Maud Land, 20° West to 45° East Long., not a sector), Chile (Antártica Chilena, sector 53° to 90° West Long.), and Argentina (Antártida Argentina, sector 25° to 74° West Long.). The overlap of the British, Chilean and Argentine sectors causes

friction. The United States has a long history of Antarctic programs; the U.S.S.R. claims early discoveries and has maintained bases in a portion of the Australian sector since the International Geophysical Year. In 1959 the States named plus Belgium, Japan and the Union of South Africa concluded a treaty in Washington (in effect from June, 1961) with mutual inspection rights and dedicating the region to scientific and other non-military purposes; nuclear explosions are prohibited; territorial claims are "frozen" for the duration of the treaty (at least 30 years). R.D.H.

Anti-Defamation League of B'nai B'rith.

Founded in 1913, to combat overt caricaturing and stereotyping of American Jews, the ADL has broadened its concerns and become an Intergroup Education agency. It is active in the civil rights field in the areas of law, discrimination, fact-finding, and the like. Programmatically, the ADL has a variety of services and materials, including a number of publications, films, and other audio-visual items, as well as extensive consultative services to colleges, schools, churches, national organizations, and civic groups. These services are offered through its twenty-five regional offices and its national staff. M.J.S.

Antifascist Bloc of Democratic Parties.

Licensed political parties (14 July, 1945) and later mass organizations in the **Soviet Zone of Germany** joined this coalition under Soviet pressure. Through the Bloc the Communistic Socialist Unity Party (SED) could force bourgeois parties to accept the **antifascistic democratic order** (1945-1950). As the influence of the SED increased and the **laying of the foundations of Socialism** began (1950-58) many of its functions were taken over by the **National Front.** E.K.K.

Anti-Federalists.

Those who opposed the ratification of the Constitution of the United States. Their objections rested on the following contentions: that the delegates to the Philadelphia Convention had not followed their instructions to revise the Articles of Confederation; that the proposed Constitution had been submitted to conventions instead of to the legislatures; that the new government would take important powers held by the states; that the Constitution seemed to be more interested in safeguarding the rights of property rather than in protecting the "rights of man," so prominent in the philosophy of the revolutionary movement; that the federal government was basically undemocratic; and the new basic law was actually restoring much of the same authority that the people had fought to overthrow. The anti-Federalists were influential particularly in Rhode Island and North Carolina, the last two states to ratify the Constitution, and they had considerable strength in New Hampshire, Massachusetts, New York, Pennsylvania, and Virginia. After the ratification of the Constitution, most of them became ardent supporters of Thomas Jefferson and joined his Democratic-Republican Party. D.C.

Anti-Masonic Party.

A short-lived (1826-1832) political movement in the United States making the plea that membership in secret societies was incompatible with good citizenship. Opposition to Freemasonry was taken up by various churches and later by shrewd politicians who used this movement to oppose the rising Jacksonian Democracy. The strong showing of Anti-Masonic candidates in the elections of 1828 may only have indicated the weakness of the National Republican party. The party came to have a national organization and a national program emphasizing domestic improvements and protective tariffs appealing to various segments of the population. In 1831 the party held a national presidential nominating convention. When a Mason, William Wirt, was nominated it suggested that opposition to Freemasonry was no longer a major factor in the party. The seven electoral votes of Vermont went with this party in 1832. By 1836 most of the movement was enveloped by the Whigs. W.D.S.

"Anti-Party" Group.

In June, 1957, Nikita Khrushchev was confronted with opposition to his policies, domestic as well as foreign, in the Presidium. Outvoted in the

Presidium, he convened a plenary session of the Central Committee of the Soviet Union Communist Party which, prodded by the Soviet military group headed by Marshal Zhukov, gave him its support. This stratagem enabled Khrushchev to oust his key opponents —Molotov, Kaganovich, Malenkov, and Shepilov—not only from the Presidium, but from the Central Committee as well. Khrushchev cited Lenin's Tenth Congress resolution on Party unity in justification of the summary exclusion of his erstwhile colleagues. The Central Committee, meeting from June 22 to 29, 1957, issued an indictment of the "anti-Party group." Specifically, the statement condemned the "anti-Party group"—its key members as well as their associates such as Pervukin and Saburov—for having opposed certain of Khrushchev's foreign and domestic policies, including the decision to cultivate the "virgin lands," the decision to establish the 105 regional economic councils, and the decision to abolish the tax on the individual peasant plot. Molotov was accused of "narrow-mindedness" in foreign policy and of having opposed the conclusion of the Austrian State Treaty, the "normalization" of relations with Yugoslavia, and the establishment of diplomatic relations with Japan. Kaganovich and Malenkov were accused of having supported Molotov on certain foreign policy issues. More likely than not, these were the men who had blamed Khrushchev for the Hungarian revolt and for the rise of Gomulka in Poland, for his secret attack upon Stalin at the 20th Party Congress of 1956 which had been followed by unrest in the Soviet bloc.

The issue of the "anti-Party group" was revived later. At the 21st Party Congress, the so-called "anti-Party group" had been humiliated and demoted. In the grand design of the 22nd Party Congress, the attack on the Stalinism of the Albanian leaders was coupled with a much broader and far-reaching indictment of the repression of the Stalinist era and Stalin's alleged accomplices, the leaders of the "anti-Party group." In the course of the Congress, one speaker after the other added details in order to illustrate Stalin's crimes and sought to implicate Molotov, Kaganovich, Malenkov, and Voroshilov in them. The violence and comprehensiveness of the charges against the "anti-Party group" went far beyond the more cautious revelations of Khrushchev's secret speech to the 20th Party Congress. Then Khrushchev had confined himself to the denunciation of his predecessor; now Khrushchev's henchmen broadened the attack in order to topple not only the effigy of the departed dictator but also those of his surviving associates who had been Khrushchev's rivals for supreme power.   R.St-H.

Anti-Rent War (1838, 1844-1845).

During the years 1838 and 1844-1845 several hundred discontented tenants on the old Patroon estates in upper New York State armed themselves and refused to pay rent on their leaseholds claiming that the purchase price of the land had been paid many times in rent and that perpetual leases were undemocratic. The anti-renters were well organized and attempted by both peaceful and violent means to persuade the landlords to sell the land. Auxiliary armies, known as Indians, were disguised and attached to most of the cell groups of the Anti-Rent Association in order to harass landlords and prevent sheriff's sales. The anti-renters succeeded in electing several state legislators and a governor who looked with favor upon their proposals and used the government to influence the landlords to sell.
                                J.A.E.

Anti-Semitism. See Appendix.

Anti-Trust Laws.
See Clayton and Sherman Acts.
ANZUS Pact.
Treaty between Australia, New Zealand and the United States signed in San Francisco on September 1, 1951. Each party recognized that "an armed attack in the Pacific Area on any of the Parties would be dangerous to its own peace and safety and declares that it would act to meet the common danger in accordance with its constitutional processes." This treaty was closely linked with the United States-Philippines Mutual Defense Treaty, signed two days previously, and the

Japanese Peace Treaty and United States-Japan Security Treaty, signed September 8, 1951. These agreements, concluded during the Korean War, were designed to guarantee against the resurgence of Japanese militarism as well as against the Communist threat in Asia. T.Mc.N.

Apartheid. (Afrikaans, separateness).
A basic feature of the race system in the Union of South Africa. It embodies the fundamental concept of the National Party and most of the Afrikaner community, namely, racial segregation, white supremacy and **baaskap** —mastership. It emphasizes differentiation of the races, not assimilation or integration. A large body of **apartheid** laws passed between 1948 and 1957 are aimed at eliminating virtually all contact between Negroes and Europeans. M.M.Mc.

"Apparatchik" (Organization Man).
Soviet term referring to those who rise in the party through absolute loyalty and obedience to the **apparat** (the organization), the party line, their superiors and through the efficient execution of assigned tasks. D.N.J.

Appeal.
In U.S. law, a procedure by which the judgment of a lower court is taken to a higher court for review. Generally, one is entitled to take an appeal (or "to appeal") only if the lower court is alleged to have erred in its interpretation or application of the law. Specific grounds for appeal, the form the appeal must take and the alternative courses available to the higher court are regulated by statute in each jurisdiction. F.H.H.

Appeasement (Munich).
From March to September, 1938, the Sudeten crisis continued to mount in intensity. The Western democracies tried to placate Hitler. By mid-September Hitler's threats against Czechoslovakia, a treaty ally of France, alarmed the British and French Governments enough to cause British Prime Minister Chamberlain to fly to Berchtesgaden. There, on September 15, 1938 Britain, France and Germany reached an agreement. The Munich Pact, ceding the Sudetenland to Germany, became the symbol of cowardly appeasement and shook the confidence of the East Europeans in the good faith of the Western democracies. R.St-H.

Appellate Jurisdiction.
The power and authority to hear and decide cases which have previously been decided by a lower court. In Anglo-American civil law the loser can appeal, but this is so in criminal cases only if the loser is the defendant. The purpose is to review and affirm or reverse the decisions of lower courts, and there are various routes and methods of appeal. Appellate jurisdiction in France is limited in scope, particularly in criminal cases. R.H.B.

Apportionment (of seats in U.S. House of Representatives).
The allocation of seats among the several states on the basis of population. Under the terms of the Constitution each state shall have at least one representative, the number of representatives shall not exceed one for every thirty thousand. As amended by Article XIV, representatives shall be apportioned among the several states according to their respective numbers, counting the whole number of persons in each state, excluding Indians not taxed. K.E.H.

Appropriations.
Appropriations are laws — national, state, or local — fixing the maximum amounts which may be expended or obligated during a limited fiscal period by a unit of government for a specified purpose. They may be either "lump sum" or "segregated" in character, the former conferring on administrative officials greater flexibility and discretion in expenditure than the latter. A public appropriation is usually based on a budget. There is a growing tendency to confer on executives a greater control over the administration of appropriation laws through item vetoes and allotment systems. H.W.

A priori.
In its classical, especially Kantian sense, the term a priori points to notions, propositions, or postulates that are considered true or necessary irre-

spective of experience or anterior to it; in other words, not derived from experience and yet considered valid ("classical, scientifically accepted, a priori"). Today the term is often used for all notions, propositions, or postulates that are extraneous to the system or method of thought under which the inquiry is conducted. Thus, in terms of modern scientific method, any proposition not introduced in line with it is a priori in this sense ("methodologically repudiated a priori" or "alien-to-method a priori"). Yet some a priori assumptions are imminent in any method of investigation, even in modern scientific method in its strictest sense (= "imminent methodological a priori"), such as "consubjectivity" (i.e. the assumption that phenomena are perceived by different persons in a similar manner), the ability of observation and reasoning to disclose "facts," some freedom of decision, some regularity in the succession of events. Other writers call a priori all things "given" ("a priori of givenness"). A.B.

Apristas.

Members of the Apra political party in Peru, or adherents of Aprismo as a political movement or philosophy elsewhere in Latin America. (See Alianza Popular Revolucionaria Americana.) M.A.

Aquinas, Thomas (1225-1274).

A Dominican monk, disciple of Albert the Great. Writer and teacher in **Paris, Rome,** other centers. Canonized in 1323, the Angelic Doctor of the Roman Catholic Church.

In political and legal philosophy St. Thomas agrees with Aristotle (whose philosophy he reintroduced, replacing the dominance of Augustinian Platonism) that man is a social and political being. The goal of government is the common good. The purpose of living in society is the attainment of God by the individual through a life of virtue. The secular government is subject to the Church to the extent that the intermediate good of the former is subordinate to the final end—salvation. Political authority involves three elements: foundation (**principium**); permanent constitution (**modus**—monarchial, aristocratic, democratic or mixed); and actual operation (**exercitium**). The ultimate foundation is God—but it is the people or the community who determine the constitution and confer, control or withdraw the exercise of power.

The requirements of law are that it should be according to "right reason" (conforming to the Divine Intellect), for the common good, and promulgated. The law derived from political authority is **human law,** one of the four types distinguished, the others being **eternal, natural** and **divine.** Custom is law since it obtains the essential characteristics.

Justice (the power to give each man his due freely) is topmost among the moral virtues; legal justice pertains to the common good of the whole community; therefore, St. Thomas values it highly.

Sections of **Summa Theologica** (his major work), **De Regimine Principium** (On Kingship), commentaries on Aristotle's **Nicomachean Ethics** and on the **Politics** contain the political and legal philosophy of Thomas Aquinas. T.P.

Arab-Israel War, 1948-49.

The war which broke out between seven Arab states and Israel the day after the establishment of the State of Israel in continuation of the hostilities initiated by the Arab states on November 30, 1947, the day after partition of Palestine was approved by the United Nations. Armies of Egypt, Iraq, Jordan, Lebanon, Saudi Arabia, Syria, and Yemen invaded across all three borders of Israel with the asserted purpose of destroying that country and reclaiming its territory for Arab possession.

Bitterly fought, the war lasted, with the exception of two truce periods, over eight months and officially ended with a series of four armistice agreements in February to July, 1949. During the war, the United Nations Security Council made several unsuccessful attempts to end hostilities. The first truce period lasted from June 11 to July 8, 1948. A second truce held from July 18 to October 15, 1948, during which period Count Folke Bernadotte of Sweden, who was United Nations Mediator, was assassinated by

Israeli terrorists in Jerusalem and was replaced by Dr. Ralph J. Bunche of the United States.

On November 16, 1948, the Security Council ordered the belligerents to enter into armistice agreements. Only Israel and Jordan complied by ending hostilities on November 30. On December 29, the Security Council passed a resolution calling for an immediate cease-fire between Israel and the other Arab states. Great Britain enlisted the support of the United States, which sent a note to Israel on January 4, 1949, asking it to comply with the cease-fire resolution and to open negotiations for an armistice. The next day, Israel accepted a proposal by Egypt, through the United Nations Mediator, providing for a cease-fire, withdrawal of forces, and negotiations for an armistice agreement.

The war with Egypt ended on January 7, 1949, and the armistice agreement was signed on February 24. This first armistice was followed by successive agreements between Israel and Jordan on April 13; and between Israel and Syria on July 20. Iraq had already withdrawn her troops without a formal agreement but had allowed Jordanian troops to take its positions. The armistice agreements, endorsed by the Security Council, provided, in addition to cessation of the war, for demilitarized areas on the borders of the armistice demarcation lines, for withdrawal of troops, and for the return of prisoners of war. The boundaries of Egypt, Israel and Jordan as changed by the war were acknowledged by the armistice agreements. Egypt had seized the Gaza Strip, which was formerly part of Palestine and allotted to the "Arab State" by the United Nations partition plan. Israel had conquered almost 2,500 square miles of territory over that allocated to her under partition. Jordan had taken about 2,200 squares miles along the west bank of the Jordan River which should have been part of the "Arab State." The El Auja zone on the border of Egypt and Israel was demilitarized.

The armistice agreement between Israel and Jordan left the City of Jerusalem divided into Arab and Jewish sectors. Old Jerusalem consists of an area little larger than one-third of a mile in which about 50,000 Arabs live under the control of Jordan. New Jerusalem covers nearly ten square miles west of the Arab sector and contains approximately 155,000 Jews under the control of Israel. In addition, there are two small enclaves within Jordan which are designated as demilitarized zones.

During the war, hundreds of thousands of Arab inhabitants of Israel fled to surrounding Arab states and settled around Israel's borders. No provisions for them were made in the armistice agreements. The agreements ended a large-scale conflict which threatened the peace of the world; but they were not followed by permanent peace treaties, nor did they result in recognition of Israel by the Arab states. Although the agreements specified that their intention was to provide a stage between truce and final peace, to this date no peace treaties have been negotiated and signed. The Arab states consider the establishment of the State of Israel an overt act of aggression, and have refused to negotiate any peace settlement with Israel which would signify direct or indirect recognition of Israel's sovereignty. A general Arab economic boycott and closure of the Suez Canal to Israeli shipping have fanned the tension. As a result of this impasse and open hostility, the war of 1948-49 appears likely to erupt again at any time. O.K.

Arab Nationalism.

Is a broad politico-cultural movement which seeks the independence of the Arab countries, the revival of Arab culture, and the ultimate unity of the Arabic-speaking peoples. The movement began in the Arab East in the early part of the Century and gained momentum after the Palestine crisis of 1948. After 1955 president Nasser of Egypt became a strong proponent of the movement. It has great appeal to the young intellectuals, but is little understood by the masses. The radical Arab nationalists call for the establishment of a Federal Arab State from Morocco to Kuwait, and the moderate among them call for an Arab entente in which the unifying norm is cultural not political. E.A.S.

Arabs.
The Arabs are ethnically the original dwellers of the Arabian peninsula who belong to the Semitic branch of the Caucasian race. The word "Arabs," however, has long since lost its ethnic connotation and become a linguistic term.

Being the language of the Muslim sacred book the Qur'an, Arabic predominated wherever the religion of Islam reached. In many countries of the Middle East and North Africa it replaced local vernaculars, and in others it greatly enriched native languages with numerous Arabic lexical items. The Arabic-speaking countries of today are: Algeria, Egypt (U.A.R.), Iraq, Jordan, Kuwait, Lebanon, Libya, Morocco, Saudi Arabia, Sudan, Syria, Tunisia, and Yemen. Arab territories include the protectorate of Aden and a number of small Sheikdoms and Emirates to the South and East of Saudi Arabia. The total Arab population amounts to approximately 80,000,000 people living in East Asia and North Africa.

The independent Arab countries are grouped together in a loose federation named "The League of Arab States," whose pact was signed on March 22, 1945. During its formative period the League of Arab States defined the term "Arab" as any individual brought up in an Arabic-speaking country, whose mother tongue is Arabic, and who desires to be identified with the Arabs regardless of his race, creed or religion. W.B.B.

Arbitration.
Arbitration, as distinct from other procedures of pacific settlement, is the submission of a controversy between states to judges of their own choice who are to decide on the basis of respect for law and whose award in the case is final. It is the free choice of arbitrators that distinguishes arbitration from judicial settlement by a permanent court established in advance of the dispute, such as the International Court of Justice.

Treaties pledging the parties to arbitration for the settlement of their disputes go back to the earliest days of international law; but it was in the nineteenth and early twentieth centuries that attention was focused on multipartite treaties, outstanding among which was the treaty creating the Permanent Court of Arbitration of the two Hague Conferences of 1899 and 1907, which set up a list of judges from which the parties might select a tribunal for the particular case, and prescribed the procedure to be followed. Among the numerous bipartite treaties the Root Treaties of 1908 were outstanding; but like other treaties they left a loop-hole of escape by making exception of disputes relating to honor and vital interests, under which might be included any dispute that the parties did not wish to arbitrate. The General Treaty of Arbitration of 1928 represented perhaps the highwater mark of efforts to establish a comprehensive multipartite treaty. More recently, resort to arbitration has lost ground in favor of the settlement of justiciable controversies by the International Court of Justice.
C.G.F.

Arcadia conference.
The first wartime conference for the planning of grand strategy in World War II, held in Washington from 24 December 1941 to 10 January 1942. Participants were President Franklin D. Roosevelt and Prime Minister Winston S. Churchill and their military advisors. Significance of the conference is that it laid the ground work for the machinery of coalition warfare which operated throughout World War II, which developed in the post World War II period into NATO. The "Declaration of the United Nations" proclaimed on 1 January 1942 by President Roosevelt and Prime Minister Churchill and signed by the ambassadors of twenty-four other nations in Washington was both the basic charter under which World War II was fought and the predecessor of the United Nations organization, further blueprinted at Dumbarton Oaks in Washington, D. C., in August 1944 and formalized at San Francisco in February 1945. T.W.

Argentina.
A Latin American state; area, 1,072,748 sq. mi.; population (1960), 20,956,000. Under the Constitution of 1853 Argentina is a federal state, but

the preponderance of power resides at the national level. There is a popularly-elected Congress, composed of a Senate and a Chamber of Deputies. The President of the Republic is elected to a six-year term by an electoral college. Leading political parties are the Intransigent Civic Union, Popular Civic Union (both formerly wings of the Radical Civic Union), Popular Union (Peronist), Popular Conservative Democratic Party, and Christian Democratic Party. The military services are a dominant force in politics. Acting President, following the military overthrow of President Arturo Frondizi in March 1962, is Jose Maria Guido. F.M.L.

Argentine Constitution.
The Argentine Constitution has a very short story. It begins after the defeat of the Rosas dictatorship, and since 1853, the year of its establishment, it has had slight amendments in 1860, 1866, and 1898.

The proclamation of the men who drafted the Constitution in 1853 reads: "men dignify themselves prostrating to the law because in that way they liberate themselves from kneeling down to tyrants."

In 1949, the constitutional text was changed by the introduction of social welfare amendments.

The September 1955 revolution which overthrew the dictatorial regime, reestablished the 1853 Constitution, which was amended later in 1957 by introducing certain social rights.

The Argentine Constitution follows in general the text of the United States Constitution, but there is a difference in their spirits and interpretations. To understand these, one must go back to the beginning of both countries: in the north, thirteen independent colonies got together in order to form a union and they did it immediately; in the old Virreynato del Rio de la Plata, most of the provinces declared themselves independent from Spain but only forty years later, after long struggles among themselves and their caudillos, did they constitute a Nation, establishing the present Constitution.

The present Constitution vests the Legislative Power in a Congress composed of two Chambers, one of Deputies representing the people of the nation and the other of Senators representing the provinces and the Federal Capital.

The executive power of the nation is performed by a citizen having the name of "President of the Argentine Nation." In case of his death, illness, resignation, absence from the Capital or removal from office, the Executive Power is exercised by the Vice President of the nation. Both are elected by electoral colleges established according to the Constitution.

Eight minister secretaries have the dispatch of the affairs of the nation and countersign and legalize the acts of the President, without which such acts shall have no effect. But the ministers can not in any case whatsoever make decisions by themselves, excepting as to matters concerning the economic and administrative policies of their respective Departments.

The judicial power of the nation is exercised by a Supreme Court of Justice and such other lower courts as Congress may establish in the territory of the Nation. The judges of the Supreme Court and those of the lower courts continue in office during their good behavior.

The Argentine constitutional political system shows a marked and strong executive preeminence both in the play of federal governmental powers and in the relations with the provincial powers. J.B.V.

Argentine Foreign Policy.
The Argentine nation was born and nourished in liberty, democracy and equality. It fought with absolute disinterestedness for the emancipation of the South American States, it has respect for the autodetermination of the peoples, and it has contributed to the formation of independent States. Its territorial disputes have been settled according to the decisions of law and justice.

The Argentine nation loathes conquest, repudiates hegemony and detests intervention, in any of its forms, unilateral or multilateral, which may diminish the States' sovereignty and considers such intervention aggression.

It respects treaties and faithfully observes them.

The Argentine people's aim is abolition of war in America and peaceful and friendly mediation. According to the doctrines of full legal content and of equity, stated by Tejedor, Yrigoyen, Calvo, Drago and other Argentine statesmen, Argentine foreign policy is recognized as proclaiming the juridical equality of all the States: the mutual respect for the personality and independence, inviolability and territorial immutability of all the States; and the right that each State has to govern itself according to the form of government best suited to its sovereignty and national interests.   J.B.V.

Argentine Political Parties.

Argentine political institutions and traditions stand for a two party system and the national political history witnesses that the people of the country were Morenists or Saavedrists, federals or unitarians, provincials or 'Portenos,' Mitrists or Alsinists, conservatives or radicals. After the turn of the 19th century, socialism sprouted in the big cities, but it did not spread out all over the country as was expected. Therefore, the tradition continued until 1945, in which year Peronism covered all the country with its marches and slogans. In spite of this emergence, the traditional two party fight stood, and in a way two political forces faced each other in the 1946 elections: Peronists v. "democratic union," which gathered all the traditional parties.

When the September 1955 revolution overthrew Peron's regime, the so called democratic parties blossomed up and many new parties reached the political arena. In the 1957 constitutional convention election more than twenty political parties, nationally recognized, participated, besides many other insignificant local parties which proliferated especially in the Federal Capital.

In the 1958 elections and in the subsequent elections the number of parties which participated in them stayed around twenty and twenty-six.

Looking at the 1962/63 panorama, one finds five different strong parties some of them being the result of national grouping of smaller provincial parties, registered under different names.

The radicalism that has characterized a vivid democratic era of the Republic did split into the two main traditional branches which have struggled through the course of the years in its ranks and files for the leadership: Yrigoyenism or Alvearism, Mayoritarios or Minoritarios, Unidad or Intransigencia. Now they have constituted two different parties sharing the basic name.

The Union Civica Radical Intransigente has fought for a leftist interpretation of the old radical program and ideals and was characterized by a marked tendency of self-destruction when it had to get rid of its permanent and fighting ideals and take another course, under Frondizi's presidency, during whose administration UCRI ruled the Argentine Congress and the provincial governments, but could not master the federal cabinet. Since Frondizi has been overthrown by the armed forces in March 1962, it seems that UCRI is recovering its once abandoned intransigent program and at the same time is getting rid of the outsiders who contributed to changing its original political, economic and social objectives.

The Union Civica Radical del Pueblo represents a more centrist point of view of the traditional radical ideals and programs. The difference between the traditional branches of the old radicalism stands more in the characterized personalities of their main leaders and caudillos rather than in the exact interpretation and exposition of the electoral platform and political ideals. Only slight differences mark both platforms and even if one scrutinizes both party leaders' discourses it is difficult to establish to which radicalism belongs the speaker, if it were not by the impersonations made and the criticism involved. It is a question of leaders' position and of personal points of view. Coolly expressed, what today is black, tomorrow is white and vice versa. Both radicalisms are alike; the radicalism is not a mere party, it is a feeling; it is a way of seeing and doing things for the Argentine people, without discriminations of any kinds or classes.

The conservative classes of the Argentine society, most of the landlords and many representatives of business and industry with open or covered links with the old British world are represented in the political arena by the Federacion de Partidos del Centro, which in 1962/63 gathers smaller and local conservative parties registered in the provinces under different names. The present Federation of Centrist Parties is the remainder of the traditional Conservative Party that ruled many years ago the country and did in the 30s its last show until the June 4, 1943 revolution. It never recovered notwithstanding some new blood injected in its rank and file after the 1955 revolution.

The Partido Democrata Cristiano was formed as a reaction of the ultra catholics towards Peron's anticatholic attacks from the government. They tried to imitate Europe's Christian democratic parties, specially those of Italy and Germany, but up to the present they have not succeeded in obtaining the support of the Argentine electorate, which is antagonistic to the meddling of the Church in politics. According to the results of March 18, 1962 elections in some provinces and later conversations of its leaders, the "Demochristians," try to get the Peronists' support with aims to next presidential and general election of 1963.

The Peronism which acts under different party names, including the neoperonism, still acts under one flag and one leader: General Peron. After the September 1955 revolution, the Peronistas have tried to recover the power lost, counting on the faithful support of the masses and the workers' union. For this purpose they have worked at first underground, plotting against the provisional government and later they made alliances with different parties, including the UCRI and allowing Frondizi to win the presidential election. Evidently Peronism has acted as a new and disturbing force of the traditional political scheme and has introduced new factors and points of view which up to now have stood firmly. In the near future and according to the present political status, the Peronist vote can again decide the next general elections. The incognita stands, for whom will they vote?

Other political parties such as the three socialist parties, the communist party, the civic independents, the progressist democrats and many others are too insignificant according to the number of votes obtained in the last elections and consequently their activities and opinions are of no importance in the Argentine political scenery.

J.B.V.

Argentine Revolutions.

Argentine normal government succession since 1853 was first broken in September 6, 1930 when the army overthrew President Yrigoyen, starting the military interference in the political affairs of the Nation and the establishment and functioning of a de facto government. The Supreme Court issued for this opportunity a special decree recognizing the existence of a "de facto government" whose title "cannot be judicially disputed."

Again in June 4, 1943 and September 16, 1935 revolutionary movements broke out that were successful and consequently were recognized by the Supreme Court according to "de facto doctrine."

In winning the March 18, 1962 elections the Peronists in twelve of eighteen electoral districts, gave place to a new military uprising that caused Frondizi to be overthrown. The Argentine armed forces did not want the return to power of the outlaw Peronists and, even if there are different points of view—as was shown last September in the clash of army cliques and lately in internal struggles among the different forces — regarding the means and ways to reach the objective of giving free elections to the people, they wish to eliminate at the same time the presence and influence of Peronists in Argentine politics. J.B.V.

Arians.

A religious sect sprung by the doctrines of Arius who denied the consubstantiality of God and Christ. Arius held that God first created the Logos (Reason, World-Spirit), which then became man in Christ. This implied a denial that Christ was a 'perfect God' since the Logos is created and a God cannot be created; it also denied that

Christ was a 'perfect man' since the Logos, of divine origin, was infused only in Christ. Arius was excommunicated in 319, and Constantine convened the Council of Nicea (325) to declare through it that God and Christ were consubstantial, a view which — after several Roman Emperors reverted back to Arianism—finally triumphed. Arianism was successful because it reconciled a Christian humanitarianism with faith in God, not unlike modern trends in Protestantism; but it unleashed a religious strife not equalled in Christendom until the arrival of the Reformation. V.Z.

Aristocracy.
1. A form of government in which rule is by a relatively small group presumed to be best qualified to rule. 2. The class which governs the aristocratic state. An aristocracy may be termed "natural," as opposed to hereditary, if those who rule do so because of their natural endowments rather than because of family affiliation.
M.J.H.

Aristotle (384—322 B.C.).
Developed the political philosophy of the city-state, ignoring the great revolution of his time: the transition to the "Hellenistic Age" with the political form of empire, planned by Philip, King of Macedon, and established by his son, Alexander the Great. Paradoxically, Aristotle was the tutor of Alexander, after studying under Plato and remaining in Plato's Academy for two decades. In his later years Aristotle opened the Lyceum, a school of philosophy, which he headed for twelve years. He died as a refugee in 322 B.C., forced to flee Athens by impending accusations against him by hostile political forces.

The most Greek of all Greek thinkers, Aristotle is one of the greatest philosophers and innovators of all times. His work in logic and ethics are complementary to his **Politics** (translated by V. Jowett, revised by W. D. Ross, Oxford: Clarendon Press, 1921). Aristotle projects man as a being who is a political animal by nature. The fullness of human life is in the political community—an organism with the attributes of a living body. Life in such a community is directed by law to the common good as well as to the individual interests. Law is the measure determining the extent and the guarantees of the good life.

As a philosopher, Aristotle recognized happiness superior to that which is attainable in the political community. The highest possession for man is truth which he can reach best in contemplative life. Thus man is able to share in what is eternal and divine.

As a political philosopher, Aristotle is concerned with the state ideally best, but as a political scientist he devotes more attention to what is practically attainable and best under existing conditions. He sees practical wisdom as the prime qualification for statesmen. He founded comparative government and politics by conducting one hundred and fifty-eight studies on different constitutions and political systems (only one, the **Constitution of Athens,** is available).

Regarding the forms of government (in **Politics,**) the strongest argument for supremacy by the multitude (restricted however to "citizens") is the assumption that in the practical order the pooling of limited individual virtues will summarily outweigh the higher virtues of the few "best" (aristocracy) or of the eminent one (monarchy). This form of constitutional government is the **polity;** in it the two principles of wealth (property) and numbers are properly mixed. A strong middle class is the backbone of this community. Among the self-seeking, perverted forms, democracy is best when compared to oligarchy or tyranny. At all events the collective body of citizens is not to govern but to control under the supremacy of law —the constitution—toward the highest good of the political community, justice. T.P.

Armistice.
An agreement among warring states to stop hostilities. It may be restricted as to area or time, or it may be general in scope and without time limit. In modern application its character depends upon the clauses of the armistice itself. The term does not suggest

a final peace treaty but rather a cessation of hostilities. H.B.J.

Arms Control.
Sometimes used synonymously for "disarmament," arms control more precisely refers to measures involving: prevention of surprise attack; designing and deploying strategic forces to decrease their vulnerability to first strikes, lengthen time available for decisions, and strengthen command and control over their operation; reassuring potential adversaries about one's intentions by taking unilateral steps along above lines, including refraining from unnecessarily provocative military policies and strategic postures, in the hope of evoking a favorable response and thus, through a tacit form of bargaining, creating an agreement — possibly unwritten — between potential adversaries, which may or may not also involve a reduction in force levels. L.P.B.

Arms Race.
The continuing contest of inventive skill, and productive capacity between and among nations in actual or potential military opposition in which defensive weapons are continually being improved to overcome enemy offensive capabilities, and offensive measures are continually being improved to nullify the effectiveness of defensive weapons. T.W.

Arthur, Chester Alan. (1830—1886).
Twenty-first President of the United States. Born in North Fairfield, Vermont, Chester Arthur graduated from Union College, taught school five years and practiced law in New York City before serving as a Civil War general with desk duties. Removed by President Hayes as Collector of the Port of New York (1871-78), Arthur then became the Republican Vice-Presidential candidate (1880) for related political reasons. He was Vice-President briefly (1881) when Garfield's death made him President (1881-85). Few thought him capable which Arthur disproved by reconstructing the American Navy, organizing Alaska, instituting U. S. Tariff Commission, vetoing Chinese Exclusion, and securing basic Civil Service Act (1883). K.E.D.

Article Nine, Japanese Constitution.
See Japanese Constitution, Article Nine.

Articles of Confederation.
For eight years (1781-89) the Articles constituted the first United States written instrument of government. Submitted to the states November 15, 1777, by the Second Continental Congress, unanimous ratification was delayed until March 1, 1781, mainly because the smaller states, especially Maryland, wanted restrictions on western land claims by larger states. Each state in the confederation, or "firm league of friendship," retained its "sovereignty, freedom and independence" and possessed all powers not expressly delegated to Congress. Lacking both a national executive and judiciary, central government powers were concentrated in a unicameral Congress composed of from two to seven delegates appointed annually from each state in a manner prescribed by their legislatures. Each state delegation voted as a unit, casting one vote. Most major decisions required concurrence of 9 of the 13 state delegations. Although the Articles helped keep divisive states united during a critical period and in some respects served as a model for the U.S. Constitution, several fundamental weaknesses caused its failure: the central government operated only through states and lacked sanction to enforce its limited authority; Congress could not raise revenue by taxation nor regulate commerce; amendments to the articles required approval by all state legislatures. C.F.N.

Art of Propaganda.
Messages which persuade people or which achieve other of their author's objectives by affecting an audience have certain distinctive characteristics. These characteristics of effective communication have been analyzed in a vast literature on rhetoric dating back to ancient Greece. Contemporary social scientists have tested many of the propositions in that literature by social-psychological experiments. The "art of propaganda" specifies the conditions under which such devices as repetition, use of example, presenta-

tion made in a one-sided versus two-sided fashion, emotionality, or the citing of distinguished authorities may affect the chances of achieving the desired results. I.d.S.P.

Aryan. See Appendix.

Asanuma, Inejiro (1899—1960).
While Secretary-General of the Japanese Socialist Party in 1959, Asanuma visited Peking and issued a statement that United States imperialism was the common enemy of the Chinese and Japanese peoples. This statement was blamed by some Socialists for the rather poor showing of their party in the 1959 elections for the House of Councillors. Asanuma was a leading opponent of the **1960** Security Treaty between the United States and Japan. In 1960 during a television debate with the heads of the Liberal Democratic and the Democratic Socialist Parties, Asanuma, then Chairman of the Socialist Party, was stabbed to death by a teen-age right-wing fanatic. T.Mc.N.

Ashanti.
The Negro inhabitants of an area of central Ghana. The people, part of the Akan family who entered between the 12th and 15th centuries, speak a Twi dialect. They were slavers, built a confederacy under a King (the Asantehene), his authority symbolized by the Golden Stool, and fought the British between 1806-1900 when the area was annexed. Integrating the Ashanti perplexes Ghana's modernist leaders. The legal area is one of the state's eight regions (9,700 sq. miles, population 1,108,548 in 1960). P.F.P.

Ashida, Hitoshi. (1887—1958).
Japanese diplomat, scholar, and politician. He entered the Diet in 1932, after a foreign service career. Following Japan's defeat, he became Welfare Minister, Democratic Party leader, and then Deputy Premier and Foreign Minister in the Katayama Cabinet until he became Premier (March 10 to October 15, 1948). He wrote voluminously on international affairs. G.O.T.

Ashwander v. TVA.
In this case, 297 US 288 (1936), the U.S. Supreme Court ruled that the government could, under the war and commerce powers, build Wilson Dam across the Tennessee River and that T.V.A. could purchase transmission lines from and sell surplus electricity produced at the Dam to the Alabama Power Co. The electricity was property of the U.S. and could be disposed of as any other property. Justice Brandeis wrote a separate opinion concurring on the constitutional questions but maintaining they should not have been passed on because plaintiffs, being stockholders in the Alabama Co., had no standing in court to question the policy of the Company. He would have dismissed the case for lack of jurisdiction. He summarized the following rules which he said the Court had adopted as guides in passing on constitutional questions:

(1) The Court will not pass on the constitutionality of legislation in a friendly, nonadversary, proceeding; (2) The Court will not decide constitutional questions unless absolutely necessary to decide a case; (3) The Court will not formulate a constitutional rule broader than required by the exact facts of the case to be decided; (4) The Court will not pass on a constitutional question if there is any other ground on which the case can be disposed of; (5) The Court will not pass on the validity of a statute at the request of one who fails to show that he is injured by it, or at the instance of one who has availed himself of the law's benefits; (6) The Court will not pass on the constitutionality of a statute if there is a plausible interpretation which will make it unnecessary. E.G.T.

As-Said, Nuri.
Leading Iraqi statesman. In World War I he broke from the Ottoman forces and joined the Arab rebellion under Amir Faisal. When Faisal became king of Iraq Nuri helped him in the organization of the state. Frequent Prime Minister and Foreign Minister of Iraq, Nuri was active in the establishment of treaty relations with Britain, and in the establishment of the Arab League. Accused by the Opposition of being a stooge of the West Nuri was murdered by a mob during the Iraqi army rebellion of 14 July

1958. He followed a moderate economic reform policy, but was accused of abusing power and jailing his enemies.
E.A.S.

Assemblee Nationale. See French National Assembly.

Assembly Government.

A version of parliamentary democracy in which both executive and legislative powers are concentrated constitutionally and actually in an elected legislature. The French Third and Fourth Republics are outstanding examples. Such legislative supremacy is based on the fact that all directly elected representatives of the people are in parliament and the chief of state is either a hereditary constitutional monarch or a weak indirectly elected president. The Prime Minister, Cabinet and other Ministers, who constitute the executive leadership (the Government), are drawn primarily from among those legislators who are able to organize a parliamentary majority. Designated officially by the chief of state because of this evidence of legislative strength, they are responsible to parliament and may be overturned either by a parliamentary rejection of a major proposal (bill) or by a parliamentary vote of lack of confidence. Since parliament frequently contains so many factions that no single party has a disciplined majority, Governments are often based upon a coalition of groups who do not agree on all major policies and hence do not provide that stable working majority necessary for effective executive leadership. Moreover, assembly government customarily does not provide the Government with real power to dissolve parliament and appeal to the public in new elections when faced with overwhelming opposition. As a result, political instability, failure to solve important national problems, and periodic overturn of governments without any evidence of popular desires are characteristic. Many countries, therefore, have abandoned this system.
D.W.

Assessment.

1. The process by which a public authority determines the value of property for taxation purposes, such value often being a percentage of the "fair value" (most commonly the "market value") of the property.

2. The value which has been assigned to a piece of property by means of the assessment process; also called the assessed valuation or assessed value.

3. The determination of the amount of tax to be paid by a taxpayer, or of the share of a tax to be paid by each of several taxpayers.

4. An entire system of taxation.

5. Fixing by a court of the amount of damages to which the successful party in a suit is entitled.
D.W.Mc.

Assessment, Political in U.S.A.

1. Solicitation of funds from government employees by party organizations. Federal legislation prohibits assessment of federal civil service employees by fellow employees, prohibits solicitation on federal premises, and forbids assessment of state and local employees paid wholly or partly from federal grants or loans. Some state legislation exists also.

2. Solicitation of political contributions by private firms or by unions from their employees, dealers, or members.

3. Other practices resemble political assessments: e.g., the solicitation of campaign contributions by government agencies from contractors, a practice prohibited insofar as it applies to federal contractors; and the collection by party committees of campaign contributions from their nominees.
D.W.Mc.

Assessment Ratio.

The ratio or percentage which is applied to the "fair value" of property in order to arrive at its assessed value.
D.W.Mc.

Assessor.

Public officer charged with locating, viewing, listing, and determining taxable value of property. Popularly elected in most counties, townships, and smaller municipalities.
P.J.C.

Assize Courts. See British Assize Courts.

Assumption.

A tentative synthetic proposition which has not yet been, and may never become, scientifically accepted as true or valid but is employed as a useful tool in the course of a scientific inquiry. What is being assumed may be a fact or event (past, present, future), a goal or purpose (as being actually pursued or being worthy of pursuit), or a universal law or regularity (e.g. causal interrelation). An assumption is often interchangeably called a "working hypothesis," especially if it refers to a goal or purpose or to a law of regular interrelations. See **hypothesis.** A.B.

Astronautics.

The science or art of making and flying spacecraft. Astronautics has significance for political science in that space vehicles, either manned or unmanned, may be used in launching weapons of mass destruction against targets on the earth or for the exploration and colonization of extraterrestrial pieces of real estate. T.W.

Aswan Dam. See Appendix.

Asylum.

Asylum consists of a state's giving sanctuary to foreign political refugees in its territory, and sometimes in its diplomatic establishments or ships. Asylum in diplomatic establishments is very rarely employed, though in Latin America it enjoys somewhat wider use than elsewhere. On warships asylum is considered proper only when the refugee is in the most imminent danger. Asylum within the territory of a state is less circumscribed and is limited only by extradition treaties which spell out extraditable offenses in detail and normally omit political offenses. H.B.J.

Ataturk. See Kemal Pasha Ataturk.

Atlantic Charter.

A declaration issued jointly on August 14, 1941 by President Franklin D. Roosevelt and Prime Minister W. S. Churchill following their meeting at Argentia Bay, Newfoundland. The statement summarized the common principles underlying the policies of the United States and Great Britain in the world crisis. These were: (1) their countries sought no territorial or other aggrandizement; (2) they desired to see no territorial changes which did not accord with the freely expressed wishes of the peoples concerned; (3) the rights of all peoples to choose the form of government under which they live; (4) equal access for all states to the trade and raw materials of the world; (5) full economic collaboration between all states for the improvement of labor standards, economic adjustment and social security for all; (6) the establishment of a peace in which all nations could dwell in safety within their own borders and which would give assurance that men may live in freedom from fear and want; (7) all men to traverse the high seas without hindrance; (8) all nations to abandon the use of force, and, pending the establishment of a wider and permanent system of general security, aggressor nations to be disarmed: lightening the crushing burden of armaments for peace-loving peoples.

Subsequently twenty-five other nations joined in the declaration. The Soviet Union agreed, subject to a reservation "that the practical application of these principles will necessarily adopt itself to the circumstances, needs, and historical peculiarities of particular countries."

The President was concerned to get public assurances from Britain which ruled out secret territorial agreements, whereas Churchill wished to make clear the unity of the United States and the United Kingdom. The United Nations' Declaration of January, 1942 pledged the signatories to support the principles of the Atlantic Charter.

C.B.J.

Atlantic Institute.

Non-governmental international organization with headquarters in Paris, set up in 1960 at the instigation of Atlantic Congress of NATO Parliamentarians (London, 1959) for the purpose of promoting closer intellectual cooperation between member countries of the Atlantic community. It serves as a clearing house for the study of problems of the Atlantic community. Henry Cabot Lodge served as its first Director-General. F.M.

Atomic bomb.

A weapon whose unprecedented destructiveness is caused by atomic fission, in which matter is converted into energy.

Spurred on by warnings from refugee scientists (including Dr. Einstein) that the Germans were experimenting in the atomic field, President Roosevelt during World War II decided upon a crash program to develop an atomic bomb. This led to the successful testing of the bomb on July 16, 1945 in New Mexico. The atomic era opened in earnest when at 8:15 on the morning of August 6 of the same year a single bomb all but destroyed the Japanese city of Hiroshima. Three days later Nagasaki suffered the same fate, and soon thereafter Japan surrendered.

The U. S. atomic monopoly ended in August, 1949, when the Soviet Union exploded its first atomic device, some three years ahead of Western expectations. This was followed four years later by Soviet testing of hydrogen weapons, tests which occurred only nine months after similar initial tests by the United States. Great Britain became a member of the nuclear club with her atomic tests in October 1952, followed in May 1957 by her thermonuclear testing in the Central Pacific. General De Gaulle's determination to create an independent nuclear striking force has come closer to realization with four low-yield French atomic explosions in the Sahara in 1960 and 1961. F.H.G.

Atomization.
As used in political science (and in line with its meaning in physics), atomization of society is the dissolution of existing groups in order to undermine the security of individuals, increase their isolation, and make them dependent on the concentrated power of the political regime. Specifically this was a technique of the Nazis during the Third Reich which was far more complete than the related technique of "co-ordination" (centralization of **political** power). Atomization accords with the emphasis of monism, and opposes that of pluralism. Yet it need not be identified solely with fascism; for example, Maritain was opposed to bourgeois liberalism because he saw it leading toward anarchical atomization of society. And certainly the Communists have adopted this policy to subordinate the individual to the party. R.B.C.

Atoms for Peace.
In 1953 President Eisenhower delivered an address before the United Nations General Assembly in which he recommended that the atom be "consecrated to man's life instead of dedicated to his death." As a result there was set up in Vienna an "autonomous member of the United Nations family"—the International Atomic Energy Agency. This Agency was to provide atomic power for peaceful purposes to the developing nations. Inspectors were to accompany the shipments in order to insure that no illegal conversion to war uses would take place. While the United States, the Soviet Union and the United Kingdom provided the Agency with source materials, most recipient nations have tended to prefer bilateral agreements. By 1963 only three applications had reached the United Nations Agency. J.G.St.

Attitude.
A predisposition to react to a given thing, situation, or idea in a given way. Attitudes are usually associated with underlying, deep-seated predispositions. They are distinguished from habits in that the latter are usually associated with overt behavior whereas attitudes also include verbal and mental responses that need not eventuate in overt behavior. Attitudes are associated with emotional responses that range from indifferent to strong attraction or revulsion. R.M.T.

Attlee, Clement Richard.
1st Earl (1883—   ), British statesman, born in London. An honors graduate of Oxford, he was admitted to the bar in 1905. Attlee joined the Labor party in 1907, was first elected to Parliament in 1921 and served in Prime Minister Ramsay MacDonald's minority Labor governments of 1924 and 1929. Having broken in 1931 with MacDonald over the latter's formation of the National Government, Attlee was elected Deputy Leader and in 1935 Leader of the Labor party. In

May, 1940, he joined Winston Churchill's Wartime Coalition Government, but he refused to continue the coalition after the defeat of Germany. As a result of the British election of July 5, 1945, Attlee became the first Labor Prime Minister commanding a solid majority of Labor Party members in the Commons (394 out of 640 members).

During Attlee's prime ministership key services and industries in Britain were nationalized, the social security system was greatly expanded, and the liquidation of the colonial empire was begun. Having lost (as a result of the election of 1951) the prime ministership to Winston Churchill, Attlee resigned in 1955 as Leader of the Labor Party, was created an Earl by Queen Elizabeth II, and entered the House of Lords.

For Attlee's non-Marxian socialist views and his reflections on empire the following of his books are characteristic: **The Will and the Way to Socialism** (1935), **The Labor Party in Perspective** (1937, revised 1949), **Twilight of Empire** (1962). G.V.W.

Attorney General.

In the U.S.A. the chief legal state officer, elected in about forty states and appointed in the others; he is charged with responsibilities similar to those of the Attorney General in the President's cabinet. His office gives legal advice to the Governor and to other administrative officials, to the legislature, and to various local officers who may request it. He represents the state in litigation and he may be charged with overall directing of local law enforcement officers.
Sp.D.A.

Auditor.

An officer authorized to check the financial operations of the executive branch and to report to the legislative branch. In the United States Government the General Accounting Office, headed by the Comptroller General, has the dual tasks of accounting and auditing. In the state governments of the U.S.A. a Comptroller or Director of Finance is a fiscal officer under the executive; and the Auditor is authorized to examine the legality and the accuracy of all financial records, reporting to the people or to the people's representatives. A similar arrangement is in effect in many cities.
Sp.D.A.

Augustine of Hippo. (350—430).

Called Aurelius Augustinus Saint, Bishop, rated both by Catholic and Protestant critics among the greatest of the Latin Fathers and Doctors of the Church, "a philosophical and theological genius of the first order" was born in Tagaste, a town in Numidia, north Africa, of a pagan father (later converted) and of a devoted Christian mother, Monia (canonized by the Church); died in Hippo during the siege of that town by the Vandals. From paganism by way of Manichaeism, Scepticism, and neo-Platonism, he made his way to Christianity being baptized at the age of 33 in Milan, Italy, by his friend and teacher, Saint Ambrose. Returning to Africa he was made presbyter (391) and consecrated Bishop of Hippo (395). Energetic preacher and controversialist, he fought vigorously against the errors of Manichaeism, Donatism, Pelagianism, and Arianism; is particularly noteworthy for his **Confessions** (397) and **City of God** (begun in 413, completed in 426).

The **Confessions**, relating the touching story of his soul, is a document of unrivalled richness and human interest. His **City of God** is rated among "the few greatest books of all time." A **livre de circonstance** it rebuts the pagan charge that Christianity caused the downfall of Roman power and the sack of the city by Alaric in 410. Admittedly a difficult work to read (22 books), yet its grand design is clear. Human history is dominated by the contest of two societies. The **Civitas Dei** originating with the creation of the angels is the kingdom of Christ embodied first in the Hebrew nation and later in the Church founded by Christ, the turning point of all history; its rival, the **Civitas Terrena**, commenced with the fall of Satan embodying itself especially in the pagan empires of Assyria and Rome. Throughout all earthly life the two societies are mingled, only to be separated at the last judgment. It is the fate of earthly dominions to pass away; thus

Rome fell, as Assyria and others before it. What society then, endures and perishes not? Only the **Civitas Dei**, the communion of the redeemed in this world and the next, answers Augustine. We are in the city of man that we may make it the city of God. Since the advent of Christianity, human salvation is bound up with the paramount interests of the Church; hence, no state can be just whose constitution withholds from God the true worship which is His due. Augustine does not deny that secular government is independent in its own proper sphere; he does stress the autonomy of the Church and the idea that the state now must be founded on the unity of the Christian faith. Augustine's **City of God** is the first Christian philosophy of history. Its influence on the theory and practice of the Holy Roman Empire and, indeed, on Church-State relations since, is clearly evident. G.A.K.

Aurelius, Marcus. (A.D. 121—180).
Full name Marcus Aelius Aurelius Antoninus, Roman Emperor (161—180), illustrious Stoic philosopher, authored twelve books, called **Meditations,** intended for himself and not for publication. Though his reign was plagued by enemy invasions, internal revolts, and serious epidemics of pestilence, he remained remarkably self-controlled and spiritual for a pagan; his death was mourned more sincerely than that of any other Roman Emperor. Unfortunately he did permit a cruel persecution of the Christians whom he regarded as "obstinately" opposed to the existing order.

While Stoics were not primarily political theorists, yet several of his ideas have special relevance to political science. "But my nature is rational and social; and my city and country, so far as I am Antoninus, is Rome, but so far as I am a man, it is the world." "Mankind are under one common law; and if so, they must be fellow citizens, and belong to the same body politic. From whence it will follow that the whole world is but one commonwealth." G.A.K.

Austinian Theory of Law.
The theory that law is law only if it is the direct or indirect command of the sovereign. This theory—known also as the command theory of law—is diametrically opposed to the natural law theory, under which the validity of a law depends upon its accord with eternal natural principles of justice. It is also in contrast with the historical theory of law, which sees law as the fruit of unconscious growth similar to the growth of language. The command theory of law, widely accepted on the continent at the time of the French Revolution, was little regarded in Britain until after the posthumous publication in 1863 of the **Lectures on Jurisprudence** of John Austin (1790—1859). M.Sp.

Australia.
A continent consisting of five mainland states: New South Wales, Victoria, Queensland, Western Australia and South Australia. The population is roughly 10 million and the capital is Canberra. Australia has a federal parliamentary form of government and is a member of the British Commonwealth of Nations as well as of the United Nations. Australia was discovered early in the 17th century but was not claimed until 1770 when Captain James Cook claimed possession in the name of Great Britain. J.G.St.

Australian Ballot.
A ballot, given to qualified voters at their polling places, listing all legal nominees and containing space for write-in candidates. The ballot must be marked in secret and deposited before leaving the polling place. K.E.H.

Austria.
A land-locked country in Central Europe with an area of 32,000 square miles and a population of 7 million with its capital at Vienna. From 1282 until 1918 the history of Austria is tied to the history of the Hapsburg family. Following World War I it became a republic and was occupied by Nazi Germany between 1938 and 1945. The Second Austrian Republic was established on 19 December 1945 but Austria remained occupied by the four Allied powers for another 10 years. Austria regained her independence in 1955 on the basis of a declaration of permanent neutrality. J.G.St.

Autarchy.
Means self-sufficiency. Some states have striven for autarchy by limiting imports and encouraging the domestic production of goods hitherto imported or the use of substitutes for goods that could not be produced within the territory of the state. J.D.

Authentication.
Proposed procedure to prevent war due to misinformation between two nations. Whenever country A suspects war preparations in specific locations of country B (and vice versa), its own inspectors are to check on suspected activities and to report findings to home government by tamper-proof, and thus authentic, radio messages. H.G.S.

Authoritarian.
Supreme political authority of one person, or a group of persons without being responsible to people under control. No legal and orderly method of terminating functions short of forceful overthrow. M.C.V.

Authority.
The legal power vested in a public agency (and its members) to execute the functions for which it was organized. J.D.

Autocracy.
A form of government in which power is held by a single person, who is independent of restraint exercised either by law or other persons. M.J.H.

Automation.
The process of using mechanical or electronic devices to do routine, repetitive work automatically, instead of employing human hands and minds. In high technology societies, especially the U.S., the adoption of automation is increasing spectacularly, eliminating the jobs of great numbers of unskilled and semi-skilled workers, and threatening to move ever higher in the levels of work it can do as devices become more capable of decision-making. It is thus creating major social and political problems (e.g., unemployment, union jurisdiction) even as it improves productivity-per-man exponentially. Among other things, education and training concepts are changing, to provide more generalist foundations for the work force, on the theory that automation will be forcing men to change their vocations wholly perhaps three or more times in a lifetime. J.B.L.

Autonomous Republics.
Administrative divisions of the USSR at the level next below the union republic. The ASSR (Autonomous Soviet Socialist Republic) is based on a particular, identifiable nationality which is different from the dominant nationality of the union republic to which the ASSR is subordinate. Among the larger ASSRs are the Bashkir ASSR (with Ufa as the capital) and the Tatar ASSR (Ufa). W.D.J.

Averroism.
An influential doctrine conceiving a double truth that philosophic reason might conflict with revealed religion was named after the leading commentator of Plato and Aristotle in the 12th Century, Abul-Walid Muhammad ibn Rushd (1126-98 A.D.). The philosophic truths which included the doctrines of the eternity of the world and of matter, the unity of active intellect for all men, and determinism should be compared with the Thomist synthesis; thirteen of his doctrines were condemned by the Church in 1270 and 219 in 1277, at which time the Aristotelianism of St. Thomas narrowly escaped suppression. In spite of condemnation, Averroes' work remained current until the sixteenth century especially in northern Italy where it provided one basis for the scientific intellectual revolution of the Renaissance. R.W.T.

Avulsion.
A sudden and rapid change in the course of a river whereby it abandons its normal channel. The boundary line remains unchanged. J.E.T.

Ayub Khan, Mohammed. (1907—).
The President of Pakistan. Ayub Khan, son of a Pathan bugler in the British Indian Army, was born at Rehana in the North-West Frontier Province of pre-independence India. After attending the Muslim University at Aligarh, he joined the Royal Military College at Sandhurst and won his

commission in 1928. He served a year with the Royal Fusiliers, and subsequently with the Fourteenth Punjab Regiment. In World War II, he was briefly a battalion commander in Burma. After the creation of Pakistan, he rose rapidly to become the Commander-in-Chief in 1951. On October 7, 1958, General Ayub forced President Iskander Mirza to abrogate the 1956 Constitution and declare martial law. Twenty days later, Ayub replaced Mirza as President. In 1962, he gave Pakistan a new Constitution, establishing a "basic democracy" under which all elections are by indirect vote, and the President holds extensive powers. While committed to the CENTO and SEATO pacts, Ayub has sought to establish friendly relations with Communist states. C.S.S.

Aztecs.

Indian tribe invading the Valley of Mexico from the northwest in 13th century A.D., after the fall of the Toltecs. Their speech was **nahuatl.** They settled in the area of Lake Texcoco, founding the town of Tenochtitlán around 1325-1350. As the civilization developed, centers of power were established until a confederacy dominated by Tenochtitlán, in alliance with Texcoco and Tlacopán, held 5,000,000 to 6,000,000 vassals, and some 75,000 square miles. This was the civilization under the Aztec Emperor Montezuma that Hernán Cortes met and subdued (1519-1521). From the rubble of Tenochtitlán arose present-day Mexico City. R.B.G.

B

Back Benchers.
Members of the British Parliament or of those based on British pattern who are not among the party leadership. The term is often applied to those who are potentially more likely than others to oppose party policies. Party leaders occupy the "front benches" or, if they form a government, the "Treasury benches." R.H.B.

Bacon, Francis. (1561—1626).
English statesman, philosopher and scientist. In politics he was a supporter of royal authority and the antagonist of Sir Edward Coke. His lasting importance lies in the realms of science and philosophy. He is acknowledged as the father of the modern inductive method. His works include **Advancement of Learning** (1605) and **Novum Organum** (1620). H.S.R.

Bacteriological and Chemical Warfare.
This term is usually expanded to "CBR," Chemical, Bacteriological, and Radiological Warfare. It designates the use of toxic weapons instead of explosive weapons against people and their animals and crops. Popular belief, especially in the Western democracies, holds CBR weapons to be especially brutal and immoral. It needs to be emphasized, however, that technological developments (and, even more, future prospects) permit much selectivity in the use of chemical and bacteriological agents so that their effects can be made to range from mildly incapacitating, through prolonged incapacitation, to the production of high fatalities. The Communist leaders have threatened that future wars may entail mass destruction through chemical and bacteriological weapons as well as thermonuclear ones. The best way, therefore, to deter the use of such weapons would seem to be the development by the Free World of advanced technological systems for both defensive and offensive use of such weapons. J.D.A.

Badoglio, Pietro (1871—1956).
Military conqueror of Ethiopia under fascism, Marshal Badoglio was Italian prime minister from July 1943 until June 1944. Appointed by the king, he signed an armistice with the Allies (September 1943), declared war on Germany (October 1943), and dissolved the Fascist Corporative Chamber. E.T.O.

Bad Tendency Test.
The English doctrine of seditious libel outlawed speech which had the **tendency** to bring the government or its officials into disrepute or public hatred because such speech bore the seeds of revolution. After use in early American history and subsequent popular disapproval, the bad tendency test was revived in **Gitlow v. New York** (1925) but today it has fallen into disuse. W.F.G.

Baghdad Pact.
Was the result of Secretary Dulles' policy of creating an alliance among the northern tier states. With American encouragement Turkey and Pakistan concluded an agreement in 1954. Iraq signed an agreement with Turkey on 24, February 1955 known as the Baghdad Pact. Pakistan and Iran entered the Pact later in the year. While Britain joined the Pact, the United States did not, satisfying itself by placing representatives in some of its committees. The Pact was designed to strengthen these states against Soviet threat. The Iraqi revolution of 1958 destroyed the Old Regime and ended Iraq's association with the Pact, which has since been called Central Treaty Organization. E.A.S.

Baguio Conference.
Seven Southeast Asian and neighboring states—India, Ceylon, Pakistan, Thailand, Philippines, Indonesia, and Australia—met to consider common problems at Baguio in the mountains north of Manila, May 26 to 30, 1950. Nationalist China was excluded from the conference and Burma absented herself at the last minute.

A central theme of the conference was the solidarity of Asian states and their strong hope of avoiding involvement in the U.S.-Soviet struggle. Final resolutions called for closer economic, social, and cultural ties among the participants.

Indian and Indonesian neutralism dominated discussion precluding a general statement on the Communist issue. The important aspect of the conference was its demonstration of regional solidarity and vaunting of purely Asian views and interests.
M.T.K.

Bail.

A person may be held in custody or in bail at the discretion of the judge after he has been arrested for a misdemeanor or felony and is awaiting information or indictment and trial. Usually a sum of money is placed with the court by the defendant or a bonding agency as a guarantee that the defendant will appear for trial. This freedom from confinement permits the defendant to have greater opportunity to prepare his defense than if he were in jail and does not place him in jail until he is proven guilty. According to the 8th Amendment of the U.S. Constitution bail may not be excessive. **Stack v. Boyle**, 342 U.S. 1 (1951), interpreted excessive as dependent upon the alleged offense, weight of evidence, and the character and financial ability of the defendant. The serving of a summons to appear in court at a future date rather than arrest and bail is often used in petty offenses.
J.A.E.

Baker v. Carr.

A 1962 U.S. Supreme Court decision holding invidious misrepresentation in a state legislature a denial of equal protection of the laws and that the Federal Courts should take jurisdiction of cases involving such misrepresentation. The case overruled earlier decisions which held that districting was a political question. The decision was followed by cases in U.S. District Courts, in state courts, and by special reapportionment legislative sessions in several states, with varying results. The apparent net result will be increased representation for cities in state legislatures.
J.E.R.

Bakunin, Michael (1814—1876).

Russian-born revolutionist, propagandist, and social theorist; noted for his advocacy of the complete destruction of the existing social and political order and replacing it with "anarchism, collectivism, and atheism;" broke away from the Marxian movement in 1872 and established an international organization for promoting universal revolution through the agency of small secret groups.
Ch.C.M.

Balance.

In economics, an equality between assets and liabilities, or between credits and debits. The best known economic "balances" are: (1) the balance-of-trade, which in case of any particular country means the difference between the money value of a country's merchandise imports and exports, (2) the balance-of-payments, that represents, in case of any particular country, the difference between the total payments made to foreign nations and the total receipts from foreign nations during a given period of time.
W.N.

Balance-of-Payments.

A summary of the money value of all exchanges and transfers of goods, services, and evidences of debt or ownership between the residents, businesses, government and other institutions of one country and the rest of the world for a given period of time. A partial international balance-of-payments would involve the transactions between one country and one or more, but not all, other countries. A persistent trend toward deficit or surplus which is not matched by long-term capital flows is evidence of balance-of-payments disequilibrium and cannot continue indefinitely.
R.J.S.

Balance of Power.

A policy aiming to prevent an upset of the international status quo. It consists of the support of the second-strongest against the strongest power if the latter tries to disturb the existing equilibrium. It became the principal guide of European statesmen with the disintegration of the medieval Christian commonwealth and was considered, until the end of World War I, a means of maintaining peace. It has presented two main difficulties: first, the frequent impossibility of ascertaining the existence of an equilibrium, especially when such imponderables as domestic consent must be considered; second, the failure to provide clues as to what aspects of the status quo are to be protected. It has fallen in disrepute since the end of World War I when President Wilson attempted to put world peace on a more secure foundation by displacing it with an international organization. However, balance of power policies, being basic to all politics, have persisted. P.J.F.

"Balance of Power" international system.

A system in which only nation states participate and in which states are predominantly security oriented. States attempt to increase their capabilities—by war if necessary; to enter into alliances to protect their interests; to shift alliances as their interests shift; to form counter-alliances against nations striving for predominance; to limit their gains in war to preserve the existence of other major nations; and to treat all other nations as acceptable alliance partners. Weapons system is conventional. M.A.K.

Balance of terror.

An international military equilibrium produced by the possession by two great powers or blocs, e.g. United States and Soviet Russia, of military striking power sufficient for mutual devastation presumably by nuclear weapons. Thus, a situation of mutual military deterrence in which neither nation directly challenges the vital national interests of the other from fear of unacceptable retaliation. H.H.R.

Balfour Declaration.

A letter sent by Arthur James (later: Lord) Balfour, British Secretary of State for Foreign Affairs, to Lord Rothschild, dated Nov. 2, 1917, as follows:

"I have much pleasure in conveying to you, on behalf of His Majesty's Government, the following declaration of sympathy with Jewish Zionist aspirations which has been submitted to, and approved by, the Cabinet. 'His Majesty's Government view with favour the establishment in Palestine of a national home for the Jewish people, and will use their best endeavours to facilitate the achievement of this object, it being clearly understood that nothing shall be done which may prejudice the civil and religious rights of existing non-Jewish communities in Palestine, or the rights and political status enjoyed by Jews in any other country.' I should be grateful if you will bring this declaration to the knowledge of the Zionist Federation."

The outcome of long negotiations carried on by representatives of the Zionist movement, foremost among them Dr. Chaim Weizmann, with the British government, the declaration had been approved prior to publication by President Woodrow Wilson and was subsequently endorsed by the French, Italian and other allied governments. Its wording was incorporated in a series of international instruments including the 1922 League of Nations Mandate for Palestine and the 1924 U.S.-British Palestine Mandate Convention. Its exact meaning became, over the years, the object of conflicting interpretations. Under the policy inaugurated by it, the Jewish population of Palestine grew rapidly, leading in 1948 to the emergence of the State of Israel. B.A.

Balkan Federation.

The ideal of establishing a federation in the Balkans was advocated from the 1840's on. Three major treaties made a start in that direction: The Balkan Alliance of 1912, the Balkan Pact of 1934, the Balkan Pact of 1953. The principal aims of these treaties were military, although the last two were intended to stimulate intra-Balkan cooperation. They all failed insofar as they did not include all of the Balkan powers, who remained divided by ideology and politics. The Yugoslav aim to create a Balkan Federation was allegedly one of the reasons for Tito's expulsion from the Cominform. G.K.

Ballot.

The object used for secret voting; at first a ball or other small article; later a slip, circulated by the candidate or his party, containing the candidate's name or those of party candidates; now, generally, a slip listing all candidates for the offices on the slip and containing space for write-in candidates. K.E.H.

Baltic States
(Estonia, Latvia, Lithuania).
Estonia. Area, 17,400 sq. mi.; population, 1,221,000; capital, Tallinn. Early Estonian history remains shrouded in mystery. Periodic migrations of Finnish, Germanic, and Slavic tribes left their mark upon the region. In 1219, the Danes conquered Estonia, founded Tallinn, and introduced Christianity. Subsequent rebellions led the Danes to sell the territory to the Order of Teutonic Knights, who ruled until 1561, when Estonia came under Swedish rule. In 1721, Russia conquered the area and kept it part of the Czarist empire until 1918.

After World War I, Estonia, like Latvia and Lithuania, became an independent state. The Bolsheviks failed to reestablish Moscow's rule, and Estonia embarked on a precarious, brief period of independence. It sought friendly relations with the other Baltic States, Germany, England, and the Scandinavian countries, and signed a non-aggression pact with the Soviet Union. During the 1920's, the country prospered, but the great depression of 1929 weakened the economic foundation of the republic and a dictatorship was established under Prime Minister K. Paets in 1935. Assigned to the Soviet sphere of influence, as were Latvia and Lithuania, by the secret German-Soviet protocol of August 1939, Estonia was incorporated into the USSR in August 1940. When Germany invaded Russia in June 1941, it occupied Estonia until 1944, when Soviet rule was again imposed. The United States has not recognized the incorporation of Estonia, or of the other two Baltic States, into the Soviet empire. (See also Latvia and Lithuania).
A.Z.R.

Banda, Hastings Kamuzu.
First Prime Minister of Malawi (Africa). R.M.

Bandung (Asian-African) Conference.
Twenty-nine African and Asian nations met between April 18 and April 24, 1955, at Bandung, 75 miles southeast of Jakarta (Indonesia) to discuss common objectives. Western powers were pointedly excluded from the invitation list although they were represented by unofficial observers.

Beyond routine resolutions on solidarity and future cooperation, the conference led, among other things, to enhanced prestige for Peking, Chinese-U.S. talks at Geneva, and the emergence of the Afro-Asian bloc in the United Nations. Through this conference representatives of over half the world's population were announcing their emergence from colonial or servile status and their demands for economic growth and political equality.
M.T.K.

Band-wagon effect (in polling).
Arises as a consequence of the publication and widespread adherence to polling survey results or from newspaper or other media in which an effect is created that a majority or preponderance of opinion favors a particular candidate, issue, or approach to government or politics. Assumedly, a number of people without strong predilections will want to be in the "majority" or to "climb aboard the band wagon" to be with the winner. The political parties emphasize those straw votes, polls or analyses which strengthen their positions or show their candidates winning or doing unexpectedly well.
M.B.D.

Bankruptcy Legislation.
Under the Constitution of the United States both State and National Governments have concurrent jurisdiction over bankruptcy. The Congress, however, has the power to establish "uniform laws on the subject of bankruptcies throughout the United States." In practice, ever since the Congressional Act of 1898 on general bankruptcy, the National laws have taken precedence, and the Federal Government has expanded its powers so as to include almost all classes of persons and corporations. Bankruptcy legislation now provides relief for the debtor even more than a method of reimbursing creditors.
R.G.S.

Bantu.
An African language or racial family prevailing in East and South Africa. There are about 250 Bantu languages, excluding dialects, among them, Swahili, Zulu, Congo, Luba-Lulua, Luganda and Nyanja. Racially the Bantus are mainly Negro with

Hamitic influences and include the Baganda, Basuto, Kikuyu, Matabele and Zulu groups. Since 1959 South African governments have sought to establish Bantustans, native reserves divorced from white society. P.F.P.

Bao Dai.
Last head of state in Vietnam before the Ngo Dinh Diem regime, Bao Dai was born October 22, 1913, and educated mainly in Paris. He was proclaimed Emperor of Annam in 1926 and ascended the throne in September 1932. Following successive periods of French, Japanese, and Ho Chih-minh domination, he abdicated under pressure from Ho in August 1945. Ho Chih-minh named him "Supreme Councillor" in January 1946, but he fled to Hong Kong in March 1948.

The French again installed him as "Chief of State of Vietnam" in April 1948, a post he held for a year and a half until power was transferred to the Government of Vietnam in December 1949. He was finally deposed when Vietnam became a Republic in October 1955.

As of July 1957 he was living at Cannes in the Chateau de Thorenc.
M.T.K.

Barres, Maurice (1862—1923).
A novelist and political writer, Barres was both an individualist and a nationalist. Following World War I he elaborated a common Franco-German tradition in **Genie du Rhin** (1921) which became a basis for the program of Action Francaise for Franco-German **rapprochement.**
R.W.T.

Barrister.
In Great Britain, a Barrister is a fully qualified lawyer who alone has the right to plead in the regular courts. Barristers must be members of one of the four Inns of Court where some of them instruct students (Readers).
R.G.N.

Basic norm.
The validity of the positive law can be derived **logically** only if the validity of a "basic norm" is assumed which prescribes that the norms contained in a country's constitution be obeyed. Much the same, the validity of (moral) natural law can be derived logically only if the validity of a basic norm is assumed which prescribes that the moral commands allegedly to be found in nature be obeyed, and the validity of divine law only if the validity of a basic norm is assumed which prescribes that the will of God be obeyed (the latter assumption is merely tautological if we mean by God him whose will ought to be done). There is no scientific necessity to presuppose a basic norm, Kelsen **says,** but without postulating it, the validity of a country's constitution cannot be **logically** derived. This is correct; but we may as well postulate a differently conceived basic norm according to which legislation in conflict with certain fundamental precepts of humanity is never legally valid, irrespective of what a country's constitution says about it.
A.B.

Bastille.
A Parisian fortress built in the 14th century, it became a prison for individuals confined by **lettres de cachet.** It was this practice rather than the fate or character of the persons confined that made the Bastille into a symbol of royal absolutism. Its capture on 14 July 1789 and subsequent destruction dramatically emphasized the end of the **ancien regime** and popularly, the beginning of the French Revolution.
K.B.

Bataan. (Area, 517 square miles; population, estimated 92,900.)
A province of western Luzon in the Philippine Islands, Bataan is coterminous with the peninsula of the same name, 30 miles long, constituting the western enclosure of Manila Bay.

Bataan was the scene of the final struggle of the U.S. and Filipino forces under General Douglas MacArthur resisting the Japanese conquest of the Philippine Islands in 1942. The northern end was occupied by U.S. forces about January 10 following the fall of Manila on January 2. These combined forces surrendered on April 9, 1942, after withdrawing southward toward Mariveles. Remnants retired to Corregidor (q.v.) continuing their resistance under General Jonathan Wainwright until their collapse on May 6. Bataan was retaken from the Japanese, February 15-21, 1945.
M.T.K.

Ba'th Party (Arab Socialist Resurrection Party).
Founded after World War II by Salah ud — Din Bitar, Michel Aflaq and others with branches in Syria, Lebanon and Iraq. The party's program pursues Arab unity and radical socio-economic reforms, which are directed especially against foreign concessionaires and Arab landlordism. Influential among urban intellectuals and younger officers of the armed services. J.D.

Bay of Pigs.
(Bahia de Cochinos, Cuba.)
Site of abortive invasion of Cuba April 17, 1961 by Cuban exiles under the sponsorship of the National Revolutionary Council (Cuban exile organization in the United States), and the Central Intelligence Agency (U.S.).
R.B.G.

Bebel, August (1840—1915).
"Kaiser Bebel" as his contemporaries called him, was for many years the most popular and influential leader of the German Social Democratic Party. He was the son of a Prussian petty officer. He learned the trade of a turner. From his early youth on he became involved in the German labor movement. First he joined the Catholic journeymen's organization of Father Kolping. Later he became acquainted with the writings of Lassalle and Marx and eventually actively participated in the **Allgemeine Deutsche Arbeiterverein** founded by Lassalle. Bebel and Wilhelm Liebknecht organized the Saxon People's Party and Bebel was elected to the Constituent **Reichstag** of the North German Confederation. In 1875 he was instrumental in bringing together the Lassallean organization with the Marxian group in the new Social Democratic Party. In 1871, Bebel was elected to the **Reichstag** and attained the leadership of the socialist faction.

In the **Reichstag** as well as through his influence within the German labor movement, Bebel strongly opposed Bismarck's fight against the Catholic Church and his militaristic policies. Bismarck's attempt to suppress the socialists brought many German socialists into jail, among them Bebel. During his confinement Bebel wrote a number of books which did not fail to make a great impact upon the German socialist movement.

Bebel was strongly democratically oriented and advocated positive collaboration of the social democrats in the Reichstag. He opposed German militarism and favored a military establishment on a broad popular basis.
E.W.

Bechuanaland.
An arid British protectorate in South Africa. Bechuanaland (275,000 sq. miles, population 337,000) dates from 1895 when chiefs obtained imperial safeguards. Important tribes are the Bakwena and Bamangwato, the latter possessing mineral lands. Tribal government is linked with commissioner rule which in 1961 introduced a legislative council with parity for Africans and Europeans. The cattle and labor-exporting economy is tied to South Africa where Afrikaners seek Bechuanaland as a native reserve. African nationalists view it as one base for ousting white rule in South Africa.
P.F.P.

Bedouins.
(Arabic, "dwellers in the open land," or "people of the tent" as Bedouins call themselves.) They are Arab nomads, originating in the Arabian peninsula, living in tribes and under their own tribal laws. Now dispersed over countries of Middle East and North Africa, numbering over 10 millions. During last decades many Bedouins have been permanently settled. E.G.

Beggars' Democracy.
This term covers politically inconsequential patterns of self-government. Such patterns occur in many spheres of multicentered societies; and in a rudimentary form they persist even under the limping totalitarianism of Fascism and the full-fledged totalitarianism of Communism. (Cf. the role played by "elders" among the inmates of concentration and forced labor camps.) But the classical locus of the beggars' democracy is Oriental (or hydraulic) society. The ruling bureaucracy of Oriental despotism, which exerted complete political power, fulfilled only limited managerial functions; hence it lacked the means to fully control all sectors of the econ-

omy, social life, and thought. Inconsequential forms of self-government were present in the Oriental villages, and also in the organizations of artisans and merchants, often referred to as "guilds." (Actually these organizations differed fundamentally from the guilds of medieval Europe, which frequently combined full self-government with some political and even military power.) Similarly, inconsequential patterns of self-government can be discerned in the kin groups, clans, etc. of Oriental society. But here, as in the case of the village communities, guilds, and tolerated secondary religions (Christian and Jewish communities under Islam), the despotic state, which permitted these groups to handle their internal affairs without bureaucratic interference, held its headman responsible for the behavior of the members and the fulfillment of the government's demands, fiscal and other. The beggars' democracies do not make Oriental despotism a democratic order, but they favor the existence of a variety of precious—if politically irrelevant — freedoms. The sharp restriction of beggars' democracies in Communist countries underlines the almost limitless extension of full-fledged totalitarian power.

K.A.W.

Behavioral Approach.
See Behavioralism.

Behavioralism.
An orientation to the study of social phenomena characterized mainly by empiricism, logical positivism and cross-disciplinary interests. Under the influence of behaviorism in psychology (see these), empiricism and logical positivism, the behavioral approach developed, mainly in the United States during the last twenty-five years. Including a variety of scholars, and defined in different ways, it is more of an orientation than a defined approach. In addition to the above-mentioned three basic characteristics, it is also distinguished by intense interest in research methodology; preference for quantification; a liking for the term "scientific," especially as used in the physical sciences; and concentration on theory on an operational level. It is mainly opposed to historicism, institutionalism, detached theory and subjectivistic methods of understanding. During its formative phases it tended to some extreme manifestations, resulting in trivial field studies, but most contemporary followers of the behavioral approach have overcome such weaknesses. Today, a majority of American social scientists accept the basic tenets of behavioralism. Modern critics accept behavioralism as contributing much to the social sciences, but emphasize the continuing importance of historic research, introspection, direct impression and similar ways to gain understanding and knowledge. Also, the basic philosophic assumptions of behavioralism are increasingly being undermined by modern thought on the extra-scientific commitments of science and by modern investigations showing the importance of implicit mental processes, such as tacit knowing. Such criticism does not impair the importance of behavioralism as an operational orientation of tremendous importance to contemporary social science, but limits it to being one of several useful ways of increasing knowledge and denies its validity as a basic philosophy of the scientific endeavor. Y.D.

Behaviorism.
An approach to psychology, developed by John B. Watson and put forth first in 1913. Watson rejected the introspective approaches to psychology and the use of concepts, such as "feeling," "imagining," etc., referring to internal mental processes. Instead, he demanded that psychology should deal exclusively with observable, external action ("behavior"), to be studied by scientific methods which can be objectively validated, similar to the natural sciences. His main model for psychological theory was S—R (stimulus—response), both conceived of as observable action. The main influence of classical behaviorism was between 1912 and 1930. Since then it has widened and developed into the rather different "behavioral approach" shared by psychology with most other social sciences. See Behavioralism. Y.D.

Beigin, Menachem (1913—   ).
Leader of Herut, second largest Is-

raeli political party; Hebrew publicist. Born Poland; studied Warsaw Faculty of Law. Settled in Palestine 1942. Commanded Irgun Zvai Leumi, underground movement uprising against British rule. Leads opposition to Mapai Government coalition in Knesset.

S.H.

Belgium.

Area: 11,799 square miles (30,507 square kilometers). Population: 1961, 9,158,154; Flemish region, 4,688,851 (51.09%); Walloon region, 3,064,765 (33.39%); Brussels district, 1,424,538 (15.52%). Population per square mile, 777.1, the densest in Europe. Belgium, an independent state since 1830, one of the smallest of European states yet highly industrialized, with a relatively stable economy and government, has held a prominent place in European affairs. A constitutional, hereditary monarchy, with a bicameral legislature, the country is divided into nine provinces, each highly autonomous: Antwerp, Brabant, East Flanders, West Flanders, Hainaut, Liege, Limburg, Luxembourg, and Namur. The king is head of state but functions through a ministry and since World War I leadership and coordination of the Government is exercised by the Premier. The ministry is responsible to the legislative branch. The legislature consists of a Chamber of Representatives and a Senate. Since 1949 the Chamber consists of 212 members popularly elected for four year terms by the D'Houdt system of proportional representation. Suffrage is universal and compulsory for all electors over 25 years of age. The Senate consists of 175 members, 106 elected directly by the same electorate choosing members of the Chamber; 46 (one for every 200,000 population) elected by the provincial councils by proportional representation; 23 elected by the other Senators. The minister of the Interior supervises local government though each unit has much autonomy. An appointed Governor is executive head of each province with legislative power residing in a provincial council elected for four year terms. Everyday administration is carried on by a **deputation permanente** elected from the membership of the council by the council. Each province is divided into districts (arrondissements) headed by a commissioner who supervises the smaller communes. Self-governing communes (municipalities) are uniformly organized. The burgomaster, nominated by the council and appointed by the king for six years, is chief administrator and president of the College of Aldermen. The Communal Council is elected for six years and determines budgetary policies, education, police protection, etc. The political parties are: Social Christian Party with Theodore Le Fevre as leader; Socialist Party with Paul Henri Spaak as leader, each having served as Premier. Minority parties are the Liberals, Communist and Christian Flemish Peoples Union. The legal system is similar to that of France. The country is divided into 26 judicial districts. Justices are appointed for life.

Belgium has been a leader in European unity and is a member of NATO, Benelux, the European Economic and Coal and Steel Community, Euratom, the Organization for Economic Cooperation and Development, the Western European Union, and the Council of Europe.

J.O.H.

Belice.

The name used in Guatemala for British Honduras, regarded as territory illegally held by Great Britain. Although from the 16th Century the general area was known to the Spaniards, no colonization was effected. British buccaneers in the early 17th Century and, later, settlers came to the area. Spain granted the English logging rights but reserved sovereignty at least until her defeat at St. George's Cay in 1798. By application of the principle of **uti possidetis** of 1821 (see **Swan Islands Controversy**), Guatemala claimed the region after independence. By boundary treaty in 1859 Guatemala conceded British sovereignty, but the **quid pro quo**, British financial and technical assistance in the construction of a road between Guatemala City and the port of Belize, was not received. The two countries differed on the implementation terms. After 72 years of substantial neglect Guatemala revived her case in 1939. Relations with the U.K. became strained. Although British **Honduras**

47

was moving toward independence, the matter remained sensitive in nationalistic circles in Guatemala.   R.D.H.

Belligerency.
The term "belligerency" was used in the nineteenth century to describe the status of political communities, colonies or other dependencies, in revolt against the state of which they were legally a part, when they had demonstrated their **de facto** character as independent communities but had not as yet been recognized **de jure,** as having separate international personality. The struggle of the Latin American colonies for independence raised the question whether they were to be allowed to exercise certain belligerent rights without being considered as pirates or executed as mere rebels. The United States and Great Britain, having ships engaged in traffic with the Latin American colonies, and being sympathetic with their cause were in favor of regarding their hostilities as acts of war when the parent state itself was exercising the right of visit and search of neutral vessels carrying contraband. The belligerent vessels themselves were expected to observe the customary laws of warfare. Belligerency was distinguished from the mere "status of insurgency," where the rebels were unable to control any large areas of territory, yet were sufficiently well organized to offer effective resistance to the parent country. Recognition of belligerency by a neutral state involves the right of the belligerent colony or community to exercise the rights of blockade, visitation, search and seizure of contraband articles on the high seas, and abandonment of claims by the neutral state for reparation on account of damages suffered by its citizens from the existence of the war. In the case of the American Civil War, 1861-1865, the status of belligerency of the Confederate States was recognized not only by neutral states but by the United States as well, the contest not being in fact a civil war but a war of secession of a part of the Federal Union from the whole.
C.G.F.

Ben Bella, Ahmed.
Born Dec., 1919, in Marnia, Western Algeria. Served in the French army during World War II. Since 1946 participated in nationalist activities. Commander of the Organization Secrete (O.S.) in the Oran district; stormed the Oran post office in April, 1949. March, 1950, imprisoned; March, 1952, condemned to 7 years' imprisonment but escaped. One of the 9 "Fathers of the Algerian Revolution" during the War of Independence, Nov. 1, 1954 to March 18, 1962. On Oct. 22, 1956, with 4 other Algerian leaders captured on their Moroccan plane flying to peace conference in Tunis, and forced to land in Algiers; liberated March 19, 1962 after the cease-fire. Threat of civil war prior to his designation by the National Assembly as the first Prime Minister of independent Algeria on Sept. 26, 1962. Pledged neutralism; adhered to the Casablanca group and enunciated friendship and sympathy for Castro Cuba. However, banned the Communist Party on Nov. 29, 1962.   C.K.W.

Bench.
A collective term for the regular judiciary. In Great Britain members of the bench are always chosen from experienced barristers (see Barrister), are appointed for good behavior and may be removed only for misconduct upon a joint address of Parliament. However, the head of the judiciary, the Lord Chancellor is a member of the government.   R.G.N.

Benelux (Economic Union).
The "fore-runner" of the European Common Market concept, the three countries of Belgium, The Netherlands, and Luxemburg joined together in 1944 to organize the "Benelux Customs Union" designed to facilitate trade among themselves. The system was so successful that they expanded into An Economic Union to cover the entire sphere of economic activities in 1948. Under this arrangement the member countries eliminated tariffs between each other, agreed to tackle economic problems jointly, and developed natural resources as a unit.
W.C.C.

Benes, Eduard (1887—1948).
Second president and first postwar President of Czechoslovakia. Although an advocate of Austrian fed-

eral reform in his doctoral dissertation (Dijon, 1908), Benes joined T. G. Masaryk in the struggle for Czech independence, serving as his chief collaborator in exile and as Czechoslovak delegate to the Paris Peace Conference. Served as Foreign Minister 1918-35; active in League of Nations. Elected President December 1935 on Masaryk's retirement, he resisted Sudeten German demands for autonomy; resigned after cession of Sudetenland. Formed Czechoslovak "exile government" recognized by Allies during World War II; made alliance with USSR December 1943 and returned as president in May 1945. Communists, following "united front" tactic outlined by Dimitrov at 1935 Comintern Congress, used coalition to which Benes had agreed as preliminary stage leading to complete takeover. In failing health, Benes yielded to Red threats in February 1948, confirming Communist Gottwald as head of "people's democratic" cabinet. Rather than approve new Communist constitution, resigned June 7; died Sept. 3, 1948. Praised as a dedicated liberal and denounced as an amoral Machiavellian, Benes has provoked much controversy. K.G.

Ben-Gurion, David (1886—   ).
Prime Minister and Minister of Defense of Israel; Hebrew publicist. Born Poland; studied Istanbul Faculty of Law. Settled in Palestine 1906; exiled by Turks 1915. In U.S. helped found Hechalutz Zionist pioneering movement and Jewish Legion. Fought under Gen. Allenby in Palestine. Leader of Mapai, Histadrut, Jewish Agency. Proclaimed Israeli statehood May 14, 1948; resigned from his position as Prime Minister June 16, 1963.
S.H.

Bentham, Jeremy (1748—1832).
English philosopher and founder of Utilitarianism, or Philosophical Radicalism. After receiving a legal education, he devoted his life to the subject of legal reform. Among his noteworthy achievements were his critique of Blackstone, his study of legal fictions, and his pioneering in the field of criminology. In politics also his interests were mainly in reform. In philosophy he was an empiricist; in ethics his main contribution was the principle of utility, the so-called pleasure-pain calculus. Bentham was a principal founder of the University of London. H.S.Th.

Bentley, Arthur F. (1870—1957).
An American writer of works in politics, sociology, and philosophy, one of which, THE PROCESS OF GOVERNMENT (1908), helped to further a growing interest in behavioral approaches to the study of politics in the 1930's. Bentley rejected metaphysical and juristic theories of politics and argued instead for empirical studies based upon the concept of the "group." E.L.

Ben-Zvi, Itzhak (1884—1963).
Second President of the State of Israel. Elected on December 8, 1952, by Israel's Knesset (Parliament) following the death of President Chaim Weizmann. Re-elected October 28, 1957, and again on October 30, 1962, for five-year terms. Born in the Russian Ukraine. One of the founders of Poale Zion (Labor Zionists) in Russia in 1904-05, he organized Jewish self-defense units in the Jewish ghettoes to fight the pogromists in 1905. He settled in Palestine in 1907 and helped found the Hashomer, the first Jewish self-defense organization in the Holy Land.

Always interested in education, Ben-Zvi established and taught at the first Hebrew high school in Palestine in 1909. In scholarship he is best known as an orientalist and historian, particularly with regard to the history and demography of the Jewish people.
O.K.

Beria, Lavrenti P. (1899—1953).
Head of Soviet secret police 1938 to 1953 and member of Presidium of Central Committee of the CPSU 1952 to 1953. Beria succeeded Yezhov during the great purges. After Stalin's death in March 1953 he appeared to be a contender for the leadership. He was liquidated in late 1953, charged with being in the employ of British intelligence. Six of his subordinates in the secret police were executed with him. W.D.J.

Berlin.
Conquered by the Red Army, May 1945. Located inside the Soviet Zone of Occupation (now called the [East] German Democratic Republic [q.v.]) but is not a part of it. Enjoys special status under basic Allied Agreement of September 14, 1944, and supplementary documents, providing for four-power joint occupation and administration. **De jure** all of Berlin has been under quadripartite Allied control since 1945; **de facto,** West Berlin (the American, British, and French sectors: population 2.2 million in 1960) has been on a tripartite, Western Allied basis while East Berlin (the Soviet sector: population 1.07 million in 1960) has been under Communist control since the Soviet representative in the Allied Kommandatura walked out in June, 1948. Legally, the door remains open to his return. Originally, the Kommandatura exercised total control over Berlin's German administration and legislation; since 1955 Western Allied control has been greatly limited, primarily to Berlin's relations abroad, demilitarization, security and immunity of Allied forces, and authority over Berlin police. Allied military occupation continues in Berlin; Allied rights of presence in and access to the city are closely related to its occupation status.

The Russian blockade (June 24, 1948 to May 12, 1949) attempted to force Soviet control of Berlin upon the Western Allies and the German population by stopping all imports of food and the other necessities of life. It was defeated by the massive American-British air-lift (277,728 flights; 2,343,301 tons of supplies) which enabled the Berliners to hold out. Free access was restored, subject to periodic harassment. In November 1958 Khrushchev declared all Soviet agreements with the Western Allies on Berlin null and void, demanded Western military withdrawal (11,000 men in July 1961), and proposed to make it a demilitarized "free city," with undefined status. If the Western Allies would not accede to Soviet demands in six months Moscow would sign a peace treaty with East Germany and turn over to it control of all access routes to Berlin. Khrushchev's ultimatum and subsequent threats were rejected by the Western powers; their counter-proposals were turned down by him. In August 1961 the East German Communist authorities erected a border wall, bisecting the city and cutting off all uncontrolled movements of persons, including East German (and East Berlin) refugees fleeing to West Berlin (2.6 million since 1949).
J.B.M.

Berlin Airlift.
The Soviet blockade of West Berlin in June 1948 led the Western Powers to initiate an airlift which supplied the beleaguered city with necessary food and materials. The airlift exemplified Western determination to stand firm in the face of Soviet pressure. Combined with the high morale of the civilian population, it enabled the city to endure the eleven months of blockade, thus thwarting Soviet efforts to gain control over all Berlin and prevent the establishment of the West German state.
A.Z.R.

Berlin Blockade. (1948).
On June 24, 1948, the Soviet Union imposed on the Western sectors of Berlin a blockade which closed the land access routes between Berlin and West Germany. The move was made initially to forestall the extension of the currency reform introduced into the Western zones of occupation to the city of Berlin. More basically, it sought to force Western abandonment of the city to Soviet rule. Confronted with a determined resistance and Allied airlift, and unwilling to risk war, the Soviets lifted the blockade on May 12, 1949.
A.Z.R.

Berlin Conference (1884—85).
To regulate European imperialism in Africa, 14 states met in Berlin and agreed to end slavery and its trade, protect Africans and foreigners, and further Western culture. The states affirmed free navigation on the Congo, Niger and allied rivers, fixed a free trade belt across Central Africa and recognized the Congo Free State. Often cited as a classic exploitive event, the Conference also evidenced benign paternalism and international law.
P.F.P.

Berlin Elections.

In 1945 the German capital Berlin was occupied by all four powers. Between 1945 and 1949 its citizens could move freely between the different sectors of occupation. Elections in Berlin were considered indicative of the German moods and aspirations, as no one power could control all means of communication.

The October 20, 1946 elections for City and District Councils are the most important and last election in all four sectors. In the Soviet Sector the Communist controlled Socialist Unity Party received 233,311 votes or 30% out of 781,562 while the Social Democratic Party emerged as the strongest single party receiving 340,572 votes or 43%; the Christian Democratic Union received 146,261 votes or 19%, and the Liberal Democratic Party 61,418 votes or 8%. Out of the 1,304,470 votes in the American, British and French Sectors the Social Democratic Party received 675,463 votes, or 52%, the Socialist Unity Party received 178,977 votes or 14%, the Christian Democratic Union received 316,204 votes or 24%, and the Liberal Democratic Party received 133,826 votes or 10%.

The breakdown of the four power control in Germany was followed by that in Berlin.

At later elections the Soviet Sector of Berlin followed closely the pattern in the Soviet Zone. That is the voters approved with virtual unanimity the Unity List of candidates prepared under the guidance of Communists and fellow travelers.

The Western Zones of Berlin follow the pattern of West Germany. The heavier industrial population in Berlin accounts for a stronger Social Democratic vote.

Berlin Elections, East.

In the election for the Third People's Congress of the Soviet Zone May 15, & 16, 1946, **The Soviet Sector of Berlin voted:**

For SED inspired "Unity List," 446,662, 51.6 per cent; Against Unity List, 322,322, and Invalid votes, 95,472, 48.4 per cent.

During East Berlin elections for District Councils on 23 July, 1957: Persons with franchise, 880,451. Votes cast, 851,625, 96.75 per cent; Invalid votes, 0.44 per cent; Valid votes, 99.56 per cent; For the SED inspired list of the **National Front of Democratic Germany,** 99.43 per cent; Against the list, 0.57 per cent.

On November 16, 1958, in the election for the People's Chamber of the German Democratic Republic, the Provincial Diets and the City Parliament of East Berlin 98.9% of the voters participated and 99.87% of these voted for the Communist sponsored Unity List.

Berlin Elections, West.

Date	Election to	Voters	Valid Votes	Per cent Participation
5-12-48	City Parliament	1,586,461	1,331,270	86.3
3-12-50	City Parliament	1,664,221	1,464,470	90.4
5-12-54	City Parliament	1,694,896	1,535,893	91.8

Division of valid votes for West Berlin City Parliament in percentage:

	SPD	CDU	FDP	DP	SED	Other Groups
1946	51.8	24.3	10.2	—	13.7	—
1948	64.5	19.4	16.1	—	—	—
1950	44.7	24.6	23.0	3.7	—	4.0
1954	44.6	30.4	12.8	4.9	2.7	4.6
1958	52.6	37.1	3.8	3.3	—	—

Identification of Parties:
SPD—Social Democratic Party of Germany
CDU—Christian Democratic Union
FDP—Liberal Democratic Party
DP—German Party
SED—Socialist Unity Party of Germany (Communist led)

E.K.K.

Bernadotte, Count Folke.

President of the Swedish Red Cross; served as intermediary between Nazi Germany and the Allied powers in the closing days of World War II; selected as mediator on behalf of the United Nations in the Palestine War in May 1948. Assassinated later that year by the Sternists, Jewish extremists. J.G.St.

Bernstein, Eduard.

Eduard Bernstein, a late 19th century German Socialist leader (b. 1850), was the leader of the right-wing of the German Social Democratic Party, called the revisionists. The author of the reformist theory in socialism, Bernstein saw his critique on Marxism ultimately adopted by the Social Democratic Party before his death in December 1932. C.R.F.

Bessarabia.

An area of 18,000 square miles and 2,526,671 population (by 1941 census) situated between the Prust and Dniester Rivers in southwestern U.S.S.R. An area of conflict since antiquity. Once part of a Roman province, it was ruled by the Turks in the 16th and 17th centuries and by the Russians from the 18th century on. Russian suzerainty over the area was formalized by the Treaty of Bucharest in 1812. During the Russian revolution, Rumania annexed Bessarabia. After World War II it became part of the Moldavian Republic of the U.S.S.R. G.K.

Betancourt, Romulo.

Latin American statesman. Born in Guatire, Venezuela, Feb. 22, 1908. Education: Liceo Caracas; law school of Univ. Central de Venezuela. Organized student protests against Pres. Juan Vicente Gomez and was exiled in 1930. Returned to Venezuela 1936, founded newspaper Orve. Exiled 1940 for agitating for social reforms. Founder of political party Accion Democratica 1941. Councilman fed. dist. 1945-48. Chief of Venezuelan delegation, 9th Inter-Amer. Conf., Bogotá, 1948. President of revolutionary junta of Venezuela 1945-47. Elected President 1958-63. M.A.

Bhutan.

(Area, approximately 18,000 square miles; population, estimated 700,000.)

A semi-independent Indian protectorate in the West Assam Himalayas, Bhutan is bordered on the north by Tibet, on the west by Sikkim, on the south and east by India. The inhabitants are a branch of Tibetan Mongolians, principally members of the "Red hat" sect of Lamaism.

The first hereditary maharajah was installed in 1907 after two and a half centuries of dual control by temporal and spiritual rulers. By a treaty of 1865, Britain undertook an annual subsidy to the Bhutan government. An amending treaty in 1910 increased the subsidy and gave Britain direction of Bhutan's foreign affairs while excluding her from internal interference. By a new treaty in August 1949, India succeeded to this same role of foreign affairs advisor and exclusion from interference in internal administration. It also increased substantially its annual subsidy to the Bhutan government.

On current Peking maps the entire Tashi-gang area of eastern Bhutan and part of northwest Bhutan are depicted as Chinese territory. M.T.K.

Bicameralism.

The term refers to the principle that legislatures should consist, and often do consist, of two houses, so-called lower and upper or second chambers. Most bicameral legislatures owe their existence to planning rather than historical evolution (British House of Lords).

Bicameralism has been defended on the grounds that it may serve either all or some of the following purposes: give representation to the constituent elements in a federal system, such as states, provinces, or cantons; permit rural areas to be represented rather than dominated by cities; assure participation of economic, vocational, and cultural groups or interests in the legislative process (Senates of Eire and Bavaria); protect and isolate the aristocratic element in society by allocating to it a separate chamber; constitute a bulwark of conservatism against the—at least potentially—more radical lower chamber; diffuse power within the legislature itself and thus introduce a modicum of limited government by acting as one of the major checks and balances (q.v.), especially in countries such as the United Kingdom where the restrictions of a written constitution, separation of powers, and judicial review are absent; combat "the propensity of all single and numerous assemblies to yield to the impulse of sudden and violent passions, and to be seduced by factious leaders into intemperate and pernicious resolutions" (**The Federalist,** No. 62), especially those harmful to private property and other rights of the individual; enlarge the number, excellence, and term of office of legislators; protect the executive against encroachments of an undivided legislature; improve legislation; and educate the public by calling attention to the dialogue between the two chambers.

Criticisms directed against bicameralism are largely identical with arguments offered in defense of unicameralism (q.v.).

While lower chambers are popularly elected, techniques governing the selection of members of second chambers vary widely. The British House of Lords is predominantly constituted upon the principle of heredity. Appointment by state governments has been the mode of selection of upper houses in Germany since 1871. In Canada members of the Senate are appointed for life by the governor-general. Universal suffrage elects senators in the United States and Italy. In France second chambers have been elected indirectly by electoral colleges since 1875.

Some second chambers, such as those of the United States, Italy, and the Soviet Union have legislative powers equal to those of the respective lower houses. Other second chambers have fallen victim to a reaction against bicameralism which began in the United Kingdom, the country of its origin, over the struggle concerning Lloyd George's budget (1909) and gained greater momentum after the First World War when second chambers were frequently declared to be incompatible with democracy. The movement resulted either in the abolishment of second chambers altogether (cf. "Unicameralism") or in their conversion into secondary chambers. By the Parliament Act of 1911, as amended in 1949, the House of Lords was virtually stripped of its power to veto money bills and retained only the power to delay the enactment of other public bills for one year. Similarly, as contrasted with their predecessors, powers of second chambers under the German Weimar Republic and the French Fourth Republic were considerably curtailed. However, under the German Bonn Republic and the French Fifth Republic upper houses were partially restored to the powers they enjoyed under the German Empire and the French Third Republic, respectively. Legislative deadlocks resulting from disagreements between the two houses may be resolved by a variety of devices, including simple or qualified majorities of the lower house to overcome the opposition of the second chamber; joint conference committees; referenda; dissolutions; and joint sessions of both houses.

In addition to legislative powers, second chambers often exercise powers not conferred upon lower houses. In the United States the Senate must consent to presidential appointments and ratify treaties; it has also the power to try all impeachments. The British House of Lords functions as a final court of appeal in many legal cases.

Whether bicameralism or unicameralism (q.v.) should be chosen, is in practice frequently decided on the basis of theoretical preferences rather than actual performance of either system.   W.F.

Bidault, Georges (1899—   ).

French statesman. Before World War II M. Bidault was a college professor who also wrote a column for a small newspaper, L'Aube. After the occupation of France by Germany in 1940 he was imprisoned but released soon afterwards. Later he became the leader of the "underground" resistance movement in Metropolitan France, contributing to the war efforts of the Free French. Between 1944 and 1959 M. Bidault served, at various times, as President of the Provisional Government of France, and as Premier or

minister in the Fourth Republic on several occasions. He is the founder of the Christian Democratic Party.
W.C.C.

Biddle, Francis (1886—   ).
Former Attorney General of the United States, U.S. Justice at the International Military Tribunal in Nuremberg (See Nuremberg Trials).
R.M.W.K.

Bierut, Boleslaw. (1892—1956).
Born near Lublin. Self-educated. Joined Communist Party of Poland in 1919. Prewar agent for Comintern. Paradropped from USSR into Poland (1943). Chairman of Communist underground parliament; president (1947-52); replaced Wladyslaw Gomulka as Party leader (1948-56); premier (1952-54). Symbol for "cult of the individual." Died in Moscow and succeeded briefly by Edward Ochab (1956).
R.F.S.

Bill.
The draft of proposed legislation at the time of introduction. In the United States before it becomes law a bill must go through certain stages including introduction and reference to a committee, committee consideration and report, three readings, debate, and vote. In bicameral legislatures, while there are some differences, the same basic steps are followed in the two houses, both of which must agree on a content before the bill is enacted into law.
W.V.H.

Bill of Attainder.
A law passed by a legislative body determining the guilt of a person or persons without judicial trial. This is prohibited by the United States Constitution, Art. I, 9, (3).
K.E.H.

Bill of Rights.
The first Ten Amendments to the United States Constitution. They were adopted in 1791, a little more than three years after the Constitution itself was adopted. The Amendments were added because many states would not ratify the Constitution without assurances that restrictions would be placed on the power of the Federal Government, which the Bill of Rights did.

The Articles deal with a variety of rights such as freedom to assemble, to petition, freedom of speech and press, of religion, trial by jury, the right against self-incrimination and to be free from unreasonable search and seizure. More recently enacted, the 13th, 14th, 15th and 19th Amendments are also considered to be part of the Bill of Rights.

Many of the rights specified in the Bill of Rights may be also asserted against the states and state officials.
M.J.S.

Bipolarity.
A balance of power system in which all units tend to gather around one of two poles monopolizing all effective power. Two camps face each other in a competitive spirit, each capable of resisting the challenge of any third power or combination of powers. While the two camps may not be perfectly integrated, satellite resistance can be broken if necessary. Decisions concerning war and peace are eminently the superpowers' responsibility. This is the condition that has prevailed in the world since 1945. The most clearcut historical example is the Peloponnesian War.
P.J.F.

Birchers.
See John Birch Society.

Birth control.
Either "natural" or "artificial" methods to limit the number of children born. Such efforts may be undertaken by single families or birth control may become a general program to reduce the birth rate for an entire nation. When birth control becomes a governmental policy a variety of direct or indirect incentives and controls may be used, ranging from making information available to enforced sterilization.
R.D.S.

Bismarck, Otto von.
("Iron Chancellor")—(1815-1898).
Prussian statesman and Imperial Chancellor from 1871 until 1890. His chief accomplishments were domestically the creation of the second German Empire and social legislation; in foreign affairs his success in securing, through victorious wars against Denmark 1864, Austria 1866, and France 1870/71, a leading position in Euro-

pean power politics for Prussia and later for Germany, which he tried to cement through friendship with Russia and international isolation of France.   P.J.F.

Black, Hugo L. (1886—   ).
Associate Justice of the United States, appointed by Roosevelt in 1937. Prior to serving in the Senate from 1927 to 1937, he was a police court judge (1910-11), county solicitor (1915-17), and practiced law in Birmingham, Alabama. In the Senate he was a New Deal stalwart, who, according to one observer, was "an absolute anomaly—an intellectual leftist liberal from below the Mason Dixon line." During the twenty-five years that he has served on the Court, he has demonstrated a devotion to the cause of individual liberty unsurpassed in the history of the Supreme Court. Despite what some consider as an extreme and untenable position pertaining to the First Amendment, he is highly regarded as a judge of unusual ability and force of mind. His basic philosophy is simply that the First Amendment means what it says: that government can pass no law abridging freedom of speech, which he believes includes all speech, even speech which is obscene or subversive. In holding this view, he rejects the position pressed by Mr. Justice Frankfurter that the right of free speech must be balanced against other legitimate public claims, such as national security.   P.B.

Black Muslims.
A cult of Negro racists in the U.S. which advocates the moral superiority of blacks over whites and complete racial separatism. The group has adopted some principal elements of the Moslem religion but rejects the brotherhood of man, polygamy, and any identity with white values and the racial integration movement.

Founded by Elijah Mohammed (the "prophet") and Malcolm X, the cult has temples in major U.S. cities and recruits largely among the lower classes and prison inmates. Vaguely resembling the Garvey Movement (1920's), it is an extremist product of racial segregation and discrimination in the U.S.   N.P.T.

Blackstone, Sir William. (1723—1780).
English jurist and author of **Commentaries on the Laws of England** (1765—1769). Blackstone received his general education at the Charterhouse and at Pembroke College, Oxford, and his legal training in the narrowly professional atmosphere of the Middle Temple. Nowhere was he offered any understanding of the relation of English law to history and philosophy. Blackstone, however, became more interested in this relation than in professional practice and abandoned the law courts in order to lecture on law at Oxford, where he became in 1758 the first Vinerian professor of English law. From the Oxford lectures evolved the **Commentaries** — the most influential legal handbook ever published. It explained English law to educated laymen in non-technical language, intelligible order and graceful style, and it also described and eulogized the constitution of England. The work became immensely popular, especially among the pre-Revolutionary civic leaders in the American colonies. The author was not, however, an analytical jurist, and his **Commentaries** suffered devastating criticism from Bentham and Austin. In the last years of his life Blackstone served as a judge of the court of common pleas.   M.Sp.

Blanket Primary.
A type of primary election, like the open primary in that the voter does not declare his party affiliation to the election official, but different in that a voter may cast votes for candidates of any party. The voter may cast but one vote for the nomination to any one office. (The blanket primary is used only in the State of Washington, which adopted it in 1935.)   T.S.

Bloc actor.
Composed of national actors. Has ultimate or effective power of decision with respect to a vital functional activity or several very important functional activities. Membership tends to remain constant, and is based on long-term interest, even at the cost of some short-term interests.   M.A.K.

Blockade.
A device of warfare whereby one state proclaims and enforces upon all

states including neutrals a restriction on trade and contact with a particular port or coast of an enemy state. A blockade must be declared and made known individually to neutral states; moreover it must be effectively maintained by a force commensurate with realistic enforcement. Ships of neutral registry caught in the act of running the blockade are subject to confiscation. H.B.J.

Bloc Voting.

By bloc voting is meant the tendency of an unusually large majority of the voters of a single class or ethnic or interest group to vote the same way. It is probably never true that **all** members of such groups react the same way to issues and candidates. But it is certainly true that being a member of such a group can influence one's political behavior, including voting. In this sense there is a farmer's vote, businessman's vote, etc., there is a Jewish vote and also an Irish, Negro, Polish, Armenian, and even a Baptist and Episcopalian vote.

Bloc voting does not mean that all Jewish voters vote for a Jew or all Catholic voters vote for a Catholic. That never happens in a national or state election. But almost any group may show a high degree of political unity in one place at a certain time, such as the Episcopalians in Connecticut in 1811, when they voted as a bloc to protest against the distribution of funds between their Bishop's fund and Yale College. If all other things are equal, a labor union member may be expected to vote for a labor union leader, an Irishman for an Irishman; but all other things are rarely equal. In local elections, ignorance or indifference to issues may promote bloc voting since party affiliation is not likely to mean as much to most voters as the group affiliations of candidates.
L.H.F.

Blucher (Bliukher), Vasily K.
(1889—1938).

Soviet Marshal. Under the alias of "Galen" Blucher served as Soviet advisor to Chiang Kai-shek from 1924 to 1927. He later commanded Red forces in the Far East and operated against the Chinese. Blucher led Soviet troops in 1938 actions against the Japanese. He was purged under conditions never made public. He was posthumously rehabilitated by Khrushchev in 1956. W.O.J.

Blue-Ribbon Jury.

A trial jury drawn from a panel of specially qualified individuals. Such juries have been criticized as not being genuinely representative but the Supreme Court of the United States, in two close decisions in 1947 and 1948, ruled that the selection of specially qualified persons to hear difficult cases was not a violation on constitutional standards of fairness unless discrimination against a class or race or creed could in fact be shown. F.H.H.

Blue-sky Laws.

A popular name given to statutes passed for the protection of the public against fraudulent sale of securities. Originating with laws passed by Rhode Island and Kansas in 1910-11, nearly all of the states in the U.S.A. now have such statutes. G.B.T.

Blum, Leon (1872—1950).

French statesman and writer. Leon Blum was a lawyer, a writer on many subjects, and a political leader of the Socialist persuasion. He was elected to the Chamber of Deputies for the first time in 1919, was the founder of the concept of "Popular Front," and was the first Socialist to serve as Premier of France. In 1936-37, in 1938, and again in 1946 he organized the French Government. During the period of the Second World War, M. Blum was imprisoned by the Vichy Regime.
W.C.C.

Board of Education.

In the United States, the educational policies on the primary and secondary level is usually the responsibility of locally selected boards of education. The members of such boards are usually elected by the voters in a school district. However, other methods of selection are also used, such as appointment by the mayor or city governing boards. G.B.T.

Board of Health.

A board invested with the function of the preservation and improvement of the public health. Nearly every state in the U.S.A. has a state board of health which has been created by state statute. Local boards are also often established by cities and counties. G.B.T.

Board of Pardon.
A board created by law in many states of the U.S.A. whose function it is to investigate all claims for clemency of persons convicted of crime. As a result of such investigations, reports and recommendations are made to the chief executive of the state. G.B.T.

Board of Review.
A quasi-judicial **ex officio** or elective body constituted to review the work of the assessor, including correction of clerical errors, addition of omitted property, and deciding whether the assessor's valuation of property is correct. P.J.C.

Boards of correctional institutions.
In the U.S.A. the function of a board of correctional institutions is to assume the responsibility for the operation of the penal institutions of the state. Various names, such as board of control or board of prisons are given to such agencies. Control of state institutions other than penal are sometimes added to their function. G.B.T.

Bolivar, Simon.
South American Liberator. Born Caracas, Venezuela, July 24, 1783. Died near Santa Marta, Colombia, December 17, 1830. Inspired by the French and American Revolutions, he swore to free Venezuela from Spain. Under the influence of Francisco de Miranda, he embarked upon the struggle. From 1812 to 1830 he endured defeat, exile at times, and hardships, but also achieved distinction in many famous battles at Boyaca, Carabobo, and Junin. After the defeat of the Spaniards, Bolivar organized Gran Colombia (Venezuela, Ecuador, New Granada) and governments for Bolivia and Peru. But as a constitution-giver and statesman he was unable to keep his confederation together, and died on his way into bitter exile in 1830. R.B.G.

Bolivia.
Capital: Sucre (legal); La Paz (seat of government). Area: 416,000 **square** miles. Population (1960): 3,462,000. The republic achieved its independence from Spain in 1825, and **was** named after Liberator Simon Bolivar. Antonio de Sucre became its first President. Political instability characterized the nation in the 19th century. In 1879 war broke out between Bolivia, allied with Peru, and Chile, over nitrate deposits. When it ended in 1883 Bolivia lost its entire seacoast to Chile. Economic domination by tin mine owners and wealthy landlords was largely unrelieved until formation of two major parties, the Revolutionary Party of the Left (PIR), **and the** Nationalist Revolutionary Movement (MNR). Violence ensued. In 1952 the MNR, under Victor Paz Estenssoro, took over, and has been in power ever since. Nationalization of tin mines resulted. See Chaco War. R.B.G.

Bolshevism.
The beliefs and methods of **radical** Russian Marxists, led to power by Lenin, and now officially identified by the Soviet government with Communism. The word itself is derived from **bolsheviki,** meaning "members of the majority faction," and also bearing the connotation of "maximalism," or carrying out measures with extreme thoroughness.

These terms were first employed in 1903, at meetings of Russian **Marxists** in Brussels and London, where the advocates of terrorist action and blindly obedient discipline happened to gain a temporary majority over the more moderate Marxists, whose leader was Plekhanov. The triumphant "all-out" faction of Bolsheviki dubbed the Plekhanovites the Mensheviki, or minority faction—though in reality the Mensheviki were the more numerous in Russia.

In the Soviet states today, **in** addition to serving as a synonym for Communist "bolshevik" implies heartiness, energy, and the like. Most of the Old Bolsheviki, however, perished **or were** sent to prison-camps during **the su**premacy of Stalin. See Communism.
R.K.

57

Bonapartism.
The system of government practiced by Napoleon I and Napoleon III, including the emergence of the "man on horseback," who holds the reins of a centralized government while receiving popular approval for his policies by frequent plebiscites. Bonapartism also refers to attachment to the fortunes of the Bonaparte dynasty.
K.B.

Bonding.
Bonding is a means for both public and private institutions to undertake indebtedness. A bond is a certificate of indebtedness indicating the principal and interest rate on the loan. A bond suggests the inability or unwillingness to finance programs out of current revenues. Several kinds of bonds are used by governments to finance "long-term" and "short-term" obligations for public improvements: (1) term or sinking-fund bonds, where a fund is established whereby both the principal and interest may be amortized at the end of the debt period; (2) serial bonds, where staggered maturity dates make it possible to pay the interest and retire a portion of the debt annually out of current revenues; (3) general obligation bonds, where the full taxing capacity of the governmental unit guarantees payment of the debt; (4) partial or limited obligation bonds, where debt amortization is guaranteed by income from specific taxes or assessments; (5) revenue bonds, where bonds are issued to finance some revenue-producing enterprise and debt payment is guaranteed only from such income. State and local governments are ordinarily limited in the amount of debt which may be incurred—usually expressed in terms of a percentage of assessed property valuation.
W.D.S.

Bonn Constitution.
Constitution ("Basic Law") of Federal Republic of Germany (q.v.). Drafted by Parliamentary Council (drawn from state diets of three Western occupation zones). In force May 23, 1949. Federal structure, with ten member-states (Laender). Lawmaking by Bundestag (q.v.) and Bundesrat (q.v.) jointly. Bundestag elects chief executive (Chancellor) upon nomination by Federal President, who in turn elected by a parliamentary body for five years; President primarily ceremonial functions. Chancellor strong position: selects and dismisses ministers; himself dismissed by parliament only upon simultaneous election of successor. Constitutional amendments by two-thirds vote of both chambers. Basic rights and liberties, protected by Constitutional Court which also possesses powers of judicial review and of outlawing antidemocratic parties.
J.H.H.

Bormann, Martin Ludwig (1900-45).
Member of Hitler's personal staff after 1938; one of his most radical and influential advisers. As chief of the Nazi party secretariat and Secretary to the Fuehrer, he handled all party and state affairs submitted to Hitler for decisions. Stressed Nazi regime's anti-Church attitude and actions. Allegedly died while trying to escape during Russian siege of Berlin.
J.B.M.

Borodin, Michael.
The Sun-Joffe declaration of January 26, 1923, opened a period of collaboration between China under Dr. Sun Yat-sen and the Soviet Union. Soviet advisers who were actually Comintern agents went to China to help the Kuomintang. Borodin was perhaps the most important among them. He became a political adviser to Dr. Sun Yat-sen and revitalized the Kuomintang party apparatus along Bolshevik lines.

At Comintern insistence, the Chinese Communists joined the Kuomintang as "individuals" and pledged to subordinate the communist objectives to those of the Kuomintang to achieve national unification and independence. Thus began an uneasy collaboration between the Kuomintang and the Chinese Communist Party. During the period of ostensible Kuomintang-Communist collaboration, the Chinese Communists infiltrated the Kuomintang apparatus and gained a considerable following among discontented industrial workers. In all probability, the Kremlin under Stalin hoped that the Chinese Communists, under Borodin's secret direction, would be able to take over the Kuomintang and use it as the spearhead

for the communist conquest of China.
In 1927, two years after the death of Sun Yat-sen, Chiang Kai-shek, who had been successful in the Northern Expedition of 1926, forced a showdown with the Chinese Communists, expelled them from the Kuomintang, killed many hundreds, broke the back of the Communist organization among the industrial workers, and ousted Russian advisers. Borodin left China in 1927, and the Soviet Government severed diplomatic relations with Chiang's government in December 1927.   R.St-H.

Borough.
A city operating under a charter granted by a state in the United States or by royal authority in the United Kingdom. The borough (or city) is authorized to have a corporate existence, to sue and be sued, to conduct elections, to make and enforce municipal ordinances, to tax and spend for local purposes, and to serve as the arm of the state for numerous functions. In Britain a city is thought of as a borough and some highly urbanized counties are designated as County Boroughs.   Sp.D.A.

Bose, Subhas Chandra (1897—1945).
Remembered in India as Netaji (Venerable Leader), Bose was born at Cuttack, son of a Bengali lawyer. After graduating from the Calcutta University in 1919, he studied at Cambridge. He passed the Indian Civil Service examination, but resigned from the service to join the **satyagraha** (q.v.) struggle. A disciple of C. R. Das, he was Gandhi's challenger and Nehru's rival. He spent seven years in prison and eight in exile or on medical treatment abroad. He resigned his second term as Congress (q.v.) President in 1939 over differences with Gandhi and founded the Forward Bloc. To seek the Axis support for Indian freedom he escaped from India in 1941. He organized the Indian National Army which briefly fought at the Burma front. In August, 1945, he died in a plane crash in Formosa. Bose believed in a strong dictatorial government, representing a synthesis of the common traits of Communism and Fascism.   C.S.S.

Boss.
A certain type of party chieftain in U.S. politics, sometimes a corrupt spoilsman. For Theodore Roosevelt the boss was "a man who does not gain his power by open means, but by secret means, and usually by corrupt means. Some of the worst and most powerful bosses in our history either held no public office or else some unimportant public office. They made no appeal either to intellect or conscience. Their work was done chiefly behind closed doors, and consisted chiefly in the use of that greed which gives in order that it may get." Bosses were described as possessing "machines." The locale of their operations was usually a city or an urban county although state bosses were not unknown. There has never been a national boss in the United States. Boss has been prefixed to the names of such men as Hague (Jersey City), Crump (Memphis), Tweed, Flynn, Platt (New York), Kelly, Nash, Cermak, Arvey (Chicago), and Long (Louisiana).
     A.G.

Bossuet, Bishop Jacques Benigne (1627—1704).
French theologian, ecclesiastic, pulpit orator, and political theorist; noted for championing the doctrine of the divine right of kings, for advocating the separation of the temporal and spiritual powers, and for his theory of the unity and continuity of history.
     Ch.C.M.

Boston Tea Party.
A group of citizens in Boston, Massachusetts, who disguised themselves as Mohawk Indians and boarded ships belonging to the British East India Company on the evening of December 16, 1773, dumping 342 cases of tea into the harbor. Action of the British Parliament (1773) giving the British East India Company a virtual monopoly of the tea trade in America aroused widespread opposition, resentment running particularly high since the duty on tea was the only remaining tax after the repeal of the hated Stamp and Townshend Acts. The raid was conducted in such an orderly manner that it was obviously a carefully premeditated act and could have been overlooked by the British government only if it was willing to waive all but

ostensible sovereignty. Reaction came in the form of the Boston Port Act which closed the port and moved the customs house to Salem, providing the colonists with even greater reason for bitterness and resistance to British rule. D.C.

Boundaries.
Boundaries are the real or imaginary lines on the Earth's surface which delimit state territory. Modern boundary lines on land are established on the basis of geographic reference points, maps, colonial and other old boundary lines, mountains, rivers, and by other natural or arbitrary means. Often these are spelled out in treaties. At the sea or ocean the boundary is at the outer edge of the state's territorial waters, a distance which is not of uniform width and about which there is considerable controversy, but which can be described loosely as varying from three to twelve miles. Special types of boundary situations exist at such places as straits, bridges, lakes, bays and gulfs. Usually treaties or prescriptive usages delimit such borders. In rivers and straits the center of the main channel, the **thalweg**, is the usual line and in mountain borders, it is the water divide, but treaties may specify otherwise.

Other very highly specialized territorial extensions which are probably outside the scope of boundaries **per se.**, include the continental shelf, polar extensions, airspace, and space. H.B.J.

Bourgeois.
Person (or person's attitude) of society's middle class, concentrating on material things and gaining or maintenance of vested interests. Often conservative, also (according to Marx) another term for capitalist. M.C.V.

Bourgeoisie.
Mostly descriptive of European middle class between nobility and working class. Has primarily functioned as group of entrepreneurs in modern capitalistic system but also as social and human institution. Spread indicated by "upper" and "lower" ("petty") bourgeoisie. M.C.V.

Bourguibah, Habib (1904—).
Studied at the University of Paris, and returned to Tunisia and to active political life. He joined the Destour Party and in 1933 broke with it and founded the Neo-Destour. During the war he refused to collaborate with the Nazis. He felt France and the Allies would give Tunisia her rights. After the war he resided in Cairo to solicit Arab League support and to publicize Tunisia's case. In 1956 his goal—Tunisian independence—was realized. With independence he set upon a course of modernization of Tunisia's institutions. The monarchy was abolished and he was elected president of the republic. His social and economic reforms are far-reaching. He follows a policy of moderation and of gradualism. E.A.S.

Boxer Rebellion.
In China, during the nineteenth Century the impact of the West and the inability of the Government to resist effectively the predatory pressures thereof gave rise ultimately to a nation-wide feeling of resentment and unrest. In the northern provinces and Manchuria, this feeling was given, in 1900, violent expression in terms especially of attacks at many places upon the persons and properties of "foreigners." Outstanding among the perpetrators were several high officials; but most conspicuous initially and in the over-all were the overt activities of a "secret society" nicknamed the "Boxers." Because of the early, picturesque, vociferous and wide-ranging part played by that society in the convulsion which eventuated in the imposition upon China of the prescriptions set forth in the Protocol of 1901, it was logical and it has been convenient to speak of that convulsion and its concomitants in terms of "Boxer": hence, variously, the "Boxer Rebellion," the "Boxer Movement," the "Boxer Year," the "Boxer Protocol," etc. St.K.H.

Brahmin.
The priestly class, the highest of four castes of the Hindu social order. The other three castes are: **kshatriyas** (rulers and fighters); **vaishyas** (artisans, merchants, agriculturists); and

shudras (manual laborers). The term also refers to a member of the Brahmin caste. **C.S.S.**

Brainwashing.

A term popularly used to describe the technique used by the Communists to extract confessions and convert enemies. It involves a combination of physical hardship and psychological pressure to attack the individual personality. Described by one authority as "The calculated destruction of men's minds," brainwashing is an essential part of the psychological mass coercion by which the Chinese Communist Party enforced their rule of mainland China. It was also used as a technique for controlling United Nations soldiers taken prisoners in the Korean War (1950-1953) and making them confess to such crimes as germ warfare. **R.L.W.**

Brandeis, Louis Dembitz (1856—1941).

Known widely as "the people's attorney," Brandeis, prior to his nomination to the Supreme Court by President Wilson in 1916, had been a successful corporate lawyer and a professor of business law at Harvard and M.I.T., as well as one of the nation's foremost defenders of civil and social rights. Often serving without fee, he was a brilliant advocate before the Supreme Court. There he successfully introduced the "Brandeis Brief" in the 1908 Oregon Wage and Hour Law for Women Case (**Muller v. Oregon,** 208 U.S. 412). It consisted of two pages of legal arguments followed by 100 pages of skillfully presented economic and social statistics. His appointment to the Court was one of the most bitterly fought in its history, all Republican Senators voting against and all but one Democrat for confirmation. Along with Justice Holmes, he became known as one of the two "great dissenters" (although he and his elder associate differed in many aspects of personal and governmental philosophy), and with Holmes, by emphasizing judicial self-restraint, was instrumental in combatting the Court's long-time adherence to "substantive due process" in economic and social laissez faire policy matters. **H.J.A.**

Brandt, Willy (1913—).

Willy Brandt has been Lord Mayor of Berlin since 1957. He was the candidate of the German Socialist Party (SPD) for the chancellorship at the federal elections in 1961 and is generally considered as the most promising leader of his party. As a very young man he joined the Social Democratic Party. Threatened with arrest after Hitler came to power, he fled to Norway, where he studied history and worked as a journalist. Throughout his emigration he kept in close contact with the German anti-Nazi resistance movement. After having been deprived of his German citizenship, he was granted the citizenship of his host country, the Norwegian government. After the fall of Norway he spent the rest of the years of his emigration in Sweden.

Following the end of hostilities he worked as a press correspondent in Berlin and Germany. In 1946 he was selected as press attache to the Norwegian Ministry of Foreign Affairs and in this capacity represented Norway on the Allied Control Council in Berlin.

In 1947 he resumed his political work in Germany after having his German citizenship restored. From 1948 to 1949 he was the representative of the Social Democratic Party's executive committee in Berlin; since 1950, member of the SPD executive committee of Berlin; 1954, deputy chairman of the Socialist Party in Berlin and since 1958 its chairman. Since 1958 Willy Brandt is also a member of the executive committee of his party on the national level. From 1949 until his election as Lord Mayor of Berlin, he also was a member of the **Bundestag.** From 1950 until 1951 he was the editor-in-chief of the **Berliner Stadtblatt.**

Both in his capacity as Lord Mayor of Berlin and as one of the leading officials of the German socialists, Willy Brandt has established and maintains important contacts with the political leaders of the West. **E.W.**

Brazil.

A Latin American state; area, 3,287,204 sq. mi.; population (1960), 65,743,000. Under the Constitution of

1946 Brazil is a federal state, but the preponderance of power resides at the national level. There is a popularly-elected Congress, composed of a Senate and a Chamber of Deputies. The President of the Republic is elected to a five-year term. Leading political parties are the Social Democratic Party, Brazilian Labor Party, National Democratic Union, and Progressive Social Party. The military services are a dominant force in politics. The President, following the resignation of Janio Quadros from the office in August 1961, was the former Vice President Joao Goulart. On April 2, 1964, in an effort to rid Brazil of Communists in governmental office, the armed services, with support of the majority of Congress, deposed Goulart prior to the expiration of his term. He was replaced by Castelo Branco. F.M.L.

Brazil. Central-West.

Largely unexplored area covering the states of Mato Grosso and Goias with 725,470 square miles or 22% of Brazil's territory and 4% of the country's population. On April 21, 1960, President Juscelino Kubitschek transferred the nation's capital to Brasilia (1960 population: 141,742), creating the new Federal District within the state of Goias, 726 miles by paved highway from the former capital of Rio de Janeiro and the coast.

East.

Composed of six states (Bahia, Sergipe, Minas Gerais, Espirito Santo, Rio de Janeiro and Guanabara), the Brazilian East covers 486,382 square miles or 15% of the national territory. In 1960 the area's population was 24.8 million, of which 3.3 million lived in Rio de Janeiro, the former capital of Brazil. The area holds two other political and economic centers: Belo Horizonte (1960 population: 693,328) and Salvador (655,735 inhabitants), respectively state capitals of Minas Gerais and Bahia.

North.

Dominated by the Amazon river system which has a 7.5 million HP hydroelectrical potential. The northern region covers 1,382,335 square miles or 42% of Brazil's total area and 3.7% of its population. Two states (Amazonas and Para) and four territories (Acre, Amapa, Rio Branco and Rondonia) make up the largely unexplored area.

Northeast.

With 15.7 million inhabitants the Northeast's seven states cover 372,742 square miles of Brazil. Economic and administrative activities are concentrated in the state capitals of Pernambuco (Recife with 797,234 inhabitants in 1960) and of Ceara (Fortaleza with 514,818 inhabitants). Over half of the Northeast lies within a drought area. The building of power plants, dams, irrigation canals and tubular wells provided initial steps toward development of a potentially wealthy area. Since 1959, industrialization has been promoted through federal and state loans, tax exemption programs and, since 1962, through U.S. Alliance for Progress funds. An official planning agency called SUDENE supervises regional development programs.

South.

Composed of the four states of Sao Paulo, Santa Catarina, Parana and Rio Grande do Sul. It covers 318,690 square miles or 9.7% of Brazil's total area and had 24.7 million inhabitants, or 35% of the country's population, and earned 51% of Brazil's national income in 1960. Most major Brazilian industrial and commercial activities are concentrated in this area, mainly in the region surrounding the rapidly growing state capital of Sao Paulo (1960 population: 3,825,351). R.R.

Brazil—Constitution.

The fifth constitution of Sept. 18, 1946, ruled that the president of the Brazilian Federal Republic exercises executive powers during his five year direct popular election term. He and the vice-president cannot be reelected consecutively. An amendment to the Constitution of Sept. 2, 1961 (see Janio Quadros), introduced the parliamentary system with prime-minister and Council of Ministers to share executive powers with the president. The Congress, holding legislative powers, is composed of the Senate (78 senators elected for eight years), the Chamber of Deputies (one deputy per

150,000 inhabitants elected for four years) and the Court of Accounts, responsible for financial control. Judicial powers are held by the Supreme Federal Court (11 nominated life-time members), the Federal Court of Appeals (9 nominated life-time magistrates), the judges, the electoral, labor and military courts. Each of the 21 states, 5 territories, the Federal District (Brasilia) and the 2,767 counties hold their own clearly defined powers.

R.R.

Brazzaville Bloc (The Union of African States and Madagascar).

A group of twelve former French colonies of Africa and Madagascar which are attempting to achieve unity mainly by cooperating in a number of specific economic, technical, and cultural projects.

The Brazzaville states consist of Gabon, Chad, the Congo (Brazzaville), the Central African Republic, Ivory Coast, Niger, Upper Volta, Dahomey, Senegal, Mauritania, the Cameroons, and the Malagasy Republic. At the urging of President Felix Houphouet-Boigny of the Ivory Coast, these states met at Abidjan (the Malagasy Republic did not attend this meeting) and Brazzaville in late 1960 and again in Yaounde in March 1961, where they established a charter which respects the sovereignty of its members, but which seeks to promote unity among them through economic and technical cooperation. The participating states, which are also members of the European Common Market, often manifest pro-Western and anti-communist sentiments and generally represent what in the African context is moderate to progressive politics.

The Brazzaville powers have often found it difficult to cooperate with the Casablanca Bloc. While preserving their own organization, however, they have become members of the Monrovian Bloc.

F.H.G.

Brazzaville Conference of 1944.

Held January 30 to February 2, 1944 in Brazzaville, French Congo. Marks major shift in the evolution of French colonial policy. Participants included Charles de Gaulle, as head of the Free French Forces and Felix Eboue, first non-European governor-general in the French Empire who, in 1940, broke with the Vichy Government and threw support behind de Gaulle. The conference was convened to gain support for the Free French cause in the African dependencies. Resolutions calling for reforms in French colonial policy included three major political recommendations. These called for an increase in the number and effectiveness of overseas representation in the French Parliament; the creation of regional and territorial assemblies in the dependencies; and stepped-up Africanization of colonial administration, to be made possible by an expanded training and educational program.

The conference recommendations were subsequently incorporated in the Constitution of the Fourth Republic (Section VIII), which reorganized relations between France and the dependencies in the new French Union.

R.L.K.

Brest-Litovsk, Treaty of.

Anxious to terminate the war with Imperial Germany, Lenin and Trotsky, in March 1918, agreed in this treaty to the independence of the Ukraine, the Baltic states, Finland, and Poland. Lenin called Brest-Litovsk a "breathing spell" which he needed to win the Civil War against the anti-Communist forces within Russia. After the defeat of Germany in World War I, the Western Allies, upon Woodrow Wilson's insistence, declared the Brest-Litovsk Treaty null and void.

J.D.

Bretton Woods Conference.

At the suggestion of President F. D. Roosevelt, representatives of forty-four nations convened at Bretton Woods, N. H., July 1-22, 1944 for the United Nations Monetary and Financial Conference. To promote post-war reconstruction and resource development and international trade and avert monetary chaos, the Conference drafted the Articles of Agreement of the International Bank and Fund to assist international capital investment and monetary stability.

F.B.G.

Briand, Aristide (Pierre Henri)
(1862—1932).

French statesman. Became a member of the Chamber of Deputies by

1902, and served as Premier, Minister of Education, Minister of Justice, and as Minister of Foreign Affairs on several occasions. His name is attached to the Briand-Kellogg Pact of 1928. W.C.C.

Bricker Amendment.
An Amendment presented to the U.S. Congress following World War II by a group under the leadership of Senator John W. Bricker, Republican, of Ohio, which would limit the powers of the Federal Government, and more specifically of the President of the United States, in the making of treaties. The Amendment would have curtailed the powers of the Federal Government as determined by the Supreme Court of the United States in the case of **Missouri v. Holland** in 1920. Under the proposal Congress could pass no law to carry a treaty into effect that it could not have passed without the treaty, and no international agreement could become effective as internal law except by an Act of Congress. The proposed Amendment failed by one vote to get the required two-thirds vote of the United States Senate in 1954. R.G.S.

Bridges v. California, and Times-Mirror Co. v. Superior Court, 314 U.S. 252 (1941).
The California courts had fined the appellants for criminal contempt for publishing comments pertaining to pending litigation. Rejecting the contention of the four dissenting justices that "Our whole history repels the view that it is an exercise of one of the civil liberties secured by the Bill of Rights for a leader of a large following or for a powerful metropolitan newspaper to attempt to overawe a judge in a matter immediately pending before him," the majority reversed the convictions as unconstitutional infringements of freedom of expression, even though Bridges' statement constituted a threat to tie up the port of Los Angeles if a new trial was not granted in an interunion suit. The sentences for contempt had not been imposed pursuant to any statute, but under a theory of inherent judicial power. The Supreme Court's assertion that due process limits all branches of government was, of course not **new;** but the only specific guarantee of "freedom of speech, or of the press," in the First Amendment, speaks only of legislative invasions of this right, and Mr. Justice Black, who wrote the majority opinion, has frequently contended that the Fourteenth Amendment makes only the **specific** guarantees of the Bill of Rights applicable to the states. In his dissent in Connecticut General Life Ins. Co. v. Johnson, 303 U.S. 77, 85 (1938) he had called upon the Court to "overrule previous decisions which interpreted the Fourteenth Amendment to include corporations." In view of the degree of corporate control over the mass media, it is not surprising that he did not vote this conviction here. J.A.C.G.

Brinkmanship.
The "art" of going up to—but not beyond—the "brink of war" in a foreign policy crisis. The object is to avoid embroilment in war, and yet to prevent an adversary from gaining his ends by "bluff" or "war of nerves." The term has sometimes been used scornfully in referring to policies thought to involve unnecessary or uncontrollable risks of war.
Origin: A 1956 **Life** magazine interview with U.S. Secretary of State (1953-1959) John Foster Dulles citing him as calling brinkmanship "the necessary art" in contemporary diplomacy, and claiming that its practice had averted war for the United States more than once in the years immediately preceding. S.L.A.

British.
Commonly used to describe anything pertaining to or derived from the United Kingdom of Great Britain and Northern Ireland. In describing people the term can be applied narrowly to those living in Great Britain, although it is often applied to those in the rapidly diminishing British Empire or in "British" Commonwealth countries. A major feature of the term is its broadness and elasticity. R.H.B.

British Assize Courts.
Most significant criminal court of original jurisdiction. Its jurisdiction extends to all major indictable crimes

such as murder, arson, and armed robbery. All indictable offenses are always heard before a jury. Britain, for the purpose of the Assize jurisdiction, is divided into circuits to which the judges are assigned from the Queen's Bench Division of the High Court of Justice. C.A.McC.

British Central Criminal Court.
The Assize Court for London, commonly known as "Old Bailey."
C.A.McC.

British Conservative Party.
The British Conservative Party, a continuation of the Tory Party that originated during the reign of Charles I, owes its aims and philosophical basis to Edmund Burke and Benjamin Disraeli. According to Disraeli, the aims of the Conservative Party, a name that was adopted in 1842, were "the maintenance of our empire, and the amelioration of the condition of the people." It is a strong supporter of traditional institutions. The leader of the Conservative Party, "the main fountain and interpreter of policy," is usually the head of its Parliamentary group. The leader is kept in touch with all sections of the party by means of an executive committee and a central council of the party which is responsible to the party's annual conference in which constituency associations are represented. The party leader makes all appointments to the central office, whose full-time workers coordinate, guide and inspire the party's work throughout the country.

Besides Disraeli, prominent leaders of the Conservative Party have been Lord Salisbury (1895), Bonar Law (1914), Stanley Baldwin (1923), Neville Chamberlain (1937), Winston Churchill (1946), Anthony Eden (1954), and Harold Macmillan (1956).
C.R.F.

British Crown Colonies.
Dependent territories of the United Kingdom scattered in different parts of the world. They vary greatly in territorial size, racial composition, religion, language, industrial growth and degree of advancement of their inhabitants. Yet for all of them the central purpose of the British colonial policy is the same, that is, to help them to attain self-government within the Commonwealth. The Colonial Office normally deals with the affairs of these territories and decides fundamental policies of their major issues. The actual administration is carried out by the colonial governments under the authority of their respective governors. S.S.H.

British High Court of Justice
(Queen's Bench Division, Chancery Division, Probate, Divorce and Admiralty Division).

The lower branch of the Supreme Court of Judicature is known as the High Court of Justice, the upper branch being the Court of Appeal. The High Court of Justice is divided into three Divisions. These are the Queen's Bench Division which is headed by Lord Chief Justice and has twenty other judges; the Chancery Division, nominally presided over by the Lord High Chancellor and there are five other judges, and the Probate, Divorce, and Admiralty Division, the head of which is the President and he is aided by seven other judges. The Judiciary Act of 1873 which established the Supreme Court of Judicature provided that any High Court judge is eligible to sit in any division and that any division may hear cases of law or equity, but in practice the various divisions deal almost exclusively with their own specialties, i.e., Queen's Bench Division in common law, the Chancery Division in equity, and the Probate, Divorce and Admiralty in the areas indicated by its title.
C.A.McC.

British Honduras. See Belice.

British Labour Party.
The Labour Party owes its origin to the spread of Socialist ideas in Great Britain, and to the rising political consciousness of the British worker.

The Independent Labour Party was founded by Keir Hardie together with Philip Snowden and Ramsay MacDonald in 1893. Ten years earlier, the Fabian Society, led by the Webbs, H. G. Wells, and Bernard Shaw, and also the Social Democratic Federation, led by H. M. Hyndman and William Morris, had begun to spread Socialist ideas. Out of these groups, in 1906, was formed the Labour Party, for the purpose of "unifying the worker's political power," under the leadership of

Ramsay MacDonald. Today the Labour Party consists of local party organizations, trade unions, and certain co-operative groups. It formed its first government in 1924. Its second government was formed in 1929, when it was the largest party in the House of Commons, and was headed by Ramsay MacDonald. Both of these governments were short-lived, and depended on the support of the Liberal Party. Despite a minor split in 1931, the Labour Party continued as a major force in British politics. In 1935 Clement Attlee became its leader, and he became Deputy Prime Minister in the coalition government of Winston Churchill during the Second World War.

In 1945 the Labour Party won its greatest triumph, and governed Great Britain for five years. Led by Morrison, Bevin, Dalton, and Cripps, the labour government carried out extensive nationalization programs. The party was re-elected in 1950, but a year later, differences caused several resignations from the Labour Government, and the party lost the election of 1951. It has since remained in opposition. The party is led by an executive committee which is elected by the Annual Conference. Major policies are also adopted by the National Council of Labour, which consists of representatives of the National Executive, the Parliamentary Party, trade unions, and the co-operatives. C.R.F.

British Liberal Party.

The British Liberal Party, which dominated English politics during the greater part of the nineteenth century, evolved out of the Whig Party. From the Whig Party it derived the principles of toleration, emancipation, free trade, and resistance to arbitrary power of the government.

The Liberal Party became one of the principal parties in Great Britain after the general election of 1865 under the leadership of William Gladstone. Aside from Gladstone and their chief thinker, John Stuart Mill, other Liberal leaders have included Herbert Asquith, Lord Palmerston, Lloyd George, Lord Beveridge and Clement Davies.

After 1915 the decline of the Liberal Party was quite rapid, and since 1935 it has never elected more than 21 members of Parliament. The major causes of this decline were the rise of the Labour Party and the Liberal Party's internal divisions.

Three elements have historically made up the aims of the Liberal Party; first, a bias against authority, second, insistence on freedom of enterprise, and third, a belief in social justice. The Liberal Party continues to combine personal freedom, economic efficiency and social justice, and these can only be fully secured in a free society.
C.R.F.

British North America Act, 1867.

The written Constitution of Canada. Originally a British statute federating Ontario, Quebec, Nova Scotia, New Brunswick. Residual powers were to vest in the central government but under judicial interpretation the pertinent ". . . Peace, Order, and Good Government" clause was held to authorize broad national powers for dire emergencies, and the provincial power to regulate, "Property and Civil Rights in the Province . . ." became a fount of implied powers. (Cf. **Russell v. The Queen,** 7 Appeals Cases 829; **Toronto Electric Commissioners v. Snider** [1925], Appeals Cases 396). Amending powers lie formally with the British Parliament but in fact with the Canadian Parliament. M.P.S.

Brook Farm.

An ideal community established near Boston, Massachusetts, in 1841 and reorganized on Fourierist (q.v.) principles in 1844; disbanded in 1846; received much attention because of the eminent literary personages associated with it. Ch.C.M.

Bruning, Heinrich (1885—   ).

German statesman. President, Christian Trade Unions, 1920-1930. Reichstag member, Center Party (1924-33); parliamentary Chairman (1929-33). Chancellor, 1930-32. Dismissed by President von Hindenburg, after having engineered his re-election; proposed agricultural reform program against rich eastern landowners. Emigrated to United States. Professor, Harvard University, until return to Germany, 1952. Professor, University of Cologne. M.C.V.

Brussels Treaty.
See Treaty of Brussels.

Bryan-Chamorro Treaty.
Negotiated between the U.S. and Nicaragua and ratified in Feb., 1916, wherein the U.S. obtained by leasehold an exclusive canal right-of-way, a ninety-nine year lease of the Great and Little Corn Islands and a naval base in Fonseca Bay. Nicaragua received $3,000,000 to stabilize its public finances. This treaty terminated the ten year old Central American Court of Justice, because the Court ruled it violated the riparian rights of Costa Rica and Salvador's territorial seas, but declined to invalidate the treaty since the Court had no jurisdiction over the U.S. M.M.Mc.

Bryce, James (1838—1922).
A British historian, jurist, and politician, Bryce is best known in America for his **American Commonwealth**, of which four editions were prepared. Based on extensive travel and observation in the United States, this work is one of the best treatises on American political institutions ever written by a foreigner. Bryce served also as British Ambassador to the United States (1907-1913). He was elevated to a peerage in 1914. Th.P.

Buchanan, James (1791—1868).
Fifteenth President of the United States. Born in a log cabin at Stony Batter near Mercersburg, Pennsylvania, James Buchanan graduated from Dickinson College (1809), was admitted to the bar (1812), and served as a volunteer in defense of Baltimore during the War of 1812. His wide experience as congressman, cabinet member, and diplomat started as a Federalist state legislator (1815-16), but he soon became an ardent Jacksonian Democrat, representing Pennsylvania in both the House of Representatives (1820-31), rising to chairman of the Judiciary Committee, and the U.S. Senate (1834-1845). Buchanan was Minister to Russia (1832-33) and Secretary of State under President James K. Polk during negotiation of the Oregon Boundary Dispute with England and the Mexican War peace settlement. Minister to Great Britain (1853-56), he participated in formulating the expansionist Ostend Manifesto (1854). Buchanan's tragedy was to be President (1857-61) at the height of the slavery controversy when strong executive leadership was desperately needed instead of his legal and constitutional concept of limited executive power. Despite great experience and integrity, he was unable to reconcile his opposition to slavery with his desire to preserve the Union, and he permitted seven states to secede.
K.E.D.

Buddha, Gautama.
Born in 563 B.C. at Kapilavastu, Gautama was the son of a Hindu ruler of the Sakya clan. He grew up amid luxury and ease, wholly oblivious of human suffering. He was in his twenties when he first learned about sickness, death, and destitution. This awareness so touched his mind that at 29 he renounced his kingdom, his wife and child, and became a recluse to discover the truth about life and death, joy and sorrow. After seven years of ascetic quest, he experienced "enlightenment" at Gaya, and became Buddha, the Enlightened One. The essence of his discovery was that deliverance from human suffering lay in complete renunciation of selfish cravings by following the eight-fold path: Right View, Right Purpose, Right Discourse, Right Conduct, Right Livelihood, Right Endeavor, Right Mindfulness, Right Contemplation. The founder of Buddhism died at the age of 80. Today, over 150,000,000 people owe allegiance to him. C.S.S.

Buddhism.
Founded in sixth century B.C. by Gautama, later called Buddha ("enlightened one"), prince of the Sakyas of Northern India. Protested formalism of the prevailing Hinduism. India's emperor, Asoka (d. about 230 B.C.), possibly the first and only ruler to renounce war as an instrument of policy, conducted zealous missionary activities spreading Buddhism beyond Indian boundaries. Buddha taught that enlightenment was attained not through worship of a god but in the knowledge of the four truths: 1) Life is painful; 2) Pain is due to the cravings of man's passions; 3) Cessation of pain results only from abandoning these cravings; 4) By following an eight-fold path of ethical prescriptions,

one can attain **nirvana**—the ultimate release from the cycles of rebirth. Two main sects of Buddhism exist today. Hinayana, the "Lesser Vehicle," closest to the original doctrine, is found mainly in Southeast Asia. Forms of Mahayana Buddhism, the "Greater Vehicle," sometimes referred to as "speculative theism," flourish in China, Korea, Japan and Tibet. The influence of Buddhism upon development of non-violent philosophy in India has been indirect but appreciable. Prime Minister Nehru has often referred to Buddha as the greatest "son of India." During the past decade, after centuries of lapse, Buddhism has been successful in gaining significant numbers of formal adherents, especially among the **harijans** (untouchables) in India. S.K.A.

Budget.

A statement of expected revenues and expenditures for a fiscal period. This annual estimate is usually compiled by the executive office of not only the amount of needed receipts but the source of those funds. The detailed expenditures outline suggests the variety of governmental programs proposed for legislative action.

W.D.S.

Bukharin, Nikolai Ivanovich
(1888—1938).

Bukharin ranks among the intellectual leaders of communism. In 1916 he edited in New York the revolutionary paper Novy Mir. Joining Lenin in the Bolshevik Revolution, he became, after Lenin's death, the chief party theoretician, member of the Politburo (1924-1929), editor of Pravda (1917-1929), No. 2 man of the Communist International after Zinoviev's downfall, and editor of Izvestia after his own decline in power. He emerged as a leader of the Right Opposition of 1928-29 to challenge the pace and direction of Stalin's collectivization and industrialization programs, but his group was defeated by the Stalinist faction. He was dropped from the Politburo as well as from the leadership of the Comintern in 1929. During the period of the Great Purge of the late 1930's following the Kirov assassination of 1934, he was arrested and executed along with most of the leaders of the former Left (Zinoviev and Kamenev) and Right oppositions (Rykov). The indictment against him embraced the usual combination of treason, espionage, diversion, terrorism, and wrecking. He wrote and translated books, pamphlets and articles on economics and political science. R.St.-H.

Bulganin, Nikolai.

Bulganin rose to the high levels of Soviet power relatively late in life. His advancement appears to represent recognition of superior administrative rather than party achievements. He began his career as an officer in the Cheka. Transferred to economic work in 1922, he made his reputation in the next decade as a major industrial administrator. He served as chairman of the Moscow Soviet from 1931 to 1937. In 1948 he became chairman of the State Bank. During World War II, he served as political commissar of the Moscow Front; the military rank of lieutenant general was conferred on him in 1942 in recognition of his important part in the defense of Moscow. In 1944 he became a full general and also replaced Voroshilov as a member of the State Committee for Defense. In 1946 he was named Minister of the Armed Forces and a candidate member of the Politburo. His promotion to full membership came in 1948. He became Premier in 1954 following the downfall of Malenkov. He deserted Khrushchev and sided for a brief moment with the "anti-Party" group in June 1957. He was forced to resign on March 27, 1958, and was later humiliated in public. He was replaced by Khrushchev. R.St-H.

Bulgaria. See Appendix.

Bull Moose.

The symbol adopted by, and the nickname applied to, the Progressive Party of Theodore Roosevelt and Hiram Johnson in the three-cornered U.S. Presidential contest of 1912. The "Bull Moose" Progressives had bolted the Republican nominating convention in protest against its domination by the conservative Old Guard supporters of President William Howard Taft. While winning only eighty-eight electoral votes, the movement split the Republican vote and resulted in the election of Democrat Woodrow Wilson.

Formed around one man's leadership, the party disbanded when Roosevelt returned to the Republican Party.
R.E.Ch.

Bunche, Ralph Johnson (1904—   ).
U.N. Undersecretary for Special Political Affairs. Born in Detroit, Mich., and educated at U.C.L.A. and Harvard U. (Ph.D., 1934), he taught government at Howard U. (1928-50), was a principal officer in the U.S. Office of Strategic Services (1941-44) and Dept. of State (1944-46), a U.N. organizer (1945-46), Director of the U.N. Trusteeships Dept. (1946-54), Professor (on leave) at Harvard U. (1950-53), and President of the American Political Science Association (1954).

An African and Middle East expert, Dr. Bunche received the Nobel Peace Prize (1950) for his role in Palestine (1948-49); and was Special U.N. Representative in the Congo (1960 and 1963). Publications include: **A World View of Race** (1936); **Africa, the War and Peace Aims** (1942), and, jointly, **An American Dilemma** (1944).
N.P.T.

Bundesrat.
German second chamber, representing member-states. Traditionally not composed of elected deputies but of representatives of state governments, instructed by these governments. Under Constitution of 1871 chief federal organ, representing ruling monarchs. Under Weimar Constitution (q.v.) called Reichsrat, less influential. Under Bonn Constitution (q.v.) represents ten Laender, each with 3 to 5 votes, depending on population. Votes cast uniformly by representatives of each state (ministers or high officials). Participates in enactment of federal statutes, either suspensive veto or full consent. Reflects party-political constellation in states, but influence chiefly bureaucratic, by adjusting bills to interests of states, which are in charge of administering most federal statutes.
J.H.H.

Bundestag.
West-German parliament under Bonn Constitution (q.v.), successor to Reichstag (q.v.). Elected for four years, half of membership from single-member districts, half from party lists by proportional representation, but parties must obtain at least 5 percent of total vote for representation. Passes federal laws and budget, elects chancellor. Convenes at Bonn. Parties organized as parliamentary "fractions"; strong party discipline. Trend toward fewer parties: First Bundestag (1949) over ten, fourth (1961) three: Christian Democrats (q.v.), 242 deputies, Social Democrats (190), Free Democrats (67). Considerable powers, but strong hold of chancellor, who appoints and dismisses ministers freely and can be forced to resign only by Bundestag electing successor at same time.
J.H.H.

Buraku.
The Buraku was a wartime revival in Japan of an old form of mutual responsibility organization which had been applied in Japan as early as the late 16th century. It was created in 1940 and was a local federation of **Tonari-gumi** (neighborhood associations). The **Tonari-gumi** were groups of from five to ten households which were mutually responsible. Every household was held responsible for the deportment of all other households of its group. If a crime were committed by one member household and not reported by the others of the group, all would be punished.

The Buraku, made up of a number of **Tonari-gumi,** served as the lowest branch of local government and operated in close relationship with the Imperial Rule Assistance Association, an organization for the preservation of domestic order. The Buraku system was dissolved in the early days of the occupation and its administrative functions taken over by the various municipal offices concerned. It is considered likely that the Buraku system is related to the traditional Chinese **pao-chia** system of group responsibility.
S.S.

Burandi.
A kingdom in Central Africa, area 10,747 square miles; population, 2,213,480 (1959 estimate). After World War I, then known as Urundi, it formed with Ruanda a League of Nations mandate, with Belgium as the mandatory power. With the supercession of the League of Nations by the United Nations it became a trust ter-

ritory with Belgium as trustee, being governed by a Vice Governor General under the Governor General of the Belgian Congo. Pursuant to a vote of the United Nations General Assembly it became, on July 1, 1962, the independent state of Burandi, being removed from trusteeship and severed from its old associate. E.V.M.

Bureaucracy.
The organization, officials, and set procedures associated with any large administrative apparatus, though especially of government agencies. Bureaucracy is designed to have the advantages of regularizing action into routine patterns, handling large volumes of work, and dealing with questions impartially and impersonally. The term bureaucracy also is often used in a negative sense with suggestions of officialism, rigidity, delay, and lack of imagination. R.D.S.

Bureau of the Budget (U.S.A.).
The principal task of the Bureau is to coordinate the monetary requests of various agencies and, after modifications by the President, to present to Congress a budget detailing proposed expenditures and sources of income. The Bureau does not merely assemble agency requests for Presidential review; it is also authorized to "revise, reduce, or increase" requests. It serves as a body of advisors to the President on matters of administrative organization, supervises financial programs, controls rates of Congressionally authorized expenditures, reviews agency programs and proposals before Congress for compatibility with Presidential policy, and prepares veto messages for financial bills unacceptable to the President.

The Bureau was created by the Budget and Accounting Act of 1921 and was attached to the Treasury. In 1939, it was transferred to the newly created Executive Office of the President and became the principal staff agency advising the President on financial matters. There is a director and five assistant directors. The staff has been expanded in size from time to time. C.R.A.

Burke, Edmund.
British statesman and man of letters (1729—1797). According to Harold Laski, "Burke has endured as the permanent manual of political wisdom without which statesmen are as sailors on an uncharted sea." Although substantially the founder of conservatism as a body of political thought, Burke also exerted, posthumously, a strong influence upon liberalism — notably affecting Gladstone, John Morley, Walter Bagehot, Woodrow Wilson, and others.

Though best known in America for his celebrated speech on conciliation with the American colonies (1775), Burke made his principal contribution to political thought late in life, beginning with the publication of his **Reflections on the Revolution in France** (1790). Abhorring the radicalism of the French Revolution, and predicting the triumph of a dictatorial regime in France, Burke defended the traditional civilization of Europe against reckless innovation.

Among Burke's chief political principles are his praise of prescription and custom; his emphasis on the continuity of human institutions; his appeal to "the true rights" of mankind in civilization, as opposed to Paine's "Rights of Man"; and his description of prudence as the statesman's principal virtue. R.K.

Burma, Republic of the Union of.
Area 261,789 square miles. Population, (1962 estimate) 20.6 million. The Union includes Burma proper with the Chin Special Division and four ethnic states, the Karen Shan, Kachin and Kayah. Karens form 10% of the population; Shans, related to the Thai of Thailand, 8½%. Arakanese want a separate state. Indians and Chinese form the largest foreign elements. Burma evolved from a first century A.D. kingdom under an Indian prince. Buddhism supplanted the Hindu way of life. From the sixteenth century, Portuguese traders, later Dutch and English rivals, strove for influence. Burma was united under Alaungpaya in 1755.

The British gained possession in stages, through three Anglo-Burman Wars, 1826-1886. Ruled from British India, Burma was denied constitutional privileges accorded India. The

Young Men's Buddhist Association (founded 1909) and the General Council of Buddhist Associations (1919) were nationalist organizations. Anti-British riots broke out in the '30s. In 1935 Burma was separated from India. The Dobama Asiayone (We Burmese Association or "Thakin" party), the Communist Party and the Freedom Bloc founded in 1939, worked for independence.

Doctor Ba Maw and Thakin Nu headed the puppet government of oppressive Japanese occupation during World War II. In August, 1944, Aung San formed the Anti-Fascist People's Freedom League (AFPFL), still the strongest political party. During negotiations with the British, Aung San expelled Communists from the Burmese Independence Army (or Burma Defense Army), he and his brother-in-law, Than Tun, had founded. Aung San and six colleagues were assassinated.

"Thakin" Nu (title now "U") became Prime Minister. U Nu built up the army and Union Military Police, revived Buddhism, and created the Bureau of Special Investigation to oppose corruption in government.

The Treaty of Independence, October 17, 1947, made with Britain's Labor Government, became effective January 4, 1948. Burma refused Commonwealth membership; joined the U.N. In 1935 the government revoked its military pact with Great Britain. It is neutral.

The 1947 constitution provided a bicameral legislature; a Chamber of Nationalities of 125 members with assured Burman dominance; a Chamber of Deputies with 250 deputies. The executive included a president, a prime minister and three deputy prime ministers. The judiciary was independent.

The economic situation was critical at independence. Two four-year plans to achieve Pyidawtha, or the Happy Land, were inaugurated, 1952-1956; 1957-1961. The first was unrealistic; benefits hardly reached the people. The second achieved more concrete results.

A split in the AFPFL caused a crisis in 1958. At the request of U Nu, General Ne Win restored order. U Nu resigned October 28; after election by the Chamber of Deputies, Ne Win became premier. Ne Win retained power after the restoration of civil law and U Nu's election, September, 1960. The chief parliamentary opposition has been the National Unity Front (NUF), organized in 1955. Communists worked through a branch of this group.

In March, 1962, Ne Win led a bloodless coup, arresting U Nu and other officials. Ne Win has announced that military rule will continue until all factions have agreed on a constitution. The foreign policy of neutralism is being continued. M.O'C.

"Business Affected with a Public Interest."

A term first used in Munn v. Illinois, 94 U.S. 113 (1877), a case involving the question of the right of the state of Illinois to set maximum charges of grain elevators. From 1877 until 1934, the United States Supreme Court consistently held that regulation of prices, rates, or hours and conditions of labor was a deprivation of liberty and property in violation of the due process of law clause of the Constitution, except in the case of business especially "affected with a public interest." The concept—actually a useful legal fiction —was never defined with precision, however, being construed on an **ad hoc** basis by the court. It was finally abandoned in Nebbia v. New York, 291 U.S. 502 (1934). C.R.A.

Business Cycle.

An important and recurrent disturbance in the level of national income; it may be considered as a process of cumulative change of a period longer than a year. During the cycle all parts of a national economy display marked changes in activity as it goes through prosperity (the high point in business activity), recession, depression (the low point), and recovery. These four phases can be measured using the appropriate indexes of the production, prices, income, employment, etc. The cycle is caused in a free enterprise system by the decisions of the enterprisers in accordance to their estimate of prospective profits and future performance of the economy. W.N.

Byelorussia.

One of 15 "autonomous Soviet Socialist Republics" in the Soviet Union, with its capital at Minsk. Theoretically Byelorussia has its own government; in practice it is an integral part of the U.S.S.R. and governed from Moscow. As a result of the Yalta Treaty, however, it and the Ukraine were given independent memberships in the United Nations in 1945.   J.G.St.

Byzantium.
Eastern, Greek or later Roman Empire, "the Roman Empire in its Christian form." Symbol of European, Christian resistance against Eastern Barbarians. Capital named Constantinople (now Istanbul); Empire called after city's original name of Byzantium. Emperor Constantine (r. 306-337) moved there capital of Roman Empire. Under Theodosius I (r. 379-395) Christianity became official and sole state religion. Empire was divided after his death into Eastern and Western Empires. Golden Age of Byzantine Empire began with Justinian (r. 527-565). He won back some of lost African and European parts and pushed back Persians. Church was put under control of government. Justinian authored last Roman law edition (Justinian code). Directed the building of Hagia Sophia, most famous of all Orthodox churches. Justinian's contributions and those of his successors (such as Heraclius, r. 610-641) were costly, since Empire became bankrupt and militarily weak. Moslems menaced Byzantium in seventh century, conquering much of imperial territory short of Constantinople. Weak period lasted until ascent of Basil the Macedonian (r. 867-886) and the Macedonian dynasty (until 1056), which developed era of wealth and strength. Constantinople became a legendary seat of culture and wealth, particularly under Basil II (r. 976-1025).

New threat from East came with Seljuk Turks during 11th century. New imperial defense plans included Western European elements and invited Crusades and, with them, internal dissent. Venetians and Crusaders (particularly of Fourth Crusade) conquered parts of Empire and finally Constantinople (1204). (Conquest considered as the end of true Byzantine Empire.) Last line of (mediocre) Byzantine rulers was started by Greek General Michael Palaeologus' conquest of Constantinople and defeat of Westerners (1261). Ottoman Turks conquered Asia Minor and all Byzantine territory with exception of Constantinople, which enjoyed a superb defensive position, during 14th century. Finally city fell 1453; last Emperor, Constantine XI, killed in battle.
    M.C.V.

C

Caballero, Largo.
Leftist socialist — but anti-Communist—leader during Spanish Civil War. He became Prime Minister of Republican ("loyalist") Spanish government in September 1936. Was deposed and prosecuted by pro-Communist Dr. Negrin on order of Soviet military authorities in Madrid.   I.D.

Cabinet Government.
A version of parliamentary democracy in which executive and legislative leadership powers are fused and concentrated in the Cabinet (Prime Minister and other chief Ministers); this despite the fact that parliament is constitutionally supreme, Cabinet members are drawn primarily from among the leading legislators, they are both individually and collectively responsible to parliament, and the Cabinet may be forced out of office by parliamentary rejection of a major Government proposal (bill) or by a vote of lack of confidence. Cabinet strength lies chiefly in the ability of its members to command a reasonably stable and disciplined working majority in parliament. Some evidence of legislative majority support was necessary initially in order for the Government to be designated by the politically weak chief-of-state (constitutional monarch or indirectly elected president). If that majority is based upon a well disciplined party or a harmonious coalition of such parties, then the Cabinet can dominate both the legislative and executive processes. It can have its policies converted into laws whose administration it supervises. Customarily, in this system the Cabinet also can have parliament dissolved and new elections called if legislative opposition becomes overwhelming and the Government does not choose to resign. The availability of this power tends to restrain indiscriminate opposition and bolsters the Government's majority. Cabinet government, therefore, can provide exceedingly strong and coordinate executive leadership within a parliamentary democratic framework. Great Britain is an outstanding example.   D.W.

Cable Act.
This act, also known as the Married Women's Citizenship Act of September 22, 1922 (42 Stat. 1021), changed and clarified the rights of women in respect to United States citizenship. Specifically it provided: (1) Women might become citizens though married to an alien, (2) Women did not ordinarily lose their citizenship through marriage to an alien, and (3) Alien women did not acquire citizenship through marriage to a citizen of the United States although some naturalization requirements were eased.
    T.C.S.

Caesarism. See Appendix.

Cairo Conference of 1943.
Conference of President F. D. Roosevelt, Prime Minister Winston Churchill and Generalissimo Chiang Kai-Shek, Nov. 23-26, 1943 in Cairo, Egypt (preceded by visits, Nov. 21 and 22). Then Russia not at war with Japan; Soviet Assistant Commissar of Foreign Affairs Andrei Vishinsky at Cairo but not participating. After meeting, Roosevelt and Churchill went to Teheran to see Stalin. Cairo Conference mapped objectives of war with Japan: stripped Japan of islands in Pacific taken since 1914; restored to Republic of China all the territories stolen by Japan since 1894 such as Manchuria, Formosa, and Pescadores; expelled Japanese from all other territories taken by violence and greed; "In due course, Korea shall become free and independent"; and to procure unconditional surrender of Japan. Together with abolition of unequal treaties by Britain and U.S. and ending of immigration exclusion law early the same year, a great boost to Chinese morale. China was then accepted as one of great powers. Military plans in Cairo Conference, less significant since Stalin made first promise to enter war against Japan in Teheran. Incorporated in Potsdam Declaration, the Cairo Declaration was accepted by Soviet Union.   C.K.W.

Calendar.
A schedule or a list of cases pending before a court, or of bills and resolutions awaiting action in a legislative

body following reports by committees on such bills. W.V.H.

Calhoun, John Caldwell (1782—1850).
Vice President, Cabinet member, Senator, Representative and state legislator, Calhoun's states' rights, concurrent majority, and nullification doctrines had marked impact on American political thought. A Yale 1804 graduate, he studied law, began practicing in 1807, and was elected within a year to the South Carolina legislature and in 1810 to Congress. A strong nationalist in his early career, he joined the "War Hawks," advocated declaring war on England, and supported vigorous prosecution of hostilities. He also favored a protective tariff, national roads, internal taxation and the Second U.S. Bank. As Secretary of War (1817-1824) under President Monroe, Calhoun extensively reorganized the army, establishing new surgeon-general, quartermaster-general and commissary-general bureaus. Elected Vice-President in 1824 and 1828, the South Carolina tariff dispute precipitated both his resignation December 28, 1832 (the only such occurrence in American history), and his immediate selection as U.S. Senator. Meanwhile, Calhoun set forth his nullification theory: if Congress exceeds constitutional authority, a sovereign state through a convention may nullify the operation of an unlawful act; ratification of a constitutional amendment granting the questioned power to the national government would justify secession from the Union. While Senator, Calhoun worked for a compromise traiff, advocated states' rights, opposed anti-slavery and abolitionist movements, and maintained the right to take slaves freely into the territories. For a year (1844-45) he served as Secretary of State under Tyler, then returned to the Senate until his death March 31, 1850. C.F.N.

Caliph.
Successor to the Prophet Muhammad in his position as the executive head of the politico-religious community, but not in his prophetic function of communicating and promulgating the divine law. His chief functions were to spread and defend the Islamic faith, to lead the community in prayer and in war and to dispense justice according to the divine law. His judicial function was to interpret the law rather than to make new law or define dogma. According to Islamic political theory, there must always be a caliph to the community of Islam, whom every Muslim is bound to obey; there shall be no more than one caliph at the same time and he must be descended from Quraysh, the Prophet's tribe. Although the powers of the caliph are derived from the divine law, his appointment was made by the people in an act of allegiance. If he failed to rule according to the law, he forfeited his right to remain caliph, and could be removed from office. Only the first four orthodox Caliphs followed the precepts of the divine law. With the spread of Islam and the expansion of the empire, election was abandoned in favor of nomination and the caliph looked more like a Persian or Byzantine Emperor than a successor to the Messenger of Allah.
F.M.N.

Caliphate (Islamic State).
The institution of the Caliphate represents the succession to the administrative authority of the Prophet Muhammad. The Caliphate became the symbol of a trusteeship of Muhummad's embodiment of all prophethood and of a perpetuation of his model rulership. It stood for the headship of an ideal empire in which the perfect combination of faith and society which the Prophet had attained would be perpetuated for all time. It was considered indispensable to the existence and continuity of a valid Islam. Under the Orthodox Caliphs (632—661) this ideal was almost fulfilled. Under the Umayyads (661—750 A.D.), the Caliphate was transformed from an elective office (in the tribal fashion) into a **de facto** hereditary monarchy with a worldly way of life and theologians and legists refused to concede to it any spiritual authority. With the Abbasids (750—1258 A.D.), the departure from the Prophet's ideal went further which led to its degeneracy. Although under the Ottomans (1517—1924) there was virtual separation between the Caliphate and Sultanate, the fortunes of the former

were tied to the destiny of the latter. On March 4th, 1924, the Turkish National Assembly led by Mustafa Kemal abolished the Caliphate as an institution and disestablished Islam as the religion of the State. Some efforts were made to resuscitate it. In May 1926 a congress attended by the religious doctors from 13 Muslim countries convened in Cairo to decide the question of the Caliphate, but it did not accomplish more than declaring the caliphate a necessity. Two other Islamic conferences were held in Mecca (1926) and Jerusalem (1931), but both failed to discuss the question of the Caliphate, an indication that it probably had become obsolete. Now that the Caliphate has been replaced by separate national expressions, no serious Muslim opinion appears to expect its revival. F.M.N.

Calles, Plutarco Elias.
President of Mexico. Born Guaymas, Sonora, September 25, 1877. Died Mexico City, October 19, 1945. Joined Mexican Revolution in 1910. Promoted to general in 1914. Governor of Sonora in 1919; Minister of Industry, Commerce, and Labor in 1919. Minister of Interior (1920—1923). President of Mexico (1924—1928). Minister of Finance (1933—1935). Exiled in the United States (1935—1941). Allowed to recover rank in Mexican army in 1942. His administration was marked by conflict with the Roman Catholic Church, the consolidation of the National Revolutionary party, and establishment of the Bank of Mexico. He supported agrarian reform and mass education. R.B.G.

Calvin, Jean (1509—1564).
French theologian and religious reformer, b. at Noyon, d. in Geneva. Having studied theology and law at the Universities of Paris, Orleans and Bourges, Calvin was forced for religious reasons to leave France in 1534 and went to Basle. In 1536, he was called to Geneva to head the reformed church but was banished from there in 1538 because of his stern religious measures. After serving as a pastor for three years to French refugees in Strasbourg, Calvin was recalled in 1541 to Geneva and continued to be there the dominant spirit till his death. The **Institutiones Religionis Christianae** (1536) are Calvin's major work. This work is important not only for its theological doctrines (such as foreordination, the division of the world between the elect and the reprobate, the individual's fate being determined solely by God's grace), but also for certain political assumptions. Secular government is a divinely ordained institution, needed by imperfect men that there "may be a public form of religion among Christians and that humanity may be maintained" among men. Individuals have the duty of passive obedience towards their rulers. Only when God sends a deliverer or some constitutional provision provides for inferior magistrates to protect the people against the oppressions of their rulers is disobedience against rulers permissible. Should, however, a ruler's commands violate God's commands then the individual has the duty of passive resistance. Therewith Calvinism provided an opening wedge for approving popular revolt against established authorities should it deem revolt against the rulers of a country in which Calvinists considered themselves a suppressed minority desirable.
G.V.W.

Calvo Clause.
A provision in the law of a state or in contracts with foreign companies requiring that aliens must resort to local judicial remedies rather than to diplomatic intervention in seeking redress of grievances. Named for Argentine jurist Carlos Calvo (1824—1906).
F.M.L.

Cambodia.
Area 66,800 square miles. Population (1962 estimate) 5 million. The first century A.D. Indian kingdom of Founan gave way to the Khmer kingdom (late sixth century) which produced the great temples of Angkor. Weakened by Cham, Vietnamese and Thai attacks, Cambodia became a French protectorate in 1863; then part of French Indo-China. Nationalism developed in the '30s. During World War II the French allowed the Japanese to build bases in Cambodia. Independence was proclaimed March, 1945. The French regained power briefly. Anti-French guerrillas,

nationalist groups, especially the Khmer Issarak led by Son Ngoc Than, the former Japanese puppet premier, and Communist bands led by Viet-Minh fought in Cambodia in 1953; regular Viet-Minh troops invaded Cambodia in 1954. In the Geneva cease-fire agreements, 1954, Cambodia promised to make no military alliances; to incorporate Khmer rebels into the nationalist army. Cambodia became a member of the U.N. in 1955.

The 1947 constitution promulgated by King Norodom Sihanouk provides limited monarchy and parliamentary government. The National Assembly comprises 91 seats. Sihanouk ruled by royal mandate from June 1952 to January, 1955. Parliament was dissolved in January, 1953. All seats went to Prince Sihanouk's Peoples' Social Community Party (or Popular Socialist Community) in the 1955, 1958 and 1962 elections. The government party works to implement the reforms of the 1947 constitution.

In order to enter active politics, King Norodom Sihanouk abdicated in 1955, in favor of his father, King Norodom Suramarit. After his father's death and a referendum in 1960, Prince Sihanouk was made Chief of State. He has proposed a neutral zone of Cambodia and Laos, guaranteed by East and West; and a Buddhist federation to include Burma.

There are outstanding border disputes with South Viet Nam. In 1962 a temple border dispute with Thailand was adjusted through the U.N. in Cambodia's favor. M.O'C.

Cameroon.
A republic in Western Africa; area 183,570 square miles; population 4,097,000 (1960 estimate). Created in 1961, and styled the Federal Republic of the Cameroon, it is composed of East Cameroons and West Cameroons, which make up a federation. East Cameroon is the former Republic of Cameroun, which had been successively a German protectorate, a League of Nations mandate administered by France, and a trust territory with France as trustee, when it was also an associated territory of the French Union. West Cameroons is the southern portion of the former British-administered trust territory of Cameroons; in 1961 it voted to join the Republic of Cameroun, while the northern portion elected to join Nigeria, with which it had been administratively associated. The President of the old republic, Ahmadou Ahidjo, is the President of the federation.
E.V.M.

Campaign.
As used in politics, effort to secure the designation or election of a particular candidate or slate of candidates or the adoption of specific changes in the social or legal system. In the United States campaigns may be virtually continuous as for the inclusion of a given matter as public policy or at periodical intervals as for the election of a government executive. There are some controls over tactics and expenditures although these are frequently evaded by campaign committees, lobbyists, or candidates. M.B.D.

Camus, Albert (1913—1960).
Algerian-born French novelist and journalist. Active and vocal in the movement for Algerian independence. Editor of **Combat** in Algeria from 1944—1945. Winner of Nobel Prize for literature in 1957. His most explicitly political works are **The Plague** (fiction) and **The Rebel** (non-fiction). His political theory calls for limited government which can insure a substantial degree of both freedom and justice in society. He rejects the validity or possibility of a society based on either absolute freedom or on absolute justice. Other major works include **The Fall** and **The Stranger.** E.R.W.

Canada.
Canada is the world's second largest country—3,845,774 square miles, but only one-third of this area has been brought under cultivation to date. Less than eight per cent of the country is classified as occupied farmland; an equal area at present unoccupied, is considered suitable for agriculture. About 24 per cent of the total area is regarded as productive forested land.

The settlement of Canada began in 1605. The first census in 1666 gave 3,215 inhabitants exclusive of aborigines. In 1961, the total population was slightly above 18 million. The largest single ethnic group in Canada consists of persons of French origin, 31 per cent; persons of English extraction make up 26 per cent of the population, while all the British Isles account for 48 per cent of the population. Over the past decade, emigration from Canada has averaged 35,000 per year, while immigration to Canada, 154,000 a year.

The system of Government that was adopted in Canada by the British North America Act of 1867 is a federal union in which certain stated authority rests with the provinces and the right to legislate on all other matters is left to the Central Parliament in Ottawa. Sixteen classes of subjects: property, civil right, health education, municipal institutions, national resources, etc., are specifically entrusted to the provinces; while twenty-nine classes of subjects: defense, banking, currency, railways and canals, external relations, etc., are specifically defined as being within the authority of the Federal Government.

Politically, Canada is divided into ten Provinces and two territories. Each of the provinces is sovereign in its own sphere, to the degree defined in the British North America Act and its amendments, and as new provinces have been organized, they have been granted political status equivalent to that of the four original provinces which united in 1867. The Yukon Territory was created in 1898, the Northwest Territory in 1905: both are administered by the Federal Government.

In each province there is a provincial legislature to which members are elected from the various electoral ridings throughout the province. In the Province of Quebec there is, in addition, an upper chamber called the Legislative Council, whose members are appointed for life. The head of the Provincial Government is the Premier, normally the leader of the political party having the support of the largest number of members elected to the Legislative Assembly. P.G.

Canon Law.

A system of Roman Catholic Church law the sources of which are, **inter alia,** the Bible, writings of the church fathers, decrees of the councils, and decretals of the popes. A codification in about 1143 by Gratian became the basic compilation to which later rulings served as modifications, and in 1918 a new code was declared in effect.

Since the canon law was respected and had temporal authority during the Middle Ages and since it came to govern various matters of international importance, it had impact upon international law. Restraining influences in warfare, solemnization of agreements, and general ecclesiastical contributions to the idea of a unified system of law and justice under a supreme deity were among the historic contributions of the canon law to international law. H.B.J.

Canton Commune.

A Chinese communist government which briefly controlled the city of Canton (from the 11th to the 14th of December, 1927). It was brought about by an uprising staged by the communists and their supporters. The uprising was timed to take advantage of the split between two Kuomintang factions in the area—the faction led by Li Chi-shen and that of Chang Fa-K'uei and Wang Ching-wei—but the communists, badly outnumbered and receiving little support from the local populace, were unable to hold their gains in the face of united opposition from the Kuomintang troops who reconciled their differences in the face of the uprising.

It has been suggested that the orders to stage the uprising came directly from Stalin who badly needed a proletarian victory in China to redeem his policy of encouraging active proletarian leadership of the Chinese Communist Party.

While in power, the Communists formed a Canton "Soviet of Workers', Peasants', and Soldiers' Deputies," which issued a manifesto calling for drastic social reform including nationalization of all big industry and reform of land.

After the Canton Commune had fallen a period of Kuomintang "white terror" followed and many outrages were inflicted on the civilian population by Kuomintang troops.

The failure of the Canton Commune caused the Comintern to reconsider its policy of encouraging proletarian uprisings in China and contributed to the subsequent fall of Ch'u Ch'iu-pai from his post as head of the Chinese Communist Party. S.S.

Cao Dai.
A religious sect politically active in South Vietnam. During World War II, it made alliances intermittently with the Japanese, the French and the Communist guerrillas. It claims a membership of more than two million persons and considers the Mekong Delta Region and Tay Ninh province its particular strongholds. It professes anti-Communism but was temporarily suppressed by the Diem regime due to its insistence on private armies. J.D.

Capitalism.
A type of economic system which is characterized by private ownership of property and freedom of enterprise, and which is based on the freedom of choice by the consumer, on business competition, and on profit motive. Forms of capitalism have been in existence since beginning of the recorded history. Adam Smith in "Wealth of Nations," 1776, defines it rather as a "natural order" of liberty; later called "laissez-faire" capitalism. In its pure form the function of political government is reduced to that of a "passive policeman." W.N.

Capital Planning.
A part of the on-going nature of fiscal planning. Capital planning asserts the possibility, indeed the necessity, of establishing timetables and priority lists for the purchase and acquisition of public lands and the construction and rehabilitation of public facilities. W.D.S.

Capital Punishment.
The governmental practice of deliberately putting to death an offender after sentence imposed by competent authority. In early societies probably it was used primarily to punish religious crimes. The modern state restricted its use to secular offenses.
Investigation has shown no significant relationship between the presence of the death penalty and the incidence of capital crime. Abolition has been achieved in about thirty countries. It has been abolished in six of the United States and is narrowly restricted in three others. W.F.G.

Capitulations.
In one usage of the term, capitulations were extra-territorial privileges formerly enjoyed by certain states (mostly Western) in the territories of various Middle Eastern and Asian states. These privileges allowed the Western states to set up courts to try their own nationals in the foreign countries in question.
In a wholly different sense the term capitulations refers to agreements by military commanders for the surrender of designated places. In this meaning, capitulations are military accords in which surrender is accepted in return for limited guarantees such as civilian protection, retention of arms, good treatment of surrendering personnel and other similar concessions by the victorious commander. The commanders can legally make such agreements only if they are endowed with sufficient authority. Accords made in excess of the commanders' authority are known as **sponsions**. H.B.J.

Cárdenas, Lázaro.
President of Mexico. Born Jiquilpán de Juárez, Michoacán, May 21, 1895. Joined Mexican Revolution against Porfirio Diaz in 1913. Became a brigadier general in 1924, and general of division in 1928. Governor of Michoacán (1928—1932). President, Partido Revolucionario Nacional, 1930. President of Mexico (1934—1940). Initiated many reforms, including land distribution to peasants, and agricultural cooperatives, credit systems, nationalization of oil properties, and extension of education. Continued to exert considerable influence in Mexican politics after his term as President. R.B.G.

Cardozo, Benjamin N. (1870—1938).
Associate Justice of the United States Supreme Court, 1932—1938. After twenty-two years in private practice—mainly as counsel for other lawyers—Cardozo was appointed in 1917 to the New York Court of Ap-

peals, and in 1926 was elected chief judge of that court. Owing to his mastery of the law and to his insight into the relation of law to life—as reflected in his opinions and his books—his court became one of the most distinguished courts in the nation. His towering reputation as a judge won him an appointment from President Hoover as Holmes's successor on the Supreme Court in 1932. On the Court he distinguished himself primarily in his dissents, which helped pave the way for a broader interpretation of the Constitution. He wrote several books, among which **The Nature of the Judicial Process** (1921) has emerged as a classic. It is a penetrating study of the task of the judge in "finding" the law. He is undisputedly regarded as one of the greatest jurists and judges America has produced. P.B.

Caretaker government.
A non-political cabinet, or "government," that carries on the necessary functions of government in the period between the resignation of a politically representative and responsible cabinet and the establishment of a new cabinet enjoying parliamentary support. A caretaker cabinet is restricted to carrying out programs and functions already approved by the parliament, and cannot properly initiate new policies nor concern itself with political questions. A caretaker government may be simply the outgoing government (as might be the case in Great Britain), or it may be a partially revised outgoing cabinet (as in France, where, after a vote of no-confidence, the President of the Assembly becomes both the Premier and the Minister of the Interior, while other ministerial offices may remain unchanged), or it may be a totally reconstituted cabinet (as in Finland, where ministers are often drawn from outside the parliament to form a non-political "government of officials"). In any case, the caretaker government is considered to be not representative of any particular political viewpoint. R.H.K.

Caribbean Organization.
Successor institution to the Anglo-American Caribbean Commission. The latter was established in 1942 as a vehicle for development of Caribbean possessions. After World War II, the French and Dutch joined Great Britain and the United States in supporting the Commission's Central Secretarial and advisory Research Council, holding occasional West Indian Conferences. In response to the growing autonomy of the territorial governments, the four metropolitan powers established in 1960 the Caribbean Organization with quasi-autonomous members (including the three Guianas) as members in their own right. At this time the headquarters of the Organization was moved from Trinidad to Hato Rey in Puerto Rico.

The Caribbean Organization devotes its energies to expediting the cultural, economic, natural resource, and social development of its members. In 1961 a Caribbean Plan was adopted by the Council of the Organization. The budget for its meetings, research, and publications was approximately $100,000 in 1961. The Secretariat of the Organization consists of about thirty professionals. One of the central functions of the Caribbean Organization is to provide representational leverage for its members in their relations with larger aid programs, such as those of the Alliance for Progress and the UN Economic Commission for Latin America. With the demise of the West Indies Federation of British islands in 1962, the Caribbean Organization may be expected to fulfill an increasingly important role in the Caribbean, as is indicated in its recent establishment of a Clearing House for Intra-Caribbean Trade and Tourism Information. H.G.

Carlyle, Thomas (1795—1881).
Scottish essayist, historian and philosopher. Although born to parents in humble circumstances, Carlyle attended the University of Edinburgh. Religious doubts led him to give up any thought of entering the ministry. He found teaching distasteful, whether as a master at a school or as a private tutor, but at first could earn little by writing. **The French Revolution** (1837) at last brought fame and an adequate monetary return. Carlyle believed in the "great man" theory of history, on which he wrote **Heroes and Hero-**

Worship (1841); and he exalted Oliver Cromwell and Frederick the Great as heroes in the biographies published in 1845 (Cromwell) and in 1858—1865 (Frederick). Although an ardent advocate of universal education, Carlyle distrusted democracy and was savagely opposed to the laissez-faire doctrines of Bentham's school. M.Sp.

Carpetbaggers.
Persons from the North who went South after the U.S. Civil War (1865-1875) were sometimes called carpetbaggers by Southerners who thereby expressed their disdain for the newcomers who supposedly were so poor that all their goods could be transported in the characteristic hand luggage of the day. The term had once been applied to bankers in the Western United States who had done temporary rather than permanent business. After the collapse of Reconstruction, many carpetbaggers returned to the North. W.F.G.

Casablanca Bloc.
An association of Ghana, Guinea, Mali, Algeria, the United Arab Republic, and Morocco dedicated to the unification of Africa.

Two weeks after a rival group of states had met at Brazzaville to establish its organ of unification, the Casablanca powers assembled on January 3, 1961 at the Moroccan capital where they passed resolutions which condemned NATO's assistance to France in Algeria, charged that Israel had sided with the imperialists, and supported Morocco in her dispute with Mauritania — resolutions at variance with those formulated by the Brazzaville Bloc. At Casablanca, at Cairo (May, 1961), and at subsequent meetings these African states established various committees dealing with economic, political, cultural, and military affairs plus a secretariat and an African military command with a permanent general staff. These organs are charged with the task of promoting unity among the members, a chore rendered more difficult by the geographic dispersal of the membership.

The unity of the Casablanca powers is strengthened by the generally leftist orientation of their foreign policies, by their espousal of political means to unify Africa, and by their critical attitude toward Western colonialism and neo-colonialism. None of these powers has joined the Brazzaville Bloc, nor has any of them become a member of the Monrovian Bloc. F.H.G.

Case, Clifford P.
Born April 16, 1904; U.S. Senate from January 3, 1955 until term ending January 3, 1967; Republican — New Jersey. R.A.B.

Case Method.
a. A monographic research method in which a delimited and interrelated set of phenomena—a "case"—is intensively studied. This research method is mainly directed at contributing to systematic knowledge through induction or deduction, direct impression, depth-understanding and comparison.

b. A teaching method in which students are confronted with a description of an episode — a "case" — and asked to discuss or manipulate it. Especially important in contemporary teaching of administration, the case method of teaching aims at increasing the skills, knowledge and tacit understanding of students through active participation, group discussions and simulated operations with abstracted reality. Y.D.

Cash and Carry.
Some legislation of the 1930's was predicated upon the theory that the United States could maintain neutrality if it required belligerents to pay cash for supplies purchased in the United States and to carry them away in foreign shipping. Actually the Joint Resolution of November 4, 1939 (54 Stat. 4) which contained the most famous version of cash and carry aided the western powers by repealing existing statutory provisions for an arms embargo. T.C.S.

Castro, Fidel.
Cuban dictator. Born on family sugar plantation in Oriente province, Cuba, August 13, 1927. Married in 1948; divorced in 1955. Led unsuccessful revolt against General Batista in 1953, but ousted Batista January 1, 1959. With his younger brother, Raul, and Ernesto Guevara, Argentine-born

Communist agent, Castro formed a governmental triumvirate. Castro designated himself premier, Raul as chief of armed forces and Guevara as unofficial executive assistant. Manuel Urrutia was named figurehead president. Most governmental posts were filled by rebels who had fought alongside Castro in eastern Cuba during 1956-58. Later Guevara was named head of the National Bank of Cuba, President Urrutia was fired for making an anti-Communist declaration, and Communists were moved into all key governmental posts. In 1962, Guevara became Minister of Industries, and Osvaldo Dorticos a figurehead president. Castro retained the premiership, named Raul vice premier, and turned over increasing economic powers to Carlos Rafael Rodriguez, president of the National Institute of Agrarian Reform, and political powers to Blas Roca, secretary-general of the Cuban Communist Party which operates under the front name **Partido Socialista Popular.** In less than four years, Castro's personal grip on all facets of Cuban public life had been transferred partially to Rodriguez, Roca, and Guevara. Oratorically, Castro still swayed Cuban emotions with his charismatic personality. But though he had captured the imagination of many revolutionary-minded young men and women throughout Latin America and the other underdeveloped nations of the world, by early 1963 Castro's popularity seems to have passed its global zenith. Major contributors to this decline were the hundreds of firing-squad executions of political opponents and the totalitarian control of Cuban mass media and daily public life. M.A.

Casus belli. See Appendix.

Casus foederis. See Appendix

Catalytic war.
Various meanings. Most commonly a hypothetical military strategic contingency in which one nation attacks another while allowing such attack to be attributed to a third nation. The country attacked would retaliate against the third party thereby precipitating counter-retaliation and war. The initiating country would hope through such connivance to emerge without suffering damage. Any attempt by a third nation, for its own purposes, to precipitate a mutually unwanted war between the two most powerful nations. H.H.R.

Catherine II, "The Great" (1729—1796).
Daughter of Prince Anhalt-Zerbst of Stettin, she married the grand-duke Peter, nephew of the Russian empress Elizabeth, and became Empress of Russia in 1762, by deposing her husband shortly after his accession to power as Peter III. Inspired by the French **philosophes,** in the early days of her reign, she believed in the ideal of benevolent rule. Her legislation, however, reflected her dependence on the nobility and Russia's general unreadiness for social reform. Her charter to the nobility (1785) not only confirmed the corporate rights of the nobles, but increased their privileges by exempting them from military service and extending their power over the serfs; she also granted them the right to participate in local self-government. Her plans for broad social reform were never realized. She became increasingly reactionary, stifling freedom of speech and the press and practicing repression of the traditional Muscovite type. Her policy of foreign expansion was conducted at the expense of Poland and Turkey. W.J.S.

Catholics in American Politics.
Although America is a predominantly Protestant nation, American Catholics, from the writing of the Constitution until the election of John F. Kennedy, have played a prominent role in politics. So great was prejudice against Catholic influence in the United States in the mid-nineteenth century that a new major political party, the Know-Nothings, emerged to stop them. But the Know-Nothings died, and Catholic influence continued to expand until the present day.

Today Catholics are in the majority and dominate the politics of several states including Massachusetts, Rhode Island, and Connecticut. Their influence in all of the major urban-industrial states is pronounced. The first Catholic politicians to rise to power in the twentieth century were usually of Irish descent, notably Al Smith, Governor of New York, who was defeated in his campaign for the Presidency in 1928 by what many believed to have been "anti-Catholic" voting. Today, there are Catholic governors and senators and scores of state legislators whose parents and grandparents came from Italy. In some big cities, there is considerable tension between Catholics of Irish and Catholics of Italian origin over control of the Democratic Party machinery.

Although Catholics are not completely unified on any important issue, there are significant tendencies for Catholics and non-Catholics to divide on some issues. The most articulate and effective support for the maintenance of religious influences in public schools as well as for the expenditure of public funds for the support of private religious schools comes from Catholics. In many communities, there is active competition between Catholics and non-Catholics for control of school boards and their policies.

John F. Kennedy, the first Catholic President of the United States, had taken a firm stand in support of separation of Church and State and against the majority of his co-religionists on the issue of religion in the schools and public support to religious schools. Kennedy's election signaled the abandonment of traditional widespread prejudice against Catholics and symbolized the fact that in a free society elected representatives are bound only by their conscience and the vote of the majority including all groups.
L.H.F.

Caucus.
An informal meeting of leaders of a party or group to select candidates or determine policy. K.E.H.

Caudillo.
Usually translated as "strong-man" or "man on horseback," the term refers to a characteristic form of political leadership in Hispanic nations, in which authority attaches to the individual, rather than to the institutions which he represents. Among the outstanding figures identified with the **caudillo** tradition are Juan Manuel Rosas and Facundo Quiroga of Argentina, Antonio Guzmán Blanco of Venezuela and Porfirio Díaz of Mexico in the nineteenth century, and Francisco Franco of Spain, Juan Peron of Argentina, Anastasio Somoza of Nicaragua and Rafael Trujillo of the Dominican Republic in the twentieth. Ch.W.A.

Causality.
Hume taught that reason alone could never establish that all events must have been caused by others or that any event actually had been so caused; we can state no more than that according to our sense experiences certain conjunctions of events do take place. Kant reversed the approach by his thesis that the human mind was unable to operate (or at any rate to acquire generalized empirical knowledge) without assuming that every change in phenomena must have a cause. More recently, microcosmic research has revealed unpredictable microcosmic events that are apparently not governed by universal laws, although accessible to statistical analysis and statistical probability calculus. Yet neither could it be scientifically established that there are any events that have no cause whatever. John Dewey saw in the concept of causation merely a "functional means of regulating existential inquiry" but maintained it as a "leading principle" for the purpose of social inquiry. Motivation is a special type of causation, distinct from physical or chemical causation by the potential interference of free will (free decision). Whether there is free will and how much of it is controversial. But, however that may be, the human will is certainly not so free as to be immune to outside influence. Research on the ways and means how human will (decisions) can be influenced (rational or irrational factors, conscious or subconscious influences, propaganda, advertising, terror, etc.) are of great significance for all social sciences. Whether "divine forces," "ends" or "purposes" set by supra-human powers cause events is a metaphysical question, which cannot be answered either affirmatively or negatively by strictly scientific methods. A.B.

Cavour, Camillo Benso di
(1810—1861).
Italian national hero. He dedicated his great diplomatic talents to achieve Italian unification. He became Prime

Minister of Sardinia in 1852 and took the country through a number of wars and diplomatic maneuvers which resulted in the proclamation of the Kingdom of Italy in 1861. G.K.

Cease and Desist Order.
In United States practice a cease and desist order is typically a command by an administrative body such as the Federal Trade Commission or National Labor Relations Board directing a party to refrain from certain conduct. Of the nature of an injunction, it is based upon the "salutory principle that when one has been found to have committed acts in violation of a law he may be restrained from committing other unlawful acts." (National Labor Relations Board v. Express Pub. Co., 312 U.S. 426, 436.)
T.C.S.

Cell.
Basic unit of the Russian Communist organization until 1939, when it was replaced by the "primary party organization." The term "cell" is still used in those Communist parties where conspiratorial tradition or need is strong. The fundamental revolutionary concept of the cell is that only one of its members (three to five) shall know the identity of a member of any other cell, thus reducing the possibility of informing. D.N.J.

Censorship.
The activities of government agencies to impose prior restraints on speeches, meetings, publications, motion pictures, plays, radio, television, and other forms of expression, based on material presumed either offensive to public morals, to incite to crime, or to endanger national security. Many prior restraints have been stricken down in the U.S.A. by the courts, but many persist under local authority. The same authority, even in more marked degree, is evident in most countries and is always intensified in time of war or national emergency. Prosecution in the courts after publication or exhibition is not regarded as censorship. Included in the concept, however, are the efforts of private organizations to ban the public distribution or showing of material offensive to them. R.B.

Censure Motion.
A motion moved by the leader of the opposition or some other opposition leader in British-type parliaments which states that a particular government policy should be disapproved. The mover of censure states the opposition's points of criticism and the prime minister or occasionally another government spokesman defends the government's policies. The government is obligated to allow time for such debate. Adoption of the motion would require resignation by the government or dissolution of the lower house. Other proposed amendments on regular legislative proposals or on government statements are similar in their effects, but they are not technically known as motions of censure. Other countries with parliamentary systems use some variety of censure motion, including Japan, India, Germany and France, but the latter two have major differences. R.H.B.

Census (to apportion representatives).
The number of persons in the United States as determined by the Federal government at first through the census office and now through the Census Bureau in the Department of Commerce. The population, as determined each ten years, is used as the basis of reapportionment of the seats in the United States House of Representatives. K.E.H.

Center Party (Zentrumspartei).
Founded to protect Catholic interests in the German Empire, it participated in the Weimar Coalition and all subsequent pre-Hitler governments. Essentially a non-ideological party of compromise, despite a general commitment to Catholic social and economic principles, it was the most stable party of the Weimar Republic, drawing support from all social and economic strata of the electorate.
C.J.S.

CENTO.
Central Treaty Organization. Originally termed Baghdad Pact by virtue of Mutual Security and Defense Agreement (later, economic cooperation) of Turkey and Iraq, Feb. 1955, joined by United Kingdom in April, Pakistan in Sept., Iran in Nov. same year. U.S.A. joined certain economic

and counter-subversive committees 1956, 1957, 1958, and sits as observer at Council meetings. Iraq withdrew in 1959 following its revolution and Headquarters were moved to Ankara.
J.P.D.

Central America.
Comprises British Honduras, Guatemala, El Salvador, Honduras, Nicaragua, Costa Rica, and Panama. R.B.G.

Central Committee of the C.P.S.U.
According to the Party Statutes the Central Committee of the C.P.S.U. directs the entire work of the party in the interval between Party Congresses. Because of its large membership (the 22nd Party Congress elected 175 full members and 155 candidate members) and its infrequent meetings(not less than once every six months), it cannot operate effectively as a policy-making body. Its real power is vested in the Presidium which it elects as the executive organ of the Communist Party and the Secretariat which it elects "to direct current work," or as in the Stalin-era, by the Secretary-General alone. However, if the party leaders on the Presidium are divided the Central Committee may overrule its Presidium. K.Hu.

Central Criminal Court.
See British Central Criminal Court.

Central Intelligence Agency (CIA).
Created as an adjunct of the National Security Council by the National Security Act of 1947, CIA superseded the National Intelligence Authority and Central Intelligence Group created by the President in 1946. Congress stipulated that CIA was to advise the NSC on foreign intelligence operations by the U.S. government, correlate and evaluate national security intelligence, perform "services of common concern" for the benefit of the many separate government intelligence units, and perform "other functions and duties" as directed by the President and NSC. The CIA has grown into a large, secret intelligence bureaucracy which by all possible means collects, evaluates and reports information to highest authority. CIA also conducts clandestine political action operations overseas. The CIA has no police, law enforcement or internal security functions in the United States. Its counter-intelligence functions are performed overseas. The Director of Central Intelligence has wide discretionary authority for maintaining secrecy for the Agency's operations, even from Congressional enquiry. Director and Deputy Director are appointed by the President with advice and consent of the Senate. H.H.R.

Centralization and Decentralization.
Centralization and decentralization are two polar ideal types, referring to complete concentration of decision-making in one person or unit and complete dispersal of decision-making between different persons or units respectively. Neither polar type exists in reality, but decision-making in various types of activity can be more centralized or more decentralized. There are three main types of centralization vs. decentralization: within a unitary organization ("delegation of authority"); between a headquarter unit and its sub-units; and between central units and autonomous lower-level units. (Some authors use the terms "concentration" and "decentralization" to refer to one or another of these types.) General political science is mainly concerned with the third type, involving the degree of local self-government vs. subordination to the central government. Administrative sciences are mainly concerned with the first and second type, involving the authority structure and decision-making system of organizations. Y.D.

Central Planning Commission or Ministry.
A body charged with socio-economic planning on a national basis. Its status may vary from that of Cabinet Ministry (as in India or the U.S.S.R.) to an adjunct bureau of a Ministry or an independent Commission. Within the context of actual administrative power, the Commissions' responsibilities within the government may vary from supervision and control (U.S.S.R.) to coordination and/or planning alone.
M.W.W.

Certiorari, writ of.
An order from an appellate court to a lower court directing that the rec-

ords of a case be sent up for review. The writ is issued at the discretion of the higher court, subject to statutory provisions. Nearly all cases reaching the United States Supreme Court do so on certiorari. The writ is in common usage throughout the Anglo-American system of jurisprudence, but it is not the only writ by which cases are brought to appellate courts.

C.R.A.

Ceylon.
Population: 8,097,895 (1953 Census). Area: 25,332 square miles. An island south of India, Ceylon was a British Colony until it became a self-governing member of the Commonwealth of Nations on February 4, 1948. Like most Commonwealth nations, its government is headed by a Crown-appointed Governor-General. He is advised by a Council of Ministers, headed by a Prime Minister. Ceylon has the distinction of having the world's first woman Prime Minister, Mrs. Sirimavo Bandaranaike. The bicameral Parliament is composed of 151 elected representatives; half the members of the upper house are nominated by the Governor-General. The parliamentary strength of political parties as a result of the March 1960 general elections is as follows: United National Party (50 seats); Sri Lanka Freedom Party (46); Tamil Federation Party (15); People's United Front (10); Equality Party (10); Ceylon Democratic Party (4); Communist Party (3). Tea, rubber and coconuts account for ninety-five per cent of the export trade and occupy two-thirds of the employed population. In 1959, Ceylon launched a Ten-Year Development Plan. Literacy and living standards are among the highest in Asia. Over seventy per cent of Ceylon's population is Sinhalese, mostly Buddhist; twenty-one per cent are Tamil-speaking Hindus, almost half of whom are resident South Indians. This has posed a serious problem for Ceylon, where Sinhalese-Tamil communal rioting periodically erupts, and political issues are affected.

S.K.A.

Chaco War.
Between Bolivia and Paraguay (1932—1935) over disputed territory in the Gran Chaco, an area of over 100,000 square miles west of the Paraguay River. American states and the League of Nations attempted to stop the fighting, but it was not until June, 1935 that the United States and several other nations in the Western Hemisphere brought about a truce. The treaty, signed July 21, 1938, gave Paraguay the major share of the Chaco, but Bolivia was granted access to the upper Paraguay River, and also use of Puerto Casado as a free port in the Paraguayan Chaco.

R.B.G.

Chad.
A republic in Central Africa; area 513,600 square miles; population 2,736,500 (1960 estimate). It was formerly a territory of French Equatorial Africa, its inhabitants being granted French citizenship in 1946. It became independent within the French Community on August 11, 1960, through an agreement between the French Prime Minister and the Prime Minister of Chad. It is virtually a one party state, with the Union pour le Progres du Tchad controlling the great majority of seats in the National Assembly. Francois Tombalbaye is now President.

E.V.M.

Chain Ballot.
A method (also called Tasmanian Dodge) used in vote buying. A corrupt politician secures an unmarked paper ballot, marks it for his candidates or party, gives it to a voter who secures an unmarked ballot from precinct election officers; in the voting booth he switches ballots, then deposits the previously voted ballot in the ballot box and returns the other to the vote buyer, receives his bribe, and the chain starts again with another voter.

J.E.R.

Chairman of the U.S.S.R. Council of Ministers.
Often referred to as the Premier of the U.S.S.R. Appointed to an unfixed term of office by the Supreme Soviet. Actually selected by the Presidium of the Central Committee of the C.P.S.U. on the recommendation of the Party First Secretary. When one individual is simultaneously chairman of the Council of Ministers and First Secretary (formerly Secretary General) of

the Central Committee, he is able to wield tremendous power over his colleagues. The Chairman recommends members of the Council for appointment by the Supreme Soviet Presidium. Theoretically, he is responsible to the Supreme Soviet for the conduct of the entire Council. May be removed from office by the Supreme Soviet. A recognized Party leader has never been removed. Chairmen have included Lenin (1917—1924), Rykov (1924—1930), Molotov (1930—1941), Stalin (1941—1953), Malenkov (1953—1955), Bulganin (1955—1958), Khrushchev (1958—   ). K.Hu.

Chamberlain, Houston Stewart (1855—1927).

An extreme advocate of Germanic-Teutonic race superiority, the British born German writer Chamberlain inspired much of the Twentieth Century German political romanticism. In **Die Grundlager des Neunzehnten Jahrhunderts** (1899) he emphasized the creative and organizing talents of the Teutons on European civilization. He felt that unless there was a restoration of Teutonic racial purity this civilization would fall like the Roman.
R.W.T.

Chamberlain, Neville.

Born 1869, died 1940. A member of a prominent British business class family, long active in politics, Neville Chamberlain was named Prime Minister in 1937. Under his administration, military preparations were accelerated while Chamberlain undertook, personally, to deal with Hitler. The Munich agreement and the policy of appeasement are associated most closely with Chamberlain's name. The early disasters of World War II caused his downfall and he was replaced by Winston Churchill in 1940. Ch.C.M.

Chambre des deputis. Chamber of Deputies. See France—Chamber of Deputies.

Chang Hsueh-liang (1898—   ).

Known as "the Young Marshal," Chang Hsueh-liang succeeded his father, Chang Tso-lin, as Commander in Chief of Chinese forces in Manchuria in 1928, when the elder Chang was assassinated by the Japanese. In 1936, troops under the command of Chang Hsueh-liang kidnapped Generalissimo Chiang Kai-shek in the celebrated Sian Incident. The object was to compel Generalissimo Chiang to fight the invading Japanese, instead of Chinese Communist forces. Negotiations at Sian effected Chiang's release and precipitated further discussions between Nationalists and Communists which ended, in 1937, in the adoption of the "United Front" agreement by which both Chinese groups agreed to cooperate against Japan. Chang Hsueh-liang has been kept in the custody of the Nationalist Government since, on the mainland, and, after 1949, on Taiwan (Formosa).
S.L.A.

Chang Tso-lin (1876—1928).

Chinese warlord in Manchuria, close to the Japanese. Created a Marshal by the Peking government in 1920, he turned against it in 1922 and took control. Driven from Peking by another warlord with Kuomintang backing in 1928, he was assassinated by the Japanese as he fled north. G.O.T.

Chapultepec, Act of.

A declaration made in Mexico City March 6, 1945 by the Inter-American Conference on War and Peace that an act of aggression against an American state during the war would be considered an act of aggression against all, and would call for joint consultation to determine common action against the aggressor. The Act also made clear that this was a regional arrangement not in conflict with the aims of the United Nations. The Act was given additional validity in the Inter-American Treaty of Reciprocal Assistance signed September 2, 1947 at Rio de Janeiro to cover peacetime as well as war. R.B.G.

Charge.

In law, the judge's instructions to the jury before it retires to deliberate. In charging the jury the judge always defines the elements of the crime (or the issues at law, in a civil case). He will instruct the jury of the legal requirements for a finding of guilt. Especially in civil cases which are frequently complex the charge may also include a definition of the issues of a

fact and a reminder to the jury about the place of the burden of proof.
F.H.H.

Charismatic leader.
A term from Max Weber, used to describe a politician to whom more than natural qualities of leadership are attributed by his followers. Weber identifies charisma as one of the three main justifications of political authority. The other bases on which people accept the legitimacy of authority over them are legality and tradition. Modern mass political parties generally require a charismatic leader if they are to maintain solidarity and discipline for they are not instruments of law and they represent a break away from traditionalistic authority.
I.d.S.P.

Charles River Bridge v. Warren Bridge.
In the Dartmouth College Case the United States Supreme Court decided that a charter granted by a state to private persons was a contract protected against impairment by the United States Constitution. The Charles River Bridge Case, 11 Pet. 420 (1837) limited this rule by applying to the contract clause the principle that public grants will not be extended by implication; rather they will be strictly construed against the grantee. This case typifies the transition from the Marshall to the Taney Court.
T.C.S.

Charter.
The organic law of a city, drafted by, or under authority emanating from, the state legislature. Normally, fixes the city's form of government, boundaries, powers, and their method of exercise, and extent of the city's jurisdiction. Sometimes understood to include pertinent judicial decisions and constitutional and statutory provisions.
P.J.C.

Charter of Punta del Este.
The major official document emanating from the special meeting of the Inter-American Economic and Social Council at the Ministerial level held in Punta del Este, Uruguay, from August 5 to 17, 1961. In it the American Republics, including the United States, agreed to establish an Alliance for Progress ostensibly designed to stimulate, improve, and strengthen democratic institutions, accelerate economic and social development, carry out urban and rural housing programs, encourage agrarian reform, assure fair wages, eliminate illiteracy, improve health conditions, reform tax laws, maintain sound monetary and fiscal policies, stimulate private enterprise and generally hasten the economic and social development of Latin America.
R.J.S.

Charter Revision.
The San Francisco Charter adopted in 1945 fell short of the expectations of the smaller nations. Article 109 of the U.N. Charter provides for a General Conference (called by two-thirds vote of the General Assembly and seven Security Council members) to prepare revision of the Charter, to be ratified by two-thirds of the membership including the Security Council permanent members. In 1955, the proposal to call a General Conference was not supported in the General Assembly and no amendments have transpired. The Organization has nevertheless developed through interpretation, non-application and supplementary agreement. Amendments concerning voting procedures, Security Council composition, General Assembly functions have been proposed ("United World Federalists" advocate radical revision creating a world legislature and executive with enforcement powers).
F.B.G.

Checks and Balances.
The term refers to the technique used by organs of government to oppose each other in the exercise of their constitutional powers so as to prevent unilateral actions which they consider either unconstitutional or undesirable as measures of public policy.

Such opposition renders the exercise of powers ineffective ("checks") or induces one organ of government to consent to sharing its power with another ("balances").

All theories of checks and balances derive from the assumption, supposedly verified by history, that, as Lord Acton put it, "political power tends to corrupt and absolute power tends to corrupt absolutely." The consequent necessity of limiting government finds its foremost expression in checks and balances. Being indispensable to constitutional government, they provide the standard equipment of every genuine constitution.

Checks and balances appear in connection with the mixed constitution; separation of powers; and independent of either system.

Historically, they seem to have been, first, linked up with the mixed constitution by which is meant a system so structured as to combine the elements of monarchy, aristocracy, and democracy by distributing political **power** more or less equally among them. In the absence of such combination, it is believed, these "pure" forms of government would degenerate into their corrupted counterparts, tyranny, oligarchy, and mob rule.

In antiquity, Polybius attributed the ascendancy of Rome to the merits of its constitution which conformed to the mixed pattern. Under it, the consul, the senate, and the people represented the monarchical, aristocratic, and democratic element, respectively. Whether under his interpretation the underlying social classes were "mixed," with each class represented by a different organ of government, or, on the contrary, only the monarchical, aristocratic, and democratic "principles," **is** disputed. In any event, it is Polybius' analysis of conflict and cooperation among the three organs of government that makes him one of the foremost expositors of the concept of checks and balances although its details may not always have corresponded to the realities of Roman constitutional life.

In modern times, British government from the Restoration of the Stuarts to the advent of democracy in the 19th century exhibited features of the mixed constitution based on the blending of social classes and supplemented by checks and balances. Ironically, even before 1660, its most eloquent defender was Charles I whom the House of Commons found guilty of erecting "an unlimited and tyrannical power." The King's position is contained in his answer to the Nineteen Propositions by **which the Long** Parliament attempted to concentrate all power in itself. He said that England enjoyed under its mixed constitution the advantages of monarchy, aristocracy and democracy, as represented by the King, the House of Lords and the House of Commons, without any of the disadvantages commonly attached to such pure forms of government. He concluded by rejecting the Nineteen Propositions on the ground that they ran counter to the system of checks and balances under which the mixed constitution operated.

Following Montesquieu, the Constitution of the United States has supplemented separation of powers (q.v.) with checks and balances among the three departments of government. However, the older concept of checks and balances supporting a mixed constitution as a system which distributes power among social classes still lingered on. John Adams was one of the most outspoken admirers of the British system and, therefore, favored bicameralism (q.v.) as a means of protecting and containing the democratic and aristocratic elements, both represented as classes in the House of Representatives and the Senate, respectively.

It is obvious that checks and balances modify separation of powers, a concept which means, among other things, that one department of government should not control or interfere with the functions of another. However, as Madison explained, the principle of separation of powers did not require that the three departments should be wholly unconnected with each other.

To the Fathers checks and balances appeared indispensable because separation of powers alone could not be relied upon to prevent too much democracy, frowned upon by the majority of the Founders, especially if it resulted in legislation adversely affecting the interests of property owners and creditors.

Checks and balances in the Constitution are familiar. Those operating on the Congress, include the power of the President to veto legislation and that of the Supreme Court to declare it unconstitutional. Among checks and balances operating on the executive are over-riding the veto by a two-thirds majority of both houses; congressional prerogative to declare war;

senatorial consent to appointments and treaties; and impeachment. The judiciary is subject to such checks and balances as the exercise of the Congressional power to determine the appellate jurisdiction of the Supreme Court; constitutional amendments reversing—in effect—the Court's decisions; and impeachment.

In addition to these "interorgan controls," some checks and balances are constituted as "intra-organ controls" (the terms are Karl Loewenstein's), such as bicameralism (q.v.).

Checks and balances which have developed as conventions of the Constitution (q.v.) include the role of parties; the committee system; the powers of the Congress to investigate; senatorial courtesy; detailed appropriations; dispensation of patronage by the President; his increasing influence on legislation; and the growing policy-making function of the Supreme Court.

Adopting a parliamentary vote of non-confidence in the cabinet to be met by the latter's counter-move to dissolve the parliament (cf. "Parliamentarism"), are typical examples of checks and balances outside the spheres of the mixed constitution and separation of powers.

In evaluating checks and balances, it may, indeed, be said that "nothing certainly would be more wrong than the belief that a well-constructed constitution incorporating a system of checks and balances is all that is needed to insure the internal stability of a country and to make it secure against any kind of violent internal upheaval" (von Fritz). Final judgment on the utility of individual checks and balances will be determined by the spirit which produced and applied them and by the nature of the social and political values they were intended to advance. **W.F.**

Chiang Kai-shek (1886—   ).
Chinese Military leader and statesman. Chiang Kai-shek was born in Chekiang Province in South China. At an early age he was sent to Japan to attend the Japanese Military Academy. While there he made the acquaintance of Dr. Sun Yat-sen and several other leaders of the Chinese revolutionary movement. After the overthrow of the Manchu Dynasty, Chiang served as Dr. Sun's military advisor. After the death of Sun in 1925 Chiang gradually emerged as the leader of the Kuomintang (the Naticnalist Party) as well as the head of the government. In 1927 he led his army in the famous North March to Nanking, and then split with several elements of the Kuomintang, among them the Communists. Between 1927 and 1937 Chiang defeated and eliminated most of the war-lords in his country. The Communists were saved only by the defection of Marshal Chang Hsieh Liang, in 1936, and by the large-scale invasion of China by Japan in 1937. In the war with Japan, Chiang was the recognized leader of China. He correctly predicted that Japan would eventually make a mistake that would prove to be her downfall. Between 1945 and 1949 his efforts to defeat the Communists failed, and he was forced to move to Formosa, where his government is now located. **W.C.C.**

Chiang Kai-shek, Mme.
(Soong Mei-ling, 1897—   ).
Youngest daughter of Chinese Christian financier Charles Jones Soong, and a Phi Beta Kappa graduate (1917) of Wellesley College, Soong Mei-ling became the second wife of Generalissimo Chiang Kai-shek in December 1927. Since then, she has written a number of books, and has served her husband as interpreter, and as goodwill emissary to the United States.

The Soongs rank as one of China's most notable families. Brother T. V. Soong has served in Cabinet level positions in the Nationalist Government of China, as has H. H. Kung, husband of sister Ai-ling. A third sister, Chingling, married Dr. Sun Yat-sen, founder of the Nationalist Party (Kuomintang), and is now a Vice-Chairman of the People's Republic of China (Red China) on the mainland. **S.L.A.**

Chief Administrative Officer.
1. An official most frequently found in large cities operating under the strong-mayor-council plan, usually appointed by the mayor and responsible to him, who commonly coordinates the work of departments and gives management and technical advice to

the mayor. Other activities carried on by some CAO's include the supervision of long-range planning by departments and the making of management surveys. In some cities the CAO has extensive appointive and removal powers.

2. A county official, appointed by the governing board, who is responsible for the general direction of county administration. Unlike a county manager, his influence in appointments and budget preparation is normally confined to making recommendations thereon to the county board. D.W.Mc.

Chief Justice.

The presiding or principal judge of a multi-judge court may be called the chief justice.

The Chief Justice of the U.S. Supreme Court presides over both the formal sessions and conferences of the Court. He assigns the writing of opinions when he is a member of the majority. His many other duties include: (1) administrative duties for the Court, (2) assignment of justices to certain courts, (3) reassignment of justices under certain conditions, (4) miscellaneous duties prescribed by Congress, and (5) serving as presiding officer of the Judicial Conference of the U.S.
W.F.G.

Chile.

A Latin American state; area, 286,397 sq. mi.; population (1960), 7,627,000. Under the Constitution of 1925 Chile is a unitary state. There is a popularly-elected Congress, composed of a Senate and a Chamber of Deputies, both elected by a system of proportional representation. The President of the Republic is elected to a six-year term. Leading political parties are the Liberal, Radical, Conservative, Socialist, Christian Democrat, and Communist. Chile is a firmly democratic nation. The President is Jorge Alessandri Rodriguez, whose term expires in 1964. F.M.L.

China, Republic of.
See Formosa.

China Incident.

On July 7, 1937, Japanese troops attacked Chinese troops at the Marco Polo Bridge near Peking. The Chinese resisted. There ensued hostilities which the Japanese chose to call "the China Incident." That designation, tacitly accepted by the Chinese, implied that those hostilities were not "war," and it served usefully to that effect for several years. The Japanese declared it their purpose to "bring Chiang Kai-shek to his knees"; and, later, to "establish a Greater East Asia Co-prosperity Sphere." Between 1937 and 1941, Japan's armed forces occupied most of the eastern part of China and disregarded in many contexts the rights and interests of other countries. In 1941 they attacked simultaneously territories in the Pacific of the United States, of Great Britain and of the Netherlands. This brought those countries into action against Japan. China forthwith declared war on Japan, and the hostilities in China became those of belligerents. Technically, those developments terminated the "China Incident": Japan's effort to conquer China had involved her in a major conflict, a war, which resulted in her defeat and emergence of her intended victim as one of the "Big Five" among the victorious allies. St.K.H.

China under the Kuomintang (1928—1949).

A combination of an uneasy coalition under Chiang Kai-shek, the Chinese Nationalists had brought national unity and economic development to mainland China until the Japanese began their large-scale invasion in 1937. The Kuomintang (Nationalist Party) achieved tariff autonomy (1930), abolition of unequal treaties (1943), balanced the Chinese budget (1932), developed education, transportation and light industry, and advanced China's international position. This benevolent oligarchy of modernizers proved the first successful government for China in the twentieth century. Subsequently in the wake of protracted war both against the Japanese and the Communists, the Nationalists lost popular support, particularly of the peasants and intellectuals. Their reforms were too late and inadequate, morale and discipline declined, and the Communists assisted by Soviet-supplied Japanese arms and their own effective organization built up during the war against Japan defeated the war exhausted armies of Chiang Kai-shek. The Nationalists moved their government to Taiwan in December 1949. R.L.W.

China—Warlords and Shadow Governments (1912—1928).
From the collapse of Manchu authority in 1912, until the reunification of China under the Nationalists, the formal government in Peking had ten heads of state and thirty-nine premierships. China itself was divided among autonomous military leaders (**tuchun**), each backed by different combinations of local interests and foreign powers. The farcical changes in Peking reflected the politics of anarchy and warlord ambitions throughout the land. The period was marked by imperialistic pressures, international intrigue (particularly on the part of the Comintern), intellectual ferment and economic destruction. Despite internal chaos, a small group of astute diplomats were able to represent China abroad as a unified country. Some advances were made in education, and a movement for national unity developed. R.L.W.

China White Paper.
Name usually given to **United States Relations with China with Special Reference to the Period 1944-1949** (Washington: U.S. Government Printing Office, 1949), Department of State Publication 3573, Far Eastern Series 30. The "White Paper," containing 409 pages of text and 641 pages of appendixes, was published in August, 1949, shortly after the Chinese Communists had conquered north China and had begun the conquest of the south. The purport of the book was that the Communist success in China was not the consequence of American policies but rather the result of political and military mismanagement, poor planning, and corruption in the Chinese Nationalist regime. The appended letter of transmittal asserted that the defeat of the Nationalists could not be attributed to a shortage of weapons or lack of American help. T.Mc.N.

Chinese Communist Five Year Plans.
See Red Chinese Five Year Plans.

Chinese Communist Party.
The Chinese Communist Party started with a handful of intellectuals in Peking University who formed a study group called the Institute of Marxism around 1919. Professors Chen Tu-hsiu and Li Ta-Chao were leaders of the group who provided inspiration for the ever-eager learners, like Mao Tse-tung, a member of the University library staff. The party was initially organized in 1921 at Frenchtown, Shanghai. Chen Tu-hsiu was elected General Secretary of the party.

Following the Peace Conference of 1919, Chinese students in Europe, like their counterparts elsewhere, were disappointed with the Versailles Treaty provisions pertaining to giving former German rights in China to Japan. As a result of these gatherings, Chou En-lai in Paris and Chu Teh in Berlin took steps to organize communist cells.

The Chinese Communist Party in its Second Congress in 1922 decided to join the Third International. Upon this entry, the Comintern ordered the Chinese Communists to join the Kuomintang. The Kuomintang-Communist "entente" lasted from 1924 to 1927.

From 1927 to 1934 the Communist Party suffered severe losses at the hands of the nationalists, but achieved success by maintaining contact with Moscow and learning mass leadership and guerrilla warfare in a small isolated region in Central China where it established a Chinese Soviet Republic under the leadership of Mao Tse-tung.

In 1934, the pressure of the Nationalist blockade of the Chinese Soviet Republic caused the "long march" to Yenan in Northwest China.

It started with 90,000 men but ended up with barely 20,000 who reached Yenan in October, 1935. Once in Yenan, they entrenched themselves among the peasantry. Since 1936 the Communists profited from Japan's effort to conquer all of China. They accepted an offer to join the Nationalist government in resisting the common enemy, and the Red forces, now named Eighth Route Army, received Central Government aid for waging guerrilla warfare behind Japanese lines.

As soon as Japan, the common enemy, was disposed of in 1945 the Communists went out of their way to court the favors of the Marshall Mission. While the Russians ostensibly kept aloof in the ensuing Chinese civil war, they saw to it, however, that the military supplies of the surrendering Japanese divisions in Manchuria would fall into Chinese Communist hands. By October 1, 1949, the Communist Party had won complete control of the mainland. L.M.L.

Chinese Communist Youth League.
See Red Chinese Communist Youth League.

Chinese People's Republic—Minor Political Parties.
At the time of the proclamation of their rule in China in 1949, the Chinese Communists sorely needed the support of the intellectuals. They therefore proclaimed a "united front" government in which eight minor political parties were to play a part. These parties represented intellectual and special interest groups: Revolutionary Committee of the Kuomintang (organized in 1947), China Democratic League (1945), China Democratic National Construction Association (1945), China Association for Promoting Democracy (1945), Chinese Peasants and Workers Democratic Party (1927), Chinan Chih Kung Tang (1926), Chiu San Society (1945), Taiwan Democratic Self-Government League (1947). Within a few years these minor parties had ceased to function except in name, and in 1957, following a period when some of their leaders dared to criticize Communist rule, they were told that if they failed to follow the directives and leadership of the Communist Party of China they were doomed to extinction. Their functions had become extinct by then anyway; for by then the united front had served its purpose. In the history of Communist rule in mainland China the minor political parties actually played an insignificant role. R.L.W.

Chinese People's Republic—Organic Law.
Adopted by the Chinese People's Political Consultative Conference in September 1949, it served as the legal basis for the organization and running of the Chinese Communist State until the adoption of the Constitution in 1954. Under the Constitution a new Organic Law was adopted and proclaimed in December 1954. This is the basis for the operation of the formal state structure. Actual control, however, remained in the hands of the leadership of the Chinese Communist Party. R.L.W.

Chinese Revolution of 1911.
At the turn of the century when the Manchu dynasty disintegrated, Tung Men Hui (predecessor of Kuomintang) agents in various centers were clandestinely active in attempts to overthrow the regime. On October 10, 1911, a plot organized in Wuchang caught fire and turned into a nationwide revolution.

The helpless Manchu regime, betrayed by its own field commanders, was forced to abdicate the "Dragon Throne."

Sun Yat-sen, leader of the revolution, having returned from abroad, was elected provisional President at Nanking. L.M.L.

Chinese Soviet Republic.
Comintern policy authorized the establishment of Soviets in China as early as 1927. The first major Soviet government to be established was set up in Kiangsi Province in 1931. In November of that year, the First All China Congress of Soviets was convened at Juichin and the Constitution of the Chinese Soviet Republic was approved. A Central Committee of 61 members with Mao Tse-tung as chairman was also elected.

The Kiangsi Soviet district consisted of about seventeen hsien along the Kiangsi-Fukien border. Its population is estimated to have been around three million. The Chinese Soviet Republic was proclaimed by the Communists to be a "democratic dictatorship of the proletariat and peasantry." A land reform program and other social reforms were carried out but the Communists moved cautiously to avoid alienating the populace.

The Kiangsi Soviet was constantly under military attack by the forces of the Kuomintang and eventually the Communists were forced to evacuate the region (in October of 1934) and to begin the "long march" to a new base in Shensi Province. S.S.

Chou En-lai.

Born in 1898, Chou En-lai came from a mandarin family of southern origin. Studied at Nan-Kai, Tien-Tsin, and in France.

One of the Communist leaders, Chou is noted for his administrative ability and diplomatic skill. When the People's Republic was organized, in 1949, he became its Premier and Foreign Minister.   L.M.L.

Chrisholm v. Georgia.

United States Supreme Court decision (1793) holding that a suit brought against a state without its consent by a citizen of another state was within federal court jurisdiction. The Constitution (Art. III) provides that judicial power of the United States extends to all controversies "between a State and citizens of another State" and that the Supreme Court has original jurisdiction in all cases "in which a State shall be Party." Several states, including Georgia, had resisted paying previously incurred British debts and refused to permit collection suits in their own state courts. Argument centered on the question whether the Constitution intended authorizing suits against "sovereign" states in federal courts. Four of the five justices writing opinions in the case agreed that states were not immune from such suits. Because of widespread adverse reaction, Congress in 1794 formulated and submitted to the states a proposed constitutional amendment which in effect reversed the decision. On January 8, 1798, President Adams announced that this amendment, the Eleventh, denying jurisdiction to federal courts of suits against a state by citizens of another state or by citizens of foreign nations, had been approved by the necessary three-fourths of the state legislatures.   C.F.N.

Christian-Democratic Union (CDU).

One of the two major West-German parties. Successor to most earlier non-socialist German parties. Backed by all strata but more strongly by middle classes than by labor, women than men, Catholics than Protestants. Strongholds: Rhineland; Bavaria (where separately organized as Christian-Social Union, CSU). Party chairman Konrad Adenauer. Chief federal government party since 1949. Stands for free market economy with traditional German welfare state features (social security); for denominational schools and education in the Christian spirit; Western-oriented, for Atlantic Alliance, Western European integration, strong German share in Western military setup. About 300,000 dues-paying members, financial support by industry.   J.H.H.

Christianity.

Christianity is the message or gospel taught by Jesus Christ in Palestine, during the reign of the Roman Emperor, Tiberius. It has been continued through history by the men he chose as apostles and their successors. The central teaching of the Christian religion is the Incarnation of God the Son, the Second Person of the Trinity. Christ proclaimed himself the Messiah and taught the people of his day the essentials of divine revelation. He died by crucifixion and rose from the dead on the third day thereafter, in proof of his claim.

Today, Christianity is divided into a number of sects which include: the various Protestant denominations, the Orthodox, and the Roman Catholics. Concern for Christian unity, one of the crucial problems of the age, is manifested in the burgeoning ecumenical movement.   Pa.B.

Christian Socialism.

A nineteenth-century intellectual movement in Western Europe which attempted to assert the relevance of Christianity to the problems of an increasingly industrialized and urbanized society. It is reflected in such nineteenth-century documents and movements as **Rerum Novarum,** papal encyclical of 1892; the English Christian Socialist movement (1848-1852) and subsequent related movements within the Church of England; and theological treatises on the continent of Europe by such writers as Friedrich Schleiermacher and Albrecht Ritschl. Common to all segments of Christian Socialism is concern for the spiritual dignity and material well-being of the individual in a capitalistic, mass-production economic system which produced sub-standard living and working conditions for the masses of industrial workers. By the twentieth century the movement had begun to take various social and political forms in various nations. Christian democratic trade unions were organized in France, Italy and Germany. Current Catholic democratic political parties include the Christian Democratic Union in Germany, Christian Democratic Party in Italy, and the **Mouvement Republicain Populaire** in France. E.R.W.

Chungking.
Has a long history since 4th century B.C.; as Yu Chow in ancient time. Built on a rocky triangle of land between Kialing River and Yangtze River; 1500 miles up the Yangtze from Shanghai; separated from the Plains of Lower Yangtze by more than 50 rapids of the Yangtze Gorges, the most beautiful natural scenery of China. The commercial center and richest city of the mountainous Southwestern China. Opened as a treaty port to outside world by Sino-British Treaty of Chefoo in 1876 and the Treaty of Peking of 1890. Became wartime capital of China, November 20, 1937 to May 1, 1946. Though "foggy" season lasted September to April, suffered extensive damages by Japanese bombings, 1938-41, which stopped abruptly after the Pearl Harbor Incident. Many lives were saved by some 1200 caves dug into limestone ridges along the river banks. Steamer navigation developed in late 1920's was a great contribution for the shift from Nanking to Chungking; and none of the steamer pilots defected to the Japanese side. Growth of population: 1927—208,294; 1950—1,038,683; 1958 — 1,700,000. Communist regime linked Chungking by rail to rest of China via Chengtu and Paoki.
C.K.W.

Church.
Church is derived from the Greek, meaning to call out or call together. It may refer to: 1) a place of worship, or 2) a body of Christians bound together by a common creed, code and cult.

For Roman Catholics, the Church is at once a visible and an invisible society; a juridical, hierarchical institution and a community of believers.

Protestant views cover a wide spectrum based on differing notions about the "unity-in-Christ" and "disunity as Churches."

The Orthodox agree with the Roman Catholics in maintaining that Christ bestowed spiritual authority upon the apostles and their successors, the bishops. They deny, however, that He gave supreme authority to St. Peter and his successors, the Bishops of Rome.

The church is distinguished from the state in origin, constitution, purpose, and the means employed to reach its end. Pa.B.

Churchill, Sir Winston Leonard Spencer (1874—).
British statesman and writer.
Winston Churchill was born into the Marlborough family, the son of Lord Randolph and his American wife. Sir Winston is considered by many to be one of the greatest political leaders of the world as well as a good writer (and a painter). He has been an "activist" ever since he was old enough to be noticed. In his early adult life he served in India, Cuba, and the Boer War. In 1900 he stood for election to the Parliament as a Conservative. Later he became a Liberal and served as the First Lord of the Admiralty in the Liberal Government during World War I. In the 1920's he returned to the Conservative fold, wrote and lectured on many topics. In the 1930's he warned against British acceptance of Neville Chamberlain's interpretation of Hitler's intentions. When the Second World War came he joined the Government to serve as the First Lord of the Admiralty again. In May of 1940 he succeeded Chamberlain as the Prime Minister of Great Britain, serving in that capacity until the end of the War in 1945. Through the darkest hours of the 1940's Churchill's determination, wit, and wisdom helped the British people see through their hardship. Several of his phrases became household words in Great Britain and elsewhere. After his retirement from active politics he turned his talents to writing (and painting). His six-volume memoirs on World War II and his **History of the English Speaking Peoples** are but two examples of his works. W.C.C.

Church of Finland.
The Evangelical Lutheran Church to which 92% of the population adhere. About 2% of the population belong to the Orthodox Church or to free churches, while about 6% are on the "civil register." The number of people belonging to no church is rapidly increasing. The supreme authority of the Church of Finland is vested in the Government and the President of the Republic. Bishops are appointed by the President of the Republic on the basis of elections held in each diocese. The bishop of Turku has the rank of Archbishop. The church has the right to collect taxes not only from all members of the church but from all corporations and other organizations. E.I.

Chu Teh (1886—).
Chairman of National People's Council Standing Committee of the Communist People's Republic of China. Born into a wealthy Szechuanese family, he received military training and joined the 1911 anti-imperial uprising. He went to Germany in 1922 where he became a Communist. Helped Mao Tse-tung organize military forces after the Communists were expelled by the Kuomintang. Leader of the Long March of 1934-6. Fought the Japanese and the Kuomintang Armies and become top military leader in the People's Republic.
G.O.T.

Cicero, Marcus Tullius (106—43 B.C.).
A Roman juris-consult who because of his ability to express himself popularized and preserved the thought of his day. Believing that a state is the property of the people and that it was created to promote justice and the common good, he made no distinction between the political and social organization. In his view, government, whatever its form may be, derives its powers from the people, and its decisions are law.

Cicero is best known for his expression of the idea of natural law. "True law is right reason in agreement with nature." Since it comes from God, it is universal, unchanging, and everlasting, and attempts to alter it are futile and sinful. One who violates it is attempting to flee from himself because it is part of nature, and for this reason he will suffer the worst of penalties even if he escapes what is commonly called punishment.

Cicero was not original in his thought, but he made the clearest and most logical presentation of the ideas that he expressed. The principal statements of his political thought are found in his **Republic** and his **Laws**.
D.C.

Circuit Courts.
Primarily state courts in the U.S., the judges of which travel on "circuit" and hold court in each of a number of counties which in 2/3 of the states make up the judicial district. In some states where there is a court in each county it is called a County Court, and in a few states it is called District Court. Number of judges in a judicial district varies according to population and amount of litigation but usually one judge is enough except in large cities. Judges are popularly elected in 36 states usually for 4 or 6 year terms. They stand above local courts and have broad original jurisdiction to handle important civil and criminal cases, as well as appellate jurisdiction of some less important cases from lower courts. They have also some administrative duties. Above these courts is the state's highest or supreme court although about 1/4 of the states have an intermediate court between the circuit and the highest court. In our federal systems of courts there are eleven circuit courts of appeal (the term "circuit" was dropped in 1948 but is still used), each consisting of from 3 to 9 judges and sitting between the District Courts and the Supreme Court. Their jurisdiction is largely appellate over federal cases, but they have some duties in connection with the work of regulatory agencies which is in the nature of original jurisdiction.
E.G.T.

Citizenship.
A citizen of a state is a person who is either born within the state, or born of parents who are citizens, or one who has acquired the status of citizen by application of the laws of the state providing for the naturalization of persons born in another state. Of recent

years the term "national" has come into use in place of "citizen," which in some states once had a restricted use.

Citizenship or nationality by birth applies without question to persons born within the state of parents who are themselves nationals of the state. The United States, Great Britain and most Latin American states adhere to the principle of **jus soli,** by which mere birth upon the soil is sufficient to confer nationality, irrespective of the nationality of the parents. By contrast, France, Germany, and other European states adhere primarily to the civil law principle of **jus sanguinis,** by which the nationality of children follows that of their parents, irrespective of their place of birth. In consequence, conflicts of jurisdiction may arise when a child is born on the soil of one state of parents who are citizens of another state. In many states both systems are held in varying degrees. Conflicts of jurisdiction are in most cases settled on the basis of giving priority to the state which, at the particular time, has **de facto** jurisdiction over the person. The conflict becomes of importance in connection with claims for injuries resulting from alleged denial of justice and in connection with the obligations of military service.

Citizenship or nationality resulting from naturalization is regulated by the law of each state in accordance with its own national interests. As a rule the national law fixes the conditions upon which citizenship by naturalization may be forfeited, as by return of the naturalized citizen to his country of birth or by permanent residence abroad.

The Act of Congress of 1922, known as the Cable Act, sought to protect American women from loss of citizenship by marriage to an alien, while providing that the marriage of an alien woman would not of itself give her citizenship. Cases of statelessness still arise by reason of varying national legislation. C.G.F.

Citizens Union of New York City.

The New York City Citizens Union, organized in 1896, is a nonpartisan political group interested in promoting efficient and honest government in New York City. Its activities include the publication of a monthly newsletter, "Across from City Hall," and an annual **Voters Directory** as well as general surveillance and persuasion of governmental officials in Albany and New York City. Membership is open to the public and the policies of the organization are determined by an Executive Committee. J.A.E.

City.

A municipal corporation occupying a definite area and serving a population concentration. While enjoying a greater degree of local autonomy than other local governments, the city is still subject to state supervision and control. G.S.B.

City Charter.

As local governments, cities in the United States are said to be "creatures of the State," and as such, their powers and rights are strictly limited. The grant of power which each city must have in order to govern itself is found in the city charter. A charter is a legal instrument enacted by the state legislature, or written by local citizens themselves in "home rule" states. This document must, with few exceptions, win the affirmative vote of a prescribed proportion of the voters of the proposed city before it becomes valid. The charter delineates the geographical boundaries of the city, describes its organization, specifies the officials who are to conduct its business, and gives explicit statements of the powers which the city legislative body may exercise. In any case involving the city charter, the courts interpret that document strictly and narrowly, following the dictates of the legal statement known as Dillon's Rule. A.E.N.

City Council.

The representative assembly of a city, chosen generally by popular election, and exercising the legislative powers of the city. Depending upon the form of government and local conditions, the council may exercise a greater or lesser degree of administrative power. Less frequently councils exercise judicial or quasi-judicial powers. P.J.C.

City-County Consolidation.
An attempt to meet mounting governmental problems by merging the governments of a city (or cities) and a county, thus reducing duplication of effort in the provision of governmental services. A rarely used device because of its unpalatability, although New York, Boston, and New Orleans were established in this manner.
P.J.C.

City-County Separation.
A device for meeting governmental problems by legally separating a city from the country in which it lies. The city will then perform some or all of the county services within the municipal boundaries. City dwellers are thus freed from disproportionate burden of cost of county services (as in Denver, Colorado).
P.J.C.

Civil Aeronautics Board.
An independent regulatory board, it owes its authority and structure to the Presidential Reorganization Plans of 1940 and the Federal Aviation Act of 1958. It is composed of 5 members appointed by the President by and with the advice and consent of the Senate. No more than three members can be of the same party affiliation.

Its prime purpose is to regulate the economic activities of domestic and international United States air carriers. In pursuance of this objective, it performs the following activities: authorizes both foreign and domestic carriers to engage in air transportation within the continental limits of the United States; regulates rates and fares charged the riding public; reviews mergers, acquisitions and working arrangements among competing airlines; controls unfair competitive practices in the industry and, finally, it issues rules and orders governing these aspects which are enforceable in the courts.

Secondarily, the Board, despite the assignment of the safety rule making function to the Federal Aviation Agency, is required to determine the probable cause of all air accidents. Its powers and decisions are not subject to review by any executive agency or department, except in the case of a grant of a certificate for foreign or overseas air transportation. Here the approval of the President is required.
B.B.

Civil Affairs Officer (United States Army or Navy).
A commissioned officer assigned to a unit charged with the military government of an occupied area, or the expediting of relations with a friendly government. Their individual specializations may embrace education, public utilities, communications, finances, medical or legal services, and other appropriate fields. Medical or Judge Advocate General officers assigned to these units, retain commissions in their appropriate services rather than in the Civil Affairs Branch.
M.P.S.

Civil Defense.
A public safety activity of governments designed in the event of an enemy attack to minimize damage, provide essential services and information, maintain law and order, and reconstruct damaged areas. Civil defense agencies operate warning systems and emergency broadcasting systems, educate the public, train and equip radiation detection monitors, and provide shelters.
J.F.Z.

Civil Disobedience.
Individual or group violation of laws, government policies or customs said to be unjust, civil disobedience is a technique of open protest used outside of courts or legislative channels. It may or may not have revolutionary intentions or results. With Gandhi, Tolstoy and Martin Luther King it is nonviolent and has a philosophy, though it may be only mechanical or condone violence.
P.F.P.

Civilization.
The sum total of intellectual, aesthetic, technological, and spiritual attainments of a particular society.
R.A.B.

Civil Law.
Civil law has several meanings. It can be used as a generic term to denote the rules of law that govern any given political community. In this sense, civil law is paramount to the concept of law itself. The term can also be used to differentiate the rules governing the private law relations be-

tween citizen and citizen from public law as a set of rules that determine the legal relations of private individuals and corporations in their dealings with the state. In this sense, the term civil law **(droit civil; Zivilrecht)** is used primarily on the European continent. To the Anglo-American lawyer civil law has yet a third meaning. It refers to the continental system of law which has taken its name **(jus civile)** and its principal elements from Roman law through the "reception" of the Justinian **Corpus Juris Civilis** that began in the twelfth century. In this sense, civil law is distinguished from the system of common law originally developed in England, and refers to a legal system culminating in and characterized by the codification of law in various countries of Europe (most famous, the French **Code Civil** or **Code Napoleon** of 1804) and other parts of the world, notably Latin America, Russia and Japan. H.R.H.

Civil Liberties.

That portion of the civil rights of citizens in a democracy embodied primarily in the principle of freedom from government interference with speech, press, association, and religion, together with freedom from unlawful searches, and with guarantees of fair trials in the courts. The concept of both civil rights and civil liberties is based on the sovereign equality of the people of a democracy as the source of governmental powers. R.B.

Civil Military Relations.

The area of study falling within the confines of both political science and military science which pertains to matters arising where military operations impinge on non-military governmental matters. Among the subjects covered by this definition are: civilian control of military forces; the role of the military in politics; military government of occupied areas; the interaction of civilian and military decision makers in foreign affairs; military participation in civilian activities such as maintenance of waterways, airways, and sea lanes; relationships between military procurement authorities and civilian officials in the economic field; relations between military procurement authorities and civilian industry; relations between the active armed services and the reserve forces of the armed services; relations between the armed services and the armed services committees of the legislative branch; and others. The element which makes civil-military relations a special field of study is the fact that in all civil-military relations there is an interaction between a more-or-less well-defined scale of military values and a dissimilar civilian scale of values.
T.W.

Civil Rights.

The body of rights of the citizen in relation to democratic governments, embodied in constitutions and laws, and presumably enforceable in the courts. In many countries, notably the U.S.A., they are constitutionally grouped in a Bill of Rights, guaranteeing freedom of the citizen against interference by the government in his political activities, with fair trials and due process of law.

In the U.S.A. the distinction commonly made between civil rights and civil liberties defines the former as racial equality before the law (the Civil War amendments to the Constitution) and the latter as the guarantees of the original Bill of Rights, particularly the first amendment, and those of the State constitutions. R.B.

Civil Service.

It comprises all the persons employed by government in a civil as contrasted with a military capacity. It is synonymous with "bureaucracy" in the European literature. In America the popular meaning is somewhat different. The term is used to include those positions in the public service which are filled and administered under the merit system as contrasted with the spoils system. Or it may be employed to distinguish those filled through open competitive examinations from those filled without competition. Elected officials are customarily excluded. H.W.

Civil Service Commission.
See U.S. Civil Service Commission.

Civil service of France.
See French civil service.

Civil Supremacy.
The constitutional principle requiring military authority to be subordinate to civilian public officials. In the U.S.A. this is effected by denoting an elected President as Commander-in-Chief of the Army and Navy and by the dependence of the military establishment upon Congressional appropriations. Concern over the merger of military and political decision-making positions arises periodically, as for example, in the present position of Supreme Commander of North Atlantic Treaty Organization forces, where diplomatic and strategic evaluations are not clearly separated. M.P.S.

Civil war.
A military conflict between two or more factions within a state seeking control of the government (e.g. Spanish Civil War) or in which a section or part is attempting to gain its independence by separating from the state (e.g. American Civil War). For civil war to be distinguished from insurrection or rebellion, the competing forces must be politically organized and able to support military forces capable of suggesting ultimate success. The outcome of civil war is either the subjugation of one or more factions, as in the American and Spanish Civil Wars; the successful separation of a section, as in the case of Belgium and the Netherlands; or a stalemate between the competing factions, as in the Wars of the Roses. C.W.B.

Class. (Stratification.)
The organization of society into vertical groupings based on one or more of the following: ownership of the means of production (Marx); income, occupation, education, power relations, kinship, race, religion; mode of life, prestige (status—Warner); ideas, attitudes and feelings towards the members of the group and those outside the group, etc. Class (stratification) theories tend to fall into two general categories: objective (point of view of the researcher) and subjective (point of view of the subject). Many modern sociologists take the position that no clear-cut delimitation of classes is possible, but that there exists a continuum based on prestige and power. D.N.J.

Class Struggle.
The theory of the existence of a permanent condition of social conflict between economic classes. The modern idea of class struggle can be traced back to the French Revolution, but the theory of class struggle is attributed to Marx and Engels, who wrote in the **Communist Manifesto:** "the history of all society up to now is the history of class struggle." Perhaps the strongest emotional appeal of Marxism has been based upon the concept of the class struggle and the impetus to action that supposedly derives from it. D.N.J.

Clausewitz, Karl von.
A 19th century German military strategist who, from 1818 until 1830, was Managing Director of the Military Academy at Berlin. His book **On War** is a classic of military strategy. In it he maintained that "war is nothing but the continuation of diplomacy by other means." He also placed great emphasis on an army's spirit and morale and held that physical forces were but the "wooden hilt," but "moral forces" were the "shining blade" of the sword. J.G.St.

Clayton Act.
Antitrust legislation by the Congress of the United States in 1914 to put teeth in the Sherman Act of 1890. The Act attempted to strengthen the Sherman Act by prohibiting price-cutting and rebates of various kinds, preventing the acquisition of stock by officials of one company in a competing company, the outlawing of interlocking directorates, and making officials of a concern liable personally for violations of antitrust legislation. The Act specified that antitrust laws should not be interpreted to forbid the operation of labor or farmer organizations as monopolies. R.G.S.

Clayton-Bulwer Treaty.
The Nicaraguan canal route controversy settlement between the United States and Great Britain, April 19, 1850, with each renouncing unilateral action or control. Abrogated by the Hay-Pauncefote Treaty. L.C.D.

Clear and Present Danger Doctrine.

A doctrine developed and used by the U.S. Supreme Court as a standard to determine the validity of the application or the constitutionality of statutes which restrict freedom of speech. The formulation of the doctrine first appeared in an opinion by Mr. Justice Holmes in **Schenck v. United States** (1919). "The question in every case," he wrote, "is whether the words used are used in such circumstances and are of such a nature as to create a clear and present danger that they will bring about the substantive evils that Congress has a right to prevent." Once the majority of the Court became aware of the implications and philosophy of the doctrine, they rejected it, leaving Justice Holmes and Brandeis to expound and develop it in their dissents. It was accepted by the Roosevelt Court and substantially extended in scope and application. However, in upholding the constitutionality of the Smith Act, the Court, in **Dennis v. United States** (1951), re-interpreted the doctrine. Since the Dennis decision, the doctrine has been eschewed by all members of the Court. P.B.

Clear and Probable Danger Test.

Dennis v. U.S. (1951) affirmed the use of the "clear and present danger" test but rejected it in principle. The Court substituted a clear and probable danger test, i.e., speech must constitute a definite and substantive danger to government but the danger need not be present in time. Speech which "is too remote from concrete action" will not be punished but speech carrying with it a future substantive danger to government constitutes sedition. W.F.G.

Clemenceau, Georges (the "Tiger") (1841—1929).

French political figure, doctor of medicine, and a militant republican in the Second Empire, member of the National Assembly in 1870, president of the Paris municipal council in 1875, and member of the national Chamber of Deputies to 1893; he was a leader of the radicals and a founder of the newspaper **L'Aurore** which defended Dreyfus after 1897; elected Senator from Var in 1902; became minister of the interior in 1906, and premier from October, 1906 to July 1909. Early in World War I he attacked national defense deficiencies; in November, 1917, he became premier and a principal architect of victory; in 1920 he was defeated as candidate for the President of the Republic, and he retired from public life. E.G.L.

Clerk.

The clerk is usually the chief recording officer of towns, cities, counties, and various special districts. In New England towns and in the counties of 25 states of the U.S.A. the clerk is elected. In cities appointment is the usual procedure. Archival and custodial duties are frequently allotted to this officer as well. New England town clerks occasionally are annually elected for over five decades. Where re-election or re-appointment is common the clerk becomes the chief repository of facts, business practices, information, gossip, and legal data for the government unit which he or she serves. A.E.N.

Cleveland, Grover (1837—1908).

A lawyer in Buffalo, New York, the twenty-second and twenty-fourth president of the United States first gained renown as reform governor (Democrat) of New York. He was twice elected to the presidency on the Democratic ticket, in 1884 and 1892. Cleveland advocated tariff reduction, opposed free silver, and supported civil service reform. A man of courage and integrity, Cleveland ranks among America's great presidents. Th.P.

Closed Primary.

The leading variation of the direct primary used in elections in most states in the United States. Some test of party affiliation is required, such as mere declaration of party preference through registration. Voting is limited to party members. Thus there is a primary election for most offices for each party. Nearly all states use the closed, rather than the open, primary for congressional nominations. About a dozen states use the open primary. The difference between the closed and open primary is not always very distinct. Sometimes the closed primary system is so loose it is nearly the equivalent of an open primary. A.G.

Closure.
A method of closing debate to secure a vote on a question. This is done by moving the previous question or by moving that "debate do now cease." Upon adoption of such a motion by the required majority of the body, debate ends, and the question is put to a vote. K.E.H.

Cloture.
Since the previous question has not been in order in the U.S. Senate since 1806 and no other method of closing debate existed from 1806 to 1917, the Senate adopted a special procedure in the latter year to close debate and stop a Filibuster under Rule XXII, commonly called cloture. The rule has been revised in 1949 and 1959 so that it now applies to all Senate measures including motions and rules and may be invoked after a petition is signed by 16 members, there is a two-day delay, 2/3 of those present and voting desire it, and time for a one-hour speech from each member is allowed. J.A.E.

Clout.
Slang. Influence with public officials, such that one who "has clout" is in a position to secure from such officials unwarranted or illegal favors (including immunity from punishment for wrongdoing). Commonly used in Chicago area. Generally synonymous with "drag" and "pull." D.W.Mc.

C.N.R.
See French resistance movement.

Coalition government.
A cabinet, or "government," made up of ministers selected from two or more minority parties in order to secure the support of a majority in the parliament. Coalition governments are usually found in multiparty systems in which no one party is able to command support of a working majority. (In time of war or other great national emergency, a **majority** party may invite minority party representatives to participate in the government in the interest of national unity and to avoid conducting elections during a time of national peril.) A coalition government tends to be unstable, vacillating and weak because of the absence of a strong and clear electoral mandate, the inherent lack of cohesiveness of its membership—reflecting as it does diverse and partisan viewpoints, and because of the need for accommodation to minority viewpoints as a price for parliamentary support. R.H.K.

Code.
A system of law; a systematic and comprehensive presentation of the law. Historically, the prototype is the Code of Justinian, the compilation of the Roman law ordered by the emperor Justinian and published in 529. Countries following in the Roman law tradition regularly embody their laws in a code. The practice also gained favor in common law countries in the 19th century and today a number of states in the United States have codes and federal legislation is periodically brought together systematically in the **United States Code.** F.H.H.

Codification.
As in domestic law practice codification in international law may mean consolidation of several instruments into one. Thus the Single Convention on Narcotic Drugs of 1961 consolidates with some significant changes nine instruments created between 1912 and 1953. Secondly, codification is also used in the sense of restatement in treaty form of existing customary international law in more systematic and precise form. Thirdly, it may also denote progressive development of international law. Usually restatement and progressive development go hand in hand as for instance in several of the early codifications (Hague Conventions of 1899 and 1907) or in contemporary efforts such as the Geneva Conventions on the Law of the Sea of 1958 or the Vienna Convention on Diplomatic Relations of 1961. Matters not regulated by the provisions of such a treaty continue to be governed by rules of customary international law. The United Nations created on November 21, 1947 the International Law Commission the task of which is to promote codification. L.G.

Cold War.
The investigation into the "causes" of the Cold War involves several factors, each important as a historical de-

terminant, though its relative significance is subject to disagreement. The expansion of the Soviet Union since 1945 into the heart of Europe has been the outstanding cause of the pervasive and irreconcilable antagonism between East and West which is now called the Cold War. The resulting tension has been further heightened by a fundamental ideological hostility between the communist camp and the Free World. Other factors have been involved as well: the challenging economic-military-political strength of the Soviet Union; the decreased international power of the Western European countries; the rise of Communist China as the leading power on the mainland of Asia; the continued division of Germany; and the difficulties and uncertainties occasioned by the postwar emergence of the politically significant underdeveloped regions. These factors have all served to exacerbate world tension and give to the Cold War its all-inclusive quality.

R.St-H.

Colegiado.

The plural executive of Uruguay, sponsored originally by the great Colorado Party statesman, Jose Batlle y Ordonez, who turned to the Swiss experience to put an end to the traditional domination of his country by the man who occupied the presidency. A controversial compromise form was tried from 1919 to 1933, and from 1939 to 1942. President Martinez Trueba revived the idea with the cooperation of the opposition Blanco Party; the 1951 Uruguayan Constitution provided for a nine-member National Council of Government (**colegiado**) and abolished the office of chief executive. The members, chosen by direct popular vote for four-year terms, are not immediately eligible for re-election. The majority party receives six of the seats; the remaining three seats are reserved for the leading opposition party, irrespective of its actual number of votes. Decision is by majority vote. Minority members have equal access to executive branch records, etc. On a rotating basis a majority party member serves for one year as chairman and titular chief of state.

R.D.H.

Coleman v. Miller.

307 U.S. 433; 59 S.Ct. 972; 83 L.Ed. 1385 (1939). Decision of the U.S. Supreme Court that in the absence of a stipulated time limit for ratification of a proposed amendment to the U.S. Constitution, Congress has the power to decide what constitutes a "reasonable" time limit. In addition, the Court upheld Congress's decision that a state may not withdraw a favorable action on an amendment, and stated that Congress also has the authority to determine the validity of state ratification after previous rejection.   R.V.A.

Collective Colonialism.

The term has become part of the Soviet lexicon since Khrushchev used it on February 26, 1960, during a visit to Indonesia. It describes the cooperative efforts of the Western Powers to preserve their foothold in Asia, Africa, and Latin America. It claims that the Western nations, no longer able individually to ensure their domination of underdeveloped areas, now coordinate their policies in order to associate the newly independent countries in military, economic, and political alliances and agreements which will be dominated by the West, and to retain a measure of control over the remaining colonial areas.   A.Z.R.

Collective recognition.

In the past the practice of recognition has followed fairly arbitrary rules of cooption which each state has developed on its own. Since the advent of the United Nations, the practice of "collective recognition" has gained currency. In the case of the birth of new states, such as Israel and Ghana, admission to the United Nations has become a kind of **imprimatur** by the world community. This rise of "collective recognition" may be a hopeful sign for the development of more uniform legal standards.   J.G.St.

Collective Security.

The guarantee of the territorial integrity and independence of each state by all states; institutions established to coordinate the common action of members in order to prevent or defeat any attack against international order. Such a system to be fully effective requires agreement on the particular status quo to be defended, acceptance of the sacrifices entailed, and sufficient power to cope with any combination of states likely to challenge the system. In addition, the system differs from an ordinary alliance in that it is directed not against a specific power but against any state which threatens the status quo. The League of Nations covenant erected such a system but, not only did it not forbid war altogether (Arts. 12, 13 [4] and 15 [6]), interpretative resolutions watered down the sanctions provision (Art. 16) in order to leave each member free to decide on its own course of action. The result was the evolution of a loose system of coordination. In direct contrast, the United Nations Charter sets up the Security Council as a powerful executive body which can determine the existence of a threat to the peace, breach of the peace or act of aggression; such determination is binding on all members and the council has the power to require the support of members in enforcing the peace. (Arts. 39-42). In practice the rule which requires the concurring votes of the permanent members of the Council (Art. 27) has produced a situation closely resembling the loose system of cooperation characteristic of the League of Nations. C.B.J.

Colombia.

Colombia is one of the biggest South American countries. Its territorial extension is 1,139,155 square kilometers and its population, according to the last census of 1951, is 11,641,586 inhabitants. The population today is calculated as 15,000,000 inhabitants. Colombia has had several names since her independence. At the time of independence, on July 20, 1810, the country was called "Nuevo Reino de Granada"; it was called "Gran Colombia," during the initial period of independence (1819—1831), at which time the territory included the present nations of Venezuela and Ecuador. Her first president was the Liberator Bolivar and the first vice-president was General Francisco de Paula Santander. It was called "La Nueva Granada" from 1831 to 1858, and "Confederacion Granadina" from 1858 to 1861, and "Estados Unidos de Nueva Granada" from 1861 to 1863, and "Estados Unidos de Colombia" from 1863 to 1886; and, finally, "Republica de Colombia" from 1886 until the present. Every period of political life of Colombia has been marked by strong social upheavals. Today, Colombia is passing through one of the most critical periods in its whole history. The present difficulties began on the 9th of April, 1948, when the liberal leader, Jorge Eliecer Gaitan, was assassinated. An attempt to solve the present social and political crisis began in 1958, with a government of joint responsibility between the conservative and liberal parties. The principal author of this solution was Alberto Lleras Camargo. B.M.P.

Colombian Political Parties.

There are in Colombia two political parties, liberal and conservative. Sometimes these two parties are divided into factions. Both political parties are said to have had their origin in the founding fathers, Bolivar and Santander. Each of the political parties has the same basic tendencies and values. The Conservative Party tends to emphasize authoritarianism and the moral values of the State. The Liberal Party tends to emphasize liberty in all aspects of political life and to regard the State as a free play of free wills. According to this interpretation, the Conservative Party tried to achieve the unitarian form of State during last century and the Liberal Party favored the Federative form. The principal leaders of the conservative party in the past were Jose Eusebio Caro, Manuel Ospina Rodriguez, Miguel Antonio Caro, Rafael Nunez, Rafael Reyes and Marco Fidel Suarez; today, they are Laureano Gomez and Mariano Ospina Perez. The principal leaders of liberalism in the past were Ezequiel Rojas, Vicente Azuero, Tomas Sipriano de Mosquera, Santiago Perez, Benjamin Herrera, Rafael Uribe, Olaya Herrera y Alfonso Lopez; today they are Eduardo Santos, Dario Echandia, Alberto Lleras Camargo y Lleras. Communism is an illegal political party. B.M.P.

Colombo Plan.

"Colombo Plan for Co-operative Economic Development in South and

South East Asia" was published in November, 1950, by the Commonwealth Consultative Committee on South and South East Asia. The original members of the Committee—Australia, Canada, Ceylon, India, Malaya, New Zealand, Pakistan, United Kingdom, British Borneo and Singapore—have since been joined by Vietnam, Laos, Cambodia, Burma, Nepal, Indonesia, Japan, Philippines and Thailand. The United States is associated with the Committee; the Economic Commission for Asia and the Far East (ECAFE) and the International Bank for Reconstruction and Development also cooperate. The Plan provides a recommended framework for development of the Committee's Asian members. Expenditure on development in the public sector of these members totalled £1,416m. in 1956 and rose to £2,019.4m. in 1961. Member countries enter bi-lateral agreements for financial aid. Technical co-operation schemes are administered by a council representing participating governments, including the United States. By 1960-61, 19,533 persons had received training under the program; up to June, 1961, technical assistance valued at £20.6m. had been provided.
S.K.A.

Colonelism.

A vestige of the Imperial National Guard of Brazil, the big proprietor or cattle-breeder is called **colonel**. Colonelism implies the ruling power of the colonels in Brazil's political life, a semi-feudal relationship between them and their dependents. These dependents provide the colonels with the harnessed vote which, in turn, allows the colonels to transcend their own proprietary realm and reach out into national affairs.
A.F.Mo.

Colonial Courts.

The courts of a British colony. Each colony has a high court and such inferior courts as its size and development necessitates. While British law and colonial statutes have precedent, the colonial courts apply for the most part native law. While many of the judges of colonial courts are Britons, the number of judges appointed from the ranks of local barristers is steadily increasing, although usually these barristers have been trained in England and have been admitted to the Bar there. Appeals may be taken from the colonial courts to the Judicial Committee of the Privy Council. Approximately a dozen appeals from the colonial courts are heard by this Judicial Committee each term.
C.A.McC.

Colonialism.

The most significant feature of colonialism is that it is difficult to define to the satisfaction of all. For example, J. A. Hobson defined colonialism as follows: "Colonialism, in its best sense, is a natural overflow of nationality; its test is the power of colonists to transplant the civilization they represent to the new natural and social environment in which they find themselves." Many writers attribute to colonialism the parent-and-offspring relationship that Hobson had in mind. E. M. Winslow, however, speaks of it as the "occupation of virgin territory in which conflict was incidental, or even unnecessary, and subordinate to the desire of Europeans to find a new place to live." While the delegates of the Bandung Conference of 1955 could all agree that colonialism was "an evil," they could not agree on what it was or where it existed. In public parlance, colonialism is fraught with the meaning of a superior-inferior relationship, of domination-subjugation. In current practice, imperialism and colonialism are used almost interchangeably.
R.St-H.

Colorado River Compact.

An agreement signed on November 24, 1922, by Arizona, Nevada, California, Colorado, New Mexico, Utah and Wyoming with the approval of the United States of America for the equitable division and apportionment of the use of the waters of the Colorado River System. Navigation was made subservient to domestic, agricultural, and power uses. Each basin may use 7,500,000 acre-feet of water per year, and the lower basin may increase its beneficial use 1,000,000 acre-feet per year. In 1948, the upper basin states agreed on a further allocation of the upper Colorado River waters.
J.E.T.

Color bar.
A barrier between races of political and economic significance, the **color bar** is usually imposed by the social or legal controls of "whites" against people of color, though it may also divide the latter. Found in many ages and places, in modern history the color bar has been conspicuous in overseas possessions of European states and the southern U.S.A. It is less evident in Latin cultures. Despite democratic, Marxist and religious disapproval, it continues to feed and is fed by personal insecurity and racial nationalism on all sides. P.F.P.

Columbus, Christopher.
Discoverer of America. Born Genoa, Italy, about 1451. Died Valladolid, Spain, May 20, 1506. His birth date and early education are controversial. Study of cosmography led him to petition the kings of England, Portugal, Spain, and the city of Genoa for aid in finding a westward route to India. His requests were finally granted by Isabella and Ferdinand of Spain. He discovered the New World October 12, 1492 at the island of San Salvador. By 1504 he had made four voyages to the Western Hemisphere. Before his death he suffered illness and humiliation through neglect by the Crown of his accomplishments. Buried in Santo Domingo. R.B.G.

COMECON.
The Council for Mutual Economic Assistance, or CEMA as the Russians call it, is an intergovernmental organization with the purpose of welding the separate national economies of the Soviet bloc countries into one commonwealth based on international cooperation and a division of labor, similar to the one sought by the EEC. It was founded on 25 January 1949 in Moscow with the following as charter members: Bulgaria, Czechoslovakia, Hungary, Poland, Rumania and the USSR. Albania joined almost immediately, and was followed by East Germany in September 1950. Since then, Albania was replaced by Mongolia. Although it was founded in 1949, as Communism's response to the United States' Marshall Plan, its activities were rather limited until the commencing of the West European Common Market in 1958. Since then, the COMECON countries have made many efforts to imitate the successes of the Common Market. However, the results are not very convincing. Whereas the EEC countries are trying to remove the national obstacles to trade within the area, such as tariffs and import quotas, and to encourage the free flow of labor and capital —the COMECON countries, where each national economy is run by central planning, are trying to coordinate their plans so as to achieve in effect, one international plan for the entire Soviet bloc without a coordinate investment program, common price structure, and the free flow of capital and labor. COMECON's titular Council consists of high-level **government** representatives of the member countries. The Council's decisions are recommendations and therefore not binding on the members until intergovernmental agreements are subsequently concluded to carry them out. In addition to the top-level Council, there is a permanent Secretariat, located in Moscow. Most of the COMECON work is accomplished through the work of a number of permanent and ad hoc commissions. P.A.T.

Cominform.
Cominform, an abbreviation for the Communist Information Bureau, was founded in 1947 at a historic meeting of communists in the little town of Miszlaw Kovince in Poland. (The chairman of the meeting was Andrei A. Zhdanov. The participating communist parties were from the Soviet Union, Yugoslavia, Bulgaria, Rumania, Hungary, Poland, Czechoslovakia, Italy, and France.) Its stated aim was to facilitate the exchange of experience of the parties and, if necessary, their cooperation. Although its decisions were not to be binding (as were those of the Comintern), and although membership in the Cominform was not obligatory for communist parties, the Cominform became a powerful instrument in the shaping of communist policy and tactics throughout the world. The first headquarters of the Cominform was at Belgrade, Yugoslavia. In 1948 the Cominform expelled the Yugoslav Communist Party, hav-

ing denounced its deviation from Marxist-Leninist orthodoxy. The headquarters of the organization were moved to Bucharest, Rumania. The Kremlin dissolved the Cominform in April 1956 partly to dissociate itself from Stalin's style in foreign policy approach and partly to accommodate Tito of Yugoslavia in its effort at "rapprochement" with Yugoslavia.
R.St-H.

Comintern.
Comintern is the abbreviated name of the Communist International (Third International), an organization founded at Moscow in 1919 with the purpose of furthering the establishment of Marxist communism in the world. It originally consisted only of the Russian and German communist parties—the only ones then in existence—and a number of left-wing Socialist splinter groups from other countries. The Comintern thus was instrumental during the early 1920's in the formation of communist parties out of the extremist groups that seceded from the more moderate elements of the world's Socialist parties. The Comintern included all communist parties, which met in Communist world congress at Moscow and coordinated their strategic and tactical policies by permanent committees. For this reason communists were actually members of a single world-wide organization. In 1943, in order to allay the misgivings of its allies in the Second World War, the government of the Soviet Union dissolved the Comintern. The widely publicized liquidation of the Comintern seemed to herald the Kremlin's abandonment of its global apparatus designed to subvert existing non-communist governments and serve Soviet interests. In the absence of conclusive evidence it is not possible to determine as to whether the Comintern actually ceased its operations or whether it continued to function in secret.
R.St-H.

Comity of Nations.
Privileges accorded to one state or its functionaries by another state as a matter of courtesy and polite deference rather than as a matter of law are spoken of as being grounded in comity.
H.B.J.

Commissaire du gouvernement.
High French civil servant designated by decree to assist a minister in the presentation of proposals to the legislative chambers.
E.G.L.

Commission.
A pattern of local government organization in which both legislative and administrative functions are unified in a small plural-member board. Each member of the board is responsible for a major administrative function in commission governed cities while the board administers functions collectively in township and county government.
G.S.B.

Commission Plan.
A form of city government which vests executive and legislative powers in elected commissioners.

The number of commissioners varies from three to seven. Each commissioner serves as head of a city department and one of their number is named the mayor although he normally has no powers beyond those of the other commissioners but does serve as ceremonial head of the city and presides over meetings of the commissioners. The first city to adopt the plan was Galveston, Texas which adopted it in 1903 after a state appointed commission of five local businessmen had served successfully as a temporary government following a disastrous hurricane in September 1900. The plan quickly became popular and by 1917 500 cities were using it. Its use has declined since that high point and only 309 cities were using it in 1960. The decline is attributable to several weaknesses of this form of local government. By elimination of the division between legislative and executive power fewer internal checks were operative in the system than is normal in American governmental institutions. Further, the system lacks both policy and administrative leadership since it is without a real chief executive.
A.K.C.

Commissioner.
Official title of a member of the general governing board in a variety of local governmental units. In county government, the term is commonly

*r*estricted to members elected to serve specifically on the county board.
G.S.B.

Committee of Supply.
In the British House of Commons this is another name for the Committee of the Whole House (see Committee of the Whole House) when dealing with appropriations. It is also called the House in Supply. R.G.N.

Committee of the whole.
The membership of a deliberative body sitting as a committee under the chairmanship of a member designated by the speaker and operating under less stringent rules than when in formal session. No roll calls are taken, and its recommendations must receive approval by the legislative body in formal session to be effective. One hundred members make a quorum for this committee in the United States House of Representatives where it is used for revenue, appropriations, and other bills. The committee of the whole is seldom used in the Senate.
K.E.H.

Committee of the Whole House.
This is the name for the entire House of Commons meeting under a slightly less formal procedure than is normal in regular meetings, and under the chairmanship of the Chairman of Committees, also known as Chairman of Ways and Means. R.G.N.

Committee of Ways and Means.
In the British House of Commons this is another name for the Committee of the Whole House (See Committee of the Whole House) when dealing with taxation. It is also called the House in Ways and Means.
R.G.N.

Committee on Account.
A standing committee of the House of Commons of Great Britain which examines in detail the report of the Auditor and Comptroller General dealing with the expenditures of the various departments and reports to the House. J.F.Z.

Committee on Committees.
A committee which nominates members of a group to other committees. Such committees are usually party committees and are found primarily in legislative bodies. W.V.H.

Committee on Intellectual Cooperation (League of Nations).
In 1922 the Council of the League of Nations appointed a twelve-man advisory committee to promote international cooperation in intellectual matters. The original committee included Albert Einstein, Henri Bergson and Gilbert Murray. Among the subjects studied by the committee were international cooperation in scientific research, inter-university cooperation, the protection of intellectual property, and the preservation of archaeological monuments. In 1931 the Committee became a part of the League's Intellectual Cooperation Organization. After World War II the Committee was replaced by the United Nations Educational, Scientific and Cultural Organization (Unesco). H.S.Th.

Committee on Local Authorities of the Council of Europe.
See Council of Europe—Committee on Local Authorities.

Committee on Standing Orders.
A Sessional (Select) Committee of the British House of Commons. When the Examiner (appointed by the Speaker) rules that a Standing Order has not been complied with in the submission of a Private Bill the report is referred to the Committee on Standing Orders for a ruling. R.G.N.

Commodity Credit Corporation.
An agency and instrumentality of the U.S. Department of Agriculture. Its principal function is the management and disposition of inventories of agricultural commodities acquired in price-support operations of the Government. This includes storage, transportation, sales, export payments, donations and financing of foreign disposal programs. The Corporation has an important effect on market prices of farm commodities and availability of storage. The management of the Corporation is vested in a board of directors. The Secretary of Agriculture is an ex officio Director and Chairman of the Board. The other six members are appointed by the President of the United States by and with the advice and consent of the Senate.
J.H.

Common Good.
The common good is the purpose for which the state exists. It consists of those conditions in society which enable the citizens to provide for their physical, intellectual and moral needs. In striving to bring about such conditions, the state exercises **protective** and **promotive** functions.   Pa.B.

Common Law.
In a narrow sense, common law means unwritten judge-made in contradistinction to statutory law as a written body of law enacted by the legislative branch of government. Common law also may be distinguished from equity as a system of remedial justice administered according to its own rules of procedure in tribunals different from the common law courts. In its broadest sense, the term common law is used to designate the whole legal system of England, the United States (with the exception of Louisiana) and most other English-speaking countries as distinguished from the civil law system of continental Europe. Of Anglo-Saxon origin, the common law developed in England after the Norman conquest as the law common to all the king's realm and administered in the king's court in contrast to the laws of local usage and custom. The true foundations of English common law were laid during the reign of Henry II (1154—1189). The common law applied in the American colonies at the time of independence. It is generally said to be in force in the United States today, in the form it had taken at the first year of the reign of James I (1603). The enduring characteristics of the common law are its method of judicial precedents, trial by jury and the doctrine of the supremacy of law (Pound). It is judge-made, relying for its force largely on the rule that judicial decisions of actual controversies in the past constitute guiding principles to be applied to similar controversies in the future. The common law rule of trial by jury, though less frequently used now in civil cases, has led to highly refined procedural rules designed to preserve the character of adversary procedure characteristic of the common law system. The common law doctrine of the supremacy of law signifies that government and citizens alike are bound to act in accordance with established legal principles enforceable before the properly constituted courts of law.   H.R.H.

Common Market.
See European Economic Community.

Common roll.
An electoral system by which all voters are listed in the same registration, and, within their respective constituencies or districts, are equally eligible to vote for the same candidates, regardless of the race or religion of the voters or candidates. In the United States and most other western democracies the principle is accepted without question, but it becomes an issue in multi-racial societies like those of Kenya, South Africa, and Tanganyika, where African voters, for example, may be eligible to vote only for African candidates, or candidates specifically designated to represent African interests. The opposing concept is communalism.   E.V.M.

Commonwealth.
A free association of the United Kingdom, Canada, Australia, New Zealand, India, Pakistan, Ceylon, the Federation of Malaya, Cyprus, Ghana, Nigeria, Tanganyika, Sierra Leone, Uganda and their dependent territories. It has no constitution or central government. Members share a broadly common pattern of political institutions but retain independence in their domestic and foreign affairs. Queen Elizabeth is the Head of the Commonwealth and the Head of State of its member States except India, Pakistan, the Federation of Malaya, Cyprus and Ghana. "The essence of the Commonwealth relationship is that it is a free association of nations with a common purpose, who belong together because they decided of their own volition to give and take their fair share in a world-wide partnership." (Lord Listowel).   S.S.H.

Communalism.
An electoral system whereby members of specified racial or religious groups vote separately for candidates

belonging to, or representative of, their own groups, with the result that responsibility is not to the entire electorate of a country, district, or geographical constituency, but only to the group electing the official. It is a phenomenon peculiar to multi-racial societies, especially in emergent areas like African countries in the final stages of colonial rule, and is typified by the Kenya constitution under which 1961 elections for the Legislative Council were held: of 65 seats, 10 were reserved for candidates from the European community, 8 from the Asian, and 2 from the Arab. Communalism is the antithesis of the common roll principle. E.V.M.

Communes.
See Red Chinese Communes.

Communication.
Communication is the exchange of information. Information is any message whose meaning is shared by the sender and the receiver. Information can be exchanged by signs and signals. Thus lovers can communicate by sighs and glances, deaf-mutes by finger movements, distant tribes by drum beats. Complex communications are usually exchanged by symbols (q.v.)—a conventionalized "language" consisting of a vocabulary (words and word-equivalents) and a grammar (rules for using the vocabulary). Whatever language is used, communication occurs only when information (meaningful messages) is exchanged. Meaningless messages, or portions of messages, may be classified as "noise."

The basic paradigm of communication involves three variables—sender, message, receiver. The analysis of persuasive communication or propaganda (q.v.) requires three additional variables—technique, policy, effect. The paradigm may be expressed (following Harold D. Lasswell) by the question: Who says what to whom, how, why, with what effect? See Propaganda. D.L.

Communication complex.
In the same sense of an industrial complex, there is a body of communication media (the press, mail, etc.), "hardware" (telephone systems, computers, etc.), traditions, practices (freedom of speech, trade secrecy, etc.), techniques, trained personnel, audiences, etc., which together form the communication complex, and subsidiary interrelated complexes at the level of a group, an organization, a city, a country, or the world community. Freedom or control of the complex, the kind of complex to be encouraged, and its uses, are central political issues because of the central role of communication in society (see Freedom of information). Indeed, the degree of freedom of individuals and institutions to use the complex for their own purposes (incuding political) may be said to be the measure of democracy, as the volume of use is the measure of technology. J.B.L.

Communism.
An ideology which, its advocates declare, will establish universal human happiness through the abolition of private property, classes and social distinctions, nearly all long-established social institutions, religious beliefs and establishments, and the state itself. Communists assert that all human longings will be satisfied through this community of goods and services, in which perfect equality of condition will prevail.

For the Marxists and certain other socialists, communism is the goal and final form of socialism, to be achieved in the fullness of time, with the destruction of the remnants of bourgeois institutions and ideas, and the withering away of the state. The present Soviet governments do not claim to have succeeded in attaining real communism as yet, but only to be making progress toward that end.

Certain classical, medieval, and renaissance philosophers advanced some communistic concepts. The theory and movement did not achieve practical importance, however, until the early years of the nineteenth century, when Saint-Simon, Robert Owen, Fourier, and other ideologues and leaders of radical reform advanced schemes for supplanting middle-class society by communistic forms of life, which would dispense with the family, the church, and the established systems of leadership and government, as well as with "capitalism."

Contemptuously calling these movements "Utopian," Karl Marx, Friedrich Engels, and their associates promulgated the **Communist Manifesto** (1848); and Marx's **Das Kapital** became their secular bible. Nearly all communist parties and factions of today claim descent from Marx and his coterie. The Marxists maintain that theirs is the only "scientific" socialism, leading eventually to the universal triumph of communism.

As early as 1848, critics of socialism like Orestes Brownson and Donoso Cortes pointed out that the communist ideology is a species of inverted Christianity, supplanting the salvation of the soul by the material redemption of the proletariat, and substituting for Heaven the earthly paradise of a classless society. Though the methods and claims of twentieth-century communists vary somewhat from country to country and year to year, the word "Communism" has become almost synonymous with Marxian socialism as practiced in Soviet Russia and Mainland (Red) China. Lenin once defined communism as "socialism plus electricity." See Bolshevism.   R.K.

Communist Front.

An organization designed to recruit non-Communists for Communist aims through the use of a special kind of unconventional channel of international propaganda. This type of channel is operated by what are known as "fronts." Some of the contemporary international (non - governmental) Communist-front organizations are: the World Federation of Trade Unions, the World Federation of Democratic Youth, the International Federation of Democratic Women, the International Organization of Journalists, the International Union of Students, the International Association of Democratic Lawyers, the International Federation of Resistance Fighters, and the World Peace Council. P.A.T.

Communist Manifesto.

(The Manifesto of the Communist League, by K. Marx and F. Engels; published in London, February, 1848.) The most influential political document written as a statement of the program and principles of Communism. It is the best known of all Communist writings, and over a thousand editions, in almost a hundred languages have been published. **The Manifesto** is divided into four parts. The first exposes the good and bad features of capitalism; the second, expounds on the role of the proletariat (the working class) in abolishing the evils of capitalism and envisions the proletariat's historical destiny; the third part, is an attack upon other "socialists" who opposed Marxism; and the fourth part, explains the necessity for the establishment of "proletarian internationalism" as a program of world order and peace and lays down the strategy to be followed by the workers in the struggle against the **"bourgeoisie,"** the capitalist ruling class. This short document closes with one of the most dynamic and often repeated exhortations in all history. "Let the ruling classes tremble at a Communistic revolution. The proletarians have nothing to lose but their chains. They have a world to win. Workingmen of all countries unite!" The important truths of the **Manifesto** are: the indictment of 19th century capitalism for the existence of millions of underpaid, unemployed and exploited workers; an irresponsible **laissez-faire** economics was the basic cause of this condition; and the failure to rectify the abysmal unchristian injustices of child labor, horrible working conditions and the emergent industrial slums. The enormous influence of the **Manifesto** finally compelled Christians in the West to introduce social reforms in behalf of justice. The basic errors of the **Manifesto** are: the theory of economic historical determinism; the false views on religion and the family; and the denial of private ownership of property.

The **Manifesto** has long out-lived its validity and purposes since 1848, and its value is chiefly historical. Both the tactical program of Marxism along with its pretentious but hollow prophecies (world revolution, demise of capitalism, "the withering away of the state," the international dictatorship of the proletariat, and the Communist world order of peace) are meaningless and no longer accepted. In fact, the **Manifesto** is out-of-date and obsolete. The world nevertheless owes a debt to the authors, for they created a movement which forced the propertied classes and Christian consciences to reform economic and social life and eliminate the vast injustice created by the Industrial Revolution under misguided and false materialistic individualism. M.M.Mc.

Communist party of France.
See French Communist Party.

Comparative Government.
Frequently, though inaccurately, used to refer to any study of foreign government and politics. True "comparative government" requires the systematic classification of political phenomena and the investigation of uniformities, differences, interrelationships among various political systems. The objective of comparative analysis is not only a more realistic understanding of alien political systems, but also the formulation of generalizations and hypotheses about universal characteristics of government. C.J.S.

Compromis d'arbitrage.
A technical phrase in international law referring to the submission of a particular dispute between states to arbitration. It is a special agreement in contrast to a general arbitral treaty prescribing the membership of the tribunal, defining the issues of the case, and lays down the rules for procedures, evidence, filing briefs, dates for hearings, place of hearings and the rules to be followed by the arbitrators in reaching their award. M.M.Mc.

Compromissory Clause.
A technical phrase in international treaty law constituting a written agreement between two or more states incorporated in a general treaty, or diplomatic and commercial treaties, stipulating compulsory arbitration of certain categories of disputes, especially those relating to pecuniary claims. M.M.Mc.

Compulsory Voting.
The practice of compelling citizens to use the franchise. In addition to dictatorships, it exists, statutorily authorized, for certain local and/or national elections in **circa** 30 non-dictatorial states, among them Australia (since 1924), Holland (1917), Switzerland (1835), Costa Rica (1889), and Brazil (1946). It was also authorized by constitutional amendment, subsequently approved by popular referenda, in North Dakota in 1900 (33,260 : 8,153) and Massachusetts in 1918 (134,138 : 128,403), but rejected by referendum in Oregon in 1920 (61,528 : 131,603). No enabling legislation, however, has been passed by the former two. Statutory penalties for unexcused non-voting vary: they include fines (e.g. Australia), periodic disfranchisement (e.g. Belgium), loss of government employment (e.g. Costa Rica, publication of offenders' names (e.g. Belgium) and imprisonment (e.g. Czechoslovakia — between-the-Wars). Enforcement is expensive, spotty, often haphazard, truly vigorous only in Australia and Belgium, especially the former which insists on absolute compliance. As a result, between 3 and 6% of compelled voters cast deliberately spoiled or invalid ballots. A legal challenge of compulsory voting occurred against a section of the Kansas City (Mo.) City Charter providing for compulsory voting; it was declared unconstitutional by the Missouri State Supreme Court **(Kansas City v. Whipple, 136 Mo. 475)** in 1896. H.J.A.

Computer Simulation.
Using a computer to represent, step by step, processes that occur in some real-world system. Each entity in the system is initially described in some alphabetic or numeric code and the description is stored in the computer's memory. Also stored is a program which instructs the computer to change the description of the entities, step by step, in specified ways. These steps usually follow a sequence representing what happens with the passage of time. Changes in stated entities in the system may depend upon outcomes of "Monte Carlo" processes thus simulating stochastic (i.e. probabilistic) variables in the real world. Changes in the state of entities in the system may depend upon the state of other entities within the system or upon exogenous forces operating upon the system.

Simulation is useful when the system and its processes are so complex that it is impossible to calculate mathematically or logically what the outcomes of particular choices or events would be.

In political science, computer simulations have been used to reproduce the behavior of the electorate under the impact of election campaigns, the behavior of combatants in international warfare, the behavior of nations in international controversy, the behavior of audiences subjected to propaganda.

I.d.S.P.

Comte, Auguste (1798—1857).

French social philosopher, some time secretary to Saint-Simon, and the founder of sociology. His major work is the **Course on the Positive Philosophy,** published in six volumes from 1830—1842, in which he advocates the virtues of a scientific approach to the study of society within the context of an evolutionary, progressive, and comprehensive philosophy of history. His later work is marked by a concern with moral and theological themes, outstanding among which is his proposal for a religion of humanity.

J.W.Ch.

Concentration (of economic power).

An increase in corporate strength and market control and/or monopoly through expansion, mergers, consolidations, combinations, trust agreements, etc. Can be vertical or horizontal; usually done to extend control over production and/or marketing in order to achieve savings in operations, intensify research, advertising, and so on. Can be due to illegal combinations in restraint of trade. W.N.

Concentration Camps (Germany).

During the regime of the Third Reich over one hundred concentration camps and similar institutions were established in Germany and Nazi-occupied Europe. Their 'legal' basis was the Decree for the Protection of People and State, issued on February 28, 1933, the day after the Reichstag Fire. It empowered the Gestapo to arrest people for an indefinite period for political reasons without judicial review. The orders of arrests, fraudulently called orders for protective custody (Schutzhaftbefehle), were issued by the Gestapo for the purpose of penalizing or exterminating alleged or real enemies of the regime. As sites of the camps, slave labor barracks, extermination installations, prison cells or old fortresses were erected or used. Among the infamous camp-names were those of Dachau, Oranienburg-Sachsenhausen, Buchenwald, Papenburg, Mauthausen-Gusen, Nordhausen, Natzweiler, Flossenburg, Ravensbrueck, Neuengamme, Niederhagen, Stutthoff, Bergen-Belsen (partly for hostages), Theresienstadt (for aged Jews), Columbia Haus, Berlin and Fuhlsbuettel, Hamburg (for 'special treatment' by the Gestapo), Drancy, France, and Westerbork, Holland (as assembly points for the death trains to the East). Extermination camps for Jews equipped with gas chambers were Auschwitz-Birkenau, Treblinka, Belcec, Sobibor, Chelmo, Poland. Mass exterminations took place also in the camps of Kowno, Riga, Lublin, Lemberg, Minsk and Gross Rosen (the latter served as execution site for Russian prisoners of war). At the end of 1944 about 600,000 persons were in concentration camps as revealed by SS Gruppenfuehrer and chief administrator of the camps Oswald Pohl, sentenced to death in Nuremberg. A total of about eight million victims were committed to camps by the Gestapo, nine tenths of them were worked, starved, shot, gassed or experimented to death. The survivors were liberated by the Allies. Rudolf Hoess of Auschwitz and Karl Koch of Buchenwald (his wife, the infamous Ilse Koch), were the most notorious camp chiefs. The population of the KZ's came from all walks of life and political or religious belief. Among them were about four million Jews, many thousand Catholics, especially from Poland and Austria — about 2,500 Catholic priests died in the camps—also many thousand Jehovah's witnesses. Tens of thousands of Gypsies, Slovenes, Poles, Russians and French were also murdered in the camps. Among the prominent inmates were Social Democratic, Communist, and Centrist politicians, such as Ernst Reuter, the late mayor of West Berlin, Ernst Heilmann, leading Prussian social democrat, Wilhelm Luebke, President of the German Bundesrepublik, Ernst Torgler and Ernst Thaelmann, Communist leaders. Other inmates

were Kurt von Schuschnigg, former Austrian Chancellor, Leon Blum, former French Premier, Martin Niemoeller, prominent Protestant leader and Carl von Ossietzky, Nobel-Peace-prize winner murdered by the Gestapo.
R.M.W.K.

Concentration Camps (Soviet Union).
See Forced Labor Camps.

Concert of Europe.
The Congress of Vienna (1814-15) established a balance of political forces in Europe. While no definite and formal provisions were ever made, it became customary in the 19th century that the final disposition of any changes in the accepted balance of power structure should be brought about only after the Great Powers were consulted (Russia, England, France, Austria, Prussia, later also German Empire, Italy, sometimes Turkey). Usually this was achieved by means of an international conference. Smaller European powers were invited to participate only when directly involved in the problems under discussion. The Concert of Europe system amounted, when effective, to a virtual collective great power hegemony. It ceased to function when the European balance of power structure disintegrated into two opposing and rigid alliance systems leading directly to World War I. On the whole the Concert of Europe did succeed to avert major wars in Europe for a century. Its basic idea of great power domination and responsibility for international peace was carried over in the 20th century into the structures of the universal international organizations where the great powers were given special prerogatives, as in the Council of the League of Nations (permanent seat) and in the Security Council of the United Nations (veto power). P.P.R.

Conciliation.
A method of settling international disputes, whereby an institution, commission, or other conciliator agreed upon or set up by the parties accomplishes an amicable solution, without the legal requirement that a specific proposed settlement be accepted. The conciliator is authorized to make findings of fact, publicize them, and recommend a solution, but the recommendations are not in the nature of an arbitral award, and the disputants retain throughout their liberty to disregard the proposals. The General Assembly and the Security Council of the United Nations may, under Chapters IV and VI of the Charter, respectively, act as conciliators, as could the Assembly and Council of the League of Nations. Settlement of the Indonesian question by the Security Council in 1949 is often regarded as a successful conciliation. A similar technique is employed in internal commercial and labor disputes. E.V.M.

Concordat.
The term denotes any agreement (coming from the Latin **pactum concordatum**) but is applied more specifically to those between the pope and a state. Such agreements define joint relationships not regulated by ordinary laws or papal decrees, such as freedom of priests from military service. Concordats have defined governmental monetary concessions to the Church, mutual rights and obligations, Church taxes, government control of the Church, and similar problems.
W.F.G.

Concurrent Powers.
In a federal system certain governmental powers may be exercised by either the national government or the state governments or both. The power to tax and the power to borrow money are examples of concurrent powers in a federal system. In the United States the delegation of powers to congress by the federal constitution does not preclude the states from utilizing these powers provided they are not exclusive federal powers and there is no conflict between the state laws and federal laws. J.F.Z.

Concurrent Resolution.
An action of one House of the U.S. Congress and in which the other concurs, but is not sent to the President and does not have the force of law. It is used primarily for administering the affairs of Congress, such as declaring legislative intent, stating an opinion or purpose of the two Houses, and fixing the time for final adjournment. Also joint committees are authorized by this procedure. W.V.H.

113

Concurring Opinion.
In the U.S.A., a separate opinion by a judge who, while agreeing with the result of the case, finds it impossible to agree with all or part of the reasoning by which the result has been reached by the court. F.H.H.

Condominium.
Joint sovereignty; joint rule of a country or region by two or more states; an area so governed. Present examples are the New Hebrides (Britain and France, since 1906); Andorra (France and the Spanish bishops of Urgel, since 1278); the isle of Pheasants in Bidassoa river (France and Spain); bays of San Juan and Salinas (Nicaragua and Costa Rica) and of Fonseca (Nicaragua, Honduras, and El Salvador); and Canton and Enderbury Islands (United States and Britain). Past examples were Samoa (United States, Britain, and Germany, 1889—1899) and Sudan (Britain and Egypt, 1899—1955). Coret claims that it was not a condominium until 1936. He also includes West Berlin because of its three-power status. H.G.S.

Confederation.
A loose association of independent states which, while not creating a single new polity, does transcend an alliance by establishing some common political institutions. Nevertheless, since the sovereign equality of member-states normally is emphasized, no truly governmental central organs exist. Thus, the customary representative assembly is essentially diplomatic rather than legislative, its members being delegates responsible to the component governments rather than real confederation law-makers. Unanimity or some other extraordinary degree of consent is usually required in decision-making and, frequently, such assemblies can do little more than make recommendations to the member-governments. Similarly, central executive and judicial agencies, if they exist, also lack the authoritative, coercive powers of government and so cannot independently impose their will on either member-states or individual citizens. No unified police or armed forces raised, equipped, and directed by central authorities exist; the confederation must depend upon military contributions by the member-governments. Central authorities, moreover, normally do not have power to tax and so are dependent upon voluntary contributions by member-states. The confederation, therefore, is most useful in promoting territorial integration only when independent states are not willing to relinquish any national sovereignty but do desire some degree of institutionalized political coordination. When the need for unity increases demonstrably, confederations sometimes have been transformed into federations (e.g., the United States and Switzerland). The technique also has been employed internationally in an effort to produce greater world political integration (e.g., League of Nations and United Nations) and can be applied to other forms of political organization. D.W.

Confederation francaise des travailleurs chretiens (CFTC).
French confederation of Christian workers, labor organization supporting the Christian Socialist viewpoint; founded in 1919, it emphasizes the Christian ethic in society, advocating the improving of the condition of the workers through social security, and planned rational use of productive facilities. E.G.L.

Confederation Generale du Travail (C.G.T.).
General Confederation of Labor largest French labor union, was created in 1895; from 1906 to World War I it was violently anti-capitalist, supporting the general strike as the revolutionary weapon of the proletariat; its leaders cooperated in the World War I effort; in 1918 it favored cooperative action with other productive forces, and urged successfully the creation of an economic council uniting labor, technicians, and government; it supported nationalization of industry. In 1921 Communist-oriented members withdrew; they rejoined the CGT in 1936 in harmony with the Moscow-approved popular front movement. In 1940 the Vichy government dissolved the CGT at well as other labor and management organizations. In 1947—1948, moderate socialists lost control of the CGT to the communists; the

socialists withdrew, setting up their own organization, the CFT (FO) (q.v.). While generally continuing to deal with government and management agencies, the CGT leaders remain militant communists. E.G.L.

Confederation Generale du Travail (Force Ouvriere).
Moderate socialist French trade union federation created in 1948 when the Communists won substantial control of the CGT. (q.v.) The CGT (FO) generally supports the evolutionary socialist parties and cooperates with government and management in solving economic problems. It is particularly strong among government employees. E.G.L.

Conference committee.
A committee, composed of members from the two houses of a legislative body, which is set up to work out a compromise between house and senate versions of a bill. The recommendation of this committee is referred back to each house for action. If either or both houses fail to adopt the recommendation, the bill will die unless further conference committees are requested and agreed to. K.E.H.

Confluent society.
A multiplex society (q.v.) whose viability stems from and results in the ability of its component organizations, institutions and individuals to somehow form a dominant confluence of opinion and action, and move in a common direction. Distinct from a society in transition, where confluence may or may not be forming; from a rigid or static (ant-like) society, and from a disintegrating or chaotic society. J.B.L.

Confucianism.
This term now embraces the substance of Confucius' thought plus the overlay of centuries of commentary, interpretation, and the rigidities of institutionalism.
Confucius' thought comprised the classical legacy of his time modified by his own creative insights. He insisted he was not an innovator, only a conveyor of established truths. But in systematizing and interpreting that legacy, he transformed it.

Confucius found in history clear signs of moral order in the natural world. The proper goal of society was to emulate the historic golden age of peace and order when leaders were virtuous and all men exemplified the ideal five cardinal relationships. Developing right relations through fulfilling the ordained roles of society would restore justice, harmony, and peace to the social order. For him, the harmonious state was the harmonious family writ large.

The classics revealed the principal human virtues of benevolence or "humanliness," sincerity, and a fundamental moral rectitude. The proper practice of ritual, ceremony, and music helped to sustain these virtues, to lend symmetry to life, and to cultivate a right sense of propriety in all relationships.

While unfailingly pious and reverent, Confucius seldom referred to or invoked the supernatural. He was more humanist than religionist. And although he was close to the common people, the main thrust of his thought was toward the truly educated and cultivated gentleman in whose leadership in public affairs lay the best hope for a good society. M.T.K.

Confucius (551—479 B.C.).
Born into the K'ung family and given the personal name, Ch'iu, China's most eminent teacher-philosopher came to be known as K'ung Fu-tzu, "Master Kung," later latinized by Jesuit missionaries as Confucius. His home was in the small feudal state of Lu in present-day Shantung province. His forebears may have belonged to the minor aristocracy, but his own family lacked both means and status. Fatherless, and perhaps orphaned, at an early age, Confucius was left to his own devices in gaining an education and planning a career.

In the light of his influence in Chinese history and culture, his own life was notably uneventful and unspectacular. Oppressed by the near-chaos of his times, he devoted his life to the restoration of peace and order. From the outset he was a singularly successful teacher. But he persisted till late in life in his fruitless efforts to gain a high political post convinced that the authority of officialdom was the necessary means for inducing political reform. He held office briefly in his own state—a sinecure post—and then spent years moving from state to state searching for leaders receptive to his ideas and for official status for himself. Few listened and even fewer responded. Ultimately he returned to his home to spend his last five years teaching and editing.

While eccentric in many ways, Confucius' qualities of intellectual force and personal magnetism and his talent for communicating ideas profoundly impressed his disciples and, through them, the whole life of China. M.T.K.

Congo, Republic of the.
Formerly Belgian Congo. Independent since July 1, 1960. Area 905,329 square miles; population (est. 1960) 13,732,000, which comprises over 200 distinct tribal groups. The most important and numerous tribes are the Ba-Kongo in Leopoldville area, the Ba-Luba in southwest and the Ba-Lunda in Katanga. These three groups are also the ones with a previous history of state organization and empire-building. The Congo lacked political unity until the creation of the Congo Free State in 1885, which in effect was an internationally sanctioned private commercial estate of Belgian King Leopold II. Direct Belgian administration was established in 1908. Belgium's Congo policy may best be described as "paternalism" in which large-scale private investments in the extractive export economy were accompanied by relatively extensive—for Africa—provision of welfare services, discouragement of European settlement, absence of a legal color bar and a total ban on political activity by any segment of the population.

Only four years of political activity preceded independence in 1960. Post independence instability led to extensive international involvement of a military, administrative and financial nature in Congolese affairs. Congolese instability is traceable primarily to the acute shortage of experienced political, administrative and technical personnel and the absence of territory-wide integrative institutions, i.e. national political parties, transportation networks, civil service, national elite. R.L.K.

Congress, Indian National.
India's premier political party. It was founded in 1885 by an Englishman, Allan Octavian Hume, with the blessings of Viceroy Lord Dufferin, to serve as a constructive channel for public unrest. For the first twenty years, it remained under the direction of moderates like Dadabhai Naoroji and G. K. Gokhale, who pressed for larger Indian role in the government. In 1905, the moderates were challenged by extremists under Bal Gangadhar Tilak, agitating for home-rule. In 1919, the Congress became, under Gandhi (q.v.), a dynamic mass organization, with **swaraj** (q.v.) through **satyagraha** (q.v.) as its objective. The **satyagraha** phase concluded with the advent of Indian independence in 1947. Since then, the Congress, led by Nehru (q.v.), has been India's governing party, winning overwhelmingly the general elections of 1951-52, 1957, and 1962. It stands for the establishment of a socialistic pattern of society, based on equitable distribution of wealth, equality of opportunity, and social ownership of the principal means of production. In foreign policy, it has advocated the **Panch Shila** (q.v.) peace concept. C.S.S.

Congressional Township System.
A system of facilitating the identification and description of real estate, devised and applied to the public lands of the United States—with few exceptions—by the Ordinance of 1785. The congressional township or "survey township" is to be distinguished from the governmental organization provided under the Northwest Ordinance. P.J.C.

Congress of Racial Equality.
Interracial organization formed in U.S.A. in 1943 to combat racial discrimination by direct non-violent action. Participants attend interracial training institutes to learn how to absorb violence and abuse, to which they must not retaliate. They then seek unsegregated service in eating places, transportation facilities, and places of recreation. Methods are intended to turn hostility into sympathetic understanding. Philosophy consists of respect for the opponent and returning good for evil as taught by

116

Jesus, Gandhi, Leo Tolstoy and others. Leadership includes nationally prominent ministers, white and colored. National Director is James Farmer. National office is in New York City.
R.E.Ch.

Connolly Amendment (or Reservation).
Article 36.2 of the statute of the International Court of Justice, the so-called optional clause, permits states to submit to the obligatory jurisdiction of the Court subject to reservations to be made by them. By such a declaration a state agrees to allow itself to be sued by a state making a similar declaration. The Senate Committee on Foreign Relations proposed a reservation, in the usual form, regarding disputes concerning matters which are essentially within the domestic jurisdiction of the United States; Senator Connolly's amendment added the phrase, "as determined by the U.S.A." Because of the principle of reciprocity this reservation may be invoked by any state against whom the United States might otherwise be able to bring suit. J.A.C.G.

Conquistadores.
The sixteenth century Spanish explorers and conquerors of Latin America. Among the more prominent members of this group are Hernan Cortes, who led the conquest in Mexico, Juan Pizarro in Peru and Pedro de Alvarado in Chile. Ch.W.A.

Conscientious objector.
A male citizen who refuses military conscription and combat on religious or moral grounds. Some governments have allowed objectors to perform non-combatant duties instead. R.R.R.

Consequences.
To examine the (actual, necessary, probable, or possible) consequences of actions or non-action in the political arena is one of the most important functions of political science, which can be performed properly only in cooperation with the other branches of the social sciences, especially anthropology, sociology, psychology, and economics. It is advisable to distinguish purely logical "implications" from empirical (causal) "consequences." That to give a dictator "unlimited power" means to give him the power to disregard human rights is an "implication"; that the adoption of Proportional Representation is likely to lead to a change in the line-up of parties is a "consequence." Actual consequences may or may not have been "intended" in whole or in part; they may or may not have been "foreseen." Changes in probabilities, especially the increase or decrease in the "risk" that undesired consequences occur, are significant subcategories of the generic category of consequences. Another significant subcategory is unintended "by-products." In disclosing implications and predicting consequences, by-products, and risks, political science can contribute significantly to the examination not only of means but also of goals. A.B.

Conservatism.
A body of political, social, and moral opinions derived from the writings of Edmund Burke and other advocates of the old and tried, as against the new and untried. As a term of politics, "conservatism" was first employed in France after the fall of Napoleon, and its usage rapidly spread throughout Europe, and to Britain and America.

According to H. Stuart Hughes, "conservatism is the negation of ideology." Believing man and society to be imperfectible, conservatives advocate prudent adherence to customs and constitutions. Freedom and authority, they maintain, always will remain in tension: a condition which is necessary to the achievement of justice. With Burke, most conservatives—including John Adams, probably the most eminent American conservative thinker—accept the need for moderate change, through which the vitality of society is renewed. But they argue that change must be harmonized with the "great mysterious incorporation of the human race," for continuity maintains civilization.

As contrasted with liberalism, conservatism emphasizes order and prescription, though — especially in the twentieth century—conservatives also defend constitutional and customary freedoms. They adhere to "organic" or "spiritual" concepts of social community, as opposed to atomic individualism on the one hand and to totalitarian collectivism on the other. R.K.

Conservative Party—United Kingdom. See British Conservative Party.

Conservative Party—U.S.A.
A minor political party formed in New York state in 1962 as a reaction against liberal tendencies within the Republican Party and particularly those of Governor Nelson Rockefeller and Senator Jacob Javits. Its candidate for governor, David H. Jacquith, received 118,768 votes in November 1962, enough to assure the party of continued legal status. J.S.S.

Consolidated city-county government.
Either by combining an entire county with a city, or by detaching a city from a county, a consolidated city-county is formed. Although the extent of administrative integration differs, most city and county functions are performed by a single government. Baltimore, Baton Rouge (La.), Boston, Denver, Nashville, New Orleans, New York, Philadelphia, San Francisco, St. Louis, and all Virginia cities having at least ten thousand population, have consolidated city-county structures. J.M.S.

Consolidation.
An attempt to meet problems of urbanization by extinguishing the existence of two or more units of local government and creating in the process a single new unit succeeding to the legal powers, duties, obligations, and responsibilities of those it replaces. (Fairborn, Ohio, U.S.A. is an example of the consolidation process.)
P.J.C.

Conspiracy.
A conspiracy is a plot to subvert or otherwise illegally do harm. Section 3 of the Alien Registration Act of 1940 of the U.S.A. (more popularly called the Smith Act), which was upheld in **Dennis v. U.S.**, 341 U.S. 494 (1951), makes it a crime to conspire to advocate, teach, print, or distribute ideas which favor the violent overthrow of the U.S. or join a group which engages in such conspiracy. J.A.E.

Constituent function.
The power to propose or adopt amendments to an organic law. Although in England an ordinary Act of Parliament may introduce constitutional changes, this is not generally the practice in other countries. More typically, it is necessary for the legislature to muster an extraordinary majority and/or to obtain the concurrence of another body.

In the United States, for example, the national legislature must share the constituent function with the states. A constitutional amendment is proposed by Congress through a two-thirds vote in each of its two chambers (or the same function may be performed by a convention requested by the legislatures of two-thirds of the states). The proposed amendment is then submitted to conventions in the 50 states, or Congress may permit the ratification question to be settled by the state legislatures. Acceptance by three-fourths of the states is required.

In France, President De Gaulle in 1962 ignored the constitutional requirement that amendments be screened by the legislature, and submitted to a popular referendum an important proposal for constitutional revision of the nation's electoral law.

The term "constituent function" is often used in another sense: to describe the personal services performed by a legislator on behalf of his individual constituents. D.M.B.

Constitution.
A written Constitution is a basic law defining and delimiting the principal organs of government and their jurisdictions, as well as the basic rights of men and citizens. It is generally regarded as superior to all other laws but only in some countries (e.g. U.S.A., Germany) can an ordinary law be held void when it is found by a court to be unconstitutional. According to the ease or difficulty with which constitutions can be amended they are sometimes divided into rigid and flexible constitutions. However constitutions may be rigid in form, but flexible in substance like the U.S. Constitution which is difficult to amend but broad enough in text to be interpreted

118

flexibly. The oldest full-fledged constitution is that of the United States. However, there are older constitutional documents, like Magna Carta (1215) and Cromwell's Instrument of Government (1653). A written Constitution may be incorporated in more than one act. See the Fundamental Laws of the Third French Republic (1875). Great Britain has an unwritten Constitution composed of customs, conventions and regular Acts of Parliament. Although all countries have written or unwritten Constitutions it is only in reasonably democratic countries that constitutions actually limit the powers of government. R.G.N.

Constitution of the Italian Republic.

In force since January 1, 1948, the Italian Constitution establishes a parliamentary government with two equal legislative chambers elected by universal suffrage, a governing Council of Ministers headed by a president (premier) and responsible to both houses, and a national President or head of state elected by parliament with regional representatives. Reflecting mainly Catholic and Communist influence and compromises in the drafting Constituent Assembly elected in 1946, it declares Italy a democratic republic based on labor. A list of fundamental principles and of civil, ethical, social, and economic relations guarantees all democratic freedoms and obligates the state to advanced social and economic responsibilities. Nineteen regional governments are envisaged; four have been created (Sicily, Sardinia, Val d'Aosta, and Trentino-Alto Adige.) A Constitutional Court rules in disputes involving the constitutionality of laws and between the national and regional governments. Amendment is possible by parliament or through popular referendum.

Much legislative implementation still pends (labor law, state reforms, regions, abrogations of all Fascist laws, some of which the Constitutional Court has found unconstitutional), and controversy exists regarding religious freedom and the special privileges reserved to the Catholic Church under the 1929 Concordat which the Constitution specifically confirms.
E.T.O.

Constitutional Commission.

In the United States a small commission of three to thirty-five members created by a state legislature and appointed by the governor to study the constitution and recommend amendments. The members of the commission usually are constitutional experts. Its recommendations serve only as the basis for amendments to be proposed by the methods authorized by the constitution. J.F.Z.

Constitutional Controls in the U.S.A.
(Congress over President).

Congress may, by a two-thirds vote, override a presidential veto. It has the power of investigation of the executive branch and may refuse to pass requested legislation. The Senate may decline approval of a treaty and thereby annul it as far as the U.S.A. is concerned. Governmental power of impeachment has never been employed since Andrew Johnson was acquitted.
M.F.

Constitutional Controls in the U.S.A.
(President over Congress).

Government in the U.S.A. is one of checks and balances, as well as separation of powers. The president must report, from time to time, to Congress, on the state of the Union. He may call the two houses into special session. He could adjourn them but this is not done in actual practice. He has the power to veto legislation. Since 1921, when the Budget System was established, he can exert his influence over financial matters through the annual Budget Message to Congress. M.F.

Constitutional Convention.

The Convention which framed the Constitution of the United States was called first by the Annapolis Convention, then by Virginia and the other states except Rhode Island, and by Congress. Its sessions manned by most of the leading men of the day ran from May 25 to September 17, 1787. Noteworthy procedures included secrecy; use of committees to agree on principles, to prepare a draft and to polish the final text; a quorum of seven states; decisions by a majority of states present. Key substantive decisions were: to devise a new frame of government with limited but plenary powers; to establish a single, strong executive; to provide through a system of separation of powers and checks and balances for interaction and harmonization of existent interests and those to arise later; and to solve the problem of the relations of the small to the large states by establishing a legislative body representing both.　　　　　　　　　　J.E.S.

Constitutional Courts.

Those courts in the U.S. created by Congress under the section of the constitution providing for the federal judicial system. (Article III). These courts are, in hierarchical order beginning with the lowest courts, the District Courts, the Courts of Appeal, and the Supreme Court, plus three former Legislative Courts recently changed to constitutional ones, but which are outside the regular court system mentioned above. The judges are appointed by the President with approval of the Senate, hold office during good behavior, and can be removed only by impeachment. Their salaries cannot be reduced while they are in office, and their jurisdiction is set forth in Article III and by Congressional acts based on this Article. This jurisdiction extends to all cases in law and equity arising under the constitution, laws and treaties of the U.S., to admiralty and maritime questions, and certain other cases determined by the character of the parties to the dispute. Their jurisdiction is thus limited to judicial functions, and they do not exercise legislative or administrative functions as do legislative courts, from which they must be distinguished, created by Congress for special purposes under its legislative power (Art. I). Judges of the legislative courts do not have the constitutional safeguards and independent status that the judges of the constitutional courts have.　　　　E.G.T.

Constitutional Dictatorship.

It occurs especially in Latin American countries in which the presidential powers and authority of the President, who most of the time emerges by way of a revolution or a military uprising, but occasionally as a result of a fair general election, are strongly exercised in an attempt to perpetuate himself in power, under the shield of the national constitution with the connivance of a weaker legislative power—almost always due to the fact that its majority belongs to the presidential party or movement with every act or action showing their solidarity—and the pressure or complicity of military cliques, confessional groups, national or foreign economic interests and the egotistic and greedy support of the workers' unions.

The "strong unipersonal executive" in most Latin American countries is traceable from the Spanish monarchy, through the adelantados and viceroys of the colonial times, the caudillos and liberators of the independence period, the governors and tyrants of the reconstruction era and the strong presidential powers elaborated in the constitutional plans.　　　　　　　J.B.V.

Constitutionalism.

The meaning of constitutionalism is very close to the meaning of the "rule of law" (q.v.). It can be defined as a determinate, stable legal order which prevents the arbitrary exercise of political power and subjects both the governed and the governors to "one law for all men." Constitutionalism is not identical with constitutions, which at times are rather meaningless paper documents, incongruous with the existing political organization and processes. An effective constitution, "written" or "unwritten," is, however, an essential ingredient of the legal order which may be called constitutionalism.
　　　　　　　　　　　　J.D.

Constitutional Law.

The branch of public law that determines the political organization of a state and its powers while also setting certain substantive and procedural limitations on the exercise of governing power. Thus, it comprises the often complex body of legal rules and principles that define the basic nature of limits upon governmental power as well as the rights and duties of individuals in relation to the state and its governing organs. Because of its position and nature, constitutional law necessarily stands legally above all other types of municipal or domestic law, public as well as private.

In the United States, with its written Constitution, Constitutional law consists of the application of fundamental principles of law based on that document, as ultimately, finally, and authoritatively interpreted by its highest judicial organ, the Supreme Court of the United States, in its exercise of judicial review. Here the Court applies the superior of two laws, that of the written Constitution, against that of lesser standing—be it statutory, common, equity, or executive and/or administrative action based upon it. But the Constitution is formally amendable by joint action of Congress and the States in accordance with the provisions of Article V.

Constitutional law is not exclusively present only in those states with a written Constitution, such as the United States or Australia, however. It prevails, too, in the United Kingdom, for example, which has no formal written Constitution, but which has an "unwritten" one, composed of great statutes, common law, custom and convention. Parliament, in its inherent power to pass or repeal whatever legislation it may deem necessary and proper is thus in a position to alter the Constitution at will. In its legislative authority it represents the main source of constitutional as well as ordinary statutory law, judicial review not being present under the British system.

A third type of constitutional law is found on the Continent of Europe, where written constitutions exist, but where judicial review is either absent (e.g. Scandinavia and the Low Countries); where it exists in a circumscribed, tangential manner (e.g. Switzerland); or where it is exercised, normally in a limited manner by judicial or quasi-judicial bodies that fall outside the regular court hierarchy (e.g. France, Austria, Italy, West Germany). H.J.A.

Constitutional limitations.
Limits placed on state authority by the U.S. Constitution in Art. I, Sec. 10. States are prohibited from entering into treaties, coining money, passing bills of attainder and ex post facto laws, impairing contracts, granting titles of nobility, and taxing both imports and exports. The Constitution further specifies that states may do the following only with congressional consent: keep troops or warships in time of peace, enter into compacts with other states or foreign governments, and engage in war unless invasion is imminent. R.R.R.

Constitutionality of Legislation.
In the U.S.A. it is the constitutional responsibility of each department of government—executive and legislative as well as judicial—to decide whether a particular act is legally valid or not. Since 1803, when Chief Justice Marshall first claimed this power as the peculiar responsibility of the judiciary in **Marbury v. Madison,** the American people have come to identify "legitimate" democratic government and the rule of law with "judicial supremacy" —with the power of the courts to decide whether governmental acts are reasonable and just and valid, or, unreasonable, unjust and unconstitutional.

Mass reverence for judicial supremacy, however, was slow in developing. This was due, in part, to the unpopularity of the Supreme Court's second attempt to invalidate an act of Congress. In the ill-fated Dred Scott decision of 1857, the Court became identified in northern minds with the sin of slavery, and, after the outbreak of the civil war, with the treason of secession.

From 1880 to 1932, the Court recaptured and reinforced its image of legitimacy as it became the defender of absolute property rights. Mass acceptance of this image became even more intense after 1925, when the Court established federal constitutional protection against unreasonable state interference with first amendment freedoms of speech, press, assembly, petition and religion. The Court's image began to fade, however, as the "nine old men" decided repeatedly that attempts of the New Deal to overcome economic chaos had no reasonable constitutional justification. Then came the President's massive attack and the Court's capitulation. The Supreme Court ultimately took on an image of subservience to Franklin Roosevelt, a loss of prestige that still haunts the Court's efforts to reestablish itself as the nation's symbol of independence, objectivity and justice.

Since 1880, the Court has invalidated some 79 acts of Congress and seventeen Presidential orders. In addition, the Court reviews state acts which involve federal statutory and constitutional questions, such as segregation, subversion control, and legislative apportionment. G.I.J.

Consular jurisdiction.
Different from the mutually enjoyed extraterritorial rights and privileges extended by all civilized states to foreign diplomats who are lawfully within their borders. Considered as "Capitulations," grants of extraterritorial jurisdiction to consuls, so that foreign nations were to be subject only to jurisdiction of their own consuls in both civil and criminal cases. These "servitudes" could be mutual: Treaty between Russia and China in 1689 granted special rights and privileges to nations of both countries when living on one another's soil. But, in China, since Sino-British Supplementary Treaty, 1843, starting consular jurisdiction, while setting up a system of foreign courts in China, granted no corresponding rights to Chinese residents in foreign states. After development of concept of territorial sovereignty, the system started with the capitulation treaty signed by Ottoman Empire with France in 1535. Later extended to nations of Near East and Far East. Japan was the first nation to end capitulations (1899), and China almost the last (1943).
C.K.W.

Consular Officers.
Consular officers are members of the foreign service of the state, but they differ in a technical sense from the diplomatic service. Generally speaking, the duties of consuls are more commercial than political in nature. Sometimes the term **consul** is used in a very broad sense to include all consular officers regardless of grade or classification, and at other times a narrow definition of the term is employed to include only officers of a particular rank. In the main, however, consuls can be divided into two classifications: **consules missi** who are professional consuls and always subjects or citizens of the sending state, and **consules electi**, who may or may not be citizens of the sending state. The general law of nations does not distinguish their status. O.S.

Consulate—France (1799—1804).
See French Consulate Period (1799—1804).

Consumers' Cooperative.
A form of organization created to save money for their members by buying direct and in large quantities, thus obtaining discounts, eliminating profits of middlemen and charges of financial institutions. The modern movement began in Rochdale, England, in 1844. The main principles of such organization usually are: open membership, one vote per member regardless of capital invested, net earnings divided among members according to patronage. Movement strong in Europe, especially in England and in Sweden. W.N.

Containment.
A foreign policy calling for the prevention, by the United States and its allies, of further territorial expansion by the Soviet Union and its allies. This policy was first enunciated by U.S. career diplomat George F. Kennan in 1947, and has constituted the basic goal of United States foreign policy ever since, despite some criticisms claiming it to be a "negative" policy. As outlined by Kennan, prolonged successful containment was expected, in the long run, to promote "either the break-up or the gradual mellowing of Soviet power." S.L.A.

Contempt of Congress.
Either House of the United States Congress may punish persons for acts or omissions which obstruct the legislative process. The antecedents of this power run through earlier American legislative bodies to the British House of Commons. By an Act of 1857 contempt of Congress which took the form of refusal to testify or produce papers was made a misdemeanor and today such contempts are punished in the courts of law. T.C.S.

Contempt of Court.
A wilful disregard of the authority or dignity of the Court as manifested in behavior calculated to obstruct and

hinder the administration of justice. The power of the courts to punish contempts has been firmly entrenched in Anglo-American law. However, the Act of 1831 limited the summary power of the federal courts to punish contempts to misbehavior "in the presence of the Court or so near thereto as to obstruct the administration of justice." Contempt power in the United States is also limited by the constitutional bar against violations of due process of law and undue interference with the rights of freedom of speech and press. See **Bridges v. California** (1941).

There are two kinds of contempt, civil and criminal. Civil contempt is an offense not against the dignity of the Court, but against the authority of the Court acting on behalf of a litigant, and may be purged by compliance to the Court order. Criminal contempt is an offense against the dignity of the Court, and a person cannot by subsequent action purge himself of such contempt. P.B.

Content analysis.
Is a research technique for the objective, systematic and quantitative description of the content of any linguistic expression. Qualitative materials (e.g. newspaper writings) are classified into appropriate categories. Comparisons can be made among materials produced at different points in time. Materials coming from different sources can be compared. The content can be evaluated against standards adopted by the investigator. Trends in communication content can be described. The international differences in communication content can be studied. The existence of propaganda can be detected. The unit of measurement and classification can be one word ("keyword"), or one sentence, or one theme or one leading article. Quantitative content analysis assigns numerical frequencies to different categories. Qualitative content analysis contains quantitative statements in rough form (e.g. one fourth). E.I.

Continuismo.
The general term for a variety of practices in Latin American politics by means of which a government in office prolongs its power beyond the legal time period. Postponement of elections because of crisis or "civic unrest," illicit or controlled amendment of the constitution, suspension of the constitution or its displacement by outright or thinly disguised dictatorship, and "re-election" by an incompetent body or irregular plebiscite are the most familiar means employed to achieve the result. The government indulging in **continuismo** often provokes violent counter action in the form of, for example, a **golpe** (q.v.) or **cuartelazo** (q.v.), because the legal manner for winning public office has been frustrated. R.D.H.

Contract.
A contract is "an agreement, upon sufficient consideration, to do or not to do a particular thing." (21 Bl. Comm. 442). It is an agreement enforceable by law. T.C.S.

Contract Clause.
The Constitution of the United States, Art. I, sec. 10, declares: "no State shall . . . pass any Law . . . impairing the Obligation of Contracts." Originally meant, probably, to protect private contracts, judicial interpretation by the Supreme Court under Chief Justice Marshall brought legislative grants and franchises, and charters of incorporation also within its scope (e.g. **Fletcher v. Peck**, 1810; **Dartmouth College v. Woodward**, 1819). The clause was highly important in nineteenth century constitutional development as a standard by which to test the legality of state action affecting private property rights; however, its importance diminished when the due process clause of the Fourteenth Amendment was judicially developed as an appropriate instrument for similar uses. Its significance, therefore, is primarily "historic."
R.H.S.

Conventions of the Constitution.
The term refers to practices, customs, precedents, and understandings which have resulted in rules concerning matters of fundamental political and constitutional importance. These conventions are not law. Yet, they are being observed as though they were laws. On the other hand, courts of

law do not take jurisdiction in a controversy alleging violation of conventions. While most of them have not been reduced to writing, some may be found in documents, such as standing orders or resolutions of legislatures, certain British Imperial Conferences, and the preamble to the Statute of Westminster (1931).

In the United Kingdom, conventions are chiefly, though by no means exclusively, employed as "rules for determining the mode in which the discretionary powers of the Crown (or of the Ministers as servants of the Crown) ought to be exercised" (Dicey). Thus, while in constitutional theory the Queen still possesses vast powers, conventions of the constitution have considerably restricted the royal prerogative or transferred its exercise to other hands. Furthermore, cabinet government in all its ramifications rests almost entirely on conventions (see Parliamentarism).

There are also conventions which either alone or in combination with law regulate relations between members of the Commonwealth and the United Kingdom. For example, changes in the position of the Governor-General were brought about by conventions. Reservation and disallowance of Dominion legislation were abolished by a combination of law and conventions.

In the United States, political parties, congressional committees, and senatorial courtesy are illustrations of the creative power conventions.

Sometimes conventions run counter to the express provisions of written constitutions. In the United States a convention has developed which, in direct contrast to the Constitution, deprives presidential electors of their unrestricted constitutional right to elect President of the United States whomsoever they please. Similarly, in France under the Third Republic a convention prevented the President of the Republic from using his constitutional power to dissolve the Chamber of Deputies.

Conventions of the constitution, then, may limit political power; effect a transfer of power from one political institution to another; supplement the constitution; or nullify some of its provisions. Their greatest importance lies in their ability to reconcile the preservation of the major structure of the constitutional system with the flexibility necessary to respond to the demands for political reform at a time when the adoption of formal amendments to the constitution might be inadvisable or impossible.   W.F.

Convertibility (of money).

The requirement that all other types of money be redeemable at par in gold, and gold (coins or bars) be redeemable at par in other types of money. It is an essential feature of any gold standard. The U.S. ceased redemption of the dollar domestically in 1933; in international payments, since 1934, the dollar can be converted at the rate of $35.00 per fine ounce, or 13.71 grains of gold for $1.00.
    W.N.

Coolidge, Calvin (1872—1933).

29th President of the U.S.; b. Plymouth, Vt., July 4, 1872; d. Northampton, Mass., Jan. 5, 1933; lawyer, Republican politician, Governor of Mass., 1918. Owing to the Boston police strike, he won the Vice-presidency because of his celebrated message to Samuel Gompers, "there is no right to strike against the public safety by anybody, anywhere, anytime." He succeeded to the Presidency upon Harding's death Aug. 2, 1923, and was elected President in 1924. The Coolidge administration was business oriented, stressing government economy and passive "normalcy" policies leading to the "Great Depression."
    M.M.Mc.

Cooper, James Fenimore (1789—1851).

American novelist, historian and political critic. Born in 1789 at Burlington, New Jersey, Cooper grew up at Otsego Hall, vast frontier estate of his man-of-fortune father who represented the Cooperstown, New York, area in Congress (1795-97 and 1799-1801). He was educated as much in the wilderness as in the village school, hardly less by the Indians than by a private tutor at Albany and the professors at Yale where he was an indifferent student and from which he was dismissed at sixteen. He went to sea for five years and then became a naval officer. After marriage at twenty-one, he left the Navy for the life of a country squire and farmer in the Lake Otsego region.

Vowing he could write a better book than an English novel that disappointed him, Cooper produced in 1820 an unsuccessful work of fiction, **Precaution,** that dealt with high English manners about which he knew little. For his second effort, **The Spy** (1821), he turned to the American Revolutionary scene and was promptly rewarded with enthusiastic acceptance. During the next three decades, he wrote, with incredible industry, more than two dozen novels and romances and many volumes of history, letters and criticism. As author of the famous **Leatherstocking Tales,** with their indigenous Daniel Boone-like hero, Natty Bumppo, Cooper was the first American novelist acclaimed widely abroad as well as at home. In **The Last of the Mohicans** (1826) he achieved his most celebrated novel, although he himself preferred **The Pathfinder** (1840). His chief historical work was **The History of the Navy of the United States of America** (1839).

While consul at Lyons and as frequent European traveler in the 1820s and early 1830s, Cooper wrote political and social criticism of Americans for Europeans and of Europeans for Americans whom he felt misunderstood each other. He was a stout patriot, but his comments on Americans displeased many of his countrymen, as did his stand on political issues in some of his novels. The result was that Cooper went from one controversy to another and through a series of lawsuits against his detractors. His chief works in this vein were **Notions of the Americans** (1828), **Letter of J. Fenimore Cooper to General Lafayette** (1831), **A Letter to His Countrymen** (1834) and **The American Democrat** (1838), although his volumes of travel and three European-based novels of the 1830s were also largely studies in society and government.

In **The American Democrat** Cooper fashioned a primer of democracy as he saw it with summaries pro and con of views of governmental concepts and forms. He preferred democracy "to any other system on account of its comparative advantages, and not on account of its perfection." Forecasting troubles for popular rule, he lamented "a disposition in the majority" to go to "extremes" and a tendency in "the minority to abandon all to the current of the day" as the surest way to "radical change." He believed "fearless truth" to be "nearly submerged" and that while "publick opinion is the moving power in this country," the press, which formulated and expressed opinion, was largely inaccurate, partisan, untrustworthy, self-serving and favor-currying—in short, "baneful" and "corrupting." He regarded "the security of property" to be "indispensable to social improvement" and looked on slavery as a state matter "over which the United States has absolutely no control." He died in 1851 at Cooperstown, much misunderstood and disliked, but also admired by leaders like Bryant, Irving and Webster. I.Di.

Cooperative Extension Service.

Federal, State, and county cooperative organization of extension service in the Uninted States. It was established in 1914 to aid in diffusing useful and practical knowledge in agriculture, home economics and related subjects. It defines its function as education for action, education to help people solve problems. Federal funds allocated to States must be matched by State and county funds provided for extension work. Extension programs are conducted in cooperation with the State Universities through specialists in a variety of fields of applied scientific research. In nearly every county there is a staff of one or more extension workers, known as county agents. In most cases, the county staff includes agricultural agents, home economics agents, and agents who work in 4-H and other youth programs. The agricultural abundance and the rapid growth in farm productivity in the United States have been largely due to the efforts of the Extension Service. J.H.

C.O.R.E.

See Congress of Racial Equality.

Core Area.
1. **Domestic.** The area of greatest commercial and population density within a city or metropolitan area.
2. **International.** A specialized meaning has developed in connection with community-building: a strong region of amalgamation (q.v.), either in the form of some one particularly large or strong political unit, or of an increasingly close-knit composite of smaller units, around which a broader community tends to form. A historical example is England, preceding England-Wales and then England-Wales-Scotland. R.W.V.W.

Corfu Channel Case.
In October 1946, two British warships were sunk by mines as they passed through the Corfu Channel in the territorial waters of Albania. Forty-four British sailors were killed, and the British Government brought the matter before the UN Security Council. A resolution which held Albania responsible for the tragedy was vetoed by the Soviet Union. Subsequently, the question of responsibility was referred by both parties to the International Court of Justice. The Court, in an eleven to five opinion, held in favor of the British contention. As a result of this opinion, the British government requested that the Court also fix the amount of damages to be paid by Albania. Although the Albanians claimed that the Court had no jurisdiction over this part of the case, the Court held that the decision of the two parties to submit the dispute gave it the right to fix the damages as well. In a ten to six opinion, the Court held that the Albanian government must have known of the existence of the mines and should therefore pay compensation to Great Britain. The amount of the damages was fixed at $2,400,000. Albania has refused to honor the decision of the Court and neither the Court nor the British government has been able to enforce the decision. J.G.St.

Coroner.
An official, usually elected in U.S. counties, whose primary function is to determine the cause of violent and extraordinary deaths. The coroner acts both as a medical officer in furnishing the state with a decision on the death, and as a legal officer where he believes there is evidence of a crime, summoning a jury of six, examining witnesses, seizing evidence, and aiding in the apprehension of the criminal. Few coroners have the necessary medical and legal qualifications. In several States the coroner has been replaced by an appointed medical examiner with nonmedical functions performed by the prosecuting attorney. J.O.H.

Corporation.
The modern corporation is a creation of the law. Chief Justice John Marshall of the United States Supreme Court in the Dartmouth College Case, 4 Wheaton 518, has defined a corporation as "an artificial being, invisible, intangible, and existing only in contemplation of law." Being an artificial person, the corporation can sue and be sued. It can make contracts the same as a natural person. G.B.T.

Corporative State.
Completed in 1939 after years of propaganda and legislative use of the term, the corporative state was Fascism's claim to a system of representation, social justice, and economic organization superior to capitalism or communism. Mussolini boasted of its universal applicability, but also linked it to a one-party totalitarian state, for its purpose and result were state control of labor and direction of the economy for military ends. The Fascist corporative structure included a Ministry of Corporations (1926) coordinating economic activity; a Labor Chart (1927) outlawing labor's free organization, activity, and movement; and twenty-two corporations (1934) combining workers and employers in defined economic activities to regulate relations and production and to form the basis of representation in the Chamber of Fasci and Corporations (1939) which replaced a Chamber of Deputies similar in composition since 1928. Neither in theory nor practice did Fascist corporativism resemble the free, self-regulating guilds envisaged in Catholic corporatism or in the syndicalism from which the Fascist system developed. E.T.O.

Corporative System.
1. A theoretical reconciliation of capitalism and proletarianism through the instrumentality of industry-wide corporations of employers' and employees' associations, all such corporations being subject to unified control and regulation by the state. 2. A state in which all persons and employments are functionally rather than territorially organized, the functions being administered through great national corporations strictly supervised and controlled by the national government. 3. Exemplifications of the foregoing in such states as Fascist Italy and Nazi Germany. Ch.C.M.

Corpus juris.
The body of Roman civil law which was compiled and promulgated under the authority of Emperor Justinian, A.D. 528—534. It systematized the existing Roman law—which was in a state of much confusion in the sixth century—into the code or codex, pandects or Digest, Institutes and Novels. It served as the foundation for the scientific study of civil law throughout the European continent, regarding the private rights of individuals, and legal remedies by action or suit in civil matters. T.P.

Corregidor.
(Area, approximately 2 square miles; population of the only village, San Jose, 5,681.)
The main island of a group including two other islets, Corregidor lies 3½ miles off the southern point of Bataan in the entrance to Manila Bay. It became a U.S. military station in 1900 and was later reinforced as a major naval stronghold.
As a key defense position in the Philippines campaign, it was the base of a protracted resistance from January to April 1942, surrendering finally on May 6. It was retaken on February 22, 1945, and ultimately became a part of the Philippine Republic in 1947.
M.T.K.

Correlation (in statistics).
A term applied to a variety of measures used to indicate the extent of relationship, or degree of correspondence, between two or more sets of observations, such as between high school and college grades. The correlation coefficient is a ratio that shows the degree of association (or the closeness of association) between any sets of observation represented by numbers. W.N.

Corrupt Practices Act.
A statute prohibiting and penalizing the corrupt use of money in public elections. Generally, it (1) regulates the size of, and prohibits contributions from certain groups, (2) limits the amount of campaign expenditures and prohibits spending for certain purposes, and (3) requires the reporting of contributions and expenditures. Such Acts, with varying provisions, have been passed in each state, by the U.S. Congress, and in most democracies. They are often ineffective.
J.E.R.

Cortes, Hernan.
One of the most prominent of the Spanish **conquistadores**, who invaded and conquered the Aztec Empire of Montezuma in Mexico. Ch.A.

Cosmology.
Philosophical investigation and formulation of the principles according to which reality is articulated.
J.W.Ch.

Costa Rica.
Population, 1,171,000; area, 23,421 sq. miles. Costa Rica has long been distinguished as one of the few consistently effective democracies in Latin America. A relatively homogeneous nation, whose population is predominantly of European stock, Costa Rica has escaped the racial cleavages between Indian and white characteristic of some nations in the region. Inequalities in income and landholding are also less marked than in many parts of Latin America. The relatively high literacy of the nation (eighty per cent) and the concentration of the population in a small intermontane valley have led to the development of a high sense of civic consciousness and national identity.
Until recently, high political leaders were generally selected by electoral means and recruited from a small group of relatively wealthy families, who followed a moderately conservative political philosophy. In 1948, following an attempt by the government

in power to annul the elections of that year, Jose Figueres led an insurrectionary movement and took power. Since that time, the National Liberation party, led by Figueres, which espouses a moderately socialistic philosophy of government, and the conservatives, under a variety of party labels, have alternated in power, succession in each case being determined by remarkably free elections.
Ch.W.A.

Cotton, John (1585—1652).
Puritan clergyman. Educated at Trinity College, Cambridge, and later at Emmanuel College, which was strongly Puritan in composition and orientation, he was forced to flee from England to the Massachusetts Bay Colony in 1633 because of his attempted Puritan "reforms" of Church ritual. His impressive Biblical scholarship enabled him to be appointed immediately to John Wilson's church in Boston, where he remained for the next twenty years. With Anne Hutchinson, he preached regeneration as the foundation for church membership. He would grant political privileges to church members only and would uphold the authority of magistrates over the charter rights of the freemen. He disliked democracy intensely and favored intolerance against Roger Williams. The state, he contended, was merely an agency for enforcing the moral laws of God and the church. On the other hand, he staunchly defended Congregationalism and the independence of the separate churches. His important theological writings include his catechism, **Milk for Babes** (1646), **The Way of the Churches of Christ in New England** (1645), and **The Way of Congregational Churches Cleared** (1648). R.F.H.

Coughlin, Charles Edward.
Born in Hamilton, Ontario October 25, 1891; ordained in 1916; pastor of the Shrine of the Little Flower in Royal Oak, Michigan since 1926. Rose to political prominence in 1936 due to his broadcasts which took a militant anti-Roosevelt line, defended the Nazi regime of Germany and after September 1939 demanded United States neutrality. His magazine **Social Justice** voiced clear pro-Nazi and anti-Semitic opinions. In 1942 Father Coughlin's broadcasts were barred by his ecclesiastical superiors who had previously reprimanded the "radio priest" on various occasions. **Social Justice** was barred from the mails under the espionage law. J.D.

Council for Cultural Cooperation.
See Council of Europe—Council for Cultural Cooperation.

Council-manager.
A pattern of local government in which legislative and policy-making functions are unified in a small plural-member board whose members are commonly elected at large and on a non-partisan basis. The executive functions are entrusted to a trained administrator appointed by and responsible to the legislative body. The plan is in wide use in American cities, in more populous townships, and in a small number of counties. G.S.B.

Council of Censors.
A "Jeffersonian" device in the Pennsylvania Constitution of 1789, which provided for an elective Council to meet every seven years to consider amendments to the constitution. The Council was authorized to publish proposed constitutional changes and to call a drafting convention. The first meeting of the Council was held in 1783. A deadlock developed among the contending factions and the Council was unable to act. The second and last meeting was held in 1789. By this time, the Federalists had come into power and there was little inclination to follow the Jeffersonian theory of adapting constitutions to the changing needs of succeeding generations. The Council device was excluded from the state's more conservative constitution of 1789. G.I.J.

Council of Economic Advisors.
In the U.S.A. a council, with a chairman and two members, appointed by the President with Senate confirmation, and created by the Employment Act of 1946. It is part of the Executive Office of the President. The Council studies the national economy and makes recommendations to the President on policies for economic growth

and stability. The Council of Economic Advisors specifically assists the President in preparing his economic reports to Congress. R.D.S.

Council of Europe.

The Council of Europe is a political institution which provides a general framework for European cooperation in all fields except defense. It was established on 5 May 1945, and its members are: Austria, Belgium, Denmark, France, German Federal Republic, Greece, Ireland, Italy, Luxembourg, Netherlands, Norway, Sweden, Turkey, and United Kingdom. The Council consists of an intergovernmental Committee of Ministers of member nations, and a parliamentary Consultative Assembly, composed of representatives of the parliaments of member nations. Although often called a "debating society," the Council has served to encourage members to work cooperatively in such fields as human rights, where other European organizations were not active. P.A.T.

Council of Europe—
Committee on Local Authorities.

The Committee on Local Authorities was created by the Consultative Assembly of the Council of Europe in 1952 to assure the participation of local authorities in the achievement of the aims of the Council of Europe and to keep local authorities informed of the work of the Council of Europe towards European integration and unity. The Committee reflects the structure and membership of the Consultative Assembly. Each Member State appoints the same number of delegates and substitutes as it nominates to the Assembly. It meets in the House of Europe at Strasbourg, France Its subcommittees include: general affairs, economic and social matters, local finance, cultural matters, housing and town and country planning. Its budget and secretariat are provided by the Council of Europe.
B.J.L.S.

Council of Europe—
Council for Cultural Cooperation.

In 1949, the Consultative Assembly of the Council of Europe made a number of recommendations to consider "European culture" which was defined as having its sources in "the thought and work of free peoples based on centuries of tradition." The Committee of Ministers of the Council of Europe convened a Committee of Cultural Experts who prepared the **European Cultural Convention** which came into force May 5, 1955. Every Member State of the Council of Europe (except Cyprus) ratified the Convention. Spain and the Holy See deposited instruments of accession. By this Convention the European States agreed to study the languages, history, civilization of the others, and of the civilization which is common to them all. To this end the **Council for Cultural Cooperation** was set up with a delegation from each government, three members of the Consultative Assembly, two representatives of and two observers from the European Cultural Foundation and the chairmen of three named committees to be set up on higher education and research, general and technical education, and youth, physical education and adult education. The first meeting of the CCC was at Strasbourg January 10-13, 1962. UNESCO, EEC, ECSC, Euratom, and OECD were represented by observers. B.J.L.S.

Council of Europe—
Resettlement Fund.

Instituted by the Council of Europe on April 16, 1956, to facilitate the solution of European refugee and surplus population problems through the provision for floating guaranteed loans..
B.J.L.S.

Council of Revision
(New York, 1777—1821).

The New York constitution of 1777 provided that the Governor, the Chancellor, and the Judges of the Supreme Court should constitute a Council with a qualified veto over all legislative enactments. During its 44 years it returned over 150 bills with objections, many on constitutional grounds; but about a third were repassed by the necessary 2/3 vote of each house. First Randolph, then Wilson and Madison, proposed a similar council for the new national government, but the plan was defeated in favor of an executive veto. J.A.C.G.

Counterforce.
A military strategy which aims at hitting and taking out (eliminating or neutralizing) an enemy's striking force. It implies a certain balance of forces through the maintenance of an active defense of interception missiles and aircraft and also through the protection of people by means of shelters. Counterforce also implies that the striking force of the country adopting such a strategy is capable of accepting a first, or surprise, blow. The accepting striking force must, therefore, have sufficient survivability to be able to take out the total striking forces which an enemy possesses.   J.D.A.

County.
The largest subdivision for local government in most American states. The unit serves primarily as an administrative unit for state services and programs, but has increasingly taken on features of a municipal, as well as those of a quasi-municipal, corporation. Such units are known as parishes in Louisiana, boroughs in Alaska, and do not exist in Connecticut and Rhode Island.   G.S.B.

County Borough.
One of the two main units of local government in the United Kingdom under which the larger towns and cities are governed. The 83 units of this type are all-purpose governing authorities with no subdivisions, and their councils are responsible for all local government functions in the area covered. Similar units in Scotland are known as burghs.   R.H.B.

County Committee.
Executive group in a political party, which, under the leadership of a chairman exercises supervision over party activities in a county; recruits candidates for public office, conducts election campaigns, raises money, makes patronage recommendations for jobs at all levels of government in the U.S. (Federal, State, and local).   J.O.H.

County Courts (United Kingdom).
Local courts empowered to hear civil cases. England and Wales is divided into geographical districts (circuits) so as to insure that local courts are available to hear minor civil suits throughout the country according to the needs of population. These circuits are no longer related to county boundaries, although the courts still retain the title County Court. The County Court Judges Act of 1950 authorized sixty-five County Court Judges who are appointed by the Lord Chancellor from amongst the ranks of barristers having at least seven years standing before the Bar. They are restricted to common law suits not in excess of 200 pounds and equity cases not in excess of 500 pounds.   C.A.McC.

County government.
A general term embracing government in these political subdivisions which are legal agents of the state and are primarily responsible for providing services prescribed by the state. Basically, they serve rural areas but provide certain types of services for residents of incorporated areas lying within their boundaries. The organizational varieties of county government are many, but the two basic patterns are the county supervisor and county commissioner plans, both of which are characterized by a plural-member governing board and a number of independently elected row offices.   G.S.B.

County—Manager Plan.
An administrator appointed by a small policy-making body of a county, charged with appointment of department heads, budget preparation, and oversight of day-to-day operations of county government.   P.J.C.

County Office Manager.
The chief administrative officer of the Agricultural Stabilization and Conservation Service (ASCS) of the U.S. Department of Agriculture on the county level. He is responsible to the county farmer committee for the execution of farm programs, provides advice and assistance to the committee and the farmers, conducts instructional meetings in the county, and employs personnel for the office and field work. The manager is hired by the county committee, subject to minimum qualifications set down by the ASCS State

committee. The managers and other ASCS county office staff are organized in the National Association of County Office Employees. J.H.

Coup d'etat.
A sudden decisive overthrow of a government, frequently by use of force (e.g., Napoleon Bonaparte's action on 9 November 1799; Louis Napoleon, 2 December 1851). Legitimization of the **fait accompli** frequently requested by a plebiscite. K.B.

Court of Chancery (British)
1474—1875, A Court of Equity.
This court was developed in the 15th century to hear petitions arising out of the inadequacies of the common law courts. The principal deficiency of the common law courts was the inability to distribute justice equitably. These petitions of distress were referred to the Chancellor, who at that time was the monarch's Chief Secretary of State. In time the procedures developed by the Chancellor to handle these petitions were formalized into a system of law which is now known as **Equity**. The court of Chancery itself was, however, abolished by the reform of the British legal system by the Judicial Acts of 1873-75. Today all that remains of this famous court is the Chancery Division of the High Court of Justice and the special Chancery Courts of Lancaster and Durham (see High Court of Justice). C.A.McC.

Court of Petty Sessions.
Local British court to try minor criminal cases without a jury and is composed of two or more justices of the peace. C.A.McC.

Court of Quarter Sessions.
A British court to hear indictable offenses committed within the county or borough in which it is located and which offenses are not of such serious nature that they **must** be tried in the Assize Court. The Court of Quarter Sessions is served by all or most of the Justices of the Peace within its area. As the name implies, it meets four times a year and it hears cases before a jury. C.A.McC.

Court of Sessions (Scotland).
Highest civil court in Scotland. Appeals may be taken to the House of Lords, not however, from the High Court of Justiciary, the highest criminal court in Scotland. C.A.McC.

Courts.
Special social organs authorized to apply the law to concrete cases. In modern democratic societies, their main characteristics tend to include: 1) formal authority to "determine" the law; 2) considerable independence; 3) basic professional character; 4) lack of self-activation, i.e., courts operate only after some outside application to them; 5) considerable formalization; 6) possibility of appeal to higher court, but only limited subordination. Some kind of "courts" or "quasi-courts" are a functional need in all societies, but in primitive societies, totalitarian states and development states various variations from these characteristics appear. Courts can be classified by different criteria, such as jurisdiction, procedure, authority, specialization and level. Of special political significance are the scope of constitution-interpreting authority and of actual law-innovating predisposition and power. Y.D.

Court system of France.
See French Court System.

Covenanting.
The act of providing restrictions in property deeds to housing which exclude certain future uses and sale of the property. The U.S. Supreme Court has held restrictive covenants prohibiting occupancy or sale of houses to non-Caucasians unenforceable in the courts. R.R.R.

Credentials.
The documents by which individual delegates or delegations establish as legitimate their claim to sit in national, state, or local political party conventions or meetings. Each convention determines, normally on recommendation of its credentials committee, which delegates or delegations shall be seated in the event there are contests. Such decisions may affect the outcome of the convention, as was the

case notably at the 1912 and 1952 Republican National Conventions. Th.P.

Credit.
Acceptance of debt in exchange for goods, services, money or other debt; thus permitting the sale of goods without an immediate payment of money by the buyer. Therefore, it becomes at the same time an obligation to pay in the future a fixed amount of money usually plus interest. Money here serves in its function as a standard of deferred payments. W.N.

Creeping Socialism.
A term used in American politics as an election campaign slogan or a propagandistic catch-word to oppose the types of social welfare legislation sponsored by the Roosevelt New Deal and subsequent administrations, especially the Democratic Party policies. The inference is that the country is in danger of being led, either deliberately or innocently, into the adoption of an alien and unwanted system piecemeal, when it would not do so if given the square choice of adopting socialism or rejecting it. H.S.Th.

Criminal Law.
It is that part of the legal order which concerns itself with the treatment and punishment of crime. It establishes rules of conduct according to which members of the legal community are held to do certain things and to avoid doing other, and provides for sanctions or punishment against those who violate these prescribed rules of conduct. Attempts to classify violations of criminal law according to the severity of the offense as felonies, misdemeanors and petty offenses (in France: **crimes, delits** and **contraventions**; in Germany: **Verbrechen, Vergehen** and **Ubertretung**) have not been universally successful. The term crime is used generically to refer to any violation of criminal law. A crime involves a breach of a public duty owed to society, in contrast to a civil trespass which consists in the infringement of a private individual right. The right to protect a private right belongs to the injured individual; the right to indict a criminal offender and to extract punishment properly belongs to organized society, though in the case of some misdemeanors it is widespread practice in the United States not to prosecute in the absence of a complaint by the injured party. In the common law countries it is a fundamental rule of procedural criminal law to consider the defendant innocent until he is proven guilty. Most civilized societies adhere to the rule that behavior can be punished only if it was clearly defined as a crime at the time the act was committed **(nullum crimen sine lege)**, and that the type and severity of punishment may not be increased with retroactive force **(nulla poena sine lege)**. In the United States Constitution both of these principles are contained in the provision prohibiting Congress and the States from passing **ex post facto** laws (Art. I, Sect. 9 and 10).

The oldest purpose of criminal law was to render punitive justice. In primitive systems of law, criminal law often was nothing more than simply revenge; and even in the highly developed systems of modern law, retribution and deterrence were predominant forces until the nineteenth century. Under the influence of the positivist school of criminology the last century saw the statutory enactment of more humane and reasonable standards of punishment. Punishment was made to fit the crime. The twentieth century has carried this development even further. Criminal justice is now primarily preventive in nature. Reform and social rehabilitation play a vital part among its functions, and punishment has been made to fit the individual defendant by means of the indeterminate sentence, probation and parole.
H.R.H.

Criminology.
The systematic study of crime and criminal behavior. J.D.

Cripps, Sir (Richard) Stafford
(1889—1952). British statesman.
Stafford Cripps was a lawyer, a church man, and a Laborite. As a successful barrister in early life he did not officially join the Labor Party until 1929-30, and not until 1931 was he elected to the Parliament as a Laborite. (Later he was expelled from that party but was re-admitted to its mem-

bership in 1945). During the Second World War Sir Stafford served as British Ambassador to the USSR, led a mission to India, and was Lord Privy Seal in the Churchill Ministry. After the War he served under Attlee as President of the Board of Trade, as Minister of Economic Affairs, and as Chancellor of Exchequer. W.C.C.

Cripps Mission.
Sir Stafford Cripps Mission to India in March-April 1942 to seek the nationalists' support for the war effort. It proposed: Dominion Status after the war with the right to secede from the Commonwealth; after the war, establishment of a constitution-making body, comprising the elected delegates of the Provinces and the appointed delegates of the Princes; constitution so framed to be accepted by Britain, subject to the right (a) of any Province to form a separate Dominion and (b) of any State to adhere to the new constitution or not; and Britain to retain control of India's defense in wartime while Indianizing the Viceroy's Council. Rejected by all parties, the proposals implied acceptance of the Pakistan demand and paved the way for the partition of India. C.S.S.

Crisis.
In decision-making, an occasion or situation requiring a response with little or no planning, within a short period of time, and with consequences which vitally affect basic values. In medicine and psychoanalysis, the term refers to a crucial turning point in a developmental process, after which the outcome of the process is more or less certain. J.A.R.

Crisis (Economic).
Another term for recession; follows a period of prosperity in the economy. Characterized by the fact that the businessman's costs have risen faster than his selling prices, by an accumulation of inventory, by the slowing down of the rate of turnover (sale) of goods, which causes in turn the business profits to decline, disappear, or even cause losses. This postpones, and lowers the rate of, new long-term investments in the nation, and spreads unemployment which causes the decline of the national income and of the gross national product. W.N.

Croix de feu.
An extremist French political league of the Right, headed by Colonel de La Roque. After 1934 it professed as its aims to lead France from economic and parliamentary crisis to the reestablishment of order and national honor. K.B.

Cromwell, Oliver. (1599-1658).
English Parliamentarian, revolutionist, military leader, and ruler. Began career as member of Long Parliament. With revolution against Charles I, he soon lead Parliamentary military forces. In victory participated in the factional struggle between Charles, Parliament, and Army. After King's execution and establishment of Commonwealth he dissolved Parliament, became "Lord Protector" and governed under an "Instrument of Government" with a Council of State. Although his behavior foretells modern military dictatorships, he appears to have believed in constitutional government based on a written document, limited political authority, legislative representation of men of substance, and religious toleration. J.P.D.

Cross Filing. (U.S.A.)
In California elections from 1914 until mid 1959, a candidate for Federal or State office could enter more than one party primary at the same election. If successful in obtaining the nomination of the party of his registration, he could also receive other party nominations. Normally, if a candidate "swept the primary" by winning the nominations of both major parties he would run unopposed in the general election. Under cross filing most minor State officials, most legislators, two United States' Senators, a Governor and a Lieutenant Governor were "elected" at the primaries. A popularly approved law (1952) required statement of the party membership of all candidates on the primary election ballot. This party identification law combined with stronger Democratic Party campaign effort resulted in fewer multi-party nominations at subsequent primaries. The

Democratic Party won a majority of the Assembly in 1956, a majority of the Senate, the Governorship and most other Statewide offices in 1958. Cross filing, which had barely survived an initiative in 1952, was abolished by a law approved by the Governor on May 4, 1959. Thus died an election device which the Progressive Party of Governor Hiram W. Johnson created to serve it as a road back to the Republican or Democratic Party should the Progressive Party prove unsuccessful.
J.M.S.

Crossing the Floor.
The term applied in British-type parliaments when a member changes his allegiance from one party to another. With the opposing arrangement of benches in the House of Commons a member would normally have to move from one side of the house to the other in order to indicate his party affiliation and to enter the division lobby on that side of the house.
R.H.B.

Crown.
In British usage this term indicates not only the regalia of monarchy but also the institution as well. Most often, however, Crown signifies the state or the government as a whole, or executive power. One may hold a commission "under the Crown" or one may sue the Crown (with its consent). Demise of the crown indicates vacating of the throne usually by the death of the Monarch and its transfer to a successor.
R.G.N.

Cruel and Unusual Punishments.
Both the Eighth Amendment to the United States Constitution and many state constitutions provide that cruel and unusual punishments shall not be inflicted. The due process clause of the Fourteenth Amendment also includes this guarantee. What punishments are constitutionally cruel and unusual depends both upon history and the changing standards of society. Although the guarantee is rarely invoked successfully, there has been some recent effort in the Supreme Court to extend it, e.g. it is both cruel and unusual to punish for the offense of being addicted to the use of narcotics. [Robinson v. California, 82 S. Ct. 1417 (1962)]
T.C.S.

Cuartelazo.
Literally a "blow from the barracks," this term describes the most frequently employed extra-legal device for the removal from power (or the disciplining) of an existing Latin American government. A segment, or segments, of the military openly defect with or without a "revolutionary plan" and with or without collaboration from certain civilian political figures or groups. The rebel military units move forcibly against government strongholds, ordinarily including the executive palace, the police headquarters and strategically located military camps that remain loyal. Most **cuartelazos** fail; most of those that succeed are carried off by the officers and men of the Army fort located in or near the capital city, location of virtually all power.
R.D.H.

Cuba.
Capital: Havana. Area: 44,218 square miles. Population (1960): 6,743,000. Spanish colony for four centuries until 1898. Constitution of 1901 accepted United States tutelage (Platt Amendment) until abrogation in 1934. U.S. military occupation (1899-1902), and (1906-1909). Under dictatorship of Gerardo Machado (1925-1933). From 1934-1940 Fulgencio Batista controlled but did not occupy the presidency. New Constitution in 1940, and Batista elected President, serving until 1944. Followed by Ramon Grau San Martin (1944-1948), and Carlos Prio Socarrás (1948-1952). Prio displaced by Batista's coup d'etat in 1952. Batista in power (1952-1959). See Castro, Fidel.
R.B.G.

Cult of the Individual (Kult jednostki).
Identified with Joseph Stalin in the USSR. Meant absolute dictatorship and glorification of the leader. Replaced briefly after Stalin's death in March 1953 with "collective leadership" which by June 1957 had completed the circle and reverted to the cult of a new leader. The same practice was followed in Eastern Europe, especially during 1948-56. A good example was Boleslaw Bierut in Poland (see entry).
R.F.S.

Culture.
A collective term for socially acquired behavior patterns of human groups including language, traditions, folkways, customs, and institutions. Culture is transmitted by processes of teaching and learning, whether formal or informal. R.A.B.

Cumulative voting.
That system of voting which allows each voter as many votes as there are representatives to be elected from a multimember district, and permits him to accumulate these votes upon one candidate, or to distribute them among the candidates as he pleases. (In the U.S.A. this crude form of proportional representation has been used to elect members of the Illinois house of representatives since 1870.) R.V.A.

Curzon Line. See Appendix.

Custom as a source of international law.
One of the three sources, the others being treaties and general principles of law recognized by civilized nations. [See Statute I.C.J., Article 38(1).] Custom was the chief source during the early modern period. Treaties are today. Customary international law is made up of practices which are general and accepted as law. It is found by examining primarily actions and pronouncements of states and secondarily writings of experts and, increasingly, decisions of international tribunals. V.R.I.

Cyprus.
Cyprus is an island situated in the north east corner of the Mediterranean. It lies about a hundred miles south of Turkey and about a hundred and twenty miles west of Syria and Lebanon with an area of 3,570 square miles and a population of 517,000 people of which 400,000 are Greeks, 89,000 Turks and about 9,000 others.

At the dawn of modern history Cyprus was under the Turkish rule, but when the British realized that the defense of the Suez Canal required the strategic location of Cyprus, they occupied it by an agreement with Turkey in 1878. The Turks officially recognized the British sovereignty over Cyprus in the treaty of Lausanne in 1923.

Strong nationalistic sentiments rose in Cyprus after World War II among its Greek majority who were strongly opposed by the Turkish minority. The Greeks demanded union with Greece and refused self government at first. After a period of demonstrations and riots the British government invited the Greek and Turkish governments to join with her in negotiations to settle the Cyprus question. The three governments were very cooperative and serious about the success of these negotiations and could easily realize that the Greek majority of the island were devout followers of their Archbishop Makarios. They agreed on granting Cyprus independence with a Greek president assisted by a Turkish vice-president. Makarios finally accepted the principle of self rule, his Greek followers supported him, and Cyprus was announced independent on August 19, 1960. See Enosis. W.B.B.

Czarism.
Government under a czar (from the Latin, **Caesar**), the title assumed by some Mongol and Slavonic rulers, especially by Russian monarchs from Ivan the Terrible (1533-84) to Nicholas II, whose assassination in 1918 ended czarism in Russia. The term bears connotations of absolutist and autocratic rule. M.J.H.

Czechoslovakia.
Multi-national republic, composed of former Austrian lands Bohemia, Moravia, and Silesia and former Hungarian Slovakia and Ruthenia. Area (incl. Sudetenland and Ruth.) 54,240 sq. mi. Largest nat. groups Czechs (8.1 million), Sudeten Germans (1939: 3.5 million), and Slovaks (3.1 million). After T. G. Masaryk and Ed. Benes had persuaded Allies to dissolve Austria-Hungary, C.-S. independence declared Oct. 28, 1918. Wracked by inter-ethnic struggles, C.-S. lost Sudetenland in 1938 and was liquidated by Hitler in March 1939. It was reconstituted at close of World War II under Communist-infiltrated "National Front" government which ceded Ruthenia to USSR and expelled Sudeten Germans. Communist takeover completed February 1948; "socialist" constitution adopted July 1960. K.G.

D

Dahomey. See Appendix.

Dairen.
Port in NE China (pop. over 750,000, including Port Arthur). Dairen comprised part of the Kwantung territory leased from China by Russia in 1898. By the Treaty of Portsmouth (1905), ending the Russo-Japanese War, this territory was turned over to Japan. At the end of World War II, in accordance with agreements reached at the Yalta Conference, Dairen was internationalized, "the preeminent interests of the Soviet Union in this port being safeguarded." When the Soviet Union and the People's Republic of China (Red China) concluded a treaty of alliance in February 1950, the former promised to restore Russian rights in Dairen to China, by 1952. After some delay, this promise was carried out.   S.L.A.

Daladier, Edouard (1884-   ).
Remembered most as the French Premier who went to Munich with Neville Chamberlain in 1938 and engaged in appeasement of Hitler less than a week after he had declared that the entry of Nazi troops in Czechoslovakia would automatically require France to come to the aid of its ally.

Having been a member of the Chamber of Deputies since 1919 and a local mayor since 1912, Daladier had also served as Minister of War, Colonies, Public Education and Public Works, and in the 1930's had served as Minister of Foreign Affairs and of National Defense besides holding the Premiership in 1934 and from 1938 to 1940. Later in 1940 he was prosecuted by Petain at the Riom trials.

Partly because of his connection with Munich, Daladier held no governmental post since the war. In the National Assembly his branch of the Radicals opposed in 1946 the governmental leaders since the Liberation, and in 1951 refused an alliance with the RPF. His group, within the RGR, was closer to the Independents and Peasants than to the Socialists.
   R.B.C.

Dalai Lama. (1935-   )
One of six children of a peasant, the Dalai Lama was born in Chinghai. He was four years old when a party of lamas discovered him as successor to the 13th Dalai Lama. In 1940, he was enthroned at Lhasa as the 14th incarnation of Chen-Re-Zi, the patron god of Tibet. To his over three million followers, he was now the Living Buddha, the Defender of the Faith, and the Holy One. He was educated by learned monks in religion and philosophy, and in the Tantric texts of Lamaism—a variant of Mahayana Buddhism. After Peking's occupation of Tibet, a 17-point Chinese-Tibetan Treaty was signed in 1951 whereby China, in return for Lhasa's surrender of foreign affairs control, agreed to respect Tibet's autonomy and the Dalai Lama's status and function. In March 1959, Red China's repression forced the spiritual and temporal ruler of Tibet to flee to India, where he currently resides.   C.S.S.

Dante Alighieri. (1265-1321)
Italian poet, author of the **Divina Commedia**, b. in Florence, d. in Ravenna. Having served his native city as a councilor and diplomat, he was banished in 1302 by the papalist faction because of his anti-papalist leaning. In Exile, he wrote **De Monarchia**. In it he propounded that a universal temporal monarchy was necessary for universal peace—through which alone man can realize a rational life and enjoy freedom—and that the imperial authority derived immediately from God, not mediately through the pope.
   G.V.W.

Danton, Georges Jacques, (1759-1794).
French revolutionary leader during the "Terror," was a successful Parisian lawyer annd a founder of the republican Cordeliers club. An imposing figure of a man, he was a fanatical orator. He is credited with leading a Paris mob to burn the Tuileries Palace in August, 1792. He was a member of the Convention, and of the first Committee of Public Safety, and a prime mover in replacing the moderate Girondins with the even more dictatorial Jacobins in June, 1793. Later he tried to moderate the extreme terrorism, arguing that though it had been needed to destroy the

old state and institutions, it must now yield to reconstruction of a new society. His enemies, (led by his one-time friend, Robespierre) fervent partisans of continued terrorism, condemned him to death for misuse of public funds; he was guillotined on April 5, 1794, to be followed to the scaffold some three months later by Robespierre. E.G.L.

Danube Commission. See Appendix.

"Dark horse" candidate.
In the United States a presidential candidate is nominated in a political party convention. Two leading contestants may dead lock the balloting. In which case the delegates may turn to a third person, less well known, and give him the nomination as a "dark horse" candidate. M.F.

Darlan, Francois-Jean (1881-1942),
French admiral and politician, commander in chief of all French naval forces (1939-1940). Admiral of the Fleet, vice-premier and minister of defense under the Vichy government, he was in Algiers (1942) as commander in chief of the French armed forces. He negotiated an armistice with the invading allied troops. Declaring himself High Commissioner of French sovereignty in North Africa, he was shortly afterwards assassinated (December 1942). K.B.

Dartmouth College v. Woodward, 17 U.S. (4 Wheat.) 518 (1819).
The Court held that the provisions of a corporate charter may constitute a contract binding upon the government, a doctrine that assumed importance with the increasing role of corporations in American life. Its effect has been narrowed by the doctrine of "strict construction" in favor of the state and more recently by the rule that the police power overrides contracts. J.A.C.G.

Darwinism.
Doctrines derived from or based upon the theories of evolution advanced by the English naturalist Charles Darwin (1909-1882) in his book **The Origin of Species** (1859) and other writings. In political science Darwinism has been used to support the organismic view of the state and many other theories and doctrines predicated on evolutionary postulates. Ch.C.M.

Debellatio.
Is the complete defeat of a state by another state or a coalition of other states in war. It entitles the victor (or victors) to dispose unilaterally of the territory of the vanquished state which loses its character as a subject of international law. Examples prior to World War II are the annexation of Ethiopia by fascist Italy in 1936 and of Austria by Nazi Germany in 1938. W.A.

Debs, Eugene Victor. (1885-1926)
Helped organize the Socialist Party of America, of which he became the five-time presidential candidate from 1900 to 1920. Starting as a locomotive fireman, Debs became secretary-treasurer of the Brotherhood of Locomotive Firemen. In 1893 he helped form the American Railway Union, and in 1894 was imprisoned for his part in the Pullman strike. He won nearly a million votes for President in 1920 while in Atlanta Federal Penitentiary for making an anti-war speech. President Harding later pardoned him. Debs condemned violence, believing that class-conscious workers would achieve power without it. He was born in Terre Haute, Indiana. R.E.Ch.

Decembrists.
Russian conspirators who at the beginning of the reign of Nicholas I staged a military revolt on December 26, 1825 (December 14 old style), hoping to establish a liberal constitution. They belonged to two secret societies formed in the army: a Northern Society at St. Petersburg (constitutional monarchists) and a Southern Society at Kiev (republicans). The leaders included: Pestel, Ryleev, Muraviev-Apostol, Kakhovski, Borisov, and Garbachevski. The Southern Society's plans were frustrated. The Northern Society's uprising was precipitated by the interregnum after the death of Alexander I on December 13, 1825. This ill-planned operation was put down by Nicholas in one day; five of the leaders were executed and 120 were sent to Siberia. The group occupies a niche in the Russian **revolutionary** tradition. W.J.S.

Decision-making.

A process of identifying problems for decision, devising alternative courses of action, and choosing one alternative. Distinguished from problem-solving by (a) requirement that problems be sought rather than given, (b) alternatives formulated rather than given. Sometimes distinguished from policy-making by (a) presence of sanctions to compel compliance with the decision and (b) including not only policy-making in governmental or political organizations, but all kinds of decisional units. J.H.R.

Decision Theory.

An effort to systematically explain the interrelationships of those elements which influence public decision-making. The objective is a comprehensive theory which will describe, and perhaps make possible predictions of how decisions are made under a variety of conditions. A.K.C.

Declaration of Independence.

This is the document in which the British American colonists declared their intention to be separate from the government of Great Britain in 1776. On June 7, 1776, a resolution was passed by the second Continental Congress creating a committee to express the views of the colonists concerning their relations with the British government. Although the committee consisted of Benjamin Franklin, John Adams, Rogers Sherman, Robert R. Livingston, and Thomas Jefferson, the drafted document that was presented to the Continental Congress on June 28, 1776, was almost wholly the work of Jefferson, and the report was adopted without change on July 4. It contains a list of grievances against the King and Parliament of Great Britain and a justification for resistance to the acts of the British government, the justification being based on the idea of natural rights. The document announced the dissolution of all political control by Great Britain and the intention of the new nation to be independent. Although the declaration is without legal effect, the ideas of natural liberty, inalienable rights, and self-government that are expressed in it have had a deep and lasting influence on political thought in America. D.C.

Declaration of Panama.

See Panama, Declaration of.

Declaration of the Rights of Man and Citizen.

The declaration voted by the French National Constituent Assembly on 26 August 1789. Formulated after the "Great Fear" and the August 4 decrees, this document contained the principles of the Revolution of 1789, affirmed the basic inalienable rights of man and provided the basis for the Constitution of 1791, of which it became a part. The Declaration of the Rights of Man appealed to men who beyond the borders of France found an aristocratic society or abuses of royal power an obstacle to the aspirations of the rising "middle class". Though the Constitution of 1791 was short-lived, and the French Revolution changed its course, the Declaration enunciated principles which transcended its own time. European constitutions after World War II echoed the declaration of rights, to which were now added declarations of duties as well. K.B.

Declaratory judgment.

A legal proceeding by which a party to a legal controversy concerning his rights, under a statute, contract, will or other legal document, may go to court and have the court determine any question of construction or validity arising under the instrument and obtain a declaration of his rights, status or other legal relations under the document. It differs from a regular judgment in that the Declaration must stand by itself, that is, no executory process follows the judgment as a matter of course. It is not necessary in order to obtain such judgment that an actual wrong have been committed or is threatened which would entitle one to an action for damages or an injunction. Its purpose is to determine the rights of the parties before a wrong has been committed or seriously threatened and thus to prevent it from occurring. Hence its use is often referred to as "preventive" justice since sometimes justice may require that a party know his rights before an actual wrong has been committed. In order to obtain a Declaratory Judgment it is necessary that there be an actual controversy and the judgment is **res judicata** on the legal points involved in the controversy.

This institution has had a long history in Roman, European and English law and today approximately three-fourths of the American States and the National Government have statutes permitting its use. E.G.T.

Deductive reasoning.

Only that type of reasoning is truly deductive which is strictly "analytic," i.e. which makes explicit what is implied in the meaning of terms or propositions (see **analytic**). Synthetic propositions (see **synthetic**) can be won deductively only from other synthetic propositions. Prior to the development of contemporary scientific standards the terms "deduction" and "deductive" were frequently applied loosely also to derivations of synthetic propositions directly from facts, events, experiences. Although that broader use is not uncommon even today it is objectionable because it blurs the line between deductive and inductive reasoning as well as that between both these types of reasoning and that by analogy, and between all three and reasoning a priori (see a priori). A.B.

De facto recognition.
See Recognition.

De facto war.
See war.

Deflation.

A reduction in the quantity or velocity of money, with no relative decrease in the volume of business, or in quantity of goods and services produced. This causes a decrease in the general price level and an increase in the purchasing power of money. Consequently, there is a redistribution of wealth in the society, the debtors losing and the creditors, as well as people on fixed incomes, gaining. An involuntary deflation is a result of declining economic conditions; a voluntary one results from the actions of a central bank. W.N.

De Gaulle, Charles (Andre Marie)
(1890-   ). French military leader and statesman.

Charles de Gaulle is the son of a retired army officer-teacher. At an early age he decided to go to St. Cyr, from where he graduated in 1911. During the First World War he served under Gen. Henri Petain. Between 1920 and 1940 de Gaulle lived an obscure life, known only as an expert in tank warfare. In 1940 he was made a general and an official of the Ministry of War. After the surrender of France to Germany de Gaulle issued a call for continued resistance to Nazism in cooperation with Great Britain, and organized the French National Committee in London. The British Government recognized him as the leader of Free France. After the liberation of Metropolitan France in 1944-45 de Gaulle returned to his home land to become President of the Provisional Government of France. When the people voted to return to the traditional form instead of instituting a Presidential Government as de Gaulle advocated he resigned from office. Between 1947 and 1959 de Gaulle's followers organized themselves into the R.P.F. in an effort to get him back to power. However, not until 1959 did de Gaulle, with the assistance of the Army, regain political power. In January of 1959 he became President of the Fifth Republic, with strong executive powers. Since then he has been trying to restore "la grandeur de France." Some see de Gaulle as the "man of destiny"; others see him as "the cross of Lorraine". W.C.C.

De jure recognition.
See Recognition.

De jure war.
See war.

Delegation of legislative power.

The granting of authority by the legislature to some other branch of the government, usually to executive-administrative officials, to issue rules and regulations which have the force and effect of law. The courts generally deny that legislative power may be delegated, but generally uphold the delegation and the rules issued under its authority if the legislature has set some standard as a guide to the administrative official. W.V.H.

Demand and Supply.

Explain between themselves the structure of market prices. "Demand" can be defined as the quantity of an

economic good that will be bought at various possible prices at a particular time, while "supply" is the quantity of the same good that will be offered for sale at all possible prices at a particular time. The assertion is that price is a function of both and that it varies directly, but not necessarily proportionately, with demand, and inversely, but not necessarily proportionately, with supply. The actual market price is to be found at the point of equilibrium between these two; they can be plotted, as curves, in a graphic form.
W.N.

Democracy.
Rule by the people, either directly (pure democracy) or through representatives (republicanism). Democracy assumes the value and the fundamental equality of all individuals, although the precise meaning of this is uncertain and has long been debated. Democracy assumes that men are rational and have the capacity to play a part in the governmental process. Political democracy is concerned with those institutions and practices considered necessary to secure the principles mentioned above. These include, for representative democracy, secret, equal, and universal suffrage (no restrictions on the right to vote because of race, creed or color, although such qualifications as to age, residency and literacy are acceptable if equitably applied), a two- or multi-political party system (for the electorate must be presented with alternatives), a responsible government (enforced through recurring elections), majority rule (a concomitant of equality), minority rights (for both individuals and groups, including especially the right of the minority to become a majority and freedom of speech), and government by law under which all are equal. Democracy incorporates two principles, liberty and equality, which are often contradictory. Liberty for the individual may result in inequalities of wealth and power; absolute political equality may result in restrictions on the freedom of the individual to advance his self-interest. The related principles of majority rule and minority rights are often similarly in opposition, for a majority decision may infringe upon minority rights, whereas a too great emphasis upon the latter may negate majority rule. These contradictions are inherent in political democracy, and survival of democratic systems requires that a reasonable balance of them be maintained. The development of the nation-state with its complex problems in domestic and foreign affairs has raised difficult problems for democratic government. Decisions must increasingly be made by experts, and the political role of the ordinary citizen has declined. Consequently, democracy has necessarily become more representative and less direct. A representative system, however, may still be accounted democratic if the people retain control, through elections and other devices, over the governing bodies.
M.J.H.

Denazification.
Allied effort, after German defeat, to wipe out vestiges of Nazism, especially eliminate Nazis from positions of influence in public and economic life. Most systematic effort in U.S. zone: German boards put in charge of classing population in five categories, from "major offenders" to "non-affected." Partly technical, partly political difficulties led to gradual breakdown of the program and broad amnesties. Remainder, even where Nazi record, classed as mere "followers." Thus little effect on personnel in public service. But despite the dubious record of many of the older civil servants, few would wish to see abolished the rule of law (**Rechtstaat**) and the bill of rights or approve of the crimes committed by the Nazi regime. J.H.H.

Denazification (Soviet Zone of Germany).
Based on the Potsdam Agreement, persons who actively participated in the National Socialistic movement were excluded from certain professions, their property was confiscated and they were sentenced to prison terms by special tribunals. First nominal (16/8/47) then all (1952) Nazis and army officers were amnestied and given civic rights. Denazification was frequently used as a tool of communization in the Zone, allowing numerous former Nazis to become Communist functionaries.
E.K.K.

Denial of Justice.
Though states have the right to impose their own laws upon aliens residing within their boundaries and jurisdictions, they also have the correlative duty, under the law of nations, to see to it that justice is not denied. What in a given case would constitute a denial of justice is contingent upon minimum standards of international law. "A strict conformity by authorities of a government with its domestic law," wrote Commissioner Nielsen in the **Neer Case,** "is not necessarily conclusive evidence of the observance of legal duties imposed by international law, although it may be important evidence on that point." It is clear, however, that the so-called "presumption of conformity" will fail whenever denial of justice is shown.
O.S.

Denmark.
Denmark proper comprises 16,571 square miles. About 70 per cent of this area is made up of the peninsula of Jutland; the remaining 30 per cent is made up of approximately 500 islands, most of them lying between Jutland and Sweden. The Faeroes, an island group located 200 miles northwest of Scotland, constitutes a special district under Danish sovereignty. Greenland, until 1953 a colony, is now part of Denmark. The population of Denmark is estimated at over 4,400,000, exclusive of Greenland and the Faeroes. Danish political history may be divided into three periods: (1) the limited monarchy, which went through various stages of growth previous to 1660; (2) the period of absolutism from 1660 to 1849, which distinguishes Danish political history from the steady development of parliamentarism in other democratic countries; and (3) the development of modern democracy since 1849. Since 1849 Denmark has had seven different constitutions (counting the three which dealt with the duchies of Schleswig and Holstein), the last being adopted in June 1953. Although in form a hereditary constitutional monarchy (the present king is Frederick IX), Denmark has a parliamentary system of government with a unicameral legislature (Folketing) selected for four-year terms by proportional representation (P.R.).

The king, however, has the power to dissolve the legislature at any time. The constitution also makes provision for a very restricted form of the referendum. Of the 179 members in the Folketing, 135 are elected by P.R. in the country's 23 districts; 40 additional members are elected on the basis of party strength in the nation-wide voting; and two members are elected for the Faeroes and two for Greenland. Danish election law carries a minimum-voting clause which eliminated the Communist and Single-Tax parties from the Folketing in the 1960 election. The leading political parties are the Social Democrats (76 seats in the Folketing) and Radical Liberals (11 seats), both parties of the left, and the Conservatives (32 seats) and Agrarian Liberals (38 seats), the parties of the right. The Socialist People's party of Aksel Larsen, a Titoist who split with the Communists over repression in Hungary, has 11 seats in the Folketing. The Independents, a right-wing Agrarian splinter group, has 6 seats. A Social Democrat-Radical Liberal coalition formed a ministry after the election of November 1960. Jens Otto Krag, a Social Democrat, has been Premier since September 3, 1962. Denmark has a successful multiparty system based on a classic example of the list system of P.R. Parties have been able to form effective, closely balanced coalitions.
R.V.A.

Department.
In the National Government of the United States, the major executive or administrative units which are responsible to the President are called departments. Their heads are generally known as "Secretary" and collectively these secretaries form the "Cabinet." In many other countries similar units are called "ministries" and their heads "ministers." In the United States, units other than the departments, such as "boards," "commissions" and "administrations" are spoken of as independent establishments when they are responsible directly to the President and not through a department head. Such agencies usually have no representation in the Cabinet. In France the name "departement" is given to a territorial division of Metropolitan

France used for administrative convenience in decentralizing functions of the central government.   H.W.

Department of Agriculture.
See U.S. Department of Agriculture.

Department of Defense.
See U.S. Department of Defense.

Department of Health, Education, and Welfare.
See U.S. Department of Health, Education, and Welfare.

Department of Justice.
See U.S. Department of Justice.

Department of the Air Force.
See U.S. Department of the Air Force.

Department of the Interior.
See U.S. Department of the Interior.

Dependent States.
Those which are under the suzerainty or protection of other nations. The degree of dependency on the one side and control on the other may vary greatly according to the terms of treaties fixing the relationship between them. The precise juristic signification of the term also depends upon the conditions under which the protectorate is recognized by other powers. The terms **protectorate** and **suzerainty** as designations of dependent states are now less frequently used in the terminology of diplomats. The same can be said of the **mandate**, which was associated with the League of Nations. With the decline of imperialism in this century there has been a corresponding decline in the number of juristically dependent states. The so-called "satellite states" of Eastern Europe are in a very different position from **de facto** protectorates. Though they are subjected to various pressures which render their independence more fictitious than real, these states are in a legal sense fully sovereign states.
O.S.

Deportation.
The act of removing someone from a country after his exclusion or expulsion.   C.W.B.

Derivative Right.
A right not specifically guaranteed by the U. S. Constitution, but one which can be derived from one or more of its provisions. Derivative rights have received varying degrees of recognition by the courts and in legislation. One derivative right is freedom of association, derived from most of the 1st Amendment freedoms. It has received considerable recognition notably by the Supreme Court in NAACP v. Alabama, 357 U. S. 449 (1958). Other derivative rights, not very well established, include: the right of the public to be free from subjection to captive audience activities; and the "right-to-know"—the right of news media to have access to government documents.   D.W.Mc.

Desegregation.
The process of removing legal and other artificial barriers to full access to and use of all public and quasi-public facilities where systematically denied on account of race, color, religion, or national origin.
In the U.S.A., complete desegregation of such facilities is the objective of the predominantly Negro civil rights movement with the active support of the federal executive and, in large measure, the federal courts. The basic assumption, consistent with the American Creed and constitutional principles, is that racial segregation and discrimination, supported by law and public policy, is constitutionally and morally wrong.   N.P.T.

Despotism.
Governmental control by absolute, arbitrary, and tyrannical force. Frequently expressed through harshness and oppression; without concern for common good and individual freedom. Exclusive interest of despot in himself.   M.C.V.

DeStalinization.
The campaign, initiated at the Twentieth Congress of the C.P.S.U. in February 1956, of publicly exposing and condemning Stalin's tyrannical mode of rule and subordination of the Party to his personal domination. A concomitant of deStalinization has been the reassertion of the Party's primacy

in Soviet society, and the effort to regularize discussion and criticism within the Party. DeStalinization has also resulted in a general easing of terroristic police controls over the population, a new concern for legality and administrative safeguards against arbitrary arrest, and a greater willingness to reforms in the economic, administrative, and, to a lesser extent, artistic areas of Soviet life. A.Z.R.

Detente.
Term used in disarmament discussions. Slackening or easing of political and military tensions between nations. To be accomplished by such methods as non-aggression pacts, nuclear weapons test bans, summit conferences, demilitarized and/or denuclearized zones (e.g. Rapacki Plan), and partial and/or complete disarmament. H.G.S.

Deterrence Theories.
Formulations of military and diplomatic strategy designed to prevent expected international actions of opponents or allies by means of positions taken by the deterring government. Deterrence is based on the idea that a government, in calculating whether or not to undertake a certain foreign policy or a certain action, will not act if the probable outcome involves costs that will be too high compared to the anticipated gains. The advent of thermonuclear weapons and intercontinental missiles has stimulated the theorizing about deterrence. Mutual deterrence is thought to prevent general war because opposing power blocs, having modern weapons, can anticipate that any type of major attack would involve a retaliation of fearfully destructive proportions. Elaborations of the idea have produced numerous calculations of how deterrence might be made to work as a control on international politics. Graduated deterrence for example, is measured retaliation against small attacks to forestall further attacks. Ch.A.Mc.

Deutsche Demokratische Republik (DDR).
See German Democratic Republic.

Dewey, John. (1859-1952)
American philosopher, educator, and political theorist. Was born in Burlington, Vermont, graduated from the University of Vermont, and got his Ph.D. from Johns Hopkins University. Taught philosophy at Universities of Minnesota, Michigan, and Columbia, and directed the School of Education at the University of Chicago. He applied his instrumentalist philosophy to ethical, social, and political problems of his time in **The Public and Its Problems, Liberalism and Social Action, Freedom and Culture,** and **Problems of Man.** Besides helping to organize the American Civil Liberties Union and the American Association of University Professors, he aided many controversial causes. R.E.Ch.

Dharma.
The Law, or basic assumptions for conduct of the individual in Buddhist society and of the ruler in the context of the State. Within the Tripitaka or Three Baskets of the Law are contained specific sections treating the sovereign powers and jurisdiction of the State, and defining the proper attitudes of ruler to subject and subject to governing hierarchy. Relationships between the monastic order and the secular powers are also clarified and defined. M.W.W.

Dhimmi (People of the Pact).
They were the non-Muslim religious groups (chiefly Christians and Jews), also known as the 'People of the Book', living in the Islamic State but who could take no active part in its civil and political life on terms of equality. Professing a monotheistic creed, they could not be classified as 'idolaters' (although they were classified as 'unbelievers'), but they had to sign a pact, **dhimma**, according to which they had to pay a head tax, **jizyah**, in return for exemption from military service, freedom of worship, inviolability of person and property and a certain measure of self-government. The autonomous religious group, **millah**, was governed by its own ecclesiastical authorities in all matters of personal status as well as in most cases of civil and even criminal judicial procedure. Except for occasional official restrictions or popular discriminations, the **dhimmi** pursued their religious and cultural life freely. F.M.N.

Dialectic.
From the Greek DIALEGEIN, which means literally 'talking divisively' or 'collecting what is separate' (DIA—divide, separate; LEGEIN—talk, collect, explain). When it refers to discourse it can simply be recognized by its combination of opposites in whatever is proposed: 'neither-nor, but both', or 'on the one hand-on the other hand'. Heraclitus was the first to develop an entire philosophic outlook from the dialectic. The main tenets of his dialectic outlook are: 1. all things are inter-connected; 2. all things are in flux; 3. contradictions are the stuff of reality. Hegel claimed that he could incorporate every single statement of Heraclitus into his system without any difficulty, and his dialectic outlook is at the basis of the Communist ideology and the Soviet Dialectic Materialism. Particularly Engels, Marx's disciple, devoted a great deal of his time to spell out the essential components of the dialectic. Stalin's **Dialectical and Historical Materialism** (1938) incorporates in its four principles, in addition to Heraclitus' three principles, Engels' principle of quantity-quality: 1. the interconnectedness of things in nature; 2. the mobility (flux) of things and their development; 3. the transformation of quantity into quality; 4. inherent contradictoriness of reality. The fundamental notion underlying all four principles of the dialectic is the notion of "flux" or "change" which implies transformation, organic interconnectedness of even contradictories, as well as change of quantity into quality. Despite Stalin's and Engels' asseverations that this view is "contrary to metaphysics", only the wildest metaphysician would deny that things change. The principles of dialectic are little more than not very meaningful commonsense on stilts; they are completely useless as hypotheses or theories about reality. However, if the dialectic is taken subjectivistically, psychologically, its meaning consists in the notion of Revolution, the notion of a willful, collective (proletarian) transformation (change) of history. As such it has, of course, immense political significance. That this meaning of the dialectic is at the heart of Communism is clearly testified to by the early writings of Marx (1843-1846), by Lenin's **Philosophical Notebooks** (1914-1917), and by the most intelligent and erudite exposition of the Marxian dialectic in Georg Lukacs' **History and Class-Consciousness** (1923).   V.Z.

Dialectical Materialism.
A systematic theory of social change, sometimes called Historical Materialism, developed by Karl Marx. Marx agreed with Hegel that human history was a process, but disagreed on the nature of the process. According to Marx, the agents of historical change are the material means of producing goods, and the mode, or way, in which the means are used. The means are the tools and techniques, including human labor and organizational techniques, by which economic production takes place. The mode is the way in which the ruling class organizes and uses the means for its own interest. The ruling class maintains its position by its organized control over the productive mechanism of society, which also gives it control over the other social institutions. However, new means of production spring up disarranging the order and control of the established ruling class. Part of the working class learns to master the new techniques, thus establishing itself as rightful challenger to the old rulers. When this process reaches fruition, a revolution takes place and a new ruling class based on the new mode of production is established. Such was the process by which the middle class overcame the feudal landed aristocracy.

Marx also detected what he believed to be a process of simplification. Increased standardization of productive processes through division of labor and machine production meant that a few people could control increasingly large enterprises. Also, workers would increasingly become unskilled feeders of machines. Hence, instead of a hierarchy of classes, one increasingly would have a small but cohesive ruling class and a large undifferentiated working class. When, according to Marx, this working class discovers its power, the ultimate revolution will take place, and the classless good society will become a reality.　　　　　　R.M.T.

Dialectic process.
According to Hegel, the process which characterizes historical change in which there is a necessary movement from thesis to antithesis, followed by a synthesis which reconciles the two; more broadly, the uneven and tidelike character of social change.
　　　　　　　　　　　　J.W.Ch.

Diaspora. (dispersion)
Greek term referring to nation or part of a nation separated from its national territory, but preseving its national identity while scattered among other peoples. Most frequently refers to Jewish population residing outside of Palestine or Israel. Sometimes used interchangeably with Galut or Golah, "exile," of Jewish people from Holy Land.　　　　　　　　　　　　S.H.

Diaz, Porfirio.
President of Mexico. Born Oaxaca, Mexico, Sept. 15, 1830. Died Paris, France, July 2, 1915. Soldier, lawyer, and Liberal congressman. Captured Mexico City from forces of Emperor Maximilian in 1867. Unsuccessful candidate for president in 1867 and 1871. Seized the presidency in 1876, and was elected to the office in 1877. Chief Justice of the Supreme Court in 1880. Again elected President in 1884, and remained until deposed in 1911 by revolution led by Francisco Madero. His dictatorship was marked by encouragement of foreign investment and industry, with most Mexicans receiving little benefit.　　　　　　　R.B.G.

Dictatorship.
Regime of unchallenged privilege for leader or leadership group. Exaltation of leadership, supported by elite of one and only party. Dictator's will is frequently law; rule by decree in police state. "Might is right." M.C.V.

Dictatorship of the Proletariat.
Marxists profess that the historic mission of the working class is to destroy capitalism and build socialism. In the Soviet view the transformation from capitalism to socialism requires that power be in the hands of the working people, led by the working class, which is guided by the party, which in turn is led by the party leadership or, as in the days of the "cult of personality," by one leader only. Hence the Western criticism: the dictatorship is not of but over the proletariat.　　　　　　　　　　　K.H.W.

Diem, Ngo-Dinh (1901-1963).
President of the Republic of Vietnam, born at Hue in 1901. Home minister (1932), Prime minister (1954). Was elected as President (1955, re-elected in 1961). Persistent nationalist and anti-Communist. Assassinated November 2, 1963.　　　　　　　H.C.K.

Dien-Bien-Phu, battle of.
The decisive battle of bringing about the end of war in Indo-China (1946-1954). Fought between Communist-lead Viet-Minh troops, supported by Communist China, and the U.S.-backed French Allied forces of Vietnam, Cambodia and Laos. Dien-Bien-Phu was one of the most important strategic posts for both sides en route to Luang-Prabang, about 200 miles north-west of Hanoi.
It fell into Viet-Minh's hands on 17 May 1954, and an agreement (cease-fire) concluded at Geneva on July 21 divided the country into two portions (Vietnam, Viet-Minh) separated by the 17th parallel.　　　　　　H.C.K.

Dillon's Rule.
A principle of municipal corporation law which holds that a municipality can exercise only those powers that: (1) are expressly granted, or that (2) are implied in or incidental to those expressly granted, or that (3) are essential for the purposes of the municipal government. All cases of "reasonable" doubt are resolved against the municipality. The rule was first stated by John F. Dillon, a noted nineteenth-century Iowa judge. It is applied, with slight variations, in all 50 states in the U.S.A.　　　C.R.A.

Diplomacy.
The practiced art of official representation abroad of sovereign states by persons and organizations specialized in such conduct. The basic functions of diplomacy are to convey information, to gather information, to conduct negotiations, and to assist in

the formulation of foreign policies made by heads of state in matters of war and peace. Ch.A.Mc.

Diplomatic Agents.
Accredited representative of one head of state to another. Diplomats are subject to "agréments" of acceptability and subject to recall if declared "persona non grata". Diplomats obtain credentials from their governments to conduct relations, negotiate and sign agreements ("full powers"). They and their retinue enjoy privileges and immunities including inviolability of mission, archives, correspondence, immunity from civil and criminal jurisdiction and taxation. Rules governing rank and privileges of agents based on customary international law, were codified 1815 (Congress of Vienna), revised 1961 (Vienna Convention). Recognized diplomatic ranks are 1) Ambassadors and nuncios, 2) Envoys and Ministers, 3) Chargé d'affaires (accredited to Foreign Ministers only). F.B.G.

Diplomatic immunity in international law.
Extensive immunity from arrest; detention; criminal, civil or administrative proceedings; taxes and performance of services enjoyed by a diplomat, his family, staff and servants while in a receiving state and, probably, traveling to it. Also the inviolability of a diplomatic mission's premises, archives, bags, correspondence and (within limits) its members, residences. [See 1961 Vienna Convention (Diplomatic Relations), Articles 22-40.] V.R.I.

Direct Legislation.
Direct legislation allows voters to supplement the actions of a legislative body by enacting or vetoing laws. The initiative is a mechanism which enables voters to enact laws or constitutional amendments without legislative action. It has been used for many years in Switzerland and is used in twenty-one states in the United States. The referendum allows voters to pass upon proposed constitutions, proposed constitutional amendments, and statutes enacted by a legislative body. The constitutional referendum has a long history of use. South Dakota in 1898 was the first American state to adopt the statutory referendum. J.F.Z.

Directory of France (1795-1799).
See French Directory (1795-1799).

Direct Primary.
A nominating election in which voters directly choose party candidates to run for public office in final elections. First used in Pennsylvania during the 1840's and in a few other states before 1900, Wisconsin enacted the first compulsory, state-wide primary law in 1903. Within fifteen years all but four states substituted the primary for the convention. Today most national, state and local candidates are selected by some kind of primary which is regulated closely by state law and paid for by public funds. Some forty states use a "closed" version which restricts voting in specific party primaries to those previously enrolled as members or who declare (subject to challenge) party membership at the polls. An "open" system in other states permits qualified electors to vote in any primary without revealing or proving party affiliation. Where certain officers, such as judges, legislators (two states), city councilmen or school board members, are elected without party identification, the top two candidates are named by a "nonpartisan" primary. Introduced as a democratic reform aimed at eliminating political corruption and checking party machines, the direct primary has been much criticized on charges that it accomplishes neither yet is expensive, weakens party responsibility, causes internal party splits, discourages able candidates, promotes demagoguery, lengthens the ballot, complicates party platform preparation, and often fails to arouse voter interest. C.F.N.

Dirigisme.
A term appearing after 1930 in French politics to identify a system in which the State orients activity by both direct and indirect intervention, while preserving the framework of a capitalistic economy. Its success depends partly on the familiarity of the

members of the government with the economy of the country and their skill in the use of statistics. Devices used include the control of credit, money, prices, and investments, and regulation of foreign trade and of the system of social security.

Although the term is French, it appears that the essence of dirigisme was reflected in the New Deal program of the 1930's in the United States. In France after World War II the RGR conducted an offensive in 1946 against the dirigisme of the Socialist Minister of National Economy, Andre Philip. It was de Gaulle's Provisional Government that had set the pattern of dirigisme, and although his RPF later criticized it, certain parts of the Gaullist program, such as association of capital and labor and the attempt toward independent French rearmament, imply support of it. The Moderates and Radicals claimed that the results of the 1951 election condemned dirigisme. R.B.C.

Dirksen, Everett McKinley.
Born January 4, 1896; U.S. Senate since November 7, 1950; Republican—Illinois. R.A.B.

Disarmament.
An ambiguous term used to refer both to abolition of armaments and various degrees of arms reduction, limitation and control. It may be achieved by unilateral or multilateral action, by agreements which prescribe controls or not; it may be partial or may be local or general in its nature.

The Washington Naval Conference (1921-22), the Geneva Naval Conference (1927), the London Naval Conference (1930) and (1936) were general in the sense that they affected the major naval powers, partial in the sense that they covered only a fraction of one aspect of naval armaments, multilateral and uncontrolled. Even the Geneva Conference of 1932 did not attempt abolition but merely severe reduction of most categories of armaments.

The period since 1945 has seen attempts by the United States to set up an International Atomic Development Authority (the Baruch plan) with the power to control, inspect and license all atomic energy followed by the destruction of existing atomic weapons (1946). In 1951 the Atomic Energy Commission and the Commission for Conventional Armaments were merged into the United Nations Disarmament Commission, following deadlocks in both bodies which centered round the desire of the Soviet Union to seek destruction of existing atomic weapons and their prohibition before controls and a general reduction of one-third in armed forces, and a Western emphasis upon priority of controls, disclosure and verification of information as a beginning step.

In the 1952-1954 period the Western powers produced complete plans for a comprehensive balanced reduction of armaments under international control, the United States abandoning its insistence on the waiver of the veto under the Baruch Plan. The general position of the Soviet Union remained unchanged.

In the 1955-57 period both sides concentrated on partial disarmament recognizing that past production of fissionable materials could not be accounted for, and studying feasible measures to safeguard a disarmament system such as cessation of nuclear testing, defense against surprise attack and limitation of armed forces and conventional armaments. The Soviet Union suddenly altered its approach, arguing that nuclear weapons should not be eliminated until cuts in others' arms were made, proposing the establishment of an international control agency, ground inspection at ports, railway junctions, motor roads and airdromes, the dismantling of all foreign bases, a ban on nuclear weapons testing, and acceptance of force levels proposed by the Western powers. At Geneva in July, 1955 Prime Minister Eden proposed a mutual security pact in Europe, arms control in Germany and Eastern Europe under reciprocal supervision and a demilitarized area between East and West. President Eisenhower suggested mutual aerial reconnaissance as a beginning step to comprehensive disarmament. In September, 1955 the United States representative suddenly reserved all previous positions pending the outcome of studies on control techniques thus casting serious doubt on the sincerity of the Western proposals. On August 29, 1957 all Western positions were combined in one inseparable package arrangement. In November 1957 the Disarmament Commission was enlarged from 11-25 members and the Soviet Union refused to participate in the new body. The United States moved to separate the whole range of proposals and in March 31, 1958 the Soviet Union unilaterally renounced further tests. The United States followed suit. This ban was suddenly broken by the Soviet Union in the summer of 1961 with a series of tests, followed by the United States in the spring of 1962. In September, 1959 the United States, France, the United Kingdom and the Soviet Union set up a 10-member committee to consider disarmament matters.

Two technical conferences, one to study measures to prevent surprise attack and one on detection of violations of the nuclear test ban, were held in 1958. The former recessed after six weeks and did not reconvene. The latter reached agreed conclusions, and the work continued through the following year. They were broken off when the Soviet Union resumed nuclear testing.

In conclusion, constant and detailed negotiations have produced no agreements which have resulted in multilateral arms reduction by treaty. C.B.J.

Discharge Petition.
In the U. S. House of Representatives, if either a subject matter committee or the Rules Committee fails to report out a bill within 30 days and seven days respectively, a discharge petition signed by at least 219 House members carries the decision of reporting the bill to the floor of the House. Either on the second or fourth Monday of the month the discharge petition is subject to 20 minutes' debate. If the motion to discharge the committee from considering a bill passes, the bill is placed on the Discharge Calendar where it receives priority for floor consideration. J.A.E.

Discrimination.
The act of depriving an individual or a group of equality of opportunity. In the Intergroup Relations field, the term is usually applied to racial, religious, nationality, ethnic, and social class groups. The major areas of discrimination are employment, housing, public accommodations, education, and social discrimination. In the U.S.A. there have been some federal prohibitions, and many state prohibitions through the passage of laws prohibiting discrimination. M.J.S.

Disengagement.
Various schemes for limiting armed forces in the center of Europe were advanced in the years around 1960. The term "disengagement" has been used for such plans, which hopefully were intended to decrease Cold War tensions, "liberate" Eastern European countries, and unify Germany. Disengagement implies the withdrawal of foreign (Big Power) troops, while the remaining local troops are neutralized and de-nuclearized by international agreements. H.L.M.

Disraeli, Benjamin.
English statesman and novelist, (1804-1881). Although commencing political life as a Radical, Disraeli became the most successful leader of the Conservative Party, becoming twice prime minister. He was knighted Earl of Beaconsfield in 1876.

A Parliamentary leader of genius, Disraeli also was a considerable political thinker, though his ideas are to be found in his speeches and novels, rather than in formal treatises. Endeavoring to adapt the Tory interest to the modern democratic and industrial age, he was the author of various social reforms (notably the commencement of a program of housing at public expense) and was responsible for the Reform Bill of 1867—though the act, as finally passed, did not wholly accord with his views of good parliamentary selection and representation. The enlargement of the British Empire, including the coronation of Victoria as Empress of India, and his success at the Congress of Berlin (1876), were among his many achievements.

The first man of Jewish origin to hold high political office in Britain, Disraeli embellished his politics, like his fiction, with an almost Oriental imagination. Strongly condemning the evils of the early industrial era (see his novel **Sybil**, 1845), he sought to preserve the stability and justice of the old English order, including a strong element of aristocracy, and was described as "the old Jew gentleman sitting on the top of chaos." R.K.

Dissolution Power.
The power to dissolve parliament before the normal expiration of the legislative term. Dissolution is followed by general elections. In Great Britain the dissolution power is wielded by the Prime Minister although the Monarch nominally gives the order. In France the President of the Republic has this power under the 1958 Constitution. In many countries this power does not exist or is severely circumscribed.
R.G.N.

Distribution of powers.
A system of dividing governmental authority along geographical lines. The principle of division in the United States between the national and state levels is federalism. The unitary principle gives full authority to the states in their relations with local governments. Alternatives to federalism are the unitary system where authority resides in the central government (e.g., United Kingdom, France) and confederation where the local governments jointly create a central government while retaining their own sovereignty (e.g., the U.S. under the Articles of Confederation). Cf., division of powers, federalism. R.R.R.

District Attorney.
In the United States, a public officer, also called a prosecuting attorney, state's attorney, county attorney; usually elected at the county level for terms of 2, 4, 6 years. He prosecutes for the state in criminal cases and defends the state or local bodies in suits brought against them. Each Federal judicial district has a U.S. District Attorney, appointed by the President and responsible to the Attorney General for a term of 4 years. He brings evidence to grand juries for indictments and prosecutes criminal cases for violation of national law. J.O.H.

District Court.
In the United States, the trial courts of general jurisdiction on Federal questions. Each state has at least one court, some as many as four. The District of Columbia also constitutes a district, making a total of approximately 100, with 1-25 Federal District judges in each district. Each case is usually heard by one judge. Each district has a U.S. attorney. Most cases may be reviewed by the Circuit court of appeals.
In the states, the district courts (sometimes called county or circuit courts) are the general trial courts with complete criminal and civil jurisdiction. Judges are usually elected and hold court at stated times in the county court houses of the district. Appeals from Justice of the Peace Courts may be heard. J.O.H.

District Officer.
An administrative officer charged with overseeing diverse governmental functions in rural districts. As associated with the British colonial administration, an appointee of the Colonial Office (in such present or former colonial areas as Malaya, Burma and Hong Kong). In Thailand, for example, the District Officer serves subject to the control of the Provincial Governor, but as an appointee of the central Ministry of the Interior. The Officer's authority varies according to local situation or local interpretation of colonial policy, but normally entails a degree of responsibility adjunct to that of State or Provincial administrative head. M.W.W.

Divine Right of Kings.
This theory holds that royal power is like the power of God, it is unrestricted and absolute; it derives immediately from God. The theological and philosophical tenets which hold that the ultimate source of authority is the Creator are thus exploited for political purposes. Developed in the sixteenth and seventeenth centuries in opposition to the theory of contract as well as to restrictions of royal power by a parliament, the theory favors a national church under the King, and consequently denies any form of papal supremacy. Its classic

exposition is by James I of England, in **The True Law of Free Monarchy.**
T.P.

Dixiecrat Party.
States' Rights Democratic Party (in U.S.A.). Political party formed for the presidential elections of 1948. It was a reaction by southern Democrats against the increasing tendency of national Democratic leaders to support federal action in support of the civil rights of Negroes, and in particular the strong stand of President Truman and the party convention in 1948. The party hoped to bring about Truman's defeat by withdrawing southern electoral votes and possibly to control the selection of the president by causing the election to be thrown into the House of Representatives. The party was able to have its candidates, J. Strom Thurmond (Governor of South Carolina) and Fielding Wright (Governor of Mississippi) designated as the Democratic Party candidates in four states, Alabama, South Carolina, Mississippi, and Louisiana, and these were the only states where the party was successful. It received an electoral vote of 39, a number inadequate to achieve any of the party's goals.
J.S.S.

Djilas, Milovan. (1911-   ).
Former Yugoslav Vice-President, he was considered Tito's heir. A Montenegrin, educated at Belgrade University, he founded the first Communist youth movement. In 1940 he became a member of the Politburo. Since 1952 he has written critically of the regime and communism—e.g. **The New Class** (1957)— for which he was expelled from the Central Committee and jailed for disseminating "hostile propaganda." In 1962 he was sentenced again when **Conversations with Stalin** was published.
J.J.K.

"Doctors' Plot".
The name given to the incipient purge of Soviet party leaders in 1953. On January 13, 1953, PRAVDA announced the arrest of nine prominent physicians, almost all Jewish, who were charged with having murdered important Soviet personages in their care and plotting the death of still others. It is believed that the charges were fabricated by Stalin in order to eliminate Beria, Molotov, Kaganovich, Mikoyan and Voroshilov, who were to be implicated in the doctors' machinations. The purge collapsed with Stalin's death and was exposed by Khrushchev at Party Congress XX.
D.N.J.

Doctrine of implied powers.
A principle underlying the U.S. Constitution from which the Congress has inferred for itself powers not expressly delegated by the Constitution itself. Art. I. Sec. 8 enumerates powers which are explicitly delegated to the Congress to exercise. Immediately following is a clause providing that Congress may do what is "necessary and proper" to carry out the preceding list of powers. This doctrine has also been referred to as the "elastic clause." Chief Justice John Marshall and the Supreme Court validated congressional use of the implied power in the case of **McCulloch vs. Maryland** (1819), based on congressional establishment of a national bank, power to do so implied from such expressly delegated powers as coining money, taxing, borrowing, and spending.
R.R.R.

Doctrine of State Immunity.
A doctrine under the common law which holds that a state is not responsible in its own courts for the tortious acts of its agents, since the sovereign might not be sued in his own courts without his consent. The doctrine rests on reasons of public policy, logic and practicality. "It is obvious that the public service would be hindered, and the public safety endangered, if the supreme authority could be subjected to suit at the instance of every citizen. . . ." **(The Siren,** 7 Wall, 152 [1869]). There "can be no legal right against the authority that makes the law on which the right depends." (**Kawananakoa v. Polyblank,** 205 U. S. 349 [1907]).

The immunity of the United States applies to suits either by individuals or by any of the states. On the other hand, it "does not follow that because a state may be sued by the United States without its consent, therefore the United States may be sued by a state without its consent." (**Kansas v,**

United States, 204 U. S. 331 [1907]). This exemption from the judicial process extends to the property of the United States as well. (**United States v. Alabama**, 313 U. S. 274 [1941]). However, when the United States institutes a suit, it waives the exemption to the point of allowing the defendant a presentation "of the set-offs, legal and equitable, to the extent of the demand made or property claimed," and if the United States proceeds **in rem** (suits against items of merchandise or property) then it has opened "to consideration all claims and equities in regard to the property libelled," and the United States stands, with reference to the rights of defendants or claimants, "precisely as private suitors" except that the United States is "exempt from costs and from affirmative relief" against it, "beyond the demand or property in controversy." (**The Siren, ibid.**)

Under the doctrine of state immunity, there is a distinction between the United States and its government. For example, the Joint Resolution of Congress of June 5, 1933, voided the "gold clauses" in private and public contracts; but the Supreme Court held the Resolution valid with regard to private contracts, (**Norman v. Baltimore & Ohio R. R. Co.**, 294 U. S. 240 [1935]), and invalid with respect to government bonds on the ground that a government bond is an inviolable contract of the United States made by Congress under its constitutional authority to borrow money on the credit of the United States. (**Perry v. United States**, 294 U. S. 330 [1935]).

Involved also in this doctrine is the question of when is a suit against a federal officer a suit against the United States? If the officer is enforcing a law the courts hold to be unconstitutional, then the suit is against the officer as an individual and not against the United States, since the United States cannot confer authority under unconstitutional statutes. If the officer acts under a valid statute but is claimed to have acted outside the scope or in excess of his authority (**ultra vires**), then the suit, again, is against the officer as an individual and not against the United States. However, for the torts of its agents acting within the scope of their authority and under a valid law, the United States has assumed limited responsibility. Congress has from time to time permitted suits for such types of tort claims as admiralty and maritime torts, patent infringements, damages to fishing beds caused by dredging operations, and injuries caused by federal corporations performing in public interest. Generally, until the Federal Tort Claims Act of 1946 was passed, the injured individual had but two weak remedies — a private action against the federal officer concerned for damages, and a private money bill in Congress.

Consent by the United States to be sued by individuals or any of the states can be given only by act of Congress; and such statutory action must be strictly interpreted. Congress may authorize certain governmental agencies to sue and be sued and determine the extent of their liability, and to endow other agencies with immunity from suit. Under the Federal Tort Claims Act of 1946, the tort liability of the United States is limited to "damage to or loss of property or on account of personal injury or death caused by the negligent or wrongful act or omission of an employee of the Government while acting within the scope of his office or employment, under circumstances where the United States, if a private person, would be liable to the claimant for such damage, loss, injury, or death in accordance with the law of the place where the act or omission occurred." Detailed procedures were provided for allowable suits, and remedies were provided departmentally and within the system of regular courts or in the Court of Claims of the United States which was established in 1855.

Immunity was extended to the states by the Eleventh Amendment to the Constitution overruling **Chisholm v. Georgia**, 2 Dall. 419 (1793) in which the Supreme Court had held that insofar as the Union was concerned the states were not sovereign and so could be sued in the federal courts. However, the Fourteenth Amendment imposed drastic limitations on action by the states against private rights of individuals and asserted the supremacy of federal over state law. How can this supremacy be enforced if the states could not be sued in the federal courts? The Supreme Court resolved the problem by differentiating between the exercise of a corrective power to restrain state action held to violate federal law and of a constructive power to compel state action to enforce federal law. The latter power is not proscribed by the Eleventh Amendment. (**Dr. Johns Hopkins, Plaintiff in Error v. Clemson Agricultural College**, 221 U. S. 636 [1911]).

For official acts of its officers, the states are responsible under the Fourteenth Amendment, and the officers are immune from personal liability. However, for acts performed unofficially or outside the scope of their authority, such officers are liable in private suits for damages. For official actions of a state officer administering a constitutional law of his state the state cannot be sued in a federal court and also cannot be sued in any court unless it gives its consent. As a remedy in such cases, the states have created courts of claim of their own.

One state may sue another in the federal courts only in the interest of its public and not on behalf of private interests. (**United States v. North Carolina**, 136 U. S. 211 [1890]). A state, by action of its legislature, may waive its immunity from suit under the Eleventh Amendment, and may make conditions for the waiving or retract the waiver. By permitting itself to be sued in its own courts, however, a state does not automatically waive its immunity under the Eleventh Amendment.

Inroads into the doctrine of state immunity have been made by the creation of courts of claims and the passage of limited torts claims acts; but the degree of liability, at both the federal and state levels, is still far too limited. O.K.

Doctrine of Suability.

Related to the ancient concept that "a king can do no wrong" is the principle of jurisprudence that a sovereign state, as the source of all law, may not be sued without its consent. Permission to sue a state in its own courts may be granted, however, as has been done for certain purposes in the United States Court of Claims and in certain European administrative courts. Likewise, the immunity of states in the United States has been affected by the Constitution which conferred original jurisdiction on the Supreme Court over controversies between the national and state governments and between two or more states. Although the Court held very early (Chisholm v. Georgia, 1793) that citizens of one state could bring suit in federal courts against another state without its consent, the Eleventh Amendment, ratified in 1798, specifically prohibits such actions. C.F.N.

Doctrine of Vested Rights.

An idea that grew out of the doctrine of natural rights which claimed that there are some rights which, even though they are not guaranteed by the Constitution of the United States, are subject to protection by agencies of government. Among the specific vested rights were the ownership of property and the inviolability of contracts. Originally the doctrine of vested rights was an attempt to protect certain rights related to property and contracts against the actions of state legislatures. The first official reference to this idea was made in 1795 by Justice William Patterson in the Circuit Court for Pennsylvania in **Vanhorne's Lessee v. Dorrance.** The doctrine was limited in **Calder v. Bull** (1798) when Justice Iredell stated that "private rights must yield to public exigencies." However, Justice Samuel Chase supported the doctrine by saying that legislative powers in a free government do not extend to the point where they can take away personal liberty or private property since the protection of such rights are among the basic principles on which such governments are founded. Therefore, legislatures have no power to pass such acts. D.C.

Dodd, Thomas J.

Born May 15, 1907; U. S. Senate from November 4, 1958 until term ending 1964; Democrat—Connecticut; vice chairman board of review, and later executive trial counsel, office of the United States Chief of Counsel for the Prosecution of Axis Criminality at Nuremberg, Germany, 1945-1946.
R.A.B.

Dodecanese Islands.
A group of approximately 50 islands in the southeastern Aegean Sea. The population of 121,488 live on 14 of the islands; the most important ones are Rhodes, Kos (Cos), Karpathos. Seat of an ancient Hellenic civilization, the Dodecanese passed from **Greek** to Roman to Byzantine control. Seized by the Turks in 1522, they came under Italian control in 1912. Occupied by the British in World War II. Turned over to Greece by Treaty of Paris in 1947; administered by a Governor General appointed by the Greek Government. G.K.

Dollar Diplomacy.
A policy begun under President William H. Taft that encouraged United States investments in the Caribbean region and then provided protection for them by diplomatic and military intervention. F.M.L.

Dollfuss, Engelbert (1892-1934).
Chancellor of Austria and leader of the Christian Socialist Party. He took office in 1932 when Germany threatened Austrian independence. After Hitler gained power in Germany, Dollfuss ruled by decree and acted against both the left and right. He was assassinated on July 25, 1934 when the outlawed Nazi Party attempted a putsch. G.K.

Domestic jurisdiction.
In Article 15:8 of the Covenant the Council of the League of Nations was entitled to decide whether matters were "solely" of domestic jurisdiction and therefore not subject to League action. In Article 2:7 of the Charter matters **essentially** of domestic jurisdiction are excluded from "interventions" by the United Nations, the interpretation being primarily that of member states. Only enforcement action under Chapter VII is not subject to this restriction.
The old World Court found that a dispute over Tunis-Morocco nationality decrees was not **solely** of domestic jurisdiction; in contrast the new World Court refused to rule on domestic jurisdiction in the Anglo-Iranian case of 1951.
Both the clause in the Covenant and that in the Charter originated from United States suggestions (despite this the clause was the subject of a Senate reservation to the Versailles treaty). The United States has been inconsistent in its attitude toward application of the clause in United Nations cases. In accepting compulsory jurisdiction of the International Court of Justice it reserved matters of domestic jurisdiction "as determined by the United States"; otherwise it has supported interpretation of the clause by non-judicial organs of the U.N.
R.B.C.

Dominance system.
To the extent that the essential rules of the system function as parametric givens for the actors, that is, to the extent that the behavior of the individual actor does not modify the essential rules of the system, the system is said to be system dominant. To the extent that the decisions—or behavior —of the individual actor do affect the nature of the essential rules, the system is said to be subsystem dominant.
M.A.K.

Dominican Republic.
Capital: Santo Domingo. Area: 19,333 square miles. Population (1960): 3,014,-000. The Dominicans proclaimed their independence from Spain in 1821, lost it to the Haitian army in 1822, and regained it in 1844. From 1861-1865 Spain reannexed the country. The republic later asked to become a foreign protectorate under the United States, a project advanced by President Ulysses S. Grant, but the U.S. Senate failed to ratify the agreement in 1870. Political and economic instability led to U.S. control of Dominican customs in 1905. From 1916-1924 the United States provided a military government. Rafael Trujillo Molina became President in 1930, maintaining a repressive dictatorship until his assassination in 1961. R.B.G.

Dominion. See Appendix.

Dominion Courts.
Courts of the self-governing territories (Dominions) which together comprise the Commonwealth of Nations. Practically the last vestige of dominion subordination to the United Kingdom lies in the fact that certain commonwealth countries i.e., Australia, New Zealand, Ceylon, Federation of Nigeria and Sierra Leone still permit

appeals to be taken to the Judicial Committee of the Privy Council.
C.A.Mc.C.

Dorr War. (1841-1842).
From 1829 to 1841 several petitions addressed to the Rhode Island Legislature requested repeal of the state's real property suffrage qualification and adoption of reapportionment to favor the urban areas. Because these petitions were repeatedly ignored or rejected, a group composed largely of landless Providence workers led by Thomas Wilson Dorr drafted a People's Constitution, held a ratifying election, elected a slate of state officials, proclaimed a People's Government, and attempted to sustain the Government by arms. Although the superior force of the State Militia overpowered "Governor" Dorr's Army with only a few casualties, the suffrage was extended and reapportionment was adopted in a new state constitution 1843, which finally replaced the 180-year-old Royal Charter granted by King Charles II. See LUTHER V. BORDEN.
J.A.E.

Double Jeopardy.
Double Jeopardy refers to the subjection of an accused person to repeated trials for the same alleged offense. Protection of the individual from such jeopardy is found in the common law, in the Fifth Amendment of the U.S. Constitution and in numerous state constitutions. In application the definitions accorded "jeopardy" and "same offense" have been important. Thus, under the Fifth Amendment the federal government cannot appeal an acquittal to a higher court; however a convicted person who appeals and gets his original conviction set aside may be retried for the same offense at risk of a heavier penalty than before. Retrial after jury disagreement on a verdict does not constitute double jeopardy. The "same offense" protection does not preclude multiple charges arising out of the same alleged act, if such act involves multiple offenses as statutorily defined; nor does it prohibit the federal and state governments each prosecuting and punishing an individual for the same act, if the act is an offense in both jurisdictions.
R.H.S.

Double talk.
See Aesopian language.

Douglas, Paul H.
Born March 26, 1892; U.S. Senate from November 2, 1948 until term ending 1967; Democrat—Illinois; author of **The Theory of Wages, Real Wages in the United States**, and **Social Security in the United States**; awarded Bronze Star for "heroic achievement in action", World War II.
R.A.B.

Douglas, William O. (1898—   ).
Associate Justice of the Supreme Court, appointed by Roosevelt in 1939. As a Professor of Law at Yale (1928-1938) he was considered one of the most able law professors in the nation and an authority on corporate law, bankruptcy, and business regulation. He was a member and Chairman of the Security and Exchange Commission (1936-39) and a close advisor to President Roosevelt on business regulation. Almost from the outset of his appointment to the Court, Justice Douglas has consistently and outspokenly fought for a more stringent judicial interpretation of the Bill of Rights. Although Justice Black has tended to overshadow him, there is little doubt that Douglas has contributed greatly in deepening and strengthening the libertarian philosophy which both justices embrace.
Mr. Justice Douglas is author of a number of books on civil liberties and has written extensively and charmingly on nature and travel. He was seriously considered for the Democratic candidacy for Vice-president in 1944, and had some support for the presidential nomination in 1948 and 1952.
P.B.

Drago Doctrine.
The principle that a public debt of a state may not be collected by means or armed intervention by a creditor's government. Named for Argentine Foreign Minister Luis Maria Drago (1859-1921). See Roosevelt Corollary.
F.M.L.

Dred Scott case.
A Supreme Court case, Scott v. Sanford, decided in 1857, holding that a slave was not a citizen, and thus did

not have standing to sue in the federal courts under the diversity of citizenship doctrine. Dred Scott, the slave, had not become free by virtue of residence in Minnesota, where under the terms of the Missouri Compromise, slavery could not exist. Moreover under this reasoning, Congress had no power to exclude slavery from the territories, and thus the Missouri Compromise was unconstitutional. In any event, since Scott had returned to Missouri, his status as slave or freeman was determined by Missouri law, and under that law he remained a slave. G.B.H.

Dreyfus Case.

The affair **par excellence of French** history, the Dreyfus case opened in 1894 with the military conviction for espionage of a Jewish army officer, Alfred Dreyfus. One officer became convinced of his innocence and Zola and Clemenceau began a newspaper defense in support of abstract justice and the principles of the French Revolution. In 1898 the real spy confessed, another officer admitted forgeries in the case, a review court reduced the sentence to ten years from life imprisonment, and a presidential pardon was granted. In 1906 the legal aspect of the case ended when a civil court absolved Dreyfus of all charges. In the intervening years, French politics and society were torn by the case. Moreover, the political aspects endured, for the passions and issues laid bare—antisemitism, military opposition to civilian control, clerical opposition to republican democracy, and anticlericalism as a response—persisted. The affair discredited clericalist and traditionalist elements and made anticlericalist defense of the republic the motif of French politics for the next thirty years. Having first produced political antisemitism, the case relegated it in France to a fringe which, however, came to power under the Petain regime of World War II. As for the army, it showed opposition to civilian control again during the French withdrawal from Algeria sixty years later. E.T.O.

Druzes (al-Duruz)

A religious sect founded in Cairo at the time of the 6th Fatimid Caliph al-Hakim who in 1017 declared himself the incarnation of God on earth and shortly afterwards was murdered in a conspiracy engineered by his sister. His followers—led by two Persian Isma'ilite missionaries, Muhammad ibn Isma'il al-Darazi, after whom the Druzes are named, and a certain Hamzah—regarded him to be in a state of concealment whence he would return as Mahdi. Persecuted in Egypt, they found refuge among the Isma'ilites in Southern Lebanon whence they spread into Syria and Palestine. The Druze creed is built upon the belief that al-Hakim is the incarnation of the one and only God. He is not God, but he embodies the oneness **of the Divine** Essence. He is infallible and his actions are beyond human comprehension. Pending the "absence" of al-Hakim, no part of his religion should be divulged or promulgated. Only the wise have access to the esoteric teaching. The mysteries of the cult are propagated in secret meetings open only to the initiates, men and women. The Druzes, who still live under a system of feudal leadership, are characterized by intense community loyalty, high sense of solidarity, vigorous spirit of independence and endurance in the face of adversity. Communal conflicts between Christians and Druzes culminated in the 1860 massacres in Lebanon and Syria and in the intervention of European Powers At present, there are some 85,000 Druzes in Lebanon, 89,000 in Syria and 18,000 in Israel. F.M.N

Druzhina.

The volunteer squads of groups of citizens established to help the local organs of government maintain public order and social discipline. They were originally established in Leningrad in November 1958 and subsequently endorsed by Premier Khrushchev at the Twenty-first Party Congress in February 1959. Composed largely of Komsomol activists, the druzhina help fight against the growing social ills of hooliganism, drunkenness, and juvenile delinquency which do not lend themselves to formal police action. Party theorists have hailed the volunteer squads as important for the encouragement of greater citizen responsibility and for the transition to communism and the eventual withering away of the state. The regime seeks to control the activities of the druzhina, but many abuses have resulted from overzealous and arbitrary use of authority. A.Z.R.

Dual Monarchy.
The name denoting Austria-Hungary after the compromise of 1867, based on dualism between Habsburg dominions in Austria and in Hungary, united only in the person of the emperor, the ministries of foreign affairs, war and, partly, finance, and through periodical meetings of delegations of the two parliaments. It lasted till the collapse of Austria-Hungary in 1918. F.M.

Dual Nationality.
A situation in which an individual is the national of two countries at the same time. Inasmuch as individual states are free to determine for themselves the conditions of nationality, it sometimes happens that two states may claim the same person as their national, or citizen. A person may possess dual nationality without knowing it. According to the principle **jus soli,** a person born within the territory and jurisdiction of a state is a citizen thereof. While according to **jus sanguinis,** a person's nationality is determined by the nationality of the parent or parents. Thus a person born within the territory and jurisdiction of the United States, for example, is a citizen thereof, but if his father is a citizen of a foreign country, or if expatriation is not recognized by that country, the child has dual nationality. O.S.

Due Process of Law.
In a loose sense, the equivalent of the words "law of the land". More specifically, a phrase in the Fifth and Fourteenth Amendments of the Constitution of the United States which protects individuals from arbitrary governmental actions against life, liberty, or property. Although the courts have refused to define the phrase exactly, and have preferred to let specific decisions over a period of time draw the line between arbitrary and reasonable actions, it can be said that there are two categories of due process: procedural and substantive. **The** requirement of procedural due process is met when the state regulates according to prescribed forms. Substantive due process protects the individual in the enjoyment of basic personal and civil liberties. Thus the state may require licenses to fish but may not require licenses to worship. The right to worship is substantive and may not be made to depend upon any procedure, however reasonable on its face. E.L.

Duguit's Theory of Law.
A sociological theory of law propounded by the French constitutional lawyer, Leon Duguit (1859-1928) as the theory of objective law. Duguit contends that law results naturally and necessarily from the objective conditions found in any given society; he refutes as a mere myth the dogma that law expresses the command of the sovereign. Duguit's theory differs from the theory of natural law in that objective law changes with time and place, and from the historical theory in that it facilitates the adaptation of law to new conditions. M.Sp.

Dulles, Allen Welsh. (1893-   )
American lawyer, diplomat, intelligence official. Director of U.S. Central Intelligence Agency (CIA) 1953-1961. Born April 7, 1893, Watertown, New York; B.A., Princeton 1914; LL.B. George Washington University, 1926; 1916-1926 U.S. Diplomatic Corps, stationed in Vienna, Bern, Berlin, Constantinople. Adviser and delegate to various peace and disarmament conferences 1918-1933. Member New York law firm, Sullivan and Cromwell, 1926-1951. Official of U.S. Office of Strategic Services, 1942-1945; O.S.S. Chief in Switzerland. Appointed Deputy Director of Central Intelligence in 1951. President of Council on Foreign Relations in 1946; author of **Germany's Underground** (1947); co-author of other works. Brother of the late John Foster Dulles. H.H.R.

Dulles, John Foster. (February 25, 1888-May 24, 1959).
Former Secretary of State in the Eisenhower administration from January 1953 to April 1959, and for many years an important advisor on foreign

policy in the Republican Party. Educated at Princeton University, the Sorbonne, and George Washington University Law School. Mr. Dulles acquired prominence as a specialist in international law, eventually becoming senior partner of Sullivan and Cromwell. A participant in the Versailles Peace Conference of 1919 and active in international affairs between the two world wars, he was several times a member of the United States delegation to the United Nations. He was interim U.S. Senator in 1949, a consultant to the State Department, and a key person in negotiating the peace treaty with Japan in 1951. Author of several books, and an influential figure in the postwar formulation of American foreign policy, Mr. Dulles fervently opposed Soviet and Communist imperialism and was instrumental in pushing the doctrine of "massive retaliation," and in depreciating neutralism as a policy in world affairs.

A.Z.R.

Dumbarton Oaks Conference.

A meeting in 1944 at Dumbarton Oaks, a mansion near Washington D.C. It established the foundations of the United Nations. The United States, the Soviet Union, Great Britain, and China were represented. Proposals emanating from this meeting, providing for the establishment of an organization of nations dedicated to the maintenance of world peace, led ultimately to the calling of the United Nations organizational conference at San Francisco in April, 1945. R.J.S.

Dunkirk, Treaty of. See Appendix.

E

Earmarked Revenues.
The practice of requiring, by statute or constitution, that certain types of public revenues flow into segregated funds for stipulated purposes. This practice is especially prevalent in American state government in such areas as motor vehicle revenues, gasoline taxes, and fish and game licenses, and has been encouraged by interest groups seeking to protect specific public programs with which they are concerned. T.S.

Eastern Regional Organization for Public Administration.
Established in 1960 to promote regional co-operation in Asia and the Far East in the field of public administration. Membership is open to States, professional bodies and individuals. The Secretariat is in Manila, a Research, Documentation and Diffusion Centre in Saigon and a Training Centre in New Delhi. S.S.H.

East India Company.
A merchant company receiving its charter from Queen Elizabeth I on the last day of the sixteenth century. One of many East India trading companies supported by European states during the seventeenth and eighteenth centuries, the English East India Company originally aimed mainly at breaking the Dutch monopoly of the spice trade. It so exploited the political disintegration of the Mughal Empire, that in 1687 it instructed its representative in Madras "to establish such a politie of civil and military power, and create and secure such a large revenue to secure both ... as may be the foundation of a large, well grounded, secure English dominion in India for all time to come." Military and political maneuvering culminated in Clive's victory at Plassey in 1757, transforming the trading company into the foremost political power on the Indian subcontinent. The British Crown, henceforth, exercised greater control over the Company's affairs. When the Indian troops of the Company revolted in 1857, (in what English historians later called the Sepoy Mutiny, and their Indian counterparts termed the First War of Independence) the British Crown took over from the Company the direct rule of India, August 2, 1858. S.K.A.

Eban, Abba S. (1915-   )
Israeli Minister without Portfolio; President, Weizmann Institute of Science. Born South Africa; studied Cambridge. Faculty, Cambridge University and Middle East Center of Arabic Studies (Jerusalem). Political officer British army in World War II. Liaison officer, Allied headquarters in Palestine to Jewish population. 1946-48 served in Jewish Agency representing Zionist cause before the United Nations. Ambassador to U.N. and to U.S.A. 1950-59. S.H.

Ebert, Friedrich. (1871-1925)
German Social Democratic Party leader and first president of the Weimar Republic. A democratic socialist with working class, trade union background. Elected to Reichstag (1912), party chairman (1913). Influential in effecting orderly transfer of authority from imperial regime to republic (1918-1919). C.J.S.

Ecclesiastical Courts (United Kingdom).
A court of special jurisdiction which in the middle ages had considerable power in matters both civil and criminal and as late as the 19th century, had authority over Probate and Matrimonial matters which are now exercised by the High Court of Justice. The organization of the Ecclesiastical Courts provides for the Diocesan Courts of the bishops called Consistory Courts which are presided over by "Chancellors" appointed by the bishops usually from the ranks of barristers and the two Provincial Courts of the two archbishops, both of which are presided over by one judge, called the "Dean of the Arches." The present authority of the ecclesiastical courts is restricted to corrective jurisdiction over the clergy and the granting of permission to make alterations in churches and church property. C.A.McC.

Economic and Social Council.
See United Nations Economic and Social Council.

Economic determinism.
The doctrine that economic forces are either fundamental to or ultimately determinative of politics. Emphasis may be placed upon economic motivation or power, or upon natural resources or upon technology. As a form of the doctrine, Marxism asserts that forms of government are correlated with the state of technology and that political change, especially revolutionary change, is governed by technological developments as these come into conflict with established and constraining systems of property. J.W.Ch.

Economic Nationalism.
Expressions of a nation's self-determinism and independence in economic spheres through ideological assertions and policy measures. In seeking to promote the autonomy of their nation-state, decision-makers use a variety of measures to assure economic self-sufficiency: external trade is controlled by "protective" tariffs, by import-and-export quotas, and through elaborate monetary restrictions and licensing processes; supplies of raw materials are secured by attempts to monopolize access to sources and by stockpiling. All varieties and mixtures of socialist and capitalist economies seem capable of direction toward nationalistic goals. Reflecting aspects of mercantilism, the doctrines of economic nationalism of the nineteenth and twentieth centuries have focused on the desire of political decision-makers to evaluate economic measures in terms of their ability to insure advancement and the "protection" of "national interests," prominent among which is the capacity of the nation to wage war without dependence on others. H.G.

E.C.S.C.
See European Coal and Steel Community.

Ecuador.
A small South American country. Its territory, according to the Cedula Real of 1740, was 1,042,103 square kilometers. This territory was reduced by her neighbors during last century to 300,000 square kilometers. The population of Ecuador, according to the census of 1951, is 4,000,000 inhabitants.

Before becoming an independent republic, Ecuador was a part of the Spanish dominions and bore the name of **Real Audiencia de Quito.** Ecuador proclaimed her independence from Spain on the 10th of August 1809, and achieved the same on the 24th of May 1822, following the memorable battle of **Pichincha.** At first, Ecuador formed a part of New Granada which it was expected would fulfill Bolivar's dream of the **Gran Colombia.** After Bolivar's death, Ecuador separated from Colombia and became a Republic. Her first president was the Venezuelan General, **Juan Jose Flores,** instead of the Marshal of Ayacucho, **Antonio Jose de Sucre,** whom the people preferred. Flores served as president of Ecuador three times and installed a personal dictatorship. After a period of prolonged political instability, **Gabriel Garcia Moreno** seized power and set up a perpetual dictatorship which was based, nonetheless, on oldfashioned and conservative ideas. This cruel, retrograded president was assassinated by a patriotic group of university students. Hopes of liberation from the dictatorship, however, were frustrated. A new period of reactionary government ensued. In 1895 a liberal and radical leader, Eloy Alfaro, came to power through a popular revolutionary movement. This man transformed many institutions, especially those concerning education, religion, commerce and government. He is a symbol of material and spiritual progress. Liberal and radical revolution was realized only partially after a period of sterile changes of men in power, liberalism was defeated by a coalition of conservatives and socialists, under the leadership of Velasco Ibarra, in 1944. Later, Galo Plaza Lasso, son of a liberal leader and ex-president, initiated in 1948 the present period of relative political stability. B.M.P.

Ecuador—Political Parties.
Traditionally, there are two political parties in Ecuador—the conservative and the liberal—which are sometimes divided into factions under various names. The Socialist Party was founded in 1926 and the Communist Party in 1930. More recent parties are the CFP or "Concentration of Popular

Forces" and the ARNE or "Revolutionary Euadorian Action," both of which are influenced by contemporary political tendencies. The first is influenced by socialism and the second by Spanish Falangism. These two political forces, conservatism and socialism, are now fighting for control.
B.M.P.

Edict of Caracalla.
The **Constitutio Antoniana** of 212 A.D. extended the right of citizenship throughout the territory of the Roman Empire. This enactment **concluded a long process of development by which the territorial conception of citizenship replaced the earlier and Roman Republican notion of civis.** The earlier conception was that citizenship was inherited through the family **and** involved a highly communal relationship characteristic also of the Greek **polis.**
R.W.T.

E.E.C.
See European Economic Community.

E.F.T.A.
See European Free Trade Association.

Egidius Colonna (1250-1316).
This Augustinian friar first espoused in his **De Regimine Principium** (1285), the view that civil authority is not an artificial but a natural institution which exists in its own right and not as an agent of spiritual forces. He also claimed that the King is the source of civil law and therefore above it, contrary to the prevalent medieval notion which held that the King is subject to the law of the land just like his subjects. Later in his life he sided with the Pope and, in his **De Ecclesiastica Potestate** (1302), affirmed that both the spiritual and the temporal powers are under Pope's jurisdiction (the view of the Bull **Unam Sanctam**). His views were extremist when championing the Papal rights. He held that everyone, holding temporal power, can do so legitimately only if baptized; political power held by unbelievers is not legitimate. He extended this principle to property, which could be held, in his scheme, only if a man was baptized and under the jurisdiction of the Church. V.Z.

Ehrenburg, Ilya
Born 1891 Kiev. Reporter in both World Wars and Spanish civil war. For some time Soviet correspondent in Paris. First novel 1921 **Julio Jurenito.** Most novels written **in 1920's** suppressed in 1930's by Stalin's regime. 1955 **Soviet Encyclopedic Dictionary** omits his early works. 1957 Large **Soviet Encyclopedia** mentions them. Followed literary Party line 1930's-1940's. Wrote **The Thaw** 1954; defended some measure of artistic independence 1956-57, did not join Dudintsev in advocating "free art." Member of Presidium, Union of Soviet Writers' leading figure in World Peace Council.
W.A.

Eichmann, Adolf.
Chief executive officer (Referent) of the anti-Jewish Department of the Gestapo, Lt. Colonel of the SS Elite Guards, born on March 19, 1906, in Solingen, Germany, sentenced to death by the District Court of Jerusalem, Israel, for organizing the mass murder of about six million European Jews; executed on May 31, 1962.—On January 20, 1942, one of the blackest days of Jewish history, fifteen top level officials of the Third Reich, representatives of their Ministries or agencies met at a conference at the Berlin suburb of Wannsee (Wannsee Conference). In line with the policy of the 'Fuehrer', the anti-Jewish expulsion policy was replaced by the new program of biological mass extermination. Eleven million European Jews were stigmatized as genocidal victims. The conference was called by SS Obergruppenfuehrer Reinhard Heydrich, chief of the Reich Security Main Office. Eichmann, the chief of its anti-Jewish department IVB4, the leading expert in this field, was a key figure in this conference because the execution of the new program was his official domain. The diabolical plan provided as the secret conference record shows: "Under proper direction the Jews should now in the course of the final solution, be brought to the East . . . in big labor gangs, with separation of sexes, the Jews capable of work are brought to these areas and employed in road-building in which task undoubtedly a great part will fall out

through natural diminution. The remnant that finally is able to survive— . . . must be given treatment accordingly since these people, representing a natural selection, are to be regarded as a germ cell of a new Jewish development should they be allowed to go free." It was Eichmann's duty to organize and coordinate the extermination program with the various Ministries, e.g. the **Foreign Office**—because most European Jews were citizens of non-German countries—the Finance and Economic Ministries because they absorbed the Jewish property including the gold teeth of the corpses, the Transportation Ministry which provided the death trains, and the administration of the concentration camps where gas ovens, gas vans and execution squads had to be ready. Eichmann—in charge of Jewish affairs for a full decade in the Third Reich—performed his murderous 'duties' with deadly bureaucratic efficiency and zeal as numerous orders and directives show, discovered after the war by the Allies. He supervised the executions by numerous field trips e.g. to Auschwitz, and filed progress reports. He even outdid some of his superiors who tried to save their own skin by releasing a few thousand Jews during the last months of the Third Reich. At the end of the war Eichmann went into hiding, first in Germany, later in Argentina. Thus he escaped the Nuremberg justice where he had been already indicted for his genocidal crimes as an un-named co-conspirator. In Argentina Eichmann was apprehended by a task force of secret Israeli agents and brought clandestinely to Israel on May 23, 1960. He was tried under Israel's 'Law against Nazis and Nazi Collaborators' of August 1, 1950, patterned after the war crimes legislation of the Allies. (see NUREMBERG TRIALS). Israel's then Attorney General Gideon Hausner was the skillful chief prosecutor. The German attorney Robert Servatius—admitted under a special law of 1961—acted as defense counsel. The trial before the Israel District Court in Jerusalem under Supreme Court Justice Moshe Landau started on April 11, 1961 and ended on August 14, 1961. The prosecution submitted as evidence more than a thousand communications of Eichmann concerning his annihilation program. The case of the defense was primarily based on the plea of superior orders. The District Court found Eichmann guilty on all fifteen counts of the indictment and sentenced him to death on December 11, 1961. The Supreme Court of the State of Israel under President Justice Itzschak Olshan confirmed the judgment and sentence of the District Court on May 29, 1962. Eichmann himself did not deny a certain moral guilt but maintained that he had no legal responsibility having been only a minor official bound by oath to follow his Fuehrer's orders. But the Court held: 'Eichmann was the final arbiter in all matters pertaining to Jews . . . life as well as property throughout the sphere of German influence . . . It was he who was the high and mighty one, he himself propelled the machine.' R.H.W.K.

Einaudi, Luigi (1874-1961)

A distinguished Piedmontese Liberal, writer, professor of economics, and antifascist Senator, Einaudi was elected first President of the Republic in Italy after guiding postwar economic policy as Budget Minister. His election indicated the office was to be one of prestige, and his term in office (1948-1953) established precedents of strong defense of presidential powers and obligations of defense of the Constitution against legislative or cabinet encroachments. E.T.O.

Eisenhower Doctrine.

It was the American response to the growing Soviet influence in the Middle East. On January 5, 1957 President Eisenhower made his proposals to congress. The doctrine took the form of a joint congressional resolution authorizing the president:

1) to employ United States armed forces to safeguard the independence of any country or group of countries in the Middle East requesting aid against aggression from a country controlled by international communism.
2) to offer military assistance to such nations.

3) to help in the economic development of these nations and by authorizing the president to spend 200 million dollars for aiding Middle Eastern countries.

The plan was opposed by the Arab nationalists and particularly by President Nasser of Egypt. E.A.S.

Eisenhower, Dwight D.
The 34th President of the U.S. was born October 14, 1890, in Denison, Texas, but spent his boyhood in Abilene, Kansas. He was graduated from West Point in 1915, and soon married Mamie Dowd in Colorado. During World War I he trained troops in tank warfare. His army service included duty in Texas; the Canal Zone; Command and General Staff School, Fort Leavenworth, where he was head of his class; France with the Battle Monuments Commission; Army War College; Washington, on industrial mobilization plans; the Philippines under General MacArthur; and Fort Ord, California. During World War II he rose rapidly to the post of field commander of the African Invasion, 1943, and the invasion of Normandy in 1944. As Commander-in-chief of SHAEF (Supreme Headquarters, Allied Expeditionary Forces) able to coordinate conflicts and always diplomatic, he was called the most popular man in the world in 1945. After serving as Chief of Staff of the Armed Forces, he became President of Columbia University, New York, but in 1950 was called by President Truman to serve as Commander of SHAPE (Supreme Headquarters, Allied Powers in Europe) to coordinate military forces for NATO (North Atlantic Treaty Organization). In 1952 he was nominated by the Republican Party for the Presidency and elected overwhelmingly. As President he arranged a settlement of the Korean conflict, continued the containment policy of his predecessor toward Russia, and, except for Indo-China, prevented further expansion of Communist held territory. His efforts to reduce the tensions of the Cold War were unsuccessful. Under acts of Congress, he established a cabinet department of Health, Education, and Welfare, and made other governmental reorganizations and adjustments in domestic policies. In 1955 he suffered a heart attack, but in 1956 campaigned successfully for a second term in office, retiring from the Presidency in January, 1961. Since his retirement he has served as an elder statesman of the Republican Party. The Eisenhower papers are now preserved in the Eisenhower Library, Abilene, Kansas. T.K.N.

Election.
The formal process by which the electorate selects officials and determines the issues submitted to it.
C.W.B.

Electoral law of France.
See French electoral law.

Electorate.
The whole body of persons qualified to vote. C.W.B.

Elite.
Elite is a descriptive term, designating those who hold high positions in a society. Any society will have several special elites—as many as there are values widely cherished in the society. There may be special elites by virtue of their large shares in such values as knowledge, authority, wealth —i.e., those persons designated respectively as intelligentsia, bureaucracy (higher civil service), plutocracy (or, less pejoratively, the wealthy). Those with large shares in the distribution of power—whether through elective or appointive office, or indeed whether through influence exercised without office—are designated the political elite. The general elite of a society is composed of those who hold large shares in several of its major values. Membership in the general elite is usually transmitted through families, which, though emphasis may fluctuate from economic to political to intellectual activity as between generations, maintain their high position with respect to all major values at all times. Thus, all members in good standing of the Kennedy, Rockefeller, Morgenthau families today may be classified as members of the American elite.
D.L.

El Salvador.
The smallest of six Central American republics, bordered by Guatemala

on the west, Honduras on the north and east, and a 160-mi. Pacific coastline on the south. **Area:** 8,260 sq. mi. **Population:** 2,612,000 (1960 U.N. est.). **Capital:** San Salvador (pop. 161,951). **Language:** Spanish. **Religion:** Roman Catholic.

The native Pipil Indians were conquered by Pedro Alvarado of Cortes' army in 1524. A Spanish colony for 300 years, El Salvador joined the Mexican Empire (1821-23) and the United Provinces of Central America (1823-39) before achieving full independence in 1841.

The 1950 Constitution provided for a 3-branch national government and 14 local departments. A president and unicameral legislature are popularly elected. There is a Supreme Court. Universal free public education for ages 7 to 13 and qualified compulsory suffrage at age 18 are established by law. El Salvador holds memberships in the Organization of American States and the United Nations N.P.T.

Emergency Powers of the President.

Although the American constitution is admittedly one of sovereign but limited powers and although the Courts have declared that even war does not suspend its operation, the idea is widely accepted that in time of crisis there is available for the Presidents' unilateral use a special reservoir of **emergency powers** above and beyond the Constitution. Strong Presidents, such as Lincoln and the two Roosevelts, attempted to justify some of their actions by appeal to such powers. However the more acceptable constitutional theory limits the powers available to the President in emergencies to those either expressed or implied in the Constitution and those which congress may by legislation delegate to him. A.A.N.

Emerson, Ralph Waldo. (1803-1882).

American philosopher, essayist and poet. Born in 1803 in Boston, Emerson came from a line of colonial preachers, his patriot grandfather having died as a chaplain in the Revolutionary War. In school from the age of three, he worked his way through Harvard which he felt did relatively little for him. However in his third year he began the journals which he kept for a half century as the daily repository of his aphorisms, poetry, essays and philosophy. He taught and then served the ministry until he broke from his church because he decided he could observe the Lord's Supper only if the bread and wine were omitted. Even so he continued to preach frequently in different pulpits.

After European travel which enabled him to meet Carlyle and other noted writers and thinkers of the day, he settled in Concord, Mass., to read, to reflect and to write in preparation for lecture trips which became a main activity. The journals provided the platform materials and the lectures in turn became the famous essays. In 1837, he delivered the historic Phi Beta Kappa oration at Harvard entitled "The American Scholar" which O. W. Holmes praised as "our intellectual Declaration of Independence."

Loving nature and passionately devoted to individualism, Emerson had much in common with the Transcendentalists; democracy, he believed, was rooted in the sacred truth that "every man hath in him the divine Reason" which each could and should turn into his own guide in life. To him the individual was pre-eminent in every way, fully capable and self-reliant. He held that the essence of America was in its equality of opportunity for all regardless of backgrounds and he opposed nativism as in conflict with the idea of the United States as a haven for the world's oppressed peoples.

Convinced that man is born to be a reformer, he called for continuous and improving change in social and political institutions. He supported women's rights and abolition and found in the Civil War the means for restoring the "intellectual and moral power" that had declined. But he was so against all forms of coercion by the state that his views were cited to uphold **laissez faire** economics. As an editor of **The Dial** beginning in 1840, he was at the center of New England's cultural rebirth which he sought to extend widely through a society that had become, in his eyes, materialistic, barren and overburdened by institutions and traditions. I.Di.

Eminent Domain.

The power inherent in sovereignty to take private property for a public use without consent of the owner, upon just compensation. The proviso for compensation is sometimes viewed as a limitation inherent in the power, sometimes as a restriction upon its exercise acknowledged necessary in constitutional regimes. The Fifth Amendment of the United States Constitution and many state constitutions expressly forbid a taking for public use without just compensation. What constitutes a valid "public use" or "just compensation" are matters subject ultimately to judicial determination. The sovereign may delegate the exercise of the power to lesser governments or to private corporations such as utility companies which qualify under the public use test. R.H.S.

Empathy.

Empathy is the inner mechanism of psychic mobility—the personality process which accompanied the spread of physical and social mobility during the centuries that witnessed, following the disappearance of feudalism, the Renaissance and Reformation, the age of exploration, the industrial revolution. These sequences of modern history unbound man from his native soil and enabled him to move at will across the earth. Physical mobility naturally entailed social mobility. Once free of his physical place on the earth, a man was free to change his social place in the world. Freed of his native soil and native status, man soon learned to become free of his native self—the psychocultural patterning imposed upon him by the circumstances of his birth and socialization. The reshaping of one's congenital self-system we call psychic mobility and its mechanism we call empathy.

Empathy developed integrally with the rising mobility of modern society because it is the mechanism which enabled newly-mobile persons to operate efficiently in a changing world. The empathic person is distinguished by a high capacity for identification with new aspects of his environment; he comes equipped to incorporate new roles and strange situations that impinge upon him from outside his routine round of life. Empathy, to simplify the matter, is the capacity to see oneself in the other fellow's situation. This is an indispensable skill for people moving out of traditional settings. Modern society requires a high capacity for rearranging the self-system on short notice. The dynamic focus of this behavioral style is empathy. D.L.

Empiricism.

The theory that experience is the criterion of knowledge and that all ideas are finally reducible to sensations is generally traced to Hume. According to this view ideas are valuable insofar as they can be confirmed in fact or in principle by scientific method. Two modern philosophical movements are traced to Hume. James's **radical empiricism** emphasizes the meaning of experience; according to him relations between things are as much a matter of direct experience as the things themselves. Wittgenstein's **logical empiricism**, on the other hand, has been primarily concerned with the analysis of language and the unity of science. The principal empirical field of the Vienna School of Wittgenstein has been language itself. R.W.T.

Enabling Act.

Part of the procedural process for admitting new states (of the U.S.A.) into the Union. After the inhabitants of a territory petition Congress for admission, Congress passes an enabling act which authorizes the election of delegates to a convention for drafting a tentative constitution. If the constitution is ratified by the voters in the territory, it goes to Congress for review. A joint resolution by Congress admits the territory to statehood.
  R.V.A.

Encomienda.

Under the **repartimiento** system the Indians in colonial Latin America were divided into two types: some were employed in the mines, in pearl fishing, and in transport service—known as the **mita** (the worse of the two types)—and some in the **encomienda** as workers on farms and in household work. In spite of Spanish law, the Indians were thereby condemned to the status of feudal serfs.

Fear that a feudal land owning class in Latin America might challenge the Spanish Monarch, led to the abolition of the system by royal decree in 1720 and the downfall of the **encomienda**.
J.F.Me.

Enemy Alien.
An enemy alien is an alien who happens to be in another country in time of war between the two countries. On the eve of the first World War it was the general practice to permit aliens, either to depart freely or to remain in the country subject to the condition of good behavior on their part, interpreted as committing no act against the laws and in favor of the enemy. During the first and second World Wars enemy aliens were subject to numerous restrictions to prevent communication with the enemy, registration being required, freedom of movement denied, and on occasion internment in concentration camps imposed.
C.G.F.

Enforcement of International Law.
There is no universal authority to enforce international law. In the absence of a world government, States are relatively free to enforce their own rights under international law. Weaker States generally find it difficult to do so when the other parties are stronger States. The International Court of Justice now helps to enforce international law through court decisions on legal disputes between States; members of the United Nations Organization are at the same time parties to the Statute of the Court. The Security Council has the responsibility to take whatever action necessary to give effect to the decisions of the Court and secure respect of the United Nations Charter, which is itself an important part of international law. Decisions of the Security Council on matters of substance can be taken only with seven favourable votes, including those of China, France, United Kingdom, United States of America and the U.S.S.R.; parties to a dispute, if they are members of the Council, must abstain from voting. International law can be enforced to a point if this condition is fulfilled. The role of the Security Council is further weakened by the absence of an international police force to enforce the Council's own action.
S.S.H.

Enfranchisement.
The act of granting suffrage; also, the act of making free.
C.W.B.

Engels, Friedrich (1820-1895).
German philosopher. Collaborator of Karl Marx. Son of a small textile manufacturer, Friedrich Engels is known to the world chiefly for his relationship with Karl Marx, as friend, colleague, financial backer, and as editor of Marx's works. From the time he first met Marx in the early 1840's to the time Marx died in 1883 Engels and Marx were either working together or corresponding with each other. Even though not as well known, Engels was a thinker and writer on his own. Besides co-authoring the **Communist Manifesto** with Marx, Engels wrote several other books, among which are **The Condition of the Working Class in England in 1844,** and **Ludwig Feuerbach and the Outcome of Classical German Philosophy.**
W.C.C.

England (Anglia, Land of the Anglo-Saxons).
The nation-state which came to be situated in the southern two-thirds of the principal island lying approximately 21 miles off the northwest coast of France. Loosely, the island itself. Known in the period of Saxon conquest of Britain, the island is about 700 miles long and varies from 300 miles to 100 miles or less in width. It embraces an area of 89,000 square miles of verdant, wet territory, with moderate temperatures. Heavily wooded in many sections, fertile soil none the less existed and extensive deposits of lead, tin, iron, and coal were present. The northwest of the island comprises higher and more frequently broken and less fertile terrain. The Celtic invaders of England, beginning to arrive about 1000 B.C., likely from east central Europe, brought with them family organization and after settlement apparently organized into tribes, the leading male in each case becoming the king.

Celtic invasion began about 1000 B.C., but the Celts left behind no permanent political institutions. They were overrun by invading Germanic tribesmen, Angles, Saxons, and Jutes, beginning in the mid 5th century, after Roman legions had withdrawn from Celtic Britain. The Saxons brought strong local government organization, and elected kingship, which became hereditary in fact, and a tradition of individual liberty. Under the impact of Viking invasions some Saxon kings accomplished near unification of the several kingdoms on the island.

In 1066 William of Normandy defeated a Saxon army, divided much of his new realm among his chief lieutenants, vesting them with feudal tenure.

Subsequent kings sought to counteract feudalism by strengthening the power of central government. Among the devices for this purpose was the establishment of one system of law, the Common Law, to be extant throughout the kingdom. Its substance was judicially devised and it was administered by **stare decisis**, a strict adherence to precedent.

As the need for royal revenues increased the monarch summoned knights and later burghers to meet, as did those who sat as nobility or clergy in the Curia Regis, as counselors to the king. These commoners, however, were to deliberate over the financial support they could advance to the Crown. Eventually they extracted as their **quid pro quo** a role in policy formation. This represented the birth of the House of Commons, to play a greater part.

In the period 1621-1629, Protestant strength being great in England, and the Commons having grown stronger, and James I's theory of divine right being rejected, the Parliament fell into severe disagreement with the Crown. Civil insurrection arose and the resulting Puritan Revolution brought Parliamentary supremacy and the execution of King Charles the First.

After the death of Oliver Cromwell, who had headed the Parliamentary government, dissension grew and the faction favoring the restoration of the King came to the majority. In 1660 Charles II ascended the British throne. In his reign recognizable political parties came to England and the Parliamentary struggle was conducted on Whig versus Tory lines.

Again under Parliamentary impetus a revolution occurred in 1688 and James II was driven from the throne. After agreeing to accept a Bill of Rights, William of Orange was placed upon the British throne. Twice Parliament, now with an even firmer party organization, had demonstrated its capacity to control the disposition of the Crown.

The military conflicts with Scotland which mark English history and which had come to include economic competition, took the Parliament's attention. In 1707, an act of Union was effected and Scotland gained representation in the Parliament with the English king becoming also the King of Scotland, his realm becoming Great Britain.

M.P.S.

Engrossment.

The process of preparing a true copy of a bill with all amendments, so that members of a legislative body may see it as it has been developed up to that point. Sometimes this is done immediately before a bill is finally acted upon by the house where it originated. In a bicameral system if bills are not engrossed before passage in one house, this must be done before they are sent to the other house. J.E.R.

Enlightenment.

The movement of thought, from the seventeenth to the nineteenth centuries, characterized by a revolt against dogma and authority and placing positive emphasis upon the use of reason and empirical methods for the discovery of truth, the achievement of happiness, and the reshaping of institutions more conducive to social progress and harmony. Leading exponents include: Voltaire, Diderot, d'Alembert, d'Holbach, Hevetius, Rousseau, Hume, and Kant. J.W.Ch.

Enosis.

See Appendix.

Enrollment.

The process of preparing a final authoritative copy of a bill as it has been passed by both houses of a legislative body, or by a unicameral chamber. Enrolled bills are signed by the presiding officers of both houses, presented to the chief executive for his approval or veto, and are preserved as official copies. J.E.R.

Entente Cordiale.
An agreement between France and England signed in 1904 pledging their mutual support for their respective colonial and other foreign policies. The alliance was aimed at neutralizing the increasing power of Germany. In 1907 it was expanded by the inclusion of Russia. The new grouping became known as the Triple Entente and formed the nucleus of the alliance which faced the Triple Alliance of Germany, Austria-Hungary and Italy. G.K.

Epictetus. (c. 50-120 A.D.)
A Stoic philosopher and freed slave, Epictetus's teachings are found in his **Discourses** reported by his pupil, Flavius Arrianus. His ethical teaching depends on a religious Stoicism with faith in a rational God and orderly universe; since men are God's children they should love one another. He taught philosophy first in Rome, and following banishment by Domitian in Nicopolis. R.W.T.

Equality of States, Doctrine of.
The rationale upon which the doctrine of the equality of states rests is derived from the sixteenth century concept of sovereignty, as well as from a theory of natural law elaborated in the eighteenth century. All sovereigns were by definition equal, and according to the rule **par in parem non habet imperium** no state could claim jurisdiction over another. Eighteenth-century rationalism conceived of state equality as a natural right, and the reasoning was as follows: In pre-political times man was living in a state of nature in which all were free and equal. But the fully sovereign states, subject to no authority but their own will, were held to exist in a state of nature with fundamental rights including that of complete equality. O.S.

Equalization.
The process of obtaining a reasonable degree of uniformity for property tax assessments as between various assessing units (U.S.A.). The objective is to distribute a fair share of the tax load to each assessing district. If the assessing unit is less than the county the county commonly equalizes among these units. The state government, in turn, equalizes among the counties. Equalization may be accomplished by adjustment of property valuations so that they all bear an approximately equal relationship to market values. The same effect can be accomplished more simply by adjusting the tax rates. Equalization is important whenever a particular tax is spread over more than one assessing district, as when assessments for the county property tax are determined by the cities and townships within the county. It is also important when state shared taxes or grants-in-aid are based on formulas that include consideration of local assessments as a measure of ability to pay. C.R.A.

Equal Protection of the Law.
A phrase in the Fourteenth Amendment of the Constitution of the United States in which the states are forbidden to deny to any person within their jurisdiction the equal protection of the law. Originally intended to protect Negroes from racial discrimination by state authority, the guarantee of equal protection was eventually extended to all persons, including corporations. Where the classification of subjects to be regulated is based upon the existence of common and distinctive properties, the classification is said to be reasonable and not a denial of the equal protection of the law. Although dollars would seem to be uniform in appearance and in value as legal tender, increments of money at different levels of income may nevertheless be taxed at different rates because there are social differences between small incomes and large. E.L.

"Equal Rights Amendment."
A proposal, sponsored by the National Women's Party and several other women's organizations, to add to the United States Constitution an amendment to prohibit discrimination against women by declaring: "Equality of rights under the law shall not be denied or abridged by the United States or by any state on account of sex." This proposal, introduced into

every Congress since 1923, was reported out favorably by the Judiciary Committee of the House of Representatives in 1945 and in 1948, and has repeatedly received a favorable report by the Judiciary Committee of the Senate—most recently in August, 1962. The proposed amendment has never been put to a vote in the House, but was approved by a mere majority vote of the Senate in 1946, and by more than the necessary two-thirds vote of the Senate in 1950 and 1953. On these last two occasions the senatorial endorsement was vitiated, in the opinion of most of the sponsoring organizations, by the addition of language proposed by Senator Hayden of Arkansas declaring: "The provisions of this article shall not be construed to impair any rights, benefits or exemptions now or hereafter conferred by law upon persons of the female sex." The "Equal Rights Amendment" has been favored in several national platforms of both major parties, but is opposed by some influential women's organizations. M.Sp.

Equity.
In British law a form of remedial justice which is applied when there is no remedy in common or statute law or when there is danger of irreparable damage. Equity which was originally dispensed by the Lord (High) Chancellor is now administered by the Chancery Division of the High Court of Justice. Equity applies only to civil cases. In America, Federal courts have equity power where remedies at law do not exist. R.G.N.

Erie Railroad v. Tompkins.
A case decided by the U.S. Supreme Court 304 U.S. 64 (1938) in which Tompkins had sued the Railroad in a federal court on grounds of diversity of citizenship for an injury to him caused by the negligent operation of one of defendant's trains in Pennsylvania. The Supreme Court had ruled in **Swift v. Tyson** (16 Pet. 1 [1842]) that in diversity of citizenship cases the federal courts need not in matters of "general jurisprudence" apply the unwritten law of the state as declared by its highest court, as distinguished from laws "strictly local, that is to say, to the positive statutes of the state . . . and to rights and titles" to real estate. In the Erie case there was no controlling federal or state statute, and Tompkins obtained a judgment based on "general law." The Supreme Court reversed the lower court and expressly overruled Swift v. Tyson saying that there was no federal common law, that the law to be applied was the state law written or unwritten, that it was no concern of the federal court whether the State law was a statute or declared by the highest state court. Congress itself could not declare substantive rules of common law applicable to the states and neither could the federal courts. E.G.T.

E.R.O.P.A.
See Eastern Regional Organization for Public Administration.

Escape Clause.
Many contracts and treaties contain a clause permitting a party to get out of its obligations under extreme circumstances. For example, a provision introduced into the Reciprocal Trade Act in 1951 and retained in the Trade Expansion Act of 1962, permits the United States to cancel tariff reductions that had been agreed to in trade agreements negotiated with foreign countries if the prevailing rate is causing substantial injury to an American industry. The Tariff Commission holds hearings upon complaints by industries and makes recommendations which can be overruled by the President. I.d.S.P.

Espionage.
A term used in its international context to denote activity attempting to obtain information about one government for transmission to another government. The term can be used to denote any activity aiming to procure information by secret methods, as in industrial espionage. Most commonly, the act of spying, as in secretly or under false pretenses searching out information or making observations with the intention of communicating such to a country or party hostile, or potentially hostile, to the country or party spied upon. An illegal method of obtaining information which a sover-

eign nation desires to conceal. One of the oldest of several methods of obtaining information for strategic intelligence purposes. The Cold War has greatly enlarged this activity by all governments. H.H.R.

Espionage Act of 1917.

This Act was passed the year the United States entered World War I and was intended to provide the government with an effective weapon to combat espionage activities by citizens, but more especially by alien residents who favored the cause of the enemy. The Act, which consists of thirteen titles and over 10,000 words, makes it a crime to: a) gather information or pictures, on government property with the intent of using them in any way contrary to the interest of the United States; b) the transmission of such information to a foreign country in time of war; c) the circulation by mail or otherwise of false reports for the purpose of causing insubordination, disloyalty, or refusal of duty in the military or naval forces of the United States; and d) other related provisions, including conspiracy with the view of doing any of the above. Punishment for violation of the Act is severe, ranging from high fines to death. The Act was used by the Attorney General to silence and to incarcerate scores of persons, including Eugene V. Debs, who were critical of the war. The Supreme Court upheld six decisions under the Act, three unanimously in 1919 and three by a divided Court the following year. "The only proceedings in our law comparable to the Espionage Act sentences," wrote the late Professor Chafee, "are the sedition prosecutions under George III, with which so many parallels have been found." P.B.

Established Church.

Any polity which provides for an official connection between a state and a church. The term has been used particularly with reference to church-state relationships in Europe, but it is generally applicable. There is no one set of requirements necessary to the idea of an established church. Many specific arrangements have been used, including tax exemption of church property, government recognition of the church as official through ceremonial occasions, church participation in the making of public policy, government participation in the making of church policy, and tax support for church functions, especially that of education. The First Amendment to the United States Constitution forbids the Congress to pass any law "respecting an establishment of religion." H.S.Th.

Estates General.
See France—Estates General.

Estonia.
See Baltic States.

Estrada Doctrine.

The principle that states should refrain entirely from the formal act of recognition of governments in order to avoid prejudicial judgments concerning the political acceptability of a new revolutionary regime. Named for Genaro Estrada, Mexican Foreign Minister in 1930. F.M.L.

Ethics in Public Service Agencies.

Public servants, in every nation throughout history, have been under pressure to meet special expectations concerning proper patterns of behavior. Their actions are commonly subject to greater scrutiny than are those of persons not on a public payroll and they are the object of folktales, rumors, suspicions, and criticism to a much greater degree. This is true in both democratic and non-democratic nations. In general, higher standards of honesty and morality are expected of public servants than of others. Many practices common in the business world are not tolerated in the case of government officials or employees. The occasional scandals concerning improper practices usually result, not from low standards among civil servants, but from the fact that the public ordinarily accepts only the highest standards of behavior from those on the public payroll. At the same time, there is in many countries little support for high salaries and perquisites which could make the public servant less susceptible to pressure and bribery. Specialists in public administration generally agree that the honesty and morality of public bureaucracies is at least as high as in private bureaucracies and that the less prestigeful one tends to follow the patterns established by the dominant one in all nations. C.R.A.

Ethiopia.

Formerly Abyssinia. An independent, feudal, empire of approximately 21,000,000 people inhabiting an area the size of Western Europe or around 457,000 sq. miles. Except for the short Italian occupation between 1935-1941, Ethiopia has had a long and continuous history of indigenous government. Ethiopian history is largely a record of the highland, Coptic Christian, Amhara peoples conquering the Moslem or traditionalist non-Amharic peoples of the surrounding plains. Though the Amharas constitute a minority, they predominate in the contemporary political, civil and military affairs of state.

In 1955 the Emperor, Haile Selassie I, promulgated a constitution, modeled after the 1889 Meiji Constitution of Japan, providing for a constitutional monarchy and an elective legislature with advisory powers. The government however remains highly centralized under the personal administration of the Emperor. There are no political parties and high property requirements for candidacy and the suffrage effectively exclude the majority from political activity. Despite an abortive coup in 1960, the major issues in Ethiopian politics continue to be the conflict between the Amharas and the non-Amhara peoples and between the church-supported landed groups and the disaffected educated elements.
R.L.K.

Ethiopia-Somali Boundary Dispute.

The dispute dates back to the partition of the Horn of Africa at the turn of the 20th century. The boundary was delimited by the Italian-Abyssinian Convention, signed at Addis Ababa on May 16, 1908. Failure to demarcate the boundary in accordance with the provisions of the convention has been due principally to three factors. a) Discrepancies in place-names between the Italian and Amharic versions of the convention, both of which are official; b) Disagreement over the meaning of the term "tribe" as understood in Somali customary law. The boundary was demarcated with reference to "tribal" lands; c) Disagreement over the exact location of territories occupied by certain Somali lineages in 1908, who have since migrated. The absence of an agreed boundary in the area led to the Wal Wal incident in 1934, which precipitated the Italo-Ethiopian War. Inability to agree on the powers of an arbitral tribunal terminated an abortive attempt to arbitrate the dispute in the late 1950's under United Nations auspices. This dispute is to be distinguished from the Greater Somalia movement which claims substantial areas in Ethiopia far removed from the disputed boundary zone.
R.L.K.

Ethnic Minorities.

Groups of people which, differing as they do by race, language or tradition, sometimes also by religion, from the majority of a State's population, are considered a people (ethnos) or nationality apart. Though the past had known States in which ethnic minorities held a dominant position, and the phenomenon has continued well into the twentieth century (e.g. South Africa, most colonial possessions), the spread of democratic ideas has resulted in a pattern wherein political, cultural and social pre-eminence is exercised by ethnic majorities. The effect of the co-existence of several ethnic groups within a State often leads to their integration, usually at the expense of the minorities, but there are circumstances in which such co-existence results, on the contrary, in the intensification of the minority's group-consciousness. During modern times, the integrationist pattern has been more pronounced in the New World, while in Europe, under the influence of the doctrine of nationalism, popular among ethnic majorities and minorities alike, intensified group-feelings constituted the outstanding outcome. When this happens, the minority group is not content with equal rights and opportunities for its individual members, but insists, in addition, on collective rights which would best ensure the continuance of the group as such. A frequent demand is that official status be accorded to the minority's language and that the State finance a parallel network of public schools and cultural enterprises in that language for the use of the members of the minority. Often a large measure of self-government is also expected. This pattern was largely followed after World War I in a number of Eastern and Central European countries under the "minorities protection" system and was partly sanctioned by international law. Traces of the system are found in that part of the world to this day (1962) in places as far apart as Finland and Cyprus. In Cyprus, following the practice in use in Indian and other former British possessions, even political elections are held by ethnic groups separately (the so-called "communal representation" system), thus ensuring to each ethnic group a pre-determined quota of seats. A similar system, by religious rather than by national groups, is used in the Lebanon. Where ethnic groups are concentrated in a given part of the State's territory and form there the bulk of the population, a federal structure can be used to give to the group still greater influence and scope (thus: Canada, Switzerland, Yugoslavia, USSR, and to a certain extent India and Nigeria). In extreme cases, ethnic minorities, aided by a favorable international constellation, were able to bring about their complete separation from a State in which they were formerly incorporated and either united with an ethnically kindred State across the border by dint of the so-called "irredentist" movement or became fully independent. The principle under which these developments were achieved is known as "the principle of nationalities." Thus were formed among others the independent Balkan States, the smaller States of East-Central Europe, Norway, and Ireland, formerly held subject respectively by the Ottoman empire, Austria-Hungary, Russia, Sweden and Great Britain. B.A.

Ethnic Politics.
Although the leaders of ethnic groups deny it, the interests of ethnic groups have frequently had significant impact on American politics. At different times in different places a substantial portion of every major ethnic group has identified its interests with those of a political party, faction, candidate, or policy.

Scotch-Irish Presbyterians, driven to the frontier in the early decades of the nineteenth century, played a leading role in the development of what was to become the Democratic Party, feeding it with votes and leaders, some of whom reached the White House (Jackson, Polk, Buchanan).

They were soon replaced as the core group of the Democratic Party by Irish-Catholic immigrants. The early arrival of large numbers of English-speaking immigrants from Ireland enabled them to play a more important role in American politics than any other group. The Irish, who identified the opposition Yankee Protestants with the Republican Party, kept the party of Jackson alive for a half century after Appomattox.

German immigrants also made a unique contribution to the history of American political parties when a large majority of them were enlisted on the side of the new Republican Party during the 1850's and 60's over the slavery controversy. Later, their Republican affiliations were fortified by the homestead and hard-money policies of the G.O.P., and German-Americans living in the Midwest became a vital Republican core group. The arrival of one and a half million German immigrants between 1881 and 1890 probably assured Republican domination of national politics for another three decades.

With the passage of respective immigration legislation, ethnic politics has not been as significant in recent decades as previously. But the interests of ethnic groups continue to manifest themselves with astonishing persistence primarily because of the struggle of more recent immigrant groups for recognition in local politics and the involvement of even third and fourth generation Americans with foreign policy questions affecting their ancestral homelands. L.H.F.

EURATOM.
See European Atomic Energy Community.

European Atomic Energy Community.
It is the third sector of the European Community (the first being the ECSC and the second the EEC) con-

sisting of the same six countries which signed the Rome Treaties on 25 March 1957. It became operative on 1 January 1958. Euratom is developing a peaceful nuclear industry in Europe to increase energy resources and thereby raise living standards. Euratom has established a common market in nuclear materials for peaceful purposes only and therefore it has no authority to interfere in the national defense uses of fissionable materials in the Community. It also conducts research programs and promotes the diffusion of technical knowledge. Just like the EEC and the ECSC, Euratom shares with these the European Parliamentary Assembly, the Court of Justice and the Council of Ministers. It has its own administrative organ, a Commission (consisting of five members) and two consultative bodies: the Scientific and Technical Committee and the Economic and Social Committee which it shares with the EEC.
P.A.T.

European Coal and Steel Community (E.C.S.C.).

It is the first post-war European organization with authority to enforce its decisions directly upon the individual subjects (both persons and corporations) of the following six countries: France, German Federal Republic, Italy, Belgium, Netherlands, and Luxembourg. Established under a Treaty signed in Paris on 18 April 1952, the ECSC formed a single market for the nations' coal, steel, iron ore and scrap. By 1959, ECSC had eliminated all trade restrictions on these products and is now devoting its efforts to supervising the operation of this common market. It stimulates investment and research, facilitates labor movement within the area and aids workers who are threatened with unemployment through resettlement and retraining programs. It functions through an executive, called the High Authority (9 members), which is assisted by a Consultative Committee (consisting of 51 producers, consumers and workers); a coordinating body, called the Council of Ministers (6 members); a legislature, named the European Parliamentary Assembly (142 members) and a judiciary, the Court of Justice (9 members).
P.A.T.

European Convention for the Protection of Human Rights and Fundamental Freedoms.

The European Convention on Human Rights and Fundamental Freedoms came into force September 3, 1953. The Convention was drawn up by the International Juridical Section of the European Movement and the principle of "human rights and fundamental freedoms" was part of Article 3 of the **Statute** of the Council of Europe which binds each Member State of the Council of Europe to accept the principles of the rule of law and the enjoyment by all persons within its jurisdiction of human rights and fundamental freedoms. Every Member State (except France) ratified the Convention. The European Court of Human Rights and the European Commission on Human Rights were instituted to provide for the collective enforcement of the rights and freedoms specified. The competence of the court was accepted by Austria, Belgium, Denmark, the Federal Republic of Germany, Iceland, Ireland, Luxembourg, and The Netherlands. All but five of the Member States have accepted the competence of the Commission on Human Rights which to date (January 1963) has handled about 2,000 individual inter-State applications, among them a conflict between Greece and the United Kingdom concerning alleged violations of the Convention in Cyprus.
B.J.L.S.

European Economic Community, (usually called the Common Market.)

It is a customs union in the making of the ECSC countries that became operative on 1 January 1958. The objective of the EEC is to create a common market through the progressive reduction and elimination of all physical and fiscal restrictions on the free movement of goods, capital and persons between the member countries, the harmonization of their economic policies and the consolidation of their separate external tariffs into a single tariff system applicable to imports from outside the Community. These objectives are to be achieved gradually and by stages over a period of from twelve to fifteen years. The EEC does not replace the ECSC. But the EEC shares with the ECSC and Euratom the European Parliamentary Assembly, the Court of Justice and the Council of Ministers. Its chief executive organ is a Commission composed of nine members. P.A.T.

European Free Trade Association.
E.F.T.A. or the "Outer Seven" (Austria, Denmark, Norway, Portugal, Sweden, Switzerland, United Kingdom), was formed after the breakdown of negotiations to associate the EEC with other members of the Organization for European Economic Cooperation (now OECD) on 4 January 1960. The EFTA agreement provides for the gradual abolition of tariffs and quantitative restrictions among member countries by **1 January 1970, a** transition period timed to coincide with the Common Market's schedule. Although both the Common Market and EFTA have eliminated internal tariffs, the Common Market members have a common external tariff while the EFTA countries retain their independent national external tariffs.
P.A.T.

European Socialist and Social Democratic Parties.
Contemporary European social democratic parties trace their origin to the "revisionist" wing which developed within the Marxian socialist movement of the 19th century. Prior to the first world war socialist parties sought to concert their attack upon the bourgeois capitalist state system by organizing the Second International (1889). As an agency of international class solidarity the Second International failed, being split by ideological controversy and disagreement on tactics and strategy. The important revisionist movement, led by the German Social Democratic party, minimized the necessity for revolutionary overthrow of the existing order and argued for an evolutionary approach to socialism by legal, constitutional means, operating within the state rather than against it. Opposition to the revisionist wing came from the orthodox Marxists. The outbreak of the war completed the schism: the Second International dissolved; the revolutionary Marxists split off to form communist parties and become associated with the Third (Communist) International. Efforts at socialist unity across national boundaries continued after the war. The Second International was revived in 1920; in 1923 it united with a smaller labor alliance to form the "Labor and Socialist International." After the second world war, a new "Socialist International" was organized (1951).

Twentieth century social democratic parties are the heirs of the revisionist movement. No longer parties of class war or revolution, they seek social and economic reform rather than ideological goals. Repudiating doctrinaire Marxism, they address themselves to practical problems of social justice, economic security, international amity, democracy and freedom.

Divergencies and conflicts still exist among European social democratic parties. All are undergoing a period of self-appraisal and reassessment. In countries where social democratic parties have held or shared political power (principally in Scandinavia, Austria, and Britain) success in achieving the goals of earlier decades leaves the problem of formulating a program that can be distinguished from other reform parties. In France and Italy, where welfare state principles have not been fully accepted, the social democratic parties find their moderate, revisionist programs inadequate to meet the challenge of the communists. The once-powerful German Social Democratic Party has consistently suffered electoral defeat, in part because it seems unable to offer the voter anything that the existing government is not already providing. The dilemma of contemporary democratic socialism lies in the fact that it must now seek new programs and principles to justify its existence and attract non-traditional support. In the meantime, a sentimental attachment to Marxism (albeit revised) continues to alienate much of the bourgeois electorate. C.J.S.

Evian Agreement (March 18, 1962).
Cease-fire agreement reached at Evian-les-Bains, between France and the rebel provisional government of Algeria. The agreement, effective March 19, 1962, ended seven years, four months, 18 days of war. It pro-

vided for a referendum on the question of self-determination for Algeria, and for future cooperation between France and an independent Algeria. The agreement included guarantees for the rights of one million Europeans living in Algeria; an interim political regime; provisions for continued French military presence in Algeria; joint exploitation of oil and other minerals in the Sahara and Oases regions; and a broad amnesty for military and political prisoners on both sides. French military occupation forces were to be gradually withdrawn from Algeria over a 36-month period from the date of self-determination. France was granted a 15-year lease of the base of Mer El Kebir, as well as use of other military installations. E.R.W.

Evolution.
A generic term referring to processes of change whereby simple things tend to become progressively more complex, homogeneous things progressively more heterogeneous, and less organized things progressively more organic. Other kinds of change are not regarded as evolution in the strictly scientific sense. Ch.C.M.

Ex aequo et bono, decision.
A decision of an international tribunal based on equity or justice rather than law. **Ad hoc** tribunals have given such decisions but the two World Courts (P.C.I.J. and I.C.J.) have not even acceded to do so though authorized to upon request of all parties to a case. (See Statute I.C.J., Article 38 [2]). V.R.I.

Exclusive Powers.
Those powers which the United States government but not the states or those which the state governments but not the national government may exercise. Constitutional delegation of power to the national government in some cases denies to the states power to act in that area, for example, coining money, or borrowing money on the credit of the United States. Unless limited by the Constitution states may exercise any governmental power, for example, regulation concerning marriage, divorce, or the terms of office of their officials. J.E.S.

Executive.
a. One of the three basic powers of the state, assumed by parts of classic political science to engage in "implementing" the will of the legislature. It includes a political apex, such as the President in the U.S.A. and the Cabinet in Great Britain, and the civil service subordinated to it. Modern political science recognizes the essential policy-forming functions of both parts of the "executive," which are constantly increasing in most contemporary states.

b. The highest levels of the hierarchy in public and private bureaucracies. (**Caveat:** In Great Britain, the terminology is different: the highest hierarchic levels are called "administrative," while the middle levels are called "executive.") Y.D.

Executive Agreement.
While not mentioned in the United States Constitution, this method of diplomatic negotiation has seen increasing use by American presidents during the 20th century. Unlike treaties, it does not require senatorial consent. In some instances, as in the "lend lease" negotiations, such agreements rest upon authority conferred in advance by Congress. Many are concluded by presidents without such authorization. At times the device may be a means for evading senatorial consent. While such agreements have been upheld by the courts as the "supreme law of the land," the limits to which they may be carried have not been defined. R.J.S.

Executive Budget.
The principle that the chief executive or the chief administrative officer shall be vested with responsibility for the preparation and submission of a comprehensive periodic financial plan to the legislature for authorization. Major responsibility for preparing the President's budget in the United States rests with the Bureau of the Budget. More than two-thirds of the American states operate under the executive budget principle, which also constitutes an essential aspect of council-manager local government. T.S.

Executive Order.
The U.S. Congress has given the president the authority to issue rules with which to carry out general policies embodied in statutes. These executive orders have the force of law. They may come directly from the president's desk or from some administrative agency under his direction.
M.F.

Exequatur.
After his commission (**patent, lettre patente, lettre de provision, commission consulaire,** or **brevet**) from the sending state has been accepted by the receiving state, a consul receives an **exequatur** which is his authorization to perform consular duties in the receiving state. J.E.T.

Expansionist.
In the U.S.A. this term was used to identify those political leaders who wished to see the boundaries of the country expanded to reach the Pacific Ocean. M.F.

Ex Parte.
A controversy in which only one side has representation with no case presented for the opposition. J.O.H.

Expatriation.
Expatriation is the act by which a person who is a citizen of a country by birth, whether by **jus soli** or by **jus sanguinis**, abandons his citizenship in favor of that of another state, or who loses his citizenship by legislative act of the government. The United States, following the doctrine of nationality held by Great Britain, maintained in its early history the doctrine of "indelible allegiance," that no one might transfer his allegiance to another state without the consent of the state of his nationality of birth. But later, when it became necessary to protect its naturalized citizens when returning to their native country, the principle was assented in 1845 that naturalization dissolved any former tie of allegiance. The earlier doctrine of indelible allegiance of necessity gave way; but there are still numerous unsettled questions in the law, which even the Hague Convention of 1930 on Certain Questions relating to the Conflict of Nationality Laws was unable to solve. C.G.F.

Ex Post Facto Law.
A law which has the retroactive effect of making a crime an action that was not a crime when the action was performed; or which retroactively increases the degree of illegality attached to an action or the penalty attached to it; or which deprives an accused person of a protection at law previously afforded, as by changing rules of procedure so as to make his defense more difficult. The Constitution of the United States prohibits the Congress (Art. I, sec. 9) and the States (Art. I, sec. 10), from passing any **ex post facto law.** It is construed to apply only to criminal (not civil) statutes, and to prohibit only those which have punitive, rather than neutral or mitigative, effect. R.H.S.

Extra Constitutional Controls in the U.S.A.
(President over congress).
Presidential appointments are eagerly sought by members of Congress for party supporters back home. The president expects cooperation and support for this patronage. He may threaten to veto proposed legislation. He may appeal to the people via radio or television. Informal conferences, luncheons, dinners, week ends on the presidential yacht help to influence uncooperative legislators. As leader of his political party the president has great influence. M.F.

Extra-Legal Party.
A political organization formed outside the statutory party in response to a desire to overcome shortcomings of the latter. Extra-legal parties have broadly-based memberships, in contrast to the skeletal structures of statutory parties, and they are free from the legal restrictions upon expenditures and structure which inhibit the effectiveness and flexibility of statutory parties in some states of the U.S.A. Commonly, the extra-legal units are policy-oriented and make pre-primary endorsements. Notable examples include: the Republican and Democratic Parties of Wisconsin (which control and overshadow their statutory counterparts); the California Republican Assembly; and the California Democratic Council. D.W.Mc.

Extramural Jurisdiction.

The exercise of municipal authority beyond a city's borders. In the United States a number of cities are authorized by the state legislature to exercise jurisdiction over adjoining territory to protect their water supply or locate an airport, hospital, or other municipal facility. — J.F.Z.

Extraterritoriality.

Extraterritoriality refers to the right of a state under general international law or under a special treaty to carry out some of its functions within the territory of another state. Judicial rights known as capitulations were once a fairly common example. Today the term refers to exemption from jurisdiction for certain persons such as foreign heads of state, diplomats, members of the armed forces of foreign states (except when specific treaties authorize trial by local authorities) and persons who have legally obtained asylum in embassies and legations. Further examples of extraterritoriality include foreign war ships in the territorial waters of a state which are not subject to jurisdiction by the port state, and in a somewhat extended sense, foreign merchant vessels which normally enjoy a considerable degree of exemption from jurisdiction. — H.B.J.

F

Fabian Socialism.

As expressed in 1887 by the Fabian Society, proposed the use of existing party and parliamentary machinery for the realization of practical reforms which were designed to lead gradually to the elimination of poverty and the establishment of community ownership or control of land and of the means of production. In 1939 emphasis was placed upon the realization of equality of opportunity in society.
J.F.M.

Fabian Society.

Named after a delaying Roman General, was formed in London during 1884 to study conditions of poverty. Its socialist and democratic objectives, adopted in 1887, were expressed (through the efforts of the Webbs) in the 1918 Labour Party program. In 1939, when the Society amalgamated with the New Fabian Research Bureau (led by the Coles), emphasis was placed on research. Membership peaks were reached in 1918 with 2,000 and in 1948 with 8,425.
J.F.M.

Facultades Extraordinarias.

The recurring crises, especially economic or financial, which have confronted Latin American countries appear to the governments of those republics to demand state action without the delays and compromises attendant upon major policy determinations in the legislature. Therefore, it is not unusual for an administration to seek **facultades extraordinarias** ("extraordinary powers") from the national congress. When passed, these delegate extensive legislative authority to the president, usually in specified fields and for a specified period of time, such as six months. During that period the already broad decree-making power of the executive is enlarged to include the decree statute **(decreto-ley).**
R.D.H.

Fagerholm, Karl-August.

A leader of the Social Democratic Party of Finland. Born Dec. 31, 1901. Editor-in-chief of "Arbetarbladet," organ for Swedish-speaking Social Democrats, 1934-42. Member of the cabinet (as minister in social affairs) 1937-44; prime minister 1948-50 and 1956-57. Member of parliament 1930- . Speaker of parliament 1945-47, 1950-57 and 1959-61.
E.I.

Fair Deal.

The title given by United States President Harry S. Truman to his twenty-one point program which was contained in his message to Congress on September 6, 1945. The message and the title symbolized for him his assumption of the office of President in his own right. The Fair Deal was a liberal and progressive program that provided for demobilization and return to a peace time economy, without permitting large price and rent increases, or a rapid decrease of wage incomes or purchasing power.
J.R.B.

Fair employment laws.

Laws enacted by the Legislature of certain states which prohibit employers from denying job opportunities to applicants on grounds of race, religion, or national origin. Similar legislation was urged on Congress by the President's Committee on Civil Rights in 1947, and later by Presidents Truman and Eisenhower.
R.R.R.

Fair Labor Standards.

Fair labor standards are requirements established by a law passed by the United States Congress in 1938 which established minimum wages and maximum weekly hours of work for persons engaged in interstate commerce or in producing goods for interstate commerce. The law also prohibited child labor in these occupations (under 16 years, or under 18 years if the occupation is hazardous). The minimum wage level has been raised and maximum hours of work changed by amendments to the original act. Laws setting minimum wage standards and maximum hours of work, governing the employment of women, and prohibiting the labor of children except under certain controlled circumstances, are in effect in the great majority of the States.
J.R.B.

Falkland Islands Controversy.

The dispute between Argentina and the United Kingdom over the island group (called "Malvinas" by Argentina) some 300 miles east of Magellan Strait. Part of a larger controversy over "southern territories," including South Georgia and South Sandwich islands and overlapping south-polar sectors (see **Antarctic Claims**). Great Britain claims discovery (1592) and possession (1765), but the colony on West Falkland was taken by the Spanish in 1770, restored, then abandoned in 1774. The Spanish colony on East Falkland (called Soledad), received from the French in 1766, was in 1811 also abandoned. Argentines revived Soledad in 1820; however, the British have maintained exclusive occupation since 1832-33. Argentina's title is based partially on the **uti possidetis** of 1810, i.e., insisting that all Spanish territory under the jurisdiction of the Viceroyalty of La Plata passed to The United Provinces (Argentina). Spain's title is derived from Pope Alexander VI's Bulls of 1493, later treaties (including with the U.K.), rejection of the British discovery claim, English abandonment, and exercise of sovereignty until the colonies' independence. Geographical proximity and the broad extension of the continental shelf in the region allow Argentina also to argue "contiguity." Much ultranationalist literature on the topic has appeared in Argentina. R.D.H.

F.A.O.
See Food and Agriculture Organization.

Far East.
China, Korea, Japan. Some writers also include Vietnam, Laos, Cambodia, Thailand, Burma, Malaya, Indonesia, the Philippines, and even India. H.L.M.

Far Eastern Advisory Council.
A Council proposed by the United States to its Allies prior to the surrender of Japan in 1945. The proposal was made in response to the desires of the Allies to participate in the occupation of Japan. It was submitted to the United Kingdom, the USSR and the Republic of China, and stipulated that a Far Eastern Advisory Commission be created to advise the various allied governments of policies adopted to insure Japanese compliance with the terms of surrender. The Allies, however, wanted a more important part in the direction of the occupation, and a compromise proposal was worked out which resulted in the establishment of the F.E.C., which in theory had power to formulate policy, and the AJC, an advisory body. See FEC; AJC. S.S.

Far Eastern Commission (F.E.C.).
Created in December, 1945, at the Moscow Conference of the Foreign Ministers of Great Britain, the Soviet Union, and the U.S., after consultation with China. The Commission ultimately included China, France, the Netherlands, Canada, Australia, New Zealand, India, the Philippines, and, after November 17, 1949, Burma and Pakistan. The function of the Commission was to supervise the Supreme Commander of Allied Powers (General Douglas MacArthur) in his administration of occupied Japan, but in practice the Commission, based in Washington, proved unable to interfere effectively with the conduct of the American occupation authority. The United States government issued directives to MacArthur directly and at times when the FEC was deadlocked over policy decisions, as it usually was, the United States was able to act entirely on its own initiative. See AJC; F.E.A.C. S.S.

Farm Credit Administration.
The Farm Credit Administration is an independent agency of the United States government which supervises and coordinates a cooperative credit system for agriculture that provides long and short-term loans to farmers and farm cooperatives through land banks, intermediate credit banks, and cooperative banks. Loans are made to acquire farms, pay for equipment, finance crop production, and general agricultural purposes. Federal loans to farmers were first provided by the Federal Farm Loan Act, July 17, 1916; the Farm Credit Administration was established as an independent agency by Executive Order 6084, Mar. 27, 1933; merged with the Department of Agriculture under Reorganization

Plan No. 1, effective Apr. 25, 1939; and reestablished as an independent federal agency by the Farm Credit Act, Aug. 6, 1953. J.R.B.

Farmer Committee System.

A system of decentralized administration of farm programs in the United States. It was born during the Great Depression, and it became a vital tool in fostering the U.S. agriculture's economic well-being, psychological uplifting, and political stabilization. Elected local committees succeeded in securing farmers' participation in agricultural adjustment programs designed to protect and improve farm income, and during World War II played an important role in the administration of the War Boards. The farmer committee system administered a variety of farm programs authorized by law since 1945, and is still regarded as a very important part of the field forces of the U.S. Department of Agriculture. The performance of the elected community and county farmer committees has been supervised and coordinated by State committees appointed by the Secretary of Agriculture. J.H.

Farmer Fieldman.

A key link in the administrative structure of the Agricultural Stabilization and Conservation Service (ASCS) of the U.S. Department of Agriculture. He represents the ASCS State committee in a number of counties, and is responsible for the supervision and coordination of the operations of farm programs in his district. He provides advice and guidance to the farmer committees and county office managers under his jurisdiction, conducts educational and training meetings in the counties for county and community committeemen and county office personnel, and keeps the State committee advised of the effectiveness of local administration of farm programs. J.H.

Farmers Home Administration.

An agency of the U.S. Department of Agriculture. It serves eligible farmers, primarily low-income farmers, with credit and needed technical help on farm and money management problems. Loans are made only to applicants unable to obtain adequate credit from other sources at reasonable rates and terms. Loans are made for farming equipment, livestock feed, seed and fertilizer; for farm enlargement and improvement; for the purchase of family farms; for irrigation and farmstead water supply systems; for refinancing existing debts; and for the construction and remodeling of rural homes and farm buildings. This program of credit and counseling is administered through a system of county supervisors assisted by county or area committees of farmers. J.H.

Farouk (Faruq).

King Farouk is the second king to rule modern Egypt. He is the great great grandson of Muhammad 'Ali, the founder of modern Egypt. Farouk was born in 1920, became king in 1936, and was ousted by a military coup led by Naguib in 1952. The military officers spared Farouk's life. He left for Italy where he still lives.
W.B.B.

Fascism.

The principles underlying the movement inaugurated by Benito Mussolini and his followers in Italy in 1919 and later adopted, in part, by Hitler and the Nazis in Germany, Franco and the Falangists in Spain, and others. Although the varying circumstances in the countries in which it took root produced a variety of configurations of fascism, it fundamentally represented a reaction to the democracy, socialism, and communism which it opposed. There are, therefore, characteristics common to all fascist movements. Fascism rejects equality and substitutes the principle of hierarchy culminating in a supreme leader or dictator whose will is law. Fascism repudiates individualism and asserts that all values derive from the state, against which the individual possesses no rights; true liberty, consequently, is found only in subjection to state authority. The fascist state requires complete conformity, rigid discipline, and unquestioning obedience; force is legitimate which conduces to these ends. Fascism is opposed to the rationalist tradition of the West. Faith and emotion, rather than reason and reflection, are regarded as the keys to proper understanding. As against the democratic view of the state as an instrument to be used by man for his advantage, fascism regards the state as the end and man as the instrument. Since the state is the highest value, fascism ideally opposes international organizations and relies upon military solutions. Peace is thought to be corrosive and a cause of decadence. Fascism is anti-pluralistic; no organizations which compete with the state for the loyalty of the individual are permitted. Fascism seeks unity through homogeneity. In Germany this resulted in racist doctrines and the program of liquidation of "non-Aryan" elements. From the standpoint of institutions, fascism typically exalts the executive power. Legislatures become ratifying bodies. Courts lose their independence. Local governments are controlled by the central authority. Political power is in the hands of the dictator and a single political party. A major difference between fascism and the authoritarian systems of the past is that fascism strives to engender mass enthusiasm for its regime and policies. M.J.H.

Faubus, Orval E.
Governor of Arkansas (U.S.A.), during Little Rock school segregation difficulties and first governor to be elected for five successive terms.
C.W.B.

Favorite Son.
An aspirant to the presidential nomination of his party whose principal source of support lies in the backing of his home state delegation. A favorite son may emerge a "dark horse" winner of the nomination but frequently his candidacy serves chiefly to permit his delegation to delay committing itself until the prospects of the major contenders for the nomination can be gauged, thus improving its bargaining position. Th.P.

F.B.I.
See Federal Bureau of Investigation.

F.E.A.C.
See Far Eastern Advisory Council.

F.E.C.
See Far Eastern Commission.

Federal-Aid Highway Act.
See U.S. Federal-Aid Highway Act of 1956.

Federal Aviation Agency.
Established in 1958 by the Federal Aviation Act, the Federal Aviation Agency inherited the functions formerly performed by the Civil Aeronautics Administration, and the Airways Modernization Board and the safety regulation activities of the Civil Aeronautics Board. It is primarily concerned with the regulation and control of navigable airspace in the interest of safety. It conducts research and development programs with respect to air navigation facilities. In general, through investigation and regulation, it seeks to develop a coordinated system of air traffic control for both civil and military aviation. B.B.

Federal Bureau of Investigation.
The Federal Bureau of Investigation (F.B.I.) is a subdivision of the U.S. Department of Justice which investigates and collects evidence regarding violations of national laws except those which have been assigned by legislative enactment or otherwise to some other Federal agency, such as counterfeiting and internal revenue laws investigated by the Treasury Department and postal laws investigated by the Post Office Department. The jurisdiction of the F.B.I. includes such things as espionage, sabotage, treason, kidnapping, thefts in interstate commerce, or interstate transportation which aids gambling and racketeering. There are 55 field offices operating under the Director in Washington, D.C. J.R.B.

Federal Chancellor (Bundeskanzler).
Chief executive, German Federal Republic. Elected by absolute majority of the Bundestag at beginning of each new parliament. May be dismissed by parliamentary vote of no-confidence only if Bundestag simultaneously elects a successor by absolute majority ("constructive vote of no confidence"). Determines and assumes responsibility for general policy; names and dismisses cabinet ministers. Has limited "emergency powers" and restricted power to dissolve Bundestag. C.J.S.

Federal Civil Defense Administration.

The Federal Civil Defense Administration is the national agency of the United States government responsible for the development, coordination, guidance, and leadership of a national program of civil defense designed to protect the lives and properties of United States citizens from attack. Actual operations are carried out by state and local civil defense officials, and civil defense organizations are sometimes used in case of natural disasters such as floods and hurricanes. The Administration was created by Executive Order 10186 and placed within the Office of Emergency Management, Dec. 1, 1950; established as an independent agency by the Federal Civil Defense Act, transferred to the Office of Defense and Civilian Mobilization in the Executive Office of the President by Reorganization Plan No. 1, effective July 1, 1958, and placed under an Assistant Secretary for Civil Defense in the U.S. Department of Defense by Executive Order 10952, Aug. 1, 1961. J.R.B.

Federal Communications Commission.

It consists of seven members appointed by the President and Senate under the provisions of the Federal Communications Act of 1934. Its primary purpose is to regulate the "communications industries." Like other independent regulatory agencies, it holds hearings, makes policy determinations and issues regulations. It is concerned with two aspects of communication, the "wire carriers," i.e., telephone and telegraph companies and "air carriers," the radio transmissions on the airwaves.

In the case of the former, the Commission regulates rates and has the power, after a hearing, to suspend them, if it feels that they are unjust or discriminatory. It also defines unfair competition and can take the necessary steps to eliminate it. In the latter, radio transmission is regulated through the licensing power. In effect, the Government has prohibited the transmission of radio signals or the operation of radio stations, except in accordance with the conditions contained in licenses granted by the Commission. The general standard governing the issuance of such licenses is "public interest, convenience and necessity" but this power has been expanded into a whole series of regulations that now govern radio communication. B.B.

Federal Housing Administration (U.S.A.).

This agency was established in 1933 to encourage owner-occupancy of homes and to help provide housing for low-income families. It guarantees home loans to protect private lending agencies against losses ("F.H.A. mortgages"), and seeks to raise housing standards by its conditions for mortgage-guarantee eligibility and through the dissemination of technical information concerning building construction and building codes. Since 1947, FHA has been a part of the Housing and Home Finance Agency, which is also responsible for the Federal public housing program, directs mortgage loans in some circumstances, and the encouragement of local public works programs. C.R.A.

Federalism.

One principle or idea regarding the division of powers between central and regional governmental authorities is known as federalism. It differs from unitarism and confederalism. The idea is that neither the central or the regional authority is supreme. They are coordinate. Each has a respective sphere of functions. In the United States the central authority, the national government, and the regional authorities, the states, share many powers, although one or the other is predominant in certain functions. Other bona fide federal governments are usually considered to be Canada, Australia, and Switzerland. It is a type of rule which can be utilized for the self-government of large areas which desire some degree of unification or small areas where complete unification is not desired. Federalism is also often favored since the divided rule makes simultaneous tyranny at both levels unlikely. J.A.E.

Federalist Papers.

A series of eighty-five essays advocating the adoption of the present Constitution of the United States, explaining its principles, and defending the federal system. These articles were written by Alexander Hamilton, James Madison, and John Jay, under the **nom de plume** of Publius. They were published in New York newspapers in 1787 and 1788 after the Constitution had been presented to the conventions of the several states by the Philadelphia Convention. They soon became widely known and influenced the thinking of people in other states as well as in New York. Later they were bound in one volume, which has gone through several editions, usually under the title **The Federalist.** D.C.

Federal Power Commission.

This agency has a history that dates back to 1920. At the present time, it consists of five commissioners appointed by the President with the consent of the Senate. The agency through a series of statutes is empowered to grant licenses for hydroelectric projects on Government lands or on navigable streams, to regulate the transmission and sale of electricity at wholesale rates in interstate commerce. In 1938, it was given similar powers over the transportation and sale of natural gas. The Commission makes rules and regulations applicable to the electric power and natural gas industries.
B.B.

Federal Republic of Germany.

One of the two units into which Germany is divided. Established 1949 by Western occupation powers. Government regulated by Bonn Constitution (q.v.). First limited by Allied reserved powers, since 1955 (Paris Treaties) fully sovereign. Member of NATO, European organizations, most international organizations (except UN). Armed forces (1962 appr. 400,000) integrated with NATO. Population (exclusive of West-Berlin) 54 million, of which 12 million Eastern expellees and refugees. Area appr. 96,000 sq. miles. Currency D-Mark, prosperity since currency reform 1948; economic growth rate appr. 8 percent annually. Social and economic structure not basically changed since prewar. Despite failure of denazification (q.v.) political climate moderate; little leftist or rightist radicalism, major parties favoring status quo or mild reform. J.H.H.

Federal Service Entrance Examination.

Merit tests conducted by the U.S. Civil Service Commission since 1955. The FSEE is designed as a general entry to Federal career service for young people with college education. In recent years over 10,000 appointments from this examination have been made annually to around sixty different career fields. R.D.S.

Federal Trade Commission.

In the U.S.A. the function of the **Federal Trade Commission** is to aid the government in enforcing the laws regulating business activities. By its power to issue cease and desist orders it seeks to prevent misrepresentation in the branding of goods and false advertising. It also gives valuable help to the Department of Justice in antitrust actions by the gathering of evidence of violations of the Sherman and Clayton Anti-Trust Act. G.B.T.

Federated city.

Where governmental power over an urban area is divided between the principal city and its boroughs or municipalities a federated city exists. London, New York and Toronto are federated cities. In 1957 a similar structure was created with Dade County, Florida, as the area wide government. J.M.S.

Federation.

Within a state (polity), a method pioneered by the United States of structuring intergovernmental relations to reconcile both political unity and territorially rooted diversity. Governmental powers are constitutionally distributed between central and lesser political authorities so that each level is granted certain exclusive as well as concurrent powers, prohibited powers are specified, and any residual powers are allocated. The central authority is given real governmental capabilities, the exercise of national sovereignty, and control over external relations. The component territorial governments, although denied political sovereignty, are granted a measure of local autonomy whose formal removal requires a constitutional amendment. Various federations distribute specific powers differently, however, and their political systems may be either democratic (United States) or dictatorial (Soviet Union), depending upon executive-legislative-judicial relationships and the role of the people. Implementation of federalism usually necessitates some decision about the permissibility of secession from the union, the designation of one house of a central bi-cameral legislature as representative of the component units, judicial arrangements to deal with intergovernmental jurisdictional disputes, and a special constitutional amending process. The technique can create new polities composed of previously independent or otherwise culturally distinct, political entities (e.g., Switzerland) or it can provide constitutional recognition for existing internal diversity (e.g., West Germany). Its complexity and the difficulty of stabilizing the power distribution, however, also may produce administrative, financial and legal problems not normal to a unitary state. Federation may also be applied to political parties or other organizations composed of distinctly diverse elements. D.W.

Federation of Malaya.
(Area, 51,200 square miles; population, approximately 6,909,000).

A federation of eleven states in the British Commonwealth, Malaya occupies the southern half of the 1,000-mile-long Malay Peninsula and is populated by nearly 7 million inhabitants: half Malays and Malaysians, 37% Chinese, 11% Indians and Pakistanis, 1% Europeans and Eurasians.

The West first invaded Malaya when the Portuguese seized Malacca in 1511. The Dutch followed, and, in turn, the British when the East India Company purchased the island of Penang in 1786. The Company later secured Singapore (1819) and Malacca (1824), the three enclaves being united as a Crown Colony in 1867 known as the Straits Settlements, the only British territory in Malaya. Between 1874 and 1909 the nine Malay States came under British protection through treaties establishing British residents or advisers acting in the name of the several sultans as legal sovereigns within each state.

The pre-World War II political control of Malaya was a complicated arrangement of ten separate governments. The governor of the Straits Settlements was also high commissioner of the nine states. Four states (Perak, Selangor, Negri Sembilan, Pahang) formed the Federated Malay States in 1895, the other five (Johore, Kedah, Kelantan, Trengganu, Perlis) remaining unfederated. The governor ruled as a benevolent despot with the assistance of three local advisory councils.

Following a period of Japanese occupation during World War II, the British were welcomed back in September 1945. In response to nationalist demands, the British instituted an interim Malayan Union which was very shortly succeeded on January 21, 1948 by the Federation of Malaya. The Crown Colony of Singapore was not a member of the Federation although politically and economically integrated with the Federation and commonly included in the term, "Malaya." In August 1957 the Federation gained complete independence thereby becoming the eleventh sovereign member-state of the Commonwealth. Singapore —with its 224.5 square miles and population of approximately 1,640,000— gained independence on June 3, 1959.

The possibility of uniting the Federation, Singapore, and the British dependencies of Sarawak, Brunei, and North Borneo in a Malaysian Federation is under active consideration by the interested governments. M.T.K.

Federation of Rhodesia and Nyasaland.
A federation in South Central Africa; area 487,641 square miles; population 8,430,000 (1960 estimate). It consists of Southern Rhodesia, Northern Rhodesia, and Nyasaland, and is within the Commonwealth of Nations. Created by authority of the British Parliament with the announced aim of sharing economic benefits and the ultimate goal of full membership in the Commonwealth as an independent state, it has never overcome the opposition of leaders of the African population (which is in the overwhelming majority in the Federation), who fear the Federation as an instrument of European domination. There

is a unicameral Parliament with a European majority, and government powers are divided between the Federation and the three territories. The Monckton Commission recommended in 1960 that the right of secession from the Federation be recognized. The Northern Rhodesia election of 1962 resulted in a large numerical vote for Assembly candidates opposed to the Federation, and the African government of Nyasaland is also hostile, so the future of the Federation in its present form admits of considerable doubt. Sir Roy Welensky is the federal Prime Minister. E.V.M.

Feedback.
Originally an engineering concept, meaning a process by which the operation of a mechanism is self-corrected through the reporting of differences between actual and intended results (the thermostat control being a simple example). By extension, feedback is now the reflection of public opinion and, more specifically, the indicated reaction from persons affected by a given action or proposal. Ideally, feedback guides the originator of the act or proposal to make changes as may be prompted by the indicated relation. Thus, an election is feedback in a general sense, and opinion research, lobbying and riots are feedback in a specific sense. J.B.L.

Felony.
A crime classified as such by law and usually carrying a death penalty or imprisonment in a state prison. (Crimes which may be felonies in some states of the United States may be misdemeanors in others). Most frequently included are criminal homicide, robbery, burglary, kidnapping.
J.O.H.

Fence-Viewers.
A fence-viewer is an officer who is required legally to settle boundary disputes between property owners. The fence-viewer may survey the line himself, hire a surveyor, or even arbitrarily fix it on observation. However done, he is responsible for the action, and his decision is final. The office lost most of its importance with the establishment of modern surveying methods and accurate reporting, and remains as a vestige of an important ancient function. A.E.N.

Fertile Crescent Plan.
The Plan was proposed by Nuri as-Said (Iraq) in 1942 in a note to the British representative in the Middle East. The Plan envisaged the unification of Syria, Lebanon, Palestine and Trans-Jordan. This state will then federate with Iraq and thus realizing Fertile Crescent Unity within a looser confederation of Arab States. The Plan had British support, but was opposed by the nationalists in Syria and Lebanon who saw in it a British-Hashemite scheme to dominate the Arab East. The Plan was strongly opposed by Egypt and Saudi Arabia.
E.A.S.

Feudalism.
It refers to the social, economic, and political system which characterized European civilization during a great portion of the Middle Ages. It was based on the discharge of mutual obligations on the part of Lords and Serfs, the rulers and toilers, which was of a personal type. The lord relied on the serf's economic and military services; the latter depended on his lord's prestige and power in organizing protection and maintaining public order. Politically, the system was highly decentralized, headed by a monarch, as dependent on the lords' services, as the latter depended on his serfs. Economically, the system was based on land: on agriculture and barter. Socially, it was characterized by a sharp dichotomy between the manners, mores, rights, privileges, etc., of those who ruled (the aristocracy), and those who toiled (the common folk). Feudalism was transformed and superseded by the introduction of the money-economy, by the rising middle classes which pursued trade, and by the increasing socio-economic mobility which arose in consequence. The two pillars of the middle classes, urbanism and wealth, slowly transformed a feudal society based on personal loyalty and land. V.Z.

Feuerbach, Ludwig (1804—1872).
He was a famous antagonist of Hegel's idealism. His materialism profoundly influenced both Marx and

Engels. Besides Nietzsche, he may also be considered as one of the most aggressive critics of Christianity in modern times. In his **The Essence of Christianity** (1843), he claimed that 'religion is the estrangement of man from himself' and proposed 'to transform the candidates of the otherworldly (the theologians) into the students of the thisworldly,' as he put it, because 'the negation of the otherworldly leads to an affirmation of the present.' Before Marx, he maintained that 'the necessary conclusion from the existing evils and injustices of human life lies solely in the will, in the endeavour to eliminate them, but not in a faith in the Beyond which leads rather to leaving the evils as they are while placing your hands in your lap.' This is why the Russian revolutionary, Sergei Bulgakov exclaimed that "the thorough study of all three volumes of **Das Kapital** has not as much Marx in it as an acquaintance with Feuerbach." Marx distanced himself from Feuerbach's vulgar materialism. Feuerbach maintained that "if you want to improve the people, then instead of preaching against sin give them better food. Man is what he eats." Such a view negates the necessity of a revolution of society by the subjugated classes; their salvation—Marx meant Feuerbach to have implied—can be attained by feeding them well. Yet, Feuerbach's epistemology is at the basis of Marx's historical materialism and the modern sociology of knowledge; for, it is Feuerbach who first maintained that 'thought is a predicate of being,' and elaborated on this in his work. V.Z.

Fichte, Johann Gottlieb (1762—1814).
One of the most prominent exponents of German Idealism who, with his 'subjectivistic idealism,' prepared the ground for Hegel and the dialectic. While the German medieval mystic Eckhart claimed that 'through the deed man partakes of divinity,' Fichte makes of the 'Deed' and the human Will a foundation stone of a philosophic outlook that assumes for itself almost divine powers of creativity: man becomes the creator of the world which he knows. Absolutizing the methodological significance of Kant's **Critique of Practical Reason,** wherein Kant had shown how the Mind—within practical or ethical reason—can attain to a knowledge of essences by positing them in the Will, Fichte made all human knowledge develop from the Will. He made of 'activity' the sole dimension of knowledge because thus he could eliminate the subject-object duality of all knowledge which in a theistic philosophic position is necessarily dualistic. Before Hegel and Marx, Fichte developed the notion of a triadic rhythm (thesis, antithesis, synthesis), as well as the notion of five stages in history. His book **The Closed Commercial State** (1800), where he espouses a self-sufficient planned economy and a welfare state, ranks him among the forerunners of modern socialism. He probably belongs to the first thinkers who have conceived of the 'right-to-work' idea, and his speeches to the German nation on the subject of nationalism make him a philosophic forerunner of twentieth century German nationalism.
V.Z.

Fidaiyun.
Literally meaning "devotees." In contemporary use, commando-units organized by Egypt from among Palestine refugees in the Gaza strip to engage in terrorism and espionage in Israel. As part of the anti-Israeli activities, Egyptian military authorities organized the Fidaiyun and pressed young Palestinian refugees to join them. Fidaiyun terrorist activities reached their climax in 1956, being a main reason for the Israeli Sinai Campaign (see there). During the Sinai campaign the Fidaiyun units disintegrated; they have been only partly reestablished, concentrating now mainly on espionage. Y.D.

Fidelismo.
Leftwing agitation for "socialistic" regimes in Latin America, inspired by the Cuban premier, Fidel Castro. This ideology advocates expropriation of foreign businesses, collectivization of private enterprises, and blanket criticism of United States policies in Latin America. M.A.

Field, Stephen Johnson (1816—1899).
Associate Justice of the Supreme Court of the United States from 1863

to 1897. Appointed during the Civil War as a Union Democrat, Field was notable for his legal scholarship and his conservative opinions. His principal contribution to jurisprudence was his interpretation of the Fourteenth Amendment to the United States Constitution as a guarantee of general principles of laissez-faire, limiting all state social and economic legislation. These views were first expressed in dissent in **The Slaughterhouse Cases** of 1873, and were cherished by Field throughout his long tenure in the Supreme Court. An ambitious man, he had wanted to be President of the United States in 1880, and Chief Justice of the United States in 1888, but was disappointed in both these desires.
E.L.

Fifth Column. See Appendix.

Fifth Republic of France.
See France—Fifth Republic.

Figueres, Jose.
Outstanding Latin American statesman. Born in San Ramon, Costa Rica, Sept. 25, 1906. Education: student of philosophy, National Univ. of Mexico; electrical engineering, Massachusetts Institute of Technology; languages, Columbia Univ. Farmer and businessman, 1929-48. Organizer and leader of the Costa Rican revolution which overthrew pro-Communist govt., March-April 1948. President of interim govt. 1948-49. Constitutionally-elected President of Costa Rica, 1953-58. Prolific writer, lecturer on hemispheric public affairs.
M.A.

Filibuster.
To slow or stop action of a deliberative body by delaying tactics or long speeches.
K.E.H.

Fillmore, Millard (1800—1874).
Thirteenth President of the United States. Born in Locke, New York and largely self-educated, Millard Fillmore read law, was admitted to the bar (1823) and practiced in and near Buffalo, New York. He entered politics as a Anti-Masonic member of the New York State Assembly (1829-31) and protege of Thurlow Weed. While a U.S. Representative (1833-35; 1837-43), he joined the Whig Party (1834), became its floor leader, and while Chairman of the Ways and Means Committee, sponsored the high Tariff of 1842. Failing as Whig candidate for Governor of New York (1844), he became state comptroller, and received in 1848, as a Henry Clay supporter, the Vice-Presidential nomination after Zachary Taylor defeated Clay for first place on the Whig ticket. He moved from Vice-President (1849-50) to President (1850-53) upon Taylor's untimely death. As President he approved the Perry Treaty opening Japan to trade, and signed the controversial Compromise of 1850 including the harsh fugitive slave law which cost him abolitionist support of Weed and William H. Seward. Defeated for renomination, Fillmore accepted the American Party (Know-Nothing) nomination for President (1856) and ran a poor third to James Buchanan and John C. Fremont.
K.E.D.

Filmer, Sir Robert.
English political writer, oft-quoted champion of divine right of kings theory in seventeenth century, was born in East Sutton, Kent; educated at Trinity College, Cambridge; knighted by Charles I at the beginning of his reign; active supporter of Royalist cause in Civil war.

His chief work, considered a classic of the divine right doctrine, **Patriarcha; or The Natural Power of Kings**, was first published (1680) many years after his death; it attacks the social contract theory of Hobbes and others; advocates the patriarchal theory as the true origin of government by attempting to trace the kingly right by primogeniture back to Adam. In the beginning of the world God gave authority to Adam with control over his descendants, even as to life and death. This absolute power was inherited in turn by Noah and then by the patriarchs. From the patriarchs it passed on to all kings. Hence, present kings (the Stuart line specifically) "are, or are to be reputed, next heir to him (Adam the first king)." Their authority, therefore, is absolute and founded upon divine right. Filmer's theory was attacked by Sidney and by Locke, especially in the first part of his **Two Treatises of Government** (1690).
G.A.K.

Fine Gael. See Appendix.

186

Finland (Suomi).

An independent republic, Finland is situated between Sweden and the Soviet Union in an area of 130,160 square miles, with a population of 4,457,000 (1960). The official languages are Finnish and Swedish, the latter being spoken by about ten per cent of the population. Finland's political history began with the establishment of a free village society by the early Finno-Ugrians about 100 A.D. Finland increasingly came under Swedish influence after the Christian crusades of the eleventh and twelfth centuries, finally becoming an archduchy of Sweden in 1556. Following military invasion, Finland became an archduchy of Russia in 1809. The Finns generally resisted Russification efforts and were able to maintain the constitutional forms that had been established by the **Form of Government Act of 1772** and other organic acts during the Swedish period. Finland became independent on December 6, 1917, but was plunged immediately into a bloody civil war, the scars of which are still evidenced in the alignment of Finnish political parties today. The Republic of Finland was officially established on June 17, 1919.

The **Form of Government Act of 1919**, the **Diet Act of 1928**, and the **Supreme Court of Law of 1922**, constitute the main elements of the Finnish Constitution. Finland is a parliamentary democracy. The Cabinet, which is primarily responsible for the conduct of governmental affairs, is responsible to the single-chambered, popularly-elected Diet **(Eduskunta).** The President of the Republic, chosen by an electoral college of 300 members for a six year term, has powers substantially greater than usually would be expected in a parliamentary system. In part this is so because of the need for strong and urgent executive action in the frequently recurring political crises, crises that usually cannot be handled adequately by the unstable coalition governments, and also because of the tradition of a strong executive inherited from tsarist days.

Finland's political party system is characterized by multiplicity and sharp division. The various parties reflect the diversity of economic, social, cultural and ideological interests among the Finnish people. The more important parties and the primary groups they represent are as follows: Agrarian Union: farm and rural; Social Democrats: urban industrial workers of socialist inclination; Finnish Peoples Democratic Union (SKDL): Communists and fellow-travellers; Swedish Peoples: Swedish-speaking Finns bent upon preserving their cultural and linguistic identity; Finnish Peoples: originally a nationalistically oriented party, now more reflective of liberals of the professional and intellectual classes; National Coalition: a loose grouping of commercial and industrial interests.

The Agrarians and the Social Democrats have predominated in the governments in the post-war period. The Communists (SKDL) have been excluded almost entirely from participation in the cabinets notwithstanding the party's constant strength (20-25 per cent of the Diet seats) electorally. Lacking a majority party, Finnish governments have tended to be unstable coalitions with cabinets lasting less than one year on the average.

Foreign and domestic policies of the Finnish government are strongly influenced by the huge presence of the Soviet Union at Finland's long eastern border and the after effects of two military defeats at the hands of this giant. Finland has felt compelled to forego Marshall Plan aid and other forms of association with the West that might be construed by the Soviet Union as unfriendly and provocative. Though retaining her political independence and westward cultural and political orientation, Finland lives always in the shadow of Soviet power, a power that could snuff out Finland's democratic existence at any time.

R.H.K.

First Empire of France.
See France—First Empire.

First Republic of France.
See France—First Republic.

First strike capacity.

A military strategic concept denoting the capability to launch a military attack with good promise of eliminating an enemy's capacity to retaliate with an effect unacceptably devastating to the nation launching the attack.

Usually denotes a capacity to severely damage an enemy's long-range striking forces, thereby preventing his retaliation. Thus, in U.S. strategic terminology, a strong deterrent to surprise attack by an adversary nation.
H.H.R.

Fiscal Policy.
The term is derived from the writings of the English economist John Maynard Keynes. His theories called for governmental expenditures in excess of revenue during times of recession, of less than revenue during inflation. He believed the two policies would, in the long run, balance off. In practice, it has been politically more feasible to engage in deficit financing than to retire debt in times of prosperity with the result that public debts tend to increase over time. The American state governments, which have little control over their own credit or overall finance, credit, and debt management policies, have little ability to participate in fiscal management policies.

Newspapers and other periodicals frequently use the term "fiscal policy" much more loosely than do economists. Often, they mean merely "financial policy," a quite different matter, in using the term.
C.R.A.

Fishing on the High Seas.
The Geneva Fishing Convention, 1958, reiterates the general rule that fishing in the high seas is free to all, subject to treaty obligations, if any; but proposes that states co-operate in the conservation of sea resources. Such efforts include area and multi-partite agreements.

The Hague Convention on the North Sea, 1882, provided for registration of boats, reciprocal right of enforcement of the established fishing rules by visit, search, and seizure. Similar regulations for fisheries around the Faeroes Islands and Iceland were adopted in 1901.

The Whaling Convention of 1931 to protect baleen whales extends to all waters. In 1937 (amended, 1938) an agreement applying to all whales was adopted, which set closed seasons and areas and restricted the use of factory ships. The 1946 Whaling Conference treaty provides for the codification and expansion of existing regulations and for the creation of a commission which would keep regulations current. The commission sets an annual quota of whales; when this is reached, the season is closed.

The Northwest Atlantic fisheries are regulated by the Treaty of 1949, which set up a Commission to investigate stocks of fish and recommend to the parties concerned necessary regulations.

To protect fur seals, the United States, Great Britain, Japan, and Russia signed the treaty of 1911, denounced by Japan in 1940. In 1947, Canada and the United States extended the Fur Seal Agreement of 1942 which established a prohibited zone for sealing, enforceable by either, and provided for patrol of the North Pacific.

The United States and Canada have regulated sockeye salmon fisheries by the treaty of 1930 and halibut by treaties of 1923, 1930, and 1937. A commission for each fishery is provided. There are closed seasons on halibut with provision for reciprocal seizure of violators.

Japan, Canada, and the United States in 1952 provided for a commission to propose conservation measures applicable to all after approval; for abstention in certain areas which are left open to fishing by the other parties; for enforcement of the abstention and conservation provisions in the North Pacific.

The 1958 Geneva Convention of Fishing, etc., declared that all states are obligated to support measures necessary for the conservation of the living resources of the sea. If negotiations on conservation fail, Article 9 provides for compulsory peaceful, settlement of disputes.

The problem of international regulation of fishing is complicated by the growing claim of various states to regulate fisheries for an increasing distance from shore, e.g., Chile, Ecuador, and Peru for 200 miles.
J.E.T.

Floor leader.
A party member who is designated as leader on the floor of a legislative body. He tries to maintain party solidarity, carries out the party program, and indicates who will speak on certain measures. The majority floor

leader in the U.S. Senate potentially is the most powerful member of that body, though real leadership varies from time to time. In the House the majority floor leader ranks next to the Speaker in importance. W.V.H.

Fong, Hiram Leong.
Born October 1, 1907; U.S. Senate from August 21, 1959 until term ending January 3, 1965; Republican—Hawaii; vice president of Territorial Constitutional Convention 1950; Colonel USAFR. R.A.B.

Food and Agriculture Organization (F.A.O.).
Specialized agency of United Nations, successor to International Institute of Agriculture. Constitution drafted by International Food and Agriculture Conference in 1943, ratified in 1945. Purpose: universal raising of nutritional levels, improved production and distribution of food and agricultural products. Functions: research, distribution of information, promotion of improved production, distribution and conservation, and technical assistance. 150 members. H.Q., Rome.
F.B.G.

Food and Drug Administration.
The Agricultural Appropriation Act of 1928 provided for a Food, Drug, and Insecticide Administration. The name was changed to Food and Drug Administration by the Agricultural Appropriation Act of 1931. The administration, first a part of the United States Department of Agriculture, was transferred to the Federal Security Agency by President Franklin D. Roosevelt's Reorganization Plan IV, June 30, 1940, and now is part of the United States Department of Health, Education, and Welfare, which was created by President Dwight D. Eisenhower's Reorganization Plan I, April 11, 1953. The Food and Drug Administration enforces laws intended to assure purity in foods and drugs, high standards of quality, correct quantities in containers, and truthful and informative labeling of the essential commodities covered by the provisions of United States pure food and drug laws. J.R.B.

Forced labor camps.
Forced labor camps are called "corrective labor camps" by the Soviet Government. The first real forced labor camp was established by the OGPU (the Union-Republic People's Commissariat of Internal Affairs or NKVD) on Solovetsky Island in the White Sea in 1923. By 1940 a huge network of forced labor camps stretched across northern European Russia and into the far northeast of Siberia and they were managed by the "Chief Administration of Corrective Labor Camps and Labor Settlements" (GULAG) of the NKVD.

The institutions of forced labor camps were maintained by the Soviet Government for the purpose of (1) isolating and punishing political offenders and "politically unreliable elements," those purged in the 1930's, various nationality groups thought to be of dubious loyalty during World War II, Baltic dissidents after the war, groups from the East European satellites, retained prisoners of war, and criminal offenders; and (2) mobilizing quickly large pools of cheap labor for special tasks in industry and transportation.

Estimates of the Soviet population directly affected by forced labor camps vary widely. The **minimum** estimate is around three and a half millions. The post-Stalin Soviet leadership claimed that forced labor camps had been entirely abolished in the Soviet Union but this claim is doubted and disputed by many students of Soviet affairs.
R.St-H.

Foreign Policy.
Courses of action in pursuit of national objectives beyond the limits of the jurisdiction of the state. It includes objectives in the sense of specific goals, principles or guides to action and conduct, commitments or specific undertakings, and the strategy and tactics suitable to the attainment of the ends sought. C.B.J.

Foreign Service of the U.S.A.
Carries out the operations of the State Department under authority of the Foreign Service Act of 1946. Largely autonomous earlier, the Service is now under direct responsibility to the Secretary of State with a dep-

uty under secretary for administration. The wall between the diplomatic and consular services was eliminated by the Rogers Act of 1924 and the new status in the State Department strengthens this integration.

Composed of officers, reserve officers, and staff, the Foreign Service is primarily the eyes and ears of the United States abroad. It represents the entire government, performing services for many agencies. It carries out foreign policy as expressed in the directives of the Secretary of State, gathers data for American policy-makers, protects Americans and their interests in other countries, and seeks to cultivate friendly relations with other peoples through many approaches and services.   C.B.C.

Formosa (Taiwan).

"Formosa" is the name given by Portuguese explorers to the island which the Chinese and the Japanese call "Taiwan." That island is the largest of some 72 islands which, lying roughly 100 miles east of the Asian mainland, constitute the main part of the Chinese province which bears its name. That province—embracing Formosa and the nearby Pescadores—has a total area of some 14,500 square miles; has a population of more than 10,000,000 of whom all but about one percent are of Chinese racial origin; and is administered by the National Government of the Republic of China.

Historically, those islands were colonized during a period of many centuries preceding 1895 by Chinese from the mainland. Formosa was at one time occupied variously and briefly by Spanish and by Netherlands forces; it became the refuge and the base from which the last organized Chinese resistance to the Manchus was conducted; it was constituted in 1885 by the Manchu Government a province of the Chinese Empire; it was ceded in 1895 by the Manchus to Japan; it was thereafter for 50 years developed economically and militarily by the Japanese as a dependent part of their Empire; and it was effectively exploited by Japan's armed forces as a base and a staging point in their operations in and after 1937 against China and in and after 1941 throughout the Far East.

In 1943, at Cairo, President Roosevelt, Prime Minister Churchill and Generalissimo Chiang Kai-shek declared it "their purpose" that, at the conclusion of the war which was then being fought, Formosa and the Pescadores "shall be restored to the Republic of China." Later, at Potsdam, Marshal Stalin subscribed to that. In 1945, armed forces of the Republic of China occupied those islands. In September of that year, Japan gave up its title to them in favor of the Allies, and they were assigned for administrative purposes by the Commander-in-Chief of the Allied Forces to the Republic of China. Since then, the allies have not taken action toward making legally effective the purpose expressed in the Cairo Declaration, but those islands have been generally regarded as having reverted to China, and the fact that throughout the years since 1945 they have been controlled continuously by a Chinese government (the National Government) renders it unlikely that any of the Allies would seriously dispute the claim of the Chinese—Nationalists and Communists alike—that they belong to China.

The Communist conquerors of mainland China have constantly declared it their intention to take Formosa and, toward that end, have repeatedly attacked one or more of the closely off-shore islands which also are administered by the National Government and are in the eyes of the Nationalists Formosa's first line of defense. In 1950 it became a purpose of the United States to prevent conquest of Formosa by the Communists; in 1955 the United States concluded with the Republic of China a Mutual Defense Treaty; when, in 1958, the Communists bombarded Quemoy, the United States assisted the Nationalist defenders; and today, although there are differences of opinion about the off-shore islands, there is in the United States practically universal commitment to the idea that an attempt by the Communists to take Formosa would call for, warrant and make imperative an intervention by this country in support of the defenders.

By virtue of its strategic location, of the character of its population, of the fact that it is the base on which and from which China's National Government now functions, of the character of the institutions and the development in general which that government, with American assistance, has since 1949 given it, and of the fact that its orientation in world affairs is definitely and conspicuously toward and on the side of the free world—"Formosa" has become and is far more than a "little island and a handful of people in the far away western Pacific." In terms of human rights and aspirations, and in the setting of today's global conflict, Formosa looms large.

St.K.H.

Formosa (Taiwan)—Land Reform.

A "land-to-the-tiller" program carried out by the Chinese Nationalist regime following its retreat to Formosa from the Chinese mainland in 1949. The reform was accomplished in three phases: rent reduction, sale of public lands, and sale of excess acreage of large estates for which bonds and stock certificates were given to the owners. Completed in six years the reform was regarded even by some of its most severe critics as a model approach to a pressing problem in areas where outmoded land tenure systems prevent economic and social advance.

R.L.W.

Fortune Magazine (Roper).

A periodical, largely devoted to discussions and reports on significant national and international issues, which regularly reports on the attitudes of the public to important social, economic and political questions. It employs the scientific sampling methods of the Roper Poll, an organization directed by Elmo Roper. M.B.D.

Fourier, Francois Charles Marie.

Born in 1772 in Besancon, France. Died in 1837 in Lyons, France. Known for the development of a socialist system (Fourierism) which aimed at a life of utmost material and spiritual enjoyment for all members of society. Conceived the "Phalanx" as a unit of regulating hours of work, production, and distribution. J.D.

Fourteen Points.

Contained in President Wilson's address to the Congress January 8, 1918 and occasioned by the publication of the secret treaties by the Bolsheviks, the hope that Russia might be kept from a separate peace with Germany and Wilson's belief in a peace with justice: 1) open covenants of peace, openly arrived at, no private international understandings 2) freedom of the seas 3) removal of all economic barriers 4) adequate guarantees given and taken that national armaments be reduced to the lowest point consistent with domestic safety 5) impartial adjustment of all colonial claims 6) evacuation of all Russian territory and Russia to determine independently her own national policy 7) Evacuation and restoration of Belgium 8) All French territory freed, invaded portions restored and Alsace-Lorraine returned to France 9) Readjustment of Italy's frontiers along clearly recognizable lines of nationality 10) Freest opportunity for the autonomous development of the peoples of Austria-Hungary 11) Evacuation of Serbia, Rumania and Montenegro; free and secure access to the sea for Serbia; international guarantees of the political and economic independence of the Balkans 12) Non-Turkish nationalities to be assured security of life and autonomous development; free passage through the Dardanelles 13) establishment of an independent Poland including territories inhabited by indisputably Polish populations, with free and secure access to the sea 14) a general association of nations affording mutual guarantees of political independence and territorial integrity to great and small states alike.

Not until October 4, 1918, when it faced total military defeat, did the German government propose peace negotiations on these points as amplified in Wilson's subsequent speeches. Using the threat of a separate peace, the American government compelled the Allies to agree to make peace on these terms subject to two qualifications—the Allies reserved complete discretion regarding freedom of the seas (Point 2) and the understanding that compensation would be made by Germany for all damage done to the civilian population of the Allies and their property by the aggression of Germany by land, by sea and from the air. The Allies did not communicate to the German government the American commentary on the fourteen points, which did not exclude confidential negotiation, opposed restoration of German colonies and proposed autonomy for the German population in Northern Italy. The minutes of the secret sessions of the Council of Four reveal the struggle to adapt the points to the complexities of the post-war European situation.   C.B.J.

Fourth Estate.
A description of the press which came from a passage in Thomas Carlyle's **Hero and Hero-Worship,** as follows: "Burke said there were Three Estates in Parliament; but, in the Reporter's gallery yonder, there sat a fourth estate more important far than they all." Carlyle himself, in **The French Revolution,** wrote: "A Fourth Estate, of Able Editors, springs up."   I.Di.

"Fourth Force" of France.
See France—"Fourth Force."

Fourth Republic of France.
See France—Fourth Republic.

France—Arrondissement.
A district of local government in France, which has no power in policy making and little responsibility in local administration of central governmental policy. The arrondissement is a subdivision of the principal unit of local government in France, the departement. Each of France's 281 arrondissements has an elective council as well as a "sub-prefect" appointed from Paris as head administrator.   E.R.W.

France—Canton.
The district of local government in France from which representatives to large governmental units—the arrondissement and departement—are elected. The more-than-3,000 cantons in France serve primarily as administrative units for such services as tax collection, military recruitment and road inspection.   E.R.W.

France—Chamber of Deputies.
The popularly-elected half of the French legislature in the Third Republic, so powerful that it made and unmade governments almost at will. In the Fourth Republic, the chamber was renamed the National Assembly, a title continued in the Fifth Republic, in which its powers were sharply curtailed. In the Fifth Republic, deputies were elected by a single member district system. The 1958 constitution limits sessions of the National Assembly to 5½ months for limited extraordinary sessions; the government, not the legislature, fixes the major parts of the agenda of the legislature; legislative committees are reduced to 6 in number; standing orders must be approved by the constitutional court; the competence of the assembly to pass laws is limited. If it does not approve of the budget in 70 days, the government may promulgate it. The second house, the Senate, can block legislation unless the government proposes that the National Assembly vote definitively. The government must resign if a majority of the assembly members supports a motion of censure, but if the motion fails, the signers who drafted the motion may not propose another during the same session, but for the major exception that if the government stakes its life on all or part of a bill, a motion of censure is again in order.   E.G.L.

France—Commune.
Unit of local municipal government in France. Communes range in size from villages of less than fifty population to large cities such as Marseilles and Lyons. Most of the more than 38,000 communes have essentially the same governmental structure, based on the "Law on Municipal Organization" of 1884. Each has an elected council, a mayor and "adjoints" (administrative assistants). Duties of communal officials include maintaining public safety and order; administering local licensing and inspection rules and regulations, and fulfilling general "housekeeping" functions for the municipality. Elective officials in the commune are responsible to the Prefect, centrally appointed administrative head of the departement in which the commune is located. The Prefect has the power, on behalf of the central government, to dissolve communal councils or set aside ordinances of mayors.   E.R.W.

France—Conseil d'Etat.

The highest administrative court in France. This and lower administrative courts, as part of the national administration of government, are distinct from the ordinary judicial system. The Conseil d'Etat has final jurisdiction over various cases involving misuse of administrative power. The Conseil d'Etat also can investigate the bureaucracy and may call attention to need for administrative reform. In addition, it must be consulted concerning various types of legislation, including that initiated by the Government for parliamentary approval. The Minister of Justice serves as President of the Conseil d'Etat, and there are 161 subordinate members of varying levels of responsibility. E.R.W.

France—Council of the Republic.

The upper house of parliament in the Fourth Republic of France (1946-1958). Its 320 members were selected on the basis of indirect suffrage through communal and departmental bodies. The Council of the Republic had the power only to delay bills and make recommendations to the lower house, the National Assembly. All bills initiated by the National Assembly were considered by the Council. If objections were raised by the Council, the National Assembly could over-ride the objections by a roll-call, absolute-majority vote, provided the decision of the Council was achieved in the same manner. (Article 20 of Constitution of Fourth Republic.) Members of the Council of the Republic were called Senators. E.R.W.

France—Departement.

The departement is the largest geographically determined subdivision of governmental administration in France. Of the present ninety-seven, eighty-three were created in 1790 by the Constituent Assembly. Established to obliterate provincial loyalties, the departements in France bear no resemblance to previous provincial boundaries. The administrative head of each departement is the Prefect, selected by and responsible to the Ministry of the Interior in Paris. Each departement has an elective council to assist the Prefect in adapting national policies to the needs of particular localities. E.R.W.

France—Estates-General.

Assembly of the French nation, composed of representatives from the three estates or orders: Clergy, Nobility, Third Estate. The Estates-General were first summoned in 1302 by Philip IV who desired popular support for his struggle with Pope Boniface VIII. Unlike the English parliament, the Estates-General were deeply divided along social lines, the first two estates agreeing more with each other than with the Third Estate. After 1614 the Estates-General did not meet again until the resistance of the **parlements** to the fiscal reforms of Louis XVI necessitated their convocation. The Estates-General met on 5 May 1789, and immediately the Third Estate, intent on discussing not only fiscal but constitutional reforms as well, demanded voting by head instead of order. On 17 June 1789 the Third Estate proclaimed itself the National Assembly. The French Revolution had begun. K.B.

France—Fifth Republic (1958—   ).

Emerging from the May 13, 1958 insurrection (q.v.) in Algeria, it embodied General de Gaulle's ideas of a government based on universal suffrage, separation of powers, and responsibility of the government to parliament. The constitution of 1958 was written under de Gaulle's direct guidance by Michel Debre, young legal technician, and with the help of heads of the classical political parties: the Socialists, MRP, Radicals, and Independents. The constitution, approved by 79.25% of the voters on September 28, 1958, vests preponderant power in the President of the Republic. Originally the President was to stand apart from day-to-day political disputes, stepping in only to assure the continuity of the French nation. Increasingly de Gaulle intervened in daily affairs. The first National Assembly, elected in November 1958, represented continuing support for the various political tendencies of the Fourth Republic. In April, 1961, during an abortive revolt of Generals Salan, Challe, and others against the government's Algerian policy, de Gaulle invoked sweeping emergency powers under the constitution. In a referendum in October, 1962, de Gaulle's proposal making the office of President of the Republic directly, popularly elected was supported by 62¼% of the voters, with massive abstentions of 23%.   E.G.L.

France—First Empire (1804—1814).
Napoleon Bonaparte, climbing to power through leadership of the army during the last years of the directorate and first years of the consulate, declared himself Emperor on May 18, 1804 though his government was not called an empire until 1809. The personal dictatorship of Napoleon was lightly camouflaged by the elaborate constitution of the Year XII, the most important institution of which, apart from the emperor, was a Senate whose members were ultimately selected by the emperor. Less consequential were the Legislative Body, Tribunate, and Council of State, having powers similar to those of the constitution of the Year VIII. (See France—First Republic.) The Napoleonic consulate and empire left its governmental mark on France in the Napoleonic code, still the foundation of the legal system; the Council of State, a technical law and decree drafting institution and final administrative court; and local government system in which the prefect, centrally appointed and controlled, was the powerful supervisor of the department, the major local subdivision.
E.G.L.

France—First Republic (1792—1804).
Followed the fall of the constitutional monarchy. The constitution of 1793, approved by popular referendum, created an all-powerful, indirectly elected, unicameral legislative assembly and a subservient executive council. In April, 1793, the first of a series of Committees of Public Safety took power, soon using the Terror as its weapon. The conservative constitution of the Year III (1795), also popularly approved, created an indirectly elected, bicameral legislature and a five man executive directorate, which yielded power to the Consulate of September 11, 1799, under the elaborate constitution of the Year VIII, mainly written by Abbe Sieyes. Under it, a council of state prepared the bills, a tribunate discussed them, and a legislative assembly voted on them, all under the watchful eye of the three consuls, the most powerful of whom was the First Consul, Napoleon Bonaparte. A conservative Senate packed with Bonapartists, whose members served for life, made the ultimate choice of legislators, and guarded the constitution.
E.G.L.

France—"Fourth Force."
Term applied to conservative democratic parties in the Fourth Republic, notably the Independents and conservative wing of the Radical Socialists. It was proposed as a counter to the socialist "third force" and also to the extremes of the Communists and Gaullists. Conflicts over the religious issue, and particularly state aid to church schools, marred the unity of both third and fourth "forces."   J.S.S.

France—Fourth Republic (1945—1958).
On October 21, 1945, French voters decisively rejected a return to the Third Republic and elected a constituent assembly to build a Fourth Republic. The first draft constitution provided for a powerful unicameral legislature and a weak president, and was rejected by a narrow margin of popular votes on May 5, 1946. A second constituent assembly elected on June 2, 1946, wrote a constitution providing for a bi-cameral legislature consisting of a powerful, popularly elected National Assembly and a weak, indirectly elected Council of the Republic, and a ceremonial President of the Republic having powers substantially like those of his predecessor in the Third Republic, and a President of the Council responsible to the National Assembly. The voters approved this constitution on October 13, 1946, but many abstained from voting, as General de Gaulle advised. After completing the urgent tasks of reconstructing war-torn France, the government became more and more like the Third Republic; on December 7, 1954, a series of amendments strengthened the Council of the Republic and allowed the premier to be invested by plurality vote. Cabinets throughout were of brief duration because of a relatively

even balance among the same six party tendencies consistently returned by the French voters. The Fourth Republic collapsed from inability to solve the political problems raised by the Algerian war. E.G.L.

France—Leading Newspapers.
Le Monde, nonpartisan; **l'Aurore,** Radical Right; **le Figaro,** middle of the road; **la Nation,** Gaullist; **le Populaire,** Socialist; **Liberation,** "progressive"; **Combat,** Independent, left of center; **Paris Jour,** middle of the road, left of center; **l'Humanité,** Communist; **France-Soir,** moderate, anti-Communist; **La Croix,** Catholic, conservative. K.B.

France, May 13 insurrection.
It laid the foundation for de Gaulle's Fifth Republic. At 3 p.m., May 13, 1958, the National Assembly in Paris discussed investing Pierre Pflimlin (MRP) as premier; at 5 p.m., in Algiers demonstrators led by army and civilian leaders supported keeping Algeria French, opposing Pflimlin. While parachutist guards looked on, the demonstrators took over the government headquarters in Algiers. F. Gaillard, interim premier in Paris, ordered General Raoul Salan to take civil powers in Algiers and appointed General Massu his deputy. Massu, Salan, and others, meanwhile, formed a Committee of Public Safety dedicated to keeping Algeria French and demanding the creation of a similar committee in Paris. At 1:15 a.m., May 14, M. Pflimlin, invested as premier, declared he could not abandon Algeria. In Paris former ministers Georges Bidault, Andre Morice, and Jacques Soustelle, urged the creation of a Committee of Public Safety. Soustelle escaped from police guard and fled to Algiers. Committees of Public Safety sprang up in many Algerian cities. General Salan concluded an oration in Algiers on May 14, with "Vive de Gaulle!" More and more de Gaulle's name was brought into the news. On May 15, de Gaulle said he was ready to assume the powers of the Republic; on May 18 he disclaimed desiring a dictatorship, and retired to his country home, at the "disposition of the country." More and more political figures supported de Gaulle. On May 27 he said he had set in motion procedure for forming a government. On May 28 M. Pflimlin submitted his resignation; on May 29 the President of the Republic, Coty, called de Gaulle to the premiership; de Gaulle took over on condition that he be empowered to reform institutions in the direction of separation of powers and vesting great authority in the President of the Republic. On June 1 the National Assembly voted 329 to 224 to give him the powers he desired.
E.G.L.

France—Prefect.
Administrative head of the departement, principal unit of local government in France. The Prefect is appointed by governmental decree and is responsible to the Minister of the Interior in Paris. He serves both as local agent of the central government and as the chief executive of the departement. The Prefect's duties include supervision of public services on the local level, such as education; health; social insurance; census taking; and appointment of various civil service officials including school teachers, postmasters and tax collectors.
E.R.W.

France—Premier.
Head of Government in France. Officially the "president of the Council of Ministers," the Premier has less executive power under the Constitution of the current Fifth Republic than under those of the Third Republic (1870—1940) and Fourth Republic (1946—1958). In the Third and Fourth Republics, the Premier was nominated by the President and subject to approval by the lower house of the French parliament (Chamber of Deputies in the Third Republic; National Assembly in the Fourth Republic). The Premier was instrumental in formulating and presenting a legislative program to the Parliament. The lower house could remove the Premier and his cabinet from office by a vote of non-confidence or censure. In the Fifth Republic the Premier is appointed by the President of the Republic without parliamentary approval. Consequently, the executive role of the Premier in the Fifth Republic thus far has been secondary to that of the President. The French Constitution of

1958 refers to the President as the "supreme arbiter of the state," and to the Government, headed by the Premier, as determining and directing "the policy of the nation." (Articles 20 and 21.) The Premier proposes the members of his cabinet for approval by the President. However, once appointed, the Premier and Cabinet Ministers are responsible to the Parliament and can be overthrown by a vote of non-confidence or censure in the National Assembly (Article 49).
E.R.W.

France—Second Empire (1852—1870).
Inaugurated by decree of the Senate restoring the Empire, was headed by Louis-Napoleon Bonaparte as Napoleon III. At first the regime was a thinly disguised dictatorship, based on Senatorial amendments of the authoritarian constitution of 1852. Universal suffrage was neutralized by "official candidates" supported by government pressure plus skillfully gerrymandered districts. Laws originated with ministers appointed by and responsible to the emperor, then were channeled through the Council of State to be approved by the Legislative Body. The Senate, all but appointed by the Emperor, like its predecessor in the First Empire, was the guardian of constitutionality. The early years were prosperous. In 1860 after inconclusive foreign wars, Napoleon III liberalized his government, first allowing some parliamentary discussion in the hope that popular forces would support him against growing upper class criticism. In 1869 the emperor set up a parliamentary regime. The empire crumbled following Napoleon III's defeat, and his capture, at the end of the short Franco-Prussian War. E.G.L.

France—Second Republic (1848—1852).
Born in revolution at the abdication of Louis-Philippe. A constituent assembly directly elected by universal manhood suffrage drafted the constitution proclaimed on November 4, 1848. In a government based on the separation of powers, a 750 member unicameral assembly elected by direct, universal manhood suffrage shared power with a popularly-elected President of the Republic, who was to serve for four years without immediate re-eligibility. The constitution did not make clear whether the President was responsible to the assembly. The first president, elected Dec. 10, 1848, Louis Napoleon, continuously argued with the anti-republican and anti-bonapartist assembly elected in 1849. On December 2, 1851, Louis Napoleon proclaimed a plebiscite to maintain himself in power, and dissolved the assembly, taking the first steps toward the Second Empire (q.v.). E.G.L.

France—"Third Force."
Term applied to a coalition of social reform parties standing between the extremes of left and right. The idea gained currency in French politics after the Gaullist victories in the local elections of 1947 and implied government primarily by the Socialists (SFIO) and the Catholic MRP, each rejecting cooperation with the Communists and the parties of the right. The two parties did not command a majority together and the problems created by the need to attract additional support quickly drove apart the two key elements of the "force."
J.S.S.

France—Third Republic.
French governmental system from 1870—1940. Characterized by parliamentary supremacy. Major institutions were a bicameral parliament—the National Assembly, composed of the Chamber of Deputies (lower house) and Senate (upper house); premiership and cabinet of ministers; and presidency. The president, as chief of state, had as his major power the nomination of the premier, the official head of Government. The premier was selected from, approved by and responsible to the Chamber of Deputies. Bills, to become law, had to pass both houses of the National Assembly. Political instability and a multi-party system were characteristic of the Third Republic: the average life of a Government in the period 1870—1914 was ten months; 1914—1932, eight months; and 1932—1940, four months. In this unstable political situation, governmental continuity was provided by the non-political staffs of the various ministries of government. Until World War I, the Third Republic pursued a

"laissez-faire" economic policy, to the neglect of industrial development, social and economic reform and planning, and colonial expansion. In the post-World War I years, there emerged increasingly extremist political groupings on the left and right. The largest parties of the 1930's were the Radical Socialists, Communists, and Socialists. During this period, dissension within and among the major parties, as well as increasing activity and appeal of right-wing fascist groups, prevented any governmental effectiveness in attempting to cope with internal depression and the threat of external aggression. With Germany's invasion of France in June 1940, the Third Republic collapsed. It was succeeded by the authoritarian Vichy regime on July 10, 1940.

E.R.W.

Franco, Francisco. See Appendix.

Franco-Soviet Pact.

A treaty between France and the U.S.S.R., signed on May 2, 1935, whose object was joint action in case of an attack or threat of attack on either state, and which was to remain in force for at least five years. The Pact had no practical effect; it was violated by the Soviet-German pact of August 1939, and superseded by the Franco-Soviet treaty in 1944 which allied them in the war against Germany.

The Pact confirmed the French collective security policy which found its first expression in the admission of Soviet Russia to the League of Nations, a move sponsored by France. The treaty sought to strengthen the effectiveness of the League Covenant (in particular art. 10, art. 15 sec. 7, art. 16, and art. 17 of the Covenant), and expressed French desires to involve the East European countries in a mutual security system. The **rapprochement** characterized the period of inter-war diplomacy in which security was sought through a series of bilateral alliances. Co-operation with the Soviet Union was feared by many in Western Europe; these concerns led in time to widespread fears of Soviet aggression. The treaty indirectly stimulated the gradual and controlled spreading of the Popular Front.

W.J.S.

Frankfurter, Felix (1882—   ).

Prior to his appointment as Associate Justice of the United States Supreme Court in 1939 to succeed Justice Cardozo in the "Holmes Seat," Frankfurter taught administrative law at Harvard Law School; practiced private and public law; held numerous governmental positions; fought tenaciously for several controversial causes (e.g. Sacco and Vanzetti). Adviser, friend, and outspoken admirer of President Franklin D. Roosevelt and the New Deal, he is often credited with being the gray eminence behind many of the latter's policies and personalities. On the Court he proved himself an avowed and articulate champion of overall judicial self-restraint and a philosophy of "humilitanism" vis-a-vis the co-ordinate branches of government, especially Congress, not excluding the field of civil liberties, which caused a basic and much-publicized, continuous feud with the "libertarian activist" wing of the Court, led by Justice Black.

H.J.A.

Franking Privilege.

The franking privilege is the right of members of the U.S. Congress and of the executive branch of the federal government to use the United States postal service for the official conduct of business without payment of any postal charges. Members of Congress are sometimes criticized for using the franking privilege to mail large amounts of personal political campaign material. The privilege is occasionally extended by law to other persons such as members of the armed forces in war time and widows of former Presidents.

J.R.B.

Free Democratic Party.

The only third party in the Bundestag since 1957 election. Coalition partner with CDU 1949-56 and after 1961 election. Claiming descent from traditional German liberalism, it stands in opposition to the Catholic elements of the CDU and all collectivist policies, appealing to the free professions and big business for support.

C.J.S.

Freedom of Association.

A principle of democratic government guaranteeing to citizens the right to form political, economic, social, and other organizations without government interference or supervision, to promote the interest of their members in public or private affairs. The only legitimate limitations on the principle are those inherent in the right of the government to control lawlessness by overt acts against the public peace, although often extended in the U.S.A. and elsewhere by proscribing organizations for activities held dangerous to "national security." R.B.

Freedom of expression.
See Freedom of speech.

Freedom of information.
Originally in the U.S., starting in 1942, the concept that the public has the right to know everything that may affect the public interest, and that therefore the press has the right of access to information (especially to governmental sources) so it can report to the people. (Military security and personal privacy have been recognized as exceptions.) As against this concept of information as a free force in democratic decision-making, in many countries the concept has been almost reversed, buttressed by debate on the Freedom of Information Convention in the U.N., to make information a tool of government: (1) to provide safeguards (through controls) for a given government that no outside reporters will "harm" it or violate the "truth," and (2) to stress internally the "constructive" value of the government informing its people about what officials believe important to stability and development while suppressing criticism as a potential jeopardy to the country's gains. J.B.L.

Freedom of Religion.
The concept that any man may believe in the religious precepts of his choice or not believe at all. The government is not permitted any inquiry into a man's religious beliefs, nor may it force any individual to accept or reject any religious faith. They cannot force or influence a person to go or to remain away from church against his will or force him to confess a belief or disbelief in any religion. No government, federal, state or local, may assist in establishing religious groups, nor may it interfere with their activities. M.J.S.

Freedom of speech.
Conceptually the right to express one's personal opinion on matters of public concern, as a necessary part of the democratic process. Freedom of the press (q.v.) and institutional right to the freedom are but extensions or special cases of personal free speech. Libel and slander laws, and other limitations, have grown around the concept, and "freedom of expression" (first stated by Franklin D. Roosevelt in his Four Freedoms) has confused the issue. In 1948, Alexander Meiklejohn suggested a dichotomy in the U.S. Constitution which is increasingly supported. Free speech under the First Amendment is an absolute right because it deals with public policy; thus a public figure cannot claim libel in criticism of his public actions. However, personal "self-expression" is non-political, and insofar as it harms another person, it is actionable under the Fifth Amendment, since defamation of character deprives a person of property rights without due process of law. J.B.L.

Freedom of the press.
The U.S. Constitutional concept, built on English tradition, that as a safeguard against tyranny the press cannot be prevented from printing news and opinions, even if critical of the government. By extension, "press" and "printing" now include other broadcast media such as radio and TV. Restraints have lessened this negative guarantee, and it nowhere exists today in pure form. In the U.S., the general limit is now "clear and present danger" to the ordered society. Opinion is growing, aided by concept of freedom of information (q.v.), that freedom of the press really means the right of all individuals to be heard, and for the public to have the whole truth and nothing but the truth, even if government control is required to assure this. Extreme of this latter view is the Soviet concept of freedom of the press, that only when the state itself owns and operates all media of communication is the press free (on the ground that all persons thereby have

"access" to the press because the state is equated with the people); in this view, individual use of the press can only be against the people. See Freedom of speech. — J.B.L.

Free Enterprise System.

The capitalist system, characterized by: (1) private ownership and management of the means of production, capital and property; (2) investment of capital for profit; (3) freedom of the individual to engage in particular fields of economic endeavor; (4) liberty to contract with others; (5) freedom to produce goods regardless whether they are needed or whether too much of them already exist; (6) freedom to engage in or refrain from engaging in any occupation no matter how pressing the need for such engagement is; (7) freedom to buy from whoever is willing to sell, or to sell to who is willing to buy, or to refuse to do so; and (8) alternating periods of economic prosperity and depression. Under this system, self-interest is the prime motivating force; and free competition, not government, is supposed to regulate the many self-interests of individuals comprising society and to move them in such directions as to benefit mankind. Equilibrium would be achieved automatically and naturally if government would let economic enterprising and job engagement alone (laissez-faire), pose no hindrance to trade (laissez-passer), and let things take their own course (laissez-aller). Government should intervene only to protect society against violence and invasion by foreign states; to protect the individual against injustice or oppression by others; and to provide certain public conveniences, such as highways and post-offices.

In this system, production and consumption are controlled by price and the ability to pay. Neither need nor ability to use goods necessarily determines the type and amount of production or how goods are consumed. Prices of different commodities and ability of different persons to pay such prices, however, determine where goods will go and the share of each person in the output of enterprise. In addition, the ability to derive satisfaction from goods may not correspond to the capacity to pay for them; and jobs do not necessarily go to people who can best perform them.

To change this system, the proponents of free enterprise argue, would interfere with individual liberty and natural law. The individual has the greatest incentive to improve his efficiency and economic lot when he is free to compete for any job or engage in any economic endeavor which he desires and to spend his income as he sees fit. To reduce this incentive would cause production and income to decline. Extremists among the proponents are opposed to all government intervention except for the prevention of invasion, violence and overthrowal of the system. They insist that free competition would eliminate such fraudulent practices as adulterated goods and would restrain human selfishness and greed for profit. Competition is viewed as the regulative force which controls economic activities and provides the motivation in each person to observe the interests of others; for, the individual is free to go elsewhere if he is displeased.

Critics of these views of free enterprise maintain that such concepts are long obsolete and that in modern society competition cannot be relied on as the regulator. It won't eliminate the evils, especially when there is a great disparity in bargaining between buyers and sellers, or in such situations as pollution of air and streams, tubercular cattle, child labor, labor-management disputes affecting public safety, health and welfare. They assert that the free enterprise system does not of itself invariably achieve equilibrium at full employment, and consequently government must enter to provide the necessary balance through fiscal and monetary action. Competition, on the other hand, generates evils of its own, so much so that it has to be restricted by law. For example, the freedom to engage in particular fields of economic endeavor may be restricted by government for such diverse purposes as promoting public health, control of traffic, ensuring solvency of financial enterprises, prevention of fraud, improvement of public utility services, and achieving clarity of radio and television reception. As a result, such regulatory practices by government as licensing and franchising, which serve in both promotional and restrictive capacities, are generally accepted as necessary and desirable. Paradoxically, many of the proponents and critics of competition switch sides on the issue of monopoly. The former, who traditionally urge free competition and laissez-faire, support monopoly and governmental protection to prevent competition, while the latter, who urge restrictions on free competition, support greater competition in order to combat monopoly.

In our era, big business has been joined by big labor; and, in response to the demands of business, labor and the general public, there has emerged big government. Government has expanded its role today to include even the function of mediating in labor-management disputes to prevent or settle strikes and lockouts, to control picketing, boycotts, trade pressures, and union leadership and finances.
O.K.

Freemasonry.
A pattern of practices and beliefs held by Freemasons or Masons expressing a moral code through the symbols and allegories of the art of building. The secrets of Freemasonry are not divulged to nonmembers, but the fact of membership is not concealed. Within the United States, these secrets are not considered injurious to the religious or political systems.
W.D.S.

Free World.
Designation of the non-Communist countries of the world, which came into use after the second world war, especially in the U.S. and to a lesser extent in Europe. Proposals, made at various times, and aiming at setting up an institutional framework for these countries have not been implemented, largely because of the opposition of the non-aligned countries. F.M.

French and Indian War.
What began as colonial action against French settlement of the upper Ohio valley in 1754, two years later broadened into the Seven Years' War with military conflict on four continents. The defeat of France and her allies resulted in the Treaty of Paris (1763) which substantially expanded the British Empire in North America by French cession of virtually all of Canada as well as all territory east of the Mississippi River; by Spanish cession of Florida, Spain was given Cuba by Great Britain, New Orleans and the area west of the Mississippi by France. Other territorial settlements were also made. J.M.S.

French civil service.
Permanent employees in the central, interior, or exterior services of the state, governed according to a general ordinance of February 4, 1959. Higher civil servants are recruited after rigorous examinations and most are trained in the National School of Administration. The titular head is a secretary of state for public service, attached to the office of the first minister. A Superior Council of the Public Service (**Conseil superieur de la fonction publique**) consisting of representatives of government and the civil service labor unions advises on civil service affairs.
E.G.L.

French Communist party.
Organized in 1920 by those Socialists who adhered to the Third International, the Communists first treated the Socialists as enemies, but by 1936 closed neither the legal nor the revolutionary avenue to power and supported the Popular Front. Thereafter until 1958 the party lost half its adherents but only one tenth of its voters. After a strong role in the Resistance, the Communists (the choice of one fourth of the electorate) sought fusion with the Socialists in 1945, and participated in "tripartism" until expelled from the Government in 1947. On Stalin's death in 1953 they supported the election of a Socialist president of the Assembly, voted for Mendes-France in 1954, and voted confidence in Faure in 1955. Having opposed any European integration, the Communists' attitude on Hungary isolated them again, friction with Russia also developing from their continued support of "Stalinism."

A party of the masses, the Communists base their structure on cells including those in the same enterprise rather than the same locality. Party leader Thorez, in Russia during the war, returned there from 1950 to 1953, with Duclos assuming the leadership in the interim. The small inner circle of leaders has remained the same since the 1930's. **R.B.C.**

French Community (1958—).
The organization of France and her overseas dependencies, established by the constitution of the Fifth Republic and subsequent legislation as the successor to the French Union.

The Community originally consisted of metropolitan France, the Overseas Departments, the Overseas Territories, and the member states. The Overseas Departments are governed in the same basic way as the departments of the metropole. Each Overseas Territory has its own legislature and enjoys representation in the French parliament in Paris. The Community established its own common organs, which originally were given jurisdiction over foreign policy, defense, and certain economic matters.

Only Guinea of France's overseas dependencies refused in 1958 to join the French Community. The remainder of the dependencies of former French West Africa, French Equatorial Africa, and Madagascar opted to become member states in the community. Since then, however, all of these former member states have become completely independent and have been admitted to the United Nations. Only six of them (Senegal, the Malagasy Republic, Gabon, the Congo-Brazzaville, the Central African Republic, and Chad) remain affiliated with the community; and their relationship to it is regulated by special agreement, not by the constitution of the Fifth Republic.
F.H.G.

French Consulate Period (1799—1804).
The Constitution of the Year VIII (1799) which Sieyes had hoped would invigorate the republic but instead established the military dictatorship of its co-founder, Napoleon Bonaparte. As First Consul (elected for ten years) Bonaparte towered above his two colleagues, the Council of State, the Senate, Tribunate, and Legislative Chamber. Where the Directory had limited the executive power, the Consulate restrained all but the head of the government. Obtaining popular approval by plebiscite (1800), Bonaparte became First Consul for life (1802) and assumed regal splendor and authority. On 18 May 1804 the "restorer of the republic" became Napoleon I, Emperor of the French. **K.B.**

French Court System.
A centralized hierarchy of courts whose format was laid down in the Napoleonic codes. Consists of two systems, one for civil and criminal cases, and one dealing with administrative law. At the base of the civil-criminal system is the justice of peace in the canton; then the **arrondissement** courts, with sections for civil and criminal cases; then regional courts; and at the highest level the Court of Cassation in Paris which deals only with interpretation of law and not the facts of a case. The administrative courts consist of two levels, regional tribunals and the Council of State in Paris. The Fourth Republic sought to give greater independence to the judiciary by vesting administration of the courts in a High Council of the Judiciary, a body whose powers have been curtailed in the Fifth Republic.
J.S.S.

French Directory (1795—1799).
Established by the Constitution of 1795, this last government of the French Revolution operated under constitutional and political impossibilities. The executive power, vested in five directors, was completely separated from the legislative branch (Council of Ancients, and Council of Five Hundred). Forced to meet the resurgence of Royalists and Jacobins by two unconstitutional **coups** (1797; 1798), Sieyes, one of the directors, Talleyrand and others sought support for the republic from a powerful general: Napoleon Bonaparte. On 18 Brumaire (9 November 1799) their **coup d'etat** toppled the Directory which was replaced by the Consulate. **K.B.**

French electoral law.
French Constitutions have authorized "organic law" to determine the electoral system. Proportional representation with the "list" system, authorized in 1946, benefited the extreme parties, and in 1951, to overcome this, a very complicated law provided for a return to the single ballot but allowed for party alliances.

An absolute majority would give a group all seats in the voting district, to be split proportionately; if none, proportional representation would obtain (this being the **only** system in urban Seine and Seine-et-Oise departments), except that the "highest remainder" system replaced the "highest average."

Because of the complexity of the 1951 law, the Parliament of the Fifth Republic returned to the Third Republic's single-member district with two ballots if the first gave no one a majority. (Now no one gaining less than 5% of the vote on the first ballot could run a second time.) While redistricting was necessary, the Parliament of the Fifth retained the pattern of elections every five years.

The Council of the Republic of the Fourth Republic was chosen indirectly by about 100,000 electors, representing deputies and mostly local councillors, who voted for half the 320 members every three years. The Senate of the Fifth is similarly chosen. R.B.C.

French National Assembly
(Assemblee Nationale).

Name taken by French Estates General in June 1789, but later changed to constituent assembly; also the name of the assembly elected in 1871 during the Franco-German war and which laid the groundwork for the Third Republic; in the Fourth and Fifth Republics it is the popularly elected lower house of the French parliament. The Assembly is housed in the Palais Bourbon in Paris. Its powers over the cabinet, which were great under the Fourth Republic, have been severely curtailed during the Fifth. J.S.S.

French Nationalized Industries.

Ownership by the state of some industries goes back in France to the monarchy, as in the case of the Gobelin tapestries. The tobacco monopoly dates from the First Empire. Systematic nationalization of particular industries however, began with the Popular Front governments after 1936. Their most conspicuous effort was the nationalization of the railroads and also part of the armament industry. After the liberation there was strong sentiment for state ownership of key industries and coal, banking, electricity and gas, and insurance companies were taken over by the state. The objective was primarily to eliminate private monopolies in these fields, and therefore small companies were not taken over. Some companies were nationalized, notably the Renault automobile factories, as punishment for wartime collaboration with the enemy. No single system of control has been devised, some industries being run as public agencies under direct public control, others as mixed corporations with the government holding a majority of the stock, and others as syndicates. That government ownership did not provide an easy substitute for economic planning became quickly evident and plans were devised in 1946 (Monnet Plan) covering both public and private industry. J.S.S.

French parliament.

For the first time the Constitution of the Fourth Republic referred to the legislature, to be comprised of the National Assembly and the Council of the Republic, as Parliament. Organic statutes were to determine the exact structure, eligibilities and incompatibilities, and duration of powers. Accordingly the National Assembly, essentially the final authority in France of the Fourth Republic, provided for a body of 627 members (544 from "metropolitan" France) and specified for them a minimum age of 23 and a five-year term. It required them to be voters (allowing now for women), and forbade them to serve coincidentally in the Council of the Republic or the National Civil Service (exempting governmental Ministers and Secretaries, as well as teachers). The 320 members of the Council of the Republic, one half chosen indirectly every three years by thousands of electors, had fragmentary powers such as referral of bills to the National Assembly.

While the Constitution of the Fifth preserves the pattern of direct election, the new National Assembly, with 481 members (as of 1962), elected for five years, has lost crucial powers to the President. The new Senate resembles the Council of the Republic, but Senators now have a nine-year term. R.B.C.

French Popular Front.
The Popular Front was a coalition of all the left of center parties in France, formed in 1935 by the Radical Socialists, the Socialists, and the Communists. These parties formed a united front, and adopted a common program —a French "New Deal"—these reforms won wide acceptance among French voters, and a Popular Front government assumed office in 1936 under the leadership of Leon Blum.
Although it was successful in enacting a number of social innovations, the Popular Front government remained weak due to internal differences. In foreign policy, it even made concessions to Hitler Germany. The government of the Popular Front was forced to resign in June, 1937, after just one year in office. Sporadic attempts have been made, always unsuccessful, to revive this alliance.
C.R.F.

French resistance movement.
Essentially unorganized in the autumn and winter of 1940, organized resistance emerged as clandestine leaflets and tracts began to circulate, as professors, priests, journalists and other professionals organized amongst their friends, and groups began to make surreptitious contact with one another. When Hitler Germany attacked the USSR in June, 1941, the Communists too became active in the clandestine movements. Resistance members increased in November, 1942, when U.S. forces landed in North Africa. On May 14, 1943, with the founding of the National Council of the Resistance (CNR), the several internal resistance groups were coordinated, and joined forces with representatives of the external de Gaulle government. As France was reconquered, and as people in the local areas revolted, representatives of the CNR took over control of the agencies of government.
E.G.L.

French Revolution of 1789.
It swept away the autocratic power of the Bourbon kings, leading to the constitution of 1791 for a limited, parliamentary monarchy, and ultimately the first republic. A major discontinuity in French governmental evolution, it laid the ground-work for modern France, including the centralized administrative system, local government departments which replaced royal provinces, a declaration of the rights of man proclaiming civil liberties, court reforms leading to the Napoleonic code, and, intermittently, democratic governmental institutions.
E.G.L.

French Socialist party.
Organized in 1905 as the Section Francaise de l'Internationale Ouvriere (SFIO), the French Socialist party fused the theory of Guesde with the pragmatism of Jaures; the latter tendency became dominant after the withdrawal of the majority as Communists in 1920. Party alliances being authorized, Blum became premier of the Popular Front in 1936. Under Vichy he opposed Petain although most Socialists supported his request for constitutional powers.
Socialist Auriol became first President of the Fourth Republic. Although during "tripartism" Socialists received one fourth of the total vote, there was internal dissension (Mollet replaced Daniel Mayer as secretary-general), and the aging party leadership, representing militants more than parliamentarians, was stalemated between the MRP and the Communists. Engaging in coalitions until 1951, the Socialists then went into opposition until 1955 when they entered governmental leadership through Premiers Pineau and Mollet.
Although holding 107 Assembly seats in 1951, the Socialists had scarcely 200,000 members. Consistently anticlerical, but troubled by a contradiction between Marxist theory and social democratic practice, the party was split in 1958 by those hostile to Mollet, who supported the Fifth Republic.
R.B.C.

French Union (1946—1958).
A union of France and her overseas dependencies, established by the constitution of the Fourth Republic and subsequent legislation.
The French Union grouped the members of the former French Empire into several categories—such as associated states, associated territories, and overseas territories—under common organs subject to France's ultimate control. Inspired in great part by a spirit of centralization, the union did not provide for independence, but

rather held out the hope to its overseas members of equal rights and equal treatment. The associated territories and overseas territories were given representation in the National Assembly and in the Council of the Republic of the metropole, and each of them was allowed to establish its own assembly. Two of the associated states (Tunisia and Morocco) refused to join the union, but the associated territories and overseas territories won many political and economic concessions under the system. Among these were the right to join trade unions, the forty-hour week, and universal adult suffrage. The local assemblies gradually expanded their powers and developed into parliamentary bodies.

In 1958 the French Union was superseded by the French Community.
F.H.G.

Friends, American.
Members of the Religious Society of Friends (Quakers) in the U.S.A. Founded in England by George Fox in 1648, the Society includes approximately 115,000 members in the U.S. and Canada. Believing God dwells within every man, Friends historically have worked for world peace, abolition of slavery, prison reform, and civil liberty. Lay Friends are represented at the national capital by the Friends Committee for National Legislation. The American Friends Service Committee carries out Friends' concerns in areas of relief, rehabilitation, and peace education. This group, together with the corresponding body in Great Britain, was awarded the Nobel Peace Prize in 1947.
R.E.Ch.

Front Liberation Nationale (F.L.N.).
Moslem rebel independence movement in French-Algerian war of 1954-1962. FLN military methods included night raids on French military installations; terrorism in Algerian cities and towns; sabotage of European industries and non-cooperation with European enterprise in Algeria. Principal FLN leaders have included Ahmed Ben Bella; Benyoussef Ben Khedda, and Houri Boumedienne. All look favorably on highly centralized economic experimentation in communist China and Cuba as examples for Algerian development. Ben Bella, first premier of independent Algeria, has pursued a policy based on a "socialist" economic organization and a "neutralist and nonengaged" course in foreign affairs. Ben Khedda, who lost a power struggle with Ben Bella for FLN leadership in 1962, is a professed Marxist, though he has advocated a neutralist policy in foreign affairs. Boumedienne, FLN military commander during the eight-year war, views the military as having the primary task of supporting and enforcing socialistic economic and political reforms.
E.R.W.

Front of National Unity.
See Polish Front of National Unity.

Frothingham v. Mellon.
A decision of the United States Supreme Court, 262 U.S. 447 (1923), in which the plaintiff, as a taxpayer, brought action to restrain Mellon, Secretary of the Treasury, from carrying out the Federal Maternity Act under which money was provided to the states that complied with the Act to help reduce maternal and infant mortality. Plaintiff challenged the law's constitutionality, generally, on the ground that the spending of the money was for local not national purposes, thus going beyond the power of congress, and specifically on the ground that it would result in an increase in future taxation thus taking her money without due process of law. A unanimous decision by the Court held that an individual taxpayer's interest in the total funds of the government was too small and indeterminate and the effect of the expenditure on future taxation too remote and uncertain to provide a standing in court to challenge the law. The decision was therefore based on lack of jurisdiction and the constitutional questions were not reached.
E.G.T.

Frunze, Mikhail V. (1885—1925).
Soviet military leader and theorist. Frunze led Red forces on the Eastern, Turkestan and Southern Fronts during the Russian Civil War. He succeeded Trotsky as Commissar for Military and Naval Affairs. Frunze propounded the unified military doctrine which called for a proletarian, as opposed to a capitalistic, military doctrine. It stressed the offensive, speed and movement. Frunze died under

suspicious circumstances after an operation ordered by the Politburo.
W.D.J.

Fulbright, J. W.
U.S. Senator since November 7, 1944. Democrat—Arkansas; attorney, United States Department of Justice. President, University of Arkansas, prior to election to the 78th Congress in Nov. 3, 1942. R.A.B.

Full Faith and Credit.
The Constitution of the United States, Art. IV, sec. 1, requires every State to give "Full Faith and Credit . . . to the public Acts, Records, and judicial Proceedings of every other State." Congress is authorized to prescribe the manner by which these shall be authenticated and given effect. Pursuant to Art. IV, what has authority in the courts of the state of origin is required to be treated as valid in the courts of every other state, and given effect in any proceeding therein. In respect to records and judicial proceedings the constitutional obligation has been met relatively well and with few complications except in divorce actions, where some difficult problems have arisen. Less well resolved is the effectiveness of the requirement relative to public Acts (statutes). Qualifying the requirement generally as judicially defined is that it applies to civil Acts and proceedings only; no state is compelled to help enforce the criminal laws of another. R.H.S.

Functional Consolidation.
Reallocation of a governmental service or function from one or more local units to another, most frequently from a municipality to the county government. Functional transfers are usually accomplished with the mutual consent of the governments involved. Their use represents a piece-meal approach to the problem of governing a metropolitan or urban area. M.J.Sch.

Functionalism.
In international relations, functionalism is used to denote an approach to the building of a supra-national community primarily through economic integration. Since the growth of world community is often suggested as a necessary prerequisite to world peace, functionalism is a theory of achieving a peaceful world through initially non-political means. The theory of functionalism implies a strong emphasis on the economic foundation of political society, but it is not itself a Marxist position. H.S.Th.

Functional Organization.
1. International. An international organization (q.v.) whose main purpose is to perform directly a primarily non-political function. It is mainly occupied with a particular economic or social matter leading toward the betterment of material welfare, health, education, or justice rather than directly toward a political end such as the elimination of war. For example, each of the Specialized Agencies of the United Nations is a functional organization. (See also Functionalism.)
2. Domestic. A somewhat similar distinction is made in domestic government, the meaning varying with the nation-state under consideration. (See, for example, Special District, a type of functional jurisdiction in the U.S.A.) It is recognized that the distinction between political and non-political is an analytical rather than a practical one. R.W.V.W.

Furtseva, Yekaterina Alekseyevna.
Born 1910 in Vyshni Volochek, now Kalinin Oblast. Studied at Leningrad Higher Academic Courses of Civil Air Fleet 1933-35, Moscow Lomonosov Institute of Technology of Fine Chemicals 1937-42. Joined CP 1930, rose to leadership positions in Komsomol 1930-37. Regarded as a Khrushchev protege; first woman on Mausoleum reviewing stand, May Day 1955. Central Committee of CPSU since 1956; first woman member Party Presidium 1957-61. Not reelected to USSR Supreme Soviet 1962. Married to N. P. Firyubin. W.A.

G

Gaitskell, Hugh Todd Naylor (1906—1963).
British Labor Party Leader. Educated at Winchester and Oxford. Economics professor, London University (1928—1939). Co-founder, New Fabian Research Bureau. Wartime service with Ministry of Economic Warfare, Board of Trade. Elected to Parliament 1945; cabinet minister in Attlee Government. Elected Leader of Parliamentary Labor Party in 1955.   C.J.S.

Gallup Poll.
Originated by Dr. George H. Gallup of U.S., in 1935, specifically this is a measure of public opinion on voting preferences and various public issues, given national prominence by newspaper syndication. It employs the techniques of opinion research.   J.B.L.

Galvan Case (Mexico v. U.S.).
The General Claims Commission (Opinion 408, 1927) awarded $10,000 to the mother of a Mexican killed in Texas in 1921. The case against an immediately apprehended American continued in Texas from 1921 to 1927 without results.   F.B.G.

Games, Theory of.
A theoretical or normative branch of mathematics and economics in which treatment is made of conflict of interests by the formalization of strategies. Initiated by Emil Borel in the 1920's, the formulations of game theory were codified in 1944 by mathematician John Von Neumann with economist Oskar Morgenstern in their volume, **Theory of Games and Economic Behavior.** The theory of games prescribes strategies of choice which enable individuals in conflict to obtain advantageous pay-offs, given the choices open to each other. The moves may take various forms: one of particular interest is a "minimax" play in which the parties may expect to minimize losses and simultaneously to maximize gains. The pay-offs among two or more players may be arranged so as to be "strictly competitive," in which case when one player gains the others automatically lose, or they may allow "cooperative" moves, so that all players may adopt strategies which yield gains.
Game theoretic notions are applied in political science to problems of power in voting behavior, as by L. S. Shapley and M. Shubik, and to the study of political coalitions, as by William Riker. The theory of games is to be distinguished from political "gaming," a form of simulation in which participants make decisions within computer-linked models of political process. Since 1950 conclusions from the theory of games have been checked in the laboratory by experimental explicitation of the derived mathematical strategies. The empirical results obtained by human subjects are sometimes at variance with the normative derivations.   H.G.

Gandhi, Mohandas Karamchand (1869—1948).
Revered in India as Mahatma (q.v.) and as Father of the Nation, Gandhi was born in the home of a Vaishya chief minister of Porbander. He studied at the Inner Temple, London, and was called to the bar in 1891. Two years later, he went to South Africa on business and eventually became the leader of Indians' **satyagraha** (q.v.) against racial discrimination. In 1914, he returned to India and supported the war effort. The repressive Rowlatt Bills and the Amritsar massacre in 1919 turned Gandhi against Britain. Assuming the leadership of the Indian Congress (q.v.), he led nation-wide **satyagrahas** for national freedom in 1919, 1920, 1930, 1931, and 1942. These campaigns were marked by imprisonments, fasts, conferences, and efforts to end untouchability and communalism. Finally, freedom came in August 1947. Five months later, Gandhi was assassinated. The Mahatma preached and practised love, nonviolence, and brotherhood. The state, he held, should promote spiritual values, abstain from violence, and allow maximum individual freedom.   C.S.S.

Garfield, James Abram (1831—1881).
Twentieth President of the United States. Born in a farm log cabin at Orange, Cuyahoga County, Ohio.

James Garfield rose from Ohio Canal towpath boy to President. A graduate of Williams College, he served Western Reserve Eclectic Institute (Hiram College) as professor and head (1857-61). From Civil War Major-General of Volunteers directly to the U.S. House of Representatives (1863-80), he is principally important as a scholar, orator, and brilliant parliamentarian, becoming Republican minority floor leader during the Hayes administration (1877-80). Dark-horse winner of the Republican nomination, and narrowly elected President over Democrat Winfield S. Hancock, Garfield's brief tenure (1881) was marred by a bitter patronage struggle. Poor medical treatment of a shot inflicted by an office-seeking assassin, Charles J. Guiteau, caused Garfield's death, but paved the way to Civil Service Reform. K.E.D.

Garibaldi, Giuseppe (1807—1882).
Italy's great popular hero, Garibaldi earned fame with his Expedition of One Thousand which ended Bourbon rule in Sicily and Naples (1860). His career included revolutionary action in Uruguay (1840) and France (1870); Mazzinian revolts in Italy before 1860; leadership of volunteer troops in royal service against Austria (1859 and 1866); but also unauthorized action against papal territory which led to battle with royal troops once and imprisonment twice (1862 and 1866). A grateful nation granted him a pension before his death. More recently, Italian Communists used him to name their brigades in the Spanish Civil War and as electoral symbol for their Popular Front. E.T.O.

Garrison, William Lloyd (1805—1879).
Publicist, abolitionist. Born in Newburyport, Mass. At fourteen, he was apprenticed to the local paper as a compositor. Soon he was writing articles and poetry anonymously. After being editor of several unfortunate ventures, he founded the **Liberator** (1831—1865). It became the great agitating force of the anti-slavery movement in the United States. The American Anti-Slavery Society (1833) of which he became President (1843-1865) channelled an intense moral agitation; and all ministers in the North were urged to advocate abolition in their sermons. Before the War, the **Liberator** advocated secession from "slavocracy." With the return of peace, Garrison formally announced the end of his career as a reformer. His fanatical zeal and constancy of purpose, praised and denounced, had aroused the conscience of a people and was recognized and honored by President Lincoln. M.E.D.

Gasperi, Alcide de (1881—1954).
Italian political leader and statesman. Alcide de Gasperi was the leader of the Christian Democratic Party of Italy and the Premier of that country during the important period between 1945 and 1953. In the early 1920's de Gasperi was a member of the Italian Parliament. Opposed to fascism, he spent the years of the Mussolini regime as an employee of the Catholic Church in Vatican City. In 1943 he came out of retirement to take part in Italian politics again. A strong advocate of alliance with the West, de Gasperi contributed greatly to the stability of his country in the post-war period. W.C.C.

G.A.T.T.
See General Agreement on Tariffs and Trade.

Gaza Strip.
A twenty-six mile long and four to six mile wide piece of land along the Mediterranean Sea between the United Arab Republic (Egypt) and Israel. Its principal city is Gaza which is located about three miles inland from the Mediterranean coast and fifty miles southwest of Jerusalem, and which was one of the leading Philistine cities in biblical times. Part of Palestine under the British Mandate, the Gaza Strip was allotted to the "Arab State" to be created under the United Nations Partition Plan of November 29, 1947, but was seized by Egypt during the Arab-Israel War of 1948—1949. Article 6 of the Egyptian-Israeli General Armistice Agreement signed February 24, 1949, recognized Egyptian military authority over the Strip. The area was the scene of friction between the two countries from the time of Israel's establishment in 1948 until 1956 when a United Nations Emer-

gency Force was stationed in the Gaza Strip along the armistice demarcation line to maintain peace and order. It was Israel's contention that Fedayeen, organized guerrillas, had been recruited by Egypt from the Arab population in the Gaza Strip to infiltrate and attack neighboring Israeli settlements.

During the invasion of Egypt by France, Great Britain and Israel in October, 1956, Israel drove out the Egyptian military forces and occupied the entire Gaza Strip. It was relinquished following the passage by the United Nations General Assembly of a resolution on November 1, 1956, calling for a prompt withdrawal of Israeli and Egyptian troops to the armistice line set in 1949, including withdrawal from the Gaza Strip. A further resolution, on November 4, 1956, established an Emergency Force to secure and supervise the cessation of hostilities. Israel, however, did not withdraw from the Gaza Strip until March 9, 1957. The delay was caused by Israel's insistence on guarantees: (1) that the Gaza Strip would not be permitted to be used by Egypt as a base for raids against Israel, and (2) that the United Nations would control, civilly and militarily, the Gaza Strip until a peace settlement was concluded. Neither the United Nations nor the United States would give such guarantees. Instead, the United States warned that it would terminate all financial and technical aid to Israel and that Israel might be expelled from the United Nations. Israel withdrew asserting the right to take action if Egypt used the Gaza Strip as a base for infiltration raids against her.

The Gaza Strip is now administered by the United Arab Republic (Egypt), with the United Nations Emergency Force continuing to serve along the armistice demarcation line. Its population was last estimated in 1960 as approximately 300,000, of which 240,000 are Arab refugees from Palestine who are being cared for by the United Nations Relief and Works Agency (UNRWA). On March 15, 1958, a Legislative Council consisting of ten Egyptians and ten Palestinians was established to advise the Egyptian Governor of the Strip. O.K.

General Agreement on Tariffs and Trade (G.A.T.T.).

An international trade agreement among thirty-eight nations, including the United States and virtually all of the important trading nations of the free world. These contracting parties together account for more than 80 per cent of the international trade of the whole world. Essentially the General Agreement consists of three elements: (1) Tariff schedules for which specific tariff treatment has been agreed upon, with separate schedules for each participating country; (2) A code of agreed rules governing the import and export trade of contracting parties; (3) Periodic meetings of representatives of the particular states for the purpose of discussion and settlement of mutual problems of international trade. G.B.H.

General Assembly.

See United Nations General Assembly.

General Fund.

Money collected from various taxes and sources, available for disposal by legislative appropriation for expenses of government; to be distinguished from a special fund set up to receive revenues from a specific source or from which appropriation can be made only for the purpose or purposes established by the terms of the law setting up the fund. The general fund permits much legislative discretion in the allocation of appropriations, whereas the special fund limits this discretion. K.E.H.

Generalist.

As distinct from the specialist who concentrates on mastering and operating within a particular skill or discipline (or, increasingly, a segment of one), the generalist seeks to provide the bridge among specialists, and to serve as the synthesizer of new ideas and processes; specifically, or ideally, also he serves as the planner, organizer and administrator in a complex division of labor. Mostly found today (but in small numbers) in the law, government, mass communication, public relations, management and some phases of economics, science and engineering, the generalist may be expected to increase in quantity, range and power as the complexity of society grows. Whether he represents Burnham's managerial revolution is moot, depending on the given social orientation; thus generalists are coming to the fore in both the monolithic U.S.S.R. and the increasingly confluent U.S.A.   J.B.L.

General Systems Research.
An approach, presently under rapid development, for advancing scientific knowledge about the operations of very complex but non-random phenomena. Already highly advanced in the fields of electronics, biology, neurology, and military man-machine relationships, general systems analysis is also being applied in the social sciences. The fundamental concept is that the relationships of the working parts (sub-systems) of a system vary and change, not only according to their own characteristics but also according to the shifting nature of the system—a political system, for example—and to demands and conditions of the environment in which the system operates. The approach seeks to analyze and explain the dynamics, in real life operations, of the three sets of relationships of sub-system, system, and relevant environment. As empirical studies develop detailed knowledge of how political behavior takes place in the three sets of complex relationship, they establish the basis for new political theories.   Ch.A.Mc.

General Will.
Concept introduced by Diderot in his **Encyclopedia** and further developed by Rousseau, with whom generally identified, in his **Social Contract**. The idea of the G.W. undertakes to resolve the dilemma of free will juxtaposed to external standards of morality by asserting that the true and higher will of the individual is to obey the G.W., which incorporates the obligations of the Social Contract.

As developed by Rousseau, the G.W. is collectivist as a philosophic and operating principle. In sharp contrast to the "consensus of reasonable men" invoked by English philosophers, the G.W. is not the result of political compromise, but is the will of the nation as a moral person in its own right.

The **mystique** of the G.W. lends itself to totalitarian practices, and exempts the State as its executor from external moral controls. "Each of us," Rousseau writes, "puts his persons and all his power under the supreme direction of the general will . . ." Whoever refuses is to be compelled, or in Rousseau's language "forced to be free." As a compulsive sanction, the G.W. "alone legitimizes civil undertakings, which without it, would be absurd, tyrannical, and liable to the most frightful abuses."

Since Rousseau does not identify the G.W. with the transient opinion of the majority, and gives no specific clues as to how the G.W. is to be ascertained, his doctrine opens the way to dictatorship of a revolutionary assembly or a Caesar emerging from revolutionary chaos. It is evident that Lenin borrowed from Rousseau in developing the rationale of his "Dictatorship of the Proletariat."   K.G.

General Zionists.
Israeli political party, founded in 1948, now merged with Progressives to form Liberal party. Promotes private enterprise system, attraction of investment capital; opposes socialist aspects of Israel economy.   S.H.

Geneva Protocol of 1925.
The Protocol for the Pacific Settlement of International Disputes. It was aimed to require signatories to submit their legal disputes to the Permanent Court of International Justice, other disputes to arbitration if the League Council should have failed to settle them, and disputes about domestic matters to conciliation. The Protocol never came into force.
S.S.H.

Genro.
Meaning "Elder Statesmen" in Japanese, this group emerged in the middle of the Meiji Period (1868-1911) as the real power holders. Originally composed of Ito, Yamagata, Inouye, Oyama, and Matsukata, it later co-opted Katsura and Saionji (the "last Genro" who died in 1940). Formed before the Meiji Constitution of 1889, this group was "extra-constitutional." Some of its power was inherited by the **Jushin** (Senior Statesmen).
G.O.T.

Geographical representation.
An arrangement under which the member of a legislative body represents individuals in a specific territorial unit. This differs from functional representation, which assigns representatives to economic or occupational groups. Geographical representation often requires that a deputy reside in the constituency he represents. It may involve a system of single-member or multi-member constituencies, or one based on proportional representation.   D.M.B.

Geopolitics.
No universally accepted definition. Sometimes used to refer to a study legitimately based on geographical influences on politics. More popularly used to refer to a pseudo science of geographical determinism. Haushofer, a "father" of the latter theory, insisted it is a dynamic science contrasting with the "static" science of political geography and empirically and objectively oriented where opponents charge it with being value loaded. Originators and developers: Friedrich Ratzel, 1844-1904, worked out a theory of the effect of geographical factors on the life and development of states using the analogy of natural organisms whose life and growth is a struggle for existence vis-a-vis space. A people's development, he claimed, depended upon their consciousness of space necessity. Rudolph Kjellen (1864—1922), a Swedish university professor and disciple of Ratzel's, termed this theory **geopolitics** but claimed it included the total environmental influences upon a people —physical, psychological, anthropological, political, and social. His **The Great Powers,** later enlarged by Haushofer, became the Bible of German geopoliticians. Admittedly Pan-German, Kjellen claimed Germany's life and growth — **Lebensraum** — included Central and Eastern Europe, Scandinavia, Asia Minor, and Mesopotamia. Sir Halford Mackinder added the concept of world politics as a struggle between oceanic and continental peoples, claiming that a state dominating the heartland or world island—an area from the Volga to the Yangtze and the Himalayas to the Arctic Ocean— could control the world. Major General Karl E. Nikolas Haushofer (1869—1946), a Professor of Geography and History, defined geopolitics as "the science of political forms of life in their regional relationships, both as affected by natural conditions and in terms of their historical development." According to this "science," a particular race is best suited to rule a particular region, although it may not be tnere presently and may require displacement or movement. The German race, he argued, was in tune with and destined to dominate a large part of the world island, present populations not being fit. Beyond the power politics implication, this addition to the theory also suggested the dominant influence of geography on all other areas of life—ethics, art, law, etc.
   J.P.D.

German Democratic Republic
(Deutsche Demokratische Republik —abbrev. DDR).
A Soviet-sponsored "state" established by the Socialist Unity Party (q.v.)—SED—on October 7, 1949, in the Soviet Occupation Zone of Germany. Recognition granted by Communist states only; refused by (West) German Federal Republic on grounds act would legalize split of Germany. Declared People's Democracy 1952. Granted "sovereignty" by Soviet Russia 1954 but Soviet troops remain for security reasons. Member Warsaw Pact 1956. Constitution (1949) declares Germany "an indivisible democratic Republic," with Berlin as its capital, to emphasize claim of DDR to all of Germany; is a facade for the totalitarian state though its text follows closely that of the Weimar constitution. State, parliament and public life are controlled by the SED. Constitutional phraseology provides for federalism but the government is strictly centralistic. In 1952 the five states (Lander) were abolished by law and fifteen districts substituted. The 400 members of the national legislature, or People's Chamber, are elected on a "unity list" of hand-picked representatives of political parties (several sham political parties are allowed to exist) and "mass organizations" (for workers, women, youth, etc.)—each allotted a percentage determined prior to election. With the abolition of states the Chamber of States became obsolete. Since the

1960 death of President Wilhelm Pieck (q.v.), Walter Ulbricht (q.v.), longtime SED Secretary General took President's place as Chairman of the (newly created) State Council.

J.B.M.

German Party.

Minor, regional (Lower Saxony, Hamburg, Bremen) party in the German Federal Republic. To the right of the CDU with which it was closely associated; has had no federal representation since the 1961 Bundestag elections. Conservative spokesmen for commercial interests of northern port cities and farmers. Traces descent from the Hanoverian party **(Welfen)** of the 19th century.

C.J.S.

German People's Congress
(Deutscher Volkskongress)
for Unity and for a Just Peace.

Quasi-representative assembly of Soviet Zone parties and communists from West Germany. Created by the East German Socialist Unity Party without benefit of elections (Dec. 6-7, 1947) to send representatives to London Conference of Foreign Ministers. The Third People's Congress elected the so-called People's Council (5/30/49).

E.K.K.

German People's Council
(Deutscher Volksrat).

Was elected 18 March, 1948 by the Second People's Congress in the Soviet Zone. It approved (October 22, 1948) and adopted (March 19, 1949) the Constitution of the German Democratic Republic. The Third People's Congress elected (May 29, 1949) a new People's Council. Its 400 members reconstituted themselves as the Provisional People's Chamber of the German Democratic Republic and declared its Constitution to be in force.

E.K.K.

German Police Systems.

During the period of the Weimar Republic (1918—1933) the functions of the German police were limited to the maintenance of public safety and order and were subject to judicial review. All activities in the various German Laender were statutorily defined by section 14 of the Prussian Police Law of June 1, 1931. Section 14, paragraph 1, reads as follows: "The police authorities shall take the necessary measures in order to protect the general public and the individual citizen from dangers which threaten the public safety or order. They shall take these measures in accordance with the laws in effect and they shall be in duty bound to use proper discretion." Before the Nazis came to power in January, 1933, Germany had never had a federal police system, either in the Empire or in the Weimar Republic. In this period the number of police officers totaled about 200,000, the major part of these were uniformed police troopers. In addition, each German state had its detective force. With the advent of Hitler this police system was centralized into a Reich police force and the German Laender police systems were abolished. Under the National Socialist regime the police had aggrandized to itself powers unprecedented in the police history of any modern western state. It exercised unlimited and ever-expanding legislative, judicial and executive functions. The main branches were the order police (Ordnungspolizei) and the security police (Sicherheits-polizei), the latter embraced the secret state police (Gestapo). It was the security police that had the power to arrest persons without warrant and without judicial control, to search houses, and to confiscate property for a wide variety of reasons falling under the elastic heading "political." It was this branch that engineered and managed the nation-wide system of concentration camps, political prisons and "liquidations." This agency organized, coordinated, and enforced programs for the annihilation of political enemies of the Nazi regime and of minority groups, such as members of the intelligentsia, Catholic priests in Nazi occupied countries, sick people designated as "useless eaters," Jews and gypsies. The acts of the security police were not subject to judicial review. The unconditional termination of this police machinery was marked by the judgement of the International Military Tribunal stigmatizing as criminal organizations the Gestapo, the SS, and the affiliated SD (Sicherheitsdienst). The western occupational administrations and the new German Laender administrations established new police forces according to modern and demo-

cratic concepts. Besides the State police forces there exists a large number of independent municipal police systems. Only a small Federal police force exists having jurisdiction over state security matters. A Federal Office of a Criminal Police (Bundeskriminalamt) exists for police information and communication under the control of the Federal Minister of the Interior. Furthermore, a Federal Office for the Protection of the Constitution (Bundesamt fuer Verfassungsschutz) has been established as agency for collecting information on any activities endangering the German federal constitution. All acts of the police are subject to judicial review by the courts.
R.M.W.K.

German Resistance against Hitlerian System.

Rather unknown to the world at large is the fact that tens of thousands of German socialists and trade unionists continued their principled anti-Nazi resistance after 1933. In this struggle, aimed at the destruction of the Nazi regime from within, the small socialist splinter groups played a special role since unlike the Social Democratic Party of Germany they had prepared themselves for the period of illegality and underground activity. But the relentless persecution of the underground forces by the Nazi secret police coupled with ever increasing difficulties to maintain contacts with their sympathizers outside the Third Reich led to the collapse of most organized resistance by the end of 1938. The resistance movement was revived when leading members of the German army, the churches, and the civil service, aroused at first by Hitler's incompetence joined the remnants of the labor movement's resistance. The merger of the resistance groups resulted in the attempt on Hitler's life on July 20, 1944, which was designated as the signal for a general uprising. H.D.

German Trade Unions.

Developed after 1890 (1890 marks the expiration of Bismarck's outlawry of the Social Democratic Party of Germany). German trade unions developed as centralized organizations of the skilled workers differentiated by their various trades. In accordance with their political and religious outlook they were divided into three large federations allied with political parties reflecting similar outlooks: the Free trade unions (with over five million members as of 1932), the Christian trade unions (with about 1,300,000 members as of 1932), the Liberal trade unions (with about five hundred thousand members as of 1932). Following their suppression during the Hitlerian period from 1933—1945, the labor unions in the Federal Republic of Germany merged into the German Trade Union Federation (Deutscher Gewerkschaftsbund), a politically neutral trade union federation with close to six and a half million members. In the Soviet zone of Germany the "Free German Trade Union Alliance," similar to the Nazi Labor Front during the Hitlerian period, is a front organization of the Communist regime and its Socialist Unity Party. H.D.

Germany.

See Federal Republic of Germany.

Gero, Erno (1898—   ).

First Secretary of the Hungarian Communist Party at the outbreak of the uprising of 1956.

Active in the Communist movement since 1918, he participated in the events leading to the proclamation of the Hungarian Soviet Republic in 1919. In 1924 he escaped to the Soviet Union where he worked for the Comintern. Fought with the International Brigade in Spain during the Spanish Civil War. He returned to Hungary in 1944 as a Soviet citizen and occupied high posts in the Party and Government. In July, 1956, he replaced Matyas Rakosi as First Secretary of the Party. When anti-Stalinist demonstrations began in Budapest on October 23, 1956, he was on his way back from a visit to Yugoslavia. It was allegedly he and Andras Hegedus, then Prime Minister, who were responsible for calling in Soviet troops to suppress the demonstrations. On October 25, 1956, Gero was replaced by Janos Kadar as First Secretary of the Party. During the uprising, he escaped to the Soviet Union. In August, 1962, he was expelled from the Hungarian Communist Party, although it is not clear how he became a member, the Party being a new organization formed after the uprising and Gero having been barred from it already in November, 1956. I.B.

Gerrymandering.
The practice of drawing the boundaries of districts having representatives in political bodies in such a way as to work to the advantage of one group or political party. Political parties have long fixed the lines of state legislative and congressional districts without regard for compactness or approximate equality of population so as to assure party representation disproportionate to the number of its supporters. At present the most flagrant example of gerrymandering occurs when state legislatures, dominated by rural and small town members, discriminate against urban populations in the apportionment of seats to the state legislature and to the national House of Representatives. A recent Supreme Court decision, Baker v. Carr, indicates that judicial remedies may be used to modify the practice. G.B.H.

Gestapo.
Abbreviation of Geheimes Staatspolizeiamt i.e. Secret State Police Office, established on April 26, 1933 in Berlin as centralized political police agency of the Third Reich under Hermann Goering as chief and Rudolf Diels as its first executive. About one year later, Heinrich Himmler, Reich leader of the SS Elite Guards (he committed suicide after his capture at the end of World War II) became chief of the newly centralized German police system, thus also chief of the Gestapo. He appointed as executive the SS Gruppenfuehrer Reinhard Heydrich and later, after Heydrich's assassination in Prague (May 27, 1942), the SS Gruppenfuehrer Ernst Kaltenbrunner (sentenced to death on October 1, 1946 by the International Military Tribunal in Nuremberg). Before the outbreak of World War II the Gestapo had been incorporated as Bureau IV under the Bureau chief Heinrich Mueller into the Reich Security Main Office (Reichssicherheitshauptamt). In Germany and all Nazi-occupied countries this police octopus had jurisdiction over incarceration in or release from concentration camps, "liquidation" of prisoners of war and all so-called enemies of the state, deportation and extermination of Jews, etc. The activities of this agency were not subject to any judicial review. (See also German Police Systems, Concentration Camps, Eichmann.)
R.M.W.K.

Getulism.
It means the corruption of laborism in Brazil. Attributed to the person of Getulio Vargas, a caudillo, native of Rio Grande del Sul who ruled Brazil from 1930 to 1945. It was to assure the obedience of the workers of Vargas' stay in power (and after his suicide in August 1954 that of his loyal followers). Getulism is not a political doctrine, but rather a technique of transforming large segments of a population into obedient tools of the government in power. A.F.Mo.

Ghana, Republic of.
A country in West Africa with an area of 92,000 square miles and a population of approximately 6,700,000. Composed of the former Gold Coast and British Togoland, it became an independent state on March 6, 1957. Its capital is Accra.

The Portuguese were the first Europeans to establish a permanent settlement in what is now Ghana: they built a castle at Elmina in 1482. Various European countries vied over control of the coastal area until the British emerged as the predominant power in the nineteenth century. The coastal area was made a British crown colony in 1874, and in 1901 Ashanti and the Northern Territories were declared to be British protectorates. The post-World War II period has been characterized by a succession of British political concessions, until independence was achieved in 1957.

The present politics of Ghana are dominated by its dynamic president, Kwame Nkrumah, and by the Convention People's Party. The young African state stands for a strident form of Pan-Africanism, non-alignment in the cold war, and uncompromising hostility to colonialism and neo-colonialism. Ghana is a member of the Commonwealth, the Union of African States, and the Casablanca Bloc. F.H.G.

Gheorghiu-Dej, Gheorghe (1901—   ).
First Secretary of the Rumanian

Workers' (Communist) Party and Politburo member, he has been the leader of Rumania since 1945. He joined the CP before World War II and served a prison term. In 1945 he was elected Secretary-General of the CP. He was Premier and CP chief 1952-54, resigned his CP post when Rumania adopted the "collective leadership" policy in 1954, but regained it in 1955 and resigned as Premier. In 1961 he was named President of the State Council. J.J.K.

Gibraltar.
British Crown colony controlling the straits connecting the Atlantic and the Mediterranean. Area about 2 sq. miles, population about 25,000. A British possession since 1713, Gibraltar has played a major role in naval conflicts involving the control of the Mediterranean, especially with France. Spain has lately reaffirmed its claim to Gibraltar. F.M.

Gimu.
The Japanese version of the English concept of "duty." H.U.

Giolitti, Giovanni (1842—1928).
From 1900 to 1922, Giolitti, a Piedmontese Liberal, either personally or from behind the scenes ran the Italian government through shifting personal coalitions **(trasformismo)**. Fascism's rise is linked to the failure of Giolitti and other Liberals to realize the old system would no longer work with the mass ideological parties of 1919 who condemned **trasformismo** as immoral and politically meaningless. Yet the Giolitti period also brought Italy economic prosperity and an expanding suffrage and labor movement, and prepared the nation for more developed political life. E.T.O.

Giri.
A part of the Japanese moral code which controls the horizontal social relationships. It insures close ties of mutual service among relatives and friends. During the Tokagawa period it helped to strengthen the power of the Samurai. H.U.

Gizenga, Antoine (1925—   ).
Born in Kinzambi, Leopoldville Province of Ba-Pende stock. Attended and later served on the staff of a Catholic seminary. In April, 1959 helped found and became president of the Parti Solidaire Africain (PSA), a movement of small peasants and workers of minority non-Bakongo tribes in the Kwango-Kwilu region of Leopoldville. Led the PSA delegation to the 1960 Brussels Round Table Conference, though spent most of his time abroad in Eastern Europe. In the May 1960 elections, the PSA won thirteen of 137 seats in the National Assembly and 35 of 90 seats in the Leopoldville Provincial Council, thereby beating Kasavubu's ABAKO party in the region of its greatest strength. Became Deputy Premier in the Lumumba cabinet after independence. After Lumumba's downfall and arrest in late 1960, Gizenga established a pro-Lumumba government in Stanleyville, which was recognized as the legitimate Congo government by many Afro-Asian governments and the Communist bloc. Gizenga was arrested and jailed by the Central government in January 1962. R.L.K.

Gladstone, William E. (1809—1898).
British politician and statesman. Born at Liverpool and educated at Oxford, he served as a member of Parliament from 1843 until 1895 in the Commons. After periods of service as President of the Board of Trade, Secretary of State for the Colonies, and Chancellor of the Exchequer under Peel, Aberdeen, Palmerston and Russell, Gladstone succeeded Lord Russell as leader of the Liberal Party in 1867. During his service as Prime Minister (1868-74, 1880-85, 1886, 1892-94), he was associated with the disestablishment of the Irish Church (1869), the Irish land bill (1870), and Irish home rule which was defeated in 1886 and 1893. R.J.S.

Glubb, Lt.-General John Bagot.
A British officer who had gone out to Iraq in 1920 as an ordinary regimental officer in the British army. In 1926, he resigned his commission and took service under the Iraqi Government mainly to put an end to desert raiding. Having successfully achieved his mission, he was engaged in 1930 by the Government of Trans-Jordan to help put an end to bedouin raiding.

From 1930—1939, he was an officer commanding the desert area. In 1939, he assumed command of the Arab Legion, a regular military force officered in large part by British personnel and supported by annual British grants-in-aid. Under the leadership first of F. G. Peake Pasha and later Glubb Pasha, the Legion grew from a handful of policemen to an efficient military force of 23,000 men and a National Guard of 30,000. The Palestine war and subsequent political upheavals in the Arab World cast a shadow on Glubb Pasha's loyalty to Jordan and the Arabs. To the Jordanians, especially those of the West Bank, Glubb and his colleagues symbolized their defeat in the Palestine War as well as they symbolized British imperialism. After the Qibya incident of 1953, involving an Israeli raid on a Jordan village, he was accused of failing to use the Arab Legion effectively to protect the villagers. On March 1956, King Hussein dismissed Glubb Pasha under pressure from extremists thus ingloriously terminating 36 years of service in the Arab world. His dismissal was a blow to British prestige in the Middle East, and a year later the Anglo-Jordanian alliance of 1948 was ended. F.M.N.

Goa.

Population: 625,831 (1960 Census, provisional). Area: 4,194 square miles. Capital: Panjim. In 1509, Albuquerque seized Goa from the Bijapur sultans and wrote to his monarch in Lisbon: "I have burnt the city and put everything to the sword." Portuguese territory in India—Goa, Daman, Diu and smaller enclaves—lay practically within Indian states of Gujerat and Maharashtra. In 1951, Portugal amended her constitution to change the enclaves' status from that of colonies to provinces of Portugal. Diplomatic relations were severed, and Goan nationalists liberated the enclaves of Dadra and Nagar Haveli in 1954. In December, 1961, Indian armed forces occupied Goa and ended Portuguese rule. March, 1962, Indian Parliament passed bills incorporating the former Portuguese possessions into the Indian Union. The Goan population, over sixty per cent Hindu and the rest Christian, speak the Konkani dialect of Marathi. S.K.A.

Goebbels, Joseph.

Hitler's Minister for Public Enlightment and Propaganda; Born October 28, 1897 in Rheydt, Rheinland, committed suicide with his wife Magda and children on May 1, 1945 in Hitler's Fuehrerbunker in Berlin during the last hours of the Third Reich. Since 1933 he had been Hitler's Propaganda Minister, and Gauleader of Berlin. Loyal to his Fuehrer to the death, an intelligent writer and organizer, but a cynic and corrupt master liar without any moral scruples, Goebbels suppressed freedom of speech, press, thought, art and literature. He synchronized German public life and communication media completely with the Nazi-propaganda and war machine. He eliminated all anti-Nazi and Jewish writers and artists from German intellectual life. In his propaganda for a Teutonic super-race and Nazi world domination he succeeded even in enlisting as his tools high-placed persons in the Western world. In the course of his war propaganda, he incited the German population to the murder of captured Allied airmen. R.M.W.K.

Goering, Hermann.

Reich Marshal of the Greater German Reich; born January 12, 1893 in Rosenheim, Bavaria, committed suicide by taking a poison capsule from another prisoner in his Nuremberg jail cell on October 15, 1946 after having been sentenced to death by the International Military Tribunal for crimes against the peace, war crimes, and crimes against humanity such as participating in mistreatment and starving slave laborers and in the anti-Jewish extermination program. Goering's personality was a most interesting mixture of contrasts with a tremendous drive to power: the son of a high echelon German colonial administrator and a low echelon flower girl. The godchild of a Jewish doctor but in charge of the greatest anti-Jewish extermination program. The flying ace of World War I but the incapable air force chief of World War II. The good husband and father of his private and official family but the brutal co-exterminator

215

of "inferior" races. The caretaker of game in the forests but the starver of slave laborers in the pits. The gargantuan muscle man and "Chief German Hunter" but the lazy and puffy dope addict. The noble and intelligent host to foreign diplomats but the cursing orator at Nazi gatherings. The generous Maecenas to his theatrical friends but also a leading thief of art and jewelry pieces in Nazi conquered Europe. The man who wanted to be the last Prince of the Renaissance but, instead, became the evil managerial boss of a criminal gang, second in command of the Third Reich, a true paladin of his beloved Fuehrer until his idol accused him of double-crossing just before his own suicidal end.
R.M.W.K.

Goldberg, Arthur J. (1908—   ).
American labor lawyer and associate justice of the United States Supreme Court. Goldberg was born in Chicago and educated at Northwestern University, where he received the degrees of B.S.L. and J.D. In his legal practice he specialized in labor law and in 1948 became general counsel of the C.I.O. and of the United Steelworkers of America. Later he served as general counsel of the industrial relations department of the A.F.L.-C.I.O. Upon the inauguration of President Kennedy in January, 1961, Goldberg became secretary of labor and began very successful service in that post. When Associate Justice Felix Frankfurter retired from the Supreme Court in August, 1962, Goldberg was named as his successor. His appointment was speedily confirmed by the Senate, and he took his oath of office when the court convened on the first of October for the new term. M.Sp.

Goldmann, Nahum (1894—   ).
President of the World Zionist Congress, elected on May 7, 1956, to fill the post left vacant since the death in 1952 of Chaim Weizmann. Also president of the Jewish Agency for Israel. Born in Wisnewo, Poland, the son of a writer and teacher, Goldmann was raised in Frankfurt am Main, Germany, to which the family had moved when he was quite young. He attended the University of Berlin, receiving the Doctor of Laws degree in 1920, and the University of Heidelberg where he was awarded the Ph.D. degree in 1921.

In 1936 Goldmann helped organize the World Jewish Congress, became its acting president in 1949 after the death of Stephen S. Wise, and was elected president in 1953. He moved to the United States in 1940 and became an American citizen.

With the creation of the State of Israel, the role of Zionism began to be questioned by the Israeli government. After a series of meetings in 1950 in Israel between representatives of the World Zionist Organization led by Goldmann and Israeli leaders, agreement was reached on world Zionism's role in immigration, colonization, and economic development policies.

In December, 1951, in Bonn, Goldmann met with John J. McCloy, American High Commissioner for Germany, to discuss payment for property destruction or loss suffered by the Jews under Hitler's rule. As chairman of a committee representing twenty-four world Jewish organizations, Goldmann, accompanied by Israeli Foreign Minister Moshe Sharett, met with Chancellor Konrad Adenauer in Luxembourg in September, 1952, and signed an agreement under which Germany would give Israel $715,000,000 worth of goods and services and pay $107,000,000 to the Conference on Jewish Material Claims Against Germany, headed by Goldmann, for distribution to some 300,000 Jewish refugees living outside of Israel. In June, 1953, as head of the World Jewish Congress, he negotiated with Austria for similar reparations amounting to about $100,000,000. O.K.

Goldwater, Barry M.
Born January 1, 1909; U.S. Senate from November 4, 1952 until term ending 1965. Republican—Arizona; United States Air Force 1941—1945; Brig. Gen. USAFR. Leading spokesman of conservative movement. R.A.B.

Golpe (de Estado).
A frequently employed extra-legal means of achieving political power in Latin America, similar to **coup d'etat.** The **golpe** aims at a forcible eviction, or intimidation, of the chief executive. Usually the defense minister and some

of the other top officers in the armed forces (with or without the collaboration of civilian members of the cabinet) call on the president personally and demand his resignation. Ordinarily he concedes, inasmuch as he is faced with a fait accompli, cut off from the exercise of power precisely by his trusted lieutenants. His flight into comfortable exile is normally provided for. If he resists, he may be imprisoned or unceremoniously sent out of the country. Except where he may be kept on as a figurehead, his administration is ordinarily supplanted by the traditional military junta as a "provisional government." Plots to carry out golpes are often detected in advance, or suspected, and counter steps taken.

R.D.H.

Gomulka, Wladyslaw (1905—   ).
Born at Krosno near Rzeszow. Locksmith by training and active leftist at age 16. Jailed twice. Studied in Moscow at International Leninist School (1934-36). Secretary General of Polish Workers' Party (1943-48), purged for "nationalist deviation" (1948-56), and again First Secretary of the Polish United Workers' Party (see Polish Revolution of 1956).

R.F.S.

Good, highest good.
See Value.

Good Neighbor Policy.
Term applied to the policy of the United States toward Latin America during the Presidency of Franklin D. Roosevelt. The generally good relations between the continents of the Western Hemisphere during this period were implemented through such policies as the establishment of the Reciprocal Trade Agreements, the Export-Import Bank, and cooperation between the American republics in World War II.

Ch.W.A.

Goslicki (Goslicius), Wawrzyniec Grzymala. or Grimaldus (c. 1533—1607).
Polish humanist, political writer, politician, courtier (secretary to Kings Zygmunt August and Stefan Batory), and bishop after 1586. Made his name as a churchman of independent views (advocate of a national church), as a senator defending unpopular causes (such as religious toleration), as a successful diplomatic negotiator, orator and poet. As a political theorist, he championed the rule of law and the principles of equality and limited monarchy. His chief objectives were freedom of conscience and political stability. He warned against hasty innovations and argued for a gradual change within the existing social framework. In describing the character and duties of King's counsellor, he recommended training in the schools of history, philosophy, and experience. He foresaw the emergence of a truly virtuous character who would also be a man of action—the "practical philosopher."

W.J.S.

Gottwald, Klement (1896—1953).
President of Czechoslovakia, 1948—1953. Official of Communist Party since 1921; Secretary-General in 1929; elected to Parliament in 1929. Spent the war in Moscow and became Deputy Prime Minister in the post-war Czechoslovakian coalition; became Prime Minister in 1946 and Chairman of Communist Party 1946—1953. Engineered the 1948 coup which converted Czechoslovakia into a Communist state.

G.K.

Government.
The agency which administers a group of people and expresses their conduct. There is government in the family (usually a parent or the parents), in a university, a trade union, in short, in all groups. The government of the state (political government) is the agency which reflects the organization of the statal (politically organized) group. It normally consists of an executive branch, a legislative branch, and a judicial branch. These three branches (and their functions) may be separate or inseparate.   J.D.

Government Corporations—U.S.A.
Created on a national level by Congress during World War I (Emergency Fleet Corporation, etc.) as administrative and managerial devices to perform a public service normally handled by private enterprises. Like others created during economic emergencies (RFC, HOLC, etc.) war-time corporations have normally been temporary or semi-permanent only. Others (FCIC, TVA, etc.) seem to be perma-

nent. These corporations usually enjoy a relative degree of autonomy from both the executive department and Congress, even to some extent in audit control, personnel, and freedom from necessity of annual appropriations. The Government Corporation Control Act of 1945 tightened up on the budgeting and auditing system of government corporations. C.B.C.

Governor (of state).

The chief executive officer in each of the fifty states of the United States has the title of governor. As "governor" or "governor general" it is also commonly used to denominate the chief representative of the home country in each colony. In the states he is always elected for a fixed term. He has extensive powers of appointment and removal as well as authority to direct the administrative activities of the state government. He is usually the leader of his political party in the state. He also has varying degrees of control over legislation and the legislature and the power to grant clemency. He is commander in chief of the military forces of the state and prepares and presents a budget. H.W.

Governor General

(In British Commonwealth).

The British monarch is represented in each of those Commonwealth countries, which have not become Republics, by a Governor-General. Once having exercised extensive powers these officials today are primarily ceremonial chiefs of state, having no more power than is accorded the Crown within the government of the United Kingdom. This definition of status has been set forth in writing since the Imperial Conference of 1926. The Governor General today acts wholly on the advice of his government and is independent of the British Crown. While nominally appointed by the British monarch, in fact the selection of a person to hold this office is made by the government of the particular Commonwealth country concerned. His significant political task arises when it is necessary to summon a member of the Parliament to form a Government; in instances in which no clear majority leader emerges discretion is needed. Legal process, governmental decree, etc. issues either in the name of the Queen, or in other instances in the name of the Governor General. M.P.S.

Governors' Conference.

Annual conference of the Governors of the fifty States of the U.S.A. The work of the Governors' Conference to further interstate understanding is an adjunct to the efforts of the Council of State Governments. In presidential election years the Governors' Conference tends to become a proving-ground or springboard for presidential and vice-presidential aspirants. W.D.S.

G.P.U. See Appendix.

Grade.

A term used in public personnel administration to designate a group of position classes, no matter how differently the work they represent, that are compensated within the same salary range. Grades are usually designated by numbers as in the Federal Classification Act (of the U.S.A.) where 18 grades are set up under the general schedule and referred to as GS-1, through GS-18. M.J.Sch.

Grant-In-Aid.

An appropriation made in the U.S.A. by the Federal Government to the States (or by the States to local units) to assist them in performing their functions and to establish and equalize standards of governmental activities. Federal aid is specific with the States usually providing "matching-funds" for highways, Old Age Assistance, agricultural experimentation, vocational rehabilitation, etc. Through such grants the national government has greatly increased its control over many state activities. States aid local government through the return of state-collected taxes, grants for roads, education, public health, libraries, etc. J.O.H.

Grand jury.

A body of 5 to 23 persons officially constituted to determine whether evidence adduced before it by the state or assembled by its own investigations is sufficient to warrant the criminal trial of persons accused of a crime or implicated by the jury's investigations.

C.W.B.

Grant, Ulysses Simpson (1822—1885).

General and eighteenth President of the United States. Born at Point Pleasant, Ohio, Ulysses Grant graduated at West Point (1843), saw action in the Mexican War (1845-48), and peacetime duty in California and Oregon to 1854. Unsuccessful in private business, he re-entered the army (1861) and won many notable battles, became commanding field officer of all Federal forces, and received Lee's surrender at Appomattox Court House. Made General (1866) and Secretary of War (1867-68), Grant, as a Republican, was twice elected President of the U.S. (1867-77) on the strength of his war record and large Negro majorities from southern states. Personally honest and incorruptible, he proved unwise in dispensing patronage jobs, appointing old associates who imposed upon him, and made his administration one of the most scandalous on record. Adoption of the Fifteenth Amendment, settlement of the Alabama Claims with England, and the Panic of 1873 occurred during his Presidency. Following a lengthy world tour, Grant bid unsuccessfully for a third nomination, and lost his fortune through a partner's fraud, but recouped it by completing his **Personal Memoirs** just before his death from cancer.   K.E.D.

Great Britain

(England, Wales and Scotland).

The nation-state resulting from the union of England and Scotland, later embracing Ireland and then finally England, Scotland, and Northern Ireland. This is the mother country of the British Empire and Commonwealth. A vigorous and aggressive Great Britain furthered its overseas expansion and came into collision with French power. From 1756 through 1763 the Seven Years' War raged on four continents and on the high seas and resulted in extension of British power in India and in Canada. Domestically party government had already matured greatly, and with Sir Robert Walpole (1721—1742) as first Minister, standards of party discipline and of transition from control by one party to another took presently recognizable form. The industrial revolution began to transfigure the economy of Britain as steam driven machinery pumped the mines and produced textiles.

The United Kingdom of Great Britain and Ireland was formed by the Act of Union of 1800 merging the Irish and British Parliaments. Greater troubles than those Ireland offered were upon England, however, for the Napoleonic Wars had commenced. From 1793 until 1815, with limited interruption, British and French force again contended. In the midst of this the United States of America which had risen in successful rebellion against Britain in 1775, again were engaged in war with the mother country. France finally was defeated by a grand alliance of which Britain was a part and the Congress of Vienna, which designed the peace, provided a power balance preventing general war in Europe for almost 100 years.

Following this great upheaval a period of domestic reform obtained. The rotten borough system was rectified to some degree and the franchise was extended in 1832 to include all occupiers paying 10 pounds a year in rent. This did not affect most of the working class, however. There was some reduction in the corruption of local government, and a revised Poor Law was passed in 1834 with all industrial production increased and the competition for international markets advanced.

Externally the Empire increased and Englishmen enjoyed a sense of superiority. This did not compensate for the extreme depression of the lower classes, and in response to this the Labour Party began to take form, starting as the Fabian Society in 1884. The Conservative and Liberal Parties advanced programs of social reform and by 1911 an extensive plan of social insurance was made available in Britain.

With the ascent of imperial German power, internation collision occurred and Great Britain became one of the Allies in the first World War. While devoting maximum effort to that conflict Britain was faced also with another rebellion in Ireland and had to move forces there in 1916. In 1921 a treaty was negotiated recognizing Ireland as a free state in the British Empire with dominion status, Northern

Ireland being free to join Eire if she chose. Later Eire withdrew from the Empire.

The aftermath of the war brought severe economic depression to Britain and a strengthening of the Labour Party.

The resurgence of German power brought the second World War and Britain again was allied against Germany. Economically Great Britain did never fully recover from the drain of these two major wars. The Labour Party enjoyed brief power. It extended the social insurance plans and nationalized some industries. Substantially these programs continue.

At the close of the second World War many portions of the British Empire sought independence, either totally or within the Commonwealth relationship. Most significant among these was the division of India into the separate republics, in 1947, of India and Pakistan, both remaining within the Commonwealth. The Union of South Africa withdrew completely in 1961. Steadily the former imperial relationship is altering so that more of the old colonies will attain a status akin to that of Canada and Australia. The mother country is now hard pressed in the field of competition for industrial markets and while striving to retain Commonwealth bonds also wished to forge firmer economic links with the European continents. M.P.S.

Greater East Asia Co-Prosperity Sphere.

A term used by Japanese leaders beginning in 1940 to designate the projected economic and political bloc in East Asia under Japanese leadership. It would be based upon the Japanese yen and the Japanese military machine, and its ideology was embodied in the mottoes "Asia for the Asiatics" and "The Eight Corners of the World under One Roof," the latter taken from the Shinto classics and implying the hegemony of the Japanese Emperor. The Greater East Asia Ministry was established in the Japanese Government in November, 1942, placing Japan's diplomacy in East Asia under military domination. The dream was ended with Japan's defeat in 1945, but during the past few years, Japan has been recovering some of the markets embraced in the former co-prosperity sphere. T.Mc.N.

Great Leap Forward.

Chinese Communist slogan first announced in 1958. Because of slackening momentum of economic growth in 1957, Great Leap Forward was to "remake everything." Economically, policy of "walking on two legs" to coordinate efforts in industry and agriculture, countryside and city, heavy and light industry, farming and herding. Introduced backyard furnaces, close planting, and deep plowing. All persons over 9 years of age compelled to do manual labor. Ideological reliability favored over technical competence. Remolding of society to be accomplished by commune system, the basic social unit organized along military lines. Within one year, all of Great Leap Forward's programs virtually broke down: commune system abandoned in all but name, backyard furnaces discarded, industrialization drive halted. Most importantly, failure to understand peasant, still bulwark of Chinese society, resulted in "foot dragging" and eventual wide-spread food shortages. H.G.S.

Great Wall, Chinese.

The 1,400 mile wall built in the Ch'in Dynasty (B.C. 221—207) north of China almost from Tibet to the sea near Peking to hold back incursions from the steppe nomads. It represents Chinese isolationism and centralized control. G.O.T.

Greece.

A constitutional monarchy located in the southern portion of the Balkan peninsula. Population (1961 census) 8,357,526. Area (including Crete and other islands) 130,918 square kilometers (50,547 square miles). Present constitution, promulgated January, 1952, provides for the exercise of executive power by the King's ministers and for the exercise of the legislative power by the unicameral Chamber of Deputies.

Post World War II developments have been largely concentrated in the political arena, with the major task being to establish a stable national government as a prerequisite to handling the problem of left-wing rebellions, and Greek relations with Britain, Cyprus, her Balkan neighbors, and the East and West in the Cold War context.

The political conjunction of loyalist governments and outside assistance (under the Truman Doctrine initially) led to the attainment of a relatively long-lived government under Konstantinos Karamanlis (1955 to date, with but one contest in 1961). This political stabilization has enabled Greece to resolve the Cyprus problem, improve her relations with Turkey, and align herself politically with the West in NATO, OECD, Council of Europe, and the European Economic Community.

Associate membership in the EEC marks a critical achievement in that it portends increasing attention to the problems of raising the standard of living and stimulating growth and activity throughout the whole of the Greek economy. P.J.C.

Greek Catholic Church.
Popular name of the Eastern Orthodox Church, which was the eastern branch of the imperial Christian Church of Rome from the death of the Emperor Theodosius in 395 A.D. to the Great Schism in 1054 A.D.; thereafter the established church of the Byzantine Empire, the Russian Empire, and many countries of eastern Europe; has persisted in the claim that it is the original and rightful imperial church from which the Roman Catholic Church broke away; untouched by the Protestant Reformation. Ch.C.M.

Greeley, Horace (1811—1872).
American newspaper man and political leader; founder and for 31 years editor of the New York **Tribune**; first affiliated with the Whigs, then with the Republicans, and finally ran for President in 1872 on a fusion ticket of Democrats and Liberal Republicans. Greeley's political thinking and writing were much influenced by Chartism (q.v.) and Fourierism (q.v.). He held and expressed strong anti-slavery views, but was not always consistent in support of Lincoln and the Republican administration in the Civil War.
Ch.C.M.

Greenbackism.
A popular name given originally to the paper currency issued in the U.S.A. under the Legal Tender Act of 1862 to aid in the financing of the Civil War. Two third-party movements, organized to induce the U.S. Congress to issue more greenbacks, were the Greenback Party of 1875 and the Greenback-Labor Party of 1878.

Green Corn Rebellion (1917).
Named after the rebels' proposed main item of diet and its concurrence with the season of the Shawnee Green Corn celebration, the Green Corn Rebellion was a minor armed resistance against the U.S. Selective Service Act of 1917. A few hundred economically depressed southeast central Oklahoma farmers were lured into rebellion by joining the Working Class Union, which had been reactivated by Industrial Workers of the World agitators. Their goal, which was to march to Washington and take over the government in order to stop U.S. participation in World War I and halt the draft, was thwarted by the local civil law enforcement authorities. J.A.E.

Green, Thomas Hill (1836—1882).
The leading exponent of British idealist political philosophy, Fellow of Balliol, and critic of empiricism and utilitarianism. He was much influenced by the thought of Rousseau, Kant, and Hegel; in his **Lectures on the Principles of Political Obligation** he transformed Rousseau's vision of the general will into the conception of a common good in which individuals may find their full and harmonious satisfaction, and on this foundation he based his theories of rights, political obligation, and state intervention. J.W.Ch.

Greenland. See Appendix.

Gregory VII.
Belongs to the most conspicuous as well as the most significant Popes of the Church. As soon as he assumed office in 1073, he initiated a series of radical Church reforms aiming with them to eliminate corruption among the clergy and establish the supremacy of ecclesiastic over temporal power. While the second Council of his reign was in session in 1075, dealing with his ideas on Church reform, he pub-

lished his **Dictatus Papae (Pastoral Rule)** in which he articulated with lucidity in twenty-seven articles the divinity and infallibility of the Papal office and its sovereignty over the entire Christian society both secular and sacral. His uncompromising stand brought him into conflict with civil authorities. Henry IV of Germany continued to make ecclesiastic appointments, despite the fact that Gregory forbade this to civil authorities in his reforms. Gregory challenged Henry's appointments, who deposed then the Pope (1076), while the Pope—in retaliation—excommunicated Henry. This led the German princes to revolt against Henry and forced him to submit to the Pope and ask for his pardon which was granted. Henry let himself be excommunicated again in 1080. He set up an anti-Pope, besieged Rome, and forced Gregory to flee to Salerno, where the latter died. Gregory's significance lies in his strenuous attempt to reduce secular authority into an auxiliary of the Church to aid in its task of the salvation of souls, which initiated the struggle between Church and State lasting several centuries, weakening Christendom, discrediting Christianity, and leading ultimately to the Protestant reformation.
V.Z.

Gromyko, Andrei.
Born 1909 Starye Gromyki near Minsk, Byelorussia. Graduated Minsk Institute of Economics 1934, studied at Moscow Lenin Institute of Economics 1934-36. Lecturer in economics, 1937-38. Foreign Ministry posts since 1939, including Ambassador to U.S. 1943-46; participant Teheran, Yalta, Potsdam, Dumbarton Oaks, and San Francisco Conferences; representative to UN Security Council 1946-48. USSR Supreme Soviet since 1946, Party Central Committee since 1956.
W.A.

Gross National Product.
The money value of the nation's total output of final goods and services (including additions to and replacement of capital) for a given time period, usually a year. Also viewed as the total of business, household, and government expenditures, plus net foreign investment, for the final output of goods and services.
T.S.

Grotewohl, Otto (1894—   ).
Prominent Social Democrat who took decisive part in the 1946 establishment of the Communistic Socialist Unity Party (q.v.) in the Soviet Zone of Germany; co-chairman, 1946-54, member of Politburo 1946—. Minister President of (East) German Democratic Republic (q.v.), 1949—. Deputy Chairman, State Council, 1960—. In recent years lost his influence due to sickness and Social Democratic background.
J.B.M.

Group.
This word has a wide variety of uses not only in the social sciences but in other sciences as well, and it is used both as noun and verb. In political research it may be used in a categorical sense to refer to individuals linked together in accordance with one common characteristic as in a statistical table arranging people by sex or age. It may be used to arrange activities of individuals proposing a policy as in interest group. It may be used to describe a lobbying organization as in pressure group. It may be used to describe a family or other intimate face-to-face associations as in primary group. It may be used as a heuristic device to separate those who favor and oppose particular political objectives as in A. F. Bentley's **The Process of Government** (1908). It may be used to identify particular interests deserving legal representation in government as in guild socialist theory.
R.W.T.

Group Libel Laws.
Common law libel today protects such groups as corporations, co-partnerships, non-profit associations, etc. on grounds of personality and substance (property). Class defamation laws are more effective to protect religious and so-called racial groups. These statutes prohibit publication which may incite general hatred or ridicule and/or present a danger to the peace. Although a state group libel statute was upheld by the U.S. Supreme Court, these laws are characterized by their infrequent use. Only four states have such statutes while an additional four prohibit group libel under their general libel laws.
W.F.G.

Gruening, Ernest.
Born February 6, 1887; U.S. Senate from 1956 (under Alaska-Tennessee Plan) until term ending 1965; Democrat—Alaska; Governor of Alaska from 1939 until 1953. R.A.B.

Guam.
Guam is the largest and southernmost of the Marianas (Ladrones) Islands in the Pacific Ocean. Discovered by Ferdinand Magellan on his circumnavigation of the globe in 1519 and formally claimed for Spain by Miguel Legaspi in 1565. At that time Guam was 70 days sailing time from Spain and thus important as a stopover point during 333 years of Spanish rule. Wars between the native Chamorros and the Spanish reduced the population from an estimated 40,000 to 3,678 in Guam's first census of 1710.

The Spanish American War was fought in the Pacific with the U.S.S. Charleston under the command of Captain Henry Glass, U.S. Navy, leading three transports into Guam. The governor, the captain of the port, and other persons were obliged to surrender and Guam was placed under the administration of the only American (naturalized) on Guam, Francisco Portusach. Classified as an unorganized United States possession until the United States Congress passed the Organic Act (P.L. 630, 81st Congress), Section 4 (a) of which added a new section to the Nationality Act which conferred United States citizenship on the "citizens of Guam." U.S. policy has developed the people's capacity for self-government by way of a unicameral Guam Congress of 21 members popularly elected every 4 years. Administration since 1949 has been under the Department of Interior.
B.J.L.S.

Guantanamo.
United States naval base in Cuba. Under an agreement of 1903, Cuba leased without limit of time to the United States an area at Guantanamo Bay for use as a naval base. The lease provided that while the United States recognized the ultimate sovereignty of Cuba in the area, the Republic of Cuba consented to the exercise by the United States of complete jurisdiction and control over and within the area. Later, by the treaty of 1934, it was agreed that "Until the two contracting parties agree to the modification or abrogation of the stipulations of the agreement" for the Guantanamo base, the provisions of the 1903 treaty would remain in effect.
O.S.

Guatemala.
Northernmost of the Central American countries, the Republic of Guatemala has an area of 42,042 square miles and a population of approximately 3,759,000. Once part of the Mayan civilization, it was under Spanish control from 1524 to 1821. Part of Mexico for a time, Guatemala joined in forming the United Provinces of Central America, then became independent after 1838. Guatemalan political history from then until the Second World War period was dominated by four dictators: Rafael Carrera, Justo Rufino Barrios, Manuel Estrada Cabrera, and General Jorge Ubico. Juan Jose Arevalo, elected president in 1944, was beset by political and social troubles under the liberal constitution of March, 1945 but completed his term in office. Colonel Jacobo Arbenz Guzman's government, successor to Arevalo's, was reportedly communist-infiltrated and was overthrown by a Honduras-based revolt led by Colonel Carlos Castillo Armas, in 1954. His government rescinded many of its predecessor's programs, and a conservative constitution was drawn up in 1956. His assassination in 1957 made Vice President Luis Gonzales Lopez provisional president; after election troubles, General Miguel Ydigoras Fuentes became president in 1958, as leader of the Democratic Reconciliation Party. L.C.D.

"Guided Democracy."
Western democracy had been found inapplicable in Indonesia because, as President Sukarno explained, it would require a certain amount of literacy and prosperity that Indonesia did not yet possess. In 1957, he introduced the concept of Democracy with Leadership (Guided Democracy) in implementing among State organs the traditional principles of **gotong-rojong** (mutual help), **musjawarah** (deliberations) and **mufakat** (agreement after consultation). Stress was laid on guidance of the leader in reaching decisions after

consultation but without voting and on representation of "functional groups" (such as peasants, laborers, industrialists, etc.). S.S.H.

Guild Socialism.
A cooperative form of socialism combining large-scale state ownership of the means of production with their administration by guilds (trade unions). Originated in England around 1900. Its chief advocate was G. D. H. Cole (1889—1959), a member of the Fabian Society, who stressed that the "public sector" of industry "must be large enough to set the tone for the rest, leaving private industry to operate within a framework of public enterprise, rather than the other way around." J.D.

Guilt by association.
The idea of making a person responsible for his views as expressed by his close associates individually or as a group and considered to be inimical to the government. This was exemplified in the U.S.A. during the 1950's. In Adler v. Board of Education, 342 U.S. 485 (1952), the Court held that government may properly inquire into the kind of company teachers keep and may impose a requirement of nonmembership in "subversive" organizations as a requisite condition for continued public employment. B.N.

Guinea, Republic of.
A country in West Africa, with its capital at Conakry. It has an area of some 95,000 square miles and a population of approximately 3,000,000. Formerly one of the eight colonies of French West Africa and an overseas territory in the French Union, it emerged as an independent state on October 2, 1958. It has since joined the Union of African States and the Casablanca Bloc.

The French penetrated what is now the Republic of Guinea in the nineteenth century, dominating the coastal areas first and only later the Fulani, a tribe of sedentary Negroes in the Fouta-Djallon Highlands. The Fulani accepted French "protection" in 1881, and ten years later France created the Colony of French Guinea. The present boundaries of the state were fixed in 1904.

The present constitution of the republic establishes a unitary government with a National Assembly and a popularly elected president, who serves both as chief of state and as prime minister. He names the ministers, who are responsible to him; negotiates treaties; and serves as the head of the army. Effective political power resides in the **Parti Democratique de Guinee,** which is the only legal party in Guinea. Under its leadership and that of M. Sekou Toure, President of the Republic, this West African state has followed a policy of positive neutralism and strident Pan-Africanism. F.H.G.

Gumbatsu (a.f. Gunbatsu).
The military groups or cliques in Japan, referring particularly to the groups which arose between World War I and World War II. In the 1920's and 1930's groups of army officers began to play an important role in Japanese politics, culminating in the seizure of power by the military in the late 1930's. The basis of **Gumbatsu** strength partly derived from the traditional prestige of the **samurai,** or military class of pre-Meiji Japan. In the late 19th century elements of this class transformed themselves into a modern military officer class. At the same time, a system of general army conscription brought new young officers of peasant origin into the army. By the close of World War I these officers began to assume increasing roles in military politics. One of the most important groups was the League of Imperial Young Officers **(Kokoku Seinen Domei),** basically opposed to the capitalistic, commercial profiteering **Zaibatsu,** peasant-oriented, and intensely nationalistic. Their leader and idol was General Araki Sadao, a peasant who rose to be President of the Imperial Military Academy. The **Gumbatsu,** in collaboration with secret societies and other dissatisfied radical elements, engaged in acts of political terrorism and power plays, resorting frequently to assassination. In Manchuria the military cliques precipitated incidents leading to the unauthorized takeover of that Chinese province. In

1932, the Blood Brotherhood League initiated a series of atrocities involving the assassination of Premier Inukai, bomb-throwing and an attempted military takeover. Again, in 1936 a wave of terror launched by the **Gumbatsu** struck Tokyo, but as before the plot itself failed. The political repercussions, however, led to the virtual collapse of civil authority, and the Army achieved ascendancy in government.

S.S.

H

Habeas Corpus.
Literally translated, this means "you have (or should seize) the body." The concept is derived from old English law and impels law enforcement officers to bring an individual before the court to test the validity of his imprisonment or other restrictions on his freedom of movement. In essence, it provides that one may not be imprisoned for extended periods of time unnecessarily. M.J.S.

Hacha, Emil (1872—1945).
Czech jurist, elected third president of Czechoslovakia after Benes' resignation in October 1938; recognized as such by Benes who wrote official letter of congratulation. Summoned to Berlin by Hitler on March 14, 1939 and browbeaten into agreeing to the German-controlled Protectorate of Bohemia and Moravia, of which Hacha served as president. Although the record indicates that Hacha served the Czech people to the best of his ability under tragic circumstances, the Communists (with the concurrence of the non-Communist parties in the postwar "National Front") marked him as a traitor, and he was beaten to death, without trial, in a Prague jail in 1945. K.G.

Haganah (Hebrew: protection).
Secret army of self-defense and resistance to British rule in Palestine; forerunner of present Israel army after statehood was achieved. S.H.

Hague Peace Conferences
(1899, 1907).
The Tsar of Russia proposed an international conference for the agreed reduction of armaments 24 August, 1898. The conference met at the Hague (May-July, 1899) and completed three conventions and three declarations. The most important achievement was the creation of a Permanent Court of Arbitration which consisted of a panel of leading experts nominated by the signatories. Arbitration was purely voluntary, each party choosing two from the panel and the arbitrators selecting a fifth member. The use of international commissions of inquiry was recommended. A single code of land warfare was established and the Geneva Convention of 1864 applied to war at sea. Promises were made to prohibit the use of poison gas, expanding bullets and to abstain from bombing for a five-year period. The Russian proposal that existing armed forces and budgets should be limited to their existing size did not gain acceptance.

The second conference was again proposed by Russia, following an earlier initiative by President Theodore Roosevelt. The three conventions of 1899 were revised and ten new treaties signed. The subjects covered were: the pacific settlement of international disputes, the limitation of the employment of force for the recovery of contract debts, the opening of hostilities, the law and customs of war on land, the rights and duties of neutral powers and persons, the status of enemy merchant ships at the outbreak of hostilities, the conversion of merchant ships into warships, the laying of automatic submarine contact mines, bombardment by naval forces in time of war, a convention of maritime war using the principles of the Geneva Convention, the right of capture in naval war, the creation of an International Prize Court (never ratified), and the rights and duties of neutral powers in naval war.

British efforts to secure arms limitation was wrecked by German Foreign Minister von Bulow's announced decision (April 30) to veto any proposals for disarmament at the Hague. Germany also led the way in rejecting compulsory arbitration. Politically, the deadlock resulted from the German belief that a large navy was essential to her prestige as a great power and the British belief that naval superiority was essential to her superiority. The lesser powers objected to any limitations which kept them in a state of permanent inferiority. C.B.J.

Haiti.
A West Indian republic, Haiti comprises the western third of the island of Hispaniola, has an area of 10,714 square miles and a population of 3,505,000. Discovered in 1492, it was first Spanish and then French; a

226

Negro slave revolt in 1791 was led by Toussaint L'Ouverture, their famous leader, later imprisoned by Napoleon in France, where he died. Haiti became independent in 1804; Jean Jacques Dessalines, commander-in-chief of the revolt's forces, was made governor general. His assassination in 1806 resulted in anarchy and division. Haiti, later united, became burdened with external debt and internal troubles and in 1915 the United States intervened to restore order. Its military occupation ended in 1934; United States control of Haiti's fiscal affairs in 1947. The first Negro president after United States military occupation began was Dumarsais Estime, who was ousted and exiled in 1950. General Paul Magloire became president later; in 1956 he was ousted and a period of rapid governmental change ensued. Francois Duvalier became president in 1957; a new constitution was promulgated on December 19, 1957. Duvalier, having established a personal dictatorship, claimed a second term in 1961, after Assembly elections. L.C.D.

Haj Amin el Husseini.

Mufti of Palestine, Haj Amin el Husseini led the Arab nationalist fight against creation of the state of Israel. Fleeing Palestine in 1936 following widespread Moslem violence, he directed pro-Nazi and anti-Jewish propaganda to the Moslem world from Germany during World War II. In 1946 he became head of a new Arab Higher Committee which later on directed the war against Israel from Egypt. Although still active in Moslem activities, he has been eclipsed in influence by Nasser and the creation of separate independent states in the Moslem world. E.T.O.

Halifax, First Marquis of,
George Savile (1633-95).

English statesman and political thinker. Although admittedly patriotic and independent in judgment, he was colloquially termed "the trimmer" because of his pragmatic methods in practical politics. Consistently, his theory involved (1) a criticism of "fundamentals" and principles as fictions supporting selfish pressures and (2) foreshadowing the modern critics of "interest struggle politics," an attack upon political parties and democracy as "a conspiracy against the nation" because of their intensification of differences. Constructively — predating Mostesquieu — he supported the presumed mixed character of the British Monarchy as containing built-in safeguards against interest conflict.

J.P.D.

Halleck, Charles A.

Born August 22, 1900; U.S. House of Representatives from 74th Congress and reelected to succeeding Congresses; Republican—Indiana; Majority Leader in 80th and 83rd Congresses; Minority Leader in 86th and 87th Congresses. R.A.B.

Hallstein Doctrine. See Appendix.

Hamilton, Alexander (1757—1804).

Born in West Indies. Educated at King's (now Columbia) College. Served under Washington as military secretary and regimental commander during battle of Yorktown. Co-author (with Madison and Jay) of **Federalist,** a collection of articles in New York press in 1787-88 advocating ratification of U.S. Constitution. Held to be best economic interpretation of politics. As immigrant, he had no sectional ties; thus, favored strong central government, a President elected for life with veto power over all national legislation. As first secretary of treasury, most influential in shaping future national policy (cf. reports on public credit, national bank, and manufactures). But he failed to fathom American society and its democratic character. Sacrificed own reputation by opposing John Adams, very popular President. Was mortally wounded by Aaron Burr in a duel in 1804. H.G.S.

Hammarskjold, Dag
(Hjalmar Agne Carl)
(1905—1961).

Born July 29, 1905. Served as a university professor and Swedish government official rising to be deputy Foreign Minister and a Cabinet member. Elected second Secretary-General of the U.N. (1953) and reelected (1957). A skilled negotiator he increased significantly the power and prestige of the office. Died September 18, 1961.

V.R.I.

Hammurabi, Code of.

Laws and usages collected and compiled by Hammurabi, King of Babylon, about 2100 B.C. One of the principal sources of our knowledge of the nature of ancient societies. The Code of Hammurabi undoubtedly served as a model for many subsequent legal codes in the ancient world and was a potent factor in the development of legal ideas and systems. Ch.C.M.

Hand, Learned (1872—1961).

Judge of the United States Court of Appeals for the Second Circuit (1924-51); senior judge of his court (1939-51); and judge of the United States Court for Southern District of New York (1909-24). Although Learned Hand was acknowledged for many years as a great American judge, he was destined not to be elevated to the Supreme Court. Over a span of forty-two years as judge he wrote approximately 1,800 decisions, which Mr. Justice Frankfurter described as "an enduring source of truth-seeking and illumination." His contribution in the law was especially noteworthy in the fields of copyright, monopoly, and constitutional law. His reinterpretation of the clear and present danger test became the basis of the Supreme Court's decision in the key case of **Dennis v. United States** (1951). His noted stylistic brilliance is clearly manifest in his **Spirit of Liberty: Papers and Addresses** (1952) and **The Bill of Rights** (1958). The Bill of Rights are not "eternal verities," he wrote, since they "are emptied of the vital occasions which gave them birth, and become moral adjurations, the more imperious because inscrutable." P.B.

Hansard, Parliamentary Debates or Official Record.

The near verbatim record of debates in United Kingdom Parliament. This has been an official government publication only since 1909, although there was support from public funds beginning in 1855. Publication of **Parliamentary Debates** was started as a private venture by William Cobbett in 1803, and it became known as "Hansard" when T. C. Hansard became the publisher commencing with the 1813 volume. The period 1066-1803 is covered in Cobbett's **Parliamentary History**, compiled from earlier histories and other sources. Other countries with similar parliamentary systems also publish this type of record, and there is a tendency to apply the term Hansard to them even though it may not be the official title. R.H.B.

Hara, Takeshi (1856—1921).

Lawyer and journalist. In 1918 he became the first commoner prime minister. Concentrated on establishing and developing party politics in Japan. Assassinated in Tokyo on November 4, 1921. H.U.

Harding, Warren Gamaliel (1865—1923).

Twenty-ninth President of the United States. Born on a farm at Blooming Grove, Morrow County, Ohio, Warren Harding was educated at an academy, Ohio Central College (1879-82), studied law briefly, and taught school, before he bought the **Marion Star** (1884) which he edited for many years. Urged on by his wife and friends, Harding entered Ohio politics as a protege of Senator Joseph B. Foraker. State senator (1900-1904), Lieutenant-Governor (1904-06), defeated for Governor (1910), he was elected to the U.S. Senate (1915-21) as a conservative Taft Republican supporting a protective tariff and the Eighteenth Amendment. A dark-horse candidate of mediocre abilities, he won the Republican nomination (1920) and the Presidency, a post beyond his powers. As President (1921-23), he opened the first great international conference to limit armaments, but otherwise weakend the presidential office by appointing incompetent friends to high office and deferring to the Senate on foreign policy. He died suddenly while on a western speaking tour before the great scandals involving naval oil reserves, alien property, the Veterans' Bureau, and the Department of Justice, became public knowledge. K.E.D.

Hare System.

A non-partisan election system designed to provide representation proportional to the numerical weight of voting groups. Proposed in 1857 by Thomas Hare, an Englishman, it was adopted between 1915 and 1948 by approximately two dozen American cities, including Cleveland (1921-31), Cincinnati (1926-57), Toledo (1943-49), New York (1936-47), Yonkers (1938-48), and Worcester (1948-60). Ruled invalid in Michigan (Kalamazoo, 1918-20) and California (Sacramento, 1920-21), all other cities except Cambridge, Massachusetts, have now dropped the plan. Known as the "single transferable vote" system, voters express preferential choices by marking numbers on ballots opposite candidates listed alphabetically and without party designation. Each ballot finally counts for one candidate only, but those not needed to elect a preferred candidate, or belonging to candidates eliminated because of low total votes, are transferred to others according to expressed order of preferences. Proponents claim the Hare system assures better minority representation, more effective voting, greater voter interest, and reduced costs. Those opposed argue it promotes minority bloc voting, helps elect extremists, eliminates area representation, confuses voters, and delays final vote tabulation. C.F.N.

Harlan, John Marshall (1899—).

Associate Justice of the Supreme Court of the United States. He was named to the Court by President Eisenhower in 1955 to succeed the late Robert H. Jackson. He served briefly (1954-55) as Judge of the United States Court of Appeals for the Second Circuit subsequent to a distinguished law practice, highlighted by defense of the du Pont Company and the Imperial Chemical Industries, Ltd., in important anti-trust suits. During World War II he served as Colonel in the Army Air Force and was decorated several times. He is the grandson and namesake of the Associate Justice of the Supreme Court who served from 1877 to 1911 and who was the sole dissenter in **Plessy v. Ferguson** in 1896. Thus far, Justice Harlan's decisions have adhered rather closely (especially in civil liberty cases) to Justice Frankfurter's philosophy of judicial self-restraint. He wrote the Court's opinion in the key case of **Barenblatt v. United States** (1959).
P.B.

Harnessed Vote.

It is the vote given by a person for someone on whom the voter is economically dependent. In the rustic northeastern Brazilian towns the farmer (or landlord) commands such a vote either for himself or candidates of his choice. Until recently the voters were kept in a kind of corral and then taken to the ballot places to make sure that they would vote for the slate for which the landlord wanted them to vote. Unified ballot forms were for the first time used in the elections of 7 October 1962 with the names of all candidates appearing on a single sheet. Notwithstanding this precaution the harnessed vote did not disappear completely. A.F.Mo.

Harrington, James (1611—1677).

English political philosopher. Born in Rand, Lincolnshire, and educated at Trinity College, Oxford. Following several years of travel and service in the Dutch Army, he returned to England and in 1646 was appointed to the suite of Charles I, despite his republican views. After Charles' death, he wrote **Oceana** (1656), an analysis of an English utopia that displeased Cromwell although it was dedicated to him. Political topics discussed in the work include rotation in office, vote by ballot, property (particularly land) as the basis of political power, restrictions on executive authority, and special methods of distributing landed property, so that the Oceana might be "an empire of laws and not of men." Charged with conspiracy by Charles II in 1661, he was imprisoned in the Tower of London. When no public trial was granted, he escaped to St. Nicholas Island near Plymouth, where he remained until his death. He lies buried alongside Sir Walter Raleigh in St. Margaret's Church, London.
R.F.H.

Harrison, Benjamin (1833—1901).

Twenty-third President of the United States, and grandson of President William Henry Harrison. Born at North Bend, Ohio and a graduate of Miami University (1852), Benjamin Harrison was admitted to the Cincinnati bar (1853), moved to Indianapolis, and became one of America's highest paid corporation lawyers. His legal

229

practice and Civil War service as Colonel and brevet Brigadier General led to political preferment. Narrowly defeated for Governor of Indiana (1876), Harrison served one term as a Republican U.S. Senator (1881-87) advocating civil service, sound money, and big navy measures. Defeated for re-election, he received the Presidential nomination in 1888 and ousted Democratic President Grover Cleveland who received more popular votes. As President, Harrison allowed Congress to govern, signed the Sherman Silver Act and high McKinley Tariff, but the first meeting of the Pan-American Congress (1889) was the most notable event of his administration. Defeated by Cleveland for re-election, he resumed legal practice.

K.E.D.

Harrison, William Henry (1773—1841).

Major General and Ninth President of the United States. Born on Berkeley Estate, Charles City County, Virginia, William Henry Harrison attended Hampden-Sidney College, and won military fame as an Indian fighter in the Northwest Territory (1791-98) and as the Commander of the Army of the Northwest in the War of 1812. He won victories at Tippecanoe (1811) and the Battle of the Thames (1813). Aided by his military record, Harrison launched a political career as Secretary of the Northwest Territory (1798), Delegate to Congress (drafting Land Law of 1800), and first Governor of Indiana (1801-12), before service as U.S. Representative (1816-19), Senator (1825-28), and Minister to Colombia (1828-29). Defeated for President (1836) by Martin Van Buren, Harrison in turn defeated Van Buren (1840) and became the first Whig President, but died of pneumonia after one month in office, the shortest term on record. K.E.D.

Hartford Convention.

A meeting of delegates at Hartford, Connecticut, December 15, 1814, to discuss the protection of New England interests in relation to the War of 1812. The convention opposed the war, the federal naturalization policies and the ease with which new states were being admitted to the Union by the U.S. Congress. It proposed that the defense of each state be left to the state itself and suggested seven amendments to the Constitution. It did not suggest that the Union be dissolved.

J.E.R.

Hassan II, King of Morocco.

First son of King Mohammed V, he was born in 1928 and educated in his country and France. He became army chief of staff after Morocco's freedom in 1956, vice-premier in 1960, and king as well as premier after his father's death in 1961. An uncertain neutralist in foreign affairs, in 1963 he shifted his base from the Istiqlal Party to a Royalist Front to combat the right and left and to maintain his place as a nationalist king. Constitutionally, he supports a mixture of representative, plebiscitary and monarchical principles. P.F.P.

Hawaii.

Hawaii, America's fiftieth and newest State, was an independent kingdom in 1893 when occupied by American naval forces through the connivance of local American residents and the United States Government. Until annexation in July of 1898, Hawaii was governed as a republic under the leadership of local Americans.

From 1900 until statehood in 1959, Hawaii was organized as an organic territory of the United States with its own elected legislature. The Governor and other executive officials were appointed by the President of the United States. Hawaii's territorial history falls into three periods. The first, which saw waves of immigrants from the Orient and the native Polynesian population governed by a tightly knit "haole" (Caucasians of North European origin) oligarchy lasted until the beginning of World War II. Military government ruled during the second period which was ended in 1945. The postwar era was a period of transition in politics and economics resulting in the breakdown of the strong Republican oligarchical hold on the islands and the political emergence of second generation Americans of Asian ancestry primarily through the Democratic Party.

In the 1950's two-party competition became a reality with a slight majority of voters tending to favor the

Democrats. Politics in Hawaii today is influenced by a strong labor union, the International Longshoremen's Workers Union; the large financial companies known as the Big Five, who still control the sugar, pineapple, and major shipping interests; the new and burgeoning middle class composed of haoles from the mainland, and second and third generation Asian-Americans; and new economic forces such as tourism, military expenditures, and light industry. L.H.F.

Hawley-Smoot Act of 1930.
A tariff schedule which raised duties on many items to their highest point in United States tariff history. The Act was outstanding also in the protection afforded agricultural products. More than a thousand economists urged President Hoover to veto the legislation, but the President signed it into law, hoping to remedy the worst features through certain flexible clauses it contained. Within two years 45 foreign countries raised their tariff rates, largely in retaliation against the Hawley-Smoot Act. Many economists have asserted that the Act hastened and deepened the effect of the world-wide depression of the 1930's. G.B.H.

Haya de la Torre, Victor Raul.
Latin American statesman. Born in Trujillo, Peru, Feb. 22, 1895. Education: Univ. de San Marcos, Univ. de Cuzco, Oxford, and London School of Economics. President of university student federation in Lima, 1919. Founded the American Revolutionary Popular Alliance (Apristas), a political movement in Mexico City in 1924. Co-founder, Center for Latin American Studies in Paris. Candidate for Presidency of Peru, 1931. Political prisoner in Lima, 1932-33. Candidate for Presidency, 1936. Apristas outlawed as an aftermath. During 1936-45, Haya led Aprista clandestine opposition to the Lima government. In Oct. 1948, dictator General Odria began jailing all Apristas. Haya received asylum in the Colombian Embassy in Lima 1949-54. Candidate for Presidency, 1962. Indecisive vote led to military rule. M.A.

Hayes, Rutherford Birchard
(1822-1893).
Nineteenth President of the United States. Born in Delaware, Ohio, Rutherford B. Hayes graduated valedictorian at Kenyon College and received a Harvard law degree (1845). Practicing in Fremont, and Cincinnati, Ohio, before entering the Civil War and becoming a brevet Major-General, Hayes rose from City Solicitor to the U.S. House of Representatives (1865-67), and Governor of Ohio three times (1868-72; 1876-77) before his unique single electoral vote victory over the Democrat Samuel J. Tilden made him President (1877—1881). His strong, able, independent administration restored honesty to government, removed the last federal troops from the defeated South, re-established a sound monetary policy, asserted U.S. vital concern for a Central American canal, deployed federal troops in a railway strike, dealt fairly with Indian tribes, and deliberately forfeited second term prospects. Hayes was noted as a philanthropist, and a prison and educational reformer. K.E.D.

Hay-Pauncefote Treaty.
The second, and effective, of two treaties was signed on November 18, 1901 by the United States and Great Britain, superseding the Clayton-Bulwer Treaty and facilitating United States isthmian canal plans. L.C.D.

Headman.
In the village context, the liaison between the populace and Central Government's local representative (usually the District Officer). The Headman's degree of responsibility varies from mere conveyance of information on governmental policies to quasi-judicial and quasi-administrative functions, under the general supervision of the district administrator. The Headman may be selected either by vaguely democratic procedures within local social context (as in Thailand) or by direct appointment. M.W.W.

Hearing.
Originally the term applies to equity procedure and signifies the argument and consideration, preliminary ("interlocutory") or final, of a case.

Modern usage transfers this meaning of the term to proceedings before administrative agencies and tribunals, on the one hand, and to criminal proceedings on the other hand. In either case, the parties must be apprised of the nature of the cause, must have an opportunity to prepare their side of the case and be given a fair chance for presentation of that case. F.H.H.

Heartland Theory.
A political geographical concept that the nation which controls the heartland of Eastern Europe and Central Asia, an area encompassing 2/3 of the world's land mass, will command the world island of which it is the core area. Australia and the Americas were thus regarded as outlying islands. This concept of an empire based on land power, introduced by Mackinder, was developed and distorted by **Dr. Karl Haushofer** into the German **Geopolitik** with its emphasis on a propaganda for **lebensraum.** The theory is said to have influenced Hitler's policies as set forth in **Mein Kampf.**
R.J.S.

Hegel, Georg Wilhelm Friedrich.
Hegel was born, 1770, and raised in Stuttgart, Germany, the son of a minor public official. He received his doctorate degree in 1790 and a theological certificate in 1793 both from the University of Teubingen. He served as private tutor in Bern, then in Frankfort, until 1801. During this period he published a number of essays on Christianity which showed Kantian influence. From 1801 to 1807 he taught at the University of Jena and published the **Phenomenology of the Mind.** From 1801 to 1807 he was principal of a gymnasium in Nuremberg. While there he published his seminal **Science of Logic** (1812—1816) which contained his conception of the dialectic. During 1817 he was a professor at Heidelberg, publishing there the **Encyclopedia of the Philosophical Sciences.** From 1818 until his death in 1831 he lectured at the University of Berlin on the philosophy of history, religion, and art. In 1821 he published his **Philosophy of Right.** But the **Philosophy of History** and works on art and religion from this time were completed after his death from notes left by him and collected from students.

Hegel's contribution to political philosophy was based on his logic. According to the dialectic of history each civilization contains the seeds of its own negation and transcendence. Thus, social life is a continuing, restless process. In this process thought partakes, having relevance for that civilization. Like civilization itself, this thought is transcended by the new, passes into history, and becomes, then, the object of idle curiosity. Modern thought, in its concern with process and its emphasis on the historical contingency of all thought, is Hegelian in genesis. R.M.T.

Heimatrecht (Right of Homeland).
Right of the individual to his home and native land, a principle which forbids forced expulsions and mass deportations. Originally stated in the Charter of the German Expellees adopted in Stuttgart on August 5, 1950, Heimatrecht has been expounded as a principle of international law by German scholars, who point to provisions of the 1949 Geneva Convention and the United Nations Universal Declaration of Human Rights prohibiting expulsions such as took place at the close of World War II. The principle of **Heimatrecht** found widespread international support at the Saloniki meeting of the World Society of Refugee Affairs in October 1961.
K.C

Helvetius, Claude Adrien (1715-71).
A French philosopher, Helvetius advocated a form of utilitarianism and a theory of education which argued that genius could be developed by a system of rewards and punishments. His **De l'esprit** (1758) opposed Rousseau's ideas, and it led to conflict with the Church as well. It was censured by the Church, the Sorbonne and the Parlement de Paris in 1759 after which it was burned. R.W.T.

Henlein, Konrad (1898—1945).
Gymnastics teacher, founder and leader of Sudeten German Party, which polled 2/3 of the German vote in the 1935 Czechoslovak parliamentary election. Originally moderate in character, the S.G.P. came under increasing Na-

tional Socialist influence. Henlein fled to Germany during the Sudeten crisis of 1938 and was subsequently appointed **Gauleiter** of the Sudetenland. Committed suicide while in American custody in 1945. K.G.

Henry, Patrick (1736—1799).

Noted lawyer, orator and statesman, Patrick Henry led Virginia opposition to pre-revolutionary repressive British measures. Born May 29, 1736, in rural Virginia, Henry had brief farming and store-keeping careers before entering law practice at age 24. His insistence (Parson's Tobacco Case, 1763) on Virginia's law-making authority gained him early prominence. Elected in 1765 to the House of Burgesses, his resolutions condemning the Stamp Act for violating fundamental rights of self-taxation were in essence adopted later by the Stamp Act Congress. As delegate to both the First and Second Continental Congresses, Henry advocated raising armed forces. He briefly held a military commission. After helping frame the new Virginia Constitution, he served twice (1776-79 and 1784-86) as state governor. Henry declined participation in the 1787 Federal Convention and bitterly attacked the proposed new Constitution at the Virginia ratifying convention. In later years he appeared as counsel in many cases, including the famous **Ware v. Hylton** (1796). Death on June 6, 1799, prevented his return to the Virginia Assembly, to which he again had been elected. C.F.N.

Herriot, Edouard (1872—1957).

This "grand old man" of French politics served as mayor of Lyons from age 33 until his death (except for World War II). A Senator at 40 and premier thrice (1924, 1926, 1932), he helped introduce the Geneva Protocol to the League, and during his last premiership cancelled German reparations to France. In the Petain cabinet from 1940 to 1942, Herriot was finally arrested by the Nazis when he declined Laval's offer to form a provisional government.

Having been president of the Chamber of Deputies in 1925 and from 1936 to 1940, Herriot served in the Fourth Republic as president of the National Assembly from 1947 to 1953, and thereafter was honorary president. As president of the Radical Socialist party since 1945 he leaned toward the Socialists and opposed any reconciliation with the Gaullists. Herriot favored a president who would not be a puppet, bitterly opposed the plan for a European Defense Community, and sought to prevent secession within the French Union. R.B.C.

Hertzog, James Barry Munnik (1866—1942).

He was born in the Cape Colony and became a judge in the Orange Free State. During the Boer War he was a general and was hostile to any British relationship. He served in the Union cabinet until 1912 when he organized the National Party and demanded South Africa's independence. Hertzog was prime minister in several coalition governments from 1924 to 1939, when he resigned because his efforts to stay out of war failed.

J.F.M.

Herut.

"Freedom," second largest Israeli political party, headed by Menachem Beigin. Founded 1948 as outgrowth of Irgun Zvai Leumi, anti-British underground movement. Pursues non-socialist, militant, foreign policies, including territorial demand for Israel on both banks of Jordan River. S.H.

Herzl, Theodor (1860—1904).

Founder of modern political Zionism and first president of World Zionist Organization. Born Budapest; dramatist and journalist, residing principally in Vienna. His **Jewish State** (1896) revolutionized Jewish world, led to convening of First World Zionist Congress in Basel, in 1897. The "Basel Platform" called for creation of a Jewish National Home in Palestine secured by public law. Conducted numerous negotiations until his death to achieve a Charter for a Jewish State guaranteed by the Great Powers. In accordance with his wishes, Herzl is buried on one of the hills (Mount Herzl) of Jerusalem. S.H.

Hess, Moses (1812—1875).

He is one of the initiators of Zionism. He propagated a spiritual type of socialism which first attracted Marx strongly, only to be soon opposed by the latter in favor of materialism. Hess proposed the establishment of a Jewish commonwealth in Palestine "in order to realize the historical ideal of our people, an ideal which is neither more nor less than the reign of God upon earth." V.Z.

Heuss, Theodor (1884—1963).

Dr. Heuss was twice elected to the presidency, the highest office of the Federal Republic of Germany and served as the first Federal President for ten years (1949—1959).

Theodor Heuss received his degree (Dr. rer.pol. 1905) at the University of Munich. Throughout his life he worked as journalist, editor, and during the Nazi era as a freelance writer and contributor for the Frankfurter Zeitung. From 1920 until 1933 he also was a lecturer in modern history and political science at the German Academy for Political Science. The Nazis dismissed him from the teaching profession because of his political affiliation and his service as a German Democratic Party member of the **Reichstag** (1924—1928 and 1930—1933).

After the collapse of the Third Reich he resumed his political activity and assisted in the building up process of the Free Democratic Party. In 1945 he became Minister of Education in Wuerttenberg-Baden and served in this capacity until the end of 1946. From June of 1946 until his election to the Presidency he was a member of the **Landtag** of Wuerttenberg-Baden. In 1947 he also was appointed as professor of political science and modern history at the Stuttgart Institute of Technology. In 1948 he was elected first chairman of the Free Democratic Party in West Germany and Berlin. He also served on the Parliamentary Council at Bonn which prepared the constitution for the Federal Republic.

Professor Heuss was a very prolific writer and has over forty books to his credit. E.W.

Heydrich, Reinhard (1904—1942).

Nazi leader and SS (Schutzstaffel) General. He joined the SS in 1931 after a brief military career. His ruthlessness brought him to Himmler's attention and to top positions in the Nazi police and intelligence network. In 1941 he was appointed Protector of Bohemia and Moravia and served until his assassination in 1942. G.K.

Hickenlooper, Bourke Blakemore.

Born July 21, 1896. U.S. Senator since November 1944; Republican—Iowa; Lieutenant Governor of Iowa 1938—1942; Governor of Iowa 1942—1944. R.A.B.

High Commissioner. See Appendix.

High Court of Justice.

See British High Court of Justice.

Himmler, Heinrich.

Born 1900, committed suicide 1945. Active Nazi since 1923. Headed SS (Schutzstaffel—black-uniformed "Protective Force," the terror backbone of the Nazi regime) which he used 1934 to suppress the SA (Sturmabteilung—Storm Troops), and the Gestapo (Secret Police), later all police forces. Responsible for the organized mass murder of Jews and other marked groups; controlled all concentration camps. J.B.M.

Hindenburg, Paul von (1847—1934).

German field marshal in World War I. Victor over the Russians at Tannenberg. President of Germany from 1925—1934, he appointed Hitler Chancellor of the Reich on January 30, 1933. R.A.B.

Hinduism.

Less a religion, more a way of life, Hinduism, which has existed for over four thousand years, defies precise definition. Its over four hundred million adherents, the majority of whom live in India, worship and believe in a variety of gods who form the Hindu pantheon, or in no god at all. Hindu schools of philosophy range from materialism to pantheism. Sacred books, e.g., the **Vedas,** the **Upanishads,** the **Ramayana** and the **Bhagavad Gita** illustrate the range of philosophical thought and guides to behavior. Hinduism's resilience and basic tolerance have enabled it to survive by incorporation of dissent rather than by combativeness. It was not as successful in its contact with Islam and Christianity. Especially under the pressure of militant attacks from Islam and Christian missionary activity, Hindu-

ism has undergone periodic reformist phases. Most important have been reformist movements founded in the nineteenth century by Ram Mohan Roy and Dayananda Sarasvati. Sarasvati's Arya Samaj achieved remarkable organizational and propaganda strength by the 1920's, at which time it linked itself with the independence movement. Many religious evils such as untouchability, discrimination based on caste have been abolished in the Constitution of independent India. Opposition still exists to these reforms, but the ground was prepared by Gandhi, and the inexorable trends of industrialization and urbanization are likely to radically affect Hinduism's remaining rigidity. A major contribution of Hinduism to political theory and policy is Kautilya's treatise, **Arthasastra** (c. 321—296 B.C.).
S.K.A.

Hirohito (1901—).
Formally installed as Crown Prince in 1916. In 1921 he became regent for his father. On December 25, 1926 he became the 124th Emperor of Japan.
H.U.

Hiroshima.
City in southwestern Japan. The first atom bomb used in warfare was dropped on Hiroshima by the United States Army Air Force on August 6, 1945, resulting in 78,150 persons killed, 37,425 injured, and 13,083 missing out of a population of 343,969. Two days later the Soviet Union declared war on Japan. On August 9 the United States dropped an atom bomb on Nagasaki, and on the following day the Japanese government offered to surrender.
T.Mc.N.

Hiss case.
Alger Hiss, at one time a high official of the U.S. Department of State, entrusted with responsible governmental missions, was accused in 1948 by Whittaker Chambers, a former Communist writer who had broken with the Communist party and become an editor of **Time**, of having transmitted classified information to agents of the Soviet Union. Under the statute of limitations, barring prosecution for acts committed more than six years prior to the indictment, Hiss could not be prosecuted as a spy. He was, however, convicted of perjury and sentenced to five years in prison.
J.D.

Histadrut.
"General Federation of Jewish Labor in Israel," founded 1920. Now largest labor, social welfare, mixed economic enterprise entrepreneur in country. Mapai, a political party, has largest representation in its membership.
S.H.

Historical Materialism.
It is that branch of the Marxist-Leninist Weltanschauung which offers a comprehensive theory of civilization and culture. It is defined by the Soviets as the application of dialectic materialism to society and history. Marx developed this view or theory from Hegel who made of history an all-embracing context of human activity, and from Feuerbach who maintained that "thought comes from being, not being from thought." In his **Paris Manuscripts of 1844** Marx (combining Hegel with English Economics) showed that the determinative dimension of human action in history is economics. In his **The German Ideology** (1846) (following Feuerbach), he declared that "life is not determined by consciousness but consciousness by life." In Marx's classic formulation of historical materialism (Preface to his **Critique of Political Economy,** 1859) "life" is economic activity. His disciples distinguished, rather crudely, between the economic "base" (production relationships) and the "superstructure" (culture, politics, philosophy, language, literature, etc.). Determinism was thus infused into Marx's outlook, although one could equally well show that the "base" is the expression of human labor (activity), the essence of **homo faber** as Marx sees him, which would make Marx's theory voluntaristic rather than deterministic. Engels' formulations followed the deterministic line of interpretation and remained the authentic source of Soviet Marxist philosophy. Stalin, in his **Five Letters on Linguistics** (1950), modified somewhat this determinism by developing the notion of an active super-structure, as well as exempting the Russian language from the super-structure. Stalin's modifications of historical materialism only increased the confusion.
V.Z.

Historic County.
A unit of local government in England and Wales which performs mainly judicial and ceremonial functions. In most cases boundaries are similar to those of the administrative counties. These were the Saxon shires, and that term is still commonly applied to them. R.H.B.

Hitler, Adolf.
Reich Chancellor and Fuehrer of Nazi-Germany (1933—1945), born on April 20, 1889 in Braunau am Inn, Austria, committed suicide with his wife Eva Braun on April 30, 1945 in his Fuehrerbunker in Berlin during the last hours of the "Third Reich,"—created by him on January 30, 1933 and destroyed through his megalomaniac wars of aggression for the purpose of subjugating Europe. The onetime Austrian paperhanger and corporal of World War I made his political career through a relentless and poisonous propaganda against the alleged world-wide conspiracy of international Jewry, Roman Catholics, Anglo-Saxons, and Bolshevists, allegedly aimed at the destruction of Germany. During the period of depression and unemployment in the Weimar Republic he organized "The National Socialist German Workers Party." Its program and his book "Mein Kampf" became the blueprint for his plan to gain political power. Hitler, though uneducated, had an outspoken gift for mass hypnosis by misusing constitutional rights under the democratic German system. He paired this instrument with the establishment of two huge paramilitary organizations the brown-shirt stormtroopers (SA) and the black-shirt elite guards (SS). The period of the abortive Bierhallen-Putsch in Munich (1923) was followed by his relentless propaganda for votes to the German Reichstag and the State legislatures. During this decade, Hitler succeeded to get political support from the army of unemployed, millions of middle class German burghers, low-echelon civil servants and ex-soldiers. But he could also enlist ultra-nationalistic and anti-democratic university professors and teachers as well as industrialists who did not want to miss the marches and bandwagons to the promised Greater German Reich. In his battle for power he was joined by such political "wizards" as the former Reich Chancellor Franz von Papen, former Reich Bank President Hjalmar Schacht and even non-German politicians who fought for their own political future. On January 30, 1933 the then German Reich President, aged former Field Marshal Paul von Hindenburg, appointed Hitler as Reich Chancellor. Other National Socialist leaders became cabinet members such as Hermann Goering (for Prussian State and Air Force), Wilhelm Frick (Interior), and Joseph Goebbels (Propaganda). For the sake of balance some cabinet posts went to members of other right-wing parties, among them to Franz von Papen (Vice-Chancellor), Konstantin von Neurath (Foreign Affairs), Lutz Schwerin von Krosigk (Finance), Alfred Hugenberg (Economic Affairs); —but they were dismissed in due course.

On February 27, 1933, the Reichstag was set on fire by Marinus van der Lubbe, an imbecile Dutch vagrant, but the real actors came from the ranks of the storm troopers—as Goering almost confessed in a secret Nuremberg interrogation. The Reichstag fire served Hitler as pretext—because of an alleged Communist threat—to abolish civil rights, political parties, labor unions, judicial review of arrests and searches. The all-powerful secret State Police (Gestapo), the SS Elite Guards, the massacre of political enemies as on June 30, 1934, and the concentration camps became the administrative tools of Hitler's dictatorial Fuehrer State. After the period of inner consolidation (1933—1938) and the preparation for the "Final Solution of the Jewish Question," Hitler started his plan to create the Greater Germar Reich: first the annexation of Austria (1938), the Sudetenland (1938), and the death coup against Czechoslovakia (1939). Then followed his wars of aggression against Poland, England, France (1939), Denmark, Norway, Holland, Belgium, Luxembourg (1940), Yugoslavia, Greece (1941). The aggression against the Soviet Union in 1941 was preceded by the Hitler-Stalin Pact (August 23, 1939) when both dictators tried to double-cross

each other in order to gain time. With Hitler's declaration of war against the United States (December 11, 1941), the Allied landing in North Africa (November 7, 1942) and the end of the battle of Stalingrad (January 31, 1943) Hitler's tide for conquest vanished. But before his suicide on April 30, 1945 millions of Allied and German soldiers had to die, six million European Jews were murdered—according to a plan laid down on January 20, 1942—more than 3000 Catholic priests in Europe were sentenced or deported to death, several thousand anti-Hitler Germans—among them the participants of the July 20, 1944 anti-Hitler plot—were sent to the gallows.
R.M.W.K.

Hlinka, Msgr. Andrej (1864—1938).

Slovak patriot priest and national hero. Active in struggle against Magyarization, he supported creation of Czechoslovakia, but later turned against the Prague government because of its centralist policies. As leader of the Slovak People's Party, sought fulfillment of 1918 Pittsburgh Agreement, in which Masaryk promised Slovakia legislative as well as administrative autonomy. This was achieved after Hlinka's death under his successor Msgr. Jozef Tiso. K.G.

Hobbes, Thomas (1588—1679).

English philosopher, b. at Westport, d. at Harwick. He was brought up by an uncle, a wealthy glover, at Malmesbury, and received his M.A. degree from Oxford in 1608. Hobbes earned his living as a tutor and travel companion of the sons of wealthy noblemen. In 1640 he left England to take up residence near Paris, where from 1646 to 1648 he tutored in mathematics the prince later to become Charles II. Having made peace with Cromwell, Hobbes returned to England in 1651. When the Stuarts were restored in 1660, he again came into favor with Charles II from whom he received a small pension which augmented the one awarded to him by another of his former students, the Earl of Devonshire.

Hobbes sought to explain man and society by the same principles of scientific explanation as were applicable in the world of nature, that is by the movement of particles according to deterministic mechanistic laws. Actually, he was unsuccessful in this endeavor. For in his numerous political writings, the best known of which is **The Leviathan, or the Matter, Form and Power of the Commonwealth, Ecclesiastic and Civil** (1651), he arrives at his deterministic scientific conclusions by a quite different method, that of psychological introspection. Among these conclusions were the following: Men are by nature so equal and motivated by such a restless desire for power that this state of nature leads to a war "of every man against every man," and to mutual self-destruction. To escape from this dire consequence men are forced to enter into a social contract in which every member declares: "I authorize and give up my right of government to this man or to this assembly of men on the condition that you give up the right to him, and authorize all his actions in like manner." Man's innate tendency to self-destruction can only be held in check by a government with absolute powers, one that itself is limited by no legal obligation, since it was no party to the legal social compact, but is merely its beneficiary.
G.V.W.

Ho Chi-minh (1890—   ).

(Originally—Nguyen Tat Tan, later changed to Nguyen Ai Quoc), is one of the founders of the Communist Party of Indo-China, President of the Democratic Republic of Vietnam (Northern Vietnam, dominated by the Communist Party). Ho Chi-minh was born in 1890 in Central Vietnam. During 1913—1916 Ho worked as a stevedore and seaman on French and English ships. In 1916—1917 he lived in England, and in 1917—1919 in the U.S.A. In 1924 he went to Moscow, and in 1925, while in Canton, where he joined the staff of Borodin, he founded a Communist oriented revolutionary Vietnamese organization, called the "League of Revolutionary Youth of Vietnam." In 1931 Ho was arrested by English police in Hong Kong and sentenced to 2-years imprisonment. In 1941, at the time of the Japanese invasion of Southeast Asia, Nguyen changed his name to Ho Chi-minh. He became chairman of the united front for the liberation of Vietnam. This unified Democratic front was named "Viet-Minh." After the collapse of Japanese rule, Ho Chi-minh's "Viet-Minh" started an armed struggle against the French in Indo-China. In 1951, the two leading organizations of Vietnam—the Viet-Minh and the more conservative Lien-Viet united into one Lien-Viet Front to continue the fight against the French. The Geneva Foreign Ministers conference in April-July, 1954 resulted in an agreement to cease fire in Indo-China, and on the division of the country into North and South Vietnam. Ho Chi-minh, Chairman of the Vietnam Workers' Party (heirs to the Communist Party of Vietnam), was also elected to the post of Secretary General of the Party, in 1956. V.P.P.

Holbach, Baron d', Paul-Henri Dietrich (1723—1789).

Political and social philosopher of German birth who settled in France; one of the leading encyclopaedists; patron of arts and sciences; intimate friend of Diderot, Buffon, Condorcet, Helvetius and Rousseau; translator of contemporary German scientific and technical writings. D'Holbach departed from Cartesianism by professing a dynamic theory of matter and life derived from Leibniz and Diderot. With Helvetius he contributed to the 18th-century materialist movement. As an atheist, he sought to eliminate religion from social and philosophical thought; as a sensualist-materialist and advocate of naturalism, he explained both the moral and social order by self-interest manifested in the general quest for pleasure and the tendency to avoid pain. His political system, which was erected on a legal code based on the social contract, attempted to provide for universal human needs. W.J.S.

Holmes, Oliver Wendell (1841—1935).

Associate Justice of the Supreme Court of the United States from 1902 to 1932. Distinguished in legal learning, intellect, and literary style, Holmes was the author of a number of dissenting opinions in the Supreme Court that later became the law of the land. Although his personal economic and social philosophy was conservative, his opinions often favored liberal state legislation because he was unwilling to substitute his judgment for that of state legislators on matters of social policy in the absence of a clear violation of specific language in the Constitution. After the middle 1930's the Supreme Court came to accept his view that legislatures should be allowed by the justices to experiment with social and economic legislation, but that they should be closely restrained in the regulation of civil liberties. E.L.

Holy Alliance.

Declaration of Christian principles signed September 26, 1815, by Austria, Russia, and Prussia, and later acceded to by all European rulers except the Pope and the Sultan. Though devoid of intrinsic significance, its importance derived from the application of the name to the international organization subsequently created by the great powers, by means of which the latter exercised a virtual government of Europe that preserved the peace for 100 years. P.J.F.

Holy See.

The Apostolic Seat in Rome. The Italian annexation of the Papal States in 1870 put an end to the temporal power of the Holy See, which had been exercised for more than 1,100 years. As a result of the extinction of its territory, the Holy See could no longer be regarded as a state. But on February 11, 1929, a treaty was signed between the Holy See and the Kingdom of Italy by whose terms the Vatican City was constituted as a territory under the sovereignty of the Holy See. Though the Lateran Treaty returned the Holy See to the society of nations, it is difficult to decide whether the statehood in this case is vested in the Holy See or in the Vatican City. It would appear, however, that the Lateran Treaty did create a new state and that the incumbent of the Holy See is its head. O.S.

Home Office.

A major department of the British central government headed by the Home Secretary, whose full title is Secretary of State for the Home Department. Its areas of administration include parliamentary elections, police supervision, citizenship applications, and review of by-laws enacted by local governments. R.H.B.

Home Rule.

The power, in the U.S.A., of municipalities (and in a few states, counties) to determine their own forms of government. Usually under provisions in State constitutions municipalities and counties may (1) draft, adopt and amend the charters providing for the organization and functions of government as desired by the people of the area; (2) with a minimum of state interference, exercise control over matters of local concern. Better drafted charters, more flexible government and lessened domination by rurally-elected legislatures have resulted.
J.O.H.

Homestead Act.

Signed by Lincoln, May 20, 1862, this first major domestic act of the Civil War Congress culminated movement that went back to colonial gifts of free land. Millions of acres were distributed in the old Northwest Territory after 1783 and Kentucky, Tennessee and other states sold land at low prices. In 1825 Senator Thomas Hart Bent of Missouri asked Congress to study the donation of land to new settlers. The Preemption Act of 1841 provided for the acquisition of land at about $1.25 an acre. Agitation continued in Congress with the result that homestead bills were introduced in 1846 by Andrew Johnson of Tennessee and Felix G. McConnell of Alabama. In 1848 the Free Soil party moved onto the national scene with a platform for free land for settlers as a public benefit. Four years later the Free Soilers asserted that ownership of "a portion of the soil" was "a natural right of all men." Meantime the popularity of the homestead idea was displayed unmistakably in 1849 when Senator Stephen A. Douglas of Illinois presented a bill to give 160 acres to any head of a family who would cultivate them for four years. Southern interests opposed the movement as a potential dilution of their political strength through immigration to new areas. Also many Easterners were opposed because of the prospective drain on the economy of their older region. Conversely anti-slavery forces, labor leaders and reformers, such as Greeley, threw themselves into the homestead cause. The Johnson bill was passed by the House as early as 1852 but the Senate, influenced by the older states' conservatism, blocked approval until 1860. Then Buchanan vetoed it as not only unconstitutional but also unfair to existing settlers and residents of the older states, and also as an invitation to vast speculation. Lincoln made Buchanan's veto an issue in the 1860 campaign and when Secession removed the Southerners from Congress, the free soil advocates renewed their long fight, this time behind an administration measure. It provided that 160 acres in free land could be acquired by actual settlers who lived on it for five years, terms which were somewhat liberally interpreted by local land officials. The Homestead Act made possible the rapid settlement of new areas to the west and thus was a major factor in developing the nation geographically, economically, socially and politically. I.Di.

Honduras.

A Central American republic with an area of 43,227 square miles and a population of 1,950,000, Honduras was discovered in 1502 and under Spain until 1821. Annexed by Mexico, and later a part of the United Provinces of Central America, Honduras became an independent republic in 1838. Honduras, El Salvador and Nicaragua joined in a confederation from 1849 to 1863. Subsequently, Honduras was involved in British-American rivalry in the area, and troubled by internal strife. Often subject to outside influences, Honduran political history has been turbulent. The administration of Tiburcio Carias Andino, longest in the country's history, ran from 1933 through 1948; his successor, Juan Manuel Galvez, retired in 1954. Julio Lozano Diaz assumed the presidency, and was ousted in 1956 by a three-man military junta. A new constituent assembly made Ramon Villeda Morales president; he took office in 1957. L.C.D.

Hook, Sidney (1902—).

Sidney Hook of N.Y.U. is by profession a philosopher who has contributed greatly to the discussion of political theory both through his studies of Marxism, socialism, and Soviet ideology and through his examination of the implications of loyalty and heresy. His **Heresy, Yes — Conspiracy, No** (1953) expresses the latter theme, while his concerns with socialism support the development of a pragmatic "revisionism" in which doctrinal Marxism is severely criticized.   R.W.T.

Hooker, Richard (1553—1600).

An Anglican churchman who in his treatise, **The Laws of Ecclesiastical Polity,** grafted upon the teaching of St. Thomas Aquinas on law and government the Anglican position on church-state relations under a national monarch. Intended as a tract against the Puritans, this became a major work bridging medieval and modern political thought.

State and government Hooker saw with St. Thomas, arising from the social nature of man. Political obedience is founded on the consent of the governed—with some allusions to a governmental contract. Positive human law is an extension of the natural law which in turn is derived from the eternal law of God. In opposition to the Thomist position, however, he would see the ecclesiastical law of England as having the same ultimate source, with the King as its mediator.

Against the Presbyterians and other non-Anglican Protestants, Hooker maintains that church and state are merely two aspects of a complete society. Therefore lack of acceptance of the power of the King in ecclesiastic as well as secular matters amounts to civil disobedience. Also, he is opposed to the Catholic dichotomy of Church and state as two distinct societies, for this tenet has the potential for ecclesiastical supremacy. Hooker saw no need of universal religious institutions transcending state boundaries as a requisite of true Christianity.   T.P.

Hopkins, Harry Lloyd.

b. Sioux City, Iowa, Aug. 17, 1890; d. Jan. 29, 1946. First met F. D. Roosevelt in 1928. As head of federal relief, 4½ years since 1933 (Federal Administrator of Emergency Relief, 1933; Works Progress Administrator, 1935-38). Secretary of Commerce, 1938-40. Lend-Lease Administrator, 1941. Special assistant to the President, 1941-July, 1945. On special diplomatic missions, 1942—1945. Subject of "more criticism and controversy than all other New Dealers combined," but had Roosevelt's absolute confidence. Sold President the idea that the unemployed must be fed and given work. Handled the draft-Roosevelt movement in 1940. Persistent ill-health for nine years. Died of hemochromatosis.
C.K.W.

Horizontal Federalism.

In a federal system of pluralistic governments many situations arise where the regional governments may conflict or cooperate with one another. These intergovernmental relations are sometimes referred to as horizontal federalism in order to prevent confusing them with international relations and because they are viewed as relations among governments on the same level. States of the United States have certain prescribed relations under the U.S. Constitution and have developed some outside the Constitution. Those under the Constitution include adjudication of disputes by the Supreme Court; making interstate compacts; giving full faith and credit to the public acts, records, and court proceedings of other states; not denying privileges and immunities to citizens of other states; and rendering up fugitives. Those relations which have developed outside the Constitution include the adoption of uniform state laws and reciprocal and retaliatory legislation and the creation of such organizations as the Council of State Governments.   J.A.E.

Horner, Henry.

First Democratic governor of Illinois in more than a generation. Probate Judge, Cook County 1914—1933. Elected governor of Illinois 1933, 1937. Born, Chicago, November 30, 1878; died, October 6, 1940. Became governor as Boss Cermak's man, but asserted his independence from Cermak's successors, The Kelly-Nash machine.
A.G.

Horthy, Nicholas (1868—1957).

Admiral, Regent of Hungary 1920—1945.

Served in the Austro-Hungarian

Navy; distinguished himself in sea operations along the Italian coast during World War I. Before the end of World War I, was in command of the Imperial Navy. In 1919, organized and commanded the Hungarian forces which overthrew the Hungarian Soviet Republic established by the Communists under Bela Kun. Elected Regent of the Kingdom of Hungary in 1920. His regime was considered moderately authoritarian: between 1920 and 1944 there was in Hungary a multi-party system, an active parliament with a strong opposition of Social Democrats, Farmers ("Smallholders"), and Hungarian National Socialists. Horthy's foreign policy of balance between German economic and political pressure and pro-Western sympathies ended in conflict with Nazi Germany. He was detained by force in Germany in March, 1944, when Nazi forces occupied Hungary. Signed an armistice with the Soviet Union on October 15, 1944, which led to his arrest and internment in Germany. Freed by U.S. troops in 1945. Screened for war crimes by U.S. authorities, but released without charge. Lived for a time in Bavaria, later in Portugal. Died in 1957. I.B.

Hostilities and State of Hostilities.

"Hostilities" is a term occasionally used in place of the term "operations." The term, if employed in a rule of law, must be understood in the light of the intent and purpose of such a rule. Its meaning is apt to vary from rule to rule. There can be no "state of hostilities" (hostilities in "the" legal sense) for the same reasons which stand in the way of the expression "state of war" (war in "the" legal sense). F.G.

Hot Pursuit in international law.

A state's right to pursue onto the high seas and arrest ships (excluding warships and perhaps other public ships) disobeying its laws. Pursuit, using ships or aircraft, must begin within the pursuer's internal waters, territorial sea or perhaps its contiguous zone; continue uninterrupted; and stop if the pursued enters its own, or a third state's, territorial sea. (See 1958 Geneva Convention [High Seas], Article 23.) V.R.I.

Hottentots.

An aboriginal people of South and South West Africa also called Namas, the Hottentots were among the least developed of the Africans encountered by the original Dutch colonists. Many became servants and some contributed to the mixed Cape Colored community. In the Cape area they are tied to a European society but in South West Africa they are closer to traditionalism. Linguistically, Hottentots are part of the Khoin or Khoisan family. P.F.P.

Houphouet-Boigny, Felix.

President and Head of Government of the Ivory Coast, co-founder and president of the **Rassemblement Democratique Africain**, and a leading statesman in West Africa.

Born in 1905 at Yamoussokro in the Ivory Coast, Felix Houphouet-Boigny attended the Medical School at Dakar, after which he practiced medicine for fifteen years. In 1945 he organized the **Parti Democratique de la Cote d'Ivoire**, which dominates politics in the Ivory Coast, and a year later he helped found, and has since served as president of, the **Rassemblement Democratique Africain**, the most influential inter-territorial party in French Africa. Elected to the French Parliament, he adopted a leftist orientation and openly cooperated with the communists in Paris and in Africa. After a series of disturbances in his native land, he broke with the communists after 1950 and has since pursued moderate policies. He has held several French cabinet posts, and has become the President of his country.

Under Dr. Houphouet-Boigny's leadership, the Republic of the Ivory Coast has taken a leading role in the formation of the Council of the Entente and of the Brazzaville Bloc. This West African state has followed a generally moderate course, espoused a functional approach to African unity, and manifested a friendly attitude toward France and the West. F.H.G.

House of Commons.

Called the "lower house" of the British Parliament it is in fact the house which counts the most. Its exact origin cannot be established with certainty but it was first mentioned in the reign of Edward III (1327—1377). It is presumed that it was in that period that the representatives of towns and villages (communes, Latin communiates — hence the name) appeared before the bar of Parliament of which they were not yet members (see House of Lords) and that they were asked to withdraw and deliberate separately. They then appointed a "speaker" to represent them before the bar of Parliament. In the 16th century the division between the House of Lords and the House of Commons became official. Members of Parliament (M.P.) the title by which members of the House of Commons are usually known, are elected in single-member districts on the basis of plurality and without run-off. The presiding officer of the House of Commons is the Speaker who divests himself of his party affiliation once elected and who is customarily re-elected with little or no opposition as long as he wishes to serve. Because there is no written Constitution (see Constitution) the legislative power of Parliament is theoretically unlimited and Walter Bagehot has coined the famous expression that "Parliament can do anything except make a woman a man or a man a woman." Actually the powers of Parliament are limited by political realities and by the fact that almost all legislative initiative emanates from the Cabinet (see Cabinet). Because of the peculiar nature of House of Commons committees (see Committees) the technical contents of bills can only be discussed on the floor of the House. But there is not sufficient time for this and hence discussion tends to regard the policy of the government rather than the exact text of a bill. This is particularly true in the case of "Budget Day" which holds the most encompassing discussion of general government policy. Theoretically the House of Commons can overthrow a government by a vote of censure or non-confidence but as governments usually have solid majorities such an event is very rare and no government which entered the House with a majority has been overthrown since 1866. While the main function of the House of Commons is the passing of legislation, another important item of business is the "Question Period" during which Members may bring grievances to the attention of the government and hear the reply of the minister concerned. Parliamentary debates are now officially published but are still popularly referred to as "Hansard" after the printer who was first authorized in 1809 to publish these debates. Contrary to most parliamentary assemblies in the world the chamber of the House of Commons is oblong with the government party and the opposition facing each other across a large table on which lies the mace, the symbol of parliamentary power. This arrangement emphasizes the prevailing two party system. The vote, called "division," is taken by the Members filing into one of two lobbies.

R.G.N.

House of Lords.

Originally Parliament was composed only of the House of Lords which emerged from the Grand Council (Magnum Concilium) and the Royal Court (Curia Regis). Even after the emergence of the House of Commons and the separation of the Houses in the 16th century (see House of Commons) the House of Lords remained powerful for a long time and some of its members actually controlled seats in the House of Commons whose constituencies had become depopulated ("rotten boroughs") and whose incumbents were often little more than retainers of some noble lord. In the 19th century the power of the House of Lords declined. It was drastically curtailed by the Parliament Acts of 1911 and 1949. Until 1958 the House of Lords was an all-male assembly composed of seven classes of peers (lords), the princes of the blood royal whose membership is largely nominal and who take no part in the discussion of controversial issues. The hereditary peers form the largest group (over 800) and are composed of barons, viscounts, earls, marquises and dukes. They are either the descendants of peers or newly created lords. Hereditary peers are either English or United Kingdom peers. Scottish and Irish lords do not sit unless they are designated "representative peers" by their own group of peers. Twenty-six archbishops and bishops of the Church of England sit as "Lords Spiritual" during their terms of ecclesiastical office. There are also nine "Lords of Appeal in Ordinary" popularly known as "Law Lords" who sit as the supreme court of the United Kingdom under the chairmanship of the Lord Chancellor. They are appointed peers for life. Another group of peers for life (non hereditary) was created in 1958 and only in this group may women be found, who sit in the House of Lords. A woman who inherits the title by right of descent may not sit in the House of Lords. Although largely a hereditary chamber few titles in the House of Lords go back farther than the 18th century. Over half of the titles were created in the 20th century and the House of Lords represents wealth more than "blue blood." Since 1949 the House of Commons may override a veto of the House of Lords if the Commons pass the bill three times and maintain an interval of one year between the first and the third passage. However, as a wide use of this suspensive veto would undoubtedly lead to further legislation curbing the powers of the Lords or even abolishing the House of Lords, such vetoes are rare. However, the House of Lords has many former high government officials and other men of considerable experience and hence the level of debate is often very high and the expertise rather than the power of the House makes itself felt. The House of Lords is presided over by the Lord Chancellor who is also a member of the cabinet. Its procedure is far more informal than that of the House of Commons. R.G.N.

Housing Authorities, U.S.A.
Public authorities, "corporate and politic," organized under State statutes usually on the municipal level to plan, develop, own, and operate projects for urban and rural slum clearance and redevelopment and for the construction of low-cost housing. Under the Federal Housing Act of 1949 the housing authorities are authorized to issue tax-free revenue bonds for their projects, which bonds are supported by the Federal Government. R.G.S.

Hoxha, Enver (1908—   ).
First Secretary of the Workers' (Communist) Party and Politburo member, he is the Albanian leader. He has led the CP since its founding in 1941, fought in the resistance movement, and was elected President of the Committee of National Liberation (1944). He was Premier (1944-54), Minister of Defense (1946-53), and Minister of Foreign Affairs (1946-53). He is General of the Army and President of the Democratic Front.
 J.J.K.

H.U.A.A.C.
See U.S. House Un-American Activities Committee.

Huber, Max.
Born on December 28, 1874, in Zuerich, died on January 1, 1960. Attended universities of Lausanne, Zuerich and Berlin (J.U.D., 1897). 1902-21, full professor for public, church and international law at U. of Zuerich. 1907, Swiss delegate to the second Hague Peace Conference. 1918, consultant to the Swiss Federal Council in connection with Switzerland's entry into the League of Nations. In the twenties repeatedly Swiss delegate to the Assembly of the League of Nations; 1931-32, delegate to the Geneva Disarmament Conference. 1923-52, Swiss member of the Permanent Court of Arbitration, and member and president of numerous international commissions for the pacific settlement of international disputes. 1922-30, member 1925-27, president and 1927-30 vice president of the Permanent Court of International Justice. 1923-45 member, 1928-44 president and 1945-60 honorary president of the International Committee of the Red Cross. During World War I deputy of the Judge Advocate General and later, as a colonel, member of the Court of Cassation of the Swiss army. Important business enterprises sought his collaboration. He thus was a member of the administrative board of the Swiss Reinsurance Corporation, vice-president of the administrative board of the **Neue Zuercher Zeitung**, president of the administrative boards of Oerlikon Machine Manufacturing Corporation and of the Swiss Aluminium

Industry Corporation. An imposing list of publications reveals his manifold interests and activities. Honorary doctorates of the universities of Geneva (philosophy), Edinburgh, Upsala, Oxford, Paris, Lausanne, Munich, Amsterdam, Louvain (law), and Zuerich (medicine and theology) testify to the high regard for Max Huber.
F.G.

Hughes, Charles Evans (1862—1948).

Chief Justice of the Supreme Court, 1930—1941. Hughes began his rich and diverse career as professor of law at Cornell University, becoming Governor of New York in 1906, and Associate Justice of the Supreme Court in 1910. He resigned his post in 1916 to run unsuccessfully on the Republican ticket against Wilson for the Presidency. From 1920—1925 he was Harding's Secretary of State, and in 1930 Hoover named him Chief Justice of the Supreme Court. His more well known opinions include his dissent in the MacIntosh case (1931) involving an oath to bear arms in case of war, his strong declaration in **DeJonge v. Oregon** (1937) against guilt by association, his upholding freedom of the press in the Near case (1931) and Negro rights in the Scottsboro case (1932). As Chief Justice he was a notable success, exercising skill and resourcefulness of leadership, and commanding respect and affection from members of a sharply divided court. He especially excelled during Roosevelt's attack upon the Court, achieving a united front within the Court against the Court-packing Bill, while at the same time exerting his influence to shift the Court's tack to a more liberal course and thus outmaneuver the President.
P.B.

Hugo, Victor-Marie (1802—1885).

Man of letters, most illustrious of French poets of 19th century. Son of a Napoleonic general, Victor Hugo's political concepts ranged from support of monarchy to the radical democracy of the Commune of 1871. Member of the Constituent Assembly after the Revolution of 1848, and of the Legislative Assembly of the Second Republic, he was forced into exile after the **coup d'etat** of 1851. An inveterate opponent of Napoleon III whom he dubbed "Napoleon the Little," he returned to France after the fall of the Empire and participated in the Assembly at Bordeaux. Member of the French Senate (1876). In **The Rhine** (1842) Hugo advocated a Franco-Prussian alliance predicated on French possession of the Left Bank of the Rhine and Prussian annexation of Hanover and Hamburg.
K.B.

Huguenots.

Between 1562 and 1598 in France an important political movement developed challenging the absolute monarchy. In part this conflict was between Protestants and Catholics; in part it was a struggle between the middle class and the King. In the St. Bartholomew Massacre (1572) 30,000 Huguenots lost their lives. In the Edict of Nantes (1598) Henry of Navarre—later Henry IV—granted the Protestant Huguenots a measure of religious freedom. However religious strife continued and resulted in 1689 in the Revocation of the Edict of Nantes. This led to exile for a great many skilled Frenchmen particularly to Germany.
R.W.T.

Hull, Cordell (1871—1955).

United States Secretary of State, 1933—1944. As President Franklin D. Roosevelt's first Secretary of State, Hull helped formulate two important New Deal programs: the promotion of reciprocal trade agreements and the "Good Neighbor Policy" toward Latin America. An advocate of post-war international organization, he received the Nobel Peace Prize in 1945 (Roosevelt called him the "father of the United Nations"). Hull served as Secretary of State longer than any other man. Before assuming the office, he had sat for 22 years in the House of Representatives and for six years in the Senate, representing his native state of Tennessee.
D.M.B.

Humanism.

Sociologically, the tendency to extend such ideals as kindness, loyalty, voluntary service, normally prevailing in primary groups (e.g. the family) to non-primary groups, such as the state.
J.D.

Humanitarianism.
Any view or program which emphasizes the centrality of human values. Humanitarianism frequently involves an emotional dedication to social reforms.   J.D.

Human Rights.
The broad concept of the natural rights of all human beings to life, liberty, and equality before the law, first politically formulated in modern times by the French Revolution in 1789, and later embodied in the laws of other countries. The Charter of the United Nations, unlike that of the League of Nations, asserts them as a basis of a peaceful world order, later spelled out in the Universal Declaration of Human Rights (1948), adopted by the General Assembly of the United Nations, without an opposing vote, but with several states expressing reservations through abstentions. The document covers not only the traditional civil and political liberties characteristic of Western democracies, but also more modern economic, social, and educational rights. (The principles are the basis of many international covenants, studies, and resolutions adopted by the United Nations with a view to creating a world wide "rule of law" for the protection of the individual. They are also the basis of provisions for human rights in the constitutions and laws of many states achieving their independence from colonial rule.)
                                                            R.B.

Hume, David (1711—1776).
Philosopher, librarian, member of England's Tory party, diplomat, Under-Secretary of State. Characterized as the precursor of positivism, Hume rejected the traditional concept of causality and stressed that the connection of one occurrence with some other is not the result of rational knowledge but rather of a habit of expecting the perception of the second occurrence after having perceived the first. He shared Spinoza's view of human nature which de-emphasizes foresight on man's part in pursuing his interests. Common interests Hume regarded as a body of conventions, a sort of language rather than a rational truth. Legitimate government—in contrast to the usurpation of political power—he defines as a government deriving its authority from conventional rules and formal enactments.   R.A.B.

Humphrey, Hubert H.
Born May 27, 1911, U.S. Senate; Democrat—Minnesota; Senate Majority Whip 1961—; leading member of American Political Science Association.
                                                            R.A.B.

Hungarian Revolution of 1956.
After the imposition of the "Dictatorship of the Proletariat" upon Hungary in 1949, the Communist Party in that country was bound to face the opposition of the population and a struggle for power within the Party. The split in the Party became evident in 1953, when Imre Nagy, as Prime Minister, initiated the liberal "New Course" policy, but Matyas Rakosi, as First Secretary of the Party, was able to retain the Stalinist policy of repression within the Party. The forced resignation of Nagy from his office of Prime Minister in February, 1955, did not slow down the process of the Party's disintegration. The "Petofi Circle," a debating society of Communist students and intellectuals, continued its work for humanitarian socialism and national sovereignty. The split in the Party came into the open again after the 20th Congress of the Soviet Communist Party (February, 1956), when the condemnation of Stalin in the USSR was interpreted in Hungary as meaning the end of Rakosi's political career and the return of Imre Nagy's "New Course" policy.

From this point on, events in Poland and Hungary followed a similar course. In Budapest the Party leadership was publicly blamed for the hardships of the past and demands were voiced for full rehabilitation of persecuted Party members. The rehabilitation of the Polish leader Wladyslaw Gomulka and the successes of the Polish Communists in emancipating themselves from Soviet tutelage (October 19, 1956) was greeted in Budapest with public manifestations of sympathy organized by the Communist youth organizations and the Writers' Union before the monument of the Polish general, J. Bem, hero of the Hungarian War of Independence of 1848-49. On October 23, 1956, at the

Bem monument, a resolution of the Writers' Union was read to some 50,000 assembled youth, intellectuals, workers, soldiers and a large delegation from the Military Academy. The resolution called for an independent Hungary, true socialism, the reinstatement of Imre Nagy as Prime Minister, and the removal of Rakosi and his associates from political life. At 7:00 p.m. that same day, Erno Gero, then First Secretary of the Hungarian Communist Party, broadcast a speech over Budapest Radio in which he condemned the demonstrations and repudiated the points of the resolution. Even as he was speaking, the demonstrators were growing in number and moving to Parliament Square and the Stalin Monument, which was demolished. A group of writers and students went to the Radio Building demanding that the resolution be broadcast. It was at this point that the Security Police (Political Police) opened fire on the assembled group and the demonstrations became a revolution. Demonstrators dispersed all over town to disarm members of the Political Police. Regular police and soldiers either joined the demonstrations or handed over their equipment. Workers captured stores of firearms kept at various factories.

During the night of October 23-24, Erno Gero called in Soviet troops against the demonstrators. At 7:00 a.m. October 24, Budapest Radio announced that Imre Nagy had been appointed Prime Minister and that he and his associates had been elected to the Party's Central Committee. In the meantime, however, armed clashes between the population and the Soviet troops and Political Police were already taking place in various parts of Budapest and also in the larger industrial cities in the provinces. On October 25, Gero was replaced as leader of the Party by Janos Kadar. As the fighting continued, Nagy promised the withdrawal of Soviet troops and the institution of a program of reforms.

Workers throughout the country organized themselves into Workers' Councils and joined the local Revolutionary Committees. Similarly, the Hungarian Army either joined the uprising or refrained from participating in the armed clashes. On October 26, Imre Nagy pledged formation of a new government, acceptance of the demands of the Workers' Councils, and amnesty for participants in the fighting. On October 28, the Government announced a ceasefire, and the immediate withdrawal of Soviet troops from Budapest and the dissolution of the Political Police. This was followed on October 30 by the announcement of the abolition of the one-party system and the withdrawal of Soviet forces from Hungary. Sporadic fighting continued against units of the Political Police. On October 31, the Soviet government declared that relations between the USSR and the nations of Eastern Europe would be based upon new principles. Thus, in Hungary the victory of the anti-Stalinist forces was complete. On November 1, the Hungarian government proclaimed Hungarian neutrality and withdrawal from the Warsaw Pact. But Soviet tanks appeared around Budapest and the main airfields and new troops were also arriving in Hungary from the USSR. On the following day (November 2), the Hungarian government informed the United Nations about the troop movements and requested the Great Powers to recognize Hungary's neutrality. On November 3, the Soviet troops moved to strategic positions in various areas of the country, and on Sunday, November 4, before sunrise, the onslaught against Budapest began, with heavy fighting developing between Hungarian Army units and Soviet tanks.

Armed resistance to Soviet troops continued until November 14, 1956, when it was turned into a general strike. In the meantime, a self-appointed "revolutionary worker-peasant government" with Janos Kadar as Prime Minister was formed outside Budapest and moved into the city. Imre Nagy and members of his government sought asylum in the Yugoslav Embassy. For a while, the Kadar regime promised that all resolutions of the Nagy government would be fulfilled, but, as time went on, and the new regime was consolidated, the promises were withdrawn.

It is still too early to form a clear picture of the developments during October and November, 1956, or to draw final conclusions. The developments in Hungary must be related to developments elsewhere, especially to those in Poland, in Yugoslavia, and, above all, in Suez and in the United Nations. Future evaluations must recognize that the events in Hungary took place in distinct phases: not all of the events should be considered revolutionary. The Revolution ended with the acceptance by the Nagy government of the demands of the National and Workers' Councils. From October 28 on, the conflict was restricted to the legal Hungarian government on one hand and the Soviet Union on the other. The intervention of Soviet troops on November 4th was directed against a legal government and, therefore, the ensuing fighting was a War of Independence, and not a revolution. I.B.

Hungary.
The modern Hungarian nation is descended from a semi-nomadic tribal federation of Finno-Ugric Magyars and Turkic Onogurs, which occupied the Carpathian Basin c. 900 A.D. King St. Stephen (997—1038) converted his nation to Christianity and replaced the tribal federation with a patrimonial kingdom based on a centralized government. A century later, Croatia was joined to Hungary as an associate kingdom. During the eleventh and twelfth centuries, the nation successfully resisted the attempts at subordination by Byzantine or German Imperial rule. In the thirteenth century, the Kingdom of Hungary expanded its influence and increased its international prestige by creating a chain of feudal buffer-principalities around the country. A short period of Tartar invasions (1241-42) devastated the country, but reconstruction was fast, both of material losses and of political prestige. A slow weakening of the nation's international position, however, resulted from the unsettled internal conditions created by the conflicting systems of royal succession (Western **primogeniture** versus Oriental **seniorate).** This constitutional weakness allowed the lords to gain influence and to claim territorial jurisdiction. The unity of the administration and of the state was saved by the new Anjou dynasty, successors of the Arpads, the last of whom died in 1301.

The two kings of the House of Anjou, Charles I and his son, Louis I, defeated the dissident lords and based their rule on cooperation with the lesser nobility. Under their rule Hungary became one of the great powers of Europe. After Louis I, the crown went to Sigismund of the House of Luxembourg, who married the daughter of Louis I. Although his claim to the crown was based on dynastic rights, he had to be elected to the throne by the nobility and, thus, in 1378 Hungary made the transition from the medieval patrimonial kingship to an elective kingship. The parallel transition from the concept of kingdom as patrimonium toward the modern concept of state was achieved by the symbolic use of St. Stephen's Holy Crown as the only proprietor of the land and by the elected king's exercising the rights of the Crown in cooperation with the whole nation, represented by the Estates. King Mathias of Hunyad (1458-1490) was the first king who was elected from the nobility. He strengthened the international position of the country and fought successful wars against the Turks, who were menacing the land from the south and east. His unfortunate wars with Austria, Bohemia and Poland on issues of dynastic succession weakened the state and led, after his death, to a growing disintegration of the country by both internal and external strife.

In 1526, the Turks defeated the Hungarians at Mohacs and occupied the central part of the country for some two centuries. The western and northern parts, nominally a kingdom, became part of the Habsburg sphere of influence. Transylvania in the east became a principality under the suzerainty of the Turks. It was in Transylvania that the Hungarians were able for centuries to maintain political selfgovernment, promote the cultural development of the whole nation and assure tolerance for the adherents of various Protestant movements of the 16th-17th centuries. After Sobieski's victory at Vienna (1683), the Turks were pushed back by the Habsburgs from Western and Central Hungary, but the sovereignty of the nation was not restored. This happened only after the unsuccessful uprising led by Ferenc Rakoczy (1703—1711). A reconciliation between the Hungarians and the Habsburg dynasty took place under the rule of Maria Theresa (1740-80). Her successor, Joseph II, implementing his ideas of enlightenment, attempted to create a centralized state based on a single language. The opposition to this policy led to the Hungarian national revival, usually connected with the names of I. Szechenyi and L. Kossuth; but, at the same time, the Hungarian patriotism antagonized the national minorities of the lands of St. Stephen's Crown.

The Hungarians were also influenced by the ideas of the French Revolution, and a strong liberal and national movement developed, culminating in the War of Independence of 1848-49. This war ended with a victory of the Habsburgs supported by Imperial Russian troops. A short period of Habsburg despotism was followed by a reconciliation in 1867 assuring the Hungarians of equality in a dual monarchy. This system collapsed with the defeat of the Austro-Hungarian Monarchy at the end of World War I. In 1919 the Communists formed a "Soviet Republic of Hungary," but were soon defeated and the Kingdom was reestablished. As the Habsburgs were prevented from returning by the opposition of the socalled Succession States, a regent was elected in 1920 (Nicholas Horthy).

In the Peace Treaty of Trianon (1920), the principle of national self-determination was applied, but without a plebiscite, and the lands of the Hungarian Crown were partitioned, large territories being given to Czechoslovakia, Rumania and Yugoslavia. Hungary retained only 29% of her former territories and lost 61% of her population, including three million Magyars. These losses in territory and population accounted for the consolidation of the conservative forces in Hungary. The main force of internal coherence and the main objective in foreign policy was the idea of a peaceful revision of the Peace Treaty of Trianon. This policy found support with Italy and later with Germany. The two Vienna Arbitrations (1938, 1940) restored parts of the disputed areas to Hungary. These territories were lost again, however, after World War II, in which Hungary participated as a reluctant ally on the side of Germany against the Soviet Union.

In March, 1944, Hungary was occupied by Nazi Germany. In 1944-45, Soviet troops entered the country, and a democratic coalition government took over the administration. In the first free elections (1945) the Farmers Party (Smallholders) received 59.9% of the votes and the Communist Party only 17.11%. The Kingdom was replaced by a Republic in 1946. As the Communists held the key positions in the government, e.g. Ministry of Interior (including Police), they were able to intimidate the whole population by terror, false indictments and arrests. By 1948-49 the Communists were in full power and most of the leaders of the democratic parties were imprisoned or forced into exile. With the introduction of the single-list electoral system in 1949, political freedom and a multi-party system were gone. The implementation of the Stalinist policy of M. Rakosi, Communist dictator of Hungary, no longer had any legal controls. His policy, unmodified even after Stalin's death, led directly (interrupted only for a short period by the New Course Policy of Imre Nagy, 1953-55 to the Hungarian Revolution of 1956. I.B.

Husain Ibn Ali (Grand Sharif and Amir of Mecca).

A scion of the Hashemites, the noblest of all Arab families, for they traced their descent in the male line back to the Prophet's daughter. As Grand Sharif and Amir of Mecca, he conducted in 1914-15 secret correspondence with Sir Henry McMahon, British High Commissioner in Egypt, in which the British Government promised to support him in a revolt against the Turks and to champion the cause of Arab independence in case of victory. In November 1916, four months after the declaration of the Arab Revolt, Husain was proclaimed "king of the Arabs," a premature and unwise move that irritated Britain and France who recognized him only as "king of the Hijaz." Two of his sons founded new royal dynasties—Abdullah in Jordan, and Faisal in Iraq. In March 1924, immediately after the abolition of the Caliphate in Turkey, he untactfully lent himself to a hastily improvised proclamation of himself as Caliph, without ascertaining Muslim opinion at large. Accused of subordinating the "Arab Cause" to his personal ambitions, discredited in the eyes of his officials and foresaken by the British, he was forced to abdicate in favor of his eldest son Ali. This did not deter the Wahhabis of Ibn Saud taking over the Hijaz in October 1925. After a number of years in exile on the Island of Cyprus, Husain was allowed to go to Amman to end his days near his sons. He died in June 1931, and was buried in the sanctuary area in Jerusalem. F.M.N.

Hyde Park Declaration.
An understanding between President Franklin D. Roosevelt and Prime Minister W. L. Mackenzie King—set forth in a press release dated April 20, 1941—that, in mobilizing the resources of North America, the United States and Canada should each "provide the other with the defense articles which it is best able to produce . . . and that production programs should be coordinated to this end." The agreement eased Canada's dollar-shortage problem and set the stage for close Canadian-American economic cooperation not only during the war but also in the post-war period. W.W.

Hyper-accountability.
The child of a legal principle **nullum crimen sine poena** accepted in the communist system of justice, according to which no crime must remain unpunished regardless of who pays the penalty. Hyper-accountability is a means of restoring equilibrium in a communist state and a potent element in the operation of its economic system.

Equilibrium is maintained by threatening officials with a purge, and inflicting terror and misery on the masses. Any easing of conditions may lead to instability. When terror lessens, the pressure of economic factors on the workers tends to increase and may drive them to revolt against their local communist leaders. The latter, in accordance with the rules of hyper-accountability, must be punished by the Party, because they did not inspire enough terror to prevent the riots.

Hyper-accountability was acutely felt during the Stalinist era and less strongly afterwards, mainly at the level of industrial managers. It involves severe punishment for negligence, errors in calculation, the actions of subordinates, inability to meet deadlines, crop failures, etc. It is an outcome of planning, yet it leads to uneconomic results. It encourages illegal practices (producing the wrong assortment of goods, incorrect accounting of goods in process, lowering the quality of output, misappropriation of funds) as well as administrative sins, such as the wide use of "pull" with higher officials in order to obtain favorable allocations of raw materials and funds. W.J.S.

Hypothesis.
The assumption made in the course of a scientific inquiry that something is, was, or will be (1) an actual fact, event, cause, or (2) a valid norm, or (3) a valid law of interrelations (esp. causal interrelations) between events, is often called a h., especially if used as the basis for logical deductions, predictions, and tests. The h. may have been formed a priori, intuitively, or by induction from observed individual cases (see a priori, inductive reasoning). If in case (3) the validity of the h. is accepted as firmly established it is sometimes referred to as a universal "law." Often, however, a h. is meant to serve as a mere "working hypothesis" not yet accepted even by the scientist who uses it. All empirical hypotheses, whether fully accepted as established "laws," or tentatively accepted, or used as mere "working hypotheses," are provisional only in the eyes of prevalent contemporary scientific thought; they must be abandoned or modified if contradicted by opposing experiences (pre-arranged tests or unarranged occurrences).
A.B.

I

Ibn Saud, King Abdul-Aziz (1880—1953).

Son of Abdul-Rahman of the House of Saud of Central Arabia. His great-great-great grandfather, Muhammad ibn Saud (1747-65), married the daughter of Muhammad ibn Abdul-Wahhab, founder of the Wahhabi movement, and became the leader of the movement. Since that time, the House of Saud and the Wahhabi movement shared the same fate. The first Wahhabi State of Nejd was politically destroyed at the hands of Ibrahim Pasha between 1811—1818. It was left to Ibn Saud to restore the prestige and power of his dynasty and ultimately unify most of the Arabian Peninsula under his reign. After the surprise attack on Riyad in 1912, his power grew, and by an audacious coup in 1913 he put an end to the Turkish occupation of al-Hasa. During the First World War Ibn Saud signed a treaty of alliance with the Viceroy of India and received recognition and a subsidy from the British Government. Rivalry with the Sharif of Mecca led to a series of clashes, and in December 1925, the Wahhabi armies forced King Ali to evacuate the Hijaz. On January 8, 1926, Ibn Saud was proclaimed King of the Hijaz. Devout, shrewd and generous, Ibn Saud ruled Arabia according to the Islamic divine law and in a patriarchal manner. Open-minded to the challenges of the 20th century, Ibn Saud encouraged Western oil companies to exploit the wealth of the desert. In 1942 he met with Churchill and Roosevelt thus becoming a figure of world stature. The name "Saudi" Arabia is a tribute to the man who created it. F.M.N.

Icarianism.

1. A program of utopian communism proposed in a romantic book **(Voyage to Icaria)** by Etienne Cabet (1788—1856), a noted French social reformer. 2. A descriptive term applied to certain 19th century Cabetian colonies in Texas, Illinois, Missouri, and other sections of the United States.

Ch.C.M.

Iceland.

An island republic in the North Atlantic, just below the Arctic Circle, between Greenland and Norway but nearer Greenland. It has 39,600 square miles and had 157,000 inhabitants in 1955. The island may have been visited by Greeks and Romans and there was probably an Irish settlement there prior to 800 A.D.

In the 9th century, Scandinavian vikings began to explore Iceland and the first permanent settlement was made by Norwegians about 870 A.D. A parliament (Althing) was established in 930 A.D. This is the oldest surviving democratic legislative assembly in the world.

In 1262, Iceland fell under the domination of Norway and later (1381), of Denmark, but never completely lost its political independence. In 1800 the Althing was abolished but it was reestablished in 1843. In 1874 Denmark granted home rule to Iceland. During World War I, Iceland was isolated from Denmark and after the war a treaty recognized Iceland's independence and made the King, when functioning as King of Iceland, King of Iceland and Denmark. In 1940, after the German invasion of Denmark, the British landed a force in Iceland and fortified the country against possible German attack. A 1941 treaty with the U.S. gave U.S. military protection to Iceland, recognized Iceland as a free and sovereign state, and agreed to insist, after the war, that she should be so recognized in any peace treaty.

In 1944, a referendum was held in which the people of Iceland voted overwhelmingly for a republic. Shortly after that the present form of government was established. There is a President, chosen by popular vote for a four year term. He governs with a cabinet approved by the Althing and headed by a Prime Minister. The Althing, consisting of two chambers, is the legislative assembly. The judicial function is performed by several local courts and a Supreme Court with five judges. There is freedom of speech, press and religion. J.E.R.

Idea. See Appendix.

Ideology.

A systematic set of arguments and beliefs used to justify an existing or desired social order.

The term appears to have originated with Destuit de Tracy at **L'institut national** in 1796. His five volume work, **Les elements d' ideologie**, was published in Paris between 1801 and 1815. His friends and followers played a role in the politics of the day and were known as ideologues.

Destuit de Tracy used the term to denote his systematization of Enlightenment ideas on thought. He believed that all thought was the result of sense perception. Thought, then, was radically dependent on the fields of anthropology and psychology. Once this was understood, rational application of empirical knowledge gathered in these disciplines could be made to the fields of ethics pedagogy, legal and political science. In this sense, then, ideology would denote rational application of principles derived from practical experience.

Karl Marx popularized the term by applying it to the thought of the ruling class in society. In doing this he followed the principle laid down by de Tracy that all thought was based on sense perception. However, Marx was concerned to show that this thought consisted of arguments and justifications used by the ruling class to defend the existing social system. From this it was but a short step to use the term to denote any partisan body of argument for an existing or desired social system. R.M.T.

Ikeda, Mayato (1899—).
B.A. Kyoto University. Member of Parliament. President of Liberal-Democratic Party. Prime Minister in 1961. H.U.

Illiberal.
Displaying excessive reliance upon authority and distrust for human rationality and freedom. J.W.Ch.

I.L.O.
See International Labor Organization.

Immigration.
The entrance into a country of which one is not a citizen for the purpose of permanent residence. C.W.B.

Immobilisme.
A French term denoting the frequently recurring periods of immobility or stalemate in governmental affairs resulting from the failure of the French government to inaugurate positive legislative policy. This condition results, on the one hand, from the reluctance of the vacillating and unstable coalition Governments (Cabinets) to propose timely and vigorous legislative policies to the National Assembly for fear that such proposals if vigorously pushed might provoke a governmental crisis that would culminate in the downfall of the Government. On the other hand, the Assembly is often unable or unwilling to initiate or approve measures that are necessary to the welfare of the nation because of the uncompromising and negative attitudes of some of the important parliamentary groups, whose support is needed. Periods of **immobilisme** often have been followed by grants of decree-making power, in the form of "decree-laws" **(decrets-lois)** or "framework laws" **(loi cadre)**, to such an extent that the Assembly has shifted much of its legislative authority to the Government (and, in practical effect, to the Civil Service), thus defaulting in its own legislative responsibilities and weakening the democratic principle of accountability.
R.H.K.

Immunity.
The status of immunity implies the suspension of application and execution of local laws in order to enable the agents of international intercourse residing or traveling in foreign territories to carry out the essential functions of their missions. Diplomatic immunities are those accorded to representatives of other nations (ambassadors, ministers, etc.) in the territory of the receiving nations, while the term international immunities refers to the analogous regime accorded to the officials of international organizations. Specific immunities are also granted to the Heads of State travelling abroad, state ships in foreign ports and armed forces of one nation stationed in the territory of another.
P.P.R.

Immunity Bath.
In U.S. law, a statutory provision designed to obtain testimony from a witness who might otherwise claim

the protection of the Fifth Amendment's prohibition against compulsory testimony (and of comparable guarantees in the state constitution). The witness, under such a statute, may be required to testify but is granted immunity from prosecution.   F.H.H.

Impeachment.
A formal written accusation made against a civil official, charging such official with treason, bribery, or other high crimes or misdemeanors. In the United States the charges are made in the lower house of the legislative body (except in Nebraska) and are presented in the form of "Articles of Impeachment" to the upper house which conducts a trial. Conviction requires an unusual majority, such as a two-thirds, vote. If an individual is found guilty he may be removed from office. An impeached person may also be tried and convicted in a court of law.   W.V.H.

Imperfect war.
See war.

Imperial Rescript.
See Japanese Imperial Rescript.

Implied Powers.
Governmental powers may be broadly classified as **expressed** or **implied**. The former are declared in specific words, the latter are logical deductions or natural inferences from the wording and purpose of **expressed** powers. For example, the congressional authority to incorporate a bank is inferred from such expressly delegated powers as "to lay and collect taxes, to coin money and regulate the value thereof . . ." Discussing the bank issue in Washington's Cabinet Jefferson and Hamilton debated the scope of powers implied in "the necessary and proper clause." This issue was definitively settled in favor of the broad Hamiltonian interpretation by the Supreme Court in **McCulloch v. Maryland** in 1819.   A.A.N.

Import Bank of Washington.
A banking corporation first organized in 1934 under the laws of the District of Columbia, but reincorporated under a federal charter in 1947. A five-man board of directors, appointed by the President with the advice and consent of the Senate, not more than three of whom may be members of the same political party, supervises its affairs. The Bank is authorized a capital stock of $1 billion and may borrow from the U.S. Treasury on its own obligations not more than $6 billion outstanding at any one time. The primary purpose of the Bank is to aid in financing and to facilitate exports and imports between the United States or any of its possessions and any foreign country or agencies or nationals thereof. The Bank's policy is to supplement, not to compete with private capital.   G.B.H.

Incas.
The Indian builders of the South American Andean empire which extended from southern Colombia to southern Chile when conquered by Pizarro in 1532. Noted for their authoritarian social and political organization, the Incas were ruled by a semi-divine emperor supposedly descended from the sun god, a circle of high officials, and a host of lesser officials. The capital, Cuzco, was the center of a system of roads, many paved or rock-hewn.   L.C.D.

Incomplete war.
See war.

Incorporation.
Creation by law of a legal entity or "artificial person"—either private, as a business; or public, as a municipality—with certain specified authority including the power to sue and be sued. Corporate charters were formerly granted by special act of the state legislature. Today, general statutes vest authority in certain public officials to issue charters upon application of the interested parties. The U.S. (national) government has also established public corporations such as the Federal Deposit Insurance Corporation.   H.J.Sch.

Independent Voters Association (I.V.A.).
A political organization formed in North Dakota in 1918 by conservative Republicans and Democrats to oppose the Nonpartisan League (NPL). After

recalling three NPL state officials from office in 1921, the I.V.A. continued to exist as the conservative faction of the Republican party until it suffered a crushing defeat in the 1932 Republican primary. R.V.A.

Indeterminate Sentence.
A commitment to prison for a period of indeterminate duration, only the minimum and maximum term being fixed by the court, the power to set at liberty being vested in an independent agency, usually the parole board. The majority of the states (of the U.S.A.) have enacted indeterminate sentence laws. On the federal level, the parole board has the power to release a prisoner on parole after he has served one-third term, or fifteen years of a life term, thus in effect creating an indeterminate sentence situation. F.H.H.

India or Bharat.
Area 1,259,983 square miles (provisional, 1961 survey); population c. 438 million (1961 census, incomplete, estimate). Republic with president, prime minister and council of ministers; bi-cameral legislature, the 236 Council of States (Rajya Sabha) and the 526(7)-member House of the People (Lok Sabha). There are sixteen states, originally divided into three classifications, and fourteen official languages. India is a member of the U.N. and the Commonwealth of Nations.

Independence was achieved August 14-15, 1947. The Congress Party, founded in 1885, which led the struggle for independence, has won every national election since 1947. Jawaharlal Nehru, Gandhi's chosen successor, has been Prime Minister since 1947, and leader of the Congress Party with one brief interruption, when a reactionary Hindu movement opposed to his socialist-secularist program captured the Congress Party presidency.

The transfer of power from Britain was effected before adequate preparations could be made. Clashes between Hindu and Muslim groups resulted in almost a million deaths. The new government was faced with the restoration of order and the refugee problem. The exchange of population between India and Pakistan (q.v.) has been judged one of the largest population shifts in history. It continues, with mutual denunciations. The allocation of the Panjab Canal waters, and the Kashmir question further strained relations. Economic war raged between November, 1947 and February, 1951. Relations have improved under President Ayub Khan's government of Pakistan. The Indus Waters Treaty of 1960 bettered the economic situation of both nations.

The integration of 562 princely states, free to opt for India or Pakistan, was achieved largely through persuasion; in some instances, by force. Junagadh, with a Muslim prince who chose Pakistan, and the large, centrally located state of Hyderabad under its Muslim Nizam, were the most difficult. Kashmir-Jammu, with a large Muslim majority, was brought into India by an ineffective Hindu prince. The decision was contested by warring neighboring tribesmen, supported by the Pakistan government. The Indian Air Force conducted an air-lift operation before roads were built. The U.N. obtained a cease-fire line, but its attempts to arrange a plebiscite have met with refusal from India.

India was united politically only three times before in its long history; under Asoka, in the fourth century B.C.; under the Mughals, from the sixteenth to the eighteenth century; under the British. The linguistic problem which has plagued India since independence bespeaks long cultural differences. Hindi is the official language, with English as a second language in the transitional period. The other languages recognized in the constitution have formed the basis of boundary changes of former British and French provinces, and of the princely states; or at least the weakening of central government. Hill tribes denied local autonomy or parliamentary representation, ruled by a governor appointed by the federal government, are becoming more self-conscious and pushing for recognition. The Naga tribes of the Northeast Frontier secured statehood in 1962. The Sikhs are agitating for an independent state to include Sikhs now within Pakistan. The government has been severe in dealing with these movements and with labor unions sympathetic to separatists.

India invaded Goa, Diu and Damao in December, 1961, and easily captured the last Portuguese possessions. Negotiations for a peaceful adjustment had been conducted unsuccessfully over a long period. France ceded Pondicherry peacefully in September, 1962; India had administered the area by an agreement with France from November 1, 1954.

Communist China claims 12,000 square miles of Indian territory. Its seizure of Tibet and influence in Nepal give it invasion routes into the subcontinent. Serious border clashes and countless press broadsides enliven the exchange of diplomatic notes.

The Communist Party of India, which grew during World War II when Congress leaders were political prisoners, has lost much prestige through China's aggressiveness. The CPI forms the main opposition bloc in the Lok Sabha. It has been strong in some of the larger cities and in Kerala. Defeated in the 1962 elections, it won a larger number of votes than before; in many areas it chose to support Congress candidates known for leftist sympathies. Split into "Soviet" and "China" blocs and divided by the linguistic issue, it reorganized after the 1962 elections.

India has inaugurated a series of Five-Year Plans, 1950-1955, 1955-1960, 1960-1965. The objectives were increased agricultural production, industrialization, increase of capital investment, of employment, of per capita income, and self-sufficiency. Education and health improvement are reaching many of the villages. To help implement these plans, the government has revived the **panchayat** or village council, a democratic institution which existed from ancient times until the British unwittingly destroyed it. The UN, U.S.A., Britain, the Commonwealth—especially Colombo Pact countries, West Germany, the U.S.S.R. and many private foundations have supplemented government funds. Private capital, both in India and abroad, feared to invest in the early years, but is now more confident of India's success. Without renouncing its socialist orientation, the government has made provisions to attract and reassure private capital.

As the largest free Asian country, with an ancient, great culture, India is eagerly watched by emerging countries. She has exercised moral leadership and is a strong neutral force for peace in the U.N.   M.O'C.

India, Princely States.

When India gained Independence in 1947, 552 semi-autonomous states remained within her borders. Ruled by rajas, maharajas and nawabs, some states merely were a few acres, others were larger than many European nations. All had had direct treaty relationships with the British Crown. Sardar Patel, Deputy Prime Minister of India, warned princely rulers that "the alternative to co-operation in the general interest is anarchy and chaos"; by diplomacy, pressure and coercion, he directed an unparalleled operation of political integration completed in less than three years. Military action was necessitated only in the cases of Hyderabad and Kashmir, the rest acceding peacefully.   S.K.A.

Indian National Congress.

See Congress, Indian National.

Indians in Spanish America.

Heavily concentrated in Mexico, parts of Central America, and the Andean area of South America, the Indians have been and are a significant part of the area's total population. Although some have mixed with other groups, the identifiably Indian portion of the population may become increasingly important in the future.   L.C.D.

Indirect Rule.

The practice of a power ruling a colonial territory, of utilizing existing indigenous governmental institutions to control and administer the territory. In relatively undeveloped countries it means the virtual transformation of chiefs and similar local notables into civil servants. Another facet of indirect rule is the official recognition of local tribunals and the appointment of local inhabitants to seats on councils and commissions. The classic example of indirect rule is the policy of Sir Frederick (later Lord) Lugard, High

Commissioner of Northern Nigeria before 1906, in utilizing the Muslim emirs as rulers in the name of and as representative of the British crown. Indirect rule has been praised as a device which safeguards customs of the people ruled but condemned as an obstacle to democratic and national movements.   E.V.M.

Individualism.
This is the doctrine which holds that the chief end of society is the promotion of individual welfare, the recognition of the dignity of man and the moral obligation of the State to help him achieve his highest capability. The development of individualism was based on: (1) the concepts of Christianity which were dramatically renewed during the Reformation, (2) the right, justice and equality of the common law, and (3) the establishment of an economic system based on exchange. The term was first used in English by Henry Reeve in his translation of Alexis de Tocqueville, **De la democratie en Amerique** (1840) from the French word, **individualisme.**

The direct relation between the individual and God was clearly implied in the Gospels with many references to the fatherhood of God and the equality of men such as: "Inasmuch as ye have done it unto one of the least of these my brethren, ye have done it unto me" (Matthew xxv:40). The supreme worth of the individual is emphasized throughout the New Testament. This is the great contribution of early Christianity to individualism. With the beginning of the Reformation people were encouraged to think for themselves, to pray alone to God, and to seek salvation alone without the intermediary of the Holy Church. Religion was based on faith of the individual in his creator and through this faith he became a member of the Church Invisible which was a personal matter. Martin Luther (1483—1546) translated the Bible into the German vernacular so that the people would have easy access to reading it without benefit of clergy.

As the Reformation was a revolt against the established Church it was not long before revolt came against government or arbitrary power especially by religious reformists. Nicholas of Cusa in his statement at the Council of Basel (1433) recognized the need of the consent of subjects. But it was in the anonymous Huguenot pamphlet, **Vindiciae Contra Tyrannos** (1579) that the theory of resistance was expanded. It stated that the ruler was the servant of the community and hence the community could do whatever its life required. Under the Social Contract, the people set the conditions the King was bound to fulfill or the Compact became void. Although this justified resistance by a corporate entity further expansion of the idea of the Social Contract stressed the position of the individual as did John Milton (1608—1674) and John Locke (1632—1704). They both justified rebellion against a sovereign who was a tyrant on the basis of the rights of the individual under Natural Law. On the other hand, Thomas Hobbes (1588—1679), also devoted to Natural Law, gave impetus to the modern view of **individualism** by his insistence on self-interest as the dominant motive in human behavior.

The most exalted statement of **individualism** came in the American Declaration of Independence (1776). Thomas Jefferson expressed the philosophy of Locke when he wrote: "We hold these truths to be self-evident, that all men are created equal, that they are endowed by their Creator with certain unalienable Rights, that among these are Life, Liberty, and the Pursuit of Happiness. That to insure these rights, Governments are instituted among men deriving their just powers from the consent of the governed."

Although **individualism** developed politically through the philosophy of Natural Law and the Social Contract, Sir Edward Coke (1552—1634) laid a firmer foundation by his emphasis upon the Common Law. As Chief Justice of England he dared to oppose the extension of the royal prerogatives of James I. In one of his famous decisions he said that, "the King cannot create any offense by his prohibition or proclamation which was not an offense before." The rights of individuals were protected not by the flimsy figment of the Social Contract but by the laws of the land. This was finally transmitted into the American Constitution as, "no one shall be denied life, liberty or property without due process of law." An added guarantee was given in the Fourteenth Amendment that no one be denied "equal protection of the laws."

The development of the concept of **individualism** gained little by the contradictory writings of Jean Jacques Rousseau (1712—1778). His defense of the common man was completely contradicted by the tyranny of his **volonte generale.**

Probably the greatest influence on the development of **individualism** was the free enterprise system based on free exchange and banking which came out of the Industrial Revolution. But without first, the emerging of a code of laws to protect private property and contracts, private enterprise could not have flourished. Capitalism grew by the ability and the ingenuity of the individual entrepreneur. In the amazing period of its growth (1750—1900) individualism reached its zenith. M.E.D.

Indoctrination.

A form of communication distinct from education or propaganda. It aims to instill or inculcate doctrine or dogma into its objects. It presents only information which supports or furthers such ideas, beliefs, programs or ideologies, rather than offering all relevant information. It is not a relatively neutral process as is education. By contrast, it does not aim merely to present information while encouraging the reaching of independent conclusions. It is a method used for communicating religious beliefs, revealed dogma, political ideology and the multiplication tables, as well as one which is typical of commercial advertising. It is distinguished from political propaganda in that it does not have to resort knowingly to untruths. It is not appropriate for the communication of ideas, for political debate, or for "education" in a free society. A.G.

Indonesia.

A state in Southeast Asia, occupying the greater part of the Malayan Archipelago and consisting of the Greater Sunda Islands, Lesser Sunda Islands, Molucca Islands, and others. The country, located on no less than 2,000 inhabited islands, has an area of 583,000 sq. miles. The population of Indonesia, according to the U.N. estimates of 1961, equals 94.5 million people, of which more than half live on the Island of Java (58 million people). The population of the country is mainly Indonesian, predominantly of Malayan origin, divided into a large number of ethnic groups. The second largest group is the Chinese—1.2 million people. Next comes a group of Europeans—240,000, and 70,000 Arabs. The country is densely populated, especially Java, where the average density is more than 1,100 persons per 1 sq. mile. Many dialects are spoken by the people of Indonesia, but the most widely used is the Malayan dialect of Sumatra, which has been adopted as the state language of Indonesia. In the 16th century, prior to the arrival of the Portuguese conquerors, the islands were divided into several small principalities ruled by princes. The Portuguese were pushed out by the Dutch at the end of the 16th century. Dutch colonial rule began with the consolidation of several trading companies into one, the East Indian Company, in 1602. The East Indies, as Indonesia was called under Dutch rule, was captured by the Japanese during World War II. On August 17, 1945, after the defeat of the Japanese, Indonesia declared its independence. After prolonged fighting the Dutch finally transferred authority to the new Republic of Indonesia on December 27, 1949. Sukarno became the first President of the new republic. V.P.P.

Inductive reasoning.

That type of reasoning is inductive which tries to reach generalizing propositions (classes, universal laws, general hypotheses) from individual facts, events, cases. Inductively reached generalizations are never quite certain to be true or valid; they may be corroborated or proven false by subsequent observations. Yet they often constitute very useful tools as premises for deductive reasoning, tests, corroboration, or falsification. Inductive reasoning followed by deductive reasoning and testing is characteristic of modern science as distinct from scientific methods that are based on reasoning a priori (see rational—**rationalism, a priori**). Attempts to justify inductive reasoning logically, range from the axiomatic assumption of the world's being governed by universal laws (J.S. Mill) to the cautious acceptance of rules of scientific procedure reached from experience (Felix Kaufmann).

A.B.

Industrial Democracy.

Can be defined as the active participation of employees (and their representatives) in the policies of industrial enterprises as far as conditions of work and their economic development are concerned.

"Co-determination" was granted to the employees in Article 165 of the Weimar Constitution. After the downfall of the Weimar Republic the Third Reich annulled both the intent and scope of Article 165. On February 4, 1946 a shop steward law (followed by the "co-determination" law of 1951 for the mining, steel, and iron industries) introduced into the Federal Republic of Germany a new era of industrial democracy. Apart from the ferrous industries employee "co-determination" in the Federal Republic is, however, rather limited.

W.A.

Inflation.

An increase in the quantity or velocity of money with no relative increase in the volume of business, or in quantity of goods and services produced. An increase in general price level and the reduction of the purchasing power of money are the primary consequences. These in turn cause a redistribution of wealth in the society; the losers being persons on fixed income and the creditors, the businessmen and the debtors being the ones who gain. It is usually associated with peaks of prosperity of a nation; can also be caused by excessive creation of money and credit by governments and business.

W.N.

Influence.

Influence is a kind of power, indirect and unstructured. If power is understood in behavioral terms as manifesting itself in the conformance of persons (and groups) to the preferences, whether express or implied, of another person or group, then influence refers mostly to situations where such power is wielded without any commands or other explicit orders being given. Influence is of vast scope and frequently serves to adjust an institutionalized system of rule to the actualities of politics. New groups and formally deprived persons, such as slaves, usually depend upon influence for participation in the game of politics to a greater or lesser extent. The means employed may be psychic, economic or even physical; Aristophanes made the refusal of sexual intercourse the key weapon of the women who wanted to prevent war (Lysistrata).—Influence rests upon the capacity of human beings to imagine and hence to anticipate the reactions of those who are affected by their actions. Hence the mutuality of the power relations is often due to the presence of a certain amount of influence. Political theory has paid relatively little attention to influence, because of its elusive quality; in recent years terms such as "informal government" and "informal organization" have had a certain vogue, suggesting the increasing recognition of influence. Because of the tendency of influence to hide, political science must turn to the historian who can, as hidden influences are revealed by the discovery of documents, show its role in a variety of contexts. Access to the power-wielder has in this connection been recognized as an important factor in permitting influence.

The interaction of consent and constraint in power situations provides a clue for the nature of influence. By anticipating the reactions of the power-wielder, the person subject to his power yields to his influence. Whether the power expresses itself in commands, favors or other kinds of conduct, it will influence conduct. From this operational observation a rule for discovering influence has been derived: any political context in which reversals of decisions occur is likely to be influenced by those who caused the reversal.

C.J.F.

Inherent Powers.

Powers essential in the nature of government is a doctrine concerning the power of the government of the United States directly contrary to that generally accepted by students of constitutional history and by the Supreme Court. However such men as James Wilson, Lincoln, Theodore Roosevelt, Truman and even the Supreme Court itself (Curtiss-Wright, 1936) have declared its validity. Regardless of the theory, presidents with the support of the judiciary are likely to use it in emergencies. J.E.S.

Initiative.
A proposed constitutional amendment or legislative act, drawn up by qualified voters and submitted through petitions containing a specified number of signatures. This number may be fixed by law or be determined from a percentage of the total votes cast at a preceding election (for example, for Governor or other officer). Some states permit the Legislature to enact the proposed measure, if it so desires, while others make it mandatory to submit the measure to a vote of the people. This, in effect, becomes both Initiative and Referendum. Sp.D.A.

Injunction.
A court order, or writ, requiring the person or persons to whom it is issued to do, or (usually) to refrain from action which may violate the personal or property rights of others. Temporary injunctions, issued at the beginning of a suit, prevent acts which might prejudice final results. Permanent injunctions are issued at the end of a suit when the case has been fully heard and decided. Violation of an injunction is considered a contempt of court punishable by fine or imprisonment. Injunctions are frequently used in the U.S. to obtain a judicial review of an administrative act. J.O.H.

Innocent Passage.
The right of surface ships, probably including warships, to traverse territorial seas and international straits. They cannot threaten the peace, order or security of a coastal state and must obey its laws though these must fall within established limits. (See 1958 Geneva Convention [Territorial Sea and Contiguous Zone], Articles 14-23.) The phrase has also been used to describe certain somewhat analogous rights including rights of aircraft and diplomats. V.R.I.

Inonu, Ismet (1884—   ).
Chief of staff under Mustafa Kemal Ataturk 1920—1922. Prime minister 1925—1937. President of Turkey after Kemal Ataturk's death in 1938. Promoted the appearance of a party of opposition, the Democratic Party, to his own Republican People's Party and resigned after the electoral victory of the Democratic Party in 1950, thereby assisting in the democratization of the new Turkish state. R.A.B.

Inquisition.
In general any quasi-judicial prosecution using cruel and arbitrary procedures. Specifically a special tribunal of the Roman Catholic church for the punishment of heretics. Most frequently it refers to the Spanish national inquisition founded in 1480 by Ferdinand and Isabella. F.M.

Inspection.
Examination of various conditions, services, commodities, and items by public authorities to assure their conformity to standards provided by law for the protection of the general public. Inspection has long been upheld by the courts as a proper exercise of the police power of the state and its subdivisions. H.J.Sch.

Integration.
The process of assimilating formerly separate or segregated elements or entities into a single, undifferentiated whole. It involves the elimination of irrationally distinctive and discriminatory status and treatment of individual and class components.
Political integration assimilates formerly sovereign or subordinate communities into a single major unit. **Economic integration** combines national or regional economies or their major elements into an undifferentiated economic union. **Cultural integration** assimilates and adapts diverse cultural elements into one common culture complex. **Racial integration** means according the same personal and civil rights of access and enjoyment which accrue to the dominant racial group.
N.P.T.

Integrism.
Integrism is less of a social movement than a doctrinal attitude whose principal characteristics are: strict

obedience to papal teachings; opposition to a separation between the state and the church; open hostility against progress, secularism, socialism and most propositions that may imply change. It may take the form of doctrinal integrism and in a rejection of any reinterpretation of the church's attitude towards labour, women's status, the role of languages other than Latin, etc. It may also, in ethical integrism, lead to puritanical intolerance. Political integrism is usually an attitude based on an acceptance that absolute monarchy or corporatism, are the only valid forms of government, and political legitimacy is only given by the church. P.G.

Intellectual.
A reflective, reasoning person or person of superior intellectual capacity, who devotes himself to study and reflection, especially about abstract or profound issues; a person who is guided primarily by the intellect rather than by emotions; a person who engages in mental or creative work particularly in scientific, literary or artistic fields rather than in manual labor. Also used in a derogatory sense to describe people who engage in empty theorizing without proposing sensible solutions to practical problems. K.Hu.

Intellectualism.
The epistemological theory that knowledge is derived or deduced from reason alone; the metaphysical theory that the idea or the intellect constitutes ultimate reality or at least that the universe is intelligible through the use of the intellect; the psychological theory that cognition is a more fundamental function than feeling or volition. The term is sometimes applied in a derogatory way to the tendency to overemphasize cognition in comparison to volition, feeling, sensation and intuition. K.Hu.

Inter-American Conferences.
The first was the Congress of Panama of 1826; the "modern" series began with the First International Conference of American States, Washington, D.C., 1889—1890, at which the International Union of American Republics and the International Bureau of American Republics were formed. The Second, at Mexico City, 1901—1902, discussed international legal questions, arbitration, and hemispheric peace. The Third, at Rio de Janeiro, 1906, considered the forcible debt collection question and the Drago and Calvo Doctrines. The Fourth, at Buenos Aires, 1910, discussed economic and cultural questions and changed the International Bureau of American Republics to the **Pan American Union**. The Fifth, at Santiago, Chile, 1923, considered reorganization of the PAU and possible modification of the Monroe Doctrine, and resulted in the so-called Gondra Treaty. The Sixth, at Havana, 1928, discussed intervention, as did the Seventh, at Montevideo, 1933, which resulted in the "Convention on Rights and Duties of States." The Inter-American Conference for the Maintenance of Peace, at Buenos Aires, 1936, considered hemispheric security and the nonintervention principle. The Eighth, at Lima, 1938, considered relations with Europe, resulting in a declaration of American solidarity and provision for emergency meetings of consultation by American foreign ministers. The Inter-American Conference on Problems of War and Peace, Mexico City, 1945, considered possible postwar problems and promulgated the Act of Chapultepec. The Inter-American Conference for the Maintenance of Continental Peace and Security, Rio de Janeiro, 1947, developed the Inter-American Treaty of Reciprocal Assistance. The Ninth International Conference of American States, Bogota, 1948, resulted in the Charter of the Organization of American States, the American Treaty on Pacific Settlement, the American Declaration of the Rights and Duties of Man, and the Economic Agreement of Bogota. The Tenth, at Caracas, 1954, discussed hemispheric policy toward communist intervention in the hemisphere and economic assistance for Latin America. An Eleventh has been scheduled for Quito, Ecuador. In addition to the major conferences, meetings of consultation of American foreign ministers have been held in times of emergency since 1939; many specialized and technical conferences also have been held through the years.
L.C.D.

Inter-American Development Bank.

Bank established by the United States Congress with the International Development Bank Act of 1959. It officially began operations in 1960. By February, 1961, it had authorized its first loan. The Bank has utilized its ordinary capital resources and its Fund for Special Operations to help accelerate the process of economic development in its Latin American member countries. All power is vested in the Board of Governors composed of regular and alternate representatives from each member country. A Board of Directors is responsible for the conduct of Bank operations. In 1961 the Bank made loans to the equivalent of $293,695,118. R.J.S.

Inter-American Mutual Assistance Treaty.

Signed in Rio de Janeiro on September 2, 1947. Its essential elements are the following: a) waiver of war b) the undertaking to submit controversies to peaceful settlement methods c) the obligation to extend immediate assistance in case of individual or collective aggression d) the determination of the area within which any armed attack may command measures of self-defense e) the establishment of a consultation body to be composed by Foreign Affairs Ministers.

The Conference for the Maintenance of the Peace and Security of the Continent was held in Petropolis from August 15th to September 2nd, as stipulated under the Chapultepec Charter of 1945. T.C.

Inter-American Regional Security.

Regional security first took shape in the Inter-American system with the signing of a treaty at Buenos Aires in 1936 which pledged the twenty-one members, in the event of a threat to the peace, to consult together to determine what measures to take under the circumstances. The treaty marked the abandonment by the United States of the so-called "international police power" proclaimed by President Roosevelt in 1904 as a necessary corollary to the Monroe Doctrine. At the Conference of Lima in 1938 the procedure was adopted of calling a Meeting of Foreign Ministers. At Havana in 1940 the obligation was made more specific by the adoption of a resolution that an attack upon one by a non-American state would be considered as an attack upon all. At the Conference at Mexico City in 1945 the American States reaffirmed the pledge of 1940 and extended it to an attack by any state against an American state, thus completing the area of regional security. At San Francisco, a month later, the American states obtained the insertion in the Charter of Article 51, providing that nothing should impair the inherent right of individual or collective self-defense until such time as the Security Council has taken measures to maintain the peace, thus offsetting the possibility of a veto by the Soviet Union.

On September 2, 1947, the final step was taken of incorporating the existing obligations of regional security into a formal treaty and specifying in greater detail the scope of the obligation. A distinction is made between an armed attack of one state against another, in which case the obligation of mutual assistance applies immediately, and an act of aggression short of an armed attack but serious enough to threaten the independence of the state. Since the ratification of the Rio Treaty it has been applied, notably in the case of the dispute between Venezuela and the Dominican Republic over the alleged complicity of the latter in the attempted assassination of President Betancourt. The treaty recites the sanctions that may be applied against an offender by a two-thirds vote, but makes the obligation to use armed force dependent upon the will of the individual state. In the case of the threat to the peace caused by the domination of Cuba by the international communist movement, the Meeting of Foreign Ministers at Punta del Este in January 1962 excluded the existing government of Cuba from participation in the inter-American system on the ground that its identification with the Marxist-Leninist system was incompatible with the principles and objectives of the inter-American system. C.G.F.

Interdependence.

The mutual need of individuals and institutions, once high technology has

made the human environment dominant over the natural environment, for the support, supply and service which other individuals and institutions provide in a complex division of labor. Distinct from dependence, which implies that some of the population are self-contained and self-reliant and in a position to sustain (or refuse to sustain) the dependent without themselves being equally dependent on others. Conscious interdependence has the political effect of moving peoples toward cooperative activities and compromise, whereas dependence breeds apathy or friction, class struggles, etc.
J.B.L.

Interest Group.
An organized group of people seeking to use its influence to promote a common interest. Also called a pressure group. Political interest groups seek to influence parties, legislators, and administrators to adopt their view on legislative or administrative action. The group must be organized for the title to apply. Sporadic and spontaneous action, such as unsolicited letter writing and visits to congressmen by constituents, would not be considered interest group activity. But if the petitioner claims to speak for the body of people with a similar interest, he thereby expresses a purported common interest, hence, is making a claim of speaking for an interest group.
R.M.T.

Inter-governmental Maritime Consultative Organization.
Established in 1959 as a UN specialized agency. Promotes international cooperation in maritime navigation, encourages the adoption of highest standards of safety in navigation. The Secretariat is in London and operates with a budget of around $750,000.
W.C.R.

Intergovernmental Relations.
The formal and informal relationships among governmental jurisdictions.
All national governmental systems divide power between a central government and various kinds of local governments. The power possessed by the local units may be a constitutional grant, as it is with the states in the American system, or it may be power granted through legislation by central, state, or provincial governments. Whatever the form of the grant the local units usually serve as administrative arms of the central government as well as possessing power of initiative in local matters.
In the United States and many other countries significant aspects of these relationships are based on financial grants-in-aid from the central, state, or provincial jurisdiction to local governments. These grants normally impose performance standards on the local units and often require matching funds be provided by the local units. As the functions of government become more complex these relationships are becoming characterized more by interdependence than independence.
A.K.C.

Internal communication.
In technical sense, the overt process by which the various parts of an organization are made aware of developments, facts, plans and ideas considered to be of general or mutual concern, for such purposes as efficiency, morale, status or political and economic indoctrination. Normally, it is instituted by top management, but to be effective it usually provides for feedback (q.v.) and even for origination of communication from all levels and all sides. Often it is handled as a public relations matter but if the process is made manipulative, it usually fails its ostensible and necessary purpose of information. The "grapevine," i.e., unofficial word-of-mouth rumor and leaked information, exists outside the system, to counter it or anticipate it. Operational communication—e.g., sales reports—is not considered internal communication.
J.B.L.

Internal Security Act of 1950.
An Act of the U.S. Congress (64 Stat. 987), popularly called the McCarran Act, aimed primarily at restricting Communist activities in the United States. All "Communist-action" and "Communist-front" organizations and the individual members thereof must be registered and are subject to a number of restrictions.
C.W.B.

Internal Waters.
All waters lying within a state's land area (lakes, rivers etc.) or between its land area and its territorial

261

sea (harbors, some bays etc.). As a rule states have complete jurisdiction over these waters and no right of innocent passage through them exists.
V.R.I.

International Administration.
The art and science of management as applied to the operations of an international organization (q.v.), especially a public international organization employing international civil servants. The term may also include operations carried on jointly by two or more states not forming an international organization. As with domestic administration, international administration involves planning, organizing, directing, staffing, budgeting, and coordinating—in short, operating. "Administration" here embraces both the British and U.S. meanings of both the terms "executive" and "administrative." It covers headquarters operations and field operations.

Although policy-making cannot be excluded entirely from any level of administration, the general distinction between administration and non-administration is that administration is not primarily policy-making in the legislative sense. Even in international administration the chief executive (administrative) officer may be quite influential in making legislation; in executive policy he is the chief maker. Diplomacy, even parliamentary diplomacy, is not considered to be administration, even though administrators must practice this art in their operations. In such international organizations as possess the crude equivalents of legislative, executive, and judicial branches, international administration is the leadership and operation of the "executive branch." For example, the Secretariat constitutes the administration (executive branch) of the United Nations, to illustrate oversimply.

Erroneously, overseas administration by a single nation is often called international administration. For example, the operations of the U.S. Agency for International Development are not properly international administration but operations extra-nationally (in foreign territory) of a national executive (administrative) agency.
R.W.V.W.

International Bank for Reconstruction and Development.
Established under 1944 Bretton Woods, N. H., Agreement, ratified 1945. Purpose and functions: Assist capital investment or reconstruction or development of productive facilities by direct loans or private loans guaranteed by governments. Voting in Board of Governors weighted according to member's contribution to funds. Thirteen Executive Directors elected by Board and five appointed by contributors. 75 members. H.Q., Washington, D.C.
F.B.G.

International Boundary Commission: United States-Mexico.
This commission was created by the Treaty of March 1, 1889, and actually set up in 1894 to administer the Treaty of 1884 which established for the water boundary between the two countries the generally accepted rules of accretion, avulsion, and the **thalweg**. It later also was made responsible for the land boundary and for carrying out the treaties of 1933 on rectification of the Rio Grande, of 1905 on banco elimination of the Rio Grande, and of 1906 and 1944 on water apportionment between the two countries.

It consists of two sections: one American and one Mexican. Each section has an engineer commissioner, engineers, a legal adviser, and a secretary, all entitled to the privileges and immunities of diplomatic officers in the other country.

Since 1944 the Commission has been called the International Boundary and Water Commission.
J.E.T.

International Civil Service.
Refers to employees of international organizations who are appointed by the secretary-general of the UN and who, in the words of the UN charter, "Shall not seek or receive instructions from any government" and "shall refrain from any action which might reflect on their position as international officials responsible only to the organization." The United Nations has over 5,000 employees and other organizations in the United Nations system have about 9,000.
W.C.R.

International Court of Justice.
The principal judicial organ of the

United Nations, composed of fifteen judges elected by the General Assembly and Security Council for nine-year terms. Only states may be parties before the court which possesses voluntary and compulsory jurisdiction, under an "Optional Clause" of the court statute, and jurisdiction which states may confer by ordinary treaties and conventions. The court has the important power to determine whether it possesses jurisdiction. It may give advisory opinions on any legal question authorized by the General Assembly or Security Council. Soviet resistance to use of the court, the reservation of cases within domestic jurisdiction by signators of the "Optional Clause," and lack of confidence by new states have stultified use of the court, although it has decided some important cases. D.P.

International Crises.

Episodes in the foreign affairs of states which invariably involve conflict between two or more national governments and which arouse unusual attention, concern, and activity in the parties involved. Most of the contemporary relations between nations and their governments are carried on without great difficulty or significant friction. Some transactions develop into serious international conflicts, however. Of the latter, a few periodically flame into great affairs. National security and prestige are perceived to be at stake and emotions of fear, hate, and self-preservation are aroused and widely distributed through the mass media. The fear or expectation of the outbreak of general war usually has been connected with these crises. Recent research on international crises has attempted to analyze their patterns of developing action, to measure their emotional levels, and to determine their periodicities. Improved knowledge of crisis behavior should strengthen the chances of peace and contribute to the calculated control of these acute conflicts between nations.

Ch.A.Mc.

International Development Association.

Established in 1960 as an affiliate of the International Bank for Reconstruction and Development, a specialized agency of the United Nations. Makes loans on terms more flexible than the Bank's conventional loans. Concerned with financing infrastructure of underdeveloped countries. Makes loans for highways, water supply, and sanitation projects which are not revenue producing or directly productive.

W.C.R.

International Exchange Programs.

These programs of international travel are distinguished from ordinary travel in that the travel arranged under the program is designed to promote a deliberate purpose of the sponsor rather than merely the interests or desires of the traveller. One of the most common purposes is to promote sympathy for and appreciation of the policies of the host country. Countries have long made a practice of inviting visits by influential persons on the assumption that the visitor would become a useful friend of the host upon his return to his homeland. Since World War II such programs have assumed massive proportions. The Smith-Mundt and Fulbright programs are outstanding American examples, though numerically more exchanges have been brought over by the armed services and by foreign aid programs for technical training. The purpose of the sponsor may also be to educate the traveller in ways other than in appreciation of the host country, e.g., to train exchangees in skills. Some exchange programs, such as the Experiment in International Living, Crossroads Africa, etc., are private in sponsorship and support. I.d.S.P.

International Finance Corporation.

An affiliate of the UN International Bank for Reconstruction and Development. Established in 1956 to help finance productive private undertakings in the less-developed areas of the world. Has loaned money when sufficient private capital is not available on reasonable terms. Serves as a catalyst and as a clearing house for investors and business men needing funds.

W.C.R.

International Labor Organization (ILO).

Instituted in 1919 as autonomous institution associated with League of Nations. Its constitution formed part of Treaty of Versailles. Purpose: improvement of labor conditions and achievement of social justice essential to international peace. In 1948 ILO revised constitution and signed agreement with United Nations becoming Specialized Agency responsible for labor and social conditions. Tripartite representation (one labor, one management, two government votes per member) in policy-making Conference drafts international standard labor conventions binding upon Governments upon ratification. 102 members. H.Q., Geneva.   F.B.G.

International Law.

International law may be defined as the body of general principles and specific rules which the members of the international community consider binding upon them in their mutual relations. Until the nineteenth century these rules were based largely upon custom, the traditional practices of Western Europe that had been developing over the years and had come to be regarded as legal obligations. With the beginning of the twentieth century multipartite treaties or conventions have come to play the leading part in the development of the law, and the Charter of the United Nations now represents the most significant part of the body of the rights and duties of states. Outstanding among the objectives of international law is the problem of national security, which until 1920 was left to the individual states, each state being the judge in its own case when there were conflicts of interest and each state left to defend itself against attack, with only the protection of the unorganized public opinion of the community. Treaties of arbitration were relied upon for the settlement of disputes, but the obligation to arbitrate was in most cases optional.

The Covenant of the League of Nations introduced the principle of collective security, the responsibility of the whole community for the protection of its individual members; but the failure of the United States to take part in the League was in part responsible for its inability to enforce its principles. The new Charter of the United States reestablished the principle of collective security; but almost immediately a conflict of fundamental principles developed between the states of Western Europe and the Soviet Union, which by 1950 had reached the tense situation of a "cold war." The United States, as the leading member of the North Atlantic Treaty Organization, has sought to maintain the principle of self-determination and the traditional right of the sovereign state to choose its own national government by democratic procedures, and the Soviet Union has followed the policy that Communism must achieve worldwide domination if it is to fulfill its destiny.

Apart from the failure of the international community to establish collective security the progress of international law in other fields has been significant, notably in the admission of African and Far Eastern states into the United Nations, the declaration of fundamental human rights, and the development of the law of territorial waters. The International Law Commission of the United Nations has contributed a number of valuable studies on particular problems, such as the responsibility of the state. Within the regional system of the American States the work of the Inter-American Council of Jurists and of its technical committee, the Inter-American Juridical Committee, has contributed significantly to the development of inter-American regional law.

C.G.F.

International Law Commission.

A fifteen member body subsidiary to the United Nations General Assembly. Established in 1947, it is charged with promoting the progressive development of international law and its codification. Members serve as experts rather than as representatives of governments. One session of eight to eleven weeks is held annually, usually in Geneva. It has prepared draft conventions on arbitral procedures and diplomatic intercourse and immunities. Other activities have dealt with the rights and duties of states, principles of international penal law, offenses against the peace and security of mankind and the law of the sea.   W.C.R.

International Monetary Fund.

Established under 1944 Bretton Woods Agreement, ratified 1945. Purposes and functions: Promotion of international monetary cooperation and currency stability by establishment of "par values" of currencies, the use of a fund to support weak currencies and members' acceptance of restrictions on currency value modification. Twelve Executive Directors elected by Board of Governors and five appointed by largest contributors. 76 members. H.Q., Washington, D.C. F.B.G.

International Organization.
Two categories: public and private. 1. A public international organization is a cooperative arrangement between two or more sovereign nation-states, having (a) an expectation of long continuity, even permanence, and (b) a continuing secretariat with (c) an operation to perform. These organizations come in a great variety of strengths and sizes, with no necessary correlation between those two attributes. The chief example is the United Nations, having all attributes in ample measure. More modest examples are the Arab League and the Organization of American States among the primarily political organizations, and the International Labor Organization and the Universal Postal Union among functional organizations (q.v.). International public unions (q.v.) are a type of public international organization. An example of an international organization having the minimum membership and a narrow function is the International Joint Commission for the U.S. and Canada. Examples of international arrangements that were not international organizations are the Concert of Europe in the early nineteenth century and the Council of Foreign Ministers after the second World War. A few very rare types of international organization border on the supranational: the European Coal and Steel Community is probably the nearest. 2. A private international organization is an association of individuals or non-governmental groups across national boundaries, normally considered as excluding international business corporations. Examples are the International Red Cross and the International Chamber of Commerce, among hundreds of others.
R.W.V.W.

International Police Force.
The Charter of the United Nations, in its article 51, permits states to fight aggression, and also requires states to use force against aggressors, but under the auspices of the United Nations. By this, the Charter of the United Nations, apparently commits the United Nations to the maintenance of international peace, including military action, if necessary. This task is entrusted to the Security Council. The first real test was during the Korean conflict, which began in 1950, when there was collective military action against North Korean aggression. Results perhaps were negligible since the situation in Korea changed little as a result of the conflict. Next came the Suez Crisis, which involved the armed attack of the United Kingdom, France, and Israel upon Egypt. In the Suez case the United Nations did not have to resort to force, since both France and the United Kingdom withdrew their forces promptly enough to make it unnecessary to consider formal sanctions against them. Israel was slower, but eventually it also gave way to pressures from the United Nations. The United Nations Emergency Force was sent to the Egyptian-Israel border, especially to the Gaza strip, to see that no new incidents took place. The 1956 uprising in Hungary against its communist rulers was another test for the efficiency of the United Nations sanctions. On this occasion the Soviet Union, which sent its military forces to crush the uprising, refused to obey the injunction of the General Assembly, and the United Nations accepted this defiance with regret without trying to enforce its decisions. Thus it came about that the United Nations Emergency Force (UNEF) was recognized as sort of a quasi-military organization, designed not to fight an aggressor but to act as an instrument for the pacific settlement of disputes. It is interesting that the UNEF consists of military contingents from the countries other than the Great Powers. Another, new, use of the UNEF arose in 1960 in the Congo, where the situation became critical in the newly independent country. While in the Suez case the role of the international force was to stabilize the re-

lations of the states involved in the conflict, the problem in the Congo has been to cope with the state of internal anarchy, and at the same time to stop foreign intrusions. V.P.P.

International propaganda.
Often considered iniquitous, it is nevertheless practiced by virtually all national governments in one or more of these political ways: (1) "information" programs to create good will and understanding, and to counter "false propaganda"; (2) use of the UN as a platform to appeal to and influence "world opinion"; (3) targeted efforts to bolster alliances and weaken opposition; (4) support and sometimes guidance for "cells" and other favorable forces in neutral or enemy countries; (5) advertising and promotional efforts to increase trade when pursued as high national policy. All techniques are used, often through specially developed media; where mass media are under government control, these are likely to be used also. Action programs such as foreign aid programs are sometimes considered at least partly for propaganda. Private efforts on behalf of such causes as religious conversions, population control or even peace are usually not within the term except insofar as they mask official efforts. (See psychological warfare.) J.B.L.

International Red Cross.
Efforts of Mon. Dunant led to the Geneva Convention of 1864 for the care of wounded soldiers in the field (revised 1906, 1929 and 1949). Compliance with the Convention was to be through a neutral "Protecting Power," as well as the International Red Cross. The International Committee of the Red Cross is a private organization composed of Swiss nationals exercising certain functions under the Prisoners of War Convention concluded at the Geneva Conference of 1929. F.B.G.

International relations.
Relations existing between sovereign nations. They are intergroup relations and must be thus distinguished from relations that exist between men who are members of the same primary group, nation-state, with which they are apt to identify themselves and to which they owe their first and foremost allegiance. International relations, in a strict sense of the word, are carried on only between the official representatives of sovereign nations either through the regular diplomatic representations, or by means of direct personal contacts between chiefs of state and main executive officers of states, or through contacts that are established among many nations at international conferences and in international organizations. Since nations are sovereign, that is independent and equal to each other, their relations must be carried out on a basis of mutual respect and in observance of the accepted rules of international law. In reality nations pursue in their mutual relations primarily their own national interests. Only rarely higher objectives, such as the general welfare of all nations, have an influence. In a negative sense, war and international hostilities are also international relations. They represent the breakdown of peaceful relations among nations. In a broader sense, the relations that are carried on by private individuals, organizations and companies with the governments and individuals belonging to another nation are also sometimes referred to as international or at least as transnational, especially if they are of a quasi-public nature. Throughout the last few centuries we can witness an ever increasing volume of international relations. The basic reason for this must be sought in the fact that no individual group or nation can be entirely self-sufficient either in the material or moral aspect. For proper development and growth the nations need communications and reciprocal exchanges of goods and services with other nations. The official international relations between the governments are thus in reality just the reflection of this wider international social process. P.P.R.

International Society.
A natural community of states which today finds partial juridical organization in the United Nations. The increasing interdependence of states leads to the formation of regional and international groupings which carry on

military, economic, social, technical, administrative, and sometimes, political functions. Pa.B.

International Telecommunications Union.
Founded in 1865 in its original form, now a specialized agency of the United Nations. Allocates frequencies for radio broadcasting in order to avoid interference. Promotes cooperation between nations in the use and running of telegraph and telephone services and offers technical assistance. Like the Universal Postal Union, has nearly all nations as members. The Secretariat is in Geneva and the budget is (as of 1961-62) around one and a half million dollars. W.C.R.

International Trade Organization.
Envisaged in the early life of the UN system as a companion to the International Monetary Fund and the International Bank for Reconstruction and Development. A Charter was approved at the United Nations Conference on Trade and Employment at Havana, November 1947—March 1948, but too few countries accepted it. With the decision in 1954-55 to establish an administering organization for the General Agreement on Tariffs and Trade (GATT) there was tacit recognition that ITO had been abandoned. L.P.B.

International treaties and agreements.
Contractual understandings among nations are called by various names, such as treaties, agreements, protocols, pacts, acts, charters, etc. There are no prescribed forms for such engagements but all imply the voluntary consent of the participating states to a set of mutually acceptable rights and obligations that will come into force because and by virtue of the particular understanding. The rule of **pacta sunt servanda**, i.e. agreements must be faithfully observed, is one of the fundamental rules of the general international law. While free consent is essential in private contracts, international law considers certain treaties, such as peace treaties, valid even if one or more of the states — parties to the treaty — were under duress to agree to the terms that were favorable to the victorious party. In concluding a treaty or agreement the contracting states follow usually certain well defined steps. First the general outlines of the understanding are discussed through regular diplomatic channels. The text of a treaty is then agreed upon, drafted and signed by specifically empowered plenipotentiaries. In case of multilateral treaties this is usually accomplished through an international conference convened for such a specific purpose. Once signed a treaty as a rule does not become binding upon the parties until it is officially ratified by the respective Heads of State and until these ratifications are officially communicated or exchanged between the parties. Most treaties are today also registered with the Secretary General of the United Nations. — The Constitution of the United States requires that a treaty can be concluded by the President only with the advice and consent of the Senate. The President, therefore, cannot ratify a treaty until and unless he receives this consent. There are, however, matters where the President may contract with other nations or with international organizations without having to obtain the consent of the Senate. These engagements are referred to in American practice as the Executive Agreements. Both treaties and agreements are equally binding under international law. P.P.R.

International Waterways Commission.
A commission of six members, three from the United States and three from Canada, created by agreement between the United States and Great Britain in 1902. Its purpose was to investigate and report upon the "conditions and uses of the waters adjacent to the boundary." The commission's restricted terms of reference soon led its members to recommend the establishment of a new and permanent body with judicial powers. The result was the Boundary Waters Treaty of 1909, creating the International Joint Commission. W.W.

Inter-party competition.
The extent to which the vote cast for or the control of a given position is divided between two political parties. Different formulae have been adopted to measure the degree to

which a two-party system exists, but the formulae vary with the research problem and the peculiar conditions of the area investigated.   J.A.R.

Interstate citizenship.
Privileges of citizenship granted by the 14th Amendment to the U.S. Constitution. Prior to its adoption U.S. citizenship was considered incidental to state citizenship, but the amendment confers U.S. citizenship to all persons born in or naturalized by the U.S. and "subject to the jurisdiction thereof." Cf., privileges and immunities.   R.R.R.

Interstate Commerce Commission.
First of the large, independent establishments, it was created in 1887. It is independent in two respects: its members hold office for a term longer than the President; and the chief executive's power to remove them is limited, for he can do so only for reasons specified in the statute creating the agency. The Commission consists of 11 members chosen by the President by and with the consent of the Senate.

Under a succession of statutes (the Transportation Act of 1920, the Motor Carrier Act of 1935 and the Transportation Act of 1958) the Interstate Commerce Commission has the responsibility for the regulation of rail, water and motor carriers in the public interest. Specifically, it issues rules and orders concerning such matters as (1) reasonable and nondiscriminatory rates (2) extension, continuance or discontinuance of routes (3) consolidations and mergers (4) issuance of securities by carriers (5) uniform accounting records and (6) safety regulations.
B.B.

Interstate Compact.
A political agreement between two or more states of the United States which has been approved by Congress. Non-political compacts can be entered into without the consent of Congress. Compacts usually are concerned with boundaries, elimination of water pollution, flood control, protection of wildlife, regional educational institutions, and port facilities.   J.F.Z.

Interstate Rendition.
In the United States the term refers to the return of a fugitive from justice to the state from which he has fled by direction of the governor of the asylum state. Although the act of Congress dealing with interstate rendition appears to require the governor of the asylum state to return a fugitive, the United States Supreme Court has ruled that the return of a fugitive is not mandatory. On a few occasions governors have refused to return a fugitive.   J.F.Z.

Interstate Transportation.
Transportation is a part of commerce. In the U.S.A. doctrines concerning its regulation have been developed, therefore, under the commerce clause of the Federal Constitution. The operations of carriers of persons or property in interstate traffic or in matters having such a close and substantial relation to it that their control is "essential or appropriate to the security of that traffic" are subject to Congressional control. But such operations, depending upon their character and other circumstances, may also be subject to regulations by the states in or through which they are carried on. Criteria relevant to the constitutionality of state regulation include: (1) whether the subject is of a character requiring uniform treatment, or, in the absence of a uniform rule is amenable to a diversity of treatment without undue burden arising therefrom, (2) whether such national regulation as may exist preemptively occupies the field, (3) whether national and state regulations are conflicting, compatible or complementary, (4) whether the state regulation is an appropriate exercise of power or a subject of legitimate state concern.   R.H.S.

Intervencion.
The practice in Latin America of replacing the normally constituted authorities of a provincial government, a public utility, a university, etc. with specially appointed officials (interventors), often military and responsible to the national executive. The justification given for **intervencion** is ordinarily corruption within the entity or adherence to a party or policy deemed inimical to the national interest. The national interest is not infrequently equated with the program of the group

in power. After a successful ouster of a dictator or any government of pronounced political leanings, the successor administration is likely to employ **intervencion** as an indispensable part of a general purging of the former leader's influence and partisans. Example: The scores of institutions intervened by Peron upon his rise to power in Argentina; the hundreds of **intervenciones** necessary when he was deposed in 1955, in order to rid the schools, the labor unions, the newspapers, the state governments, etc. of Peronist domination. R.D.H.

Intervention.
Manifests itself in efforts of coercing an offending state into modifying its domestic or foreign policy. Intervention (or interference) in the internal or foreign affairs of another state is a measure short of war and conceived as an extension of the intervener's right of self-defense. J.D.

Intolerable Acts (1773).
British statutes closing the Boston harbor to all trade except in basic necessities, making the upper house of the Massachusetts Assembly appointive by the Crown, and authorizing provincial governors to requisition inns and unoccupied buildings for possible quartering of British soldiers. R.F.H.

Intolerance.
The refusal to accept all people as basically equal, instead identifying them on a superficial basis as good or evil. Intolerance should be viewed as being on a continuum which includes progressively negative prejudicial attitudes and increasing willingness to commit acts of discrimination. M.J.S.

Involuntary Servitude
(Thirteenth Amendment).
The Thirteenth Amendment, approved in 1865, prohibits any compulsory labor (slavery, peonage, etc.) imposed by governmental or private action within the United States or its possessions, except as court-imposed punishment for crime. This Amendment does not prevent imposition of military service by Congressional Act. Selective Draft Law Cases, 245 U.S. 366 (1918). The Supreme Court early decided that the Amendment did not protect civil rights from discrimination. J.M.S.

Iran (Persia).
Physical and Economic Life: Boundaries: North — Caspian Sea, USSR; East—Afghanistan, Baluchistan; South —Persian Gulf, Arabian Sea; West— Iraq, Turkey. Area: 628,000 square miles. Population: 20,678,000. Terrain —Interior Plateau 3,000-5,000 ft. high with large salt swamps, encircled by mountains and table lands. Generally arid. Agriculture: largely pastoral, little continuous cultivation; Northwest —fruits, cereals; East — dates — the principal source of food; Caspian Sea —fishing; mountains—forestry. Industry and export: major—oil; minor— textiles, rugs. Principal imports — industrial machinery, vehicles, electrical goods. Land largely owned as "villages" by a few feudal families. Recent attempts at ownership dispersal and economic development not a spectacular success. Ethnic base: central plateau—an Iranian or Irano-Afghan subrace; Turki-(Mongoloid) Afghan groups strong throughout. Language: Persian, an Indo-Aryan language, official; Kurdish dialects in some regions; English and French known by educated. Religion: generally Islam. History: Persian Empire established ca. 550 B.C. by Cyrus. Thence empire conquered Babylon 539 B.C., Egypt 525 B.C. Halted by Greeks at Marathon 490 and Salamis 480. Overthrown by Alexander 331 B.C. and at his death divided among his generals, one Seleucis ruling Persia proper. Local nomadic forces ruled from 175 B.C. to Arab conquest in 637 A.D. Re-emerged as political entity 16th century with Ismail Safari 1502-24 laying modern foundation. From 1700 on was subject to British, Russian attempts at influence and control, often successful because of sale of the economy, customs, etc., by corrupt court. Nationalist agitation brought semblance of constitutional monarchy in 1906, abdication of Shah in 1909, a coup d'etat in 1923 by military leader Reza Khan who took crown, 1925. Although ruling autocratically latter established a more independent government and economic policy but during World War Two forced to abdicate to his son due

to Allied pressure to secure country against Germans and control communications. Following World War Two, government secured withdrawal of Russian troops, but under Prime Minister Mossadegh tried unsuccessfully to nationalize oil industry. Conflict led to domination of government by Shah largely supported by U.S. military and economic aid. Although officially ruling through a prime minister approved by **majlis** (national consultative assembly), Shah can dissolve Parliament and postpone elections indefinitely. Territorial provinces are responsible to central government.
J.P.D.

Iraq.
Area—653,151 sq. km.; Population (1959)—6,413,658. A part of the Ottoman Empire before World War I; mandated to Great Britain in 1920; recognized as a kingdom by Britain in 1922; and admitted into the League of Nations in 1932. Since 1943 fought on the side of Great Britain during World War II. Dominating, 1943-1958, was Nuri es-Said Pasha, premier for six times. Participated in the Baghdad Pact against the Soviet in 1955, and formed the Arab Federation with Jordan in rivalry with the United Arab Republic in February, 1958. Both were repudiated by General Abdel Karim Kassem after his successful revolution of July 14, 1958 in which King Feisal II, his uncle and Crown Prince, Prince Abdulillah, and Premier Nuri were killed. Since then, internationally, neutralist but slightly toward the left; Iraqi Communists, heavily controlled and disciplined; and people, closely controlled and censored. Oil was discovered in 1927. Engaged ever since in large-scale economic development, especially flood control and irrigation projects. In June, 1961, made a futile attempt to seize the oil-rich Kuwait, claimed to be an "integral part of Iraq." Later, the Kurdish revolt in northeastern Iraq was incompletely suppressed by the Army.

Premier Kassem's regime was overthrown on February 8, 1963 by a military coup d'etat. On the next day Kassem died before a firing squad. The new junta reportedly pro-Nasser and anti-communist is headed by Abdul Salam Mohammed Aref as President, formerly a Vice-Deputy under Kassem who had been involved in an assassination attempt on Kassem but whose life had been spared by the latter.
C.K.W.

Ireland. See Appendix.

Iron Curtain.
Expression coined by Winston Churchill as symbol of demarcation between the "free nations," particularly in Western Europe, and those countries within the Soviet Orbit. In a speech delivered March 5, 1946, at Fulton, Mo., Churchill said, "From Stettin in the Baltic to Trieste in the Adriatic, an Iron Curtain has descended across the Continent."
F.B.G.

Iron Law of Oligarchy.
A doctrine advanced by Roberto Michels (q.v.) that self-government is realizable only in very small groups; never is possible in large and complex organizations; and hence that leadership always falls into the hands of a few, thus tending to become a specialized activity in which the rank and file cannot participate and therefore tending eventually to be more concerned with the exercise and retention of power for its own sake than for the ends for which the organization basically exists. Deduced from this is the Iron Law of Oligarchy, which may be stated thus: Society requires organization; organization requires leadership; leadership inevitably becomes oligarchical; oligarchy always becomes self-centered.
Ch.C.M.

Irrationalism.
The doctrine that thought and behavior, both moral and political, neither are nor should be governed by rational considerations. Reliance is placed upon emotional and intuitive processes for the appraisal of values, and the possibility of a harmony of interests is denied. The sources of irrationalist political theory include the works of Schopenhauer, Nietzsche, Bergson, Freud, and Sorel.
J.W.Ch.

Islam.
The term is used to denote a system of beliefs and practices as well as a cultural complex embracing specific political structures and legal and social traditions. As a religion, Islam consists of five **pillars** based on the

Koran stressing faith and works: 1. **shahadah** (profession of faith), 2. **salat** (prayer), 3. **zakat** (almsgiving), 4. fasting of **Ramadan**, 5. **Hajj** (pilgrimage to Mecca). Islam (literally: submission to God) was revealed to the Prophet intermittently between 610—632 A.D., in Mecca and Medina of the Arabian Peninsula. With fervor and determination the Prophet spread the word of God by persuasion and the sword; and by the time of his death the whole Arabian Peninsula had been united and infused with the new faith. Under the Orthodox Caliphs (632—661) most of the Middle East and a large portion of Africa were incorporated within the Islamic State, and under the Umayyads (661—750) and the Abbasids (750—1258), the Muslims had built a great empire spreading from the shores of the Atlantic to the borders of China. In 1258, the Mongolian Hulaku captured Baghdad, killed the caliph and abolished the caliphate, a blow from which the Muslim world did not recover until the beginning of 16th century when the Islamic State restored its power and prestige under the Ottoman Turks. There are no accurate statistics for the number of Muslims in the world today. Estimates range from 350-450 millions mainly in Asia and Africa.

F.M.N.

Isma'il, Khedive of Egypt (1863—1879).

Grandson of Muhammad Ali (1806-1849), founder of modern Egypt. His reign was an essential phase of Egypt's revolutionary attempts to modernize itself. Aspiring to identify Egypt's fate with Europe, he became the god-father of the Suez Canal, the "Maecenas of Aida," and the champion of adventurous projects. His reign saw the beginning of public education, a rapid development of public works, and the convening in 1866 of a Chamber of Deputies, which served as a nursery of Egyptian nationalism. He founded a national library and museum, was a patron of the theatre, encouraged journalism and may be credited for the freedom given to a Press which was then in its infancy. But his "gullibility," "speculation," "vanity" and "extravagance" made him a victim of European financial and diplomatic adventurers. Geared more towards grandeur than welfare, his policy of modernizing Egypt led to financial imperialism and to a nationalist reaction culminating in the Arabi Revolt of 1882 and the British occupation of Egypt. F.M.N.

Isolationism.

A political attitude or opinion opposing involvement in the affairs of other nations. Classic American statement in George Washington's "farewell address" warning against "foreign entanglements." Historically, directed more at Europe than at the Far East and South America. In more recent times, expressed in terms of opposition to American entry to World War I and II and to participation in the United Nations. Often associated with ethnic backgrounds. Classic confrontation was between America First Committee (isolationist) and Committee to Defend America by Aiding the Allies (interventionist) before U.S. entry into World War II. Also applied to British foreign policy and political attitudes before 1939. W.C.R.

Israel, State of (Medinat Israel).

An independent republic at the eastern end of the Mediterranean Sea. Area 7,993 sq. mi.; total population (census, May 1961) — 2,170,082, of which 1,932,536 Jews, 170,000 Muslims (mostly Sunnis), 50,000 Christians composed of 20,000 Greek Catholics (Melkites), 17,00 Greek Orthodox, 7,000 Roman Catholics (Latin), 3,000 Maronites and others. The Druzes numbering about 18,000 are recognized as a special community. Capital — Jerusalem. Israel proclaimed its independence on 14 May 1948 with the termination of the British Mandate of Palestine, after a resolution of the UN General Assembly of 29 November 1947 that a Jewish state and an Arab state be established in (Western) Palestine. Israel's relatively long international land boundaries (590 miles) were determined by the armistice agreement signed with its Arab neighbor states (24 February 1949—Egypt; 23 March—Lebanon; 3 April—Jordan; 20 July —Syria) whose armies invaded the country on the day of its establishment. Israel was admitted as

59th member of the UN on 11 May 1949.

Since its establishment Israel's population has more than trebled, mainly through mass immigration **(aliya)** of Jews under Law of Return (1950) which guaranteed every Jew the right to immigrate to Israel. Bulk of immigrants were remnants of European Jewry left after the Hitlerian massacres and Jewish refugees from Middle Eastern and North African countries. Resultant economic, social, cultural and political problems of absorption were satisfactorily solved, partly with help of generous foreign aid, including German reparations and financial assistance of Jews of Western World as well as U.S. governmental and UN resources.

The Arab population of Israel participates in and benefits from these developments with steady increase in standard of living. It fully keeps its national and religious autonomy. The rather severe travel restrictions imposed for security reasons on border regions mainly inhabited by Arabs have gradually been relaxed and the functions of the Military Administration over these areas drastically curtailed.

Israel has a parliamentary system of government with a unicameral legislative called **Knesset** (Assembly) of 120 members elected for four years by universal suffrage of all citizens over 18 years of age on the basis of a rigid party list system of proportional representation with the whole country serving as one multi-member constituency.

The party composition of the Fifth **Knesset** (elected 15 August 1961) is as follows: Mapai—42 seats (34.7% of total votes); Herut—17 (13.7%); Liberals—17 (13.6%); National Religious Party—12 (9.8%); Mapam—9 (7.6%); Ahdut Ha'avoda—8 (6.5%); Communists—5 (4.1%); Agudat Israel—4 (3.7%); Arab lists (associated with Mapai)—4 (3.5%); Poalei Agudat Israel—2 (1.9%).

The President of the State is elected by the Knesset for five years. The first President, Dr. Chaim Weizmann, onetime President of the World Zionist Organization, died in office—1952; his successor, Mr. Itzhak Ben-Zvi, was re-elected for a third term of office in 1962, but died April 23, 1963. He was succeeded by Zalman Shazar, former Minister of Education.

The Cabinet (composed of about 16 ministers who usually are, but do not have to be **Knesset** members and headed by the Prime Minister) takes office on receiving a vote of confidence by the **Knesset** and is collectively responsible to it. The Cabinet may resign and must do so after new elections, after the resignation of the Prime Minister and upon a vote of non-confidence, but in each case it continues in office with full powers until a new cabinet is constituted. As no party has so far commanded an absolute majority, all Cabinets have been coalitions, all of them based on Mapai, the largest party with a majority within the Cabinet. Upon Ben-Gurion's resignation, June 16, 1963, Moshe Sharett, former Minister of Finances, became the Prime Minister.

E.G.

Istiqlal.

Istiqlal (Arabic for independence) party is the heir and successor of the National Party of 1937. It is opposed by PDI (Party of Democratic Independence). The Istiqlal has a strong base throughout Morocco with regional councils and a National Council at the summit. In January 1959 Ben Barka split the party by announcing his intention of establishing the "true" Istiqlal party. Istiqlal leader Al-Fassi was given emergency power. The Istiqlal collaborated with Sultan Muhammad V for the realization of Moroccan independence, and it remains after independence the predominant political force in the country appealing to modern and traditional elements alike.

E.A.S.

Italian Christian Democrats.

Largest postwar Italian party (receiving 40% of the vote), Christian Democracy is a highly organized party whose official ideology, derived from Catholic moral teachings and papal social encyclicals, also includes the method of freedom, left-of-center policies, and independence from clerical control. It is actually rent by internal divisions and influenced by church and conservative interests which support it as leader of Italian anticommunism. Backbone of all Italian governments since 1945, it established constitutional government, economic recovery, and restored international prestige under Alcide de Gasperi's leadership (1945—1953). From 1953 until 1960, internal dissension rendered it immobile until Amintore Fanfani steered its organization and government policy leftwards. E.T.O.

Italian Communists.

The Italian Communist party, established in 1921 by revolutionary Marxist Socialists under Bolshevik tutelage, is the largest communist party in the free world. Under Palmiro Togliatti, it has been loyal to Soviet direction and interests, but its political strength rests on flexible exploitation of specifically Italian conditions. Until ousted in 1947 from the six-party coalition which ruled Italy immediately after fascism, the Communists posed as a great national party of democracy and compromise, even a friend of the Catholic Church. Since then it has been the chief opposition party and, by controlling roughly 35% of the national vote when united with the Italian Socialists, it has exerted a conservative and negative influence on Italian politics by limiting the possibilities of choice of voters, government, and parties. Its vote, a heavy majority in some north-central areas and approximately 23% nationally when unallied, comes from its leadership in the wartime Resistance against Nazis and Fascists; its vigorous anticlericalism; and labor leadership of class-conscious industrial and agricultural workers in a country of great poverty and glaring inequalities. Well-financed, manned by dedicated, disciplined workers, and acting through a vast network of party units, front organizations, recreation facilities, schools, and propaganda media calling for peace, jobs, and democracy, the party maintained its voting strength even after it was shaken internally by the 1956 Khrushchev denunciations of Stalin and the revolt in Hungary. In recent years, Togliatti has become expounder of a policy of "polycentrism" which has implied greater independence from Soviet direction for national parties and which has provoked some opposition within his party but has been well-suited to maintaining strength with non-party voters. E.T.O.

Italian Constitution.

See Constitution of the Italian Republic.

Italian Democratic Socialists.

Middle-class reformists, the Italian Social Democrats united in 1951 several groups which had abandoned the Communist-dominated Socialists. Until 1958, when it began earnestly to work toward unification with larger parent body, the party alternately joined and abstained from what it considered conservative and clerical Christian Democratic governments. E.T.O.

Italian Liberal Party.

Successor to the loose coalitions and personal groups of liberals who ran pre-Fascist Italy, the Italian Liberal party today is a grouping of economic conservatives rather than a modern party. It has become the spokesman of Italian business and property and, until alienated by economic reform programs, was one of the lay parties which supported Christian Democratic governments. It receives about 4% of the national vote. E.T.O.

Italian Monarchists.

The monarchy lost the 1946 referendum by only 10 to 12 million votes. But its supporters now vote mainly for Christian Democrats and the Monarchists, whether united or split into separate parties by personality differences, have had voting support like the Neofascists whom they resemble also in policy. E.T.O.

Italian Neofascists.

The neofascist Italian Social Movement, combining since 1947 former fascists and followers of the "Republic of Salo," feeds on past glory, bitterness, and anticommunism. Its support, 5% nationally, is concentrated in the south and islands, where it has formed local governments with Christian Democrats. Such support has been refused the neofascists at the national level. E.T.O.

Italian Radical Party.

Newest and smallest of Italian political groups, the Radical Party was established by a few distinguished intellectuals and journalists who, bolting the Liberal Party in 1956 because of its conservatism, hoped to create a lay "third force" between Catholicism and Marxism. E.T.O.

Italian Republican Party.

Mazzini's heir, the Italian Republican Party was a largely regional party which lost its meaning after the establishment of a republic. Tiniest (with 2% of the vote) of the center coalition parties, it is, like the democratic socialists, a lay party advocating economic and social reform. E.T.O.

Italian Socialists.

A revolutionary Marxist party created in 1892, the Italian Socialist Party was spokesman of the northern working class and free Italy's largest party until 1948 when it lost both its independence and leadership under a Popular Front with the Communists. Its vote, nearly 35% in 1919 and over 20% in 1946, has fallen to about 12-14%. The motives of leader Pietro Nenni—whether he was a Communist "Trojan horse" or sincere in refusing to split working class ranks—dominated Italian postwar speculation because the Communist-Socialist alliance stalemated democracy. In 1956, Nenni began to detach himself from the Communists, eventually breaking the Popular Front and then ceasing to oppose the center government. By 1962 hints at government participation opened the possibility that at least part of the Italian working class would break its historical isolation from and opposition to the state and its government. E.T.O.

Italy.

The Italian Republic occupies a peninsula extending from the Alps into the Mediterranean and includes the islands of Sicily and Sardinia. Her 116,246 square miles, generally mountainous with impoverished soil and scant resources, carry a population of 50,000,000 (1960 est.). Despite heavy emigration before 1920 and a declining birth rate recently, unemployment is chronic. The modern industrial north, prosperous even in its Po Valley agriculture, contrasts sharply socially and culturally with the impoverished and backward agrarian islands and south.

Italian history encompasses republican, imperial, and Christian Rome; cultural and economic leadership and self-government in the late Middle Ages and the Renaissance; and a thousand years of foreign invasion and dominion and of papal-antipapal struggles. The legacy for modern Italy has been divisions between regions and classes and on the clerical issue. Napoleon's conquest was followed by both restoration of papal, Austrian, Bourbon, and French dominion and the **Risorgimento**, a political, literary, and idealistic movement for national unity and independence. Despite the appeal of a Mazzini or Garibaldi, the Italian people as a whole did not participate in unification. Italy was created by the prime minister of Savoy, Cavour, through diplomatic and military action and unions ratified by popular plebiscite. The new united kingdom, proclaimed in March 1961, acquired its chosen capital when royal troops entered Rome in 1870, at the cost of papal hostility lasting until World War I.

Despite its relative poverty, divisions, and limited suffrage, Italy progressed in most respects. It acquired a North African empire before 1900 and emerged one of the victorious allies from World War I. Yet a climate of post-war economic dislocation, frustration over failure to acquire Italian areas which had belonged to Austria, and political changes under universal suffrage contributed to the fall of democracy. Parliament's hostile and suspicious groups — large disciplined Socialist and Catholic (Popular) parties who refused to compromise their principles and unorganized prewar Liberal personalities unable to adapt to new conditions—could create no stable government. Socialist workers inspired by the Russian revolution resorted to direct action; then Fascist squads, benefitting from a red scare among conservatives, spread havoc and violence in the north. Rather than invoke martial law, the king appointed Fascist leader Mussolini prime minister in 1922. By 1926, a totalitarian dictatorship was entrenched and lasted until July 1943 when, after Allied invasion of Sicily, the Grand Council of Fascism forced Mussolini to resign. After this Italy was split between the Allies and an antifascist royal government in the south, and German occupation, a puppet Fascist Republic, and partisan Resistance in the north. In 1946 the Italian people voted to end the monarchy and elected an assembly to write a new constitution. Until 1947 governments included all antifascist parties. Since then they have been led by the Christian Democrats who, with smaller democratic parties, maintain a bare majority between a Communist-dominated (until 1960) left and a monarchic and fascist right. Virtually all government policy, including agrarian reform, development programs for the south, and Western European economic integration and defense, is dominated by desire to cut domestic Communist strength. Except for the dispute with Yugoslavia over Trieste, resolved in 1954, when the city returned to Italy, there have been no outstanding foreign policy issues once decision to join in NATO and European economic integration was made. E.T.O.

Item Veto.
The power possessed by the governor of forty-one states of the United States to refuse to approve items contained in appropriation bills. In the state of Washington he may veto items in general bills. In six states the governor may reduce the amounts of items in appropriation bills. The item veto may be overridden by the same procedure as an ordinary veto. J.F.Z.

I.T.O.
See International Trade Organization.

Ito, Hirobumi (1841—1909).
Leading statesman in the Meiji Period. Prime minister four times between 1886 and 1901. Appointed Governor-General of Korea after the annexation of Korea by Japan in 1906. Assassinated at Harbin on October 26, 1909. H.U.

Ius gentium.
Originally in Roman law the term **ius gentium** referred to the body of private law common to all nationalities and communities of the diverse Roman empire. It was based on common sense and customs and was distinguished from civil law **(ius civile)** which applied only to the citizens of Rome proper. In the Middle Ages and in the early Modern Age **ius gentium** meant the law governing the relations among nations, deriving its principles from the law of nature and from customs established among nations. It was translated into English mostly as the **Law of Nations.** During the 19th century these terms were gradually replaced by the term **International Law.** The latter represents the positivistic conception of law as based on consent of and coordinating relations among independent nations. P.P.R.

Ivory Coast.
An independent state on the west coast of Africa between Ghana and Liberia, comprising 115,558 square miles and having 2,661,000 inhabitants in 1956. The French acquired trading settlements here prior to 1842 when treaties asserted French rights. After 1882 the French occupied and actively developed the territory and in 1899 attained complete control by subjugating native tribes.
The Ivory Coast became an autonomous republic within the French community in 1958 and an independent state in 1960. There is a President, popularly elected for a five year term, who has strong executive power. Legislative power is vested in a 70 member assembly, elected at the same time and for the same term as the President. There is an independent judiciary headed by a Supreme Court. J.E.R.

Izvestia ("News").
The daily organ of the Soviet government (as opposed to PRAVDA, which represents the Communist party). I. is generally regarded as the second most important newspaper in the U.S.S.R. I. was first published on March 13, 1917, and until the October Revolution, it was under Social Revolutionary and Menshevik control. In the Khrushchev period, I. came under the editorship of Aleksei Adzhubei, Khrushchev's son-in-law, who has tried to increase reader interest by enlivening the newspaper's style. D.N.J.

J

Jabotinsky, Vladimir (1880—1940).
Born Russia; educated there and in Italy.
Lawyer, poet, linguist, journalist, Zionist leader.
Candidate to Czarist Duma; founder of Jewish self-defense in Russian pogroms of 1905-06.
Organized Jewish Legion under Gen. Allenby in World War I and defense of Jerusalem in Arab pogroms of 1920. A member of World Zionist Executive, he opposed policies of Weizmann as pro-British and insufficiently militant. In 1935, his World Union of Zionist Revisionists left World Zionist Organization to pursue independent course toward statehood. President, Brith Trumpeldor, Revisionist Zionist youth movement. Author of numerous works. S.H.

Jackson, Andrew.
b. March 15, 1767, in South Carolina. Died June 8, 1845 at his home, The Hermitage, in Nashville, Tennessee. He was the seventh president of the United States (1829-1837), the first Democrat and the first from the West. His military record made him a popular hero. He defeated the British at New Orleans. He took Florida from the Spanish. He ran for president in 1824, with a plurality of the electoral vote, but lost to John Quincy Adams by vote of the House of Representatives In 1828 and 1832 he had an overwhelming majority in the electoral college. He believed any person should have a right to hold public office. His veto killed the National Bank. M.F.

Jackson, Robert H. (1892—1954).
Associate Justice of the United States, appointed by Roosevelt in 1941. He practiced law in Jamestown, New York (1913—1934) before coming to Washington as General Counsel for the Bureau of Internal Revenue (1934-36), was Assistant Attorney General (1936-38), and Solicitor General (1938-39). He strongly supported New Deal legislation and before joining the Court wrote a brilliant tract against judicial excess in a democracy. During his early years on the Court, he took a moderately liberal position in civil liberty cases and a moderately conservative one on matters pertaining to labor and business regulations. In the post-war period he became more strongly inclined toward Mr. Justice Frankfurter's philosophy of judicial self-restraint. His slight volume, **The Supreme Court in the American System of Government** (1955) is an insightful analysis of the role of the Court in maintaining an equilibrium of power in the federal system. P.B.

Jacksonian democracy.
Pertains to Andrew Jackson, a leader of the Democratic party and seventh President (1829-37) of the United States, who led the movement that witnessed the political and social rise of the common man in America. Jackson's views and policies were based upon faith in the common man, belief in political equality, belief in equal economic opportunity, and hatred of monopoly and special privilege.
R.V.A.

Jamaica.
A British dependency in the West Indies, with an area of 4,411 square miles and a population of 1,607,000, Jamaica was discovered in 1494 and was under Spanish control until taken by the English in 1665. Jamaica became a member of the West Indies Federation in 1958 and was to receive independence in 1962. In 1961, however, Jamaican voters indicated preference for leaving the Federation and gaining separate Commonwealth status. Great Britain has indicated that Jamaica would be granted independence and be sponsored by Great Britain for full Commonwealth membership. L.C.D.

Japan. See Appendix.

Japanese-American Security Treaty.
The original security treaty between Japan and the United States was signed, with the peace pact, in 1951. It was designed for "the maintenance of international peace and security in the Far East" (Article 1); but it provided no prior consultation in case American forces based in Japan were used outside the country. A revised treaty was signed in Washington in January, 1960. Both parties agreed to

consult if the security of Japan or the Far East were threatened (Art. 4). Nevertheless, demonstrations against the revised treaty in Tokyo were so grave as to lead Japan, on June 16, 1960, to postpone the scheduled visit of President Dwight Eisenhower. Under severe pressure, the Japanese Diet finally approved the treaty and exchange of ratifications took place in Tokyo, June 23, 1960. For the purposes of the treaty, the United States was granted continued use of areas and facilities for forces in Japan (Art. 6).
A.W.B.

Japanese Constitution.
Article Nine.

The most unusual and controversial feature of the new (1946) Constitution of Japan is Chapter 2, Article 9. By this provision, the Japanese aspire to peace and "forever renounce war as a sovereign right of the nation and the threat or use of force as means of settling international disputes." Originally, the article was interpreted to mean that land, sea and air forces, as well as other war potential, would never be maintained. The provision has by usage been reinterpreted to prohibit offensive armament, to be used outside Japan, but to permit the Self-Defense Forces, used inside Japan. In 1959, the Supreme Court ruled that American forces based in Japan did not constitute "war potential" under Article 9.
A.W.B.

Japanese Diet.

The Japanese legislative body under the contemporary constitutional structure (since 1947), consisting of a House of Representatives (467 members elected for a 4 year term) and a House of Counsellors (250 members, 100 elected at large and 100 from prefectural districts, one half every 3 years). The Diet is convoked by the Prime Minister and may be dissolved upon a vote of no-confidence by the Prime Minister and Cabinet. The lower house controls the budget and approves treaties with foreign powers.
M.W.W.

Japanese Emperor Concept.

The concept of the divinity and divine origin of the Japanese Emperor and Imperial family, traceable to the mythological creation of the Japanese islands and foundation of the royal house by union of the deities Izanagi and Izanami. The Imperial house is also closely associated with the practice of Bushido, or the social custom of ancestor veneration and familial honor. The post-World War II "MacArthur Constitution" and subsequent governmental evolution legally divested the Emperor of his divine prerogatives and the substance of such real authority as he possessed prior to 1945.
M.W.W.

Japanese Government.

The present Japanese Constitution, which was drafted in the Headquarters of the Supreme Commander for the Allied Powers and passed with minor changes by the Japanese Diet in 1946, became effective in 1947. The Emperor is the symbol of the State and of the unity of the Japanese people with whom resides sovereign power. The Prime Minister is elected by the Diet. (If the upper and lower houses disagree, the decision of the latter prevails.) The House of Representatives (lower house) is made up of members elected from multimember districts in which each voter votes for only one candidate. If the Representatives pass a resolution of no-confidence, the Cabinet must either resign or dissolve the house within ten days. The House of Councillors, which may not be dissolved, consists of 250 members serving for six-year terms; half of whom are elected every three years. One hundred fifty of the members represent prefectures, 100 members are elected by the nation at large. A bill may be enacted over the veto of the upper house if repassed by a two-thirds majority in the lower house.

The Supreme Court consists of fifteen Judges designated by the Cabinet. The appointment of each (except the Chief Judge) is subject to approval by the voters at the next general election and every ten years thereafter. The Supreme Court has the final determination concerning the constitutionality of laws and executive acts. The system of government is unitary rather than federal. According to the current interpretation of the Constitution, which bans war and armaments, the Self-Defense Forces may not be used outside of Japan and are permitted only defensive weapons. Since 1955, the conservative Liberal Democratic Party has held about two-thirds of the seats in both houses of the Diet, and its party presidents have successively served as Prime Ministers.

T.Mc.N.

Japanese Imperial Rescript.

An edict handed down and proclaimed by (or in the name of) an emperor. It is a document intended to carry with it the full weight of Imperial authority and will. In Japan, following the Meiji Restoration, the nominal position of the Emperor was restored and he was elevated to an **appearance** of real and direct authority. It became the practice of the government thereafter to cause important policies and directives to be issued by the Emperor. Among the more important Rescripts issued in the 19th century were those dealing with education and particularly the important Parliamentary Rescript of October 12, 1881, establishing a Parliament in Japan by royal will. The Japanese Constitution was handed down to the people as an Imperial gift, imparting the sense that it was **for** the people, but by no means **of** or **by** them. This was not merely an example but a positive factor in limiting the development of popular and democratic tendencies in Japan. The most significant Imperial Rescript in the 20th century was that issued by Emperor Hirohito on January 1, 1946, in which he formally declared that he was not divine, and that Imperial divinity was a false conception based on ancient myths and legends. He also stated at that time that the dogma which held that Japan was destined to rule the world and that the Japanese were a racially superior people was untrue. But perhaps the most important effect of this Rescript was that it signified that government belonged to the people through their legislature and that the use of Imperial Rescripts had become meaningless for the future.   S.S.

Japanese Politics.

In the fourth century the united Yamato state was supposedly established by the ancestors of the present imperial family in the western part of Honshu after an approximate hundred years' absorption and conquest of smaller tribal states. Borrowing Chinese legal and Buddhistic moral concepts, a centralized state was established under the absolute authority of the Emperor. Three centuries of peaceful rule followed—known as the Heian period. In the tenth century the Fujiwara family, who rose from the bureaucracy, seized power and governed under the name of the Emperor. During their dominance, there was a preference for the arts and luxurious life rather than political development. Consequently, the warrior class, originating as local police units, became independent. It utilized power conflicts among the aristocrats to make inroads into the central political arena. One of the police units established an independent government at Kamakura and by the end of the twelfth century it replaced the central government. This marked the first warrior government (Bakufu), and it also marked the beginning of the feudal society which continued through the Edo period (see Tokugawa period). The feudal period ended with the collapse of the Tokugawa Bakufu, and the Meiji period began (see Meiji Constitution). The state, depending upon the absolute power of the Emperor rather than the people's will, was effective for strengthening Japan industrially against foreign imperialistic powers. At the same time, intellectuals were inspired by Western democratic thought, especially British utilitarianism and the writings of Jean-Jacques Rousseau. They insisted upon a popularly elected Diet as opposed to the ruling groups who aimed at a weak Diet. The intellectuals succeeded in establishing a party system of politics, which reached its peak in the period of "Taisho Democracy" (1918—1925). In the economic depression socialistic sectors of the Labor movement joined the democratic forces. Thus Japanese democracy, based on western liberalism, socialism, and even some concepts of anarchism, developed until the militaristic groups became dominant by assassinations and coups d'etat. They entered into imperialistic ventures despite the opposition of the Emperor, the liberals and others who desired to maintain peaceful relations with the foreign powers. After the alliance with Germany and Italy in 1940, the militarists proceeded with little resistance and suppressed any possible opposition through stringent police tactics.

Since the end of the Pacific War, Japan was democratized as part of the occupation policy. All social and political institutions underwent a process of reform. Nevertheless, many Japanese have become doubtful as to the stability of their western inspired democracy.   H.U.

Japanese War Crimes Trials.

At the International Tribunal for the Far East in Tokyo beginning on May 3, 1946, representatives from eleven leading Allied powers sat in judgment on twenty-eight major war criminals including Hideki Tojo. In November 1948, all of the accused were found guilty of planning a war of aggression. Through the two years of trial much significant historical material was made public. In addition, various nations carried on their own independent trials against Japanese who had committed war-connected atrocities.   G.O.T.

Jaures, Jean.

Jean Jaures, the father of French socialism, was a professor of philosophy at the University of Toulouse. Turning to politics in the late 1890's, he was elected a deputy from Toulouse in 1898 and by 1904 he had united numerous socialist groups in France. That same year he founded the then reformist and evolutionist socialist newspaper **Humanité**. Jaures, a great idealist, pacifist, internationalist, a fluent orator and writer, was assassinated on July 31, 1914.   C.R.F.

Javits, Jacob K.

Born May 18, 1904, U.S. Senate from November 6, 1956 until term ending 1963; Republican — New York City; attorney general of New York in 1954 for a 4-year term. Reelected to U.S. Senate in 1962.   R.A.B.

Jefe Maximo.

In Latin American politics the embodiment of all power in the person of one charismatic leader — literally a "maximum boss," the extreme manifestation of paternalistic **personalismo** (q.v.). The **jefe maximo** is looked upon by his followers with adulation, virtually as a secular Prophet or Messiah; near-miraculous deliverance from the bonds of poverty and oppression are expected at his hands. Only he can command; only he can decide. His speech is inspired and to be preserved for posterity. Tremendous energy is made available to the **jefe's** movement by the faithful, but once in office megalomania, lack of sophistication in social engineering and, eventually, corruption, have always impeded actual accomplishment of heralded transformations. The popular impatience, the regime's mistakes and scandal bring disenchantment and then oppression as the **jefe's** cohort attempts to maintain power. Notorious examples: Juan Peron (Argentina); Fidel Castro (Cuba.) Also: **jefe supremo**.   R.D.H.

Jefferson, Thomas (1743—1826).

Born of a marriage of yeomanry and Virginia aristocracy, Thomas Jefferson was reared on the frontier but also mingled with the first families. Educated at the College of William and Mary and a lawyer by profession, he married Martha Skelton and lived at Monticello, a magnificent dwelling which he designed and labored for a generation to complete. After six years of service in the Virginia House of Burgesses, Jefferson was elected to the second Continental Congress in 1775. Here, as a member of a select committee, he drafted the immortal Declaration of Independence.

For the next fourteen years Jefferson pursued a varied career which included service in the Virginia House of Delegates, as governor of Virginia, and as Minister to France. In 1790 he reluctantly accepted appointment as Secretary of State in Washington's first Cabinet. He differed seriously with Hamilton about public policy, and both men eventually left the government. Jefferson was vice president (1797—1801) after losing the presidency to Adams by a narrow margin in 1796.

Jefferson's two terms as president, beginning in 1801, launched a Republican era in politics. Despite his earlier differences with Hamilton, Jefferson continued many Federalist policies. Laying constitutional scruples aside, Jefferson negotiated the Louisiana Purchase. He maintained neutrality in the Napoleonic wars, but at the high price of the controversial Embargo Act.

A student and statesman of incredible versatility, Jefferson was one of America's greatest presidents. Diffident by nature, lacking a colorful political personality, he succeeded through industry, study, and a consummate skill in dealing with men in small groups. Throughout his life Jefferson retained a profound faith in freedom, in the need for education, and in the virtues of a rural life. No other American deserves more than he to be called the prophet of the American dream. Th.P.

Jeffersonian Democracy.
Jeffersonian democracy recognized the natural rights of man and believed it wrong for the state to intervene in human affairs beyond the necessities of peace and order in society. There is recognition of the dual hazards of weak government and strong government—both may fail to adequately protect the individual. If there were possible abuses in democracy, the cure was more democracy. The goal was to place the control of government as completely as possible in the hands of the people. John Taylor became the real philosopher of the movement as he produced systematic and comprehensive arguments. The practical politics of Jeffersonian democracy included the freedoms of speech, press, and religion, local self-government, universal free education, universal adult male suffrage, and political and popular election of executives, judges, and legislators. W.D.S.

Jesus.
1. Greek equivalent of the Hebrew **Yeshu**, which was a corruption of **Yehoshua**, the Hebrew equivalent of the English **Joshua**. 2. The messiah of the Christians and a major prophet of the Muslims; dates of his life usually given as 4 B.C. to 29 A.D.; gospels of Mark and Luke present him as an apolitical personage who said, "Render unto Caesar the things that are Caesar's, and unto God the things that are God's," which passage of Scripture became the basis of the political doctrine of the separation of church and state. Ch.C.M.

Jewish Agency for Israel.
Authoritative body, founded 1920, representing Zionists and non-Zionists in immigration, colonization and related matters in pre-statehood Israel. Forerunner of Israeli government, now mainly supports Israeli economic development, quasi-governmental functions of overseas immigration, fundraising. S.H.

Jews in American Politics.
Since the beginning of the Republic, American Jews have exercised their political interests in a vigorous way. They played a crucial role in supporting Thomas Jefferson in New York City, Philadelphia, and other large towns, siding with the secular, humanist, and liberal forces of the day. Even well-to-do Jewish merchants tended to side with Jefferson, Jackson, and other Democratic candidates against the more conservative candidates and policies of the Federalist and Whig parties.

The emergence of the slavery issue and the new Republican Party found German-Jewish-Americans abandoning the traditional Jewish preference for the Democrats. The memory of Lincoln, the absence of liberal-conservative ideological issues as perceived by Jews, and the identification of the Democrats as the party of slavery kept most Jews in the Republican fold until 1928, when a significant shift to the Democrats, already begun in the mid-1920's, took place.

The Jewish response to Franklin D. Roosevelt was phenomenal with more than ninety percent of the voters of Jewish background casting ballots for Roosevelt in 1940 and 1944 because of the President's strong internationalism-liberalism and defense of the Jews against Hitler. Most Jews developed a strong attachment to Democratic candidates at the very time they were advancing up the economic-class ladder, going against general class tendencies in American politics. The reason appears to be that Jews, as a group, are unusually issue-oriented, and have tended to identify their group interest in advancing liberalism and internationalism with Democratic success. The issue-orientation of Jews shows itself in political independence in state and local politics since no group splits tickets, votes for third-party candidates, or switches major party loyalties more than the Jews.

American Jewish pressure played a significant role in the recognition of the new state of Israel by President Harry S. Truman in 1948. Jews also played an important part in the election of President Kennedy in 1960. Many Jews have been governors, congressmen, and cabinet members. Individual Jewish contributions have been most significant in the Supreme Court through the dissents and decisions of three of the great figures in the history of American jurisprudence, Nathan Cardozo, Louis D. Brandeis, and Felix Frankfurter.   L.H.F.

Jihad (Holy War).

Jihad is the term used by Muslim jurists to describe all forms of "exertion" against the infidels. It does not necessarily mean war or fighting: the believer could discharge his jihad obligation either by his heart; his tongue; his hands; or by the sword. The main thing is to spread God's word supreme, no matter how. As such, jihad is regarded as **bellum iustum,** "a litigation between Islam and polytheism," a noble activity with religious merit. It follows that jihad is a doctrine of a permanent state of war, if not of continuous fighting, until the House of Islam (peace) supersedes the House of non-Islam (war). In Sunni Islam jihad is a collective, and not an individual, obligation; a community and, consequently, a state instrument. The Kharijites were the only sect which regarded jihad as an article of faith incumbent on every individual believer. The concept, has undergone certain changes in its meaning as a result of changes in Islam's political and social conditions. With the rise of the modern state system and the advent of nationalism, religious solidarity has given way to national interests.   F.M.N.

Jim Crow.

Based upon a 19th-century American song-and-dance act, Jim Crow refers to thestereotyped Negro and particularly the segregation of Negroes from whites in social, commercial, and educational facilities. In the southern U.S., tradition and even restrictive legislation (Jim Crow Laws) have attempted to separate the races. See PLESSY v. FERGUSON, 163 U.S. 537 (1896), and BROWN v. BOARD OF EDUCATION, 347 U.S. 483 (1954).   J.A.E.

Jinnah, Mohammed Ali
(1876—1948).

The founder of Pakistan. The eldest son of a Khoja merchant, Jinnah was born in Karachi. His studies took him to England, where he qualified as a barrister at Lincoln's Inn. Returning home, he established a good practice at the Bombay bar. In 1906, he entered politics as secretary to Dadabhai Naoroji, President of the Congress (q.v.). This brought prominence in Congress ranks. As a staunch nationalist, Jinnah condemned communalism and advocated Hindu-Muslim unity. In 1920, he opposed Gandhi's satyagraha (q.v.) and resigned from the Congress. Hereafter, **he became chief** spokesman for Muslim interests, especially on his election as permanent President of the Muslim League in 1934. He transformed the League into a mass organization and became its Qaid-i-Azam (Great Leader). In 1940, he led the demand for a separate Muslim state, Pakistan. Seven years later, Pakistan was established. Jinnah became its Governor-General and held the post until his death in September 1948.   C.S.S.

Jiyu Minshuto.

Liberal Democratic Party of Japan. Following World War II, the Liberal Party, which included many former Seiyukai people, was organized by Hatoyama Ichiro, and the Progressive Party (later renamed the Democratic Party) was formed under the leadership of Premier Shidehara Kijuro. Following General MacArthur's purge of Hatoyama, Yoshida Shigeru became the leader of the Liberals, and his governments ruled in 1946—1947 and 1948—1953. The depurge of many former politicians, the end of the Allied occupation, and a conservative reaction against occupation reforms favored the Democratic Party, which came to power under Hatoyama, who had left the Liberals. In 1955, the two conservative parties merged to form the present-day Liberal Democratic

Party, of which Premiers Hatoyama, Ishibashi, Kishi, and Ikeda have served as presidents. The party holds about two-thirds of the seats in each house of the Diet and supports alliance with the United States, rearmament for defense, private enterprise, various social security measures, and trade expansion. T.Mc.N.

Joan of Arc (1412—1431).

French saint and symbol of French national unity. The daughter of a well-to-do peasant family of Domremy, the Maid of Orleans reached adolescence in a disunited France at war with England. Prompted by piety and saintly voices, she embarked on her mission of instilling in Charles VII confidence in the justice of his claim. Joan successfully led French troops against the English besiegers of Orleans, 8 May 1429. On 7 July 1429 she saw Charles VII crowned and anointed at Rheims. Captured in 1430 by the Burgundians, she was sold to the English, who turned her over to the inquisition for trial as a heretic. Her condemnation and sentence to be burned at the stake, 30 May 1431, was more a political than an ecclesiastical decision, since she had surrounded Charles VII with the aura of divine approbation. This union of faith and loyalty, if not yet of altar and throne, prepared the way for royal absolutism. Charles VII belatedly recognized his debt to Joan in 1455. She was canonized in 1920. Since 1919 the second Sunday in May is a French national holiday in her honor. K.B.

Joffe, Adolf Abramovich (1883—1927).

Life-long supporter of Trotsky and Soviet diplomat of the post-Revolutionary period. Joffe, one of the few Bolsheviks to undergo psychoanalysis (by Alfred Adler), met Trotsky in Vienna. Sent by Trotsky to organize the underground in Russia, he was immediately arrested and remained in Siberia until 1917. After the Revolution, he was for a time the chief of the Bolshevik delegation at Brest-Litovsk and later was given important revolutionary and diplomatic assignments in Germany, China, Austria and Japan. Already dying of tuberculosis and polyneuritis, he committed suicide in 1927 in protest against Trotsky's ouster from the party. D.N.J.

John Birch Society.

American political association founded in December, 1958 by retired candy manufacturer Robert H. W. Welch, Jr., and dedicated to combating what it perceives as the pressing danger of Communist internal subversion of the United States. Members, estimated at approximately 100,000 at the end of 1961, have been politically active in local and national campaigns to repeal the federal income tax, reduce alleged Communist activities in American churches, schools and colleges, and to impeach federal government officials such as U.S. Chief Justice Earl Warren. The society was named posthumously after a fundamentalist Baptist missionary who served as a U.S. intelligence officer in China during World War II, and, according to the society, was killed by Chinese Communists at age 27, ten days after the end of the war.

Mr. Welch has expressed the view that all of the Presidents of the United States since 1932 (Roosevelt, Truman and Eisenhower) were dedicated tools of Communism. They, therefore, according to Welch, contributed to the enactment of social legislation which threatens to so alter the political and economic structure of the United States as to enable it to be integrated into the Soviet Union without armed conflict.

The John Birch society itself admits to being organized along authoritarian rather than democratic lines. S.L.A.

John of Salisbury.

Born in England about 1120, died as Bishop of Chartres, France. in 1180. His Policraticus (Statesman's Book, transl. John Dickinson) is one of the foremost medieval writings on politics. An ecclesiastic with extensive church and secular political experience, he studied under Abelard in Paris and was an intimate co-worker of Thomas Becket. He enjoyed ties of friendship with Pope Adrian IV, the sole English pope in history. The French King, Louis VII, made him Bishop of Chartres in 1176.

The struggle between ecclesiastic and secular power in his native England influenced his political philosophy. Two notable elements: the organic analogy and tyrannicide. He held that a well ordered constitution consists in the proper apportionment of functions to members of the body and in the proper condition and strength of each member. The church is the soul, "the prince of the body," God must be preferred before any man on earth and the secular ruler is subject to God and to those who "represent Him on earth." Pleading for moral supremacy, he does not advocate temporal power over state government and administration for church and clergy.

His emphasis on law is the basis for tyrannicide. The tyrant rules by force while the King rules by law, the former turns against God while the latter preserves the liberties of the people. But the slaying of a public tyrant must not be precipitately adopted. T.P.

Johnson, Andrew (1808—1875).

Seventeenth President of the United States. Born at Raleigh, North Carolina, apprenticed to a tailor at age ten, Andrew Johnson escaped to Tennessee (1826). Self-educated, effective in stump oratory, and courageous, he had a remarkably long public career in the Democratic Party starting as alderman and mayor of Greenville, Tennessee (1830-33), Tennessee Legislator, U.S. Representative (1843-53), Governor of Tennessee (1853-57) and U.S. Senator (1857-62 and 1875). He championed the poor and urged liberal land policies. As the only southern Senator to repudiate his state's secession, and support the Union, Lincoln named Johnson military governor of Tennessee (1862-65). Elected Vice-President with Lincoln on the Union Ticket, he served briefly (1865) before Lincoln's assassination made him President (1865-69). Impeached by Radical Republicans for violating the Tenure of Office Act by removing Secretary of War, Edwin M. Stanton, Johnson was acquitted by a single vote. A moderate, like Lincoln, he believed Reconstruction to be an executive and not a legislative function. Despite his hot temper, impatience, blunt manner, and lack of finesse with Congress, he is remembered for his vigorous defense of presidential power and devotion to the Constitution. K.E.D.

Johnson, Lyndon Baines.

Born August 27, 1908; U.S. Senate from November 2, 1948 until term ending January 3, 1961; Democrat—Texas; elected Democratic Whip 1951; elected Democratic leader 1953; elected U.S. Vice President November 8, 1960 and became President on the assassination of John F. Kennedy, November 22, 1963. R.A.B.

Joint Resolution.

A statement in the form of a resolution requiring the approval of both Houses of the U.S. Congress, and, with the exception of proposing constitutional amendments which are submitted to the states for acceptance, the approval of the President. A joint resolution for most purposes is the same as a bill. It deals with either incidental or unusual legislation, such as making minor changes or correcting an error in existing legislation, proposing constitutional amendments, admitting new states, or declaring war. W.V.H.

Jordan.

The Hashimite Kingdom of Jordan is located east of Israel between Syria and Arabia.

At the beginning of World War I, the British won the cooperation of Sharif Husayn of Mecca against the Turks who held official hegemony over most of the Arab territories in the Middle East. Sharif Husayn hoped with British cooperation to establish an Arab kingdom that would include Syria, Iraq, and Arabia including Transjordan. However, at the close of the war, 'Abd al-Aziz Sa'ud was fighting Husayn in Arabia, and the French dismissed his son Faysal from Syria. The British who had promised Husayn's family their support, helped in installing Faysal as king of Iraq, and agreed to install his brother Abdulla ('Abd Allah) as Amir of Transjordan. In April 1921, the first government of Transjordan was formed in a territory which included the eastern part of the river Jordan. In 1923, the British recognized a limited independence of Transjordan under Amir Abdulla; and in 1946, it recognized its full independence. Amir Abdulla was then proclaimed "King of the Hashimite Kingdom of Transjordan."

Upon the cessation of Arab-Israeli hostilities in 1948, an armistice was signed leaving an Arab section of Palestine west of the Jordan under the suzerainty of Transjordan. In April 1949, King Abdulla annexed this territory to his kingdom and proclaimed himself "King of the Hashimite Kingdom of Jordan." W.B.B.

Jordan, Elijah (1875—1953).

Jordan's **Forms of Individuality** (1927) and **Theory of Legislation** (1930) attempt a radical reconstruction of politics and social theory on metaphysical-positivistic lines. In opposition to prevailing individualism as well as alternative totalitarianisms, his theory locates will in institutional growth guided by intelligence. His corporate theory seeks to relate principles and human sentiments with action; he explains that individuals think while institutions act. The cause of current political and theoretical difficulties he finds in the subjectivisms which ground will in individuals or groups. The Jordanian legislative class, always concerned with action and creation, is implicated in the metaphysical foundations of life and is responsible for the explicit formulation of cultural ideals which experimentally may lead to appropriate institutional development. R.W.T.

Jouhaux, Leon (1879—1954).

French politician and labor leader. Secretary-general of the C. G. T. since 1909, he established the non-communist C. G. T.—F. O. (Force ouvriere) in 1947 and was elected its president. Member of the International Labor Office, he was elected vice-president of the World Federation of Free Trade Unions (1945). He represented France at the UN, was president of the Economic Council of the French Parliament (1947), president of the International Council of the European movement (1949). Recipient of the Nobel Peace Prize (1951), Jouhaux founded the movement of "Militant Democracy" (1952). K.B.

Judaism.

Religion of the Jewish people, oldest of the monotheistic religions which both Christianity and Islam regard as their source. It is committed to the belief that a transcendent, omnipotent Creator who is also Supreme and Righteous Judge of all the earth intervenes in the lives of individuals and nations. He chose Abraham and his seed to be a blessing to all the earth and several times covenanted with them to give them a land as they undertook forever to be His people and obey His law. The record of the covenants, their development and everything pertaining to them, are called Torah which encompasses both a Written Law (the Old Testament) and an Oral Law (later compiled and edited in a vast body of literature consisting of two Talmuds—Babylonian and Palestinean, Codes, Responsa, Commentaries, Midrashim, et al.). The sects of Judaism—in ancient and modern times—differed in their attitudes toward Torah, its scope, the measure of its binding character, and the manner of legislating or innovating within its frame. Because of the centrality in Judaism of a people and a land, and because it projects God's justice at least as significantly as His love, Judaism is more preoccupied with the legal order it ordains than with its theology. Thus its jurisprudence is incomparably rich as it encompasses every aspect of man's relationships with God and his fellow-man. In addition to an all-pervasive code affecting dress, food, sexual intercourse, sabbaths, festivals, ritualistic observances and offerings, there are codes affecting kings, judges, war, peace, marriage, divorce, crimes, torts, contracts, property, partnership, capital, labor, zoning, building regulations — virtually every branch of the law presently existing. Its political orientation is generally anti-monarchical. Sovereignty is never vested in human beings—God alone has it and He divides and diffuses its exercise among kings, priests, judges and the people. The king is never the source of the Law nor the head of any system of land tenure. Only in emergencies does he have broad powers. Human rights are zealously safeguarded for next in importance to the doctrine that God alone is Sovereign is the doctrine that man's personality is sacred since man was created in the divine image. From this doctrine there flowed many considerations which inspired philosophies of democracy in modern times. Except for comparatively brief periods of Jewish history there was neither an organized "church" nor any religious hierarchy. Authority was generally in the Rabbis —doctors of the Law — who were principally teachers with none of the hereditary position or sacerdotal powers of priests and their authority derived from the people's acceptance of them as such. Judaism is optimistic with regard to man's hopes on earth and its Messianic vision of a future in which there will not only be peace on earth and universal justice among the nations but also the end of death and other imperfections in nature. Zionism is regarded as a first stage of this vision's fulfillment. E.R.

Judd, Walter H. (1898—   ).
Medical missionary in China. U.S. House of Representatives from 78th Congress (1942) through 87th Congress. Republican — Minnesota. Congressional delegate to Council of Europe. Congressional delegate to World Health Assembly of World Health Organization, 1950 and 1958. United States delegate to United Nations General Assembly, 1957. Congressional delegate to Conference on Peaceful Uses of Atomic Energy, 1958. Left public office after twenty years of devoted patriotic service with the statement: "I would rather lose living by the things I believe in than win by departing from them." J.D.

Judicial Behavior.
An approach to the study of U.S. public law which emphasizes the analysis of the decision-making behavior of judges. Underlying this approach is the assumption that discoverable uniformities in political behavior with predictive value exist at least in a statistical sense and also that ethical evaluation and empirical explanations must be kept separate. The "scientific approach," systematization, integration with other social science techniques, and quantification are stressed. W.F.G.

Judicial Review.
The examination of Federal and state legislative statutes and the acts of executive officials by the courts to determine their validity according to written constitutions. The authority of the United States Supreme Court to exercise the power of judicial review under the Constitution of the United States was forecast by Alexander Hamilton in **The Federalist Papers,** Number 78, and was specifically set out by Chief Justice John Marshall in **Marbury v. Madison** (1803). The Supreme Court declared only two Congressional statutes unconstitutional in the first seventy years of the Federal Republic, and seventy-seven such statutes unconstitutional in the period between the Civil War and the Second World War. E.L.

July 4, 1776. See Appendix.

July 14, 1789. See Appendix.

July 20, 1944.
It marks the date in Germany on which Count Schenk von Stauffenberg made an attempt on Hitler's life in the "Fuehrer" headquarters. Planned by a group of army officers, among them Major General Ludwig Beck, civil servants, among them Lord Mayor Karl Goerdeler, representatives of the churches, as well as the illegal Social Democratic Party, the rebellion did not succeed, and Hitler emerged with but a minor wound. As a consequence, thousands of men and women, suspected of participation in the plot, were hanged, shot, or imprisoned. Most of the members of the resistance movement (see German Resistance against Hitlerian System) hoped to restore pre-Hitler conditions in Germany and Europe and effect an honorable peace with the United Nations. H.D.

Jurisdiction.
From the Latin "ius dicere," the right to speak. Ordinarily, the right to adjudicate concerning the subject-matter in a given case. In a broader sense, the word becomes virtually interchangeable with "authority," especially when it refers to territorially limited authority or control. F.H.H.

Jury.
A varying number of persons chosen according to law to make legal findings on the basis of evidence submitted to them. A petit or trial jury is most commonly composed of twelve persons and usually requires a unani-

mous verdict, although in the American states the trend is toward fewer jurors and away from the requirement of unanimity. Trial by a jury of one's peers or equals has long been considered to be a major British right, but the jury is now used mainly in particularly important cases. Both in Britain and the United States the choice of using or not using a jury is often left to the defendant in a criminal case or the parties in a civil case. A grand jury is formed to hear evidence submitted by the state and to determine if it is sufficient to bring an indictment against a defendant. The term is derived from the fact that it is usually larger than a petit jury. It is characterized by the secrecy of its proceedings, by the absence of any requirement of unanimity, and by the fact that its findings do not determine guilt or innocence. The United Kingdom discontinued its use in 1933, and the United States shows an increasing tendency to use indictment by "information." R.H.B.

Jus Sanguinis. (Law of the blood).

A person gaining citizenship by **jus sanguinis** does so by reason of being born to parents who are citizens, regardless of the place of birth. This principle is applied in the nationality laws of most Continental European states. In the United States the Congress has adopted the rule of **jus sanguinis** for special cases: e.g., one may be born abroad and still be a United States citizen provided that at least one of his parents is a citizen, and provided that he later meets certain residence requirements. R.E.Ch.

Jus Soli. (Law of the land).

A principle of international law under which the place or country in which a person is born determines his citizenship. This is the principle applied in the nationality laws of Great Britain, the United States, and many other countries. The Fourteenth Amendment to the U.S. Constitution adopts this rule. In special cases Congress has adopted the rule of **jus sanguinis.** R.E.Ch.

Justice.

A standard for judging the legal and moral order for the mutual relations of men. When satisfied, it is regarded as achieving social happiness in a context of social order. The problem is posed as to what differences are relevant in arriving at a kind of relative equality, but then equality before the law should exist. Absolute standards may be erected by philosophic or religious ideologies. Nature, reason, and social contract have been connected at different times with the origin of standards. Ideas of justice may be traditional, accepting existing institutions, or may go beyond them to criticize in accordance with changing moral or political values. In the state, legal justice refers both to the making of laws and their application. The modern period has seen a movement within the state from stress upon individual rights to greater stress upon collective welfare, and among states to an achievement of greater equality. D.P.

**Justice of the Peace.
(United Kingdom).**

The crown acting through the Lord Chancellor who, in return, generally accepts the advice of the Lord Lieutenant of the county concerned and appoints in each county Justices of the Peace who are empowered by commission to maintain the King's Peace. These Justices need not be trained in law, and in times past, were usually county squires. However, in recent times, the "J. P." have been drawn from a wider cross section of society. When a Justice of the Peace sits alone, the court is limited to hearing cases in which the fine could not exceed 5 pounds nor the jail sentence be greater than 14 days. When two or more Justices of the Peace sit together, the Court is known as the Court of Petty Sessions and slightly higher penalties may be imposed. There are approximately 19,000 Justices of the Peace, about 20 per cent of them being women. Mayors of cities are usually ex-official Justices of the Peace for the duration of their office.

C.A.McC.

Justice of the Peace (U.S.A.).
See Appendix.

Justiciable question.

Questions which are proper or appropriate for examination in courts of justice are justiciable. In determining justiciability, United States courts decide "whether the duty asserted can be judicially identified and its breach judicially determined and whether protection for the right asserted can be judicially molded." (Justice Brennan in Baker v. Carr, 369 U.S. 186 [1962]). Justiciability is to be distinguished from jurisdiction, the power of the court to hear the case. T.C.S.

Juvenile Delinquency.

May be defined as any youthful behavior considered offensive by a community or state and warranting placing the youth under the jurisdiction of a juvenile court. Technically he must have violated a law or ordinance to be in this category; practically, however, the term is popularly used to include those children who are considered to have failed to meet community standards of behavior. As delinquent behavior is generally defined by the individual state or community, what is considered delinquent in one community may not be so considered in another. Adequate comparisons are, therefore, difficult. Children under seven years of age are usually considered incapable of delinquency. The upper age limit is generally eighteen, although some states consider it sixteen or seventeen, and two states rule it to be twenty-one. In some areas girls are given a higher age limit than boys. Before the twentieth century the police and courts generally did not distinguish between youthful and adult offenders. In the U.S.A. the first Juvenile Court was established in Chicago in 1899, and special and more informal court procedures were initiated for children. Today all states of the U.S.A. have juvenile courts, with varying procedures and degrees of adequacy. Witnesses often are not required, defense attorneys may be lacking, social workers may report their court-directed investigations; the whole child and his family are considered. Court decisions are intended for the child's welfare rather than as punishment; the use of probation may be liberal. Special places of detention and custody have been developed for children and youthful offenders. Children's shelters may house both children facing court action and others who are lost, deprived of parents by accident or misfortune, or otherwise needing protection. Not all cases brought to a juvenile or children's court may be delinquent in a legal sense; some may be brought for disposition of the child. Most court facilities are not adequate for the demands placed upon them: the judges, attendants, probation officers, and police may have had no special training or experience, and the facilities may be overcrowded, causing haste and, sometimes, carelessness. In most states facilities for the rehabilitation of the youthful offender seem meager. Reformatories and industrial schools may be overcrowded and wretched places; when investigations or exposures lead to reforms, these may be only temporary. A few, however, are outstanding exceptions. The causes of delinquency follow well-defined patterns of unfavorable neighborhoods, broken families, apathetic parents, dull schools, and neurotic behavior patterns of the child. Children of immigrants often provide the largest single group of delinquents in proportion to their numbers. T.K.N.

K

Kadar, Janos (1912—   ).
Hungarian Communist.
Active in the Hungarian Communist Party since 1931, holds high party offices and government posts since 1945. Elected to Parliament in 1945, Minister of Interior in 1948. Arrested and jailed by the Stalinist regime of M. Rakosi in 1951; rehabilitated in 1954 by the government of Imre Nagy. In July, 1956, elected to the Party's Central Committee and to the Politbureau. During the October Revolution of 1956, he sided with the supporters of Imre Nagy and on October 25 replaced E. Gero as First Secretary of the Communist Party. On this day he announced that negotiations for the withdrawal of Soviet troops would be initiated. Became member of Nagy Government on October 30, 1956. On the following day, he declared that the Party would be reconstituted under a new name. When the fighting was over (November 1), he asserted: "We can safely say that those who prepared the uprising were recruited from our ranks. Communist writers, journalists, students, the youth of the Petofi Club, workers, peasants . . ., we are proud that you have stood your ground honestly in the armed uprising." On the eve of the Soviet intervention (November 3), he disappeared from Budapest, returning as head of a self-appointed "revolutionary government." After the crushing of the Nagy Government and of the armed and passive resistance, he relinquished the office of Prime Minister in favor of Ferenc Munnich in January, 1958. He became Prime Minister, again, in September 1961. He is also the First Secretary of the newly organized Communist Party.   I.B.

Kaganovich, Lazar.
Born 1893, Kabany, Kiev Province. Jewish. Unskilled laborer, age 14; little formal education. Joined Bolsheviks 1911, became trade union organizer. Political Commissar during Civil War. Member of abortive Constituent Assembly 1918. Member of Party Central Committee 1918—1957, and of Politburo (called Party Presidium since 1952) 1930—1957. Chairman of Party Control Commission mid-1930's, associated with purges. Ousted 1957 from Party posts for "anti-Party" activities. Relieved as Minister of Building Materials, assigned to obscure post.   W.A.

Kamakura Era.
The Kamakura Era in Japan was begun by Minamoto no Yoritomo when in 1185 he established a government at Kamakura after defeating the Taira forces in that same year. The Kamakura government was simple in form. At the apex of the political system was a heritary Shogun. Under him was a class of provincial administrators, the **shugo**, who oversaw a large number of **jito** (stewards), each of whom had the responsibility of overseeing the operation of one of the great estates which constituted the economic foundation of the government. The entire system was held together by the loyalty of the various retainers to their Shogun. Under this system martial bravery and feudal loyalty were strongly stressed.
The Imperial establishment at Kyoto continued to exist during this period but without any real political power.
Culturally, the period saw a flowering of Buddhism and a proliferation of its sects. The Pure Land sect, the True sect and Zen all developed in the first part of the era. Buddhist sculpture reached a high level of development and a robust form of literature developed.
In the early 13th century, control over the Shogunate passed into the hands of the Hojo family on the extinction of the Minamoto line. During this period the two Mongol invasions of 1274 and 1281 were repulsed.
The Kamakura Era came to a close when, in 1333, Kamakura fell to rebel forces who had rallied around Emperor Daigo II.   S.S.

Kambatsu.
A Japanese term meaning, "the bureaucratic clique," **kambatsu** is derived from the words **kan-ryo** (bureaucracy) and **-batsu** (clique). In prewar Japan the **kambatsu** thought of themselves as direct servants of the emperor and as guardians of the na-

tional polity. Of all pre-war cliques—the aristocracy, the military, the **zaibatsu** (finance clique), and the bureaucracy—the **kambatsu** was the last to change under impact of Occupation and post-Occupation reforms. Under the new Constitution, the civil service is responsible to the Cabinet, which in turn is responsible to the Diet.

A.W.B.

Kamenev, Lev Borisovich
(real name—Rosenfeld)
(1883—1936).

One of the leading communists of the Soviet Union, who was prominent in the Bolshevik faction of the Socialist Democratic Party, headed by Lenin. Kamenev, perhaps, was the best educated and most intellectual of Lenin's colleagues. He was related to another communist leader Trotsky, whose sister he married. Kamenev was exiled to Siberia for his revolutionary activity in Tsarist Russia in 1915, and returned to Petrograd after the February 1917 revolution. With the advent of the Bolshevik regime in Russia, Kamenev played an important role in the Soviet government and communist party. From 1918 he was president of the Moscow Soviet, and in 1922 became vice-chairman of the Council of Peoples' Commissars (Sovnarkom). At the time of Trotsky's factional struggle within the communist party in 1923, Kamenev sided with Zinoviev and Stalin against Trotsky. However, in 1926, he and Zinoviev joined the opposition, which resulted in his expulsion from the party. However, he held important posts with the government until 1932, when he was finally relegated to a minor post. The murder of Kirov in 1934 brought about Kamenev's arrest, and two years later, after a public trial with other leading communists, Kamenev was executed on August 26, 1936.

V.P.P.

Kansas v. Colorado.

A 1907 case (206 U.S. 46) in which the United States Supreme Court declined to accept the theory that Congress possesses inherent authority over matters of national scope. The Court held that powers not delegated to Congress by the Constitution are "reserved to the people of the United States," even though the powers may involve matters that are national in character. This constitutional doctrine today possesses little but historical interest. See, e.g., Wickard v. Filburn, 317 U.S. 111 (1942).

D.M.B.

Kansas-Nebraska Act.

A statute, enacted by the United States Congress in 1854, repealing the Missouri Compromise of 1820, under which slavery had been banned in much of the area acquired from France through the Louisiana Purchase. The Kansas-Nebraska Act abandoned this prohibition on slavery in favor of an authorization to the new territories of Kansas and Nebraska to decide for themselves whether they wanted to tolerate the institution. The new arrangement inflamed abolitionist feeling, exacerbated North-South relations, and helped bring on the Civil War.

D.M.B.

Kant, Immanuel (1724—1804).

German philosopher, was the son of a saddlemaker at Koenigsberg (East Prussia). A true son of the Age of Reason, he was also its greatest critic who undertook in a number of famous works to delineate the limits of reason. These works, notably **The Critique of Pure Reason** (1781), **The Critique of Practical Reason** (1788), and **The Critique of the (Power of) Judgment** (1790), undertook to show that reason in the sense of rational demonstration had definite limits and that it was unreasonable to expect more from it than it could do, and that the result must be skepticism and despair. But apart from this strictly philosophical enterprise which certainly had political implications, Kant was also very directly interested in political questions. In fact he is next to Hobbes the most concerned in politics among the great European philosophers. Indeed, a political problem would seem to be central to his entire philosophical work, namely how beings as nasty as men demonstrably are manage to live in peace and concord with each other. It is a problem to which he returns in all his major works and to which he gives a rather conventional answer: by subjecting themselves to a government. Unlike Hobbes and other writers in the tradition of state and sovereignty, however, Kant favored a constitutional order which he called a republic, whether the order was monarchical or not. He was pre-occupied with insisting upon the rule of law and in this connection developed what has been called the most influential philosophical jurisprudence (Pound). The work for which Kant is most universally admired in the field of politics is his essay **On Eternal Peace** (1795). In this brief book he undertook to apply his general views on peace to the international scene. Squarely basing his argument on the proposition that the moral law, i.e. the categorical imperative commanded that "there shall not be war," he proceeded to outline a plan for an universal order under law which would consist of a loose confederation of republics — the kind of order the United Nations would be, if all its members were constitutional regimes. Though such an order could only be achieved in slow steps, it is possible and all men have the duty to promote it. C.J.F.

Kaplan, Fanya (Dora) (1888—1918).

Russian Social Revolutionary who shot at and wounded Lenin in Moscow on August 30, 1918. Three days later she was executed by the Cheka. For many years the Bolsheviks circulated the rumor that she had been spared by Lenin's personal intercession. D.N.J.

Kapp-Putsch.

Rebellion by rightist elements against the Weimar Republic in March 1920 under leadership of the Marine Brigade Ehrhardt which occupied the government buildings in Berlin. The members of the Reich's government were forced to flee from the capital. While the Reichswehr (army) preserved an attitude of neutrality, the General Strike on the part of all organized workers led to the defeat of the rebellion. H.D.

Karelian Refugee Problem.

Following defeat in the Russo-Finnish War (1939-40; 1941-44) and consequent concession of 17,800 square miles of her territory to the Soviet Union, Finland had to resettle some 450,000 refugees, mainly from Finnish Karelia and the Karelian Isthmus. The effort presented several formidable problems. The very great number of refugees—12 per cent of the Nation's population — posed a revolutionary threat to the nation if resettlement was delayed. Being primarily farmers, effective resettlement meant that a majority of them had to be resettled on farms. But Finland's farms were already small and near-marginal, and the acquisition of farm lands would have to come mainly from these already crowded farms. Financing the effort was especially onerous because of the bad condition of the economy as a result of the war effort, costs of reparations, and the severe losses of territory and resources. Psychological adjustment was difficult, Karelia being the original source of **Kalevala**—the great national epic of Finland — and therefore the spiritual home of the Finns. The resettlement was largely and successfully accomplished by mid-1950, with some, but tolerable, infringement of private property rights and losses financially to some individuals through inflation. R.H.K.

Kashmir.

Officially the state of JAMMU and KASHMIR (area, 86,024 square miles; population, estimated 4,410,000: 77% Moslem, 20% Hindu).

Bordering China on the north and Tibet on the east (the frontiers have not been defined), the state of Jammu and Kashmir in north India became a part of the Mogul Empire under Akbar in 1586, and in 1819 was annexed to the kingdom of the Punjab. Jammu in 1820 and Kashmir in 1846 were made over by treaty to the control of the ruler, Gulab Singh.

Following the partition between India and Pakistan, the two countries contested the control of Jammu and Kashmir. The Maharajah acceded to the Dominion of India in October 1947 whereupon armed forces from both countries entered the state. The portion under Indian control was incorporated as its seventh republic in January 1957.

A United Nations cease fire came into effect in January 1949, both sides agreeing to a plebiscite in its area. However, conflict over details of the plebiscite have never been resolved. Pakistan presently controls about one-third of Kashmir (northern and extreme western sectors) while India holds the remainder. M.T.K.

Kassem, Abd-al-Karim.
Born in Baghdad, 1914, Brigadier General and Prime Minister of Iraq. He is the leader of the revolution of 14 July 1958 which ended the monarchy and introduced the republican regime into Iraq. A quiet, and mystic, soldier Kassem distinguished himself during the Palestine war of 1948. He follows a policy of neutralism in international affairs. Kassem is involved in a battle of rivalry with Nasser for leadership in the Arab East. His military dictatorship is committed to reform, to the liquidation of the feudal class and to the modernization of Iraq. The multiple sects and races of Iraq intensify his problems, and indicate the precarious balance that he must keep. E.A.S.

Katyn Incident.
When the Soviets occupied Eastern Poland immediately after the Hitler-Stalin Pact of 1939, they interned, among others, some 15,000 Polish officers and men, the elite of the defunct Polish army. In Stalin's view, these Polish officers, who were strongly imbued with the idea of Polish independence, represented a special menace to the new dominant Soviet power and had to be liquidated summarily. The execution of these Polish officers, when disclosed many years later, created an international uproar known as the Katyn incident.

In April 1943, the Nazis reported the discovery of the mass graves of Polish officers in the Katyn Forest and placed the blame for their murder on the Soviet government. With the resumption of Soviet-Polish diplomatic relations in July 1941, the Polish Government-in-exile, London, repeatedly requested an impartial investigation of the Nazi allegation. Stalin severed diplomatic relations with the Polish Government-in-exile over the Katyn Forest controversy, asserting that Polish belief in the Nazi accusation indicated a lack of faith in the integrity of the Soviet Government; he also charged the Poles with exploiting the Nazi scandal in order to force a restoration of their 1939 frontier with the Soviet Union. A few days later, he announced the establishment of an organization known as the "Union of Polish Patriots" which later became the Soviet puppet Lublin Government. Soviet officialdom still maintains an ominous silence about the Katyn incident, analyzed in detail by J. K. Zawodny in **Death in the Forest,** a Notre Dame publication. R.St.-H.

Kautsky, Karl Johann
(1854—1938).
German-Austrian Socialist leader, close associate of Engels, and leading interpreter of Marx after Engels' death. In 1891 the German Social Democratic Party adopted Kautsky's Erfurt Program, which retained Marx's economic doctrines but rejected the necessity for violent revolution and made political democracy the workers' first goal. For this Lenin termed him the "renegade Kautsky." In 1919 he published an expose, **The Origin of the War,** based on official German documents. When Hitler took over Austria, Kautsky fled to Holland, where he died. R.E.Ch.

Keating-Owen Act.
A statute, enacted by the United States Congress in 1916, barring from interstate or foreign commerce any goods produced through the use of child labor. By a 5-4 vote, the Supreme Court invalidated the statute in 1918, in Hammer v. Dagenhart (247 U.S. 251). The Court's argument was that the commerce power of Congress could only be employed to regulate the transportation of products harmful in themselves (e.g., adulterated drugs). In this view, only the police power of the states could reach an aspect of the manufacturing process, such as the use of child labor. Beginning in 1937, the Supreme Court discarded this approach. It substituted a broader interpretation of the commerce power and sanctioned congressional action designed to advance social purposes. See, e.g., United States v. Darby Lumber Company, 312 U.S. 100 (1941).
D.M.B.

Kefauver, Estes.
Born July 26, 1903; U.S. Senate from November 2, 1948 until term ending January 3, 1967; Democrat—Tennessee; Democratic nominee for Vice President, 1956; member of the 76th-80th Congresses; author of **Crime in America** and co-author of **20th Century Congress.** R.A.B.

Kekkonen, Juho Kaleva
(1900—   ).
President of the Republic of Finland. Born in Finland. Legal education and early experience as a legal officer in various municipal and national government offices. Minister of Justice, 1936-37; 1944-46. Minister of the Interior, 1937-39. Speaker of the Diet, 1948; 1949. Prime Minister, 1950-53; 1954-56. Minister of Foreign Affairs, 1952-53; 1954. Member of Parliament, 1936-56. Elected President of the Republic in 1956; re-elected in 1962 for a second six-year term. Member of the Agrarian Party. Particularly noted for his continuance and elaboration of the "Paasikivi Line," a guiding principle in Finnish foreign policy that recognizes the need for maintaining amicable relations with the Soviet Union as a matter of national survival and welfare. Consequently, President Kekkonen has enjoyed the favor of the Kremlin, and has been a central figure in the resolution of the Russo-Finnish crises of 1958 and 1961-62.   R.H.K.

Kelly, Edward Joseph.
Mayor of Chicago 1933-1947. Chieftain of the Kelly-Nash machine. Appointed mayor upon death of A. J. Cermak, 1933. Elected mayor 1935, 1939, 1943. Democratic National Committeeman, 1940-44, 1948-50. Born, Chicago, May 1, 1876; died, October 20, 1950. He was the chief heir of Cermak to the conquering Chicago and Cook County Democratic Party Organization.   A.G.

Kemal, Mustafa (Ataturk).
"Father of the Turks." (1881-1938). Creator of modern Turkey. Organized military and political resistance against Treaty of Sevres of August 10, 1920 which reduced Turkey to the status of a minor state and subjected her to severe limitations of her sovereignty. Following the expulsion of the Greeks who had landed their troops in Asia Minor at the end of World War I and the over-throw of the Ottoman Sultanate, he became president of Turkey and leader of the Republican People's Party which in the "six principles of Kemalism" dedicated itself to the regeneration and democratization of the Turkish polity.   J.D.

Kempner, Robert M. W.
Born on October 17, 1899, Freiburg i. Br., Germany, U.S. citizen, member of the German Bar, formerly Chief Legal Advisor of the pre-Hitler 76,000-men Prussian Police Administration; suggested Hitler's deportation as undesirable alien. In the U.S. he served as expert to Federal agencies and courts in foreign agents' and espionage trials. From 1945—1949 he was prosecutor at the Nuremberg Trials first on Justice Jackson's staff, in charge of preparing trial briefs against the individual defendants, and prosecuted Hitler's Minister of the Interior, Wilhelm Frick, who was sentenced to death. During the subsequent trials Dr. Kempner was U.S. Deputy Chief of Counsel in charge of the so-called Wilhelmstrassen Trial against Hitler's cabinet members, such as the Ministers of Finance, of Agriculture, of the Chancellery and against such Nazi diplomats and State secretaries as Ernst von Weizsaecker, Adolf von Steengracht, Wilhelm Keppler, Wilhelm Stuckart. They all were sentenced to prison terms mainly for their participation in the anti-Jewish extermination program and other crimes against humanity.   J.D.

Kendall v. United States.
An 1838 United States Supreme Court case (12 Pet. 524) upholding use by the judiciary of the power of mandamus to force a Cabinet officer, regardless of the President's wishes, to perform a ministerial duty imposed on him by Congress (as distinguished from a discretionary function). The decision meant that Congress might delegate authority directly to subordinate executive officials. An important result was the diminution of the President's constitutional responsibility to assure that the laws are faithfully executed.   D.M.B.

Kennedy, John Fitzgerald
(1917—1963).
Became 35th President of the United States in 1960 at age of 43, youngest man and first Catholic ever elected to the office. Elected as a Democrat with narrow margin of 118,263 popular votes; received 300 of 537 electoral votes after a history-making series of

television debates with Vice-President Richard M. Nixon, his Republican opponent. Graduated from Harvard, 1940; served in U.S. Navy, 1941-1945; served three terms in House of Representatives, 1946-1952; elected to Senate, 1952 and 1958. Wrote Pulitzer-prize-winning biography, **Profiles in Courage.** Modeled his "New Frontier" administration after "New Deal" and "Fair Deal." Assassinated in Dallas, Texas, November 22, 1963. R.E.Ch.

Kentucky and Virginia Resolutions.

Sets of resolutions adopted by the Kentucky and Virginia legislatures in 1798-99, protesting the constitutionality of the Alien and Sedition Acts of the U.S. Congress. The Virginia Resolutions were drafted by James Madison. Those of Kentucky by Thomas Jefferson. They were based upon the theory of strict construction of the Constitution, and reflected the states' rights theory in extreme form by declaring the Acts null and void, and asking other states to join in nullifying them. They were the first effort at nullification. J.E.R.

Kenya.

A British East African colony and protectorate since 1895. Area 224,960 sq. miles; population (est. 1960) 6,550,700, which includes 174,300 Asians, 67,700 Europeans and 38,600 Arabs. Kenya's political problems stem largely from her multi-racial population. Three key issues continue to dominate Kenya politics: the future status and role of the immigrant communities, the issue of land alienation to European settlers, and the question of unitary vs. federal governmental structure, which is related in part to relations between the dominant Kikuyu people and less numerous Masai, Nandi, Abaluhya and other groups. Constitutional developments have lagged because of these multiple cleavages and the inability of African leadership to create a single political movement.

The 1960 Kenya Constitutional Conference saw the final abandonment of the multi-racial principle in favor of African majority rule. The new constitution allocates legislative council seats as follows: Africans 37, Europeans 14, Asians 11, and Arabs 3. Two parties dominate Kenya politics: the leading Kenya African National Union (KANU) led by Jomo Kenyatta and Tom Mboya, with support among townspeople and the settled agricultural groups and the lesser Kenya African Democratic Union (KADU) which draws strength in the south and east among largely pastoral peoples.
R.L.K.

Kerala.

Population: 16,875,199 (1961 Census, provisional). Area: 14,992 square miles. Capital: Trivandrum. Its density of population, 1,125 per square mile, is highest of any Indian state. It has the largest Christian population in India. It also has the highest literacy rate, nearly fifty per cent. In April, 1957, the Communist Party of India won the general elections of Kerala, attaining the only communist ministry in India, and the first democratically elected communist government in the world. Despite strict constitutionalism and "general aim of respectability," Congress-Communist tensions resulted in eventual imposition of Presidential Rule followed seven months later by a non-Communist coalition government elected in February, 1960.
S.K.A.

Kerensky, Aleksandr F. (1881—).

Head of Provisional Government in Russia from July 1917 until the Bolshevik seizure of power in November 1917. Kerensky attempted, in vain, to rally the Russian Army at the front and to restrain the disruptive, revolutionary activities of the Communists at the rear. He fled to Paris in 1917 and emigrated to the United States in 1940. W.D.J.

Keynes, John Maynard (1883—1946).

Economist, born in Cambridge, England, June 5, 1883; died in London, April 21, 1946. He was the most influential economist in the non-communist world in the first half of the 20th century and founded the "expansionist" school of economics, which was based on public works programs to overcome unemployment and deflation. Franklin D. Roosevelt's New Deal stemmed in part from his views. Keynes' two great treatises, comparable to the works of Smith and Ricardo, are **Treatise on Money** (2 vols., 1930),

and **The General Theory of Employment, Interest and Money** (1936). The conceptual reconstruction of economics is his most important claim to fame, including the necessity of planned economic policy. He was raised to the First Baron Keynes of Tilton.
M.M.Mc.

Keynote speaker.
A party leader possessing oratorical flair chosen by his party's national committee to deliver the keynote speech at the national party convention. Customarily, but with recent exceptions, the keynote speaker is expected to flail the record of the opposition party while praising the achievements of his own party, thus kindling enthusiasm among delegates and party supporters.
Th.P.

Kharijites (Seceders).
One of the earliest sects in Islam noted for its puritanism and fanaticism. It originated in 657 A.D. in the conflict between Caliph Ali and the Umayyad Mu'awiyya over the caliphate. Ali's consent to submit the conflict to arbitration had compromised his cause in the eyes of these nomads. The Caliphate could not be made the object of bargaining. They were uncompromising fanatics who insisted on "works" as the sole criterion of faith and branded as apostates worthy of excommunication or death all those who deviated from the letter of the law. Their dogma sanctioned not only individual murder but also open revolt against any authority that did not conform to its doctrine. Being nomads and religious puritans, they asserted the equality of all believers and the right of any Muslim, even a slave, to become a caliph. Some anarchists among them maintained that no caliph was needed. The Kharijites symbolized the anti-aristocratic patterns of the desert, and in their condemnation of the laxity of the rulers a social revolt was concealed. The more moderate leaders formulated systems which had survived in small puritanical communities in Southern Algeria, Libya, Oman and Zanzibar.
F.M.N.

Khanh, Nguyen. See Appendix.

Khrushchev, Nikita Sergeevich.
Now Premier of the Soviet Union and First Secretary of the Soviet Communist Party, Khrushchev was born on April 17, 1894, in Kalinovk, a village in Kurst Province on the borders of the Ukraine. His political career followed the traditional course of upward mobility through the Party apparatus. As a matter of fact, he was the first worker to become head of the Party and government in the Soviet Union and also the first member to be admitted to Stalin's inner circle (the Politburo) who had entered the Party after the Revolution.

A coal miner and the son of a coal miner, he joined the Party in 1918 at the age of 24 and enrolled in a Rab-Fak or Workers' Faculty, which was established to prepare adult workers for subsequent higher training. Upon graduation, he was assigned to the Ukraine Party organization. In 1929 he was sent to the Industrial Academy of Heavy Industry for training as a future industrial executive. After the completion of his course at the Academy, Kaganovich, then the head of the Moscow Party organization, chose him as his second secretary. In 1934, he succeeded Kaganovich as first secretary the next year. In 1938, he was shifted to Kiev to assume the duty of First Secretary of the Ukraine Party organization. The following year he was admitted to the Politburo. He remained in the Ukraine until December 1949, when he was appointed as one of the secretaries of the All-Union Central Committee. He assumed the post-Stalin leadership of the Soviet Communist Party with his elevation to the rank of First Secretary in September 1953. By the end of 1957 he had virtually eliminated his rivals from the "collective leadership" circle and asserted a well-knit system of personal rule over the Party and the government. Following the 20th Party Congress of 1956 he emerged not only as the undisputed master of the USSR but also assumed the role of chief strategist and theoretician of the international Communist movement.
R.St-H.

Kibbutz (and Kvutza)
(pl. Kibbutzim, Kvutzot)
(Hebrew "group").
An Israeli communal or collective village on national lands. Property is collectively owned and work is organized on collective basis. Consumption

is based on principle of satisfying individual needs within available means. Governed by the general assembly of all members it bears responsibility for housing, health, education and other services. The family is a social but not an economic unit. Predominantly agricultural, many kibbutzim and kvutzot also run industrial enterprises. The initial differentiation between **kibbutz**, characterized by a relatively large membership (up to 1000) and the smaller **kvutza** (up to 100 members) has disappeared. The several Kibbutz movements are affiliated with various political parties. In 1961 230 Kibbutzim had an aggregate membership of 78,000 (4.1% of the total Israeli population). E.G.

Kilpi, Juho Eino.
A leader of the Peoples Democratic Union (Communists) of Finland. Born June 7, 1889. Member of parliament 1930-33 and 1948-61. Member of the cabinet 1945-48. A candidate for election of president of the republic in 1956. E.I.

King, Martin Luther, Jr.
(1929—   ).
Leader of Gandhian type, non-violent resistance movement against racial discrimination in the U.S.A. Born in Atlanta, Georgia, King attended Boston University, then became pastor of a Negro Baptist Church in Montgomery, Alabama. In 1955—1956 as President of the Montgomery Improvement Association, he led the Negroes of Montgomery in a 351-day boycott of city buses which ended in their desegregation by a federal court order. He helped to establish the Student Non-Violent Coordinating Committee to guide the sit-in demonstrators. He maintains in his autobiographical **Stride Toward Freedom** that love is a stronger force for social change than hatred. R.E.Ch.

Kiraly, Bela (1912—   ).
General, leader of the Hungarian military resistance against Soviet intervention in 1956.
Career officer since 1935, fought against the Red Army 1942-44, was active in the Hungarian resistance movement against Nazi Germany 1944-45. After World War II, joined the Communist Party and received a commission in the new Hungarian Army. By 1950 was General and Commander of the Hungarian Infantry. Was arrested and sentenced to death in 1951 for resisting the sovietization of the Army. Sentence was commuted to life imprisonment. Paroled during the wave of rehabilitations in September, 1956, he joined the ranks of those Communists who wanted reform. On October 28, 1956, he was made Chairman of the Revolutionary Committee of the Hungarian Armed Forces. On October 30, 1956, the government of Imre Nagy appointed him Military Commander of Budapest. During the Soviet intervention he assumed the leadership of all Hungarian military resistance. Resides at present in the United States. I.B.

Kirov, Sergei Mironovich
(real name—Kostrikov)
(1886—1934).
Soviet political leader. Kirov was born in 1886, in the town of Urzhum, Viatka Province, now renamed Kirov Province. He received vocational training in the Kazan Technical School, graduating in 1904. At the end of 1904 Kirov moved to the western Siberian city of Tomsk, where he joined the Bolshevik faction of the Social Democratic Party. From this moment he became a professional revolutionary, taking part in armed uprisings, which were followed by numerous arrests. After the revolution, at the conclusion of the Polish-Soviet War in 1920, Kirov headed the Soviet Russian delegation at the Peace Conference in Riga. In 1925, Kirov was sent to Leningrad to replace Zinoviev, and to suppress the "Trotskyite-Zinoviev gang." The following year, 1926, Kirov became the secretary of the Leningrad Committee of the party. He became a full-fledged member of the ruling Politburo in 1930, and a secretary of the Central Committee of the All-Union Communist Party (Bolsheviks) in 1934. Kirov was shot and killed by Nikolayev, a Communist Party member in the Smolny Palace, Leningrad, on December 1, 1934. Recent disclosures implicate Stalin in Kirov's murder. V.P.P.

Kishi, Nobusuke (1896—   ).
After a distinguished record at

Tokyo Imperial University, Kishi entered the Ministry of Agriculture and Commerce. He served as Vice Minister of Industry in the Manchukuo government and in 1941 was Minister of Commerce and Industry in the cabinet of General Tojo, which declared war on the United States. After the war, he was arrested, but not tried, as a war criminal. Following his release from prison, Kishi promoted the merger of Japan's two conservative parties to form the Liberal Democratic Party. As Prime Minister (1957—1960), he signed the United States-Japan Treaty of Mutual Cooperation and Security, and his supporters passed the treaty in the lower house during a boycott by the Socialists. In protest against this highhandedness, strikes and street demonstrations demanding Kishi's resignation and the dissolution of the Diet broke out throughout the country. Consequently, the projected visit of President Eisenhower to Japan was "postponed" and Kishi resigned in July, 1960. Kishi's original name was Sato; Kishi is the family name of his adoptive uncle and father-in-law. Kishi's brother, Sato Eisaku, leads one of the most powerful factions in the Liberal Democratic Party.   T.Mc.N.

Kleemola, Kauno Antero.
A leader of the Agrarian Party of Finland. Born July 5, 1906. Agronomist. Member of parliament 1939-44 and 1948-. Member of the cabinet 1950-57. Speaker of parliament 1962.
                                          E.I.

Knesset (Assembly).
Israeli multiparty unicameral legislature of 120 members. Elects President of the state, ratifies and controls Cabinet tenure under parliamentary system. Elected by proportional representation, party list systems, universal suffrage.   S.H.

Knights of Labor.
An organization of American trade unions; existed as a secret society of craft unions from 1869—1881. The Order grew rapidly after 1880 to a membership of nearly 1,000,000. The Order of the Knights of Labor aimed at a cooperative society rather than a competitive one. Their program included equal pay for women, eight hour day, public ownership of utilities, abolition of child labor, reorganization of currency and banking systems, and educational methods of dispute settlement. During the eighties the Knights conducted a series of strikes for higher wages. The organization of the Knights of Labor was not able to reconcile the interests of both skilled and unskilled workers. The Knights of Labor lost membership to the growing American Federation of Labor, but continued activities until 1917.
                                      W.D.S.

Know-Nothing Party.
This was the better-known name of the American Party which was founded in New York in 1849 and flourished in the 1850s. It began as a secret patriotic society called the "Order of the Star-Spangled Banner" (also tagged "The Sons of '76") and mushroomed between 1852 and 1854 when a national organization was launched. Members, clandestinely initiated and sworn to secrecy, committed themselves to vote for only native-born citizens for public office, to support a campaign for a 21-year period of probation for immigrants as a condition to admission to citizenship, and to oppose the Roman Catholic Church as a menace to American democracy. The stock answer of a questioned member on the movement and its purposes was: "I know nothing about it." From this came the common designation of adherents as "Know Nothings" and their organization as the Know-Nothing Party. Political conditions favored an interim party as the Whigs were breaking up and the Republican Party was not yet effectively organized. By avoiding the slavery issue in their early years, the Know Nothings attracted many voters who did not want to become involved in the struggle over servitude. Campaigning on the slogan, "Americans must rule America," Know-Nothing candidates won many races in 1854. But by 1856 slavery had to be faced and that caused a party split which shattered the Know Nothing performance in the presidential election of that year. The party's nominee, ex-President Millard Fillmore of New York, carried only Maryland notwithstanding Whig in-

dorsement. As the sectional breach deepened, the Know-Nothing Party declined and in 1860 many of its members joined with former Whigs in forming the Constitutional Union Party which placed John Bell of Tennessee against Lincoln, Douglas and Breckinridge for the presidency.
I.Di.

Kodo ha (Imperial Way faction).

A radical group in the Japanese Army which engineered the February 26, 1936, mutiny in Tokyo, in which a number of members of the Cabinet were assassinated and the mutineers held control of the central part of the capital for three days until ordered to surrender by the Emperor. The **Kodo ha** was opposed to democracy, individualism, and capitalism and advocated the replacement of civilian parliamentary government by military dictatorship. General Araki Sadao (Minister of War, 1931—1934, and Minister of Education, 1938—1939) was affiliated with the Imperial Way faction, and Kita Ikki, a national socialist writer, was an ideological mentor of the group. The **Tosei ha** (Control faction), in which General Tojo figured, was more conservative in its social views but equally militaristic and imperialistic. The effect of the terrorist activities of the Imperial Way faction was to frighten the Japanese ruling cliques into giving increasing authority to the Control faction of the Army.
T.Mc.N.

Kokutai.

A Japanese term literally meaning, "the national polity," the **kokutai** was traditionally regarded as located in the "line of emperors unbroken for ages eternal" (Meiji Constitution, 1889, Chap. I, Art. 1). Although the concept thus underwrote autocracy, it did allow room for a major debate, in 1912, over the organic theory of the Japanese State. In 1945, despite assurances by Japanese leaders that the surrender left the national polity unbroken, in acceding to Allied terms Japan did fundamentally affect the traditional **kokutai**. Under the new Constitution of Japan, drawn up in 1946, the emperor became "the symbol of the state and of the unity of the people, deriving his position from the will of the people with whom resides sovereign power" (Chap. I, Art. 1). A.W.B.

Kolkhoz.

Soviet collective farm; a farmers' cooperative established by voluntary or forced participation. Administered by a chairman, elected by the general meeting of members upon the recommendation of the party and government. Payment of members according to workday credits depending upon the type of work, and the productivity of the kolkhoz. Extra bonus paid for over-fulfillment of the plan, fines paid for under-fulfillment. Kolkhozniky (members) allowed to have private garden plots to supplement their incomes.
K.Hu.

Kollontai, Aleksandra Mikhailovna (1872—1952).

Follower of Lenin in the October Revolution, later Bolshevik diplomat. Mme. Kollontai, the daughter of a tsarist general, entered the revolutionary movement in the 1890's, but joined the Bolsheviks only in 1915. In 1917 she returned from exile to take an active part in the Revolution and the establishment of the Soviet Government. But three years later she became one of the leaders of the Workers' Opposition, arguing that the Bolsheviks were favoring the new bourgeoisie and the wealthy peasants against the interest of the workers. Mme. Kollontai managed to escape the purges of the Workers' Opposition of the 1920's and 1930's, but she never again became politically important in the Soviet Union. From 1923 until 1945 she represented the Soviet Government in Norway, Mexico and Sweden and is widely regarded as the first woman ever to be accredited as minister to a foreign country. Mme. Kollontai was a strong advocate of women's rights and took a leading role in the post-Revolutionary onslaught on traditional standards of family law.
D.N.J.

Komsomol.

The All-Union Leninist Communist League of Youth, a Soviet youth organization for ages 14 to 26. Established in 1918. Membership over 19 million. Organizational structure corresponds to the Communist Party. Activity supervised by the party. Purpose: teaching Marxism-Leninism, Soviet citizenship, discipline and love for work, effective participation in the economy, training of builders and defenders of communism, preparation of qualified applicants for the Communist Party, and utilization of the energy, enthusiasm, and idealism of youth to further goals of the party. K.Hu.

Korea (North and South).
Total area of 220,230.83 square kilometres; population 35,023,371. North covers 120,538 sq. km. with 10,029,254 inhabitants (1960 estimate). South, with population of 24,994,117 (1960 census; aliens included), covers 98,431 sq. km.

Following Japanese surrender in 1945, American and Russian troops divided the country into two portions separated by the 38th parallel. War between South and North (1950-1953). The United Nations intervened and Communist China entered the war.

Russians established Communist-led Korean "Provisional Government" in North which evolved into the "Democratic People's Republic of Korea" in September 1948 with Kim, Il-Sung as Premier.

South Korea held a general election in May 1948 for a National Assembly which adopted Korean Constitution and elected Dr. Syngman Rhee as President, and proclaimed the "Republic of Korea" in August. Economic Aid Agreement concluded with U.S.A. in December. U.S. forces were withdrawn in June 1949 and a Mutual Defense Treaty concluded in 1953. Syngman Rhee's government collapsed in 1960 during a students' rebellion. In May 1961, Lieutenant-General Pak, Chung-Hee, through a military coup d'Etat, established a Military Revolutionary Government. North and South Korea are developing different patterns of organization, particularly in the economy, thereby impeding reunification, the most outstanding "postwar problem" of Korea. H.C.K.

Korean politics, fundamental ideas of.
Today use and meaning of the Korean word "Chung-Chi" resembles use and meaning of Anglo-American "politics," primarily linked with contemporary party politics. The fundamental ideas of Korean politics, however, should be found in the context of Korean social mores and heritage. The meaning of the word politics—"Chung-Chi" — in oriental Confucian thought connotes the word "Jung-Chi" which means the King governs his subjects with justice (righteousness). "Chung-Chi" therefore includes the concept of statesmanship based on personal character and genuine leadership qualities. (This is why Syngman Rhee was considered by the people of Korea as "national father"). Which "party" governs is actually less significant from traditional Korean point of view and largely a procedural issue.
H.C.K.

Korean War (1950—1953).
On June 25, 1950, North Korean Communist forces invaded the Republic of Korea (South Korea), beginning what became an undeclared "limited war" in which almost 6,000,000 American troops were to be engaged and over 140,000 American casualties suffered. Total casualties suffered by all participants in this conflict, probably the most unpopular in modern American history, have been estimated at approximately 2,500,000. The Korean War also marked the first (and, as of 1962, the only) occasion when large scale military action was undertaken through the United Nations, with sixteen member states contributing armed forces.

Divided into Communist and non-Communist components, along the thirty-eighth parallel, as a result of administrative arrangements at the close of the Second World War, Korea remained divided, despite efforts at peaceful reunification under U.N. auspices, until the North Korean attack. When a cease-fire order by the United Nations Security Council was ignored by Communist forces, the United States decided to commit American sea and air forces to the defense of South Korea. Shortly afterwards, following the adoption of a Security Council recommendation that U.N. members aid South Korea, the United States also undertook massive intervention with ground forces. After driving invading forces back to the thirty-eighth parallel, the U.N. decided, on October 7, 1950, to continue operations in an effort to unify all of Korea. This led to intervention by Chinese Communist forces, a highly frustrating military stalemate, and, after prolonged negotiations, the signing of an armistice agreement (July 27, 1953) which left Korea divided along the battle line, generally slightly north of the thirty-eighth parallel. Subsequent attempts to arrange a political settlement have proven fruitless. S.L.A.

Kornilov, Lavr G. (1870—1918).
Russian military leader. Kornilov served as commander in chief of the Russian Army under Kerensky from the March revolution until September 1917. He was dismissed by Kerensky after an abortive attempt to seize power. Kornilov was arrested but escaped after the Bolsheviks seized power. He led the White Army in the Kuban in actions against the Red Army until his death from wounds in 1918.
W.D.J.

Kosygin, Aleksei Nikolaevich (1904—   ).
Leading member of the Soviet managerial bureaucracy during the late Stalin and Khrushchev periods. Kosygin received the specialized political-technical training that the party provided in the '20s and early '30s for the likely members of its then-building new elite. He came under Mikoyan's wing. Like many others now prominent in the U.S.S.R., he advanced rapidly during the purges and World War II. In 1946 he became a candidate member of the Politburo and has been in and out of the top party group since that date. Kosygin serves in the Government as First Deputy Chairman of the Council of Ministers (Sovmin). His particular areas of responsibility appear to be domestic policy, generally, and economic planning, in particular.
D.N.J.

Kozlov, Frol.
Born 1908, peasant family, Loshchinio, now in Ryazan Oblast. Worker age 15, joined Komsomol. Studied at Mining Institute, graduated metallurgical engineer Kalinin Polytechnic Institute, both in Leningrad. Member of Central Committee of CPSU 1952; member of Party Presidium 1957. Government posts have included USSR Supreme Soviet since 1950; RSFSR Supreme Soviet; Chairman RSFSR Council of Ministers; Presidium USSR Supreme Soviet; First Deputy Chairman USSR Council of Ministers since 1958. Mentioned as possible successor to Khrushchev. W.A.

Kronstadt Rebellion.
A mutiny by the sailors of Kronstadt in February 1921 demanding an end to the dictatorship of the Communist Party (Bolshevists) in the USSR and freedom for workers and peasants to choose their own representatives. Denouncing the rebellion as a "white Guardist conspiracy" Lenin suppressed the rebellion with Red Army contingents. Realizing the need for some concessions, he, however, introduced the New Economic Policy (NEP).
J.D.

Kropotkin, Prince Peter (1842—1921).
Born in Moscow, a "scientific" anarchist. Joined the International Workingmen's Association in 1872. Imprisoned in several countries. Lived in England, 1886—1917. Returned to Russia in 1917—played no part in the revolution. Maintains that the law of natural evolution applies to society as well as to physical nature. However, revolution must speed up the evolutionary progress. Cooperation, "mutual aid," characterizes evolution rather than competition, conflict. The three hindrances to progress: the state, property rights, organized religion. Evolution (aided by revolution) will replace these by voluntary groups and associations of groups. Pure communism will eliminate ownership both in production and consumption; distribution will take place according to personal needs, with the goal of living in "comfort." Social morality will be the universal religion, consisting of the instinctive habits of self-sacrifice, mutual support and desire to work for the "well-being for all." T.P.

Kruger, Stephanus Johannes Paulus (1825—1904).
K. was born in the Cape Colony and had little formal education. In 1836 he went on the Great Trek. He became a general in the Transvaal in 1864 and was dismissed when he opposed British annexation. Kruger was president of the Transvaal Republic

from 1883 to 1900. He wanted an independent Afrikaner state and refused political rights for "Uitlanders" — a major cause of the Boer War.
J.F.M.

Krupskaya, Nadezhda Konstantinovna (1869—1939).

Lenin's wife. Though born to a noble family, Krupskaya was already a Marxist when she met Lenin in 1894. Four years later she joined him in exile in Siberia. She became his wife, secretary and constant companion for the remainder of his life. It was probably due to Stalin's constant affronts to Krupskaya that Lenin turned against him in 1923. After Lenin's death, Krupskaya opposed Stalin, but in 1927, fearing an open split in the party, she broke with the Opposition. Her own professional interest was in education.
D.N.J.

Kubitschek de Oliveira, Juscelino.

Brazilian politician born Sept. 12, 1902, worked as telegraph operator, obtained M.D. in 1927. Was twice elected federal deputy (1934 and 1946), became mayor of Belo Horizonte (1940) and governor of home state Minas Gerais (1950). Served as President of Republic during 1956-61 term distinguishing himself as economic planner and founder of new capital Brasilia. In 1961 was elected senator for the state of Goias.
R.R.

Kuchel, Thomas H.

Born August 15, 1910; U.S. Senate from January 3, 1953 until 1962; Republican — California. Reelected in 1962.
R.A.B.

Ku Klux Klan.

A secret society of Southern whites organized at the end of the Civil War. The KKK was only one of several secret associations organized to resist the Congressional plan for reconstruction (1865—1876), and to protest against governments dedicated to emancipation and Negro suffrage. Numerous Southern whites took part in the activities of the Ku Klux Klan or one of the other societies. The whole movement was more or less successful, while provoking widespread condemnation in the North. In some Southern communities, leadership of the Klan fell into hands of men devoted to anarchy and violence in opposition to civil law and civil authority.
W.D.S.

Kun, Bela (1886—1939).

Hungarian Communist leader. Studied law, became a journalist, and after 1912 was active in left-wing political movements. Originally a member of the Social Democratic Party, he became a Communist in Russia in 1916 while a prisoner of war. In Russia closely associated with Lenin and Trotsky. Returned to Hungary in 1918 as a Communist agitator. Arrested in February, 1919, only to be appointed Prime Minister in March after the fall of the moderate left-wing government of Mihaly Karolyi. Under Kun's leadership a Hungarian Soviet Republic was proclaimed. His regime was defeated by popular uprising, Rumanian intervention, and the anti-Communist military units led by Nicholas Horthy. In August, 1919, Kun fled to Austria and thence to Russia, where he fought in the Red Army in 1920. As agent of the Comintern, he was active in Germany in 1921, in Austria in 1928. He died in 1939 in the Soviet Union, probably a victim of one of Stalin's purges. No reference to him was made in the Hungarian Communist press until after the death of Stalin and the XXth Soviet Party Congress.
I.B.

Kuomintang.

The Nationalist Party responsible for the overthrow of the Manchu Empire and the establishment of the Republic of China in 1912. The party at first was a secret society known in 1895 as Hsin Chung Hui (Revive China Society). Sun Yat-sen was the guiding spirit of the movement. His ultimate aim was the adoption of Western democratic institutions. In order to achieve this goal, the Manchu dynasty would have to be liquidated, and new members were also needed to strengthen the movement. The name of the society was changed to Tung Meng Hui (Combined League Society). Fresh and bold tactics were employed by the society in different sectors of the realm. A local incident at Wuchang, Central China on October 10, 1911 unexpectedly turned into a nation-wide revolution. The Manchu empire collapsed and the Republic was proclaimed in the following year. But the society, now an open political party, did not gain control of the government. Therefore, another change was in order. New dissident elements were taken in and the party was now known as Kuomintang (Nationalist party).

During the period of 1912 and 1924 Kuomintang did a good deal of introspection and conceptual expansion. Sun Yat-sen provided the party with its basic principles known as San-Min-Chu-I, namely nationalism (Min Chu), democracy (Min Chuan), and livelihood (Min San). Political strategy of the party was to proceed in three different stages: (1) military rule, (2) political tutelage, and (3) constitutional government. In 1924 the party underwent its final reorganization. Also a major decision was made to open its membership to individual communists.

The death of Sun Yat-sen hastened the party to launch the much-talked about northern expedition. Literally, the marching nationalists swept everything before them. By March 1927 they reached the fertile Yangtze Valley. It was at this juncture that a split with the communists took place. Chiang Kai-shek employed drastic measures to purge the communists from Kuomintang.

By January 1928 the nationalists reached Peking. Simultaneously Marshal Chang Hsueh-Liang of Manchuria raised the nationalist flag. Soon other regional leaders decided to join the fold. Thus, the nationalists virtually unified the whole country at the end of the year and Chiang Kai-shek became the virtual leader of the nation, although not without some dissidence.

The party decided to move the capital from Peking to Nanking. The nationalist government was to be organized on the basis of the five-power theory as expounded by Sun Yat-sen in his San-Min-Chu-I. The idea was to place two more powers, examination and supervision, on the same level with the traditional tripodic arrangement. The government in its first ten years made considerable progress in most areas. Perhaps the most prominent success was the standardization of national currency with an almost incredible record of a balanced budget for 1936.

Meanwhile, the government had to cope with two difficult problems. Internally, the communist party posed a constant threat to the party in power whether in opposition or collaboration. Externally, Japan was an insatiable aggressor. In fact, her appetite grew with eating. A full scale war finally flared up in July, 1937.

In spite of a second rapprochement reached with the communists in late 1936 so as to present a united front against Japan, the cooperation did not prove to be any more lasting than the first one in 1924—1927. For as soon as Japan surrendered in 1945 civil war broke out again. Even with the earnest attempt of the Marshall mission to form a coalition, it was soon found out to be futile. However, to the disinterested, this effort on the part of the Marshall Mission was like trying to reconcile the irreconcilable.

Under circumstances of its own manufacture as well as over-anxious impositions by friendly nations, Kuomintang obviously was unable to capitalize on a major victory, which the Chinese so valiantly fought to achieve. Instead it became a victim of this situation and was forced to retreat to Formosa. The party's record in Formosa over the past twelve years has been on the whole creditable. However, its future lies solely in its ability to fulfill the ardent wish of Sun Yat-sen in establishing a genuine constitutional government. L.M.L.

Kurds.

Kurds inhabit the oil-rich area known as Kurdistan. This area covers south-eastern Turkey, north-eastern Iraq, western Armenia and north-western Iran. There are approximately four million Kurds. They are tribal, proud and warlike. Their four dialects express a rich and colorful folklore. The Kurds do not constitute at present a homogeneous entity. Their ethnic origin is shrouded with ambiguity. With the rise of Islam and their subsequent acceptance of the faith they entered modern history. The great Saladin was a Kurdish soldier, and a defender of Sunni Islam. The Ottomans exploited the Kurds as buffers

against Persia. In the new order succeeding the First World War Kurdish representatives petitioned the League of Nations for the establishment of a Kurdish State. Kurdish nationalism is opposed by the governments of the above states, but seems to have the encouragement of the Soviets.
E.A.S.

Kuusinen, Otto Wilhemovitch (1881—).

Soviet politician, historian, ideologist, author. Born in Finland. Graduate of the University of Helsinki. Leader of the left-wing faction of the Social Democratic Party, 1908-17. Editor of the **Socialist Journal**, 1906-08, and the **Worker**, 1907-17. Minister of Education in the Finnish Socialist government, 1918. Leader of the newly-formed Communist Party of Finland, 1918, and active revolutionary. Citizen of the Soviet Union since fleeing from Finland in 1918. Secretary of the Executive Committee of the Comintern, 1921-23; continued as a member until 1939. Chairman of the aborted Finnish Democratic Republic of 1939-40 (a puppet government of the Soviet Union established at Terijoki during the Winter War). Chairman of the Presidium of the Supreme Council of the Karelo-Finnish Socialist Soviet Republic and Deputy to the Supreme Soviet of the USSR, 1940-56. Member of the Presidium and Secretary of the Central Committee of the Communist Party of the Soviet Union, 1957 to the present. Member of the Central Committee, CPSU, since 1941.
R.H.K.

Kuwait.

About 6000 square miles. Its population prior to the discovery of oil was about 150,000. It has now doubled. Kuwaitis were good sailors, traders and boat builders. Its strategic location on the top of the Persian Gulf explains why it was contested by the Portuguese, the Spaniards and later by the British. Since the end of the Nineteenth Century Kuwait became a British protectorate. In 1961 it was granted independence and consequently joined the Arab League. Iraq's claim to Kuwait created a tense political situation which has not yet eased. Kuwait's large income from oil administered by the Shaykh and his Sabbah relatives has been chiefly responsible for the economic and cultural development of the country.
E.A.S.

Kyoto.

Japan's ancient capital (794—1868), this old-world city was first poetically called the Capital of Peace **(Heiankyo)**; later, Imperial Capital **(Miyako)**; and now, Capital City **(Kyoto)**. Under the Tokugawa Shogunate, with the effective administration of the country removed to Edo (now Tokyo), Kyoto lost most of its brilliancy. In 1868, the capital was formally moved to Tokyo. Nevertheless, Kyoto remains the classical capital, since there the ceremony of Enthronement of successive emperors takes place. Now Japan's fifth largest city (1960 census: 1,284,818), Kyoto-**fu** is ranked as a metropolitan prefecture.
A.W.B.

L

Labor Zionism.
Branch of Zionism which integrates the national aspirations of the Jewish people as embodied in Zionism with a socialist ideology. Includes a Marxian, economic-materialistic variety, first developed by Ber Borochov (1881—1917) and organized in Europe and America around **Poale Zion** (Workers of Zion) as well as an idealist theory first envisaged by men like Nahman Syrkin (1867—1924) and A.D. Gordon (1856—1922), which centered, in Palestine, around **Hapoel Hatzair** (The Young Worker). In Palestine this movement created the cooperative sector of the economy, including the collective settlements and the all-embracing **Histadrut** (General Federation of Labor). At present it is grouped around the three Israeli labor parties, **Mapai, Mapam,** and **Ahdut-Haavoda,** which have related groups in other countries.   E.G.

Labour Party—United Kingdom.
See British Labour Party.

Ladakh.
(Area, approximately 45,672 square miles; population, estimated 195,430; 79% Moslem, 20% Buddhist.)
Ladakh is a frontier district in the state of Jammu and Kashmir constituting the entire eastern half of Kashmir and including the tehsils of Ladakh, Kargil, and Skardu. It is bounded on the north by China (Sinkiang) and on the east by Tibet. Allied ethnologically and geographically with Tibet, it has often been known as Indian Tibet.
Following the advent of Islam into Kashmir, the western area became Moslem while the eastern sector is predominantly Buddhist. It was invaded periodically by Moslems after 1531 during the period when it was nominally a dependency of Tibet.
The Ladakh area was annexed to Kashmir in the middle of the 19th century. The area north of Kargil has been held by Pakistan since 1948. Because an indeterminate area (India asserts 12,000 square miles) is currently occupied by Communist Chinese forces, it is one of the centers of acute tension between India and China.   M.T.K.

Lafayette, Marie Joseph Gilbert du Motier, Marquis de
(1757—1834).
When he was nineteen years old, independently wealthy, a captain of the dragoons, Lafayette went enthusiastically to help the American revolutionists, arriving in Philadelphia in 1777; after some discussion in Congress, he was named a major-general and put in command of a division; after a short visit back to France, he took part in the battle of Yorktown in October, 1781, then returned to France. He urged Louis XVI to convoke the Estates General of which he afterwards became a member; after the fall of the Bastille he was elected colonel-general of the revolutionary Paris National Guard. Until the execution of the royal family in 1793, he tried to urge moderation in an increasingly violent situation. Declared a traitor by the Jacobin assembly in 1792, Lafayette fled to Liege, where he was imprisoned by the Austrians as a revolutionist, to be released five years later at the intercession of Napoleon. From 1818 to 1824, and from 1831 to his death, he served as a deputy from Meaux.   E.G.L.

La Follette, Robert Marion
(1855—1925).
Lawyer, politician. Born in Duane Co., Wisconsin. Graduating from U. of Wisconsin (1879) he was admitted to the bar (1880) and began his practice in Madison. His life was devoted to public service. He was elected to Congress (1885—1891), to the governorship (1901—1905), and to the U.S. Senate (1905—1924). His creed was liberal Republicanism, pacificism, and the public interest. As Governor, he broke the power of the bosses in the State, regulated the railroads and utilities, reorganized the tax system, established an industrial commission and introduced the direct primary. Disappointed with the Taft Administration, and in the tradition of the Populist movement, he organized the Progressive Republican League (1910) and was looked upon as their candidate in the next presidential campaign. But he collapsed while making a

speech (Feb. 2, 1912) and his support vanished overnight. Some years later he co-operated with labor, farmers, and socialists to form the Conference for Progressive Political Action (1922) which continued the tradition of western discontent, and was nominated as their candidate for the presidency (1924). His progressive platform included public ownership of natural resources, fixing railroad rates, legislation for Congressional veto of decisions of the Supreme Court. He polled nearly 5 million votes, and carried Wisconsin but the Republican Party won the victory and the CPPA disbanded. La Follette represented the rebellious, reform movement of the West but was ahead of his time for practical politics. M.E.D.

La Guardia, Fiorello Henry
(1882—1947).

Lawyer, politician was born in New York City, son of an Italian bandmaster serving with the U.S. Army. After his father's death he went to Europe to visit relatives and his first position was with the American Consular Service in Central Europe (1901-1906). Returning to N.Y. he became interpreter at Ellis Island while studying law at night at New York U. and received an LL.B. degree (1910). As a Republican, he was elected to Congress (1916) but a year later joined the U.S. Air Service and was assigned to North Italy. By the end of the War, he had been decorated and promoted to rank of Major. Again elected to Congress he served several terms (1921—1933). But his contribution to politics was on the local level. At a critical time, following the Tammany scandals exposed by the Seabury investigations, he was elected mayor on a Republican-Fusion ticket (1933—1945). He was one of the most colorful and popular figures in the City's history and was fond of saying that he could be elected on a laundry ticket. He declined to run for a fourth term. During his administration, he obtained a new charter for the City (1938), balanced the budget, worked for slum clearance, and better sanitary conditions. His last public service was as Director General of UN Relief and Rehabilitation Administration. M.E.D.

Laissez-Faire.

Economic and political doctrine dominant in Europe and United States during 19th century. Arose around 1800 in Europe as reaction against excessive government regulation of industry. As political doctrine, it can be equated with individualism. Helped in bringing about greater political democracy by abolishing religious discrimination, broadening the voting franchise, and improving judicial procedures. Chief exponents were Bentham, the two Mills, and Spencer. According to Bentham's hedonistic calculus, if each man is given complete freedom to seek maximum happiness, the best possible society would emerge. Held social and economic legislation to be inherently evil. Government to be only "keeper of the peace." Spencer's extreme concept was similar to Godkin's anarchism. After 1870, laissez-faire in Europe was gradually modified by collectivism. In United States, became dominant as strongly conservative doctrine and known as Social Darwinism. Chief exponent was Sumner. H.G.S.

Lakewood Plan.

Lakewood, a council-manager city of over 67,000 people, contracts with Los Angeles County, California, for the performance of most municipal services and functions. The extent of county provided services and the compensation paid are determined by city-county contracts which may be terminated by either party. The Lakewood city council retains its legislative, budgetary and planning powers. Some administration is carried on by the city, but most is done by county departments. J.M.S.

Lame Duck Amendment (Twentieth).

The amendment to the United States Constitution changing the date of taking office of the President from March 4 to January 20 and of congressmen from March 4 to January 3, and providing for succession to the presidency. This eliminated the session of Congress, starting in December of the even year and ending March 4, in which members who were not re-elected participated, because their terms had not yet expired. K.E.H.

Landrum-Griffin Act
(Labor Management Reporting and Disclosure Act of 1959).

The first major revision of United States labor law since the Taft-Hartley Act was passed in 1947. The law sought to raise standards of responsibility and conduct in trade unions, primarily through stricter regulation of internal union affairs. It required detailed disclosure of union finances, established standards and procedures designed to prevent abuses in the use of union funds, provided for democratic procedures in union elections and hearings, and attempted to insure that international unions do not illegally force their wills upon the local branches. T.S.

Laos.
Area 91,000 square miles. Population (1961 estimate) 3,000,000. The area became a French protectorate in 1893. May 11, 1947, the king promulgated a constitution providing a constitutional monarchy. The fifty-nine member National Assembly is elected by universal suffrage.

Laos became an independent state within the French Union, July 19, 1949. Viet-Minh and Pathet Lao (Communist) troops headed by Prince Souphanouvong, invaded Laos in April, 1953. In the Geneva cease-fire agreements, July 21, 1954, the Pathet Lao received two provinces. Its forces were to be incorporated into the Royal Laotian Army. Laos entered the U.N. in December, 1955.

After two years of negotiation, Prince Souvanna Phouma set up a neutral government in the fall of 1957. It was overthrown in May, 1958. Fighting has continued between leftist and rightist blocs. The U.S.S.R. has supported leftist forces by an airlift and air-drop and charged the United States with giving rightists military aid through Thailand. Premier Phoui Sananikone led a loose anti-communist coalition government January 16—December 30, 1959, with a special mandate to govern without the National Assembly.

A revolutionary junta was replaced August 29, 1961, for four months by Prince Souvanna Phouma and an attempted neutral government. Prince Boun Oum and his deputy General Phoumi Novasan had financial support from the United States for their government. Their forces lost much strategic territory to the Pathet Lao. They were forced to agree to a coalition government.

A second international conference begun in May, 1961, resulted in a second Geneva cease-fire agreement, signed by eighteen nations, stipulating the removal of all foreign troops. Prince Souvanna Phouma, Prince Souphanouvong, and Prince Boun Oum head the resultant Government of National Union effected June 24, 1962. M.O'C.

Laski, Harold J. (1893—1950).

British university professor, political theorist, writer, and Labor Party leader; frequently lectured in universities in Canada and the United States; was associated as a political thinker with pluralism, socialism, trade unionism, pragmatism, and social Darwinism; prolific author of articles and books, such as **Authority in the Modern State** (1919), **Political Thought in England from Locke to Bentham** (1920), **Grammar of Politics** (1925), **Liberty in the Modern State** (1930), **Democracy in Crisis** (1933), **The State in Theory and Practice** (1935), **The American Presidency** (1940).

Ch.C.M.

Lassalle, Ferdinand (1825—1864).

Ferdinand Lassalle, son of a prominent German-Jewish family, studied at the University of Berlin and came there under the strong influence of Hegel. He joined the group of Young Hegelians and started out on a scholastic career. In 1852 he published a study of the philosophy of Heraclitus in 1859 a pamphlet on "The Italian War and Prussia's Mission," and in 1861 a treatise on property, **"Das System des erworbenen Rechts."** The impact of Hegelian philosophy never left Lassalle although he adopted some of Marx's ideas. In 1862 he began to call upon the workers to fight for their political and economic emancipation.

Lassalle was a splendid orator and capable pamphleteer and he utilized these advantages to arouse the workers from their apathy. "The Working

Man's Program" (1862) and "The Open Letter" (1863) were the most important publications during this period. In 1863 he founded the **Allgemeine Deutscher Arbeiterverein,** one of the two major groups which later at the unity congress at Gotha in 1875 formed the Social Democratic Party of Germany. In contrast to the Marxist groups he advocated immediate reforms such as universal suffrage and the establishment of producer's cooperatives.

On the more personal side, Lassalle became a trusted friend of Countess Hatzfeld and supported her in her many lawsuits against her husband. He died as a result of a duel. E.W.

Latifundismo.
System of large landed estates widely prevalent in Latin America. As a heritage from Spanish and Portuguese colonialism these landholdings are usually self-contained economic units consisting of the owner, his family, and many families of peons. The estates are known as **haciendas** in most of Spanish America, although in Argentina and Uruguay, they are called **estancias,** and in Brazil, **fazendas.** In most instances a very small percentage of the upper classes owns most of the best land in each country, and the tendency is toward economic, political, and social monopoly by the landed elite. R.B.G.

Latin America.
L.A. is a collective name used for 20 nation-states which dot the map between the southern borders of the U.S.A. and Cape Horn. Of these states seven are part of North America; three are island states in the Caribbean; the rest cover the South American continent. The name is derived from the Latin-based languages and cultures of Spain and Portugal which had a decisive influence on the political, economical and cultural development of the Latin American states. The centers of Spanish settlement (during the 15th and 16th centuries) were in Mexico, Peru, Guatemala, Colombia and Paraguay. The centers of Portuguese colonization were chiefly in what is today Brazil. Most Latin Americans have Spanish, Portuguese, Indian or Negro ancestry. The mestizos, people of mixed white and Indian descent, form the largest population group. Roman Catholicism, to which most of the native Indians were converted, is the leading religious faith. There are also about 5 million Protestants in all L.A. (3½ per cent of the total population) and about 600,000 Jews (a fraction of one per cent). Independence movements, inspired by the example of the British colonies in North America, became effective after Napoleon's invasion of the Iberian Peninsula in 1808. Argentina achieved her independence from Spain in 1816. Brazil declared her independence from Portugal in 1822. In 1824 Guadalupe Victoria was inaugurated as the first president of an independent Mexico. (For the political development of these and other L.A. countries as well as for such peculiarly L.A. institutions as the caudillo system see special entries.) J.D.

Latvia.
Area, 24,800 sq. mi.; population, 2,142,000; capital, Riga. Also subjected to periodic migrations of Finnish, Slavic, and Teutonic tribes, the Letts were converted to Christianity by German missionaries in the twelfth century. Riga was founded in 1203. For several centuries German influence was predominant. The Swedes ruled for a short time, until Peter the Great made Latvia part of the Czarist empire in 1721.

Latvia became independent in 1918, when the Czarist empire collapsed. It managed well until the 1930's. Economic distress created political unrest which culminated in the establishment of a dictatorship under Prime Minister Karlis Ulmanis in 1934. With the coming of war, Latvia experienced Soviet absorption in 1940, German occupation from 1941 to 1944, and incorporation into the USSR in 1944.
A.Z.R.

Lausanne, Treaty of July 24, 1923.
The Treaty replaced the abortive instrument signed three years earlier at Sevres. It established peace between the Allies and Republican Turkey. Turkey renounced its rights over its non-Turkish provinces. The capitulations were abolished. Freedom of transit and of navigation in the straits was recognized. The straits were to be gov-

erned by an international supervisory commission under the permanent presidency of Turkey. The Treaty then recognized the republican regime in Turkey and defined the status of the former provinces of the Ottoman Empire. E.A.S.

Laval, Pierre (1883—1945).
French politician and collaborationist. Pierre Laval was the son of an inn-keeper and schoolmaster. In his youth he was a student of Edouard Herriot. Known to be outspoken, aggressive, and impatient to "get somewhere," Laval switched political affiliations several times in the course of his life. Before the Second World War he served as Premier and minister in several governments. With the defeat of France he became a collaborationist. In the Vichy Government of Marshal Petain Laval was second in importance only to the Marshal, and considered himself the link between the German Government and Vichy, holding in his hands vast powers. After the War he was tried and convicted of the crime of collaboration, for which he paid with his life in 1945. W.C.C.

Law.
In natural sciences, a report of observed frequencies of physical properties or behavior, and in social sciences also, a basis for generalization about human beings and their behavior. As a code of conduct, law is established and enforced by the state or between states, replacing or supplementing custom and moral codes characteristic of primitive societies. Law implies a standard and enforcement, and views differ whether some parts of it are beyond man's control, either fixed by nature ("natural law") or by divine intervention ("divine law"). Legal positivists hold that recognition by the government of a sovereign state establishes law and hence divine law and natural law are not recognized as sources of law. Law may be private or public dependent upon whether it affects private relationships only, or the state. Public law may be administrative, criminal, or constitutional. Municipal law is the law within a state, and international law, the law between states. Some contend the latter is in the realm of morality rather than law, in the absence of a world state. D.P.

Law Enforcement.
In any governmental system laws must be obeyed. Their violation is usually met with punishment. In the U.S.A. the president is responsible for the enforcement of federal law. He makes use of the Justice Department, the Federal Bureau of Investigation, the Secret Service and the Coast Guard, to seek out the offender and to see that he is tried by the courts. If found guilty he will be subject to penalties such as financial fine, imprisonment or execution. M.F.

Law of Diminishing Administrative Returns.
Important aspect of the Law of Changing Administrative Returns, which correlates administrative cost (in personnel and material) and the advantages gained by those who determine the character and size of the administrative effort. At the start the administrative enterprise may find itself in a position in which revenue, power, prestige, and services outweigh cost. Later the administrative returns and cost may balance. Still later the returns may diminish to the point where no additional administrative advantage accrues. The Law of Changing Administrative Returns is operative in private enterprise. In government it assumes a different, but highly significant, form. The administrative activities of limited governments are influenced by recognized political and social forces whose differing strengths differently affect government budgeting. Under the two major types of total power—Oriental despotism and Communist totalitarianism — administrative plans are determined exclusively by the ruling bureaucracy, which combines the desire for a maximum of power and revenue with the determination to keep the population politically atomized. Under Oriental despotism, the regime's ability to exert economic, social and ideological control is limited by its limited managerial functions. Under Communist totalitarianism, the establishment of a total managerial economy (a nationalized industry and a collectivized agriculture) enables the bureaucracy to

manipulate increasingly the population's economy, social life, and ideas. The Law of Diminishing Administrative Returns still asserts itself consequentially in agriculture where the many dispersed and intermittent activities make on-the-spot supervision overwhelmingly costly. This latter fact accounts for the low agricultural productivity in the USSR and the countries of Eastern Europe that have collectivized their agrarian economy; it affects agricultural productivity even more seriously in countries with an intensive irrigation economy, such as China and North Vietnam. K.A.W.

Law of the Sea.
It is clearly established that though the high seas are exterior to the sovereignty of states, they are not without law. A large number of international conventions have been concluded, setting down certain rules and regulations with respect to such topics as safety, salvage, rules of the road, submarine cables, fisheries, and collisions at sea. Apart from such conventions there are certain rules of law which are universally recognized, such as those appertaining to the use of a nation's flag. It is also well established that every state has a right to seize pirates on the high seas and to punish them, on the ground that pirates are enemies of the human race, **hostes humani generis.** O.S.

Leadership.
A behavioral process consisting of stimulating persons, called "followers," to act integratively toward the achievement of group goals. It is primarily a function of the situation within which it occurs, though significantly influenced by personal traits and status-role. Traditional conceptions overemphasize heroism ("The Great Man Theory") or universal traits and types.

The study of leadership requires recognition of the primary importance of **the situation;** the distinctions between actual, potential, and **pseudo** leaders; variations in technique and roles; projected images; and the character and responses of non-leaders.
N.P.T.

League of Nations.
International organization, intended to be universal in scope, established at the instigation of President Wilson in conjunction with the peace settlement following World War I, aiming to eradicate war through collective security. The desire to confine the ruthless power struggle into an organizational framework had been prevalent ever since the breakup of the medieval Christian commonwealth. Further impetus was given by the professed belief that World War I was a war to end all wars, based on the expectation that force could be eliminated in international relations if definite and stable institutions could be substituted for the tenuous stability formerly provided by the balance of power.

The main organs were the Assembly, composed of all members having an equal vote, exercising mainly advisory functions; the Council, made up of a small number of permanent (the great powers) and rotating members, invested with executive, administrative, and supervisory powers as well as the authority to settle conflicts; and the Secretariat, consisting of an international Civil Service. Attached to the League was the Permanent Court of International Justice as the organization's judicial organ lacking, however, compulsory jurisdiction.

The efficacy of the League fell far short of its goal. Only once did it attempt enforcement action against a declared aggressor, i.e. Italy in the Ethiopian War of 1935-36, which, however, remained ineffective. With the rise of totalitarian dictatorships in the 1930's the League was completely bypassed. Its main shortcomings lay partly in the unrealistic conception of politics held by its founders and partly in the failure to materialize as planned. On the one hand, the implicit analogy of international "society" and domestic society, evoking the expectation that power could be eliminated from international as it had been from domestic conflicts, was improper and resulted in nothing but perilous illusions. It was patently absurd to treat war as a criminal disturbance in a world made up of sovereign states. On the other hand, the principle of collective security, by means of which an overwhelming balance was to be automatically created against any would-be aggressor, was better theory than practice. Not only was it frequently impossible to ascertain when aggression had occurred or to exclude emotion-based sympathies from deliberations, but states also tended to resist involvement in a war of enforcement that was incompatible with their particularistic interests. Hence, as early as 1921 the Collective Security Article 16 of the Covenant was reinterpreted so as further to reduce the feeble obligations it imposed. In the same vein, England and France supported only half-heartedly the economic sanctions against Italy in 1936. The League was also handicapped by the miscarriage of its universalist aspirations through the failure permanently to include such great powers as the United States, Russia, and Germany.

Although the League ceased to be a factor in international relations with the outbreak of World War II, its underlying ideas were revived through the United Nations, for which it served as a model. P.J.F.

League of Women Voters.

A nonpartisan organization designed to promote political responsibility on the part of all citizens, although active membership in the League is limited to women. An outgrowth of the movement for women's suffrage, the League was founded in 1920, the year the 19th Amendment to the U.S. Constitution, giving women the right to vote, was ratified. R.V.A.

Lebanon.

Physical and Economic Life: Boundaries North and East—Syria; South —Israel; West — Mediterranean Sea. Area: 4,015 square miles. Population 1,644,000. Terrain: West—broken flat coastal strip; Central—mountains cut through by trough-like valley, the Bekka. 52% of land is mountain, desert and swamp, 23% cultivated, 17% cultivable. Rainfall: coast 30-40 inches; mountains 50, Bekka 15. Agriculture: vineyards, olives, cereals, cotton. Industry: oil refining, food processing, sugar refining, textiles, cement. Beirut: finance capital of Middle East, a free market, large air commerce, center of banks and insurance. Ethnic base: Levantine-Arab, including mixed group who are descendants of Crusaders; Armenoid. Language: Arabic; English and French (leading European languages). Religion: one-half Christian, one-half Muslim, scattering of minority religions. History: In ancient world, Lebanon appears simply as part of Palestinian area much sought by the empires for its cedar, copper, and iron. Gradually it developed a kind of integrity as a refuge of minorities, becoming also largely Christianized. It is doubtful thus that Arab conquest included it, although Islam penetrated gradually and in 11th century Druse won a foothold. The crusaders established strongholds there and during Turkish Mamluk period local rulers played outsiders against each other. In the 16th century Turkish influence became stronger and eventually the Shihab Amirs succeeded in consolidating power over most of country until Bashir II (1788-1840) was overthrown for supporting Ibrahim Pasha of Egypt and the Ottomans assumed more direct control. Strife between the Druse and the Maronite Christians, revolt and massacre led to French intervention in 1864, and an organic statute establishing Lebanon as an autonomous province under a non-Lebanese Christian governor appointed by Sultan with Great Powers' approval. Prosperity followed. Turkey's defeat in World War One led to creation of State of Greater Lebanon (under French Protectorate) and Constitution of 1932 provided for a Parliamentary government, with a President (conventionally Christian) and Prime Minister (Muslim). After World War Two Lebanon became completely independent but increasing economic difficulties, Arab nationalism, the refugee pressure led to an imbalance of factions, the crisis of 1958, and landing of American Marines under Eisenhower doctrine. Constitutional reforms ensued, designed to quiet factional pressure but politics remain unsteady.

J.P.D.

Leftist.

Term originating in French Chamber, where Republicans, Socialists, and later Communists sat to left of President. The term L. is properly used to refer to those who would reform society and man through institutional measures, and who support extensive gov-

ernment activity directed at human betterment. The range would run from moderate interventionism to Communist. In politics, "Leftist" has become an epithet implying extreme radicalism or Communism. Some writers would do away with the terms "Right" and "Left" as vague or meaningless.
K.G.

Legation Asylum.
The practice of giving asylum to political refugees within the precincts of a foreign embassy. It is clearly recognized in international law that every state has a right to grant asylum to political refugees, i.e., a place of shelter, security, and protection within its jurisdictional area or territory. Whether this right extends to embassies and legations abroad is, however, doubtful and is certainly not universally recognized. The United States in signing the Havana Convention of 1928, by which the 21 American republics agreed to grant asylum to certain political offenders, reserved the right not to recognize the so-called "doctrine of asylum."
O.S.

Legislative caucus (at state and national level in U.S.A.).
Meetings of state or national legislators of a given political party designed to formulate policy and to make committee assignments. In the early nineteenth century in the United States, the legislative caucus was also utilized to select candidates for statewide or national positions but was replaced by the convention system. During the heyday of "King Caucus," the proclamation signed by the legislators which "recommended" candidates for the party was tantamount to nomination.
M.B.D.

Legislative day.
The period which commences after a legislative body meets following an adjournment until the time it adjourns again. Thus a legislative day may extend to several calendar days when either chamber of a legislative body recesses rather than adjourns. This procedure permits the body to continue its work without interruption, which would not be true if it followed the regular order of business following an adjournment.
G.B.H.

Legislative Investigation.
For a unanimous Court, Mr. Justice Van Devanter wrote, "The power of inquiry—with process to enforce it—is an essential and appropriate auxiliary to the legislative function." (**McGrain v. Daugherty,** 1927). In addition to being essential to the legislative process, the investigating committee has traditionally served two other functions: to hold administrative officers to strict accountability, especially with respect to the expenditure of public funds; and to influence public opinion. In regard to the latter, Woodrow Wilson once said that the informing function of Congress was even more important than legislation. However, while the power of investigation is inherent in the legislative process, it has, especially since World War II, been abused; individual rights have been infringed and unpopular opinion silenced. Constitutional limitations on the power of investigation are, practically speaking, not great. Investigations must be related to a legitimate legislative task; they cannot be instituted for the purpose of punishing those investigated or for the aggrandizement of the investigators. If, however, the latter are the by-products of a legitimate investigation, the courts have not been prepared to stand in its way. On the other hand the courts have insisted that the enabling act of the investigating committee be clear and that the committee's questions be germane in terms of it.
P.B.

Legislative leadership.
In Britain and in other countries with the cabinet system of government, leadership in initiating legislation and in guiding it through the parliamentary process is usually in the hands of the cabinet and in particular the prime minister. In the French Fifth Republic, however, it has been the President who has exercised primary leadership, although in form he has worked through the premier and the cabinet. In the United States, the separation of powers and the absence of party responsibility militate against the existence of a unified focus of legislative leadership. As a consequence, power is usually fragmented, notably among the President, committee chair-

men of Congress, and the elected leaders of the congressional parties.

D.M.B.

Legislative Liaison Officer
(In United States Army).

A commissioned officer assigned to assist in communicating the Army's needs and problems to the Congress and to presenting the military viewpoint. He is also charged with conveying Congressional responses to military officials and aiding members of the Congress in all appropriate ways. This duty is one of the career specializations available to U.S. Army officers.

M.P.S.

Legislative Reapportionment.
State constitutions require that State legislative bodies be redistricted after each decennial census. Districts are usually determined by the legislature itself, although this function is done by a designated commission or official in some States of the U.S.A. The main constitutional considerations in delimiting legislative districts are population, or combined population and area. Creation of districts in order to markedly diminish the number of legislators who would normally be elected by one party is called "gerrymandering." Although the Tennessee constitution required reapportionment after each decennial census, the legislature failed to redistrict after 1901. The U.S. Supreme Court upheld Federal court action to compel Tennessee to redistrict in Baker v. Carr, 369 U.S. 186 (1962).

J.M.S.

Legislative Reference Bureau.
An office serving the State Legislature, in the U.S.A., charged with gathering and editing information on many problems, standing ready to assist the legislators with advice on bill drafting, and maintaining a file of data on other states. The library services of the Bureau may be available to the public.

Sp.D.A.

Legislative Reorganization Act of 1946.
A law passed by the U.S. Congress and designed to improve legislative procedure by reorganizing the committee system through a reduction in the number of standing committees in the House and Senate, outlining the jurisdiction of each committee, limiting the number of standing committees on which each member may serve, providing for legislative aids, and requiring the registration of lobbyists.

W.V.H.

Lend-Lease Act, March 11, 1941.
Passed by the United States Congress to promote American defense. It authorized the President to sell, transfer, exchange, lease, lend, or otherwise dispose of any defense article, i.e., goods, weapons, services, etc., to any nation fighting the Axis, thereby making the United States the arsenal of the free world.

Executive agreements negotiated in the name of the President by the State Department were carried out by the Office of Lend-Lease Administration.

J.E.T.

Lenin, Nicolai.
Pseudonym of Vladimir Ilyich Ulyanov (1870—1924), since 1903 leader of the Bolshevik faction of the Russian Social Democratic Party, renamed in 1918 the Russian Communist Party of Bolsheviks. B. in Simbirsk, d. in Moscow. The son of parents both of whom were school teachers, he attended high school in Simbirsk, the Universities of Kazan and St. Petersburg, and in 1892 was admitted to the bar. A revolutionary ever since (in 1886) his oldest brother Alexander had been hanged for complicity in an abortive plot against Tzar Alexander III, he spent years under police surveillance and in prison, and in 1897 was exiled to the Lena region of Siberia—from which he derived his pseudonym "Lenin"— and where he married a fellow revolutionary, Nadezhda Krupskaya. After his release from Siberia in 1903, Lenin lived abroad, returning to Russia only on sporadic clandestine visits, as during the revolution of 1905. When the March revolution of 1917 had overthrown Tzardom, Lenin arrived from Switzerland in Petrograd on April 6, 1917 and set himself the task to overthrow the Provisional Government which aimed at establishing in Russia a constitutional democratic system. By staging the November revolution of 1917, Lenin succeeded in establishing in Russia the dictatorship of the Russian Communist Party, with himself as Chairman of the Council of People's

Commissars, a position he continued to hold until his death. Lenin revived the revolutionary trend of Marxian Socialism, and sought to adapt Marxian theory to the conditions of industrially underdeveloped, predominantly agrarian societies, like the one Russia presented in the early 20th century. Lenin advocated: (1) a small party consisting of dedicated revolutionaries fully conversant with conspiratorial methods; (2) an alliance between the industrial proletariat and the masses of poor peasants, the former, however, remaining in full control of such a coalition; (3) a close collaboration between the Communists and the colonial national movements that resented the exploitation of their countries by the "Imperialists."

Influenced by certain views expressed in the "Study of Imperialism" (1902) by the British Liberal J. A. Hobson, Lenin developed the theory that in the final stage of monopolistic capitalism, in the stage of Imperialism, proletarian revolutions do not necessarily occur in the industrially most advanced nations but in countries that, for a variety of reasons, happen to be the "weakest link" in the chain of world wide monopolistic capitalism. Thus Lenin really abandoned the Marxian deterministic theory of revolutions being the result of the economic forces of production.

Among the best known of his numerous writings are: **What Is to Be Done?** (1902); **Imperialism—the Highest Stage of Capitalism** (1916); **State and Revolution** (1918).   G.V.W.

"Leningrad Affair."

The purge of the Leningrad Communist party apparatus in 1949—1950, following the death of Andrei Zhdanov. The "Leningrad Affair" was probably planned by Malenkov in conjunction with Beria in order to eliminate the associates of the late Zhdanov, who had been Malenkov's chief rival for Stalin's favor. Among those who lost their lives in the purge were Politburo member and noted economist Nikolai Voznesensky and A. A. Kuznetsov, a leading member of the chief party secretariat.   D.N.J.

Leninism.

Lenin's writings, though distinguished by clarity, began to be interpreted variously by different communist groups, notably, in the past, the Trotskyists and the Stalinists, and, later, the Soviet Union Communist Party under Khrushchev and the Chinese Communist Party under Mao Tse-tung (especially in connection with the Sino-Soviet ideological conflict which erupted in 1961). Each group has maintained that **its** interpretation is the pure Leninist doctrine. Lenin elaborated on the teachings of **Marx** through his analysis of imperialism and by his belief that the revolution of the proletariat, though historically inevitable, must be prepared and guided by a strongly organized and well trained communist party (the concepts of the "vanguard of the proletariat" and "democratic centralism"). One of the greatest and most practical revolutionists of all times, Lenin favored opportunistic compromises if they were certain to further the ultimate establishment of "socialism" (actually communism). His doctrine, however, remained always revolutionary and opposed to all gradualism and revisionism.   R.St-H.

Lesseps, Ferdinand de (1805—1894).

Originally a member of the French diplomatic service, originator and builder of the Suez canal, completed in 1869. He headed the French company organized to build the Panama canal, but had to abandon the project in 1888 when it ran into financial and technical difficulties.   F.M.

"Let a hundred flowers bloom."

A celebrated phrase used by Mao Tse-tung in a speech delivered to a closed session of the Supreme State Conference, Peiping, Feb. 27, 1957, entitled, "On the Correct Handling of Contradictions Among the People." Referred to as the "Hundred Flowers" address and regarded as the high water mark in the Chinese experiment of relaxation in the post-Stalin thaw, Mao's slogan is now believed to have been a ruse. He spoke in favor of "letting a hundred flowers bloom" and "a hundred schools of thought contend," thus, encouraging criticism by the Chinese intellectuals. A veritable flood of abuse and polemics ensued, attacking the Chinese Red leadership and Communism itself. Mao reacted to this development with extreme harshness by what he called a "rectification campaign," leading to the belief that the famed speech was an enormous blunder. The intellectuals were disciplined **en masse,** and more than one million government officials were removed. M.M.Mc.

Letter of credence
(lettre de creance).
Document by which the Head of State accredits his diplomatic envoy to a foreign country. In it he requests that "full credence" be given to what the envoy may say on behalf of his country. J.E.T.

Levellers.
Mainly a political movement of democratic radicalism in the Cromwellian Revolution; zenith 1647-50. Members largely came from less prosperous middle-class small owners and tradesmen and were confined to rank and file. While agreeable to private ownership Levellers objected to monopolies in trade or profession. Immediate aims a failure but philosophy predated American colonists a century later: natural law as natural rights of individuals and rule by consent expressed in written contract creating limited government; representation in Parliament based on men, not interests or land, and selected by widespread suffrage. J.P.D.

Levi, Paul (1883—1930).
German socialist leader. For some time a student and follower of Rosa Luxemburg, founder of the Spartacus League and the Communist Party of Germany. Paul Levi resigned in 1921 from the chairmanship of the Central Committee of the Communist Party of Germany and joined the Social Democratic Party. Being the leader of its left-wing, he represented the Social Democratic Party in the Reichstag from 1921 to 1930. One of the greatest orators of his time, Levi did much to show the subservience of Communist Parties throughout the world to the Moscow center and the brutal cynicism of Communist leaders regarding the welfare of the working man.
H.D.

Libel and Slander.
From time immemorial a person's right to his reputation has been protected by law against defamatory actions. Libel (written) and Slander (Oral) are the two major forms of character defamation. Each involves the publication of information which demeans a person in the esteem of his fellowmen. This may be achieved by exposing him to ridicule or hatred or by imputing to him criminal actions and thus adversely affecting his character or trade. **Libel** may be either a tort or a crime. **Slander** of itself is not criminal. The truth of the statement is usually considered an absolute defense. A.A.N.

Liberalism.
Although the term has undergone changes in meaning it has generally been concerned basically with the spiritual freedom of the individual and hence identified with the broadening of the Middle Class. As a School of Philosophy it followed Natural Law which was based on intuition or right reason. It may be said that while Natural Law and Natural Rights was the revolutionary creed of the 18th century, **liberalism** spearheaded the constitutional change of the 19th century.

The break with Natural Law began in England with David Hume (1711—1776) whose influence was apparent in the great treatise by Adam Smith, **The Wealth of Nations** (1776). Smith urged the end of restraint by government (mercantilism) and the establishment of a simple system of natural liberty with every man left free to pursue his own interest in his own way to bring both his industry and capital into competition with those of any other man. This **laissez faire** philosophy influenced all of western Europe and America but the most characteristic development took place in England and the United States. **Liberalism** may conveniently be divided into economic and political thought and its 19th and 20th century variants.

Economic Liberalism in the 19th century was aided by the decline of the landed gentry and the coming of the industrial revolution which needed freedom to develop. As the theory was expanded by such writers as David Ricardo (1772—1823), and John Stuart Mill (1806—1873), it meant liberty to choose one's employment, free competition, free trade, free banks, and a free competitive rate of interest. Mill urged resistance to all State intervention saying, "every restriction of competition is an evil."

Political Liberalism in the same period was an adaptation of the autonomy of the individual from authority but pertained to his political and civil rights under a government of law based on the consent of the governed. This concept was best expressed by Jeremy Bentham (1784—1832). Believing in the essential goodness of man, he postulated on the hedonistic idea of pain and pleasure, that the best government provided the greatest happiness to the greatest number with each person himself deciding on his own happiness. The link was formed between free individual initiative, free competition, free suffrage and free elections. The Liberal Party of England was rooted in liberalism and the philosophy of Bentham and Mill. It arose with the Reform Act (1832) and blossomed under the leadership of William Ewart Gladstone (1809-1898). The party stood for progressive legislation and claimed to represent government by the people in opposition to vested interests.

Liberalism received a revision toward the end of the century from the doctrine of free competition through the writings of T.H. Green (1836—1883), the philosophical supporter of Gladstone's Irish Land Bill (1881). He held that there was "political obligation" for the general good, such as legislation for public health and public education. Seeing a relationship between the individual and the social community, he believed that liberalism must include the moral dignity of man. Green became the channel of transition between liberalism of the 19th century and the 20th century.

In the 20th century, liberalism acquired new meanings in response to changing economic and political conditions. In the United States, two great changes came in the economic structure. Business grew beyond the individual, competitive companies into giant corporations with ownership diffused among thousands of stockholders, and with a hired manager. Their bigness and power sometimes threatened the public interest. Industry had reached maturity. On the other hand, a new class had come to power, labor. A three-fold conflict of power resulted: industry, labor and the public interest. Early in the century, the concept of a free, competitive society began to give way to government regulation. Theodore Roosevelt (1858—1919) secured the Hepburn Act (1906) to regulate railroad rates in the "public interest." Woodrow Wilson secured the Adamson Act (1916) limiting to eight hours work on the railroads. Franklin D. Roosevelt sponsored the Security and Exchange Act (1934) to regulate the stock market, and the Utility Holding Company Act (1934) to limit corporate financial structure. In the public interest, John F. Kennedy used his power to force the U.S. Steel Corporation to rescind an announced price increase in steel (1962). All of these restrictions and many more have been described as liberalism, or in the best interests of the people. To relieve the harshness of rugged capitalism, the Social Security Act was passed (1935) to provide unemployment insurance, and old age and survivor insurance. Although often referred to as the "welfare state" few denied that this too was liberalism.

Lastly, the rise to power of the monolithic State since World War II has had an impact upon the trend of government today to impose its will upon society in the public interest.

M.E.D.

Liberal Party—United Kingdom. See British Liberal Party.

Liberal Party—U.S.A.

A minor political party in New York state which normally does not nominate candidates of its own for office but rather nominates the candidate of one of the major parties, usually the Democratic. By threatening to withdraw its support the party seeks to influence the major party's choice in the direction of liberal candidates. This action is made possible by New York election laws which permit multiple nominations. The Liberal Party

was formed in 1944 as a reaction against the domination of the American Labor Party by the Communists. Its principal support comes from David Dubinsky and the International Ladies' Garment Workers Union.
J.S.S.

Liberia.
The oldest African republic, located on the west coast of Africa, with an area of 43,000 square miles and an estimated population of some 1,500,000. The American Colonization Society established a government of immigrant Negro Americans over the back country tribes beginning in 1816, and relinquished its political control in favor of an American-styled constitution in 1847. But the adoption of a presidential type of government with a legislature divided into a house of representatives and a senate did not ensure constitutional government along American lines. Legislative or judicial checks and balances on the personal authority of the president are virtually non-existent. For over 85 years Liberia has been governed by the True Whig Party. Opposition groups have been fragmentary, and none has persisted for long. The party itself is confined largely to a hereditary caste of around 15,000 descendants of Americo-Liberians. The present chief executive, W.V.S. Tubman, was first elected in 1943, and seems likely to continue his presidency for as long as he lives. Although Liberia has internal problems of administrative inefficiency and corruption, autocracy, caste rule, poverty, and illiteracy, some reform measures have been adopted during the presidency of Tubman. R.V.A.

Libya.
Its area is about 810,000 square miles, consisting of two fertile strips and a vast desert, with rich oil deposits. Its population is estimated between one and two million, predominantly nomads and peasants. Since 642 the Libyan region fell to the Arabs, and became an integral part of Islamic politics. From the 16th to the beginning of this century, Libya was formally under the rule of the Ottoman Turks. In 1911 it fell under Italian occupation. It was liberated by United Nations forces and was declared independent by the United Nations, in December 1951. Libya is a United Kingdom under the crown of Sayyid Muhammad Idris al-Sannusi. It is a member of the Arab League and of the United Nations. E.A.S.

Licensing.
The process, in the U.S.A., by which a state or local unit of government grants authority to conduct a business, professional or trade activity. State governments, through special commissions, prescribe qualifications and conduct examinations prior to entry into specified vocations (physicians, pharmacists, attorneys, teachers, electricians, plumbers, etc.). Local governments control entry into and continuing regulation of various types of business enterprise (hotels, barbershops, laundries, bowling alleys, movie theaters, etc.). Fees and excise taxes concomitant with licensing may also provide control and revenue for the governing body. J.O.H.

Lidice Massacre.
On June 10, 1942, Lidice, a small mining town near Kladno in Czechoslovakia, was completely destroyed by SS Elite Guard detachments on order of Hitler, executed by his deputy in Prague Karl Hermann Frank — sentenced to death after the war — and Police General Kurt Daluege (committed suicide in the Nuremberg jail). All buildings of Lidice were levelled to the ground and the name of the village abolished. 199 men and boys over 15 years were shot. 200 women were deported; seven of them later shot in Prague, the rest murdered in Ravensbrueck and Auschwitz concentration camps. 91 children were deported; 82 of them murdered, the remaining 9 "Germanized" but only two allegedly survived. The massacre was a barbarous act of revenge for the assassination of Reinhard Heydrich, Hitler's Reich Protector of Bohemia and Moravia who had been shot on May 27 and died on June 4, 1942 in Prague. The assassins were Czech patriots; they had no connection whatsoever with the population of Lidice. But its inhabitants had to die in order to instill fear into the Czech people and bring them to their knees. The world answered by giving settlements and gardens in many countries the

name "Lidice" and by helping to rebuild the town after the war. On the twentieth anniversary of the massacre representatives of the German Bundesrepublik expressed deep shame over the terrible crime. A similar action as in Lidice took place in the French city of Oradour. R.M.W.K.

Lie, Trygve Halvdan.
Born July 16, 1896. A lawyer and politician he served Norway as Foreign Minister, helped found the U.N. and became its first Secretary-General. (Elected 1946; term extended, effective, 1951; resigned, effective, 1953.) He endowed the office with a tradition of strong active leadership but was increasingly immobilized by Russian opposition after the Korean War began. See his autobiographical work In the Cause of Peace (1954). V.R.I.

Liebknecht, Karl (1871—1919).
Liebknecht was one of the leading elements of the extreme left-wing of German social democracy. He was a lawyer by profession. In 1912 he was elected to the Prussian Chamber of Deputies and in 1912 he became a member of the German **Reichstag**. Liebknecht advocated forceful and revolutionary actions against the German government and its militaristic policies. When World War I broke out, he strongly opposed the war and the approval of appropriation for the war effort. Only under the pressure of his social democratic fellow-members of the **Reichstag** did he vote in favor of the initial war credits, although still in the same year, in December of 1914, he opposed as only **Reichstag** member further military appropriations.

He published together with a few other revolutionary socialists the anti-war and anti-militaristic "Spartacist Letters." This group became later known as the Spartacist League, the forerunner of the German Communist Party, which maintained contact with foreign revolutionary groups. Liebknecht was strongly opposed to the official policy of the German social democrats.

In order to neutralize Liebknecht's anti-war propaganda, the German government drafted Liebknecht into the military service. This, however, did not prevent him from continuing his work. On May 1, 1916, he participated in a street demonstration against the continuation of the war. He was subsequently arrested and sentenced to four years imprisonment. An amnesty in 1918 set him free.

During the German November Revolution of 1918, Liebknecht and his small group of revolutionaries attempted to guide the spontaneous anti-war revolution further to the left. He proclaimed the German Socialist Soviet Republic. However, the moderate socialists in the Provisional Government, who followed after the abdication of the Kaiser, foiled his attempt.

In January of 1919 Liebknecht led the Sparticists, who participated in the insurrection in Berlin which was nurtured by the left-wing of the Independent Socialists and the Revolutionary Shop Stewards. This uprising was suppressed; Liebknecht was arrested and brutally murdered by members of a military volunteer corps.

His main impact upon the German socialist movement was due to his revolutionary actions which brought him not only into conflict with the German government but also with the moderate Majority Socialists. E.W.

Liebknecht, Wilhelm (1826—1900).
Wilhelm Liebknecht studied at the Universities at Giessen and Berlin and was dismissed from the latter because of his socialist sympathies. After a short stay in Switzerland, he attempted to organize a republican corps in Paris with which he intended to invade Germany in 1848. This effort, however, failed. Liebknecht with a group of volunteers moved across the Rhine and proclaimed a republic in Baden. After the collapse of this adventure and his imprisonment, he found asylum in London where he remained for thirteen years. In London he maintained a close association with Karl Marx, although he disagreed with him on many fundamental issues. He stressed more peaceful social reforms and democratic institutions.

The 1861 amnesty in Germany permitted him to return and in 1862 he became editor of the **Norddeutsche Allgemeine Zeitung,** but when the paper came under the influence of Bismarck he resigned. Liebknecht joined the **Deutsche Allgemeine Arbeiterverein** of Lassalle. In 1865 he was expelled from Prussia and settled in Leipzig. Since the Lassallean group favored Prussian policies, he founded together with August Bebel in 1869 the Social Democratic Labor Party. The Unity Congress of Gotha in 1875 finally brought the two groups together under the name of Social Democratic Party of **Germany**.

In 1867 Liebknecht was elected to the **Reichstag** of the North German Federation. His strong opposition to Prussian militarism and to the deliberate wars conducted by Bismarck brought him into conflict with the authorities. Even a two year prison sentence could not silence him. From 1874 until his death he was a member of the **German Reichstag**.

Liebknecht's great influence in the German socialist labor movement is evidenced by the general reference to him as the founder and leader of the German Social Democratic Party.

E.W.

Lieutenant Governor.

Lieutenant governors are now elected by thirty-nine states of the U.S.A. Historically this officer presides over state senates, voting only on ties, and succeeds to the governor's post upon the latter's death, resignation or involuntary removal. Some states authorize the lieutenant governor to act as chief executive when the governor is either incapacitated or absent. He appoints senate committee members in about one-third of the states, often serves ex-officio on various boards and commissions, and occasionally, as in Indiana, may head an administrative department. Although this office resembles in part the vice-presidency of the United States, methods of selection sometimes result in choosing lieutenant governors unsympathetic with or even politically hostile to an incumbent governor's policies. C.F.N.

Lieutenant-Governor

(In British Commonwealth).

An official of Canadian provincial and Australian state governments bearing the same relationship to those territorial subdivisions as the Governor General does to national government. The title of this ceremonial chief in Australia is Governor, while it is Lieutenant-Governor in Canada. An Australian Lieutenant-Governor is actually a deputy to the Governor. A Canadian Lieutenant-Governor is appointed by the Governor General of Canada and is responsible to him in his political roles, which are more extensive than those of the latter official in national government. Canadian Lieutenant-Governors have disregarded cabinet advice and appointments, refused dissolution of provincial Legislatures, and refused assent to legislative acts. Australian Governors are appointed by the state Premiers, and are independent of the Governor General. Partisan affiliations are significant for appointment in Canada and of growing significance in Australia.

M.P.S.

Lima, Declaration of, 1938.

Adopted by the Eighth International Conference of American States meeting in Lima, Peru. It reaffirmed their continental solidarity and decision to defend their principles against foreign intervention. In case the peace, security, or territorial integrity of any republic was threatened, consultation of the ministers for foreign affairs would determine what collective action was needed. Each government would act independently. J.E.T.

Limited Government.

One of the two basic patterns (the other being absolutist government) into which the various forms of government may be classified. It is characterized by significant institutionalized restraints on political power which transcend those unavoidable social and cultural restrictions to which even the most absolute of rulers must make some occasional concessions. It imposes on rulers some measure of political responsibility to a large segment, if not all, of the citizenry. Normally, this takes the form of reasonably meaningful elections which provide the basis for the selection and removal of top political leaders and their policies. Application of the principle of **rule of law** also is an important feature. It assures that government will be conducted under laws applying equally to governors and governed, permits the accused his day in court, and provides some guarantee that punishment can be prescribed only in accordance with existing and publicly promulgated laws. Limited government is not synonymous with democracy, however, although the latter constitutes its maximum application since governmental responsibility is based upon universal suffrage and the greatest guarantees of liberty are given the entire population. Apart from democracy ("representative" as well as "direct"), limited government has functioned throughout history in the form of limited monarchy (Great Britain from 1688 to the last half of the nineteenth century) and limited republicanism (the American system from the Revolution until the gradual establishment of universal suffrage). Many similar, partially democratic but firmly non-dictatorial states also exist today. D.W.

Limited voting.

That system of voting by which each elector votes for less than the total number of representatives in a multi-membered body. This gives minority representation, but not necessarily in any systematic proportion. Some cities in the United States (including New York, Boston, and the present Philadelphia charter) tried the system. R.V.A.

Limited War.

An armed conflict in which the immediate military goal of the participants is something less than the destruction or unconditional surrender of its opponents. Thus a limited war is usually (1) restricted to a particular geographic area not including the bulk of the territory of some or all of the main participants; and/or (2) restricted in the sense that some or all of the main participants fail to utilize the most potent military weapons at their disposal. The "classic" modern example is the Korean War (1950—1953), in which actual engagement of forces was restricted to the territory of Korea, despite the massive participation of both United States and Chinese Communist military forces operating out of so-called "privileged sanctuaries" in Japan and Manchuria, respectively. For political rather than military reasons, moreover, the United States declined to use nuclear weapons in this conflict.

The term "limited nuclear war" has also been used, by statesmen, diplomats, and scholars, to refer to hypothetical conflicts involving the use of small-scale ("tactical") nuclear weapons aimed at specific military targets, but not of large scale nuclear weapons directed primarily against civilian populations. S.L.A.

Lincoln, Abraham (1809—1865).

Sixteenth President of the United States. Born in a log cabin at Hodgenville, Kentucky, largely self-educated, Abraham Lincoln moved to Indiana (1816) and to Illinois (1830). While a resident in New Salem (1831-37), he clerked in a country store, surveyed, managed a mill, split rails, and served as Postmaster, and a Captain in the Black Hawk War. Admitted to the bar (1836), he removed to Springfield (1837). Lincoln entered politics as a Whig member of the Illinois legislature (1834-41). He served a single term as a Clay Whig in the U.S. House of Representatives (1847-49) where he opposed the Mexican War. In the following decade, he won distinction as a circuit-riding lawyer, joined the new Republican Party (1856), nearly became John C. Fremont's running mate on the first Republican presidential ticket, and lost (54-46) his bid in the Illinois legislature for the U.S. Senate seat held by Stephen A. Douglas (1858). Nevertheless, his seven memorable debates with Douglas crystallized the slavery issue for the entire nation and elevated Lincoln to national prominence as a Republican spokesman. Nominated for President at Chicago (1860) over William H. Seward and others, Lincoln was elected President (1861-65) by a popular vote plurality over Douglas, John C. Breckinridge, and John Bell. Faced with a secession crisis, Lincoln moved to reprovision Fort Sumter, South Carolina, but the shelling of the supply ship opened the Civil War. Though opposed to slavery, Lincoln's primary goal was to preserve the Union, and only in the midst of the War (1863) did he issue the Emancipation Proclamation as a means of mobilizing world opinion against the South. Lincoln demonstrated great skill in forming and controlling his strong, able Cabinet, handling his Generals, and dispensing the patronage in the interests of both his party and the nation. Though guilty of unconstitutional actions, his magnificent faith and courage in the face of tremendous obstacles saved the Union. Beloved for his compassionate humanity, lack of vindictiveness, and sense of humor, Lincoln achieved literary immortality by his Gettysburg Address (1863) and Second Inaugural (1865). His plans to heal the wounds of war ended with his assassination in Washington's Ford Theatre by John Wilkes Booth, only a few weeks after his second term began. Lincoln is buried in Springfield, Illinois. K.E.D.

Line agency.
Agencies, ministries, or departments which are engaged in the main work of government. They accomplish the major substantive purposes of government—carry out the primary objectives for which government exists. Examples would be the British Ministry of Health, the American Department of Commerce, the French Ministry of Interior, and the USSR Ministry of Culture. These are in contrast to "staff agencies." R.D.S.

Liquidation.
As generally used in business, the conversion of assets into cash. Usually means giving up business operations and effect liquidation of assets for payment of debts and final distribution among owners of whatever assets remain. By analogy the term "liquidation value" refers to the process of ascertaining the true value of things.
In Soviet terminology the term is also applied to the elimination of certain classes of society, witness the famous and bloody "liquidation" of Kulaks ("rich" peasants) in Russia by Stalin in 1930's. W.N.

List System of Voting.
A system of proportional representation in which the voter marks his ballot for one of the lists of candidates presented by the various political parties with candidates elected according to their order on the list and in proportion to the votes cast for each party. The voter is allowed varying degrees of choice in departing from party lists. For the Swiss National Council there is complete freedom to change lists or compose an independent list. For the Bundestag of the Bonn Republic the voter must vote for one of the lists as they appear on the ballot. The chief methods of counting are the highest average and the highest remainder. Under the former each seat is allocated in turn to the party which would have the highest average of votes per seat if it were to win the seat being allocated. Under the latter a quota is determined by dividing the total votes cast by the number to be elected. Each party with votes in excess of the quota is given a seat, the quota is subtracted from the votes of such parties, and the remaining seats are allocated in descending order to the parties with the highest remainder of votes. In the Bonn Republic the list system with the greatest average method of counting is used for approximately half of the Bundestag seats and the plurality and single-member district method is used for the other half. R.H.B.

Listers.
The term "lister" is used in Vermont (U.S.A.) to designate the official ordinarily called an assessor in other states. The town meeting annually elects one lister of a three-member board for a three year term. The three listers are required to "view" property and appraise it at its "fair market value." One percent of this total appraised value is set down as the "grand list" which serves as the basis for levying property taxes. A.E.N.

Literacy test.
A means of determining that a person desiring to qualify as a voter can read or write. C.W.B.

Lithuania.
Area, 31,600 sq. mi.; population, 2,800,000; capital, Vilnius (Vilna). Despite successive intrusions by Slavic, Teutonic, and Viking tribes, Lithuania, unlike Estonia and Latvia, maintained its independence and traditional ways for many centuries. A powerful Lithuanian empire flourished in the fourteenth and fifteenth centuries. In 1386, Grand Duke Jagela embraced the

Roman Catholic religion and combined the crowns of Poland and Lithuania through marriage to a Polish princess. By 1500, the Lithuanian and Polish nobility had intermarried and established a rigid feudal system. In 1569, Lithuania was made part of Poland, losing its separate political identity. With the partition of Poland in the late eighteenth century, Lithuania was incorporated into the Russian empire. Despite repeated repressions, national feelings revived in the nineteenth century. After 1904, the Czar was forced to grant a measure of autonomy.

Lithuania regained its independence in 1918, but border disputes with Poland and Germany plagued efforts to establish a viable democratic state. A series of military coups and domestic troubles further weakened the country. In 1940, 1941, and 1944, it experienced a fate similar to that of Latvia and Estonia. At the present time, all three Baltic States are constituted as union-republics within the Soviet Union. A.Z.R.

Little Rock.

Capital of Arkansas in which severe rioting over the desegregation of a high school in 1957 led President Eisenhower to send in Federal troops and to nationalize the Arkansas National Guard. C.W.B.

Liu Shao-ch'i (1900—).

"Chairman of the Republic" (Head of State) of the People's Republic of China (Red China) since 1959, and top-ranking vice-chairman of the Politburo and Central Committee of the Chinese Communist Party, Liu Shao-ch'i is generally considered the man most likely to succeed Mao Tse-tung as number one leader of China's 700,000,000 people. Prior to 1959, Liu held other top Party and Governmental posts including those of Vice-Chairman of the Republic (1949-1954) and general secretary of the Party Central Committee.

Born of a moderately well-to-do peasant family in Mao's home province of Hunan, Liu spent the 1921-22 academic year studying in Moscow, where he was recruited into the Chinese Communist Party which had just been organized at Shanghai. For many years an underground trade union agitator, he has held since 1943 key administrative positions in the Chinese Communist Party, with, apparently, special responsibility in matters pertaining to party discipline and organization. He has also written a number of "classic" treatises on these subjects, including "How to Be a Good Communist" (1939) and "On the Party" (1945). S.L.A.

Livermore, Mary Ashton Rice (1821—1905).

Reformer, publicist, author, lecturer. Was born in Boston and studied at the Female Seminary at Charlestown, Mass. After teaching French and Latin and conducting her own school at Duxbury for three years, she married Daniel Parker Livermore (1845), a Universalist minister. Upon moving to Chicago (1857) she was active in civic affairs and church work and with the coming of the Civil War she was appointed agent of the North-western branch of the Sanitary Commission. This work projected her into the woman's movement. She was the first President of the Illinois Woman's Suffrage Assn. and established the **Agitator** (1869) devoted to woman suffrage which within the year was merged with the **Woman's Journal** of Boston. Moving to Boston she continued editorial work on the combined paper for several years but then gave it up to lecture on the need for higher education and professional training for girls. She was President of the Massachusetts Woman's Suffrage Assn., the American Woman's Suffrage Assn., the Mass. WCTU, and the Woman's Congress. M.E.D.

Lloyd George, David (1863—1945).

b. at Manchester. Age one when father died; raised by mother's brother, a village shoemaker. Entered parliament as a Liberal in 1890. A leader of the Welsh party and a champion of weak and poor. As President of Board of Trade (1905) and Chancellor of Exchequer (1908), accomplished more than anybody else for social betterment and social security with "War Budget" against poverty in 1909 and National Insurance Act, 1911. As Prime

Minister (December, 1916 — October, 1922), sent reinforcements to forestall Italy's defeat, Oct., 1917; provided transport for carrying 2,000,000 American soldiers across Atlantic, April and May, 1918; secured unified command of Entente armies, Aug. 1917; and negotiated Treaty of Versailles, 1919. Since General Election of 1922 took little part in political life. Elevated to peerage as Earl Lloyd George of Dwyfor at end of 1944. C.K.W.

Loaded question (in polling).
In the polling of attitudes, the questions to be asked of the respondents may be so devised as to more likely secure answers desired by the questioner than the real feelings of the people being polled. M.B.D.

Lobbying.
The practice of applying pressures on legislators to influence the legislation before them. (Sometimes applied to comparable activities in the executive branch.) In a multiplex society (q.v.), it is not only legal but necessary for organizations to make their opinions felt in this kind of direct communication, and most large organizations in the U.S. operate openly to affect legislation on behalf of their members. Otherwise, in the glut and confusion of the multiplex process (and especially mass communication) there would be no real way for legislators to understand the full effect and implications of many measures. Lobbying, however, is often considered evil and degrading because it is misused to bring undue pressure (and bribes) which distort the true issues involved and give unwarranted weight to the unscrupulous. J.B.L.

Local Federalism.
A term employed to designate the division of governmental powers or service responsibilities at the local level. Based on the familiar principle of federalism as applied to the national and state governments (in the U.S.A.), local federalism describes the functional relationship between municipalities and the county or other area-wide governments. Many experts maintain that government in a metropolitan or urban area can best be carried out if functions of a "local" nature remain in the hands of individual municipalities while those of "area-wide" character are administered by governments with broader territorial jurisdiction.
H.J.Sch.

Local government.
A generic term pertaining to political subdivisions, which are created at the pleasure of the state and exercise duties and responsibilities within a framework of state constitutional provisions and legislative enactments. Both municipal corporations, those with a considerable degree of autonomy, and quasi-municipal corporations, those which serve primarily as administrative units for state services and enactments, are included within its meaning. G.S.B.

Lochner v. New York
(198 U.S. 45, 1905).
A case in which the U.S. Supreme Court invalidated a New York statute pertaining to a maximum working day, stating that this statute interfered with the freedom of contract protected by the due process clause in the Fourteenth Amendment.
In Bunting v. Oregon (243 U.S. 426, 1917) the U.S. Supreme Court reversed the decision of 1905 by upholding a similar Oregon statute and asserting that the law had to be considered as a legitimate exertion of a state's police power. J.D.

Locke, John (1632—1704).
English philosopher of late seventeenth century. His rationalism and individualism were influential among French thinkers of the Enlightenment and American revolutionaries of the eighteenth century. His major political works are the **Two Treatises of Government**. The **First Treatise** was designed to refute Sir Robert Filmer's theory of the divine right of kings; the **Second Treatise** explained the origin, authority, and purpose of civil government. Locke proposed that men in nature are equal and possess rights which are inadequately protected. Society results from a compact among men; government is then established as a trust to protect individual rights. The people may remove a government which violates its trust. Locke emphasizes property rights. His view of

321

property as a natural right leads to capitalist economics; his contention that private property originates in labor, which also gives property its value, leads to socialist economic thought. M.J.H.

Lodge, Henry Cabot (1850—1924).

American lawyer and statesman. Lodge served one term in the Massachusetts House of Representatives, three terms in the national House of Representatives, and almost thirty-two years until his death in the United States Senate. He served as a member of the Alaska Boundary Commission in 1903, and of the U.S. Immigration Commission of 1907. He was one of the most prominent Republicans serving three times as the permanent chairman of Republican National Conventions. Lodge became one of the principal critics of the foreign policies of President Woodrow Wilson after 1914. Lodge led the opposition to Wilson's Caribbean and Mexican policies. He called for support of the President's war program after U.S. entry. In 1915 and 1916 Lodge advocated a league of nations and compulsory arbitration between nations, but later changed his mind. As Republican Senate floor leader, Lodge emerged as the successful leader in the opposition to Wilson's peace policies. Lodge's tactics to separate in Senate consideration the League of Nations from the Versailles Treaty and to attach reservations to the treaty were successful. His influence waned under Republican President Harding. W.D.S.

Log-Rolling.

A practice most often used in legislatures in the United States, especially in regard to appropriations for public works. Legislators frequently decide upon projects on the basis of "deals," "spoils," compromises and adjustments, instead of using the criterion of the public interest. Public funds are often regarded as a "pork-barrel" from which each legislator attempts to get a lion's share. Log-rolling is the trading of votes or support in order to get the "pork." "I will help roll your log (an appropriation for a dam — sometimes on a non-existent river) if you will help me roll mine (perhaps a grandiose new post-office)." A frequent synonym is "back-scratching." The practice is not unknown elsewhere, although the terminology varies. A.G.

London and Westminster Review.

Originally the **London Review**, founded by John Stuart Mill and Sir William Molesworth, first number issued in April, 1835; it was managed by Mill and became the leading organ of radical and utilitarian opinion.
J.W.Ch.

London Conference of 1908—1909.

This conference grew out of an attempt at the Second Hague Conference in 1907 to establish an international prize court. The conference which met on December 4, 1908 consisted of the major naval powers in Europe plus Japan and the United States. On February 26, 1909, its work was completed with the signing of the Declaration of London comprising 71 articles, grouped under the following headings: blockade in time of war; contraband of war; unneutral service; destruction of neutral prizes; transfer to a neutral flag; enemy character; convoy; resistance to search; compensation; and final provisions. This was the first attempt in history to codify the law of prize, and was remarkable in its regard for neutrals. It failed of ratification, however, and never came into effect. O.S.

London, government of.

A special system similar to the administrative county. It is composed of the County of London, the City of London and 28 metropolitan boroughs, all of which have their own councils. There are special agencies, such as the Metropolitan Police District, which extend beyond the boundaries of the County of London into greater London. R.H.B.

London Round Table Conference (1930—1932).

Initiated by the MacDonald Labor government to study Indian constitutional reforms, this conference of British and Indian delegates showed imperial adjustment to Indian nationalism, but also the distance between the two. The Congress party boycotted the first session, but sent Gandhi

322

to the second. His call for immediate responsible government met British refusal; and his claim that the Congress represented all Indians alienated minorities and conflicted with British safeguards for them. Deadlocked, he returned to India and jail. Cooperative Indians participated in all three sessions. Overall, federalism and dyarchy received support from the conference which contributed to the India Act of 1935. P.F.P.

Long, Huey Pierce (1893—1935).
Louisiana politician, known as "the Kingfish," who asserted a more active and broad purpose for state government and who built a political machine bordering on a dictatorship and family dynasty unique in United States history. Long was elected to several political offices with heavy support from "backwoods" Louisiana districts: 1918, to the Louisiana Railroad Commission; 1928, Governor; 1930, United States Senator. Long's highway building and Share-the-Wealth programs were enticing to the depression-ridden people of the early 1930s. In 1935 Huey Long was assassinated in the Louisiana capitol at the peak of his political power by Carl Weiss, the son of a political enemy. W.D.S.

Long, Russell B.
Born November 3, 1918; U.S. Senate from November 2, 1948 until term ending 1963; Democrat—Louisiana.
R.A.B.

Loose bipolar system.
A system in which national actors and universal actors, such as the United Nations, participate. National actors participate as bloc members or as uncommitted states, in addition to their functions in the universal actor. Blocs perform the major peace-keeping function and act to increase their own capabilities at the expense of the other bloc. No effort to maintain existence of other bloc. Uncommitted—or nonbloc member—national actors and universal actors perform predominantly mediatory functions. Military capabilities are predominantly those of the blocs and, if nuclear, reinforce a stalemate that otherwise would be tenuous.
M.A.K.

Lopez, Mateos, Adolf.
Latin American statesman. Born in Atizapan de Zaragoza, Mexico, May 26, 1910. Education: law degree, Toluca Institute. Instructor, later director of studies, Toluca Institute. Federal Senator, 1946-52. Minister of Labor, 1952-58. President of Mexico, 1958-64. M.A.

Lord Chancellor.
The presiding officer of the British House of Lords, head of the judicial system and a member of the cabinet. As a presiding officer he lacks the extensive power over the House of Lords which the Speaker has over the House of Commons, and he can take part in partisan debates. He is head of the Law Lords, who compose the highest appeal court, head of the Court of Appeal for civil cases, head of the Chancery Division of the High Court of Justice, and head of the Judicial Committee of the Privy Council. He appoints County Court judges and recommends appointments of members of the High Court and Justices of the Peace. Through the operation of several committees he is responsible for rules of procedure and proposals for legal reform in the area of civil law. He is the chief legal adviser of the government and is custodian of the great seal. In earlier days he was the principal officer of the king, and it was from his role as "keeper of the king's conscience" that chancery or equity law developed. R.H.B.

Lord Mayor.
The special title of the mayor in British historic cities. The title carries greater honor, but does not imply a difference in functions. It is used in cities such as London, York and Manchester. R.H.B.

Lords of Appeal in Ordinary
(Law Lords).
To assure that there would be competent members of the House of Lords to carry out its judicial function, the Judiciary Act of 1871 provided for the appointment to life peerages of persons who have held high judicial posts for two years or who are eminent barristers who have practiced for a minimum of fifteen years. The law now

provides for the appointment of nine "Lords of Appeal in Ordinary." Therefore, at the present time the composition of the House of Lords when acting as a court of law consists of the Lord Chancellor, ex-lord Chancellors, and the Lords of Appeal in Ordinary and any other peers who have held or are holding high judicial office. The House of Lords so constituted is the ultimate appellate court for England and Wales for both criminal or civil cases. However, it will hear appeals in civil cases only if the right to appeal is granted by the Court of Appeals or by itself, and in criminal matters only if a certificate of appeal is granted by the Attorney General, who will grant such a certificate only if the case "involves a point of law of exceptional public importance and that it is desirable in the public interest that a further appeal should be brought."

C.A.McC.

Lorimer Scandal.
In 1909 Republicans in control of the Illinois Legislature deadlocked for five months over the election of a United States Senator. Albert J. Hopkins held the seat but he had fallen in favor with Chicago's "blond boss," William Lorimer (1861—1934) then United States Representative. On the 95th ballot, taken May 26, Lorimer himself received enough votes for election. The fact that Democratic legislators cast 53 of Lorimer's 108 votes brought on an investigation by the **Chicago Tribune,** which, on April 30, 1910, disclosed that Democratic legislator Charles A. White of O'Fallon, took $1000 to vote for Lorimer. Three other Democrats made similar sworn statements. This created a sensational situation in the Senate where Lorimer promptly introduced a resolution calling for an investigation of the charges. A Senate Committee conducted hearings and then reported against unseating the Illinois Republican. However one dissenting member of the committee, Albert J. Beveridge of Indiana, pushed through to a vote on his resolution to declare Lorimer "not duly and legally elected." This was defeated 46 to 40, March 1, 1911. But the scandal which rocked the country was far from closed. The **Chicago Record-Herald** implicated a group of business men and industrialists in a Lorimer pay-off fund of $100,000. Meantime President Taft went to work against Lorimer. When the new Congress met in 1911, Senator Robert M. LaFollette of Wisconsin sponsored a resolution for a reinvestigation. Again the committee sided with Lorimer, but the minority succeeded in taking the issue to the Senate floor for a new vote, July 13, 1912. In an impassioned speech, Lorimer defended his seat, but Senators newly elected in 1911 in the place of defeated pro-Lorimer Senators, plus Republican Senators who reversed themselves, including Lorimer's Illinois colleague, Shelby M. Cullom, joined to produce an overwhelming 56-to-28 vote for unseating. Lorimer sought vindication by seeking a Senate seat in 1916 and his old House seat in 1918 but each time he failed in the primary. The scandal, one of the worst in American political history, gave rise to the term "Lorimerism." Between the first and second votes on unseating Lorimer, Congress submitted for ratification by the states, the Seventeenth Amendment which took the election of Senators away from the Legislatures and entrusted it to the people.

I.Di.

Losonczy, Geza (1907—1958?).
Communist ideologist, member of the Nagy government during the Hungarian Uprising of 1956.

Active in the Communist underground in Hungary before and during World War II, he was editor of the clandestine CP newspaper "Szabad Nep." Imprisoned on various occasions for Communist agitation before 1945. Deputy Minister of Education between 1949 and 1951. Arrested and sentenced in 1951 for criticizing the excessive industrialization. Freed and rehabilitated in 1954 during the New Course policy of Imre Nagy. On October 30, 1956, during the Hungarian Uprising, he became a member of the Nagy government. After the Soviet intervention on November 4th, he sought refuge in the Yugoslav Embassy together with Imre Nagy and many others. Granted safe conduct by the Kadar regime, he departed for Rumania. Later arrested, he was brought back to Hungary, where he died while awaiting trial. His alleged anti-state crimes and his death were announced on June 17, 1958. I.B.

Lotus Case.
A legal action between France and Turkey adjudicated by the Permanent Court of International Justice at The Hague in 1937, involving a collision on the high seas of the French Steamship **Lotus** and the Turkish collier **Boz-Kourt.** The main question to be determined was whether or not international law would prevent Turkey from instituting criminal proceedings against the French officer, Lieutenant **Dumons,** under Turkish law. The Court found that, apart from certain special cases which are defined by international law, vessels on the high seas are subject to no authority except that of the state whose flag they fly. It was only natural, the Court said, that each state should be able to exercise jurisdiction and to do so in respect to the incident as a whole, and that therefore this was a case of concurrent jurisdiction. O.S.

Lowell, James Russell (1819—1891).
American poet, editor, political observer and diplomat. Lowell was born in Cambridge, Mass., in 1819, of an old New England family. He attended Harvard where he was class poet. His distinguished career in scholarship and literature included professorships of languages and belles-lettres at Harvard in succession to Longfellow and editorships of the **Atlantic Monthly** and the **North American Review.**

In these influential seats, as well as on the lyceum platform, Lowell became a leader of liberal utterance and criticism in religion, letters and politics. A broad-ranging reformer, he was a passionate abolitionist who used his pen against slavery in both verse and prose before and during the Civil War. In the **Biglow Papers** he described war as murder, but after Appomattox, in his celebrated "Ode Recited at the Harvard Commemoration," he glorified the heroism of men who lost their lives on the battlefield.

Lowell was a delegate to the 1876 Republican National Convention that chose Hayes over Blaine. He declined to be a congressional candidate but served in the Electoral College where he supported Hayes on all the tests against Tilden. The next year he received a presidential appointment as minister to Spain and in 1880, although previously critical of Britain, was named minister to the Court of St. James's, where eventually he served the cause of Anglo-American relations most effectively. By 1886 he was distressed at the "new dry rot" he found separating scholarship from culture and political life. His intense feeling for liberty was expressed in his lines: "They are slaves who dare not be in the right with two or three." He died in historic "Elmwood," the house in which he was born. I.Di.

Loyalty Oath.
American experience with loyalty oaths goes back to the days of the Revolution. Pennsylvania's loyalty oath created considerable hardship for Quakers, while in Massachusetts they were exempt from the oath. During and immediately after the Civil War a number of states and the Federal Government enacted loyalty oaths designed to bar those who had aided the South in the war from practicing law, the ministry and other professional pursuits. The Supreme Court held these laws to be Bills of Attainder and hence unconstitutional. A rash of loyalty oaths were evidenced after World War I and again, but on a considerably wider scale, in the 1940's, persisting to the present. Unlike former laws, which simply required an oath affirming attachment to the Constitution, the modern oath requires a declaration from the individual that he is not, nor has been, a member of the Communist Party or any subversive organization. Such oaths are in effect in virtually all states. The Federal loyalty program covers not only government employees and those who perform services under government contract, but also such persons as labor leaders, scholarship students and scientists who receive services or funds from the government. Except for oath statutes which do not require scienter, the Supreme Court has upheld as constitutional both state and federal oath laws on the ground that a declaration of loyalty is a reasonable requirement for public employment. P.B.

Lubke, Heinrich (1894—).

In September 1959 Heinrich Lubke succeeded Theodor Heuss as President of the Federal Republic of Germany. At the time of his election by a federal convention which met in Berlin, Lubke was Minister of Agriculture in Chancellor Adenauer's cabinet, although not a widely known personality in the Federal Republic.

Heinrich Lubke, born in Westphalia, attended the University of Berlin; he graduated in geodesy and soil cultivation. During World War I he served as a lieutenant. After the war he directed a German agricultural organization **(Deutsche Bauernschaft)**. As a representative of the Catholic Center Party he was elected in 1931 to the Prussian legislature.

After the ascendance to power by Hitler, Lubke was arrested several times. From 1937 he worked in a housing construction organization. In 1945 he joined the Christian Democratic Union and in January 1947 became Minister of Food and Agriculture in North-Rhine Westphalia. In October 1953 he was appointed as Minister of Food, Agriculture, and Forestry in Adenauer's second cabinet. He is credited with initiating the so-called "Green Plan," a plan designed to modernize agriculture in the Federal Republic.   E.W.

Luxembourg, Grand Duchy of.

Situated between Germany, France, and Belgium. Capital Luxembourg. Area 999 sq. mi. Population (estimated): 320,000.

Founded 963 as minor principality. Holy Roman Emperor Charles IV (one of four emperors from Luxembourg) made country into duchy (1354). Held successively as province of Spain (1506—1714), Austria (1714-1795), and France (1795—1815). Made a grand duchy by Congress of Vienna and assigned, as an independent state, to King William I of the Netherlands (1815). Declared independent and neutral (neutrality abolished since 1948) by Treaty of London of 1867.

Constitution of 1868 revised three times. Constitutional and hereditary monarchy. Ruler Grand Duchess Charlotte (r. since 1919); her son, Prince Jean, installed as Lieutenant-Representative (to exercise all powers possessed by ruler) since May 4, 1961. Executive power shared by ruler and Minister of State and at least three ministers. Legislative power in Chamber of Deputies, now comprising 52 deputies, elected for five years by citizens of 21 years. Multi-party system.   M.C.V.

Luxemburg, Rosa (1870—1919).

Rosa Luxemburg was born in Russian Poland and became during her youth an active worker in the Polish socialist movement. In order to avoid arrest by the Tsarist police, she fled to Switzerland. There she studied law and economics and became a Marxist. In 1896 she settled in Germany, obtained German citizenship, worked with socialist newspapers, and became the leading theorist of the revolutionary left-wing of the German Social Democratic Party. Luxemburg stressed mass spontaneity, the general strike as the most meaningful revolutionary weapon, and the seizure of political power by force. Some of her views brought her into fierce conflict with Lenin.

After the outbreak of World War I, Rosa Luxemburg was arrested for inciting to rebellion and sentenced to one year imprisonment. She spent, however, the entire war in protective custody. Together with Karl Liebknecht she published the "Spartacist Letters" and supported from her confinement the founding of the Spartacist League. The Revolution of 1918 freed her. However, her months were numbered. In connection with the Spartacist League's participation in the abortive insurrection in January of 1919—incidentally Luxemburg was opposed to the Spartacists' taking part in this revolutionary adventure led by the Revolutionary Shop Stewards and left-wing Independent Socialists—Rosa Luxemburg was arrested and brutally murdered by members of a military volunteer corps.   E.W.

Lysenkoism.

The Communist theory of genetics developed by the Soviet horticulturist, Trofim D. Lysenko (1898—), who maintained that hereditary characteristics can be changed by human intervention, through the organism's response to a changed environment, and that these changes will be passed on to succeeding generations. As an antithesis to the Mendelian ("bourgeois") laws of heredity, Lysenko's genetics became the only permissible theory in the Soviet Union since 1948, when the Communist Party of the Soviet Union outlawed Mendelianism and exalted Lysenkoism as "the materialist science which is developing as the science of control of heredity and its variability, as the science of control of the processes of evolution in the interest of society." Since that time, Lysenkoism in the West was popularly called "party science." P.A.T.

M

MacDonald, James Ramsay
(1866—1937).
British Labor party leader and Prime Minister of two minority Labor Governments (1924, 1929-31). Was denounced and expelled from his party for joining with the Conservatives to form a "national government" (1931—1935). Entered Parliament in 1906, becoming Leader of Parliamentary Labor Party in 1922.   C.J.S.

Machetismo.
Violent method of political change in Latin America characterized by the use of the **machete**, a hatchet-knife widely used by peons for farm work and in support of rebellion.   R.B.G.

Machiavelli, Niccolo (1469—1527).
Florentine statesman and philosopher. In Machiavelli's time the mainstream of historical development in the West was toward consolidation of nations by force under the direction of powerful monarchs. Disunity in Italy, which consisted of five city-states, prevented a similar evolution there. Machiavelli, passionately nationalistic, attacked those, mainly the nobility and the Pope, who barred the path to Italian unification. His major political works, **The Prince** and **The Discourses,** consist chiefly of advice to prospective rulers on how to establish and maintain a state. Machiavelli believed that rulers must ignore individual morality in pursuing their ends, although a stable state would be impossible unless subjects were "virtuous." Machiavelli is best known for his advocacy of a complete subordination of means to the end of national unity, or, in subsequent and less accurate usage, to any political end.
    M.J.H.

Machine Politics.
Typical of a highly organized political organization which is called a "machine." The "machine" is presumably most effective, ruthless, impersonal, interested only in results rather than in forms or programs and political ideology. It is organized into tight-knit, well-disciplined hierarchic structure usually under the command of a boss. Machine politics is the politics of spoils, pelf, patronage, pork-barrel, power, preferment and money. Spoils, favors and patronage supply the "oil" for the machine and ruthless, often lawless men, "the muscle." (Politics of the Kelly-Nash or Hague machines are examples.)   A.G.

Mackinder, Sir Halford J.
(1861—1947).
English geographer who advanced the idea in 1904, as part of a paper, "The Geographical Pivot of History," that much European history could be explained by the pressure of landlocked peoples in Eastern Europe and Central Asia, identified as the "heartland," upon coastal peoples. Mackinder regarded the heartland, which includes 2/3 of the world's land area, as the core of the world island. While the theory that the nation which commands the heartland will dominate the world island is striking, Mackinder's main contribution was the spur which he gave to geographical studies.
    R.J.S.

**MacMahon, Patrice Maurice de,
    Duc de Magenta** (1808—1893).
Marshal of French Army in Franco-Prussian War (1870-71). Suffered defeat at Sedan, 1870. Commanded government troops against Paris Commune. President of Republic after Thiers, 1873. Monarchist, conservative. Dismissed Premier, J. Simon, May 16, 1877; dissolved Chamber of Deputies. Resigned 1879. No President of Third Republic used again power of dissolution.   M.C.V.

Macmillan, Harold (1894—   ).
British Conservative Party leader. Educated at Eton and Oxford. Entered Parliament (1924); openly opposed Chamberlain's Munich settlement. Held various wartime government posts. In successive postwar Conservative ministries, becoming Prime Minister in 1957. Made bid for British membership in European Economic Community.
    C.J.S.

Madariaga, Salvador de
(1886—   ).
Spanish diplomat and historian, Minister of education and of justice in Republican regime of Spain 1934, Director of the Disarmament section of

the League of Nations, Spanish Ambassador in Washington and Paris. He fled from Franco's Spain and settled in England. After the war he became one of the founders of the European movement. He has written numerous books in the fields of history (especially of South America and of Spain) and politics.　　　　　　　　　　　　F.M.

Madero, Francisco I.
Intellectual leader of the Mexican Revolution of 1910 and first Revolutionary president of that nation from 1910—1912. A political moderate, he conceived of the revolution primarily as a means of terminating the long regime of Porfirio Diaz rather than as a movement for large scale social reform.　　　　　　　　　　Ch.W.A.

Madison, James (1751—1836).
Educated at College of New Jersey (now Princeton). Delegate to Virginia Convention, first Assembly of Virginia and to Continental Congress. Member of Annapolis Convention (1786) and Constitutional Convention in Philadelphia (1787). In latter, his influence was so great that often called "chief architect of American Constitution." Co-author (with Hamilton and Jay) of **Federalist,** a collection of articles in New York press in 1787-88 advocating ratification of U.S. Constitution. Held that a viable union must have central government able to act upon individuals, not just states. Yet, after ratification, interpreted Constitution narrowly and thus opposed many of Hamilton's measures, e.g. funding the national debt. Member, House of Representatives, 1789-97. Led fight for "Bill of Rights" (first ten amendments to Constitution). In 1801, returned to Washington to serve as secretary of state, then, from 1809 to 1817, as fourth President of the United States.　　　　　　　　　　　　H.G.S.

Maghreb.
The term meaning West, was used by the Arab conquerors of the 7th century to describe their territories in the north-western part of Africa. The area covers Morocco, Algeria and Tunisia. Sometimes Libya is included. Since the 7th century the area fell under Islamic rule. In the 19th century and the early 20th century European, mainly French, colonialism swept the area. The decline of France after two world wars, the rise of a significant intellectual class, and the exigencies of World politics brought about the independence of the Maghreb states. Algeria gained its independence in 1962 after a war with France that lasted eight years.　　　　　E.A.S.

Maginot Line.
The line of defensive fortifications constructed by France following World War I to guard against an armed attack from Germany. In the German "blitz krieg" offensive of May 1940 the Maginot Line was outflanked and breached, with the result that the term has since come to symbolize a type of thinking in which rigid, permanent, fixed fortifications are blindly considered to be adequate to contain a determined imaginative, flexible, powerful assault.　　　　　　T.W.

Magna Carta.
Signed by King John at Runnymede, England, June 15, 1215. The foundation of English feudal law as a system of agreements based upon custom. King John brought on a baronal revolt by violating this system. The Charter, drawn up by the barons, was simply an articulation of existing feudal law. In essence **Magna Carta** declared that even the king was bound by the law and could be forced to observe it. The provisions of the charter, however, did not extend beyond the aristocracy. Historically, **Magna Carta** is important as a symbol of legitimacy —of the subordination of governmental power to law and fundamental principles of justice.　　　　G.I.J.

Mahatma.
Great soul or self; the magnanimous, august; the sage; an individual with superhuman faculties. Title of reverence, as given to Mohandas K. Gandhi (q.v.).　　　　　　　　　　　C.S.S.

Maimonides (Moses ben Maimon) (1135—1204).
Born in Cordova, Spain, forced to emigrate, at first to Morocco, then to Egypt where he earned his livelihood as Saladin's court physician. According to popular tradition, Maimonides was buried in Tiberias, Israel. Considered

the greatest thinker of the Jewish people in the diaspora, he is known for two monumental works: **Mishneh Torah** (the Code of Law), a systematized summary of the laws and ethical teachings of Judaism, and **Moreh Nebuchim** (Guide for the Perplexed), a commentary on Jewish religious philosophy. At a time when Judaism, Christianity, and Islam were equally exposed to the challenge of an alleged antagonism between "revelation," as taught by religion, and "reason," as propounded by philosophy, he used the works of Aristotle, and, to a lesser extent, those of Plato, to demonstrate that the teachings of Judaism are in harmony with the results of best philosophical thought, and beyond that, offer insights which reason alone cannot obtain. Viewing state-building as one of the aspects of the divine endowment of man, Maimonides saw the function of the state in the establishment of "the best possible relations among men" and stressed that in order to promote the common welfare, the state must "possess the power of enforcing the dictates of legislation."

A contemporary of the Islamic philosopher Averroes, whose double standards (one for theology and another for philosophy) he rejected, Maimonides influenced a number of Christian philosophers, foremost among them Albertus Magnus, Thomas Aquinas, and, through him, all medieval and modern Thomists. J.D.

Maine, Sir Henry (1822—1888).

British professor of law, civil servant, and historical jurist; a pioneer in the comparative study of law and other social institutions; often regarded as skeptical of democracy and all doc-doctrines of popular rights; author of **Ancient Law** (1861), **Early History of Institutions** (1875), **Popular Government** (1885), **International Law** (1888). Ch.C.M.

Malagasy Republic.

Formerly Madagascar. An independent republic of 5,200,000 people inhabiting an area slightly larger than France. Capital in Tananarive. The Malagasy people are of mixed Bantu and Indonesian origin and their language and culture possess numerous Malaysian traits. Of the nine major ethnic groups in the island, the most numerous are the Merina of the central highlands (1,200,000) and the Betsimisraka of the east coast (750,000). Before 1885 the Merina Empire controlled most of the island and was recognized as a state by Britain. Between 1896 and 1958, Madagascar was a French colony.

At present, Malagasy is governed by an indirectly elected president, M. Philibert Tsiranana, chosen for a 7 year term in 1958 and a 107 member Assembly, in which the ruling right-of-center Social Democratic Party has 75 seats. The remaining 32 seats are shared by 6 parties. The major issues in Malagasy politics are related to the enduring divisions between the coast and the highlands, which coincides with the cleavage between the formerly dominant Merina and the subject non-Merina peoples. Since independence in 1960, Malagasy has pursued a western-oriented policy of close ties with France, membership in the moderate Monrovia group of African states and domestic policies favorable to private enterprise. R.L.K.

Malan, Daniel Francois (1874—1959).

Born in the Cape Colony, studied ministry at Stellenbosch and Utrecht. After 1918 he became editor of **Die Burger** and a National Member of Parliament. He served in the Cabinet from 1924 to 1933 when he sought to strengthen the National Party rather than join the coalition. He was Prime Minister from 1948 to 1954 and urged nationalist policies including apartheid. J.F.M.

Malawi. See Appendix.

Malenkov, Georgi.

Born 1902, middle class family, Orenburg, now Chkalov. Red Army volunteer 1918. Moscow Higher Technical School 1921-25. Stalin's secretary 1930's—1940's. Orgburo of CP 1939. Presented Central Committee report 19th Party Congress 1952 as Stalin's heir apparent. Chairman USSR Council of Ministers 1953 after Stalin. Succeeded by Bulganin 1955 but remained in Party Presidium, Central Committee, and government Presidium. Ousted from all Party and government posts 1957 as member "anti-Party group." W.A.

Maleter, Pal (1917—1958).
Major-General, Hungarian Minister of Defense in the Government of Imre Nagy in 1956. A career officer in the Hungarian Army, he fought during World War II against the Red Army. At the close of the war, he joined the Hungarian partisan movement against Nazi Germany. After 1945, he became a Communist and served in the new Hungarian Army. During the revolutionary events of 1956, he was ordered to combat the uprising, but, instead, joined the anti-Soviet forces. On November 3, 1956, was appointed Deputy Minister of Defense in the Imre Nagy Government, and shortly afterwards, Minister. He was abducted while on his way to discuss details of the announced withdrawal of Soviet troops from Hungary. Sentenced to death together with Imre Nagy and others in a secret trial. The sentence and the execution were simultaneously announced on June 17, 1958.
I.B.

Mali, Republic of.
A country of West Africa of 465,000 square miles with a population of approximately 4,900,000. Formerly the French Sudan and later temporarily united with Senegal in the abortive Mali Federation, Mali became a separate, independent republic in 1960. Its capital is Bamako.

The territory of this republic is rich in history, having been host to several ancient Sudanese kingdoms (it is named after one of them) and possessing a number of old cities, including Timbuktu. Conquered by French arms in the latter part of the nineteenth century, it was declared a French colony in 1904. The Upper Volta was separated from it in 1919. Post World War II politics have been characterized by keen competition between the moderate **Parti Soudanais Progressiste** and the radical, anti-colonial **Union Soudanaise**. The latter emerged victorious, and it has become the only political party in Mali. After the death of Mamadou Konate, the founder of the **Union Soudanaise**, Mobido Keita became its leader, and he now serves as the President of the Republic.

Although affiliated with the European Common Market, the Republic of Mali adamantly opposes Western colonialism and neo-colonialism and stands for political Pan-Africanism. It is a member of the Union of African States and of the Casablanca Bloc.
F.H.G.

Malik, Charles.
Born in Btirram, Lebanon in 1906, of the Greek Orthodox Faith, studied philosophy at the American University of Beirut and at Harvard. Taught philosophy at American University of Beirut until called by his government to serve as first Lebanese Minister to Washington in 1945. Dr. Malik played a dominant role in the United Nations and was active in the formulation of the United Nations Declaration on Human Rights. He served as Lebanon's foreign minister during the civil conflict of 1958. In 1959 he was elected president of the United Nations General Assembly. He is known for his staunch opposition to international communism. At present Malik is a distinguished professor of philosophy at the American University of Beirut.
E.A.S.

Malinovsky, Rodion.
Born 1898, workers' family, Odessa. Drafted 1916, sent to France 1917, anti-war agitation among Russians. Returned 1918, Red Army commander during Civil War. Graduated Advanced Training School for Officers; Frunze Military Academy 1930. In World War II his commands included Stalingrad, Ukraine, Balkans, operations against Japanese. Officially rated sixth in military contribution to victory. Joined CP 1926; member Party Central Committee since 1956. Party liner, close to Khrushchev.
W.A.

Malta.
Largest of the three Maltese Islands (122 sq. miles, 330,000 population) in the central Mediterranean, Malta gives its name to the British dependency. It is a major port and naval base. A rich history includes rule by knights of St. John (1530—1798) and British title since 1814. Partial self-government came in 1947 and receded in 1958. The 1961 constitution gives internal self-rule and concurrent power with the Governor in foreign affairs and defense, the Crown prevailing in disputes. A bitter campaign between the Mintoff-led Laborites and Catholic-

backed parties in 1962 defeated the former, the Nationalists winning legislative plurality. P.F.P.

Management of Public Affairs.
This term is synonymous with administration (i.e., the fulfillment of public policies). It is to be distinguished from executive and legislative functions as it lacks the power to determine public policy. It is also to be distinguished from judicial functions as it operates with a comparatively greater freedom from procedural rules.
J.D.

Manchu Dynasty (1644—1911).
This last of China's imperial dynasties was established when armies from eastern Manchuria invaded China and wrested power from the declining Ming dynasty between 1644 and 1661. Applying their knowledge of the Confucian bureaucratic state, the already Sinocized Manchus selected the dynastic title, Ch'ing (pure), and instituted joint Manchu-Chinese control within the traditional bureaucratic framework of Confucian-style government.

During its peak years the dynasty consolidated its frontiers, developed widespread external relations, and reached a high level of literacy, artistic, and technical achievement. Its decline was hastened by rapid population growth, inept economic policies, and the jarring impact of the West in the 18th and 19th centuries. Last minute reforms failed to arrest the decline. Sun Yat-sen's revolutionary activity provided the occasion, in 1911-12, for the dynasty's demise. M.T.K.

Mandamus.
A court order compelling a designated official to perform a specific action, e.g., granting a license or permit to a person legally entitled to it. The power to issue the writ of mandamus is usually given only to the highest court under provisions in the constitution of a state in the United States. It cannot be used to compel an officer to take action where discretion is permissible by law. J.O.H.

Mandate.
(1) An expression of popular opinion through the electoral process that serves to direct or guide elected officials in the determination of public policy. It may vary in definiteness from an instruction as to a specific public policy issue to an expression of popular opinion as to the general direction that governmental policy should take. A clear and definitive mandate, once given, enables the majority political party to organize and control the legislative branches of government and to initiate and implement policies and programs consonant with the mandate.

(2) An order or commission issued by the League of Nations under Article 22 of the Covenant to a member nation authorizing and directing it to administer a dependent territory on behalf of the League. The mandate included guardianship and tutelage of the dependent people until such time as they were able to establish responsible self-government. The "mandate system" had valuable application in resolving the problem of what to do about the former colonies and conquered territories of defeated Germany. In 1945, the mandate system was replaced by the trusteeship system of the United Nations. R.H.K.

Manicheism.
This synchretistic version of Christianity, Buddhism, and Zoroastrianism was initiated by a Persian monk Mani (216—277) who propagated salvation through knowledge without rituals which he espoused in systematic writings ("Treasure of Life," "The Book of Mysteries," "The Writings of the Giants," etc.). Manicheism was hierarchically organized in a Church headed by a "King of Religion" with 12 apostles, 72 bishops, 63 priests, and numerous auditors. They had weekly confessions, fasted regularly, and greeted each other by saying "peace" and shaking the right hand. They differentiated sharply between good and evil, spirit and matter, light and darkness, out of which man was created through a struggle waged by the "Father of Greatness" against the "Prince of Darkness," which man then continued to wage led by the "elect," the Manicheists, to liberate himself from evil. They believed that fasting, asceticism, and general abstention from flesh, would aid this struggle by purifying man. They were a menace to

332

"the powers that be" which they rejected as the forces of Satan; this led to their persecution. They had a far-reaching and long-lasting influence; especially scholars and teachers were under their influence, and they spread into Western Europe and into the Far East. They continued to exist until the thirteenth century or so, and, especially in the West, gave birth to a variety of heresies, such as the Albigensi, Kathars, and Bogomils. V.Z.

Mannerheim, Carl Gustav Emil (1867—1951).

National hero of Finland; soldier; statesman; explorer. Born in Finland. Officer in the Tsarist army, 1889-1917; active in the Russo-Japanese War of 1905, and on the Rumanian front in the First World War. Returned to Finland to become Commander-in-Chief of the White Guard forces in the Finnish civil war of 1918. The Red Guard forces were defeated and thousands of leftist supporters were executed or starved to death in the "White Terror" that followed. Regent of Finland for six months until defeated in his bid for the presidency in 1919. Retired to private life until recalled in 1931 to be the President of the Council of Defense. Appointed Field Marshal in 1933, he was chiefly responsible for the development of the Finnish military forces and the erection of the Mannerheim Line, which figured prominently in the Finnish defenses in the Winter War of 1939-40. Commander-in-Chief of the Finnish forces from the period of the Winter War until 1944. President of the Republic, 1944-46. R.H.K.

Mansfield, Michael J.

Born March 16, 1903, U.S. Senate from November 4, 1952 to January 3, 1953, from 1958 until term ending January 3, 1965; Democrat—Montana.
R.A.B.

Mao Tse-tung.

Born in 1893 in a village in Hunan Province, China. Claims peasant descent, but the evidence suggests a business and marginally "gentry" background. After the victory of the anti-Manchu rebellion (in the fall of 1911), Mao joined the regular army for half a year. He graduated from a teacher's college in 1918, held a lowly job in a university library in Peking, and was the principal of a primary school in Changsha, Hunan, in 1922/23. Mao was one of the founders of the Chinese Communist Party (CCP) in 1921. During the first United Front (1924/27) he performed a number of relatively important functions in the Kuomintang (KMT) and in the CCP, applying the Leninist peasant policy hesitatingly prior to and immediately after the collapse of the KMT-CCP alliance. During the subsequent civil war period (1928—1934) he occupied positions of varying importance in the Red Army and CCP, among them the chairmanship of the Central Chinese Soviet Government from 1931—1934. Compelled to leave Central China, the Communists undertook their Long March (1934/35), during which Mao became the undisputed head of the CCP, a position he has held ever since. In Northwest China—capital first in Paoan, then in Yenan — he became head of the Chinese Communist Government. Pressured by Moscow, he called for a second United Front with Chiang Kai-shek since March 1936. The resulting second alliance persisted formally from 1937 to 1945; it was badly shaken during the Stalin-Hitler Pact and it decayed after Stalingrad. From 1944 Mao strove for a coalition government with the Nationalists. But following Stalin's speech in February 1946 the Chinese Communists again resorted to civil war, from which they emerged as victors in 1949. In October of that year Mao became the chairman of the Chinese People's Republic, the junior partner in the Sino-Soviet axis. Since Stalin's death, Mao, as the elder statesman among the top-ranking leaders of world communism, has at times taken an independent line, first in the matter of Stalin's image and recently in international policy. In the winter of 1953/54 he began the collectivization of agriculture; after the Hungarian revolution he unleashed and then quickly crushed the criticism of the non-party intellectuals (the "hundred flowers" and the "hundred schools" of thought). He tried to counter the growing agrarian crisis (key problem: the "labor shortage," due to the poor quality of the incentive-deficient work in China's intensive agriculture) by the

Great Leap Forward (early in 1958) and by the organization of "Communes" (since August 1958). After a disastrous decline in agricultural productivity—and open criticism by Moscow—Mao made far-reaching internal concessions, which he sought to veil by emphasizing international "contradictions" (theoretically: by stressing the tendency toward war inherent in the "imperialist" camp; practically: by his border strife with India). Mao has made no major contribution to the basic theoretical and strategic concepts of Communism, but he has specified the "contradictions" under socialism and significantly elaborated the principles of Communist guerrilla warfare in agrarian and "colonial and semi-colonial" countries. Until the forties he was politically cautious. Since the fifties he has shown increasing symptoms of irrationality ("the growing megalomania of the aging autocrat"), which thus far, however, as in the case of the aging Stalin, has remained a controlled irrationality. Mao's guerrilla strategy has greatly influenced the methods of the (totalitarian) revolutionary elements in many "underdeveloped" countries. K.A.W.

Mapai.
"Jewish Labor Party of Israel," founded 1930. Moderate labor party, headed by Ben-Gurion, since 1948 in control of government. Promotes planned mixed economy, ingathering of Jewish people, social-democratic society, agricultural collectives and cooperatives. A member of the Second (Socialist) International. S.H.

Mapam.
"United Workers' Party of Israel." Leftist socialist labor party founded 1948. Sometimes in coalition with Mapai, pursues socialist economic and social goals, neutrality in cold war, Arab-Jewish working class solidarity. A major factor in kibbutz (agricultural collective) movement. S.H.

Maquis.
The name given to French partisan or guerrilla soldiers operating both from partisan-controlled areas in France during World War II and "underground" in German-occupied areas. By mid-1943 most of the Maquis had pledged their loyalty to General Charles de Gaulle's Free French Army operating in North Africa, coming officially under his command with the designation of French Forces of the Interior, or "FFI." Technical, logistical and other types of support were officially provided to the FFI thenceforth by the armed forces of the United States.
T.W.

Mara.
In Hindu mythology, the concept of evil, embracing the actions of an all inclusive spirit of evil and its relationship to the World Soul and the individual soul. Its relationship to the body politic must be construed in terms of its effect upon both ruler and subject in the social and behavioral context.
M.W.W.

Marat, Jean Paul (1743—1793).
Was a French revolutionary leader and a medical doctor, for a time a court physician; in 1789 Marat turned political pamphleteer, and published a newspaper until September, 1792. He was a deputy of the Convention. He was completely suspicious of nearly all the leaders of the constitutional monarchy and afterwards, of the republican revolutionaries. After helping bring about the fall of the Girondins in June, 1793, he was stabbed to death by Charlotte Corday on July 13, 1793.
E.G.L.

Marbury v. Madison (1803).
One of Chief Justice Marshall's greatest opinions, was designed to protect the political power of the judiciary in the U.S.A. by insisting that the courts had the constitutional authority to invalidate unconstitutional acts of the government. In claiming this power for the judiciary, Marshall syllogized as follows: 1) the Constitution is a precise, unchanging and paramount "law," which is designed to limit the powers of the government—especially those of the legislature; 2) it is the province of the courts to say what the law is; and 3) acts in conflict with that law should be invalidated by the judiciary.
This decision provided the rationale for what has become the traditional American method of defending judicial supremacy against the charge of judicial oligarchy. This orthodoxy, often called "mechanistic jurisprudence," al-

leges that judicial discretion is controlled by the precise nature of the binding legal "rule" and its analogical extension to new fact situations. To this mechanistic theory of the constitution and the judicial process Marshall added a similarly non-relative or absolutist conception of separation of powers. The end product was the judicial supremacy of **Marbury v. Madison.**

Ironically enough, the power of judicial review, generally defended by Marshall's federalist friends and opposed by his Jeffersonian enemies, was not mentioned in the Constitution as one which had been specifically and precisely delegated to the judiciary. At the time of ratification, no doubt this "golden silence" about the extent of judicial power contributed to the constitution's acceptance by the contending factions. Scholars, nevertheless, disagree over the extent to which the founding fathers intended to incorporate judicial review in the Constitution. G.I.J.

Marcel, Gabriel (1889—   ).

French philosopher, whose social and political views involve a critique of the technological basis of contemporary western society. He feels that the individual is in the process of becoming little more than a tool of modern industrial methods — called "technics" which have been applied increasingly to all facets of man's existence. In Marcel's view, this situation has tended to sap the individual of initiative and creativity. His major works include **Man Against Mass Society; The Mystery of Being;** and **Existentialism.** He won the 1948 Grand Prize for Literature awarded by the French Academy. E.R.W.

March on Rome.

The term used to imply Fascist seizure of power in Italy, the "march on Rome" (October 28, 1922) by Fascist squads was essentially unguided and unopposed. Mussolini, while on his way to catch up with his followers who had camped outside the city, was to his own surprise sent a royal invitation to become prime minister. The Fascists paraded peacefully through Rome on October 31. E.T.O.

Marco Polo Bridge Incident.

On July 7, 1937, Japanese military forces at Lukouchiao, in North China, staged military maneuvers and attacked the Chinese garrison there at the strategic Marco Polo Bridge. This marked the beginning of the Sino-Japanese War (1937—1945) and thus of what later became the Second World War. Previously, in 1931, Japan had invaded the Chinese territory of Manchuria, and set up the puppet state of Manchukuo. But this and further Japanese incursions onto Chinese territory were not met with organized Chinese armed resistance until the Marco Polo Bridge incident.
S.L.A.

Maritain, Jacques.

A foremost contemporary French philosopher, residing in the United States, whose intellectual development has been greatly influenced by the philosophy of St. Thomas Aquinas. Born in Paris (1882) Maritain studied under Henri Bergson at the Sorbonne. A friend, Leon Bloy, turned him to Catholicism.

Maritain's **new humanism** is opposed to the materialistic approach to social and political problems. His political philosophy centers around the **person** whose whole being is rooted in spirituality, ordered to a "good" or end superior to temporal values. Man—endowed with intellect—has dignity and rights. The **natural law** is his norm of action; its dictates are the principles of morality. The moral act is a free act, and thus **liberty** is linked to morality in the framework of social living.

The **body politic** integrates community and society. The **community** is like an organism, a work of nature; **society** is a work of reason. The body politic is the "whole" tending to the **common good,** containing the requirements of nature and reason. The **state** is a part of the body politic—the topmost part—for law and order. While authority rests on the natural law, **sovereignty** interpreted as complete autonomy is a misconception.

Pluralism characterizes today's world regarding religious societies and cultural organizations — but these are united in the practical order by the common good. However, the indirect authority of the **Church** is upheld where spiritual matters become part of the temporal concern of the body politic.

In setting the pattern for Christian **democracy,** Maritain finds it organic, pluralist, personalist, and theocentric.

Major political works: **Freedom in the Modern World** (1931); **True Humanism** (1938); **Scholasticism and Politics** (1940); **Ransoming the Time** (1941); **The Rights of Man and the Natural Law** (1945); **Christianity and Democracy** (1945); **The Person and the Common Good** (1947); **Man and the State** (1951). T.P.

Marriage and Divorce Laws.

Marriage, the establishing of a husband-wife relationship, is universal among human societies as a stabilizing procedure for family life and the protection of children. United States laws vary as to who may be legally married. Usually parental consent is required for males between 18 and 21 and females between 16 and 18. In half the states first cousins may not marry; closer family relationships are generally barred from marriage, in some states even when no blood relationship exists. In some states whites may not marry Negroes. Blood tests to demonstrate freedom from disease and waiting periods between the license and the wedding, generally three days, are often required. The ceremony of marriage may be performed by a civil official or a religious leader of recognized authority. Common-law marriages, without ceremony, based on private agreement, are legal in eighteen states. Cohabitation for a period of time as man and wife may also be recognized as a marriage. A marriage may be void, or annulled, within a state if the requirements for marriage have been violated.

Divorce, the legal dissolution of marriage, ranges in various societies from simple repudiation of the marriage to complex restrictions involving settlement of property, rights of various adult family members and care of children. Most modern societies have devices for terminating marriage. Italy, Spain, Eire, Chile and Argentina, however, prohibit any divorce. Other nations have regulations of varying severity. In Belgium and Luxemburg mutual consent is acceptable. In the United States divorce is universally granted for adultery, which is the only legal basis in New York State. Desertion, mental or physical cruelty, habitual drunkenness, conviction of a felony, postmarital insanity, and non-support are legal causes in most of the states. Legal residence requirements for divorce vary from five years in Massachusetts to six weeks in Nevada, Idaho, and the Virgin Islands. Although proof of recrimination (mutual guilt), collusion, connivance, or condonation may prevent dissolution of a marriage, most divorces are only nominally, not actually, contested, and the reasons given in court may be far removed from the actual causes. The divorce rate in most nations permitting divorce has risen through this century; in the United States the high point in the divorce rate was one divorce in four marriages in 1946.

T.K.N.

Marseillaise.

The national anthem of France. Composed in Strasbourg (25 April 1792) by C.-J. Rouget de Lisle, a Lieutenant of Engineers, as the **Song of War for the Army of the Rhine.** Paris, hearing it sung for the first time by the federated troops arriving from Marseille, gave it its present name. The martial fervor and stirring music of the **Marseillaise ("Allons enfant de la patrie"**—"Advance children of the Fatherland") found great appeal. Intended by its author as a patriotic song, the **Marseillaise** became identified not only with the French revolution but with revolution per se.

K.B.

Marshal.

In U.S. law, an officer, appointed by the President to serve a judicial district of the federal court system as process server and in other capacities generally similar to those discharged by a sheriff. Marshals may also be found in some local court systems, e.g. in some courts in the city of New York. F.H.H.

Marshall, John (1755—1835).

Chief Justice of the United States from 1801 to 1835. Basic tenets in his constitutional philosophy were the doctrine of judicial review, the supremacy of the Federal Constitution, the sanctity of contracts, the liberal construction of grants of constitutional authority to the Federal Government, and the limitation of state powers when in conflict with valid Federal power. A man of great personal influence and prestige, Marshall dominated the Supreme Court as Chief Justice, established the practice of single opinions for the majority view in Supreme Court cases, and was in dissent from other members of the Court only once on a constitutional issue (**Ogden v. Saunders**, 1827). Perhaps his best known decision was **Marbury v. Madison** (1803) which explicitly set out the doctrine of judicial review. E.L.

Marshall, Thurgood (1908—   ).
Judge, U.S. Court of Appeals, 2d Cir. Born in Baltimore, Md., and educated at Lincoln U. (Pa.) and Howard U. (LL.B., 1933), Marshall became the foremost civil rights lawyer in the U.S. during the 1940's and 1950's.

He became NAACP Special Counsel and Director of its Legal Defense and Education Fund, Inc., in 1940, after four years assisting Charles Houston, first full-time NAACP Counsel. He argued successfully such cases as **Smith v. Allwright** (1944), **Shelley v. Kraemer** (1948), and **Brown v. Bd. of Education** (1954) during the planned legal assault on racial segregation.

In 1961, he received an interim appointment to the federal bench and was confirmed by the U.S. Senate in late 1962, the first Negro to hold a U.S. Circuit Court judgeship. N.P.T.

Marshall Mission to China (1945—1947).
At the end of 1945, when it appeared that major civil war would erupt between Chinese Nationalists and Communists, President Truman dispatched the respected American General George C. Marshall to China to attempt to bring about a peaceful settlement and, if possible, to effect a coalition government of Nationalists and Communists in China. On January 10, 1946, Marshall arranged a cease-fire agreement, but subsequent developments indicated that both sides regarded it only as a convenient pause. After more than a year of fruitless effort, Marshall was recalled on January 6, 1947 to become Secretary of State. The following day, in a final Statement to the President, Marshall blamed both the Chinese Government and the Communists for the renewed hostilities and the failure of his mission. He concluded that hope for the future of China lay in a liberal third-force. R.L.W.

Marshall Plan.
A policy of the United States, based on a proposal by Secretary of State Marshall at Harvard University in 1947, of extending economic aid to European countries to facilitate restoration of their war-torn economies. Although aid was offered also to East European countries including the Soviet Union, all of whom rejected it, the Plan was designed to arrest the political advance of communism in West and Central Europe. P.J.F.

Marsilio of Padua (1278—1343).
A student of medicine, politics, philosophy, law and theology, b. in Padua, d. in Bavaria. Marsilio, having first studied, and qualified for medicine in Padua, then studied at the University of Paris where he earned a Master of Arts degree. In 1326, he moved to the court of Emperor Lewis IV of Bavaria with whom he sided in the latter's conflict with Pope John XXII who had backed another contestant for the imperial crown. Marsilio accompanied Lewis on a Roman expedition (1327—1330) during which Lewis sought to have an anti-pope elected; and he was appointed by Lewis Imperial Vicar of Rome.

In the **Defensor Pacis** (1324), Marsilio's major political treatise, and in a later shorter political treatise, the **Defensor Minor** (1342), views were advanced which were at variance with the dominant medieval climate of opinion and foreshadowed certain aspects of political thought that were to come to the fore during the ensuing centuries.

The main cause of political discord, Marsilio held, was the pretension of the pope. Yet, in matters of this world the church is but a department of civil society, subject to its laws, whereas in otherworldly matters, in matters of faith, not the pope but a General

Council of the Church, consisting of both ecclesiastics and laymen, are the legitimate authority. Divine law may have a bearing on the individual's fate in life to come. In this world, however, only human or positive law, not divine or natural law prevail. Yet human law, in order to be regarded as the command of civil society, requires the consent of the entire body of citizens or its "Prevailing part," both the "number and quality in the community being taken into account." Moreover, the "Pars Principans," the executive as we might say nowadays, derives his authority from the election by the "legislator" and is accountable to him. G.V.W.

Martial Law.
The term denoting military rule in domestic areas. This law applies to all persons within the given area in which suspension of municipal law has been declared. While predicated upon the discretion of a military commander, and not upon fixed principles, it none the less, must be administered in conformity to the United States Constitution; for example, habeas corpus cannot be suspended at the will of a military officer. M.P.S.

Martin, Joseph William, Jr.
Born November 3, 1884; U.S. House of Representatives from 69th Congress (1924) through 87th Congress; Republican—Massachusetts; elected minority leader 76th to 85th Congresses except the 80th and 83rd in which he was elected Speaker; permanent chairman of the Republican National Conventions of 1940, 1944, 1948, 1952, and 1956. R.A.B.

Marti y Perez, Jose Julian.
National Hero of Cuba. Born January 28, 1853 in Havana. Died May 19, 1895. Widely known throughout Latin America as a poet, journalist, diplomat, and revolutionist. While in exile in the United States (1880—1895) Marti wrote for leading newspapers in New York City and Latin America, and became the major interpreter of the United States to Spanish-speaking peoples during this period. His fame is derived from his decisive efforts to promote Cuban independence from Spain, his elevation to political sainthood in Cuba, and his contributions in poetry to modernism in Spanish American literature. R.B.G.

Martov, L. (Yulii Osipovich Tsederbaum) (1873—1923).
Russian revolutionary leader, journalist, mouthpiece of the moderate Menshevik opinion, and opponent of Lenin and Trotsky; laid the theoretical foundations of the Bund by urging the creation of a Marxist mass party of Jewish workers; an editor of the Marxist paper **Iskra** (The Spark) (1900—1905) which became the official organ of the Russian Social Democratic party; since 1903 a leader of the Menshevik faction; urged a democratically-run proletarian party against Lenin's Bolshevik conception of a highly-centralized organization; during World War I one of the leading "internationalist" socialists advocating "peace without victory"; after the Russian Revolution led an unsuccessful campaign to form a coalition government of all socialist parties, denounced Bolshevik terrorism and urged the need for democratizing the Soviet system; as an exile in Berlin, founded and edited **Sotsialistichesky Vestnik** (Socialist courier) (1921—1923). W.J.S.

Marx, Karl (1818—1883).
Political writer and founder of "scientific" socialism. Born in Trier, Marx became involved in liberal and radical causes in journalism early in life, leaving Germany after 1842 and becoming a cosmopolitan political agitator and writer, residing at various times in Paris, Brussels, and London. For the League of Communists, he and his collaborator Friedrich Engels wrote **The Communist Manifesto** (1848), the famous revolutionary declaration of that year of insurrection.

In London, where Marx's later years were spent, he organized the First International, and wrote and published his principal work, **Das Kapital** (first volume published in 1867). Though frequently denouncing Hegel—as he condemned nearly all other philosophers—Marx actually was strongly influenced by Hegelian doctrines. He aspired to sweep away both "capitalism" (a term coined by Marx) and "Utopian" socialism, supplanting such systems by a "scientific" socialism on materialistic and deterministic principles. Various writers have noted Marx's inversion of Christian symbols and concepts: thus, for instance, supernatural salvation is replaced by the earthly redemption of the proletariat, in his system.

Twentieth-century communist parties are dogmatically bound to Marx's writings, and most modern socialist factions, including to some extent even the British Labour Party, remain indebted to him. R.K.

Marxism.
A body of political and economic doctrines founded upon the writings of Karl Marx, and forming a set of secular dogmas for modern communist parties, as well as strongly influencing most twentieth-century socialist factions. Marxist writers and leaders desire to establish an egalitarian social condition upon principles of "scientific" materialism, dedicated to the improvement of the material condition of the laboring masses.

Challenging the institutions of nineteenth- and twentieth-century industrialism, "capitalism," and representative democracy, the Marxists advocate revolution, to be followed by the "dictatorship of the proletariat," and eventually by a changeless and classless society, communism. Absolute equality of economic and political status is their objective — though, as Marx wrote, "in order to establish equality, we must first establish inequality."

Collective ownership of all means of production, economic arrangements which dictate "from each according to his ability, to each according to his need," and the abolition of "bourgeois" morality are conditions necessary for the achievement of communism, the Marxists argue. In theory, they desire the "withering away" of the state, although in practice Marxists have established, when in power, governments with immense authority—and, in the case of the Soviet regimes, totalitarian orders. R.K.

Masaryk, Jan (1886—1948).
Son of Thomas G. Czechoslovak career diplomat, Foreign Minister of World War II exile "government" in London; Foreign Minister of "National Front" government 1945-48. Killed in fall from window after Feb. 1948 Communist takeover; whether suicide or murder remains mystery. K.G.

Masaryk, Thomas G. (1850—1937).
First president of Czechoslovakia. Of Slovak, Czech, and German descent, M. took Ph.D. at Vienna and in 1882 became Prof. of Philosophy at Czech univ. in Prague, where he championed liberal "realism" against romantic Czech nationalism. Although M. wrote against dissolution of Austria-Hungary in 1908 (in **The Czech Question**) and urged federal reform of the Empire in his last speech in the Austrian parliament in 1913, he cast his lot in favor of Czech independence upon the outbreak of World War I. Aided by the brilliant and unscrupulous Dr. Eduard Benes, he founded the Czechoslovak National Council in Paris and persuaded the Allies to support creation of a C.-S. Republic. Elected president in November 1918, M. served until December 1935 when he was succeeded by Benes. K.G.

Mass.
In modern political sociology, it constitutes a phenomenon of the greatest importance in view of the increasing participation of the people in the democratic process. Although it has not always attained a high degree of political development, the mass possesses sensitivity and demands corresponding to its needs. Communication facilities and new methods of propaganda permit the integration of the masses into the political system, but they have characteristics of their own that rather than being lost are placed at a greater value by the numeric expression of voters. The mass should not be considered as an inorganic social structure, but as a phenomenon inherent in the extension of the democratic integration process as opposed to concepts of "elites" and "leading classes" (Mosca) which, for this very reason, have already adjusted to the new social structures. T.C.

Mass communication.
The process, made possible by high technology, through which the whole public is reached with news, opinion, and service information (e.g., weather

reports). Generally an information or opinion-influencing function is implied, as distinct from entertainment, even though the mass media (q.v.) sometimes contain a preponderance of such material to attract and hold audiences. In democratic countries, the concept implies private and free-speech channels, based on subscription or advertising (or, as in the English BBC, a specific tax), as distinct from government-controlled information, however "mass" the broadcast. J.B.L.

Mass media.

The agents in mass communication (q.v.), generally daily and weekly newspapers, open and usually large circulation magazines, radio and television stations, sometimes books (especially paperbacks) and motion pictures when considered beyond their entertainment function. Specialized, trade and professional communication media are normally distinguished. The singular, medium, applies to one kind of the media, e.g., newspapers, as well as to a particular newspaper. J.B.L.

Massive Retaliation.

A threatened military response involving destruction on a large scale, as by use of atomic or hydrogen weapons. This term was applied to the posture assumed by the United States in 1954 and publicly announced by Secretary of State John Foster Dulles. Based upon assumption that future general war or large-scale limited war involving the United States would be waged with nuclear weapons. A declaratory policy, derived from the political desire for economy and the military requirement for security, stating that the United States would reserve the right to meet future aggressions "by means and at places of our own choosing," i.e., implying the threat of massive retaliation against local aggression at the source of the aggression. Since 1954 this policy has evolved into more refined concepts of deterrence. H.H.R.

Matteotti, Giacomo (1885—1924).

The death of Socialist leader Matteotti, coming after his criticism of Mussolini in parliament in May 1924, has come to symbolize the death of Italian opposition to fascism. Following his death, all anti-fascists withdrew from parliament to protest his suspected murder on Mussolini's orders. Early in 1925, Mussolini not only admitted his responsibility but acted soon after to ban all opposition parties and consolidate his dictatorship.
E.T.O.

Mau Mau.

A term variously applied to a violent anti-British uprising in Kenya between 1952—1956 and to a secret society composed of Kikuyu, Meru and Embu tribesmen in Kenya. Generally attributed to land shortage among the Kikuyu, the Mau Mau rebellion must be viewed as an "irrational" nativistic movement without "rational" nationalistic goals, program or leadership. Characterized by extreme violence, oath-taking and other atavistic traits, the main fury of the Mau Mau was directed at other Africans. During the four year emergency, it is estimated that 2,451 persons were killed by the Mau Mau. This includes a total of 95 European casualties, of which 32 were civilians. In turn, it is estimated that a total of 11,000 Kikuyu were killed by British security forces. R.L.K.

Maurer, Ion Gheorghe (1902—   ).

Prime Minister (since 1961) and Politburo member of the Rumanian Workers' (Communist) Party (since 1960), he served as defense lawyer for the Communists before World War II. Elevated to the Central Committee after the War, he worked in the economic ministries under CP leader Gheorghiu-Dej. From 1948 until 1954 he held minor positions, but in 1957 became Minister of Foreign Affairs, in 1958 full member of the Central Committee, and during 1958-61 served as President of the Grand National Assembly. J.J.K.

Mauritania.

An Islamic Republic in Africa, located between latitudes 15° and 27° N., on the West African coast. Its neighbors are Spanish Sahara, Algeria, Mali and Senegal. The area of this new independent state is equal to 416,216 sq. miles, and its population is about 650,000 people. The Dutch, English and French struggled for possession of its coastline, and finally in the mid-

dle of the 19th century the French came to stay. The interior of Mauritania was gradually penetrated by the French and the whole region fell under French rule by 1914. Mauritania became a French colony in 1920, and forty years later, in 1960, it was declared an independent republic. Attempts to bring Mauritania into the United Nations were blocked by the countries of the Soviet bloc, which wanted to bring Outer Mongolia into the U.N. A compromise was finally reached, when both Mauritania and the Mongolian Peoples' Republic were simultaneously accepted as full members of the U.N. A large portion of the country is desert and it is poor in natural resources; at present its greatest economic resource is its livestock. There are indications that Mauritania is rich in iron ore and copper ore. Iron ore found near Fort Gouraud has an iron content of 63 to 70 percent.
V.P.P.

Maverick.

A politician having the characteristics of an unbranded calf on the Western range country. In the United States the maverick is very often a legislator who bolts his party to set an independent course or to join the opposition on several legislative issues.
W.D.S.

May Fourth Movement.

Originally a students' movement in Peking, with students of National Peking University as the nucleus, on May 4, 1919 against the Treaty of Versailles. They attacked three members of government, dubbed as pro-Japanese traitors. Later extended to students' demonstrations, merchants' closing of their shops, and workers' strikes in leading cities of China. Encouraged by this unprecedented manifestation of public opinion, Chinese delegates in Paris Peace Conference declined to sign the Treaty which through the support of Britain, France, and Italy (Britain was an ally to Japan and all three had given secret promise of support in 1917) and reluctant consent of U.S., recognized claim of Japan to former German holdings in Shantung Province, chiefly port of Kiaochow and Tsingtao-Tsinan Railroad which Japan had held after its declaration of war on Germany, Aug. 13, 1914. China's claim was: its declaration of war on Germany, Aug. 12, 1917 automatically canceled all the German rights in Shantung. Avoiding direct negotiation with Japan, China finally through the "good offices" of U.S. and Britain succeeded in negotiating a treaty with Japan during but outside the Washington Conference, 1922 for the return of Shantung. The May Fourth Movement of 1919, coupled with the Literary Revolution started two years earlier, became the vehicle for expression of Chinese nationalism and paved the way for Nationalist Revolution, 1927-28. C.K.W.

Mayflower Compact.

When the Pilgrims on the "Mayflower" reached the coast of North America in the bay at the tip of Cape Cod in late 1620, they drew up a written agreement whereby they planned to govern themselves. Forty-one members of the group signed the document known as the Mayflower Compact. Statements in the agreement such as ". . . solemnly and mutually in the presence of God and of one another covenant and combine ourselves into a civil body politic for our better ordering and preservation . . .," ". . . just and equal laws . . .," and ". . . unto which we promise all due submission and obedience" indicate this as probably the first written provision for a democratic government in America.
W.D.S.

Mayor-council.

The oldest and predominant pattern of city government in the United States. Patterned somewhat after the plan of federal government, the legislative power is vested in a plural-member council elected at large, by wards, or by a combination of the two bases, and the executive power is exercised by a mayor who is either popularly elected by the voters or selected by the council from its own membership. Depending on the powers of the mayor, the form is known as a weak or strong mayor-council form. G.S.B.

Mazarin, Jules (1602—1661).

Cardinal and French statesman, successor of Richelieu as first minister of France (1641—1661). An Italian by birth, Mazarin left a military career for the papal diplomatic corps and served as nuncio in Paris (1634—1636). A man of ability and subtlety, cardinal (1641) though never a priest, he crushed the last resistance of the nobility (Fronde), scored diplomatic successes against the Empire (Peace of Westphalia, 1648) and against Spain (Peace of the Pyrenees, 1659). He had the full confidence of Anne of Austria and her son, Louis XIV, the latter becoming his own minister after Mazarin's death. K.B.

Mazzini, Giuseppe (1805—1872).
Great propagandist and revolutionary of the Italian **Risorgimento,** Mazzini sought national unification through popular participation and as part of a new democratic Europe. Through the secret society **Young Italy,** he sparked uprisings throughout Italy. At the end he accepted monarchist unification, but his ideals inspired afterwards a republican party and the goals of self-government and European unity. E.T.O.

McCarran Act of 1950.
Congress passed the Internal Security Act of 1950, popularly called the McCarran Act after its sponsor, Senator Pat McCarran of Nevada, "to protect the United States against certain Un-American and subversive activities by requiring registration of Communist organizations, and for other purposes." President Truman vetoed the bill on the grounds that it "puts the United States in the thought-control business." The veto was overridden, and the law quickly became a leading center of controversy. Amendments in 1954 defined three categories of Communist organizations as "Communist-action," "Communist-front" and "Communist-infiltrated." After nearly a decade of litigation, the registration requirement was narrowly upheld by the Supreme Court in 1961 **(Communist Party v. Subversive Activities Control Board,** 367 U.S. 1). I.Di.

McCarthy, Eugene J.
Born March 29, 1916; U.S. Senate from January 3, 1959 until term ending 1965; Democrat—Minnesota; member of 81st to 85th Congresses; author of **Frontiers in American Democracy.**
R.A.B.

McCarthy, Joseph Raymond (1909-1957).
U.S. Senator (Republican) from Wisconsin, 1947-57. Noted for his energetic exposure of Communists and pro-Communists within the U.S. Government, which earned him the bitter enmity of the Communist Party and of liberal advocates of "coexistence." Although controversies persist concerning some of McCarthy's public statements, the vast majority of persons accused by him resigned or were removed following investigation; many invoked the Fifth Amendment on their Communist connections. Following a collision with General Zwicker concerning the promotion to Army major of a Communist dentist named Peress, the Department of the Army published charges against McCarthy and members of his staff. There followed two series of hearings culminating in the censure of McCarthy by a vote of 67 to 22, all Democrats and half the Republicans voting for censure. McCarthy performed a valuable public service by focusing public attention on the genuine problem of Communist infiltration; but he was frequently undiplomatic and crude, unwise in delegating authority to staff members, and he weakened his case by overstating it. K.G

McCarthyism.
Utilization of the political tactics of Joseph R. McCarthy, U.S. Senator (R., Wisc.), 1909—1957. As chairman of the Senate's subcommittee on investigations, Senator McCarthy charged many U.S. Government officials and private citizens with Communist leanings and disloyalty to the United States. His opponents considered these charges unsupported by adequate proof and politically-motivated; and believed his investigative techniques to be unfair and demagogic. The term McCarthyism seems most often used by critics of Senator McCarthy's methods, and therefore usually implies irresponsible or "politically"-motivated accusations of disloyalty or Communist leanings. S.L.A.

McClellan, John L.
Born February 25, 1896; U.S. Senate from January 3, 1943 until term ending January 3, 1967; Democrat—

Arkansas; prosecuting attorney of the seventh judicial district of Arkansas 1926—1930; member of 74th and 75th Congresses. R.A.B.

McCulloch v. Maryland.

Landmark Supreme Court decision (1819) which firmly established constitutional principles of implied powers and intergovernmental tax immunity. A Baltimore branch of the second United States Bank issued notes without paying a Maryland tax imposed on all banks not chartered by the state. Chief Justice Marshall's opinion, adopting the Hamiltonian broad construction theory, held that Congressional power to establish a bank could be implied from its delegated powers to collect taxes, borrow money, raise an army and regulate commerce. Under the necessary and proper clause Congress could choose any appropriate but not prohibited means to achieve legitimate ends. Because Congressional acts pursuant to the Constitution are supreme, no state could impede or control the operation of national law. Ruling that the "power to tax involves the power to destroy," the Court declared the Maryland tax unconstitutional as a burden on a legitimate instrumentality of the Union. C.F.N.

McKinley, William (1843—1901).

The twenty-fifth president of the United States was a Civil War veteran and practiced law in Ohio. He served six terms in the U.S. House and was governor of Ohio. Elected to the presidency as a Republican in 1896 and 1900, McKinley was an ardent protectionist and launched America as a world power in the Spanish-American War. He died in 1901 from wounds inflicted by an assassin. Th.P.

Meany, George.

President, American Federation of Labor—Congress of Industrial Organizations, since 1955. Born New York, N. Y., August 16, 1894. Educated pub., elem. and high schools. Married. Catholic. Democrat. Local (plumber's), State union official before election as AFL secy-treas. 1940 — 1952, AFL president 1952—1955. Member, Nat. War Labor Board, 1942—1945. Delegate, twelfth U.N. General Assembly. J.M.S.

Measurement (of public opinion).

In the area of public opinion primarily an analytical device to assess the attitudes and responses of the people to actual or potential commercial or governmental policies and practices. Among the leading measurement or polling organizations are the American Institute of Public Opinion (Gallup) and Fortune Magazine (Roper). M.B.D.

Measures Short of War.

There is much dissension among writers on international law as to the meaning of the expression "measures short of war." The core of the objections against the dissertations on "measures short of war" lies in the fact that their authors invariably adhere to the state-of-war theory or theory of war in "the" legal sense. Since the meaning of the word "war" cannot be squeezed into a mold of a particular size and shape, the expression "measures short of war," as such, is legally meaningless. It immediately raises the question "short of war in relation to and in the meaning of which rule of law on war?" Yet, there is no practical need for stating that such and such a measure is short of war in the sense of some rule of law on war, of Article I, Section 8, Paragraph 11 of the Constitution of the United States, for instance. Such a statement is the same thing as the statement that Article I, Section 8 Paragraph 11 of the Constitution does not apply. On the other hand there is, of course, no objection to "measures short of war" as an expression in common parlance. It may be so used like "war," "peace" or "act of war." The lend-lease aid extended by the United States to various countries in the course of World War II thus can be appropriately termed a "measure short of war." As a technical, legal term, however, the expression "measures short of war" ought to be sponged off the slate. F.G.

Media.

See mass media, and media of information.

Media of Information.

Communication takes place either face-to-face between individuals or is conveyed to the audience via mediating equipment such as printed pages, radio sets, etc. The latter are media of information. The word media is most often applied to the mass media (newspaper, radio, television, etc.) through which a spokesman simultaneously addresses a large number of individuals unknown to him. There are also media which are not mass media such as the telephone and mails. The growth of mass media is one of the things which most sharply distinguishes modern society from its predecessors. I.d.S.P.

Mediation.

One of the means for solving international conflicts regulated by the Hague Conventions for the Pacific Settlement of International Disputes of 1899 and 1907, now in force for some 20 or 35 countries, respectively, including the U.S. Mediation consists in an attempt by a third party to reconcile the opposing claims of the parties in conflict by making a non-binding proposal to that effect. It differs from **good offices** which merely intend to bring the parties together without concrete proposals for the solution of the conflict, and from **conciliation** which involves also an investigation of the facts of a case and the independent submission of a proposed solution. Mediation is mentioned in Article 33 of the UN Charter among the peaceful means of their own choice by which the parties to a serious dispute shall first seek a solution. If they fail to settle it by such means, they shall refer the dispute to the Security Council (Article 37). S.E.

Meiji Constitution.

The first constitution written in the style of the Occident. Promulgated under the Meiji Emperor on February 11, 1889 and put into force on November 29, 1890. Consisted of seven chapters and seventy-six articles. A compromise between imperial absolutism and democracy, it recognized the Diet (legislature) but insisted on the principle of the Emperor's sovereignty. (The Emperor was considered the chief of state and source of all governing power. Areas of the imperial rule were excluded from legislative controls.) H.U.

Mencius (c. 372 B.C.—c. 289 B.C.).

b. in the state of Tsau, Chou Dynasty. Most renowned Confucian, second only to Confucius himself. Wandered more than 20 years in search for a prince who would consent to govern according to principles of benevolence and righteousness instead of oppression and war as a path to universal sway by which rulers and people of other states would willingly submit to his rule. Unable to succeed, passed last 20 years to perfect philosophy and to train disciples. Believed that nature of man was good and emphasized that this "child's heart" should be further developed. Developed to the full the conception of government for the people, though not that of government by the people. Thought that the people were the most "precious" element in a nation, the government ranked next, and the monarch was the "lightest." Counselled rebellion against unworthy rulers or even putting them to death by the nobility but did not rule out the possibility that Heaven would raise up some one, other than a noble, for the task. C.K.W.

Mendes-France, Pierre (1907—   ).

French politician. Deputy from the L'Eure, 1932-40, 1946-58, defeated for re-election in the Fifth Republic. Under-secretary of state for the treasury, ministry of Leon Blum, 1938, minister of national economy, DeGaulle ministry, September 1944 — April 1945. Prime minister, June 19, 1954—February 5, 1955, noted for his vigorous efforts to solve France's economic and colonial problems by ending ministerial **immobilisme**. While he succeeded in ending the war in Vietnam, negotiating Moroccan independence, and laying the ground work for the Tunisian settlement, he aroused at the same time enough animosity among conservative forces to end his ministerial career. A prominent member of the Radical party in the Third and Fourth Republics, in the Fifth Republic he gave his allegiance to an independent Socialist group. J.S.S.

Menon, Vengalil Krishnan Krishna (1897—   ).

Son of a Nair lawyer, Menon was born at Calicut, Kerala. At 27, he went to Britain and studied at the London

School of Economics, London University, and qualified for the bar at the Middle Temple. During his thirty-year stay in England, he campaigned for Indian freedom as secretary of the India League, and won the friendship of Nehru (q.v.). In 1947, Premier Nehru appointed friend Menon as High Commissioner to Britain. After 1952, Menon emerged as Nehru's chief foreign policy spokesman at the U.N. and elsewhere. In 1957, he became Defense Minister. "Liberating" Goa on the eve of 1962 elections, he defeated his opponent for the Parliament seat, and emerged as Nehru's likely successor. He was ousted from the Nehru Cabinet in November 1962 when the Chinese attack on India revealed shocking weaknesses in Indian defenses. C.S.S.

Merit system.

The approach in the public service where personnel are recruited, appointed, and retained strictly on the basis of their ability to perform their administrative functions efficiently and impartially. This system, when complete, essentially includes all personnel other than a few of the highest policy-makers. Service is on a permanent professional career basis with removal only for incompetence or unethical conduct. Personnel are insulated from partisan pressures, and the merit system serves succeeding political leaders impartially. It is the opposite of a "spoils" or "patronage" public service. R.D.S.

Messianism.

Stems from the Jewish **Mashiah**, meaning the anointed, the redeemer, the one chosen by God, or Christos in Greek. Some scholars claim that authentic messianism always demands a personal savior or redeemer. The term, however, may justly be used more loosely to characterize religious and political movements which espouse the necessity of redemption from the prevailing situation perceived as intolerable. In both of its senses the term denotes a world-wide phenomenon, present in many cultures. In Zoroastrianism, for example, a future savior (Saosyant) is expected, and in Buddhism a Buddha (Maitreya) is expected to descend upon earth, bring about a Kingdom of God and redeem man from his evil situation. Messianism is characteristic of primitive civilizations (Africa, for example) as well as advanced civilizations, such as Christianity. Both nationalism and communism as political ideologies have strong overtones of messianism where the personal savior is superseded by a collectivity, which in nationalism is of a parochial type while in communism of a more universalist type. In some messianic movements redemption and salvation is conceived under the aspect of renewal of the original past paradisiacal age. V.Z.

Metropolitan area.

Commonly defined in terms of specific population requirements, the term is more realistically defined as a large geographic territory, usually surrounding an old and congested city, characterized by the existence of a number of suburban or surrounding units of government which are politically independent of but have social and economic ties with the core city. G.S.B.

Metropolitanism.

The interrelationships and internal processes which occur within and between metropolitan areas.

These areas are densely settled places possessing a central city surrounded by less densely populated but non-agricultural areas. Significant economic, governmental, and social interrelations characterize these areas which contain within their limits numerous governmental jurisdictions including cities, counties, villages, towns or townships, and special districts. The geographic limits of these areas depend on the criteria selected for measurement. Such criteria include: population total and density, market characteristics, commutation patterns, newspaper circulation areas, transportation facilities and financial transactions. The definition most widely used is that of the U.S. Census Bureau which defines a "standard metropolitan statistical area" as consisting of a central city of 50,000 or more population and the county (town in New England) in which it is located plus those contiguous counties (towns in New England) which possess extensive economic and social contacts with the central county and city. By their defi-

nition, the Census Bureau in 1960 identified 212 metropolitan areas in the United States. They contain 63 percent of United States population. Almost 85 percent of the total population increase between 1950 and 1960 occurred in the "standard metropolitan statistical areas"; but the relative increase in the suburban ring was almost five times that of the central cities.
A.K.C.

Metropolitics.

In an age of urban-suburban sprawl has come the vocabulary of the new age, including standard metropolitan statistical area, megalopolis, and metropolitics. Metropolitics deals with the social, economic, and political challenges of overlapping and duplicating governmental units. It seeks interaction among the elements of the metropolitan area. It looks beyond special districts for special problems in the direction of metropolitan answers and metropolitan organization for metropolitan problems. W.D.S.

Mexico.

A Latin American state; area, 760,337 sq. mi.; population (1960), 34,626,000. Under the Constitution of 1917 Mexico is a federal state, but the preponderance of power resides at the national level. There is a popularly-elected Congress, composed of a Senate and a Chamber of Deputies. The President of the Republic is elected to a six-year term. The leading political party is the Institutional Revolutionary Party (PRI), which wins almost a totality of the elective offices at the national and state levels of government. Minor parties are the National Action Party and Popular Socialist Party (Communist). The President is Adolfo Lopez Mateos, whose term expires in 1964. F.M.L.

Michels, Roberto (1876—1936).

Italo-Swiss university professor, sociologist, and political theorist; author of **Political Parties, A Sociological Study of the Oligarchical Tendencies in Modern Democracies** (1915), the thesis of which was that leadership is of necessity oligarchical and that this cannot be prevented or corrected by any system of constitutional contrivances or controls. Ch.C.M.

Michurin, Ivan Vladimirovich (1855—1935).

Soviet horticulturist and sometime geneticist whose adaptation of the Lamarckian doctrine was established by Stalin as a fundamental truth of Soviet science. Michurin's chief interest was in the hybridization of plants, and it was his achievements in this area that brought him to Lenin's attention. But he also held that acquired characteristics were transmittable through inheritance. In 1948, Stalin, interested in Michurin's statements in this field by T. D. Lysenko, decreed that Michurinism had replaced Mendelian genetics. Stalin's interference in this matter severely hampered the work of Soviet biologists for most of the following decade. D.N.J.

Middle East.

Syria, Lebanon, Israel, Jordan, and Iraq constitute the core area of the Middle East, but Iran, Egypt, Cyprus, and Saudi Arabia are usually included, while some writers also include Turkey, Afghanistan, W. Pakistan, Libya, and Sudan. H.L.M.

Midway, Battle of.

Japan's two serious attempts to capture Midway: 1. Evening of Dec. 7, 1941, Japanese warships shelling American installation on Eastern Island, repulsed with heavy losses. 2. The Battle of Midway, June 4-7, 1942 (following the Battle of the Coral Sea, May 7 & 8, 1942), fought almost entirely by carrier-based planes 700 miles west of Midway. Well alerted, American bombers and torpedo planes put Japanese fleet to rout after sinking four enemy aircraft carriers, two cruisers and several other vessels and destroying 250 planes. The first really smashing defeat of Japanese Navy and the turning point of war in Pacific. Japan, forced on the defensive, cancelled plans for conquest of Fiji, New Caledonia and New Zealand.
C.K.W.

Mikhailovitch, Draja (Mihailovic, Draza) (1893—1946).

Yugoslav General. After the defeat of Yugoslavia in 1941 Colonel Mihailovic gathered remnants of the Yugoslav Army and organized the largely Serb **Cetnik** movement. The Royal

Yugoslav Government in exile promoted him to General and Minister of Defense. His forces engaged both the Nazis and the Communist Partisans and he lost domestic and foreign support. He was tried and executed by Tito's regime for alleged war-time collaboration. G.K.

Mikolajczyk, Stanislaw (1901—   ).
Born in Westphalia of Polish migrant workers. Since 1930, a leader of the Peasant Party. Succeeded General Wladyslaw Sikorski (q.v.) as premier of the exiled government at London. Resigned to join communist-dominated coalition in Warsaw. Ten months after fraudulent election of 1947, fled to the United States. Currently chairman of Peasant (Green) International. R.F.S.

Mikoyan, Anastas.
Born 1895, worker's family, Sanain, Tiflis. Graduated Armenian Theological Seminary, Tiflis, joined Bolsheviks 1915. Imprisoned during Civil War, escaped 1919. Member CP Central Committee since 1923, Politburo (called Party Presidium since 1952) since 1935. Member Central Executive Committee (called Supreme Soviet since 1937) since 1919. Ministerial posts in foreign and domestic trade. USSR Council of Ministers. Known for foreign trade negotiations. One of few old Bolsheviks to survive Party leadership struggles 1920's, 1930's, and 1950's. W.A.

Militarism.
The term militarism was first used in France about 1860. The concepts as well as the practices which give content to this term, however, date back to the earliest time of political history. Militarism strongly influenced the behavioral pattern of most ancient primitive societies.

In its broadest sense militarism refers to a policy which on one hand places great emphasis upon so-called military virtues such as personal courage, strength, endurance, discipline, obedience within an established and rigid hierarchy and readiness for self-sacrifice as an end in itself. On the other hand, it underscores the role of military force and preparedness in the conduct of international relations as the most significant single factor. An outstanding example of a genuine militaristic spirit is provided by classical Sparta. In this ancient Greek community militarism was the all-permeating concept which dominated the entire political, social, and economic structure of community life and provided the basis for most of the values of the Spartan society.

Militarism as a term is often falsely applied to describe a situation which is marked by a conscious effort of military preparedness for defense purposes or by the existence of strong national armed forces. As long as the militaristic spirit and values are not superimposed upon the civilian sector and do not overrule civilian concerns about non-military methods in dealing with social and political problems within the domestic or international spheres, militarism in its true connotation is not applicable to describe the situation. Although, it must be recognized that especially during prolonged periods of crisis, the unchecked influence of the military leaders might lead to militarism through their effort to militarize society and through the glorification of the forceful struggle and the natural selection through war. The upshot of the militarization of society is characterized by the general acceptance of military values also for the civilian sector of day to day life. Hitler's Third Reich with the strict application of the leadership-principle furnishes an example of this type of militarized society.

Militarism finds its most ardent supporters within the group of strong traditionalists and authoritarians who frequently follow still the outdated patterns of the alleged static feudal society in which every man had his due place assigned within the social and political hierarchy.

Militarism is also often confused with practices which can be found in all military establishments, also in those which are under effective civilian control. Thus the use of ceremonies, decorations, symbols and rank designations do not in themselves constitute visible signs of an existing militarism.

Militarism as a policy and military dictatorship as a form of government generally endanger the maintenance of peace as many historic events have demonstrated. The most powerful obstacle to militarism is an effective civilian supremacy which must not only provide political leadership but also the guiding values for the community. E.W.

Military Courts.
Tribunals commonly called Courts-martial are established to conduct the trials of members of the armed forces accused of violating military law. The Constitution of the United States divides authority over these courts between Congress and the President. Although military courts are authorized to impose the death penalty, they do not participate in the judicial authority of the United States. They proceed without a jury, and are not bound by the same rules of evidence as American criminal courts. Courts-martial are designated "Summary," "Special," or "General." The decisions of these courts require the approval of an appropriate commanding officer, and are subject to a Review Board. Since the enactment in 1950 of the Code of Military Justice, under specific conditions an appeal lies to the Court of Military Appeals. A.A.N.

Military Government.
The military control of civilian occupants of conquered territory; also embracing analogous activities in friendly territory within a theatre of military operations. American military government power stems from Presidential authority over conquered territories and Constitutional or statutory guarantees of the United States do not apply to the conquered people. Military government as well as civil affairs units are required to expedite the overall military aims of the armed forces by relieving the tactical units of the problems of caring for and coping with civilian personnel. In friendly territory within a theatre of operations, however, the emphasis, on the basis of World War II experience, is placed upon the reestablishment of stable economic and political conditions, not only to relieve conquering armed forces from the problems that arise in periods of instability, but also to assist friendly powers in recovery from the effects of war, hence, increasing their ability to offer assistance.

The task of military government in conquered Germany was of greater magnitude than was met in Japan, for in the former case the total reconstitution of a civilian body politic and economy was undertaken and most institutional arrangements were dealt with by military government. In Japan an operating political structure was modified and subordinated to new authority. M.P.S.

Military in Latin American Politics.
Traditionally part of the ruling "triumvirate" (along with the landed aristocracy and the Roman Catholic clergy) and in modern times the most powerful pressure group. With few exceptions and in spite of unequivocal constitutional provisions to the contrary, the colonial experience of autocratic and quasi-military rule was carried over. Civilian control of the state was not established. Military pomp and ceremony fascinated or intimidated the many; the special privileges and rewards of the officer class attracted ambitious and self-seeking individuals. The result has been frequent military dictatorship by a "man on horseback" (caudillo; see **Personalismo** and **Jefe Maximo**). The notorious irregularities in Latin American politics almost always involve the armed forces, directly or indirectly (see, e.g., **Golpe** and **Cuartelazo**). The officers witness the corruption and the irresponsible excesses of their civilian counterparts with consternation. Most have little patience with parliamentary procedures; the poorly-trained police are incapable of preserving public order or commanding public respect. Repeated military interventions have failed to solve the countries' chronic problems; on the other hand, civilian administrations are rarely capable of securing the cooperation of the many factions. In most of the Republics the armed forces are accepted in fact as the final arbiter of national policy. The ideological disputes of the day are of prime concern to such political armed forces. Junior officers particularly are ashamed of social injustices or frustrated over their country's economic stagnation. Officers constitute a high percentage of the trained administrators, especially in remote regions. R.D.H.

Military Law.

That branch of the municipal law regulating the military establishment of the state, and embracing members of the armed forces, captured enemies, and, under certain conditions, civilian employees of and persons accompanying the armed forces. Military law is applied through courts martial or military commissions. United States military law is authorized by Constitutional delegations of power to the Congress, and the authority vested in the President, as well as a provision of Amendment V. M.P.S.

Militia.

The volunteer military forces retained by each state to maintain internal order. The 2nd Amendment to the U.S. Constitution guarantees each state the right to keep their own militias. In peacetime militia units are under the direction of the governor who appoints their officers and who may dispatch them to protect persons and property in time of disaster, labor disputes, etc. The militia is today known as the national guard and is financially supported largely by federal funds. In wartime, the state militia may be called into federal service. R.R.R.

Mill, John Stuart (1806—1873).

The last of the great English utilitarians and the author of English classics on liberalism. John Stuart Mill, eldest child of the utilitarian economist, James Mill, was subjected from the age of three to an exacting private education by his father, assisted later by Bentham and Austin. His indoctrination is apparent in the first editions of his **Logic** (1843) and **Principles of Political Economy** (1848), but he modified his early views in later revisions of these important works. John Stuart Mill's lasting fame is due mainly to the persuasiveness and literary charm of his more popular later writings. The chapter on freedom of discussion in **On Liberty** (1859) has superseded Milton's **Areopagitica** as the English classic on freedom of the press; **Considerations on Representative Government** (1861) is even today one of the strongest endorsements of representative democracy against autocracy; **Utilitarianism** (1863) modified Benthamism and made it far more palatable. Like his father before him, the younger Mill earned his living in responsible posts in the India House. After the India Act of 1858 caused his retirement on a generous pension, he was elected in 1865 to a single term in the House of Commons. Here he seriously proposed a woman suffrage amendment to the Reform Bill of 1867. His indignation at the position of women in English law led him to publish **The Subjection of Women** (1869). M.Sp.

Millah (Millet).

A term used in the Koran for religion, and subsequently in the caliphate of the Arab states of the Middle Ages to designate certain non-Muslim minorities **(dhimmis)**, mainly the Christians and Jews, which constituted self-governing communities on the basis of their own canon law and under the control and jurisdiction of their ecclesiastical authorities. The Ottomans incorporated the system **(millet)** into the public administration of their Empire. The nationality of every subject was the particular religious denomination to which his **millet** belonged. They were also called "nations" and considered as individual nationalities. The political identity (citizenship) of the Sultan's subject was Ottoman and his "nationality" was the religion of the community to which he belonged, i.e., his **millet**. Until the end of the 19th century the **millets** conducted their affairs through their communal councils free from outside intervention, in contact with the central government only through the intermediary of their spiritual heads. Matters of personal status and family law survived the reforms of the late 19th century and continued to be the reserve of the religious courts of the different communities. To this day, most Near Eastern countries find it more convenient to leave these matters to the religious courts. F.M.N.

Miller, Jack Richard.

Born June 6, 1916; U.S. Senate from January 3, 1961 until term ending in 1967; Republican—Iowa. R.A.B.

Millerand, Etienne Alexandre (1859—1943).

French political figure. A lawyer, he

was elected a socialist deputy in 1885; minister of commerce, 1899—1902; minister of public works, 1909; under Briand, minister of war, 1912—1913; and from August, 1914 to October, 1915; in January, 1920 he became premier and minister of foreign affairs; in September, 1920, elected President of the Republic, from which position he tried unsuccessfully to exercise real political influence; he resigned in June, 1924 when socialists and radicals attacked him as a renegade. E.G.L.

Milton, John (1608—1674).

English poet, litterateur, political publicist, republican. Most memorable tract—"Areopagitica" (1644) a classic statement of freedom of speech and intellectual liberalism: with freedom of both thought and expression, truth will prevail over error. He also defended tyrannicide, arguing from natural law, the laws of England and Scripture; believed the origin of government rested on mutual defense of natural freedom; argued that the separation of religion and the state was necessary pragmatically as well as theoretically. Distrusting the masses, he rested his republican case against formal monarchical inheritance upon the natural moral and intellectual superiority of certain men to rule. J.P.D.

Mindszenty, Jozsef (1892—   ).

Cardinal, Archbishop of Esztergom, Primate of Hungary. Ordained priest in 1915, he became Bishop of Veszprem in 1944, Archbishop of Esztergom in October, 1945, and was created Cardinal of the Roman Church in February, 1946. As Archbishop of Esztergom, he is Primate of Hungary. Was imprisoned during the Nazi occupation of the country for demanding human liberties. After World War II, was arrested by the Communist regime during the Christmas holiday of 1948 and sentenced to life imprisonment for "espionage, illegal currency dealings, etc.", but in reality, for resisting the sovietization of education and public life. Consistently refused offers of cooperation with the Communist regime. In 1955, during the "New Course" policy of the first Nagy government, his prison term was commuted to indefinite house arrest. Was freed on October 30, 1956, when the government of Imre Nagy was in power. The Soviet intervention on November 4, 1956, and the return of the radical Communists with J. Kadar to power forced him to seek refuge in the U.S. Legation in Budapest, where he remains virtually cut off from contact with his subordinate clergy and with the population. I.B.

Minifundismo.

System of land tenure in Latin America in which very small farms are contrasted with the large landed estates known as **latifundios**. Economically unproductive, the **minifundios** consist of large families of farmers who eke out a pitful existence marked by disease, hunger, and privation. They are mainly in private hands, but their owners do not have economic, social, or political standing in their respective countries. R.B.G.

Ministrable.

A French term identifying a parliamentary deputy who has the requisite personal and political qualifications for ministerial appointment. Personal prestige and popularity, keen political judgment, and a compromising and undoctrinaire attitude are some of the essential qualities of a **ministrable** if he is to function effectively in the customarily unstable coalition French cabinet. The **ministrables**, reflecting the leadership element of the National Assembly and comprising about one-tenth of its total membership, constitute an informal pool from which ministerial candidates, including the Premier-designate, are likely to be drawn. R.H.K.

Minority presidents.

Presidents who failed to secure an absolute majority of the popular vote, although with the exceptions of Jefferson (1800) and John Quincy Adams (1824) every American president has received an absolute majority of the electoral vote. Minority presidents since the Civil War have been Hayes, Arthur, Cleveland, Harrison, Wilson and Truman. Hayes and Harrison received fewer popular votes than their respective opponents. The term's significance is political rather than constitutional. Th.P.

Minor parties (general definition and example for U.S.A.).

Generally, political organizations which have little or no expectation of electing candidates in a particular campaign but view their role as innovation, presentation of new ideas or compelling concepts, educational, with principle as the motivating force rather than political expediency. They have been instrumental in the United States for suggesting varying solutions to public problems, "trial balloons," and for representing pressure groups in the form of protest politics as against the major parties. In a few instances, a minor party has secured enough support to decide the election outcome for the major party candidates. In many instances, such third party planks have been adopted by one or both major parties after proving to have widespread popular support. Among the innumerable minor parties have been such significant ones as the Liberty, Greenback, Populist, Native American, Progressive, and Farmer-Labor. M.B.D.

Minuteman.

A three-stage, solid propellant intercontinental ballistic missile (ICBM) weapon system assigned to the Strategic Air Command equipped with an inertial guidance system, range of 6000 miles, speed of 15,000 mph and a capability to be stored at-the-ready for instantaneous use in hardened, blast-resistant underground launch silos.
T.W.

Mirabeau, Honore Gabriel Riquetti, Comte de (1749—1791).

After an early career as a literary figure and scandalous blade, he was elected to the Estates General in 1789 as a member of the Third Estate. He argued persuasively for creating a constitutional monarchy after the English model but based on wider suffrage. From May, 1790 to his death in April, 1791, he was discreet adviser to the Bourbon court in its relations with the National Assembly. In foreign relations he tried unsuccessfully to prevent foreign sovereigns from intervening in French affairs. He died after a short illness on April 2, 1791. E.G.L.

Misdemeanor.

A violation of criminal law of less serious consequence than a felony, usually punishable by confinement in a local prison or by fines. Traffic offenses, nuisances, breaches of the peace, etc., may be misdemeanors.
J.O.H.

Missile Gap.

A concept first advanced in 1959 that there was an important "gap" between the United States and the Soviet Union in ICBM's. It was argued that the USSR was definitely superior to the U.S. in intercontinental ballistic missiles. The "missile gap" was apparently a misconception brought about by the tendency of U.S. evaluators to take exaggerated views about Soviet ability to produce ICBM's. This may have been aided by Khrushchev's claim (14 November 1959) that one plant produced in one year "250 missiles with hydrogen warheads." Perhaps because of past intelligence difficulties, we tended to overestimate Soviet ICBM capabilities. By 1961 revised intelligence evaluations indicated that there was no "gap." The "missile gap" controversy demonstrates the dangers inherent in guess-estimates at relative strengths (especially vis-a-vis the USSR) whether the guess-estimates be over-pessimistic or over-optimistic as might be the case with some projections today. J.D.A.

Missouri Court Plan.

A plan for choosing judges, used for certain courts in Missouri since 1940. A commission consisting of a judge, lawyers and laymen recommends three persons to fill any vacancy on the bench. The Governor appoints one of the three. After at least one year, the people vote to retain or remove the appointee. If retained, he serves a full term; if removed a vacancy is created and the process starts again. Similar plans are in effect in California, Alaska and other places. J.E.R.

Missouri v. Holland.

A case decided by the United States Supreme Court in 1920 which sustained the powers of the Federal Government over those of the States in regard to the making and enforcing treaties. The treaty involved had been made in 1916 between the United States and Great Britain to provide for the mutual protection of migratory birds between the United States and Canada. The States had complained of the enforcement of the Treaty by the Federal Government as an invasion of the rights of the States. Justice Holmes, for the Court, said: "It is not lightly to be assumed that . . . a power which must belong to and somewhere reside in every civilized government is not to be found." R.G.S.

Mithraism.
Ancient Persian religion based on worship of Mithras, god of light and truth. Spread with Persian conquests, became well established in Assyria. First brought to Roman empire in first century B.C. and became dominant among the army and merchants in second century. Its attraction lay with hopes of immortality and with a high moral standard. Like Christianity, it made the military the champion of good over evil. Received imperial backing because it supported the idea of divine right of rulers. Organization of Mithraism consisted of 7 degrees; mystics within the first 3 degrees were called servants indicating that they were still not full-fledged members. The Mithraic community had both spiritual and temporal powers; the latter included the right of holding property. Began to lose its importance in 275 when Roman empire lost Dacia. Christianity also made inroads upon Mithraism; while both religions were amazingly similar in many respects, Christianity was more inclusive (women were not considered by Mithraism). H.G.S.

Mixed Constitution.
This term is also referred to as mixed government. See Checks and Balances.

Mizrachi.
Now called National Religious Zionist Party of Israel. Pursues legislative goals based on Laws of Torah, ethical and social values of Judaism in national life; opposes "secularist modernism." Supports religious education system, social services, settlement of religious collectives and cooperatives.
  S.H.

Mob violence.
Illegal, destructive acts performed by a crowd which has been incited by demagoguery and symbolic manipulation by speakers. The rights of assembly and free speech stop short of incitement to riot and commission of illegal acts. R.R.R.

Moch, Jules (1893—).
French Socialist political leader. Born into a French Jewish family with a strong military background, he trained as an engineer and enjoyed a brief but successful career in that field. In 1928 he was elected to the chamber as a Socialist and during the 30's he rose as a protege of Leon Blum, and served as minister of public works in the second Blum cabinet, 1938. One of the 80 deputies who voted against granting Petain unlimited powers he was arrested by the Nazis, released and eventually made his way to De Gaulle's Free French forces. A member of the post-war constituent assemblies and also a deputy throughout the Fourth Republic he was a cabinet minister continuously from 1945-50. During the 1947-8 disturbances caused by a strike wave and Communist-led riots against the Marshall Plan he was Minister of the Interior and was credited with the strong actions taken. Again, in the Pflimlin government at the close of the Fourth Republic in 1958, as Minister of the Interior he was credited with maintaining order in Paris. Since 1950 he has been a member of the Socialist Party executive committee. J.S.S.

Model State Constitution.
A document prepared by the National Municipal League in the U.S.A. and revised at about ten year intervals. It sets forth in relatively brief form the features of state government of a constitutional nature, as recommended by the composite judgment of many state officials and laymen. Sp.D.A.

Moderator.
The term Moderator is used in New England as the name of the presiding officer at Town Meetings. Ordinarily the first official chosen at the annual gathering he presides over that session and any special meetings called during his term of office. His personality and his skill in parliamentary law determine the tone and quality of the Town

Meeting and are undoubtedly major factors in the unique reputation of that body. A.E.N.

Molotov-Ribbentrop Pact.
See Nazi-Soviet Pact.

Molotov, Vyascheslav M.
Now around seventy-four years old, he has been an active professional Communist since 1905. His career conforms to the pattern of the perfect Bolshevik apparatchnik. He is a man of energy and ability but without claim to ideological and political leadership. In early 1912, **Pravda** made its appearance as the Bolshevik newspaper of Moscow. Stalin and Molotov were among its first editors. In 1920, Molotov became secretary of the Ukraine Communist Party and secretary to the Central Committee of the Soviet Communist Party in 1921. From 1925 at least, but probably earlier, he was associated with Stalin's personal entourage, and was his most reliable administrative agent. In 1925 he was elevated to the Politburo as a reward for his service in the Party apparatus and undeviating loyalty to Stalin. He served as premier (chairman of the Council of People's Commissars) during the period between 1930 and 1940. From 1940 to 1949 he served as foreign minister. In 1949 he was replaced by Andrei Vyshinsky but became again foreign minister after Stalin's death in 1953. In July 1957, Molotov strove for the overthrow of Khrushchev as leader of the Communist Party in collaboration with Malenkov, Kaganovich and others. He failed. The official communique of the Central Committee of the Soviet Communist Party and the Khrushchev faction accused him of having been one of the "anti-Party" group. He was excluded from the Committee and the Presidium (former Politburo). He was not, however, expelled from the Party, nor was he arrested. He became ambassador to Outer Mongolia and the chief Soviet delegate to the International Atomic Energy Agency in Vienna. He was demoted and humiliated both at the 21st and 22nd Party Congresses. At the 22nd Congress of 1961, he was charged with personal responsibility for sanctioning Stalinist repression and crime. R.St-H.

Monaco.
An independent principality in the southeast of France bordering on the Mediterranean. (Area 0.578 square miles; population of 22,297.) The Grimaldi Family ruled the principality almost continuously since 968. Sardinia acted as a protecting power from 1814 until France took over in 1861; France annexed Nice and some adjoining territory. In 1911 the ruling prince accepted a Constitution which provided for an elected National Council with which he shared legislative authority; the Council was suspended in 1959. The executive branch consists of a Ministry and a Council of State. Monaco's main economic activities lie in the realm of tourism and commercial activities largely based on Monaco's tax exemption. G.K.

Monarchy.
Originally, a government in which sovereignty was vested in a single person, thus government by the absolute rule of one. The term now, however, applies mainly to "limited" or "constitutional" monarchies, in which the authority of the ruler is shared with and often subordinated to other agencies of government, such as a parliament. Monarchy may be either elective or hereditary; in modern times the latter is generally predominant. M.J.H.

Mongolia (Outer Mongolia or Mongolian Peoples' Republic).
A large sparsely populated country of 591,119 sq. miles, between the Soviet Union and China. Population is about one million. It is about 90% Mongols, predominantly Khalkha Mongols. Other Mongols are Ojrats and Buryats. Mongolia in the past had its share of glory and decline. At the time of the T'ang Dynasty (618—907 B.C.) Mongols were known as the **Mong-ku** invaders. Mongolia's greatest conquests were at the time the country was consolidated and ruled by Genghis Khan. It reached its zenith under the rule of Kublai Khan in the 13th Century. The decline of Mongolia came with the ascent of the new Manchu Dynasty in China, when Mongolia formally accepted Manchu rule, which lasted until the Chinese revolution of 1911. In 1911 the northern princes of Outer Mongolia de-

clared their independence, with the Living Buddha as ruler of the country. The 1915 Russo-Chinese-Mongolian agreement made Mongolia an autonomous part of China. In 1919, the Chinese general Hsu Shu-tseng abolished Mongolian autonomy. In Oct. 1920, Mongolia was invaded by the White Russian Army, under Baron Ungern von Sternberg, who occupied Urga in Feb. 1921. In July 1921, Soviet armies invaded Mongolia, expelled White Russian forces and recognized Mongolian independence. In 1924, the Living Buddha died, and the pro-Communist revolution established the Mongolian Peoples' Republic. Its independence was recognized by Nationalist China only after World War II, October 20, 1945. In October 1961, the Mongolian Peoples' Republic became a member of the United Nations on the condition of the simultaneous acceptance of Mauritania. V.P.P.

Monism.
The political and juridical doctrine that unity of authority is essential to a social order, and that this involves a uniformity of law throughout the whole social system together with a supreme and final determiner of the validity of law; the opposite of pluralism, which holds that human society is too heterogeneous for real political unity. Ch.C.M.

Monnet, Jean (1888—   ).
French economist and financier, member of cognac producing family, participated in allied economic planning and resources allocation in both world wars, served as deputy secretary general in the first years of the League of Nations, initiating several of its economic actions for monetary stabilization. During the two world wars he headed several important firms of investment bankers in the U.S. and in Europe. During world War II, he became commissioner of armaments, supply and reconstruction in the Free French organization, and later head of the French general plan for industrial modernization. One of the original proponents of the European Steel and Coal Community and of the European Economic Community. F.M.

Monnet Plan.
Plan devised to bring about French economic recovery after World War II. Named for Jean Monnet, head of the planning commission. Starting in 1946 the plan called for a series of investment priorities over a four year period, particularly in six key branches of the economy: coal, electricity, steel, cement, transportation, and agricultural machinery. The plan covered both private and publicly owned industries. In 1948 the plan was extended and redesigned to take into account American Marshall Plan aid. Many of the goals were achieved by 1952 and the plan was extended. J.S.S.

Monopoly.
A grant of privilege or exclusive right to provide, produce, or sell certain goods or services. These conditions bring about artificial conditions of competition (note possibility of oligopoly) or the absence of competition—complete monopoly is not necessary to the exercise of monopolistic power. There may be private monopolies the result of exclusive grants of privilege by government (copyright or patent privileges) or by business arrangements limiting competition in production or prices. There may be public monopolies in the exclusive franchises in the utilities field.
W.D.S.

Monroe, James.
b. March 28, 1758, in Virginia. Died July 4, 1831. Fifth president of the United States (1817—1825). Studied law. He and R. R. Livingston negotiated the treaty with Napoleon I which obtained Louisiana for the United States. Elected president in 1816 and in 1820 with only one electoral vote cast against him. In 1823 he issued the famous Monroe Doctrine which stated that the western hemisphere was not open for foreign interference. M.F.

Monroe Doctrine.
On December 3, 1823, President Monroe, confronted by what he believed to be the threat of the Holy Alliance to assist Spain in recovering the Latin American colonies which had recently won their independence, declared first that the American continents were "henceforth not to be considered as subjects for future col-

onization by any European Powers," thus disposing of further efforts to secure a foothold upon the continent on the ground of its being unoccupied territory. Then while declaring that it did not comport with our policy to take any part in the wars of the European powers in matters relating to themselves, and that the political system of the allied powers was essentially different from ours, to the defense of which the whole nation was devoted, President Monroe continued: "We owe it, therefore, to candor, and to the amicable relations existing between the United States and those powers, to declare that we should consider any attempt on their part to extend their system to any portion of this hemisphere as dangerous to our peace and safety." Then, while disclaiming any intention to interfere with the existing colonies or dependencies of any European power, the President declared: "But with the governments who have declared their independence and maintained it, and whose independence we have, on great consideration and on just principles, acknowledged, we could not view any interposition for the purpose of oppressing them, or controlling in any other manner their destiny, by any European power, in any other light than as the manifestation of an unfriendly disposition towards the United States."

The Monroe Doctrine was thus, in spite of its crusading character, fundamentally a doctrine of self-defense, of self-protection against the too-near presence of European powers whose political system was "essentially different" from that of the United States. But when, in 1904, President Roosevelt interpreted the principle to justify the assumption of a unilateral police power, on the ground that if European powers were to be kept out of America someone must keep order in America, the Roosevelt Corollary was sharply attacked by the Latin American States, and the doctrine of "non-intervention" was asserted in opposition to the policy of the "Big Stick." It was this extension of the Monroe Doctrine that was abandoned in 1936 when a treaty was signed at Buenos Aires pledging the American States to consultation in the event of a threat to the peace, a pledge confirmed by specific obligations to take measures of collective security by the Treaty of Reciprocal Assistance signed at Rio de Janeiro in 1947.

As a doctrine of self-defense and limited to that objective, the Monroe Doctrine is still as valid as when first proclaimed. But in view of the changed conditions that have led the United States to take part in measures of collective defense with the North Atlantic Treaty Organization, the present validity of the doctrine has been questioned. As a doctrine of self-defense the principle underlying the doctrine still holds. C.G.F.

Monrovian Bloc.
An association of twenty African states, dedicated to the unification of the continent and open to all independent African states under indigenous rule. Its present membership (based on the Lagos Conference of January, 1962) consists of the twelve members of the Brazzaville Bloc (Ivory Coast, Niger, Upper Volta, Dahomey, Senegal, Mauritania, the Cameroons, the Malagasy Republic, Gabon, Chad, the Congo-Brazzaville, and the Central African Republic); four other states from West Africa (Liberia, Nigeria, Togo, and Sierra Leone); three states from East Africa (Ethiopia, Somalia, and Tanganyika); and the Congo-Leopoldville. Despite urging from many quarters, the six members of the rival Casablanca Bloc have not joined.

The resolutions adopted at its major founding conferences (Monrovia in May of 1961 and Lagos in January of 1962) reflect the generally moderate political orientation of the members. The organization has adopted functionalism as the means of unifying Africa. While recognizing the political identity and sovereign equality of each of its members, it seeks to promote their unity through cooperation in specific technical, economic, and cultural matters. The establishment of a regional customs union, a development bank, and a joint shipping company have been proposed. The creation of overall coordinating organs has been accepted in principle, but their formation awaits final approval. F.H.G.

Montes, Ismael.

Latin American politician. Born in La Paz, Bolivia, in 1861; died in 1933. Education, preparatory school, La Paz. President of Bolivia in 1904 and again in 1913. Created the Bolivian national bank (Banco de la Nacion). M.A.

Montesquieu.

Charles-Louis de Secondat, Baron de le Brede et de Montesquieu, son of a nobleman, born at Brede, 1689, and trained in the classics, spent his early mature years administering justice in Bordeaux. In 1716 his uncle died bequeathing him his office of chief justice. In 1721 Montesquieu published **Persian Letters,** a witty satire on French clericism and manners. In 1728 he was elected to the French Academy. From 1729 to 1731 he traveled widely in Europe, spending more than a year in England. Because of his interest in and contributions to the field of natural science he was elected a member of the Royal Society. In 1734 he published **Considerations on the Greatness and Decline of Rome.** This was followed in 1748 with his greatest work, **The Spirit of the Laws.** He died in 1755.

In his major work Montesquieu returned to the concern of classical thought for the variety of conditions and development of people to whom political principles were to be applied. This gives his work a cultural and anthropological basis that contrasts strikingly with other political works of the time. He is best known for his concept of the separation of power with its claim that liberty could be preserved only if a proper limit and balance were achieved between the three branches of government.

R.M.T.

Montreux Convention.

Revision favoring Turkey, and to a degree Russia, of the Lausanne Convention of 1923 internationalizing the Turkish Straits. Britain, France and Russia were the major actors at the 1936 conference which ended the international Straits commission, allowed Turkey to militarize them and to exercise greater control over passing warships, and gave Russian Black Sea fleets increased security. The convention grew from new Turkish and Soviet power and an Anglo-French need for friends in the East. In 1945 Russia tried unsuccessfully to revise the convention and secure mastery over the Straits. P.F.P.

Mooney Case.

Thomas J. Mooney, contributor to the anarchist paper **Blast** and active leader during several violent labor struggles in California, was convicted in 1916 for the bomb killings during the San Francisco Preparedness Parade. In 1913 he had been acquitted of unlawful possession of explosives during a strike. The case aroused international interest partially because it was discovered that some of the trial evidence was perjured. In 1918 Mooney's sentence was commuted from death to life imprisonment and in 1939 he was pardoned. W.F.G.

Moral Law.

The moral law is implanted in the reason of man. It is that part of the eternal law which applies to the free acts of man. It is, thus, not made by human reason but discovered by human reason. The ultimate standard of right and wrong is the "Reason of God." Because there is such a thing as human nature which is the same in all men, there is an order which reason can discover and according to which the human will must act in accordance with the ends of the human being.

The idea of natural moral law is a heritage of classical and Jewish-Christian thought, stemming from the great moralists and poets of antiquity, through Cicero and the Stoics, St. Paul, Augustine, Maimonides, Aquinas, Grotius. Pa.B.

Morale.

The moral or mental condition of the individual or group with respect to courage, discipline, confidence, enthusiasm, and willingness to endure hardship or sacrifice. It depends in part on an awareness by the individual or group that contributions are both recognized and appreciated. It is a matter of attitude, opinion, and belief which involves group spirit and a sense of pride in common activities of those in the same group or community. R.J.S.

Morale Building.
The creation of an awareness of the purpose and objectives which an organization or community seeks to achieve and of their essential social value. An effort to create a sense of the "worth-whileness" of one's work. Success is largely predicated on the degree of confidence of the rank and file in the integrity, good intent and fairness of associates and supervisors as well as their willingness to recognize the contributions and achievements of individual members of the group. Both morale and morale building are undermined by feelings of insecurity in the individual and the group. R.J.S.

Morality.
The code of human conduct which sets standards for the individual or group in relation to other individuals or groups. Differing from custom, it implies conscious recognition or acceptance of a desirable value. The code may include law, but it goes beyond law and may serve to evaluate law. Law brings in the sanction of the state for the sector of conduct it encompasses. No sanction exists for a moral code outside law, other than individual conscience or group pressure, except for those who accept "divine" or "natural law" as forming a basis. For the latter, divine or religious sanction exists. Public and private morality are sometimes separated, but they may be viewed as different levels of problems, involving expanded or more complex considerations, when the state is concerned.
D.P.

Moreno, Gabriel Garcia
(1821—1875).
Was born in Guayaquil, the son of a Spanish adventurer and an Ecuadorian mother who was herself a descendant of Spanish nobles. Following private studies at home, he studied humanities in the Jesuit College in Quito and jurisprudence in the University of Quito. His political career began while he was a young man. He governed the country autocratically for fifteen years, from 1861 to 1875. Religious ideas prevailed over civic, patriotic interests. For example, public instruction and culture were under clerical supervision. This man's great political opponent was Juan Montalvo who opposed him in his capacity of journalist and writer. A group of young men, incited by Montalvo, assassinated Garcia Moreno on the 6th of August 1875 in Quito. The Conservative Party regards Garcia Moreno as a martyr. B.M.P.

Morgenthau Plan.
A scheme promoted by Henry Morgenthau, Jr., Secretary of the Treasury, to disarm Germany in depth by eliminating or drastically reducing the industrial might of that country. A developing concept, this "plan" at different times called for: 1) the denial of all industry to Germany; 2) the removal of all heavy industry from her control; or 3) the removal of a portion of heavy industry from German control. The scheme was to be implemented mainly by the removal of factories and the separation of industrially-rich regions from the victim state.

The Morgenthau approach was accepted in principle by President Roosevelt and Prime Minister Churchill at the Second Quebec Conference in 1944 and by the Big Three at Yalta and Potsdam, and the thinking of the Secretary of the Treasury inspired the drastic four power level of industry plan of April, 1946. Numerous revisions, however, greatly altered this drastic instrument — at least in the Western Zones. Although industrial equipment was removed from 706 plants in these zones, many companies soon thereafter replaced the missing equipment and resumed operations. The deindustrialization carried out by the Western occupation powers has not prevented the German Federal Republic from regaining its prewar industrial pre-eminence. The Soviet Union pursued a more ambitious program in its zone, but Soviet actions can hardly be attributed to the influence of Mr. Morgenthau. F.H.G.

Morocco.
Its area is about 190,000 square miles, and its population is estimated around 10 million. The capital is Rabat. The people are Muslims. The language is Arabic, though the Berber tongue is spoken by 35 percent of the population. Morocco fell to the Arab conquerors in the 7th century and sub-

sequently adopted their religion and their language. On March 30, 1912 Morocco fell under the "protection" of France. French colonialism introduced the country to Western civilization and produced the modern Moroccan nationalists. Morocco under the leadership of its Sultan Muhammad V, attained its independence on March 2, 1956. It joined the Arab League and the United Nations. Moroccan Government is autocratic, but democratic reforms are gradually introduced. Culturally it remains very much under the influence of France. E.A.S.

Morse, Wayne.

Educator, specialist in labor relations, and United States Senator from the state of Oregon. 1929—1944, Professor and Dean of the University of Oregon Law School. Prior to 1944, Wayne Morse accepted appointment as labor arbitrator for the government on the west coast and served as a member of the War Labor Board. In 1944 and 1950, Morse was elected to the United States Senate as a Republican. In 1955 Morse formally broke with the Republican Party. Then in 1956 and 1962 Morse was re-elected to the Senate as a Democrat. Morse's name has appeared on presidential preference primary ballots of both the Republican and Democratic tickets as a candidate for President of the United States. In the Senate he has been noted for his efforts on the Foreign Relations Committee and as one of the most verbose of the Senate floor speakers in defense of the public interest. W.D.S.

Moscow-Peking Axis.

A partnership created by Stalin and Mao Tse-tung in a treaty of alliance between the Soviet Union and the Chinese People's Republic of February 14, 1950. Communist China became a junior partner-leader in the international Communist movement. The axis was based on the mutual goal of world-wide Communist victory, common hostility toward the West, and initial economic agreements. Following Khrushchev's February 1956 denunciation of Stalin, whom Mao admired, the Hungarian revolt later that year, and the differing assessments of Western strength during Mao's visit to Moscow in 1957, significant strains and differences developed between the axis partners. Chinese national interests, economic problems (particularly population growth), bid for leadership of the underdeveloped areas, and accent on military solution for international problems were at variance with the Soviet line. Major differences between the two Communist partners emerged into the open in June 1960, at a conference in Bucharest and later at the gathering of 81 Communist Parties from all over the world in Moscow from October to December that year. Despite intensification of strains, mutual Communist interests continued to cement the axis. R.L.W.

Moses.

Legendary leader, prophet, and lawgiver of the ancient Israelites; significant in political science chiefly because of the laws and legal institutions ascribed to him, particularly the Decalogue and the Mosaic Law. Ch.C.M.

Moshav (pl. moshavim).

(Hebr. "settlement"). There are various types of agricultural settlements in Israel. The **Moshav** is a smallholders' settlement; the **Moshav Ovdim** (Hebr. "workers' settlement"), is a workers' cooperative smallholders' settlement based on principles of mutual aid, individual holdings of national land, but cooperative purchasing of equipment etc., and marketing of produce; the **Moshav Shitufi** (Hebr. "cooperative settlement") is based on collective economy and ownership but individual family housing. In 1961, the 365 **moshavim** had a population of 120,000 (6.3% of total Israeli population). E.G.

Moshava (pl. moshavot).

(Hebrew "colony", "settlement"). In Israel it is the term for an agricultural village, in which farming is conducted on individualistic lines (privately owned land, private profit, etc.). The first moshava was established in 1880. Some moshavot have expanded to towns or become partly urbanized. E.G.

Mossadegh, Mohammed.
Iranian statesman. Born 1879. Served with finance ministry but fled country because of opposition to shah. After return, became minister of justice (1920), of finance (1921), and of foreign affairs (1922). 1923-27, member of Teheran majlis but because of opposition to new shah, was forced to resign. 1944-51, as member of majlis, studied problem of foreign oil concessions. March 1951, oil nationalization act passed; April 1951, Mossadegh elected premier. August 1953, tension between shah and Mossadegh resulted in overthrow of Mossadegh. Brought to trial and imprisoned for treason. Has lived in retirement since release in 1956.
H.G.S.

'Most Favored National' Clause.
A major principle embodied in the international trade agreements of the United States. Adopted in 1933 as a general policy, it calls for any benefits or concessions granted to a given country, to be automatically extended, without specific concessions in return, to all other countries; thus it makes the U.S. bilateral trade agreements multilateral in practice. The President of the U.S. can withhold this concession from certain countries that discriminate against American commerce, etc. Thus this clause is currently (1962) not applied to agreements with communist-controlled countries. W.N.

Motion.
1. A formal proposal by a member of an organization, body or group to secure action. 2. An application to a court for an order or ruling. K.E.H.

Mouvement Republicain Populaire.
This "party of the Fourth Republic", created in 1944, is the most recent representative of French political Catholicism. Composed mostly of "practicing Catholics", it seeks to be separated at least in name from the church. These Christian Democrats opposed both communism and capitalism, but swung toward the right, after the Pinay Government of 1952. Again moving left at the beginning of the Fifth Republic after the Bidault faction, insisting on "Algerie francaise", split off, the MRP has given qualified support to De Gaulle.

With about one fifth of the total vote in 1946, the MRP participated in "tripartism", but its membership was sapped by the RPF in 1947. Firmly attached to a parliamentary regime, it refused to help overthrow governments until its political enemy, Mendes-France, came into power in 1954, removing the MRP from the Foreign Ministry, which its leaders Bidault and Schuman had held for ten years.

The MRP lost power primarily on the issues of Indo-China policy and the European Defense Community. This "European party", however, was the primary instrument through which European integration was commenced in the Schuman Plan. Five party leaders resigned from De Gaulle's government in 1962 on the issue of European integration. R.B.C.

M.P.
Abbreviation for Member of Parliament. Although used in several countries and appropriate translations, the designation M.P. is commonly associated with the British House of Commons. R.G.N.

Multicentered societies.
An institutional order in which political decisions are made by a supreme authority restricted by recognized subsidiary political forces (estates, guilds, parliaments, political parties, an indepented public opinion), or by societal forces that, while not primarily political, unofficially and/or indirectly influence the government. Tribal societies comprise a variety of primitive political orders, many of them characterized by such forces. Complex multicentered configurations appear above the tribal level. In the city states of Homeric Greece monarchical, aristocratic, and plebeian forces asserted themselves with subsequent developments favoring varying combinations of aristocratic and plebeian forces. Republican Rome took a similar course, without going to plebeian extremes. In feudal Japan two major power centers emerged, the national government (the emperor and his shogun) and hundreds of vassals; temporarily certain Buddhist temples also exercised considerable influence. Medieval Europe moved from a simple to a complex feudalism

with four major recognized political forces: 1) the ruler and his representatives; 2) the nobility; 3) the Church; and 4) the non-aristocratic and non-clerical townspeople organized in guilds and enjoying varying degrees of self-government. (Cf. the classical manifestation of Europe's multicentered society: the Magna Carta.) Under post-feudal absolutism the central government tended to monopolize political power, but even when the subsidiary forces did not officially influence the regime's decision-making, the government had to take their interests into account. (The central governments of Western and Japanese absolutism were able to abolish the institutions of entail and primogeniture; and they could not tax the population generally as did Oriental despotism.) Among modern representative governments, the multicentered societies of the West and Japan have assumed new forms. Large units—big industry, big labor, big agriculture, big education, etc.—interact with differing strengths but effectively, and within some of these units the shrinking influence of the lower stratum (the shareholders in large corporations and the rank-and-file members in large trade unions) is partly counterbalanced by the lateral influence which the various units exert upon one another. Recent Fascist and Communist developments show that the elimination of one or two major countervailing forces may endanger, and even destroy, the multicentered character of the whole society.

K.A.W.

Multi-party System.

A number of political parties of relatively equal popular support and electoral strength compete for political power. Where these parties are legally permitted to function effectively, the system becomes associated with some measure of political democracy. In the multi-party system, the fact that all competitors have some chance of gaining a share of legislative seats makes them seek electoral victory actively rather than function merely as critics, as do many minor parties in the two-party system. Nevertheless, since the development of a multi-party system normally results from the existence of significant societal fragmentation on a socio-economic, ideological and possibly constitutional basis, the various parties tend to have a more well-defined doctrinal and program positions than do the major parties of a two-party system. Quite often, some of the parties may resemble special interest groups rather than truly national parties. Customarily, the multi-party system prevents any single party from gaining a legislative majority and so fosters coalition government. This, in turn, may produce political instability and, when occuring in a parliamentary system, tends to foster assembly government; the French Third and Fourth Republics and the German Weimar Republic being outstanding examples. Where the number of parties is limited and societal fragmentation is not excessive, however, the multi-party system can also produce reasonably stable coalition government; the Scandinavian countries being excellent examples. Generally, the multi-party system tends to represent a country's internal diversity and disagreement so well that national unity and effective political leadership may be seriously weakened.

D.W.

Multiplex society.

Usually a high-technology society undergoing change, in which modern pluralism (q.v.) has been developed into the distinguishing element, i.e., the society's decision-making and productive processes are carried out primarily by an inter-working and balancing of great numbers of varied and usually specialized institutions and organizations (e.g., political, social, religious, economic, industrial) dependent and impinging upon one another in many directions at many levels. (Formal political processes, such as elections, and governmental functions are but parts of the inter-working and balancing.) Distinct from centrally planned, monolithic societies. See confluent society.

J.B.L.

Mundt, Karl E.

Born June 3, 1900; US Senate from 1948 to January 3, 1949, from 1954 until term ending January 3, 1967; Republican-South Dakota; member of 76th-80th Congresses.

R.A.B.

Municipal Administration.

The application of policy to specific

cases within an urban governmental system.

Municipal administration has the same characteristics as general public administration except that it is sometimes argued that the central function of city government is administration. This argument holds that policy-making is much less important at the city level than other levels of government (state and federal) and that the prime need of cities is efficient administration. It is maintained, for example, that there is no Republican or Democratic way to build a street, simply a right way. This point of view has come under increasing attack in recent years. The attack centers on the need for effective political leadership and argues that there are important policy questions at this level of government. The retort to "the right way to build streets" argues that there may not be a Republican or Democratic way to build streets but that there is an important issue as to whether expenditures should be made for streets or for some other alternative purpose. As with administration at other levels of government there is in municipal administration the usual staff and line differentiation, although it is most pronounced in the largest cities. The role of staff (personnel, budgeting, planning, public relations, and organization and methods) has been increasing in the larger cities as the functions of city government become more complex. In general city governments have been following the lead of federal and state governments in making the administrative arm of government increasingly responsible to the chief executive. There remain, however, more independent and semi-independent administrative units at this level of government than at the state and federal level. A.K.C.

Municipal Government.

The government of municipal corporations which have been established to provide general local government for a specific population concentration in a defined area. Known variously as cities, boroughs, villages or towns (except in the New England states), such corporations generally employ one of three basic patterns of government— the mayor-council, commission, or council-manager plans. G.S.B.

Municipal Home Rule.

Municipal home rule is the right of a local government to draw up, validate, and amend its own charter, but this right is limited by the constitutional grants or legislative enactments which authorize home rule. In 1960, 23 states of the United States had effective constitutional validation for home rule. Seven other states had rescinded or never made use of similar grants of power. Each home rule charter represents an abdication of power by the legislature, and requirements that these charters be accepted by the legislature shows the reluctance with which that body accepts this fact. Each home rule charter is drafted by an official citizens' group and must be accepted by a prescribed majority of the voters involved. At one time hailed as the final answer for good city government, home rule charters are today no longer so regarded. Slightly over one-fifth of the cities in the United States which are eligible for home rule charters actually have them. A.E.N.

Municipio.

The basic administrative unit of local government in Latin America, with geographical boundaries similar in size to a county in the United States. Municipio is translated as "municipality," but it includes not only its headquarters or principal city, called a **cabecera**, but also one or more other villages, towns, or small population clusters. M.A.

Munnich, Ferenc (1886-).

Communist functionary, member of the government in Hungary.

Received University degree in Law in 1915. As prisoner of war in Russia in 1915, joined the Bolsheviks and fought in the ranks of the Red Army. Returned to Hungary in 1918 and participated in formation of the Soviet Republic of Hungary in 1919. After the collapse of the Communist regime, he escaped to Austria and later was politically active in Germany. In 1922 he settled in the Soviet Union, where he became a Soviet citizen. In 1936 he participated in the Spanish Civil War. In 1941 he returned to the Soviet Union and fought again in the Red Army.

After World War II, he assumed high Party and Government functions in Hungary. Ambassador to Finland, Bulgaria, Soviet Union, and, in 1956, to Yugoslavia. During the revolutionary events of October, 1956, he supported the government of Imre Nagy and became Minister of Interior on October 27. Resigned from his office and disappeared from Budapest on November 3, 1956, the day before the Soviet intervention. Returned to Budapest as Minister of Armed Forces and Public Security in the government formed by J. Kadar in Szolnok. After the overthrow of the legal government of Imre Nagy and the liquidation of armed and passive resistance, Munnich became Prime Minister in January, 1958. He held this office until September 1961, when he was replaced by J. Kadar. He is a member of the Politbureau of the new Hungarian Communist Party. I.B.

Munoz Marin, Luis.
Latin American statesman. Born in San Juan, Puerto Rico, Feb. 18, 1898. Education: Georgetown University, 1912-16. Sec'y. to resident commissioner for Puerto Rico in Wash. 1916-18. Editor, **Revista de Indias,** 1918-19. Publisher **La Democracia** 1920's. Member of constitutional assembly for Puerto Rico 1951. Elected first governor of Commonwealth of Puerto Rico for terms 1953-56, 1957-60, 1961-64. M.A.

Muskrat v. United States.
A 1911 decision by the United States Supreme Court which reinforced the Court's prior position that, by the words of the Constitution, it may hear only "cases and controversies." Here Congress had authorized certain named Indians to sue the United States and the law specified that the Attorney General of the United States should defend the suit. The purpose was to test the validity of some other Acts of Congress which restricted the conveyance of land to Indians. The Supreme Court held that there was legitimate conflict of interest between the United States and the Indians: the fact that Congress had stated the issue and designated the parties did not create a case or controversy. (219 U.S. 346). F.H.H.

Muslim Brotherhood (Ikhwan al-Muslimin).
A politico-religious revivalist association founded in 1929 in Ismailiya (Egypt) by Shaykh Hasan al-Banna, a former school-teacher and a watchmaker. Its ideology was based on the thesis that **Shari'a** (Divine Law) had established for all times the most perfect guidance in private as well as in public life. The Islamic State envisaged by al-Banna would be neither **Commu**nist nor Capitalist but one governed according to the **Shari'a** which is superior to all western ideas and institutions. Combining religious fanaticism with nationalistic fervor, opportunism with efficiency of organization, the Association spread all over Egypt and the rest of the Arab World. Religious indoctrination soon gave way to political agitation and terrorism. In 1948, the Egyptian Prime Minister, Nuqrashi Pasha, was murdered after decreeing the dissolution of the party and the confiscation of its property. Al-Banna, the Supreme Guide, was murdered a few weeks later, and the Association suffered a great loss in prestige and leadership. It was revived in 1950 to be finally liquidated by the Nasser Government after it had tried to infiltrate the militias created by the new regime and turn to its profit the revolutionary victory. A daring attempt on the life of President Nasser in October 1954 sealed its fate. Forced underground, the Association remains a force to be reckoned with, but time is running out with the forces of modernization taking over in the world of Islam as a whole. F.M.N.

Mussolini, Benito. (1883-1945)
Head **(Duce)** of Italian Fascist Government (1922-1943). Working class origin; socialist journalist until World War I when he became right-wing nationalist. Founded Fascist Party (1919); established dictatorship following "March on Rome" (1922). Deposed by Fascist Grand Council (1943); created fascist republic in north Italy; was captured and executed by Italian partisans. C.J.S.

M.V.D. See Appendix.

Mystique.
The French contrast "mystique" with

"politique" and tend to identify these, respectively, with **theory** and **practice** in politics. But a comparison is hard to make. **Mystique** relates to the specific ideological appeal of a political group (perhaps a sort of **Weltanschauung**). **Politique** relates to day-to-day policy in politics. The MRP mystique, for example, revolves around Christian humanism; the Gaullist mystique concentrates on the "eminent and exceptional destiny of France." R.B.C.

Myth.
Traditionally an explanation of first things in terms of good and evil personalized forces. In political philosophy, an explanation of first things that cannot be proven, yet fits in with the known facts. In recent political sociology, the underlying unquestioned explanations, usually emotion-laden, which are used to defend an existing or potential social and economic system. R.M.T.

N

N.A.A.C.P.
See National Association for the Advancement of Colored People.

Nagasaki.
City in southern Japan atom-bombed by the United States Army Air Force on August 9, 1945, three days after the atomic attack on Hiroshima. Out of a total population of 252,630, 73,884 persons were killed. Kogura had been the original target, but was obscured by clouds. The Japanese government offered to surrender to the Allies on the following day. During Japan's "Christian Century" (1549-1650), the Nagasaki area became the principal center of Christian activity, and from 1640 to 1859 Nagasaki was the only city in Japan open to foreigners, but only Dutch and Chinese were permitted access. When Christianity was made legal in the 1860's, several thousand Japanese were discovered to be worshipers of Christ notwithstanding two centuries of suppression of the faith.
T. Mc. N.

Naguib (Najib).
General Muhammad Najib was the leader but not the author of the military coup which ousted King Farouk from Egypt on July 26, 1952. A difference of opinion between him and Nasser (the revolution's actual engineer) resulted in Naguib's resignation and Nasser's assumption of complete control.
W.B.B.

Nagy, Imre (1896-1958).
Communist leader, Prime Minister of Hungary 1953-55, 1956.

Hungarian prisoner of war in Russia during World War I, he joined the Bolshevik revolution there. Returned to Hungary as a convinced and active Communist. Avoiding arrest, he fled to the Soviet Union in 1929, where he became a Soviet citizen and worked as an agricultural expert. In 1944 he returned to Hungary, becoming a prominent member of the Communist Party and of the Government: Minister of Agriculture in 1944, Minister of Interior in 1945, Speaker of Parliament in 1947, Deputy Prime Minister in 1952. In June, 1953, he replaced Matyas Rakosi as Prime Minister. His name is associated with the liberal policies known as the New Course: more consumer goods, retreat from forced collectivization of Agriculture, rehabilitation of political prisoners (Communists and former Social Democrats). He was ousted from office by the radical Stalinist group of Rakosi in April, 1955, and soon afterwards was expelled from the Party. Was readmitted to the Party during the new wave of rehabilitations in October, 1956. Appointed Prime Minister on October 24, the day after the first armed clashes of the Hungarian Uprising. Demanded and received the promise that Soviet troops would be evacuated from Hungary (October 30, 1956). The subsequent Soviet intervention (November 4, 1956) and unsuccessful resistance forced him to seek refuge in the Yugoslav Embassy in Budapest. Granted safe conduct by the Kadar regime, he sought asylum in Rumania. Later arrested, he was sentenced to death in a secret trial. His execution was announced on June 17, 1958. I.B.

Nansen Passport.
A travel document issued by the League of Nations for stateless people following the displacement of thousands of Europeans following World War I, named for the distinguished Norwegian arctic explorer, Fritjof Nansen, who was appointed commissioner for the resettlement of stateless persons in other lands than their own. R.B.

Napoleon I (1769-1821).
French military leader and Emperor.

Napoleon Bonaparte was born in Italy where his father was serving the French government in Corsica. At the age of sixteen he was made an officer of the French Army. His promotion to the rank of general came in 1794 and, by 1796, at the age of 26, he was made Commander-in-Chief of the Army of Italy. His campaigns in Italy and Egypt were successful. In 1799 he was named First Consul of the Republic; later he was named Consul for life; finally, in 1804 he was named Emperor of France. To counter the attempts of other European powers trying to encircle France, Napoleon instituted the "counter blockade". In 1812 he started his famous Russian Campaign which ended in total failure. By April, 1814, Napoleon was forced by the Russian-Prussian-Austrian-British allies to leave France and take up residence on the Island of Elba. Later he attempted a come-back in 1815, but met his Waterloo at the hands of the British. His legal reforms are significant contributions to civilization. W.C.C.

Narodnaya Volya (People's Will).
Russian terrorist group of the early 1880's. Narodnaya Volya was one of the successor organizations to Zemlya i Volya. Convinced that the assassination of the tsar would unleash a wave of reform, Narodnaya Volya made half-a-dozen attempts upon the life of Alexander II, before it succeeded in killing him on March 1, 1881. However, the assassination of Alexander resulted not in liberal changes, but in harsh repressive measures, including the destruction of Narodnaya Volya itself. D.N.J.

Nasser (Nasir).
Col. Jamal 'Abd al-Nasir rose to sudden fame after planning a military coup in July 1952 to oust King Farouk. The coup succeeded under the leadership of General Naguib (Najib). In the following years Nasser was successful in quietly ousting Naguib from the leadership of the revolution of which he became the sole leader to the present time. During this period Nasser effected the British evacuation from Egypt, nationalized the Suez Canal which precipitated the Suez invasion of 1956. Later he formed the United Arab Republic which united Syria with Egypt in 1958. When Syria severed this union in 1961, Nasser concentrated his efforts on establishing a Socialistic-Democratic-cooperative society in Egypt which might be a model for other Arab states. W.B.B.

Nation.
A derivative of natio (people) and nasci (to be born). Since the French Revolution nation connotes the concept of people who are conscious of their common historical and cultural background and who wish to perpetuate this background politically, i.e. within the framework of a state. J.D.

National Association for the Advancement of Colored People.
Founded in 1909 in U.S.A. by white and colored citizens with the goal of obtaining full citizenship rights and equality of opportunity for American Negroes. Numbers 350,000 members. Its methods have been those of militant propaganda, lobbying, mass pressure, and legal action. By its many Supreme Court victories it is responsible, more than any other group, for the increasing legal support of Negro rights. Roy Wilkins is Executive Secretary; the national office is in New York City; it publishes **The Crisis** and the **N.A.A.C.P. Bulletin**. R.E.Ch.

National Association of Soil Conservation Districts.
A nation-wide organization of Soil Conservation Districts and their State associations in the U.S.A. Soil Conservation Districts are instrumentalities of State Government. They are established to promote the conservation and orderly development of soil and water resources with maximum local participation. The National Association pools District experience and participates in the development of national policies affecting soil conservation. It exerts a significant influence on behalf of Districts, and is the most articulate voice for the exercise of grass roots responsibility in conservation and resource development. J.H.

National Committee.
See U.S. National Committee.

National Communism.
A post war variant of Marxism. Installed by Tito in Yugoslavia it was branded as a "heresy" and denounced as deviationism. Titoism manifested an ideology corresponding to the identification of the leadership principle with national aspirations, very similar to the **fuehrership** of Nazism and **caudillismo** of Spain and Latin America. National communism had its roots in Lenin's New Economic Policy (NEP) of 1921. During World War II, significantly named by Stalin, "The Great Patriotic War", Greek Orthodoxy was re-established for nationalistic purposes. Oppo-

sition to national communism as invalid deviationism arose very early under Trotsky and old line Bolshevists who considered it a betrayal of Marxism. But sheer survival was the main objective of this revisionism. Nationalism was considered a necessary tactic ultimately to be abandoned when communist strategy could be free to establish a world order. Titoism changed all this in 1948, and the Cominform was created to combat the new heresy. Yet it is a fact that the Communist Parties throughout the world, especially in the newly emergent African-Asian states and Latin America are still encouraged to employ nationalism to provoke disorders and civil wars. In the bloody Hungarian purge of 1956, the Soviet Red Army smashed the nationalist uprising. Recently Albania, Red China and Cuba are cited as examples of growing national communism. M.M.Mc.

National convention (of parties in U.S.A.)
A group of party members, elected for the purpose, to adopt a political platform and to nominate candidates for the presidency and vice-presidency. Meeting every four years, it is theoretically the highest governing body of the political party. M.B.D.

National Council of Farmer Cooperatives.
A nation-wide organization of farmer-owned and farmer-controlled business associations in the United States. Affiliated with the Council are local, State, regional, and national cooperatives engaged in the marketing of agricultural commodities or the purchasing of farm production supplies, or both. They range in size from a few hundred members to several hundred thousand. The Council exerts a significant influence on national legislation and government policies affecting cooperatives and their members, and participates in development of agricultural and economic policies of a national and international nature. J.H.

National Democracy.
First enunciated by Premier Khrushchev during a major foreign policy speech on January 6, 1961, the term refers to non-Communist, neutralist underdeveloped countries that pursue anti-Western, anti-imperialistic foreign policies, that adopt domestic programs deemed socialistic, rather than bourgeois or capitalistic in character, and that are considered likely to move closer to the socialist camp and eventually to constitute themselves as People's Democracies. National democracies are thus used to describe a transitional stage of political development in neutralist countries whose nationalist leadership is regarded as showing a "progressive" or pro-Communist orientation. In early 1963, Cuba, Ghana, Indonesia, and Mali, for example, were so categorized by Soviet writers. A.Z.R.

National Farmers Union.
A farm organization in the U.S.A. Formally designated as the Farmers' Educational and Cooperative Union. Founded in Point, Texas, in 1902, membership gradually spread north through the Midwest, but today its members (about 750,000) are mainly located in the Great Plains wheat belt. Its views are primarily oriented to the family-sized farm. It works for the economic interests of small farmers, farm tenants, and agricultural laborers and has sponsored a program of cooperative endeavors. C.W.B.

National Front.
(of German Democratic Republic.)
Soviet Zone mass movement founded (7/10/49) by the People's Congress to further German unification. Its member organizations aim to spread communism in Germany. Its basic units are House or Farm Communities. Its highest organ is the National Council headed by Erich Correns. It is staffed on all levels by communist functionaries. E.K.K.

National Grange.
A farmers' organization in the U.S.A. Originally founded as the Patrons of Husbandry in 1867 to give farmers an opportunity for social intercourse and intellectual advancement. The Grange achieved great strength as the spearhead of the agrarian revolt, but in recent years it has had somewhat less influence in farm politics. In general, the Grange works for price support policies and other governmental pro-

tections for its half million members, who are located primarily in the New England states. C.W.B.

National Interest.
In the "realist" (e.g. Hans Morgenthau) view of international politics, the national interest is the important guide to wise statesmanship. The concept of national interest contains two elements: "minimum requirements," involving the nation's physical, political, and cultural identity and integrity; "variables," depending on the political circumstances and traditions, the "total cultural context" within which a nation formulates its foreign policy. In the nuclear age it is imperative, according to Morgenthau, that a nation's national interest is defined by its statesmen in terms compatible with other nations' national interests. The continuous conflicts of national interests must be minimized by continuous diplomatic action. H.L.M.

Nationalism.
A modern political ideology focused upon the nation as the perfect community and stipulating the coincidence of a state's jurisdiction with the area inhabited by a compact nation as the ideal form of political organization. Beginning as an intellectual and cultural movement during the 18th Century, it developed into a conscious political force during the French Revolution when it became the basis of claims for political self-determination of nations, thus challenging the claims of ruling dynasties. Postulating self-determination as the right of all nations, and considering the nation merely a stepping-stone toward a cosmopolitan humanity, early nationalism became the standard liberal doctrine in the 18th and early 19th Centuries. Nevertheless, the nation eventually became the supreme object of adulation, displacing the earlier cosmopolitan goal. By the end of the 19th Century nationalism had become "integral" and was adopted as the ideology of conservative and other right-wing movements.

The international repercussions of nationalism have been varied. It has been responsible for the disintegration of multi-national empires as well as for the unification of formerly independent ethnic units. Moreover, intolerance and self-glorification have led to the assumption of a divinely ordained hierarchy of nations justifying encroachments of presumed superior nations upon the rights and freedoms of others. Because of the excesses perpetrated in the 20th Century in the name of the nation, nationalism has come to be widely frowned upon as the main source of the world's ills.

Despite the decline of the nation-state as an effective political unit, nationalism has received further impetus by World War II and is now professed with equal ardor by leftist and rightist movements. Closely associated with democracy, it has been an especially potent force in the newly emerged Asian and African states where it frequently precedes the existence of a nation. P.J.F.

Nationalistic Universalism.
The term is used to denote a change in the nature of nationalistic feeling in the twentieth century. Whereas the liberal nationalism of the nineteenth century looked only to the freedom of nations from alien rule, contemporary nationalism tends to impose its way on other nations. Its principal effect is a tendency to aggrandize; hence it has a divisive and unsettling effect on international relations. H.S.Th.

Nationalized Industries of France.
See French Nationalized Industries.

National Liberation Wars.
Soviet term for internal wars, usually waged by irregular, insurgent forces. Khrushchev has stated that such wars are inevitable and to be welcomed. The Program of the Communist Party of the Soviet Union (1961) states that such wars will be supported by all the means at the disposal of the Soviet bloc. Examples of national liberation wars, cited by Soviet sources, are the Castro revolution, the Algerian actions and the Viet-Cong insurgency.
W.D.J.

National Mental Health Act of 1946 (U.S.A.).
Provides for a number of grants-in-aid, particularly to encourage the hiring of state personnel for rehabilitative programs, to underwrite mental health

research, and to provide for psychiatric services at the community level.
C.R.A.

National Municipal League.
A private citizens' organization, founded in 1894, devoted to the improvement of state and local government and intergovernmental relations. From headquarters in New York City, it publishes the **National Civic Review** (formerly the **National Municipal Review**) and a wide range of model laws, constitutions, charters, and other publications dealing with reform of state and local government.
T.S.

National People's Congress.
See Red Chinese National People's Congress.

National Security Agency (NSA).
United States secret communications, cryptographical and intelligence agency, established on November 4, 1952, by Presidential directive, replacing the Armed Forces Security Agency established by the Secretary of Defense in May 1949. One of the most secret of government agencies, it has two primary missions: (1) protecting the world-wide American government secret communications and (2) producing intelligence information derived from its surveillance of secret communications of all foreign nations. Headed by a Director under the jurisdiction of the Secretary of Defense, it serves as the principal secret code-maker and code-breaker of the United States government. Headquarters at Fort George G. Meade, Maryland.
H.H.R.

National Socialism.
Ideology and movement created by Adolf Hitler (q.v.) in early Twenties in control of Germany 1933-45. Doctrine based on extreme racism: History viewed as struggle between superior and inferior races. "Aryan" nations, as highest groups, facing danger of racial mixture and of Jewish world control. Jews sapping strength of host nations through liberal-democratic ideas and institutions, which lead to (Jewish) capitalist-plutocratic rule, and through Marxism, which, through class struggle, divides nations and, as Communism, likewise means Jewish rule. Mission of National Socialist movement to wipe out divisive forces, establish genuine "people's community" under strong leadership, rearm nation, unite all Germanic people in a Greater Germany, defeat hostile West (especially France), finally conquer "living space" for German master race in East.

Movement built up as "National Socialist German Workers Party" under strict one-man (Hitler's) leadership, with fighting formations (SA: Storm Troopers, SS: "Protective Formations"), attracting nationalists resenting "fetters" of Versailles, small traders and professionals resenting Jewish competitors, savers having lost under inflation, unemployed under depression, finally financial backing by business fearful of left. Propaganda through emotionalism, symbolism (Swastika emblem, brownshirts, etc.), terrorizing opponents. Strongest inroads among non-Catholic middle classes, but never majority in nationwide free election.

After take-over establishment of totalitarian control: Hitler sole leader, unlimited powers, controlling all organizations including Nazi party (Gauleiter regional chieftains). Bureaucracy and courts coordinated under Nazi leadership. Elective institutions and freedom rights abolished, complete control of information and opinion, education, cultural activities. Opposition suppressed by secret police (Gestapo) with power to place anybody into "concentration camps." Major social groups Nazified (e.g., "Labor Front", "Hitler Youth"). Churches intimidated (but resistance, e.g., of Protestant "Confessional Church"). Economy regulated for rapid rearmament and war. Foreign-policy gains step by step, powers appeased through profession of peaceful intentions. Racial policy: Eugenic program ("mercy killing" of feebleminded); "non-Aryans" (Jews) forced to emigrate, remainder, together with millions of Jews from occupied Europe, deported to and gassed in "annihilation camps." National Socialist institutions spread over occupied Europe either through direct rule of party formations or through collaborationists ("Quislings"). In history unequalled in cruelty and fanaticism.
J.H.H.

N.A.T.O.
See North Atlantic Treaty Organization.

Natural Law.
It may be defined as a system of rules and principles for the conduct of human affairs independent of any positive legal enactment and deriving its existence from the rational intelligence of man that grows out of his nature as a rational and social being. The true significance of natural law lies in the function it has performed since classical antiquity as a moral standard with which to measure the actions of men and of governments, rather than in the legal doctrine itself.

The earliest notions of natural law can be traced to the Greek sophists of the fifth century B.C.; and in form of immutable principles of natural justice that govern man and society, the concept of natural law as a moral ideal can first be found in Plato. As an individualistically founded belief that all men are equal members of a universal society governed by the law of nature as the common possession of all mankind, natural law found mature philosophical expression with the Stoics, in this form, was given juristic definition by the Roman lawyers of the period immediately preceding our era as true law or right reason in accordance with nature, with universal application, unchanging and everlasting (Cicero). The jurists of the Digest of the Justinian Code recognized **jus naturale** in addition to **jus civile** (civil law) and **jus gentium** (the law of nations or, more accurately, the law common to all nations) as one of the three sources of law.

The Middle Ages gave to the idea of natural law a Christian spiritual foundation. In the writings of the early church fathers, natural law is explained as an expression of God's will for the providential government of man, revealed as an act of grace (St. Augustine). The Stoic notion of the universal brotherhood of all men becomes the belief that all men are the children of God and equal in the eyes of their creator. St. Thomas Aquinas, in his effort to synthesize reason and faith, defines natural law **(lex naturalis)** as the reflection of divine reason **(lex aeterna)** which God permits man to share through the faculty of natural reason.

With the secularization of natural law in the seventeenth century (Hugo Grotius), the concept finds a rationalist explanation and gives rise to the assertion of natural rights. The seventeenth and eighteenth century theory of natural law becomes in fact a doctrine of natural rights. From **jus naturale** signifying the objective ordering norm of things, the emphasis shifts to the subjective right of man to act in accordance with his nature. But natural law and natural rights are not antithetical (Hobbes), but correlative (Locke). There is a "right" in as much as there is a law (D'Entreves, **Natural Law**). The unalienable rights of man find expression in the American Declaration of Independence and in the French Declaration of the Rights of Man; but the Constitution of the United States is an expression of the fundamental or "higher law" (Corwin) ideal which has always been the essence of natural law.

Because of the ambiguities that it contains, the natural law concept has always been subject to challenge. Hume attacked it on the ground that it proceeded from a logically unsound conception of reason. In the nineteenth century the idea of natural law came generally into disuse. The historical school of jurisprudence (Savigny) criticized it for being historically ill-founded, and the views of the analytical school (Austin) and the positivist legal theories of the later nineteenth century, who conceived all law in terms of the sovereign will of the state, left no place for the natural law notion that law was above law-making. The social and political turmoil of the twentieth century, in particular the substitution by totalitarian dictators of their arbitrary will for the rule of law, has brought about a noticeable revival in natural law thinking. H.R.H.

Naturalization
The process by which a state grants citizenship to persons who have not acquired it by birth. C.W.B.

Navigation Acts (1651 on).
Laws of the British Parliament to stimulate shipbuilding throughout the Empire. British, American, and Irish ships were granted a monopoly of trade between England and the Colonies. Raw materials needed by English manufacturers which the Colonies might export to England only were enumerated. This policy of giving special trading privileges to England encouraged colonial smuggling.   R.F.H.

Nazi-Soviet Pact.
Non-aggression pact concluded on August 23, 1939 between Stalin and Hitler. It was signed in Moscow late at night by Molotov, newly-appointed Soviet Commissar of Foreign Affairs, and Ribbentrop, the Nazi Foreign Minister who had arrived by air during the day. The USSR was given a free hand in areas generally east of the 22d meridian and Germany in areas to the west. The pact was ratified on August 31 and Germany invaded Poland the next day.   W.D.J.

Necessary and Proper Clause.
The last paragraph (Clause 18) in Article I, Section 8 of the U.S. Constitution, grants to Congress the power "to make all laws which shall be necessary and proper for carrying into execution the foregoing powers, and all other powers vested by this Constitution in the government of the United States, or in any department or officer thereof." This clause, sometimes called the "elastic clause," is the basis for the implied powers exercised by Congress, which in turn has given the Constitution the flexibility necessary to permit the national government to handle the problems of an expanding nation.
     R.V.A.

Nehru, Jawaharlal. (1889-1964)
Prime Minister of India. Son of a wealthy Kashmiri Brahmin (q.v.) barrister, Nehru was born at Allahabad in 1889. At 15, he went to England, studied at Harrow, Cambridge, and the Inner Temple, where he qualified for the bar. Returning home in 1912, he began law practice. Eight years later, he joined the **satyagraha** (q.v.) struggle and eventually emerged as Gandhi's heir. He served nine prison terms totalling 3262 days. He was President of the Indian National Congress (q.v.) in 1929, 1936, 1937, 1946, and 1951. After a year as Vice-President of the Interim Government, he became India's first Premier in 1947, and retained this office till his death. At home, he instituted planned socialistic economic development, pushed through progressive social legislation, and created a secular democratic republic. Abroad, he has advocated non-alignment based on the **panch shila** (q.v.) concept. This policy has been put to a severe test by the Chinese incursions into India since 1959.   C.S.S.

Nenni, Pietro (1891-   ).
Leader of Italian Socialist Party. In early life Nenni was a journalist. After Mussolini took over the Italian Government he went to live in France. At the end of the Second World War he returned and served in the coalition government of De Gasperi. Towards the end of the 1950's the Italian Socialist Party was split into a left and a right wing. Nenni became the leader of the left wing but refused to accept dominance by the Communist Party.
     W.C.C.

Neo-colonialism. See Appendix.

Neo-Destour.
Organized by Habib Bourguibah after his disenchantment with the traditional order represented by the Destour Party. The Neo-Destour is progressive and western in its philosophy. Its organization is modelled after the most efficient western style party. Through its numerous cells it reaches every corner of Tunisia and thus orients the people to its philosophy. The party has organized "Destour Youth Associations" to indoctrinate the youths and to mobilize them into "action groups". The party has a president (elected by the members), a political committee, and a national council. A national congress is called every two or three years.
Since independence the Neo-Destour has functioned as the right arm of the regime. The party has become virtually coterminous with the population.
     E.A.S.

Neo-Hegelianism.
Term used to refer to British philosophical movement, beginning in the middle of the nineteenth century and continuing into the twentieth, the leading exponents of which were F. H.

Bradley and Bernard Bosanquet. The former advanced as an alternative to utilitarian ethical theory the doctrine of "my station and its duties" which he derived from his beliefs in the absolute and internal relations; the latter, in his **The Philosophical Theory of the State** and other writings, attempted to treat the state as an instance of concrete universality. J.W.Ch.

Neo-Kantianism.

Term used to refer to German philosophical movement of the late nineteenth and early twentieth centuries and marked by an attempt to ground in reason ethical, legal, and political principles. Among its leading exponents are Rudolph Stammler, who advanced the concept of a "community of free-willing men" as the test of legal validity, and Ernst Cassirer, whose work is distinguished by concern for rationality and moral freedom. J.W.Ch.

N.E.P.

See New Economic Policy.

Nepal.

(Area, approximately 54,360 square miles; population, estimated 8,475,000).

An independent kingdom on the southern slope of the Himalayas, Nepal is bounded on the north by Tibet, on the east by Sikkim and West Bengal, on the south and west by Bihar and Uttar Pradesh. Basically Mongolian with a considerable admixture of Hindu blood from India, the Nepalese were originally divided into many small clans and principalities. One of these, the Gorkha or Gurkha, gained predominance about 1770 giving its name to all inhabitants of the country.

From 1846 to 1951 the country was ruled by the Hindu Rajput Rana family which continuously held the Prime Minister's office and relegated the kings to a status of virtual prisoners. The Rana tenure ended on February 18, 1951, when the King proclaimed a constitutional monarchy and eight years later promulgated a constitution establishing the monarchy. In December 1959, however, he dissolved parliament and assumed sole leadership in order to establish "basic democracy."

Britain recognized Nepal's independence in a 1923 treaty. India also recognized her independence in a treaty signed in 1950. As the largest and most important of the three border hill-states (Nepal, Sikkim, Bhutan), Nepal receives a large annual subsidy from India plus extensive assistance in other forms. In September 1956 Nepal established diplomatic relations with China opening the country to vigorous Chinese economic and cultural activity. Nehru warned, in November 1959, that an attack on Nepal would be regarded as an attack on India. M.T.K.

Nepotism.

Literally, "nephewism." It refers to the practice of persons controlling political patronage to hire their own relatives. Although such a relative may be highly qualified or totally incompetent, the public generally assumes the latter. Legislators at the state and national levels not infrequently engage in nepotism, in part because of their lack of confidence in professional specialists who might not support the legislators' position. C.R.A.

Netherlands, Kingdom of the.

Consists of the Netherlands, the Netherlands Antilles, and Surinam. The Netherlands proper is located in Northwestern Europe, bounded by Germany, Belgium, and the North Sea. Capital: Amsterdam. Area: 12,528 sq. mi. Population (estimated 1963): 11,800,000.

Several duchies and counties, founded in the Low Countries by local noblemen after Charlemagne's death, were acquired by the Dukes of Burgundy in the 15th century and passed to the House of Habsburg (1477). They became Spanish through inheritance; by the end of his reign, Charles V was master over the Low Countries (1555). His son, Philip II, sent the Duke of Alba to check Dutch political and religious liberties. William the Silent, Prince of Orange (assassinated 1584), became leader of 17 rebelling provinces, comprising the Low Countries. By 1579, the northern seven provinces formed new union of United Provinces (Holland was leading province) and repudiated allegiance to Spain (1581). During the 17th century, its "Golden Age," the country enjoyed naval, economic, and artistic pre-eminence, and prospered by settlements in the East Indies and South America. France conquered the territory in 1795. Napoleon's brother, Louis, became King 1806 and abdicated 1810. The country was liberated in 1813. The Congress of Vienna, in 1815, set up the Kingdom of the Netherlands, composed of the United Provinces and the Southern Provinces (former Spanish Netherlands) under King William I of the House of Orange. The Southern Provinces rebelled in 1830 and set up the new Kingdom of Belgium.

The country's constitution, promulgated 1814, has been often revised. The country is a hereditary, constitutional monarchy. The monarch is Queen Juliana (since 1948, when Queen Wilhelmina abdicated). Executive power is in the hands of the Crown and the Cabinet under a Prime Minister. Legislative powers are shared by the Crown and the bi-cameral States-General, consisting of the First Chamber (with 75 members indirectly elected for 6 years, one-half every three years, by provincial legislatures) and the Second Chamber. It consists of 150 deputies, elected for four years directly by all Dutch citizens over 23 years (compulsory voting) through proportional representation. Ministers cannot be members but may attend the sessions of the States-General in advisory capacity. The country has a multi-party system, partly based on religious differences. A Council of State, appointed and chaired by the Sovereign and consisting of not more than 15 members, may be consulted on legislative matters.
M.C.V.

Neuberger, Maurine Brown.
Elected to the U.S. Senate (1960) after the death of her husband, Richard L. Neuberger (q.v.). Taught in Oregon public schools, served three terms in Oregon state legislature. Democrat, interested in protection of consumers and assistance to low income groups. First woman senator from Oregon.
F.M.

Neuberger, Richard Lewis.
(1912-1960).
U.S. politician and author. Democrat, Oregon state senator 1949-1954, U.S. senator from Oregon 1954-1960, proponent of planned development and conservation of natural resources in the Pacific Northwest of the U.S. Among his books are: **Our Promised Land, The** Lewis and Clark Expedition, Adventures in Politics—We Go to the Legislature. Prolific contributor to national magazines on political, historical and regional issues. Married (1945) Maurine B. Neuberger (q.v.).
F.M.

Neurath, Baron Constantine von
(1873-1956).
German Ambassador, Copenhagen, Rome, London (1919-30). Minister of Foreign Affairs under von Papen, von Schleicher, Hitler; dismissed 1938 (Successor von Ribbentrop). President, Secret Cabinet Council. Protector for Bohemia and Moravia, 1939; after sick-leave (1941) resigned 1943. Sentenced to 15 years at Nuremberg War-Criminals Trial. Released 1954.
M.C.V.

Neutralism.
From the Latin "neuter", meaning not to take sides, the adoption of an attitude of impartiality. The behavior of states professing such a policy varies from one of relative withdrawal or isolation to a policy of independent action and the avoidance of alliance arrangements. Hence the use of such terms as "positive" neutralism. A political concept, not to be confused with the legal concept of neutrality.
C.B.J.

Neutrality.
The legal and political condition of a state which adopts an attitude of impartiality toward belligerents. This attitude of impartiality creates rights and duties between impartial states and belligerents as follows: first, neutral states must not take sides in the war or assist either participant; secondly, neutral states have the right and duty to prevent their territories being used as a base for hostile operations and thirdly, neutral states must agree to certain restrictions imposed by belligerents on peaceful intercourse between their citizens and their enemies, particularly limitations of freedom of the seas. Unless expressly stipulated otherwise in a treaty, no duty exists for states to remain neutral upon the outbreak of war. The rights and duties of states in respect of neutrality are called into existence when the outbreak of war becomes known, when third states declare their intention to remain neutral, and when belligerents acquiesce in their choice.

These rights and duties expire with the termination of the war. Even signatories of the United Nations Charter can remain neutral if the Security Council is unable under Chapter Seven to arrive at necessary decisions regarding acts of aggression. C.B.J.

New Deal.
The phrase "New Deal" was used by President Franklin D. Roosevelt in his speech accepting the nomination at the Democratic National Convention in Chicago, Illinois, July 2, 1932, when he promised "a new deal for the American people." After his inauguration, Mar. 4, 1933, his administration proposed measures which were enacted into law which considerably increased governmental regulation of economic affairs and greatly expanded national welfare programs. It was partisan and controversial and included such laws as: The National Labor Relations Act (July 5, 1935), the Fair Labor Standards Act (June 25, 1938), the Social Security Act (Aug. 14, 1935), the Agricultural Adjustment Act (Feb. 16, 1938), and the Tennessee Valley Authority Act (May 18, 1933). J.R.B.

New Delhi.
Population: 124,000 (1951 Census). Capital of Republic of India. Sir Edwin Luytens designed the plan for the city, which was inaugurated the capital of British India in 1929. S.K.A.

New Economic Policy. (N.E.P.)
The Civil War which followed the Bolshevik Revolution in Russia resulted in the complete collapse of the nation's economy. New Communist Government regulations in agriculture took away all incentives for cultivating the land. The result was that while the 1916 harvest produced 74 million tons of grain, the 1919 harvest accounted for only 30 million tons. The droughts of 1920 and 1921 cut down harvest to a mere 18 million tons, which resulted in widespread famine. During these famine years more than 5 million people died of malnutrition. Lenin, here, proved his abilities and willingness to put the road to communism into reverse gear. A New Economic Policy was proclaimed in the spring of 1921 to save the sinking economy of the Soviet state. Peasants were suddenly permitted to sell their surplus produce on the open market, and this soon led to free trade, which was a limited form of capitalism. This New Economic Policy or N.E.P. was necessary to gain the confidence of the peasantry, to retain the communist power, and to increase the quantity of products. This new policy made it possible to supply agricultural products to the urban population, and also to produce raw materials for consumer goods. In 1929, when N.E.P. outlived its usefulness and the country's industrialization was on its way to success, it was abolished. V.P.P.

New England Town Meeting.
The Town Meeting is an annual gathering of all the eligible voters in a town, called for the purpose of electing town officers, deciding policy issues, and voting the taxes to pay for the town services. All qualified freemen can (and many, though not all, do) convene in response to a warrant of warning which specifically states each item of business to be discussed.

The New England Town Meeting originated in Massachusetts around 1630, and was originally open only to a limited segment of the male population of the town. In 1778, Vermont permitted all adult males who were not insane or in prison to participate and vote in town meeting. During the 19th Century the other New England states gradually adopted the same rules, but it took the Nineteenth Amendment to give women the same rights.

Under the original individual town charters, and the subsequent general state statutes which superseded the original documents, each town was an autonomous governing unit. While often eulogized as an example of pure democracy, actual practice often found a local rural boss making the decisions, while the Town Meeting under the domination of his henchmen docilely acquiesced. The Town Meeting often created and filled unique offices of local interest of which that of Hearse Warden is an example.

Today a very large population in a few towns has forced the adoption and use of a Representative Town Meeting with elected delegates, a new institution which has retained the form of the early town meeting while destroying the spirit. Elsewhere, except in very small rural towns, the Town Meeting has become a weak, attenuated reflection of its former robust self, and generally today it is often only the name which links the meetings in the six states, since each state has followed its own pattern. A.E.N.

New Jersey Plan.

During the formation of the Constitution of the United States, the small states urged revision of the Articles of Confederation to strengthen Congress' tax and commerce powers, the creation of a federal judiciary, and the Congressional election of a plural executive. Consideration of it revealed adjustments necessary to small-state acceptance of a strong government.
J.E.S.

Newtonianism.

The analogizing of Isaac Newton's mathematical, mechanical interpretation of physical phenomena to social and political institutions. Newton's contribution to physics, i.e., that phenomena follow uniform and knowable patterns, was extended by European philosophers and men of letters to fields other than physics. Eighteenth century philosophy, law, history, economics, and belle-lettres exhibited analogies to a mathematical interpretation of the non-physical world. The extension of Newtonianism was more prominent in Europe than American political theory; according to the analogy there are laws of politics as discoverable and regular as laws of physics. J.A.R.

New York School Prayer Case.

A case tried before the Supreme Court of the United States in 1962, in which the Court decided that the prescribing of a prayer in publicly-supported schools was a violation of the first clause of the First Amendment to the Constitution, as constituting an establishment of religion.

The prayer in question, drawn up by the New York Board of Regents, ran as follows: "Almighty God, we acknowledge our dependence upon Thee, and we beg Thy blessings upon us, our parents, our teachers, and our country." Recitation of the prayer was not compulsory upon students.

Five parents in New Hyde Park, Long Island, brought suit against the Regents, arguing that this prayer infringed the rights of their children. Although the New York Court of Appeals rejected this plea, the parents appealed to the Supreme Court of the United States, which in June ruled in their favor, by a vote of six to one.

The dissenting justice, Potter Stewart, wrote in his opinion, "I cannot see how an 'official religion' is established by letting those who want to say a prayer say it." Justice Black's majority opinion appeared to be a further step by the Supreme Court, in decisions extending over the preceding decade, toward a more distinct demarcation between the state and religious belief.
R.K.

New Zealand.

A British Dominion of 103,416 sq. miles. It has a length of 1000 miles long, and 180 miles wide. It is situated in the S. Pacific 1,200 miles S.E. of Australia. It comprises the North Island (44,280 sq. miles) and South Island (58,100 sq. miles). These are the two principal islands. Each island is about 500 miles long. Cook Strait which separates them, at its narrowest part, is only about 16 miles wide. Other islands are the Stewart Island (670 sq. miles) and Chatham Island (370 sq. miles). The principal cities are Auckland (the largest), Wellington (the capital), Christchurch (stock-raising) and Invercargill. The language spoken is English.

New Zealand has many lakes and rivers. The N. Island contains the Wanganue which is 150 miles long; the S. Island contains the Wairau, 100 miles long. Lake Taupe is in the N. Island and is 1,211 feet above sea level and 238 sq. miles in area; in the S. Island there are Te Anau (132 sq. miles) and Wakatipu (112 sq. miles) lakes. Mt. Cook (12,349 feet) is the highest peak.

New Zealand has a marine climate due to the narrowness of the island. Fogs are widespread and persistent. The annual temperature in Wellington is 54.8 F. and in Auckland it is 59.0 F. The chief port is Auckland and among the exports are: meat, wool, dairy products, wheat and fruit. Principal mining is coal, iron, mercury, manganese ore, sulphur and asbestos.

There is free public education with a minister of education. New Zealand universities comprise: Otage University (Dunedin, 1869), Canterbury University College (Christchurch, 1873), Auckland University College 1882, and Victoria University College (Wellington, 1897).

The estimated population of 1960 is 2,403,488. Two thirds of the New Zealanders live on the N. Island and one third live in Auckland and Wellington on the N. Island and Christchurch and Dunedin on the S. Island.

There are nine provincial districts: Auckland, Taranaki, Nelson, Marlborough, Otago, Hawk's Bay, Wellington, Westland, Canterbury. These districts are used for census purposes.

New Zealand was discovered in 1642 by A. J. Tasman (Dutch), visited by Captain Cook in 1769, by missionaries in 1814, and in 1841 New Zealand became a separate British colony. In 1907 it became a British Dominion.

The sovereign is Queen Elizabeth the Second. There is a Governor-General. There is a parliament consisting of a House of Representatives and a Legislative Council. Members of the Government are elected every three years. The Maori (who represent about 6% of the population) are represented in parliament by their own leaders and hold office by custom in the cabinet—but without portfolio. By the New Zealand Citizenship Act of 1948, New Zealanders also have status of British nationality. New Zealand is closely allied with G.B. and the Commonwealth. It is a member of SEATO and ANZUS.

There are two parties in the House of Representatives: the National Party with 46 seats and the Labor Party with 34 seats. The National Party was in office from 1949 to 1957 and won again in 1960. The party stands for property-owning democracy. It favors social legislation. The Labor Party governed from 1935 to 1959 and 1957 to 1960. It introduced much social legislation. It supports New Zealand's foreign commitments under SEATO and ANZUS and UN as well as international agreements to abolish nuclear weapons and other weapons of mass destruction.

In 1907, New Zealand adopted a national infant welfare system. In 1938 a comprehensive social security law was adopted, followed, in 1941, by a program of broad socialized medicine.

A number of outlying islands belong to New Zealand. Western Samoa is under a New Zealand trusteeship. Nauru is held jointly by New Zealand, Great Britain, and Australia. New Zealand administers the Ross Dependency of 175,000 sq. miles of ice-covered land in Antarctica.   J.F.M.

Nicaragua.

Population, 1,475,000; area, 57,145 sq. miles. Three themes dominate the political history of Nicaragua. First is the record of continual friction and civil strife between the Liberal Party, concentrated in the province of Leon, and the Conservatives primarily represented by the first families of Granada. Second, Nicaragua has historically experienced a succession of strong-man dictatorships, which have brought a modicum of stability at the price of suppression to a nation torn by factional conflict. Third, the country located athwart one of the principal sites of an interoceanic canal has always been an object of great power diplomacy, and has experienced a high degree of foreign intervention in her internal affairs.

During much of the twentieth century, Nicaragua was a virtual dependency of the United States. American marines were landed in 1910, to protect United States interests in the nation which primarily resulted from loans granted to relieve Nicaragua of large debts owed European creditors, accumulated during the fiscally irresponsible Zelaya regime of the turn of the century. The marines were not finally removed until 1932. In 1937, Anastasio Somoza came to power to rule the nation in strong-man fashion until 1956. Upon his assassination in that year, his son, Luis Somoza, assumed power. Elections are scheduled for 1963 to select a successor to the Somoza family which has dominated Nicaraguan politics for a quarter of a century.   Ch.W.A.

Nicholas of Cusa (1401-64).

An outstanding 15th century thinker, Nicholas of Cusa contributed to theology, science, politics, and church reform. His most important contribution was an elaboration of the conciliar theory in **De Concordantia Catholica** which was presented to the Council of Basel in 1433. Harmony rather than authority was the theme of this work. While this left in doubt the question of papal or conciliar authority, his later support of Pope Eugene IV resolved this question in favor of the papacy. However, his writing emphasized the principle of consent for "by nature men are equally strong and equally free." Scientifically he emphasized going to sources; consequently, he questioned the Donation of Constantine and the Decretals of the pseudo-Isador. R.W.T.

Nietzsche, Friedrich. (1844-1900)

German philosopher, psychologist, and moralist. He held that the "will to power" is the most basic human drive and capable of sublimation in artistic achievement and moral grandeur, or perversely in an ethic of resentment, which he identified with Christianity. His own ethic is fundamentally Aristotelian, although he depreciated reason. His work was admired by Freud and continues to influence existentialist thought. J.W.Ch.

Niger.

A republic in north-central Africa which achieved internal autonomy from France in 1958, and gained full sovereignty and membership in the United Nations in 1960. Area, 458,993 sq. mi.; pop. (est. 1960) 2,850,000; capital, Niamey. The legislative power rests with a popularly elected assembly of 60 members. A chief executive (President of the Council) is elected by an absolute majority of the assembly. The constitution provides for an independent judiciary. Niger cooperates with neighboring African republics in a variety of social and economic matters, including a customs union. The republic maintains close cultural and economic ties with France. T.S.

Nigeria, Federation of.

Area, 338,593 square miles; Population (UN est., 1960) 34,296,000; Capital, Lagos.

The first British Colony in Nigeria was established in 1861, and most of the territory was under British control by 1894. Negotiations with the British for Nigerian independence occupied a large part of the 1950's. By 1960 the Federation became independent and a member of the British Commonwealth.

Interest groups are in a transition stage and include religious, tribal and regional groups, women's organizations, and the more recently established trade union federations.

Major federal parties include the National Council of Nigerian Citizens (NCNC) from the Eastern Region and the Northern Peoples Congress (NPC) representing the most populous region; both of the parties participate in a federal coalition. During 1962 a state of emergency was declared in the Western Region when a struggle developed between two factions in the Action Group which was the federal opposition party and also had control of the government in the Western Region.

The Constitution for Nigeria establishes a parliamentary system in which the Governor-General (now Nnamdi Azikiwe, NCNC) serves as the Crown's representative, and the Prime Minister (now Alhaji Sir Abubakar Tafawa Balewa, NPC) is the member of the House most likely to command majority support. The Federal Parliament consists of a Senate with 52 members selected mainly by regional legislatures, and of the House of Representatives with 305 members directly elected from single member constituencies. An Election Commission supervises the establishment of constituencies and registration. All adults have voting rights except in Northern Nigeria where only males vote. The Federal Supreme Court can hear disputes between the Federation and Regions, appeals over constitutional interpretations, and can give advisory opinions.

Nigeria has a federal system, with three regions and the federal territory of Lagos. Each region has a Governor, Premier, and bicameral legislature with an elected Assembly and a House of Chiefs. The regional governments are concerned with social services, agriculture, education and local roads. In 1962 Six Years' Development Programs were major parts of federal and regional legislation. J.F.M.

Nkrumah, Kwame. (1909-)

The President of Ghana and life chairman of the Convention People's Party. Nkrumah was born in 1909, the son of a goldsmith, in Nkroful, Gold Coast. After having attended Catholic mission schools and the Government Training College in Accra, he taught school until in 1935 he began an extended sojourn in the United States. Having studied theology, economics, sociology, and education in several American universities, he travelled to England, where in 1945 he attended the Sixth Pan-African Congress. At this congress the future President of Ghana organized the West African National Secretariat, which the following year resolved to promote a west African federation as a step toward the unification of all Africa. Summoned by the leadership of the United Gold Coast Convention to become secretary general of this party, he arrived home in December, 1947 after a twelve year absence. Two years later, he formed the Convention People's Party, a mass party which under his dynamic leadership led Ghana to independence in 1957. As the ruler of Ghana, President Nkrumah has promoted Pan-Africanism, advocated neutrality in the cold war, and has tirelessly opposed colonialism and neo-colonialism. F.H.G.

"No Taxation without Representation."

A slogan of the American colonists prior to the Revolutionary War which was based upon the belief that Parliament had no right to levy taxes on the colonies since they were not represented in Parliament. The colonists maintained that the colonial legislature was supreme in the matter of taxation of the colonists. J.F.Z.

Nomination.

The naming or designating of a person for an elective or appointive office. The nomination may be partisan or nonpartisan, and is a preliminary part of the selection process. W.V.H.

Non-Aggression Pact (Soviet).

On 23 August 1939, Ribbentrop and Molotov, the then Foreign Ministers of Germany and the USSR respectively, signed a ten-year nonaggression pact. The agreement obliged each partner to absolute neutrality "should one of the high Contracting Parties become the object of belligerent action by a third power." In reality, it set the stage for Hitler's invasion of Poland and the partition of Poland between Germany and the Soviet Union. The secret protocol called for the partition of Poland and placed Estonia, Latvia, Finland, and Bessarabia within the Soviet sphere of influence, assigning Lithuania to Hitler's Germany.

The Nazi-Soviet non-aggression pact of 1939 differed in two notable ways from previous non-aggression pacts signed by the Soviet Union. First, it had no stipulation that "if one of the contracting parties should commit an act of aggression against a third party the other contracting party would be entitled to denounce the pact." Second, the last article of the Treaty stated that it was to "enter into force as soon as it signed," an unusual diplomatic provision. These departures from tradition constituted a tacit Soviet acknowledgement of the character of Nazi intentions—indeed, they openly encouraged Germany's aggressive designs. R.St·H.

Non-alignment.

"Isolationism," "neutralism," "positive neutrality," "neutrality," and "non-alignment" are names give by different nations at different times to largely corresponding policies. The common thread of these policies is freedom from entangling military alliances. While "neutrality" has been applied to the slightly different postures of Switzerland, Sweden and Austria, "neutralism" was the term applied by underdeveloped nations of Asia and Africa to their post-war policies of freedom from either of the bi-polar military blocs associated with the U.S. or the U.S.S.R. When this policy was castigated as immoral, it was replaced by the more descriptive "non-alignment." R.W.T.

Nonbelligerency.

An expression which in 1939, at the start of World War II, was coined by the Italian Foreign Office, if not by Mussolini himself. It was adopted in 1940 by the government of Turkey and in 1941 by the governments of Spain and Argentina. The meaning of the expression varied. It meant a wait-and-see attitude of temporary neutrality in the case of Italy; "benevolent" neutrality toward France and the United Kingdom and, after the fall of France, a pious reference to the remaining alliance with the United Kingdom, in the case of Turkey; clandestine disregard of the rules of neutrality in favor of the Axis Powers and an open breach of neutrality toward the U.S.S.R., in the case of Spain; a short-lived partiality pure and simple in favor of the United States in the case of Argentina. F.G.

Non-immigrant visitors.
Aliens visiting the territory of a state temporarily for business or pleasure without intent of seeking permanent residence. C.W.B.

Nonpartisan.
1. Pertaining to an entity (e.g., election, ballot, person, group, attitude, or policy) not characterized by recognition of a political party or of its interests as such. This term is relative. For example, an administration may be conducted in a way which recognizes not only the interests of the chief executive's party, but also, in some degree, those of opposition parties—sometimes designated a "quasi-nonpartisan" administration; e.g., the governorships of Lausche in Ohio and Warren in California.

2. The same meaning as (1), but applied to political ideology. Term used in this sense describes a virtually non-existent situation.

3. A person who is nonpartisan. D.W.Mc.

Nonpartisan Ballot.
A ballot which contains no party designations after the names of candidates. D.W.Mc.

Nonpartisan Board (or Commission or Committee).
In the case of an appointive board, a governmental body whose members are not formally designated as belonging to certain parties. In the case of an elective board, a body whose members are elected without designations of their party affiliations appearing on the ballot. However, with both types, nonpartisanship is frequently only nominal—the appointing authority may allocate a certain number of memberships to each party, and the voters may be aware of the party affiliations of board candidates. D.W.Mc.

Nonpartisan Election.
1. An election wherein party affiliations of candidates do not appear on the ballot. However, in some jurisdictions, party organizations endorse and support some or all of the candidates, and the public is aware of their affiliations; e.g., in England (candidates for the House of Commons), and Chicago (candidates for alderman). Widely used in the U.S. to select local officials, and, in Minnesota and Nebraska, to choose legislators.

2. A state or local election wherein candidates do not bear the labels of national parties. Technically inconsistent, as this term does not imply exclusion from the ballot of state and local party designations. D.W.Mc.

Nonpartisan League (NPL).
An organization formed in North Dakota (U.S.A.) in 1915 as a nonpartisan body to reform the system of marketing farm products through public ownership of public necessities. Although organized later in about a dozen midwestern states, it achieved political power only in North Dakota. After its defeat in the recall election in 1921, the NPL continued to exist as the liberal faction of the Republican party. It filed its candidates in the Democratic primary in 1956, later merging with the Democrats to form the NPL-Democratic party. R.V.A.

Nonpartisan Primary.
A primary election wherein party designations of candidates do not appear on the ballot. Consequently, no test of party affiliation need be met by voters. The highest vote-getters among the candidates, numbering twice the number of offices to be filled, become candidates at the general election. In some jurisdictions, any candidate who receives a majority of the total vote cast for an office in the primary is declared elected. Generally found in the same jurisdictions as the nonpartisan election. Party influence may also be present. D.W.Mc.

Nonpartisanship.
The practice of being nonpartisan,

or the quality of possessing nonpartisan characteristics. Syn. nonpartisanism.
D.W.Mc.

Non-Party System.
A pattern of political life within a jurisdiction characterized by the absence of parties. Where such a system prevails, the choice of officials is based far more on their abilities or their efficiency and honesty in carrying out policies widely approved by the citizenry than upon their policy declarations or decisions. A government operating under such a system may be called a non-party or nonpartisan government.
D.W.Mc.

Non-Violent Protest Action.
The use of organized civil disobedience to protest and compel remedy of political, economic, and social suppression and discrimination with emphasis upon determined avoidance of violence.

Mahatma Gandhi's India independence movement is the classic modern example. Gandhi stressed moral suasion, mass strikes, and other obstructionist demonstrations against British rule, rejecting violence even in retaliation or defense.

In the U.S., Southern Negro college student-led desegregation efforts use this approach exclusively. The techniques employed include the "sit-in," "Freedom Rides," and economic boycotts with federal executive protection and support. Dr. Martin Luther King Jr. is the movement's symbolic leader.
N.P.T.

Non-voting.
Failure of eligible voters to exercise their franchise. May be due either to a rational rejection of the choices presented or to a weak sense of involvement in the political system. Groups which have a higher proportion of nonvoters than their counterparts are: those with low incomes, unskilled workers, those with few years of formal education, young voters, women, persons cross-pressured by membership in groups with different partisan positions, those with no membership in voluntary organizations, and those with weak or no partisan attachments.
J.S.S.

North Atlantic Treaty Organization.
An organization of states formed in 1949 at the instigation of the United States for the protection of West and Central Europe against the extension of Soviet control. Its membership comprises the United States, the United Kingdom, Canada, France, West Germany, Italy, Portugal, Denmark, Norway, Iceland, Belgium, Holland, Luxembourg, Greece, and Turkey. Resting on the principle of collective security, it has a considerably more effective military organization than the U.N., including a permanent military headquarters, Supreme Headquarters Allied Powers Europe (SHAPE), under the command of an American general. In order to render the organization more enduring than earlier offensive alliances and thus equip it for a protracted Cold War, military cooperation has been accompanied by attempts at some measure of economic and cultural integration. In assuming the leadership of a peacetime alliance, the United States has responded to the consolidation of Soviet control in Eastern Europe by abandoning its traditional isolationist policy.
P.J.F.

Northern Ireland—Supreme Court.
Under the Government of Ireland Act of 1920 there was established a Supreme Court of Judicature composed of two branches, a Court of Appeals in Northern Ireland and a High Court of Justice. In 1930 a Court of Criminal Appeal was established to parallel the Court of Appeal in Northern Ireland. In certain instances, a further appeal may be taken from the Supreme Court of Northern Ireland to the House of Lords.
C.A.McC.

Northern Tier.
A geo-political concept of the Cold War that Turkey, Iraq, Iran and Pakistan form a natural grouping for Middle Eastern defense. Growing from a British need to restate its relations with Iraq and from Turkish and American desires to provide regional defense, the idea became concrete in the Baghdad Pact of 1955 among the northern tier states, plus Britain, with American aid but not membership. Egypt and other Arab nations denounced the pact and Iraq withdrew after the 1958 **coup d'etat.** The pact continues as CENTO. The concept may derive from Sir Olaf Caroe's **Wells of Power.**
P.F.P.

Northwest Ordinance.

Was enacted by the Congress of the United States in 1787 for governing territories north of the Ohio and east of the Mississippi rivers. Representative government, religious freedom, jury trial, public education, admission of new states into the Union were among its principles. This set the government pattern for other territories.   J.E.S.

Norway. See Appendix.

Nuclear deterrents.
(nuclear deterrence.)

The doctrine that the possession of a significant nuclear capability (or more accurately, of a significant capability in weapons of mass destruction) by more than one state has abolished all-out war among possessing states; or that this condition has rendered such warfare less likely; or that it will do so, if the nuclear nations act rationally. Exactly what is deterred besides all-out war is a disputed point.

This doctrine assumes that even a surreptitious, counterforce nuclear attack by one of the possessing powers could not deprive another such power of the ability to retaliate with a devastating riposte. Realizing this, nuclear statesmen take all measures necessary to prevent such a suicidal attack, and adopt the defensive strategy of threatening to retaliate if another possessing state uses the big bombs first. The result is stalemate, imposed by the logic of the nuclear age.

This optimistic doctrine has gained wide currency in the West since 1954. Skeptics (Soviet writers are included in this category.) deny its validity, either because they question the military assumptions upon which it is based or because they deny that the big bombs act as a restraint upon nuclear statesmen. Pessimistic observers warn of the possibility of mistakes, the unsettling effects of a technological breakthrough in weapons technology, and the increased dangers of the future dispersal of nuclear weapons. F.H.G.

Nuclear Pause.

A Cold-War strategy in U.S. military-political policy. The hypothesis of the policy is: given an attack by Soviet conventional forces, U.S. defense would be limited to counter-conventional forces. The theory is that such confinement to defensive conventional weapons—in view of a conventional attack—would create a military stalemate during which time both sides would have political negotiating possibilities to prevent the use of atomic weapons and nuclear war.   R.A.B.

Nuclear stockpile.

The stock of atomic and hydrogen weapons at the disposal of the nuclear powers, which at present consist of the United States, the Soviet Union, the United Kingdom, and France.

Much evidence indicates that the United States has reached a position of nuclear abundance. Representative Bruce Alger of Texas in November, 1961, estimated the U.S. nuclear arsenal at 35,000 to 40,000 weapons with a total explosive force equal to 35 billion tons of TNT. The Atomic Energy Commission spent $516,000,000 for nuclear weapons in fiscal 1961; and in May, 1962, the U.S. government reduced its procurement of some types of nuclear warheads, because of an adequate supply of them. U.S. stocks consist not only of high yield strategic weapons to be transported to their targets by bombers, missiles, and submarines; but also lower yield tactical weapons. The latter include short-range missiles, atomic artillery, and a bazooka-type rocket operated by one infantryman.

The Soviet stockpile is generally considered to be inferior to that of the United States. The Soviet tests in the fall of 1961 revealed, however, that the U.S.S.R. has developed a hydrogen device of some 55 to 60 megatons and that the Soviet Union may have surpassed the U.S. in certain categories of weapons. The British stockpile includes atomic and hydrogen weapons, the French only the former. Neither of these Western European states has attained the nuclear position of the two superpowers.   F.H.G.

Nuclear weapons.

Weapons whose energy is derived either from the fission of heavy atoms (atomic weapons) or from the fusion of light atoms (hydrogen weapons).

A distinguishing feature of nuclear weapons is their lethal efficiency. Approximately 30 per cent of the inhabitants of Hiroshima were killed by one atomic bomb, contrasted with a one per cent urban morbidity rate caused by all conventional raids on German and Japanese cities during World War II. Casualties result from the blast, heat, and radiation of the nuclear devices: radiation is particularly dangerous in the case of large hydrogen bombs. Nuclear weaponry has advanced from the Hiroshima-Nagasaki type of atomic bomb of twenty kilotons (with a blast effect equivalent to 20,000 tons of TNT) to the 1961 Soviet thermonuclear test devices of approximately fifty-five to sixty megatons (with a blast effect equivalent to from 55,000,000 to 60,000,000 tons of TNT). A major step in this development was the fabrication of hydrogen devices by the U.S. in the fall of 1952 and by the Soviet Union nine months later. Besides providing a whole spectrum of high-yield strategic weapons together with heavy bombers and missiles for their delivery, military technology is developing a number of tactical weapons for use against enemy combat troops. F.H.G.

Nuncio.

The representative of the Holy See (now in some 30 states). According to the Vienna Protocol of 1815 the apostolic nuncio has the rank of ambassador. He customarily is the dean of the diplomatic corps. S.E.

Nuremberg Trials.

An Inter-Allied Declaration signed by nine European countries at St. James' Palace, London (January 13, 1942) marked the beginning of a program for bringing war criminals to justice "through the channel of organized justice." Similar announcements by President Roosevelt and the British Lord Chancellor Viscount Simon (October 7, 1942) and at the Moscow Conference (October 30, 1943) followed. The final result of Inter-Allied negotiations was the 'London Agreement for the Prosecution and Punishment of the Major War Criminals of the European Axis' and an annexed 'Charter of the International Military Tribunal' signed on August 8, 1945 by the representatives of the United States, France, Great Britain and the Soviet Union. The following acts came within the jurisdiction of the Tribunal: Crimes against peace, such as planning, etc., of aggressive wars, furthermore war crimes such as murder, ill treatment of prisoners of war and civilian population, etc. (finally crimes against humanity, namely mass murder, exterminations for political and racial reasons). Thus, a new judicial organization in the field of international criminal justice came into being. Its main architect was America's representative, the late Associate Justice of the U.S. Supreme Court, Robert H. Jackson. As his biographer Eugene C. Gerhart states in 'America's Advocate: Robert H. Jackson': "he had the faith to believe that his tremendous task was of the highest value to the world and he had the courage to confront appalling difficulties and triumph over them all." The City of Nuremberg (in German: Nurnberg) was selected as site of the Tribunal; Jackson, the one-time U.S. Attorney General was appointed Chief American Prosecutor by President Harry Truman. Francis Biddle became the American Justice and Judge John J. Parker his alternate. The other justices were: Lord Justice Lawrence, and his alternate Justice Birkett for Great Britain, Le Professeur Donnedieu de Vabres and his alternate Conseiller R. Falco for France, and Major General I. T. Nikitchenko and his alternate Lieutenant Colonel A. F. Volchkov for the Soviet Union.

The defendants before the IMT were: Hermann Goering, Rudolf Hess, Joachim von Ribbentrop, Wilhelm Keitel, Ernst Kaltenbrunner, Alfred Rosenberg, Hans Frank, Wilhelm Frick, Julius Streicher, Walter Funk, Hjalmar Schacht, Karl Doenitz, Erich Raeder, Baldur von Schirach, Ernst Sauckel, Alfred Jodel, Martin Bormann (in absentia), Franz von Papen, Arthur Seyss-Inquart, Alfred Speer, Constantin von Neurath, Hans Fritsche.

After the end of the trial before the IMT on October 1, 1946 twelve subsequent trials have been held against other major war criminals at Nuremberg before courts each composed by three American judges. The judicial basis was Control Council Law No. 10, patterned after the London Agreement. Brigadier General Telford Taylor was appointed Chief Prosecutor and filed twelve indictments against members of the following agencies or organizations: 1. Doctors of infamy; 2. Air Force Field Marshal Erhard Milch; 3. Jurists who had perverted justice; 4. Officers of the economic administration of the SS; 5. Officers of the Flick industrial empire; 6. Officers of IG Farben, 5 and 6 mainly for spoliation and slave labor; 7. Army generals mainly accused for crimes against humanity in South Eastern Europe; 8. Officers of the Race and Settlement Office of the SS for crimes against humanity; 9. Officers of the special task forces because of mass murder of Jews and other minorities in the East; 10. Officers of the Krupp munitions empire for spoliation of slave labor; 11. Wilhelmstrassen case the most important trial after the IMT Trial against Hitler's cabinet members and diplomats as well as officials of its economic administration, for participation in genocidal actions, spoliation and similar crimes; 12. Members of the High Command of the Wehrmacht for war crimes and crimes against humanity.

A total of 199 defendants were in the Nuremberg docks, 38 have been acquitted, 36 sentenced to death, about two thirds of them executed; the rest received prison terms but all were released from prison under heavy German pressure until about the year of 1951. Only in the year 1958 a newly created Central Office of the German States started series of war crimes prosecutions before the German courts mainly against chiefs of concentration camps and officers of the so-called Einsatzgruppen. R.M.W.K.

O

Oder-Neisse Line. See Appendix.

OECD. See Organization for Economic Cooperation and Development.

Office block ballot.
A form of ballot used in about twenty states of the United States in which names of candidates with or without party designations are grouped under the office for which they are contending. This has tended to discourage straight party voting and compels the elector to note the names of persons for whom he is voting. B.N.

Office of Emergency Planning.
In the U.S. national government, located in the Executive Office of the President. This small coordinating and planning agency assists the President in developing policies for emergency use of strategic resources, facilities, and manpower. It also develops policies for civil defense (actual operations are in the Defense Department) and post-attack requirements of the government and civilian economy. Created in 1961, the OEP is the successor to the National Security Resources Board (1947-1953), the Office of Defense Mobilization (1950-1958), and the Office of Civil and Defense Mobilization (1958-1961). R.D.S.

Offshore Islands.
See Quemoy and Matsu.

Offshore Oil Controversy.
A federal-state dispute in the United States, in which the states had the support of oil producers, concerning jurisdiction of the continental shelf between the low water mark and the three-mile limit. Historically, the national government exercised few controls over these lands. The Supreme Court in 1947 and 1950 found federal jurisdiction paramount. The issue was settled by the Submerged Lands Act of 1953 which quitclaimed to the states the offshore areas for three miles. T.S.

Oficial Mayor.
In Latin American governmental ministries or agencies, especially Mexico, the manager of housekeeping functions of the ministry and the supervisor of various units of the agency, directly responsible to the subminister or undersecretary, sometimes the third or fourth ranking official of the ministry or agency. M.A.

Ogdensburg Agreement.
The joint declaration — enunciated August 18, 1940, as a brief press release — by President Franklin D. Roosevelt and Prime Minister W. L. Mackenzie King, at Ogdensburg, New York, that the United States and Canada would set up at once a Permanent Joint Board on Defense "to consider in the broad sense the defense of the north half of the Western Hemisphere." The agreement not only contributed greatly to the winning of the war but also marked the opening of a new era in Canadian-American relations.
W.W.

Old Age Assistance (U.S.A.).
Financial aid for elderly persons ("old age pension") provided partly by state governments and partly by the Federal government under the Social Security Act of 1935. This grant system is one of the so-called "categorical aids" established by the act. It is a form of **public welfare** and, as such, is to be distinguished from Old Age and Survivors' Insurance ("social security"), which is financed largely through contributions of employers and employees, and is thus a form of retirement **insurance**. Assistance is based on need, insurance on a right established by the payment of premiums. C.R.A.

Oligarchy.
1. A form of government in which rule is by the few, who govern in their own interest. 2. Those who govern an oligarchy. 3. Those who do not possess official authority but whose power enables them strongly to influence the conduct of governmental affairs.
M.J.H.

Ollenhauer, Erich (1901-1963).
Erich Ollenhauer was the present leader of the German Socialist Party (SPD) and also headed the socialist opposition in the **Bundestag**. He occupied these positions since the death of Dr. Kurt Schumacher in August of 1952. Mr. Ollenhauer had been connected with the German labor movement since

his youth. He was from 1920 until 1928 editor of the **Arbeiterjugend,** the organ of the Socialist Youth organization whose chairman he became in 1928 until its enforced dissolution under Hitler in 1933. He also served as secretary of the International Socialist Youth Organization from 1921 until 1945.

During the Third Reich he lived in the emigration in Prague, Paris, and London remaining active as a member of the executive committee of the German Socialist Party in exile.

After the Second World War he assisted in the reconstruction of the German Socialist Party and was elected at the first Party Congress in May 1946 as Vice-chairman of the party. Since the establishment of the Federal Republic of Germany in 1949 he was a member of the **Bundestag.** E.W.

On.

A part of the Japanese traditional moral code which controls the vertical social relationships. Developed in the Tokugawa period, it established the power of the father over the rest of the family. H.U.

On New Democracy.

A policy statement written by Mao Tse-tung, chairman of the Chinese Communist Party, in 1940, which announced a program that envisioned an alliance of all "revolutionary classes" in China, including the "progressive bourgeoisie", under the leadership of the Chinese "proletariat". This joint revolutionary force was to carry out a "bourgeois - democratic revolution" which would merely be the first stage in the ultimate development of a Communist state. The state produced in this stage of the revolution would be a transitional form of government—the New Democracy—standing between the old "feudal, semi-colonial and colonial" regime and the Communist order to follow.

The New Democracy was to take the form of a republic under the dictatorship of all anti-feudal and anti-imperialist people embracing Dr. Sun Yat-sen's "Three Peoples Principles" and his Three Great Policies. Under the New Democracy government all large enterprises were to be nationalized and land reforms were to be implemented. The peasantry was assigned a large role in the revolutionary movement.

On New Democracy was perhaps intended as an enticement to the Chinese bourgeoisie to participate in the Chinese Communist movement, or at least to split them from the Kuomintang. The concept of a multi-class revolutionary front under the leadership of the proletariat became a basic doctrine for the Chinese Communists. The work was widely published and distributed and is considered today to be a major document in the history of Chinese if not world Communism. S.S.

One-Man Command (edinonachalie).

Principle introduced into the Red Army to replace the previously existing principle of political commissars. One-man command makes the military unit commander responsible for both the military and political training of his outfit. The principle has been suspended several times in the past but is currently in effect in the military and other (e.g. industrial) areas.

W.D.J.

One-Party System.

One officially sanctioned political party is authorized a legal monopoly of all formally organized political activity. Since this monopoly eliminates that political competition essential to Western democracy, the one-party system is characteristic of modern authoritarianism and particularly of modern totalitarianism. In this system, the single party customarily functions as a political elite whose membership is restricted to persons meeting certain ideological and other standards. Employed by the regime to indoctrinate, discipline, organize and test the loyalty of the masses as well as to provide political guidance to the bureaucracy and armed forces, the single party is either an important control device of a personal dictator or the ruler of the state under its own supreme leader(s). Where the single party is not only a control agency but also a primary leadership source (as in modern totalitarianism), it will customarily conduct political training schools at age levels ranging from childhood to adulthood whose purpose is both to indoctrinate and to create future leaders for the regime. In such circumstances, criti-

cism of or opposition to the party may be equated with treason to the state, punishable by state agencies, and non-party members find it extremely difficult to obtain important positions in government, the economy, or society. Justifications normally provided for the one-party system are that one particular party alone has a monopoly of political truth while all others are either disruptive or treasonous. Outstanding examples of this system are Nazi Germany, Fascist Italy, and the contemporary Communist states.
D.W.

Open Door Policy.
Pertains to U.S. claim to a full share in the trade with China at the end of the Nineteenth Century. It is credited to John Hay, U.S. Secretary of State, who enunciated this policy in identical notes sent to the governments of those countries, foremost among them Britain and Japan, which seemed to be bent on carving out monopolistic trade areas for themselves and in the process destroy all vestiges of Chinese sovereignty.
J.D.

Open Primary.
The type of direct preliminary election used to nominate candidates in about thirteen states in the United States. Voters are permitted to decide on primary election day in which party primary they wish to vote. Only after they are in the privacy of the voting booth do they have to choose among the parties whether paper ballots or voting machine are used. Washington State uses the blanket or wide-open variation of this. There, voters not only may choose the party in whose primary they wish to participate, but may change their choice from office to office.
A.G.

Opinion research.
Technique of determining the opinion of a "universe" (any defined group, including the general public) on any given issue, set of candidates for office, etc. Originally, this was done entirely by probability sampling of small numbers of "respondents," either through personal interviews (as in the Gallup Poll, q.v.) or mailed questionnaires asking objective questions carefully controlled to avoid "bias." Increasingly other techniques, notably depth interviews, which may reflect a subjective influence by the interviewer but which are more illuminating of underlying factors, are being added to the methods available. As distinct from a "random" sample, selecting persons to interview simply by chance, the probability sample is designed by determining the number of persons of each pertinent characteristic (e.g., sex, age group, income bracket, geographical location, etc.) which must be balanced into the total sample, before selecting the particular respondents of each type by random methods.
J.B.L.

Opium War. (1840-1842).
Named for the Chinese at Canton burning British opium imported from India, this war arose from the British desire to reduce the heavy Chinese restrictions on trade and intercourse. China was forced to accede at Nanking to her first "unequal" treaty.
G.O.T.

Optional Charter.
Drafted by the state legislature. Alternative organic acts of government available to cities of a certain classification. City may choose "cafeteria style" from among a series of prepared charters, but cannot draft its own charter as can home rule cities.
P.J.C.

Optional Clause.
Set forth in Art. 36 of the Statute of both the old Permanent Court of International Justice under the League of Nations and the International Court of Justice under the United Nations, calling for compulsory jurisdiction of the Court in all legal cases. Some thirty-five member states are now bound by the optional clause, but lacking universality and owing to inimical reservations by the Great Powers its effectiveness has been gravely weakened.
M.M.Mc.

Ordinance.
In the U.S.A. presidential or administrative orders are sometimes called ordinances. Congress will pass a skeleton bill; the president, by ordinance, will fill in the details. A state governor has similar authority to expand the scope of a general statute passed by the state legislature. The laws of a

city council are called municipal ordinances. M.F.

Organic theory of the state.
Two contrasting views: 1. The **biological** organic view, exemplified by Herbert Spencer who applied the evolutionary theories of Darwin and Lamarck, drawing far reaching analogies between the biological and social organism. "Mechanistic" in its philosophy, it devalues the role of intellectual and moral forces. 2. The metaphysical organic theory, based on Aristotle and St. Thomas Aquinas, emphasizes unity, continuous interaction and interdependence of the whole and its members. The state is a moral organism, "everyone for the common good and the common good for everyone." Private and public associations and institutions present a "genuine" pluralism which does not dissolve the unity of the state. Constitutional democracy corresponds to this theory of the state. T.P.

Organization.
A bounded sub-set within a society of interdependent relations among individuals, who interact with each other both directly and in mediated ways. The term "institution" is often applied to organizations of stability and endurance, such as churches, business enterprises, and governmental entities. At times the term "organization" is employed narrowly to designate the central machinery involved in the functioning of a political party.

Sometimes there is singleness of purpose among members of an organization as to goals; other times there is little consensus with respect to desired outputs of the organization. The interrelations among such individuals, who at the moment have various degrees and kinds of membership in the organization, differ in their formality and explicitness. Often an organization has social sub-structures within its boundaries, consisting of specialized roles and face-to-face groups. Social differentiations within the organization, such as its status system, often incorporate cultural patterns similar to those found within the society at large. At times special social norms may develop to govern particular aspects of organizational life, such as the administrative regulations which develop within bureaucracies. Many organizations have authority structures for the exercise of control over their members and material resources. The degree of involvement of members in their organizations varies from quite occasional participation in voluntary groups, such as political parties, to complete, total inclusion of the members, as in prisons. Inasmuch as membership may change over time, eventually all individuals may be replaced by others without discontinuity in the existence of the organization itself. H.G.

Organization Armee Secrete. (O.A.S.)
Extremist organization organized in March 1961 for the purpose of actively opposing Algerian independence. Its public leadership was provided by former French military generals Raoul Salan and Edmond Jouhand. Using terroristic methods, the OAS was active primarily in Algiers and Oran. Membership included European colonists, as well as minority elements of the French army and the French Foreign Legion. Its most concerted effort was an April 1961 uprising which collapsed after four days. In spite of OAS activities, the French Government and the Algerian rebel provisional government reached the agreement of Evian-les-Bains in March 1962, which provided a cease-fire leading to Algerian independence. E.R.W.

Organization for Economic Cooperation and Development was established on 14 December 1960 to harmonize member countries' economic policies, to promote worldwide economic growth and to coordinate and increase the flow of assistance to the underdeveloped countries. It replaces the 13-year-old OEEC, set up to coordinate the European recovery program after World War II, and links the United States and Canada with 18 European nations: Austria, Belgium, Denmark, France, German Federal Republic, Greece, Iceland, Ireland, Italy, Luxembourg, Netherlands, Norway, Portugal, Spain, Sweden, Switzerland, Turkey and United Kingdom. Apart from its major concern with economic development, OECD promotes multilateral world trade on a nondiscriminatory basis. Its supreme body is the Council, which is in fact a permanent conference constantly reviewing economic problems of the member countries. It appoints its chairman who is also secretary-general of a Secretariat assisting the Council and other bodies of the Organization. P.A.T.

Organization of American States.

The Organization of American States is the successor in law and in fact to the Union of American Republics created at the Conference held in Washington, 1889-1890. At the Conference of American States at Mexico City in 1945, in advance of the meeting to be held at San Francisco to adopt the Charter of the United Nations, the American States recognized the need of reorganizing the inter-American system in order not only to establish the relation of their regional system to the new international organization, but also to make it a more effective instrument to meet the changed conditions with which they were confronted.

In consequence, after securing the incorporation in the Charter of the United Nations of the status of "regional arrangements" in relation to the powers of the Security Council, the American States met at Bogota, Colombia, in 1948 and drew up the Charter of their own regional system, designated as the Organization of the American States. In a succession of articles the Charter first sets forth the Nature and Purposes of the Organization, its Principles and the Fundamental Rights and Duties of States, provisions for the settlement of disputes and for collective security, repeating on this last point the principles of the Treaty of Reciprocal Assistance signed at Rio de Janeiro a year earlier. Then follows a specification of the organs of the Organization, the Inter-American Conference, the Meeting of Consultation of Ministers of Foreign Affairs, the Council, the Pan American Union, acting as General Secretariat, and the Specialized Conferences and Specialized Organizations. While the Conference, meeting every five years, is declared to be the "supreme organ", the Meeting of Foreign Ministers has in fact the more important task of meeting threats to the peace and taking action in regard to problems of an urgent nature. The Council exercises the functions of a permanent executive committee, and the Pan American Union those of a working secretariat. The Specialized Conferences and Specialized Organizations deal with matters of a technical nature. In 1962 the "present government of Cuba" was excluded from membership because of its identification with the Marxist-Leninist system. C.G.F.

Organization of Central American States.

This represents the culmination of a century of unsuccessful attempts to unify an area which was a single entity in Spanish colonial times. The charter, providing a loose association of the republics of Costa Rica, El Salvador, Guatemala, Honduras and Nicaragua, was proclaimed at San Salvador in October, 1951. It did not begin to function until 1955. It seeks to strengthen the bonds among the nations, to further peaceful settlement of disputes and to promote economic, social and cultural development. The five national presidents comprise the supreme organ. A secretariat and a budget based on proportional contributions by the five states are provided.

R.J.S.

Organized Labor.

A combination of workmen either on the basis of craft, trade, or occupation (called craft unions, such as those constituting the American Federation of Labor), or on the basis of industry in which all workers of a given industry can belong regardless of craft, trade, or occupation (such as those constituting the Congress of Industrial Organizations). See Trade Unionism.

C.B.C.

Oriental Despotism.

A regime different from European and Japanese absolutism in that it not only exerts total political power, but also prevents the emergence of countervailing societal forces such as a feudal aristocracy, an independent church, or power-endowed guilds. The peculiarities of Oriental despotism were dimly recognized by Hippocrates and Aristotle; they were outlined by Montesquieu and institutionally defined by the classical economists, including Marx. Today the underlying concept is obscured by the Marxist-Leninists, because it leads to an interpretation of Tsarist autocracy as an Oriental despotism and of Communist totalitarianism as a stronger Oriental despotism. Oriental despotism flourished most significantly to the east of Europe (hence the designation "Oriental"), but it also occurred in pre-Spanish Meso-America and the Andean zone of South America (hence the recently suggested alternative terms "agro-managerial" or "hydraulic" despotism). Oriental despotism emerged in water-deficient areas where effective farming and safe living required irrigation and flood control through government-managed large water works. The hydraulic efforts stimulated other government-managed constructions: great walls, highways, monumental palaces, temples and tombs; it involved general census-taking and taxation, a centralized army, and usually also a state post and a far-flung intelligence system. The resulting power structure—a state stronger than society, run by a monopoly bureaucracy and headed by an autocratic rule—persisted without a hydraulic economy in post-Mongol Russia, middle and later Byzantium, Maya society, and elsewhere. Being semi-managerial, the total power of Oriental despotism was limited to the political sphere; it permitted politically inconsequential forms of self-government—"Beggars' democracies" and a variety of economic, social, and ideological freedoms. Communist totalitarianism, like Oriental despotism, is characterized by a ruling bureaucracy. But since it exerts total managerial control, it tends much more than did Oriental despotism to exert total control also over the entire economy and the population's social life and ideas. K.A.W.

Oriental Society.

A term used by the Classical economists to designate the distinctive combination of institutional features which they found in the civilizations of the Near East, India and China. The term was generally used interchangeably with "Asiatic Society" (see also, Oriental Despotism). The "despotic strength" is the most prominent feature which these societies shared. The term has recently been given renewed importance through the writings of Karl August Wittfogel, who stresses the "hydraulic" features or origins of such societies. In all of the areas mentioned large water works were maintained for irrigation, communication and flood control. Further, everywhere in the Orient the government was the biggest landowner.

Karl Marx recognized the existence of a distinctive form of social organization which he termed "Asiatic Society". He outlined Asiatic Society as being characterized by extensive artificial waterworks. Such water control necessitated, according to Marx, the interference of the centralizing power of the state, since the civilization was too low and the territorial exent too vast to call into life voluntary association. Thus, it was the need for government-directed water works that gave rise to the Asiatic State, and the "dispersed" condition of the "Oriental People" and their agglomeration in "self-supporting" villages (combining small scale agriculture and domestic handicraft) that permitted its agelong perpetuation. Marx viewed India, China and Russia as being examples of Asiatic Society.

Wittfogel has found conditions characteristic of Oriental Society in the pre-Columbian civilizations of America and elsewhere. Many Marxists, including Lenin and more recent groups, have repudiated the concept of Oriental Society as a threat to the unilinear concept of societal development and more particularly as a reflection on conditions in Czarist and Soviet Russia. S.S.

Original Jurisdiction.

It is the authority of a court to exercise judicial power in regard to persons and/or subject matter in a specific case. Jurisdiction is twofold, **Original** and **Appellate,** the former is the power to hear and determine a case in the first instance, i.e., before it has been heard in another court, the latter is the power of a higher court to review the decision of a lower court and to confirm or reverse it. Some courts, i.e., trial courts may exercise only **Original** Jurisdiction, others only **Appellate.** The Supreme Court of the United States has both. A.A.N.

"Original" states.
Those English colonies which joined in support of the Declaration of Independence and later became the first member states of the United States of America through ratification of the Constitution between 1787 and 1790. Delaware, Pennsylvania, New Jersey, Georgia, Connecticut, Massachusetts, Maryland, South Carolina, New Hampshire, Virginia, New York, North Carolina, Rhode Island. Cf., "admitted" states. R.R.R.

Orlando, Vittorio Emanuele.
(1860-1952).
Italian Prime Minister in 1917; led his delegation to the Versailles Peace Conference but failed to obtain concessions promised Italy by Great Britain and lost office. Elected President of the Chamber of Deputies and resigned in 1928. Retired from politics. Elected President of the Chamber of Deputies 1944-1946 and served as member of Constituent Assembly. G.K.

Osterholm, John Emil.
A leader of the Swedish National Party of Finland. (1884-1960). Member of parliament 1919-60. E.I.

Otis, James. (1725-1783)
American colonial lawyer and statesman, best known for his opposition to the writs of assistance in 1761. The writs, sought in the courts of Massachusetts on the claim that they were sanctioned by British law, were designed to make it easier to search private premises for smuggled goods. As attorney in opposition to the writs, Otis argued that a law contrary to constitutional principle was really not law and courts must so declare. This was to become a basic principle of American government. Later, as legislator and pamphleteer he opposed British policy in regard to the colonies and advocated human rights and limited government. J.E.R.

Outdoor Relief.
A somewhat outmoded term (U.S.A.). It refers to the provision of aid in kind, or the granting of a monetary allowance, to persons who reside in private dwelling places. In contrast, "indoor relief" provides for care of the indigent and incompetent within public institutions. C.R.A.

Overkill.
That amount of thermonuclear power available to a state which is above the required nuclear force needed to obliterate an enemy's population. Overkill represents therefore the ability of one state—in terms of its nuclear power—to kill a population "many times over." R.A.B.

Overseas Chinese.
Refers to the "hua-chiao" (literally, Chinese visiting abroad), the estimated twelve to thirteen million Chinese residing outside of mainland China, Taiwan, Hongkong and Macao. Approximately ten million live in the countries and islands of Southeast Asia. In Singapore they constitute about eighty percent of the total population, in Malaya about 35%. The majority of the Overseas Chinese maintain their Chinese cultural identity, consider themselves to be Chinese, and by Chinese law and custom are generally acknowledged by Chinese governments as being, in fact, Chinese, despite naturalization or birth in other countries.

Large communities of Overseas Chinese exist in the Americas, particularly in San Francisco, New York, Vancouver (British Columbia) and the West Indies, but the most important aggregations are in Southeast Asia where, as in Singapore, Malaya, Thailand, the Philippines, and Indonesia they possess great economic power. To these nations they present great problems owing to their slow rate of assimilation, questionable loyalty and insistence on maintenance of their own language and cultural traditions. Moreover, since the rise of the Chinese Communists to power they have been considered to be particularly susceptible to Chinese Communist influence. In Malaya, for instance, some 80% or more of the Communist terrorists were ethnically Chinese. The Overseas Chinese continue to send remittances to the mainland, and are urged by the rival Chinese governments to invest in their respective enterprises. The Chinese engage both in local and international trade, and have produced a sizeable group of business tycoons in

Southeast Asia. Their hold on the rubber industry and banking has produced considerable anxiety on the part of host governments. As a result periodic waves of repression have been experienced by the Chinese, the most recent having been in Indonesia and Thailand. For the purpose of controlling and protecting the Overseas Chinese, all recent Chinese governments have maintained Overseas Chinese Affairs Commissions. S.S.

Owen, Robert (1771-1858).

British industrialist, reformer, and utopian socialist; leader in the founding of a model community at New Lanark, Scotland, in 1799; founded an ideal community at New Harmony, Indiana, in 1825; helped organize the Grand National Consolidated Trades Union in 1833; author of **A New View of Society** (1813) and **A Report to the Committee for the Relief of the Manufacturing Poor** (1817). Ch.C.M.

P

Paasikivi, Juho Kusti. (1870-1956)

Statesman; "peacemaker"; banker. Born in Finland. Member of Parliament, 1907-13. Minister of Finance, 1908-09. Prime Minister briefly in 1918. Head of the Finnish delegation that negotiated the Treaty of Dorpat, 1920, which delineated the Finnish-Soviet border. Minister to Sweden, 1936-39. Chief negotiator in the Moscow discussions in September, 1939, prior to the outbreak of the Winter War. Member of the Finnish-Soviet Peace Commission that negotiated the Moscow Treaty of 1940, which terminated the Winter War. Minister-without portfolio, 1940. Chief negotiator in the Finnish-Soviet armistice discussions of 1944. Prime Minister, 1944-46. President of the Republic, 1946-56. Originator of the "Paasikivi Line"—the basis of Finland's foreign policy since 1944, which recognizes the centrality of Soviet power in Finland's foreign relations and the need for accommodating Finnish policy to that power. Affectionately known as the "Grand Old Man of Finland." R.H.K.

Pacifism.

While almost all people prefer peace to war, pacifism is a term which is properly confined to those who oppose any use of military methods for dealing with international conflicts. Pacifists are divided into three groups. Followers of Tolstoy or the Mennonites believe in non-resistance to evil. Followers of Gandhi and A. J. Muste advocate non-violent resistance to evil. Quakers and many modern pacifists, although they approve to some degree the first two approaches, emphasize the importance of establishing satisfactory political and legal institutions to resolve conflicts through legislation, administration and adjudication at all levels of social relations. While all pacifists recognize the problem of evil, they differ regarding appropriate measures for dealing with it. Two serious areas of controversy concern the use of an international police force and the propriety of depending on domestic police and courts. R.W.T.

"Packing" of the U.S. Supreme Court.

See U.S. Supreme Court "Packing" plan.

Pacta sunt servanda.

As a fundamental customary principle of international law it is used in either of two senses: one, that legally binding precepts may be created by means of treaties in the broadest sense and second that valid treaties ought to be executed. Whether, when, to what extent and for whom a treaty is binding, are questions relating to the validity of the treaty itself. Once these questions are resolved it follows necessarily that the treaty must be carried out in good faith. This principle is not inconsistent with the seemingly contrary principle of **rebus sic stantibus.** Both principles, one standing for stability and the other for change form part of international law. Thus a treaty may be revised or terminated by the will of the parties or it may cease to be binding by operation of the law e.g. in case of a bilateral treaty, the outbreak of war or disappearance of one of the parties.

L.G.

Paderewski, Ignacy Jan. (1860-1941).

Born in Podole province. Pianist and composer. Premier and then foreign minister in first Polish coalition government after World War One. Resigned after Allied Supreme Council refused Poland's demands. In 1940, accepted presidency of parliament in exile. Same year returned to United States. Buried at Arlington National Cemetery. R.F.S.

Paine, Thomas (1737-1809).

Pamphleteer, agitator, philosopher. Born in England. Although of meagre education he was employed briefly in the excise. Encouraged by Benjamin Franklin, he came to America (1774) and promptly adopted the revolutionary cause of the colonies. Within two years his pamphlet, **Common Sense,** was published. It crystallized the arguments for separation from England and also aroused national fervor by first using the term, "free and independent states of America." It is one of the greatest calls to revolution of all times. Basing this argument upon Natural Law he held that the origin of government rested on the Social Contract and sovereignty in the majority will. He ranks as the most important philosopher in the colonies of the period. As his popularity ebbed, he returned to England (1787) to oppose the policy of William Pitt and wrote the **Rights of Man** (1791). Indicted for treason, he escaped to France and participated in the Revolution. He was elected from Calais as a member of the French Convention. Voting against the execution of Louis XVI, he aroused the enmity of Robespierre who had him imprisoned. While in prison, he wrote the **Age of Reason,** an attack on revealed religion. After the fall of Robespierre, he was released from prison. The publication of an angry letter to Washington for refusal to force France to release him from prison as well as his attitude toward religion, destroyed his popularity in the United States. Nevertheless, he came back to New York (1802) to claim the estate at New Rochelle which a grateful legislature had given him. M.E.D.

Pakistan.
Area 364,737 square miles. Population (1961 census, provisional), 93,-812,000. Pakistan was constituted a separate nation just before India (q.v.) became independent of Great Britain, August 15, 1947. Pakistan is a member of the U.N., the British Commonwealth of Nations, CENTO and SEATO. East and West Pakistan are separated by over a thousand miles of Indian territory. English is the official language. National languages are Urdu in West Pakistan; Bengali in East Pakistan. Though East Pakistan has only 54,501 square miles to West Pakistan's 310,236, she comprises over half the population.

The capital was moved in 1959 from Karachi to Rawalpindi. Nearby Islamabad is under construction as the new capital. The National Assembly meets in Dacca.

The Muslim League, founded in 1906, worked to protect Muslim interests in India, by securing separate electorates. From 1940, under the leadership of Mohammed Ali Jinnah, the League pressed for a separate nation. Pakistan, with a population 85% Muslim, offered an opportunity to form a Muslim polity. Divisions between the devout and secularists caused the government to operate as a sovereign nation under the Government of India Act (1935) until 1956, when the first constitution of the "Islamic Republic of Pakistan" was adopted.

The 1962 constitution has dropped "Islamic" from the nation's title. Its preamble retains the assertion that sovereignty over the universe belongs to Allah alone; the authority exercised by the people is a sacred trust. The "Guiding Principles" of the constitution declare unconditionally that "no law should be repugnant to Islam." The interpretation of this principle is now left to the National Assembly, constitutionally the sole judge of its own actions. Earlier there had been pressure to refer laws to the ulama.

The religious and cultural rights of minorities are guaranteed. Communal electorates have been retained; in East Pakistan high caste Hindus are further separated from the scheduled castes.

Jinnah served as the first governor-general of Pakistan. Acknowledged as founder of the nation, and given the title "Quaid-i-Azam" (**Great Leader**), he exhausted himself in its service and died September 11, 1948. Jinnah's friend and lieutenant, Liaquat Ali Khan, succeeded as head of the government. He continued Jinnah's policies, successfully repressed the Rawalpindi plot, and fell before an assassin in 1951. The loss of these leaders was a severe blow to the stability of the young nation. The Muslim League lost control, and leaders of new parties and factions succeeded one another until Field Marshal Mohammed Ayub Khan staged a bloodless coup in October, 1958. Martial law was enforced until June, 1962. A sweeping land reform was carried out. Corrupt officials of former governments were allowed to resign or to retire from public life. President Ayub Khan instituted "basic democracies" at the village level, to train citizens in the democratic process.

The 1962 constitution provides a strong president, indirectly elected by an electoral college of 80,000. Central and provincial legislatures are indirectly elected. Building on the basic democracies, five governmental tiers combine popularly-elected and government-appointed officials in union, tehsil/thana, district, divisional, and provincial development advisory councils.

The economy and communications were severely disrupted by the division of India (q.v.) the refugee problem, and the cost of war in Kashmir. The immediate necessity of adequate communication between the two wings of the country brought about the development of commercial airlines, a merchant marine, and new ports. Railroads and highways have been developed in both wings. Canal and river transportation is the predominant pattern in East Pakistan.

Fifty-five per cent of the national income still comes from agriculture. Industrial growth is accelerating. The First Five-Year Plan, 1955-1960, was to increase national income by 15%; which, allowing for population increase, might have yielded a per capita increase of 7.5%. The plan fell short of expectation: 11% national increase; 4% per capita increase were achieved.

The Second Five-Year Plan (1960-1965) hopes to increase national income by 24%; per capita income by 13%; production of food-grains by 21% or self-sufficiency; industrial production by 50%; exports by 15%; to improve the balance of payments and increase capital savings investment; to increase employment; accelerate economic growth in Pakistan's less developed areas; to expand educational health, and social welfare facilities; to increase lower income housing.

Pakistan is the fifth largest nation in the world, in population. It is the largest Muslim nation and the only major Asian nation firmly committed to the free world. Its border difficulties with Muslim Afghanistan are significant for its defenses and its influence in other Muslim countries. Some emerging nations have agreements to share its training programs for military and administrative personnel.

M.O'C.

Palestine Mandate.

This was one of the so-called A Mandates established under Article 22 of the League of Nations Covenant. The Mandate of July 24, 1922, as defined by the League Council, confirmed Great Britain as the Mandatory for the former Turkish territory of Palestine. It entitled the Mandatory, with the consent of the Council, to postpone or withhold in the territories lying between Jordan and the eastern boundary of Palestine, application of such provisions of the Mandate as he considered inapplicable. The Council approved a separate regime for Transjordan in September 1922 which was followed in 1923 by the recognition of an "independent Government" and in 1928 by a treaty between Great Britain and Transjordan. The Mandate made the Mandatory responsible for securing "the establishment of the Jewish national home" in Palestine without prejudice to the "civil and religious rights of existing non-Jewish communities" as stipulated in the Declaration of 1917 made by the British Government (Balfour Declaration) and adopted later by the Principal Allied Powers. Under the Mandate an "appropriate Jewish agency" was to be "recognized as a public body for the purpose of advising and co-operating with the Administration of Palestine" in matters affecting said Jewish national home. This Jewish Agency for Palestine was formally set up in 1929. Largely under Arab pressure the Mandatory restricted Jewish immigration to Palestine. In 1947 the Mandatory brought the Palestine question before the United Nations. In its resolution of November 29, 1947, the General Assembly took note of the Mandatory's declaration to complete the evacuation of Palestine by August 1, 1948 (later advanced to May 15, 1948) and recommended the adoption of a Plan of Partition with Economic Union. On May 14, 1948, a Provisional Council of State proclaimed the establishment of the State of Israel in part of Palestine.

S.E.

Palmach.

(Synthetic word derived from Hebrew: Plugat Mahatz); Jewish mobile shock troops in Palestine during later years of British mandate. Served principally to protect Jewish colonists against Arab violence. Dissolved by Israeli government after statehood.

S.H.

Pan-Africanism.

A political and cultural movement which has strived to obtain equal rights, self-government, independence, and unity for African peoples. Under the inspiration of the tempestuous Marcus Garvey, it took the form of a "back to Africa" movement for American Negroes. It extolls African history and culture and encourages the development of African literature and distinctiveness.

During the first decades of its existence, the Pan-African movement was controlled by Negroes of the Western Hemisphere, notably Dr. W. E. B. DuBois, the "father" of Pan-Africanism. Under their auspices, five Pan-African congresses were held in New York and in Western European capitals between 1900 and 1927. These congresses passed "reformist" resolutions calling for protection of African rights, equal treatment, and self-government. The sixth Pan-African Congress held in Manchester in 1945, however, was dominated by African leaders, including Kwame Nkrumah and Jomo Kenyatta, and this congress endorsed "autonomy and independence" for Black Africa.

The postwar movement has been controlled by African leaders. It has tended to divide into two tendencies: the first which advocates direct political unity (see the Union of African States and the Casablanca Bloc); and the second which holds that African unity will be reached gradually by cooperation in specific economic, technical, and cultural projects (see the Brazzaville and Monrovian Blocs).
F.H.G.

Panama.
Population, 1,053,000; area, 28,576 sq. miles. Panama was a province of Colombia until 1903, when a revolution brought about its independence from that nation. This revolution was apparently encouraged and supported by the United States, which prevented Colombian troops from landing to suppress the rebellion.

As an independent nation, Panama is virtually dependent upon its receipts from the canal. It has few other sources of wealth, and remains quite undeveloped economically. See also Panama Canal Zone. Ch.W.A.

Panama Canal Zone.
By treaty of 1904 between the United States and Panama, a ten mile wide strip of land through the center of Panama was ceded to the United States for the purposes of construction of a canal. The precise legal status of the zone remains unclear. The United States has long claimed full sovereign powers in the area, while Panama insists that American jurisdiction extends only to those measures necessary for the construction and maintenance of the canal. In recent years, this dispute has caused considerable friction between the two nations. At present the U.S. has agreed to fly the Panamanian flag together with the American in the zone, as a symbol of residual Panamanian sovereignty.

Under the terms of the original treaty, Panama received an annual rental of $250,000 from the canal rights. This payment was raised to $430,000 in 1936, and revised to $970,000 in 1956.
Ch.W.A.

Panama, Declaration of (1939).
Adopted by the first Inter-American Consultative Conference of Foreign Ministers on October 3, 1939. It declared that the American Republics for continental self-protection are of "inherent right" entitled to be free from hostile acts by land, sea, or air by any non-American belligerent in a zone of security beginning in Passamaquoddy Bay and going east, south, west, and north around the western hemisphere to the strait of Juan de Fuca.

Collective or individual action could be taken to secure compliance with this declaration. J.E.T.

Pan American Union.
In popular understanding the Pan American Union stands for the Union of American Republics established in 1890 at the First International Conference of American States and for its successor, the existing Organization of American States established at the Conference of Bogota of 1948. Technically, however, the Pan American U. did not receive its legal status until a conference held at Buenos Aires in 1910, when it was recognized that the permanent Commercial Bureau created in 1890 had grown in functions and come to be popularly regarded as the original parent Union.

When the inter-American system was reorganized at Bogota in 1948 the name "Organization of American States" was given to the Union of

American Republics of 1890, and the name "Pan American Union" was assigned to the General Secretariat of the Organization, an indirect tribute to a name that had been associated with inter-American relations for so many years, although the Conference was unwilling to use the term "Union" in connection with the inter-American system in its entirety. The Pan American Union is described in the Charter of the Organization as its "central and permanent organ", paralleling in its activities the Secretariat of the United Nations, and directed by a Secretary General who may participate with voice, but without vote in the deliberations. C.G.F.

Pan-Arabism.

While Pan-Islamism was confronting strong opposition from the local rulers within the Ottoman Empire who aspired to become independent, Pan-Arabism aiming at the unification of the Arabic-speaking communities of the Middle East found its way gradually within the ranks of Arab politicians. Several attempts were made to unify the Arab world and sever it from the Ottoman domain. Muhammad Ali's campaigns in Syria and Palestine led by his son Ibrahim Pasha in the middle of the 19th century were advanced under the banner of Pan-Arabism. Although these campaigns ended in failure, nevertheless the distinction between Arabs and Turks continued to grow until World War I when the Arab world finally decided to throw its lot against the Turks and side with the Allies. The chief promotor of Pan-Arabism during this period was Sharif Husayn of Arabia who was looking forward to an Arab kingdom in the Middle East to be established after the war.

The Allies, however, disappointed him and divided the Arab Middle East into territories under British and French mandates. In so doing, they were appealing to local nationalisms within the Arab world. Pan-Arabism became almost dormant until World War II and the rise of the state of Israel, when it was revived under its present name, Arab nationalism. Although there are certain influences which might weaken the possibilities for Arab unity, yet the unifying bonds among the Arabs (namely religion, language, culture, history and economy) are clear and undeniable and will continue to keep the torch of Arab nationalism burning for a long time to come. W.B.B.

Panchayat.

Literally, a council of five. It refers to a village council or court of elders, entrusted with executive and judicial powers for the governance of community affairs. This institution, which flourished in many parts of India in the past, is now being revived as the basic administrative unit of government. The Constitution of India provides for the organization of village **panchayats** with necessary powers to function as units of self-government. By the end of 1966, almost all the villages are expected to be included in the **panchayat** system. The creation of village councils is also provided for in the 1962 Constitution of Pakistan.
C.S.S.

Panch Shila.

Five Principles (of Peace), which were enunciated in the Sino-Indian Agreement on Tibet, April 28, 1954, as follows: mutual respect for each other's territorial integrity and sovereignty; mutual nonaggression; mutual noninterference in each other's internal affairs; equality and mutual benefit; and peaceful co-existence. They were subsequently incorporated into India's treaty relations with several states. They formed the basis of the Bandung declaration on international peace and cooperation in 1955. The **Panch Shila** theory suffered a severe setback with the progressive worsening of Sino-Indian relations after 1958. C.S.S.

Pan Europe.

An Austrian writer, Count Richard Coudenhove-Kalergi, vigorously promoted the idea of a federation of Europe during the decade of the 1920's. His efforts led, in 1926, to the calling of a large conference held in Vienna, and to the founding of the Pan-European Union. Coudenhove-Kalergi became President of this organization and attracted the support of many distinguished Europeans. Only the general idea of uniting Europe (Pan Europe) was advanced; no practical steps were possible at that time. Ch.C.Mc.

Pan-Islamism.

The French campaign in Egypt could be said to have awakened the Muslims of the Middle East from a cultural slumber of about three hundred years. Few years after 1798, Muslim intellectuals attributed the deterioration of the Islamic domain under the Ottomans to the lack of piety of the Ottoman rulers and the numerous superstitions which fogged the bright light of the pure Islamic doctrines.

From 1871 to 1879, al Afghani was preaching a reformation among the Muslims and called for a spiritual as well as a physical unity among all the Islamic states, including Turkey. However, by that time most of the Arab territories were pulling away from the Ottomans, and therefore Afghani's call for Pan-Islamism did not find much response from governing authorities. Muhammad 'Abdu and his disciple Rashid Rida continued the struggle of Pan-Islamism after the death of Afghani, succeeding only in arousing the emotions of the Muslim intellectuals without any appreciable response from local governments.

Recently in 1928, the Muslim Brotherhood was founded in Egypt under the leadership of Hasan al-Banna. This organization drew a strong following and spread its message of Pan-Islamism in many other Arab countries. However, in Egypt where they were strongest, they have been outlawed by the Nasser regime and forced to go underground.

At present, there is no doubt that many individual Muslims believe in Pan-Islamism as the only remedy for the deterioration of the Muslim community. It is yet to be seen whether religion or language will finally succeed in stabilizing national sentiments in that vitally located region of the Middle East.   W.B.B.

Panmunjon Truce.

Peace discussions in the Korean War began in July, 1951. The truce, negotiated at Panmunjon, finally (prisoner repatriation issue!) came on July 27, 1953. It called for a cease fire, a neutral zone at the battlefront (slightly North, as a whole, of the 1945 demarcation line, latitude 38°), no reinforcements for either side, a UN Neutral Nations Supervisory Commission (Sweden, Switzerland, Poland, Czechoslovakia), and a political conference to discuss a general settlement of Korean and related problems. Commission removed in 1956, due to its inability to exercise adequate supervisory powers in North Korea. Attempts at political settlement have made no progress.   H.L.M.

Pan-Turanianism.

A supernational propaganda and a political program to unite all the Turkish-speaking peoples, in Turkey, Russia, Persia, Afghanistan, and China, in a single state. Nationalistic and modernist forces combined to encourage in the latter part of the 19th, and the first part of the 20th century, the growth of this political movement based, not on a dynasty, a faith, or a state, but on a people—the Turkish people, in its vast territories extending from Europe to the Pacific. In Ziya Gokalp's poetry we find the most eloquent exposition of this doctrine. Turkey's defeat in World War I, the fact that two-thirds of the Turkish-speaking peoples of the world were to be found within the frontiers, not of Turkey but of Russia, the religious differences between the Turkish-speaking peoples, and the rise of the Kemalist movement with its emphasis on Anatolian Turkey, all of these forces cooperated to discourage Pan-Turanianism. In May 1944, Pan-Turanian groups were discovered in Turkey. Proved to be fascist organizations with racist doctrines bent on bringing Turkey into the war on the side of Germany, they were tried and condemned in September of the same year.   F.M.N.

Papen, Franz von. (1879-   .)

Conservative Center Party member of Prussian Diet, 1921-32; owned party's leading newspaper **Germania**. While short time Chancellor without parliamentary support suppressed Social Democratic government of Prussia, 1932. Intriguing, paved Hitler's way into power, believing he could be controlled. Vice-Chancellor, 1933. Negotiated concordat with Vatican, Hitler's first foreign policy success, 1933. Criticized Nazi suppression in Marburg University speech, barely escaped murder by SS, 1934. Ambassador to Vienna and Ankara, 1934-44, serving Hitler's purposes. Acquitted at Nuremberg War Crime Trials; served part of denazification tribunal sentence in labor camp. J.M.B.

Paraguay. See Appendix.

Pardo, Jose.
Latin American politician. Born in Lima, Peru, Feb. 24, 1864; died in 1947. Education: law degree, Univ. de San Marcos, 1887. Prof. of politics, Univ. de San Marcos. Minister of foreign affairs, 1903-04. President of Peru 1904-08 and 1915-19. M.A.

Pardon.
In the U.S. system of checks and balances the president has the power to issue pardons to all offenders against the United States, except those convicted by impeachment. A pardon restores the person who receives it to his former freedom. A state governor has similar power in connection with convictions made by state courts. M.F.

Pareto, Vilfredo (1848-1923).
Italian engineer, sociologist, economist, and political theorist; noted for his mathematical formulation of a theory of economic equilibrium, for his differentiation between logical and non-logical social behavior, and for his theory of the circulation of the elites: author of **Manual of Political Economy** (1906), **Treatise on General Sociology** (1916), and **The Mind and Society** (1935). Ch.C.M.

Paris Commune.
Revolutionary government established in Paris in 1871 (18 March) after the Peace of Frankfurt had been signed and Prussian troops had lifted the siege of the city. Fears that the National Assembly at Bordeaux would restore the monarchy, the physical suffering of the siege, and the imminent disbandment of the National Guard, caused the latter to revolt. The Commune seized hostages against expected attacks from the Assembly and established a Committee of Public Safety (1 May). Troops from the Assembly, concentrated at Versailles, entered Paris on 21 May. The week that followed deserved the title "Bloody Week," for before the Commune was destroyed (28 May), the barricades had to be stormed street by street. The killing of hostages, the fires set to buildings as the revolutionaries retreated, were matched by the severe punishment meted out by the victors. K.B.

Parish.
The smallest unit of rural local government in England and Wales. Parishes are subdivisions of the rural districts, which are the main rural subdivisions of the administrative counties. The larger parishes have councils, and the others have parish meetings which all voters may attend. In the United States the term parish is applied to the units of local government in Louisiana which are known as counties in the other states. R.H.B.

Parliament.
The bicameral legislature of England, consisting of popularly elected representatives in a lower house (Commons) and "lords spiritual" and "lords temporal" in an upper house (Lords). The term—derived from the French **parler** (to speak)—was used in England as early as the 13th century, originally describing the vassals and representatives of the counties and towns who were summoned by the King to consent to taxation measures and to act as a consultative and deliberative body. In time, Parliament insisted upon the right to exercise general law-making authority as the price of its cooperation in financial matters. Today the Parliament of the United Kingdom of Great Britain and Ireland exercises legislative powers limited only by tradition. In practice, the existence of a disciplined majority power usually guarantees the enactment by Parliament of measures proposed by the cabinet.

Many other countries, particularly those associated with England in the commonwealth of nations, have given the name "Parliament" to their national legislatures. D.M.B.

Parliament of France.
See French parliament.

Parliamentarism.
In its general meaning, the term embraces all aspects of the activities of law making bodies, including rules of procedure governing their business and the conduct of their members.

At its best, parliamentarism refers to "the gentlemanly character of (British) politics" (Joseph Dunner). It is a code which embodies the principles of scrupulous fairness and impartiality to all. It operates in a climate of mutual respect and utmost courtesy which members have been carefully trained to accord to each other. It constitutes the framework within which great orators and statesmen have acted, inspired their countrymen and sent their historic messages to the world.

At its worst, parliamentarism is a term of derision. It is identified with inefficiency resulting from the parliamentary process itself which by its nature is time-consuming, given to emphasize procedural details, and delaying action. Parliamentarism is also associated with openly flouting representative government, as illustrated by individual members engaged in mocking speeches, table pounding, and rattling desk lids. Finally, parliamentarism is remembered as one of the vehicles on which, after the First World War, extremist parties, hostile to constitutional government, rode to power; by obstructing the parliamentary system they hastened its demise.

As a term used in political science, parliamentarism, or parliamentary government, denotes a political system which "makes the executive dependent upon and responsible to a majority in the representative assembly" (Carl J. Friedrich).

Parliamentarism originated in Britain as a consequence of the Glorious Revolution of 1688.

While details of the system differ from country to country, the following features may be considered typical. With few exceptions, ministers are members of the party or coalition which commands a majority in the parliament. Their leader, the prime minister, is either **primus inter pares** or **luna inter stellas minores.** The head of state is, as a rule, bound to accept the cabinet as the highest policy-making body. The parliament, on the other hand, is not so bound. Its most drastic method of invoking and enforcing ministerial responsibility is the removal of the cabinet altogether. This may be accomplished by passing a vote of non-confidence or censure; rejecting a vote of confidence; defeating measures considered vital by the government; and, in Britain, moving an amendment to the Address from the throne.

To achieve an equilibrium or balance between the parliament and the executive, parliamentarism usually accords the latter some "checks and balances" (q.v.) to counter the destructive measures of the former. Most prominent among these checks is the dissolution of the parliament by the executive.

Since the second half of the nineteenth century dissolution has become a formidable weapon in the hands of the British Government. It happened a number of times (for example, in 1857, 1868, 1886, and 1924) that a Prime Minister, having been defeated in the Commons, refused to resign. Instead, he requested the monarch to dissolve Parliament which he did. Ultimately, then, the electorate would function as an arbiter between the Cabinet and the majority of Parliament. However, the mere threat or possibility of such dissolution with the risks and inconveniences of ensuing general elections has frequently been sufficient to unite the Prime Minister's party solidly behind him. "It is significant that resignations and dissolutions due to the defeat of the Government in the House of Commons have been rare in the twentieth century" (Sir Ivor Jennings). With the Parliament thus having been deterred from enforcing ministerial responsibility, the balance of power has decidedly shifted to the Cabinet. Because of this far-reaching change in the relations between Parliament and Cabinet, parliamentarism in Great Britain is appropriately referred to as Cabinet Government. It rests almost entirely on conventions of the constitution (q.v.).

The remarkable success of this version of parliamentarism consists in harmonizing strong executive leadership with democratic responsibility and protection of individual liberties. The achievements of British Cabinet Government have been fairly well matched in some other countries, for example, the Commonwealth nations. However, if, as in Western Europe, some of the conditions for success were absent, such as the two-party system with its strict party discipline; agreement on political fundamentals; collective responsibility of the Cabinet to the lower house of parliament; power of dissolution of the Prime Minister; freedom of the Cabinet from intervention by the head of state; considerable experience with this type of government; and tradition with its invaluable guiding precedents, then in some continental countries parliamentarism could not fail to fall short of the British standards and performance.

Advantages of parliamentarism include control of all acts of the executive by the legislature and preventing deadlocks between them. The greatest disadvantage of continental-parliamentarism is political instability, due to overturning governments or dissolutions.

Since parliamentarism means the fusion of legislative and executive functions, there is no room for it in the United States where government is established on the basis of separation of powers. W.F.

Parliamentary diplomacy.

The special practices of intergovernmental multilateral negotiations and discussions. It is carried out in the continuing international organizations, such as the General Assembly and the Council of the United Nations, under the conditions of public debate and formal rules of procedure that are in themselves subject to tactical manipulation to advance or oppose a point of view. The result is usually a formal conclusion of debate, expressed in resolutions that are reached by a majority vote of one or the other magnitude. The whole process is somewhat analogous to the parliamentary processes in national legislatures. Unfortunately the practice of parliamentary diplomacy is employed primarily to achieve for a nation or group of nations a favorable position of political prestige. Only seldom actual solutions for pressing international problems or binding international agreements are achieved in this way. P.P.R.

Parliamentary government.

A system of government which vests political leadership in a legislative body (parliament) which, in turn, selects the executive (cabinet) entirely or largely from its membership. In accordance with the British prototype, disagreement on major issues of public policy between parliament and cabinet results either in the selection of a new cabinet or election of a new legislature. See Parliamentarism. J.D.

Parole.

The placing of a person under supervision following the serving of part of a sentence upon condition that he or she live up to certain requirements for a stated period of time and report regularly to his or her supervising officer. K.E.H.

Parti Republicain de la Liberte (PRL).

A minor French political party created within Parliament in 1946 by some who, not discredited by Vichy ties, were opposed to the government leaders since the Liberation. Laniel and Michel Clemenceau (son of the "Tiger", who ran for President in 1947) helped organize it, but few leaders joined this right wing party whose hopes were mainly destroyed by the organization of the RPF in 1947. The PRL tolerated double membership with the RPF, but its own Montel resigned in 1948 as vice-president of the Gaullist "Intergroup", and associations were generally severed in 1949. In that year two PRL government ministers who refused to resign their posts were expelled.

In 1946 the Radicals and PRL had divided departments. But 30 PRL deputies in the first Assembly were merged after 1951 in a National Union which also included Independents and Peasants.

The PRL, closely linked to business, opposed "dirigisme" and had campaigned against the nationalization program. Conservative in economic policy, it was not pro-clerical but opposed secularization of schools. As part of the National Union it opposed giving the Council of the Republic more power. R.B.C.

Partial war.
See war.

Partisan.

Name applied to anti-German guerrilla forces operating in the German-occupied areas of Europe during World

War II. Although such forces operated on a large scale in Russia, Poland, France and Italy, the term is frequently used to refer particularly to forces operating in Yugoslavia where two major groups of partisan forces fought each other as well as the Germans: Communist partisans under Marshal Tito and royalist partisans under General Mihailovich. T.W.

Partition of Palestine.

Plan adopted by the United Nations General Assembly on November 29, 1947, incorporated in Resolution 181 (II) calling for: (1) termination of the Mandate for Palestine and withdrawal of the British armed forces as soon as possible but no later than August 1, 1948; (2) establishment of an "Arab State," a "Jewish State," and a special international regime for the City of Jerusalem administered by the Trusteeship Council of the United Nations, two months after evacuation of the Mandatory armed forces but no later than October 1, 1948; (3) entry by the two states into an economic and transit union for promoting joint economic development in irrigation, land reclamation and soil conservation; operating inter-state railways, highways, communications, seaports, and airfields; instituting a joint currency system and a single foreign exchange rate; and creating a joint customs union; and (4) formation of a Palestine Commission of five member states to ensure peaceful execution of the partition plan. The Resolution required also that the two states to be created in Palestine each establish a provisional council of government to maintain law and order, prevent frontier clashes, regulate land, control immigration, and conduct a democratic national election for a constituent assembly which would draw up a constitution providing for a regular structure of government.

The partition plan actually divided Palestine into seven sections, three of which were to form the "Jewish State," three the "Arab State," and the seventh section—the City of Jerusalem—was to be an enclave within the "Arab State," but under the supervision of the United Nations and free to the inhabitants of either state to visit. A jigsaw arrangement made possible movement throughout the "Jewish State" without ever touching "Arab" territory, and similar movement throughout the "Arab State" without having to touch "Jewish" territory. Jews traveling to Jerusalem, however, would have to cross through the "Arab State." Although the three sections allocated to the "Jewish State" amounted to about 55 percent of the total area of Palestine, and the "Arab State" was given nearly 45 percent, more than half of the territory assigned to the "Jewish State" was to consist of the Negev, an arid, bare and largely uncultivable desert area in the south bordering Egypt and Jordan.

Immediately after the Resolution was adopted, the delegates of Iraq, Pakistan, Saudi Arabia, Syria, and Yemen announced they would not consider their nations bound by the General Assembly's partition action and would not take part in the creation of the Palestine Commission. Members elected by the General Assembly to the Palestine Commission were representatives of small neutral nations—Bolivia, Czechoslovakia, Denmark, Panama, and the Philippines.

The day following the Resolution's passage, the Arab countries began hostilities to prevent partition. An Arab general strike was called in Palestine, followed by an armed invasion by an "Arab Army of Liberation." In May, 1948, however, the Jewish defense forces had driven the invading Arab armies out of Palestine.

On May 14, 1948, as the Mandate ended and the British military and administrative forces departed from Palestine, the State of Israel was proclaimed, whereas the "Arab State," has never been established. Instead, Jordan annexed the major portion of the "Arab State" territory, and Egypt seized control of the Gaza Strip.

Partition of Palestine was a provocative issue from the moment it had been proposed and discussed. The United Nations Special Committee on Palestine (UNSCOP), which had studied the history of the Mandate, visited Palestine and the surrounding Arab countries, conducted hearings with Arab and Jewish organizations, and investigated displaced persons camps in Europe, agreed on termination of the Mandate, withdrawal of British civil authorities and military forces, and independence of Palestine; but it was divided on the question of what kind of independence—partition into two states—one "Arab" and the other "Jewish" with Jerusalem to be an international trusteeship—or a single federal state composed of "Arab" and "Jewish" provinces with Jerusalem as the state's capital. A majority of the eleven-member Special Committee favored partition, while the minority supported the federal state idea. The General Assembly took up the issue in September, 1947. Great Britain, backed by India and Yugoslavia, opposed partition. The Arab states rejected any solution other than a unitary Arab state. The Soviet Union favored partition; and the United States, after wavering for a time, supported partition and exercised influence among the Latin American nations to win enough votes for a two-thirds majority in its favor. On November 29, 1947, the U.S.S.R. moved to put the partition proposal to a vote; and partition was approved, 33 for, 13 against, and 10 abstentions. The thirteen opposing votes were cast by ten Arab and Moslem states, Cuba, Greece, and India. Great Britain was among the abstainers.

The dilemma of Palestine has not been finally solved. Partition and the creation of the State of Israel came about as a result of world reaction to the mass slaughter of millions of Jews by the Nazis. The problems of the Arab refugees, the never created "Arab State" in Palestine, and Arab-Israeli distrust and hostility caused by partition have yet to be resolved.　　O.K.

Party Competition. (U.S.A.)

The level of party competition in a constituency is the likelihood that a party other than the incumbent will capture the office in the next or succeeding elections. In the individual states (U.S.) the competitive level varies in that in some states one party is in complete control of all offices while in others there is a high rate of party alternation. Sectional party attachments and a homogeneity of interests within a state are the major reasons for lack of competition. Population mobility, and growing economic diversity in the various regions of the United States appear to be providing a base for increasing levels of competitiveness.　　J.S.S.

Party Platform.

One of the major mechanisms for formulating and declaring the policies of a political party. It is an official statement of party principles, policy, and programs. In the United States party platforms are adapted in party conventions—national, state and local. In Britain the party conference fulfills a similar function. It formulates the party creed, a basis upon which it seeks the support of the electorate. Party platforms and individual "planks" in them are usually vague and ambiguous in order to appeal to the widest possible clientele. In the United States, they do not bind the party's candidate very much because United States parties are not highly "disciplined". In various other countries "disciplined", centralized, integrated and responsible parties attempt, with varying degrees of success, to have all members accept the party's statement of programs, and to implement it in a serious fashion.
　　A.G.

Party Primary.

The most important device used to nominate party candidates for public office in the United States. Most states use some variety of the party primary (and for some local offices the nonpartisan primary) to make nominations for state and local offices. It is used almost universally for the nomination of United States Senators and Congressmen. Less than half the states also utilize the primary to select delegates to the parties' presidential nominating conventions. The remainder use the convention system for choosing such delegates as well as for making party nominations for other public and party offices (such as state or national committeemen).　　A.G.

Pascal, Blaise. (1623-1662).

A brilliant mathematician who preceded Leibniz and Newton in the invention of the integral and differential calculus, but also a famous philosopher who may be considered a forerunner of contemporary existentialism. He lived at a time when science strongly challenged the authority of religion, and yet he remained a devout Catholic while being a scientist. He became a member of the famous Port-Royal circle which was the seedbed of Jansenism in France, a movement in Catholicism which demanded renunciation of the world. Jansenists were fiercely attacked by the Jesuits who championed orthodoxy and who—following their philosopher Molina (1535-1601) — sought to establish a harmony between worldly morality and Christian faith. Pascal, in his brilliant **Provincial Letters,** defended the Jansenists from the Jesuit accusations, and attacked the Jesuit 'casuistry' so effectively that the Society of Jesus has not quite recovered from Pascal's critique of its ethos. Pascal remained a Catholic after Jansenism was proscribed by the Church, and he spent his last years in meditation and seclusion, suspending entirely his intellectual activities. V.Z.

Paternalism.

A social system characterized by the predominance of the prestige of the elder or of the one that holds a personal influence over the system of selection of merits and values. Literally, it is connected with the idea of "paterfamilias", whose influence exceeded the limits of the natural society based on a strictly family group. It is a political system to be found in less developed social groups, where individuals seek to approach those of greater political and social prestige. The expression is taken by analogy from the patriarchal society. T.C.

Pathet-Lao.

The struggle of the peoples of Indo-China for their independence from French rule resulted in the creation of three states: Vietnam, Cambodia and Laos. During this struggle a national liberation army was organized in Laos, which received the name of Pathet-Lao. In August 1950 a national congress of various groups of the Laos population formed the Pathet-Lao government, which pledged itself to fight French rule. During the period of struggle and later independence, three Royal half-brothers emerged in Laos, of which two were the more prominent: Prince Souvanna Phouma of neutralist tendencies, and the pro-communist Prince Souphanouvong, who became leader of the Pathet-Lao. During the internal strife the pro-communist Pathet-Lao gradually gained control over a considerable part of Laos. In 1953, it had control over two Northern provinces, Phong Saly and Sam Neua, and in 1954, by the time the Geneva agreement was signed, a considerable part of Laos was under control of the Pathet-Lao. In spite of the agreement, the Pathet-Lao, however, continued its attacks on the loyal forces. In March 1956 the new government of Prince Souvanna Phouma made an attempt to come to terms with the Pathet-Lao. The fluid situation in the country, with constant pressures from the Pathet-Lao and occasional fighting, resulted in the loss of a large portion of the territory by the loyal forces. By the middle of 1961, an international conference in Geneva agreed upon a coalition neutralist government headed by Prince Souvanna Phouma, although more than half of the territory was in the hands of the Pathet-Lao rebels.

V.P.P.

Patrimonialism.

Max Weber described patrimonialism as a political system based on a political-administrative organization staffed by civil servants. Such a system is said to have its origin in small localized patriarchal structures. It knows but little separation of public from private spheres of life. The administrator considers himself the owner of his administrative function. There is also no difference between private and public revenues. In Brazil patrimonialism is intimately associated with colonelism. A.F.Mo.

Patronage.

One of the key elements of the spoils system. It refers to public employment or appointments which are available for distribution by public officials, political parties or politicians. Used to reward faithful party workers and to create effective political organizations or machines. The "merit system", has greatly reduced "federal patronage" although most diplomats, all postmasters, all federal judges, collectors of customs, United States attorneys and marshals, fall into this category, as do the highest ranking policy-making officials. Patronage is used much more widely on the state and local level in the United States, especially in counties. Nearly all state government jobs in Pennsylvania (40,000-50,000) are patronage appointments. This practice is not restricted to the United States.   A.G.

Pauker, Anna (1893-).
Rumanian Communist of Jewish extraction. An important personality in the Comintern, she spent the war years in the Soviet Union and returned to Rumania with the Red Army. She reputedly engineered the conversion of Rumania to communism in 1947, became Foreign Minister and participated in the organization of the Cominform. Dismissed from office in 1952.   G.K.

Paul, Saint.
Only Jesus is more important in Christianity than St. Paul. Born in Tarsus of Jewish parents, he distinguished harshly between Judaism and Christianity and was at first one of the fiercest antagonists of Christ who —with his Gospel of love—negated the fundamental relevance of the Jewish law. He experienced a sudden conversion to Christianity after Christ appeared to him in a vision while he was on the road to Damascus prepared to continue there his merciless persecution of Christians. From then on Paul travelled tirelessly all over the Roman Empire, undergoing infinite privation and sufferings, but gathering converts whom he organized into churches. His life is vividly depicted in his epistles which are of immense value for reconstructing his missionary activities and his views, and which are comparable in their significance only to the epistles of Plato or Cicero. His Epistle to the Romans is beyond any doubt the most influential political document of the New Testament, if not of Christianity. Therein Paul exhorts Christians that obedience toward 'the powers that be' is the only attitude compatible with their faith, because the magistrates are commissioned by God, and to oppose them is to oppose God. This doctrine of the duty of civic obedience on the part of Christians, is founded in a respect toward the office of the magistrates, not necessarily the particular person who happens to occupy this office.   V.Z.

Paulus, Friedrich von. (1890-1957.)
Field Marshal; as head of the German Sixth Army surrendered at Stalingrad, January, 1941. In Russian captivity joined Soviet-sponsored National Committee Free Germany. Returned to (East) Germany 1953; engaged in some anti-West propaganda.
  J.B.M.

Pavelic, Ante (1889-1959).
Croat political leader and founder of the terrorist **Ustashi** who received his training in medicine. In 1934 he fled to Fascist Italy after alleged participation in the assassination of King Alexander. He returned to defeated Yugoslavia with the Italian occupiers in 1941 and became **poglavnik** (Fuehrer) of the puppet Croat state.   G.K.

Pax Britannica.
The years from 1815 to 1914 which were the most peaceful in western history since the **Pax Romana.** During them Britain used the great power flowing from her early industrialization and naval dominance to stabilize the European balance of power and police her vast empire and much of the remaining non-European world.   V.R.I.

Pax Romana.
A period in western history most commonly said to have lasted from about 27 B.C. to 180 A.D. During these years imperial Rome dominated the western world which was prosperous and largely free from civil war and external threats.   V.R.I.

Peace Corps.
Established March 1961 as an agency within the U.S. Department of State. At the request of newly developing nations, arranges for placement of U.S. volunteers to help fill critical needs for skilled manpower. After ten weeks or more of training, usually at American universities, volunteers serve for period of two years abroad. Over fifty per cent of volunteers are in teaching. A rapidly expanding program, the Corps had nearly 3,000 volunteers in training or abroad at the end of its first year of operation.   W.C.R

"Peace, Order, and Good Government".
A statutory recital frequent in British 19th century Imperial legislation delegating power to colonial or dominion governments. These general words, regularly followed by specific, enumerated powers, were meant to designate the locus of residual power. (See also British North America Act, 1867.) M.P.S.

Peaceful Change.
The resolution of social problems, normally by institutionalized procedures, without resort to large-scale physical force. The term is used especially at the international level and refers to the process by which conflict is settled between states by any non-violent method, with "violence" used in the sense of "physical force". Even more specifically, it refers to settlement of international tensions (especially disputes) according to the rules of international law, which are themselves changed by non-violent means. The "peaceful change article" in the Covenant of the League of Nations is Article 19, and the one in the Charter of the United Nations is Article 14. R.W.V.W.

"Peaceful Co-existence".
The slogan of "peaceful co-existence" is Nikita Khrushchev's contribution to the semantics of Soviet foreign policy. In order to understand Soviet foreign policy, it is therefore essential to examine carefully Khrushchev's own definitions of "peaceful co-existence."

"Peaceful co-existence" does not signify a Soviet retreat or an attempt to stabilize communism but is, on the contrary, an expression of an even greater dynamism—militant and aggressive strategy that accords fully with the requirements of the changing international scene (i.e., the existence of the "balance of terror"). For example, the communist manifesto issued during the Moscow Conference of 1960 stated that "should the imperialistic maniacs start war, [the communists] will sweep capitalism out of existence and bury it." Then follows the blunt admission that "peaceful co-existence of states does not imply renunciation of the class struggle." On the contrary, "co-existence of states with different social systems is a form of the class struggle between socialism and capitalism."

In other words, the Free World if it were to presume that "peaceful co-existence" will mean "live and let live," would succumb to a very dangerous illusion. The communist manifesto implies that "peaceful co-existence" between communism and the Free World signifies a gradual and preferably non-military though ruthless campaign to force the surrender of the Free World to the communist system. Apparently, the communists have no doubts that they will "bury" the Free World in any case.

In this respect, the Chinese Communist view of the inevitability of war with the West and the Soviet view that such a war is avoidable because Communist goals can be achieved through a "peaceful co-existence" with the Free World, are both equally militant and aggressive. The difference is one of tactical emphasis concerning the best means to be employed for the annihilation of the opponents of Communism. R.St-H.

Pearl Harbor.
Early on the morning of December 7, 1941 Japanese navy planes surprised and devastatingly attacked U.S. naval units and installations at the Pearl Harbor base in Hawaii. Vice-Admiral Chuichi Nagumo commanded the Japanese task force of several cruisers and a half-dozen small aircraft carriers. U.S. forces were under Admiral Kimmel and General Short.

Within two hours, 105 Japanese planes put out of action half the capital ships of the U.S. Navy plus three cruisers, three destroyers, and assorted small craft. Most of the American planes based at Pearl Harbor were destroyed on the ground. American casualties included 2,340 dead, over 1,270 wounded, and 960 unaccounted for.

Whereas the blow was staggering, it failed to paralyze the U.S. as the attackers assumed it would. The U.S. promptly entered World War II as a full-fledged participant. M.T.K.

Peiping.
Capital city of Northern China since early 10th century (Liao and Kin Dynasties) and of unified China since

1267 (Yuan Dynasty, most of the Ming Dynasty, Ch'ing Dynasty and the early Republican period) under different names. Both the early Ming Dynasty (1368-1421) and the Nationalist Government (since 1928) named it Peiping (Northern Peace) with Nanking (Southern Capital) as their capital. The name "Peking" (Northern Capital) adopted by Ming Dynasty in 1421 was revived when the Japanese puppet government (1937-45) and Communist China (since 1949) used it as capital. Only 35 miles from the Great Wall built against "Tartars" in Mongolia and Manchuria, ever a crucial region in relations of China Proper, Mongolia and the Northeastern Provinces. Much admired by Marco Polo in 13th century. Bones of "Peking Man" of Paleolithic period, discovered at Choukoutien, 37 miles southwest of Peiping. Sino-Japanese War (1937-45) started at Lukochiao, just south of the city. Most renowned and most beautiful city in China; though scenery like palaces and temples, essentially man-made. Also the cultural center and railway hub of China. "Peking Opera" and "Peking duck," perhaps most famous; "Peking dust", the chief drawback. Prior to 1949, 273 sq. mi. with population of 1,700,000. Expanded by the communists to 6,500 sq. mi.; said to contain over 6 million people.
C.K.W.

Pendleton Act.

American national government legislation passed in 1883. This Act initiated the major transition in the U.S. from the politically dominated (and often corrupt and inefficient) "spoils system" to a "merit system" based on professional competence and divorced from partisan political influences. The Act created the U.S. Civil Service Commission, the agency responsible for directing, expanding, and improving the merit system in the national government's public service.   R.D.S.

Peninsulares.

White persons born on the Iberian peninsula, for whom the highest posts were reserved in the administration of the Spanish Empire in the Americas. Occupying the best positions in the army, Church, business establishments, and society, they also enjoyed many special privileges, such as exemptions from the general application of the laws. White persons born in the New World were known as **criollos**, and were considered as lesser nobility.
R.B.G.

Pentagon.

A five-sided structure completed on January 15, 1943 on the Virginia side of the Potomac River adjacent to Washington, D.C. is the locus of authority for and houses the principal executive offices of the United States Department of Defense, including those of the Army, Navy and Air Force. Also called the National Defense Building, it contains 17 miles of corridors and has provided office space for as many as 32,000 persons. Official address is Washington 25, D.C.   H.H.R.

Peonage.

The form of employer-employee relationship characteristic of the great estates or **latifundia** in Latin America. The semi-feudal character of this relationship, in which the worker is virtually attached to the estate, derives from the **encomienda** system of the Spanish colonial period. The traditional obligation of the worker to labor on the lands of the estate has in recent times been supplemented by various forms of debt slavery.   Ch.W.A.

Peoples' Courts.

See Soviet Peoples' Courts.

People's Democracy.

A "People's Democracy" is an authoritarian state organization introduced by the Soviet Union in the countries of Eastern Europe after World War II (1945-1947). Since democracy means "rule of the people," "people's democracy" is a tautological term. In the view of Soviet scholars, "people's democracy" should not be confused with "proletarian democracy," the latter being identical with the dictatorship of the proletariat which does not share its power with any other class. (This, presumably, is the case in the Soviet Union.) In turn, the concept of "people's democracy" is meant to distinguish Communist government from "capitalist party democracy," i.e., representative government based upon parliamentary institutions. The concept of a "people's democracy" was elaborated as a theoretical framework to legitimize Soviet-imposed regimes in Eastern Europe. According to this theory, these countries were administered by "coalition" governments, composed of bourgeois, petty-bourgeois, peasant, and proletarian elements, the latter dominating the "coalition." A theoretical explanation was needed in order to justify the inclusion of non-Communist parties in these peculiar regimes. According to this theoretical contrivance, "people's democracies" represent a transitional, though hybrid, form in the evolution from a "capitalist democracy" to true "socialism." This evolutionary process usually begins with the formation of a "popular front," i.e., the alliance of the non-Communist socialist and the Communist factions. During this transitional stage on the road to "Socialism," the opposing bourgeois and peasant parties are being either destroyed or included, usually upon having been purged of refractory elements, in the new government. Moscow-oriented Communist elements exercise complete control over the government so constituted. During this intermediate stage, the nationalization of the means of production is incomplete and the existence of several parties is still being tolerated. Thus a "people's democracy," desirable as it might be as an opportunistic device, must be considered, according to Communist doctrine as an "inferior type" of democracy, compared with the "highest form," such as "democracy" prevailing in the Soviet Union. R.St-H.

People's Republic of China.
See Red Chinese "People's Republic."

Performance Budget.
Every governmental budget carefully estimates the anticipated revenues and projected expenditures for a fiscal year or biennium. A performance budget divides disbursements into functions, activities and projects. Thus an education department budget would tell how many students at specific grade levels would be taught, given auxiliary services, etc. Although some program type budgeting always existed, it gained further recognition when the Hoover Commission (1949) advocated that the United States government adopt it. J.M.S.

Permanent Joint Board on Defense.
A Canadian-American board of ten members created in conformity with the agreement reached by President Franklin D. Roosevelt and Prime Minister William Lyon Mackenzie King at Ogdensburg, New York, on August 18, 1940, to establish a Permanent Joint Board on Defense to "consider in the broad sense the defense of the north half of the Western Hemisphere." As an advisory agency, the board rendered useful service during the war and has continued to keep under review the task originally assigned to it. W.W.

"Permanent Revolution."
The much-discussed and confused theory, explicit in Marx, that the proletariat must relentlessly push the bourgeoisie in the direction of the proletarian revolution. After 1905, Trotsky regarded it as his own contribution, a usurpation that was concurred in by others. In the post-Lenin period, Trotsky was attacked by Stalin through "permanent revolution", which stood in opposition to Lenin's and Stalin's more conservative theory of "socialism in one country." Stalin at that time falsely asserted that "permanent revolution" had been a major source of contention between Lenin and Trotsky in the pre-Revolutionary period.
D.N.J.

Peronismo.
The movement composed of the followers of Juan Peron, president of Argentina 1946-1955 (see **Jefe Maximo**). Its slogans and activities gave "dignity" to the workers (dubbed **descamisados**, "shirtless ones"). Peron's political theory was called **Justicialismo**, or "era of justice." It purported to combine the best of capitalism and Marxism into a third way (not just a compromise between the two). Social justice was "assured" for all: Capital was at the service of the economy, which was at the service of society, creating a new relationship to the law and the first **true** "democracy." Thinly disguised neo-fascism permeated policies and practices, **e.g.**, all individuals were organized into interest-group associations (corporate

government was instituted as an experiment in one province); the State was the highest integrating unit, although Peron was above the State; the "New Argentina" and Juan and Eva Peron were glorified everywhere; the "Twenty Fundamental Truths" were promulgated in 1950. Eva Peron became, after death, the "spiritual chief of the fatherland." A golpe (q.v.) was precipitated in Argentina in March, 1962, annulling the electoral successes of the Peronistas (allowed to run candidates the first time since Peron's ouster); they won 35% of the total vote cast. Juan Peron continued in exile in Madrid. R.D.H.

Perry, Matthew Calbraith.
American naval officer (b. 1794, d. 1858). His most notable exploit was the opening of Japan in 1854. Entering the Navy at the age of fifteen he saw service in the War of 1812, and later saw service in African and European waters. During his period of shore duty from 1833-43 at the Brooklyn Navy Yard he made important contributions to the development of steam squadrons. Thus the issue of coaling stations for the East Asian Squadron assumed growing importance in his mind. After a tour of sea duty with the African Squadron, and action in the Mexican War, he again returned to the Brooklyn Navy Yard.

In 1852 he was appointed to command of the East Asia Squadron. Plans had already been made to effect an opening of Japan. Perry's predecessor, however, became involved in a disciplinary action and was replaced before he could visit Japan. In taking over command of the East Asian Squadron, Perry wrote his own orders to give effect to his assignment. He carried a letter from President Fillmore to the Japanese authorities requesting the opening of Japan to American commerce and other privileges. In July, 1853 Perry sailed with part of his squadron into Tokyo Bay, and against this background of force delivered the letter. After returning to Chinese waters for the winter he proceeded once more to Japan in February, 1854, where he entered into negotiations. On March 31, he concluded the Treaty of Kanagawa, thereby "opening" Japan to trade at the ports of Hakodate and Shimoda.

During his stay in Chinese waters Perry made observations on the Taiping Rebellion than raging in China, expressing sympathy with the rebels, and hostility toward the Manchus, thereby antagonizing the State Department's Minister Humphrey Marshall. In 1856 he published an account of his mission in the three volume **Narrative of the Experiences of an American Squadron in the China Seas and Japan.** S.S.

Persona non grata.
This term is usually applied to a diplomatic official who is not acceptable to the government to which he is sent.
R.A.B.

Personal liberty.
The privileges and immunities of the individual protected against both governmental and private infringement by the Constitution and legislation. A continuing problem of democratic government is the reconciliation of personal liberty and governmental authority.
R.R.R.

Personal Union.
A loose form of union between states with the governmental forms of monarchy; two hitherto separate states come under one dynasty. The states remain distinct legal persons in national and international matters. The only bond of union is the common Sovereign. Example: the union of England and Hanover between 1714 and 1837. T.P.

Personalismo.
The Latin American political habit of deference to and dependence upon personal authority, dating back to four centuries of Spanish colonial rule in the Americas which concentrated governmental, economic, and religious powers in a handful of officials. Electorally, personalismo usually denotes that a candidate for public office attracts followers with his personality rather than with a political party platform or through an established political party membership. M.A.

Petain, Henri Philippe (1856-1951).
French military leader and politician. Petain was known for his "prudence"

and ability to conduct "defensive" wars. He became a world figure in 1917 when, after winning the Battle of Verdun he was made Supreme Commander of the French Army and a Marshal. After the First World War, Marshal Petain "played" politics from time to time. In 1940 when France was defeated by the Germans he advocated a policy of disengagement. In June of that year he organized his government, with Pierre Laval as his deputy, for the specific purpose of negotiating peace with Nazi Germany. His regime, which lasted until the invasion of France by the Allies in 1944, was known as the "Vichy Government". After the War he was tried and sentenced to die, but the sentence was reduced to life imprisonment by President Charles de Gaulle. W.C.C.

Peter I, "The Great" (1672-1725).

Emperor of Russia, launched a ruthless policy of westernization and opened Russia to Europe; built a new capital, St. Petersburg, in 1703; proclaimed Emperor of All the Russias in 1721, thus inaugurated the Russian Empire. Europeanized Russian administration, central and local institutions (in 1711 an "Administrative Senate", consisting of 9 of the Czar's appointees, replaced the traditional council of the boyars), church administration (in 1721 "the Holy Synod", composed of bishops presided over by a lay procurator, replaced the patriarchate), social manners, dress habits etc. He adopted measures regardless of the enormous human and financial sacrifices which they entailed. His actions divided the Russians into Westerners, who approved of his policies, and Slavophiles who, intent on preserving the traditional Russian way of life, condemned his reforms. Opposed to reliance on foreign specialists, he trained a new class of military men and administrators and scores of specialists in various fields and trades. He upset the class system by turning the peasants into serfs, recruiting a new nobility from among his military leaders, and making merit the criteria for social advancement.

He won hegemony of the North from Sweden as a result of the Great Northern War (1700-1721); from Persia he wrested the provinces to the west of the Caspian Sea. He left an enormous war machine of 126 army regiments and 48 ships of the line.
W.J.S.

Petition.

(1) Right of petition is the guarantee that the individual may freely take his viewpoint before governmental officials. The 1st Amendment to the U.S. Constitution includes the right to petition Congress for a redress of grievances, which is the basis of widespread interest group activity in politics known as lobbying. (2) Any written or verbal request for particular action directed toward a governmental official or body. Petitioners frequently seek to show broad support for their requests by circulating their petitions widely for signatures. (3) A written request bearing a required number of signatures to place a candidate's name on the ballot or to set in motion the processes of initiative, referendum, and recall available in some states of the United States. R.R.R.

Petition of Right.

An important document in English constitutional development listing the rights of the English people in a formal request presented by Parliament to King Charles I and signed by him on June 7, 1628. R.A.B.

Petofi Circle.

A debating society organized in 1955 by Hungarian intellectuals and students, all of them Communists. Members discussed theoretical and practical problems of Communism as applied to the Hungarian society and state. The Circle stood for humanism, freedom of opinion, and national sovereignty. It became famous after the 20th Soviet Party Congress, when the abuses of the Communist government under M. Rakosi were openly criticized. There were public sessions of the Circle discussing mistakes in economic policy, the falsification of national history, the distortion of Marxist philosophy. Six thousand persons took part in the session devoted to freedom of the press, where abuses of the Communist press were criticized (June 27, 1956). Although the Circle was a Party outlet, it was condemned by the Central

Committee; and its leaders, poets and well-known writers, were expelled from the Party (June 30, 1956). In the ensuing controversy within the Party's leadership, M. Rakosi was replaced as First Secretary by E. Gero, and the Circle was again free to pursue its activities. Similar debating circles were formed in several university and industrial centers. The circles became a major force driving for reform and national independence. Conflict within the Party led to the events of October, 1956, and to the clashes with the Political Police and Soviet troops. I.B.

Pflimlin, Pierre. (1907-)

French Premier at the time of the May 13, 1958, revolt of colonists and army units in Algeria. Pflimlin was the last Premier of the French Fourth Republic before General Charles de Gaulle assumed the office June 1, 1958. He then became a Minister of State in de Gaulle's cabinet. Now a deputy to the French National Assembly from the Alsatian department of Bas-Rhin, Pflimlin is principal spokesman for the Mouvement Republicain Populaire, liberal Catholic party formed at the close of World War II. His government posts have included those of Undersecretary of National Economy, 1946; Minister of Agriculture, 1947-1949 and 1950-1951; Minister of Overseas Affairs, 1952-1953. Pflimlin's publications include **Cours d'Economie Alsacienne** and **Perspective sur Notre Economie**.
E.R.W.

Philadelphia Convention of 1787.

Called by the delegates who had convened at Annapolis in 1786, for the purpose of revising the Articles of Confederation. Due to the impossibility of amending the Articles of Confederation in such a way that a stronger union would be effected, agreement was reached for the creation of a new basic document. The U.S. Constitution which resulted from the deliberations was signed in September 1787.
R.A.B.

Philippines.

The Philippines, a 7,100 island archipelago north of the equator and off Asia's southeast coast, has a land area of 115,758 square miles and a population (1960) of 27,455,799. Several ethnic strains are represented, but Malay ethnic and linguistic patterns predominate. English is widely spoken also.

Moderately advanced civilization existed prior to Western contact and small principalities constituted the governmental framework. Western influences began with the Spanish conquest following 1521. The Spanish era lasted until 1898. Catholic Christianity became predominant and a facade of European civilization became widespread. Moreover, a sense of nationalism emerged and by the late 19th century a reformist ethic existed, symbolized by the versatile Jose Rizal. A serious revolt in 1896 was nominally settled, but was renewed by informal alliance in 1898 with the American command in the Spanish-American war.

American acquisition of the islands was resented by the Filipinos and war broke out in 1899. It was largely a guerrilla conflict and lasted until 1902. Prior to this war a government under Emilio Aguinaldo was formed and just before hostilities began the short lived First Philippine Republic was charted.

The American era witnessed rapid change. Education, public health, transportation, agriculture, and trade were benefitted, and rudiments of Filipino political participation began under a government with an appointive Governor and Commission. In 1907 an elected Assembly shared influence with the Commission and an era of rapid tutoring in government began. Independence sentiment was strong but not belligerent. The Jones act in 1916 promised independence and a Senate replaced the Commission. In 1934 the Tydings-McDuffie Act was passed and in 1936 the Commonwealth government was inaugurated. Independence was promised for 1946. Under this government an elected President and Congress dominated the archipelago with foreign relations under American control. Manuel Quezon and Sergio Osmena of the Nationalist Party were elected President and Vice President.

In World War II the Philippines suffered invasion and severe damage. Filipino units fought the Japanese, and guerrilla activity continued during the occupation. Nevertheless, a Japanese sponsored Republic existed under

409

President Jose Laurel which perhaps mitigated wartime hardships.

Following liberation, the new Liberal party emerged successful in the 1946 election electing Manuel Roxas as President. Vice President Elpidio Quirino, who became President upon Roxas' death in 1948, was reelected in 1949. Taxing post war problems prevailed and corruption was widespread. The Huk rebellion was very serious in many areas. This was quelled by Defense Secretary Ramon Magsaysay who broke with Quirino over inadequacies in social-economic reform and ran victoriously for President in 1953 on the Nationalist Party ticket. Magsaysay attempted changes and urged honesty in government. The administration was dynamic and some rural and economic reform was accomplished. Magsaysay died in 1957 and was succeeded by Vice President Carlos Garcia who was reelected in 1957. Garcia continued Magsaysay's policies seemingly with less vitality and there appeared to be increased difficulties with corruption. The 1961 election saw the Liberal party victorious and Diosdado Macapagal became president.

Since independence, progress has been made in education, public health, road building, agricultural reform, industry, community development, etc. Dissident activity is minimal and many democratic procedures are in evidence including a vigorously free press. The Philippines is allied with the United States and has received considerable aid. Government is vested in an elected President, Vice President and a bicameral Congress. The state is unitary with national field services, but with elements of provincial and local self-government.   H.B.J.

Pieck, Wilhelm. (1876-1960).
Joined Social Democratic Party 1895. Member of the Central Committee of the newly founded Communist Party in Germany 1918. Member Prussian Diet 1921-28, Reichstag 1928-33. Prominent in Comintern. Lived in Soviet Russia, 1934-45. Chairman of the Communist Party in the Soviet Zone, 1945-46. Co-chairman Socialist Unity Party (q.v.), 1946-54. President (East) German Democratic Republic, 1949-60.   J.B.M.

Pierce, Franklin.
Born in Hillsboro, New Hampshire, November 23, 1804. Died October 8, 1869. He was the fourteenth president of the United States, (1853-1857). He was graduated from Bowdoin College as a lawyer. He served in the state legislature and in the United States Senate. He was an officer in the Mexican War. In 1852 he was nominated, on the forty-ninth ballot, as Democratic candidate for president. He defeated the Whig candidate, General Winfield Scott. Although not a pro-slavery man he supported slavery interests in the Kansas-Nebraska controversy.   M.F.

Pilate, Pontius.
Roman procurator of Judea (26 to 36 C.E.) whose administration was characterized by corruption, illtreatment and wholesale massacre of the people, the toleration of idolatry, and continuous executions without due process. In the New Testament his part in the crucifixion of Jesus is that of a wretched coward but this does not agree with his character as recorded in other sources.   E.R.

Pilsudski, Jozef. (1867-1935).
Born at Zulow, near Wilno. Polish socialist leader. Jailed five years in Siberia. Organized sharpshooters (**Strzelcy**) in World War One. First chief of state in Poland. Successful coup in 1926 led from retirement. Refused the Presidency but took War Ministry and chairmanship of Supreme Army Council. Last five years in semi-seclusion.   R.F.S.

Pitsinki, Kaarlo Vilhelmi.
A leader of the Social Democratic Party of Finland. Born December 27, 1923. Member of parliament 1958- . Secretary General of Finnish Social Democratic Party 1957- .   E.I.

Pivotal state.
In a United States presidential election a populous state where the party vote is fairly evenly divided or a doubtful state having a large number of electoral votes. A state that is "safe" as far as party voting is concerned is not pivotal. New York and Ohio exemplify pivotal states in having produced many successful candidates for the Presidency.   B.N.

Planning.

The process whereby governments attempt to anticipate and prepare for future needs and developments. Although the term also applies to economic and social programs, it is most commonly employed in connection with land use. In this sense, it indicates the efforts of communities to plan for their future growth and development in an orderly fashion by designating the uses to which land can be put. For this purpose comprehensive plans are prepared marking out areas for residential, commercial, and industrial use and indicating needed public facilities. Such plans are enforced and carried out through zoning codes, subdivision regulations, building and housing codes, and capital improvement programs.

H.J.Sch.

Plato. (428/427-348/347 B.C.).

The son of a distinguished Athenian family, he came early under the influence of politics. In the power struggle between democratic and oligarchic factions, at first Plato hoped for the restoration of Periclean democracy. The unjust treatment of Socrates by democratic leaders, and his ensuing death, disillusioned Plato and he temporarily left Athens. At a later time Plato served as the tutor of the future King of Sicily, Dionysius II, invited to educate the young prince for constitutional rule. Sicily's seizure of Syracuse and the assassination of Dion, his friend and uncle of Dionysius II, occasioned some shorter writings.

Plato was the founder of the Academy, a center for the study of philosophy and the sciences. On a problem posited by the Master, the solution was sought by joint effort with the students. Reflecting this method, his principal writings are in the form of dialogues. His chief political dialogues are **The Republic** (on man and the state), **The Statesman** (on the art and science of ruling), **Laws** (on the rule in an imperfect state). In the last two of these works, his low esteem of democracy—inspired by the fate of his beloved Socrates—is somewhat mitigated.

The Republic is the fullest expression of Plato's ethical and political ideas applied to the community. Justice—identified with morality—is the highest virtue, and is regulative of all other virtues. Justice restrains, and to achieve the common good individual action needs to be restrained. Man is a social being who submits to the moral law and forms political associations. The task of the ruler is to maintain conditions most conducive to the individual development of virtues. Political unity is a universal requirement of any kind of state—but none achieves it perfectly.

The ideal state is a class state, in which the rulers, the fighters and the producers constitute separate communities. Superiority in virtue (wisdom and justice) is the qualification of the ruling class. Nature makes man unequal, the aptitude for full human virtue is reserved to few. Philosophers are in a special class to govern, since they are alone in possession of the true knowledge of the good. They know the Idea of the good, not needing instruction by the law. The philosopher is above the law, he is the source of law. The guardian class consists of warriors distinguished by the virtues of courage and temperance. To be fortified by education against temptations they must be freed from the possession of property and of family. (Plato's novel idea of "communism" among the guardians.)

The state is analogous to a person: where wisdom (justice), courage and temperance prevail—the state is most excellent. This is an Aristocracy, the rule of the philosophers. Where the military rules, the state is a Timocracy; where the merchants govern (the Plutocrats) Oligarchy is the political form. A further deviation from the best form is Democracy; here political power is with those who have no virtues to govern. But the worst is Tyranny where an irresponsibly and unqualified person holds total power at will.

T.P.

Plato's "Republic".

Plato's "Republic" is representative of an idea which explores the concept of "justice". Status in Plato's "Republic" is determined by natural aptitudes:

". . . yet God has framed you differently. Some of you have the power of command, and in the composition of these he has mingled gold, wherefore also they have the greatest honour; others he has made of silver, to be auxiliaries; others again who are to be husbandmen and craftsmen he has composed of brass and iron . . . ". . . when a man of brass or iron guards the State, it will be destroyed." (Book III).

Each Platonic citizen is a functional unit whose raison d'etre is service to the state. B.J.L.S.

Platt Amendment.
Amendment to a bill in the United States Congress, accepted as an annex to the Cuban Constitution of 1901, and incorporated in a treaty between the United States and Cuba in 1903. It provided that Cuba was not to sign any treaties impairing her territorial integrity or independence, nor was Cuba to contract any debts that could not be paid from regular sources of revenue. Article II gave the United States the right to intervene for the preservation of Cuban independence and the maintenance of a government for the protection of life, property, and individual liberty. Abrogated in May, 1934. R.B.G.

Plebiscitarian.
1. Pertaining to or based upon a plebiscite.
2. One who advocates plebiscites or a plebiscitarian government.
3. Pertaining to a government, state, or system, wherein the electorate gives up its voice in policy-making, retaining the function of giving inspired support for the attainment of very general goals (such as freedom and security). In return, the electorate is assured by an elite, which assumes the policy-making function, that the general will, which it is supposedly capable of divining, will be implemented. A state enjoying this system, where elections and political parties are free, may be called a plebiscitarian democracy, although the plebiscitarian feature reduces its democratic character. A plebiscitarian state without these characteristics would be a plebiscitarian dictatorship. D.W.Mc.

Plebiscite.
A vote by the people of an area to express their will (1) leading toward independence, or (2) fixing their allegiance to one country or another, or (3) establishing its form of government. An example is the decision of the Saarland favoring Germany rather than France; another example is a vote within the cantons of Switzerland on some question of national policy.
Sp.D.A.

Plekhanov, Georgy Valentinovich.
(N. Beltman) (1856-1918).
A leading Marxist theoretician; the ideological father of the Russian labor movement, in particular of the Marxist group for the 'Emancipation of Labor' formed in Geneva in 1883; spent 40 years abroad; directed from Geneva the Russian Social Democratic party; one of the founders (in 1900) and editors of **Iskra** (the Spark) and the founder in 1917 of **Edinstvo** (Unity) in which he attacked Lenin's totalitarian politics; co-author (with Lenin) of the program of the Russian Social Democratic party adopted in 1903; later he worked mostly with the Menshevik group in the party although occasionally he would form alliances with the Bolsheviki; a vigorous publicist, he disputed with various Marxist revisionists including Bernstein, the Russian 'economists' in the labor movement, the 'reformists' such as Struve and Tugan-Baranovsky, Bogdanov, Lunacharsky and others. Noted for his theory of art. Critical of the facile interpretations of Marx, he rejected the simplified view of the connection between economics and art as a mere linear cause and effect relationship.
W.J.S.

Pleven, Rene Jean (1901-   ).
Formerly with De Gaulle on the French Committee of National Liberation and as Minister of Colonies in the Provisional Government, Pleven became Minister of Finance in 1945, and since then has been a deputy in the Assembly from Cotes-du-Nord. As Minister of Defense in 1949 Pleven was official author of the plan for a European Defense Community. In late 1950 and late 1951 Pleven served twice as premier. He was first defeated because of opposition to a newly proposed electoral law under which in 1951 he led a center alliance in Cotes-du-Nord to victory. Socialist opposition led to his second defeat on a strict vote of confidence (second and last time this occurred in the Fourth Republic).

A leader of the UDSR, Pleven was personally popular with the Left, but his economic policy was orthodox. As premier he sought a team spirit among the major parties, and favored delegated legislation (lois Cadres) to lighten the Assembly's load. Pleven resigned from the UDSR when it opposed the De Gaulle constitution in 1958. R.B.C.

Pluralism.

First developed by Durkheim, von Gierke, and certain guild socialists and syndicalists, political pluralism is variously associated with the individual conscience and the need for variety of self-expression, with the power of interest groups, and with a multi-party system. But all pluralists oppose the pre-eminence of state sovereignty; in fact pluralism dates back to the Middle Ages when states were embryonic. Power should be distributed among the natural groups that compose society; no single body can represent the whole community. Implicit is the concept of countervailing power, with the general interest emerging from a balance of partial interests. Yet Laski attacked the American political party as an organization of interests. Certainly American politics is pluralistic, as were such leaders as Jefferson and Calhoun.

In part pluralism rationalizes collective bargaining in an industrial society in which Durkheim found a democratic structure inadequate. It was Aristotle who argued that a naturally pluralistic community might attain such unity that it would lose its character.

In contrast to the neat monism of Nazism, pluralism is "untidy", but is developing through metropolitan authorities, continental European national economic councils, and functional European organizations such as the Coal and Steel Community. R.B.C.

Pluralistic Security-Community.

A security-community (q.v.) which retains the legal independence of separate units without any merger, so that more than one supreme decision-making center exists. Example: the combined territory of Canada and the United States. R.W.V.W.

Plurality Voting.

A term which signifies a relative majority secured by a political candidate in an electoral contest. Under plurality voting the candidate who has polled votes in excess of those cast for every one else wins a seat in the legislature or a public office although he may not have obtained an absolute majority.

In Anglo-Saxon countries plurality is usually sufficient for election. Seats in the British House of Commons have been frequently won by a mere plurality of votes cast under the single-member district system. Conservative victories were due to heavy concentration of labor votes in some districts and the addition of the Liberal Party.

In the United States a candidate for president, while he needs an absolute majority of the Electoral College, has frequently polled not more than a plurality of the popular vote (e.g., Taylor, Buchanan, Lincoln, Garfield, Cleveland, Wilson, Truman, and Kennedy).

Primary elections in the American states are also largely governed by plurality. However, most of the Southern states require a second primary if no candidate received a majority; this run-off primary is a contest between the two highest competitors in the first primary.

Although plurality voting brings about the victory of a minority, a wide consensus on political fundamentals assures the acceptance of the outcome of a plurality election.

On the other hand, intensity of disagreement on political fundamentals in countries outside the Anglo-Saxon tradition tends to militate against the adoption of plurality voting. For example, on the continent of Europe minorities have often been opposed to being outvoted by another though larger minority than they constitute themselves and have, therefore, insisted on majority voting, proportional representation (q.v.), or other electoral systems. Yet, even in these countries plurality voting is by no means unknown.

Half of the membership of the German Bundestag (Bonn Republic) is elected in single-member districts with a plurality of votes being sufficient for election. While the deputies of the lower house of the Parliament of the French Fifth Republic are also elected from such districts, the candidates must receive a majority of the votes cast provided these votes are equal to at least 25% of the voters registered in the district; in the absence of such a majority a run-off election is held, a plurality this time being sufficient for election. Furthermore, in both Germany and France the President of the Republic may be elected by a plurality of votes of the Federal Convention and the Electoral College, respectively, should he fail to be elected by an absolute majority on the first ballot. In addition, in the absence of a majority, the Chancellor of the Bonn Republic may be elected by a plurality unless the President prefers to dissolve the Bundestag.

Plurality voting is, where it exists, not so much the result of philosophical speculation but simply the expression of the conviction that it is second best to voting by an absolute majority.
W.F.

Plutocracy.
1. A government dominated by the wealthy. 2. The class which dominates by virtue of its wealth. M.J.H.

Pocket veto.
In the U.S.A. the term is used to define the result when a president fails to sign a measure passed by both houses of Congress and Congress adjourns **sine die** within the ten day period. It results in absolute veto.
M.F.

Poincare, Raymond (1860-1934).
French political figure, a lawyer, was elected deputy in 1887; active parliamentary figure and orator; in 1893, minister of public instruction; 1895, minister of finance; 1896, minister of public instruction; 1906, minister of finance; in 1903 he was elected Senator. In 1912 he became premier and foreign minister, dealing with the Agadir crisis. In 1913 he was elected President of the Republic, serving during World War I. In 1921 he was again elected Senator, and in 1922-1924 was premier, noted for ordering the French occupation of the Ruhr to force German war debt payments. From 1926-1929, he was again premier, heading a national coalition, reestablishing the collapsing franc. E.G.L.

Poland.
Area of 120,359 sq. miles. Located between 14°07′ and 24°08′E. (440 miles); 50°50′ and 49°N. (405 miles). Seacoast of 320 miles along Baltic. Boundaries with East Germany (285 miles) on W., Czechoslovakia (808 miles) on S., and USSR (826 miles) on E., for a total of 1,919 miles. Territorial changes in 1945 moved country westward with annexation of former German lands east of Oder and W. Neisse Rivers. Not recognized **de jure** by United States. USSR seized Eastern Poland (46% of country) up to Curzon Line after 1939 Hitler-Stalin Pact.

Population in 1962 was over 30 million, with 15,524,000 or 51.5% rural and 14,609,000 or 48.5% in towns. Capital city Warsaw has 1,171,000. Due to postwar changes, about 98% of people ethnically Polish. Language is Western Slavic with Latin alphabet. No official statistics on religion, but over 95% Roman Catholic.

Political History. Piast dynasty united Polish tribes, with Mieszko I introducing Roman Catholicism (966). His son crowned king. Conflict next 300 years with Germans, Eastern Slavs, and Mongols. Polish-Lithuanian union (1386) from Baltic to Black Seas and start of Jagiellonian dynasty. Teutonic knights defeated at Battle of Grunwald (1410). Golden Age is sixteenth century. However, elective throne after J. dynasty and political power centered in parliament (see entry **Sejm**). Turks defeated at Vienna by King Jan III Sobieski (1683). After weakening of state, three partitions end of eighteenth century started 125 year occupation. Only in Galicia, some autonomy under Austria. Uprisings in 1830 and 1863 against Russian oppression. Control by Prussia worst, due to fanatic depolonization drive **(Kulturkampf)**.

Independence after World War One (see entries Sikorski, Paderewski, Pilsudski). German and Russian invasions of September 1939. Exile government in France and then England, with armed forces on all fronts and underground. Tremendous losses included over six million killed out of 30 million population; 2½ million deported to German and 1½ million to Russian forced labor; over 500,000 permanently crippled; and over $50 billion in property losses.

In July 1944 Communists from USSR (See Beirut) established the Polish Committee of National Liberation at Chelm, then Lublin, and later becoming the government at Warsaw. Initially a coalition (See Mikolajczyk), since the falsified elections of 1947 it has been controlled completely by the Communists, although two stooge parties are allowed to function (See Polish United Workers' Party, Polish Road to Socialism, **Sejm**). R.F.S.

Polaris.

The world's first underwater-to-surface intercontinental ballistic missile capable of being fired from a submarine with a missile range of 1500 to 2500 miles, speed of 8000 mph. T.W.

Police.

The police is responsible for the maintenance of public order and the protection of persons and property from unlawful acts. Many nations, such as Eire, Denmark, Norway, and France, centralize police organization into a national agency. In the United States, however, there are about 40,-000 police jurisdictions, with functions locally assigned. The typical municipal duties include neighborhood patrol, traffic regulation, criminal investigation, and such specialized activities as control of narcotics, liquor, prostitution, gambling, and juvenile delinquency. Rural townships and the counties may have their own sheriffs or constables. States also have police for highway patrols and criminal apprehension. The Federal Bureau of Investigation (FBI) engages chiefly in criminal detection and apprehension but also serves as a crime reporting service. The Coast Guard serves the coastal areas in maintenance of regulations of commerce, and sea safety and rescue. Other federal agencies, such as the Post Office or the Treasury, maintain investigators. In other nations police activities may also include such functions as supervision of domestic health and sanitation, scavenging, and maintenance of census records. In authoritarian states police may be used to support the government in power and suppress opposition movements, usually as an organization entirely separate from the civil police, having the power to arrest and confine any citizen suspected of being a threat to the state. In most democratic nations, however, police functions are strictly limited to civil order as opposed to political control. T.K.N.

Police Power.

The power of a state to make regulations to promote the health, safety, morals, and general welfare of its inhabitants. It is the general power of government possessed by the states before the adoption of the Constitution of the United States, and retained by them subject only to the limitations of that document. It is in the exercise of the police power that the states enact such diverse regulations as child labor laws, limitations on the hours of employment of women, standards of weights and measures, and laws governing the quality and sale of food and liquor, the use of automobiles, the vaccination of children, and the taking of fish and game. E.L.

Policy.

The objectives or goals which a group (organization, state, nation, international organization) sets for itself plus the means adopted toward the postulated goal. Also see decision, administration. J.A.R.

Policy-Approach.

An applied approach to knowledge emphasizing its direction at understanding and improving public-policy-making. Political science has a long history of presumed action-orientation, renewed after some extreme positivistic and "value-free" intervals by recent increasing interest among scientists in social problems, well expressed by Harold D. Lasswell's call for "policy orientation" and "policy science." Achievements lag radically behind presumptions and needs, political science —like most other social sciences with the exception of economics—having as yet in fact little substantive knowledge directly useful in public policy making. Y.D.

Policy-making.

The process of formulating both ends and means to the ends, including the selection of problems for attention, devising alternatives to meet the problems, and prescribing one alternative over others. Formerly distinguished clearly from administration (as in the writings of Woodrow Wilson and Frank Goodnow), but now recognized to include the execution of an alternative as well as the process of selection. Sometimes distinguished from decision-making by (a) the absence of sanctions to compel compliance and (b) by being confined to governmental or political decision-making. J.A.R.

Polish Front of National Unity (FJN —Front Jednosci Narodowej).

Established prior to the October 1952 unopposed election in Poland; only one candidate was allowed to run for each seat on a so-called coalition basis. The FJN also operated in the 1957 and 1961 elections, with the Communists obtaining absolute majorities every time at the expense of the two stooge parties (see **Sejm**). R.F.S.

Polish Revolution of 1956.

Misnomer for events during October 1956 which brought Wladyslaw Gomulka (see entry) back into power at eighth plenum of Central Committee, Polish United Workers' Party. An uninvited Russian group (Khrushchev, Molotov, Kaganovich, Mikoyan, Konev) arrived in Warsaw on October 19 and attempted to interfere with the election of Gomulka. No comparison should be made with Hungary, where an uprising took place. In Poland, what occurred was only a change in Communist leadership.

The Warsaw regime did win these concessions from the USSR: Konstantin K. Rokossovsky (see entry) withdrawn as Defense Minister; the status of forces agreement revised in Poland's favor; debts cancelled in return for coal deliveries (1946-53) below cost; a new 700 million ruble loan; and promise of 1.4 million tons of grain in 1957.

Gomulka announced internal ban on force in collectivization (the system immediately collapsed), slowdown in the rapid rate of development for heavy industry, and restoration of "Socialist legality" as well as intra-Party democracy. He promised a higher living standard, more personal freedom, and greater independence from the Soviet Union. This apparently sufficed to avert more riots, like those at Poznan (see entry).

Perhaps one of the reasons why the Poles were more cautious than the Hungarians and refrained from crossing the point of no return in 1956 can be discovered in their past experiences. October 1939 had brought defeat at the hands of Germany after six weeks of heroic fighting against two enemies (the Red Army struck from the East on September 17th) without any aid from either Britain or France, other than declarations of war but only against Germany.

Again in July-September 1944, there occurred the 63 day Warsaw uprising against the German occupants which the Red Army watched from across the Vistula River without making a move to assist the insurgents. These two events, and the firsthand acquaintance with the Soviets during their 1939-41 occupation of Eastern Poland as well as that toward the end of the Second World War, have familiarized the Polish nation only too well with the USSR. R.F.S.

Polish Road to Socialism. (polska droga do socjalizmu).

Term identified with Wladyslaw Gomulka and 1956 development, although he discontinued its use as of 1958. The main difference from the Soviet pattern is that the Polish peasantry and Church are not completely dominated. In 1962, over 95% of the population was still Roman Catholic and 91% of the land under private cultivation. R.F.S.

Polish Socialist Party. (PPS-Polska Partia Socjalistyczna).

Movement established toward end of nineteenth century under foreign occupation; split in 1906, with left wing opposing Jozef Pilsudski's "revolutionary faction" and independence plank. Recognized political party until forced fusion with Communists on December 15, 1948 and extinction of right wing (see Jozef Cyrankiewicz). R.F.S.

Polish United Workers' Party.
(PZPR—Polska Zjednoczona Partia Robotnicza).
Name of the Communist Party since the December 1948 fusion with the Socialist left wing. Original predecessor was the Communist Party of Poland (1918-38), dissolved by the Comintern. Agents, paradropped from Moscow, organized the clandestine Polish Workers' Party (PPR) on January 5, 1942 in Warsaw. Membership has grown from 20,000 in 1945 to 1.3 million in May 1962.   R.F.S.

Political Behavior.
The behavioral approach to politics, stressed in recent years by many political scientists, is a way of investigating political data; it is not a field of political science such as constitutional law or international relations, but an approach which can be applied to any of the traditional fields by asking **why** judges, precinct captains, and nations **behave** the way they do. The stress **on why** or on the ecology and etiology of politics as distinguished from an emphasis on **how** or description and classification of political phenomena, is what marks the behavioral approach.

Political behavior leans heavily on anthropology, sociology, and psychology. Studies on the politics of underdeveloped areas stress the relatedness of politics, the systems of property, family, and sex. Studies of voting behavior in the United States emphasize group influences such as the political behavior of labor union members, Negroes, or Westerners. Recent political biographies explain political styles and crucial decisions by an analysis of early childhood relationships or other psychological factors.

The major methodological problem of political behaviorists is the same as that faced by other behavioral scientists—the difficulty of controlling the many variables which influence human action. The science of human behavior including political behavior is still crude, but advancing, and while it may never, or some would say, should never, be able to predict behavior with certainty, it is likely to yield significant information concerning the nature of political man which cannot be discovered through the purely descriptive or speculative approaches.   L.H.F.

Political Community.
A social group with a process of political communication, some machinery for enforcement, and some popular habits of compliance. A political community may or may not be a security-community (q.v.).   R.W.V.W.

Political Geography.
The study of politically organized areas, especially of the states. The physical environment, such as geographical location, boundaries, surface configuration, resource endowment, general climatic conditions, has a definite relationship to the development of states and their population, and to the general strength and weakness that states have in relation to other states. Sensible political leadership must always take note of the relevant environmental factors though these should not predominate in political decision making as this happened to some degree in Hitler's Germany under the influence of the geopolitical school.   P.P.R.

Political machine.
The organization of a faction within a political party which dominates party matters with machine-like precision. Its aim is to control political and governmental affairs of an area such as a city or state through patronage, obedience, and at times through corrupt practices. One strong political personality or a coterie of such personalities direct the machine's efforts. The Byrd organization of Virginia in the U.S.A. represents a state machine today, while Tammany Hall of New York City represents a long-operating machine.
    B.N.

Political Party.
The largest mass organization of voters in modern governments. The most famous definition is Edmund Burke's: "a body of men united for promoting by their joint endeavors the national interests upon some particular principle on which they are all agreed." This definition is not widely accepted today because it does not distinguish party from pressure group. A party is rather a group following a leader or leaders who desire to gain and maintain control over governmental power. Political power may be desired for public ends or to distribute power,

wealth and influence among party leaders and members. The party permits voters to select public officers and influence policy and the party undertakes to operate the machinery of government. It also stimulates voters to participate in politics and educates them.
A.G.

Political rights.
The implicit rights of citizens in a free society to participate in governmental procedures. This infers the influencing and controlling of public policy and the conduct of public affairs through the franchise and through access to seats of authority.   B.N.

Political Science.
See Introduction: The Meaning and Scope of Political Science.

Political theory.
Generally the entire realm of thought concerning the origin, form, and behavior of the state. It may be subdivided into political philosophy, which is closely related to moral philosophy or ethics; legal political theory, dealing with the nature of the positive law, the concept of sovereignty and legal controls for the exercise of political power; scientific political theory, consisting of empirical observations of political events and efforts to arrive at generalizations.   J.D.

Political Theory of Law.
Law consists of those norms which are rendered binding upon people and institutions by state authority or international accord. Excluded from this usage are such terms as law of gravity, laws of physics, laws of God, etc. But implicit in the term is the idea of a governmental entity which enjoys rule making authority of binding character.

It may be objected that law should not be identified solely with state institutions, and indeed an attempt to do so with absolute precision is never quite satisfactory. Nevertheless, the term law as usually employed in political science concerns itself with the state in one or another of its manifestations, and it is in this context that it can be most usefully identified.

Within this framework (and also in other contexts), a political definition of law merely postulates that rules of law reflect the dominant forces of a society. Hence this writer has suggested that law is a formalized derivative of politics, and the Chilean publicist, A. Alvarez, observed that law takes politics and the psychology of peoples into account, and, in the case of international law, they form or constitute the law and give it direct and spontaneous birth. Finally, some writers view law as consisting of those norms which the ruling group wishes to enforce. (While only peripherally relevant to law **per se** it is useful to note that this relationship applies equally well to non-state norms. Hence the rules of fraternal society, a church, a vocational association, a sewing circle, or a PTA can be said to reflect their internal politics.)

This is not to suggest that concept of justice, certainty, predictability, etc. are irrelevant, but rather to emphasize the more transcendent consideration that the norms themselves reflect these concepts only to the extent that they are the prevailing components within the political forces.   H.B.J.

Politician.
A term derived from the Greek designating a person devoted to the service of the **polis** (or city-state). Present day meaning: a person active in public affairs and skilled in the formation of public policies. (When used in a disparaging sense, the word "politician" connotes a party "boss" or other manipulator of public affairs for private gain.) See Statesman.   J.D.

Politics.
An activity which expresses the wills and interests of individuals in the ordering of their public affairs. The term is derived from the Greek word polis (or city state). The objective of politics (or man's political activities) is policy, i.e. a certain conduct in public affairs.   J.D.

Polity.
Broadly, a politically organized community or a state. Also, the constitution or the organization of government. As an Aristotelian concept, it is the constitution (or form of government) that places the power to govern in the entire body of citizens which uses this power unselfishly for the common wel-

fare, benefiting individuals and social groups equitably and proportionately according to their contributions to common ends. T.P.

Polk, James Knox.
Born in North Carolina, November 2, 1795. Died June 15, 1849, buried on capitol grounds in Nashville, Tennessee. He was the eleventh president of the United States, (1845-1849). He was graduated from the University of North Carolina. He served in the Tennessee legislature and in the lower house of Congress. For three years he was Speaker. In 1844 he was nominated for the presidency as the first "dark horse" candidate. He won as a Democrat and an expansionist. In 1845, during his administration, the Mexican War occurred. As a result of the peace treaty The United States secured California, Utah and New Mexico by cession from Mexico. M.F.

Polling.
Any technique by which an alleged and predetermined fair sample of the population is selected and questioned on some public issue, and from which the tabulated results are claimed to provide an accurate representation of the opinion of the total population. Polling may range from man-in-the-street impressions to highly sophisticated population analysis. Elections are a special form of polling used for electing public officials or determining certain public issues. R.M.T.

Poll Tax.
A direct tax levied at so much per head. (Its payment is still a requirement for voting in five states of the U.S.A.) C.W.B.

Polybius (appr. 201-120 B.C.).
A diplomat and statesman of the Achean League, is best known for his writings of history to which he gave a new — scientific and philosophical direction. His contribution to politics is chiefly in the analysis of the Constitution of Rome. As an early exponent of Realpolitik, Polybius is basically concerned with state power. What made Rome the ruler of the world? In part, its mixed constitution. He admires the able blending of monarchical and democratic elements; the administrative powers of the consuls, and the power of the purse, war powers and foreign relations in the hands of the Senate representing monarchy. Meanwhile, democracy found expression in the People's power in matters of capital punishment, deliberations on war or peace, ratification of treaties and the like — resulting in balance of the power structure. Beyond the constitution, Polybius believed, the growth of the state depends on the quality of the people, particularly that of the leaders. His initially pragmatic approach brings him closer here to Plato and Aristotle. He emphasized the importance of state religion for integrity in public affairs. Professing the cyclical revolutions of the state, (a state will return after progress to its original form) he admonished that democracy will decay to mob rule when political glory vanishes.
T.P.

Poor Law Act.
This law, dating from Tudor Times, placed the responsibility for the administering of poor relief upon the British parishes. The Poor Relief Act of 1601 created "overseers of the poor" who were subject to the control of the justices of the peace. The law required that all paupers had to be either set to work or provided with aid from a new local tax — the "poor rate." Poor law administration, which was almost entirely in the hands of the justices, was removed from them and placed in the "Poor Law Commission" by the Poor Law Amendment Act of 1834. The Poor Law Commissions were later replaced in 1847 by the Poor Law Board. The antecedents of present welfare legislation, which recognizes the responsibility of the state for the welfare of its members, may be seen in the Poor Laws of the 17th century and the Poor Law Amendment Act of 1834.
C.A.McC.

Popular Front.
See French Popular Front.

Popular Sovereignty.
System of government in which the people are the source of all legitimate governmental power. The American Declaration of Independence (1776) affirms this principle as a justification for the American Revolution. The principle is asserted in the preamble to the

419

U. S. Constitution and in all of the 50 state constitutions. Thirty-nine of the state constitutions specifically go on to recognize the right of the people to alter their government. W.F.G.

Population.
An aggregate of individuals defined with reference to geographical locale, political status, and similar specific conditions. The growth and decline of populations, immigration, emigration, optimum size, over-population or under-population as against available means of sustenance are of vital interest to the political scientist. J.D.

Population explosion.
The rapid increase in a nation's population often associated with the first several decades of industrialization. It is also aided by the drastically lowered death rates due to modern medicine and sanitation. Rapid population increase may indicate vigor in a society and dynamic growth in the economy. However, if population already is dense and if resources are meager or untapped, population explosion may actually reduce living standards. China, India, and Egypt are countries where population explosion may have serious internal and international consequences. R.D.S.

Port Arthur.
Naval base in NE China (pop. over 750,000, including Dairen). Port Arthur was part of the Kwantung territory leased from China by Russia in 1898. By the Treaty of Portsmouth (1905), ending the Russo-Japanese War, this territory was turned over to Japan. At the end of World War II, in accordance with agreements reached at the Yalta Conference, the Russian lease of Port Arthur was restored. When the Soviet Union and the People's Republic of China (Red China) became allies, in 1950, arrangements for restoring Port Arthur to China were agreed upon, and, after some delays, implemented. S.L.A.

Port of London Authority.
Organized in 1909 by an Act of Parliament as a self-governing trust to control the whole of the tidal reaches of the River Thames from the Estuary to Teddington. It is governed by a Board of appointed and elected representatives of the interests of the Port. One of the appointed members is nominated by the Admiralty, two by the Ministry of Transport, four by the London County Council, two by the Corporation of the City of London, and one by the Corporation of Trinity House. Eighteen others are elected by shipowners, merchants, and other users of the Port. The Authority's rates and charges are designed to cover the costs of its operations. R.G.S.

Port of New York Authority.
Created by an interstate compact between New York and New Jersey in 1921 as the first large interstate public authority in the United States, after the model of the Port of London Authority. Its purpose is to coordinate the planning and development of the Port of New York within an area roughly twenty-five miles in radius about the Statue of Liberty, known as the "Port of New York District." This is a multi-purpose public corporation financing itself through issues of general-purpose revenue bonds and collections of tolls and other fees. Governed by six Commissioners from New York State and six from New Jersey appointed by the respective Governors. R.G.S.

Portsmouth, Treaty of.
September 5, 1905.
Negotiated through American good offices, it settled the Russo-Japanese War of 1904-5 by Russia conceding former rights in Manchuria and Sakhalin and recognizing Japan as "paramount" in Korea. China agreed to this settlement in December. By it Japan became a continental Asian power. G.O.T.

Portugal.
Portugal has an area of 35,490 sq. miles and a population (1960) of 9,149,000 people. The capital is Lisbon and the language is Portuguese. It is situated in the western part of the Iberian Peninsula and faces the Atlantic on the West and South and Spain in the East and North. It produces wine, cork, fish, and some mining is important. Its overseas colonies—called territories since 1951—include the Cape Verde Islands, Angola, Timor, Mozambique, Guinea, S. Tome and Principe Islands, Macao. It is a predominantly Catholic country. A concordat was

signed with the Vatican, May 7, 1940 which provides for the relations of Church and the State. A census showed that (1950) 60% of the population over seven years of age was literate. There has been compulsory education since 1911. There are three universities: at Lisbon (1911), at Coimbra (1290), and Oporto (1911). There is also a Technical university in Lisbon (1930).

Portugal's President, Admiral Americo Deus Rodriques Thomaz, was elected in June, 1958 for a term of seven years. The cabinet, reorganized in 1961, is non-partisan. Its premier is Dr. Antonio de Oliveira de Salazar. There is a Parliament composed of a Corporative Chamber and a National Assembly. The members of this Corporative Chamber are appointed for 4 years; they represent various economic and social groups. Their number is 185. The National Assembly was last elected in November, 1961 for 4 years. It numbers 130 deputies.

Portugal is a unitary corporate republic whose constitution was adopted in 1933 and revised in 1959. The Corporate Chamber acts as an advisor to the National Assembly. There is a Council of States consisting of: the Premier, the President of the National Assembly, the President of the Corporate Chamber, the President of the Supreme Court and the Attorney General. The Council of State renders opinions and controls elections when the National Assembly is dissolved. The President of the State appoints the Premier. He, in turn, selects a cabinet which is not responsible to the National Assembly.

There are no political parties as they are understood in the United States or similar democracies. There does exist a semi-official political association, the National (pro Government) Union. Opposition groups such as the Movement of Democratic Unity and the National Democratic Movement were outlawed as communist fronts.

Despite its authoritarian character—a "personalism" which resembles that of various Latin American states, Portugal is allied with the West. It is a member of the North Atlantic Treaty Organization. It has long been an ally of England; and the United States has had military bases on its territory.

J.F.M.

Position Classification.

The grouping of positions or jobs into classes or categories according to their duties, responsibilities, and qualification requirements. By means of position classification, a variety of occupations with approximately equal duties can be subjected to common treatment with respect to selection, compensation, and other employment processes.

H.J.Sch.

Positive personnel administration.

An approach to American (and in other countries) personnel practices emphasizing aggressive development of new and improved techniques. Examples of this positive approach are using professionally staffed personnel offices, operating vigorous recruiting campaigns, and conducting imaginative in-service training and career development programs. An earlier "negative" or "passive" approach gave most attention only to keeping out the obviously unfit, incompetent, or dishonest candidates as well as assuring the political neutrality of the public service.

R.D.S.

Potsdam Declaration.

Policy statement on control and treatment of Germany issued by Allied leaders (Stalin, Truman, Attlee; Potsdam Conference, July - August 1945) to implement general agreements reached at previous wartime meetings (Moscow, 1943; Yalta, 1945). **Political Principles:** To disarm, demilitarize, denazify Germany; prepare for the eventual reconstruction of German political life on democratic basis by reform of educational, legal, judicial system; no central government to be permitted for the time being; local self-government to be developed under supervision; **Economic Principles:** To dismantle war industries; decentralize the economy; productive capacity to be controlled with emphasis upon peaceful domestic industry and agriculture; Germany to be treated as a single economic unit. **Reparations:** To be paid by plant removals, capital equipment and external assets, leaving only enough to enable Germany to attain minimum living standard. **Boundaries:** Koenigsberg and vicinity ceded to Russia; Russo-Polish boundary adjusted westward along old Curzon line; former German territory east of Oder-Neisse line placed under Polish administration "pending further determination." **War Criminals:** To be tried by an international tribunal. **Population Transfers:** German population remaining in Poland, Czechoslovakia, Hungary to be resettled in Germany. C.J.S.

Poujadist Party.
(Union for the Defense of Tradesmen and Craftsmen.)

Small, reactionary French party led by Pierre Poujade, an anti-tax demagogue. Briefly significant in the 1956 National Assembly (52 seats), it disappeared after winning only one seat in the 1958 elections. Antiparliamentarian and undemocratic, its principal support came from discontented small shopkeepers and businessmen. C.J.S.

P.O.U.M.

A Spanish Trotskyite party whose members had broken with the Comintern and the Spanish Communist Party in the late 1920's. It played a significant role in the Spanish Civil War against Franco and his fascist allies. Its leader Andres Nin was murdered by members of the Soviet Russian Secret Police (NKVD) whose delegation controlled the "loyalist" government in Madrid under Dr. Negrin since the summer of 1936 and used its power to liquidate those Trotskyites and socialists who refused to accept Communist domination. J.D.

Power.

1. Participation in making decisions; 2. Force or ability to get another party to do one's will; 3. The probability that A can get B to do M minus the probability that B would have done M if A had not intervened. 4. In various usages it sometimes implies sanctions while in others it does not. 5. Usage varies in the inclusion of legitimacy in the definition. See influence, authority; also see balance of power. J.A.R.

Power Economy and Subsistence Economy.

A country's power economy comprises operations of production, communication, credit, and distribution that serve the government's internal and international purposes. Its subsistence economy provides the population with food, clothing, shelter, and other consumer goods. Agriculture predominantly feeds the people, and the production of arms predominantly cements political power; yet neither the subsistence nor the power economy is tied exclusively to any specific branch of the economy. In the 19th century American heavy industry served only in small degree the government's defense and internal security. In certain pastoral societies such activities as fast riding, disciplined camping and moving, and hunting, which immediately satisfied the needs of subsistence, were also essential to the tribe's military power. The relation between the two economies varies with the institutional order in which they occur (e.g., a multicentered or single-centered society), with the order's international conditions (weak or strong neighbors), political developments, and the character of the leading personalities. The economy of Genghis Khan's Mongols produced few calories, but it had an enormous potential for aggression and conquest. Modern totalitarian states have systematically subordinated their subsistence economy to their power economy under such slogans as "guns for butter" and "the hegemony of heavy industry." To the conventional patterns of a power-oriented economy the Communists have added new types of expenditure: funds for Communist parties and fellow-traveling groups throughout the world, cultural propaganda, guided tours, politically impressive forms of economic aid, etc. The systematic restriction of the totalitarian subsistence economy tends to produce frustrations and discontents among large sections of the population. On the other hand, spectacular developments in particular sections of the power economy (missiles, space vehicles, etc.) augment the totalitarian regime's actual military strength and—skillfully utilized—even more the image of its striking power. Such developments are among the most effective material and psychological weapons for furthering the Communist strategy of total expansion.

K.A.W.

Powers (Francis Gary) Case.
Francis Gary Powers was born in Camden, Kentucky, August 17, 1929. He was a former United States Air Force pilot employed by the U.S. Central Intelligence Agency who flew a U-2 espionage aircraft downed on an intelligence reconnaissance mission some 1,200 miles within Soviet territory on May 1, 1960. He was tried for espionage, pleaded guilty, expressed regrets to Soviet authorities, and was convicted and sentenced to 10 years of confinement by the Military Division of the U.S.S.R. Supreme Court in August 1960. Was released on February 10, 1962 and returned to the United States in exchange for a Soviet agent, Rudolph Abel, imprisoned for espionage in the United States. A special Board of Inquiry appointed by CIA cleared Powers of suggestions of improper conduct, although full circumstances of incident were not disclosed. See U-2 Affair. H.H.R.

Power Structure.
The distribution of influence among persons, institutions, organizations, and ideas within a defined political or social community.

Influence is the ability to have public decisions within the community reflect one's wishes and interests. Measurement of amounts of influence possessed is difficult and there is considerable difference of opinion among scholars in the field as to the chief characteristics of power structure in American communities. One of the chief points of disagreement centers around the degree of pluralism possessed by these structures. One group argues that power is monopolized by a relatively few leaders who sit at the top of a stable power structure while another group believes that the system is much more pluralistic than this with many groups possessing differing amounts of influence in different fields of public policy. A.K.C.

Poznan Riots.
(June 28-29, 1956).
Started as peaceful strike against unbearable living conditions by ZISPO factory workers. After police fired at demonstrators, attack on prisons, Communist Party offices, and police headquarters. Troops sided with population, but special security forces rushed from Warsaw. Officially 53 dead and over 300 wounded, with 323 arrests. Regime shaken (see Polish Revolution of 1956). R.F.S.

Pragmatism.
Term invented by C. S. Pierce to describe his operational theory of meaning and used by William James and John Dewey to refer to their theories about truth, that which has good experimental consequences. It is more generally used to characterize any position which lays emphasis upon results and depreciates reliance upon rules and principles. In politics it refers to an empirical and experimental outlook. J.W.Ch.

Prague Coup d'Etat of 1948.
Forcible seizure of power by the Communist Party of Czechoslovakia in February 1948 after the resignation of non-Communist ministers from the postwar coalition government established by President Eduard Benes. The coup marked the beginning of complete communization of the country. F.M.

"Prairie Fire".
The designation of rapidly spreading grass-roots support for a relatively unknown candidate. (Example: J. Howard Edmondson; 1958 Oklahoma governor's race.) P.J.C.

Prasad, Rajendra. (1884-)
First President of the Republic of India, Prasad was born in Bihar, the son of a wealthy landlord. He earned an M.A. and M.L. from Calcutta University, and his LL.D. from Allahabad University. After several years' law practice, he joined Gandhi (q.v.) in Champaran **satyagraha** (q.v.) in 1917. Three years later, he took charge of **satyagraha** in Bihar. Subsequently, he emerged as one of Gandhi's most devoted lieutenants. He served several prison terms for his role in the nationalist movement. Prasad was President of the Indian National Congress (q.v.) in 1934, 1939, and 1947. Besides a year as Minister for Food and Agriculture in Nehru's Cabinet, he was President of the Constituent Assembly, 1946-1949. He was inaugurated Presi-

dent of India in 1950 and retained this position till 1962. C.S.S.

Pravda ("The Truth").
The official daily journal of the Communist Party of the Soviet Union. PRAVDA is the Soviet Union's most important, authoritative and widely read newspaper (A circulation of greater than five million daily copies is claimed). In PRAVDA is to be found the party's statement of its line and usually the first indication of any change to be made in that line. PRAVDA is edited in Moscow and printed almost simultaneously through the use of matrices in more than a dozen other cities across the Soviet Union. PRAVDA was first published in St. Petersburg on May 5, 1912 (now celebrated throughout the U.S.S.R. as "Press Day"), and was suppressed by Tsarist officials and started up again, usually under another name, on almost a score of different occasions before 1917. Among PRAVDA's editors have been Stalin, Molotov, Kamenev, Bukharin, Sverdlov, Kalinin, Gorky, Suslov.
D.N.J.

Pre-audit.
Determination by an authorized finance officer of the availability of appropriations and the legality of the claim before a warrant is issued. This function in the United States traditionally rested with officers independent of the executive; today the trend in American national, state, and municipal government toward placing this function in the hands of the chief executive is well established. T.S.

Precinct.
A minor governmental division for election purposes or for police administration in a city of the U.S.A.
C.W.B.

Precinct Caucus.
A basic unit of political party organization in the United States. It is a closed meeting of party members within the precinct to discuss party policy issues, to elect party leadership for the precinct level (precinct committeeman or captain, and possibly committeewoman), to elect delegates to city or county party caucuses or conventions, or to endorse party candidates. In the 20th century the caucus-convention system has given way to the primary system, but may still be found in operation separately or in conjunction with the primary system.
W.D.S.

Preferential Voting.
Election system using additional choices and weighted votes in attempt to provide majority rather than plurality election when more than two candidates contest for the same office. Under the Bucklin plan, adopted first (1909) in Grand Junction, Colorado (in the U.S.A.), voters express preferences by traditional marks in parallel columns to indicate first, second and third choices. Any candidate receiving an absolute majority of first choices is declared elected and other preferences are disregarded. Otherwise, second and third (if necessary) place votes are added to first choices to obtain a majority candidate. Failing the latter, the candidate with the largest plurality wins. To offset giving all choices equal value, the Nanson plan counted second and third place votes arithmetically worth half or one third the weight of first choices. The Ware system eliminated lowest first choice candidates and redistributed votes according to next choices. Although adopted in some form by more than fifty cities, many with commission type government, very few now use preferential voting. C.F.N.

Prejudice.
Generally considered to be prejudgment of an individual based on his racial, religious, nationality or ethnic grouping, without a sufficient quantity of facts. It is usually considered to be a set of attitudes, beliefs, values, emotions or feelings relatively unrelated to reality, or at most, based on limited experiences or facts out of proportion to their real meaning. Prejudice is distinguished from discrimination in that it is not an act. M.J.S.

Premier.
See France—Premier.

Premiers Conference.
An annual or special meeting of the Prime Minister of Australia and the six state premiers for the purpose of discussion of and possible agreement on problems of policy. The regular

annual meetings take place in conjunction with meetings of the Loan Council, a formal body which agrees on the borrowing programs of the national and state governments. The Premiers Conference must reach agreement on distribution of uniform tax receipts, usually by compromise. Past conferences have with mixed success and failure handled such problems as railway unification, economic problems during the great depression, marketing of agricultural products, and development of natural resources. R.H.B.

President of the United States.
(as a managerial functionary).

Among the various duties of the President of the United States is the demanding one of serving as the General Manager of a vast enterprise employing over four million persons (civil and military) and spending over eighty billions of dollars per year. If he is to discharge this obligation faithfully, he must coordinate the plans and activities of ten major departments and more than fifty important independent establishments as well as many other minor ones. As the Brownlow Commission pointed out and President Franklin D. Roosevelt agreed, the administrative task of the President has become an impossible one. The President has been given many staff assistants to help in this work, but much more reorganization is needed if the presidency is not to be overwhelmed or dissolve into futility. H.W.

President of the United States.
(as a political leader).

The President plays many roles, one of the most important of which is that of the leader of his political party. He names or has a great influence in the choice of the Chairman of the National Committee. He has a principal role in determining political strategy. He often lends his influence to his supporters in securing election or reelection and exerts a negative influence in the defeat of those who oppose his policies. He uses political patronage to reward his supporters and punish his enemies so far as he can within the scope of the Civil Service Act. He may appeal to the people against the action or inaction of Congress. His position as chief executive, chosen indirectly by the voters, gives him great prestige and makes politically noteworthy his every word and action. H.W.

President pro tempore.

An officer of the United States Senate who is chosen to preside during absences of the Vice President. In the event that the vice presidency is vacant, the president **pro tempore** becomes the President of the Senate. The president **pro tempore** is chosen from the ranks of the majority party, and ordinarily is the senior member of his party in point of service in the Senate. Th.P.

Presidential electors.

These officials are chosen by American voters at the general presidential election held in November every four years. Collectively, the electors become the Electoral College (535 members) which actually elects the President of the United States. This function has become **pro forma**, and the discretionary role of the electors practically eliminated, since the rise of political parties. Each state receives one elector for each member of its Congressional delegation. Th.P.

Presidential Government.

A system or form of government, usually democratic, based upon separation of powers, especially between the legislative and executive branches. Thus, legislative and executive powers are exercised by different persons. For example, the members of the U.S. Congress cannot at the same time be members of the executive branch, and the President and cabinet members cannot be members of Congress. Further, the chief executive is not chosen by, is not responsible to, and may not be removed by Congress (except, of course, through the impeachment procedure). W.V.H.

Presidential Inability.

If the President of the United States is incapacitated the Vice President shall "act as President . . . until the disability be removed or a President shall be elected." (Art. II, Sec. I) No Vice President has acted. To clarify the Constitution both President Eisenhower (in 1958) and Kennedy agreed with their Vice Presidents: The President shall, if able, decide his own disability; otherwise the Vice President shall decide; the President alone shall decide when his disability ends. T.C.S.

Presidential Inauguration Day.
Prior to the adoption of the 20th amendment to the United States Constitution in February, 1933, the President assumed office on March 4 of the year following election. Under the 20th amendment, the presidential inauguration day was established on January 20 following election. Inauguration day has come to be a gala festival day in Washington, D. C. The new President is first greeted in the streets as he proceeds to the "swearing-in" ceremonies. The Constitution requires the following oath to be taken: "I do solemnly swear (or affirm) that I will faithfully execute the Office of President of the United States, and will to the best of my Ability, preserve, protect and defend the Constitution of the United States." The President's Inaugural Address is important in all world capitals. The day ends with the Inaugural Ball. W.D.S.

Presidential lobby.
Efforts of the president of the U.S.A. to secure the enactment of his program into law are aided by lesser administrative officials whose relations with Congress include providing information, explanations and persuasion in behalf of the president's measures. Many administrative agencies employ full time people who cultivate close relations with members of Congress.
M.F.

Presidential primary.
A nominating procedure which enables voters to participate more directly in the selection of their party's presidential nominee. Now employed in about one-third of the states, the presidential primary requires both the expression of voter preference among candidates who are entered (the "popularity contest") and the selection of delegates to the national convention. Such delegates may or may not be committed to the candidate who wins the preference vote. Th.P.

Presidium of the Supreme Soviet.
Elected by and accountable to the Supreme Soviet, it is like a miniature Supreme Soviet in continuous session. Consists of a chairman considered to be the titular head of the state, fifteen vice-chairmen, one for each Union Republic, by custom always the Chairman of the Union Republic's Presidium of the Supreme Soviet, a secretary and sixteen members. Referred to as the "collective president." It includes important party leaders. It issues legislative decrees, interprets the laws of the U.S.S.R., convenes the sessions of the Supreme Soviet, releases and appoints ministers of the U.S.S.R. on the recommendation of the Chairman of the U.S.S.R. Council of Ministers and performs other executive functions.
K.Hu.

Press.
Originally printed organs of news and opinion (including pamphlets), today by extension, especially in terms of U.S. constitutional guarantee, includes all the mass media (q.v.). Also refers to personnel involved, generally limited to those producing news and opinions; "working press" still more limited to those actually performing news gathering, writing and editing functions. "Members of the press" are often referred to as "the Fourth Estate" (after clergy, nobility, elected representatives) in recognition of their political power. J.B.L.

Pressure Group.
An organization of people, with a certain amount of formality, based upon some sort of common interest or a set of closely related common interests, which attempts to influence government. It attempts to control or influence the formulation and execution of policy and the making of public decisions in order to protect and enhance its interest. Pressure groups vary greatly in terms of size, influence, interest, location, leadership and techniques. Among the most powerful pressure groups in the United States are the National Manufacturers Association, the United States Chamber of Commerce, the American Federation of Labor-Congress of Industrial Organizations, the American Farm Bureau Federation, the American Legion. A.G.

Prestige.
A policy of prestige is one of the ways in which nations may attempt to

carry out their foreign policies. It can be executed through the display of military or economic power, or through the insistence on certain aspects of diplomatic ceremonial (such as the choice of a capital for international conferences). Its purpose is to impress others with one's national power, real or simulated. H.L.M.

Preventive War.
The launching of a military assault on a hostile power in the belief that unless beaten to the punch he will in time attack with the benefit of concealment, surprise, and possibly superior strength. A doctrine occasionally advocated by some military commentators in post-war America in light of the Sino-Soviet military build up, but consistently repudiated by official spokesmen. The historically slow-motion version of "pre-emptive" or "spoiling" attack. L.P.B.

Price Support.
Any action by government to raise, maintain, or stabilize the price level of goods or services for sale by producers and distributors through parity payments, restricting production and marketing, buying of surpluses, or other means. The most pervasive and expensive price support programs in the United States relate to agriculture. T.S.

Prime Minister.
Title of the head of government in Great Britain and many Commonwealth countries. Under the constitution of the Fifth French Republic (1958) the head of that government is also called Prime Minister (premier ministre). Although the British Prime Minister is nominally appointed by the Monarch it would be more correct to say that he is elected by the people as the voters know with certainty that by voting for the one or the other party they are voting for the leader of their party as Prime Minister. However, if a Prime Minister leaves office through death or resignation it is the leadership of his party which in fact selects his successor who is then formally appointed by the King or Queen. Both as leader of the majority party and as head of the government the Prime Minister has an exceedingly strong position. He determines the outline of policy and all important decisions of other ministers are cleared with him first. He can reshuffle cabinet seats practically at will and constitutionally he is the principal advisor of the Monarch who must accept his advice. It is also the prerogative of the Prime Minister to have the House of Commons dissolved (see Dissolution). Because the Prime Minister must be in a position to defend the record of his government in the House of Commons it is politically impractical for a Lord to become Prime Minister. The last Lord to be Prime Minister was Lord Salisbury who retired in 1902. In 1922 Lord Curzon was not chosen Prime Minister because he was a peer. R.G.N.

Primitive Political Systems.
The institutions and processes of authoritative social control in non-bureaucratic societies. As such, the term is generally applied to the traditional and customary political structures of pre-literate and pre-industrial societies. At present, numerous such societies still survive within the boundaries of modern states in the Americas, Africa, Asia and Australia.

The major distinguishing characteristics of most primitive political systems is the absence of specialized social institutions and organizations with specific political functions. The vital functions of social control, social mobilization and conflict resolution are diffused, in varying degrees, in other social institutions such as the family, lineages, clans, age-groups, age regiments or ad-hoc councils. While there have been many examples of centralized chiefdoms and monarchical states, especially in traditional African political systems, these have been generally rare. The study of primitive political systems has until recently been the exclusive preserve of anthropologists. Political scientists are increasingly considering their study to be essential for comparative political analysis and the development of a general theory of politics. R.L.K.

Princely States of India.
See India, Princely States.

Prisoners of War.
The relevant law was first codified in the Hague Conventions of 1899 and 1907 (War on Land) and further de-

veloped in the Geneva Convention of 1929 which is now replaced by the Geneva Convention of August 12, 1949, relative to the Treatment of Prisoners of War. As of 1963 the latter was binding for close to 90 States, including the U.S., United Kingdom, U.S.S.R., and France. In addition to the provisions which shall be implemented in peace time, the Convention applies in all cases of: declared war; of any other armed conflict even if the state of war is not recognized by one of the parties; and of partial or total occupation even in the absence of armed resistance. It also applies between the parties thereto although one of the powers in conflict is not a party thereto. It applies also in relation to the latter if the latter accepts and applies its provisions. In case of an armed conflict not of an international character occurring in the territory of a party, each party shall apply certain minimum provisions. The different parts of the Convention deal with general protection, conditions and termination of captivity, information bureaus and relief societies, and the execution of the Convention.   S.E.

Private Law.

In the common law system, the term private law is used sometimes to distinguish the branch of law concerned with the definition, determination and enforcement of private rights and duties from criminal law. In the countries of the continental European legal system, the concept of private law **(droit prive; Zivilrecht)** includes civil law; but also extends beyond the conception of the latter specifically as the law of the various civil codes, to include all other legal norms (e.g., the law of negotiable instruments) which outside the civil codes proper govern the legal relations between private citizens. In this sense, private law is used in contradistinction to public law. See Civil Law, Public Law.   H.R.H.

Privilege.

A benefit or immunity conferred by authoritative action on a person or group. Although no complete listing has been made, privileges may be comprehended as: protection by government; pursuit of life, liberty, and happiness; and the acquiring and possessing of property with only such restraints as government may justly prescribe for the general good.   B.N.

Privy Council.

Historically, the Privy Council was the term given to the group of private advisors to the Monarch. As membership in the Privy Council is for life, that body is a very large one indeed, including all past and present cabinet members, certain high administration officials, heads of the Church of England, and other distinguished persons who have been honored by their appointment. The council as a whole only meets for ceremonial functions. Its real significance lies in the fact that the British Cabinet receives its constitutional mandate to govern as a subdivision of the Privy Council. Also important is the "Judicial Committee of the Privy Council," which is composed of the Lord Chancellor, the Law Lords in Ordinary, and other Privy Councillors who hold or who have held high judicial office in the United Kingdom or in the Commonwealth or colonies. Its most important function is hearing appeals from the Dominions and Colonies. However, since the passing of the Statute of Westminister, 1931, a number of the self governing commonwealths have exercised the right granted by that act to abolish the right of appeal to the Judicial Committee of the Privy Council. Thus its jurisdiction, while still important, is decreasing.   C.A.McC.

Privy Council Appeals.

Although by the end of the medieval period the king's council was coming to be mainly an executive body, it retained extensive legislative and judicial powers. As the court of last resort over colonial courts, it exercised a broad appellate jurisdiction over those of the American colonies. Some such appeals, e.g., Winthrop v. Lechmere (1727), refused enforcement to colonial statutes found to be in conflict with charter provisions, thus laying the groundwork for the development of judicial review under the state and national constitutions. Since 1833 the judicial work of the Council had been handled by a Judicial Committee, composed of persons holding or who have held high judicial office. Post-World War II developments have virtually ended this jurisdiction. Decisions have always taken the form of advice to the crown, hence no diversity of opinion even has been revealed. J.A.C.G.

Probate Court.
A special court, in many of the states of the U.S.A., charged with the establishment of wills and supervision over the administration of estates. Historically, these special courts assumed a function originally vested in the ecclesiastical authorities. Frequently, today, the probate court is only formally distinct and the office of probate judge is held by a judicial officer also charged with other responsibilities (e.g. juvenile court, county court, family court, etc.). F.H.H.

Probation.
The placing of a person under supervision following suspended sentence. The person agrees to live up to required conditions for a stated period of time and to report regularly to his supervising officer. K.E.H.

Procedural rights.
The orderly and established processes which guarantee those protective rights to an accused person before he can be deprived of his life, liberty or property. Some of these include: the availability of counsel, the privilege of the accused to hear the nature of evidence against him, the certainty of an impartial trial, and a verdict before being sentenced. B.N.

Process.
Interaction of variables or changes within a variable over time. Introduced by Bentley (1908) to emphasize the dynamic and changing qualities of government, including the influence of non-governmental factors on political decisions. Usage is now broader, as in the phrases, legislative process, judicial process, decision-making process, etc. J.A.R.

Procurator (Prosecutor).
The advocate of the Soviet state in judicial proceedings. At the republic level and above, the procurator also supervises all judicial proceedings to guarantee that both state and defendant receive just treatment. In theory, the procurator is immune to government pressures, being outside its organization. D.N.J.

Procurator-General (Prosecutor-General).
Chief legal executive of the Soviet state. The procurator-general has the responsibility for public prosecution, for the supervision of the civilian courts and often of local state organizations, and for the appointment of procurators at the **republic, krai** and **oblast** levels. The procurator-general, who is appointed by the Supreme Soviet for a seven year term, is almost invariably a legal specialist. D.N.J.

Producers' Cooperative.
A form of organization of the members, who pool their funds to own and operate the enterprise in which they work. Earnings are divided among worker-owners according to an agreed scale. This type of cooperative movement is the oldest; mainly influenced by ideas of Robert Owen, Saint-Simon, Louis Blanc and Fourier. Used to be a very strong movement in France; presently 90% of the agricultural production in the USSR is organized on this basis. W.N.

Productivity.
A rate at which goods are produced; thus we speak of 'labor productivity,' or the quantity of goods produced per worker per unit of time. It increases with an increased assistance from capital goods and investments, and with increased skills and specialization of the labor force. The assertion is that only the increases in productivity will provide the working class with higher real wages and more, and cheaper, goods. W.N.

Progressive Party.
Three separate American third party movements in the twentieth century have labelled themselves "Progressive Party." In 1912, Theodore Roosevelt's Progressive Party candidacy for the presidency measurably aided the Democrats. Neither a Progressive Party which nominated Senator Robert LaFollette for president in 1924, nor a Progressive Party which nominated Henry Wallace for president in 1948,

had any appreciable affect on national election results. The last Progressive Party campaigned unsuccessfully in 1952. Th.P.

Prohibition.
In the U.S.A. this term applies to legal prohibition of the manufacture, sale or use of alcoholic beverages. In 1919 the Eighteenth Amendment to the Constitution of the U.S. went into effect. It made the country "dry," i.e. no spiritous liquors were allowed to be manufactured, transported or sold. Violations were frequent and opposition widespread. In 1933 the Twenty-first amendment repealed the Eighteenth Amendment. Conventions in forty-six states approved the repeal. M.F.

Proletarian, Proletariat.
Proletarian, as an adjective, is used more loosely than the denotations of its noun (proletariat) would permit. Many things are termed proletarian (culture, society, etc.) which are not of the proletariat. Originally denoting the poorest among the Roman cities, today we designate with the term proletariat the industrial workers who sell for a set time their labor in exchange for wages to employers, entrepreneurs, capitalists, and enterprises, who mobilize this labor for the performance of specific but mechanical manual operations in large industrial establishments. Students of economic history, and Marx among them, trace the origination of the proletariat from the industrial revolution which began mainly with large-scale 'enclosures' in sixteenth, seventeenth, and eighteenth century England displacing peasants from the land now 'enclosed' and turned to pasture for grazing sheep to feed with wool the mushrooming and expanding textile mills offering wages in exchange for labor to masses of landless, impoverished peasants. Socially from the lowest stratum, politically diffident and impotent, lacking a consciousness of a common identity mainly because unaware of the nature and significance of the socio-economic forces that brought it into being, the proletariat could not organize to defend its rights and interests. The attainment of a consciousness of their common identity came gradually and mainly through the intellectual movement of socialism which expressed their grievances and demanded social justice in their name. This enabled workers to organize more effectively and to assert their interests in a program based on an outlook. Karl Marx's **Das Kapital** makes of the proletariat a demiurge of capitalist civilization, laboriously showing that this civilization is a product of human labor, the labor of the proletariat. His ideas gave tremendous confidence and selfconsciousness to the proletariat. It is for this reason that Marx's ideas eventually came to dominate all the movements which sprung up in the name of the proletariat to assert and advance their rights and interests. The term proletariat, when used loosely or propagandistically, is also meant to include members of other classes, particularly agricultural laborers. V.Z.

Proletarian Military Science.
Theory advanced by Frunze in debates with Trotsky in the USSR in 1922. Frunze argued that the Red Army should have a military science different from that of the capitalistic armies. He said it should be characterized by the offensive, speed and movement. Trotsky held that the military art is universal and not dependent on class. Lenin apparently supported the Trotsky view. The debate was broken off in 1922 without decision. W.D.J.

Propaganda.
Propaganda is persuasive communication—the technique of transmitting messages designed to influence human behavior. Verbal propaganda usually is interwoven with some form of supporting action ("propaganda of the deed"). In such commercial usage as advertising, verbal publicity is accompanied by **promotion** (manipulation of the publicized product). In such military usage as psychological warfare, verbal "output" is accompanied by combat activity (e.g., "psychological operations"). In the political arena, "information" is accompanied by legislative or administrative activity. The Bolsheviks stressed the special importance of this interaction, for revolutionary politics, in their phrase **agitprop** (agitation and propaganda). All of

these variants express the propagandist's recognition that persuasive communication requires the close coordination of words and deeds.

As a technique to serve a purpose (policy), the propagandist goes beyond the basic communication paradigm (who says what to whom?) and asks: how, why, with what effect? See Communication.   D.L.

Property qualifications.
A restrictive requirement for voting. In colonial America it was expressed in landed property, e.g. Pennsylvania (50 acres) or land value, e.g. Massachusetts (£40 or 40 shillings a year) and later in tax payments. Its aim was to limit the franchise to a specific minority. By 1822 general property requirements for voting had disappeared in all but four states of the United States.   B.N.

Proportional Representation.
P.R. is an electoral system which ensures that each political party, especially a minority group, will obtain a number of legislative seats in proportion to the number of votes cast for it.

Proponents of P.R., such as John Stuart Mill, consider it "contrary to all just government" if electors are represented by someone not chosen by themselves. Both majority voting and plurality voting (q.v.) fall under Mill's stricture, the former leaving a minority, the latter even a majority without representation of its own choosing.

P.R. proposes to do away with such injustice. Its technical requirements include the substitution of the general ticket system for the single-member district system; the return of at least three members to the legislature; and an electoral area, usually larger than that of the one-man constituency.

The main types of P.R. are two: the Single Transferable Vote, developed by Thomas Hare first in 1857, and the list system.

Under the Hare system, voters may express their preferences for individual candidates on the ballot by numbering them as first, second, and third choices, etc. A candidate will be declared elected when the first choices on his behalf equal or exceed the electoral quota. The latter is determined by dividing the total number of valid ballots cast in the area by one more than the number of seats allocated to it and by adding one to the result. The votes in excess of the electoral quota are counted with respect to their second, third, etc. preferences to fill the remaining seats. Countries which use the Hare system include Eire and the Commonwealth of Australia to elect the Dail Eireann and the Senate, respectively. A few city councils in the United States are also elected under this system.

While the Hare system is based on the voter's interest in candidates, the list systems attract those whose allegiance lies primarily with parties. Though the P.R. list system vary widely, all provide for lists, prepared by the party organizations themselves, for which the electors must vote. In some states, once the electoral quota has determined the number of seats won by each party, the voter is permitted to exercise full freedom of choice among the candidates; however, under most P.R. list systems choice among candidates is limited. Among the nations which employ the list system are the European democracies—West Germany, Italy, Switzerland, the Scandinavian and Low countries—and Israel.

P.R. could claim gains after both world wars. However, after the Second World War in some countries a reaction against P.R. set in which either led to the outright abolition of the system, as, for example, in some cities of the United States, Greece, the Union of South Africa, and the French Fifth Republic; or brought about its modification, as in West Germany where one half of the lower house is elected under the single-member district system and plurality voting (q.v.), and the other half by a list system of P.R.

Some of the reasoning in favor of P.R. emphasizes organizational advantages, such as the elimination of primaries, run-off elections, and gerrymandering; also, under the list system, bringing men of distinction into the legislature who, often lacking popular appeal, would not be voted for in a regular election. However, the gist of the arguments favorable to P.R. derives from Mill's invoking the causes of individualism and justice on behalf of those remaining unrepresented (see above).

Critics of P.R. who, following Walter Bagehot, adopt a functional rather than individualist approach, insist that what really matters is the effect of P.R. on the operation of the governmental process. To the critics, P.R. appears as a method which destroys the intimate contact between the representative and his constituents; strengthens the party bureaucracy; limits voters' participation in the selection of legislators; encourages multiplicity of parties; creates splinter parties; makes it difficult to rally a majority behind the government; leads to coalition governments which, because of the ideological differences of the participating parties, often fall apart; undermines the two-party system which is the foundation of parliamentarism; and obstructs both the location and enforcement of political responsibility.

Experience has not always confirmed the validity of these arguments. It is true that P.R. contributed to political disunity in the German Weimar Republic and the French Fourth Republic. On the other hand, multiple party systems existed in France and Germany even before the advent of P.R. Coalition governments were quite common under the French Third Republic although P.R. was employed only in the general elections of 1919 and 1924. In Eire P.R. brought a majority party to power which held on to it for a long time. Finally, in Scandinavia P.R. has proved its ability to effect stable coalitions and co-exist with parliamentarism (q.v.). "But the proportional enthusiast, who would argue from the relative success of proportionalism in some small countries that we should try it in Great Britain and the United States, goes wrong" (Carl J. Friedrich). In the United States, P.R. may encourage religious or racial groups and economic interests to form militant third parties which would not necessarily be disposed towards compromise and, therefore, tend to widen existing social and political cleavages. In Great Britain, both Parliament and the electorate may find it difficult to perform their traditional function to constitute the government on the basis of stable party support and, subsequently, to cast an unequivocal verdict as to whether such support of the government should be continued.

P.R. must be viewed from the standpoint of individual characteristics, needs, and objectives of each political system rather than exclusively from that of abstractions. W.F.

Proprietary colony.
A colony established under a royal grant to a proprietor, who was authorized to govern the colony as a feudal lord and was obligated to return certain dues to his sovereign. This grant might also contain provision for an assembly, selection of officials, and rights and liberties of subjects. Pennsylvania, Delaware, and Maryland were proprietary colonies. E.V.M.

Protectorate.
A form of political entity lacking the attributes of sovereignty yet recognized as a subject of international law. A protectorate usually results from a contractual relationship by which a weaker state or political entity places itself under the protection of a more powerful state, and accepts the direction of its foreign affairs by the latter. A protectorate or a protected state retains some powers of self-government under its own administration. Historically protectorates have usually resulted from expansionist policies by great powers, and the term has been most often used in European colonial rule in Africa and Asia. Relationships of widely different nature have been called protectorates. This type of political relationship seems to be disappearing from the post-World War II world. H.S.Th.

Proudhon, Pierre Joseph.
Born in 1809 in Besancon, France. Died in 1865 in Passy, France. Founder of the theory of anarchism in his treatises **Qu'est-ce que la propriete** and **Systeme des contradictions economiques ou la philosophie de la misere.** Seeking a free society, he attacked Marxism as "the tapeworm of socialism" and warned that the "dictatorship of the proletariat" would in reality lead to serfdom. J.D.

Prussia, dissolution of.
The Allied Control Council of Germany (Law #46, 25 Feb., 1947) requested that the State of Prussia be dissolved. This measure was approved by the Moscow Conference of Allied Foreign Ministers (March 10, 1947).
The Soviet Military Administration (Order #5, July 9, 1945) unified the territories of Soviet Zone **Laender** and provinces without regard to Prussia's boundaries. Following a resolution of the **Landtage** (Diets) of the former Prussian provinces of Saxony-Anhalt and Brandenburg, the Soviet Military Administration for Germany (Order #180 of July 21, 1947) declared them to be **Laender**, (States).
In the British Zone the **Laender** Schleswig-Holstein, Hannover, and Nordrhein-Westfalen were created (Ordinance #46 Aug. 23, 1946) on former Prussian Territory. In the U.S. Zone the Prussian provinces Hessen-Kassel and part of Nassau were absorbed by Land Hessen, (Proclamation #2, 19 Sept., 1945 and Report Aug. 20, 1945 of the U.S. Commander-in-Chief), while in the French Zone former Prussian possessions (e.g. Hohenzollern), were incorporated (1945) into five districts, predecessors of **Laender**. E.K.K.

Psychological mass coercion.
A totalitarian technique for governing and controlling masses relying on the methods of modern psychiatry. Developed by the Communists in China, it involved the fusion of two traditional Chinese institutions (mutual responsibility and the insistence on conformity) with the Leninist techniques of self-criticism and the democratic centralism of a militarized Communist Party. The key factor is the small "study group" into which people are organized. The study groups help to guarantee that no unofficial group activity or contacts exist among the people. Through full development of this technique the Chinese Communists were able to extend their control over the whole of the Chinese mainland in record time. Continuation of psychological mass coercion depends upon a monopoly of communications, the disciplined cadres, a series of drives and the ever-present threat or use of force. As developed in Communist China beginning in 1949, psychological mass coercion represents a new dimension in political power and control. R.L.W.

Psychological operations.
This term includes psychological warfare, and, in addition, encompasses those political, military, economic, and ideological actions planned and conducted to create in neutral or friendly foreign groups the emotions, attitudes, or behavior favorable to the achievement of national objectives. T.W.

Psychological warfare.
Planned use of propaganda and exploitation of other psychological techniques by which a belligerent nation works to influence the opinions, emotions, attitudes and behavior of enemy officials, troops and civilian populations, based on trained analysis of weak points, susceptibilities, etc., to create dissidence and disaffection and to build cadres behind enemy lines who can further both "psych war" and direct military objectives. It deals, therefore, with political ideals, ideologies, value systems, and communication techniques and hardware, as well as such motives as saving one's own skin. Cold war activities of a related nature are technically known as "psychological activities," and the military term for these and "psych war" together is "psychological operations." J.B.L.

Public Administration.
It is the activity of a governmental unit in carrying out the public policy declared in the laws. It is also a field of professional study through which preparation for public managerial positions is secured. John Vieg defines it as "determined action taken in pursuit of a conscious purpose." Pfeffner and Presthus call it "the organization and direction of human and material resources to achieve desired ends." E. N. Gladden thinks that the arts of policy making should be excluded from the definition. Leonard White would include them, as would Marshall Dimock. Perhaps the definition is still in an amorphous state, awaiting agreement among scholars. H.W.

Public Administration Clearing House.
1931-1956.
Established to serve as an exchange

for information, experience, and ideas among organizations of public officials and others in the United States and Canada engaged in the active work of planning for improvements in the administrative techniques of government. Its principal activity was the bringing together of several existing national organizations of local, state and federal governmental officials; the creation of several others not then in existence, and, after 1937, their establishment in one building at 1313 East 60th Street in Chicago, adjacent to the campus of the University of Chicago. It also provided several joint services for those organizations which included: a personnel exchange; a joint reference library; and various administrative and clerical services. Louis Brownlow served as director until 1945 when he was succeeded by Herbert Emmerich. During its lifetime, PACH exerted a profound influence on the improvement of the quality of public administration in American local, state, and national government and international organizations. W.C.R.

Public Authorities.

Semi-autonomous bodies, "corporate and politic," usually exercising powers of government, but operating outside the normal structure of government. They finance their operations by revenue-bond issues and by the collection of tolls and other fees for the use of their facilities. They generally are single-purpose, and frequently have jurisdictional boundaries coterminous with those of municipalities or counties; some, however, are multi-purpose and function on a regional and even an international basis. They are proliferating throughout the world. R.G.S.

Public Defender.

In the U.S.A., a public official whose duty it is to defend in court persons accused of crime who lack the means to retain counsel of their own. Although widely advocated by legal reform groups, only a few states (notably California and Illinois) authorize communities to establish public defender offices. Efforts to enact legislation to create a public defender system for the federal courts have (as of 1962) not met with success. F.H.H.

Public Employee Associations.

Voluntary associations or unions of governmental employees organized to improve working conditions and to protect employment rights of their members. In the United States, public employee organizations are generally permitted to affiliate with outside labor unions. The American Federation of State, County, and Municipal Employees, an affiliate of the AFL, is an example of such an association.

H.J.Sch.

Public Law.

It connotes the existence of a dualism, if not with regard to the objective legal order so at least in the enforcement of subjective legal rights, between public law as a legal sphere dominated by the state in contrast to private law as the body of legal rules which governs the legal relations of individuals and non-public corporations with each other. Such a distinction between public law (**droit public; offentliches Recht**) and private law is clearly recognized in the continental European legal system. It is facilitated there by the existence—in addition to the ordinary or civil courts of special tribunals of administrative jurisdiction and, more recently, in some countries also by the institution of special tribunals with exclusive jurisdiction over constitutional disputes. There is disagreement, though, as to the exact line of demarcation between public and private law; and the criteria of jurisdiction, **viz.** administrative and constitutional tribunals versus civil courts, provides only a rough test. Legal and political theorists have attempted to explain the dualism of public and private law in terms of external and formal criteria, **i.e.**, whether the state appears as a party, or whether the civil courts or special tribunals are competent to take jurisdiction; in terms of the special "interest" of the state or the "power" of governmental authority which attach the character of public law to all legal relations directly involving the state; and in terms of the "social" foundation of all public authority in contrast to the private nature of individual interests.

Legal system and theories based upon an integrated or monistic conception of the legal order deny the dualism of public and private law. They consider the enforcement of subjective rights as well as the sum total of objective legal norms in terms of a unified legal order in which the state either dominates all legal relations by impressing upon them its public will, or in which the state is subject to the same rules and to the same forms of legal action characteristic of the legal relations of private individuals. In the first case, all law is public law (the Communist theory of law); under the second system all legal relations are expressed in categories appropriate to private law. This second position corresponds to the traditional common law point of view and has been re-enforced by the absence in the Anglo-American legal system of separate tribunals of administrative jurisdiction. While the common law thus asserted the unity of the legal order under the primacy of private law, in more recent developments of American law, the public law character of those branches of the legal order that govern the organization of the state and the relations between the state and individuals has become increasingly recognized. It is now common usage to apply the term public law to constitutional, administrative and criminal law in the United States, and there is some authority to suggest that other branches of the law, like procedural and labor law, should be included in the same category. See "Civil Law," "Private Law," "Common Law." H.R.H.

Public opinion.

The formed predominant attitude of the (large) group concerned with a given issue. Sometimes equated with a public expression, as in a riot or a newspaper editorial claiming to reflect public opinion. Opinion research (q.v.) has demonstrated a general validity in measuring at least some forms of public opinion, although the shifts and imponderables of "the collective mind" leave room for varied assessments in most political situations: Does a riot represent the showing iceberg of deep general resentment or the full fury of only the small group involved? The power of public opinion, therefore, rests on the political leaders' estimates of the prevalence, direction and intensity of feeling on a particular issue; except (perhaps) in a strong and ruthless police state, no political action can stand against great and sustained public disapproval. J.B.L.

Public policy.

A fixed plan and pattern of behavior by a government toward an issue confronting it. If reduced to writing it is normally couched in broad terms, so as to allow flexibility and freedom of maneuvering. In policy areas of the greatest significance it is the product of numerous minds, making their contributions at various levels of the administrative hierarchy, and subject to constant analysis, review, modification, and clearance. In such fields as foreign and defense affairs elaborate machinery has been set up in most states to insure the acquisition of relevant information and the presentation of the problem in its clearest and most precise form to the ultimate policy determiner—the President, Prime Minister, or other Head of State of Government. The machinery for formation of public policy has reached a very high state of development in the National Security Council of the United States in the Eisenhower Administration (1953-1961). E.V.M.

Public relations.

In professional terms the function through which public and private organizations and institutions seek to win and retain the understanding, sympathy and support of their present or potential "publics" i.e., those groups with whom they are or may be concerned, such as voters, stockholders, directors, government officials, employees, customers, suppliers and the general public. To date, this consists primarily of informing the publics of the institution's actions, usually explaining them in palatable or persuasive terms, although candor about unpleasant events is a professional hallmark. Increasingly, in an interdependent society, public relations involves also internal efforts to influence the institution's actions to meet more directly the needs of the publics, and to develop a mutuality with the general public interest, often after feedback from opinion research. J.B.L.

Public Utilities.
Businesses or services which supply the public with such commodities and services as electricity, transportation, water, gas, telephone or telegraph which affect the community at large rather than a particular class. These utilities must be ready, able, and willing to serve the public without discrimination. Synonymous with public use, in which the public generally or that part of it which has accepted the service has the legal right to demand that the service shall be conducted, so long as continued, with reasonable efficiency under reasonable charges.
C.B.C.

Public Welfare.
An inclusive term, which, however, is generally restricted to refer to tax-supported activities of a state or federal government for the relief of groups and persons who are in need. These activities may include child welfare services, institutions for delinquents and criminals, veteran services, aid to the blind, training programs for the handicapped, general relief, and assistance to the aged. The state may also supervise standards and performance of private and semi-private agencies or work in cooperation with them.
T.K.N.

Publicity.
In technical sense, originally paid advertising, now free notice in press of attitudes, actions or products of a person or institution, obtained or induced for the benefit of the name so mentioned. Reinforced by **promotion** (the active creation of interest), publicity is used primarily by the entertainment and sports industry and by marketers of products, although political figures, ideas and organizations benefit from "exposure." Public relations (q.v.) includes a press or news function to provide news and answer questions for the press, but in advanced usage at least, these are not primarily for publicity purposes. An early sense of the term publicity as airing bad conditions for public correction—e.g., the press exposing corruption in government—is used decreasingly.
J.B.L.

Puerto Rico. See Appendix.

Pure Theory of Law.
The legal theory of Hans Kelsen, an outgrowth of the Vienna Circle of logical positivism. The adjective "pure" stands for the exclusion, on grounds of being value judgments, of presupposed ideas of justice or other required content. "Pure" also reflects the rejection of sociological, historical and other approaches. Kelsen, while emphasizing the fruitfulness of enquiries by such methods, regarded it as improper for the jurist or legal scholar to blur the lines between a normative science and the study of human behavior qua behavior (rare instance of a theorist restricting the scope of his own discipline). The proper province is those **norms** belonging to a positive, coercive order; the two spheres of "is" and "ought" meet only in the ultimate question of effectiveness. Kelsen later became familiar with the Analytical School of Jurisprudence. He was struck by the similarity, but concluded that the Pure Theory carried forward the analytical method more consistently than had Austin or his followers. Based on the Kantian idea of **Sollen** (Ought), the Pure Theory conceives of legal norms not as commands of the political superior, but as expressing the proposition: "If A occurs, then B **ought** to follow" (A is the proscribed behavior, B is the prescribed sanction). The legal order is conceived as constituting an integrated, hierarchical system of norms in descending order of particularity, a monist position. The States necessarily receive their jurisdiction ("spheres of validity") by delegation from international law (which stands above domestic orders as the legally harmonizing element), inasmuch as Kelsen found sufficient evidence to regard international law as law properly so-called. At the fountainhead of the system is the Basic Norm (**Grundnorm**), admittedly extra-legal and formal. Thus, the Basic Norm may be expressed as: "The States ought to behave as they customarily have behaved." The traditional duality of law and state is rejected as a vestige of animism. A particular state is, scientifically speaking, nothing more than a relatively centralized legal order.
R.D.H.

Puritanism.
A religious movement of the sixteenth and seventeenth centuries in

England and the United States that attempted to refine, purify, and further "moralize" Reformation doctrines. Insisting on the paramount authority of Holy Scripture in personal ethics and doctrinal disputes, it condemned ritual, vestments, teachings of the Church Fathers, and the traditional hierarchical organization of churches. Its adherents came primarily from the rising, urban middle classes, who emphasized the importance of a hard-working and righteous life for the individual. During the reigns of Elizabeth I and the Stuarts, the Puritan members of Parliament were the most outspoken defenders of parliamentary rights and the most determined opponents of established power in religion, politics, and commerce. Early New England was colonized principally by Puritans. Initially stringent controls imposed on individuals in the interests of survival gave way in time to extreme individualism, and the view that membership in the state was automatically membership in the church was gradually weakened. In the development of modern American business, Puritan emphasis upon the thrifty, disciplined, and industrious individual is clearly evident. R.F.H.

Pushtunistan.
The Pushtu speaking, semi-nomadic Pathans (about 9 millions) are divided by the Afghan-Pakistan border dating from the 1893 Durand Line. Since 1947 Afghanistan has backed the independence of the 5 million Pathans in Pakistan, which implies all of its area west of the Indus (Pushtunistan), arguing that the Durand Line is inoperative since Britain's withdrawal, the Pathans are mistreated and they deserve self-rule. In the Cold War Russia backs Afghanistan's thesis and India is sympathetic, while the SEATO powers support Pakistan which upholds the Durand Line and periodically checks Afghan ambitions with economic pressure. P.F.P.

Q

Quadros, Janio da Silva.
Brazilian politician born Jan. 25, 1917, accomplished spectacular career from Sao Paulo city councillor (1947), state deputy (1951), mayor (1953), governor of Sao Paulo State (1954-58) to federal deputy (1958). With record landslide was elected president of Republic in 1960. His unexpected resignation on Aug. 25, 1961, led to amendment of Brazil's constitution (q.v.), from presidential to parliamentary system. In the 1962 elections for Sao Paulo governorship Quadros lost to long-time opponent Adhemar de Barros. R.R.

Qualification.
A requirement of eligibility for an office or for voting and the like; generally relates to minimum age, citizenship, and residence; there may be also educational requirements. In addition to the usual legal qualifications there may be others of a practical political nature, such as availability and experience. W.V.H.

Quarter Sessions.
See Court of Quarter Sessions.

Quasi-Nonpartisan.
Somewhat nonpartisan or seemingly nonpartisan. See Nonpartisan.
D.W.Mc.

Quasi-Party System.
A party system which cannot reasonably be classified as a multi-party, two-party, one-party, or non-party system. For example, on the municipal level, a party system characterized by the activity of only one party, which, at most recent elections, has won a substantial proportion of the vote, but not a majority of the offices (most offices having been won by non-party candidates). The term can be considered a transitional one, pending the formulation of a more precise classification scheme. D.W.Mc.

Quasi war.
See war.

Quatorze juillet.
Fourteenth July, French national holiday celebrating the anniversary of 14 July 1789. On that day occurred the first Parisian insurrection of the Revolution of 1789. The people searched for arms to defend themselves against the royal troops surrounding Paris, in the wake of Necker's dismissal (11 July). The Bastille was conquered; its fall serving as the popular symbol of the beginning of the Revolution. K.B.

Quemoy (Kinmen) and Matsu.
Two groups of islands occupied by Chinese Nationalist forces a few miles off the coast of mainland China. These islands are part of Fukien Province and, unlike Taiwan and Penghu (Pescadores) were not Japanese possessions before 1945; they are therefore of diplomatic as well as strategic significance. Some Western diplomats have urged that Chiang Kai-shek withdraw his forces from these islands (as he had withdrawn from the Tachen Islands in 1955), because they are difficult to defend, are unnecessary to the defense of Taiwan, and their occupation by Chiang is a provocation to the Communists. In 1954 and again in 1958 these "offshore islands" were subject to heavy bombardment by the Chinese Communists, apparently in preparation for an assault, and American logistical aid was extended to the islands. It remains unclear, however, whether the American commitment to Chiang to aid in the defense of Formosa includes the offshore islands. The issue was raised during the Kennedy-Nixon television debates in 1960, when Kennedy suggested that the Nationalists should withdraw from the islands. T.Mc.N.

Quid Pro Quo.
Favor, privilege, or aid given by one person or group to another person or group in return for some kind of assistance received by or promised to the giver. For example, where a legislator who votes for a pressure group's bill in return for the group's contribution to his campaign fund (actual or promised), the lawmaker's vote is the **quid pro quo** for the group's contribution.
D.W.Mc.

Quisling.
Those who willingly collaborated at

the political, economic, intellectual, or social level with an enemy occupation power, have been called quislings (after Vidkun Quisling, Norwegian Nazi and head of the German-sponsored Norwegian government during the occupation). At the end of World War II, liberated countries faced major problems in taking appropriate action against masses of quislings whose crimes could not be adjudicated by regular judicial processes. The resulting "purge" has often been criticized as being too soft—or too severe.
H.L.M.

Quorum.
The minimum number of members of an organization required to be present for the transaction of official business. A simple majority (just over half) of the members of an organization is usually acceptable as a quorum. The rules of an organization may specify otherwise. For example, only one hundred members of the United States House of Representatives are required for a quorum in the committee of the whole, whereas a majority of the membership is required for a quorum to transact regular business. K.E.H.

Quota system.
A means by which a state (e.g. the U.S.A.) restricts the volume and quality of its immigrants by allocating a specific number of the annual total to different countries. C.W.B.

Quwatli—Shukri al.
First president of the republic of Syria after its independence in 1943. Soon after, the political balance in Syria became disturbed and several military coups followed each other until 1956 when Quwatli was again made president. He was a great believer in Arab unity and negotiated with Nasser of Egypt the formation of the United Arab Republic of Egypt and Syria in 1958. W.B.B.

R

Race.
The anthropological term denoting a large group of persons distinguished by significant hereditary physical traits. There are three broad groupings: Caucasoid (white), Mongoloid (yellow), and Negroid (black). Each contains several sub-races and some groups defy precise classification. A common misconception is that cultural traits sufficiently differentiate races.

The political implications are that race and misconceptions about race are the bases of systems of slavery, segregation, economic discrimination, and deprivations of human and civil rights. Such systems magnify and distort racial differences, supporting scientifically inaccurate conceptions of an inherent superior-inferior relation between certain races.   N.P.T.

Racism.
The deliberate and ruthless exploitation of particular racial or cultural groups to effect some political, economic or social advantage. Based on scientifically unsound notions of racial superiority, popularized in modern form by De Gobineau, racism has been an element in Negro slavery, Western colonialism, Nazi anti-semitism, Japanese imperialism, South African apartheid, African nationalism, and national immigration policies.

It involves inflaming passions, inciting violence and persecution, and racial exclusion; and is characterized by extreme antirational, antiliberal, authoritarian behavior.   N.P.T.

Radek (Sobelsohn), Karl B.
(1885-1947?).
Radek returned to Russia from exile on the famous "sealed train" that carried Lenin to the Finland Station. He was then active abroad in the service of the Communists. He became Secretary of the Comintern in 1921. During the purge trials, Radek apparently avoided the death penalty by implicating others, especially military leaders. Radek received a prison term and apparently died in prison, possibly as late as 1947.   W.D.J.

Radical Socialists.
Neither radical nor socialist, this French political party, organized in 1875, represents the moderate center. In political power from 1898 to 1912 and from 1924 to 1926. The party program demands personal and political freedom in juxtaposition with economic laissez-faire and the separation of state and church. Negatively expressed, it opposes political authoritarianism and all economic collectivization, be it through socialistic nationalization or the concentration of private capital in trusts and / similar monopolies. Best known among the leaders of this party are Clemenceau, Herriot, and Daladier.
J.D.

Radio Free Europe (RFE).
Private broadcasting organization beaming radio programs to Czechoslovakia, Poland, Hungary, Bulgaria and Rumania, with operational headquarters in Munich, Germany. Sponsored by the Free Europe Committee located in New York, with the bulk of its financial support collected in the U.S. through the Crusade for Freedom. Its main purpose is to broadcast information not provided by the communist-controlled radio stations of the target countries.   F.M.

Raeder, Erich. (1876-1960.)
Headed German navy, 1935-43. First Grand Admiral since von Tirpitz, 1939. Member Secret Cabinet Council, 1938-43. His warships assisted Franco in Spanish Civil War. Received life sentence at Nuremberg War Crimes Trial, 1946; released because of poor health, 1955.   J.B.M.

Raison d'Etat.
The doctrine invented by Machiavelli and developed by Hobbes and Hegel that the security and advantage of the state justifies disregard of morality and obligation.   J.W.Ch.

Rakosi, Matyas (1892-   ).
Communist Party leader and member of Government in Hungary between 1944 and 1956.
In 1910 he joined the Social Democrats. In Russia as prisoner of war (1915-1918) he became a Communist. After his return to Hungary in 1918,

440

he and Bela Kun organized the Hungarian Communist party. Chief of the Hungarian Red army in the Hungarian Soviet Republic of 1919. After the collapse of the Republic, escaped to Austria, whence deported to Communist Russia. Between 1920 and 1924 was member of the Executive Committee of the Comintern. Returned to Hungary to organize a new Communist party. Was arrested in 1925 and tried for subversion, and after eight years in prison was sentenced again for crimes committed in 1919. In 1940 handed over to Soviet authorities in exchange for Hungarian national flags captured by Russians in 1849. Returning to Hungary in 1944, he was (until 1953) in virtual command of the political and economic life of the country. In June, 1953, he was replaced as Prime Minister by Imre Nagy, but remained First Secretary of the Party. In 1955 he was able to oust Nagy and to implement again his Stalinist policies. Completely discredited after the 20th Congress of the Soviet Communist Party, he was replaced by Gero as First Secretary of the Party in Hungary. Left the country for the Soviet Union during the summer of 1956. Was expelled from the Hungarian Communist party in August, 1962.   I.B.

Ramadier, Paul (1888-).
French Socialist leader and former premier. Son of a psychiatrist and trained in the law he entered politics as a general councillor and mayor of the town of Decazeville in 1919, a position he retained until 1959. He was elected a deputy from 1928 to 1940 and after serving in the two postwar constituent assemblies was a deputy from Aveyron 1946-1958. He served in the Popular Front cabinet of Blum (1936-37) as well as in those of Chautemps and Daladier (1938-40). Within the Socialist Party he stood for cooperation in government as distinct from systematic opposition. From January to November 1947 he was premier, a critical period which saw the Communists withdraw from government, partly in protest against his anti-inflationist policies. He served subsequently as Minister of Defense (Queuille, 1948-49) and as Finance Minister (Mollet, 1956-57).   J.S.S.

Ranke, Leopold von (1795-1886).
Noted German historian. Professor of History, University of Berlin after 1825. Member, Prussian Council of State. One of founders of historical-critical method. Stresses primacy of foreign policy. Sees in the state the essence of history.   M.C.V.

Rapacki Plan.
A proposal submitted to the U.N. on December 2, 1957 by the Polish Foreign Minister Adam Rapacki to prohibit the production and distribution of atomic weapons in the Federal Republic of Germany, the Soviet zone of Germany, Poland, and Czechoslovakia.   R.A.B.

Rapporteur.
A French term identifying the reporter appointed by a French parliamentary committee (**commission**) from its own membership to guide a legislative proposal through committee deliberations and subsequent debate in the Assembly. He conducts a study of the proposal, makes recommendations, drafts the final report of the committee, and presents it to the Assembly. Debate in the Assembly is often focused on this presentation, which may be at variance from the Government's position. (The Constitution of the Fifth Republic requires that debate be held on the Government's text, whereas in earlier practice the text as revised by the committee was used.)
The important Commission of Finance appoints a **rapporteur general** to supervise and coordinate the work of the various **rapporteurs speciaux** (special reporters), who are responsible for consideration of the respective departmental budgetary, tax, or appropriation proposals, and who exercise supervisory control over departmental expenditures and public accounts.   R.H.K.

Rassamblement des Gauches Republicains (RGR).
A French political center group created in 1946 and originally composed primarily of some Radicals (the Daladier faction but not the Herriot faction) and the UDSR, although some RGR candidates had no separate party allegiance. Persisting as an alliance until 1955, and strong in Correze and Alpes Maritimes, the RGR shared constituencies with the Moderates. Until

1949 26 RGR members were part of the Gaullist "Intergroup" in the Council of the Republic. Although the weakest of the major political groups, the RGR had 43 members in the first Assembly of the Fourth Republic, and while losing votes after 1951 secured 90 seats as a result of the electoral law.

Having opposed "dirigisme" in 1946, the RGR favored a "liberal economic policy." In 1951 it split over the issue of school subsidies for Catholics. When Premier Edgar Faure was expelled by the Radicals for dissolving the Assembly in 1955, he became a candidate of the RGR (abandoned by Radicals and UDSR), seeking to make of it a new liberal party. But when in 1958 an Assembly rule required 28 deputies for a parliamentary "group," the RGR and UDSR reunited. R.B.C.

Rassemblement du Peuple Francais. (RPF).

Organized in 1947 as a non-party group in the French Fourth Republic, the RPF reflected autocratic centralization, with decisions coming from a Council and a Secretariat but in practice representing the will of De Gaulle. Claiming 800,000 members, it secured 28% of the vote in six months, and its Intergroup attracted especially many members of the MRP. With 20% of the seats and 22% of the vote, it became the largest political group in the second Assembly of 1951.

Parliamentarians had a minor role in creation of RPF policy, which was vague but included corporative tendencies. De Gaulle accepted the profit-sharing schemes of Capitant and Malraux, but was non-committal during growing internal tension after 1951. Refusing to cooperate with parties, the RPF organized youth, veterans and sports groups.

Friction had arisen in 1948 between "clericals" and "neutrals," and after a split over Pinay in 1952, the RPF was dissolved in 1953 by De Gaulle, most of its deputies being absorbed by the new Social Republicans, a party by 1955. When De Gaulle returned to power in 1958, the Union for the New Republic (with 35% of Assembly seats) was in effect if not in fact a relaunching of the RPF. R.B.C.

Rathenau, Walther (1867-1922).

Son of founder A.E.G. (largest German electrical concern); President, 1915. Organized during World War I Germany's raw materials supply. Although he opposed surrender in 1918, he became one of the leading Weimar exponents of policy of fulfillment of Versailles Treaty. Foreign Minister 1921; negotiated Rapallo Treaty with Russia, 1922. Assassinated by extreme nationalists. Authored many (often critical) books of socio-economic nature and a volume dealing with his position as a German and a Jew.

M.C.V.

Ratification of a treaty.

The issuance of a formal declaration (i.e. ratification), usually by a Head of State (often after legislative authorization), confirming the acceptance of a treaty. Some treaties concerning minor matters or containing appropriate stipulations become operative when signed. Most others become operative when a minimum number of states, specified in them, subsequently exchange or deposit centrally their ratifications. The American President ratifies treaties after submitting them to the Senate and gaining approval from 2/3 of the members present. [See U.S. Constitution, Article II, Section II (2).] V.R.I.

Rational—Rationalism.

These terms are used with various, often mutually contradictory meanings, which must be carefully distinguished. 1. "Rationalism" in philosophy denotes a type of thought prevalent in late medieval and early modern philosophy, according to which human reason is capable of finding ultimate, absolute, truth without reference to empirical grounds and experimental tests. This approach, originally closely associated with Christian religion, culminated, after the separation of philosophy from religion, in the limitless trust in reason during the 18th century (Age of Enlightenment). It was radically criticized by Hume and sharply reduced also by Kant who, however, maintained the belief in the capability of pure reason to establish the truth of some types of synthetic propositions "a priori" (see a priori). The opposite of this kind of rationalism is reliance on empirical science and experiments

(Galileo, Newton, modern scientific method) or, on the other hand, on Scripture rather than reason (Reformation). 2 "Rational" in modern usage is the pursuit of attainable, prudently selected goals with adequate means capable of reaching them according to the laws of cause and effect. In this sense Galileo and Newton acted rationally. The opposite here is "irrational" behavior. 3. In still another sense "rationalism" is used as a derogatory name for the reliance on utopian or ideological political theories. Its opposite then is an approach grounded on tradition, especially on traditional values. A.B.

Rationalization.
A word with many meanings. 1) The giving of reasons for doing something which are not the real reasons but which will be more socially approved than the real reasons. In this sense the word rationalization is usually used to imply that the person giving the "good" reasons is fooling himself, not consciously lying. 2) Organizing an activity in such a way as to achieve its explicit ends with maximum efficiency. Thus in the economic field, rationalization of an organization would be arranging it so as to produce maximum profit regardless of the consequences for any other latent functions that the organization may have. I.d.S.P.

Reaction. See Appendix.

Reading by title.
The official reading of the descriptive title of a bill. This occurs the first time at introduction. However, the listing of the bill at introduction may be considered sufficient for first reading by title. The second reading, customarily in full, may be by title if so ordered. The third reading is by title in most states. K.E.H.

Reading in full.
The official reading of the entire bill, including the descriptive title, the enacting clause, and the body of the bill. This occurs at second reading or in the committee of the whole. It may be dispensed with if so ordered by the legislative body. The third reading may be in full if requested by the number of members required by the rules of that body. Such action is usually a delaying tactic or an attempt to kill the bill. K.E.H.

Realism.
Unlike the connotations this term has had in metaphysics and epistemology, in politics it has generally denoted a reaction against idealistic thinking, understood as thinking centered on ethical ideals or principles. Modern political realism stands in the tradition of Machiavelli. In 19th and 20th century political thought realism has had close associations with positivism and pragmatism, and has shared with them an orientation around the scientific method. In the 19th century **Realpolitik** meant a foreign policy based on prudential calculations of national interests, devoid of sentimentality or ideology. The possession and use of power, usually military power, was a prime consideration. H.S.Th.

Real Union.
A union between states under the same monarch. The member states retain their own constitution, however, they establish common authority in certain governmental functions. Example: Austria-Hungary according to the Compromise of 1867. The Emperor of Austria was also the King of Hungary. Common Ministries of Foreign Affairs, War and Finance were established. Ministers were responsible to Delegations which were nominated from the separate parliaments of each state. The Delegations determined the needs of the common services, dependent on legislative implementation by the separate parliaments, and assessments and collection of financial contributions by executive agencies of the individual governments. T.P.

Reapportionment (of seats in the United States House of Representatives).
The process of reallocation of seats in the House among the several states taking into consideration provisions of the Constitution and changes in population. (See apportionment.) Reapportionment shall take place within every term of ten years. Art. I, Sec. 2, cl. 3, as amended by Art. XIV. K.E.H.

Rebus Sic Stantibus.
In general, an explicit or tacit condition attaching to an agreement or

promise to the effect that the latter retains its validity only so long as conditions have not substantially changed. Specifically, a doctrine in international law which holds that a tacit **rebus sic stantibus** clause attaches to all treaties.
D.W.Mc.

Recall.
A method of removing a public official from office before the expiration of his term by petitioning for a special election to decide his continuance in office. It appears to have originated in Switzerland. In the United States Los Angeles in 1903 was the first city to adopt it and Oregon in 1908 was the first state to adopt it. The recall usually cannot be used to remove a public official from office during the first few months of his term. J.F.Z.

Recess Appointment.
Appointments made by the president of the U.S.A. during a period when the Senate is not in session are called recess appointments. The official has the same authority as he possesses after senatorial approval. If the Senate should refuse to confirm the appointment the person would have no salary for his interim service. M.F.

Reciprocal Trade Act.
A 1934 amendment to the Smoot-Hawley Tariff Act which in effect reversed American protectionist policies and permitted large scale reductions of American tariffs by executive agreements. The President was authorized to negotiate trade agreements under which American tariff rates are reduced in exchange for reciprocal reductions by foreign countries. The President's initial power was limited to a 50% reduction, but on successive renewals of the Act, further reductions were authorized. The most favored nation clause of the Act provided that reductions extended to one country would be extended on the same terms to virtually all, thus changing the whole American rate-structure whenever a trade agreement was signed with any one country. The Act was finally replaced by the Trade Expansion Act of 1962 (q.v.). I.d.S.P.

Reciprocity.
A term used in international relations and trade, designates an agreement between two or more trading countries to exchange definite tariff reductions or other concessions on specific articles entering into trade by one of the trading partners, in return for similar reductions or concessions by the other(s) country(ies). One of the biggest agreements of this kind is the General Agreement on Tariffs and Trade (GATT) negotiated in 1947 in Geneva between more than twenty nations, including the U.S. W.N.

Recognition.
This has been a controversial concept and no generally accepted understanding has emerged. Generally this term relates to the decision of an established Government to enter into relations with a new State or new Government. When such new entities result from constitutional process no problem arises: the new State or Government is "recognized" as a matter of course and the manifestation of this act is the exchange of regular diplomatic missions. Many of the new States in Africa and Asia were so recognized. In case of new Governments or States issuing from revolution, the practice distinguishes between de facto and de jure Government and States as well as between de facto and de jure recognition. There is no consistency in this matter. The situation can be still further complicated by the refusal of a revolutionary Government to honor the international obligations of its predecessor—as was done by the Bolshevik Government in 1917—or when the old Government continues to exist as is the case in China. Granting or withholding recognition usually has significant consequences in the domestic courts of the non-recognizing State such as denial of access to its courts but from the point of view of international law the new State or Government acquires juridical personality from the moment of its effective establishment and succeeds to the rights and obligations of its predecessor. The Governments of many Members of the United Nations issued from revolutions such as the Government of Fidel Castro in Cuba and there was no question of their representing the State in the United Nations. The denial of representation to the Communist Government of

444

China is largely based on considerations unrelated to recognition.   L.G.

Recognition, diplomatic of the Republic of China and its Government.

Diplomatic recognition is an affirmative manifestation by the government of a sovereign state of an intention on its part to deal with a political entity external to it as a **state** or to deal with a particular group exercising jurisdiction within such entity as that entity's **government.**

In American theory and practice, diplomatic recognition is accorded or is withheld on a basis of political considerations and in service of political objectives.

The government of the United States accorded diplomatic recognition in 1913 to "The Republic of China" and in 1928 to the "National Government" of that Republic. When, in October, 1949, the leaders of the Communist Party in China announced the setting up by them of "The People's Government of the People's Republic of China," all Communist governments accorded diplomatic recognition to that government; and then and since then various **non-Communist** governments have done likewise. Not however, the government of the United States and the majority of other governments.

It became in 1950 the opinion of the American government, and it has been since then the opinion of subsequent Administrations, that continuation by the United States of its recognition of the Republic of China and of that country's National Government (which show respect for established principles of international conduct) and withholding of recognition from the People's Republic and its government (which utterly flout those principles) would best serve the interests of the United States, of the people of China, and of the "free" world.

As matters stood in August 1962, of the then 104 members of the United Nations, 55 maintained diplomatic relations with the National Government, 38 had recognized the "People's Government," and 10, neither.

The suggestion that there be created, be recognized and be seated in the United Nations "two Chinas" did not originate in the United States and has not been sponsored as a formal proposal by any government. Among the Chinese, both the Nationalists and the Communists are firmly opposed to it. In discussion of it there are advanced, on the one hand, arguments of expediency; there are cited, on the other hand, historical, ethnic, social, economic, political and psychological considerations; and there is asked: by what processes could it be implemented and, if implemented, to whose advantage and for how long?   St.K.H.

Reconstruction Finance Corporation.

A government corporation established by Congress in 1932 as an emergency agency to bolster the faltering economy with authority to make loans in many different areas. Eventually the Corporation lent billions of dollars to banks, railroads, schools, business firms, insurance companies, and state and local governmental units.

RFC is credited with saving many banks and businesses from bankruptcy. RFC's life was extended beyond the depression period and it played an important role in financing war industries in World War II. In the early 1950's congressional investigating committees uncovered several cases of maladministration in the lending of funds in the post-war years. A reorganization of the agency followed. RFC was abolished in 1957 with its remaining functions transferred to other agencies.
   G.B.H.

Red Chinese Communes.

In 1958, the Communist Party of China began to organize its 500,000,000 peasants into new political, social, and economic units called communes. In these large administrative units, averaging about 25,000 persons, all the labor resources of the countryside were mobilized in an effort to maximize agricultural production, facilitate labor-intensive "spare-time" projects, and increase the political control of the Communist regime over the rural people. Private property was virtually abolished, and Communal mess halls, nurseries, and old age homes released hundreds of millions of women to work full time in the fields. By 1960, virtually all of rural China had been communized, and communes were beginning to be set up in urban areas, also.

Chinese Communist spokesmen claimed the communes to be a new advance toward the building of perfect communism. Though results appeared good at first, peasant resistance later induced the regime to retreat on a number of points. Eating at public mess halls became optional; incentive pay was restored; and peasants were granted the privilege of cultivating private garden plots and selling the produce from these plots in a limited "free market." Though the communes were retained as an administrative unit, important administrative responsibilities were shifted to the smaller "production brigades" and "work teams." Development of the communes remained an ongoing process in the early 1960's.

S.L.A.

Red Chinese Communist Youth League.

One of the most important of the mass organizations utilized by the Government of the People's Republic of China to build support for official policies, the Communist Youth League (formerly the New Democratic Youth League) also serves as key training ground for future leaders. By 1956, it claimed 20,000,000 members between the ages of 14 and 25. In addition, its subsidiary, the "Young Pioneer Corps," claimed over 30 million members of ages 9 to 15.

S.L.A.

Red Chinese Five Year Plans.

In nations in which the economy is controlled by the state, the quantities of goods to be produced and the ways in which these goods will be distributed must be planned by the government. The People's Republic of China (Red China) is one of the nations which uses Five Year Plans for this purpose.

Communist China's First Five Year Plan, covering the 1953-1957 period, was less a real plan for coordinated economic development than a set of target figures for economic growth. Investment was concentrated heavily in the industrial sector, with the development of a modern industrial base the main goal. By limiting public consumption severely, the Government seems to have succeeded in raising China's Gross National Product at the impressive average annual rate of about 7 to 8 percent, according to Western estimates.

The Second Five Year Plan (1958-1962), however, has proved less successful. After an initial "leap forward" in 1958, a succession of bad harvests—due to faulty planning as well as to bad weather, in the opinion of Western observers—led to a severe food shortage, a downward revision of many Five Year Plan target figures, and the rechannelling of investment formerly earmarked for industrial development into the lagging agricultural sector.

S.L.A.

Red Chinese National People's Congress.

Nominally the ultimate source of governmental authority in the People's Republic of China (Red China) under the constitution adopted in 1954. "Elected" indirectly for four year terms on a one-candidate-per-office basis, the National People's Congress is empowered to choose the Head of State, enact laws, amend the constitution, etc. In practice, however, it is an unwieldy body (over 1000 members), which meets only for a few weeks once a year, and serves primarily as a sounding board for policies determined by the Communist Party and as a channel for disseminating these policies to the elite and the masses.

S.L.A.

Red Chinese "People's Republic."

(4,000,000 sq. mi.; pop. 700,000,000). Inheritors of one of the world's oldest and highest civilizations, the leaders of the Communist Party of China have undertaken the most sweeping transformation Chinese culture has experienced since the third century B.C.

A century of agonizing reappraisal of basic cultural values induced by forced contact with Western science, technology and commercial and military aggressiveness culminated in the establishment of the People's Republic of China at Peking on October 1, 1949. The Nationalist Government headed by Chiang Kai-shek, which had governed China since 1927, was forced in quasi-exile on the island of Taiwan (Formosa).

Though nominally "democratic," the People's Republic was organized along classic "democratic centralist" lines, similar to those used by the Soviet

Union. The new Government undoubtedly exercises more effective administrative control over the Chinese people —down to the village level—than any predecessor. The most powerful figures in the new regime are Communist Party Chairman Mao Tse-tung, Chairman of the Republic Liu Sho-ch'i, Premier Chou En-lai and military chief Chu Teh. Willingness to sacrifice present consumption standards in the name of future industrial trial development has made possible considerable strides in national economic growth and military power, since 1949, despite widespread food shortages in the early 1960's. (See Red Chinese Five Year Plans.) Virtually all industrial and agricultural enterprises are state-controlled, with most of rural China, and many urban areas, organized into communes.

Concerted efforts to reduce the cohesiveness of the family system—cornerstone of China's traditional way of life—have also wrought a social and moral revolution. Women are granted legal equality with men, and youths with their elders, for the first time in Chinese history. Art, literature and religion have been harnessed for state purposes, and intellectuals who fail to appreciate the virtues of the new order are "reeducated" via "thought reform."

Devoted to the cause of world Communist revolution, Chinese Communist leaders have proved to be so militantly hostile towards the West as to provoke a breach between themselves and the leaders of their ally, the Soviet Union. Their other major foreign policy goals seem to be regaining territories traditionally belonging to China—especially Taiwan—and rewinning for China its too long lost place of equality and honor among the great nations of the world. S.L.A.

Referee.
In the U.S.A. a person appointed by a court to perform certain functions for the court. These may range from the taking of testimony to the rendering of judgment. In some states (and in the federal courts), the referee may be designated a "special master" or "commissioner." F.H.H.

Referendum.
A vote by the people of a nation, state, province, county, district, or city on a question of public policy, such as an amendment of the constitution or an act of legislation or the authorization of a bond issue or merely an advisory preference. An amendment may be submitted by a convention or a legislature or popular petition known as the Initiative; and a law may be offered by legislative will or forced to a Referendum vote through properly submitted signatures of voters. Such a measure may become effective upon approval of the people by simple majority or the requisite fraction such as three-fifths or two-thirds. Sp.D.A.

Reformation.
A religious movement in Europe that may be said to have begun formally in 1517, when the Wittenberg monk Martin Luther published his **Ninety-Five Theses,** which condemned the sale of indulgences by agents of the Pope and repudiated the sacrament of penitence. It contested the supremacy of the Roman Catholic Church and ultimately eliminated that church's paramount ecclesiastical control in Europe. In its Lutheran form, it was clearly involved in politics by virtue of Luther's association with German princes because of his need of their assistance in opposing papal claims. Its adherents were drawn primarily from the guild, whereas Roman Catholic power was concentrated in the aristocracy and in the priesthood. Embryonic national capitalism, which abetted economic and social mobility, gave impetus to Reformation growth. Yet purely spiritual factors, such as Luther's repudiation of old dogmas, insistence on justification by faith alone, and firm commitment to the teachings of the Bible, were basic to the prescription of Reformation creed. The prescription was given its most logical and systematic expression in John Calvin's **Institute of the Christian Religion** (1536) directed initially to the citizens of theocratic Geneva. Besides the Lutherans and Calvinists, other significant Reformation denominations included the Zwinglians, Socinians, and Anabaptists. R.F.H.

Reformism.
This is Eduard Bernstein's critique

of Marxist orthodoxy. Bernstein pleaded for evolutionary socialism through legislation, democratic reforms, and personal rights rather than revolution. He rejected the "dictatorship of the proletariat."

Moreover, Bernstein argues that "we have to take working men as they are. And they are neither so universally paupers as was set out in the Communist Manifesto, nor so free from the prejudices and weaknesses as their courtiers wish to make us believe."

Bernstein's Reformism defined socialism as a co-operative scheme of production. As far as he was concerned, the interests of society were above class considerations. C.R.F.

Refugees.

A refugee may be defined as a person fleeing his homeland for reasons of persecution or the fear of persecution. The problem has existed since antiquity. In the 20th century, World War I was responsible for the displacement of Russian and Balkan refugees and World War II dislocated a total of approximately 60 million people. The combined efforts of the United Nations Relief and Rehabilitation Administration (UNRRA) and the International Refugee Organization (IRO) managed either to repatriate or to resettle approximately two-thirds of these uprooted people. However, the refugees created after World War II added to the problem: the independence of India and Pakistan made 15 million people homeless; roughly 600,000 Palestine refugees left the new state of Israel; the Korean War produced 2 million refugees; the Indo-Chinese wars 2 million; close to 3 million have escaped from Communist China; a steady flow of refugees escape from Iron Curtain countries in Europe; Jews have become refugees from North Africa; French from Algeria; and, most recently, the refugee problem has moved into Africa as a result of unrest in Angola and in the Congo.

The only United Nations agencies in existence to deal with the mounting problem are the United Nations High Commissioner for Refugees (UNHCR) and the United Nations Relief and Works Agency (UNRWA) for the Palestine refugees. It is estimated that the number of uprooted in the world today approaches 25 million. J.G.St.

Regional Development.

Regional development is the establishment of a program for the most efficient, esthetic, and productive use of the facilities and resources of a contiguous part of a country, and the governmental implementation of that program. In the United States regional development is most often carried out at the state level and around metropolitan areas. The federal government sometimes develops the given region such as the Tennessee River Valley.

J.R.B.

Regional Organization.

A relatively new term in political science and international organization. According to Hintze, it was first used in poetry to describe subsections of the nation state, such as French Brittany. In the U. S. it became a common reference for the Deep South, the Midwest, New England, etc. Since 1890 the term has had greater usage in international relations and was employed descriptively to refer to a group of nations, generally neighboring states, but not in all cases, desirous of international co-operation along political, economic and cultural lines. Some notable examples are: the Organization of American States, the North Atantic Treaty Organization, the Common Market, Southeast Asiatic Treaty Organization, the Warsaw Pact, the Arab League and the British Commonwealth of Nations. In practice, this is an attempt to subdivide the world itself. More confined in scope than universalism (United Nations), it amounts to selected multilateralism and rejection of bilateralism. Wirth defines regionalism within a state as a "high degree of conformity between geographic, economic and cultural contour lines." But a definition for regionalism in international relations is almost impossible along geographic lines. As noted in the example of international regionalism, there is only a limited geographical validity to the instances cited. The weight of evidence sustains the view that although an exact definition of regionalism is lacking in international affairs, it is to be largely defined in political terms, with emphasis on the practice of states in creating alliances custom unions, etc. In international organization, the assumption in the practice of states reflects interests and not geography as the basic objective.

Most universalists maintain that regionalism is impracticable, especially for the promotion of world peace. Yet, the successes of some regional organizations merit strong consideration. Changing international conditions, the convergence of national policies, required institutionalized joint decision-making, and to some extent the melioration of national unilateralism by the substitution of new forms of collectivism, all, seemingly suggest the necessity of regionalism. Finally, regionalism as an instrument of consolidation for peaceful cooperation can properly be considered as a stepping stone to a more workable universalism. Hence, the growth of regionalism is not to be construed as incompatible with universalism, but a complementary development which the Charter of the United Nations reflects in Article 52, approving of "regional arrangements . . . consistent with the Purposes and Principles of the United Nations." M.M.Mc.

Regionalism.
The concept that existing entities—be they units of a federal government or nation-states—may function as more closely integrated groupings, because of their economic, social and/or political characteristics. At the intra-national level in the United States, it is suggested that the present 50 states might be amalgamated into eight or so districts or regions, as has been proposed for the territories serviced by the Tennessee Valley Authority. At the extra-national level, the regional groupings may be based on geographic proximity, as is the case of the Organization of American States. Sometimes "regional" organizations are integrated in part on ethnic and religious ties, as in the case of the Arab League, and thereby fail to include proximate units, as Israel. In both the East and West there has been a tendency to build functionally specialized groupings for politico-military purposes (as in the North Atlantic Treaty Organization—"NATO"—and the Eastern European Mutual Assistance Treaty—"Warsaw Pact") —separately from the regional organizations concerned with economic activities (the Western European Economic Community—"Common Market" —and the Eastern Council for Mutual Economic Assistance—"Comecon").

See also Regional Organization.
H.G.

Registration.
The system used to identify those qualified to vote. In general, a voter must appear before the proper officials some days in advance of the election and establish his qualifications. Registration lists are used as an official check list at the polls in order to prevent fraudulent and repetitive voting.

In the U.S.A. every state but Arkansas, North Dakota, and Texas now require some type of registration in connection with virtually all elections.
R.V.A.

Regulation of parties.
(In U.S.A.—by states and federal government).

Political parties have come increasingly under state control and can no longer be regarded as purely voluntary associations. The control process started in 1888 when some of the states legislated the use of the secret (Australian) ballot and of the method by which party candidates appear on the ballots, followed in subsequent years by regulating party nominations by conventions and primary elections, by controlling party machinery, and by regulating campaign financing and procedures. The national government has followed by regulation of the parties in congressional and presidential campaigns.
M.B.D.

Regulatory Commission.
Independent agency of government created to regulate a specific sector of industry or type of economic activity in order to correct or prevent socially harmful behavior and to promote desirable economic action or relationships. It differs from the ordinary executive agencies in three major respects: (1) it is headed by a group of people instead of one person; (2) it exists primarily to make policy rather than to execute programs, and it therefore requires a smaller working force; and (3) its acts with regard to the public are the decisions of the officers at the top of the organization rather than the activities of employees at its bottom.

The regulatory commissions are called independent because they are outside and independent of the organizational structure of the executive departments. Members of such commissions are called commissioners and, at the federal level, are appointed by the President with the advice and consent of the Senate for varying terms of office as determined by Congress. They exercise quasi-legislative and quasi-judicial powers as distinguished from ordinary administrative officers who exercise purely executive or administrative powers. Because of this difference, the courts have decided that, unless the statutes provide otherwise, regulatory commissioners may not be removed by the appointing authority without cause. The President, for example, may remove appointive officers in the ordinary executive agencies at his pleasure **(Myers v. United States,** 272 U. S. 52 [1926]); but, with regard to the regulatory commissioners, Congress establishes the causes for their removal and removals are limited to the specified causes **(Humphrey's Executor v. United States,** 295 U. S. 602 [1935]).

Regulatory commissions exist at all levels of government. At the federal level in the United States there are nine such bodies all created by Congress. The first to be established and the largest is the Interstate Commerce Commission, created in 1887, which regulates interstate common carriers—buses, railroads, ships, and trucks—with respect to rates, services, financial structure and records, and public interstate transportation policy. This Commission influenced the later development of additional commissions. In 1913 the Federal Reserve Board was established to control money and credit and supervise member banks. The following year the Federal Trade Commission was created to restrain unfair methods of competition. Originally formed in 1920 as an inter-departmental committee, the Federal Power Commission was converted into an independent regulatory commission in 1930 with authority to regulate interstate transmission of electric energy, and in 1938 was given the additional responsibility of regulating interstate gas pipe lines. In 1934 Congress created the Federal Communications Commission to regulate radio, telephone and telegraph. The same year the Securities and Exchange Commission was formed to regulate stock exchanges and dealers and to prevent malpractices in the securities and financial markets. The next year Congress established the National Labor Relations Board to regulate labor-management relations. In 1936 the U. S. Maritime Commission was created to regulate rates, conditions of service and the grant of subsidies to ship companies. Reconstituted in 1940, the Civil Aeronautics Board regulates air carrier operations and determines the probable causes of major air accidents.

These commissions are not the only governmental agencies exercising regulatory power; but they are different in that they are independent of departmental and presidential control and their membership is generally bipartisan. In addition, overlapping terms of members assure some degree of continuity and expertness. The regulatory commission is not solely a federal phenomenon. Commisions of a similar nature exist also at state and local levels.

It was during the depression period (1929-1941) that the greatest number of independent regulatory commissions came into being. In some instances, the laws establishing the commissions were hastily drawn to meet emergency situations and failed to provide adequate safeguards for the protection of individual rights. It became increasingly evident that the regulatory commission was a special type of agency which violated the separation of powers doctrine in that it combined executive, legislative and judicial functions in the one body. As a result several inquiries were made into the commissions. In 1937, the President's Committee on Administrative Management viewed with alarm this "headless 'fourth branch' of the government, a haphazard deposit of irresponsible agencies and uncoordinated powers." Congress, it argued, had found no way of supervising them, nor could the President control them even though he was held responsible by the people for the acts of government in the expanding field of economic regulation; and they were answerable to the courts only in respect to the legality of their activities. The Committee recommended that all the independent regulatory commissions be placed within the regular executive departments to the extent such departments have functions relevant to those of the commissions. In being put into the departments, the commissions were to be divided into two sections. One would be the judicial section, which was to be independent of the department except for administrative housekeeping, and which would handle the judicial aspects of regulation. Its members were to be removable by the President only for incompetence or misconduct; and its decisions would be unreviewable by the department head or the President. The second section, an administrative one organized as a bureau or division in the department and fully responsible to the head of the department and the President, would perform the administrative functions.

Opponents of the Committee's proposals objected on the grounds that, if placed within a department, the judicial section could not avoid being influenced by the department's top officials and the President, and that the traditional principles of judicial independence and constitutional checks and balances would be violated. The Committee's recommendation was not generally adopted. In one case, however, it was attempted. This was in 1940 in regard to the Civil Aeronautics Authority which consisted of the Civil Aeronautics Board and the Civil Aeronautics Administration. The Authority was placed within the Department of Commerce according to the Committee's proposal. It was not a wholly satisfactory affair; and in 1958, Congress reaffirmed the Civil Aeronautics Board's full independence and transferred the functions of the Civil Aeronautics Administration to a new, independent administrative body—the Federal Aviation Agency.

In 1949, the Commission on Organization of the Executive Branch of the Government (Hoover Commission) also studied the regulatory commissions. It recommended that: (1) all administrative responsibility be vested in the chairman of the commission; (2) all regulatory commissioners be removable only for cause; (3) salaries of commissioners and staff members be raised in order to attract high caliber personnel; (4) statutory amendments be made to permit the delegation of preliminary and routine work to staff members; (5) measures be taken to speed up the disposition of controversies before the commissions; (6) all commissions be represented bipartisanly; and (7) all commissions avoid becoming too engrossed in case-by-case activities to the point of neglecting planning and promotional activities. Congress acted upon a number of these proposals; but the demands for further reform have been persistent. Currently popular is the old recommendation of the President's Committee on Administrative Management for increased control over the regulatory commissions by the President. O.K.

Regulatory Immunity.

Regulatory immunity, in American constitutional doctrine, relates to the exemption of the federal government and persons acting under its authority from compliance with state and local laws or regulations, otherwise of general applicability, if such compliance would result in an interference with or burden upon federal functions. Thus, Maryland could not require a Post Office employee to obtain a state driver's license in order to drive a mail truck on its highways (**Johnson v. Maryland,** 1920). The immunity conferred upon a person so acting is not a general and presumptive one, however; the same case did not settle whether local authorities might have punished him for violating their traffic regulations. If federal regulations governing the conduct exist, they prevail; in their absence it may be that obedience is owed to local regulations which do not materially interfere with the federal activity (Ibid.). R.H.S.

Reichstag.

Name of German parliament in the Hohenzollern empire of 1871 and under the Weimar Constitution (q.v.). Sole popular organ under the Hohenzollern system, deputies elected by universal manhood suffrage from single-member district. With Bundesrat (q.v.) power to adopt federal budget and enact federal laws, but no control over executive (chancellors and aides) who are responsible only to emperor. Major parties Conservatives (authoritarian-agrarian), National Liberals (business), Center (Catholic), Social Democrats (Labor, Marxist). Under Weimar elected by proportional representation, government responsible to it. Major parties: German Nationalists (monarchical-rightist), People's Party (big business), Democrats (republican), Center (Catholic), Social Democrats (moderate Labor), Communists; toward end National Socialists (q.v.). J.H.H.

Relativism.
1. A generic term to characterize any doctrine that denies either the existence of absolute truth, goodness, beauty, etc. ("philosophical r.") or the ability of science to make scientific statements of absolute validity on some or any subjects ("scientific r."). R. has played a role in physics (relativity of movement, Einstein), the theory of history (historical relativity, historicism), the theory of evolution (evolutionary relativity, Auguste Comte, Julian Huxley), Marxism (relativity of ideas to the stage of production and the class struggle), sociology (sociological relativity of knowledge, Hans Mannheim), and law (relativity of the positive law to the legislation of the respective country, relativity of justice to goals). 2. Of particular significance to political science is that type of r. which is best called "scientific value relativism" or "scientific value alternativism." It says not that there is nothing of absolute value (God, morals, highest goods) but only that the existence of absolute value judgments cannot be established through purely scientific methods. Scientific statements on values, it says, can only be made with reference to the usefulness of some alleged value for attaining another alleged value (ulterior, ultimate value) or to human ideas on values ("evaluations") and on their rank. However, science can nonetheless make important contributions in the area of values and evaluations by examining opinions actually held by people, the meaning of evaluations, their origin (historic, biologic, biographic, religious, etc.), alternative evaluations (actual or imaginable), any objective elements that have entered evaluations, and especially the logical implications and the practical consequences and risks involved in the pursuit of certain values at the cost of other values. Science may also attempt to find universal and invariant elements in all human evaluations. A.B.

Religious Factors in Politics.
Religious values cut across public policy issues on such questions as federal aid to education, prohibition, divorce legislation, birth control, prayers in the public schools, and censorship. There is no monolithic Catholic, Protestant, or Jewish position on these issues but there is a tendency for Americans to divide along Catholic and non-Catholic lines.

Religious factors have also manifested themselves through prejudice in the nineteenth century and nativist movements directed against Catholics. Later the restrictive immigration of the early 1920's was directed primarily against the same group. While Protestant power in national politics has often exploded against Catholics, Catholic power in many cities and towns has also been used to discriminate against Protestant and Jews in public employment. The interests of religious groups are sometimes stirred by foreign policy issues, too. Notable examples would include Catholic intervention in behalf of Franco of Spain during the Spanish Civil War; Protestant opposition to President Truman's attempt to appoint an Ambassador to the Vatican; and the role of Jews in influencing American-Israeli relations. L.H.F.

Religious test.
Article VI of the United States Constitution states, ". . . No religious test shall ever be required as a Qualification to any Office or public Trust under the United States." In 1961 this clause was substantiated by the Supreme Court's holding in Torasco v. Watkins, 367 U.S. 488 that a Maryland religious test which required its state officials to make a declaration of belief in God was an unconstitutional invasion of freedom of belief and religion. However, covert pressures within specific localities in the United States still breach the intent of this constitutional stipulation. B.N.

Rendition.
The constitutional obligation that each state "render" fugitives from justice when sought by another state. The act is executive, granted by the governor of the state where the fugitive has found haven.

Art. IV, Sec. 2 of the U.S. Constitution reads that rendition is mandatory, but in practice rendition has sometimes been denied on grounds that the fugitive is not wanted on bona fide criminal charges or that he has led an exemplary life since his alleged crime and should not be further punished. Cf., extradition. R.R.R.

Reparations.
See Soviet Reparations in Germany.

Representacao (Representation).
A judicial procedure utilized in Brazil as an appeal to the Federal Supreme Court to have it decide upon the constitutionality of an act of the Federal or State governments when the said act violates any of the fundamental principles of the Federal Constitution, such as the separation or independence of powers, the autonomy of states, the democratic system, the transitoriness of elective functions, the independence of the judiciary power, the autonomy of the states, etc. The appeal is made by the Attorney General of the Republic, the decision being compulsory and permitting the resort to Federal troops. The first case of the kind came up in 1947. A Southern State had adopted a parliamentary constitution that was contrary to the Federal System. The Supreme Court held that the law approved by the State chamber (Rio Grande do Sul) and which amended the State Constitution was unconstitutional. There have been many cases of representation ever since. T.C.

Reprisals.
A term occasionally used by governments to style operations of their armed forces for one of the following purposes: to characterize them as being limited and for the purpose of retaliation only; to proclaim them as serving a just cause; to camouflage illegitimate operations as being legitimate.

As far as the **law** is concerned one must not lose sight of the one basic fact that positive rules of law on reprisals are extremely rare in municipal law and completely absent in modern international law. Article I, Section 8, Paragraph 11 of the Constitution of the United States contains a rule of law on reprisals and a perfectly obsolete one at that. It gives to Congress not only the power to declare war, but also the power to grant "letters of marque and reprisals." The same cogent reasons which prevent the achievement of "the" legal definition of war likewise prevent the achievement of "the" legal definition of the term "reprisals." The expression "state of reprisals" (reprisals in "the" legal sense) is a mocking term like the expression "state of war" (war in "the" legal sense). A legal definition of the term must relate to some specific rule of law on reprisals in the same way as a legal definition of war must relate to some specific rule of law on war. There hence exists a variety of legal definitions for the term "reprisals." Textbook definitions of the term are useless.

A **special** "letter of marque and reprisals" was a document granted by a sovereign to an individual who had been injured abroad and was unable to get redress there. Such a document authorized the bearer to capture at sea an equivalent for his losses from any of the subjects of the State that refused to grant redress. The word "marque" (German, **die Marken**) indicated the permission to pass the jurisdictional limits of one's sovereign and the word "reprisals" the permission for a taking in return. This crude mode of redress through self-help flourished chiefly from the thirteenth through the sixteenth century. It began to disappear when State navies began to assume control of the seas.

The words "letters of marque and reprisals" in Article I, Section 8, Paragraph 11 of the Constitution of the United States meant **general** "letters of marque and reprisals:" A commission issued by Congress to a privately owned, fitted-out, armed and manned ship which was called either, like her commission, a "letter of marque and reprisals" or a "letter of marque" or "privateer." A ship called a "letter of marque and reprisals" was an armed **trading** vessel that was authorized to capture ships and cargoes belonging to citizens of a third State. A "letter of marque" or "privateer" did no trading at all, but was commissioned to serve solely as a cruiser. The United States never employed "letters of marque and reprisals," but did employ "letters of marque" or "privateers" in the course of the American naval operations against France in 1798-1800 and in the war of 1812. The parties to the Declaration of Paris of April 16, 1856, evidently intended to suppress the employment of both types of ships when in its first article they declared: "Privateering is and remains abolished."

Great Britain, in modern Orders in Council, has been using the term "general reprisals" as meaning the operations of the British fleet for the purpose of seizing all enemy ships and goods.

F.G.

Republic.

Section 4 of Article IV of the United States Constitution obligates the national government to "guarantee to every State in this Union a republican form of government." A **republic** is a form of government which derives all its powers, directly or indirectly, from the great body of politically vocal people (i.e., those who vote and who are qualified to vote) and which is administered by persons who hold their offices for limited periods or during good behavior. The essence of the American concept of a **republic** is that those who govern are chosen by and responsible to those whom they govern.

B.J.L.S.

Republican form of government.

A system of government wherein laws are enacted by elected representatives of the people. Used synonymously with "representative democracy." Frequent elections result in a broad electorate giving limited authority to elected lawmakers, who then exercise this authority until the next election either returns them with a vote of confidence or replaces them. This indirect method of legislation became a necessity with the expansion of political jurisdictions from the limited city-state, where direct democracy was possible, to nation-states with vast populations. Art. IV, Sec. 4 of the U.S. Constitution guarantees to each state a republican form of government, but efforts to distinguish what may be unrepublican aspects within particular states have been brushed aside by the U.S. Supreme Court as political questions and not justicable.

R.R.R.

Republican Organizing Committee (R.O.C.).

A political organization formed in the state of North Dakota (U.S.A.) in 1943 by conservative Republicans to oppose the Nonpartisan League (NPL) in the Republican primary. Nomination in the biennial NPL-R.O.C. primary fight was tantamount to election in a one-party state. When the NPL filed its candidates in the Democratic primary in 1956, the R.O.C. and "Old Guard" Leaguers formed a United Republican party.

R.V.A.

Reserved Powers.

In a federal system of government the powers are often divided between the central and regional authorities by delegating certain powers to one and reserving certain powers to the other. In the United States many powers are delegated to the national government in Article I, section 8, of the U.S. Constitution; and those powers which are not prohibited to the states in Article I, section 10, or preempted by the nation through Article VI, paragraph 2, are reserved to the states by the 10th Amendment of the U.S. Constitution.

J.A.E.

Residence requirement.

A person must be domiciled in good faith in a particular place considered as one's abode for a specific time in order to exercise the voting privilege. It usually means one to two years' residence in a state and several months residence in a subordinate governmental unit.

B.N.

Residual Power.

Connotes those powers not delegated to the United States by the Constitution, nor prohibited by it to the states; according to the Tenth Article of Amendment, they are reserved to the states respectively or to the people.

Sp.D.A.

Responsibility of States.

State responsibility is the collective liability of the people of a State for acts and omissions of individuals imputable to the State and constituting violations of international law. It exists in the case of acts and omissions of State organs within the sphere of their jurisdiction. It also exists in the case of acts and omissions of State organs outside their jurisdiction and even in the case of private individuals but in these two cases only if the competent State organs did not apply the necessary diligence to prevent the violation or to punish the violator and have him repair the damage. The problem of State responsibility is under discussion before the International Law Commission of the United Nations.   S.E.

Ressentiment.
Friedrich Nietzsche (1844-1900) used the term in his **Beyond Good and Evil** (1885) and his **Toward a Genealogy of Morals** (1887) to describe with it a sensitive yet powerful form of resentment coupled with a desire for revenge which—unable to find a chance for discharge—effects a subtle transformation of outlook among those who entertain or experience it. Nietzsche claimed that Christian love is an inverted, transformed type of 'ressentiment' experienced by Jews and Gentiles after their conversion to Christ. Max Scheler elucidated the term further in his famous essays "Das Ressentiment im Aufbau der Moral" (1915), (Engl. ed. by Free Press, 1961), and developed with it a brilliant psychology of outlook and evaluation which is destined to have a lasting significance for developing a psychology of ideologies.
V.Z.

Retaliation.
A strategic concept of checking aggression by the threat (to be followed by the execution, if necessary) of measures involving unacceptable losses to an aggressor, possibly measures against his own territory. The term is usually associated with "massive retaliation."
"Massive retaliation" first came into prominence in a speech made by Secretary of State John Foster Dulles on January 12, 1954. He stated that "local defenses must be reinforced by the further deterrent of massive retaliatory power" and went on to say that "the basic decision was to depend primarily upon a great capacity to retaliate, instantly by means and at places of our own choosing." Mr. Dulles and other members of President Eisenhower's administration later modified the concept of "massive retaliation" by stressing the "means and at places of our own choosing" part of the strategy and pointed out that it provided not one but several choices of response to aggression. Essentially, then, the policy was not simply total nuclear attack, but a selection from several responses (of which nuclear response would only be one) with the aim of warning an aggressor in advance that he would stand to lose more than he would gain. Hence the strategy was one of deterrence.
J.D.A.

Reuter, Ernst. (1899-1953)
Reuter became especially known as the courageous Lord Mayor of West Berlin during the Soviet blockade of this city. He was elected to this position in 1947 but could not take office because of a Russian veto. He served as a city councillor until the 1948 elections and then became mayor, a position he held until his death in 1953. The reason for the strong Soviet opposition to Reuter goes far back into his personal history.

Reuter, who was educated at the Universities of Marburg and Munster, joined the Social Democratic Party in 1912 and served as Secretary of the **Bund Neues Vaterland** until 1916. During World War I he served in the German Army, was captured on the Russian front and as a prisoner worked in the coal mines. He was liberated through the Bolshevik Revolution with which he sympathized and served as a political commissar in the Volga German Republic from 1917 until 1918. Back in Germany he became General Secretary of the German Communist Party in 1920. However, he soon rebelled against Moscow's domination and left the party and returned into the fold of the social democrats. In 1921 he became a member of the Berlin City Council. From 1922 until 1926 he was the editor of the official organ of the Social Democratic Party, the **Vorwarts**. He became greatly interested in communal projects. From 1931 until 1933 he was the Lord Mayor of Magdeburg. As a member of the **Reichstag** he fought against the anti-democratic forces on the extreme left and right. After Hitler's ascendance to power, he was sent to a concentration camp. Later he was released and went first to England and then became adviser to the Turkish Ministry of Economics and professor of public administration at the University of Ankara (1935-1939). Throughout World War II he remained in Turkey and returned to Germany after the collapse of the Nazi regime.

In addition to his influential position as Lord Mayor of Berlin he also was a social democratic member of the German **Bundesrat** (Federal Council).
E.W.

Reuther, Walter Philip.

Vice president, American Federation of Labor—Congress of Industrial Organizations since 1955. Born Wheeling, W. Va., September 1, 1907. Married. Student Wayne U. three years. Advanced from apprentice tool and die maker to foreman. Three years' travel abroad, including sixteen months' employment in Russian automobile factory. Leader of United Automobile, Aircraft and Agricultural Workers of America; founder-president of local 174, director of General Motors Division since 1939, international vice president 1942-1946, international president since 1946. President, Congress of Industrial Organizations, 1952-1955.
J.M.S.

Reverse veto.

An exception to the rule that the veto is the prerogative of the executive. By the Reorganization Act of 1939 the President of the United States was authorized to propose to Congress plans for reorganizing executive departments, to become effective after sixty days unless opposed by a concurrent resolution. The 1945 Act extended this power, but in 1949 Congress provided that only one house need oppose a plan; this arrangement is still in effect. A majority of the entire membership of the house is required, and proposals may be debated but not amended.

No similar mechanism is yet to be found elsewhere than within the United States. The closest to this in England is the provision that "statutory instruments" (delegated legislation) to be in effect must lie before the House of Commons for forty days without a "negative prayer" (motion to annul). This is significant since only about 4% of all such "instruments" have to be expressly approved by Parliament.
R.B.C.

Revolution.

A fundamental change in the political principles and institutions of a state as the result of popular opposition. A revolution may begin as a rebellion, e.g., the American Revolution, or with demands for changes in the constitution, e.g., the French Revolution (1789), without effecting an immediate change in the government. In contrast to a **coup d'etat**—a sudden change in or by the government—a revolution represents a desire for change by masses of the people. K.B.

Revolving Fund.

Money appropriated or set aside for a purpose or money received from its use which may continue to be used for that purpose without reappropriation or reapproval by the original authority.
K.E.H.

Reynaud, Paul (1878-).

A French deputy representing Basse-Alpes and Paris in the Third Republic, and Nord in the Fourth Republic since 1946. The last premier of France in 1940, he was prosecuted by Petain during the Vichy regime at the Riom trial. Having served as Minister of Colonies, Justice, National Defense and Foreign Affairs, as well as Deputy Premier in 1953, Reynaud is most noted for his three periods as Minister of Finance, especially during the Fourth. Although personally friendly with Socialist Premier Blum in 1947, as Finance Minister the following year Reynaud proposed reorganization of nationalized industries and of social security, and suppression of subsidies but encouragement of agriculture through import of equipment and guarantee of prices. An Independent politically and a convinced liberal, Reynaud favored fiscal austerity and sought reforms through government decree power.

Although questioning the efficacy of the European Defense Community project, Reynaud was an enthusiastic federalist as early as 1948, pressing for direct election of a European constituent assembly within the year. In 1949 he was a French delegate to the Council of Europe. At the age of 84, Reynaud led the parliamentary overthrow of DeGaulle's premier, Pompidou, in 1962. R.B.C.

Reza Pahlevi.
Shahinshah (Shah) of Iran. In Iran usually referred to as Mohammed Reza Shah. Born October 26, 1919. Studied in LeRosey, Switzerland and returned to Iran in 1937. When his father, Reza Khan Pahlevi, was forced to abdicate in 1941, he ascended the throne. In 1949, the constitution was revised to give the Shah certain veto powers; also a Senate was created of which the Shah appoints half of the members. In August 1953, he fled the country but returned to Iran within a week after the government of Dr. Mohammed Mossadegh was overthrown. His third and present wife is Farah Diba.
H.G.S.

Rhee, Syngman (1875-).
Eminent Korean statesman, ex-President, born at Hwanghae-Do in 1875, Princeton University education (Ph.D.). After Korean annexation by Japan (1905), exiled in America. President of "Korean Provisional Government" (1919) in Shanghai. Conducted Korean independence movement in America (1921-1945). President of the Republic of Korea from 1948 to 1960 (re-elected in 1952, 1956); exiled in Hawaii thereafter. H.C.K.

Rheims Surrender.
Was signed on May 7, 1945 (2:41 a.m.) at Rheims, France by Colonel General Jodl for Germany. It was one of a series of armistice agreements between the German Army and the Allied Expeditionary Forces to terminate fighting in World War II. Armistice terms such as, "unconditional surrender" do not prejudice subsequent peace treaties to be concluded by diplomatic representatives. E.K.K.

Rhodesia and Nyasaland.
See Federation of Rhodesia and Nyasaland.

Ribbentrop, Joachim.
Received prefix 'von' by adoption— Hitler's Minister of Foreign Affairs (1938-1945); born April 30, 1893 in Wesel, Rheinland, sentenced to death by the International Military Tribunal in Nuremberg on October 1, 1946 for crimes against the peace, war crimes, and crimes against humanity. The former champagne salesman started to work for the Nazis in 1930 by extending his business connections to political circles. In his home in Berlin-Dahlem the decisive meetings took place between the representatives of the German Reich President Paul von Hindenburg and the heads of the NSDAP who had prepared the entry of Nazis into power on January 30, 1933. Thereafter, Ribbentrop became Hitler's advisor on foreign policy, (1933), was appointed Ambassador to London (1936), and finally Foreign Minister (February 1938) as successor of Konstantin von Neurath. He also became a Gruppenfuehrer in the SS Elite Guards. He geared the Nazi diplomatic machine for the Anschluss of Austria (1938), prepared the extortion procedures against the Czechoslovak President Hacha (1939) and played a particularly significant role in the diplomatic activity which led to the attack on Poland (1939). He regarded the Hitler-Stalin Pact of August 23, 1939 as his own idea and masterpiece aimed at "securing the neutrality of the Soviet Union in case of a German-Polish conflict and as balance against anti-German plans of the Western powers." Ribbentrop was also very active in deceiving the Holy See about the Nazi treatment of prisoners of war, participated in the murder of the French General Maurice Mesny — a German PW — and assisted by "diplomatic" communications in the annihilation of Jewry. Ribbentrop was the most stupid foreign minister ever member of a European cabinet. His stupidity was only surpassed by his vanity and cadaver obedience to the Fuehrer. He was afraid to lose his job in 1942 because — Germany might not need diplomats any longer after the conquest of the whole world. R.M.W.K.

Ricardo, David (1772-1823).
English economist, was born of Jewish lineage, in London, Apr. 19, 1772, died in Gatcombe Park, Gloucestershire, Sept. 11, 1823. Follower of Adam Smith, but abandoned Smith's realism in economics for highly abstract rationalism. His theory of rents and labor theory of value had enormous influence in the development of modern economics. George's single tax and Marx's

theory of surplus value owe much to Ricardo. The odious iron law of wages is a Ricardian postulate based upon the doctrine of scarcity of economic goods. He wrote a number of celebrated studies on money and trade, but his chief work was **Principles of Political Economy and Taxation**, (1817).
M.M.Mc.

Richelieu, Armand du Plessis.
(1585-1642).

Cardinal and French statesman. Bishop of Lucon (1607), Richelieu was brought to the Court in 1614, when he became almoner of the queen regent. After Louis XIII assumed the reins of government, Richelieu created cardinal in 1622, joined the royal council and from 1624 until his death was first minister of France. His aims were to make the monarchy supreme in France by subduing the nobles, eliminate the Huguenot state within a state, and instruct every subject in his duty. He developed the system of intendencies, prohibited duelling, reduced the political though not the religious privileges of the Huguenots, and led France into Thirty Years' War against the Empire of Spain. Richelieu founded the French Academy (1635). More minister than cardinal, Richelieu depleted the French treasury but left to his successor, Mazarin, a well-fashioned absolute monarchy.
K.B.

Ridgway, Matthew Bunker.

Born March 3, 1895, Ft. Monroe, Va. Graduated, West Point, 1917. 1942-44 Commander of 82nd Division; airborne invasion of Sicily, Italy, and France. 1944-45 in Belgium, France and Germany as Commander of 18th Airborne Corps, which captured 500,000 German prisoners. Communist counteroffensive serious, December, 1950, appointed Commander of American 8th Army and UN ground forces in Korea. April 11, 1951, at Gen. MacArthur's summary dismissal by President Truman, succeeded as Comdr. in chief Far East Command, Comdr. in Chief UN Command, and Supreme Commander for Allied Powers; inflicted heavy losses so as to force Chinese Communists to negotiate. May, 1952, replaced Gen. Dwight D. Eisenhower as Supreme Commander Allied Powers Europe. Aug., 1953, as U.S. Army Chief of Staff. Retired in June, 1955.
C.K.W.

Right.

A just claim, either moral or legal, upon the society. A freedom to act or not to act in a particular fashion. It involves duty to permit the same freedom to others. Fundamental rights are variously derived, according to different schools of thought, from a state of nature prior to the state, a social compact, the deity, social customs and mores, or formal legal recognition. Certain natural or "inalienable" rights are proclaimed in the Declaration of Independence of the U.S.A., whereas certain legal rights are conferred by the bill of rights found in numerous national constitutions, and by ordinary legislation.
R.E.Ch.

Right to Counsel.

In the U.S., Amendment VI to the Constitution states that "in all criminal prosecutions, the accused shall enjoy the right . . . to have the assistance of counsel in his defense." Originally, this meant only that an accused's counsel could not be barred from the trial. Since 1938 **(Johnson v. Zerbst)**, a criminal trial in federal court is void unless the accused is represented by counsel (which must be supplied him if he is a pauper) or has intelligently waived his right to such assistance. However, this absolute requirement does not apply to state courts.
F.H.H.

Right to peaceable assembly.

A guarantee to the individual found in the 1st Amendment to the U.S. Constitution is the right to assemble for peaceful purposes. The exercise of this right has led to the formation of a multiplicity of groups with political goals, and the right is closely dependent upon other 1st Amendment guarantees as free speech, press, religious conscience, and right to petition Congress. Peaceable assembly is permitted and is distinguished from prohibited assemblies having as their purpose to commit illegal acts.
R.R.R.

Right to Work Laws.

General term used by its proponents to describe state laws which make the union shop illegal. Under the provi-

sions of the Labor Management Act of 1947 (Taft-Hartley Act), the closed shop was made illegal and the union shop is legal only if the state law does not prohibit it. There are close to twenty states with right to work laws. These states are mainly in the South.
G.B.T.

Rightist.
Term originating in French Chamber (See Leftist), where Conservatives and Monarchists sat on right of President. The term R. designates conservatives who emphasize human weakness rather than human perfectibility, and supporters of prescription or legitimacy as a political principle. Since Communism is popularly identified as "Leftist," the term "Rightist" is often misused as a generic label for anti-Communists. This practice has the confusing effect of lumping collectivists such as the National Socialist Hitler in the same category with constitutionalists and libertarian conservatives.
K.G.

Rio Grande Compact.
Was signed at Sante Fe, New Mexico, United States of America, on March 18, 1938, by Colorado, New Mexico, and Texas; and approved by the three state legislatures and Congress in 1939. It provides for the equitable apportionment of the water of the Rio Grande among the three states, replacing the preliminary compact of 1929.
The Rio Grande Compact Commission, consisting of a representative from each of the three states, administers the compact.
J.E.T.

Risk.
See Consequences.

Robespierre, Maximilien Francois Marie Isadore de. (1758-1793).
French revolutionist, was a lawyer, literary and society figure before the revolution. He was a member of the Estates General. In the constituent assembly he was a most vociferous and effective supporter of the extreme left, and an active Jacobin. A member of the Committee of Public Safety in July 1793, and in many ways its master, he at first tried to restrain the use of terror for political objectives. Later he employed it ferociously in the hope of establishing a Rousseauist state. Feeling his power slipping and his goal vanishing, on July 26, 1794, he harangued the convention to end the terror, punish the deputies guilty of excesses, and replace the members of the Committee of Public Safety. Two days later the Committee and the Convention decreed his death on the guillotine.
E.G.L.

Rokossovsky, Konstantin Konstantinovich. (1896-).
Born at Warsaw of Polish parents. Career officer 32 years in Red Army, when sent as Defense Minister and Politburo member in 1949 to Poland. Symbol of Russian domination. Returned to Moscow in November 1956 as USSR Deputy Defense Minister and Marshal of the Soviet Union.
R.F.S.

Rollback.
A foreign policy calling for positive United States action to bring important areas of the world taken over by the Communists since World War II out of Communist control, presumably by force if necessary. Eastern Europe and China have been the areas most frequently referred to in this connection. Rollback (sometimes called "liberation") has been put forward as an alternative to the allegedly negative policy of containment pursued by the U.S. Government since 1947.
Though important Republican Party leaders publicly advocated a policy of rollback before 1953, the Eisenhower Administration's actions toward Nationalist China and during the Hungarian uprising of 1956 made clear its unwillingness to accept the risks implicit in the active pursuance of such a policy.
S.L.A.

Roman Catholic Church.
Western branch of the imperial Christian Church of the Roman Empire from about 476 A.D. to the Great Schism of 1,054 A.D.; separately and independently governed and administered since 1,054, but maintaining the claim to be the true lineal descendant of the original Roman Church; once the established and only lawful church in many countries of western Europe; disestablished in many countries since the Protestant Reformation (1517-1555).
Ch.C.M.

Romulo, Carlos Pena.

One of the most prominent figures in Philippine international affairs since World War II, Romulo was born January 14, 1901 at Manila. He was an influential editor and publisher before serving as an aide to General MacArthur in Bataan, Corregidor, and Australia (1941-44).

From 1944 to 1946 he was Resident Commissioner of the Philippine Islands to the United States and in 1946 headed the Philippine delegation to the UNO conference at San Francisco and the UNRRA conference at Atlantic City. Nine years as permanent Philippine representative at the UN were followed in 1954 by a brief period as Personal Envoy of President Magsaysay to the U.S. He became Ambassador to the U.S. in September 1955, serving until his appointment to the chancellorship of the University of the Philippines at Manila in 1962. M.T.K.

Roosevelt Corollary of the Monroe Doctrine.

Theodore Roosevelt in a Presidential message in 1904 transformed the Monroe Doctrine into a justification for intervention in Latin America. While the original Monroe Doctrine held that the Western Hemisphere and Europe constituted separate political spheres, the 1904 Corollary held that the U.S. should intervene to prevent chronic bankruptcy of Latin American States which might involve these states with Europe. The occasion of this policy followed the peaceful elimination of a British, German and Italian blockade of 1902 to enforce private claims against a Venezuelan dictator. The Roosevelt Corollary was subsequently used to justify U.S. intervention policies; however, it was greatly qualified during the administrations of Hoover and Franklin Roosevelt. Since the formation of the Organization of American States in 1948 the United States has been specifically committed to multilateral approaches in Latin America; President John F. Kennedy regarded the whole Monroe Doctrine as a "weak reed," and U.S. commitments to the United Nations deny the basic assumptions of both the Doctrine and its Corollary. R.W.T.

Roosevelt, Franklin Delano.

32nd President of the U.S., was the only President to be elected for four successive terms, 1933-1949, but died in office April 12, 1945. Born January 30, 1882, in Hyde Park, N. Y., he received an upper-class education in sports, travel, and schooling. He was graduated from Harvard in 1900 and from Columbia Law School in 1904. In 1905 he married Anna Eleanor Roosevelt, his sixth cousin and a niece of President Theodore Roosevelt. As a Democratic New York State Senator he early showed his interest in progressive and reform legislation. From 1913 to 1921 he was a vigorous Assistant Secretary of the Navy. In August, 1921, he developed polio-myelitis, from which he never fully recovered. In 1928 he became Governor of New York, and in 1933 President of the United States, entering office as a member of the Democratic Party in a severe economic depression with business largely idle and banking on the verge of collapse. In his first month in office, through legislation passed by Congress, he restored confidence in the banks, initiated relief of distress, reformed investment and securities procedures, and set up public works programs. Although much of what he did was temporary and experimental, he established a social security system for old age pensions and measures intended to stabilize the fluctuations of business cycles. He is remembered chiefly for his achievements in social welfare, his informal messages to the American people, and his leadership in preparation for and during World War II, when he established personal relationships with the Allied leaders and developed a framework for the United Nations, which he wanted established before the end of the War. Always purposive and adaptable, he died just before the close of the War. T.K.N.

Roosevelt, Theodore. (1855-1919).

Writer, statesman, 26th President of the U.S. was born in New York City. Graduating from Harvard College (1880) he was shortly elected to the New York Legislature (1881-1884). Because of poor health he bought a ranch in Dakota Territory where between riding the range he wrote several biographies and therewith decided upon a literary career. This happy occupation was interrupted when he was appointed (1889-1895) to the Civil Service Commission, and later as President of the Police Board of N. Y. City. With the new Republican Administration he was appointed Assistant Secretary of the Navy (1897). Devoted to the theories of Captain Alfred Thayer Mahan, Roosevelt had become an ardent expansionist. Largely due to his efforts in the Navy Department, as soon as the Spanish American War was declared, Admiral Dewey was in a position to defeat the Spanish squadron at Manila. At the opening of the Spanish American War, he resigned (1898) to organize the 1st U.S. Volunteer Regiment, the Rough Riders, for service in Cuba, and won fame in the battle of San Juan Hill. Returning home a hero, he was elected Governor of New York (1898). Two years later he was elected Vice President of the U.S. which many hoped would be his political oblivion. With the assassination of President McKinley, Roosevelt became President (1901), the youngest person to hold that high office. He was elected a second term (1904).

Roosevelt was essentially a moralist and looked upon politics as a "jolly good pulpit." The right to regulate wealth in the public interest he said was "universally admitted." In the anthracite coal strike (1902) he brought management and labor to the White House and forced a settlement. Instructing the Attorney-General to enter suit (1902) against Northern-Securities Co., a consolidation of the Hill-Morgan and Harriman railroads, to stop the process of further mergers he declared a policy of greater supervision of Government over big business. He asked Congress to approve a Department of Commerce and Labor (1903) and a Bureau of Corporations to investigate business practices. As early reforms he secured the end of railroad rebates (Elkins Act, 1903) and fixed rates (Hepburn Act, 1906). He also extended Government supervision over drugs and food, especially meats which affected the packing industry. In short he used the "big stick."

His knowledge and love of the West as shown in his seven-volume work on **Winning of the West,** gave him a special interest in the conservation of natural resources such as soil, water, mines and forests for the use of all people. This was one of his leading policies and resulted in the Reclamation Act (1902), the Inland Waterways Commission (1907) and the establishment of the National Conservation Association (1909). He also set aside over 100 million acres of land as national forest reserve.

In international affairs, he promoted the expansion of the United States in the Caribbean area. When negotiations with Colombia over a zone for the Panama Canal lagged, he promptly recognized the rebels who proclaimed (1903) the Republic of Panama and gave the U.S. the desired zone. He bluntly added a corollary to the Monroe Doctrine that the U.S. would not permit any European nation forcibly to collect debts in the Western Hemisphere and therewith he occupied Santo Domingo (1905) to straighten out its tangled financial affairs and pay its debts.

By his offer of mediation, he brought an end to the Russo-Japanese War. For this, he was the first American to be awarded the Nobel Peace Prize. Called upon to assist in the settlement of the First Algeciras Conference, he proposed an "open door policy" which was accepted. Finally, he sent the American fleet around the world (1908) to show the power of this country, especially to Japan who was beginning to have delusions of grandeur.

Although he could have been reelected President (1908), he chose to leave his unfinished reforms to another and went to Africa. Returning home two years later he was astonished at the conservatism of the Administration and he applauded the insurgent Republicans who had organized the "Progressive Republican League." Disappointed with the outcome of the Republican National Convention (1912), he bolted his party and with the help of the PRL organized the Progressive Party with its bull moose symbol and himself as presidential candidate. In this campaign, his announced creed was the New Nationalism. It was a platform for increased government powers to effect such reforms as national regulation of business, legislation to benefit labor, inheritance and income taxes, and public welfare. At the same time he talked much about the "square deal." In the election, he carried 27% of the votes and six states with 88 electoral votes, making the Progressive Party second.

He has been criticized for his secession from the Republican Party and then dumping the Progressive Party in the 1916 campaign leaving it without leadership. It is charged that he thereby weakened the Republican Party for a generation and smothered the liberal reform within the party.

From a constitutional viewpoint, his greatest contribution is to be found in his concept of presidential leadership of Congress. A decade before Woodrow Wilson asserted his view of legislative leadership, Roosevelt had already made himself the Leader of Congress, of the Republican Party and of public opinion.
M.E.D.

Rousseau, Jean-Jacques. (1712-1778).
A French philosopher who in his **Social Contract** and other writings contributed to the idea of liberal democracy. Beginning with the thesis that man is "naturally" good and that only the existence of social institutions has made him bad, he attacked the institutions that existed in his day. Rousseau thought that man possesses liberty as part of his nature and cannot relinquish it permanently any more than he can relinquish his humanity. He explained the existence of government on the basis of a social contract whereby man, innocent, good, and free, had moved toward civilization by giving up his liberties to society collectively, not to a political superior. (Giving up one's liberty did not mean losing it, since it was not given to any particular individual but to the group as a whole.) Every man is part of the corporate body thus formed, and sovereignty (the power that exists in a state) consists of the **general will**—that is, the will of the people on matters of common concern. Obedience to the state can be demanded only when the state acts in accordance with the will of the people. All phases of life that are not part of the community interest must be reserved to the individual as his rights. The objective of the community organization is to protect its members and to promote their prosperity and happiness.

Coming at a time when people in Europe were attracted to the ideas of liberty and equality, Rousseau gave people a theory that they were anxious to accept regardless of the weaknesses in parts of its logic.
D.C.

Royal Commission.
A special investigating body used in the United Kingdom and other Commonwealth countries. The commission is appointed by the Crown, sometimes as a result of parliamentary initiative. Those appointed may include Members of Parliament, government officials and private individuals. The commission is intended to be nonpartisan and to gather evidence both from experts and from the general public, and it may make legislative recommendations.
R.H.B.

Rule-making.
Action by chief executives and administrative agencies of government in interpreting and executing legislation calling for the enforcement of benefactory, fiscal, police, political, and proprietary functions affecting the interests of the public in general or particular sections of the public. It is a form of administrative action that is called also administrative or delegated legislation, ordinance-making, quasi-legislation, and "filling in legislative details."

In the U.S.A. the Federal Administrative Procedure Act of 1946 — passed to eliminate the confusion, duplication and extreme variations in procedure and forms for administrative agencies to take action and to ensure that administrative action is taken with adequate regard to due process of law — defined "rule" as follows: "the whole or any part of any agency statement of general or particular applicability and future effect designed to implement, interpret, or prescribe the organization, procedure, or practice requirements of any agency and includes the approval or prescription for the future of rates, wages, corporate or financial structures or reorganizations thereof, prices, facilities, appliances, services or allowances therefor or valuations, costs, or accounting, or practices bearing upon any of the foregoing." Rule-making was defined as "agency process for the formulation, amendment, or repeal of a rule." The **Attorney General's Manual on the Administrative Procedure Act,** issued in 1947, emphasized that the definition of "rule" was not limited to substantive rules, but embraced also interpretive, organizational and procedural rules, and these rules applied either to a group or a single person. A key factor in rule-making is future effect. The rules must implement or prescribe future law. Some rules go into effect only when certain circumstances exist. These are called "contingent rules."

Rules are more easily amended than statutes. On the one hand rules free the legislature to concentrate on policy, and on the other they give the administrator a freer hand to enforce the statutes. The technical expert — the administrator — is given the authority to develop the rules best calculated to achieve the statutory objectives.

Two categories of rules were acknowledged by the above Act: (1) those which implement, interpret or prescribe law or policy, and (2) those which describe the organization, procedure or practice requirements of an agency. The first category generally relates to substantive statutory provisions applied to individuals, and involves: giving specific meaning to such general legislative standards as "reasonable rates" and "unfair methods of competition"; furnishing the facts on which the enforcement of statutes is based; and prescribing the classification of persons, organizations, or things affected by the statutes concerned. Accordingly, rule-making agencies become associated with the legislature in both the formulation and enforcement of legislative policy. The second category of rules aims at providing uniformity and certainty to the administration of statutes, and includes rules of a managerial nature — such as those governing veterans' benefits and subsidies — and rules which govern the adjudication of cases.

A "rule" differs from an "order" in that the former is essentially legislative in nature, and has general and continuing applicability. An "order" is the result of a procedure essentially judicial in nature, and applies to a particular and individual situation.

Rule-making powers have two sources — constitutions and statutes. It is those rule-making powers delegated by statute which have at times provoked political and legal controversy. Rule-making powers may be classed in three categories: (1) discretionary elaboration of rules; (2) interpretation of statutes; and (3) determining that the conditions exist which make a contingent statute's provisions operative. Obviously, discretion is a strong element in the rule-making process. However, this is its point of weakness as well. Where the statutes may not adequately limit discretion, the courts may attempt to do so. Yet, effective operation of modern government, and especially in times of emergency, necessitates a broad application of discretion. How much discretion becomes a key problem.

With regard to delegation of legislative powers to the President or other administrative officers, the Supreme Court has acknowledged such delegation as essential for modern government to function, but it has distinguished between valid and invalid delegation. Until the depression period and the New Deal program, the Court upheld every delegation as valid. In 1935 in **Panama Refining Co. v. Ryan,** 293 U. S. 388, and **Schechter v. United States,** 295 U. S. 495, and in 1936 in **Carter v. Carter Coal Co.,** 298 U. S. 238, the Supreme Court declared the delegations involved in these cases unconstitutional and laid down the following requisites of valid delegation: (1) Congress itself must have the power to regulate in the matter concerned; (2) Congress must provide definite limitations to the delegation by defining the subject of the delegation and by providing a primary criterion or standard to guide the rule-making officials; (3) a finding must be required in the case of contingent legislation; (4) the delegation must be to public officials, not private individuals or groups; and (5) Congress must provide the penalty, if any, for violation of the rules.

Congress alone, not the administrators, may provide that violations of rules under its delegations are indictable penal offenses. However, the administrators may define the elements which constitute the criminal offense;

but the penalty will be set by Congress. (**United States v. Grimaud**, 220 U. S. 506 [1910]). This is generally true also at the state level. O.K.

Rule of Four.
If four members of the United States Supreme Court, one less than a majority, vote favorably, a writ of certiorari will issue. While most members of the Court seem to agree that, except under unusual circumstances, once the writ is granted, they should hear the case on the merits, Mr. Justice Frankfurter felt much freer in voting to dismiss the writ as improvidently granted. T.C.S.

Rule of law.
A significant Anglo-American doctrine, which in the words of A. V. Dicey, means that "no man is punishable or can be lawfully made to suffer in body or goods except for a distinct breach of law established in the ordinary legal manner before the ordinary courts of the land." J.D.

Rule of reason.
A doctrine first enunciated in 1911 by the U.S. Supreme Court in cases against the American Tobacco Company and the Standard Oil Company, stating that the Sherman Anti-Trust Act — aimed at protecting trade and commerce "against unlawful restraints, and monopolies" — applied only to business arrangements which could be considered "unreasonable" restraints of trade, and which, therefore, constituted unfair competitive methods. J.D.

Rule of War.
Varied in accordance with political objectives of wars in the course of history. H.C.K.

Rules, Committee on.
A very important standing committee, which proposes the rules under which the legislative assembly operates, and which proposes the rules to take up legislation out of its regular order. This second function of determining the time that bills are to be discussed tends to give it the powers of life and death over many issues and adds greatly to its power as a committee. K.E.H.

Rumania.
Rumania has an area of 91,700 square miles. Its population is around 18,700,000, about 9% being ethnic Hungarians. The predominant religion is Orthodox.

Rumania's history begins with the Roman colonization in the second century A.D. Withdrawal of the Romans in the third century was followed by a succession of invasions. In 1003 the Magyars subjugated Transylvania. In the 13th century the principalities of Walachia and Moldavia were established but came under Turkish suzerainty in 1476 and 1513. The Treaty of Kuchuk Kainarji (1774) gave Russia influence over them. In 1812 Russia acquired Bessarabia.

The Congress of Paris (1856) placed Walachia-Moldavia under the guarantee of the European Powers. Under Alexander Cuza they united (1861) as Rumania. Rumania obtained its independence from Turkey in 1878 and proclaimed a kingdom under Carol I in 1881. It entered the Second Balkan Wars (1913) and obtained southern Dobrudja. In World War I Rumania, with Ferdinand on the throne, acquired Transylvania, Banat, Bessarabia and Bukovina.

In 1927 Ferdinand died. Carol II returned in 1930, acquired dictatorial powers in 1938, and was deposed in favor of son Michael in 1940 when Ion Antonescu became dictator and German troops entered the country. Also in 1940 Rumania lost territories and the following June, Antonescu declared war on the USSR. In 1944, following a coup by Michael, Rumania joined the Allies. With Soviet assistance a Communist led coalition government was established in March 1945 and Michael abdicated in December 1947. By the Paris Treaty of 1947 Rumania recovered all territories except Bessarabia, north Bukovina and south Dobrudja.

The constitution of 1948 (superseded in 1952) proclaimed Rumania a People's Republic. Legislative power is vested in the unicameral Grand National Assembly, elected every four years from a single ballot. The Council of Ministers, headed by the Premier, is the highest executive body. The judiciary consists of people's courts, regional courts, and the supreme court; all are elected or appointed for fixed terms. The only party permitted is the Rumanian Workers' (Communist) Party. Rumania is closely allied to the USSR and the other Communist-dominated states through the Warsaw Pact and the Council for Mutual Economic Assistance. J.J.K.

Run (on banks).
A special type of panic on the part of the public; wholesale withdrawal of deposits from banks by its clients, forcing the banks into an illiquid position. Caused by the fear that banks are, or will be, not able to meet their obligations to pay cash on demand. Consequently forces the banks to suspend payments temporarily or permanently. The biggest runs on the banks in the U.S. were in 1907 and in 1933, causing in each case a revision by the Congress of the American banking system. W.N.

Run-off primary.
This is a United States election device used especially in southern states to prevent minority nominations. The run-off occurs when no candidate receives a majority of the votes cast in the "first" primary. The candidates with the highest and next highest vote are the only competitors in the "run-off" or "second" primary. B.N.

Rural government.
A generic term pertaining to government in less heavily populated areas with 2,500 the point of division between rural and urban established by the Bureau of the Census. Broadly, the term is used to include county and township government in the United States as well as the rudimentary governmental system in unincorporated communities. G.S.B.

Rush-Bagot Agreement.
An agreement, effected by an exchange of notes between Sir Charles Bagot, the British Minister in Washington, and Richard Rush, the Acting Secretary of State, (April 28, 1817), putting into effect a lakes naval limitation arrangement. The agreement — frequently cited as a symbol of Canadian-American friendship — while imposing no limitations on land fortifications — limited the respective naval forces of Canada and the United States to one vessel each on Lake Ontario, two on the Upper Lakes, and one on Lake Champlain. W.W.

Russell, Bertrand (1872-).
British philosopher - mathematician, for many years associated with Cambridge University. In the course of a long career of university lecturing and writing, he achieved distinction as a logician, mathematican, and political essayist. Among many technical works, he is perhaps best known as the co-author, with A. N. Whitehead, of **Principia Mathematica** (3 vols., 1910-1913). In political philosophy, Russell stands in the traditions of empiricism and liberalism, which to his thinking are related. His political tenets include a firm belief in democracy, support for collectivist solutions to social problems, and an outspoken attack on the problem of war. This latter concern has involved pacifism, support for world federalism, and in the post-World War II period, advocacy of nuclear disarmament. In 1950 Lord Russell was awarded the Nobel Prize in literature. H.S.Th.

Russo-Finnish War.
(1939-40; 1941-44).
A two-phased war. The first phase— the Winter War—began on November 30, 1939, when the Soviet Union launched a major attack following Finland's refusal to make territorial and other concessions that had been demanded in the preceding year. Finland capitulated on March 20, 1940, after an heroic struggle against overwhelming odds. Finland ceded 16,000 square miles of her territory and made other important concessions to the Soviet Union as the price for peace. In the second phase, Finland, this time in a relationship of cobelligerency with Nazi Germany, was able to regain her lost territories when hostilities with the Soviet Union were renewed as a consequence of the German invasion of the Soviet Union in June of 1941. Defeat in 1944 again led to important concessions, including the valuable mining area of Petsamo and the payment of burdensome reparations to the Soviet Union. Notwithstanding the great burdens of military defeat and economic loss, Finland has been able to preserve her free political institutions and con-

tinues to maintain her westward orientation.   R.H.K.

Russo-Japanese War.

The Russo-Japanese War grew out of a struggle between the two countries over rights in Manchuria where both had extensive commercial interests. It was precipitated by a Japanese surprise attack on Port Arthur, February 8, 1904. War was declared on February 10. Subsequently, Japanese armies landed in Manchuria. The Russians were unable to repulse the Japanese forces and were gradually forced away from the coast. On January 2, 1905, Port Arthur fell to the Japanese giving them a significant strategic advantage.

In May of 1905 the Russian Baltic fleet was almost destroyed in the Sea of Japan with only minor Japanese losses.

Japan, despite her victories, was feeling the strain of the war. Her economy was unable to sustain a long war effort. Consequently, she solicited the good offices of President Theodore Roosevelt to arrange a peace treaty. Treaty discussions were held at Portsmouth, New Hampshire, and a treaty was signed by the belligerents on September 5, 1905.

Under the provisions of the treaty, Japan acquired the southern part of the Chinese Eastern Railroad (formerly controlled by Russia), the Laotung leasehold, and other privileges in Manchuria. In addition, Russia ceded Japan the southern part of Sakhalin Island in lieu of an indemnity and agreed to respect Japan's interests in Korea and not to interefere with whatever measures she took there.   S.S.

Rwanda.

A republic in Central Africa; area 10,169 square miles; population, 2,634,451 (1959 estimate). Along with Urundi (now Burandi), and then known as Ruanda, it formed a League of Nations mandate, Ruanda-Urundi, with Belgium as the mandatory power, after World War I. In 1946 Ruanda-Urundi became a United Nations trust territory with Belgium as trustee, being governed by a Vice Governor General under the Governor General of the Belgian Congo. A United Nations sponsored plebiscite in 1961 abolished the monarchy of Mwami Kigeri IV. In 1962 the trusteeship was terminated and the old Ruanda was severed from its associate, becoming the separate independent state of Rwanda, by vote of the United Nations General Assembly.   E.V.M.

S

Saar.
Rich coal mining area between France and Germany, southeast of Luxembourg. Capital: Saarbrucken; area: 988 square miles; population: 1,060,500 (1960). Historically, possession of the area has been disputed by both France and Germany. Following World War I it was separated from Germany by the Versailles Treaty and placed under League of Nations administration; the coal mines were awarded to France as reparations; political status to be finally determined after 15 years' time by plebiscite. The plebiscite (1935) returned an overwhelming majority for unification with Germany. Following World War II, the Saar came under French administration; it was separated **de facto** from Germany by economic union with France. With the restoration of West German sovereignty (1954) France and Germany began to negotiate a final settlement of the Saar's status. The first proposal, the Saar Statute to "Europeanize" the region was defeated by the Saar population in a plebiscite (1955). After further negotiations a new accord was reached (1956) whereby France agreed to the political unification of the Saar with Germany in return for certain economic rights. On January 1, 1957, the Saar became a **Land** of the Federal Republic. C.J.S.

S.A.C.
See Strategic Air Command.

Sacco-Vanzetti Case (1920-27).
The leading American **cause celebre** took its name from a pair of alien Socialists, Nicola Sacco (b. 1891) and Bartolomeo Vanzetti (b. 1888), both natives of Italy. They were charged with killing the paymaster of a shoe factory in South Braintree, Mass., Apr. 15, 1920; tried before Judge Webster Thayer in Dedham, May 31-July 14, 1921; found guilty of first-degree murder, sentenced to death and electrocuted, Aug. 23, 1927. Eye-witnesses said the fatal shots — a payroll guard was also killed — came from two men of foreign description.

The brutal crime took place during a wave of post-war feeling against radicals and agitators and speedy retribution was demanded. But the arrest and prosecution of "a good shoemaker" (Sacco) and "a poor fish-peddler" (Vanzetti) raised many doubts as to the justice of the proceedings. Neither the get-away automobile nor any of the payroll loot of $16,000 was connected with the accused men. The flimsy evidence against them was identification of Sacco and Vanzetti as participants and their false statements to police. The prosecution made much of their evasion of military service and their anarchistic views, obvious irrelevancies, but all efforts by the defense for a new trial failed, even after a condemned criminal, Celestino Medeiros, in 1925, said that Sacco and Vanzetti were not guilty of the murder. The Medeiros statement led to an investigation which indicated that the crime might have been perpetrated by a robber band from Providence, R. I.

When William G. Thompson, eminent Boston lawyer, took over the defense, and Harvard law professor Felix Frankfurter began to write about the contradictions and confusions, the case became an international affair with protest meetings around the world and petitions from Anatole France, Romain Rolland, Albert Einstein, Thomas G. Masaryk and other noted figures. After imposition of the death sentence, Apr. 9, 1927, demand for a review grew so great that Gov. Alvin T. Fuller of Massachusetts appointed a three-man advisory committee, including Harvard president A. Lawrence Lowell, which found no reason for executive intervention. The federal courts also declined to entertain the case.

Demonstrations, including bombings of American embassies and consulates, occurred in many countries and pickets were arrested at the Massachusetts statehouse. The executions took place with Boston under heavy police protection. Poems, plays, stories and novels all have made the Sacco-Vanzetti case a part of American literature as well as an ugly black question mark in our criminal law. I.Di.

Safety commissioner.
The urban counterpart of the sheriff in rural areas. While commonly limited

to the officer with police and law enforcement responsibilities, the term is sometimes used to connote the officer in charge of both police and fire functions in some cities. G.S.B.

S. A. G.
(Sowjetische Aktiengesellschaften). Soviet (U. S. S. R.) Corporations in the Soviet Zone of Germany (SMA Order 167-1946). 213 seized plants were operated by 13 corporations. Locally subsidized they produced for export to the Soviet Union, employed about 550,000 workers (1952), and produced 32% of the Zone's industrial output. The U. S. S. R. sold these enterprises to the German Democratic Republic (31-12-1953) for $1.4 billion.
E.K.K.

Saint Simon, Claude Henri, de.
Chief founder of French Utopian Socialism. Born in Paris of impoverished noble parents, he fought in the American Revolution. He contributed to such modern political thought as positivism, technocracy, and internationalism. He sought a supranational cult of the positive sciences for the purpose of directing and improving man's social relations. Workers were to submit voluntarily to a benevolent hierarchy of industrialists ruling for the benefit of all according to the social ethics of Christianity. His influence spread through such men as Comte, Bismarck, Rodbertus, and the socialists. His doctrines are found in his **Reorganization of European Society, L'Industrie**, and **Nouveau Christianisme**. R.E.Ch.

Sakhalin.
An island in North Pacific, opposite to mouth of Amur River in Siberia; 586 m. long, 15 to 96 m. wide; area, 24,560 sq. m.; population, 500,000. Under Chinese dominion till 19th century. Japanese-Russian joint possession by treaty of 1858. Treaty of 1875; Russia retained the whole of Sakhalin; the Kurile Islands went to Japan. By Treaty of Portsmouth, (N.H.), 1905, southern half ceded to Japan by Russia. Later, oil was discovered in northern half. 1920, Japanese seizure of northern portion; for withdrawal, Japan was granted in 1925 concessions in oil (50%), timber, and fishing. Oil production, 4 to 5 million barrels annually.

Sakhalin and Kuriles promised to Russia at Yalta Conference, and occupied by Russia in 1945. By Peace Treaty of 1951, Japan renounced right to those islands. C.K.W.

Salan, Raoul (1899-).
Commander - in - Chief of French troops in Far East, 1948. Inspector-General of French National Defense, 1954. Commander of French troops in Algeria, 1956-58. Joined Algerian revolt, 1958. Military Governor of Paris, 1959. Leader of OAS in Algeria. Declared war against De Gaulle March 1962. After capture sentenced to life, May 1962. M.C.V.

Salazar, Antonio de Oliveira.
Born April 28, 1889. Graduated from Coimbra University in 1914 with degree in economics and joined its teaching staff. Left Coimbra University in April 1928 and since then has been an acknowledged leader of Portugal's political affairs. Salazar was instrumental in the adoption of Portugal's Constitution adopted March 19, 1933, and revised August 29, 1959. Formulated according to Dr. Salazar's principles, the Portuguese government is a unitary corporative republic with a National Assembly of 130 members who are elected every four years and most of whom adhere to the principles of the semi-official Uniao Nacional (National Union) headed by Salazar. A Corporate Chamber is composed of representatives of economic and cultural associations and serves to advise the National Assembly.

Salazar became Premier on July 5, 1932. In the November 1961 election Henrique Galvao's Anti-Totalitarian Front attempted to present a "Democratic Opposition." But it evaporated before the election was held. In the Spanish civil war of 1936-1939, Dr. Salazar followed a policy of non-intervention. He recognized the regime of General Franco of Spain and in a Protocol to a Treaty of Friendship and Non-Aggression signed July 29, 1940, he and Franco agreed to a policy of neutrality in World War II. In 1949, Dr. Salazar effected Portugal's entry into NATO. In 1961, his colonial policy was challenged in Angola, Mozambique and Portuguese Guinea. In the same year Goa was lost to India after 451 years of Portuguese rule. B.J.L.S.

Salt March.
Dramatic march of Mohandas K. Gandhi in 1930 to obtain salt, a British monopoly in the Indian Empire. The 200-mile journey from Ahmedabad to Dandi took 24 days and stirred public opinion. Breaking the salt laws by obtaining salt from the sea, Gandhi and his followers stimulated additional civil disobedience and world sympathy for nonviolent, Indian nationalism. P.F.P.

Saltonstall, Leverett.
Born September 1, 1892; U.S. Senate from November 7, 1944 until term ending January 3, 1967; Republican-Massachusetts; speaker of the Massachusetts House of Representatives, 1931-1936; Governor of Massachusetts 1938-1944. R.A.B.

Samaritans.
Ancient religious sect separated from Judaism around 400 B.C. Centered in Nablus (Jordan), with nearby Mt. Gerizim as its sacred mountain, headed by High Priest. Some 150 Samaritans live in Israel. E.G.

Sanctions.
In a narrow sense, the jural penalties that are provided for violations of law such as fines, imprisonment, and capital punishment. More broadly, the term includes all forces, such as social disapprobation and public opinion, that induce observance of law or community mores. In the international field, sanctions refer to measures that are taken by nation states to enforce international law, including severing of trade relations, withdrawal of diplomatic recognition, blockades, and war. M.J.Sch.

San Francisco Vigilance Committee of 1856.
Aroused by San Francisco's record of lawlessness and ballot-box stuffing and the killing of a popular newspaper editor, a secret organization known as the Vigilance Committee of 1856 was formed by William Coleman and others who had been associated with a similar group in 1851. With 15,000 members enrolled and one-third of them potentially under arms the Committee controlled law enforcement in San Francisco from May to August of 1856 when they voluntarily disbanded. Altogether the Committee hung four, caused one death by suicide, banished several undesirables, and prevented the landing of many persons with a criminal record. J.A.E.

San Martin, Jose de.
South American Liberator. Born February 25, 1778 in Argentina. Abandoning royal army of Spain, he joined Argentine revolution in 1812, and prepared for liberation of Chile and Peru from Spain. Chile freed by San Martin's army at Chacabuco, after heroic Andes crossing in 1817. Declining high office, he proceeded to the partial liberation of Peru at the battle of Maipu in 1818. Became "Protector" of Peru in 1821, but conflict with Simon Bolivar over final liberation and government of Peru led to his selfless withdrawal to Europe in 1824. Died in Boulogne, August 17, 1850 in obscurity. R.B.G.

Santa Anna, Antonio Lopez de.
Mexican general and President. Born in Jalapa, Veracruz, February 21, 1794. Died Mexico City, June 21, 1876. Dominated Mexican politics (1828-1855). Supported the Plan de Iguala, instrument of Mexican independence in 1821. The empire of Agustin de Iturbide that followed was not to his liking, and he gave his support to its overthrow. He repelled a Spanish invasion in 1829, and maneuvered behind the scenes until he himself became President in 1833, as head of the Centralist party. Destroyed the Alamo in Texan revolt in 1836. Later was captured and recognized Texan independence in return for his release. Repudiated by Mexico. Regained favor, and continued his stormy career as President and soldier-antagonist of the United States. Exiled in 1855. Condemned for treason, but permitted to return to Mexico after General Amnesty of 1874. R.B.G.

Santander, Francisco de Paula.
Colombian patriot and President. Born Rosario de Cucuta, New Granada, April 2, 1792. Died Bogota, May 6, 1840. Brigadier general under Simon Bolivar. Vice-President of New Granada in the Republic of Gran Colombia

(New Granada, Venezuela, and Ecuador) 1819-1821. Became Vice-President of Colombia in 1821, and re-elected in 1826. Serving as acting President in absence of Bolivar, whom he later opposed. Exiled in 1828. In 1830 Gran Colombia broke up, and Santander served as President (1832-1836) of New Granada. He was a senator at the time of his death. R.B.G.

Saragat, Giuseppe (1898-).
Italian Social Democratic Party Leader. A democratic socialist who resided abroad during the Mussolini period, Saragat returned to Italy in 1943. Because of his unwillingness to follow the lead of the Italian Communist Party he left the Italian Socialist Party and organized his own group, called at first the Socialist Labor Party and now the Social Democratic Party. The Social Democrats have cooperated with the Christian Democrats in the government on several occasions.
W.C.C.

Sarit Thanarat.
Prime Minister of Thailand since 1958, Sarit was born in 1908 and educated largely in Western Europe. Marshal Sarit participated in the coup of 1932 which led to the establishment of the constitutional monarchy; later increased his authority and became a member of the governing triumvirate (with Prime Minister Phibul Songram and Police General Phao Sriyanond) until he led a successful coup in 1958 and assumed control of the state. His regime has been characterized by moderation, increased attention to economic development and alliance with the West. M.W.W.

Satellites.
See Soviet Satellites.

Satyagraha.
It means firm adherence to the Truth, and is freely translated as Soul-Force, Love-Force, or Truth-Force. It refers to Gandhi's philosophy of action, used successfully for the attainment of Indian freedom. Its basic tenet is nonviolence—the only way for the realization of Truth or God. It seeks to conquer evil by good, hatred by love, falsehood by truth, deceit by honesty, and violence by nonviolence. As practically applied against the British rule, satyagraha entailed: nonviolent non-cooperation; civil disobedience; boycott of British goods, political institutions, and schools; patronage of home-made articles; resignation from government service; surrender of titles and honors; fasts; and imprisonment.
C.S.S.

Saudi Arabia.
The Arabian Peninsula is about a million square miles, most of which are desert. Saudi Arabia occupies most of the Peninsula. Its population is approximately 5½ million. It includes the two Holy cities of Islam, Mecca and Medina. The Peninsula flourished during early Islamic expansion, but soon fell into conflict and oblivion. In the Eighteenth Century the Saudi family in alliance with the Wahhabi religious movement imposed peace on the tribes. In the 1920's Ibn Saud defeated his enemies and unified Nejd and Hijaz under his leadership. The present government under his son Saud is a traditional monarchy. The government applies Islamic law. Income from oil comprises more than 85 percent of Saudi budget. E.A.S.

Savigny, Friedrich Karl von.
(1779-1861).
German professor of law and juristic scholar; exponent of historical analysis of law; critic of statutes, codes, and other legislative enactments; author of **Of the Vocation of Our Age for Legislation and Jurisprudence** (1814), **History of Roman Law in the Middle Ages** (1815-1831), **System of Contemporary Roman Law** (1840-1849), **Contracts** (1853). Ch.C.M.

S.C.A.P.
See Supreme Commander for the Allied Powers.

Schacht, Hjalmar Horace Greeley.
Born on June 22, 1877 in Tingleff, Schleswig, one-time Reich Bank President of the Weimar Republic (1924-1930) and again under Hitler (1933-1939), also Economic Minister of the Third Reich (1934-1937), now owner of a Bank for foreign trade in Duesseldorf, Germany. Schacht, a former director of private banks, assisted as high financial official of the Republic in the re-stabilization of the German Mark after World War I. However, in the

early thirties, the one-time democrat promoted Hitler's accession to power and became his Reich Bank President. In this capacity, he supported the Nazi rearmament by unscrupulous financial maneuvers. Later he broke with the Hitler regime, participated in the anti-Hitler conspiracy of 1944 and was put in a concentration camp. Indicted for alleged participation in the preparation of aggressive wars at the International Military Tribunal in Nuremberg, Schacht has been acquitted against the votes of the American and Soviet judge. As Justice Francis Biddle revealed in his book **In Brief Authority** (1962): "To the English he was a respectable man, a banker, not like these other ruffians; and they finally persuaded Donnedieu de Vabres (the French justice) to go along with them, against the Russian view, which I shared, that Schacht had been active in the preparation for aggressive war, a powerful and necessary link in the chain which he helped Hitler forge, and that he should receive a severe sentence. It was then agreed . . . that Schacht should receive a term of eight years. But the next day Donnedieu de Vabres announced that he had changed his mind. Obviously the British had persuaded him. The vote being a tie, Schacht was acquitted." He lived thereafter as private banker and served as an advisor to various governments in Asia vexed by financial troubles. R.M.W.K.

Scheler, Max (1874-1928).
A follower of Edmund Husserl with whom he founded the phenomenological movement which inspired contemporary European philosophy. He taught philosophy at Jena, Munich, and Cologne. His voluminous **Der Formalismus in der Ethik und die materiale Wertethik (1916)** is probably his most important work. In it he developed a theory of human personality within a Christian frame of reference criticizing Kant's formalism and modern utilitarianism. His essay on "Ressentiment" (1915) is one of his most interesting contributions to the psychology of knowledge, wherein he followed up on Nietzsche's insights in the latter's **Toward a Genealogy of Morals** (1887). His **Die Wissensformen und die Gesellschaft** (1925) is one of the foundation stones of the sociology of knowledge. Scheler stimulated contemporary thought in many directions. He was critical of bourgeois morality, of democracy, and of capitalism as inimical to the development of the highest types of values. V.Z.

Schelling, Friedrich Wilhelm von. (1775-1854).
One of the leading German Idealists (Kant, Fichte, Hegel) who was first a follower of Fichte, then inspired by the somewhat older Hegel, only to be opposed soon by Hegel. His philosophy drifted into a mysticism inspired mainly by the German mystic Jacob Boehme and the neo-Platonist Plotinus. V.Z.

School districts.
Independent units of government found in most of the States of the United States which provide education on the elementary and secondary levels. They enjoy financial autonomy in that their budgets are not subject to review by another local government. Their boundaries frequently are coterminous with those of a municipality, but increasingly in rural and suburban sections of the country they are becoming regional. R.G.S.

Schopenhauer, Arthur. (1788-1860).
Belongs to the most lucid of German philosophers, despite the fact that he was a mystic. Blending Kant with Indian mysticism of the Upanishads, he took Kant's "thing-in-itself" as a veil hiding true reality which lay in Will the affirmation of which is the source of all evil. He bifurcated thus Kant's dualism between the phenomenal and the noumenal world even more into a type of dualism that led him to demand extinction of reality (Will) through Nirvana (nothingness) as a state of bliss. Although he lived most of the time the lonely life of an angry misanthrope, hating women in general, his mother in particular, and waging quixotic battles against academicians, he did not follow up upon his purposeless philosophical asceticism: he liked sensual pleasures, good food, and even women. His book **The World as Will and Idea** (1818) began its influence only after 1848, when revolutionary optimism suddenly waned and "historical consciousness" declined.

He exercised as great an influence on Nietzsche as Rousseau did on Kant. He pioneered in the discovery of the sub-conscious. V.Z.

Schumacher, Kurt. (1895-1952)

Dr. Schumacher's outstanding contribution toward the development of democracy in Germany falls into the period of his chairmanship of the German Social Democratic Party (SPD) from 1945 until his death in 1952. Following the defeat of Nazi Germany he devoted his entire energy to rebuild social-democratic movement and to strengthen the new German democracy. It was under his leadership that the socialists refused the fusion with the German Communists as requested by Moscow. Schumacher's opposition to any form of totalitarianism dates back to the German Revolution of 1918-19 when he fought against the establishment of a Soviet style dictatorship. When the Communists and Nazis during the Weimar Republic endangered with their para-military formations the very existence of the democratic institutions, he founded the social democratic militant organization **Reichsbanner Schwarz-Rot-Gold.** From 1930 on, he also served the cause for the preservation of the Republic as SPD member of the **Reichstag.** Because of his strong opposition against the Nazis, he was arrested after Hitler came to power and spent ten of the following years in various notorious concentration camps. When he was liberated by Allied forces, he was a physical wreck and almost blind. As a result of the maltreatments suffered, he contracted thrombosis and his left leg had to be amputated. He had lost his right arm during World War I. As a young man he had volunteered for the military service.

Dr. Schumacher studied at the Universities of Halle, Leipzig, Berlin and Muenster and obtained a degree in jurisprudence. After World War I he worked in the Reich Ministry of Labor (1920). In 1924 he became editor of a daily socialist newspaper, a position which he held until 1933. In 1924 he was elected to the **Landtag** in Wuerttenberg and in 1930 to the **Reichstag.**
 E.W.

Schuman Plan.

A popular name for the treaty establishing the European Coal and Steel Community, ratified in 1952 by Belgium, France, (West) Germany, Italy, Luxembourg and the Netherlands; named after Robert Schuman, prominent French politician and its main proponent. It is a customs union, in operation since 1954, limited to coal, iron ore and scrap, steel and steel alloys. Immediately eliminated all import duties and quantitative restrictions on these products between member states. In 1958 common tariff duties on these products from other countries were imposed. The High Authority, its executive organ, also regulates competition and concentration of ownership within the community. It has been a focal point of the new European spirit and a stepping stone towards greater unity in the form of the Common Market. W.N.

Schuman, Robert (1886-).

Lawyer and French political figure. He was deputy from the Moselle from 1919 to 1940, and from 1945; premier from November, 1947 to July, 1948; Minister of Foreign Affairs, 1949-1953; Minister of Justice, 1955-1956; he is a major architect of the European Coal and Steel Community, and a member of the Catholic Popular Republican Movement. (MRP). E.G.L.

Schuschnigg, Kurt von (1897-).

Austrian Chancellor and leader of Christian Socialist Party. He became a deputy in 1928, held cabinet posts until the Dollfuss assassination in 1932, when he became Prime Minister. He tried to preserve Austrian independence against the rising tide of Hitlerism. The Germans interned Schuschnigg after occupying Austria in 1938. G.K.

Scientific Freedom.

The absence of restraints permitting scientists to engage in their work without interference. The greater the interference, the lesser the freedom. There is, however, no absolute scientific freedom in reality because every society — democratic or undemocratic — imposes certain restraints (laws, customs, habits, etc.) on its members thus making scientific freedom subject to these restraints. Hence we speak of scientific freedom in the United States, the Soviet Union, Germany, and so on. The quantity or quality of scientific freedom depends therefore on the relative value of the answer to this question. What is it that scientists would like to do and what does society permit them to do? P.A.T.

Scott, Hugh.
U.S. Senate from November 1958 until term ending 1965; Republican, Pennsylvania; National Chairman, Republican Party, 1948-1949; on Eisenhower's personal staff, 1952; NATO Parliamentary Conference 1961; author of **How To Go Into Politics,** 1949.
R.A.B.

Scottish Committee.
A Standing Committee of the British House of Commons dealing with all public bills relating exclusively to Scotland, regardless of the bills' subject matter. R.G.N.

Scrutin d'arrondissement.
System of electing French deputies, used during the Third Republic, 1875-1885, 1889-1919, and 1928-1940. It has been revived during the Fifth Republic. Deputies are elected in single-member districts, and as applied in the Third and Fifth Republics, a runoff election is held if no candidate has won a majority of votes cast. The candidate with a plurality wins the second election. The runoff election permits the parties to realign their forces and make strategic withdrawals in favor of parties allied with them. The precise impact of the electoral system on party structure is not clear, although much of the fractionated character of parties in the Third Republic was attributed to it. J.S.S.

Scrutin de liste.
A form of ballot for electing several delegates from one electoral district; the converse of a single member district (called, in France, the **scrutin uninominal**); in France, deputies were elected by **scrutin de liste** from 1849-1852; 1870-1875; 1885-1889; between 1919-1927 the **scrutin de liste** was combined with a form of proportional representation, as it was from 1948-1958. E.G.L.

Scrutin publique.
Method of recording publicly votes in the French National Assembly. Used if requested by the government, the interested commission, the president of a group of at least twenty-five deputies, or by any twenty-five deputies. Deputies need not be present but may turn over their votes to a party member or **boitier,** except when a vote **a la tribune** is called for, in which case only members present vote. The latter method was abolished in 1952 except for formal votes of confidence after it had been employed as a dilatory tactic by the Communists. Public votes are recorded in the parliamentary debates. J.S.S.

Search and Seizure.
Terms concerned with the problem of protecting the rights of the individual from arbitrary governmental action in making arrests and searching for evidence of crime. The conflict between governmental power and individual freedom has had greater legal significance in England and the U.S. than in other countries. The Fourth Amendment to the U.S. Constitution, adopted in 1791, provides that the people shall be free from "unreasonable searches and seizures" and that "no warrant shall issue but upon probable cause, supported by oath or affirmation, and particularly describing the place to be searched and the person or things to be seized." This Amendment resulted largely from the struggle of the American colonists against the British use of vague and indefinite writs of assistance in enforcing the trade laws against the colonies. The U.S. Supreme Court has given meaning to the Amendment by applying it to individual cases. In the first case before the Court (**Boyd** v. **U.S.**, 116 U.S. 616 [1885]) it declared unconstitutional a congressional act permitting the seizure under a Court order of a man's private papers to be used against him because it constituted the essence of an unreasonable search and seizure. Later it ruled that information obtained through an unreasonable search by federal officers, (**Weeks** v. **U.S.**, 232 U.S. 383, [1914]) or by state officials, (**Elkins** v. **U.S.** and **Rios** v. **U.S.** 364, U.S. 206, 253 [1960]), was inadmissible as evidence in federal courts; nor can evidence illegally secured by state of-

ficers be used in a state court because of due process clause of the Fourteenth Amendment, (**Mapp v. Ohio** 367 U.S. 643 [1961]). It has, however, permitted the use of evidence gained by tapping telephone wires (**Olmstead v. U.S.** 277 U.S. 438 [1928]) and by using sound instruments (**On Lee v. U.S.** 343 U.S. 747 [1952]). (Wire tapping is now prohibited by a 1934 Congressional statute.) A legal search for evidence requires a valid warrant, **Johnson v. U.S.** 333 U.S. 10 (1948), **McDonald v. U.S.** 335, U.S. 45 (1948), except under special circumstances, e.g., the search of an automobile on the highway. **Carroll v. U.S.**, 267 U.S. 132 (1924). The Amendment and the Courts' use of it is the American way of applying the principle that "a man's home is his castle." E.G.T.

S.E.A.T.O.
See South-East Asia Treaty Organization.

Second Empire of France.
See France—Second Empire.

Second Republic of France.
See France—Second Republic.

Secretary of State.
In the U.S.A. the top ranking member of the President's Cabinet, responsible for the conduct of the foreign relations of the United States. Originally the office was charged with maintaining contact with the several states in the Union, as well as conducting foreign affairs. For this reason the term "State" replaced the previous designation of "Foreign Affairs," as employed during the government under the Articles of Confederation. This officer is third in line of Presidential Succession after the Vice President. Sp.D.A.

Secretary of State, or Secretary of the Commonwealth.
In the U.S.A. an officer charged with keeping state records, certifying official communications, and sometimes supervising various activities such as conduct of elections and issuance of licenses and permits. He is elected in about three-fourths of the states, appointed by the Governor in most others, and elected by the legislature in three states.

In Hawaii the duties of this office are performed by the Lieutenant Governor. Sp.D.A.

Sector Principle.
A method, first advocated by Canada and later subscribed to by the Soviet Union, by which sovereignty in the Arctic is claimed within an area circumscribed by a base line connecting the meridians of longitude, marking the limits of the eastern and western frontiers, and the projection of those meridians to their point of intersection at the North Pole. O.S.

Security-Community.
A group of people which has attained, within a territory, a "sense of community" and a set of institutions and practices strong enough and widespread enough to assure, for a long period of time, dependable expectations of "peaceful change" (q.v.) among its population. For this purpose, "sense of community" is defined as a belief on the part of individuals in a group that they have come to agreement on at least one point: that common social problems must and can be resolved by processes of "peaceful change." It may be an amalgamated security-community (q.v.) or a pluralistic security-community (q.v.). In different words, a security-community is one in which there is real assurance that the members of that community will not fight each other physically, but will instead settle their disputes in some other way.
R.W.V.W.

Security Council.
See United Nations Security Council.

Security Program (in U.S.A.).
Current program to assure the loyalty of Federal employees, designed to safeguard the national government against security risks. In 1947, President Truman prescribed a loyalty test for all federal employees (Executive Order 9835, 12 **Federal Register** 1935 [1947]). This test was later stiffened (Executive Order 10241, 16 **Federal Register** 3690 [1951]). Finally, the emphasis passed from loyalty to security under President Eisenhower (Executive Order 10450, 18 **Federal Register** 2489 [1953]). Security risks included personal indiscretions which might subject a person to blackmail by enemy agents.

A later modification included only persons in "sensitive" positions. (**Cole** v. **Young**, 351 U.S. 536 [1956]). W.F.G.

Security risk.

The term applied to an individual who could be denied employment or removed from employment in the U.S. Government on the basis of potential or actual disloyalty. The concept was first used by President Harry S. Truman in an executive order which was later superseded by one issued by President Dwight D. Eisenhower. If there is reasonable doubt about the loyalty of the person involved to the government of the United States on the basis of all the evidence, he can be discharged. Such evidence has to do with his activities and associations related to sabotage, espionage, spies or saboteurs, treason or sedition or their advocacy, advocacy of revolution or force or violence to alter the constitutional form of the U.S. Government, unauthorized disclosure of confidential or non-public documents or information, performing his duties or otherwise acting so as to serve the interests of another government in preference to U.S. interests, or membership or sympathetic association with persons or groups designated by the Attorney General as totalitarian, fascist, communist or subversive. M.J.S.

Sedition Act of 1918 (U.S.A.).

Convinced that the Espionage Act of 1917 did not go far enough in preventing disloyal propaganda, the Attorney General recommended that a more stringent statute be passed. The Sedition Act of 1918 added nine new offenses to the original statute, the most important being: 1) saying or doing anything with intent to obstruct the sale of United States bonds; 2) uttering, printing, writing, or publishing any disloyal, profane or abusive language intended to cause contempt, scorn or disrepute as regards the form of government of the United States; 3) or the Constitution; or 4) the flag. Coupled with the Espionage Act of the previous year, the statute — until its repeal in 1921 — was the center of a storm of controversy regarding its effect on civil liberties in the United States. Over the strong dissent of Mr. Justice Holmes, the Supreme Court, in **Abrams v. United States** (1919), upheld a conviction under the statute. See Espionage Act of 1917. P.B.

Segregation.

Racial separation enforced by public authority in the use of common facilities such as public schools, public means of transportation, and public places of amusement, comfort, and convenience. Until 1954, such segregation in U.S.A. was regarded as constitutional so long as the facilities, although separate, were equal. In 1954, however, the U.S. Supreme Court held that segregation in the public schools was a denial to Negroes of the equal protection of the laws guaranteed by the Constitution of the United States. All segregated schools were ordered to end racial discrimination with all deliberate speed. E.L.

Sejm.

Historic name of Polish parliament. Since 1946 referendum, unicameral. Results of fourth postwar elections on April 16, 1961: Polish United Workers' Party, 254 seats (55.4%); United Peasant Party, 117 seats (25.4%); Democatic Party, 39 seats (8.5%); the so-called independents, 49 seats (10.7%) which includes five from Roman Catholic **Znak** (Sign) organization (see Poland). R.F.S.

Select Committees.

In the British House of Commons they are composed, as a rule, of 15 members and are created from time to time to report on specific subjects on which legislation is pending or contemplated. When appointed for an entire session of the House they are called Sessional Committees. They have no right of subpoena unless specifically so authorized. R.G.N.

Selectmen.

Selectmen are the present day descendants of the "selected men" of Massachusetts Bay towns of 1630. Three or five are chosen for overlapping terms by the town meetings in New England. Collectively the selectmen are responsible for the conduct of town affairs between town meetings. They levy taxes, fill officer vacancies, remove officers when necessary, borrow money for town purposes, pay bills, and issue the official warrant or warning for the annual Town Meeting. The selectmen are frequently re-elected for periods of several decades. A.E.N.

Self-Criticism in the U.S.S.R.

A sacred duty of every party member is to criticize not only the shortcomings of others but also his own. Errors may be admitted at party meetings, places of work or in a letter to the press. Self-criticism must not compromise party policy; rather it is to be aimed at the administration of policy only. Although self-criticism may be based on either belief or expediency, it is sometimes arranged by the party. Purpose: to curtail bureaucratic practices, and keep the party well informed about every aspect of life in the U.S.S.R. K.Hu.

Self-determination of Nations.

The right of nations to independence and to determine their own government. Also the right of the inhabitants to decide, usually by plebiscite, to which of two or more states their territory should belong. One of the most notable examples of the use of plebiscite was when, in conformity with the Versailles Treaty of 1919, the eligible voters of the Saar after fifteen years under the administration of the League of Nations elected to return to German sovereignty. The United States throughout its national history has been a great champion of self-determination, even though in 1916, in connection with the transfer of the Danish West Indies, a plebiscite was refused by the United States. President Wilson, however, was to become the greatest advocate of this doctrine in regard to a number of territorial problems following the First World War. O.S.

Self-Incrimination.

The forcible disclosure of testimony from a witness that may then be used to convict him of crime. The Fifth Amendment of the Constitution of the United States provides that no person "shall be compelled in any criminal case to be a witness against himself." Although originally a limitation on the Federal Government only, the protection has been extended to the states, where it may be narrower. The protection against self-incrimination is available to natural persons but not to corporations, may be invoked only for one's self and not for the benefit of others, and is limited only to those statements that might lead to a prosecution for crime. The protection does not extend to statements that may have the effect merely of tending to degrade the witness or to cause him to suffer a loss of reputation. E.L.

Senatorial Courtesy.

Appointments made by the president of the U.S.A. must be confirmed by the Senate. If an office is to be filled in a state having a senator (or senators) of the president's political party the president will consult with the senator before placing a name in nomination. If the senator approves the Senate will confirm the appointment. If the senator objects the Senate will refuse confirmation.

A second use of the term applies to the willingness of the Senate to confirm the nomination of any senator to any position which the president designates. M.F.

Seneca, Lucius Annaeus.

(4 B.C.-65 A.D.).

A Roman philosopher, tutor to Nero, the chief minister to the emperor, and the leading literary figure of his age. His philosophy is an eclectic one in which stoicism predominates.

Although Seneca did not write a single purely political essay, he expressed a social ideology that was popular for a while during his lifetime and widely acclaimed in later eras. Writing during the early years of the empire when despotism had replaced self-government and when the state was no longer viewed as a moral being nor an agent for moral advancement, Seneca thought that the good man still had a moral responsibility to society. However, he did not identify society with the state, asserting instead that society is the universal fellowship of man which nature arranged in the development of the first communities. Greed and selfishness had destroyed these communities, causing poverty and suffering, but men continued to return to the laws of nature. Strong men ruled the weak, and, when people submitted to rule by the man who was stronger and better, they were happier. In such a society the ruling was a service that was essential to the happiness of the society. Natural fellowship of man was merged with the political organization.

Reflecting the pessimism of his times as well as the ideology, Seneca thought that the golden age of man had passed and that political society existed in a debased form, but there still existed the natural society of humanity as a whole. Service to this society was man's moral duty and the most good could be accomplished by service to the state.

The earlier Stoics had usually remained apart from public life, not only because the civic ideal was too narrow for their concept of a universal society but also because they felt that participation in political affairs posed a threat to spiritual self-mastery. Seneca, however, believed that, since the golden age was past and political society existed in a debased form, man's moral duty of service to humanity as a whole could best be performed through holding public office. D.C.

Senegal.
Once a member of the French Colonial Empire and its center of West-African expansion is to-day an independent republic on the West Coast of Africa. Its population, over 3,000,000, occupies an area of some 76,084 square miles. **Senegal** gained autonomy in 1958, joined the Mali Federation in 1959 and seceded from it in 1960. In this year it elected its first President, Leopold Senghor, and joined the United Nations. Tension over public policy between the President and Premier Mamadou Dia continues to exist. Dakar, the capital, has an excellent harbor, intercontinental airport, and university. Principal products are peanuts, millet, rice, beans. Industries include phosphate mining and textiles. Exports (1960) were $112,900,000, imports $172,100,000. A.A.N.

Seniority System.
A system in which status, priority, or precedence is based on length of service in a given job. Under a "rule of seniority" the eligible person with the longest service is automatically awarded the promotion. The system prevails in the United States Congress where committee chairmanships are awarded on a seniority basis. The majority member of longest continuous service on a committee will almost as a matter of course be put up by the party nominating authority for the chairmanship. R.J.S.

"Separate but Equal" Doctrine.
The doctrine of American constitutional law that originated in the 1896 decision by the Supreme Court of the case of Plessy v. Ferguson. The question before the Court was the validity of a state statute requiring separate railroad cars for white and Negro passengers despite the clause of the Fourteenth Amendment that forbids any state to "deny to any person within its jurisdiction the equal protection of the laws." The statute was sustained on the ground that separate but equal accommodations furnished the equality demanded by the constitutional amendment. The Supreme Court followed this "separate but equal" doctrine for more than fifty years, but with increasing insistence that Negro schools and "Jim Crow" cars must be really equal to the schools and cars used by whites. In 1954, in the opinion supporting its unanimous decision of **Brown v. Board of Education**, the Court renounced the doctrine and declared that racially separated schools cannot be equal. M.Sp.

Separation of Church and State.
The First Amendment prohibits any law "respecting an establishment of religion, or prohibiting the free exercise thereof." It also prohibits any religious test for holding public office. Thomas Jefferson viewed this clause against the establishment of religion by law as erecting a "wall of separation between Church and State." This principle was later adopted by the U.S. Supreme Court. Establishing religion means the setting up or recognition of one or more churches by the state or the granting to one church of special favors and advantages which are denied to others.

This does not mean that the government should be required to oppose religion and religious practices carried on in the home or in the church. On the contrary, this concept is based on the conviction that religious beliefs can best flourish under a system in which the government does not get involved in religious matters. M.J.S.

Separation of Powers.

A concept which developed from the natural right theorist's concern with the selfish or self-seeking nature of man. Since these theorists held man to be essentially individualistic and self-seeking by nature, any centralization of political power in one man, or a single body of men, would lead to tyranny.

John Locke distinguished the executive from the legislative power and suggested the desirability of separation. But he insisted that ultimate authority rested with the legislative body as the representative of the people. He could argue thus in that each person had a natural right to defend his liberty and interest. Hence, the representative body of the people, being subject to electoral approval, could be trusted with the highest authority.

Baron de Montesquieu, drawing inspiration from what he believed to be English practice, distinguished three powers of government, executive, legislative, and judicial. He not only believed that each should be separated from the others, but that no single body should be superior to the others in power. Hence, each would act as a check on the other two. In this way, self-seeking men in any branch would be blocked by jealous men in the other branches. Liberty and the public good would prevail. The fact that such an arrangement might cause the government to be weak and act slowly and painfully was of little concern, for, with most others of the natural right school of thought, Montesquieu believed that the government that governed least governed best. R.M.T.

Separatism.

At the basis of separatism lies that principle of nationality which was developed in eighteenth century Europe: the principle that national and political frontiers should coincide. Separatism also finds justification in the principle of democracy, for it takes as its starting point the principle of self-determination of people, and the conviction that the sovereignty of a state over a given territory is legitimate only when it results from the consensus of opinion of the people who live in it. Since democratic doctrine regards the state as an institution of national self-organization, ethnic homogeneity and cultural consensus become the ideological elements for asking for a separation of a territory into its components so as to give stability to the state and satisfaction to the demands of the people. P.G.

Serraj, 'Abd al-Hamid.

Chief of the second bureau of the Syrian army during the formation of the United Arab Republic which united Syria with Egypt in 1958. Subsequently he became Syria's minister of Interior in the U.A.R. government and helped greatly in maintaining order in Syria during its unity with Egypt. Early in 1961, however, he was given a high government post in Cairo, Egypt; but he soon resigned and went back to Damascus. During a successful military coup which severed Syria from the United Arab Republic in 1961, Serraj was arrested, then released and allowed to go to Egypt. W.B.B.

Servitudes.

By analogy with the corresponding Roman Law institution servitudes are obligations concerning the territory of one State in favor of another State which are not affected by changes in the territorial jurisdiction of either the "servient" or the "dominant" State. The applicability of this private law concept to international law is questionable. Such obligations, whether created by treaty or custom, would seem to be cases of obligations **en faveur et a la charge** of third States. The question came up **inter alia** in the **North Atlantic Coast Fisheries, Wimbledon, Free Zones,** and **Aaland Islands** cases. S.E.

Sevres, Treaty of 10 August, 1920.

The Treaty was imposed on the Ottoman Sultan by the Allied Supreme Council after Britain and France had settled their differences over the mandated areas. The Treaty deprived Turkey of all the non-Turkish provinces

and much of Anatolia. The capitulatory regime, and the traditional minority rights were restored. An international commission was to control the straits. Reluctantly signed by the Sultan's representatives, the Treaty never came to effect, due to the successful opposition of Mustapha Kamal, the founder of modern Turkey. Mustapha denounced the Treaty, deposed the Sultan, and asked for the negotiation of a treaty commensurate with Turkish rights.
E.A.S.

S.F.I.O.
See French Socialist Party.

Shakaito.
The Socialist party of Japan. In 1947 the Socialists won a plurality of the seats in the lower house of the Diet and formed a government under Katayama Tetsu in coalition with the Democratic and People's Cooperative parties. The coalition was embarrassed by bickering both among and within the government parties concerning key legislation and resigned in 1948. There has not been a Socialist Prime Minister since. The party split into a Right Wing and a Left Wing in 1952, when the former supported the San Francisco Japanese Peace Treaty but opposed the Security Treaty with the United States and the latter opposed both of the treaties. In 1955, the two wings united to form a single Socialist party, but disputes over doctrine, tactics, and personalities continued to plague the party, and in 1960 secessionists formed the Democratic Socialist party.

Today Socialists occupy 145 seats in the House of Representatives and 66 seats in the House of Councillors, and with their allies are able to prevent the revision of the Constitution, which requires two-thirds majorities. The Socialists opposed the 1960 security treaty with the United States, nuclear weapons and tests, the revision of the Constitution, and the adoption of the single-member-district electoral system, and favor the recognition of Communist China and a four-power security treaty with the Soviet Union, Communist China, and the United States. The pary advocates the achievement of a socialist revolution by winning a majority in the Diet, but has not unequivocally renounced the use of extraparliamentary devices such as street demonstrations and political strikes to attain its goals. It is greatly dependent upon financial and electoral support from the General Council of Trade Unions of Japan (Sohyo). In recent years, secretary-general Eda Saburo has advocated "structural reform," the improvement of the lot of the worker under capitalism pending a socialist take-over.
T.Mc.N.

Shamoun, Camille.
President of the republic of Lebanon in 1952. Although he believed in Arab unity, he bitterly opposed Nasser's leadership. This caused considerable friction which divided the Lebanese people themselves among whom were numerous admirers of Nasser. In 1958 when Shamoun announced his desire to run again for the presidency, his opponents joined hands with Nasser's admirers against him. As civil war was threatening American marines landed to be on guard. Finally Shamoun gave up the idea of a second term if a compromise president was elected. General Shehab accepted the presidency, and thus ended Lebanon's serious crisis.
W.B.B.

Shared Taxes.
A tax collected by one level of government which allocates part of the proceeds to another level of government. Shared taxes are distinguished from grants-in-aid in that conditions usually are not imposed upon the recipient government. Efficiency in tax collection is the reason for the use of shared taxes.
J.F.Z.

Shari'a (Sacred Law of Islam).
A system of rules comprising every aspect of a Muslim's life including economic transactions, marriage and divorce, charity and the rituals of prayer, i.e., the principles of his moral and social existence. It is a system of obligations which help to show the **right path (shari'a)** to be traveled by the believer during his life sojourn in order to achieve salvation. Apart from the Koran and Prophetic Tradition, **Qiyas** (analogy) and **Ijma'** (consensus) constitute the sources of the Law. As a divinely-revealed law, valid for all times and all people, the **Shari'a** not only ensures observance but it also

guarantees perfection. At the same time a law and a faith, it ensures justice in this world and salvation in the next. Authoritarian and totalitarian in character, the **Shari'a** must serve as the source of all legislation in all Muslim States. In fact, there can be no legislation strictly speaking but only elaborations in conformity with the Law. However, during the last few decades most Muslim countries have moved away from the **Shari'a** except in matters of personal status. Even here modifications have been made by Turkey, Egypt and Tunis. F.M.N.

Shastri, Lal Bahadur.
Installed as Prime Minister of India following the death of Nehru in June, 1964. Born in Benares, Shastri grew up in Allahabad and later worked with Nehru in India's struggle for independence, spending nine years in British jails. When independence arrived in 1947, Shastri became a Congress Party leader in Allahabad. Shortly thereafter he was summoned to New Delhi by Nehru and named Minister of **Transport.** Later, as Home Minister, he worked with great effectiveness to hold India together against the pull of linguistic, communal and religious separatism. His elevation to the Prime Ministership was not unexpected and was applauded throughout the western world. J.D.

Shaw, Anna Howard. (1847-1919).
Methodist minister, physician, reformer, lecturer. Born in England. Brought to this country as a small child she grew up in Massachusetts. She studied at Albion College, Michigan, and later graduated from Boston U. of Theology (1878), and also took a medical degree at Boston U. (1885). She was pastor of the Methodist Episcopal Church at Hingham, Mass. (1878) but received ordination in the Protestant Methodist Church (1880). Attracted by the rising woman's movement, she resigned her pulpit (1885) to lecture for the Mass. Woman Suffrage Assn. and the following year became the Superintendent of Franchise of the National WCTU. About the same time she was appointed lecturer of the National American Woman Suffrage Assn., and became its President (1904-1915). During World War I, she was named chairman of the Woman's Committee of the Council of National Defense for which she was awarded the Distinguished Service Cross. Ardent for a peaceful world, she campaigned (1919) with William Howard Taft and A. Lawrence Lowell of Harvard for the League of Nations.
 M.E.D.

Shays' Rebellion.
An agrarian uprising in 1786-87 in western Massachusetts under the leadership of Daniel Shays, a Revolutionary War captain. It was due to discontent arising from economic distress. The brief struggle alarmed conservative circles and served as a catalyst for the movement toward revision of the Articles of Confederation. R.V.A.

Shehab, Fu'ad.
Lebanese statesman. When in 1958 civil war threatened to tear apart the small peaceful republic of Lebanon, only one Lebanese could command the respect of both Shamoun and his opponents — Fu'ad Shehab, then commander and chief of the Army. He accepted the presidency, and thus ended Lebanon's serious crisis.
 W.B.B.

Shehu, Mehmet. (1913-).
Prime Minister of Albania (since 1954) and Politburo member of the Workers' (Communist) Party (since 1948), he fought in the resistance movement, and became Army Chief of Staff (1946). He was dismissed as Chief of Staff and from the CP Central Committee in February 1948 because he opposed Tito's demand to station two Yugoslav divisions in Albania. Following Tito's ouster from the Cominform, he became Minister of Interior, Deputy Premier, and CP Secretary. J.J.K.

Shepilov, Dmitri.
Born 1905, Ashkhabad. Studied law and agriculture in Moscow. Scholarly career in agriculture, early 1930's, participating in collectivization drive. Joined CP 1926. Positions in departments of Party Central Committee since 1935. In World War II Major General; associated with Khrushchev. Central Committee 1952-57; editor Pravda 1952-56; USSR Supreme Soviet 1950-58. Prominent in foreign affairs mid-1950's as Khrushchev's strength grew; replaced Molotov as

Foreign Minister 1956. Ousted from Party and government posts in 1957 for "anti-Party" activity. W.A.

Sheriff.
The chief law enforcemnt officer in American counties. Commonly elected, his principal duties are to conserve the peace, keep the county jail, and serve as an officer of the county courts.
G.S.B.

Shi'a (Shi'ites).
The partisans of Ali, a schismatic group whose origin is rooted in the question of succession to the Prophet. The Alid party claimed that the Caliphat belonged to Ali, cousin and son-in-law of the Prophet, and his offspring. Shi'ism began as a political movement amongst the Arabs themselves. Gradually this political aspiration created for itself a doctrinal basis, opposed to the accepted doctrine of the community. Schismatic in character, Shi'ism appealed to disaffected groups, and became a symbol around which many new teachings were developed. With the deification of Ali and the tenet of the divinely-appointed **imam** fused the notion of the immunity from death, impeccability and infallibility. Shi'ism endows the **imam** with spiritual and political powers which are lacking in his Sunni counterpart. While the Sunni Caliph is democratically elected, and rules under the law, the **imam** is above the law and he can change it at will. This super-human character of the **imam** is universally recognized by all Shi'ite sects. Shi'ite religion was centered on a principle of absolute personal authority, foreign both in politics and religion to the orthodox theory. So many esoteric and schismatic movements flourished under the cover of Shi'ism, but three major Shi'a sects remain. 1. Zaidis, still dominant in Yemen, stand closest to the old legitimist Shi'ism and to Orthodox Sunni Islam. 2. The Twelvers of Imamis, now the official religion of Persia, recognize 12 **imams**. They do not accept the principle of **Ijma'** (consensus), and in the absence of the **imam**, the leading theologians, called **Mujtahids**, exercise an extensive authority in religious and legal matters. 3. The Isma'ilis, the most extreme group. F.M.N.

Shinto.
Literally, the "way of the gods," so called to distinguish the cult of the indigenous Japanese deities from the Buddhist faith, which was introduced into Japan from Korea in the sixth century, A.D. Shinto includes many primitive superstitious beliefs and practices, possibly akin to the shamanism of north central Asia, whence much of Japanese culture may have originated. The pantheon and mythology of Shinto bear some striking parallels with Greek paganism. Shinto has no moral code. The Sun Goddess of the Shinto religion, Amaterasu, is considered the ancestress of the dynasty of Japanese emperors according to the Shinto scriptures, **Kojiki** (712 A.D.) and Nihongi (720 A.D.). Shinto was disestablished as the state religion of Japan during the Allied occupation, but the Emperor, in his private capacity, continues to perform rituals in honor of his divine ancestors.
T.Mc.N.

Shogunate.
A type of government by the warrior class (Samurai or Bushi warriors) which wrested political power from the court aristocracy and whose power was later legitimized by the powerless Emperor. The Shogunate prevailed during the Kamakura period (12th-13th century), the Muromachi period (14th-15th century) and Tokugawa period (17th-19th century). H.U.

Short ballot.
The condition in which the number of public offices filled by election has been greatly reduced. C.W.B.

Shvernik, Nikolai.
Born 1888, workers' family, St. Petersburg, now Leningrad. Joined CP 1905, often arrested before 1917. Political commissar in Civil War. Orgburo 1930; candidate member of Politburo 1939-52 and Party Presidium 1953-57. Full member of Party Presidium since 1957. High trade union posts. Government positions have included membership of various Republic Supreme Soviets. Chairman, Presidium RSFSR Supreme Soviet in 1940's. Chairman, Presidium USSR Supreme Soviet 1946-53. Chairman, Party Control Commission since 1956. Reelected USSR Supreme Soviet 1962. W.A.

Sierra Leone (Lion Mountain).

So named by the fifteenth century Portuguese, Pedro de Centra, Sierra Leone is an area of 28,000 sq. miles with a population of 2,500,000 on the southwest coast of Africa. Freetown, its capital, has one of the largest natural harbors in the world and is the center of the Creoles, its leading citizens. **Sierra Leone** from its humble origin as a British settlement for emancipated slaves became a Protectorate in 1896, elected its first cabinet in 1960 and under the leadership of its first Prime Minister, Sir Milton Margai, an African statesman, became in 1961 an independent State of the British Commonwealth and a member of the United Nations. Agricultural products: rice, the dietary staple, cassava, peanuts, cocoa, ginger and grains. Exports: Palm kernels, iron ore, chrome and diamonds, its greatest source of wealth. Its system of education; privately controlled but aided by the government includes 550 primary schools, 28 secondary, several technical ones and 6 teachers' colleges. Exports (1958) were £19,613,058, and imports £23,-903,129.   A.A.N.

Sikorski, Wladyslaw. (1881-1943).

Born at Tuszow, near Sandomierz. Graduate of Lwow polytechnicum. An Austrian army officer, he transferred to the Polish legions. Important role in battle for Warsaw (1920). Held posts as Chief of General Staff, Premier, Interior and War Minister. Retired to write (1926). Premier and Commander-in-Chief at Angers and later London (1939-43). Killed in air crash at Gibraltar.   R.F.S.

Simple Resolution.

A formal statement requiring only the approval of one legislative House and expressing the sense of that House on some issue or action before it. Thus, a simple resolution may be used for a variety of purposes, such as to create a select committee, to express sorrow or sympathy, or to call upon an executive official to submit a report.   W.V.H.

Simulation.

The construction and manipulation of operating models of individual and social processes by means of computers or man-computer systems. In political science, simulation is seen as an extension of verbal theories and mathematical formulations for purposes of encompassing more adequately the complexities of political phenomena, from voting behavior as in the all-computer "simulmatics" project of Ithiel de Sola Pool to the man-computer "inter-nation simulation" system of Harold Guetzkow. Once basic variables and their interrelations have been posited, the simulation may be operated to explore the consequences of differing initial conditions. En route, it is possible to examine the effects of intervention in the simulation run. In addition to its heuristic use as a research tool, simulation is employed as a training instrument for decision-makers, as in diplomatic games through which foreign affairs officers may be instructed in international relations.

Although having existed in rudimentary form for centuries in the form of war-gaming, political simulation has derived contemporary impetus from the fruitfulness of experiments in social psychological laboratories and from the spectacular increase in the use of miniature models in the physical sciences (as the wind-tunnel).   H.G.

Sinai Campaign. (1956)

The fall 1956 invasion of the Sinai Peninsula by Israel. Following the Egyptian blockade of the Gulf of Aqabah, reception of Russian heavy military equipment, military entrenchment in the Sinai Peninsula and an increase in Fidaiyun terrorist activities (see "Fidaiyun"), Israel invaded the Egyptian Sinai Peninsula on October 29, 1956. Next day, Great Britain and France — agitated by the Egyptian seizure of the Suez Canal Company in July 1956 and having apparently been informed in advance of the Israeli invasion — issued an ultimatum demanding withdrawal of forces to 10 miles from the Canal and agreement by Egypt to Anglo-French occupation of positions in the Suez area. After rejection of these demands by Egypt, Anglo-French forces began on October 31 to bomb Egyptian bases and invaded on November 5 the northwestern end of the Suez Canal area, making slow progress against stiff Egyptian resistance. In the meantime, Israel overran the Sinai Peninsula, reaching the Suez Canal from the East. Complicating the international situation, the Russian liquidation of Hungarian autonomy took place at the same time. The United Nations General Assembly held special meetings, demanding on November 7 immediate withdrawal of all invading forces and setting up a special emergency force to police the Egyptian-Israeli border. Following strong U.S. and U.N. pressure, Israel, Great Britain and France agreed to withdraw. The Anglo-French forces withdrew by December 3 and the last Israeli forces withdrew by March 8, 1957. The Suez Canal was reopened on April, 1957. The main consequences of the Sinai Campaign were some improvement in Israel's position involving opening of the Gulf of Aqabah to Israeli goods, a decrease in Egypt's military prestige, and an end to Fidaiyun terrorist activity, some economic repercussions both in Egypt and Israel, and permanent policing of the Israel-Egypt border by the U.N. Also, there was some deterioration in Great Britain's and France's relations with the United States, a break in their relationships with Egypt and changes in the leadership of the Conservative party in Great Britain. Y.D.

Sinclair, Upton Beall. (1878-).

American writer whose novels of social protest place him among the "muckrakers." A perennial Socialist Party candidate, Sinclair in 1934 turned Democrat, entered the direct primary contest of that party in California and won the gubernatorial nomination. He campaigned for his EPIC plan to "End Poverty in California" through "production for use" by the unemployed. He was narrowly defeated in the stormiest campaign in the state's history. In 1943 he won the Pulitzer Prize for the novel **Dragon's Teeth.** Born in Baltimore, he was educated at the College of the City of New York and at Columbia University.
R.E.Ch.

Sinecure.

Formerly an ecclesiastic office without parishioners, now an office with rank and emolument but without any specific duties. In Great Britain the positions of Lord Privy Seal, and of the Chancellor of the Duchy of Lancester are called sinecure offices. The Lord President of the (Privy) Council is also sometimes counted in this category. Holders of these offices are frequently high ranking cabinet ministers who are thus freed from departmental responsibilities in order to devote themselves to special tasks. R.G.N.

Sine Die.

Meaning without day. In the U.S.A. the term is used to refer to final adjournment of a session of a legislative body. M.F.

Single-centered Societies.

An institutional order in which, over time, all societal power is concentrated in one supreme authority. To be distinguished from conspicuously multicentered societies and also from societies in which a substantially pluralistic order is temporarily shackled by a dictatorial regime. Pastoral nomads of the cavalry type occasionally approached single-centered forms of control. Agricultural tribes with communally managed irrigation works, such as the Pueblo Indians of New Mexico, developed genuinely single-centered patterns of authority. Above the tribal level the two major forms of a single-centered society are the agro-despotic (Oriental, hydraulic) state and the industry-based modern totalitarian orders of Fascism and Communism. Under Western absolutism the strength of the central government at times obscured the multicentered character of the society; and under Oriental despotism the prominence of the priesthood of the dominant religion and the influence of non-officiating notables (a "gentry") at times obscured the single-centered character of the society. But under Western absolutism several organized non-governmental forces could act effectively; under Oriental despotism the dominant religion remained administratively subordinated to the secular regime (no independent church being tolerated), and the bureaucratic "gentry" was significant only because of its relation to the government. Under Fascism significant elements of a multicentered society persisted, particularly private-property-based business communities, big landowners, and non-Fascist members of the officer corps. However, success in destroying some major pluralistic elements encouraged further encroachments. When the war reached a critical point, the Fascist power-holders aimed at nationalizing the landed estates and at subordinating industry. Communist totalitarianism from the start aimed at dominating all major means of production. Communist countries that have nationalized industry and collectivized agriculture exert an almost complete control over the social and intellectual life of the population. They constitute the most comprehensive forms of single-centered societies in the history of man. K.A.W.

Single member district.
An electoral district which returns one member chosen by a plurality to a legislative body such as the Congress or a state legislature. This means the candidate with the greatest number of votes is chosen regardless of the fact that there may be others receiving almost as many votes. Therefore, the elected person may represent a minority of the total vote cast in the district. B.N.

Sino-Indian Border.
The border's demarcation by the McMahon Line drawn at the Simla Convention of 1914 is formally disputed by China. The Chinese representative had initialed the Convention, although formal ratification had never followed. The McMahon Line is recognized by the United States as "the accepted boarder and is sanctioned by modern usage." Nineteenth century Indian administrative and legal documents specifically deal with areas China now claims. The Government of India Act of 1935 and the Indian Constitution of 1950 similarly attest to the disputed area as lying within Indian territory. Sino-Burmese Agreements of 1960 accepted the Burma sector of the McMahon Line as the traditional boundary. But during the fifties, China moved into the Ladakh region of India in order to assure a strategic link between Sinkiang and Tibet. In October, 1962, Chinese troops penetrated deeply into Indian territory, and India turned toward the West for arms to meet aggression. An uneasy cease-fire, unilaterally imposed by China, prevailed in December, 1962. S.K.A.

Slansky, Rudolf. (1901-1952).
Czchoslovak Communist since 1921 who held various Party positions. Elected to Parliament in 1935; spent war in Moscow until the 1944 Slovak uprising. Secretary-General of the Communist Party from 1946-1951; became Deputy Prime Minister in charge of economic affairs in 1951. Executed in 1952 for high treason and Titoism. G.K.

Slovak Republic.
Independent Slovak state, founded March 14, 1939. Hitler, determined to liquidate Czechoslovakia, summoned Slovak leader Dr. Tiso to Berlin and offered him Slovak independence or annexation by Hungary; Slovak parliament naturally chose former. In contrast to Nazi-controlled Bohemia-Moravia Protectorate, S.R. was independent in law and fact. Judgment of Select Committee on Communist Aggression (House of Rep's., 83d Cong.) was "not a perfect democracy in the traditional sense" but "in general . . . an expression of the self-preservation instinct of the Slovak Nation." Although Slovakia was re-annexed to C.-S. under Soviet auspices in 1945, anti-Communist Slovak exiles carry on tradition of Slovak Republic. K.G.

Smith, Adam. (1723-1790).
Political economist and author of **Inquiry into the Nature and Causes of the Wealth of Nations,** generally known as the **Wealth of Nations.** He was born at Kirkcaldy, Scotland, June 5, 1723, and died there July 17, 1790. Smith was the first systematic economist. The impact of his authority is still considerable. His theory overthrew feudal economics — the medieval guilds and mercantilism — and the division of labor in production processes was the forerunner of present day mass production. Smith is referred to as the founder of the classical school of economics. M.M.Mc.

Smuts, Jan Christian (1870-1950).
Smuts was born in the Cape Colony and studied law. He worked for self-government of the Transvaal, and cooperation with the British. After

Botha's death, Smuts, a founder of the South African Party, became Union Prime Minister until 1924. In the 1930's he worked with the United Party. He supported South Africa's entrance in the Second World War and was Prime Minister from 1939 to 1948. He served in both world wars and in the Second became a field marshal. J.F.M.

Soblen Case.

Fugitive spy case which created international sensation, nearly caused a cabinet crisis in Israel, and raised fundamental questions relating to the rule of law for the three countries involved — Great Britain, Israel and the United States. The central figure was Dr. Robert A. Soblen, a psychiatrist who was born in Lithuania in 1900, came to the United States in October 1941, and became an American citizen in 1947.

Suffering from leukemia, Soblen was arrested in 1960 and convicted in 1961 for conspiracy to spy for the Soviet Union before and after he had gained American citizenship. Refusing to cooperate he was sentenced to life imprisonment. The chief witness against him was his younger brother, Jack Soblen who was arrested in 1957 and confessed that he and his brother had become Communists in 1919 and had agreed in 1940 to spy for the U.S.S.R. against the United States in exchange for permitting fifteen members of their family to escape from Europe by way of Vladivostok and Shanghai.

Out on bail of $100,000, Soblen was due to surrender in New York City on June 26, 1962, to begin serving the life sentence. Instead, he flew to Israel entering on that day as a tourist under an assumed name and with false papers, particularly his dead brother's Canadian passport. His identity discovered two days later, he was arrested and detained by the police. The United States asked Israel for his return even though a negotiated extradition treaty between the two countries had not yet been ratified; and even if it had it would not have made espionage an extraditable offense. An order for Soblen's expulsion was issued by the Minister of the Interior under the Entry into Israel Law; and on July 1 Soblen was placed on an Israeli plane which flew to Athens, where he was transferred to another Israeli plane bound for the United States. On the first airliner an American marshal took custody of Soblen. As the plane approached London, Soblen stabbed himself with a steak knife. Taken off the airliner, he was hospitalized under guard.

A London court granted Soblen's application for a habeas corpus hearing; and remaining in detention, he legally sought for nine weeks to prevent his removal to the United States and asked for political asylum. The British Home Secretary rejected his request, and the British courts ruled that he was illegally in England. The Home Secretary thereupon directed that Israel should fly Soblen to the United States. The Home Secretary's order for the removal of Soblen to New York by El Al, the Israeli airline, which had brought him to London, was in accordance with British law, but Israel complained that it would constitute a violation of Israeli law.

The speed and secrecy with which Israel expelled Soblen, without granting him his day in court, and acting subserviently to American pressure by placing him on a plane one of whose passengers was known to be a United States marshal, aroused severe political opposition. However, on July 11, the Knesset rejected three non-confidence motions against the Government on its behavior in the case; and on July 29, the Cabinet decided unanimously that it did not consider the Law of Return applicable to Soblen because he had been properly tried by the democratic American courts and was a fugitive from justice, and denied his application for an immigrant's visa. Israel's Government had been so bitterly criticized internally over its handling of the case, it directed El Al not to transport Soblen to America. Instead, it offered to carry Soblen back to Israel. From Israel he could then have been given sanctuary by Czechoslovakia which had granted him a visa. Soblen's lawyers in England argued that if he were placed on an airliner other than Israel's, it would constitute deportation rather than refusal of entry. They did not deny that Soblen could be ordered out of Britain as an illegal entrant; but their contention was that to expel him to a specific country was an abuse of executive power since the Home Secretary had never been given such authority in deportation proceedings.

While Soblen was in England, his lawyers in Israel petitioned the courts to force the Minister of the Interior to grant him entry into Israel under the Law of Return which ensures Jews the right to immigrate to Israel unless they are deemed to menace the health or security of the nation. Since Soblen's single crime, his lawyers maintained, was espionage, and his background did not point to criminality, the Law of Return had been infringed.

Theoretically, a person denied entrance into a country is on his own. He should be permitted to go where he wishes. Nevertheless, the laws of most countries permit the responsible authorities to direct him to some particular place. This is so under British law. Consequently, the British government maintained that Soblen had never received permission to land in England; and, although, he had been taken, for humanitarian reasons, to a London hospital, he was considered simply as "in transit." Although an extradition treaty has existed between Great Britain and the United States, Soblen's offense — espionage — is not among the extraditable crimes listed therein. Hence, Soblen could not have been extradited from Great Britain. The same applied in the case of Israel. Furthermore, Britain refused to deliver Soblen to any Israeli airliner or any plane Israel would have arranged for in transporting Soblen if it suspected that Soblen would not have been returned to the United States. Israel, on the other hand, insisted it would not be a party to carrying Soblen to America.

Finally, the British Home Secretary decided to deport Soblen to the United States in a non-Israeli plane. On September 6, while being driven in an ambulance to a London airport enroute to the United States, Soblen collapsed from the effects of an overdose of barbiturates he had mysteriously obtained and was taken to a London hospital where he died five days later.

O.K.

Social Contract theory.

Epicurus, who founded his school of philosophy at Athens in 306 B.C., taught that men enter into a tacit or at times even outspoken agreement to form a state which is to protect each member against the selfishness of the others. This theory, basing the origin and justification of the state on a contractual agreement, we call today the Social Contract theory. It was developed further by Thomas Hobbes, a follower of Epicurus, in the **Leviathan** (1651) and, for differing reasons, by John Locke in his two treatises **Concerning Civil Government** (1690), and Jean Jacques Rousseau in **The Social Contract or Principles of Political Right** (1762). If man was to free himself from the chains in which, Rousseau opined, he was held in nearly every statal organization (after leaving the "state of nature"), the problem was to devise "a form of association which will defend and protect with the whole common force the person and goods of each associate, and in which each, while uniting himself with all, may still obey himself alone, and remain as free as before." To solve this problem, Rousseau, a highly eclectic writer, transformed Spinoza's concept of the "will of the whole body" into the "general will" and grafted on it Plato's organismic theory of the state. The outcome of this potpourri was Rousseau's statement that "if the state is a moral person whose life is in the union of its members, and if the most important of its cares is the care for its own preservation, it must have a universal and compelling force, in order to move and dispose each part as may be most advantageous to the whole." To make sure that there could be no misunderstanding as to his intention to give the state every possible coercive power over any non-conforming individual or group, Rousseau added that "whoever refuses to obey the general will shall be compelled to do so by the whole body. This means nothing less than that he will be forced to be free." Here, then, we have the paradox of a popular political theorist who started out with the challenging idea to liberate man from the demands of political society and who ends by putting him in chains in order "to be free." Instead of using the social contract concept to lay the foundations of personal and political freedom, as John Locke had done, Rousseau turned the social contract into a vindication of such absolute power of the state over the individual as even Hobbes, who exempted some areas of private and business life from the intervention by the Leviathan-state, might have considered too enslaving.

Nearly one hundred years before Rousseau led the social contract theory ad absurdum, Spinoza had already warned that this explanation of the origin of the state was at best a myth which had no foundation in history and which could easily be used to endanger human liberty. A "compact," Spinoza wrote in the **Theologico-Political Treatise** (1670), "is only made valid by its utility, without which it becomes null and void.... For this reason government which attempts to control minds is accounted tyrannical ... and it is considered ... a usurpation of the rights of subjects, to seek to prescribe what shall be accepted as true, or rejected as false, or what opinions should actuate men in their worship of God.... The object of government is not to change men from rational beings into beasts or puppets.... In fact, the true aim of government is liberty." Unlike Locke, who also stressed man's moral and religious freedom, Spinoza questioned altogether the validity of the social contract theory as an explanation of the state. For while a contract is a voluntary agreement which a person is free to conclude or reject, the state, being a historically grown and world-wide institution, leaves him no such choice. (Even if an individual should decide to leave a particular state, he is compelled to enter another.) Moreover, a contract, unlike the state, cannot possibly bind the descendants of the original contractual partners.

Frequently the "Mayflower Pact," concluded by the Puritan Pilgrims in 1620, is quoted as a social contract for the creation of a state. The very text of this pact, drawn up by the 41 Pilgrims on board the ship Mayflower en route to North America, demonstrates, however, that these men had not just left a pre-political "state of nature" to form a state. They were obviously accustomed to political government and merely transferred their European experience to their new abode. J.D.

Social Darwinism.
1. Ideologies resulting from transferring the biological concepts of Charles Darwin (q.v.) to ethical, political, economic, and sociological fields. 2. A body of literature on the evolution and social significances of races, cultures, and institutions. Ch.C.M.

Social Democratic Party of Germany.
The Social Democratic Party of Germany **(Sozialdemokratische Partei Deutschland** — SPD) is presently the major opposition party in the Federal Republic of Germany. In the last federal elections in September 1961, the SPD obtained 36.3 per cent of the votes. In some of the **Laender** (states) the SPD is the strongest party and has participated or is participating in the state governments. In the so-called German Democratic Republic (Soviet Zone), the SPD was forced by the Soviet Military Administration to merge in 1946 with the Communist Party to form the Socialist Unity Party.

The present SPD is a well organized party and strongly oriented toward social reforms. At the Party Congress at Bad Godesberg in 1959 the SPD dropped entirely its traditional socialist goals such as the nationalization of industries as a matter of principle. However, the SPD is still primarily a workers' party and thus has difficulties in making substantial inroads into other social and economic groups.

The historic origin of the SPD goes back to two socialist movements: the **Allgemeine Deutscher Arbeiterverein** founded by Ferdinand Lassalle in 1863 and the Social Democratic Labor Party founded by Wilhelm Liebknecht and August Bebel in 1869. Both groups joined forces at the Unity Congress of Gotha in 1875 and soon thereafter took the name **Sozialdemokratische Partei Deutschland.**

Chancellor Bismarck's anti-socialist laws forced the party underground from 1878 until 1890 and also caused a radicalization process among some of its adherents. At least in theory the SPD adopted stronger revolutionary concepts. After the re-emergence of the party into legality a Marxist program was adopted at the Party Congress at Erfurt in 1891 although in practice the SPD continued to advocate a peaceful reform program.

Within the SPD three factions emerged. On the right were the Revisionists led by Eduard Bernstein who for all practical purposes determined the official party policy. The center was occupied by Marxists who followed Karl Kautsky's evolutionary interpretation of Marx and Engels. On the left was the radical and revolutionary faction of Karl Liebknecht and Rosa Luxemburg.

During World War I a split occurred between the moderate Majority Socialists (SPD) and the Independent Socialists (**Unabhaengige Sozialdemokratische Partei Deutschland** — USPD) who also harbored the revolutionary left, the **Spartakusbund,** which on December 31, 1918 formed the German Communist Party. During the 1920's most of the Independent Socialists returned to the fold of the SPD; the rest joined the communists.

From 1919 to 1933, the period of the Weimar Republic, the SPD was one of the main supporters of the republic. Hitler's Third Reich forced the party underground. Some of its leaders (e.g. Erich Ollenhauer, Wilhelm Sollmann, Frederic Stampfer, went into exile abroad); others were murdered by the Nazis or spent the Hitlerian years in concentration camps. In 1945, under the leadership of Kurt Schumacher, the SPD was reconstituted and took a very active part in the foundation of the Federal Republic of Germany.
E.W.

Social Security.

This term refers to specific community or state protection for individuals or families who are in need or distress. In the United States the interpretation of social security as an aspect of the broader term of public welfare is a development of the 1930's. The federal Social Security Act of 1935 provided old-age insurance, assisted the states in unemployment insurance, and aided the blind, the aged, and dependent children. These activities were previously developed by the various states. Social security may also include aid to the disabled, the handicapped, and certain other welfare activities for persons in need.
T.K.N.

Socialism, Burmese Way to.

Policy goal promulgated on April 30, 1962 by Revolutionary Council of Burma, headed by General Ne Win. Said to be only alternative to parliamentary democracy which failed in Burma. Backbone of socialist state to be peasants and workers controlled by mass organizations. No restrictions on religion. Unity among ethnic groups to be achieved first. Will avoid "deviation towards right or left," i.e. will take ideas, theories, and experiences from any and all countries. Transition marked by reorientation of popular views. Manual labor to be cherished by all. Aims at planned, proportional development of all national productive forces. Agriculture, transportation, and external trade to be nationalized, i.e. owned by state, cooperative societies, or collective unions. Private enterprises contributing to national productive forces will be permitted with some restrictions. Compensation on basis of "from each according to his ability, to each according to his output." Equalitarianism in Burma held impossible but gaps between incomes to be held to minimum.
H.G.S.

Socialist and Social Democratic Parties.

See European Socialist and Social Democratic Parties.

Socialist Competition (Soviet style).

To increase productivity and enthusiasm in Soviet enterprises socialist competitions are held between brigades, shops, plants, kolkhozes, mines, railroads, etc. The objective of the competition may be the best quality, greatest quantity, lowest cost, or a combination of all. Prizes and distinctions are given to the management and the workers of the winning enterprises. The best working methods of a victorious enterprise are made known for adoption by others.
K.Hu.

Socialist Democracy (Soviet style).

Presupposes an economic, social and political equality in a classless society. At the present time it is a "directed democracy" guided by the Communist Party and the state to build socialism and communism. The party claims to represent the will of the masses. In the Soviet view party restrictions and democracy are compatible. K.Hu.

Socialist Unity Party.
(Sozialistische Einheitspartei Deutschlands, abbrev. SED).

Result of forced merger of Communist and Social Democratic Parties in Soviet Zone of Germany and East Berlin (rejected by Social Democratic Party membership plebiscite of West Berlin), 1946. Leadership originally fifty-fifty Communist and Social Democratic; party is now all-Communist-directed. Aims to "build Socialism," after Soviet model, in (East) German Democratic Republic (q.v.) and, later, all of Germany. Controls state, economy, law, culture, etc., and "mass organizations" (workers, women, youth, etc.) through inter-locking directorate of key positions. Elaborate party structure controlled by Walter Ulbricht (q.v.), First Secretary, Central Committee. J.B.M.

Socrates (c.469 B.C. to 399 B.C.).
Athenian teacher and philosopher whose analytic method of searching for truth marks the beginning of systematic philosophy among the ancient Greeks. Not primarily a political thinker, he nonetheless exerted a great influence on the subsequent political theorizing of Plato, Aristotle, and many other Greek philosophers. Ch.C.M.

Soil Conservation — U.S.A.
Under Soil Conservation Service of U.S. Department of Agriculture and state and local officials; determines solutions to problems of land needs, conservation, erosion damage, and increased productivity. Extends over 1,600,000,000 acres, 4,500,000 farms and ranches in U.S., Puerto Rico and Virgin Islands. C.B.C.

Soka Gakkai.
"Value-Creating Society."
A lay religious organization in Japan affiliated with the Nichiren Shoshu sect of Buddhism. The movement traces its origin to the bronze Nichiren, who was born in 1222 and claimed to be the true Buddha. Nichiren blamed the evils of his day on the existence of heretical sects and emphasized the teachings of the Lotus Sutra. The discipline and aggressive evangelism of the adherents of the Soka Gakkai have raised its membership to over 2,800,000 households in 1962. In recent years, it has supported its own candidates for local assemblies and the national Diet and now holds fifteen seats in the House of Councillors (upper house), where it is the third largest parliamentary group. Its membership is largely lower middle class and it opposes labor strikes and nuclear weapons. Some twenty Soka Gakkai leaders were imprisoned for their beliefs during World War II, and the group opposes any amendment of the present Constitution which would permit government subsidies to the Shinto faith. T.Mc.N.

Japanese militant, lay-Buddhist organization which has recently entered the political scene. It emphasizes massive athletic competitions for the physical strengthening of the Japanese population and demands an end to all cultural vulgarity. Its strength can be deducted from the fact that its thrice-weekly newspaper boasts a circulation of 2.5 million. J.D.

Sokolovsky, Vasili Danilovich.
Marshal of the Soviet Union 1947, Deputy Minister of Defense 1948, Chief of Army-Navy General Staff 1952, Hero of the Soviet Union, Deputy to the Supreme Soviet. In World War II he was commander of the Byelorussian, Ukrainian Front. Subsequently he became Deputy Commander in Chief, Soviet Forces of Occupation in Germany and representative in the Allied Control Commission for Germany.
E.K.K.

Solicitor.
In Great Britain a Solicitor is a fully qualified lawyer in general law practice who deals directly with clients and prepares cases to be pleaded by a barrister (See Barrister) but who does not himself plead in court.
R.G.N.

Solicitor General.
In the U.S.A., the third-ranking officer in the Department of Justice, appointed by the President with the

advice and consent of the Senate. He has special charge of the business of, and appears and represents the Government in the Supreme Court. When requested by the Attorney General, the Solicitor General may conduct and argue any case in which the United States is interested, in any court, federal or state. No appeal is taken by the United States to any appellate court without the authorization of the Solicitor General. F.H.H.

Somalia.
Independent republic in Northeast Africa, formed on July 1, 1960 by the merger of the former Italian trust territory of Somaliland and the British Somaliland Protectorate. Area 265,936 sq. miles; population (est. 1960) 2,047,000. Unique among its neighbors for its ethnic and linguistic homogeneity, Somalia is generally considered one of the poorest of the new African states. With a majority of its population engaged in pastoral nomadism, the country's major problem is the absence of exploitable natural resources for taxation and foreign trade, except for some Italian owned banana plantations in the south.

The government, modelled on a cabinet-parliamentary system, is controlled by the dominant Somali Youth League, the spearhead of the independence movement. The major issues of Somali politics are: a) the problem of expanding tax resources; b) the relations between the more numerous nomadic Somali clans of the north and the less numerous but more productive agricultural Sab clans of the south; c) the problem of political and administrative integration of the former British and Italian areas; d) relations with Ethiopia regarding the undefined common boundary. R.L.K.

Soplones.
In Latin America, especially Mexico, the name for informers, i.e., those who give inside information to politicians, police, and other governmental authorities. M.A.

Sorel, Georges. (1847-1922).
French political philosopher, noted for his **Reflections on Violence,** published in 1906, in which he attempts to display the irrational character of political behavior, presents a theory of political myth, and asserts the efficacy of the syndicalist myth of the "general strike." J.W.Ch.

Soustelle, Jacques (1912-).
Of a Protestant family and with a Ph.D. from the University of Lyons in 1937, Soustelle was a Resistance intimate of De Gaulle, holding posts for the Free French in London and Algiers. He served as Minister of Information and Colonies in 1945 and 1946, and was Secretary-General of De Gaulle's RPF from 1947 to 1949.

As secretary-general of a French antifascist organization prior to 1940, and as a founder of the UDSR, Soustelle was close to the Left, but moved right in politics while an Assembly deputy from 1951 to 1959. As Governor-General of Algiers from 1954 to 1955 he became a firm "integrationist," and was political adviser to those who organized the 1958 coup in Algiers. He helped organize the UNR and served De Gaulle as Minister of Information until the latter's decision to disavow "integration" led to a split. Out of France by 1961, Soustelle has served temporarily as U.N. correspondent for L'Aurore, and has published a book on his specialty as an anthropologist, the Aztecs. R.B.C.

South Africa, Republic of.
Area, 472,358 square miles; Population (census 1960) 15,841,128 including about 3,067,000 Europeans; Administrative Capital, Pretoria; Legislative Capital, Cape Town.

On May 3, 1961 the Union of South Africa, established in 1910 as a self-governing British Dominion, became a Republic and left the Commonwealth. The new constitution provided for a president (now Charles R. Swart, the former Governor-General) to be selected by an electoral college of a joint session of the Parliament. Parliamentary features were retained in provisions for the Prime Minister (now Hendrik F. Verwoerd) to come from the majority party of the House. The House of Assembly consists of 160 members and the Senate of 54 members. Judicial powers reside in a system of courts which include a Court of Appeals whose membership and powers were redefined in Acts of 1954 and 1956. The Republic does not have a true federal system, but has four provinces with assemblies to handle local affairs. The administrators of the provinces are nominated by and responsible to the government of the Republic.

Some effective interest groups during the century have included the Afrikaner cultural organizations, the Chamber of Mines and the South African Federated Chamber of Industries. In addition the white workers have at times enjoyed strong organizations, yet during the 1950's at least five different labor federations existed.

In the 1961 elections the National Party obtained 105 seats in the Assembly while the opposition United Party received 49. Other minor parties have existed since the Second World War, but none has been able to retain representation in the Assembly due partially to changes in constituencies sponsored by the National Government. Since 1912 a section of the National Party has continued with its Afrikaner nationalist strain, even when at times a major part of the party joined with more moderate groups. The United Party, formed in 1934 after the coalition of the South African Party and a section of the National Party, has continued to represent the views for cooperation with the British, and a less extreme course for native affairs. The National Party has maintained a majority in Parliament since 1948 and has proceeded with apartheid policies. The first Bantu self-governing authority was established in Transkeian during 1959. J.F.M.

South-East Asia Treaty Organization.
It was set up in 1955 to provide the collective defense in the treaty area — Pakistan, Thailand, the Philippine Republic, North Borneo, Brunei, Sarawak, Singapore, Australia, the Trust Territory of New Guinea and Papua. Each of the signatories — Australia, France, New Zealand, Pakistan, the Philippine Republic, Thailand, the United Kingdom and the United States of America — recognized that aggression by armed attack in this area against any party, or against any State or territory would endanger its own peace and safety and agreed that it would, in that event, act to meet the common danger in accordance with its constitutional processes. S.S.H.

Sovereignty.
In the political sense, it is one of the characteristics of a state in international law. It is the quality of independence from the control or interference of any other state in the conduct of its international relations. Each sovereign state theoretically is equal to every other in international law, regardless of its population, area, or economic wealth. It is thus the basis for equality of representation and voting strength in international bodies such as the General Assembly of the United Nations. This aspect of a state is known as external sovereignty, first described systematically as to modern nation-states by Grotius.

Sovereignty also has an internal aspect. In this sense it relates to the power and authority of the state over individuals and groups. John Austin considered it indivisible and although it originated with the people it was exercised in their name by the government which they established. This monistic view is denied by the pluralists, such as Leon Duguit, who consider the power exerted by organized groups in the state over their members an exercise of sovereignty. Few would deny that sovereignty is divided in a Federal State, such as the United States or Canada.

Many political theorists have contributed to the formulation of the concept of internal sovereignty. Among the more important are Jean Bodin, John Milton, Thomas Hobbes, Richard Harrington and John Locke. In their writings one may trace the evolution of the idea from its use as a support to absolute monarchy to its modern form as popular sovereignty.

Prudent observation and reflection clearly show that neither internal nor external sovereignty is or can be absolute. They are continually changing. The question is not whether a nation shall surrender sovereignty to some international community or to its people, but only how much. This process already has proceeded far through the practice of treaty making. H.W.

Soviet Military Administration in Germany. (SMAD).
Was established (1945) in Berlin-Karlshorst, to head the Military Government in the Soviet Zone of Occupation and to carry out the policy of the Allied Control Council.

When the German Democratic Republic was established its functions were ostensibly turned over to German authorities but in reality were exercised by the new Soviet Control Commission (11-11-49). E.K.K.

Soviet Military Reforms.
Program instituted by Frunze in 1924-25, designed to transform the Red Army from the irregular outfit of the Civil War into a more regular, professional organization. The reforms, carried on by Voroshilov after Frunze's death, involved the organization of the armed forces on a mixed (regular and militia) basis and the integration of the industry of the USSR into military production. Military ranks and discipline were also introduced. W.D.J.

Soviet-Nazi Pact of Non-Aggression.
See Nazi-Soviet Pact.

Soviet of Nationalities.
With the Soviet of the Union forms the U.S.S.R. Supreme Soviet. Elected on the basis of 25 deputies from each Union Republic, 11 deputies from each Autonomous Republic, 5 deputies from each Autonomous Region and 1 deputy from each National Area. The number of deputies is not affected by the size of the area or the population of the republic or region. The Soviet of Nationalities is designed "to give every nationality representation" in the Supreme Soviet. K.Hu.

Soviet of the Union.
With the Soviet of Nationalities forms the U.S.S.R. Supreme Soviet. Elected by the Soviet citizens voting by election districts on the basis of one deputy for every 300,000 of the population. Deputies are expected to inform their electorate about their work and the work of the Supreme Soviet despite their full-time employment in production or other work. K.Hu.

Soviet Peoples' Courts.
The lowest level of elected courts in the Soviet system. The peoples' court in session consists of a judge and two lay members known as peoples' assessors, all of whom are elected for three year terms. The judge is a full-time official, but the peoples' assessors, of whom there may be as many as 75 per raion, are supposedly limited to a maximum of ten days' service per year. In practice, the judge is generally able to lead the lay assessors in the direction he favors. D.N.J.

Soviet Reparations in Germany.
Reparations were taken as a compensation for damages caused by the German forces in W. W. II, and to limit German industrial and war potential. The Soviet troops seized and, with bank notes they had requisitioned or printed, purchased goods and industrial equipment for export to the Soviet Union, cutting production of the Soviet Zone to one half. Some plants were operated by Soviet Corporations in Germany, (see SAG). By 1953, when the Soviet Union "renounced all reparations" it had taken $28 billion worth of goods and services, that is $18 billion more than it originally demanded. E.K.K.

Soviet Satellites.
The defeat of Germany in World War II and inter-allied agreements presented the Soviet Union with immense opportunities to extend its power westward. For the first time since the abortive attempt to communize Europe in 1919, "objective factors," i.e., the military situation and the severe curtailment of economic productivity, seemed to favor the revolutionary transformation of European society. The immediate objective of the Soviets was the consolidation of their military conquests. After the success at Stalingrad (if not earlier) the Soviet leaders, despite their preoccupation with the winning of the war, turned their thoughts to the postwar prospects of a Soviet-dominated system of communist states in Eastern Europe. Under the euphemistic label of "people's democracy," all Eastern European countries as well as East Germany were yoked with totalitarian rule administered by communists at the order of Moscow. The features common to all satellite states are the abrogation of personal and political freedoms; ad-

justment to the Soviet economic, social and cultural system; complete subordination to the aims of Soviet foreign policy; and severance of virtually all ties with the non-Soviet world. In Asia, the Soviet satellite empire includes North Korean and Outer Mongolia; in America, Cuba has been reduced (by political penetration rather than by military occupation) to satellite status. R.St.H.

Soviet Union.
The Union of Soviet Socialist Republics (U.S.S.R.) is a **federal state** composed of Russian Federative, Ukrainian, Byelorussian, Azerbaijan, Georgian, Armenian, Kazakh, Turkmenian, Kirgiz, Tadshik, Uzbek, Estonian, Latvian, Lithuanian, and Moldavian Soviet Socialist Republics. The Soviet "Republic" is less autonomous than any of the 50 states of the United States; for the central government of the U.S.S.R. has the power to amend the Soviet constitution without the consent of the individual Soviet Republics.

The U.S.S.R. distinguishes between "union republic" and "autonomous republic." A "union republic" has (on paper only) the power to secede from the U.S.S.R. if it is a "border republic." The nationality which gives its name to the "union republic" must constitute a more or less compact majority within that republic. The population of a "union republic" must be not less than a million.

The administrative structure of the U.S.S.R. is characterized by three types of ministries: (1) the all-union ministries which operate from Moscow down to the local level with vertical lines of responsibility; (2) union-republic ministries which operate from Moscow through the corresponding ministries in each republic with both vertical and horizontal lines of responsibility; and (3) republic ministries which are not connected with Moscow. B.J.L.S.

Soviet Union — Economic Planning.
The unsuccessful attempt to create full communism in one sweeping gesture during the years 1917-1920 ("war communism") led to the "new economic policy" (NEP) of the years 1921-1927. Money, abolished during the previous period, was again brought into use, private trade permitted, and some industrial concessions were granted to foreign capitalist interests. In 1928 Stalin adopted a centralized approach to the building of a "socialized" economy, establishing top priorities in production and allowing concentration of resources on certain sectors of the economy in order to provide for, and speed up, the economic growth. Thus in the centralized plans of future economic performance heavy emphasis was laid on industry in general — at the expense of the consumer sector, and on production of steel, heavy machinery and equipment at the expense of the light industry in particular. Since the beginning of the planning era, the Soviet Union has launched six Five-Year Plans, four of which have been declared completed: The first (in four years), second, fourth, and fifth. Two plans have been discontinued: the third, interrupted by Second World War, and the sixth, abandoned in 1958 by Khrushchev who replaced it with the first Seven-Year Plan (1959-1965). There is an abundance of materials released by the Soviet Government on the first and second Five-Year Plans, but not on the others. The data available for the Seven-Year Plan give only key output targets and various growth rates by products, industry and sectors. Recently the Soviets are using more extensively the input-output matrix and the linear programming techniques in their planning. Out of sheer physical impossibility of scheduling and coordinating the production of thousands and thousands of various products in existence, the Soviet planners restrict themselves to the rationing and allocating of the output of "key" commodities, (the so-called "funded" commodities), manpower and construction. The two main soviet central planning agencies are: (1) Gosplan state planning commission, presently limited only to the development of operational one-year plans within the framework of the more general Seven-Year Plan that is prepared by (2) Gosekonomsovet state economic science council. In 1958 some decentralization of the economy took place by the creation of "regional economic councils" (Sovnarkhozy) and abolishing most of the trade and industry ministries in Moscow. W.N.

Sovkhoz. (Pl. Sovkhozy).
State farm like an agricultural factory—State-owned and -operated. Although state-owned farms are a theoretical ideal in a socialist (Soviet style) society, in the U.S.S.R. there are many more kolkhozy than sovkhozy. Workers are paid fixed wages based on skill required for work done, with a bonus for outstanding quantity or quality. Workers are permitted use of individual plots and rent state-owned houses for a minimal fee. K.Hu.

Sovmin (Soviet Ministerov).
The Council of Ministers.
According to the Soviet Constitution of 1936, "the highest organ of state power in the U.S.S.R." In practice, the Sovmin is subordinated to the Presidium of the party Central Committee, the chief policy-making body in the Soviet system. The Sovmin is made up of some sixty members and is headed by its own Presidium. The Chairman of the Presidium, usually the First Secretary of the party, as well, is commonly referred to as the Premier of the Soviet Union. D.N.J.

Sovnarkom (Soviet Narodnykh Komissarov, SNR).
Council of People's Commissars, the supreme administrative body of the Soviet governmental apparatus until 1946. Sometimes referred to as "the Soviet government." The Sovnarkom was established by the Second All-Russian Congress of Soviets on November 8, 1917, with Lenin as chairman. Its name was changed to Sovmin (Council of Ministers) by Stalin in 1946. D.N.J.

Spaak, Paul-Henri (1899-).
Belgian statesman, active for many years in the Belgian socialist movement, served as minister of transport, posts and telegraphs, and of foreign affairs in various Belgian governments, as well as Prime Minister. Was president of United Nations general assembly in 1946, president of the Organization of European Economic Cooperation 1948-1950, Secretary General of NATO 1957-1961. Vigorous proponent of European and Atlantic unity. He opposed his concept of a federal union of Europe to Gen. de Gaulle's concept of a "Europe of states." F.M.

Space Jurisdiction.
Since 1919 it has been universally recognized that every state has complete and sovereign jurisdiction over its super-jacent airspace. In quite recent years the question has seriously arisen as to the extent to which areas beyond airspace might become, or be excluded from becoming, part of the national domain.

Ancient theory prescribed land rights as extending "up to the heavens," but today this highly unscientific position is not taken seriously anywhere. Instead various theories have been advanced to govern the upper extent of state jurisdiction. Prominent among these are distances believed to limit the extreme potential extent of flight based on aerodynamic lift (expressed as from forty to sixty miles above the Earth's surface); at points where the gravitational pull of the earth is offset by other gravitational forces; according to various atmospheric criteria; at a specific distance reflecting the upper trajectory of intercontinental missiles; and, more generally, in conformity with realistic effective control.

It has been suggested that a general accord among the major states might fix such a line, and a variety of speculation has considered problems resulting (or which may be expected to result) from space traffic, "junk" in space, exploration of space and heavenly bodies, and even what rules might apply to relations with thinking beings from non-Earth sources. Such considerations remain speculative at the present writing. H.B.J.

Spain. See Appendix.

Spartacus Rebellion.
An armed rebellion of leftist Berlin workers in January 1919 against the provisional government of Germany. It was provoked by the dismissal of a leftist socialist from his position as president of the Berlin police forces. While the Communist party (an offspring of the Spartacus League) seemed to have no share in the planning of the rebellion, it nevertheless gave it its full support. W.A.

Speaker.
The presiding officer in the lower house of the legislatures in the United

494

States, Great Britain, and other English-speaking countries. As presiding officer the Speaker recognizes members who wish to speak, interprets and applies the rules of procedure, and signs bills, resolutions, and other proceedings. In Great Britain the Speaker is nonpartisan, but in the United States he early became a party leader. The Speaker of the House of Representatives follows the Vice-President in the order of succession to the Presidency.
W.V.H.

Special Assessment.

A levy by public authority against a restricted group of properties in the immediate vicinity of a proposed improvement for the purpose of paying part or all of the cost of such an improvement, justified by the presumption that such properties will gain special benefits from the improvement.
D.W.Mc.

Special District.

An organized governmental entity established to provide one or more specific services, such as fire protection or sewage disposal, for a local area. Exclusive of school districts (a type of special district) approximately 14,500 such units exist in the United States. Although there is no consistent pattern in their structure and organization, special districts are generally characterized by a considerable degree of fiscal and administrative independence from other local units. Their governing body is either popularly elected or appointed by officials of other governments.
H.J.Sch.

Special Municipal Corporation.

Special districts organized as bodies "corporate and politic" to handle either single functions or closely related functions of local government. They operate within areas of jurisdiction often coterminous with those of a municipality, but sometimes more or less extensive in scope. They have the power to levy taxes and usually to issue revenue bonds. They are semi-autonomous units of local government.
R.G.S.

Special order.

In the United States House of Representatives, a device through which a bill that has been approved by a standing committee may be scheduled for floor consideration with regard to its calendar status. A special order, establishing the amount of time to be allowed for debate on the measure and the policy on accepting amendments from the floor, must be recommended by the Rules Committee and then approved by the House. It is extremely difficult to bring a bill to the floor without a special order.
D.M.B.

Special Welfare.

All military and paramilitary measures and activities related to unconventional warfare, psychological operations and counterinsurgency operations.
T.W.

Specialized Agency.

Term denoting an international, intergovernmental organization related to the United Nations, but independent and autonomous in its organization, e.g. the World Health Organization, the Food and Agriculture Organization, the International Bank for Reconstruction and Development, the International Monetary Fund, UNESCO or International Labor Organization.
F.M.

Spencer, Herbert. (1820-1903).

British social and political thinker, notable for his attempt to derive ethical conclusions and political prescriptions from evolutionary principles combined with his belief in the inheritance of acquired characteristics. In political theory this led him to an extreme version of contractualism, and in economics to the advocacy of **laissez-faire.** He regarded state intervention as an enemy of individuality and the prime threat to the progressive development of humanity.
J.W.Ch.

Spengler, Oswald. See Appendix.

Spheres of Influence.

Refers principally to agreements reached by European colonial and imperial powers with respect to the enjoyment of economic and political privileges and rights in China during and after the late 19th century. The term has also been used for similar arrangements or claims in other areas of Asia and Africa. The growing overseas ambitions of Germany and Russia at the close of the 19th century, and the rise of Japan as a competitor for rights in China, led the European powers to reach a "gentlemen's agreement" under which China would be divided into "spheres of influence." The Chinese have described this as "the cutting of the melon." Each of the powers concerned, Great Britain, France, Germany and Russia was to enjoy monopolistic privileges in commerce and in the development of resources in the area that it dominated with no interference from the other European powers. In some cases the powers appropriated for themselves certain political functions and usurped Chinese authority in their "spheres." The principal areas which European powers considered to be "spheres of influence" were as follows: Britain to have principal power and influence in the Yangtze Valley (in addition to the maintaining of a Colony in Hong Kong and a lease on Kowloon); France was paramount in the Chinese territories bordering on Indo-China; Russia had special rights in Manchuria and the Northeast; Germany had a special position in Shantung Province with a treaty port at Tsingtao.

Following the Sino-Japanese War, and later the Russo-Japanese War (1906) Japan contested Russia's rights in the Northeast Provinces, and until her defeat in 1945 asserted her own claims to wide spheres of influence in Northern and Eastern China. As a result of these divisions China was reduced to what Sun Yat-sen termed a "hypo-colony." Only after the rise of the Nationalists and World War II were Chinese rights gradually regained.

S.S.

Spinoza, Baruch (Benedict de).
(1632-1677).

Portuguese-Dutch-Jewish philosopher whose works offer intellectual grounds for political liberty apart from establishing the first scientific basis for the evaluation of moral behavior. Born on November 24, 1632 in Amsterdam, where his parents had sought refuge from the Inquisition in the Iberian Peninsula, he received his formal education in a Jewish high school (Heder). Harboring rather unorthodox views with regard to the scriptural traditions, Jewish and Christian alike, he was excommunicated by the Amsterdam Jewish authorities in 1656. But he remained a Jew in his philosophical and theological thinking, albeit "un juif protestant" as he was called by his contemporaries, or a reform Jew, as he would be probably called today. Having learned the art of polishing optical glasses, he earned his livelihood as a lens-grinder, a manual trade which afforded him the privacy and quiet for writing **The Ethics, A Short Treatise on God, Man and His Well-being, Tractatus Theologico-Politicus, Tractatus Politicus,** and other books, all of them classics today in philosophy and political science. In 1673 he was offered the chair in philosophy at the University of Heidelberg—a unique event—since Jews in those days of the ghettoization of European Jewry were excluded from all universities. But since the letter of invitation expressed the hope that Spinoza would say and write nothing which could be considered critical of the "established religion," he rejected the offer. Although he tried to see all natural phenomena **sub specie eternitatis**, he was essentially a political moralist who searched for the "good life" on earth. With Aristotle he viewed man as a political animal always in need of external help. Hence, he insisted, man's well-being is best promoted by cooperative social efforts, and a reasonable man will desire nothing for himself that he does not desire for others. Against the contention of the Sophists that morality is just a social convention and that "might makes right," Plato and Aristotle had already established certain universal principles of justice which man, by virtue of his reason, can discover if he so desires. The Stoics who substituted for the ancient polis the cosmopolis or citizenship of the world, added, that the individual achieves serenity by comprehending the inevitability of natural causation. But it was not before Judaism taught the world the great message of its prophets that man learned to recognize history not as a meaningless and repetitious cycle but rather as the march of humanity toward the Messianic Age, the kingdom of God on earth. While this concept was obscured by the Christian over-emphasis on "original sin," Spinoza, in the foot-steps of Maimonides, promises man salvation not by unquestioning faith in any doctrine, not by adherence to any church, however powerful, but by the intellectual search for God, by a steadily progressing understanding of his natural environment and of himself. While writing the final chapters of the **Tractatus Politicus,** "wherein is demonstrated how society should be ordered so as not to lapse into a tyranny," Spinoza, at the age of 44, died of consumption. J.D.

Splendid Isolation.
Aloofness of a major power from defensive and offensive alliances, associated especially with England from the 16th until the beginning of the 20th Century. The self-imposed isolation did not, however, imply indifference toward European politics. On the contrary, England thereby preserved its freedom to throw in its weight where it was needed to maintain or restore the status quo. Its position of a balancer was the basis for England's dominant position in European politics. P.J.F.

Split Session.
Practice of dividing legislative sessions into two parts with intervening recess period. Used in California (1911-58), West Virginia (1920-28), New Mexico (1940) and occasionally a few other states. Typically provides preliminary 30 day assemblage for organizing legislature, appointing committees and introducing bills, followed by adjournment for like period to study proposed measures and consult constituents. Proponents maintained legislators would be better informed on issues and could enact bills during the post-recess session without the usual rush and accumulation during the last few days, but experience did not support these claims. C.F.N.

Spoils System.
Selection of government officials and employees on a party basis rather than on merit. The use of offices as rewards for party service and loyalty. It was perfected during the Jacksonian era and is still used today, although much less. Used in contrast to "merit system." Also, the practice of utilizing political appointments, with some or little regard for efficiency or fitness, as technique for building party factions or machines. It is also used to refer to other perquisites, emoluments, favors, preferments, honors, and distinctions which are distributed by political parties, public officials or politicians frequently independent of merit in order to strengthen, politician, party, faction, or official. A.G.

Sputnik.
Russian word for "companion" or "satellite"; the name given to the first successful space vehicle in human history launched by the Russians in October 1957. The achievement of this magnificent technological "first" by the Soviet Union came as a tremendous psychological shock to the non-Communist world. As a result the word "Sputnik" became a symbol of the tremendous technological, industrial, and scientific advances in the field of military hardware possible under a Communist system, which advances the United States and the rest of the non-Communist world would have to match lest it court military defeat at Communist hands. T.W.

Staff Agency.
It is a term borrowed from military organization where each commander of a large military unit has in his command not only line or combat elements but also staff or advisory elements. He is advised by the staff, but he alone issues orders to the line. In civil administration, the concept suffers some modifications; staff advice is more often in the form of evaluation of alternative courses of action. Because staff and line elements and tasks are not often carefully separated in civil government, there is a tendency to speak of staff functions rather than staff agencies.
H.W.

Stakhanovism.
A term coined in the U.S.S.R. in 1935, based on the name of a Don basin miner, Alexei Grigorevich Stakhanov; a new form of division of labor introduced in industry and agriculture which seeks to exploit technological devices and the worker's individual experience to achieve greater productivity; a system — developed as a movement — in which the worker is goaded into maintaining an output considerably greater than the "norm" through incentives of status, higher pay (often several times above average), and fringe benefits such as priority to 'rest homes' and sanatoria. An objective is the creation of a labor elite which, by constantly

outperforming other workers, exercises an upward pressure on productivity quotas. W.J.S.

Stalin, Josef.
(Josef Vassarionovich Dzhugashvili).
(1879-1953).
Son of cobbler. Expelled as revolutionary from theological seminary, 1899. Member, Russian Social-Democratic Party; joined Bolshevik faction, 1903. Member, Central Committee, 1912. Exiled to Siberia several times.
Returned to Petrograd 1917. Commissar of Nationalities, 1917. Secretary-General, Communist Party, 1922. After Lenin's death fight against party's "left" and "right" oppositionists, particularly Trotsky. Developed concept of "Socialism in one country," Five Year Plans, collectivization of agriculture. Initiated "great purges" leading to the "liquidation" of many of Lenin's most trusted co-workers, the "Old Bolsheviks"; proclaimed in 1936 the so-called Stalin Constitution. Chairman, Council of People's Commissars (Ministers), 1941. Marshal, Supreme Commander, Red Army, 1941. M.C.V.

Stamp Act (1765).
Bitterly opposed British statute (for revenue, defense) requiring American Colonies to place revenue stamps on newspapers, business instruments, playing cards, legal documents. Repealed, 1766. R.F.H.

Standard of living.
A measurement of the level of welfare and comfort prevailing in a given area or country, usually by comparison with some other area or country. A number of statistical and other devices have been used to make data non-subjective and comparable. F.M.

Standard Metropolitan Statistical Areas. (U.S.A.)
The Standard Metropolitan Statistical Area was created so that all Federal agencies would use identical urban geographical units when reporting general purpose statistics. The Bureau of the Budget recognizes 215 such areas (1961). Each contains at least one American city of 50,000 population as well as the adjoining urbanized territory which is socially and economically related to it. J.M.S.

Standing Committee.
A regular, as distinct from a special, and permanent committee of a legislative body. In the United States the standing committees are appointed at the beginning of each new Congress and have jurisdiction over all bills pertaining to certain subject matter. Seniority is the main factor in determining committee assignments. W.V.H.

Stare Decisis.
The judicial practice of abiding by cases previously decided. A precedent is created when the principle of law is applied in a particular way to a certain pattern of facts, and later cases will usually be decided in the same way. It is a major principle of Anglo-American law. R.H.B.

State.
The state is that particular, subsidiary, functional organization of the body politic which has for its proper object the promotion of the temporal common good. The essential physical attributes of the state are: 1) people; 2) territory; 3) government, i.e., the agency through which the policies of the state are formulated and carried out; 4) sovereignty, i.e., supreme power, both internal and external, including the authority to make final legal decisions and the physical power to enforce them. The state is distinguished from the nation, which is a human community based on the fact of birth and lineage and a common historical tradition and culture. Pa.B.

State Aids.
State aids are financial assistance sometimes given in the form of subsidies, but most often as grants-in-aid, by the United States federal government to the States. The federal portion of a grant-in-aid is matched in part by state appropriations. Examples of grants-in-aid are the federal-state highway building program and the federal-state old age assistance programs. Aids for building purposes are sometimes granted directly to municipalities.
J.R.B.

State Central Committee.
See U.S. State Central Committee.

State civil service commission.
In the U.S.A. state civil service com-

missions have the function of administering the merit systems of their respective states. The commissions are usually composed of three or five members appointed by the governor. They are responsible for the recruitment and job classification of state employees.
G.B.T.

State Constitutions.
Written constitutions establishing and controlling government exist in all states of the United States. Although earliest state constitutions stressed fundamental principles and basic structural features, addition of detailed directives and limitations made many of them lengthy and complex. Only three current state constitutions date prior to 1800, nearly three-fourths were framed in the nineteenth century, and a dozen were written since 1900. Despite differences and exceptions, most state constitutions contain several similarities: preambles setting forth aims and purposes; bills of rights enumerating liberties; articles outlining the organization and powers of legislative, executive and judicial branches; provision for general revision and piecemeal amendment; sections on taxation, education, elections, municipal corporations and other areas subject to state regulation. Although many experts have long advocated reforms, only a few states have revised extensively their basic charters in recent decades.
C.F.N.

State convention (in U.S.A.).
A deliberative body of elected members to propose or adopt a new or revised state constitution or, for party purposes, to adopt a political platform and designate state-wide candidates. The latter has been superseded by the direct primary election in virtually all states. Where it still remains it is preceded by a primary election of delegates.
M.B.D.

Statelessness.
A condition in which, for one reason or another, an individual is destitute of nationality. It is precisely this lack of bond between the individual and the state which not only places him outside the pale of international law, but also deprives him of the diplomatic protection of any state as well. It is this latter fact which renders the position of a stateless person most precarious.
O.S.

State of Siege.
A legal condition in most countries under Roman civil law under which the free movement of persons and communications is suspended, and the civil law equivalents of habeas corpus, freedom of speech, freedom of assembly and freedom of the press are suspended. A state of siege is usually decreed by the chief executive of a country or political sub-division thereof (or by a person assuming the chief executive's authority) when a military coup d'etat or condition of mass lawlessness or other civil disturbance is expected or underway. During the state of siege movement of persons on streets and highways is limited to persons possessing passes issued by the decreeing authority, and telephone and telegraph communications and radio and press announcements are limited to those approved by the decreeing authority.
T.W.

State of the Union Message.
The U.S. Constitution directs the President of the U.S. to inform the Congress on the state of the nation and to recommend measures for its consideration. By custom this message is given early in each session of Congress. It was sent in written form from 1809 to 1913, when President Wilson went personally before a joint session of Congress and read his message. Television and radio facilities are used to familiarize the people with the views and wishes of their chief executive.
M.F.

State of War.
See War.

Statesman.
A successful leader in public affairs, particularly the affairs of the state as a whole, who in the creation and guidance of public policy displays careful preparation, wisdom, and personal integrity. (A prominent politician meriting the above description is, therefore, frequently called a statesman.) See Politician.
J.D.

States' Rights Doctrine.
See U.S. States' Rights Doctrine.

499

Statute Law.

That form of law which is expressed by an act of the legislature (Congress, Parliament). It is distinct from such other forms of law as Common Law and Equity. In America self-executing treaties are equal to statute law but in Great Britain legislation is necessary to give the same effect. R.G.N.

Statute of Limitations.

A law establishing a termination period for legal action in certain civil or criminal cases. After the time limit has passed all legal rights and remedies are barred. The statute of limitations gives the individual protection from law suits in which, because of lapse of time, evidence is difficult to produce. Each state of the U.S.A. sets time limits for a variety of claims. J.O.H.

Statute of Westminster.

This is a document adopted in 1931 which gave effect to some resolutions passed by the Imperial Conferences of 1926 and of 1931. The Statute defined the relations between Great Britain and the Dominions — Canada, Australia, New Zealand, South Africa, Ireland, and Newfoundland. The Statute asserted the equality of the members of the present Commonwealth of Nations, united by common allegiance to the symbol of the crown. It stipulated that laws made by the British Parliament could no longer extend to any Dominion, and thus it gave the Dominions complete independence in law-making. C.R.F.

Statute-making power.

The power of a legislature to make laws of a general or specific character and to enact revenue or appropriation measures. Although a legislature generally possesses other functions (e.g., supervision of executive administration, participation in the constitutional amending process), the authority to enact statutes is its most significant power. Present-day statutes are often phrased in general terms, with administrators empowered to fill in details and thus exercise a type of delegated legislative authority. In the United States, both Federal and state statutes are subject to judicial invalidation should they be found to conflict with the Constitution. D.M.B.

Statuto of 1848.

Granted by royal decree to the Kingdom of Sardinia and applied to unified Italy through popular plebiscite, the **Statuto** was Italy's fundamental law until 1946. It called for individual rights, a royal-appointed senate, and a chamber based on limited suffrage; cabinet responsibility to parliament rather than king developed early. Never repealed during fascism, it permitted royal dismissal and arrest of Mussolini after the "revolt" of the Fascist Grand Council on July 25, 1943. E.T.O.

Statutory Construction.

Owing to the inherent deficiencies of human language most laws, even those drafted with precision, often raise questions as to their meaning when applied to a concrete set of circumstances in a legal case. The art of ascertaining their applied meaning is called **statutory construction**, which is a difficult but important function of the Courts. In construing a statute the Court is required to consider such elements as the obvious or technical sense of words used, the intent of the legislature, the evil to be remedied by the law and other well established principles of legal interpretation. A.A.N.

Stavisky Affaire (France).

Serge A. Stavisky, suspected of elaborate swindles involving high political and other personages, was pursued by the police and found shot to death in January, 1934, some alleging that he was a suicide, others that he had been shot on government order. In the aftermath, on February 6, 1934, militant right wing organizations demonstrated in favor of overthrowing the government while the police tried to control the demonstration and defend the Chamber of Deputies building. Some twenty people were killed, and many more were wounded. Left wing organizations countered with other demonstrations. The Radical Socialist Daladier government resigned, yielding to a government of national union, headed by Gaston Doumergue, excluding only the Communists and the Socialists. E.G.L.

Steering Committee.

A party committee in a legislative body composed of members of the majority party to manage the party program and to facilitate the enactment of legislation advocated by the party. The floor leader serves as chairman and the whip as an **ex officio** member. Sometimes the minority party also has a steering committee. W.V.H.

Steffens, Lincoln. (1866-1936).
American journalist and "muckraker," author of **Shame of the Cities** (1904), **The Struggle for Self-Government** (1906), **The Uplifters** (1909), and **Autobiography of Lincoln Steffens** (1931). In books, newspaper and magazine articles he and other "muckrakers" exposed corruption and graft in the government of many large American cities and contributed to municipal reform. J.E.R.

Stereotype.
A stereotype is an image of a class of objects which incorporates what is believed to be its most typical characteristics and which disregards the variability within the class. For example, the stereotype of a nationality is the image of a supposedly typical person of that nationality. The stereotype of a South European in many people's minds is a passionate person, whereas the stereotype of a Scandinavian is of a reserved person. Stereotypes are often grossly inaccurate. Even where they are accurate, however, they inevitably grossly misrepresent the large proportion of deviants from the central tendency in any group. However, it is to some extent impossible to think without stereotyping since in the absence of knowledge (and we often act in the absence of knowledge) the best gambling guess about an individual is to assume that he has the model characteristics of his group. Despite its inevitability, stereotyping has been widely criticized as unfair, as indeed it is if the central tendency is mistaken for a fixed rule. I.d.S.P.

Stevenson, Adlai Ewing.
Born, Los Angeles, February 5, 1900. Democratic candidate for President, 1952, 1956; Chief United States delegate to United Nations, 1961-; Assistant to Secretary of the Navy 1941-44; Advisor, United States delegation to Conference on International Organizations, San Francisco, 1945; Governor of Illinois 1949-1953; Author of several books; lawyer. A.G.

Stimson Doctrine.
A designation given in many contexts to the essence of an utterance by the American government in 1932 in terms of identical Notes to the governments of Japan and of China to the effect that the American government could not admit the legality of any situation and did not intend to recognize any treaty or agreement which might impair the treaty rights of the United States or its citizens, or to recognize any situation, treaty or agreement brought about by means contrary to the provisions of the Pact of Paris (1928).

This designation attributes to Secretary of State Stimson credit for the enunciation of the "doctrine" implicit in the notification. Another designation, the "Hoover Doctrine," attributes to President Hoover that credit.

Regardless of accrediting, the Notes of January 7, 1932 were drafted in the Department of State, and for the principle of non-recognition which is their essence the idea and the pattern were derived from study made of action taken by Secretary of State Bryan in 1915 (of which Stimson makes appropriate mention in his **The Far Eastern Crisis**). St.K.H.

Stipendiary Magistrate.
(United Kingdom).
In certain urban areas, the Justices of the Peace have been replaced by full-time paid magistrates appointed by the crown acting through the Lord Chancellor from the ranks of barristers. They usually sit alone. Increasingly, because of the increased complexity of the law, magistrates have been replacing J. P.'s. C.A.McC.

St. Lawrence Seaway.
A navigable waterway of North America connecting the Great Lakes with the Atlantic Ocean. The waterway, with 15 locks — each 800 feet long, 80 feet wide, and 30 feet deep — has a minimum depth of 27 feet and a length of 2350 miles. Its most recently completed navigation works — along with a related New York-Ontario power project — were constructed

through the cooperative efforts of Canadian and American engineers and were officially opened to ocean-going vessels on June 26, 1959, by Queen Elizabeth and President Dwight D. Eisenhower. W.W.

Stockpiling of strategic materials.

The practice of producing or buying and storing in the continental United States in peacetime raw materials or finished products expected to be in critical supply in the event of war. Examples of stockpiled materials are: lead, copper, aluminum, uranium, titanium, tungsten and other metals, raw materials and ores not sufficiently abundant in the United States to sustain a major war effort; machine tools and plant capacity adequate for the production of airplanes, tanks, ships, electronic equipment, etc., and other implements of war; pharmaceuticals and medical supplies for use in the event of nuclear attack. T.W.

Stocks.

Represent part-ownership in a corporation; thus have no maturity date and profits divided (dividends) are not guaranteed. On the other side they do carry the right to vote for directors and thus the control power over the corporation. In case of liquidation the stockholders have only a residual claim against the remaining assets, after all the other claims have been satisfied. The value of a share of stock fluctuates in response to its prevailing demand in supply on the market, which in turn depend on the profits and earnings of the corporations, as well as on the general business and political situation, and future expectations. W.N.

Stoicism.

Zeno, the founder of stoicism about 300 B.C., taught in a colonnade at Athens, known as a **stoa** from which the philosophy took its name. Being a Persian in a Greek city-state, Zeno was anxious for the Hellenic society to adopt a philosophy that would not exclude foreigners **per se**. He taught that there should be no difference between states or people. All men should be fellow citizens and there should be one life and order based on common law. Men have little need for institutional government, for nature provides the rules by which they should live together. All people, regardless of wealth, social position, or sex, should be considered equal; only moral good or evil should determine differences in value. The best known tenet of stoicism is self-discipline. Emphasis on the willpower of the individual and on the right to exercise one's own moral choice was central to stoic philosophy.

The influence of stoicism had a great effect on the moral and legal thought of Rome. The stoic conception of the common law of nature became the **jus naturale** in Roman jurisprudence, and the influence of the stoic principle of equality caused Roman lawyers to hold that all human beings were equal before the law. In the French Revolution liberty, equality, and fraternity were proclaimed as the universal inheritance of all mankind, and this idea of the free man equal to his fellows and united in a common brotherhood of men was an essential part of Zeno's thought.

D.C.

Stolypin, Peter Arkadievich.

(1863-1911).

A gifted Russian statesman, Stolypin was born in Baden-Baden in 1863, and received his education in St. Petersburg. He was appointed to the post of Minister of Internal Affairs in April 1906, and a few months later, became Chairman of the Council of Ministers. Stolypin is known for his sweeping reforms in Russian agriculture. Russian peasantry freed from serfdom in 1861 was still tied to the village communes, and the majority of peasants did not possess individual farms. Stolypin's decree of Nov. 22, 1906 dissolved the peasants' communes and gave the peasants the right to leave the communes and apply for the individual ownership of a farm. A direct result of Stolypin's reform was that the peasant communes started to disintegrate. 5,000,000 households left the communes by 1913 and applied for their individual allotments. To enable peasants to purchase Crown lands, Stolypin took measures to finance the peasants through the Peasants Bank. His other measures were to encourage the re-settlement of peasants from poor communes in European Russia and to provide them with land in Siberia and the Far East.

In September 1911 his career was abruptly terminated by a bullet from the assassin, M. Bogrov, an agent provocateur. Stolypin was assassinated in a theater in Kiev, during a performance attended by Emperor Nicholas II and other dignitaries. V.P.P.

Strategic Air Command.
A specified combatant command of the United States Air Force, a one-service command, with a line of control from the President through Secretary of Defense direct to Commander, with a mission of being prepared to conduct strategic air operations on a global basis so that, in event of sudden aggression, the command can immediately attack and destroy the vital elements of the aggressor's war-making capabilities, to the extent that he will no longer have the **will or ability** to wage war—a deterrent force to general all-out war. T.W.

Strategic bombing.
The military bombing of selected targets considered by the attacker to be vital to the war-making capability of an adversary nation. Thus, for example, it could include cities — to destroy the enemy's will to fight; ball-bearing factories — to eliminate a basic industry; or intercontinental missile sites — to take out retaliatory capacity. Early advocates of this concept were Giulio Douhet, Italy; Hugh Trenchard, Great Britain; and William Mitchell, United States. Strategic bombing became a part of basic U.S. Air Force doctrine; was applied in World War II with debatable results. H.H.R.

Strategic Intelligence.
Information pertaining to the capabilities, vulnerabilities and probable courses of action (or reaction) of foreign or enemy nations, used in planning national strategy, carrying out national security measures, in conducting foreign policy, or in conducting military operations. Term normally used to denote information needed by high-level policy makers, strategic planners of national governments or general military planning staffs. In an age of total war and Cold War the informational needs of national decision makers are boundless, so that what once might have been considered tactical intelligence can today be of strategic importance. Includes information on military geography; transportation and communication; psychological and sociological factors; subversion, economics, science, armed forces and biographical data. Distinct from tactical (combat) intelligence or counter-intelligence (police) functions. H.H.R.

Strategic materials.
Generic term applied to raw materials and semi-manufactured products indispensable for the successful prosecution of war, especially under modern technological conditions. The availability of strategic materials, or the ability of insuring their supply by stocking, substitution, or other means constitutes a major component of national power. F.M.

Strategy.
The art and science of making general plans for the purposeful, coherent and deliberate use of resources, or any form of power, towards the attainment of specified objectives. Distinguished from **tactics** which refers to execution of strategic plans in an operational sense. Strategy is most commonly used in a military sense, but also in connection with politics, marketing, courtship, etc. Originally, from the Greek, "the art of the general." More recently distinctions are made between "higher," "grand," or "national" strategy and military strategy. Demarcation line between national strategy and military strategy becomes increasingly blurred in an age of an accelerating technology and total war. The "Cold War" has broadened the scope of national strategy to the economic, propagandistic, diplomatic and coalition as well as military fields of governmental activity. Events have also blurred some of the former distinctions between policy and strategy. H.H.R.

Strauss, David Friedrich.
(1808-1874).
Hegelian humanist and critical theologian, noted for his **Life of Jesus**, published in 1835, in which a naturalistic account is offered of biblical history. J.W.Ch.

Straw Vote.
A straw vote is a poll (q.v.) done before an election with the objective of determining how the vote would go were the election held right then. Straw votes have a history going back long before scientific methods of public opinion polling. Candidates used them in the 19th Century to assess their chances. Many straw votes have been conducted with return post cards or by telephone or by street corner interviewing. More reliable straw votes are now regularly conducted by all the major public opinion polling organizations. With the use of scientific sampling they usually anticipate election outcomes closely although it is always possible for the electorate to shift after the straw vote has been taken.
I.d.S.P.

Streicher, Julius.
Hitler's foremost Jew baiter; born February 12, 1885 in Fleinhausen, Bavaria, sentenced to death by the International Military Tribunal in Nuremberg on October 1, 1946 for incitement to murder the Jews of Europe. He had been editor of the Jew-baiting Nazi weekly 'Der Stuermer' and publisher — in Nuremberg — of anti-Jewish books with pornographic slant. In addition he had been Hitler's Gauleader of Franconia where he displayed his psychopathic traits noticeable enough for commitment to an insane asylum in any normal society.
R.M.W.K.

Stresemann, Gustav (1878-1929).
Significant statesman and Foreign Minister of Weimar Republic. Member of Reichstag since 1906. Leader, National-Liberal party, 1917. After advent of Republic leader of (conservative) German People's Party. Chancellor and Foreign Minister, 1923; Foreign Minister until death. Instrumental for Locarno Pact, 1925. Nobel Prize for Peace, 1927.
M.C.V.

Strike.
A concerted stoppage of work by a body of workers usually for the purpose of expressing a grievance or of forcing management to comply with their demands. Government employees in the United States are usually restrained from striking by law, public attitudes, or by the constitutions of civil service unions.
T.S.

Sturzo, Luigi (1871-1959).
Sicilian priest and theoretician of Christian Democracy, Sturzo founded the Popular Party when the papal ban on Catholic political activity in Italy was lifted (1919). Under him, Italy's second-largest party sought political, economic, and social reforms aimed at greater democracy and social justice. Insistence on state recognition of church schools prevented coalition government with other, anti-clerical anti-fascists. In 1924 Fascist pressure on the Church led to his retirement and exile. He was elder statesman and gadfly of the postwar Christian Democrats and was appointed (1952) one of the Republic's lifetime senators.
E.T.O.

Suarez, Francisco. (1548-1617).
The last of the great scholastic philosophers, he ranks with Thomas Aquinas. With his **Tractatus de Legibus ac Deo Legislatore** (1679), he belongs to the founders of modern International Law. He was also among the first Catholic thinkers to expound the notion of consent of the governed which was so popular especially with Protestant thinkers. He opposed not only royal absolutism, but also the doctrine of tyrannicide. He taught theology in Spain as a Jesuit, and his influence on modern neo-scholasticism is considerable.
V.Z.

Subpoena.
A writ or order requiring a witness to appear in court or before a legislative committee. The subpoena may require the witness to bring with him certain specific evidence (documents, papers, etc.).
J.O.H.

Subsidiarity.
The principle of subsidiarity means that the smallest unit of society which can properly perform a given function, should be allowed to do so. A larger organization should not take over a task which can be adequately accomplished at a lower level. Thus, the State should not interfere unless individuals and private groups are unable to perform their work for the general welfare.
Pa.B.

Subsidy.

Refers in its broadest meaning to an infinite variety of loans, grants, and allowances in money or in kind by one governmental unit to another governmental unit or to private or corporate individuals. As commonly used by social scientists in the United States, subsidy means a gift of money or property made by a government to assist an individual or other private party in the establishment or operation of a service, or the production of a commodity deemed beneficial to the public at large. Examples of federal subsidies would include land grants to railroads, financial aid for the construction of merchant marine ships, and guaranteed price supports for agricultural products. G.B.H.

Substantive due process.

A concept in American jurisprudence by which legislation is judicially tested to determine whether it arbitrarily or unreasonably restrains the liberty involved on the grounds of its contents or nature, as distinguished from procedural due process, i.e. the process by which it was enacted or administered. C.W.B.

Substantive rights.

The protection of property rights and vested interests from state police power action or federal social legislation by judicial interpretation of the reasonableness or arbitrariness of the wording of the challenged statutes. Since 1937 the United States judiciary has retreated from such interpretations. B.N.

Succession.

Succession is one of the serious problems confronting any political order. It was much neglected during the Liberal age, because it was generally believed that the forward march of constitutional democracy would provide a universally satisfactory answer. For under a constitution the succession is usually provided "for all times." The rise of totalitarianism has once more highlighted the significance of the issue; with succession unprovided for in these regimes the question of: who will succeed Stalin? or: who will succeed Hitler? was revealed in its cataclysmic potentialities. But even in constitutional regimes, the predominance of a leader such as Roosevelt, Adenauer or de Gaulle helps to focus attention upon the importance of succession. Provisions or traditions of succession are closely linked to the type of regime of which they form a part. Hobbes went so far as to claim that "there is no perfection of government, where the disposing of the Succession is not in the present Sovereign," which is in line with his radical absolutism. Constitutionalism is based upon precisely the opposite notion, namely that good government requires the fixing of the succession by the constitution. Historically considered, we might say on an overall view that succession may be based upon the following five major grounds: (1) charisma, (2) heredity, (3) wealth or some other "objective" possession, (4) election, (5) force. These five types of succession often occur, however, in combinations, such as the hereditary wealthy class in Venice, or the combination of election and force in totalitarian systems. A problem at all levels of government and in all organizations, it is most serious at the apex of the hierarchy. The exclamation: le roi est mort — vive le roi! is symbolic for the universal concern over succession.

Besides the succession of rulers, the succession of "states" is a significant issue; elaborate doctrine has been developed in international law concerning it. The establishment of a new state or a new regime, or the acquisition by an existing state of new territory involve such succession. Derived from Roman Law, the doctrine was introduced by Grotius, but no single principle suffices to deal with the several situations. C.J.F.

Sudan, Republic of (Jamhuryat El-Sudan).

A federal republic in northeast Africa, bordered by Egypt on the north; the Red Sea and Ethiopia on the east; Kenya, Uganda, and the Republic of the Congo on the south; and the Central African Republic, Chad, and Libya on the west. **Area:** 971,450 sq. mi. **Population:** 10,262,674 (1960 U.N. est.). **Capital:** Khartoum (pop. 82,000). **Language:** Arabic. **Religion:** Moslem.

Formerly a land of small kingdoms, the Sudan was alternately controlled by Egypt (1840-85); Britain (1898 and 1924-36); Britain and Egypt, as the

Anglo-Egyptian Condominium (1899-1924 and 1936-53). By unilateral Egyptian action (1953), later agreed to by the British, independence was achieved Jan. 1, 1956. The Sudan joined the Arab League (Jan., 1956) and the United Nations (Nov., 1956).

The federal state consists of 9 provinces and 69 departments. The President of the Supreme Council for the Armed Forces, Lt. Gen. Ibrahim Abboud since 1958, is the head of state. The Council is the highest constitutional authority and possesses law-making power.
N.P.T.

Sudeten Germans.
Name applied after World War I to Germans of Bohemia, Moravia, and Austrian Silesia incorporated in new state of Czechoslovakia. In fall of 1918 S. G.'s, demanding self-determination, set up Austrian provincial governments, which were liquidated by Czech military, who provoked bad feeling by killing 54 unarmed German demonstrators for self-det. on March 4, 1919. Later, parties representing majority of S. G.'s adopted policy of "activism," i.e. co-operation with Czechs, but their demands for regional autonomy and ethnic equality were repulsed. With Hitler in power in Germany, continued refusal of concessions by Prague drove many S. G.'s into Henlein's nationalist S. G. Party, which eventually came under National Socialist domination. An anti-totalitarian movement led by the Social Democrats Ernst Paul and Wenzel Jaksch fought Nazism in the Sudetenland until its annexation by Germany; its leaders, in exile during World War II, attempted to secure reconciliation with the Czechs. Benes, however, had decided to reannex the Sudetenland and expel the S. G.'s to Germany, which was done with great brutality and many casualties in 1945 and 1946. The S. G.'s in the Federal Republic have formed the **Sudetendeutsche Landsmannschaft** and the **Sudetendeutscher Rat,** bodies which assert the **Heimatrecht** (right of return) of the S. G.'s while seeking a federal relationship with the Czechs and other peoples of Central Europe.
K.G.

Suez Canal. See Appendix.

Suffrage.
The privilege of participating in the determination of political matters submitted to the electroate; voting. As suffrage is regulated by legal enactments, it is not an inherent right.
C.W.B.

Sugar Act (1764).
British statute (for revenue, trade restrictions) imposing duty on sugar, molasses, etc. imported by American Colonies from foreign plantations of West Indies.
R.F.H.

Sukarno, Achmed. (Soekarno). (1901-).
The Indonesian leader, who became the first President of the Indonesian Republic. Sukarno was born in 1901 in Surabaya, on the Island of Java, and received his education at the Bandung Institute of Technology, where he received a degree in Civil Engineering. He began his political activity while still at the Institute, and was one of the original founders and chairman of the Nationalist Party of Indonesia. After completing school, he was very active in the anti-Dutch movement and in 1928 was arrested by the Dutch authorities. In 1932 after his release from prison, he became chairman of the new Indonesian Party, founded on the basis of the old Nationalist Party. He was again arrested in 1933 and exiled to Flores Island, from which he was transferred to Southern Sumatra in 1938, where he remained until 1942, when he was released by the Japanese, during World War II. Sukarno actively collaborated with the Japanese occupation authorities, allegedly with his nationalist interests in mind. After the defeat of Japan, Sukarno's adherents declared Indonesia's independence on August 17, 1945, and he became the first president of the country. On April 18, 1955 he opened the Bandung Conference of Asian and African countries, playing the role of a neutralist and independent leader. In 1957 internal strife forced Sukarno to embark on a new "guided democracy" policy, in which the presidential power became stronger with closer governmental supervision over political parties.
V.P.P.

Summitry as an Instrument of Diplomacy.
Summitry refers to meetings of heads

of state or government for the resolution of issues that have defied their subordinates or emissaries. Historically, such meetings were ceremonial, with such notable exceptions as the Congress of Vienna, Versailles, and, one war later, Casablanca, Cairo, Quebec, Yalta and Potsdam.

With the discredited 1955 Summit, the unedifying spectacle of the 1959 General Assembly, and the torpedoed May 1961 meeting, has come a reversion to move conventional levels of diplomacy, punctuated by such mutual feeling-out exercises as the 1961 Kennedy-Khrushchev meeting in Vienna and the urgent exchanges in the 1962 Cuban crisis. L.P.B.

Summons.

A judicial order served by an authorized officer, requiring a person (usually a defendant) to appear in court. The summons must state the purpose for which one is expected to appear.

J.O.H.

Sun, Yat-sen (1866-1925).

Founder of the Republic of China. Dr. Sun Yat-sen was born in Canton Province in South China. He attended schools in Hawaii and Hong Kong, where he acquired a degree in medicine. Believing that China was in danger of being colonized by the World Powers, he joined several others in an attempt to introduce drastic political-social reforms in China. When convinced that the Manchu Government would not accept these reforms, he began to agitate for revolution. He traveled abroad, lectured on the need of China, and solicited support for his cause. In 1911 his supporters successfully staged a revolution, and China became a republic. Soon after the Revolution China became divided with many warlords exercising control over different parts of the country. Discouraged by these events Dr. Sun decided to organize a military force of his own in Canton. But before trying to unite the country by force he made a last attempt to solicit voluntary cooperation among its many factions. He died in Peking in 1925. His doctrines are embodied in the book **Three People's Principles** (nationalism, democracy, and economic well being). W.C.C.

Sunakawa Case.

A legal controversy in Japan arising from the arrest of demonstrators opposing the enlargement of an American air base at Sunakawa, near Tokyo. The Tokyo District Court determined that under Article 9 of the Japanese Constitution, which renounces war and armament, the U.S.-Japan Security Treaty of 1951 was unconstitutional and therefore invalid. The issue was immediately appealed to the Japanese Supreme Court, which unanimously found that the Security Treaty was constitutional, but did not rule on a more controversial subject, the disputed constitutionality of Japan's Self-Defense Forces. The Court also asserted that unless a treaty is "obviously unconstitutional and void, it falls outside the purview of the power of review granted to the court." T.Mc.N.

Sunnis (Sunnites).

Followers of the orthodox **Sunna**, or path, of the Koran and the Prophetic tradition. Originally, the term was applied to the general body of 'orthodox' Muslims who adhered to the 'usage of the Community' as it developed in diverging directions after the Muslim conquests. Theologians later maintained that the term Sunna could be properly used only of the usage set by Muhammad himself, either in the form of definite prescription or prohibition or by example. Their opponents, the Shi'ites, gave the same allegiance to the Sunna of the Prophet, but held the subsequent conduct of the Community to have been illegal. Unlike Shi'ism, Sunnism believes in the validity of the historic caliphate and rejects the notion that the **Imam** is the mediator of the Muhammadan revelation without whom its relevance cannot be known. According to Sunni political theory, the Caliph is preeminently a political functionary, a guardian of the divine law, but he is in no sense an authority in doctrine. Unlike the Sunni Caliph, the Shi'ite **Imam** is the leader and teacher of Islam by virtue of personal qualities given to him by God. He is the heir of the Prophet's Ministry. All differences between Sunnism and Shi'ism originated from their different understandings of the role of leader of the Islamic politico-religious community. The majority of Muslims are Sunnites. F.M.N.

Superintendent of Public Instruction.
Administrative officer for a state school system in the U.S.A., elected in almost half the fifty states and appointed in others — most often by a governing board for a department of education but sometimes by the Governor with the State Senate or both houses confirming. Duties are numerous, generally of a supervisory nature in relation to local schools. Educational standards may be established by an administrative board and put into effect through the various offices working under the Superintendent.
Sp.D.A.

Supervisor.
Official title of a member of the general governing board in some counties and townships. In county government, the term is commonly restricted to members of boards originally elected as township supervisors who sit on the county board in an ex officio capacity.
G.S.B.

Supranational.
The term "supranational" has been used to characterize certain organizations, particularly the European Coal and Steel Community, which have gone beyond the traditional international organizations in their exercise of powers over national governments. The organs of supranational organizations are more independent from national governments than the organs of international organizations, and their sphere of jurisdiction is more penetrating and concrete. The supranational executive has direct authority over private individuals, including the power of taxation, while the supranational court enjoys compulsory jurisdiction over states and individuals. H.L.M.

Supreme Commander for the Allied Powers (SCAP).
The title held by General of the Army Douglas MacArthur from the beginning of the Allied occupation of Japan in September, 1945, until his dismissal in April, 1951, when he was succeeded by General Matthew Ridgway, who served as SCAP until the end of the occupation on April 28, 1952, when the Japanese Peace Treaty became effective. The Moscow Conference of Foreign Ministers of December, 1945, set up the eleven-power Far Eastern Commission and the four-power Allied Council of Japan to formulate Allied occupation policy. However, the United States held a veto power in the former and the latter was reduced to a purely advisory role, so that American policy, as interpreted by General MacArthur, prevailed during most of the occupation. T.Mc.N.

Supreme Court of Judicature.
The Judiciary Acts of 1873-75 carried out the task of reorganizing and simplifying the complex and bewildering systems of courts in Great Britain. The Supreme Court of Judicature consists of two branches, the Court of Appeals and the High Court of Justice. The upper branch of the Supreme Court of Judicature is the Court of Appeal, a bench composed of eight Lord Justices of Appeal and over which the Master of the Rolls presides. Its jurisdiction includes the power to hear appeals in **civil** matter only. A Quorum for the Court of Appeals is three judges, but it is possible for more than three divisions to sit simultaneously as the Lord Chancellor may require any High Court Judge to sit in the Court of Appeals if necessary. A parallel court to the Court of Appeals is the Court of Criminal Appeal which, as its name implies, is authorized to hear **criminal** cases on appeal from the courts of Assizes or Quarter Sessions. This court is composed of the Lord Chief Justice of England and Judges from the Queen's Bench Division of the High Court of Justice. A quorum is three judges, but more may sit provided there is an uneven number of judges presiding. C.A.McC.

Supreme Court of Northern Ireland.
See Northern Ireland — Supreme Court.

Supreme Soviet (Council) of the U.S.S.R.
Described by the 1936 Constitution as "the highest organ of state power," it consists of two chambers with equal rights and powers, the Soviet of the Union and the Soviet of Nationalities, each elected for four years. Meets regularly for approximately one week,

twice each year. Extraordinary sessions may be called. Almost 1400 deputies. Sometimes called the Soviet Parliament. Although it has the constitutional right to exercise exclusive legislative power, in reality it performs little original legislating. Most laws are initiated by the Party and issued as legislative decrees by the Presidium of the Supreme Soviet or as orders by the Council of Ministers. Subsequently they are ratified by the Supreme Soviet, usually by a unanimous vote. K.Hu.

Suslov, Mikhail.

Born 1902, Shakhovskoe, Saratov Province, now Ulyanovsk Oblast. Joined CP 1921. Graduated 1928 Plekhanov Institute of National Economy, Moscow; taught at Moscow University. Party Control Commission 1930's; Central Committee since 1941. Succeeded Zhdanov as Cominform head in 1948, led ouster of Tito. Editor **Pravda** 1949-50. Member of Party Presidium since 1955. Presidium USSR Supreme Soviet 1950-54; reelected to Supreme Soviet in 1962. Appeared in Budapest during suppression of Hungarian revolt 1956. W.A.

Swan Islands Controversy.

Honduras claims the small islands of Great Swan and Little Swan some 110 miles north of the Honduran coast, although only United States interests have occupied them and engaged in commercial exploitation (insignificant; originally guano). The United States alleges discovery plus continuous possession since 1857. Honduras maintains that the islands were originally discovered, mapped and controlled by Spain. Honduras' title derives from the application of the controversial principle of **uti possidetis** of 1821, i.e., all territory administered by Spain through the Kingdom of Guatemala at the time of the colonies' break passed automatically to the Central American Federation; when Honduras became independent in 1839, she succeeded similarly to certain territory, including Swan Islands. With the establishment on Great Swan of "Radio Swan" in 1960 (to oppose the Castro dictatorship in Cuba) the nationalist, anti-**yanqui** issue was seized upon by pro-Castro elements in the entire region. In Honduras the dispute became so sensitive and distorted that rational settlement became impossible. R.D.H.

Swaraj.

Self-government; self-determination; independence; government by the consent of the people. It was proclaimed in 1921 to be the goal of the Indian National Congress (q.v.). Subsequently, the goal became **purna swaraj** (complete independence) rather than Dominion Status within the British Commonwealth. C.S.S.

Sweden.

With an area of 173,649 square miles Sweden has a population of 7,495,129 (November, 1960), or a density of 43.2 per square mile. Ancestors of present Swedes lived in Sweden at least 5,000 years ago, although the earliest historical mention of Sweden was in Tacitus's GERMANIA (98 A.D.). Olaf Skottkonung established a Christian stronghold in Sweden in the late 10th century. Then in 1397 an initial union was made with Norway. Christian II of Denmark conquered Sweden in 1520, and the "Stockholm Blood-Bath" followed. Gustavus Vasa (1523-1560) broke from Denmark and created the modern Swedish state. Sweden, active in the Thirty Years' War, obtained western Pomerania and some neighboring territory on the Baltic by the Treaty of Westphalia (1648). In the eighteenth century Sweden was forced to relinquish Livonia, Ingria, Estonia, and parts of Finland after Russia, Poland, and Denmark united against her.

Sweden gained Norway from Denmark in the Napoleonic wars, and also emerged with a new royal dynasty stemming from Marshal Bernadotte of France who became Swedish king Charles XIV (1818-1844). The union with Norway was dissolved in 1905. Sweden remained neutral in the first and second world wars and follows a policy of neutrality in the Cold War.

A constitutional monarchy, Sweden's fundamental laws are: The constitution of June 6, 1809; the Parliamentary Act of June 22, 1866 (modified in 1902, 1921, 1949); the law of Royal Succession of September 26, 1810; and the Law on the Freedom of the Press of April 5, 1949. Parliamentary government as finally established in 1917 has a Diet of two chambers. The first (Forsta Kammaren) consists of 151 members elected by provincial and municipal councils for eight years; the second chamber (Andra Kammaren) has 232 members popularly elected for four years. Election to both chambers is proportional and regulated by special law.

Executive power is in the hands of the king, who must be a member of the Lutheran Church. He acts under the advice of a Council of State, the head of which is the Prime Minister. Public administration is characterized by an unusual amount of decentralization. The administration of justice is entirely independent of the executive and legislative arms. The kingdom has a Supreme Court of Judicature and is divided into six high court districts and 159 district court divisions.   C.B.C.

Switzerland.
41,295 square kilometers. 5,429,000 inhabitants (1950). Capital: Bern. A federal State consisting of 25 Cantons. In 14 Cantons the language is German, in 3 French, in one Italian, in 3 German and French, in one German, Italian and Rhaeto-Romansch. In 1950, 3,400,000 inhabitants spoke German, 957,000 French, 279,000 Italian and 49,000 Rhaeto-Romansch. In linguistically mixed Cantons no language is given a privileged position. Under the Federal Constitution German, French, Italian and Rhaeto-Romansch are "national" languages. The official languages of the Federal State, however, are German, French and Italian. 57% of the population are Protestants, 41% Roman Catholics. 31% work in industry, 21% in agriculture, the rest in other occupations, among which the hotel industry is of particular importance. To grant asylum from political persecution is an old Swiss tradition. During World War II, Switzerland granted asylum to about 300,000 political refugees.

Switzerland, with the exception of the short period from 1798-1803, was from its beginnings in 1291 up to 1848 a confederacy. The present federal Constitution dates from 1874. The structure of this federal State rests upon the principle of an extensive decentralization. Administrative authority rests mainly with the Cantons, each of which has its own parliament and government. (In five **Landsgemeinde** Cantons the annual open air meeting of all citizens exercises the main functions of a parliament). The question of how to distribute governmental powers between the Cantons and the federal State constitutes the main political problem in Switzerland. Federal law supersedes cantonal law. Cantonal laws which contradict the federal Constitution or statutes are invalid.

The Federal Assembly, the federal parliament, consists of two houses, the National Council and the Council of States. The National Council consists of 200 members and is elected by the people on the basis of proportional representation. The Council of States represents the Cantons. Nineteen "full" Cantons delegate two representatives each, six "half" Cantons delegate but one representative. The procedure of electing State Councillors and their terms of office are decided by the Cantons. For the making of federal laws the consent of both houses is required.

The federal government is called the Federal Council. It consists of seven members, elected by the Federal Assembly for four years. Each Federal Councillor administers a federal department. The chairman is called Federal President. Both he and the vice chairman are elected by the Federal Assembly for one year. Head of State is the Federal Council in corpore, not the Federal President. Switzerland has no parliamentary system of government. The Federal Council cannot be overthrown by a vote of non-confidence in the Federal Assembly.

The federal Constitution can be changed only through a consenting majority of both the voters and the Cantons. Direct democracy in federal affairs is provided for by the rights of referendum and of initiative. The right of referendum, i.e. of a national vote on federal laws, is facultative. It depends upon a demand made by at least 30,000 voters or eight cantonal governments. Treaties concluded for a duration of more than 15 years or without fixed duration are also subject to the right of referendum. Through the right of initiative constitutional law only can be made, not statutory law. The complete revision of the Constitution or specific amendments thereto may be proposed in petitions bearing at least 50,000 voters' signatures.

As early as the beginning of the 16th century Switzerland chose and ever since has adhered to **permanent neutrality** as the guiding principle of her foreign policy. Only once, during the Napoleonic wars, was Switzerland unable to enforce her neutrality. As a permanently neutral State Switzerland is not a member of the United Nations.

The main political parties in the National Council in 1959 were: Liberals 51; Catholic Conservatives 47; Social Democrats 51; Farmers 23; Independents (Liberals promoting the interests of consumers) 10.

The Swiss State rests not upon a common language but on political ideas evolved in the course of Swiss history: far going democracy, good fellowship and fruitful collaboration among different linguistic groups and peaceful neutrality within the family of nations.
F.G.

Sykes-Picot Agreement.

Is a secret understanding among Britain, France and Russia for the partition of the Ottoman Empire. The agreement was finalized by exchange of eleven letters in the summer and fall of 1916. France was to have a strong hand in the coastal areas of Syria and Lebanon. Britain was to have a strong hand in Palestine and Iraq. Russia was to control northeastern Anatolia. An independent Arab state or a confederation of Arab states were to be recognized in the region where the allies did not make claims. Though the Agreement was not strictly adhered to, it had greatly influenced the post-war political frontiers in the Fertile Crescent. E.A.S.

Symbol.

A symbol is the conventionalized sign of some person, object, event, idea or relationship. In ideographic or pictographic languages, the symbolic unit is a picture. In mathematical language, letters and numbers (and conventional marks denoting relationships among the letters and numbers) are the symbols. In verbal languages, the symbolic units are words — phonetic and phonemic arrangements of letters whose meanings are conventionalized by usage and stabilized by dictionaries and grammars.

In an older usage, antedating the emphasis on referential symbolism of modern linguistics, the allusive characteristic of symbols was stressed. The symbol, in this usage, was assigned "deeper and broader meanings" than its purely referential function. This usage persists in such contemporary utterances as, for example, "De Gaulle is the symbol of France!" D.L.

Symington, Stuart.

Born June 26, 1901; U.S. Senate from November 4, 1952 until term ending January 3, 1965; Democrat — Missouri; Assistant Secretary of War for Air; Secretary of the Air Force.
R.A.B.

Syndicalism.

A movement of labor unions, at one time particularly strong in France, Spain, and Italy, favoring "direct action" by sabotage, boycott, and the "general strike" which was to lead to the socialization of the means of production. J.D.

Syndicat.

A term sometimes used to describe a French labor union; French syndicalism traditionally advocates making labor unions the foundation of the economic system. E.G.L.

Synthetic.

A proposition is synthetic if it **adds** something to the meaning of a given term or proposition that cannot be analytically deducted from it." All men are mortal" is a s. proposition unless the condition of death had been incorporated in the definition of "man." Any s. proposition is subject to scientific challenge on the ground that it has been or will be falsified by experience (pre-arranged tests or unarranged occurrences) or that it is incapable of being either verified or falsified. Classical rationalism assumed that some synthetic propositions are certain to be absolutely true independently of all experience (a priori). Kant reduced the vague generality of this doctrine in his **Critique of Pure Reason**, but still maintained it for a few types of s. statements. Mathematical operations, to which he and others referred in this context, are not synthetic, however, as he believed, but purely analytic. The few synthetic basic postulates of

511

mathematics are not a priori absolutely true but either based on experience (classical geometry, the practical necessity of counting, etc.) or arbitrary (and in this case either useful or useless). A few borderline questions are still open to controversy. A.B.

Syria.

Physical and Economic Life: Boundaries: North — Turkey; East — Iraq; South — Jordan; West — Israel, Lebanon and Mediterranean Sea. Population: 4,839,237. Area: 72,000 square miles. Narrow fertile coastal strip, abundant rainfall, bounded by Lebanon mountains from which increasingly arid land slopes eastward, part steppe, part desert, cut by Euphrates Valley, where there is irrigation. Country thus one-third desert and mountains, one-third suitable for nomads, one-third cultivable. Agriculture: Olives, soft fruit, cotton, tobacco, cereals, stock-raising — all exportable, including wool and hair. Industry — major: textiles, cement, sugar refining, vegetable oil, glass, pipe lines, small oil refining. Ethnic base: mixed — Nomads, a Mediterranean type; also Armenoids, Druse. Language — Arabic, Kurdish, Aramaic. Religion: Muslim, Christian. History: In Ancient period Syria was subject to immigration of Canaanites, Phoenicians — 3rd millennium; Hebrews, Armenians — 2nd; nomads from Arabia, Egyptians, Assyrians, Hittites, Persians, Greeks invaded until conquest by Rome in 1st century B.C., which was succeeded by Byzantine-Greek Empire and the Arab conquest, 6th century A.D. Arabic became official language and new Umayyad dynasty replaced Byzantine bureaucracy with Syrian Muslims and Christians. Syria became presently heart of Arab Empire but for ensuing 200 years turned into pawn of Arab politics as Abbasid rulers succeeded Umayyads and transferred imperial capital to Iraq. Struggle for Syria swayed between Baghdad and Cairo. In 10th century Byzantines temporarily regained control in North; in 11th the Seljuq Turks secured a temporary hold. The next 200 years is the story of crusaders; at close the Egyptian Mamluks fought the Mongols, finally repelling them in 1303. During Mamluk rule conditions declined and did not improve greatly under direct Ottoman control (from 1516); office holding was by bribery and exercise of office by extortionate taxation. Temporary Egyptian control in 19th century saw beginning of modern administration until ended by intervention of Great Powers. Nationalism increased and Syria demanded independence at close of World War One, being denied freedom as France secured mandate control lasting until World War Two and the establishment of an independent republic. Subsequent events have been the ill-fated Egyptian union and coup d'etats of 1961 and 1962. J.V.D.

Systems theory in international politics.

Oriented to theoretical — not descriptive — models of international politics. Abstracts from historical reality a small set of key variables which are then related theoretically. These variables include the number of actors, type of actors, style of behavior, motivation, and economic and military variables. Variations of the variables produce different kinds of international systems, e.g., "balance of power," loose bipolar, tight bipolar, universal, hierarchical, and unit veto, international systems. Variations in boundary conditions produce a transformation from one type of system to another. Specification of key boundary conditions permits engineering the systems to historic specificity. M.A.K.

T

Tactical Air Command.
A unified combatant command of the United States Air Force with a mission to provide fast-reacting, combat-ready tactical air power for employment anywhere in the world on short notice to operate unilaterally or in concert with other military forces in support of both strategic and defensive operations — a deterrent force for limited wars. T.W.

Tactics.
(1) Methods designed to achieve a given objective; (2) that part of the art of war which is determined primarily by local military factors, embracing the theory and practice of fighting battles, cooperation between units, the use of various arms on the battlefield, the disposition of troops and the execution of their movements. A distinction has been made between grand tactics, the concern of commanders, and minor tactics, the concern of lower ranks. The objective of military tactics is to defeat the enemy with minimum losses. Tactics is distinguished from strategy, which is wider in scope and requires consideration of political, economic, additional military and other factors. Etymologically, strategy means "the art of generalship" (from the Greek **strategus**). It is the planning of a war as a whole, including the direction and coordination of campaigns, the distribution of armies and many other aspects. The meanings of 'tactics' and 'strategy' overlap to some extent. Jomini, the noted 19th-century French military theorist, placed 'grand strategy' as lying between policy and strategy, and 'grand tactics' between strategy and tactics. Currently, the term 'operational strategy' is used with reference to the distribution of larger units (corps and divisions) before battle. Tactics and strategy are distinguished from 'logistics,' the term invented by Jomini to cover problems of moving, quartering and supplying troops. Waging wars being comparable to the struggle for social control, by analogy the term "tactics" is applicable to political processes. W.J.S.

Taft, Robert Alphonso (1889-1953).
Son of William Howard Taft, 26th President of the United States, graduated from Yale-1910 and Harvard Law School-1913. Served in Ohio Legislature 1921-1926; 1931-1932. Elected to the U.S. Senate in 1938, Robert A. Taft soon became known as an outstanding expert on financial affairs. In 1947, together with Representative Fred A. Hartley, he sponsored the Taft-Hartley Labor Act, also known as the Labor-Management Relations Act, which qualified and amended much of the National Labor Relations Act of 1935. Among other things, the Taft-Hartley Act provided that a union or an employer must give notice to the other party before terminating a collective bargaining agreement, it gave the Federal Government power to obtain an eighty-day injunction against any strike which could be said to endanger national health or safety, it outlawed the closed shop, limited the union shop agreement to one year and prohibited jurisdictional strikes and secondary boycotts.

Known in his later years as "Mr. Republican," Robert A. Taft was a contender for the Presidential nomination of the Republican Party in 1936, 1940, 1948 and 1952. While he advocated isolationism in the post-First World War period, he backed the U.S. war effort in World War Two and U.S. participation in the U.N. Widely admired for his personal and political integrity, he is frequently quoted as an example for the qualities befitting a Congressional lawmaker. J.D.

Taft, William Howard. (1857-1930).
President of the United States from 1908 to 1912 and Chief Justice of the United States from 1921 to 1930. Taft was one of the two Presidents in the first six decades of the twentieth century to receive only one term when, in 1912, the Republican Party he headed was split by the defection of the "Bull Moosers," thus making possible the election of the Democratic candidate, Woodrow Wilson. As Chief Justice of the United States, Taft presided over a Supreme Court that was notable for the conservative views of a majority of its members in matters of social and economic policy. E.L.

Tai Ping Rebellion.
A tragic episode in China in which, a hundred years ago, there was given a demonstration of what can come of a combination of a fanatical effort on the part of a self-confident personality and eagerness on the part of the masses of humanity to believe in and follow a leader who proclaims a gospel of Heaven on Earth.

A young man who had repeatedly failed to pass the state examinations, gained a smattering knowledge of Christianity, began to talk about a Heavenly Kingdom, and soon gained enough followers to launch a "movement" directed toward seizure by himself and his aides of temporal and spiritual authority. Half-hearted efforts on the part of the Manchu government to quash this movement were defeated, and before long the Tai Pings had produced an armed force which advanced upon and took the city of Nanking. Thereafter, for a period of twelve years, there was fighting between the Tai Ping forces and government forces, in the course of which innumerable atrocities were inflicted upon the populace and large areas in southern China were devastated. When in 1860, Shanghai was threatened by the rebels, an American private citizen, Frederick T. Ward, organized an armed force and in several encounters defeated the rebel forces. In his command of "The Ever Victorious Army" Ward was succeeded first by another American, Burgevine, and, in 1863, by a British officer, Charles George Gordon (later Gordon of Khartoum). Gordon, given support by the Imperial Government, defeated rebel forces repeatedly and disposed of most of them. The rebels held out in Nanking until, in July 1864, they were defeated there, many of their leaders were executed, and their anointed ruler committed suicide. Finally, in 1865, the great Chinese Viceroy Tseng Kuo-fan destroyed the last of them.

The "Heavenly Kingdom" had at no time had any close resemblance to a Christian regime. The movement had at the outset given some promise of bringing about reforms and achieving political and economic improvements, but in its late years it degenerated into a savage tyranny. It left nothing but a record of countless deaths, widespread destruction, and long-persisting devasation. St.K.H.

"Taking the Fifth Amendment."
A journalistic term for a witness's refusal on the ground of possible self-incrimination to answer a question asked him by a court, legislative investigating committee or other authority. The privilege against self-incrimination is based, as far as federal inquiries are concerned, on the clause of the Fifth Amendment to the United States Constitution that stipulates that no person "shall be compelled in any criminal case to be a witness against himself." The term "taking the Fifth Amendment" came into use with reference to witnesses before state as well as before federal authorities in the 1950's, when congressional and state legislative investigating committees subpoenaed hundreds of witnesses suspected of present or past membership in or association with the Communist party. A witness's refusal to answer a question was seldom excused unless he claimed his constitutional privilege against incrimination. Any one who consequently "took the Fifth Amendment" was widely regarded as having admitted Communist affiliations. M.Sp.

Talleyrand-Perigord, Charles-Maurice de (1754-1838).
Prince de Benevent, French statesman and diplomat. An aristocrat of ancient lineage, he supported the Revolution; as Bishop of Autun, champion of the Civil Constitution of the Clergy, Minister of Foreign Affairs under the Directory (1797), he intrigued against it. Foreign Minister of the Consulate and Empire (until 1807), Talleyrand, clairvoyant or bending before the storm, prepared the end of Napoleon I. He represented France at the Congress of Vienna and by his principles of legitimacy made his defeated country the equal of the victors. After 1815 he gradually opposed the Bourbons, participated in the Revolution of 1830 and as French envoy in England brought about the **entente cordiale.** Counseling political moderation, he exercised little restraint in private life. Talleyrand was a diplomat who by his brilliant wit and fulsome flattery manipulated men and

events, surviving them all with imperturbable self-control. K.B.

Tanaka Memorial.
A memorial purportedly written by Prime Minister (Baron) Tanaka of Japan and supposedly presented to the Emperor in the course of or following an important conference on Far Eastern affairs between June 27, and July 7, 1927. All important military and civil officials concerned with the topic attended. The memorial was reputed to represent the results of this conference, and was first published by the Chinese in 1929. Doubt exists as to whether such a memorial ever was presented to the Emperor, and there is some question as to whether it was a working paper or even a skillful forgery. It may be considered, however, a good summary of opinions which took hold in Japan in the late 1920's and which were to dominate during the following decade.

The memorial briefly summarized the strategic advantages of possession by Japan of Mongolia and Manchuria. It warned of the increasing restiveness of the Chinese officials in the Three Eastern Provinces, the threat of Chinese industrial competition in that area, and the implications of the Nine Power Treaty which limited Japanese rights in the region. It was pointed out that Manchuria was also important to Japan for raw materials and as an outlet for excess population. The U.S. and Great Britain were shown as attempting to displace Japan in China and establish themselves as colonial powers. The memorial advocated a "positive policy" toward Manchuria. By a policy of "blood and iron" Japan was to enlarge her rights in Manchuria and China, and using these as a base establish her preeminence over all of Eastern Asia with nothing to fear from the Western Powers. The penetration by Japan was to begin with Manchuria.

In 1929, unable to control the military, Tanaka's government fell. S.S.

Taney, Roger Brooke. (1777-1864).
Chief Justice of the United States from 1836 to 1864. Although Taney did not diminish the supremacy of the Federal Constitution and laws nor the security of property as established by the decisions of the Marshall Court, his constitutional philosophy permitted somewhat freer scope for state actions not in direct conflict with explicit Federal law. The slavery question complicated many of the cases in the Taney Court, and split the judges into dissident factions. Perhaps the most notorious of these was **Dred Scott v. Sanford** (1857) which was eventually reversed by the Fourteenth Amendment to the United States Constitution, in the clause making all persons born in the United States and subject to the jurisdiction thereof, citizens of the United States and of the state wherein they reside. E.L.

Tanganyika.
A republic in southeast Africa; area 361,800 square miles; population 9,238,-000 (1960 estimate), of which over 98% is African. A German colony prior to 1918, it was made a League of Nations mandate with Great Britain as the administering power, and in 1946 it became a United Nations trust territory with Great Britain as trustee. A Legislative Council was set up in 1926 but Africans were not elected to it until 1958. Tanganyika achieved independence within the Commonwealth on December 9, 1961, with Julius Nyerere, leader of the multi-racial Tanganyika African National Union, as the first Prime Minister. The next year it became a republic, with Nyerere as popularly elected President. In the future, under the present constitution, the President will be elected by the National Assembly, candidates for which are expected to announce, prior to their election, their choice for the presidency.
E.V.M.

Tannu Tuva.
The Tuvinians, a Turkish-speaking people, have long been closely associated with the Mongols. Up until a generation ago Mongolian was their literary language. In 1960, about 50,000 lived in the Tuvinian Autonomous Oblast (formerly the Republic of Tannu Tuva), on the Mongolian border east of the Atlai Mountains. It is estimated — no accurate census figures having been published — that several thousands are settled in the People's Republic of Outer Mongolia.

The region of Tannu Tuva is largely mountainous, but there is sufficient grassland suitable for large scale cattle raising. The Chinese and Russians long contended for the domination of Tannu Tuva. Annexed by Russia in 1914, the country, given independence after the Bolshevik revolution, tended to gravitate toward Outer Mongolia. The Soviet regime, seeking to counter this secessionist trend, placed Moscow-trained communists in control of Tuvinian affairs. A Tuvinian alphabet with Latin and, later, Cyrillic letters was devised; newspapers, which had formerly been published in Mongolian, were converted to Tuvinian. In 1944 the Republic of Tannu Tuva was incorporated into the Soviet Union.

R.St.-H.

Taoism.

Founded by Lao Tzu in sixth century, B.C., Taoism flourishes among Chinese communities. An essentially passive philosophy, it maintains that one universal principle, the Tao, is the origin and essence of all which exists. The political implications of Taoism are evident in the principle of **wu-wei**, stating that forces of nature should not be manipulated, but should be allowed to work themselves out. Taoist metaphysics, ethics and philosophy are contained in **Tao Teh Ching**, a compilation attributed to Lao Tzu. In its most popular manifestations, Taoism has survived as a dominantly mystical and superstition-laden religion. The Communist Chinese regime has sought to obliterate Taoism, partially because of its apparent traditional relationship with Chinese secret societies. S.K.A.

Tariff.

Used as a general term the word tariff means a schedule of rates or charges. A customs tariff is a duty levied on imports or exports when they pass the border of a political unit, although modern usage normally refers to import exactions alone. Customs duties may be of the **ad valorem** (according to the value) variety, or specific charges based on some unit of measurement, i.e., pound, gallon, yard, etc., or a combination of the two. Tariffs may be levied primarily for revenue, to protect domestic industries, or as a retaliatory measure against the trade policies of another nation. G.B.H.

Tariff protection.

Frequently a primary purpose of tariffs, i.e., customs duties, has been to afford protections of various types to domestic producers whether private or governmental. One common justification for a protective tariff is to shelter a newly-developing industry from more efficient foreign competition. High tariffs may enable a domestic industry to gain a larger profit in the domestic market long after the original purpose of protection during the development stage of the industry has been served. Anti-dumping duties may be levied to protect a domestic producer from unfair foreign competition. Protective tariffs may be so high as to be prohibitive, a type sometimes employed to assure continued high revenues from the sale of items produced by governmental monopolies. G.B.H.

Tawney, Richard Henry (1880-).

An intellectual leader of British socialism, Tawney wrote **The Acquisitive Society** (1921) which many regard also as a classic of English literature. This volume defines industry as "nothing more mysterious than a body of men associated in various degrees of competition and co-operation, to win their livelihood by providing the community with some service which it requires." While the function of industry is "service," under capitalism legal property concepts have developed which make possible income and power without service. This "functionless property" is "the greatest enemy of legitimate property." He proposes that industry be subject to public and democratic control. R.W.T.

Tax Abatement.

Tax abatement is the procedure for forgiving the non-payment of certain taxes and excusing the delinquent taxpayer for his neglect or inability to pay. Real property taxes remaining a first lien upon the property involved, tax abatement ordinarily applies only to capitation taxes and personal property taxes. At a prescribed time each year a statutory, ex-officio body in the local government involved meets and is presented with a list of the delinquent taxpayers. The board, after deliberation, proceeds to cancel the taxes of those who are known to be truly poor, or who have had extraordinary financial disasters. The board also cancels taxes which are non-paid for a fixed period, usually seven years, by persons who have left the community, or who have died without sufficient estate to pay taxes due. In a very few cases the board will abate taxes for low income delinquents who are so far in arrears that they can never pay the back taxes and penalties without pauperizing themselves. These procedures clear the town tax rolls. A.E.N.

Tax Immunity.

The principle of intergovernmental tax immunity in the United States, by which the concurrent taxing powers of the national and state governments are denied exercise against each other, derives from the concept of federalism as a system of dual sovereignties. The immunity of national instrumentalities from state taxation was established by **McCulloch v. Maryland** (1819), wherein Chief Justice Marshall coupled the proposition that "the power to tax involves the power to destroy" to the constitutional design of national supremacy in case of conflict with state power. Subsequently the immunity principle was given reciprocal effect, and broad application, reaching even to exempt the salaries of state employees from federal income taxes and vice versa. The judicial tendency since the late 1930's, however, has been to restrict the sphere of immunity to the possessions, institutions and activities of the governments proper and, with respect to the states, to only those activities deemed essential. R.H.S.

Taxpayer's Suit.

An action by a member of the public to counsel or to restrain official action, on the grounds that his interest as a taxpayer is affected. In the U.S.A. taxpayer's suits are not available as a means of attack on federal statutes. Some of the states specifically recognize the taxpayer's standing in court though in a few states the taxpayer's suit is available only against municipal and other local officials but not against state officials. F.H.H.

Taylor, John. (1753-1824).

American statesman and political theorist. A Virginia planter, member of its Bar, sometime legislator in his State and in the United States Senate (where he served at three different periods but never for a full term) and prolific author, Taylor was both a prominent advocate and leading philosopher of Jeffersonianism. In numerous works he championed an agrarian liberalism against the Hamiltonian vision of a rising industrial, capitalist nation and defended strict-constructionist, states-rights constitutionalism against centralizing tendencies within the Union. Important among his works are: **An Inquiry into the Principles and Policy of the Government of the United States** (1814); **Construction Construed and Constitutions Vindicated** (1820); **New Views of the Constitution of the United States** (1823). R.H.S.

Teapot Dome Scandal.

One of the most flagrant instances of political corruption in United States history had its origin when Harding's Interior Secretary, former New Mexico Senator Albert B. Fall, who entered the presidential Cabinet in 1921, persuaded Naval Secretary Edwin Denby to give up authority over great oil reserves set aside previously and by design for future needs of the navy. Harding, who signed the Executive Order for the transfer said: "I guess there will be hell to pay." There was.

Fall quickly leased Teapot Dome reserves in Wyoming to Harry F. Sinclair and the Elk Hills reserves in California to Edward L. Doheny. Both oil men had contributed heavily to the 1920 Republican campaign. Doheny's son promptly delivered to Fall a "little black bag" containing $100,000 in cash as a "loan" not in any way part of a bank transaction.

Similarly more than $200,000 in Liberty bonds owned by Sinclair's dubious Continental Trading Company (Canadian charter) were turned over to Fall's son-in-law from whose hands they somehow reached Fall. The cabinet officer most concerned with conservation of the public domain received other rewards from Sinclair and Doheny each of whom looked ahead to corporate profits of some $100,000,000 from the transfers and leases.

The tipoff was the new prosperity at

Fall's dilapidated ranch on which taxes had gone unpaid for nearly 10 years. Senators LaFollette of Wisconsin and Kendrick of Wyoming sought a thorough explanation of the leases with the result that a full-scale investigation, headed by Senator Walsh of Montana, was ordered. The shocking revelations led to charges of bribery and conspiracy. Doheny and Sinclair escaped on the main counts but the latter was fined $1000 and jailed for three months for contempt of the Senate. Sinclair also served six months for contempt of court because his detectives shadowed the jurors when he was on trial for fraud. Fall resigned in disgrace, was found guilty of bribe-taking, imprisoned for a year and fined $100,000. The leases were annulled through suits that went to the Supreme Court where the defendants were declared guilty of "fraud and corruption" in the Elk Hills case and of "collusion and conspiracy" in the Teapot Dome case. Complete restitution for the illegal use of government property was required of the leaseholders. At the time the Department of Justice was so untrustworthy that independent prosecutors were appointed (Owen J. Roberts and Atlee Pomerene). I.Di.

Technological Change and Politics.

In a high-technology society, continuing change is likely to be a matter of degree, and thus absorbable by the general political system, although in a market economy automation tends to create a dislocation of employment that can become explosive politically. Whether, in the long run, increasingly complex interdependence requires a more centralized government, and individual freedoms must be surrendered for common security, is being debated, but the trend is in those directions.

In underdeveloped areas, technological change is central to the on-going revolutions in ideas, goals and institutions; politics, albeit sometimes supported by force, is the overt way of managing the decisions which must be made. Political realities such as the resistance of powerful elites to change can block the development at times, although once technological change begins what they more often seem to do is pervert it. The need for some kind of stability in the midst of change, reinforced by the needs of a technological society itself for stability (e.g., fulfillment of contracts, punctual delivery, safety for investments), creates its own version of the tendency to strong central government, so that often in the name of efficiency and necessity, democratic processes are threatened or subverted (if they exist at all) and the "public sector" far overbalances the "private sector" in both economic and political terms.

On the world scale, the cumulative technological change has created a profoundly altered political situation, and seems certain to affect it still more fundamentally. Instant communication, jet transportation, world markets for raw materials needed by technology, medical and other technologies which have created the population explosion, the development of weapons which can reach anywhere on earth and destroy all life, have made the world's people substantially interdependent today. This is reflected in changing international political arrangements already, and a world multiplex society seemingly must become a confluent society or perish. A time bomb exists: the peoples of the underdeveloped areas have awakened to the need and potentiality of sharing equally the fruits of technology, and both political and economic accommodations will have to be made peacefully to these aspirations, or the now-submerged peoples — goaded by the population explosion — will erupt into more violent forms of politics than the technologically-created recent breakdown of the colonial system.

Whether a confluent society of roughly present sovereignties can be realized; whether the dangers will prompt a super-sovereign state, perhaps by strengthening the U.N.; whether the pressures plus the Cold War will divide the world into permanent opposing blocs; whether the exponential increase of technological complexity will some day shatter the whole society into chaotic splinters, or whether nuclear accident or policy will blow civilization to death is but one set of questions which arises from technological change. J.B.L.

Technology.

In the academic sense this involves

the scientific study of the practical or industrial arts. The term may also be used to apply to the practical and in-industrial arts collectively. As applied to a particular community or nation, it is concerned mainly with the general level of development and the system of control organization with respect to industrial and natural resources. R.J.S.

Teheran Agreement.
Churchill, Roosevelt, and Stalin met at Teheran, Iran, from November 28 — December 1, 1943. Discussion focussed more on winning the war than planning for peace, although such issues came up as the future of Germany and Poland, Russia's needs for warm-water ports, and the postwar world organization. After lively debate (Churchill's plans for Aegean operations!), May 1944 was agreed on as the time for a two-way invasion of France, across the Channel and in the South. It was obvious at Teheran that Russia wanted to extend its frontiers and would insist on friendly neighbors, but Roosevelt and Churchill had reason to believe that postwar cooperation with the Soviet Union could be achieved on reasonable terms. H.L.M.

Tenno.
(Literally, Lord of Heaven.) The Emperor of Japan. Japanese tradition, especially as reflected in the **Kojiki** (712) and the **Nihongi** (720), has held that the Emperors of Japan are of a single dynasty directly descended from the Sun Goddess, Amaterasu. The present Emperor is 124th in the line, of which the first sixteen are legendary or semi-legendary. The 1889 Constitution stated that the Japanese Empire was "reigned over and governed by a line of Emperors unbroken for ages eternal," but in his 1946 New Year's Rescript, Emperor Hirohito denied the "false conception that the Emperor is divine." The 1947 Constitution provides that the Emperor is "the symbol of the State and of the unity of the people, deriving his position from the will of the people with whom resides sovereign power." T.Mc.N.

Territorial Air.
That portion of the atmosphere or airspace which is superincumbent on the land and water territory of any state. The Aerial Navigation or International Flying Convention, signed in Paris on October 13, 1919, and the Convention on International Civil Aviation, signed in Chicago on November 1, 1944 in almost identical language stated that every power has complete and exclusive sovereignty in the airspace which lies over its land and sea territories. The territorial air of any state, according to the Chicago Convention, must be considered as coterminous in all directions with the earth's atmosphere. O.S.

Territorial Cession.
A bilateral transaction by which territorial sovereignty is transferred by one state to another. It has been classified as a derivative mode of acquisition, as title to such territory is always derived from the state which was the previous sovereign. Whatever the provisions of municipal law may be as regards cession, they are without direct effect upon established rules of international law. Yet any action with respect to territorial cession, on the part of the agents of a state, which is in contravention of constitutional provisions cannot stand. On the other hand, such action on the part of a responsible state official may create certain international obligations. O.S.

Territorial Sea.
A band of water along a state's coast. Claims concerning its width, normally measured from the low water line, range from three nautical miles (U.S. and Britain) to two hundred. They probably should not exceed twelve. The adjacent state has sovereignty over this water (including air above and bed below) but must allow innocent passage through it. [See 1958 Geneva Convention (Territorial Sea and Contiguous Zone), Articles 1-23.] V.R.I.

Territorial Waters.
Waters surrounding parts or the whole of the land of a State which do not lie completely within its national boundaries. Coastal States normally extend jurisdiction to their territorial waters, especially in matters of public order, fishing rights, coastal trade, navigation, customs duties and sanitation.

Foreign merchant ships may, in time of peace, claim the right of inoffensive passage through these waters. No general agreement has been reached on the breadth of territorial waters; leading maritime States traditionally favor the 3-mile limit. S.S.H.

Territory.
A land area designated by natural or conventional boundaries. A state is characterized, inter alia, by its territory which marks both the limits of the property rights of the state and its jurisdiction over persons. J.D.

Test Act.
A provision that only persons with certain religious beliefs or affiliations should be admitted to public office or employment. Acts of this kind were passed at various times in the British Isles during the 17th Century, the most important of which was the Test Act of 1672 (25 Car. II, c. 2), which required every person filling any civil or military office to adjure the doctrine of transubstantiation and to receive the sacrament of the Church of England within three months after assuming the office. All have since been repealed. In the United States, religious qualification for federal office is prohibited by Art. 6, Sec. 3 of the Constitution. Many states have similar constitutional prohibitions, and in 1961 the United States Supreme Court outlawed all religious tests for state offices (Torcaso v. Watkins, 367 U. S. 488, 6 L. ed. [2nd] 982, 81 S. Ct. 1680). E.V.M.

Texas.
Area, 263,513 square miles. Census population April 1, 1960, 9,579,677, an increase of 24.2% over 1950. An independent republic from 1836, Texas entered the American union in 1845. Texas joined the Confederacy in 1861. Influences of the Civil War and Reconstruction have continued in Texas government and politics. The government operates under a constitution adopted in 1876 but frequently amended since. Texas has had the Democratic one party system of the South although by 1962 the Republican Party seemed to be establishing itself as a serious contender. T.C.S.

Thailand.
(198,456 sq. mi.; 25,519,965 inhabitants).

Officially, the southeast Asian country of Thailand, which was known as Siam until 1939, has been a constitutional monarchy since 1939. However, since 1958 internal unrest sparked by the fires of communist aggression in bordering Laos has led to virtual one-man rule. Field Marshal Sarit Thanarat rules the country but allows the King, a twelve-man cabinet, and a 240-man legislature to continue as symbols. The principal exports are rice, rubber, corn, and tin. Most of the people are Buddhist. Bangkok is the capital and chief commercial center. Thailand is a signatory of SEATO and the Joint Protocol on Laos. J.A.E.

Thalweg.
German term meaning the downway. It is used to describe the boundary in a navigable river. Normally, the deepest channel, it is the principal artery or channel of commerce; it is commonly called the "middle of the main channel." J.E.T.

Theocracy.
1. A government directly conducted by divine beings. 2. A government under ecclesiastical authority as exercised by a church, a priesthood, or a body of clergymen. 3. A state having a theocratic system of government. Ch.C.M.

Theories of International Relations.
The immense detail in the reporting and describing of international events and the great expanse of the subject material included in international relations preclude a direct comprehension by any individual or group of what is going on in the relations between peoples, societies, states, and economies. Thus, systems of simplification are required. Theory, in its broad meaning, refers to such orderly schemes of simplification. The development of coherent and relevant theory is important because it provides a general guide to what research needs to be done. In the study of international relations, recent theoretical work has begun to show significant progress. Two broad families of theory have taken form, one of which concentrates on the phenomena of the national unit in action (the

international actor; foreign policy) and the other of which concerns the interacting of national units (the international system; patterns of international relations). Concepts of power and of decision-making are current approaches to actor-foreign policy theory. Balance of power, social modernization, system-transformation, and deterrence systems are names which stand for clusters of contributing ideas toward theory in the second category of patterns-international system. There is general agreement that international relations theory must advance to a more precise and more sophisticated level. Ch.A.Mc.

Theory.
In the narrower sense of the term a theory is a proposition (or a set of propositions) that tries to "explain" something. The explanatory theory may be "scientific" or "nonscientific." A "scientific theory" tries to explain something in line with scientific standards of procedure. It will, as a rule, refer to some alleged universal law or to the tentative hypothesis that such a law operates, or it will propose such a hypothesis. But the theory itself is neither a law nor a hypothesis; it merely uses them for the purpose of explanation. Often the term theory is used in a broader sense so as to designate the entire system of thought on a certain subject or area, as in speaking of "the political theory of Plato"; it then includes, in addition to explanatory propositions, the presentation of facts and the proposal of goals and of moral principles. In modern technical use it is preferable to distinguish (1) descriptions of facts and events, (2) proposals of goals, valuations, moral principles and the like, and (3) theories in the first (narrower) sense that try to "explain" the facts (events) or the necessity or advantages of the proposed goals, valuations, moral principles. A theory may be correct or incorrect; it is not advisable to limit the term to correct propositions only. A.B.

Theory of the Five-Power Constitution.
Sun Yat-sen's theory to divide governmental powers into legislative, executive, judicial, examination and control, each to be exercised by a separate department **(yuan)**. The Examination Yuan has primary responsibility for conducting civil service examinations as an effective and impartial means of recruiting government officers through competitive examinations. The main function of the Control Yuan is to impeach government officers for misconduct and corruption. It is believed that the principle of checks and balances can thus be better practised than in countries adopting the theory of separating government powers merely into legislative, executive and judicial.
S.S.H.

Thermonuclear War.
A war in which the phenomena of atomic fission and fusion would be employed as weapons. Weapons which use a fusion process develop enormous yields as compared to atomic weapons which use a fission process. Since the explosion of two atomic bombs in the last phases of World War II, the destructive power of nuclear weapons has grown geometrically. Soviet Premier Khrushchev boasted of a 100-megaton bomb, for example, in a speech on January 16, 1963. The development of multi-megaton bombs does not mean, however, that a thermonuclear war is inevitable since an aggressor must accept the consequences of reprisal. A number of authorities have argued that because of the importance of the reprisal factor, a peace-loving nation can only keep a thermonuclear war from occurring by being fully prepared for waging it. It should also be noted that the selective employment of low-yield nuclear weapons, for example, would not make inevitable the much feared escalation into a general thermonuclear exchange. J.D.A.

Third Force.
Tendency of uncommitted powers in a bipolar world to resist involvement in the struggle between two competing blocs, normally resulting in an international organization of powers so inclined although such a position is occasionally assumed by an individual power. A case in point is India's post-World War II policy of maintaining friendship with both the United States and the Soviet Union while refusing to commit itself to either. P.J.F.

"Third Force" of France.
See France — "Third Force."

Thomas, Norman Matoon. (1884-).

Leader and six times presidential candidate of the Socialist Party of America, 1928-1948. A graduate of Princeton and of Union Theological Seminary, Thomas resigned his Presbyterian pastorate in New York City in 1918 to devote full time to socialist, labor, peace, and civil liberties activities. He helped to found the American Civil Liberties Union and the Fellowship of Reconciliation. He also helped the Southern share-croppers to organize the Southern Tenant Farmers Union. Thomas has resolutely opposed cooperation between Socialists and Communists. His numerous writings include: **Is Conscience a Crime? What is Our Destiny?** and **A Socialist's Faith.**

R.E.Ch.

Thorez, Maurice (1900-1964).

French politician, secretary-general of the French Communist Party since 1930. During World War II in the U.S.S.R., Thorez returned to France in 1944, was a member of the Constituent Assembly, a member of de Gaulle's provisional government (1945-1946), as well as of the ministries of Gouin, Bidault, and Ramadier (1947). In Russia between 1950 and 1953 for "reasons of health." K.B.

Three-mile zone.

The zone of territorial waters lying between the shore and the high seas, also called the territorial belt. The sovereignty of a nation extends over this zone yet by international law the innocent passage of foreign ships, both merchantmen and warships, must be tolerated. This rule does not apply to the passage of airplanes in the air above the territorial belt. The territorial waters begin on the sea shore at the low water mark, or at the outermost harbor installations, or at the baseline that is drawn between headlands of narrow bays or connecting the outermost points of island groups close to the shore. Harbor waters and sea inside the baseline are internal waters, completely under the jurisdiction of the shore state. The traditional width of the territorial belt was three miles, a limit to which today still adhere the big naval powers such as the U.S.A. and the United Kingdom. Recently several nations began to press for an extension of the territorial belt in order to increase their exclusive fishing areas and for other advantages. Some other nations have also historically claimed wider limits, often up to 12 miles. The recent United Nations Conferences on the Law of the Seas at Geneva, 1958 and 1960, were unable to agree on a commonly accepted limit, though the tendency was to admit at least a six-mile zone of territorial waters next to which a contiguous zone of not more than 6 miles could be established where a nation would exercise only certain prerogatives. P.P.R.

"Three People's Principles."

"Three People's Principles" is an English rendition of the Chinese San Min Chu I. Literally, it is as follows: San — three; Min — people; Chu I — principle. It is the title of a series of sixteen lectures given by Sun Yat-sen in 1924. They are grouped in three parts: Min-Chu (people's national — consciousness), Min-Chuan (people's power), Min-sheng (people's livelihood).

Sun's major objective was that the Chinese people must unfetter themselves of foreign concessions and be their own master. Chinese nationalism could then be achieved through their own effort.

Sun Yat-sen envisaged a China that would adopt the best Western democratic institutions and at the same time preserve the best Chinese usages. In this connection, he was most ingenious in adapting two Chinese traditions, the examination and control systems, to a modern governmental structure.

Sun unfolded a rather comprehensive economic plan for China.

The "Three People's Principles," have become the ideology of the Kuomintang and they are recognized as the political philosophy of the Republic of China. L.M.L.

Thurmond, Strom.

Born December 5, 1902; U.S. Senate from November 2, 1954 until resignation April 4, 1956, reelected 1956 until term ending January 3, 1967; Democrat — South Carolina; Governor of South Carolina 1947-1951; States' Rights Democratic candidate for President of the United States in 1948 (carried four states, receiving 39 electoral votes).

R.A.B.

Tibet.
South Asian land (ap. 470,000 sq. mi.) higher above sea level than any other comparable area in the world. Its approximately 2,000,000 residents possess a distinctive political, cultural and religious heritage, based on Lamaism, an offshoot of Buddhism. Alternately autonomous and subject to Chinese imperial suzerainty during various periods in its history, Tibet was invaded by Chinese Communist forces in 1950 and integrated into the People's Republic of China as a supposedly "autonomous" area. Tibetan resentment of Chinese control erupted into violence in 1960. Tibet's religious leader, the Dalai Lama, fled the country as Chinese forces suppressed the revolt.
S.L.A.

Ticket.
A slate of candidates for public office endorsed by a particular political party.
C.W.B.

Tiso, Msgr. Jozef (1887-1947).
Leader of Slovak People's Party after Hlinka's death. Premier of autonomous Slovak government formed at Zilina in October 1938 but dissolved by President Hacha of Czechoslovakia on March 9, 1939. After Slovak parliament had, on March 14, 1939, declared independence, it elected T. president of the Slovak Republic. Tiso and his moderate supporters resisted efforts of pro-Nazi extremists; there were no political executions under T.'s presidency. Although unable to forestall Hitler's program for "resettling" Slovak Jews in Poland, T. succeeded in stopping the deportations in 1942 after learning that the Jews were in fact being exterminated. Fled to Bavaria to escape Russians in 1945, but U.S. occupation forces, on Washington orders, turned him over to Communists. Tried in "National Court" before a judge who swore publicly before the trial to "hang Tiso." Hanged April 18, 1947; revered by Slovaks as national hero and martyr.
K.G.

Tito (Josip Broz). (1892-).
President (since 1943) and Communist Party chief (since 1937), he has been the leader of Yugoslavia since World War II. A Croatian, he fought in the Russian Civil War. Appointed to the Politburo in 1934, he worked for the Comintern. He fought against the Germans (and Mihailovich's Chetniks) after Germany attacked USSR. After World War II he established a communist dictatorship. His differences with Stalin led to Yugoslavia's expulsion from the Cominform in 1948. "Titoism" has become synonymous with "independent road toward socialism."
J.J.K.

Titoism.
The nationalistic response of the Yugoslav Communist elite to Soviet efforts at imperial domination. In June 1948, Yugoslavia, hitherto Stalin's most zealous supporter, and the Soviet Union split over the issue of the degree to which national communist parties must unquestioningly subordinate themselves to Moscow's will. Titoism represents a fusion of nationalism and communism into an ideology and a movement having as its goal the acceptance by Moscow that each Communist country must be permitted to seek its own "road to socialism" and to retain political autonomy over its own Party apparatus.
A.Z.R.

Tocqueville, Alexis de. (1809-1859).
French statesman and author, b. in Verneuil, d. in Cannes. The son of a French prefect and the scion of the oldest Norman nobility with a tradition of public service, he embarked at the age of twenty-one on a judicial career. From 1839 to 1849 he served as a member of the Chamber of Deputies and in 1849 for a few months as Foreign Minister. After Louis Napoleon assumed dictatorial power, he resigned from public service.

In retirement he wrote **L'ancien regime et la revolution** (1856) in which he showed how the administrative system of the **ancien regime** survived the French revolution.

Tocqueville's most famous book, **De la democratie en Amerique** (1835-1840), was the result of a nine-month trip to the United States undertaken in 1830-1831. Reputed to be the best work ever written by a foreigner on the United States, it not only describes with deep insight the American scene, but it develops the thesis that the characteristic feature of the age is the increasing urge for equality, even though at the expense of liberty, and that this can be discerned best in the United States where the craving for equality has led to the tyranny of public opinion and increasing governmental centralization. On the other hand, Tocqueville contemplates "A state of equality is perhaps less elevated, but it is more just."

Democracy in America, as the work is called in its English translation, contains among its many famous passages especially one that has been quoted time and again since the end of the second World War: "There are at the present time two great nations in the world . . . I allude to the Russians and the Americans . . . each of them seem marked by the will of Heaven to swing the destinies of half the globe." G.V.W.

Togliatti, Palmiro. (1895-).
Leader of Italy's Communist Party. Engaged in Communist activities since Party's founding in 1921. Forced to flee Fascist Italy in 1926, he was an active Comintern agent in Europe throughout the 1930's and was widely known under the pen name of Ercoli. He returned to Italy in 1944 to join the provisional government and to lead the Communist Party. G.K.

Togo Republic.
Area, 21,893 sq. mi.; population (1954), 1,029,946. 3/5 of former German Togoland, 1885-1914. The German colony, seized by British troops in Aug., 1914. In 1922, split into 2 Class B mandates of League of Nations: British and French. 1946, British and French UN Trusteeships. British Trusteeship: area 13,041 sq. mi.; population, (1954) 423,000, landlocked; no railway; by UN sponsored plebiscite in May, 1956 (92,775 to 66,500 votes), integrated with Ghana (independent, March, 1957). In 1958, UN General Assembly approved independence of French Trusteeship as Togo Republic, April 27, 1960. The new republic: coast line of Gulf of Guinea but no good harbors; Lome as capital and seaport, 3 railroads, 242 miles, radiating from it; principal exports: coffee, 45%, cocoa, 30%. President Sylvanus Olympio, London-educated economist, pro-Western, with "most efficient and economically run bureaucracy in West Africa." Pres. Nkrumah of Ghana covets Togo as 7th province of Ghana under the Ewe reunification movement.

Sylvanus Olympio, distinguished for his resistance to Ghana's attempts to annex Togo, was assassinated on January 13, 1963 outside U.S. Embassy. C.K.W.

Tojo, Hideki. (1884-1948).
Graduated from the National Military Academy in 1905; served as provost marshal, Vice-minister of War, and War Minister. War-time prime minister from 1941-1944 and a General of the Imperial Army. Executed as a war criminal in 1948. H.U.

Tokugawa Period.
When Teyasu Tokugawa (1542-1616), the first Tokugawa Shogun, established his government in Edo (the old name of Tokyo) in 1603, the Baku-han regime — the political system in which the Bakufu (central government) controlled all Han (fiefs of the Daimyoo feudal lords) — was also inaugurated. While it seemed to be a system of decentralization, the power of the Bakufu was unquestionable. An efficient system of spying and police inhibited the political and economic power of the Daimyoo. In this period there prevailed fixed status differentiation — warrior, farmer, artisan, and merchant — in order to maintain the social structure which allowed Samurai rule. Confucianism was adopted as the leading principle of the Japanese state. But gradually the power of the Samurai was severely limited by their indebtedness to the merchants whose influence extended even into the Tokugawa family. The status structure underlying the Shogunate system was finally undermined by the introduction of national discipline and Western culture patterns. Japan was obliged to open trade to foreign powers and forego its former policy of isolation. This new situation gave the lower Samurai their chance to overthrow the Bakufu and to return nominal governing power to the Emperor. H.U.

Tokyo.
The world's largest city, Tokyo-to (Tokyo Metropolis) is the capital and the hub of political, economic, and cultural activities of the new Japan.

According to the official 1960 Census, the total population of Tokyo Metropolis was 9.67 million (unofficial estimates of 1962 put the population at over 10 millions). Tokyo sits on the Kanto Plain, at the upper end of Tokyo Bay, and anchors the **Kei-Hin** (Tokyo-Yokohama) metropolitan area. The urban center consists of 23 wards; outskirts embrace 10 cities, 23 towns, 10 villages, and offshore islands. The entire area is about 790 square miles. The Metropolitan Government combines the powers of a capital of an urban prefecture, and of a large city. The Governor is popularly elected (4-year term); the elected Assembly has 120 members (4-year term); there is a complex of commissions to aid the Governor. A.W.B.

Toledo War. (1835).
A boundary dispute between Ohio and Michigan Territory, called the Toledo War, arose because the survey was indefinite; the terms of the Northwest Ordinance, the Ohio Constitution, and Michigan Territorial Act were ambiguous and conflicting; and Toledo on Lake Erie at the mouth of the Maumee River was a desirable port. Since it appeared as if Congress would not settle the controversy over the "Toledo Strip" five to forty miles wide, both Ohio and Michigan Territory attempted to exercise jurisdiction over the area and enforce their authority with arms. The opposing militias did not meet in combat although both were massed for attack in 1835. The U.S. Congress finally awarded Ohio the "Strip" and Michigan was admitted to the Union with the Upper Peninsula. J.A.E.

Tolerance.
A generally outmoded term in the Intergroup Relations field which implies acceptance of a person on his individual worth, merit, dignity, and honor. At one time used rather widely, it has fallen into disrepute because of the implications that one who is tolerant of someone else "tolerates" that person or group, rather than accepting him as an equal. M.J.S.

Tolerationism.
The adoption of a policy of toleration for purely political ends; distinguished from both religious tolerance and toleration.

Tolerance is a philosophical principle implying moral virtue of the kind defended by the 16th-century advocate of genuine religious tolerance, Sebastian Castellion (1515-1563), and in the following century by Pierre Bayle (1647-1706), the "philosopher of Rotterdam," who was one of its first modern champions. But whereas Castellionism was "irrational" and provided an argument for tolerance based on the plea for truth, Bayle's rationalism and skepticism suggested to him that, assuming honest motives, to persecute truth was as justifiable as to persecute error, and thus made him reject all religious persecutions as nonsensical.

If tolerance was in the nature of an ideal and had strong theoretical connotations, toleration was more practical. It had legalistic qualities implying freedom for dissenters within the framework of legal measures, and as such it was desired by the party of **Politiques** and practiced by Chancellor de l'Hopital and King Henry IV.

Tolerationism was cunningly used by Cardinal Richelieu (1585-1642). It accepted toleration of the Huguenots as a measure of temporary political expediency and was sustained by the political goal of ultimately eliminating the Huguenot minority. W.J.S.

Tories.
A term applied to the British Conservative Party. Prior to the use of the latter term in the early nineteenth century, this was the main group opposing the Whigs. It is derived from an Irish word meaning robber or bandit. It was first used in 1679 to describe those who favored the accession to the throne of the future James II, a Roman Catholic. British Conservative Party members now make common use of the term. R.H.B.

Tort.
A wrongful act resulting in injury to a person, his reputation or his property. The injured person has a right to compensation for the injury, which may be secured through law suit. If the wrongful act constitutes a crime, as in criminal assault, criminal prosecution may be instituted also. Tort actions are common in cases of assault, conversion, libel, negligence resulting

in accident, trespass, etc. Breach of contract is not **per se** a tort, but a contract may be tortious. J.E.R.

Totalitarianism.

It is the theory and practice of a particularly virulent form of autocracy, made possible by modern technology as a perversion of Western party democracy. It is often referred to in political writings as "tyranny" (q.v.), "despotism" (q.v.) and "absolutism" (q.v.), but these earlier forms of autocracy lacked some of the most characteristic features of totalitarianism. A secular ideology of messianic expectations, demanding a total destruction of the existing society and its replacement by a utopian order, coupled with the monopolistic centralization of all power in a single party inspired by this ideology are perhaps the most outstanding features of such totalitarian regimes. In the long run, however, the monopoly of control and direction of mass communications, of all organizations and groupings, whether economic or other, and an elaborately developed system of secret police operations (terror) would appear to be equally significant. Certainly the first two, if not the third, distinguish totalitarian regimes from older forms. Totalitarian regimes are usually referred to as dictatorships in the West, although they prefer to speak of themselves as democracies; both terms are anachronisms resulting from the ideological antecedents in Marx who spoke of the dictatorship of the proletariat as leading to the democracy of socialism (q.v.), but of the two, dictatorship is more appropriate, since it highlights the predominant role of the leader who typically wields dictatorial power at the head of the ruling party hierarchy. Two distinct forms of totalitarianism have made their appearance: Communist and Fascist; of these the original Communist form has proved decidedly more viable. It is still spreading, although not as rapidly as it did after World War II when the Soviets were able to fill substantially the vacuum caused by the defeat of Nazi Germany and Japan. Close comparative analysis has shown these two forms of totalitarianism to be very much alike in all but ideology. Communist totalitarianism is, however, still evolving and may eventually achieve a stable structure. C.J.F.

Toure, Sekou. (1922-).

President of the Republic of Guinea and Secretary General of the **Parti Democratique de Guinee,** the only legal party in that country.

M. Sekou Toure was born in 1922 in Faranah (Guinea), studied at a Koranic school before attending a French elementary school, and obtained his secondary education by correspondence. He served as a clerk for a business firm and later became an employee of the postal and telecommunications service. Demonstrating a keen interest in the labor movement, he rose by 1956 to the position of President of the **Confederation Generale du Travail** in Africa, only to break with it the following year to form a separate African organization, **L'Union Generale des Travailleurs d'Afrique Noire.** With the strong support of the Guinean labor movement, M. Toure became the Mayor of Conakry, a founding member and leader of the left wing of the **Rassemblement Democratique Africain,** and in 1958 the President of the Republic of Guinea.

M. Toure is a convinced Marxist, but he denies the existence of the class struggle in his native land. A hero of young radicals in Africa, he is a dedicated Pan-Africanist and a foe of colonialism and neo-colonialism.

F.H.G.

Town. (U.S.A.)

The governmental subdivision of the country or the principal units of local government in the New England states, characterized by the town meeting form of government. The term is also used to designate small municipalities in a number of states. G.S.B.

Townsend Plan.

Formally, Old Age Revolving Pensions, Inc., organized in 1934 in U.S.A. Dr. Francis E. Townsend's idea for stimulating the economy and ending the Great Depression by paying each retired citizen over sixty years of age a pension of $200 monthly. This had to be spent within thirty days and was to be financed by a two per cent tax on all business transactions. Promoters organized Townsend Clubs, which at their height claimed two and a half million members, and published the **Townsend National Weekly.** The Plan was defeated in the U.S. House of Representatives in 1939. R.E.Ch.

Townshend Duty Act (1766).
British statute imposing on the American Colonies a duty on imported tea, glass, paper, and lead, and authorizing writs of assistance (general search warrants). R.F.H.

Township. (U.S.A.)
The rural governmental subdivisions of the country outside the New England area. The term also embraces the congressional township, a geographic area concept used in surveying land, and the urbanized township, a unit of urban rather than rural government.
G.S.B.

Trade Expansion Act of 1962. (U.S.A.)
This Act retains the pattern of Executive tariff making adopted under the Reciprocal Trade Act (q.v.), but extends still further the President's power to modify existing tariff rates. For limited classes of goods (e.g., tropical products and goods for which 80% of the free-world trade originates in the United States and the Common Market countries) the President can negotiate a tariff rate of zero. The Trade Expansion Act authorized negotiated cuts in other tariffs by 10% a year, or 50% in total below the 1962 rates. I.d.S.P.

Trade Unionism.
A combination of workmen of the same occupation of several related trades for the purpose of united action in securing the most favorable conditions regarding wages, hours, and conditions of labor. Principally through collective bargaining, the trade union seeks to promote and protect the welfare, interests, and rights of its members. See organized labor. C.B.C.

Tradition.
Ideas, principles, knowledge, and usages transmitted from generation to generation over a long span of years; though held by some to embrace only oral transmission, now generally extended to written transmission as well.
Ch.C.M.

Traditionalism.
A political and juristic doctrine based upon the belief that the individual is but a link in an endless series of generations, and, consequently, that wisdom of all policies and laws should be judged by the criterion of the historical whole rather than that of the current and momentary situation. A corollary of this is the belief that the human mind itself is so much a product of countless generations of historico-psychological conditioning that truly rational thinking is impossible without taking account of the whole tradition of a people. Ch.C.M.

Treason.
In general, the offense of attempting to bring about the overthrow of the government of the state to which allegiance is owed. In monarchies, the definition may also include attempts on the life of the sovereign. In the U.S., treason is narrowly defined in the Constitution (Article III, section 3) to consist only of levying war against the United States, "or in adhering to their enemies, giving aid and comfort to them." F.H.H.

Treasurer.
An elected or appointed officer at any level of government in the U.S.A. entrusted with funds collected from taxes or other sources. This money is to be disbursed upon order of an appropriating body when countersigned by an authorized person such as a Comptroller or Director of Finance. A Treasurer may be a bonded officer — i.e., his financial accountability is supported by a bond executed with a company or a fund fully able to cover possible losses or shortages.
Sp.D.A.

Treaties.
Treaties are agreements between states and other subjects of international law. Like international custom and the general principles of law recognized by civilized nations, treaties are a source of international law (Article 38 [1] of the Statute of the International Court of Justice), i.e., a means of creating rights and obligations under international law. They may be general or particular in scope or in parties (multi-, pluri-, bi-partite) and create

obligations for one or more of the contracting parties (multi-, pluri-, bi-, unilateral), regardless of the name used (treaty, convention, agreement, protocol, declaration, note, etc.). There are thus no "law-making" treaties as opposed to "treaty-contracts." Their relations inter se and with regard to the other sources of international law are determined by the principles of **lex posterior derogat priori** and of **lex particularis derogat generali**. Possible exceptions are the Covenant of the League of Nations and the Charter of the United Nations which, in the interest of international peace and security, claim universal application and superiority to conflicting treaties (cf. Articles 17 and 20 of the Covenant and Articles 2[6] and 103 of the Charter). These are examples of treaties creating obligations for third parties, as there are treaties creating rights for third parties. The law of treaties is under discussion before the International Law Commission of the United Nations.
S.E.

Treaty of Lausanne.
See Lausanne, Treaty of July 24, 1923.

Treaty of Trianon.
See Trianon, treaty of 1920.

Treaty of Versailles (1919).
See Versailles Treaty of 1919.

Trial by jury.
A formal procedure before a competent judicial body for determining the guilt or innocence of a person accused of a crime, or for examining and deciding the justiciable issues in a case or controversy, in which a properly constituted body of impartial laymen determine questions of fact. C.W.B.

Trianon, Treaty of 1920.
Concluded between Hungary and the Allied Powers on June 4, 1920. Large territories were ceded to Czechoslovakia, Yugoslavia and Rumania which reduced Hungary to one-third of its pre-World War I population and to one-fourth of its territory. The Treaty also provided for war reparations to the successor states. G.K.

Tripartite Declaration of May 25, 1950.
An agreement in the form of a three-point declaration entered into on May 25, 1950, by France, Great Britain and the United States after the Foreign Ministers Meeting in London. Its immediate purpose was to warn the other Arab states to refrain from attacking Jordan or from resuming their war against Israel. Its long-range objective was to prevent aggression and to control the arms race developing between the Arab countries and Israel.

As history has shown, the Declaration was based on an assumption which proved fallacious — that France, Great Britain and the United States controlled the flow of arms to the Middle East. The Soviet-bloc sale of arms to Egypt seriously upset the balance of power in favor of Egypt and enabled the U.S.S.R. to establish itself as an influence in the Middle East. Quickly the U.S.S.R. denounced the Tripartite Declaration as the symbol of Western imperialism and monopoly.

The formation of the Baghdad Pact and the Czech-Egyptian arms agreement, both in 1955, precipitated a large-scale arms race in the Middle East. Friction between Egypt and Israel grew. Twice that year, Great Britain and the United States offered to guarantee any territorial settlement agreed to by Israel and the Arab nations. On February 1, 1956, Britain and the United States issued a joint communique warning that the Tripartite Declaration provided for action inside and outside the United Nations in the event of aggression in the Middle East. Visiting the United States early in 1956, Sir Anthony Eden proposed that teeth be put in the Tripartite Declaration. The United States did not go along and agreed only to the establishment of a tripartite working group to plan military measures in the event of a crisis. No announcement or evidence of the existence of joint plans for action was ever made; and the Suez invasion of 1956 by two of the signatories — France and Great Britain — nullified any substantial effectiveness the Declaration might have had.

In 1957, during the crisis created by the conflict between Jordan and Egypt, with Syria allied with the latter, President Eisenhower called attention to the Tripartite Declaration and the Eisenhower Doctrine as instruments under which the United States could act if Jordan were attacked. It appears, however, at this writing, that neither Israel nor the Arab states have derived any real feeling of security from the Tripartite Declaration. O.K.

Troika.

The demand, made initially on September 23, 1960 by Premier Khrushchev before the U.N. General Assembly, for the replacement of the Secretary-General by a three-man directorate. It further insists that all positions and power in internal secretariats be apportioned to accord with the three political groupings — Soviet, neutralist, and Western. Khrushchev's proposal constitutes an assault on the office of the Secretary-General and on the concept that there can be an impartial international civil service. It would extend the Soviet veto into the Secretariat, thus enabling Moscow to thwart the will of the General Assembly. A.Z.R.

Trotsky, Lev Davidovich.

(Real name—Bronstein) (1879-1940).

The Soviet political leader and associate of Lenin, Trotsky was born in 1879, near Elizavetgrad. He received his education at the University of Odessa, and early in his life plunged himself into the political struggle against the Tsarist regime. Trotsky was arrested and exiled to Siberia in 1898. but soon managed to escape to England on a forged passport, issued in the name of Trotsky. In 1905, he returned to Russia, was arrested and again exiled to Siberia, from which he again escaped, this time to Vienna, where in 1908 he became the editor of "Pravda." When World War I began, Trotsky went to Germany to agitate against the war, and was promptly arrested for his active opposition to the war. Next, he went to France, where he was arrested in 1915 for the same anti-war opposition. In 1916 he was expelled from the country. In January 1917. he came to New York via Cuba, and became the editor of the Russian Socialist newspaper, Novyi Mir. When the February revolution occurred in 1917, Trotsky immediately sailed for Russia, but was taken off the ship by the British authorities at Halifax. Finally he arrived in Petrograd. In his political life before the Russian revolution, Trotsky wavered between Menshevik and Bolshevik factions, but joined Lenin's Bolsheviks, when they took over from the Provisional Government of Kerensky. Trotsky became the People's Commissar for Foreign Affairs, and played an important role in the Bolsheviks' signing of the Brest-Litovsk Treaty with Germany. Next he was appointed Commissar for War and is credited with organizing the Red Army, in the reorganization of which he used the experience of former officers of the Tsarist Army. During the Civil War and in the post-war years while at the helm of government with Lenin, Trotsky proved to be a ruthless leader, who had no qualms about sending thousands of people to death to preserve Soviet rule. As a result of Trotsky's opposition to communist party policy and his factional activity, he was relegated to minor posts in 1925-1926, expelled from the party in 1927, and exiled to the city of Verny (now Alma-Ata) in Central Asia in 1928. Finally, he was banished from Russia in 1929, and settled on the Island of Prinkipo, a suburb of Istanbul, where he lived four years. Next he went to France, then in 1935 to Norway, from where in 1937 he was forced to go to Mexico, where on August 20, 1940, he was killed with an ax by a man who posed as a "friend" and "Trotskyite" who actually was a Stalinist agent, dispatched from Moscow to murder him. V.P.P.

Trotskyism.

A body of thought, highly critical of Stalin's corruption of Marxist-Leninist ideas and policies, that developed from the most powerful faction of the Left Opposition in the 1920's against the "bureaucratic degeneration" and propeasant tendencies of the Communist Party. With Stalin's triumph, this faction, expelled from the Party, formed abroad the Fouthr International which promulgated Trotsky's ideas of the permanent revolution (in contrast to Stalin's position that socialism could be built in isolation in one country), and of the need to reestablish democracy within the Communist Party and institute workers' democracy. Trotskyism survives politically as a minor Communist faction in a few countries, such as the United States, Japan, and Ceylon.   A.Z.R.

Trud (Labor).
Soviet daily newspaper, voice of the trade union organization, the All-Union Central Council of Trade Unions. Trud was first published February 15, 1921.
D.N.J.

Truman Doctrine.
In 1946 the Soviets tested Western determination in two areas, through diplomatic moves in Turkey and through a Communist-led guerrilla movement in Greece. As the British withdrew from their traditional responsibilities in the region, President Truman took the initiative for the United States. On March 12, 1947, he requested (and obtained) 400 million dollars from Congress for aid to Greece and Turkey. At the same time, he proclaimed the "Truman Doctrine," which pledged world-wide American support to "free peoples who are resisting attempted subjugation by armed minorities or by outside pressures."
H.L.M.

Truman, Harry S.
33rd President of the U.S., was born May 8, 1884, in Lamar, Mo., but spent his boyhood on a small farm near Independence, Mo. He served in France in World War I, where he was promoted to Captain in the Army. He married Bess Wallace in 1919, entered the haberdashery business unsuccessfully, then received a series of positions, both appointive and elective, from Democratic Boss Thomas J. Pendergast. From 1926 to 1934 he was a presiding judge in Missouri. He was elected U.S. Senator from Missouri in 1934 and re-elected in 1940. During the war he became nationally known because of his "watchdog committee" that investigated and exposed graft and collusion in military contracts. In 1944 he was nominated and elected Vice-President of the U.S. On April 12, 1945, he succeeded Franklin D. Roosevelt, as President, and promptly declared a continuation of Roosevelt policies, backing the formation of the United Nations and insisting on unconditional surrender of Germany and Japan. Under his administration the occupation policies of West Germany and Japan transformed these nations from destitute enemies to prosperous friends. In February 1947 he initiated the "Truman doctrine" by supplying military and economic aid to Greece and Turkey, following this with the European Recovery Program (Marshall Plan), and a series of military and political alignments throughout the world to contain the military aspirations of the U.S.S.R. This was a striking reversal of the traditional foreign doctrines of neutrality and isolation. In China, on the advice of General Marshall, he withdrew military and economic aid to the Nationalist Government of Chiang Kai-shek, contributing to the loss of China to the Communist leader Mao Tse-tung. When North Korean Communists attacked South Korea in June 1950, he sent U.S. troops to South Korea, but upon the conquest of North Korea, in an effort to contain the war, refused to support General MacArthur's plan for bombing supply lines in China, and this reduced the military action to a stalemate.

His domestic policies, which he called the Fair Deal, were blocked by conservative elements in both the Democratic and Republican parties, and served as a minor background to his foreign policies. He retired from active politics in January 1953 and has since served periodically as a senior statesman in the Democratic Party. The Truman papers are now preserved in the Truman Library in Independence, Mo.   T.K.N.

Trust Territory.
See United Nations Trust Territory.

Trusteeship Council.
See United Nations Trusteeship Council.

Tshombe, Moise Kapende (1919-).
Leader of secessionist government of Katanga since July 11, 1960. Born to a wealthy, plantation-holding family of the Lunda tribe. Primary and secondary education in American Methodist missionary schools. Member, Katanga Provincial Council, 1951-53. Helped found the **Confederation des Associations du Katanga** (CONAKAT) in 1959, which he represented at the 1960 Brussels Round Table Conference. Political support comes mainly from

fellow Lunda tribesmen and European enterprise in Katanga. Tshombe's CONAKAT has never received majority support in Katanga. In May, 1960 elections, CONAKAT won eight of 137 seats in National Assembly and twenty-five of sixty seats in the Katanga Provincial Council. Tshombe has been the leading exponent of a confederate solution to constitutional crisis in the Congo, barring which he has demanded an independent Katanga. In 1964 appointed Prime Minister of the Congo republic. R.L.K.

Tukhachevsky, Mikhail N. (1893-1937).
Soviet marshal. He held various command positions in Russian Civil War and led the Red Army in an abortive invasion of Poland in 1920. Tukhachevsky headed the Staff of the Red Army from 1925 to 1927. His chief theoretical work is **Voina klassov** (The War of Classes) which urges that the Red Army be regarded as the general staff of world revolution. He was the highest officer liquidated in the great purges, being executed in 1937. W.D.J.

Tunisia.
The population of Tunisia is slightly over four million, 90 percent of whom are Muslims. Tunisia's history like that of North Africa is part of the story of the Phoenicians, the Carthaginians, the Romans, the Vandals, the Byzantines and the Arabs. Its Berber population had been largely Arabized. In 1881 Tunisia became a French protectorate. The new Tunisian Elite under the leadership of Bourguiba negotiated in 1955 and in 1956 a treaty with France establishing Tunisia's independence. Tunisia is a constitutional republic. It is a member of the Arab League and of the United Nations. It follows a westernizing course and a moderate role in international politics. It stands officially for the unification of the Maghreb, and for closer collaboration among the Arab States. E.A.S.

Turgot, Anne Robert, Baron de l'Aulne. (1727-1781).
Encyclopaedist, close to physiocrats. One of the first scientific exponents of "political economy." Spokesman for freedom of enterprise and competition. His **Reflections sur la formation et la distribution des richesses** (1766) preceded Smith's **Wealth of Nations.** Minister of Finance of Louis XVI, 1774-76. Favored political and economic reforms. Liberated grain trade from internal tariffs. M.C.V.

Turkey. See Appendix.

TV Debates.
Discussion of issues over television by candidates in a political campaign. The practice received its greatest impetus during the 1960 U.S. presidential campaign in four debates between Vice-President Richard M. Nixon and Senator John F. Kennedy. In subsequent campaigns the device has been used by candidates for Congress, Governor, and other offices. Debates are usually moderated and leading questions asked by TV news personnel.
J.O.H.

Two Chinas policy.
The proposal that both the Communist regime on the Chinese mainland and the Nationalist regime in Taiwan be diplomatically recognized and/or admitted to the United Nations. The military and naval stalemate between Communist China and the United States in the Formosa Strait appears to make it unlikely that the Communists will "liberate" Taiwan or that the Nationalists will recapture the mainland in the foreseeable future. The two Chinas policy, it is asserted, would contribute to peace and stability in the Far East and provide a compromise settlement of the question of Chinese Communist representation in the United Nations. The principal obstacles to the realization of the two Chinas policy are the apparently inflexible attitudes of the Nationalist and Communist governments, which both advocate the liberation and unification of all China (each on their own terms), and of the United States, where public opinion is reluctant to "make a deal" with Communism. However, economic, diplomatic, and strategic considerations may induce the parties concerned to arrive at a compromise which would recognize **de facto**, if not **de jure**, the two Chinas.
T.Mc.N.

Two-party System.
Two major political parties dominate in the electoral process and, hence, in the allocation of political positions (elective and appointive) within all

organs of government. If both parties are legally permitted to function effectively, their competing programs and leadership teams inevitably require some measure of political democracy. A two-party system does not automatically imply the existence of only two parties, however, and a number of minor parties normally exist. Nevertheless, the great popular support accorded the two leading parties assures that one will almost always gain a legislative majority or near majority while the other will lead the opposition. Similarly, political positions in the executive will also be filled by leaders of one of the two major parties. In such circumstances, the minor parties tend to express the views of special, relatively small segments of the population and concentrate on criticism of the program inconsistencies and inadequacies of the "big two." The latter, seeking majority support, make broad programmatic appeals designed to accommodate diverse interests and emphasize common aspirations. Proponents of the two-party system acclaim the relative decisiveness of elections (customarily based upon single-member districts and plurality) and the fact that legislative majorities promote political stability. Critics decry the various distortions of public will introduced by the sometimes artifical manufacture of majorities. The English-speaking countries are outstanding users of the two-party system, which normally develops only where a relatively high degree of societal agreement on major constitutional, socio-economic and political questions prevails. D.W.

Two Swords.

Authoritatively stated by Pope Gelasius I at the close of the fifth century, the doctrine claims for the Church exclusive authority in spiritual matters. Simultaneously, the doctrine acknowledges the supremacy of civil authority in matters of public peace and order. One significant consequence of this doctrine was, for example, that civil courts could not try ecclesiastics for breaches of peace on violation of public order: they had to leave their trial to ecclesiastic courts. The doctrine may well be considered an early institutionalization of constitutionalism through an imposition of limitations upon the internal jurisdiction (sovereignty) of civil authority. V.Z.

Tyler, John.

B. March 29, 1790 in Virginia. Died January 18, 1862. Tenth president of the United States, (1841-1845). Tyler was graduated from William and Mary, 1807. He served in the Virginia legislature, as governor of Virginia, in the lower house of Congress and as a United States senator. He was elected Vice President in 1840 with President William H. Harrison. When Harrison died in 1841, Tyler was the first vice president to succeed to the presidency. Elected as a Whig he soon turned away from their program. Later he sat in the Confederate Congress, having been a strong supporter of secession. M.F.

Tyrannicide.

The propriety of murder of evil rulers has been a constant problem of political theory. Particularly significant discussions appear in the late Middle Ages, the Reformation, and the late Nineteenth Century. John of Salisbury and St. Thomas dealt with this subject in the earlier period, while George Buchanan and Mariana argued in favor of tyrannicide during the Reformation. Anarchist arguments in favor of political murders and an incident led to their exclusion under an Immigration law adopted in 1903 by the United States. However, Criminal Anarchy statutes adopted by many states have not been primarily directed toward anarchists. R.W.T.

Tyranny.

Coercive, arbitrary government uncontrolled by prescription. The term had its origin in ancient Greece.
R.A.B.

U

Ukase.
Formerly a decree issued by the Czar in Russia. Now an edict from the party Presidium in the Soviet Union. While having the force of law, it is not formulated by democratic legislative means but rather by party leadership dictum. Example: the ukase terminating the state of war between the Soviet Union and Germany in 1950. R.A.B.

Ulbricht, Walter. (1893-).
Originally a Social Democrat, joined the newly founded Communist Party in 1919. Member of its Central Committee, 1923; represented it in Comintern, 1923-26. During Hitler regime in Moscow. Rebuilt Communist Party in Soviet Zone of Germany, 1945-46. Deputy Chairman of the Socialist Unity Party (q.v.), 1946-; Secretary General 1950-; Secretary of Central Committee, 1953-. Deputy Minister President of the (East) German Democratic Republic (q.v.), 1949-60. Took place of its deceased President as Chairman of the (newly created) Council of State, 1960. Is recognized boss of the GDR, subject to Moscow directives. J.B.M.

'Ummah (Islamic Community).
The religious community which includes all Muslims irrespective of race, color or status. Membership in the 'ummah is a matter of faith and not of race or nationality. Envisaged by a Divine Law **(Shari'a)**, it assumes a predominant role in guiding the personal and communal life of its members. It is sometimes called the community of Muhammad **('ummat Muhammad)** or the community of God **('ummat Allah)**. The Prophet referred to the Believers as 'my community.' The "Witness" (that there is no God but Allah and Muhammad is his Prophet) binds the Muslims together. Since the **'ummah** comes into being by divine action, it engulfs the whole life of the individual. He has no meaning outside it, and his judgment cannot run counter to its moral precepts. The **'ummah** provides him with social and spiritual security. F.M.N.

Unam Sanctam.
The Bull of Pope Boniface VIII, issued in 1302 when a Council was assembled at Rome to discuss the political problems the Church faced in its struggle for supremacy with Phillip the Fair, King of France. The Bull developed a version of the Two Swords doctrine according to which the temporal power is entirely subordinated to the spiritual. Its ultimate justification rests in its function to aid in the salvation of souls which is the primary concern of the Church. The Bull also espoused Papal supremacy in the Church. V.Z.

Unanimous Consent.
The method by which a legislative body may proceed contrary to a rule or rules if no member objects. In the United States House of Representatives, on the first and third Mondays, bills may be taken from the Consent Calendar for immediate consideration if no member objects. During its so-called "morning hour" the Senate takes bills from its calendar in the order listed if no member objects. K.E.H.

U.N. Atomic Energy Commission.
See United Nations Atomic Energy Commission.

Unconditional Surrender.
Termination of armed conflict among nations on a basis allowing the victor(s) legally unlimited authority to subsequently impose upon the defeated state(s) such terms and conditions as the former may deem appropriate. Most frequently used to describe the policy of unconditional surrender applied by the Allied forces against the Axis powers in the Second World War. The first public use of the term to describe Allied objectives in the Second World War was by U.S. President Franklin D. Roosevelt at the Casablanca Conference in January, 1943. The policy was subsequently criticized by some as prolonging the war, and/or as contributing to the perceived necessity for using the first atomic weapons against Japan in August, 1945. S.L.A.

Unconventional Warfare.
Bernard Baruch used the term "cold war" to designate the uneasy truce that followed the Second World War. Gen-

eral William J. Donovan, World War II Chief of the Office of Strategic Services, believed that a more all-embracing term should be used rather than "cold war." Hence he began using the term "unconventional warfare" in order to describe the new, post-World War II pattern of neither peace nor war. "Unconventional warfare" included a broad spectrum of conflict techniques, but did not include general or limited war. Rather it embraced the lowest intensity of conflict methods to and through sub-limited warfare. It included propaganda, economic warfare, sabotage, espionage, subversion, strikes, civil disturbances, terrorism, political warfare, and guerrilla warfare. Other terms used to describe the dimensions of the blending of peace and war in the present era of world politics are: "special warfare"; "protracted conflict" (adopted from the writings of Mao Tse-tung); "the new warfare" (Brigadier Barclay, British Army); and "polyreconic warfare" (James D. Atkinson). It should also be noted that the term "unconventional warfare" is used in a very specialized sense. The United States Department of Defense defines it as covering evasion and escape, subversion, and guerrilla warfare. J.D.A.

Underdevelopment.

Underdeveloped, or bluntly "backward," is a relative term frequently referring to the economic rather than cultural development of a country. To a certain extent every nation in the world is underdeveloped. Economists usually explain "underdevelopment" as poor economic performance evidenced by a low standard of living. The most impressive characteristic of the underdeveloped areas is an almost shocking waste. Human and cultural resources are employed in an inefficient manner; labor is low in cost and is used at an extremely low level of productivity. These factors produce populations that are poverty-stricken, uneducated, disease-ridden, and apathetic. Approximately two-thirds of the Free World's people live in economically less well developed areas that span most of Asia, the Middle East, Africa and much of Latin America. They produced in 1955, on the average, only about $100 worth of goods and services a year, compared with $2,000 in the United States. The industrial nations, primarily the Western nations which comprise only 14 per cent of the world's population, enjoy 55 per cent of the world's income.
P.A.T.

U.N. Emergency Force.
See United Nations Emergency Force.

Unequal Treaties.

Unequal treaty system started with defeat of China by Great Britain in the "Opium War," 1839-42. Until 1943, the treaties of Nanking (1842) and The Bogue (1843) with England, those of Wanghia and Whampoa (1844) with U.S.A. and France respectively contained basic principles that were to govern China's international status. Most important provisions were loss of tariff autonomy, grant of consular jurisdiction, and imposition of the most-favored-nation treatments. Later treaties between China and foreign nations modified or amplified these provisions so as to include navigation rights in inland rivers, "concessions" (foreign settlements) in big cities, leased territories and rights of building railways, "spheres of influence," establishment of foreign banks and great business concerns, and use of Englishman and Frenchman as Customs Inspector-General and Deputy Postal Inspector-General respectively. Called by Chinese the unequal treaties because of their character of one-sided privileges. Same impositions existed in other states, but magnitude and elaborateness of impositions in China were unique. Abolition of the system was considered to be completed with signing of treaties by China with U.S.A. and Great Britain in 1943, though equal treaties were signed either before or after this date (with Germany, Austria, and Hungary after World War I, with Russia in 1924, and with Japan in 1952). C.K.W.

UNESCO.
See United Nations Educational, Scientific and Cultural Organization.

Unicameralism.
The term refers to the principle that legislatures should consist, and sometimes do consist, of one house or chamber rather than two,

Arguments in favor of unicameralism include the following:

It permits exact location of legislative responsibility rather than shift such responsibility from one house to another. Thus, legislation becomes better accountable to the public than under bicameralism.

From the standpoint of organization unicameralism is approved because it develops no frictions, rivalries or deadlocks, promotes policy decisions to be made in the open rather than in the secrecy of bicameral conference committees, prevents objectionable deals between two houses, does away with delays so typical of bicameralism, and is less expensive than the latter.

Unicameralism is said to eliminate certain obstacles to effective government. It does this, for example, in the case of cabinet government should the cabinet be responsible to both houses of the legislature, as illustrated by the French Third Republic and republican Italy. Similarly, unicameralism removes obstacles to the proper working of party government which cannot operate effectively if one chamber is not truly representative or if different parties dominate the two houses. In general, defenders of unicameralism agree with Benjamin Franklin, who is said to have compared a double-chambered legislative assembly to a cart "with a horse hitched to each end, both pulling in opposite directions" (James W. Garner).

The case for unicameralism is also stated by the attempt to show that bicameralism has become unnecessary. Wherever the same voters elect members of both houses, some of the original objectives of bicameralism, representation of classes or territorial subdivisions in their corporate capacity, have become impossible of attainment. Furthermore, in view of such limiting devices as the executive veto and judicial review, a second chamber as one of the major checks and balances (q.v.) can be dispensed with. Finally, advocates of unicameralism agree with the Abbe Sieyes that "if a second chamber dissents from the first, it is mischievous; if it agrees with it, it is superfluous," a view which, according to James Bryce, overstates the case on behalf of unicameralism:

"A second chamber may do work involving neither agreement nor disagreement with the other house, and it may where it agrees in aims, suggest other and better means of obtaining them."

This criticism and others directed against unicameralism are largely identical with arguments offered in defense of bicameralism (q.v.).

Efforts to establish unicameral legislatures did, on the whole, not materialize until the twentieth century. The universal influence exercised by the mother of parliaments, that at Westminster, organized as a bicameral legislature, proved too powerful to make establishments of unicameral systems, often adopted in the wake of upheavals, such as the Puritan, American, and French Revolutions, anything but short-lived experiments.

The movement for unicameralism was stimulated by a reaction against bicameralism after the First World War. The policy to "make the world safe for democracy" had its repercussions on the domestic scene where demands for abolishing second chambers were justified on the ground that they were undemocratic. Among the countries which since that time have introduced the unicameral system are the German states, with the exception of Bavaria's advisory senate; Israel; Indonesia; South Korea; South Vietnam, New Zealand, and Denmark. The Soviet satellites, except Yugoslavia, have also instituted unicameral legislatures.

In the Western hemisphere, the Canadian provinces, except Quebec, and most of the Central American states are unicameral. In the United States, the adoption of unicameralism by the state of Nebraska in 1937 has largely remained an isolated incident; only on the level of municipal government, unicameral city councils have been adopted. However, in 1953 a Report of the Committee on American Legislatures of the American Political Science Association came out in favor of unicameralism in the American states, among other things, on the grounds that the system had operated satisfactorily in Nebraska and the American cities, and, after all, had been in existence not only in some of the American colonies but also in three American states, Pennsylvania, Georgia, and Vermont (in the latter for 59 years).

Regardless of the actual performance of unicameral legislatures, increasing democratization and centralization of government may well strengthen the movement toward unicameralism. Conversely, defenders of limited government may be expected to oppose such trend and continue to support bicameralism. W.F.

U.N.I.C.E.F.
See United Nations Children's Fund.

Union Democratique et Sociale de la Resistance.

Formed from Resistance groups, this loosely organized minor French party, with 30 members in the Constituent Assembly, was composed of new political figures many of whom (e.g. Soustelle) were personally attached to De Gaulle. In 1948 some joined the RPF's Group, but soon UDSR deputies were forbidden to join such groups without party authorization. This cost the party 12 of its 26 deputies in the Assembly.

In 1946 the UDSR had allied with Radicals in the RGR, remaining in the alliance until 1955. Also a parliamentary alliance was formed with Houphouet-Boigny's leftist African party.

Mitterand's socialistic policy clashed with the later rightist leadership of Pleven in the UDSR. The failure of the European Defense Community weakened its originator, Pleven, and Mitterand returned to the presidency in 1953. When the National Congress of 1958 demanded opposition by party members to the De Gaulle constitution, Pleven resigned. Born with the Fourth Republic, the party in effect died with it, losing all its Assembly seats in 1958. R.B.C.

Union of African States.

An association of Ghana, Guinea, and Mali considered by its members to be the nucleus of a United States of Africa and open to every African state or federation of African states which accepts its aims and objectives.

In November of 1958, one month after Guinea had refused to join the French Community, President Toure and Prime Minister Nkrumah agreed to form a union **a deux** as a nucleus for a union of West African states. Measures to strengthen the ties between Ghana and Guinea were taken later in 1958 and again in 1960. The third member, the Republic of Mali, expressed her desire to adhere to the union in a tripartite declaration of December 24, 1960, after the attempt to form the Mali Confederation had failed. On July 1 of the following year the charter of the union went into effect. It calls for cooperation in the areas of domestic and foreign policy, defense, and economic and cultural affairs; and looks forward to the establishment of organs to promote this cooperation.

The unity of the three partners is enhanced by their generally leftist political orientation, their dedication to a strident form of political Pan-Africanism, and their opposition to colonialism and neo-colonialism. Ghana, Guinea, and Mali are also members of the Casablanca Bloc, but are not affiliated with the Brazzaville or Monrovian Blocs. F.H.G.

Union of South Africa.
See South Africa, Republic of.

Unitary State.

Probably the most widely used method of organizing the territory of a state to produce a particular pattern of relationships and geographic distribution of powers between the central (national) government and lesser territorial units. In the unitary state, the central government alone determines the distribution of political power among the various governmental levels (e.g., provinces, municipalities, towns, and villages, etc.). Since the lesser governmental units are essentially creatures of the central government and have not constitutionally sanctioned exclusive powers, they act as its administrative agents. In addition, they exercise any local self-government powers which may be granted by the central government. The unitary method simplifies national constitution-making and economic planning, maximizes governmental ability to deal with national problems uniformly throughout a country, can reduce administrative costs by the elimination of duplication and jurisdictional disputes among various governmental levels, and can clarify political responsibility by concentrating it primarily at the national level. It may also be associated with excessive centralization and the denial of all local self-government. As a method of geographic integration, however, the unitary state is not automatically associated with either democracy or dictatorship, this being determined by the distribution of powers among executive, legislative and judicial organs of the central government and their degree of responsibility to the public. Similarly, whether it condones or rejects local self-government depends upon the policies of the central government. Thus, democratic Britain (traditionally committed to local self-government) as well as Nazi Germany (1933-1945) are examples of the unitary state. D.W.

United Arab Republic (Egypt).

Physical and Economic Life: Boundaries: North—Mediterranean; East—Israel (and Gulf of Aqaba), Red Sea; South—Sudan; West—Libya. Population: 26,000,000. Area: 386,200 square miles. Present fertile area—trough-like valley 2-10 miles wide (excepting delta) cut by Nile plus oasis depressions with fresh water such as Fayoum. Generally arid—3 inches annual rainfall, land requiring irrigation by damming flood waters of Nile. Agriculture: cotton—large production as cash crop for export and foreign exchange—many food crops—wheat, maize, dates. Rice and sugar sometimes exported. Industry: textiles, phosphates, fertilizers, iron and steel, oil, cigarettes. Ethnic base: a Mediterranean subrace built on early Nile population, Arabs, Sudanese. Language: Arabic, with educated speaking French and English. Religion: Majority, Islam; minority, Coptic Christians. History: Begins with legendary Menes 4,000 B.C. Old Kingdom zenith in 3rd millennium 4th Dynasty, capital at Memphis. Decline. Resurgence, 2,000 B.C. 11th-12th Dynasties. Zenith in New Kingdom at Luxor and Thebes 18th Dynasty. Decline under Akhenaten; restoration by Rameses II, 1300 B.C. Soon divided into Upper and Lower Egypt. 671 B.C. temporary Assyrian Conquest, followed by Persian 525 B.C. and Alexander 332 B.C. Latter's general, Ptolemy, established royal line ending with Cleopatra's suicide and Roman rule 30 B.C. continuing under Byzantine Empire until Arab Muslim Conquest in 7th century. Thence ruled with varying degrees of freedom from outside control by Muslim Arab or Turkish rulers until establishment of U.A.R. under Nasser. Thus period of considerable independence and prosperity under Salah Al-Din 12th century, governed by Mamluk Sultans (slave soldiers of Ottomans) from then to Napoleon, 1798, and their massacre by Muhammad Ali, an Albanian Muslim officer representing Turkish Sultan, 1811, who established a royal line ending with Farouk in 1952. Muhammad Ali laid foundation of modern Egypt, his descendants witnessing building of Suez Canal but permitting public debt to lead to international control and establishment of British Protectorate in 1883, ending with withdrawal of last British troops from Suez, 1956. Revolution of 1952 ended the monarchy and established a provisional republic. Recent history has been marked by the nationalization of the Suez Canal; British-French-Israeli invasion and U.N. intervention; the creation of the temporary union of Egypt and Syria (1958-61); the building of the High Dam at Aswan. J.P.D.

United Front.

Refers to efforts made in the decade following the mid-1930's to unify Communist and non-Communist socialist and democratic forces in opposition to the growing strength of Fascism, National Socialism and Japanese militarism on the world scene. While Communist Parties, following the policies of Stalin, attempted to rally opposition to Franco in Spain, and Litvinov vainly sought "collective security" against Germany, mass movements were organized throughout the world. In China this led to the National Salvation Movement of the mid-thirties, in which the Kumintang was urged to abandon its struggle with the Communists and resist Japanese encroachments upon Chinese territory. Chiang Kai-shek, leader of the Nationalists, preferred, however to "exterminate" the Communists before turning to the Japanese invaders. In the fever pitch of public enthusiasm, and undoubtedly under the influence of the Communists, the Manchu warlord, the "Young Marshal" Chang Hsueh-liang, who had been assigned to fight the Communists, instead kidnapped Chiang Kai-shek and forced him to meet with the Communist representative, Chou En-lai.

Chiang was released after several weeks, apparently on orders from Stalin, without making any definite public commitment. But in February, 1937, his Kuomintang agreed to enter into a United Front if the Chinese Communist Party would comply with the following conditions: 1) abolition of its separate army and its incorporation under a united command; 2) dissolution of the Chinese Soviet Republic; 3) cessation of Communist propaganda; 4) termination of the class struggle. In the Spring of 1937 an agreement was worked out whereby the Communists would cease land confiscation and modify their propaganda, while the Kuomintang agreed to convene a National Congress in November 1937, to formulate a new Constitution.

The United Front in practice amounted to little more than a cessation of actual hostilities during the period of Japanese invasion despite several severe violations which resulted in virtual breakdown of cooperation after 1942. For good reasons there was little trust on the part of either party and the alliance fell apart completely upon the defeat of Japan in 1945. S.S.

United Kingdom.

The United Kingdom of Great Britain and Northern Ireland, thus including England, Wales, Scotland, and Northern Ireland. It also includes many smaller islands, including the Isle of Wight and the Scilly Islands as part of England, Anglesey as part of Wales, the Orkney, Shetland and Western Islands as part of Scotland, and Rathlin as part of Northern Ireland. The Channel Islands and the Isle of Man with their own legislatures have a special status. The term Britain is often used as meaning the United Kingdom, even in official publications. R.H.B.

United Nations.

An international organization, successor to the League of Nations, designed to aid in maintaining world peace and security, and to promote international cooperation. With an international legal personality, it is not a world state, nor may it invade the domestic jurisdiction of any state. It may operate military forces to uphold the charter, but development of a world moral force and provision of opportunities for preventive diplomacy remain basic characteristics. It has been a strong influence promoting change from colonial status, and has assumed responsibility for transitional government in such areas, and for promoting economic growth. Ideological differences between the Soviet Union and the West affect structure, finances, and exercise of powers, and threaten its survival. The General Assembly, Security Council, Secretariat, Economic and Social Council, Trusteeship Council, and International Court of Justice are principal organs (q.v.). A number of specialized international agencies operate in agreement with the organization. D.P.

United Nations Atomic Energy Commission.

Established in 1946 by the General Assembly of the U.N. at the instigation of the United States, the United Kingdom and the Soviet Union for the chief purpose of making proposals for effective disarmament in nuclear weapons. Its membership includes ahe members of the Security Council and Canada. P.J.F.

United Nations Charter Revision.

See Charter Revision.

United Nations Children's Fund. (UNICEF).

Established in 1946 at the General Assembly's first session as an operating agency within the U.N. Gives direct aid to children in less-advanced areas by providing food and medical supplies. Also helps governments develop national services in child health, nutrition, and welfare. Has directly served over 55 million children and mothers in more than 100 countries and territories. Financed entirely from voluntary contributions from governments, private groups, and individuals. Governed by a thirty-nation Executive Board and

administered by an Executive Director from headquarters in New York.
W.C.R.

United Nations Conference on International Organization (UNCIO).

Following the Yalta Agreement and Dumbarton Oaks Proposals, delegates of 50 states met at San Francisco April 25-June 26, 1945 to draft the Charter of the United Nations and Statute of International Court of Justice. While the sponsoring powers (U.S., U.S.S.R., U.K., China and France) maintained the veto in the Security Council, the smaller states obtained a greater role for the General Assembly and the establishment of the Economic and Social Council and Trusteeship Council. The Charter was unanimously adopted and came into force October 24, 1945.
F.B.G.

United Nations Economic and Social Council.

A principal organ of the United Nations which studies, investigates, and coordinates a variety of social, cultural, educational, health, and related matters, including the new program of a Development Decade and an illusory Declaration of Human Rights. The Council is composed of eighteen members, elected for three-year terms by the General Assembly, in practice including states which are permanent members of the Security Council, and operates under the authority of the General Assembly. It has established a number of functional commissions and four regional commissions for Europe, Asia and the Far East, Latin America, and Africa. Considerable confusion and overlap of powers of the Council with other United Nations activities exists, but the regional commissions have been useful.
D.P.

United Nations Educational, Scientific and Cultural Organization.

It is one of the specialized agencies of the United Nations mentioned in Article 57 of the U.N. Charter, and like the others, is organizationally separate. It has its own constitution, membership budget and staff. Its work is coordinated with that of the other specialized agencies and the United Nations organs through the United Nations Economic and Social Council. By 1962 the membership of Unesco (113) had become substantially universal and nearly identical with that of the United Nations itself. Unesco was organized by the victorious powers in World War II at a conference in London in 1945, and began functioning officially late in 1946. Its headquarters is in Paris. Unesco culminated a quarter century of efforts to put international cooperation in the fields of education and culture on a footing of international public organization. The League of Nations' Committee on Intellectual Cooperation was a forerunner. The work of Unesco has covered a broad spectrum, and has included such things as fostering international private organizations in several scholarly and cultural fields, promoting the training of teachers in under-developed countries, sponsoring international conferences, and a wide range of publications.
H.S.Th.

United Nations Emergency Force.

UNEF was created by the General Assembly in November, 1956. This "para-military" force was to "secure" the withdrawal of Anglo-French and Israeli troops from Egypt. Its further duties consisted of the temporary occupation of the Gaza Strip, the occupation of the Sharm el Sheikh area at the entrance to the Gulf of Aqaba, and the patrolling of the Israeli-Egyptian armistice line. By March, 1957, Hammarskjold's first "truly international force" consisted of 5,840 soldiers from ten countries, not including the Big Five.
H.L.M.

United Nations General Assembly.

A quasi representative, legislative body of the United Nations, with equal representation and voting power for all members, meeting annually. Decisions are by a majority or two-thirds vote, depending upon importance of the question. In matters affecting international peace and security, its role has expanded due to decline of the Security Council blocked by the veto power of permanent members. The General Assembly has powers of recommendation only, but it serves as a world forum with moral power. It may promote a wide range of economic and social matters, consider human rights and questions of colonial administration, and may institute studies. It appoints the Secretary-General

and admits new members following recommendations of the Security Council, and approves the United Nations budget and allocates expenses. Growth of membership has made it unwieldy, and ideological conflicts have made it a stage for bloc politics.
D.P.

United Nations Financing.

The overall costs of the United Nations system are roughly $500 million a year for 1963. These are broken down into: (a) the regular budget of $80 million; (b) the ten Specialized Agencies costing another $80 million; (c) the voluntary programs — the Expanded Program for Technical Assistance, the Special Fund, refugees programs and the Children's Fund — cost $200 million a year; and (d) the two peace-keeping operations in the Middle East and in the Congo amounting to $140 million.

The costs of the two peace forces have brought the United Nations to the brink of bankruptcy. The Soviet Union and France refuse to pay and over half of the membership are either unwilling or unable to pay. In December 1961 the General Assembly authorized the subscription of $200 million of United Nations bonds and requested an advisory opinion of the World Court on whether the costs of the two peace-keeping operations were considered to be legally binding obligations. Roughly $150 million of the bonds have been purchased but this amount is already owed; on July 20, 1962 the World Court, in a 9 to 5 opinion, answered the question put to it in the affirmative, but the Soviet Union and France have refused to abide by the opinion.

The finances of the United Nations continue to be precarious. J.G.St.

United Nations Human Rights Commission.

A standing commission of the United Nations under the Economic and Social Council specializing in developing the program of the United Nations to protect and extend human rights as embodied in the Charter and Universal Declaration. Composed of eighteen members elected annually from as many member States, it meets in annual sessions to prepare recommendations to the Economic and Social Council. It has no power to hear grievances or to deal with violations of human rights in any member State. Such grievances are within the sole jurisdiction of the General Assembly and the Security Council on complaints by member States. R.B.

United Nations International Court of Justice.

See International Court of Justice.

United Nations Operations in the Congo.

Established by the U.N. Security Council on July 14, 1960. Its commission was defined as "complete restoration of law and order in the Republic of the Congo." Law and order in the area began to deteriorate almost immediately after independence from Belgium was gained on June 30. U.S. Air Force planes made available to the United Nations began flying contingents from member states into the Congo within twenty-four hours after the U.N. action. Over two dozen countries contributed over 20,000 troops. Cost of the operation averaged about 10 million dollars per month causing a serious crisis in United Nations financing. This was temporarily alleviated by a U.N. bond issue. Prevented a possible confrontation between the Soviet Union and the United States in the heart of Africa. W.C.R.

United Nations Preparatory Commission.

Established by the United Nations Conference on International Organization at San Francisco in 1945. From headquarters in London, the Commission prepared for the first session of the General Assembly which began January 10, 1946. W.C.R.

United Nations Relief and Rehabilitation Administration. (UNRRA).

Predecessor of the specialized agencies of the U.N. (q.v.), established in 1943, and liquidated in 1947, by 48 member governments for the purpose of providing postwar economic aid through supplies of basic commodities and services, as well as assistance to displaced persons, health and social welfare services and industrial as well as agricultural rehabilitation. Programs were limited to allied countries which had been invaded. Total aid distributed amounted to about $4,000,000,000, of which 75% was contributed by the U.S. At the peak of operations the agency had about 13,000 employees. Main recipients were East and Southeastern Europe and China.　　F.M.

United Nations Secretariat.

The international civil service of the United Nations, headed by a Secretary-General who is appointed by the General Assembly on recommendation of the Security Council for a five-year term open to renewal. As chief administrative officer of the organization, with power to perform functions entrusted to him by United Nations organs, and authorized to bring to the attention of the Security Council threats to international peace and security, the position has been enhanced by dynamic use of the office. Substantial field and military operations by the Secretary-General have been undertaken in recent crises. Strong Soviet opposition has resulted from these developments leading to its proposal of a collective executive, the "troika," extending the veto principle to the Secretariat. Enlarged membership of the United Nations has also led to reexamination of the relation of geographic distribution of staff appointments to assessed budget contributions.　　D.P.

United Nations Security Council.

Intended to operate as the executive organ of the United Nations with primary responsibility for the maintenance of peace and security, and formulation of plans to regulate national armaments. A condition of stalemate has resulted from the veto power given to permanent members on substantive questions due to the struggle between the Soviet Union and the West. Five of the eleven members are permanent (Republic of China, France, Soviet Union, United Kingdom, United States of America), and six are elected for two-year terms. The Security Council has available a number of techniques for pacific settlement, including investigation, conciliation, and interposition. Lack of agreement on composition has prevented implementation of charter provision for a permanent military force. The Council may order members to take political, economic, or military measures to give effect to its decisions. Efforts to enlarge the Council have failed due to differences over China's membership and the Soviet Union's desire to put into effect a "troika" principle, a balance of three blocs.　　D.P.

United Nations Special Committee on Palestine (UNSCOP).

Established in May, 1947, by the first special session on the General Assembly to investigate, and make recommendation on the Palestine Question. The minority of UNSCOP (the representatives of India, Iran and Yugoslavia) recommended an independent federal Palestine, with an Arab and a Jewish State. The majority, however, (representing Canada, Czechoslovakia, Guatemala, the Netherlands, Peru, Sweden, Uruguay), proposed partitioning Palestine into an Arab and a Jewish State, with an economic union between the two, and Jerusalem becoming a trusteeship, administered by the UN, a proposal that was adopted by the General Assembly on November 20, 1947 by a vote of 33 for, 13 against, with 10 abstentions.　　G.V.W.

United Nations Strategic Trust Territories.

Article 82 of the Charter provides for the designation within a trust territory of a strategic area or areas. In such cases the trusteeship functions of the United Nations are exercised by the Security Council instead of the General Assembly and the permanent members thus have the power of veto over the adoption, alteration or termination of agreements. The only trusteeship agreement of this kind is that of the Pacific Islands, administered by the United States.　　L.P.B.

United Nations Sub-Commission on Prevention of Discrimination and Protection of Minorities.

The only sub-commission of the U.N. Human Rights Commission, composed of fourteen members serving as individual experts (with the approval of their governments) meeting annually to carry on studies in its field and to report its recommendations to the

Human Rights Commission. Its worldwide surveys have covered racial, religious, political and other discriminations, with recommendations for action designed to reduce them. It has not so far dealt with the "protection of minorities" because of the indefiniteness of the term. R.B.

United Nations Technical Assistance Board.
(TAB) Coordinates the U.N.'s expanded program of technical assistance (ETAB). Created in 1949 at U.S. initiative and paralleling the beginning of U.S. "Point 4" programs. Comprised of the executive heads of participating organizations (most of them U.N. specialized agencies). W.C.R.

United Nations Truce Supervision Organization.
An organ composed of international observers and headed by a chief of staff. Formed in 1949 at the time of the first Palestine crisis. The chief of staff supervises the implementation of the armistice agreements between Israel and the Arab states and reports as need arises to the Security Council. W.C.R.

United Nations Trusteeship Council.
A principal organ of the United Nations, successor to the League of Nations mandate system, designed to oversee administration of trust territories under authority of the General Assembly, except for strategic areas which are under the Security Council. Pressure of the Council is moral, issuing questionnaires and receiving reports from administering powers, accepting petitions, and visiting the territories. As the Council has achieved independence of trust territories, its responsibilities have declined. Membership is a compromise between administering and non-administering states, including all administering states, all permanent members of the Security Council, and such additional members elected by the General Assembly as create a balance. D.P.

United Nations Trust Territory.
A non-self-governing area which is governed by a state under trust arrangements with the United Nations, as provided by Chapter XII of the United Nations Charter. As the successor to the League of Nations mandates system, the Trusteeship system carries forward the ideal of national self-determination and the idea that the trustee power will act as protector and tutor to the trust territory to lead it in the direction of self-government. According to the United Nations Charter, trust territories should include territories previously held under League mandate, territories detached from enemy states by the victorious powers in World War II, and any other territory voluntarily placed under the Trusteeship system by an administering power. H.S.Th.

Uniting for Peace Resolution.
A resolution adopted by the General Assembly of the United Nations on November 3, 1950, at the height of the Korean War. The resolution maintained that the General Assembly may become responsible for maintenance of peace and security and thus can make recommendations to member nations for actions against an aggressor in case the Security Council is unable to exercise its primary responsibility in this field. The aim of the Resolution was to circumvent the deadlock created in the Security Council by the use of the veto power by the Soviet Union. While the General Assembly can not make legally binding decisions it can achieve its objectives through recommendations. If the latter are backed by an impressive majority of the member-nations they have a substantial moral and political weight. Thus member-states could proceed voluntarily to various recommended peaceful and military actions against an aggressor. The Resolution was specifically designed to provide the necessary backing to continued participation of the United Nations in the Korean War. In the long run the effect of the Resolution was to shift the main scope of the activities of the United Nations from the Security Council to the floor of the General Assembly. A preponderant influence in the entire U.N. system thus gradually accrued to the various big voting blocs of nations which were able by means of various combination to marshall the necessary two thirds majority, while in the Security

Council the veto power of the permanent members dominated.　　P.P.R.

Unit veto system.
A system in which national actors or blocs of national actors possess second-strike nuclear forces. Except for weapons, the system may be similar to "balance of power" systems, but this weapons difference also produces behavioral differences, e.g., reducing the value and hence the frequency of alliances.

Essential rules of the system: Those rules which, although based on the motivation or interests of the actors in the international system, are necessary to preserve the system from major change.　　M.A.K.

Universal Declaration of Human Rights.
Became operative on December 10, 1948, when it was adopted by the General Assembly of the UN. Since it is not a treaty and imposes no legal obligations, it did not have to be submitted to the members for ratification. It is intended to lay down "a common standard of achievement for all peoples and all nations" in the sphere of civil, political, social, and economic rights.　　H.L.M.

Universal Postal Union.
Founded in 1875, it became a specialized agency of the United Nations in 1947. Makes possible the free movement of mail throughout the world and is one of the most widely accepted international organizations. Acts as a research and information center and as a clearing house on inter-governmental postal accounts. Based on a convention and seven accessory agreements. Headquarters are in Berne. The annual budget is slightly over $600,000.　　W.C.R.

U.N.R.R.A.
See United Nations Relief and Rehabilitation Administration.

UNSCOP.
See United Nations Special Committee on Palestine.

Upper Volta.
(105,839 sq. mi.; 3,635,000 inhabitants).
The west African nation of Upper Volta emerged as an independent republic of the French Community with "special relations" status in 1960. Before then, this area had spent two years as an autonomous republic, was part of France's colonial possessions, was partitioned by its neighbors — Niger, Sudan, and Ivory Coast, and was the Kingdom of Ouagadougou under the protectorate of France. Its president is elected by the 75-member National Assembly which is chosen for five-year terms by universal suffrage. The capital city, Ouagadougou, is located at the end of the Abidjan-Niger railway. Export trade in livestock, fish, and groundnuts has been principally with Ghana.　　J.A.E.

Urban Agent.
An outgrowth of a movement to extend the scholarly resources of state universities to local communities in an organized and continuing manner, the urban agent or "urban scientist" is a "resource" person, broadly trained and versed in local community problems, and also a "catalyst" motivating communities to help themselves.　　P.J.C.

Urban County.
An American county, possessing traditional powers of county government, yet endeavoring to respond governmentally to burgeoning urban and suburban population growth. Located generally in metropolitan areas. Such counties offer a wider range of services than traditional, and utilize various methods — contracts, informal agreements — of coping with growing problems of urbanization.　　P.J.C.

Urban Renewal.
In the U.S.A. a comprehensive term that relates to the combination of public and private action that seeks to eliminate and prevent urban blight and slums. The program includes (1) slum clearance or total demolition and the redevelopment of the cleared land by private or public agencies; and (2) conservation and rehabilitation or the improvement and upgrading of deteriorating neighborhoods in which the majority of structures are capable of being saved. The Federal Housing Act provides for grants to communities to help finance the cost of acquiring and clearing blighted areas.　　H.J.Sch.

Uruguay.

Population, 2,700,000; area, 72,172 sq. miles. During the nineteenth century, Uruguay's political history was as chaotic as that of any other Latin American nation. The factional feuds between the Colorado and Blanco parties were reinforced by the nation's position as a buffer state between Brazil and Argentina. The transition of the nation to one of the more politically mature nations in Latin America in the twentieth century is largely due to the efforts of one man, Jose Batlle y Ordonez.

Batlle initiated the experiments in governmental structure and social welfare which have given Uruguay its unique characteristics. The first welfare state in the Western Hemisphere, Uruguay was among the pioneers in such policies as the eight hour day, workman's compensation, and other social reform programs. The constitutional system of Uruguay is also somewhat unusual, the nation being governed by a plural executive of nine members, based on a modification of the Swiss model. Ch.W.A.

U.S. Army Special Forces.

Military personnel with cross training in basic and specialized military skills, organized into small, multiple-purpose detachments with the mission to train, organize, supply, direct and control indigenous forces in guerrilla warfare and counterinsurgency operations, and to conduct unconventional warfare operations. T.W.

U.S. Civil Service Commission.

Created by the Pendleton Act of 1883, and serves as the highest personnel agency of the U. S. national government. The three members are appointed by the President with Senate confirmation for six year staggered terms; no more than two members may be of the same political party. The Commission administers and coordinates most of the merit system and civil service laws of the national government. In recent years considerable decentralization of personnel functions to the major departments has been encouraged; this has brought increased efficiency, flexibility, and cooperation while still retaining ultimate control with the Civil Service Commission.
R.D.S.

U.S. Democratic Party.

One of two major present American political parties. It traces its beginnings to the early 1800s and Thomas Jefferson. The party has traditionally been associated with American rural democracy, the South, and more recently has gained important urban and labor group support. However, strength comes from all regions and classes in the country. The Party program is broadly based and sometimes inconsistent; groups within the Party have quite varied political philosophies. Recent leaders have been Franklin D. Roosevelt, Harry S. Truman, and John F. Kennedy. R.D.S.

U.S. Department of Agriculture.

Established by an Act of Congress in 1862, it was administered until 1889 by a Commissioner. In that year Congress made it the eighth Department of the Federal Government and designated the Commissioner as the Secretary of Agriculture with cabinet status. Its purposes are: to acquire and disseminate useful information on agricultural subjects, to administer the national forests, to supervise the inspection of meat, to assist in the prevention of floods, to administer programs to dispose of surplus farm commodities, to cooperate with the States in a national school lunch program, to make loans to farmers for farm operations and to allow tenants to buy their lands, to cooperate with farmers' cooperatives and other non-profit organizations in financing electric and telephone facilities in rural areas.
R.G.S.

U.S. Department of Defense.

A principal department of the Executive branch of the Federal Government with the responsibility, under the President, for policy determination, and management of the military establishment including, since 1961, civil defense functions, of the United States. Established by the National Security Act of 1947, the department was originally designated "National Military Establishment;" redesignated Department of Defense in 1949 in major reorganization. Other reorganizations in 1953 and 1958 strengthened the authority of the

Secretary of Defense for centralized military planning, management and control, although the Army, Navy, Air Force and Marine Corps have maintained through 1962 a statutory independence and separateness. The Defense Department thus has remained a confederation of separate armed services, each represented on the Joint Chiefs of Staff by the Chief of each military service. Headquarters: the Pentagon on the Virginia side of the Potomac River. Address: Washington, 25, D.C.   H.H.R.

U.S. Department of Health, Education, and Welfare.
Formed on April 11, 1953, to combine several previously scattered federal activities into a single Department of Cabinet rank in the U.S. Government. The oldest federal activity is the Marine Hospital Service established in 1798 for sick seamen. This gradually expanded in functions to include quarantine and sanitation. It became the Public Health Service in 1912, with the National Institutes of Health and scientific research organizations under its jurisdiction.

The Office of Education, dating in function from 1867, collects and disseminates information on educational activities and methods throughout the nation and supervises federal funds allocated for educational needs, programs, and research.

The Social Security Administration, created to administer the Social Security Act of 1935, operates old-age and survivors insurance, public assistance, maternal and child health and welfare programs, and federal credit unions. It also administers the Children's Bureau, which is concerned with child welfare. Many of the Social Security programs are federal-state cooperative activities, with standards set by the federal government for matching state funds.

The Food and Drug Administration enforces federal standards for purity and quality, interstate transportation, and trade practices of foods, drugs and cosmetics. The Office of Vocational Rehabilitation establishes standards for federal grants to states that operate restoration to employment of the handicapped. The Department also operates a printing plant for the blind and two colleges, Gollandet College and Howard University.   T.K.N.

U.S. Department of Justice.
An executive department of the U.S. Government, headed by the Attorney General, who, assisted by the Office of Legal Council, gives legal advice and prepares opinions for the President and all U.S. agencies. The Solicitor General represents the U.S. in Supreme Court cases. Also in the Department are eight divisions: (1) Antitrust — enforces Federal antitrust laws; (2) Civil — responsible for all civil matters except those specifically delegated to other divisions; (3) Civil Rights — enforces all laws relating to Civil Rights; (4) Criminal — enforces Federal criminal law and supervises U.S. district attorneys; (5) Internal Security — enforces criminal laws relative to subversive activities; (6) Lands — supervises civil matters relating to U.S. real property interests; (7) Tax — represents the U.S. in civil and criminal cases arising under the internal revenue laws; and (8) Administrative — responsible for business management operations of the Department. Other agencies in the Department are the F.B.I., Bureau of Prisons, the Immigration and Naturalization Service, the Board of Immigration Appeals and the Parole Board.   J.E.R.

U.S. Department of State.
See Department of State.

U.S. Department of the Air Force.
Established as an Executive Department of the Army and the Navy. Congress took no action on a subsequent Joint Resolution proposing an Amendment to the Constitution of the United States to provide for an Air Force, apparently feeling that the Constitutional provisions for military power and national defense, particularly through the use of the "necessary and proper" clause, made such an Amendment unnecessary. The Air Force Academy was created in 1955 at Colorado Springs as a counterpart to the Academies at Annapolis and West Point.   R.G.S.

U.S. Department of the Interior.
Created in 1849, this Department

absorbed the General Land, Indian Affairs, Pension, and Patent offices, and assumed jurisdiction over public buildings, Penitentiary of D.C., census, accounts of marshals and other U.S. Court officers and over lead and other mines and other institutions. Formerly a general housekeeper, the Department today is more a custodian of natural resources, including petroleum and gas, solid fuels, electric powers, fishery commodities or products, metals and minerals, and scenic and historic areas. Its jurisdiction extends over the continental U.S., Caribbean and South Pacific Islands, and lands in the Arctic Circles, and over U.S. trust territories. This includes a special jurisdiction over Indians, Eskimos, and Aleuts in Alaska.

C.B.C.

U.S. Federal-Aid Highway Act of 1956.

(70 Stat. 374).

The Federal-Aid Road Act of 1916 (39 Stat. 355) and the Federal-Aid Highway Act of 1950 (64 Stat. 785) have been amended by the Federal-Aid Highway Act of 1956 and subsequent acts to expand and accelerate the Federal-Aid Highway Program. A sum of $36,685,000,000 was authorized to be spent by the national government on the construction of the Interstate System and other projects from 1957 to 1971 for the purpose of promoting local and interstate commerce and national and civil defense. In order to help finance the program the Act amends the Internal Revenue Code of 1954 by increasing taxes on motor fuel, tires, trucks, and buses.　　　　　　J.A.E.

U.S. House Un-American Activities Committee.

A committee of the United States House of Representatives created in 1938 under the chairmanship of Representative Martin Dies of Texas to investigate subversive or un-American activities; originally known as the Dies Committee, it was made a permanent committee in 1945 and named the Committee on Un-American Activities.

W.V.H.

U.S. Intelligence Board.

An interdepartmental American governmental body representing the major U.S. agencies having intelligence responsibilities. U.S.I.B. serves as a "Board of Directors" of the intelligence community. Replaced the Intelligence Advisory Committee in 1958. The Director of Central Intelligence serves as chairman and its membership includes representatives from Central Intelligence Agency, Departments of Defense (Defense Intelligence Agency) and State, National Security Agency, the Army, Navy and Air Force, Atomic Energy Commission and Federal Bureau of Investigation. Functions as advisory body to Director of Central Intelligence. Participates in making National Intelligence Estimates for the President and other high officials.

H.H.R.

U.S. National Committee.

Principal continuous governing agent of the national political parties in the United States. Composed of one man and woman from each state as well as from the dependencies. The Republican committee, in an attempt to provide a more accurate reflection of party strength, has since 1952 added a third representative — the state chairman — from those states demonstrating in one of several ways electoral victories for the party. While formally chosen by the national convention, the members are chosen by the states in various ways, either by direct primary, state conventions, state committees, or by the state delegation to the national convention. As committees they are most important in making plans for the national conventions and also in filling vacancies in the post of national chairman when the party is not in control of the presidency. They also take charge of the electoral campaigns for the presidency. Individual committeemen may enjoy some control over national patronage in their home states, particularly when the party has no senators.　　　　　　　　　　J.S.S.

U.S. Political Parties.

National political movements in the United States have their origins in the complaints of the frontiersmen against the indifference to their problems displayed by the Colonial rulers as well as those of the merchants against the burdensome commercial regulations of the home country. This combination, plus some landowners and many artisans, spurred on by Tom Paine's **Common Sense** and the Declaration of Independence, constituted the Revolutionary Party. Those whose dissatisfactions were not sufficient to dissuade them from adherence to the Empire were the Loyalists.

With the achievement of independence, a group of the Revolutionaries organized as the Federalist Party, pressed for the creation of a centralized governmental system and were joined by those Loyalists who had not migrated. The opposition to centralization, the anti-federalist farmers and artisans, functioned as the Whig or Patriot Party until the adoption of the Constitution and afterwards coalesced with the Jeffersonian Republicans.

The Federalists in control of the national administration under Presidents Washington and Adams, stressed the strengthening of the national government's powers, protection through tariffs of domestic industries, creation of a national bank, and assumption of the debts of the States.

The Republicans, favoring state and individual rights, won in 1800 and remained in control for a generation. The Federalists lingered on but the party's opposition to the War of 1812 destroyed its influence and it finally expired in 1820. Within the one remaining really major party, factionalism inevitably developed and the so-called era of good feeling was marred by various factions nominating their own presidential candidates to succeed President Monroe in 1824. The defeat of President Adams in 1828 by Jackson and his Democratic wing of the party led to a political realignment, the supporters of Adams designating themselves as National Republicans and some years later as Whigs. The example of a minor party that afterwards merged into the Republicans, the Anti-Masonic, in holding conventions instead of relying on the caucus for nominating candidates was adopted by both Democrats and Whigs, marking the death knell of "King Caucus."

Party organization and machinery were enormously strengthened under both groups, the Whigs for example instituting a vigorous and effective as well as successful campaign in 1840, including the initiation of mass meetings, processions, and torchlight parades.

The issues of slavery emerged in the 1840's as crucial for the parties. The Democratic convention of 1844 repudiated President Van Buren because he opposed the annexation of Texas as a slave state. Henry Clay, the Whig nominee, was regarded as insufficiently forthright against annexation to suit the abolitionsts who organized themselves under the Liberal Party banner. In New York, their vote was sufficiently strong to divide the anti-annexationists and throw the electoral vote and the election to the Democratic candidate, James K. Polk.

The Whigs returned to power in 1848 but sectional rivalries began to supplant the national party structure. The Democratic Party secured its greatest support in the south, picking up the Southern Whig vote and winning the election of 1852. The Whigs alienated their anti-slavery adherents and steadily lost ground, almost disappearing even before the establishment of the Republican Party in 1856. The issues of slavery, agrarian reform, tariffs, labor, migration, and others divided the country and led to a proliferation of minor parties. The Republicans were in effect a combination of many of these nativist, patriotic, labor, farmer, temperance, free soil, and abolitionist groups.

The Democrats could not resolve the slavery issue and split into several opposing factions that managed in part to reunite for the election of 1860 but failed to stop Lincoln from winning the Presidency. The much weakened party gave little opposition to the Republicans in the post-Civil War period but rather fastened upon an insurgent movement, the Liberal Republicans, in the election of 1872. The depression in the following year revived Democratic hopes and made the recovery of the party possible, culminating in the election of its presidential candidate in 1884. While the Republican Party thereafter dominated the national scene generally, the Democrats managed to provide a substantial opposition. With the split of the Progressives, the Theodore Roosevelt partisans, in 1912 from the Republicans, the Democratic candidate, Woodrow Wilson, was elected President.

Republican control was reinstituted in 1920, after the first World War, to give way a decade later because of the great depression. The Democrats, at a low ebb in the 1920's, had even found that many of their followers deserted them and supported the National Farm-Labor slate in 1924 but charged back to power in 1932 with Franklin D. Roosevelt, thereafter reelected for an unprecedented four terms. A greater degree of political balance, however, emerged with the elections of 1940. The Republican presidential candidate won in 1952 and again in 1956 although, as in some previous periods, the opposition frequently controlled one or both the houses of Congress and a majority of the states' chief executive posts. A close election in 1960 saw the first Catholic president and presaged a new era in American politics. M.B.D.

U.S. Republican Party.
One of two major present American political parties. First organized in the late 1850s, it gained national power in 1860 under Abraham Lincoln. Traditionally strongly supported in the Midwest and by eastern business interests, it nonetheless draws considerable strength in all areas (though still quite weak in the South) and from all classes. Though normally preferring a conservative philosophy, the Party in its programs is likely to be pragmatic and flexible; also some Republicans have been progressive or even radicals. Recent Republican Presidents have been Herbert Hoover and Dwight D. Eisenhower. R.D.S.

U.S.S.R.
See Soviet Union

U.S.S.R.—Chairman of the Council of Ministers.
See Chairman of the U.S.S.R. Council of Ministers.

U.S.S.R. Council of Ministers.
Described by the 1936 Constitution as the "highest executive and administrative organ" of the state. Consists of over 60 members: the chairman, first vice-chairman, vice chairmen, ministers, heads of important institutions such as the State Planning Committee and the State Bank, and **ex officio,** the chairmen of the Councils of Ministers of the fifteen Union Republics. The chairman and vice-chairmen, important party leaders, make the political decisions; the rest of the ministers are experts and/or competent administrators. Function: directs the All-Union and the Union-Republican Ministries, economic planning, state budget, public order, foreign relations, and defense.
K.Hu.

U.S.S.R.—Supreme Soviet.
See Supreme Soviet of the U.S.S.R.

U.S. State Central Committee.
Sometimes called State Executive Committee. The principal governing agency of state political parties in the United States. They are regulated by state law and vary greatly in size, composition, and powers. Some are chosen by direct primary election in congressional or legislative districts; some are composed of officials in the county organizations; some are chosen by county or state conventions. A committee's importance is greatest in carrying out party activities not otherwise provided for by law, such as the conduct of electoral campaigns, party finance, and planning for state conventions. Control of the committee may also be of national significance when it chooses delegates to the national convention. J.A.S.

U.S. States' Rights Doctrine.
The doctrine that the member states of the American union retain sovereignty over their internal affairs — especially over race relations — in spite of the clause in the United States Constitution that makes the Constitution itself the supreme law of the land. Advocates of states' rights at one time claimed that a state might secede from the union — as from a confederacy — but the outcome of the Civil War brought that idea to an end. The states' rights outcry is today, however, as loud as it ever was against "usurpation" by the Supreme Court of final authority to interpret the text of the Constitution. To some exponents of states' rights, racial segregation in public schools, etc., is beneficial and constitutional, no matter what the Court may say to the contrary. M.Sp.

U.S. Supreme Court — analysis of decisions.
Today qualitative and quantitative

methods are used to study public law. Of the former, the case method is most widely used. It originated with C. C. Langdell in 1871 as a revolt against the older methods of training. (Instead of relying on general rules from unexamined sources of authority, the student must formulate the general rules for himself.)

Some significant quantitative methods are as follows: (1) "Box score" analysis, used by C. Herman Pritchett (1948), which isolates various majority and minority voting patterns. (2) "Guttman Scale" analysis, used by Jessie Bernard (1955) but perfected by others, which uses a method of cumulative scaling borrowed from psychology. This method indicates whether a single dominant variable is present in a set of cases. (3) "Factor analysis," used by Thurston and Degan in 1951, which isolated the major variables affecting court behavior but those variables defied identification until Glendon Schubert's work (1962).

W.F.G.

U.S. Supreme Court "Packing" plan.

Refers to President Roosevelt's recommendations to Congress (1937) of a measure to improve and expedite the administration of justice by the Federal courts. The most controversial provision was the request for presidential authority to appoint one new judge to any court for each judge who had served ten years, who had reached the age of 70, and who within 6 months thereafter did not take advantage of present laws to retire on a pension. A total of only 50 judges could be so appointed, and the size of the Supreme Court could not be enlarged beyond fifteen members. This provision was to enable "new blood" to be infused into the federal judiciary because many judges failed to retire at 70 and stayed on the Court after their mental powers had declined, or their thinking on social problems had become obsolete.

The Supreme Court had already declared unconstitutional a number of New Deal laws and the Plan was attacked as being politically motivated; also it was opposed as striking at the independence of the judiciary. The Plan was killed by the Senate but only after the Supreme Court had in recent decisions indicated a more liberal attitude toward the New Deal.

E.G.T.

U.S. Tariff Commission.

A six-man body, established in 1916, for the purpose of investigating and reporting upon tariff and foreign trade matters, as required by statute. The members are appointed by the President and confirmed by the Senate for six-year over-lapping terms, with no more than three members being from the same political party. The President, either house of Congress, the House Ways and Means Committee, and the Senate Finance Committee can request the Commission to investigate and make reports on tariff and foreign trade matters. On its own initiative the Commission conducts studies concerning the operation of U.S. custom laws, the relations of foreign and domesic tariffs, and the costs of foreign and domestic production. In certain instances the President is required to ask the Commission for studies before he raises or lowers tariffs under reciprocal trade agreements.

G.B.H.

U.S. v. Butler.

297 U. S. 1 (1936).

Although the Court invalidated the AAA (1935) as constituting a regulation of production, the opinion's permanent importance lies in its endorsement of the Hamiltonian view of the spending power of Congress as one not limited to the direct grants of legislative power but extending to "the general welfare."

J.A.C.G.

U.S. Veterans Administration.

See Veterans Administration (U.S.A.).

Utilitarianism.

A philosophical movement prevalent in Great Britain from the late 18th to the mid-19th centuries, also called Philosophical Radicalism or Benthamism. Its founder was Jeremy Bentham, and other prominent names were James Mill, John Stuart Mill and John Austin. It was a part of the broad stream of liberal social and political thought. Its inspiration came from the French rationalists, but it was characterized by empiricism, individualism and attention to practical problems.

Its economic side favored laissez faire capitalism, though this was modified near the end by John Stuart Mill. Its most famous principle was that of utility, which was to be the standard to supplant all other standards.

H.S.Th.

Utopianism.
1. The social, economic, and political system described by Sir Thomas More (1475-1535) in fictional work entitled **Utopia**, a Greek word meaning nowhere. 2. Any ideal society of a socialistic or communistic nature. 3. A philosophy of social perfectionism.

Ch.C.M.

U-2 Affair.
On May 1, 1960 a Lockheed high altitude, low-speed jet reconnaissance aircraft operated by the U.S. Central Intelligence Agency and flown by Capt. F. Gary Powers, was downed some 1,200 miles within Soviet territory, near Sverdlovsk. Plane was flown from Peshawar, Pakistan, intending to land at Bodo, Norway after photographing military and industrial establishments and recording electronic signals in the U.S.S.R. Incident caused disruption of a Big Four summit conference in Paris and, after considerable confusion in Washington, prompted an unprecedented acknowledgment by the U.S. President that the U.S. was engaged in intelligence gathering by all possible means as defense against surprise attack. That U-2 flights were later continued, at least along Soviet borders, was indicated by a Soviet protest on September 4, 1962 about an overflight of Sakhalin Island, which the U.S. acknowledged as unintentional, and the use of U-2s in the fall, 1962, crisis over Soviet arms in Cuba.

H.H.R.

V

Value.
In abstract use, the noun "value" has tended to replace the noun "good" in political science (as it has in philosophy, psychology, sociology) since the end of the 19th century, especially in connection with terms such as "judgment" (value judgment), "ulterior," "ultimate," "highest." The capability of science to "set" values, to demonstrate the validity of absolute value judgments, or to establish a hierarchy of values in absolute terms is in dispute. Claimed by the "natural law" school of thought it is denied by "scientific value relativism." The former refers to nature, reason, intuition, and self-evidence as sufficient grounds for valid statements in this area; the latter declares the validity of "ultimate" values or standards of value, unless they are self-contradictory, to be beyond the reach of science (in its strict sense of **scientia transmissibilis**). Instead, it sees the proper function of science in this area in the scientific examinaton of the implications, consequences, risks involved in evaluations and in actions based on them, of the biological, psychological, etc. roots of evaluations, and of the methods through which evaluations can be influenced and changed or attempts to influence or change them be counteracted. However, scientific value relativism does not deny that there **may** be goods of absolute value (God, the pursuit of moral goals) nor the right of theology and philosophy to deal with them, provided that no scientific demonstrability is claimed. See Relativism. A.B.

Van Buren, Martin. (1782-1862.)
Eighth President of the United States. Born in Kinderhook, New York, Martin Van Buren received a common school education, was admitted to the bar (1803), practiced law, and meanwhile entered politics. Elected state senator (1812-20) and state attorney-general (1815-19), he became a prominent New York Democrat and leader of the "Albany Regency," forerunner of modern political machines. U.S. Senator (1821-28), briefly Governor of New York (1829), Jackson's Secretary of State (1829-31) and Vice President (1833-37), Van Buren assumed the Presidency (1837-41) in difficult circumstances inheriting the Panic of 1837 as an aftermath of poor financial policies by Jackson, but he did create the Independent Treasury System (1840) and establish a ten-hour day on public works. Defeated for re-election as the Democratic choice (1840), he lost again as the Free Soil candidate (1848) but his third party strength enabled the Whig nominee Zachary Taylor to defeat the Democrat Lewis Cass. K.E.D.

Vandenberg Tradition of Bipartisan Foreign Policy.
Policy associated with Senator Arthur H. Vandenberg of Michigan, a member of the isolationist bloc of Republicans who opposed a revision of the Neutrality Act of 1939. He subsequently became the leader of the internationalist wing of the Republican Party and advocated, with President Franklin Roosevelt, a bipartisan foreign policy program which subsequently supported the Truman Doctrine and the Marshall Plan. R.J.S.

Vargas, Getulio.
President of Brazil from 1930-1945, 1950-1954. The Vargas regime in Brazil has sometimes been described as an "easygoing tyranny" more in the pattern of the Latin American **caudillo** heritage than the thoroughgoing suppression of the Fascist model from which Vargas borrowed many of his concepts of government. The Vargas philosophy of **O Estado Novo** (The New State) was essentially ultra-nationalistic, with a component of social and labor reform, and attention to the industrial development of the nation. Ch.W.A.

Vatican.
The residence of the Pope and also, since the Lateran Treaty of 1929, the State of Vatican City. Last vestige of the Papal States, it has an area of 107.8 acres within Rome and a population of one thousand. It is the headquarters of two supreme and distinct authorities, ecclesiastical and civil. The Pope, as Supreme Pontiff of the

Catholic Church, administers its operations through committees called Roman Congregations, and judicial commissions called the Rota and the Signatura. The Pope, as sovereign, governs the civil state. His Cardinal Secretary of State supervises relations with other civil governments. Treaties made with these are called Concordats. The Vatican maintains diplomatic relations with 59 countries; its ambassadors are called nuncios. 48 Countries have ambassadors or ministers accredited to the Vatican. As a neutral state and as an authorative center for a Church embracing over 537 million people in virtually all nations, the Vatican exercises a significant role in international affairs and other social developments. A.A.N.

Venezuela.
Population, 6,700,000; area, 352,150 sq. miles. Until recent years, Venezuelan history has read as a succession of strong-man dictatorships. Antonio Paez, the lieutenant of Bolivar, dominated the nation's politics during the early independence period. The turn of the century brought such figures as Cipriano Castro and Antonio Guzman Blanco to the presidency of the nation. In the twentieth century, the "Tyrant of the Andes," Gomez, was the dominant figure. Since 1945, however, the development of the moderately socialistic party Democratic Action, led by Romulo Betancourt, has provided a countervailing force to the tradition of military and paramilitary dictatorship.

The exploitation of the petroleum resources of the nation, beginning in the 1930's, and the more recent development of iron and bauxite, have made Venezuela one of the wealthiest nations in Latin America. However, this income was poorly distributed among the nation's population. While the city of Caracas became a glittering metropolis and an indigenous upper class achieved opulence, the mass of the people continued to live in poverty. Since the fall of the Perez Jiminez dictatorship in 1958, the Betancourt government has been taking steps, through agrarian reform and social welfare projects, to correct this imbalance in the nation's economic life.
Ch.W.A.

Venizelos, Eleutherios. (1864-1936).
Greek Prime Minister from Crete and leader of the Liberal Party. In 1916 he established a pro-Allied government in Salonika against the opposition of King Constantine, and then took Greece to war against the Central Powers. His last term of office came between 1928-1932 when Greece was a republic. G.K.

Vereador (Alderman).
In Brazil, the member of municipal chambers. The expression comes from the old Portuguese terminology of colonial days. Aldermen are always chosen by election. At first they were chosen from among the citizens of good standing; today they are voted for according to the system of proportional representation. The existence of a Chamber of Aldermen constitutes one of the guarantees of the political autonomy of municipalities. T.C.

Verification.
Term used in disarmament discussions. Evaluation and formulation of conclusions based on information supplied by inspection system. First mentioned in disarmament resolution of UN commission for control of armaments and armed forces, January 11, 1952. To be applied after each stage of proposed total disarmament. H.G.S.

Versailles Treaty of 1919.
One of five peace treaties that terminated the First World War. It was signed on June 28, 1919 by the representatives of Germany, on the one hand, and those of the Allied and Associated Powers (except Russia) on the other. According to its terms Alsace-Lorraine was restored to France; the Rhineland was demilitarized; the government of the Saar was placed in the hands of a commission of the League of Nations for a period of fifteen years. The treaty also provided for an independent Poland; the loss to Germany of her overseas possessions; Germany accepted the responsibility for causing the war, was deprived of her general staff, and her armed forces were drastically reduced. The Covenant of the League of Nations constituted an integral part of the Treaty of Versailles. O.S.

Vested Interest.
This term is applied in politics to a person, group or institution actually in possession or control, or enjoying the benefits of a situation. It is a conservative force in politics, of a type which has been called "possessive conservatism." In law vested interest is a present right to a thing whose enjoyment or use might lie in the future. It is distinguished from contingent interest, and in some respects from future interest. H.S.Th.

Veterans Administration (U.S.A.).
This agency, headed by an Administrator, was created in 1930. Under other names and within various organizations, it has a number of predecessors. Veterans organizations have insisted that the Administration be kept independent of other Federal agencies. This serves to maximize their influence upon its policies and to keep Congressmen aware of the political influence of veterans. The agency provides a large number of services to veterans, including educational and retraining subsidies, the guaranteeing of home and farm mortgages, provisions of medical care in about 170 Administration hospitals, special unemployment and burial benefits, and pensions for those with service-connected (and some non-service-connected) disabilities. C.R.A.

Veto.
The right to oppose the execution of a decision. Internationally it is vested in certain countries as a political instrument against the decision of an assembly. Under internal law the veto is part of the legislative process permitting the Head of the Executive Power to prevent partly or in whole the passage of a bill. In most countries, the veto is again submitted to the approval of the House of Representatives, who may decide, by a special quorum, on the approval or rejection of the veto. As long as no decision is taken, regarding the veto, the law remains in force. T.C.

Vice-President.
The presiding officer of the United States Senate. He succeeds to the Presidency in the case of a vacancy in that office. He also has the title of President of the Senate. He is not a member of the Senate and has a vote only in the case of a tie; the Vice-President may be invited to attend cabinet meetings and be given special assignments by the President. W.V.H.

Vichy regime.
The authoritarian government of southern France during World War II. The capital was in Vichy (Allier). On July 10, 1940, Marshal Philippe Petain, Vichy Chief of State, was given full provisional powers of government by the French National Assembly. The following month he abolished the National Assembly and, thereafter, ruled by decree. The Petain government had jurisdiction over the unoccupied southern portion of France. The Germans occupied the northern part of France on the basis of the German-French armistice of June 21, 1940. The dividing line ran from the Swiss border near Geneva to a point twelve miles east of Tours, then southwest to St. Jean Pied de Port. Petain's regime was filled with Nazi sympathizers, including Pierre Laval, who had the title of "chief of government." Included among Vichy policies were anti-semitism; dissolution of trade unions; outlawing of strikes; strict censorship; and favoritism toward big business and the Catholic Church. E.R.W.

Vienna Congress (1814-15).
Conference of European powers aiming to restore the balance of power, which had been profoundly disturbed by the Napoleonic wars. The arrangements made produced a system that was to maintain European peace for 100 years until the outbreak of World War I. The Congress was remarkable also as a last determined effort to secure the principle of hereditary succession, referred to as "legitimacy," against the challenge of the new legitimizing principle provided by nationalism. P.J.F.

Vietnam, Democratic Republic of, (North Vietnam).
Area (estimate) 62,000 square miles. Population (1960 estimate) 16 million.
The Lao Dong, (Workers' Party) controls the government. Constitutions, 1946, 1960. Ho Chi Minh, veteran na-

tionalist and Communist leader, has been president since 1945.

Ho's Viet-Minh was the best organized independence party with effective military support. In opposing the Japanese, it joined with other political groups in a Popular Front. Independence came August, 1945. The Viet-Minh was recognized as the legitimate government by the Allies. When France refused to grant political autonomy, Ho led the revolt that became the "Indo-China War." In the Geneva cease-fire agreement, 1954, the 17° N. parallel was recognized as the dividing line between North and South Vietnam until a plebiscite could be arranged.

Openly Communist, receiving aid from the U.S.S.R. and China, Ho maintains greater freedom of action than any "satellite" leader, as he established his regime independently. War rages between the DRV and South Vietnam, though the DRV insists that it is a civil war in South Vietnam.

Ho had strong popular support in anti-imperialist campaigns. His program of collectivization and religious persecution still meets strong resistance. M.O'C.

Vietnam, Republic of, (South Vietnam).

Area (1960 estimate) 65,000 square miles. Population (1960 estimate), c. 13 million. Vietnam was a Chinese conquest in the second century B.C.: independent from 939 to mid-nineteenth century; the French took over its divisions as protectorates and a colony: included Vietnam with Cambodia and Laos in French Indo-Chinese Union. Vietnam was occupied by the Japanese in 1940; became independent in 1945. The "Indo-China War" ended in independence from France, but a divided state. (**Cf.** Democratic Republic of Vietnam). As South Vietnam had not been a party to the Geneva cease-fire agreements, it has refused to accept the proposed plebiscite.

A referendum deposed Emperor Bao Dai, October, 1955. Ngo Dinh Diem became Chief of State; President under the constitution of October, 1956. Universal suffrage and a secret ballot elect the 123-member National Assembly. The political power of the Cao Dai and Hoa Hao sects was broken by the government in 1955-1956. Following assassination of Diem in 1963 a military junta reorganized the government.

The army is trained by United States officers and aided by American volunteer paratroop corps. The campaign against guerrilla Viet Cong, supplied by the Viet-Minh, often through Laos, was stepped up in 1962. M.O'C.

Viet-Minh.

In 1941, while Indo-China was under Japanese domination, several political and other parties of the region decided to unite into one organization, which they called the Democratic Front of the Struggle for the Liberation of Vietnam. This organization became known by its short name — Viet-Minh. From the beginning it was under the influence of communist elements headed by the present leader of North Vietnam, Ho Chi-Minh. It united, in addition to the communist party, also representatives of various professional, peasant, youth, and women's organizations, as well as some religious Catholic and Buddhist groups. By the end of 1944 seven provinces of North Vietnam were infiltrated by the Viet-Minh and were ruled by this organization. In February 1951, Viet-Minh joined another major organization of Vietnam, called the Lien-Viet, the membership of which consisted of more stable groups of people, such as the intellectuals, bourgeoisie, and even some landowners and clergy. Lien-Viet was formed in 1946 for the purpose of fighting the French. The United Nationalist Front of Viet-Minh and Lien-Viet, became known as the Lien-Viet. V.P.P.

Village.

A term without precise meaning but used generally to connote a small municipality with simpler governmental organization and less extensive powers than larger municipalities known as cities. G.S.B.

Vindiciae Contra Tyrannos (1579).

A book presenting systematically the arguments of the French Huguenots and their allies on religious and political subjects which were current in the sixteenth century. The identity of the author of the work is subject to much debate. The assumption underlying the entire work is that the religion of the ruler affects the welfare of his subjects, that religion and politics are closely related, bypassing thus the possibility of isolating one from the other. The work espouses a twofold contract or compact, one between God and the King and people, the other between the King and the people, bringing thus man's relationship to God into the domain of politics. While the work gave a strong impetus to the 'contract' doctrine of modern political thought, it affirmed the divine origin of the monarch's authority, an authority which could not be challenged unless the religious conscience of his subjects was repeatedly violated. Thus the work envisaged limits to the monarch's authority, especially insofar as the religious rights of the people were concerned, and recognized the right of tyrannicide residing in the whole community. The work contrasted rather strongly with political theorizing prevalent at the time which espoused absolutism. The work had more influence in seventeenth century England than in France of its own time. V.Z.

Virginia Plan.
A proposal for the form of government that the American states should adopt for their union. The plan was presented by Governor Edmund Randolph of Virginia on May 29, 1787. This proposed form of government was made after the delegates decided to rewrite the Articles of Confederation to provide for a stronger national government, and along with the New Jersey Plan the Virginia Plan was the most important plan suggested.

The Virginia Plan consisted of a bicameral legislative body with the first house elected by popular vote and the second house elected by the first from lists of nominees submitted by state legislatures. The plan also proposed that the legislative branch elect a single executive for one term and that a national judicial system be established with supreme and inferior courts. Judges were to be elected for life tenure by the legislative assembly.
D.C.

Vlasov, Andrei A. (1900-1946).
Soviet general. Vlasov served as military adviser to Chiang Kai-shek, 1938-1939. He led Soviet units in the defense of Kiev and Moscow. Captured in 1942, Vlasov became chairman of the "Committee for the Liberation of the Peoples of Russia" (KONR), a Nazi-sponsored anti-communist group among Soviet prisoners of war. Vlasov commanded some KONR troops in actions near the end of the war. He was captured by Americans and turned over to the Soviets who executed him.
W.D.J.

Vocational Rehabilitation.
A term applied to the training of physically or mentally handicapped to enable them to be socially useful. The United States government, through the Department of Health, Education and Welfare, provides a number of grant-in-aid subsidies to the states to promote such programs. The U.S. Veterans Administration has a program for its clientele. C.R.A.

Volga Germans.
Descendants of German settlers who came to Russia in the eighteenth century. Inhabitants of the Volga German Autonomous Soviet Socialist Republic (vicinity of Saratov) were deported by Stalin to Central Asia at the start of World War II. The entire ethnic group may have perished. Certain other deported groups (e.g., Chechen-Ingush and Karachai-Balkars) are reported to have been returned from their places of exile, but the Volga Germans have not been mentioned. W.D.J.

Volkskongress.
See German People's Congress.

Volksrat.
See German People's Council.

Voluntary Associations.
Groups of individuals who have freely joined together for a common purpose. Particularly prevalent in the U.S.A. where it is estimated that there is one such association for every 100 persons. Also common in Northwestern Europe and Scandinavia.

Some definitions exclude churches, trade unions, and trade associations, because membership in such groups is not always completely voluntary. Approximately 40 per cent of the U.S. population belongs to one or more associations although active participation may be as low as 10-20 per cent. There are over 1,000 international associations usually composed of affiliates from individual nations. Purposes range through civic and public affairs, professional and vocational, health and medical, sports and hobbies, veterans and patriotic and welfare. Politically, they distribute power broadly, give individuals satisfaction with the democratic process and provide a mechanism for social change. W.C.R.

Voroshilov, Klimenti.
Born 1881, working class family, Verkhnee, Yekaterinoslav Province, now Dniepropetrovsk, Ukraine. Original member of Bolshevik faction in 1903. Member of Constituent Assembly 1918. Red Army Civil War commander. On CP Central Committee since 1921. Member of Politburo (called Presidium since 1952) 1926-61. USSR Defense Commissar (Minister) 1925-40, made Marshal of the Soviet Union in 1935. Poor performance in early World War II. Chairman, USSR Council of Ministers 1953-60, retired. Denied 1961 charge of "anti-Party" activity. Reelected USSR Supreme Soviet and Presidium in 1962. W.A.

Voting machine.
A mechanical device used at the polls in lieu of paper ballots for casting, and automatically tabulating, votes in an election. C.W.B.

Voting Turnout.
The proportion of eligible electors who vote in a given election. The actual proportion varies greatly from country to country and according to type of election. Turnout is highest in totalitarian countries running to over 95 per cent; in major parliamentary elections in western Europe it runs around 70 to 80 per cent; and in recent American presidential elections to around 60 per cent. Turnout tends to be higher in national than in local elections; in periods of crisis than in calm; in competitive than in one-party constituencies. J.S.S.

Vyshinsky, Andrei. (1883-1954.)
Born in Odessa, studied law at Kiev University. Joined Mensheviks 1903, fought in Bolshevik ranks during Civil War, joined CP 1920. Member of Party Central Committee 1939-54. His **Soviet State Law** 1939, (translated 1948 as **Law of the Soviet State**), is a polemic against "bourgeois" legal systems and against earlier official view of Pashukanis (purged 1937) and others that law will wither away gradually as socialism displaces capitalism. Vyshinsky argued that socialist law is distinctive and must be strengthened. He was professor of law 1920's, state prosecutor of purge trials 1936-38. Entered Foreign Commissariat (Ministry) in World War II; became permanent UN representative. Foreign Minister 1949-54. W.A.

W

Wahhabism.
A movement of religious reform in Islam led by Muhammad Ibn Abd al-Wahhab in the middle of the 18th century. Its inspiration came from the puritanical Hanbalite School and the teachings of the theologian Ahmad ibn Taimiyya (14th century). Ibn Abd al-Wahhab achieved his initial purpose of propagating his new teaching by alliance with the house of Sa'ud. Wahhabism called for a return to a literal interpretation of the Koran and the Traditions of the Prophet and for the restoration of the simplicity and austerity in public and private life in conformance with the example set by the Prophet and the first caliphs. It insisted upon the prohibition of intoxicating drinks, smoking, dancing and music and condemned all luxury in habitation, dressing and food and even the adornment of mosques. Fanatic and militant, the first Wahhabi State was politically crushed. Wahhabism had a spiritual and political renaissance at the beginning of 20th century under the leadership of Ibn Sa'ud. Most revivalist movements in Islam today trace their origins to the Wahhabism of 18th century Arabia. F.M.N.

Waite, Morrison Remick. (1816-1888). Chief Justice of the United States from 1874 to 1888. Waite's tenure in the Supreme Court covered a decade and a half of great social and economic change in the American society, generated by new industrial technology in the aftermath of the Civil War. His Court added substantive restraints to the procedural limitations embodied in the concept, "due process of law," extended the guarantees of the Fourteenth Amendment to the United States Constitution to corporations, formulated the concept of the "police power" as a validation of social and economic regulation by the states, and substantially curtailed the presumed power of Congress to protect the civil rights of Negroes by positive legislation. One of Waite's best known cases, **Munn v. Illinois** (1876), established the authority of the states to regulate the rates of public utilities and of businesses said to be affected with a public interest. E.L.

Walker, Edwin A. (1909-).
Formerly Major General, U.S. Army. As commander of 24th Division in Germany, instituted "pro-blue" troop education program on Communist methods and how to combat them; the American heritage and how to preserve it; and duties toward and benefits from the NATO shield. He was removed from command April 17, 1961, on charges of using materials published by the John Birch Society and Americans for Constitutional Action. According to evidence assembled by Senator Strom Thurmond (Democrat, S. C.) and private researchers Walker's removal was part of a concerted policy to weaken anti-Communist education programs. Since leaving the 24th Division, Walker resigned from the Army and ran (unsuccessfully) for the Governorship of Texas. K.G.

Wallace, Henry Agard.
Born, Adair County, Iowa, October 7, 1888. Vice-President of the United States 1941-45; Progressive Party candidate for President, 1948; Secretary of Agriculture 1933-40; Secretary of Commerce 1945-46; Editor, **New Republic**; Associate Editor, **Wallace's Farmer**, 1910-24. Editor, 1924-29; Editor, **Wallace's Farmer** and **Iowa Homestead**, 1929-33. Author of more than ten books, including **Century of the Common Man**. A.G.

War.
There are writers who contend that there is a generally accepted definition of war in the legal sense — a **de jure** war. Almost every writer on international law, however, has a definition of his own. The truth of the matter is that there can be no such definition in the legal sense, to wit a definition in the sense of all the rules of law on war, both municipal and international. The rules of law on war are not all made with one and the same intent and purpose. The particular rules are calculated to serve particular functions. Thus, what has to be looked for is not one over-all legal

definition of war, but a variety of legal definitions, each made in the light of and in relation to the particular intent and purpose of the rule which happens to be under consideration.

It is important to note that it is also impossible to define the expression "state of war," because it is but a substitute for the expression "war in **the** legal sense." Each legal definition of war has its counterpart in a corresponding legal definition of **peace.** The narrower the definition of war in the sense of a particular rule, the broader the corresponding definition of peace. The wider the definition of war, the narrower the corresponding definition of peace.

The definitions of war required by the various rules of law on war vary greatly in their respective latitudes. Some rules, the "laws and customs" of war on land or at sea, for instance, spring into life at the slightest provocation. Others are less likely to become applicable. Such, for instance, is the case with certain rules respecting the conduct of neutral powers. Still other rules call for a very narrow definition of war. Such rules, therefore, remain dormant while most other rules apply. Article I, Section 8, Paragraph 11 of the Constitution of the United States is a rule in point. There is no reason why Congress should enact a declaration of war as long as operations are instituted by Congress itself and not by the President in his capacity as Commander in Chief of the Army, Navy and Air Force.

Every single characteristic of a legal definition of war depends upon the intent and purpose of the rule concerned. The most often recurring themes in the definitions of war in **the** legal sense are to the effect that the parties to war are States and that its essence is an armed sruggle. Not even that much ought to be taken for granted.

There exists a marked difference between the meaning of the word **war** as used in common parlance and various legal meanings of war. Common sense sometimes does not recognize as war what must be considered as war in the sense of some rule of law on war. Common sense, on the other hand, sometimes, does not recognize as war what cannot be considered as war in the sense of some other **rule.**

History shows that States employ their armed forces in a great variety of modes, usually against another State or States. In spite of the great variety of modes, historians in general do not find it difficult to give some name to each concrete mode. In general they accept without hesitation the appellation which one or the other party employs officially. The military operations of the Powers in China in 1900-1901, for instance, went down in history not as a **war,** but as an **expedition** because the allied governments had styled them an **expedition.**

The task of the lawyer is of a different nature. Unlike the historian he is not concerned with adequate appellations, but with finding out whether a concrete mode of employing the armed forces of a State constitutes war in relation to and in the sense of some rule of law on war, and whether, in consequence, such rule applies or not.

Reasonable questions as to whether certain operations constitute war must needs relate to some rule of law on war, if the questioner expects a **legal** answer. Unrelated questions are unanswerable, because they leave the person to whom they are addressed in the dark about the rule of law in relation to which he might either assert or deny the existence of war.

Because there can be no such notion as a **state of war** or war in **the** legal sense, there can likewise be no such thing as a **state of peace** or peace in **the** legal sense.

The assertion that certain operations are an **act of war** or **de facto war,** in order to make sense **legally,** must relate to some rule of law on war. There is no potency in these terms irrespective of the intent and purpose of a rule of law on war.

Expressions like "imperfect state of war," "limited state of war," "partial state of war," "incomplete state of war" and "quasi state of war" stand and fall with the expression "state of war."

The expressions "imperfect war," "limited war," "partial war," "incomplete war" and "quasi war" likewise are useless as far as the law is concerned. The expression "partial war," for instance, tells nothing. It immediately raises the question: "partial" in relation to and in the meaning of which rule of law on war? There is, however, no need of stating that certain operations do not have all, but only a part of the characteristics required for the application of some rule of law on war. Such statement would be tantamount to stating that the rule concerned does not apply. Rules of law either apply or do not. There can be no "partial" application.

F.G.

War of Liberation.

According to Premier Khrushchev, addressing on January 6, 1961 the party organizations of the Higher Party School, the Academy of Social Sciences and the Institute of Marxism-Leninism, local war (limited war), is a military operation undertaken by "capitalist-imperialist" (Free World) forces short of global war, most probably for the purpose of putting down Communist guerrillas and insurrectionists. For example, an American military operation in a country outside the Communist Bloc would be considered a local war. A similar military operation by the Soviet Union or by Communist forces in the same country would be described not as a local war but as "war of liberation." Such a Communist military intervention would be justified as support of "liberation." Khrushchev acclaimed liberation wars not only as "just wars," but also as "sacred." He said: "We recognize such wars," which means that the Soviet Union is prepared and willing to fight wars of this type. Notwithstanding the points-at-issue in the Soviet ideological controversy, Khrushchev agreed with the Chinese Communists that such "just wars" are "inevitable" so long as imperialism and colonialism exist.

Under modern conditions practically any war can be described as a "war of liberation." In his January 6, 1961 speech, Khrushchev declared that the Soviet Union would help all those people who are "striving for their independence." In another passage, passing over the difference between national liberation wars and uprisings, he joined together the struggle for independence and self-determination with the struggle for social and national development; i.e., the struggle for communism. Thus, the Communists are free to justify any type of war as a liberation war. Khrushchev argued specifically that uprisings differed from "wars among states" and "local wars," but he did state that they should not be identified with liberation wars.

R.St-H.

War of Roses.

(England — 1455-85).

Intermittent non-idealistic factional and dynastic struggle between Houses of York (symbol: White Rose) and Lancaster (mistaken symbol: Red Rose; actually not used until 16th century). Closing Battle of Bosworth Field, Aug 22, 1485, called a "bleeding operation performed by the nobility upon their own body" (Smith, **History of England)**, marked a strengthened monarchy with the ascent of the Tudors and the final death of feudal anarchy and medieval England.

> Abate the edge of traitors,
>   gracious Lord
> That would reduce these
>   bloody days again
> And make poor England weep
>   in streams of blood.
>
> **(Richard III)**

J.P.D.

War Powers of the U. S.

President: The president is commander-in-chief of the armed forces of the U. S. A. and of the militia of the several states (when called into actual service of the United States). He has the power to enforce all laws. Troops may be sent anywhere. Executive orders may supplement acts of Congress. Public proclamations may be issued. Hostilities cease officially only after presidential order.

Actual declaration of war is the prerogative of the U.S. Congress.   M.F.

Ward (in U.S. politics).

A basic political division in the United States politics, usually consisting of the district from which a municipal, county, or other local official is elected. It is generally organized into voting subdivisions known as election districts or precincts. The ward, e.g., ward politics, frequently carries a connotation of close control by a power-oriented, patronage-minded or corrupt political boss.   M.B.D.

Warlords.
Term used to designate independent Chinese military commanders exercising **de facto** political authority in the regions of China occupied by their forces, during periods when there was no strong central government in effective control of China. The period from 1916-1927 is often referred to as the "warlord" period of modern Chinese history. The term "tuchuns" is also sometimes used to refer to warlords.
S.L.A.

Warren, Earl. (1891-).
Chief Justice of the United States since 1953. The Warren Court has been most notable for the development of new law concerning the civil rights of Negroes, the prosecution of defendants accused of subversion, the rights of witnesses in Congressional hearings, passport regulations, and state representative apportionment systems. One of the most famous cases in the Warren Court was **Brown v. Board of Education** (1954) which held that racial segregation in the public schools was a violation of the equal protection of the laws guaranteed by the Fourteenth Amendment to the United States Constitution.
E.L.

Washington, George. (1732-1799).
America's first president ranks second only to Lincoln in greatness among U.S. presidents. Planter, soldier, and statesman, Washington attained an unparalleled place in American history because of his granite-like character, rather than because of any other single attribute of excellence. Orphaned at eleven and with limited formal education, Washington grew to manhood among the Virginia aristocracy, from whom he acquired devotion to principle, the concept of **noblesse oblige,** and an imposing character.

Washington's mettle was tested early in life as a surveyor on the frontier and as a soldier in the French and Indian War. In 1759, he married Martha Dandridge Custis and lived at Mount Vernon, an estate whose holdings he so augmented and so managed that he became one of the wealthiest men in America.

Washington's fame rests upon three extraordinary achievements — his military leadership in the American Revolution, his work at the Constitutional Convention and his accomplishments as president. He took command of the American armies in 1775 and led them to victory over the British. He returned to Mount Vernon after the Revolution as the most famous man in America. Four years later, in 1787, his presence at the Constitutional Convention as its chairman, together with his pre-eminent stature, aided immeasurably in the successful completion of its work.

The unanimous choice of the Electoral College as first president, Washington served two terms, but declined a third. Major achievements of his administrations included his proclamation of American neutrality upon the outbreak of war in Europe, the establishment of American sovereignty over the territory within her boundaries, the institution of sound fiscal policy, and the construction of a superlative administration system. Of Washington, Jefferson wrote "that never did nature and fortune combine more perfectly to make a man great."
Th.P.

Water Apportionment, United States-Mexico.
Under the Treaty of 1906, Mexico was allotted 60,000 acre-feet of water annually from the upper Rio Grande for irrigation purposes in the Juarez Valley, between Acequia Madre and Fort Quitman, Texas. The Treaty of 1944, after setting up the order of preferences for utilization of international waters allocated to Mexico 1,500,000 acre-feet annually from the Colorado River plus, if available, 200,000 acre-feet; and divided between the United States and Mexico the waters of the lower Rio Grande and its tributaries. The International Boundary and Water Commission administers this allocation.
J.E.T.

Water Conservation — U.S.A.
In the U.S.A. under the direction of Department of Interior and states and local government. Involves storage, diversion, and development of waters for purposes of reclamation. flood control, hydroelectric power, and for municipal, domestic, and industrial use.
C.B.C.

Way of Life.
A set of socially accepted values and of institutional means for their pursuit and attainment, together with a set of established or emerging habits of behavior corresponding to them. To be distinctive for a group of people, a "way of life" must include at least some major social or political values and institutions that are different in time from those existing in the past or different in place from those prevailing among other groups of people, or both. R.W.V.W.

Wazir (Vizier).
The title of a minister of State in the Arab countries. The word is of uncertain origin. However, the office had existed under the Prophet. From secretary and adviser the Wazir, in close relationship with the Caliph, stood behind all the departments of government. With the Abbasids the function of the Wazir as the highest state and court dignitary was introduced under Persian precedent. The importance of the office fluctuated according to the personality of the Caliph and the official himself. Normally, the Wazir exercised a general supervision over the affairs of the empire. His position was comparable to that of a modern prime minister. The office was temporarily suspended during the period of the decline of the caliphate when the Wazir was overshadowed by the rising power of Buwayhid princes. It was restored to its former importance under the Fatimids in Egypt and the Wazir became the commander of the Armies as well as the director of civil administration. In the Ottoman Empire the Grand Wazir was chief in every department of the State, and had charge of all its affairs. He was the only person who had unrestricted access to the Sultan whose seals he held. During the Sultan's absence in war the Wazir presided over the **diwan**, a sort of council of state, which ran the affairs of the government. In the modern Arab world the title is used in the same sense as ministers in Western Governments. F.M.N.

Webb, Sidney and Beatrice.
(1859-1947; 1858-1943).
The Webbs provided an extraordinary intellectual and research partnership which through the Fabian Society contributed to a reconstruction of the British economy on socialist lines. Their studies of labor unions, cooperatives, local government, and of politics provided much of the ground for the development of the Labour Party, and Sidney Webb's **Labour and the New Social Order** (1918) provided the first program for gradual democratic socialism of the B.L.P. This program advocated an economic minimum standard of living, democratization of finance, nationalization of industry and land, and "surplus for the common good."
R.W.T.

Webster, Daniel. (b. 1782; d. 1852).
Constitutional lawyer, Congressman, Senator, twice Secretary of State, Webster greatly influenced public affairs until mid-19th century. Born January 18, 1782, in New Hampshire, he attended Phillips Exeter Academy and Dartmouth College. Admitted to the bar in 1805, he practiced at Portsmouth, N. H., for some years. As a Congressman from 1813 to 1816, he strongly attacked the administration's war program. After resuming law practice in Boston, Webster appeared as counsel in the Dartmouth College, McCulloch, Gibbons and other famous cases. Elected to the House again in 1827. An earlier tariff opponent Webster now became a protectionist and supported strong central government. Debating Hayne in 1830, Webster eloquently pleaded for constitutional supremacy and the cause of union and denied a state's right to nullify Congressional Acts. Sponsored by Massachusetts Whigs Webster carried only his own state in the 1836 presidential election. President Harrison named him Secretary of State in 1841, a post he retained also under Tyler until 1843. Again elected in 1844 to the Senate, Webster became involved in the dispute over slavery in the territories, favoring the Wilmot proviso. Regarding slavery as wrong, he argued that peaceful secession was not possible, and advocated moderation. President Fillmore appointed Webster Secretary of State again in July 1850, a position he occupied until his death October 24, 1852. C.F.N.

Wedemeyer, Albert Coady.
Born July 9, 1897, Omaha, Nebraska.

Graduated from West Point, 1918. October, 1943, as American deputy Chief of Staff of Southeast Asia Command. October, 1944, Gen. Joseph Warren Stilwell, recalled at demand of Generalissimo Chiang Kai-shek of China differing on cooperation with Chinese Communists; Wedemeyer succeeded as Commander of China Theater and Chief of Staff to Chiang. Stayed clear of Chinese politics; established better relations; helped to relieve China's "darkest hour." Remained in China till summer of 1946. Report on the fact-finding mission to China and Korea, July & Aug., 1947: for "drastic, far-reaching political and economic reforms in Chinese Government," placing Manchuria under trusteeship of China, Russia, U.S.A., Britain and France, and urging American forces stay in South Korea. Retired, July, 1951.   C.K.W.

Weimar Constitution.
Republican-democratic constitution of Germany 1919-1933; named after town where National Assembly adopted it. Provided for popularly elected parliament (Reichstag, q.v.), President elected by people for seven years, Government, consisting of chancellor and ministers, appointed by president, requiring confidence of Reichstag majority. Federal structure, member-states (Laender). Laender governments represented in Reichsrat. Laws enacted by Reichstag and Reichsrat jointly, occasionally by plebiscite. President emergency powers, could suspend comprehensive catalogue of basic rights and liberties. Multiparty sytem. Parliamentary processes functioned until 1930. 1930-33 presidential control, chiefly through emergency powers. 1933 replaced by Nazi dictatorship but not formally repealed.   J.H.H.

Weizmann, Chaim. (1874-1952).
Chemist, Zionist leader. Born Poland; studied Berlin, Freiburg. Professor, Geneva, Manchester. Director of British Admiralty Laboratories 1916-1919; discoveries in production of acetone were significant to Allied war effort in World War I. A member of World Zionist Executive from 1898, formulated "synthetic Zionism"—combination of political Zionism with agricultural pioneering activities in Palestine. His negotiations in England led to 1917 Balfour Declaration promising a Jewish National Home. Headed Zionist delegation to Versailles Peace Conference and negotiations for British Mandate in Palestine under League of Nations. President, World Zionist Organization and Jewish Agency for Palestine, Daniel Sieff Institute of Chemical Research, Weizmann Institute of Science, Hebrew University (which he founded in 1918). Key role in establishment of Israel and twice elected as its first president, 1948-1952.
   S.H.

Welensky, Sir Roy.
Prime Minister of the Federation of Rhodesia and Nyasaland since 1955. Born in 1907, he early became active in railroad trade union activities. As a member of the Northern Rhodesia Legislative Council he advocated amalgamation of Northern and Southern Rhodesia, with freedom from the British Colonial Office, but later, with Sir Godfrey Huggins (now Lord Malvern), then Prime Minister of Southern Rhodesia, worked vigorously for the formation of the Federation, composed of the Rhodesias and Nyasaland, which came into being in 1953. Succeeding Huggins as Prime Minister, he has championed Federation independence, and his insistence that the government should be in "responsible hands" has aroused the hostility of African nationalists, as well as his utterances on "partnership," which they assert is a blind for white domination. He is the leader of the United Federal Party in the Federation and despite attacks on the Federation remains strongly opposed to the secession of any territory from it, and points to economic advantages resulting from it.   E.V.M.

Welfare State.
A concept of government which, in the past three decades, has assumed an increasingly significant place in the socio-political thinking of many nations, including the United States, and has profoundly influenced the fiscal policies of government at all levels. Its viewpoint and terms of reference are broad in nature and are focused on social values, stressing social good while minimizing personal accumulation of wealth and economic power.

The welfare state undertakes to provide equality of opportunity and burden; to combat monopoly and curtail power; to encourage competition and aid small business; to distribute income equitably; to conserve the natural and human resources; to attain full and useful employment of capital, labor and resources; and to develop social security of an all-inclusive nature. Its method consists of governmental regulations of the economy, planning for economic and social development, expanding civil liberties and civil rights, and raising the standards of health, education and welfare of the people. It calls for governmental aid for education, government-sponsored health programs, public housing, old age pensions and survivors insurance, assistance to the blind, unemployment compensation and public works programs to prevent or relieve unemployment, child care, youth guidance, and other similar subsidies.

The welfare state reflects a shift in the concept of government from the negative role of maintainer of law and order to the positive one of large-scale promoter and dispenser of social services to the individual and his family. For example, the welfare state believes the government has the duty not only of compensating the unemployed but also of finding jobs for them. This change is the result of a combination of factors beginning with the industrial and technological revolutions and accelerated by urbanization, depressions and ravaging wars. The major accelerating factor was the economic depression of 1929-1941. As a result, public confidence in existing institutions was shaken, and government was compelled to step in when private enterprise failed to cope with the severe economic problems.

Inevitably, the welfare state impels governmental growth; and since the difficulties which the welfare state aims to remedy are generally broad, nation-wide in scope, the results are: (1) the growth of government and the greater centralization of political, economic and social power in government, especially at the national level; (2) increased taxes; (3) wider fiscal powers for government; (4) shorter work-week and more leisure for all; (5) the requirement of democratically minded administrators for welfare programs; and (6) the need for cooperation between capital and labor. Government is the essential instrument for maintaining the economy in a state of balance under conditions of persistent demands for additional economic and social reforms, increasing workloads, complexity of operations, and bureaucracy.

The economy of the welfare state is accordingly a mixed one. It is not laissez faire capitalism since the key element in providing the social welfare programs is government exercising dispensing and regulatory powers. Neither is it pure socialism since the essence of full socialism is total state control of, if not also total ownership of, all production, capital, land, resources and property.

In the United States, the New Deal of President Franklin Delano Roosevelt (1933-1945) and the Fair Deal of President Harry S. Truman (1945-1952) are principal periods of the welfare state concept in operation. Other countries, such as Australia, India, Israel, the Scandinavian states, and the United Kingdom are, to various extents, also examples of this movement.

Proponents of the welfare state characterize it as the answer to predatory capitalism on one hand and to regimenting socialism on the other. Opponents characterize it either as "outright socialism," or "a prelude to socialism," and warn that such huge expenditures for social welfare will destroy individual initiative, coddle the people, and bankrupt the nation.   O.K.

Welles, Sumner (1892-1961).

United States Under Secretary of State, 1937-1943. Welles spent one-quarter of a century in the diplomatic service, specializing for much of that time in Latin American affairs. It was he who originated the term "Good Neighbor Policy" to describe Franklin D. Roosevelt's rejection of "dollar diplomacy" and the use of armed intervention in United States dealings with Latin America. Friction with Secretary of State Cordell Hull led to Welles's resignation from the State Department in 1943.   D.M.B.

West Irian Conflict.
Jurisdictional conflict over the sovereignty of Western New Guinea. A Dutch territory (Netherlands New Guinea), the government of Indonesia laid claim to the colonial area following the struggle for independence (1949). Under the transfer of sovereignty the question of control was to have been discussed in 1950, but the joint committee charged with the task was unable to resolve the deadlock.
M.W.W.

Whampao Academy.
Set up in 1923 at Whampao, near Canton, by Sun Yat-sen for training a Chinese officer corps under Soviet advisers. Its graduates formed the nucleus of a new Kuomintang army under Chiang Kai-shek, the Academy's first President. At first Communists were also present, including Chou En-lai.

Whigs.
A term applied to the British Liberal Party. Prior to the use of the latter term in the nineteenth century the Whig Party was the main group opposing the Tories. It was originally a term of attack and its meaning included country bumpkins, cattle and horse thieves, and insurgent Scottish Presbyterians. It was first used politically in 1679 to designate those who favored the exclusion from the throne of the future James II, a Roman Catholic. In the United States the Whig Party was formed in the 1830's in opposition to Jacksonian policies, but the controversy over slavery produced dissension among the various Northern and Southern interests which had created the party.
R.H.B.

Whip.
A party member of a legislature who serves as an assistant floor leader. He keeps in touch with his partisan colleagues, canvasses their views, reminds them to be present when important votes are needed, and arranges "pairs" for absent members.
W.V.H.

Whiskey Insurrection (1794).
The militias of New Jersey, Pennsylvania, Maryland, and Virginia were combined and marched to western Pennsylvania in the summer of 1794 in order to quell the violence which had erupted by the refusal of many small distillers to pay the 1791 Hamiltonian Excise Tax on whiskey. The reluctance to pay the tax led to protest meetings, harassment of collectors, intimidation of other persons, and destruction of property. When it appeared to President Washington that civil authority alone could not enforce the law and that the insurgents would not submit, he overawed the rebels with such a large force no combat occurred.
J.A.E.

White, Walter Francis. (1893-1955).
Executive Secretary of the National Assn. for the Advancement of Colored People, 1931-55. Born in Atlanta, Ga., and educated at Atlanta U., Walter White, of Caucasian appearance, joined the NAACP staff in 1918 principally as an investigator of lynchings and race riots.

An affable personality, public relations skills, a sense of timing, and organizational politics facilitated his rise to executive leadership and to national prominence in politics and intergroup relations. The able lobbyist had easy access to U.S. Presidents F. D. Roosevelt and Truman but was highly controversial within and outside the NAACP. He published works on lynching, and autobiography **(A Man Called White,** 1948), and an award-winning review of U.S. race relations **(How Far the Promised Land?,** 1955, posthumously).
N.P.T.

White primary.
A political party's nominating election in the U.S.A. from which Negroes were excluded on the grounds that the party's choice of its candidates is private and not state action. Outlawed by the U.S. Supreme Court in 1944.
C.W.B.

Whitley Councils.
Named after the chairman of a British ministerial committee (1916), these councils were originally formed to settle grievances in wartime industries but have become associated with the Civil Service. Departmental and National Whitley Councils have been instrumental in setting standards of work and redressing grievances in the British Civil Service.
R.G.N.

Whitlock, Brand (1869-1934).

American municipal leader, diplomat and author. Born in 1869 in Urbana, Ohio, Whitlock transferred from daily journalism in Chicago and Springfield, Illinois, to secretarial service with Gov. John Peter Altgeld and Senator John M. Palmer, both of Illinois. In 1897 he began legal practice in Toledo, Ohio, of which he was elected mayor in 1905 in succession to "Gold Rule" Jones. Re-elected three times, he became known in his eight-year tenure as a friend of the underprivileged and for his handling of new and perplexing municipal problems he was widely studied and reported. In 1913 Wilson appointed Whitlock minister to Belgium where presumably he would enjoy leisure to work at his avocation of novelist. But with the outbreak of World War I in 1914 and the invasion of Belgium by the German army he soon became a world figure. Staunch champion of the civilian victims, many of them women and children, he organized an international relief program for food, clothing and shelter; as on-the-ground administrator he saw that the assistance reached those in dire need. He issued a report on the execution of English war nurse Edith Cavell which provoked German demands that he be withdrawn from Belgium. He died in Cannes, France, where he spent his last years writing, and was buried there. His autobiographical **Forty Years of It** (1914) is a classic account of imaginative, humanitarian municipal administration. I.Di.

Whitman, Walt. (1819-92).

American poet and editor. Son of a farmer-carpenter, Whitman was born in 1819 on Long Island, N. Y. He quit school early and was an office boy at eleven. In his thirteenth year he became a printer's devil at the Long Island **Patriot**. From then until publication of his classic volume of poems, **Leaves of Grass**, in 1855, he was engaged mostly in newspaper work. He wrote editorials for the Brooklyn Daily **Eagle**, 1846-48, and the Brooklyn **Daily Times**, 1857-59. He also edited **The Freeman**, a Brooklyn paper of the Barnburner Party, 1848-49. His sympathies were against slavery and he favored emancipation on a gradual basis, but he objected to the extremist course of the abolitionists. Urging territorial expansion, he was a patriotic nationalist. Yet he was opposed to nativism as in conflict with democracy whose virtues he praised editorially and sang in poetry. Against capital punishment, he called for prison reform and criminal rehabilitation. He strongly advocated free public education and better working conditions for laborers. Above all he sought through his writings to be the spokesman for the common people and their hopes and ambitions. After the Civil War, in which he cared for casualties, he was dismissed from a clerkship in the Department of the Interior for having written a "scandalous" book. This brought on a public controversy with pamphlets in support of Whitman and a vindicating appointment in the Attorney General's office. In later life, he was disturbed by increasing materialism and corruption which he believed had put democracy on trial. When Whitman died in 1892 in Camden, N. J., he was already a mystical, legendary figure.

I.Di.

Willard, Frances Elizabeth. (1839-1898).

Educator, reformer, lecturer. Born at Churchville, New York, but grew up on a farm at Janesville, Wisconsin. After graduating from the North Western Female College at Evanston, Ill. (1859), she began teaching and she became President of the Evanston College for Ladies (1871), and first Dean of Women at Northwestern U. With enthusiasm she joined the new temperance reform called the WCTU and was its Secretary (1874) and President (1879-1898). Under her dynamic leadership the Union grew to 10,000 local units with a paying membership of 250,000 women enlisted in 39 departments for "Home Protection" including suffrage. It was the great woman's movement of the period and formed an effective pressure group before state legislatures for temperance and women votes. At her death, Congress extolled her as, "the first woman of the 19th century." M.E.D.

Williams, Roger (1603-1683).

Puritan minister and founder of Rhode Island. Fleeing from England to Boston in 1631, he became a separatist, arguing for Puritan withdrawal from the Church of England. Denying that the state has any authority over religious matters, he was expelled from Massachusetts Bay Colony in 1636. The English Puritans, who were in general agreement with his radical writings, granted him a charter for the founding of Rhode Island, the first American colony to tolerate complete religious freedom. In Providence, he established the first Baptist Church. Deriving his political ideas from his religious thought, he believed that all religions stand as equals before the law, that religious liberty demands limitations on political authority, and that the economic policies of a state, no matter how opprobrious, are not the province of the church to condemn. It was Williams who gave articulate expression to the revolutionary sentiments of lower middle class sects, assisting in the overthrow of the Massachusetts oligarchy. R.F.H.

Willkie, Wendell. (1892-1944).

Lawyer, industrialist, politician. Born at Elwood, Indiana. He studied at U. of Indiana receiving a law degree (1916) and entered industry from the legal department of Commonwealth and Southern Corporation becoming President (1934). Attacking the New Deal, especially TVA, he was a favorite speaker at financial meetings. He achieved national prominence by his debate at Town Hall Meeting of the Air (1938) and his appearance soon after at the N. Y. Herald Tribune Forum. **The New York Times** (Feb. 23, 1939) suddenly boomed him for President. He warmed the hearts of millions by being on the radio program "Information Please" (April 9, 1940). Thereafter, independent Willkie Clubs sprang up all over dedicated to his candidacy. At the Republican National Convention in Philadelphia (1940) he was nominated presidential candidate on the 6th ballot. Despite his ebullient personality he was defeated in the ensuing campaign chiefly because of the "Battle for Britain" and his lack of political experience. Although 22 million people voted for him, the Electoral College result was 449 to 32. Resented by the professional politicians, he was nonetheless the conscience of his party and lifted it to new goals. As the self-styled Leader of the Loyal Opposition, he visited (1942) the USSR and China on a 31,000 miles flight to show American unity. On this mission he travelled as the emissary of the President and held diplomatic rank. He carried the message of Global Unity and brought closer the friendship with China as he was instrumental in ending extra-territoriality and Chinese exclusion. M.E.D.

Wilson, (Thomas) Woodrow. (1856-1924.)

Twenty-eighth President of the United States. Born at Staunton, Virginia, Woodrow Wilson received an exceptional education He graduated from Princeton (1879), attended the University of Virginia Law School (1880), and received a Ph.D. from Johns Hopkins in 1886. Meanwhile he was admitted to the bar (1881) and practiced briefly in Georgia (1882). Finding law unrewarding financially and personally, Wilson began a distinguished career as an author and college professor of history and political science at Bryn Mawr (1885-88); Wesleyan (1888-90); and Princeton (1890-1902) before becoming President of Princeton (1902-1910). He resigned to enter politics, was elected Democratic Governor of New Jersey (1911-13), changed his viewpoint from conservative to liberal, and led a state administration noted for its political and social reforms. Nominated by the Democratic Convention in 1912 on the forty-sixth ballot with help from William Jennings Bryan, Wilson was elected by popular plurality to a first term as President (1913-17) with the Republicans dividing their support between President William H. Taft and ex-President Theodore Roosevelt. Wilson was narrowly re-elected President (1917-21) over Republican challenger, Charles Evans Hughes, on the slogan "He kept us out of war." President Wilson's New Freedom program dealt directly with the great issues before the country. The tariff was lowered, and a Federal Reserve Act, Federal Trade Commission Act, and Clayton Anti-Trust Act all passed, and three constitutional amendments were adopted providing for direct election of Senators, prohibition, and the right to vote for women. When war broke out in Europe Wilson attempted to keep the United States neutral in thought and deed, but the renewal of unrestricted submarine warfare by Germany prompted him to request a declaration of war (1917) to make the world safe for democracy. When the Allies won, he personally went to Paris for the peace talks and worked hard to achieve his program for enduring peace based on the Fourteen Points. Compelled to give way on some and compromise others, he did win acceptance in the Peace Treaty of his great dream for a League of Nations, but the Senate of the United States refused to ratify American membership in the League. Wilson collapsed in Pueblo, Colorado, while on a speaking tour in defense of the Peace Treaty and the League, and remained a semi-invalid the rest of his term and life. Awarded the Nobel Peace Prize (1919), Wilson died broken in body and spirit, but his eloquence and splendid ideals lived after him to become the inspiration for American leadership in forming and sustaining the United Nations. K.E.D.

Winthrop, John (1588-1649).
Puritan founder and governor of Massachusetts Bay Colony. Educated at Trinity College, Cambridge (1602-1604), he became attorney at the Court of Wards and Liveries in 1626. In 1629 he was elected governor of the recently formed Massachusetts Bay Company, and in 1630 he migrated with the Company to New England. His political ideas were based predominantly on the Bible and on Calvin's **Institutes.** He believed that there was no sanction for democracy in Holy Scriptures. Yet because the freemen of the Colony insisted on their rights under the royal charter, he compromised for a "mixed aristocracy." He regarded the Colony as a Christian commonwealth derived from a contract between God and the Colonists. Although he considered the state to be entrusted with religious orthodoxy, he would not permit the clergy to interfere in the actual governance of the colony. His important political work was the **Little Speech on Liberty,** in which he maintained the indispensable relationship of liberty and authority. In his economic thought, he argued for the medieval "just price," governmental regulation of wages, prices, and production, and a divinely decreed and hierarchical system of social classes. R.F.H.

Wiretapping.
Clandestine listening to conversation especially telephonic conversation by almost any kind of mechanical device. The Federal Communications Act of 1934 forbids the use in United States federal courts of wiretap evidence, however, this has not prevented official wiretapping. A number of states authorize wiretapping by the police under a warrant. The Supreme Court decisions on this subject have wavered between the ideals of individual privacy and the practicality of using modern techniques to fight crime. B.N.

Wise, John (1652-1725).
American clergyman and pamphleteer, staunch defender of liberty and democracy in Puritan era. Born in Roxbury, Massachusetts, and graduated from Harvard (1673), he was ordained (1683) a Congregational minister in Chebacco, a parish of Ipswich, Massachusetts, where he remained the rest of his life. Inciting the citizens of Ipswich to resist the proposed province tax of Governor Edmund Andros in 1687, he was tried, convicted, fined, removed from clerical office, and placed under peace bonds. Andros later restored him to the ministry. Wise sued Joseph Dunner, the judge who had pronounced the sentence, for refusing to grant him a writ of habeas corpus. Apparently he was awarded damages. In a pamphlet **The Churches Quarrel Espoused** (1705), he branded as reactionary Increase Mather's **Questions and Proposals,** which argued for the establishment of a church council of Massachusetts ministers that would assume the authority then exercised by the individual churches. Mather's movement was soundly defeated. The pamphlet **A Vindication of the Government of New England Churches** (1717) examined the principles of both civil and religious administration. Supporting the project of many liberal groups to establish a monetary system based on paper currency, he published the pamphlet **A Word of Comfort to a Melancholy Country** in 1721.
R.F.H.

"Withering away" of the State.

The concept was given its classical form in Engels' **Anti-Duehring** (1878); it was supposed to coincide with the achievement of socialism in which the means of production were transformed into state property, the disappearance of classes, and the replacement of the government of persons by "the administration of things." Lenin insisted that the state would disappear only after a society had passed through two stages, first the socialist and then the communist; and emphasized the great difference between these two stages. Paraphrasing Saint-Simon, he said in his **State and Revolution** (1917): "The state will be able to wither away completely when society has realized the rule: from each according to his ability, to each according to his needs." Under Stalin, the principle became "from each according to his ability, to each according to his work." The 'withering away' process was played down although never explicitly disavowed by Stalin; its postponement was justified by 'capitalist encirclement' and the need for the greatest possible industrialization. The state was to assume more power under 'socialism in one country.' The progress of 'socialist construction' was thus linked with the state's further institutionalization and the concept of 'withering away' became irrelevant. Khrushchev combined the Leninist and Stalinist viewpoints. He authorized certain practical steps toward communism through greater participation of the general public in enforcing public order and in a newly decentralized system of justice, but simultaneously he urged the immediate strengthening of the state. W.J.S.

Witte, Sergei Yulievich. (1849-1915).

A Russian statesman, who was born in Tiflis, in 1849. He received his education at the University of Odessa. An efficient administrator he was appointed Director of the Department of Railways in the Finance Ministry in 1889, and became Minister of Communications in Feb. 1892. In August of the same year he was given the post of Minister of Finance. Witte is known for his financial reform in Russia, in 1897. He devaluated the ruble, lowered its value by 1/3 and put gold into circulation stabilizing Russian currency. In 1903, Witte became Chairman of the Council of Ministers. In his foreign policy he favored a peaceful penetration of the Far East by financial and economic means. At the end of the Russo-Japanese War, Witte was sent to Portsmouth, N. H. to conduct peace negotiations with the Japanese delegates. His diplomacy at the conference led to the conclusion of a Peace Treaty without surrendering territorial concessions with the exception of the southern part of the Sakhalin Island. On his return to Russia, Witte received the title of Count. To put Russia on a sound financial basis, he negotiated a loan from France in the amount of 2.25 billion gold French Francs. In April 1906 Witte was retired and appointed to the post of member of the State Council.
V.P.P.

Woolsey, Theodore Dwight.
(1801-1889).

Ninth president of Yale College (1846-1871), outstanding Greek scholar, Congregationalist minister, historian, international lawyer, and political scientist, was born in New York City and died in New Haven, Connecticut. His **Introduction to the Study of International Law** (first edition 1860, sixth edition 1891), widely used in American colleges and at Oxford in England, gained him much fame. His two volume work, **Political Science or The State Theoretically and Practically Considered** (1877), was truly rated at the time as "the most scholarly and systematic presentation of the principles of political science" to appear from the pen of a native American. Founded on natural law principles his political philosophy is in the classical and Christian tradition.
G.A.K.

Working Class.

In Marxism, the proletariat, one of the two basic elements of dialectical materialism which explains social change in terms of class welfare; the other essential class, standing in 'contradiction' to the first, is the bourgeoisie. The working class is the foundation of the Marxist state functioning as a dictatorship of the proletariat; in the early stage of the Soviet State, it was the epitome of all civic virtues and the focus of literary and cultural activities, and served as a pretext for indirectly praising and glorifying the State. In non-Marxian terms the concept has a broader and vaguer meaning; it is lacking in self-consciousness and is generally taken to include lower economic groups in society. W.J.S.

World Government.
The concept of world government has never completely faded from Western civilization since the disintegration of the Roman Empire. In the 20th century it has been increasingly prominent as various persons have felt dissatisfaction with the national state as the basic unit of modern politics, and the doctrine of sovereignty as its legal foundation. The problem of war, exacerbated by the erosion of the international law of war, by the development of total war tendencies, and by nuclear weapons, has been a powerful stimulant to world government ideas. A number of individuals and organizations have put forward proposals and schemes to unite the world, usually under some sort of federal plan which would preserve the existing national states for some purposes. H.S.Th.

World Health Organization (WHO).
Specialized agency of United Nations, successor to health activities of League and related international health organizations. Constitution drafted in 1946 by international health conference, ratified in 1948. Purpose: universal attainment of highest health standards and complete physical, mental and social well-being. Functions: research, information dissemination, technical assistance and international standards in health fields.

109 members. H.Q., Geneva. F.B.G.

World Peace Council.
A Communist-front organization, founded on November 22, 1950 at Warsaw by the Second World Peace Congress. It claims to represent over six hundred million people through the work of 442 "representatives of all forces engaged in practical action for Peace" in 72 countries. The major objective of the Council is to gain widespread support from individuals and groups ordinarily unresponsive to Communist doctrines. By playing the role of "champion of peace," it aims to win such elements away from democratic ideology and politics to an illusory concept of neutrality which plays upon the universal desire for peace, abhorrence of warfare, and the peaceful purposes of the Soviet Union. P.A.T.

Wrangel, Baron Peter N.
(1878-1928).
Successor, early in 1920, to Denikin as leader of White forces in Russian Civil War in the Ukraine. Wrangel campaigned successfully in the Taurides for a time but eventually was forced back into the Crimea. The entire Red Army under Frunze was concentrated against him. Frunze defeated Wrangel at Perekop and Chongar in the Crimea and forced his evacuation from Russia in November 1920. He died in Belgium in 1928. W.D.J.

Write-in candidates.
While the vast majority of candidates for public or party office are nominated or elected through party petitions and primary and general elections, there are provisions in many states permitting the voter to insert in an appropriate place the name of an individual for a particular office. Such write-in candidates are nominated or elected if they secure a majority or plurality and are otherwise eligible. Successful write-ins are very rare. M.B.D.

Wyszynski, Stefan (1901-   ).
Born in Zuzela, province of Bialystok. Studied abroad and received doctorate. Known as "labor priest." Advanced to archbishop (1948), primate (1949), cardinal (1952). Arrested in Warsaw and imprisoned, 1953-56. Since then free but under constant pressure by Communists, due to strong hold of Church on the people. R.F.S.

Y

Yagoda, Henrikh Grigorevich.
(1891-1938).
Soviet **apparatchik;** sided with the Bolshevik faction of the Social Democratic party after 1907; in 1920 member of the Presidium and one of the mainsprings of the Soviet secret police **Cheka** (after 1922 known as the GPU; later reorganized as the OGPU and then as the NKVD) of which he became head in 1924. Knowledgeable in pharmaceutics he became Stalin's chief political poisoner and an originator of GPU's toxicological methods. Yagoda was made Commissar of the Interior in 1934, and was elevated to the rank of General Commissar of State Defense in 1935. He shared in the murder of Maxim Gorky and led the annihilation of the Zinoviev-Kamenev group. He fell into political disgrace in 1936. Arrested in April 1937, he was accused of conspiring against Stalin, tried in March 1938 with the "bloc of rightists and Trotskyists" (which included Bukharin, Rykov and Krestinsky) and executed.
W.J.S.

Yalta Agreement.
Churchill, Roosevelt, and Stalin met at Yalta, the Crimean resort, from February 4-11, 1945, and reached agreement on a variety of postwar issues. In the Far East, in return for the promise to enter the war against Japan within three months after the German surrender, the Soviet Union was granted basically what had been Russian before the Russo-Japanese War of 1904 (S. Sakhalin, rights over Port Arthur, Dairen, and Manchurian railroads, recognition of influence in Outer Mongolia; also, the Kurile Islands). These concessions, made at a time that the atomic bomb was still untested, were kept secret until 1946 and were granted regardless of China's reaction. As to Germany, each of the big powers (including France) was to have an occupation zone, with coordination of policies through a central control commission. Nazism and German militarism were to be extirpated, but no definitive decision was reached on dismemberment nor on the amount of reparations. As to Poland, its eastern frontier was to follow the Curzon line, thus granting the Soviet Union large territorial concessions, while territorial compensations for Poland were left for final determination at the "peace conference." In Poland and other liberated countries free elections and governments responsive to the people were to be introduced, under the supervision of the Allied power in actual occupation of the country. Finally, the Soviet Union was promised support for its "three votes" in the UN Assembly, while Stalin agreed to a very slight limitation on the Big Five veto in the UN Security Council. Several Yalta "paper" agreements were soon violated and distorted, as the realities of the location of military power made their enforcement seemingly impossible.
H.L.M.

Yankee Imperialism.
Various political groups and individuals in Latin America have throughout the twentieth century characterized the relations of the United States with that region as imperialistic in nature. Whether interpreted within the framework of Marxist thought or not, United States Latin American policy is seen as having parallels with European colonial practice, though the end of achieving a sphere of influence in this region was usually achieved without direct political control. Policies cited in support of an imperialistic interpretation of United States Latin American policy generally include: the Roosevelt Corollary to the Monroe Doctrine and the Platt Amendment to the Cuban constitution, permitting American intervention in the political affairs of Latin American nations; fiscal control and the presence of U.S. marines in the Dominican Republic, Haiti and Nicaragua from 1910-1932; the economic power of American firms operating in Latin America and the use of public policy in support of these companies; the U.S. presence in the Panama Canal Zone; and the influence of the United States in delimiting the sphere of legitimate political activity in the Hemisphere.
Ch.W.A.

Yellow-Dog Contract.
An agreement, whereby an employee as a condition of employment, agrees that as long as he is in the employment of the employer, he will refrain from

joining a labor union. The origin of the term is from the custom of laboring men in declaring that employees who sign such an agreement have no more status than a yellow-dog of uncertain parentage. G.B.T.

Yemen.
Consists of some 74,000 square miles of mountains and coastal strips. Its population is estimated at 6 million. While most of the Peninsula is Sunni Muslim, Yemen is half Zaidi (Shi'i Islam) and half Sunni. Its ruler until recently has been the traditional Imam. In October of 1962 an army revolution under strongman Sallal did away with the Imamate and declared Yemen a republic. The civil war between the republicans and the Imamites has not yet ended. Yemen has no significant oil resources, and is virtually free of the symptoms of modern civilization. E.A.S.

Yezhovshchina.
Period of intense blood purges in the USSR. So-called after Nikolai I. Yezhov who was Commissar of the Interior from January 1937 to December 1938. The purges were accomplished by Yezhov under Stalin's supervision. During the Yezhovshchina the top leadership of the Communist Party and the Red Army was virtually destroyed. Among the more prominent figures who were liquidated were Tukhachevsky, Radek, Bukharin, Rykov and Piatakov. Yezhov himself was later purged. W.D.J.

Yishuv.
Lit. "settlement"; refers to Jewish community of Palestine, primarily in pre-statehood Israel. Recognized as internally self-governing by British mandatory regime. S.H.

Yoshida, Shigeru. (1878-).
B.A. Tokyo University. Became prime minister during the post-war occupation period and until 1954. His chief concern was the reconstruction of post-World War II Japan. H.U.

Young China Party.
The Young China Party received its early impetus from the ideas of nationalism. When China, one of the Allies in World War I, was refused equal treatment at the Paris Peace Conference, nationalistically-minded students determined to redouble their scholastic efforts in order to build up a stronger state. At first they organized a Young China Learning Society emphasizing scholastic endeavors and self-reliance. But in the mid-thirties the name was changed to Young China Party. Most of its members had pursued advanced studies in Europe, chiefly in France and Germany. Their leader, Tso Shun-Sun, however, had never been abroad.
The party had participated in the Political Consultative Conference in the mid-forties and Tso Shun-Sun consequently was appointed Minister of Agriculture and Mines. L.M.L.

Yuan Shih-k'ai (1852-1916).
A native of Honan Province in China, who served as a viceroy and military leader under the Manchu dynasty in its last years. Upon the abdication of the Manchus in the wake of the revolution of October 1911, Yuan was appointed Imperial representative to negotiate an abdication settlement with the revolutionaries led by Sun Yat-sen. In February 1912, Sun Yat-sen resigned in favor of Yuan who had built powerful military and political support for himself. After an election by provincial leaders on October 16, 1913, Yuan became the first duly constituted President of the Republic of China. His plans to make himself emperor of a new dynasty, in hopes of overcoming localism and chaos in China, were ended by his early death, June 5, 1916. R.L.W.

Yugoslavia.
Yugoslavia has an area of 98,766 square miles, four-fifths mountainous, and a population of about 18,800,000. The major ethnic groups are Serbs, Croats, Slovenes, Macedonians and Montenegrins. Albanians are the largest minority. Orthodoxy and Roman Catholicism are the major religions.
The south Slavs migrated into the Balkan Peninsula in the 6th century A.D. The Slovenes in the northwest were under foreign rule from the 9th century until 1918. The Croats, between the Adriatic Sea and the Drava River, formed an independent state until defeated in 1102 by the Hungarians. The Serbs in the south were dominated by the Byzantine Empire until the 12th century when they established an independent monarchical state. Turkey

defeated Serbia at Kosovo (1389) and ruled it for nearly 500 years.

Led by Karageorge (1782-1817), the Serbs revolted against the Turks and achieved autonomy after the Russo-Turkish War (1877-78). In 1882 Serbia became a kingdom. In 1918 the Kingdom of Serbs, Croats, and Slovenes was formed and in 1929 became Yugoslavia. The pro-German regency of Prince Paul was overthrown in March 1941; Peter II was proclaimed king. Germany, Italy, Bulgaria, and Hungary invaded and partitioned Yugoslavia. Croatia declared its independence.

During World War II and the parallel Civil War, 1,700,000 Yugoslavs lost their lives. The Communist partisans, commanded by Tito, received the preponderance of Allied support by 1943. As part of the peace settlement, Yugoslavia obtained Istria and the southern part of Trieste from Italy.

After the war a Federal People's Republic was established. Belgrade's dispute with Moscow led to Yugoslav expulsion from the Cominform in 1948. Subsequently Yugoslavia received economic and military assistance from the West. Recently efforts have been made by Moscow and Belgrade for closer cooperation.

The Federal People's Republic of Yugoslavia is composed of six republics and two autonomous areas within Serbia. Legislative power is vested in a Federal National Assembly, consisting of a Federal Council and a Council of Producers. Executive power resides in the President and a Federal Executive Council. The judiciary consists of courts in the republics and the federal Supreme Court. The League of Yugoslav Communists is the only party allowed in Yugoslavia. J.J.K.

Z

Zafrullah Khan, Chaudhri Mohammed.
Pakistani statesman. Born at Sialko (Punjab), February 6, 1893. Educated at Government College, Lahore and King's College, London. Practiced law in Lahore High Court 1914-35. Member of Punjab legislative council, 1926-35; as president of All-India Muslim League, participated in Indian Round Table conferences of 1930, 1931, and 1932; delegate to Joint Select Committee on Indian Parliamentary Reforms, 1933. Member of Viceroy's executive council, 1935-41; agent-general for India in China, 1942; judge of Federal Court of India, 1941-47. Foreign minister of Pakistan, 1947-54; led Pakistani delegations to U.N., notably to Security Council on Kashmir dispute. Judge on International Court of Justice (vice-president, 1958-61), 1954-61. Since 1961, permanent representative of Pakistan to U.N.   H.G.S.

Zaibatsu.
Japanese economic monopolies. Classifications are: (1) the oldest monopolies developed from commercial capital (Mitsui, Mitsubishi, Sumitomo, Yasuda); (2) those originally started from the commercial enterprises or banking after the Meiji Restoration (Mitsubishi, Shibusawa); (3) speculative enterprises developed during the Russo-Japanese war and the First World War (Okura, Furukawa); and (4) the "new" Zaibatsu enterprises which developed after the Manchurian Incident (Nakajima, Ayukawa, Noguchi). The central government protected the Zaibatsu, who became virtually "political merchants." Although some had their origins in the feudal period, they were essential adherents of a modern aggressive militarism, as they provided reliable markets for military supplies. World War II occupation policies, like the Anti-Monopoly Law and the Economic Decentralization Law, aimed at democratizing and demilitarizing the Japanese economy, caused the weakening of the Zaibatsu. However, economic reforms were not thorough due to a change in occupation policy and the international situation.   H.U.

Zanzibar.
(1020 sq. mi.; 299,111 inhabitants.)
Less than 23 miles off the coast of Tanganyika in east central Africa are the islands of Zanzibar and Pemba, which since 1890 have composed the British Protectorate of Zanzibar. The fundamental law of the Protectorate, the Zanzibar Order-in-Council of 1924, divides the powers of legislation and administration between a hereditary Sultan and a British Resident, respectively. The seat of government is Zanzibar City. Most of the world's supply of cloves is produced in Zanzibar; and coconuts, ivory, and coir fiber are also exported. The people are predominantly indigenous African and Muslim.
     J.A.E.

Zemlya I Volya (Land and Freedom).
Russian revolutionary organization of the late 1870's. Zemlya i Volya was in the populist tradition, growing out of the ill-fated "To the People" movement of the early 70's. From the experience of that fiasco, some members of Zemlya i Volya concluded that change could be effected only through force. Disagreement over the resort to violence led to the formal dissolution of Zemlya i Volya in August, 1879.   D.N.J.

Zengakuren.
All-Japan Federation of Student Self-Government Associations. Founded in 1948, the Zengakuren soon fell under leftist leadership and became interested in political questions not directly related to student welfare. The Zengakuren was conspicuous in political demonstrations and riots in Tokyo, especially in 1950, 1952, and 1960. Zengakuren demonstrators tore up the inside of the Tokyo airport restaurant in an unsuccessful effort to prevent Premier Kishi from departing for Washington to sign the 1960 United States-Japan Security Pact. Following the passage of the treaty in the Diet during a Socialist boycott of the session, Zengakuren students participated in repeated demonstrations at the Diet building, the Prime Minister's residence and the American Embassy. Two days after the June 15, 1960, student riot at the Diet building, during which hundreds of persons were injured and a

coed was trampled to death, the visit of President Eisenhower to Japan, scheduled for June 22, was "postponed" on request of Kishi, who shortly resigned from office. The leaders of the "mainstream," a Trotskyite faction of the Zengakuren had been expelled from the Communist Party for their left-wing adventurism, but the "anti-mainstream" faction remained under Communist domination. T.Mc.N.

Zenro Kaigi.
(Zen Nihon Rodo Kumiai Kaigi).
Abbreviation for the 800,000 strong Japanese Trade Union Congress, created in 1954 by dissident groups to counter the more leftist political policies of **Sohyo** (q.v.). At its center is the **Sodomei**, a conservative labor federation from prewar days, supporting the right-wing Socialists. In 1962, **Zenro's** name was changed to the **Domei Kaigi (Nihon Rodo Domei Kaigi)**, or Japanese Confederation of Labor, with a membership of 1,408,000. G.O.T.

Zetkin, Clara.
German leftist socialist. Born July 5, 1857. Died June 20, 1933 in Archangelskoje near Moscow. Co-founder of the Spartacus League and the Communist Party of Germany. Fearlessly criticized Stalinist terrorism. H.D.

Zhukov, Georgi.
Born 1896, Strelkovka, Kaluga Province. Joined Red Army during Civil War, CP in 1919. Graduated Frunze Military Academy 1931. In World War II led thrust into Germany, captured Berlin. Officially ranked first in military contribution to Soviet Russia's victory. Lesser commands 1946-53. Member of Party Central Committee 1952-57; member of Presidium June-October 1957. USSR Defense Minister 1955-57. Reputedly supported Khrushchev against "anti-Party group" June 1957, but was ousted from all posts in October 1957. W.A.

Zinoviev, Grigori Evseyevich.
(Real name — Radomyslsky.)
(1883-1936).
Zinoviev joined the Social Democratic Party in 1901, and sided with Lenin's Bolsheviks. He became a member of the Central Committee in 1907. From 1908 to 1917 he lived in exile abroad. Zinoviev often opposed Lenin's views. In April and May, 1917, while in Petrograd, he opposed the famed Lenin's April theses. When the question of armed insurrection was debated on the eve of the "October" revolution, Zinoviev together with Kamenev sharply opposed it. After the Bolshevik revolution (November 7, 1917), Zinoviev led a zigzag career. He became head of the Leningrad Party Committee in 1917. From 1919 he simultaneously held the post of head of the Third International. Until 1926 he was also a member of the ruling Politburo of the party. He is known as the alleged author of the famous "Zinoviev letter," which contained instructions for the preparation of a communist uprising in England, in 1924. After Lenin's death, Zinoviev was a member of the ruling triumvirate, consisting of Zinoviev, Kamenev, and Stalin. Zinoviev at first sided with Stalin to unseat Trotsky from the leadership of the party, and later, in 1925, joined Trotsky's opposition fighting Stalin's domination. He was expelled from the Politburo in 1926, and lost his membership in the Communist Party in 1927. After confessing to his "mistakes," he was re-admitted into the Communist Party in 1928, to be again expelled in 1932 for his alleged conspiracy against Stalin. After the murder of Kirov in 1934, Zinoviev with Kamenev and other leading communists was accused of counter-revolutionary activity. In August 1936 Zinoviev and 15 other leading party members were put on public trial and sentenced to death. Zinoviev was executed two days later.
V.P.P.

Zionism.
Term coined 1893 by Nathan Birnbaum designating the modern ideology and movement (Zionist movement) calling for the return of the Jews to their ancient homeland, the land of Israel (also called Zion). Zionism proceeds from the assumption that the Jews form a people many of whom cannot or will not assimilate themselves to other peoples and wish to retain their identity as a national community. Zionism became an international political factor with the convening by Theodor Herzl (1860-1904) in 1897 of the First Zionist Congress in which the World Zionist Organization was founded with the program to "establish a national

home for the Jewish People in Palestine guaranteed by public law" (Basel Program).

Most opposition to Zionism among Jews subsided with the creation of the State of Israel. Today the Zionist movement is active in promoting solidarity with Israel's cultural goals among Jews not living in Israel; and under Israeli law it is responsible for the immigration and absorption of the new immigrants in the State of Israel.   E.G.

Zola, Emile Edouard Charles Antoine. (1840-1902).

French realist author active in the Dreyfus affair at the end of the nineteenth century. His letter **"J'accuse"** (I accuse), published on January 13, 1898 in *L'Aurore* denounced the government and high army and church officials for conspiring to condemn Captain Alfred Dreyfus on fabricated espionage charges. In February, 1898, Zola was convicted of libel, and in April, the Court of Cassation called for a retrial. On July 18, before the end of his second trial, he fled to England, to return almost a year later when it was clear that Dreyfus would be retried on the genuine evidence; his novel "Truth" is a partly fictional account of the famous affair.
E.G.L.

Zone of Peace.

First used by Nikita Khrushchev at the Twentieth Congress of the C.P.S.U. in February 1956, this term drew attention to the growing political significance in world affairs of the neutralist countries that were not politically or militarily aligned with either Soviet or Western blocs. It constituted a sharp departure from Stalin's bipolar approach to international relations, and heralded the intensification of Soviet efforts to cultivate closer ties with neutralist countries, encourage their continued policy of nonalignment, and enhance Soviet prestige in underdeveloped areas. It is also intended to equate neutralism with far-sighted statesmanship.   A.Z.R.

Zoning.

The legal regulation and limitation in the use to which private property may be put in specified districts of a community or area was developed in Europe in the 19th century. In the United States, New York City in 1916 enacted the first comprehensive zoning ordinance which, in addition to specifying uses of the land by areas, required a series of set-backs to buildings in order to admit light and air, but permitted unlimited height to 25% of the ground coverage. The purpose of zoning is to develop a community in an orderly way with adequate facilities for business, industry, and residential purposes. Residential areas particularly need protection from encroaching apartment houses, industry, and business establishments. As communities grow or change their character, zoning regulations are altered.   T.K.N

APPENDIX

Aden.
British crown colony and naval station in southwest of Arabian Peninsula. It is administered by a British-controlled legislative council. The surrounding territory comprises twenty-three small sultanates and sheikdoms which have the status of British protectorates.   J.D.

Algeria.
French possession in North Africa (divided into three French Departments) from 1830 to 1962. Area: about 86,000 square miles. Population: (as of 1962) 8,500,000; of which 7,500,000 are Islamic Arabs (whose ancestors conquered the area in the 8th century) and Berbers. Of 1,000,000 Frenchmen and other Europeans living for many generations in the coastal region between Oran and Constantine, only a few thousand remained after the country was granted political independence from the Fifth French Republic in 1962. A dictatorial regime, professing neutralism, yet having close ties with the Soviet Bloc, maintains itself because of substantial outside financial aid. Prior to independence the Algerian Arabs received military and propagandistic support from the Nasser regime in Egypt. Although successive French governments had granted French citizenship to an ever-increasing number of Arabs and Berbers in the area, the Islamic personal status laws (marriage, divorce) militated against the French effort to turn all Algerians into citizens of France. Another possible solution, the partition of Algeria into two zones—a French zone in the coastal region and an independent Algerian Republic in the rest of the country—proved unattainable in view of the resistance offered by both the European settlers (Colons) and the Moslems (Arabs and Berbers). Since 1954 the Moslem Front National de la Liberation (FLN) waged continuous guerrilla warfare against the French Administration. See Evian Agreement.   J.D.

Andorra.
A tiny quasi-state in the Pyrenees. Area: about 280 square miles; population: about 5,000. France and the Bishop of Urgel (Spain) appoint a governor and chief judge. These two officials are assisted by a legislative council of twenty-four members, elected by the citizenry for four years. Language and currency: French and Spanish.   J.D.

Annexation.
The absorption of new territory by an existing state which thereby extends its sovereignty to the new territory and its population. Under international law such annexation needs formal recognition by other states. It is not to be confused with a temporary occupation or a trusteeship arrangement.   J.D.

Anti-Semitism.
Although the term implies antagonism to all persons of Semitic origin and their cultures, it actually means hatred of the Jews. The first manifestations of anti-Semitism occurred in the Babylonian-Persian Captivity when Haman (pointing to the Jewish belief in one God and Jewish religious observances) accused the Jews of being a foreign and subversive element. Religious anti-Semitism was nurtured by the Greek church fathers in the Roman Empire who considered the Jews dangerous competitors in their proselytizing efforts. In modern times Karl Marx, resentful of his Jewish origin, in **Zur Judenfrage,** accused the Jews of wielding exorbitant financial power in Europe and saw in them the standard-bearers of capitalism. His attitude, devoid of facts, was echoed in an anonymous opus, **The Protocols of the Wise Men of Zion,** published in 1895, in which the Jews were accused of having plans to rule the whole world. The protocols, probably fabricated by the Czarist Ochrana (secret police), served the Russian Government in organizing pogroms against the Jews of Russia. After Hitler's advent to power in 1933, anti-Semitism was made the official policy of the German Government. Accused of belonging to an "inferior race," the six hundred thousand Jewish citizens of Germany were placed under the Nuremberg Laws and made outcasts in the country of their birth. Their possessions were largely taken from them. Their houses of worship (synagogues) were destroyed. Those

Jews who did not leave Germany before the beginning of the European phase of World War II (1939) became the victims of the Hitlerian policy to "exterminate the Jewish race of Europe." As the Hitlerian armies conquered Poland and other European countries after 1939, close to six million European Jews were murdered in Nazi concentration camps and gas chambers. The only known active resistance to this mass annihilation took place in the Ghetto of Warsaw where the remnants of Polish Jewry, with the support of the Polish underground movement, fought one of the most heroic battles of the Second World War.

Motivated by the dislike of the unlike, anti-Semitism is fanned by the jealousies of those who fear the intellectual and economic competition of individual Jews. As latent menace to Jewish security, it exists in every country in which the Jews form a defenseless minority and is prone to come to the forefront in times of psychological, economic and political crisis. While officially outlawed in the Soviet Union, it manifests itself there in the identification of Jews with Trotskyites and Cosmopolites, in vehement attacks on Zionism and Israel, and in the systematic suppression of the religious and cultural heritage of the two and a half million Jews living within the borders of the Soviet Union. Although Russian Jews, ostracized by the Czarist Government, played a significant role in the Russian revolutionary movement, although a number of men and women of Jewish origin (but disdainful of Judaism and no longer willing to identify themselves as Jews) were active in the Bolshevist-Communist Party before and after the October Revolution of 1917, it appears to be present-day Soviet policy to prevent Communists of Jewish origin from attaining positions of political influence.

Since the establishment of the State of Israel, created by Zionist Jews to develop their religious culture in freedom from persecution and the proselytizing influences of the majority cultures, anti-Semitism has become particularly virulent in those Arab-Moslem countries which were frustrated in their efforts to prevent a modern Jewish statehood in the Middle East. In several instances (Egypt, Iraq, Yemen, Syria), governmental anti-Semitism has led to the exodus of most of the Jewish citizens.
J.D.

Aryan.
Alludes to the name of groups of warriors and their languages in the north of India (about 3000 B.C.). Toward the end of the 19th century Friedrich M. Mueller, a German philologist at Oxford University, hypothesized that these groups, forming an "Aryan race," conquered all of India, Persia and Europe and were responsible for the development of the Indo-Germanic culture. While Mueller later on retracted his hypothesis and used the term Aryan only for the designation of certain language groups, Hitler in **Mein Kampf** developed the concept of an Aryan "master race," chiefly the Germanic peoples, in which he saw the sole standard-bearers of all advanced culture. By contrast he termed the Jews an "inferior race." Political expediency led him to call the non-Germanic Japanese "Aryans." Similarly, those Arabs, who under the leadership of Haj Amin el Husseini (Grand Mufti of Jerusalem between 1917 and 1939) organized an Arab legion to fight on Hitler's side against the Allies, were granted the status of "Aryans."
J.D.

Aswan Dam.
Begun in 1960 with aim of doubling Egypt's area for agricultural production and to provide additional electricity. Financed largely by credits from the Soviet Union.
J.D.

Bulgaria.
Area: about 44,000 square miles; population: about 6,500,000. Until 1908 under Turkish overlordship. During both World Wars allied with Germany (but without declaration of war on the Soviet Union during World War II). Asked United States and United Kingdom for an armistice on August 26, 1944, whereupon the Soviet Union declared war on Rumania in order to justify subsequent Soviet occupation and transformation of Bulgaria into a Communist "Peoples' Democracy."
J.D.

Caesarism.
A term to characterize the dictatorial government which Julius Caesar em-

ployed in ancient Rome. Caesarism is government by one man whose rule is not legitimized by elections or dynastic succession. The Caesarean dictator rises to political power in a successful **coup d'état**, supported by armed forces or mob violence. He frequently employs a democratic facade, plebiscites and an ineffectual parliament composed exclusively of loyal followers. J.D.

Casus belli.
Case or reason for warfare. An action by State A which State B considers as sufficient cause to declare war on A. J.D.

Casus foederis.
An event (e.g., an attack) anticipated in a treaty of alliance compelling the treaty partners to come to each other's aid. J.D.

Curzon Line.
A border line between Soviet Russia and Poland, suggested by British Foreign Minister Lord Curzon in 1920. It was rejected by Poland. In October 1939, in accordance with the Ribbentrop-Molotov Pact, the Soviet Union annexed the eastern parts of Poland up to the Curzon Line, thereby extending her sovereignty over the 4,000,000 Ukrainians, 2,000,000 White Russians and 4,000,000 Poles living in that area. The Curzon Line is the present demarcation between the Soviet Union and Communist-ruled Poland. J.D.

Dahomey.
A former West African French colony. Population: about 1,700,000. Since December 1958 an independent republic with democratic elections and a cabinet based on parliamentary support. J.D.

Danube Commission.
Created in 1856 by the states bordering the Danube for the regulation of shipping on the Danube. Renamed International Danube Commission in 1921, when the United Kingdom, France and Italy joined the successor states of Austria-Hungary, Bulgaria, Rumania, Turkey and Russia in the administration of the river. In 1946 at the Peace Conference in Paris, a "freedom of shipping" clause was inserted in the treaties with Italy, Hungary, Rumania and Bulgaria. J.D.

Dominion.
Literally: government. The term is used to designate the member states of the British Commonwealth—with the exception of the United Kingdom. The use of the term is incorrect when referring to those member states of the Commonwealth which have chosen a republican form of statehood. J.D.

Dunkirk, Treaty of.
Concluded between France and the United Kingdom in March 1947 for the duration of fifty years. It stipulates mutual assistance against an attack on the part of a remilitarized Germany. J.D.

Enosis.
"Union with Greece." Following the declaration of independence (August 19, 1960) of Cyprus, this demand led to renewed violence between its Greek and Turkish inhabitants. Involving both Greece and Turkey, it has threatened to engender warfare between these two NATO partners and allowed Soviet propagandists to fan anti-Western sentiments in Greece, Turkey and Cyprus. UN forces, stationed on the island since early 1964, have attempted pacification. While the Turks clamor for partition, the Greek followers of Enosis want to make Cyprus an integral part of Greece. In the event of Enosis, the members of the Turkish minority of Cyprus would be left with the alternative of emigrating to Turkey or becoming Greek citizens. J.D.

Fifth Column.
Term originated in Spanish Civil War (1936-1939). While Franco attacked the forces of the Republic with four military columns, his followers in Madrid and other cities held by the "Loyalists" tried to undermine the confidence of the population in the government of the Republic, spread false rumors and committed acts of sabotage. They were, therefore, called Franco's fifth column. The Communist Parties outside of the Soviet Union and Red China could be called fifth columns for similar reasons. J.D.

Fine Gael.
Means United Ireland. It is the name of a moderate Irish party led by John Costello, Prime Minister of Ireland from 1954 to 1957. J.D.

Franco, Francisco (1892—).

As Commander-in-Chief of Spanish military units in Spanish Morocco, General Franco, in July 1936, organized the military revolt against the democratically elected government of Spain. Supported by Nazi Germany and Fascist Italy, he was victorious over the government of the Republic, which during the course of the Civil War came more and more under the influence of Soviet Communism and the political and military emissaries sent by the Soviet Union to assist the "Loyalist" forces. In 1939 Franco created a fascist-type dictatorship with himself as Caudillo and the Falange Espanola as the only legally permitted political party. After the downfall of Mussolini and Hitler and due to international pressure, the Franco regime discarded many of its repressive features and allowed a minimum of political opposition. In 1948 Franco declared Spain a monarchy. A member of the Bourbon dynasty is to occupy the throne after Franco's death or resignation. J.D.

G.P.U.

Abbreviation of Gossudarstvennoie Politisheskoie Upravlenie (State Political Administration). Is the former name of the secret police of the Soviet Union (the successor of the Bolshevist Cheka during the Civil War). In 1947 the G.P.U. was integrated into the NKVD (abbreviation of the Russian words for People's Commissariat of the Interior), which, in turn, was renamed MVD (Ministry of the Interior). Organized to destroy all active and potential opposition to the dictatorship, the Soviet secret police, like the Nazi Gestapo, was also employed to murder rival factions within the ruling Party when their exponents after trying to occupy the key positions of the state happened to be defeated. Also like the Gestapo, the G.P.U. is known for the bestial brutality of its means (physical tortures followed by forced confessions used as proof of the defendant's guilt). Since Stalin's death (1953) it appears that the arbitrary power of the Soviet secret police has been somewhat curbed. J.D.

Greenland.

An Arctic island possession of Denmark. Area: about 840,000 square miles (mainly glaciers). Population: about 500 Danes and 20,000 Eskimos. Serves NATO as strategic base. In 1953 Greenland lost its colonial status and became a Danish province with two representatives in the Danish Parliament. J.D.

Hallstein Doctrine.

Formulated by Walter Hallstein, former leading official of the Foreign Office of the Federal Republic of Germany. In accordance with this doctrine the Federal Republic is to sever diplomatic relations with any country (except the Soviet Union) which grants recognition to the Soviet Zone (the so-called German Democratic Republic). J.D.

High Commissioner.

Title of a British or American official who is entrusted with the administration of a colonial possession, a mandate, trust or temporarily occupied area destined to become eventually independent. J.D.

Khanh, Nguyen.

Leader of Vietnamese military junta which was responsible for the assassination of President Ngo-Dinh Diem November 2, 1963, and who thereafter assumed the presidency. The Khanh government received immediate recognition from U.S. President J. F. Kennedy. J.D.

Idea.

An idea is a reference to something which at the moment might not be physically perceived. Plato sees in an idea the essence of things, things not as they are in their physical reality but as the mind conceives them in a supposed perfection. According to Plato, the visible world is, therefore, but a pale reflection of ultimate realities. For Locke an idea is "the object of the understanding when a man thinks" or, in other words, an idea is the acute awareness of an object. Using Locke's concept of the idea, Berkeley and Hume arrived at a subjective idealism which bases all that exists on man's ideas on such existence, i.e., on man's experiences and impressions, whereby Hume went so far as stating that even the idea of the existence of one's own personality may be an illusion. Borrowing from Plato as well as Spinoza, Hegel defined ideas as concepts of reason and regarded

the universe as an interrelated, intelligible system with every existing thing, man included, as one of its fragments.
R.A.B.

Ireland.
The Republic of Ireland or Eire (formerly: Irish Free State) was established in 1922 when Great Britain granted Ireland the status of a dominion, followed by Ireland's separation from the crown. Since 1922 Ireland comprises the provinces of Leinster, Munster, Connacht, as well as three of the nine counties of Ulster. Six of the counties chose to remain with Great Britain which, thereby, became the United Kingdom of Great Britain and Northern Ireland. The Republic of Ireland covers an area of about 26,600 sq. miles with a population of close to 3½ million. 94.3% are Roman Catholics; 4.2% are Protestant Episcopalians; 1% are Presbyterians. In addition, there are about 8,500 Methodists and 4,000 Jews. Farming constitutes the largest industry. Agricultural products form the main export item. The United Kingdom is the largest customer. It accepts ¾ of the total exports of Ireland and in return supplies Ireland with coal and raw materials for small industries.

Eire is governed under a constitution passed by plebiscite in 1937. Executive leadership is in the hands of the President of the Republic, who is elected by popular vote for a period of 7 years. He appoints the Prime Minister, who in turn selects the members of his cabinet. Legislation (and policy-making) is entrusted to a National Parliament, composed of a Senate and a House of Representatives. Some members of the Senate are appointed by the Prime Minister, most Senators are elected on a vocational basis. The members of the House of Representatives are chosen under a system of proportional representation. The Prime Minister and other cabinet members need the approval of the House of Representatives. The Senate is allowed to suggest amendments of bills but has no veto power over legislation passed by the House. Policy differences between the political parties (Fianna Fail, originally led by Eamon de Valera; Fine Gael, led by John A. Costello; a relatively small Labour Party, led by William Norton) are slight. All of these political parties demand the extension of the jurisdiction of the Republic to the six Ulster counties of Northern Ireland. While being anti-Communist, they favor neutrality and refuse to align themselves with NATO for fear that Eire's entry into NATO might be interpreted as recognition of the present borders. Ireland participates, however, in all efforts of European integration.
J.D.

Japan. (Nihon).
Is an insular country which comprises the four main islands of Honshu, Shikoku, Kyushu, Hokkaido, as well as numerous small islands in the Pacific Ocean. It has an area of about 142,798 sq. miles and a population of about 88 million (as of 1954). Shinto, Buddhism and Christianity form the three major religions. Recently, Judaism has won some 20,000 adherents, and a Jewish congregation has been established in Tokyo. Prior to World War II Shinto with its myth about the divine descent of the Japanese Emperor was sponsored as a cult of patriotism (state Shinto) and given priority over all other religious groupings. For purposes of local administration Japan is divided into forty-six prefectures. Hokkaido constitutes one such administrative unit. So does Tokyo, the capital city. (See Japanese Government and Japanese Politics).
R.A.B.

July 4, 1776.
A memorial day in the U.S.A. celebrating the signing of the Declaration of Independence in 1776.
R.A.B.

July 14, 1789.
A memorial day in France celebrating the storming of the Bastille in 1789, the beginning of the French Revolution against the Ancien Regime.
R.A.B.

Justice of the Peace. (U.S.A.).
A popularly elected law-enforcement officer in small towns and rural districts with short terms of office (usually two years). The J.P.'s jurisdiction in civil matters is limited by the monetary sum in the controversy or the amount of damages demanded. State law fixes a maximum (usually $500). Suits involving higher sums must be tried before a superior court. In criminal cases the J.P. exercises summary jurisdiction

over minor infractions of the law, such as traffic law violations and breaches of the peace. His power does not extend beyond the imposition of small fines and imprisonment for a few days. Moreover, his decisions in criminal cases may be appealed to a court of higher jurisdiction. The J.P. also determines whether evidence suffices to warrant holding accused person for further action by the Grand Jury or other authorities. In most states the J.P. is not required to have legal training—a residue from pioneering days when he was considered a kind of community patriarch whose judgment and advice seemed to be more important than his knowledge and citation of statutes and court decisions. Where he is unsalaried (as in most states), he relies on the fees which he is able to collect; and for this reason he tends to favor the plaintiff regardless of the circumstances. Some states have, therefore, introduced legally trained and salaried Justices of the Peace, thereby giving them the same status which the judges of the magistrates' (or police) courts enjoy in the bigger cities. J.D.

Malawi.
Formerly part of the Federation of Rhodesia and Nyasaland. Nyasaland, after 73 years of British rule, received independence in July 1964. Called Malawi, the new state will remain within the Commonwealth. J.D.

Malaysia.
Southeast Asian federation, member of the Commonwealth of Nations. Area: about 50,600 sq. mi. Multi-ethnic population: about 7,800,000. Major religion: Islam. Minority religions: Buddhism, Christianity and Hinduism. Producer of 32% of the world's natural rubber. Major port city: Singapore. Became independent on August 31, 1963 by agreement between Malayan Prime Minister Tengku Abdul Rahman and British Prime Minister Harold Macmillan, thereby ending former British colonial regime in Singapore, North Borneo, Sarawak, Brunei. Governmental structure modelled after that of the United Kingdom. J.D.

M.V.D.
Russian abbreviation for Ministry of the Interior. In charge of Soviet secret police. Successor of Cheka, GPU, and NKVD, the M.V.D. administers the forced labor camps (Soviet concentration camps). J.D.

Neo-colonialism.
A term used by Communist and pro-Communist politicians to denounce any agreements between newly independent African and Asian states and the Western powers. The term should be used to signify the relationship between the Soviet Union and her satellite dependencies. J.D.

Norway.
(Area: 125,064 sq. mi. Population: about 3,300,000.) Most thinly populated political unit in Europe. Constitutional and hereditary monarchy. (On September 21, 1957 King Haakon died and was succeeded by his son, King Olav V.) The endowed state religion to which the king must conform is Evangelical Lutheran. Agriculture is an important resource in addition to fisheries and industrial production. The output of electricity per capita is the highest of any country in the world. After 1945 the economy became strictly controlled and guided by the Labour Government. Quotas, price controls, subsidies and a system of licenses were used to spur development. State monopolies over grain and alcohol were established before World War II.

The Constitution (Grunnlov), adopted May 17, 1814, vests executive power in the king, who exercises this power through a council of state, composed of the prime minister and seven councilors as heads of the various ministries. The councilors sit in the parliament (Storting) but have no vote. The life of a parliament is four years. It cannot be prematurely dissolved by the king. The 150 members of the parliament are directly elected by the people in electoral districts corresponding to Norway's twenty counties (fylker). Parliament is divided into two groups: lagting, consisting of 38 members, and odelsting, consisting of the rest of the parliamentary members. Lagting introduces a bill, which, if passed, is sent to odelsting. When there is no agreement between the two groups, a joint session is called, and the issue becomes settled by a two-thirds majority vote of the whole. Bills become law without royal assent when passed by two ordinary sessions of parliament after two separate and successive elections. Budget proposals, other financial matters and political policies not in the form of a bill are considered by parliament as a single body. Political parties are: Labour (with a majority in parliament since 1945), Conservative, Agrarian, Christian People, Liberal and Communist. Districts (64 urban and 680 rural) are run by councils (kommuner), which are elected every four years and in the same manner as the parliament.

A notable feature of Norway's judicial system is that in civil law cases a suit is brought first before the town or county mediation council with appeal to town and county courts. A supreme court has final decision in all cases. (Capital punishment has been abolished except in certain military and treasonable cases).

In 1949 Norway joined NATO.
R.A.B.

Oder-Neisse line.
Since 1945 the frontier between Poland and the Soviet-occupied zone of Germany. In 1945, due to Soviet pressure, Poland received Upper and Lower Silesia, Pomerania, parts of Brandenburg, the city of Danzig and the southern portion of East Prussia in exchange for territory east of Warsaw which was annexed by the Soviet Union. The Polish occupation of the former German territories goes back to the Yalta Agreement between Franklin D. Roosevelt, Stalin and Churchill (with Churchill accepting the Curzon line as a border between the Soviet Union and Poland but protesting the Polish absorption of German territory). Detaching significant East German territories with an overwhelmingly German population (of 9 million Germans about 7 million have been forcibly expelled). The Oder-Neisse line is rejected by all Germans with the exception of the Communists. (The Communist zonal regime, headed by Walter Ulbricht, himself a Soviet Russian citizen, has recognized the Oder-Neisse line as an "eternal frontier.") The USA, the United Kingdom and France reject the permanency of the frontier and insist that the Potsdam Agreement (like the Yalta Agreement) permitted its establishment only as a temporary demarcation line subject to revision in a peace treaty with a unified Germany.
J.D.

Paraguay.
Republic in the south central part of South America. Area: 157,047 sq. mi. Population: about 1,500,000. Capital: Asuncion. Homogeneous, mostly white population. Has been a refuge for groups from foreign countries seeking to establish new communities for religious or other purposes. Constitution, adopted on July 10, 1940, grants sweeping presidential powers. President is elected by all males (18 years and over) for a five year term and is eligible for re-election. A one-chamber parliament (Congress) consists of 40 members elected for five years. The President has absolute veto power and can dissolve the Congress at will. He may issue decree-laws when the Congress is not in session—to receive legislative approval later. He may declare a state of emergency and, thereby, increases his ordinary powers. He is aided by a council of state, an advisory body (composed of cabinet members, the archbishop, the rector of the university, the president of the central bank and others chosen directly or indirectly by the President).
R.A.B.

Puerto Rico.
Smallest and most easterly island of the Greater Antilles group in the West Indies. Area: 3,314 sq. mi. Population (1958): 2,321,000. The constitution, approved by the island's electorate and ratified by the United States, was adopted on July 25, 1952. It provides for a representative government and a bill of rights guaranteeing the liberties and rights of the citizens. Amendments which do not conflict with the U. S. Constitution or the Puerto Rican Federal Relations Act are permissible. Governmental powers are divided among the executive, legislative and judicial branches. The governor is popularly elected for four years with unlimited chance for re-election. He appoints the heads of the executive departments who form his advisory council. The legislature consists of a senate and a house of representatives, both of which are elected for four

years. There are 8 senatorial (2 members each) and 40 representative districts. 11 senators and 11 representatives are chosen at large. The Constitution guarantees the representation of minority parties in the legislature through automatic appointment based on island-wide voting strength. Puerto Rico sends a resident commissioner to the US Congress for a four year term, but he has no vote. Puerto Ricans do not vote in US presidential elections and are not subjected, therefore, to federal taxes of the US. After 1956 the government's Economic Development program (one phase known as "Operation Bootstrap") caused the economy to shift from one mainly agricultural to one mainly industrial and manufacturing.　　　　　　　　　R.A.B.

Reaction.

The opposite of progress. The term is used for political parties and movements which idealize the past and radically oppose any innovations which tend to destroy their ideal. Communists and pro-Communists call anyone a reactionary who disagrees with the party dogma enunciated by the Moscow Communist center (or Peking). In Communist terminology Social Democrats and genuine liberals become, thereby, "reactionaries." Bona fide liberals will at times use the term to denounce certain conservative concepts of thought. In reality conservatism is not reaction. While stressing the civilization heritage (and rejecting the omnicompetent state, be it fascist or communist), the conservative accepts the continuity of the political process. Far from trying to turn the clock back to an idealized past, he uses man's historical experience to enhance the conditions of choice, i.e., the cause of human freedom.
　　　　　　　　　　　　　　J.D.

Spain.

Area: about 195,000 sq. mi. Population: about 30,000,000. Major possessions: Spanish Sahara, Spanish Guinea. Chiefly agricultural, the country has been known since Phoenician days as a producer of copper, mercury, lead and iron ore.

The Spanish government operates under five "Fundamental Laws": the Labor Charter of 1938, the Law of the Cortes of 1942, the Charter of Rights of 1945, the National Referendum Law of 1945 and the Law of Succession of 1947. According to the last law, Spain is defined as "a Catholic, social and representative state hereby constituted, in accordance with tradition, a kingdom." General Francisco Franco, presently head of the Spanish state, is to be succeeded by a king to be approved by a two-thirds vote of the Cortes and sworn to observe the five Fundamental Laws. The Cortes, established by a law of July 1942 as the "superior organism for the participation of the Spanish people in the work of the state", may propose laws. The head of the state (who normally initiates legislation) has a veto right. Members of the Cortes are: fifty elected representatives of the provincial municipalities, fifty delegates of the state-sanctioned employers' and workers' organizations, fifty or more appointees of the head of the state. In addition the members of the National Council of the Falangist Party (Franco's party), the provincial governors and the heads of the universities are ex officio members of this quasi-legislative body. The head of the state is advised by a Supreme Consultative Body, composed of 4 representatives of the Cortes, 3 nominees of the head of the state and 14 ex officio members. The executive functions are entrusted to a cabinet whose members are appointed by the head of the state. (The Secretary General of the Falangist Party is a cabinet minister without portfolio.) During World War II, Spain was officially neutral. A "blue division" of Spanish volunteers fought on Germany's side in the Ukraine after Hitler broke the Nazi-Soviet friendship pact of August 1939 and occupied nearly all of Soviet Russia west of Moscow. After World War II Spain was first denied membership in the UN, which in December 1946 demanded the replacement of the Spanish government by one "deriving its authority from the governed", but failed to make a similar demand from the Soviet Union, one of the UN's "Big 5." In 1951 the USA initiated discussions with the Franco Government with a view to Spanish participation in the western defense against Soviet Communist aggression. In December 1955 Spain was admitted into the UN. The terroristic features of its dictatorial regime had meanwhile been abolished. In April 1945—6 years after the end of the Civil War (1936-1939)—all political charges against former "Loyalists" were dropped and Republican exiles were invited to return. All prisoners convicted of political offenses committed during the Civil War were pardoned. But the one-party system (the Falange Espanola Tradicionalista) was maintained. J.D.

Spengler, Oswald (1880-1936).
German historian and philosopher. In his main work, **Der Untergang des Abendlandes, (The Decline of the Occident)** Spengler rejects the continuity of human progress. Instead he believes that every culture must be seen as an independent organism which grows from childhood to maturity and then gradually decays. Signs of this decay in the western world he sees in the creation of metropolitan cities with their mass populations addicted to "bread and circuses" by those who profess democracy but try to manipulate them for the sake of gaining loyal voters.
J.D.

Suez Canal.
An artificial waterway, about 100 miles long, connecting Suez in the Red Sea with Port Said on the Eastern Mediterranean. Enables shipping between Europe and Asia to avoid sea passage by the Cape of Good Hope. Constructed by Ferdinand de Lesseps and opened on November 17, 1869, the Canal was to be a neutral passage way, "free and open, in time of war as in time of peace, to every vessel of commerce or of war, without distinction of flag." (Article I, Constantinople Convention, October 29, 1888). Management of the Canal was entrusted to a board of directors (thirty-two as of 1956) representing the shareholders of the Suez Canal Company. In violation of both, the Constantinople Convention and the rights of the Suez Canal Company, the Nasser regime of Egypt nationalized the Canal on July 26, 1956, declared martial law in the Canal zone and seized control of the Company's buildings and office installations on Egyptian territory. J.D.

Turkey.
Republic in southeast Balkans and Asia Minor. Area: 296,185 sq. mi. Population: about 25,000,000. Agriculture supplies main support. Principal crops include cotton, tobacco, cereals, olives, oilseeds. Mineral deposits include coal, iron and chrome. Under the influence of the Kemalist revolution the sultanate was abolished in 1922 and Turkey declared a republic with Kemal Ataturk ("Father of the Turks") as president. An organic law, adopted in 1924, stated "the people of Turkey regardless of religion and race are Turks as regards citizenship" (until then the word "Turk" signified a Moslem subject of the sultan). In 1928 Islam ceased to be the state religion. In 1929 Latin script replaced Arabic script. In 1937 the six principles of the People's Republican Party (until 1945 the only political party) an outgrowth of Kemal's revolutionary movement, were inserted into the organic law. They were: republicanism, nationalism, state socialism (etatisme), sovereignty of the people, secularism and dynamism. In 1948 Turkey adopted the secret ballot (after having extended suffrage to women in 1934). Conceived as a party of "tutelage," the Republican People's Party gradually permitted a political opposition, the Democratic Party under the leadership of Celal Bayar. On May 14, 1950 the Democratic Party, with a program of economic liberalism, won the national elections. Bayar became President of the Republic, an office held by Ismet Inonu after Ataturk's death (1938). Suppressive measures, introduced by Prime Minister Menderes, led in May 1960 to a military revolt and the presidency of General Cemal Gursel. A new constitution was adopted in July 1961. On its basis new political parties, chiefly the Justice Party, the New Turkey Party and the National Peasant Party, replaced the Democratic Party. As Prime Minister Inonu formed a coalition government of Republican People's Party and Justice Party.

Legislative authority is vested in a Grand National Assembly, which elects the President of the Republic for a term of 4 years and a chance for re-election. A Council of Ministers (cabinet), entrusted with the executive departments, is responsible to the Grand National Assembly. In addition a Council of State forms an advisory body and judicial authority in administrative matters. Its members, attached to the office of the prime minister, are chosen from leading citizens. Since the dissolution of the Democratic Party, whose leaders were accused of financial corruption and efforts to reintroduce Islam as a state religion, the armed forces exercise considerable political power.

Neutral during the Second World War, Turkey declared war on Germany and Japan in February 1945 but did not participate in combat. Threatened by Soviet aggression it was granted US aid under the Truman Doctrine. In 1949 it joined the Council of Europe and in 1951 NATO. In the Korean War the Turkish brigade, fighting side by side with US and South Korean armies, distinguished itself by special bravery. Turkey is also a member of CENTO, which has its seat in Ankara.

J.D.